THE ROUGH GUIDES

OTHER AVAILABLE ROUGH GUIDES

NEW YORK, PARIS, MEXICO, PERU, GREECE, CHINA, BRITTANY & NORMANDY, SPAIN, CALIFORNIA, PORTUGAL, KENYA, TUNISIA, EASTERN EUROPE, YUGOSLAVIA, SICILY, SCANDINAVIA, CRETE, MOROCCO, AMSTERDAM, VENICE, ITALY, GERMANY AND IRELAND

FORTHCOMING TITLES INCLUDE

BRAZIL, GUATEMALA & BELIZE, HOLLAND, BELGIUM & LUXEMBOURG and **THE PYRENEES**

ROUGH GUIDE CREDITS

Series Editor: Mark Ellingham
Editorial: Martin Dunford, John Fisher, Jack Holland, Jonathan Buckley, Greg Ward, Richard Trillo, Jules Brown
Production: Susanne Hillen, Kate Berens, Andy Hilliard, Gail Jammy
Typesetting: Greg Ward

Many people have been involved in the production of this book, but above all the authors must thank Greg Ward and Rosie Ayliffe, along with Susanne Hillen and Robert Jones.

We would also like to record our gratitude to the many readers of the previous edition of this guide, who took the trouble to write in with their comments and suggestions, and in particular we want to thank Florica Kyriacopoulos and Peter Polish, without whose support this book could not have been written.

This 1989 edition published by Harrap-Columbus Ltd, 26 Market Square, Bromley, Kent BR1 1NA.
Reprinted 1990 and 1991.
Originally published 1986 by Routledge & Kegan Paul

Typeset in Linotron Univers and Century Old Style to an original design by Andrew Oliver.
Printed in the United Kingdom by Cox and Wyman Ltd (Reading).
Illustrations in Part One and Part Three by Ed Briant.
Basics illustration by Helen Manning; Contexts illustration by Jane Strother.

720p.
Includes index.

British Library Cataloguing in Publication Data

Baillie, Kate
The Rough Guide to France. – 2nd ed. (The rough guides)
1. France. Visitors guides
I. Title II. Salmon, Tim
914.4'04838

ISBN 0–7471–0131–0

WRITTEN AND RESEARCHED BY

KATE BAILLIE AND TIM SALMON

With additional accounts by
Nicola Baxter, Greg Ward,
Gordon McLachlan, Andrew Neather,
Robin Salmon, Ann Rook, Christine Smith,
Rosie Ayliffe, Paul Jenner, Conrad Cairns,
and Andrew Sanger

Edited by
MARK ELLINGHAM
with Rosie Ayliffe

HARRAP-COLUMBUS ■ LONDON

CONTENTS

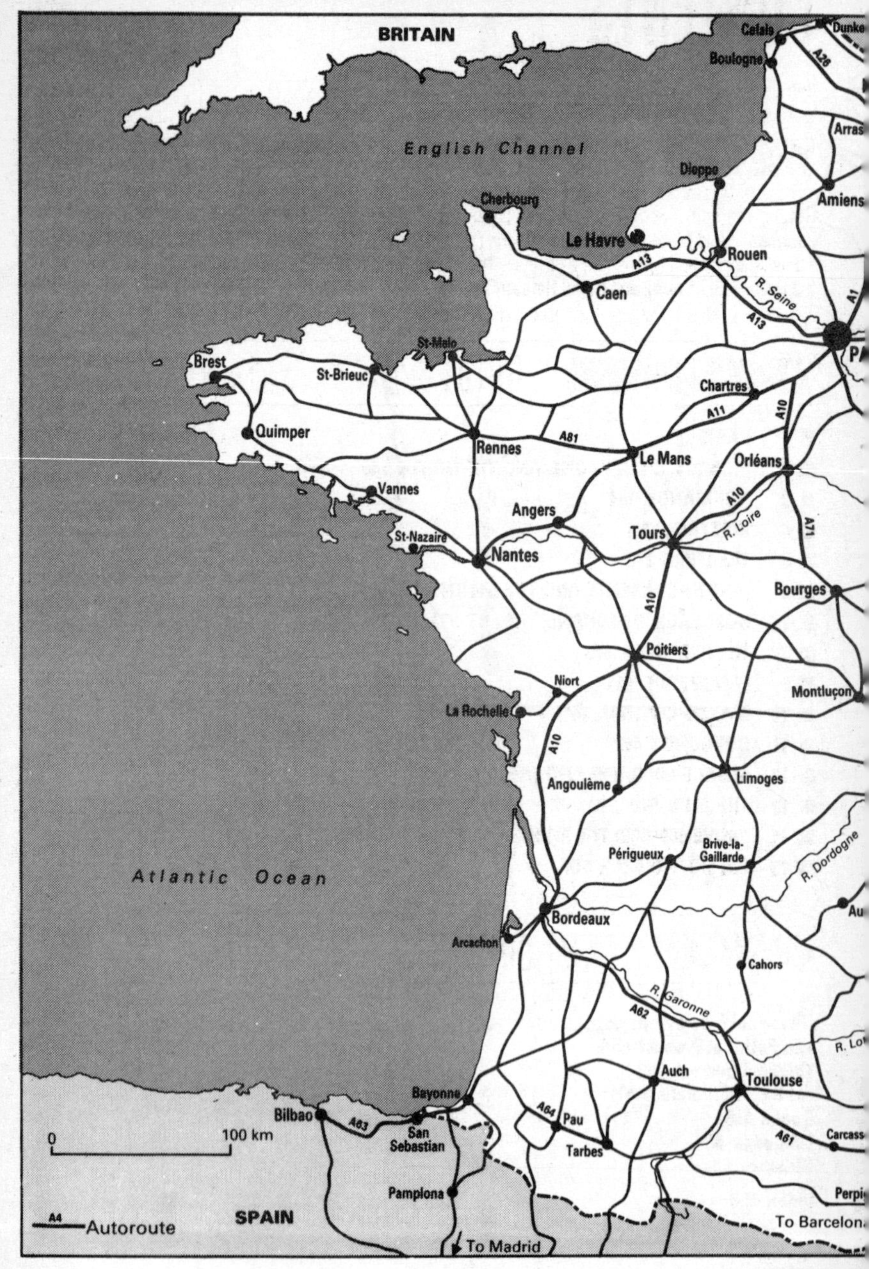
BRITAIN
English Channel
Atlantic Ocean
SPAIN
Calais
Boulogne
A26
Arras
Dieppe
Amiens
Cherbourg
Le Havre
Rouen
A13
R. Seine
Caen
St-Malo
Brest
St-Brieuc
Chartres
A11
A10
Quimper
Rennes
A81
Le Mans
Orléans
Vannes
Angers
Tours
R. Loire
A71
St-Nazaire
Nantes
Bourges
Poitiers
Niort
La Rochelle
Montluçon
Limoges
Angoulême
Périgueux
Brive-la-Gaillarde
R. Dordogne
Bordeaux
Arcachon
Cahors
R. Garonne
A62
Auch
Toulouse
Bayonne
A64
Pau
Tarbes
A61
Bilbao
A63
San Sebastian
Pamplona
0
100 km
Autoroute
To Madrid
To Barcelona

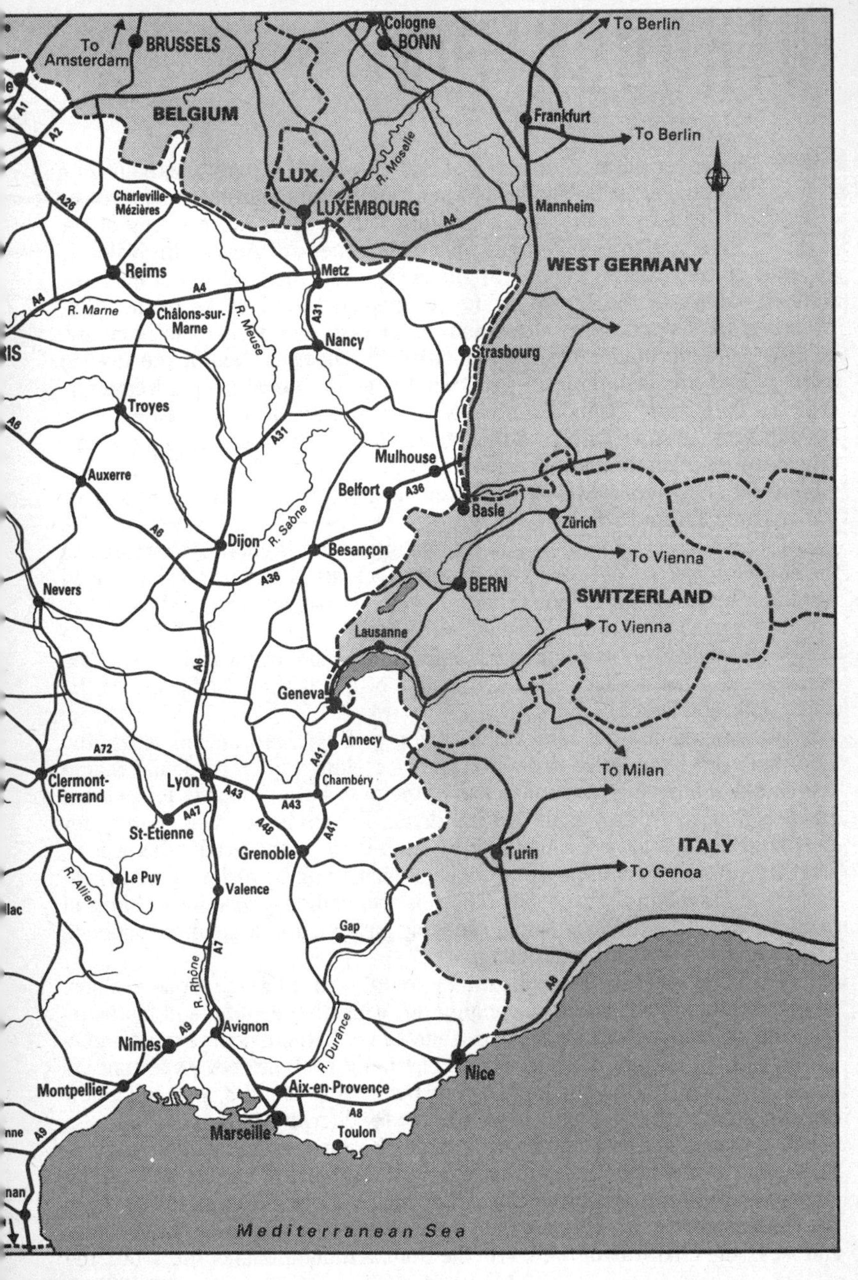

Cologne
BONN
To Berlin
To Amsterdam
BRUSSELS
BELGIUM
Frankfurt
To Berlin
R. Moselle
LUX.
LUXEMBOURG
Charleville-Mézières
Mannheim
A4
A1
A2
A26
WEST GERMANY
Reims
Metz
A4
R. Marne
Châlons-sur-Marne
R. Meuse
A31
Nancy
Strasbourg
Troyes
A6
A31
Mulhouse
Auxerre
Belfort
A36
Basle
Zürich
A6
Dijon
R. Saône
Besançon
To Vienna
A36
BERN
Nevers
SWITZERLAND
To Vienna
Lausanne
A6
Geneva
Annecy
A72
A41
To Milan
Clermont-Ferrand
Lyon
A43
Chambéry
A43
A47
A48
A41
St-Etienne
Grenoble
ITALY
Turin
To Genoa
R. Allier
Le Puy
Valence
Gap
A7
R. Rhône
A8
Avignon
R. Durance
Nîmes
A9
Nice
Montpellier
Aix-en-Provence
A8
Marseille
Toulon
A9
Mediterranean Sea

INTRODUCTION

The sheer physical diversity of France would be hard to exhaust in a lifetime of visits. The landscapes range from the fretted rocky coasts of Brittany to the limestone hills of Provence, the canyons of the Pyrenees to the Germanic picturesqueness of Alsace, the volcanic uplands of the Massif Central to the wide grain fields of Touraine, the wooded valleys of the Dordogne to the glacier-capped peaks of the Alps. Each **region** looks different, feels different, has its own style of architecture, its characteristic food, often its own patois or dialect. Though the French word *pays* is the generic term for a whole country, local people frequently refer to their own immediate vicinity as *mon pays*, and to a stranger as coming from another *pays*. And this strong sense of regional identity, sometimes expressed in the form of active separatist movements as in Brittany and Languedoc, has persisted over centuries in the teeth of centralised administrative control from Paris.

To the British eye the most striking feature of the French **countryside** is the sense of space. There are huge tracts of woodland and undeveloped land without a house in sight. Industrialisation came relatively late, and the countryside remains very rural. Away from the main urban centres, hundreds of towns and villages have changed only slowly and organically, their old houses and streets intact, as much a part of the natural landscape as the rivers, hills and fields.

Historical and cultural associations are so widely disseminated across the land that even if you were to confine your travelling to one particular region you would still have a powerful sense of the past without having to seek out major sights. With its wealth of local detail, France is an ideal country for dawdling; there is always something to catch the eye and gratify the senses, whether you are meandering down a lane, picnicking by a slow, green river, or sipping *Pernod* in a village café. There is also endless scope for all kinds of **outdoor activities**, from walking, canoeing and cycling to the more sophisticated pleasures of skiing and sailing.

If you need more **urban stimuli** to activate the pleasure buds – clubs, shops, fashion, movies, music, hanging out with the beautiful and famous – then the great cities provide them in abundance, Paris of course most particularly, with its elegant boulevards and charming back streets, its art and its ethnic diversity. And in summer, if your budget can stand it, you can follow the migration to the superchic resorts of the Mediterranean coast.

For a thousand years and more France has been at the cutting edge of **European development**, and the legacy of this wealth, energy and experience is everywhere evident in the astonishing variety of things to see: from the Gothic cathedrals of the north to the Romanesque churches of the centre and west, the châteaux of the Loire, the Roman monuments of the south, the ruined castles of the English and the Cathars and the prehistoric cave-paintings of the Dordogne. If all of the legacy is not so tangible – the literature, music, ideas and the political influence, say, of the 1789 Revolution – as much as possible is recuperated and illustrated in museums and galleries across the nation, from colonial history to fishing techniques, aeroplane design to textiles, migrant shepherds to manicure, battlefields and coalmines.

Many of the **museums** are models of clarity and modern design. Among those that the French do best are museums such as the Musée Basque in Bayonne and the Musée Dauphinois in Grenoble, i.e., those devoted to local arts, crafts and customs – another manifestation of the sense of regional identity and the deep-felt desire to stay in touch with origins. But inevitably first place must go to the fabulous collections of paintings, many but not all of which are in **Paris**. This is perhaps because the city nurtured so many of the finest creative artists of the last hundred years, both French – Monet or Matisse, for example – and foreign, such as Picasso and Picabia.

But even if you are quite untroubled by a Puritan sense of duty to improve your mind by contemplating old stones and works of high art, France is uniquely well endowed to satisfy the much maligned grosser appetites. The French have made a high art of daily life: eating, drinking, dressing, moving, simply being. The **pleasures of the palate** run from the simplest picnic of crusty *baguette*, ham and cheese washed down by an inexpensive red wine through what must be the most elaborate take-away food in the world, available from practically every *charcuterie*; such basic regional dishes as *cassoulet*; the liver-destroying riches of Périgord and Burgundy cuisine; the fruits of the sea; extravagant pastries and ice cream cakes; to the trance-inducing refinements – and prices – of the great chefs. And there are wines to match, at all prices, and not just from the renowned vineyards of Bordeaux, Burgundy and Champagne. If you feel inadequate in the face of such choice, never be afraid to ask advice, for every French person is a true devotee and ever ready to explain the arcane mysteries to the uninitiated.

The people

Visual appearance is important to the French. No effort is too great to make things look good: witness the food shops even in the poorest neighbourhoods of a city, always sparkling clean and beautifully displayed. And it is evident that the people too take pride in looking neat and sharp; they look at others and expect to be looked at. Life is theatre, lived much more in the public eye – especially in the warm Mediterranean south – than in Anglo-Saxon societies. And from the traveller's point of view it's a free and fun spectacle.

The French tend to be extremely courteous – it's not unusual for someone entering a restaurant to say 'Good evening' to the entire company – and rather formal in their manners. At the same time, if they want something, they may be quite direct. If you are feeling self-conscious about coping with the language, that can seem like rudeness. It isn't. If you observe the formalities and make an effort to communicate, you will find the French as friendly and interested as anyone else.

As for the reputed arrogance: the French are certainly proud of their culture, something which is reinforced by the education system. Artists and thinkers are held in high esteem in France and their opinions are listened to. Even prime ministers tend to be literate, often accomplished authors in their own right. But in a world dominated by commercial values and, in addition, the English language, the French – not unnaturally, for their language was once the *lingua franca* of the educated – feel this **culture** is under threat. And the desire to defend it can sometimes seem like arrogance.

Where to go and when

France is easy to travel around. Restaurants and hotels proliferate everywhere and the lower-budget ones are much cheaper than in most other developed western European countries. Rail services are highly efficient, as is the road network, especially the (toll-paying) autoroutes, and cyclists are much admired and encouraged. Information is highly organised and available from the tourist offices (*syndicats d'initiatives*), a feature of practically every place in the land, as well as from hiking, cycling, camping, hang-gliding and hitch-hiking organisations. But although these activities all have their specialist associations, they are not obtrusive; the French will not stand for regimentation, so you are left to your own devices. And such is the diversity of the country that there is something to suit every taste and interest.

There are all kinds of pegs on which to hang a holiday in France: a city, a region, a river, a mountain range, activities, cathedrals, châteaux. And in many cases your choice will determine the best time of year to go. Unless you're a skier, for example, weather will keep you out of the mountains from November to May, as well as away from the seaside, though spring on the Mediterranean coast can be very attractive and crowd-free.

Climate, otherwise, need not be a major consideration in planning a trip. Northern France, like nearby Britain, is wet and unpredictable. Paris perhaps has a marginally better climate than New York, rarely reaching the extremes of heat and cold of that city, but it is really only south of the Loire that the weather becomes significantly warmer. West coast weather, even in the south, is tempered by the proximity of the Atlantic, subject to violent storms and close thundery days even in summer. The centre and east, as you leave the coasts behind, have a more continental climate, with colder winters and hotter summers. The most reliable weather is along and behind the Mediterranean, where winter is short and summer long and hot.

The single most important factor to take into consideration in deciding **when to go** to France is tourism itself. As most French people take their holidays in their own country – and what better advertisement for its charms could there be than that? – it's as well to avoid the **main French holiday periods**. In summer this means mid-July to the end of August, with August being particularly bad. Almost the entire country closes down, except for the tourist industry itself. You can easily walk half a mile and more in Paris, for example, in search of an open *boulangerie*, and the city seems deserted by all except fellow tourists. Prices in the resorts rise to take full advantage and you can't find a room for love nor money, and not even a space in the campsites on the Côte d'Azur. The seaside is worst, but the mountains and such popular regions as the Dordogne are not far behind. Easter too is a bad time for Paris; half Europe's schoolchildren seem to descend on the city. For the same reasons, ski buffs should keep in mind the February school ski break. And no one who values life, limb, and sanity should ever be caught on the roads the last weekend of July or August, and least of all on the weekend of 15th August.

Average temperatures

	Jan	Feb	Mar	Apr	May	Jun	Jul	Aug	Sep	Oct	Nov	Dec
Paris/Ile de France	7.5	7.1	10.2	15.7	16.6	23.4	25.1	25.6	20.9	16.5	11.7	7.8
Alsace	5.5	5.3	9.3	13.7	15.8	23.0	24.1	26.3	21.2	14.9	7.6	4.7
Aquitaine	10.0	9.4	12.2	19.5	18.0	23.7	27.2	25.7	24.2	19.7	15.4	11.0
Auvergne	8.0	6.4	10.1	15.9	17.1	24.2	27.0	24.5	23.3	17.0	11.0	8.3
Brittany	9.3	8.6	11.1	17.1	16.0	22.7	25.1	24.2	21.2	16.5	12.1	9.3
Burgundy	6.1	5.9	10.3	15.3	15.8	23.8	25.8	26.1	21.2	15.5	9.1	6.2
Champagne-Ardenne	6.2	5.6	8.9	13.8	15.1	22.5	23.8	24.9	19.3	15.0	9.6	6.2
Franche-Comté	5.4	4.8	9.8	14.6	15.5	23.0	25.0	26.5	21.8	15.2	9.6	5.8
Languedoc-Roussillon	12.4	11.5	12.5	17.6	20.1	26.5	28.4	28.1	26.1	21.1	15.8	13.5
Limousin	6.1	6.1	9.6	16.1	14.9	22.1	24.8	23.6	21.0	16.2	12.8	8.5
Lorraine	5.5	5.3	9.3	13.7	15.8	23.0	24.1	26.3	21.2	14.9	7.6	4.7
Midi-Pyrénées	10.0	9.0	12.3	18.3	19.1	26.4	27.6	27.2	25.0	19.3	15.5	9.8
Nord/Pas de Calais	6.6	5.6	8.3	13.7	14.9	21.5	22.7	24.0	19.3	15.3	8.3	6.9
Normandy	7.6	6.4	8.4	13.0	14.0	20.0	21.6	22.0	18.2	14.5	10.8	7.9
Picardy	6.6	5.6	8.3	13.7	14.9	21.5	22.7	24.0	19.3	15.3	8.3	6.9
Poitou-Charentes	10.0	8.7	11.7	18.2	16.4	22.4	25.3	24.6	22.0	18.4	14.0	9.8
Provence	12.2	11.9	14.2	18.5	20.8	26.6	28.1	28.4	25.2	22.1	16.8	14.1
Rhône Valley	7.4	6.7	10.8	15.8	17.3	25.6	27.6	27.6	23.5	16.5	10.4	7.8
Riviera/Côte d'Azur	12.2	11.9	14.2	18.5	20.8	26.6	28.1	28.4	25.2	22.2	16.8	14.1
Savoy/ Dauphiny Alps	3.1	3.7	7.9	13.8	15.7	22.4	26.8	25.7	22.7	15.9	10.7	6.3
Val de Loire	7.8	6.8	10.3	16.1	16.4	23.6	25.8	24.5	21.1	16.2	11.2	7.0
Western Loire	9.9	8.6	11.3	17.7	16.7	23.3	25.7	24.6	21.8	16.9	12.4	9.5

Average sea temperatures

	May	Jun	Jul	Aug	Sep	Oct
Channel						
Calais to Le Havre	10	13	16	17	16	14
Cherbourg to Brest	11	13	15	17	16	14
Atlantic						
Brest to Bordeaux	13	15	17	18	17	15
Bordeaux to St-Jean-de-Luz	14	15	18	19	19	17
Mediterranean						
Montpellier to Toulon	15	19	19	20	20	17
Ile du Levant to Menton	17	19	20	22	22	19

All temperatures are in **Centigrade**: to convert to **Fahrenheit** multiply by 9/5 and add 32. For a recorded **weather forcast** you can phone the Paris forecasting office at ☎45.55.91.09 (☎45.55.95.02 for specific inquiries).

PART ONE

THE BASICS

GETTING THERE

FLIGHTS

Deals on flights to France change all the time. To find the best you should shop around, ideally a month or so before you plan to leave. Students and anyone under 26 can take advantage of a range of special discount fares from London to France. The main destinations for flights from Britain are Paris, Bordeaux, Toulouse, Montpellier, Marseille, Nice and Lyon; the best deals are generally those to Paris. Promising sources for checking the possibilities include the classified travel sections in the quality Sunday newspapers and, if you're in London, *Time Out*.

The cheaper choices boil down to either a charter *(Orion, Air UK* and *British Island Airways* are among regular operators), a Superapex/Late Saver scheduled ticket (on *British Airways* or *Air France*), or, often cheapest, a flight with an airline that makes a stop in Paris en route to more distant destinations (typically *Malaysian Air, Pakistan International Airlines,* or *Kuwait Air*).

Charters are supposed to be sold only in conjunction with accommodation, and if you're after just a flight it's generally a matter of luck, scrounging for whatever seats remain – often at the last minute. The *Air Europe* **Paris** flights, however, are sold regularly as flight-only deals by *Nouvelles Frontières* (for address see box); their departures are from London (Gatwick)–Paris (Charles de Gaulle), daily; current prices start at about £65 return. In summer ***Nouvelles Frontières* operates daily charter flights from Gatwick to cities other than Paris**. The destinations are Clermont-Ferrand, Toulouse, Nice, Montpellier and Perpignan. Throughout the year their charter flights from Paris to Nice can be booked from the London office.

British Airways, Air France and *Dan Air* **Superapex tickets** must be reserved two weeks in advance and your stay must include one Saturday night. Your return date must be fixed when purchasing and no subsequent changes are allowed. *Air France* feature the widest **range of French destinations**, including Biarritz, Bordeaux, Clermont-Ferrand, Lille, Lyon, Marseille, Montpellier, Nántes, Nice, Strasbourg and Toulouse; *British Airways* flies to Bordeaux, Lyon, Marseille and Nice; *Dan Air* destinations include Montpellier, Perpignan, Toulouse and Lourdes/Tarbes. *Brit Air* have regular flights to Brest, Le Havre, Quimper and Rennes. *Air France* also offer a combined flight and *France Vacances Pass* (see 'By train' below); £131 for four days rail travel and £175 for nine days.

Bargains with **long-haul airlines** are harder to predict. Like charters, availability can be chancy but a good travel agent (*STA* – see below – are specialists) should usually find you something to Paris. The drawback is that there is generally only one weekly flight, on variable days, though there's no maximum stay and you're allowed to make changes if necessary.

If you want to do the journey to Paris in style, flights from **London City Airport** with either *Brymon* (☎01/476 5000) or *London City* (☎01/511 4200) Airways have the advantages of reliability and convenience: riverbuses from Charing Cross or London Bridge leave for the airport every hour, check-in time has been cut to a minimum and tickets can be collected at the check-in desks.

STUDENT/YOUTH FLIGHTS

STA (see box) offers flights to various cities for which anyone under 26 and all students under 32 are eligible. Current return prices are: Paris £65; Marseille £126; Nice £142; Toulouse £119; Lyon £107; Bordeaux £112 Perpignan £125. For Paris the cheapest deal is the three-times weekly student charter to Beauvais. The drawback is the distance of the airport from the city, although the

70km bus ride to Porte de la Villette is included in the ticket.

If your trip is going to be a short one *Le France Pass* may well be worth considering. It's a **student and youth pass** valid for unlimited travel on internal flights with Air Inter.

GENERAL DEALS OUTSIDE LONDON

As often as not, whether you live in Birmingham or Newcastle, Manchester or Aberdeen, you will find it pays to go to London and then fly on to France from there. Scheduled direct flights from British regional airports are very expensive. Charters do exist, though availability is a big problem and prices are unfavourable in relation to London flights: even with added coach/rail travel. What is worth considering, however, is a **package deal**, which often offers exceptional bargain travel - even if you go it alone on the actual holiday. See the box below for further details.

FROM IRELAND

If you want to fly directly to France from Dublin or Belfast you'll be limited to the major destinations. *Air France Holidays* (see box below) have package deals including flights from Dublin and Belfast, and *Budget Travel* organise Charter flights to Nice from IR£179. Alternatives via Britain are unlikely to be attractive considering the additional time factor and the cost of a flight from Ireland to Britain. For up-to-date details on the situation, try contacting *USIT*, specialists in student /youth travel.

FROM AUSTRALIA AND NEW ZEALAND

It's generally easier and cheaper to fly to Britain and then make your way to France. *Qantas* don't fly directly to France at all, only via Amsterdam, London and Frankfurt. *Nouvelles Frontières* in Paris can book seats on charter flights (☎42.73.05.68; 42.60.36.37), but do not have offices in Australasia.

The French international airline, *Union Transport Aeriens* (UTA) have weekly flights from Auckland (Mon.) and excursion flights from Sydney (Fri.) which cost the same as flights via London, but it's better to book through an agent like *STA Travel* if you qualify for student or youth discounts.

PACKAGES FROM REGIONAL BRITAIN

There's a lot to be said for taking an all-in, travel plus accommodation package to France, on regional charter flights or flights from London with inclusive fares in Britain. Many companies offer flights at highly competitive rates, with a range of hotels from as little as £8 per person. The following is a selection from a very wide range of companies. More complete lists are available from the French Government Tourist Office, 178 Piccadilly, London W1V OAL. (☎01/ 491 7622)

Air France Holidays, 69 Boston Manor Road, Brentford, Middlesex (☎01/568 6981) Flights from many regional destinations including Birmingham, Belfast, Bristol, Edinburgh and Southampton.

Allez France, 27 West St., Storrington, West Sussex RH20 4DZ (☎09066/5793) Flights from Aberdeen, Birmingham, Bristol and Glasgow, mainly for short breaks, with fly-drive deals and self-catering accommodation.

Paris Travel Service, Bridge House, Ware, Herts; (☎0920/463922) Very wide range of packages from £154 for flight and three nights basic accommodation. Good for regional flights (Aberdeen, Birmingham, East Midlands, Edinburgh, Glasgow, Leeds/Bradford, Manchester) they also offer ex-London deals for rail travel from anywhere in Britain.

Sunscene Holidays, 40 Market Place South, Leicester LE1 5HB (☎0533/620644), flights from Manchester and Gatwick, 14 nights in the South of France under canvas from £150.

Travelscene 22a Cheapside, Bradford,(☎0274 392911); and 94 Baker St., London W1 (☎01/ 935 1025). Again a good range of regional flights on offer, and very flexible packages.

AGENCIES AND AIRLINES

London

STA Travel, 86 Old Brompton Rd., London SW7 and 117 Euston Rd., London NW1; ☎01/937 9927
USIT, 52 Grosvenor Gardens, London SW1; ☎01/730 8111
Nouvelles Frontières, 1–2 Hanover St., London W1; ☎01/629 7772
Air Travel Advisory Bureau, 320 Regent St., London W1; ☎01/636 5000 . Not actually an agent, but an information clearinghouse that can tell you the current best buys for any route.

Ireland

Budget Travel 134 Lower Baggot St., Dublin 2 (☎0001/613 122)
USIT, 7 Anglesea St., Dublin 2 (☎0001/778117)
Aer Lingus, 59 Dawson St., Dublin (☎0001/795030)

Australia and New Zealand

STA Travel, 1a Lee St., Sydney 2000 (☎212 1255)
STA Travel, 220 Faraday St., Carlton, Victoria 3053 (☎03/347 6911)
STS NZ, Courtenay Chambers, 15 Courtenay Place, Wellington (☎850 561)
STS NZ, 10 O'Connel St., Auckland (☎399 191)
Try also contacting UTA direct:
UTA, 33 Bligh St., Kinderfley House, Sydney NSW 2000 (☎221 3911)
UTA, 57 Fort St., Auckland (☎649/31229, 33521)

BY TRAIN

On the shortest and most economical Channel crossings the choice is between **train and hovercraft** or **train and ferry,** the latter taking between 1½ and 3 hours longer. Fare options include special deals on Eurotrain (for anyone under 26) and senior citizen reductions for those over 65. If you plan to travel a great deal in France you might also consider the *InterRail* or *France Vacances Pass*..

The **hovercraft** crossing links Dover with Boulogne. Services are frequent (up to 27 a day in peak season) and tie in well with the trains. There are substantial reductions for those over 65 or under 11 and students and anyone under 26 can buy heavily discounted *BIJ* tickets from *Eurotrain** outlets (see address below) and most student travel agents.

By **train and ordinary ferry**, the shortest and cheapest crossings are at Dover/Folkestone to Calais/Boulogne; best deals are on the very conveniently scheduled (though slightly slower) night trains. *BIJ* tickets are discounted 35% of the full fare, and senior citizens and children also enjoy similar concessions. *Campus Travel* sell *Eurotrain Explorers*, on which you can travel to and from your destination via different routes (with optional stopovers).

The **InterRail pass**, available from *British Rail* or any sizeable travel agent, currently sells at £145. For this you get a month's unlimited travel on all European railways, plus half-price travel in Britain and on the Channel ferries. The only restriction, other than maximum age of 26, is that to be eligible you need to have been resident in Europe for at least six months. The **France Vacances Pass**, available from most major travel agents offers unlimited travel throughout France for any 4 days during a period of 15 days (£64) or any 9 during a period of a month (£108) It also entitles you to a 25% reduction on Hoverspeed channel crossings.

Note. For details on the **longer ferry routes**, see'The Ferries' overleaf.

---

*At the time of writing, *Transalpino*, *Eurotrain*'s perennial rivals, are in temporary liquidation.

Addresses of agencies for train travel in London
Eurotrain/London Student Travel, 52 Grosvenor Gardens SW1, ☎01/730 8111
Victoria Station *(European Rail Inquiries)* ☎01/834 2345

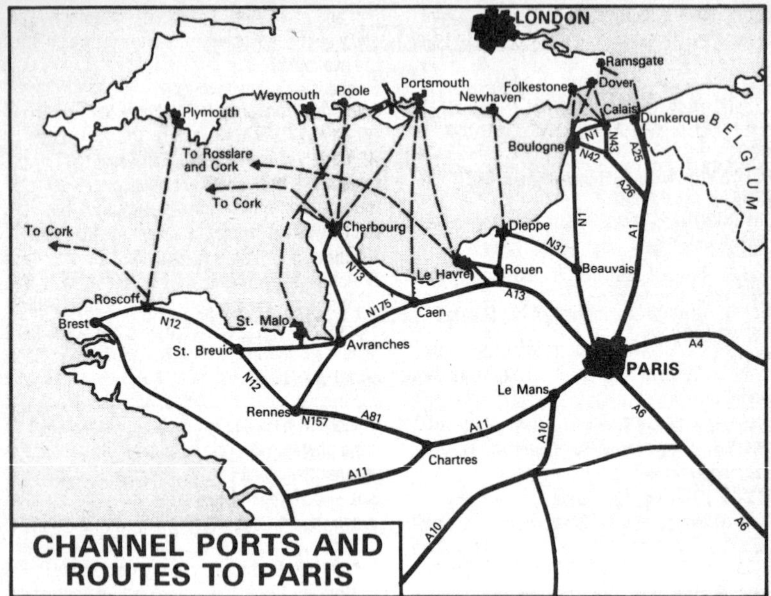

BY COACH

Again, for the shortest Channel crossing, there is the choice between bus and hovercraft and bus and ordinary ferry. Prices are very much lower than for trains, especially the hovercraft.

The coach for the **Hoverspeed City Sprint** service leaves from London's Victoria Coach Station, catching the hovercraft from Dover to Calais/Boulogne. Regular adult return £43 (student discount of £1). Tickets can be purchased through any local agent; for details call *Hoverspeed* at ☎01/554 7061.

Going via combination **bus/ordinary ferry**, the main companies are *Euroways,* (52 Grosvenor Gardens, Victoria, London SW1; ☎01/730 0202) and *Wayward Travel* (6 Westbourne Grove, London W2; ☎01/727 1898). Regular adult return fares in season are currently £43 for Paris, £47 for St.-Malo (via Portsmouth), £69 for Lyon, £70 for Orléans, £77 for Tours, £76 for Strasbourg, £90 for Perpignan and Montpellier, £93 for Bordeaux, £105 for Cannes and Nice. Student/youth tickets are often discounted.

BY CAR/HITCHING: THE FERRIES

The best cross-channel options for most travellers starting from London will be the **conventional ferry** or **hovercraft** links between Dover and Calais or Boulogne, Folkestone and Boulogne, or Ramsgate and Dunkerque. But if you intend to visit Normandy or Brittany then the ferries from the south coast ports – Newhaven to Dieppe, Portsmouth, Weymouth, or Poole to Le Havre, Caen, Cherbourg and St.-Malo and Plymouth to Roscoff – may be more convenient, and cheaper, depending on the time of year, the size of your car and the amount of petrol it consumes. The main ferry companies for Channel crossings are *Sealink, Sally Lines, Hoverspeed* and *Brittany Ferries.* While action on the part of the Seamens' Union over crew levels on *P&O Ferries* has now ended, the dispute has not been satisfactorily resolved and the union is still urging passengers to take their custom elsewhere. Current **ferry routes** from Britain are:

DOVER–CALAIS/BOULOGNE. 35–40 min., *Hoverspeed*, otherwise, *Sealink* ferries sail to Calais in 1 hr. 15 min., Boulogne in 1 hr. 40 min.

FOLKESTONE–BOULOGNE. 1 hr. 50 min., *Sealink*
RAMSGATE–DUNKERQUE. 2 hr. 30 min, *Sally Line*
NEWHAVEN–DIEPPE. 4 hr. on *Sealink.*
PORTSMOUTH–CHERBOURG. 4 hr. 45 min., *Sealink.*
PORTSMOUTH–CAEN. 5 hr. 45 min., *Brittany Ferries*
PORTSMOUTH–ST.-MALO. 9 hr., *Brittany Ferries.*
POOLE–CHERBOURG. 4 hr., *Brittany Ferries.*
WEYMOUTH–CHERBOURG. 3 hr. 55 min., *Sealink*
PLYMOUTH–ROSCOFF. 6 hr. , *Brittany Ferries*

Any competent travel agent in the UK or France should be able to provide you with up-to-date schedules and reserve space in advance (which at peak season is essential if you're driving). Or, contact the ferry companies directly (see box).

FERRIES FROM IRELAND

There are four Ireland–France ferry links: **Irish Continental Lines** from Cork to Cherbourg (20¾hr.); Cork to Le Havre (21½hr.) and Rosslare to Le Havre (17hrs). **Brittany Ferries** operate from Cork to Roscoff (13½–17hr.). While these are long crossings the routes to Le Havre and Cherbourg are again likely to prove more convenient and economical than going via Britain, especially out of season when ten-day excursion fares are available.

Frequencies are as follows:
CORK–LE HAVRE weekly
ROSSLARE–LE HAVRE daily
ROSSLARE–CHERBOURG two weekly
CORK–ROSCOFF weekly

HITCHING

Hitching from Calais or Boulogne towards Paris is notoriously difficult. If that's the route you want to take, the quicker – and only slightly more expensive – *Hoverspeed* crossings will give you a head start on the French side. If you can possibly afford one of the cheaper bus or train tickets, you'll save yourself a lot of trouble. If not, get friendly with drivers on the boat over and try to get a promise of a ride before docking. Dieppe is not that much easier to hitch out of. From Caen's port – Ouistreham – you can get a cheap local bus to the city if your thumb fails you. Hitching in Brittany is much more feasible and single passenger fares on *Brittany Ferries* are reasonable.

Coming back it may well be worth contacting the ride-share organisation *Allostop* or its equivalents which matches riders with drivers for a small fee (see 'Driving and Hitching' below).

CROSS-CHANNEL FERRY LINES

From Britain

Sealink (in Dover ☎0304/210 755; in Folkestone ☎0303/42954).
Hoverspeed (☎01/554 7061; in Dover ☎0304/214 514).

Brittany Ferries (in Portsmouth ☎0705/827701; in Plymouth ☎0752/221321).
Sally Lines (☎01/409 2240; in Ramsgate ☎0843/595 5222)

From Ireland

Irish Continental Lines 19–21, Aston Quay, Dublin 2; (☎774 331)

Brittany Ferries 42 Grand Parade, Cork; (☎215/277801)

RED TAPE AND VISAS

Citizens of EC countries do not need any visa to enter France, and can stay for up to 90 days. The British Visitor's Passport and the Excursion Pass, both obtainable over the counter at post offices, can be used as well as ordinary passports.

If you **stay longer than three months** you are officially supposed to apply for a *Carte de Séjour*, for which you'll have to show proof of income at least equal to the minimum wage. However EC passports are rarely stamped, so there is no evidence of how long you've been in the country.

If your passport is stamped, cross the border, to Belgium or Germany for example, and re-enter for another 90 days legitimately.

At present, following 'temporary' legislation in 1986, **all other passport holders** (including Australians, Canadians and Americans) must obtain a visa before arrival in France; this cannot be obtained at your destination. Obtaining a visa from your nearest French consulate is fairly automatic, but check their hours before turning up, and leave plenty of time, since there are often queues (particularly in London in the summer).

Three types of **visas** are currently issued: a transit visa, mostly intended for train passengers and valid for three days; a short-stay (*court séjour*) visa, valid for ninety days after date of issue, good for multiple entries; and the most popular multiple-stay *visa de circulation*, allowing multiple stays of ninety days over three years (maximum of 180 days in any one-year period).

FRENCH CONSULATES ABROAD

Australia. 303 Angas, Adelaide; 492 St Kilda Road, Melbourne; 10 Eagle, Brisbane.

Britain. French Consulate (Visas Section), 29/31 Wright's Lane, London W8 (☎01/937 1202). Also: 7/11 Randolph Crescent, Edinburgh (☎031 225 7954); 523/535 Cunard Building, Pier Head, Liverpool (☎051 236 8685).

Canada. Embassy: 42 Promenade Sussex, Ottawa, Ont. K1M 2C9, (☎613/512-1715). Consulates in Edmonton, Montréal, Québec, Toronto, and Vancouver.

Eire. 36 Ailesbury Road, Dublin 4 (☎694 777).

Netherlands. Vyzelgr. 2, Amsterdam.

New Zealand. corner Princes St/Eden Crescent, Auckland; c/o Teachers College, Christchurch; c/o University of Otago, Dunedin.

USA. Embassy: 4101/Reservoir Rd. NW, Washington, DC 20007, (☎202/944-6000). Consulates: 934 Fifth Ave., New York, NY 10021, (☎212/535-0100); 540 Bush St., San Francisco, CA 94108, (☎415/397-4893); also in Boston, Chicago, Detroit, Houston, Los Angeles, Miami and New Orleans.

COSTS, MONEY AND BANKS

Because of the relatively low cost of accommodation and eating out, at least by northern European standards, France is not an outrageously expensive place to visit. For a reasonably comfortable existence, including hotel room and restaurant or café stops, you need to allow about 250 to 300F (£1=10.44F at time of writing) a day per person. But by watching the pennies, staying at a hostel (between 35F and 75F for bed and breakfast) or camping (around 15F a head in the municipal sites) and being strong-willed about denying yourself cups of coffee and culture, you could manage on 150F, including a cheap restaurant meal – considerably less if you limit eating to street snacks or market food.

For two or more people **hotel accommodation** can be almost as cheap as the hostels, though a sensible average estimate for a double room would be around 120F. As for **food**, you can spend as much or as little as you like. There are large numbers of good **restaurants** with three- or four-course menus for between 45 and 75F. **Picnic fare**, obviously, is much less costly, especially when you buy in the markets and cheap supermarket chains. More sophisticated meals – **take-away** salads and ready-to-(re)heat dishes – can be put together for reasonable prices if you shop at *charcuteries* (delis) and the equivalent counters of many supermarkets.

Transport will inevitably be a large item of expenditure if you move around a lot, which makes the *InterRail* pass an attractive proposition for the restless. The standard tariff for trains is 50 centimes per kilometre (some sample one-way fares: Paris to Nice 530F, Paris to Bordeaux 286F). Buses are cheaper though prices vary enormously from one operator to another. Bikes cost about 45F per day to hire. Petrol is just under 5F a litre and most motorways have tolls. Rates vary but to give you an idea, Paris to Menton would cost you 370F just to use the *autoroute*.

Museums and monuments are likely to prove one of the biggest invisible wallet-eroders. If you're entitled to one, be sure to carry an *ISIC* (International Student Identity Card) – it will get you into most exhibitions at half-price. But, most importantly, budget-watchers need to be wary of **night life and café-lounging**.

Travellers' cheques are one of the safest ways of **carrying your money**. They're available from almost any major bank (whether you have an account there or not), usually for a service charge of one percent on the amount purchased. Some banks may take 1.25% or even 1.5%, and your own bank may offer cheques free of charge provided you meet certain conditions – ask first, as you may easily save £10 to £15. *Thomas Cook, Visa* and *American Express* are the most widely recognised brands. Alternatives for Europeans are Eurocheques, backed up with a card, which can be used for paying shop and restaurant bills in the same way as an ordinary cheque at home. **Credit cards** are widely accepted; just watch for the window stickers. *Visa/Barclaycard* – known as the *Carte Bleue* in France – is almost universally recognised; *Access, Mastercard* – sometimes called *Eurocard* – and *American Express* rank considerably lower. Also worth considering are post office **International Giro Cheques**, which work in a similar way to ordinary bank cheques except that you can cash them through post offices, more common and with longer opening hours than banks. Standard **banking hours** are 9am to noon and 2 to 4pm; closed Sunday and either Saturday or Monday. **Rates of exchange** and **commissions** vary from bank to bank; the *Banque National de Paris* usually offers the best rates and takes the least commission.

There are **money-exchange counters** at the railway stations of all big cities, and usually one or two in the town centre as well. However, it would be a sensible precaution to buy some French francs before leaving. The franc, abbreviated as F or sometimes FF, is divided into 100 centimes and comes in notes of 500, 100, 50, and 20F, and coins of 10, 5, 2, or 1F, and 50, 20, and 10 centimes.

HEALTH AND INSURANCE

Citizens of all EC countries are entitled to take advantage of each others' health services under the same terms as the residents of the country, if they have the correct documentation. So British citizens in France may expect to receive medical attention on the same terms as a French citizen, if they have with them form E111. In theory you should apply for this on Form SA30 by post, one month in advance to any DHSS office, but it's possible to get one over the counter.

Under the French Social Security system every hospital visit, doctor's consultation and prescribed medicine is charged (though in an emergency not upfront). Although all employed French people are entitled to a refund of 75–80 percent of their medical expenses, this can still leave a hefty shortfall, especially after a stay in hospital (accident victims have to pay even for the ambulance that takes them there).

As a complicated bureaucratic procedure is entailed in getting a refund, a better idea is to take out ordinary **travel insurance**, which generally allows one hundred percent reimbursement (minus the first £5 or so of every claim). Travel insurance also covers loss or theft of luggage, tickets, money etc., but remember that claims can only be dealt with if a report is made to the local police within 24 hours and a copy of the report sent with the claim. Insurance policies can be taken out on the spot at just about any British bank or travel agent. *ISIS*, originally designed for students but now available to all, is a particularly good one, obtainable at any of the student-youth companies detailed under Flights.

Non-EC members should make sure that they aren't already covered by existing policies before taking out **travel insurance**; Canadians, for example, are usually covered for medical expenses by their provincial health plans. North

American travel policies do not insure against theft, except in the case of items in possession of a responsible third party.

In serious **emergencies** you will always be admitted to the **local hospital** (*Centre Hospitalier*) whether under your own power or by ambulance, summoned by dialling ☎18. Another useful phone number is ☎17, the police/rescue service. To find a **doctor** stop at any *pharmacie* and ask for an address. Consultation fees for a visit should be between 75 and 85F and in any case you'll be given a *Feuille de Soins* (Statement of Treatment) for later documentation of insurance claims. Prescriptions should be taken to a *pharmacie* which is also equipped – and obliged – to give first aid (for a fee). For minor illnesses pharmacists will dispense free advice and a wide range of medication.

INFORMATION AND MAPS

The French Government Tourist Office gives away large quantities of maps and glossy brochures for every region of France including lists of hotels and campsites. Some of these, like the maps of the inland waterways, lists of festivals, etc. can be quite useful; others are just so much dead wood.

In France itself you'll find a *Syndicat d'Initiative*, **SI**, – or *Office du Tourisme*, as they are sometimes called – in practically every town and many villages (addresses are detailed in the guide). From these you can get specific local information, including listings of leisure activities, bike hire, launderettes and countless other things. And always ask for the free town plan. Many SI's publish local car and walking itineraries for their areas. In mountain regions they often share premises with the local hiking and climbing organisers. They are often also willing to give advice about the best places to go in addition to just handing out paper. The regional tourist offices are administrative overseers rather than purveyors of useful practical information.

PRINCIPAL FGTO OFFICES:

UK 178 Piccadilly, London, W1, (☎ 01/491 7622)

Ireland 35 Lower Abbey St., Dublin 1 (☎0001/ 30 07 77)

Australia BWP House, 12 Castlereigh St., Sydney NSW 2000 (☎612/213 5244)

Netherlands Prinsengr. 670, 1017 KX Amsterdam (☎20/24 75 34)

Norway Handelskammer 0152, Oslo 1, Dronningensgate, 8B (☎2 20 37 29)

Denmark CK 1459 Kobenhavn K, Frederiksberggad

Sweden S11146 Stockholm, Normalmstorg 1 Av. (☎8/10 53 32)

MAPS

In addition to the various free leaflets – and this guide – the one extra you'll probably want is a reasonable **road map**. The *Michelin* map no. 989 is the best for the whole country. A useful free map for car drivers, obtainable from filling stations and traffic information kiosks in France, is the *Bison Futé*, showing alternative back routes to the congested main roads.

For more **regional detail** the *Michelin* yellow series (scale 1:200,000) is best for the motorist. If you're planning to **walk or cycle**, check the *IGN* maps – their green (1:100,000 and 1:50,000) and purple (1:25,000) series. The *IGN* 1:100,000 is the smallest scale available with contours marked – essential for cyclists. The full IGN series is generally available (by mail or in person) from *Stanfords*, 12 Long Acre, London WC2; *McCarta*, 122 King's Cross Rd., London WC1; *Roger Lascelles*, 47 York Rd., Brentford, Middlesex; *Map Shop*, 15 High St., Upton-on-Severn, Worcs; and *Heffers*, Green St., Cambridge.

GETTING AROUND

With the most extensive railway network in western Europe, France is a country to travel by rail. The areas that are not well served are the mountains, both because of the ruggedness of the terrain and because there aren't many people, but often, where the train stops, an *SNCF* (the French rail company) bus continues the route. The private bus services are confusing and uncoordinated. Where possible, it is very much simpler to use the *SNCF*. Approximate journey times and frequencies can be found in the Travel Details at the end of each chapter and local peculiarities are also pointed out in the text of the guide.

TRAINS

SNCF **trains** are by and large clean, fast, and frequent and their staff both courteous and helpful. All but the smallest stations have an information desk and *consignes automatiques* – coin-operated lockers big enough to take a rucksack. Many (indicated in the text of the guide) hire out bicycles, sometimes of rather doubtful reliability. **Fares** are reasonable, at an average – off-peak – of about 50 centimes per kilometre. The ultra-fast *TGVs* (*Trains à Grande Vitesse*) require a supplement at peak times and compulsory reservation costing around 20F. The slowest trains are those marked *Autotrain* in the timetable, stopping at all stations. These are usually the only ones on which you can travel with a bike as free accompanied luggage – marked with a bicycle in the timetable. Otherwise you have to send your bike as registered luggage, which is quite safe and not expensive – around 35F. Though it may well arrive in less time, the *SNCF* won't guarantee delivery in under five days.

While *InterRail, EurRail and France Vacances* passes are valid on all trains, the *SNCF* itself offers a whole range of **discount fares** on *Période Bleue* (blue period) days – in effect, most of the year. A leaflet showing the blue, white (smaller discount) and red (peak) periods is given out at *gares SNCF* (railway stations). Under-26s can buy a *Carte Jeune* for 160F, allowing travel at half-fare on blue period days between June and September, including a free couchette on one journey. The *Carré Jeune* (same price) gives 50% (blue) and 20% (white) discounts on four journeys made during the year. Married couples can have a free *Carte Couple*, entitling one of them to a half-fare if they travel together off-peak. If you're over 65, there's a *Carte Vermeille*, for 199F, which gives you one year's half-price blue period travel. Families with several children can use a *Carte Kiwi* for which one child is the holder and pays full fare while the parents, brothers and sisters go half-fare. The card costs 350F and the rest of the family have to buy complimentary cards costing 50F each. And any passenger buying a return ticket for a total distance of over 1000km and willing to start *en periode bleue*, can have a 25% discount (*Billet Séjour*).

All tickets – but not passes – must be date-stamped in those orange machines that obstruct the entrance to station platforms. '*Compostez votre billet*', they say, in French only and it is an offence not to. Rail journeys may be broken any time, anywhere, but after a break of 24 hours you must 'compost' your ticket again when you resume your journey. On night trains an extra 80F or so will buy you a **couchette** – well worth it if you're making a long haul and don't want to waste a day recovering from a sleepless night.

Regional **rail maps** and complete **timetables** are on sale at tobacconist shops. Leaflet timetables for a particular line are available free at stations. *Autocar* at the top of a column means it's an *SNCF* bus service, on which rail tickets and passes are valid.

BUSES

With the exception of *SNCF* services, **buses** play a generally minor role. They can, however, be useful for cross-country journeys. The most frustrating thing about them is that they rarely serve the regions outside the *SNCF* network – which is

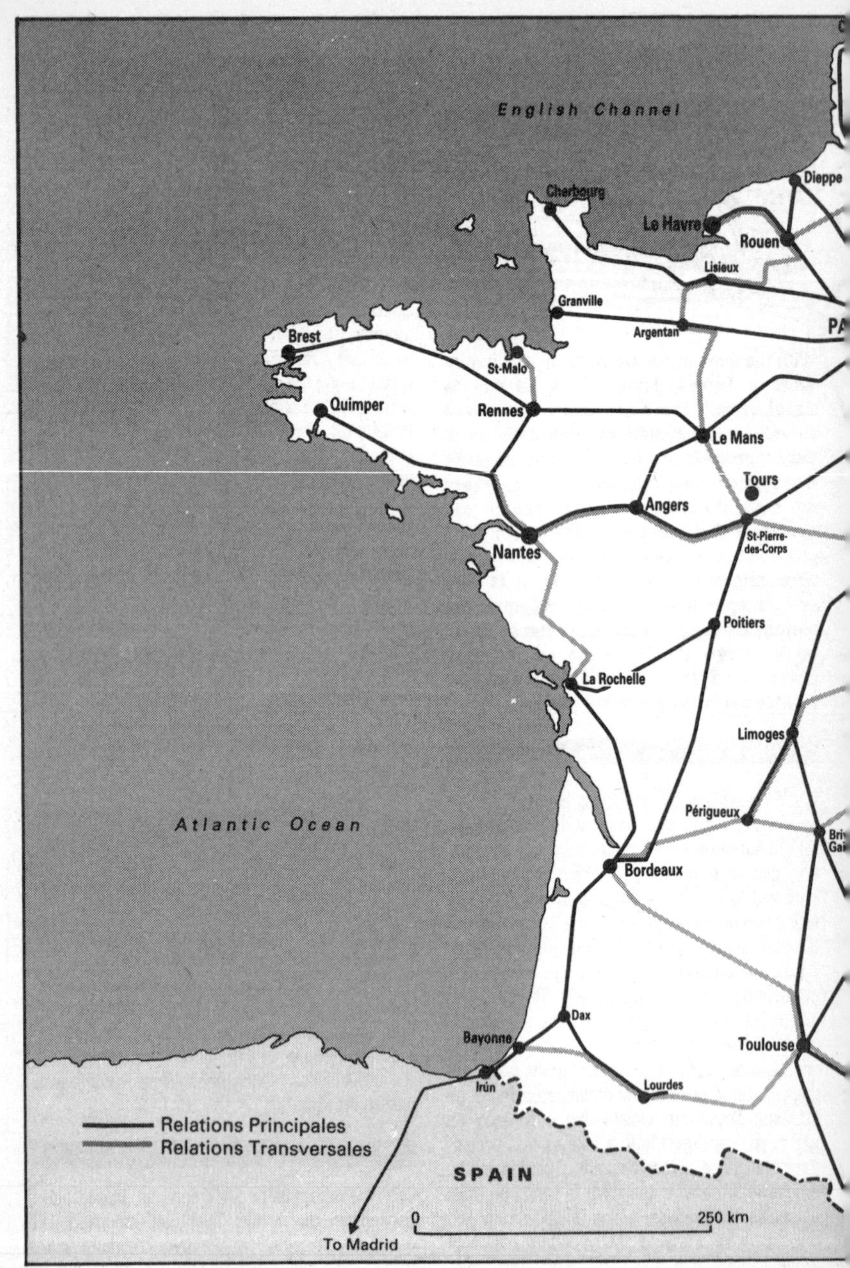

English Channel
Cherbourg
Le Havre
Dieppe
Rouen
Lisieux
Granville
Argentan
Brest
St-Malo
Quimper
Rennes
Le Mans
Tours
Angers
Nantes
St-Pierre-des-Corps
Poitiers
La Rochelle
Limoges
Atlantic Ocean
Périgueux
Bordeaux
Dax
Bayonne
Toulouse
Irún
Lourdes
Relations Principales
Relations Transversales
SPAIN
0
250 km
To Madrid

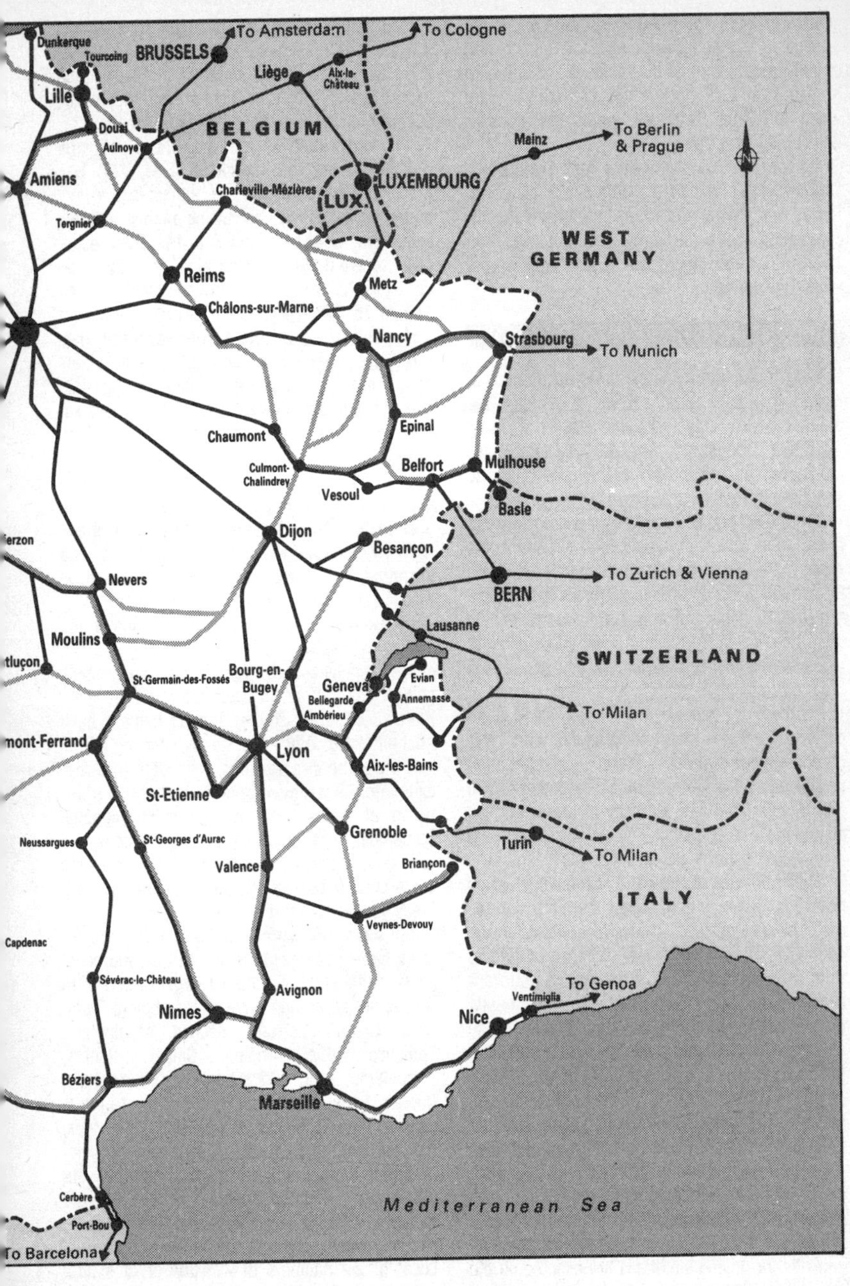
To Amsterdam
To Cologne
Dunkerque
Tourcoing
BRUSSELS
Liège
Aix-la-Château
Lille
Douai
Aulnoye
BELGIUM
Amiens
Charleville-Mézières
LUX
LUXEMBOURG
Mainz
To Berlin & Prague
Tergnier
WEST GERMANY
Reims
Metz
Châlons-sur-Marne
Nancy
Strasbourg
To Munich
Epinal
Chaumont
Culmont-Chalindrey
Belfort
Mulhouse
Vesoul
Basle
Dijon
Besançon
BERN
To Zurich & Vienna
Nevers
Lausanne
Moulins
SWITZERLAND
Bourg-en-Bugey
Geneva
Evian
St-Germain-des-Fossés
Bellegarde
Ambérieu
Annemasse
To Milan
Lyon
Aix-les-Bains
St-Etienne
Grenoble
Turin
To Milan
Neussargues
St-Georges d'Aurac
Valence
Briançon
ITALY
Veynes-Devouy
Capdenac
Sévérac-le-Château
Avignon
To Genoa
Ventimiglia
Nîmes
Nice
Béziers
Marseille
Cerbère
Mediterranean Sea
Port-Bou
To Barcelona

precisely where you need them. Where they do exist in rural areas, the timetable is constructed to suit school kids and market days – it will be a real stroke of luck if one is going where you want when you want. They are, predictably, cheaper and slower than trains.

Larger towns usually have a *gare routière* (bus station), often next to the gare *SNCF*. However, this is not always the case, for the private bus companies have difficulty coordinating their efforts. In some places not even the SI knows what they are up to.

DRIVING AND HITCHING

Taking a car gives you enormous advantages of access to remote areas. If you're camping the ability to carry equipment can make driving an attractive proposition, but you will only save money on car hire if there are several of you to share the otherwise prohibitive costs.

British, EC and U.S. drivers' licences are valid, though an *International Drivers Licence* could make life easier if you get a policeman unwilling to peruse a document in English. The vehicle registration document and the insurance papers must be carried. You should have your headlight dip adjusted to the right before you go – it's a legal requirement – and as a courtesy change or paint them to yellow or stick on black glare deflectors. All the major car manufacturers have garage/service stations in France – best get a list of addresses from the manufacturers before you go. If you have an accident or break-in, you should make a report to the local police (and keep a copy) in order to make an insurance claim.

The main **rule of the road** to remember when driving in France is that, unless there are signs to the contrary, you must always give way to traffic coming from your right, even when it is coming from a minor road. This is the law of *priorité à droite*. Except in town centres, there nearly always **are** 'signs to the contrary.' The main one is the yellow diamond roadsign, which tells drivers on main roads 'you have right of way'. More crucial, a yellow diamond crossed out means you do not have right of way. Signs saying *STOP* or *CEDEZ LE PASSAGE* also mean you must give way. Because it is one of the main causes of accidents, attempts are being made to phase it out – many traffic circles no longer operate *priorité à droite*. But in towns you must be vigilant about it.

Fines for driving violations are exacted on the spot and only cash or a French bank account cheque are accepted. The minimum for speeding is 1300F and for exceeding the drink/driving level 2500 to 5000F. Speed limits are: 130km/hr. on expressways; 110km/hr. on two lane highways; 90km/hr. on other roads; 60km/hr. in towns.

For information on road conditions call *Inter Service Route* on ☎1.48.58.33.33 (24 hr.). Motorway (*autoroute*) driving, though fast, is very boring when it's not hair-raising and the tolls are expensive. Use the Bison Futé free map, especially to avoid the endless traffic jams that build up over the weekends between July 15 and August 15. **Hitching**, you'll have to rely almost exclusively on car drivers. Lorries very rarely give lifts. And it won't be easy. Looking as clean, fresh, ordinary and respectable as possible makes a very big difference, as many a conversation with French drivers has made clear. Experience also suggests that hitching the less frequented D-roads paradoxically goes much quicker. In mountain areas a rucksack and hiking gear ensures an immediate lift from fellow aficionados. When leaving a city study the map to find a station on the road a few miles out and go there by train.

Autoroutes are a special case; hitching on the motorway itself is strictly illegal, but you can make excellent time going from one service station to another. If you get stuck at least there's food, drink, shelter. It again helps to have Michelin's *Guide des Autoroutes*, showing all the rest stops, service stations, tollbooths (*péages*), exits, etc. All you need apart from that is a smattering of French and not too much luggage. Remember to get out at the service station before your driver leaves the *autoroute*. The tollbooths are a second best (it's legal): ordinary approach roads can be disastrous.

For **safer hitching** – and sexual harassment is as bad in France as in the U.K. – you could contact *Allostop*, a national organisation with offices in seventeen towns (Strasbourg, Bordeaux, Clermont-Ferrand, Rennes, Montpellier, Toulouse, Lille, Angers, Chôlet, Nantes, Angoulême, La Rochelle, Aix-en-Provence, Cannes, Paris, Grenoble, Lyon). You pay to register with them (130F per year or 60F for long trips, 35F for short trips, plus 16 centimes per kilometre) and they find a driver who's going to your destination. *Allostop* seems like a desperate measure and lacks spontaneity, but it some circumstances may well be worth considering. Local phone numbers of *Allostop* or of similar organisations are given in the guide).

CYCLING AND WALKING

Keen **cyclists** are much admired in France. The more professional you look, the warmer your reception. Other traffic keeps at a respectful distance (save in the big cities). Restaurants and hotels go out of their way to find a safe place for your bike, even letting you take it up to your room. Most large towns have well-stocked retail and repair shops. Parts are not expensive, but if you're riding a British-made bike it's wise to carry spare tyres as French sizes are different – though most large towns will have a Raleigh stockist. It can also be difficult to find parts for low-gear machines, the French enthusiasm being directed towards racers instead.

The railways offer packages for cyclists, all of them covered by the free leaflet *Train et Vélo*, available from most stations. Basically you can take your bike free on *Autotrains*; on other services you have to pay 30F and hand your bike in well in advance (it won't necessarily travel on the same train as you, so make sure you find out when to expect it). If you're loading a bike straight on to the train at a ferry port, such as on the boat train at Dieppe, remember that you must first go to the ticket office of the station to register it – there is time. Don't just try to climb on the train with it, as both you and your bike will end up left behind.

Most *SNCF* stations also **hire** bikes. The quality is extremely variable – it can be terrific – and the cost is round 45F per day plus a deposit of about 200 to 300F or a credit card number. You can return the bike to any other station as long as you specify the place when hiring. The bikes are not insured however, and you will be presented with the bill for its replacement if it's stolen or damaged. Make sure your travel insurance policy covers you for this if you intend to hire a bike. You can also hire bikes from some SIs (tourist offices) and a fair number of bike shops (detailed in the guide). The private outlets may well be better than the *SNCF* and often no more expensive on the rental though deposits can be as high as 1000F for racing bikes.

Cross-Channel ferries take bikes free, as will *British Airways* and *Air France*. You may have to box them and you should contact the airlines first.

Particular regions for cycle touring are the valleys of the Loire, Dordogne and the Lot – not too hilly and with plenty of interesting stop-offs. The areas from Strasbourg and Alsace southwest to Dijon and Beaune, as well as Normandy and Brittany, are ideal too. If inclines don't bother you too much, Provence is one of the loveliest regions to explore by bike.

The best **maps** are the contoured *IGN* 1:100,000 series. The *Cycle Touring Club*, Cotterell House, 68 Meadrow, Godalming GU7 3HS will suggest routes and supply advice for a small charge. *Cycle Touring in France* by Rob Hunter, (F. Muller Ltd, £4.95) is a useful handbook. The Youth Hostels Asssociation also sell combined bike-hire and hostel packages; details from their main office at 14 Southampton St., London WC2 (☎01/836 8541).

Walkers are well served in France by a network of over 30,000km of long distance marked footpaths, known as *sentiers de grande randonnée* – **GR** for short. Some are real marathons, like the GR5 from the coast of Holland to Nice, the trans-Pyrenean GR10 and the *Grande Traversée des Alpes*. GR65 – the *Chemin de St-Jacques* – follows the ancient pilgrim route from Le Puy in the Auvergne to the Spanish border above St-Jean-Pied-de-Port and on to the shrine of Santiago de Compostela. GR3 traces the Loire from source to sea and there are many more.

Each path is described in a ***Topoguide***, which gives a detailed account of the route, including maps, campsites, refuge huts, sources of provisions, etc. In addition many tourist offices can provide guides to their local footpaths, especially in popular hiking areas, where they often share premises with professional mountain guides and hike leaders. The latter organise climbing and walking expeditions at all levels which are open to all. The principal French walkers' organisation, which produces the *Topoguides*, is the *Comité National des Sentiers de Grande Randonnée* (8 av Marceau, 75008 Paris; ☎1.47.23.62.32). The main climbing organisation is the *Club Alpin Français* (9 rue de la Boétie, 75008, Paris; ☎1.47.42.38.46).

Maps are listed under 'Information and Maps', but you might like to look at the specialised walking maps produced by *Didier et Richard* of Grenoble for the Alps. *Walking in France* by Rob Hunter (Oxford Illustrated) gives a general round-up of walking information for the whole country. Other titles worth looking out for include *Walks and Climbs in the Pyrenees* by Kev Reynolds; *The Tour of Mt. Blanc* by Andrew Harper; and *Walking the French Alps: GR5* by Martin Collins (all Cicerone Press). Details of particular walks are given in the text of the guide.

INTERNAL FLIGHTS

The main internal airline is *Air Inter*, though there are lots of small provincially based companies. If you want to jet-hop for a week, then *Le France-Pass* (see p.4 above) might be just the thing. Otherwise, trains are not only much cheaper, but often quicker and more convenient too.

INLAND WATERWAYS

With some 7500km of navigable rivers and canals, **boating** can be one the best and most relaxed ways of exploring France. There is no charge for use of the waterways, except on parts of the Moselle and you can travel without a permit for up to six months in a year. For information on maximum dimensions, documentation, regulations and so forth, ask at a FGTO for their booklet *Boating on the Waterways*. They will also have brochures on boating in particular regions and lists of French and British firms that rent out boats. Some are detailed in the guide; for a full list write to the *Syndicat National des Loueurs de Bateaux de Plaisance* (Port de la Bourdonnais, 75007 Paris; ☎1.45.55.10.49).

The principal areas for boating are Brittany, Burgundy, Picardy and Flanders, Alsace and Champagne. Brittany's canals join up with the Loire which is only navigable as far as Angers with no links eastwards. But the other waterways permit numerous permutations, including joining up via the Rhône and Saône with the Canal du Midi in Languedoc and then northwestwards to Bordeaux and the Atlantic. The eighteenth-century Canal de Bourgogne and 300-year-old Canal du Midi are fascinating examples of early canal engineering. The latter completely transformed the fortunes of coastal Languedoc, and in particular Sète, whose attractive harbour dates from that period. Together with its continuation, the Canal du Sète à Rhône, it passes within easy reach of several interesting areas.

The through-journey from Channel to Mediterranean requires some planning. The Canal de Bourgogne has an inordinate number of locks, while other waterways demand considerable skill and experience – the Rhône and Saône rivers, for example, have tricky currents. The most direct route is from Le Havre to just beyond Paris, then south either on Canal du Loing et de Briare or Canal du Nivernais to the Canal Latéral de la Loire, which you follow as far as Digoin in southern Burgundy, where it crosses the river Loire and meets the Canal du Centre. You follow the latter as far as Châlon, where you continue south on the Saône and Rhône until you reach the Mediterranean at Port St-Louis in the Camargue.

SKIING

Skiing - whether downhill, cross-country, or mountaineering – is enthusiastically pursued by the French. It can be an expensive sport to pursue on your own, however, and the best deals are often to be had from package operators. These you can arrange in France or before you leave, (most travel agents sell all-in packages). In France the umbrella organisation is the *Fédération Française de Ski* (34 rue Eugène-Flachat, 75017 Paris; ☎1.47.64.99.39).

The best skiing is generally to be had in the Alps. The higher the resort the longer the season and the fewer the anxieties you'll have about there being enough snow. These resorts are almost all modern, with the very latest in lift technology. They're terrific for full-time skiing, but they lack the cachet, charm or the nightlife of the older resorts such as Megève and Courchevel. The foothills of the Alps in Provence have the same mix of new and old on a smaller scale – the clientele is the Riviera residents and prices are not cheap though at least you can nip down to the coast for a quick swim when you're bored of snow. The Pyrenees are friendlier mountains, less developed – though that can be a drawback if you want to get in as many different runs as possible per day – and warmer, which means more problems with the snow.

Cross-country (*ski de fond*) is being promoted hard, especially in such smaller ranges as the Jura and Massif Central. At a basic level it's an easier sport for the less athletic and stiff-jointed. For the really experienced and fit, it can be a good means of transport, using snowbound GR routes to discover villages still relatively uncommercialised Alternatively, if you want to go for the real big time, the Plas y Brein Centre for Mountain Activities (Capel Curig, Betws-y-Coed, Gwynedd, Wales) organise summertime **ski-mountaineering** courses in the Alps, including doing parts of the High Level Route.

SLEEPING

For most of the year it's possible to turn up in any French town and find a room, or a place in a campsite. Booking a couple of nights in advance can, however, be reassuring; it saves the effort of trudging round and ensures that you know what you'll be paying. Phone numbers as well as addresses have been given in the guide and the language section at the back should help you make the call, though many hoteliers and campsite managers, and almost all youth hostel managers, will speak some English.

Problems arise mainly **between July 15 and August 15**, when the French take their own vacations en masse. The first weekend of August is the busiest time of all. Travelling during this period, hotel and hostel accommodation can be hard to come by – particularly in the coastal resorts – and you may find yourself falling back on local SIs for help and ideas. With campsites, you can be more relaxed, unless you're touring with a caravan or camper van. Big cities can be difficult throughout the year: we've given a greater range of possibilities for them in the guide and very detailed listings for Paris, the worst of them all.

HOTELS

Hotel recommendations are given in the text of the guide for almost every town or village mentioned. Mostly they are in the 80–130F price range (for a double room), though some a little more upmarket have been included when they seem particularly attractive or well priced. Full accommodation lists for each province are available from any French Government Tourist Office or from local SIs. Travelling in peak season, especially, it is worth getting hold of these, together with a handbook for the *Logis et Auberges de France*. The latter are independent hotels, promoted together for their consistently good food and reasonably priced rooms; they're recognisable on the spot by a green and yellow logo of a hearth.

All French hotels are **graded** from zero to three stars. The price more or less corresponds to the number of stars, though the system is a little haphazard, having more to do with ratios of bathrooms-per-guest than genuine quality; ungraded and single-star hotels are often very good. At the cheapest level, what makes a difference in cost is whether a room contains a shower: if it does, the bill will be round 25F more. Breakfast, too, can add 25F to 30F per person to a bill – though there is no obligation to take it and you will nearly always do better at a café. The cost of eating dinner in a hotel's restaurant can be a more important factor to bear in mind when picking a place to stay. Officially it is illegal for hotels to insist on you taking meals – but they often do and in busy resorts you may not find a room unless you agree. If you are unsure, ask to see the menu before signing in; cheap rooms aren't so cheap if you have to eat a 100F meal. Single rooms are only marginally cheaper than doubles so sharing always cuts cost considerably. Most hotels willingly provide rooms with extra beds, for three or more people, at good discounts.

In country areas, in addition to standard hotels, you will come across *chambres d'hôte*, bed-and-breakfast accommodation in someone's house or farm. These vary in standard but are rarely an especially cheap option – usually costing the equivalent of a two-star hotel. However, if you're lucky, they may be good sources of traditional home-cooking. Brown leaflets available in SIs list most of them.

HOSTELS, *FOYERS*, AND *GITES D'ETAPE*

At around 45F per night for a dormitory bed, *Auberges de Jeunesse* – youth hostels – are invaluable for single, budget travellers. For couples, however, and certainly for groups of three or more people (see above), they'll not necessarily be cheaper than hotels – particularly if you've had to pay a bus fare out to the edge of town to reach them. However, many hostels are beautifully sited, and they allow you to cut costs by preparing your own food in their kitchens, or eating in cheap canteens. Though you are meant to be a member of the YHA (main office in UK at 14 Southampton St., London WC2) you can often join on the spot. There are two rival French youth hostel associations: the *Fédération Unie des Auberges de Jeunesse* (6 rue Mesnil, 75116 Paris), which has its hostels detailed in the *International Handbook* and the *Ligue Française pour les Auberges de Jeunesse* (83 rue de Rennes, 75006 Paris). *IYHF* membership covers both organisations – and you'll find all their hostels detailed in the text.

A few large towns provide a more luxurious standard of hostel accommodation in **Foyers des Jeunes Travailleurs/euses**. These are residential hostels for young workers and students, in which for round 55F you can usually get an individual room. They normally have a good cafeteria/canteen.

A third hostel-type alternative exists in the countryside, especially in hiking or cycling areas, in the **gîtes d'étape.** These are less formal than the youth hostels, often run by the local village or municipality (whose mayor will probably be in charge of the key) and provide bunk beds and primitive kitchen and washing facilities. They are marked on the large-scale *IGN* walkers' maps and listed in the individual GR *Topoguides.* A selective list of *gîtes* and *chambres d'hôtes* is given in the booklet *Acceuil à la Campagne* which is sold by French Government tourist offices.

Mountain areas have **mountain refuge huts** on the main GR routes, open normally only in summer. They are extremely basic but invaluable if you get caught by a storm. Costs are round 40F for the night, less if you're a member of a climbing organisation affiliated to the *Club Alpin Français.*

RENTED ACCOMMODATION: *GITES DE FRANCE*

If you are planning to stay a week or more in any one place it might be worth considering **renting a house**. You can do this through the official French Government service, the *Gîtes de France,* which you can contact though the Tourist Offices. A small membership fee gets you a copy of their handbook which contains properties all over France, listed by *département.* The houses vary in size and comfort, but all are basically acceptable holiday homes. There is a photograph and description of each one and the computerised booking service means that you can instantly reserve one for any number of full weeks. The cost varies with the season from around 800F to 1600F per week.

CAMPING

Practically every village and town in the country has at least one campsite to cater to the thousands of French people who spend their holiday under canvas.

The cheapest – at round 10F to 15F per person per night – is usually the *Camping municipal,* run by the local municipality. In season or when they are officially open, they are always clean with plenty of hot water and often situated in prime locations. Out of season, many of them don't even bother to have someone round to collect the overnight charge.

On the coast especially, there are superior categories of campsite, where you'll pay similar amounts to a hotel room for the facilities – bars, restaurants, sometimes swimming pools. These have rather more permanent status than the *Camping municipal,* with people often spending a whole holiday in the one base. If you plan to do the same and particularly if you've a caravan or camper, or a substantial tent, it's wise to book ahead.

Inland, *Camping à la ferme* – on somebody's farm – is another (generally facility-less) possibility. Lists of sites are detailed in the Tourist Board's *Accueil à la Campagne* booklet. With these you should make sure of what you'll be charged before you pitch up – it's easy to get stung the following morning.

Lastly, a **word of caution**: never camp rough (*camping sauvage,* as the French call it) on anyone's land without first asking permission. If the dogs don't get you, the guns might – farmers have been known to shoot before asking any questions. In many parts of France *camping sauvage* on public land is not tolerated – Brittany is the notable exception. With beaches it's best to camp out where there are other people doing so.

FOOD AND DRINK

French food is as good a reason for a visit to France as any other. Cooking has art status, the top chefs are stars, and dining out is a national pastime, whether it's at the bistro on the corner or at a famed house of *haute cuisine*. Eating out doesn't have to cost much as long as you avoid tourist hotspots and treat the business of choosing a place as an interesting appetiser in itself.

BARS AND CAFES

Bars and cafés – there's no difference – commonly advertise *les snacks*, or *un casse-croûte* (a bite), with pictures of omelettes, fried eggs, hot dogs, or various sandwiches. And even when they don't, they'll usually make you a half or third of a *baguette* (French bread stick), buttered (*tartine*) or filled with cheese or meat.

TYPICAL FRENCH SNACKS

Un sandwich/ une baguette . . .	A sandwich	*Crêpe*	Pancake
jambon	with ham	*au sucre*	with sugar
fromage	with cheese	*au citron*	with lemon
saucisson	with sausage	*au miel*	with honey
à l'ail	with garlic	*à la confiture*	with jam
au poivre	with pepper	*aux oeufs*	with eggs
pâté (de campagne)	with pâté (country-style)	*à la crème de marrons*	with chestnut purée
croque-monsieur	Grilled cheese and ham sandwich	Other fillings/salads:	
croque-madame	Grilled cheese and bacon, sausage, chicken or an egg	*Anchois*	Anchovy
Oeufs	Eggs	*Andouillette*	Tripe sausage
au plat	Fried eggs	*Boudin*	Black pudding
à la coque	Boiled eggs	*Coeurs de palmiers*	Hearts of palm
durs	Hard-boiled eggs	*Epis de maïs*	Corn on the cob
brouillés	Scrambled eggs	*Fonds d'artichauts*	Artichoke hearts
Omelette . . .	Omelette . . .	*Hareng*	Herring
nature	plain	*Langue*	Tongue
aux fines herbes	with herbs	*Poulet*	Chicken
au fromage	with cheese	*Thon*	Tuna fish
Salade de . . .	Salad of . . .	And some terms:	
tomates	tomatoes	*Chauffé*	Heated
betteraves	beets	*Cuit*	Cooked
concombres	cucumber	*Cru*	Raw
carottes rapées	grated carrots	*Emballé*	Wrapped
		A emporter	Takeaway
		Fumé	Smoked
		Salé	Salted/spicy
		Sucré	Sweet

This, or a croissant, with hot chocolate or coffee, is generally the best way to eat breakfast – at a fraction of the cost charged by most hotels. Brasseries – which serve full meals (see below) – are also possibilities for cups of coffee, eggs, or whatever you like on their menu.

If you're standing at the counter, which is cheaper than sitting down, you may see a basket of croissants or some hard-boiled eggs (they're usually gone by 9:30 or 10am). Help yourself – the waiter will keep an eye on how many you've eaten and bill you accordingly.

Coffee is invariably espresso and very strong. *Un café* or *un express* is black; *un crème* is with milk; *un grand café* or *un grand crème* is a large cup. In the morning you could also ask for *un café au lait* – espresso in a large cup or bowl filled up with hot milk. *Un déca* is decaf, widely available.

Ordinary tea (*thé*) is Lipton's nine times out of ten; to have milk with it, ask for *un peu de lait frais* (some fresh milk).

After overeating, herb teas (*infusions* or *tisanes*), served in every café, can be soothing. The more common ones are *verveine* (verbena),

REGIONAL CUISINE

The geography of France explains much of the pride of place the country holds in European cuisines. The French can fish and breed seafood in the Channel waters, the Atlantic Ocean and the Mediterranean as well as catching freshwater fish in a thousand lakes and rivers. Mountains, forests, deltas and plains with climates ranging from the aridly sun-soaked to northern cold and wetness allow an extraordinary variety of produce. Added to this is the historical and social factor of a class of *paysans* – small-holders – who have passed down traditional methods from generation to generation. Though it is true that in recent years industrialisation has standardised and sanitised production methods, food imports have greatly increased, and pollution has taken its toll, there is still a strong connection between the countryside and the table, reflected in the different regional cuisines.

The gastronomic map of France features certain regions – Alsace, Provence, Brittany and the Pays Basques – in which the preservation of a distinctive cuisine owes much to historical separation. Burgundy, the Auvergne, Normandy and the Dordogne represent classic French cooking from different corners of the country. Lyon has a special position as the meeting place of North and South.

Below we list a small selection of typical dishes and produce from the main gastronomic regions.

Brittany

Oysters, lobster and other seafood; seafish; artichokes; white haricot beans; *crêpes* and *galettes*, wheat and buckwheat flour pancakes, with sweet or savoury fillings; *coquilles St-Jacques*; heavy buttery cakes such as *kouign-amann* and *far breton*, a prune and custard flan or batter.

Atlantic Coast

Seafood; ocean fish; eels; snails; *mouclade*, mussel soup with saffron; *chaudrée*, Atlantic fish stew; *mojette*, white beans; *pibales*, baby eels; *bouilliture*, eel stew with red wine and prunes.

Burgundy

Charolais beef; mustard; frogs' legs; snails in parsley and garlic; *coq au vin*; *boeuf bourguignon*; *jambon persillé*, ham and parsley in aspic; *pain d'épices*, spiced bread; *pochouse*, freshwater fish stew; red summer fruits; cheese.

Dordogne

Duck and goose in a myriad of forms including *pâté de foie gras*, preserves, *Cou farci du Quercy*, stuffed goose neck marinated in alcohol, and *Canard périgourdin*, duck with prunes; truffles; hazelnuts and walnuts; wild mushrooms; cheese.

tilleul (lime blossom), *menthe* (mint) and *camomile.*

Chocolat chaud – hot chocolate – unlike tea, lives up to the high standards of French food and drink and can be had in any café.

Every bar or café displays the full price list, usually without the 15% service charge added, for drinks at the bar (*au comptoir*), sitting down (*la salle*), or on the terrace (*la terrasse*) – all progressively more expensive. You pay when you leave and you can sit for hours over just one cup of coffee.

At midday you may find cafés offering a *plat du jour* (chef's daily special) between 25F and 50F or *formules*, i.e., a limited or no-choice menu. *Croque-Monsieurs* or *Madames* (variations on the grilled-cheese sandwich) are on sale at cafés, brasseries and many street stands, along with *frites, crêpes, galettes* (wholewheat pancakes), *gauffres* (waffles), *glaces* (ice creams) and all kinds of fresh sandwiches. For variety, there are Tunisian snacks like *brik à l'oeuf* (a fried pastry with an egg inside), *merguez* (spicy North African sausage), Greek *souvlaki* (kebabs), Middle

Alsace

Game; fruit brandies; cheesecake; braised pork knuckle; *choucroute*, sauerkraut with sausage, bacon and other meats; *baeckeoffe*, pork, beef and lamb stew with onions and potatoes; *tarte flambée* or *flammekueche*, cream, bacon and onion flan with pizza-like pastry; *madeleines*, lemon teacakes beloved of Marcel Proust; bilberry tart.

Normandy

Oysters, mussels and other seafood; cheese; cream; apples and pears; *pain brié*, saltless bread; tripe, in sausages or *à la mode de Caen* which means cooked with Calvados and cider or white wine; *sole Normande*, sole with mussels, shrimps and mushrooms; *poulet vallée d'Auge*, Pays d'Auge chicken in cream and cider; *agneau pré-salé*, lamb grazed on salt marshes; *douillon*, whole pear cooked in pastry.

Lyon

Sausages; smoked meats; tripe; chitterlings; cheese; *quenelles*; *poulet au vinaigre*, chicken in sour cream and vinegar; *salade Lyonnais*, green salad with croutons, bacon and runny egg; *tarte Lyonnais*, custard flan with kirsch and almonds.

Auvergne

Sausages; lentils; bilberries; morel mushrooms; salmon trout; cheese; rye bread; garlic soup; *aligot*, mashed potato, cheese curds and garlic; *potée auvergnate*, cabbage, pork and bean stew; *tourte au Cantal*, Cantal cheese tart.

Pays Basques

Bayonne ham; white tuna; sheep's milk cheese (*brebis*); pimentoes; corn bread; wild pigeon (*palombe*); *gâteau Basque*, black cherry cake; *agneau chilindron*, sautéd lamb with potatoes and garlic; *tourtière landaise*, apple and prune strudel.

Languedoc

Rocquefort cheese; anchovies; Bouzigues mussels; *cargolade*, grilled snails and sausages; *boule de Picoulat*, beef, pork, egg and garlic meatball; *crêpes languedociennes*, rum flambéed pancakes filled with vanilla cream.

Provence

Olive oil; garlic; basil; melons; early fruit and vegetables; citrus fruits; lavender honey; pasta; sea fish soups served with *rouille*, a red pepper and garlic mayonnaise; goats cheese; fish grilled in fennel or *herbes de Provence*; *aïoli*, salt cod with garlic mayonnaise; *mesclum*, a salad mix of several plants; *estocaficada*, stockfish and tomato stew; *gardiane*, bull meat stew from the Camargue.

Eastern *falafel* (deep-fried chickpea balls with salad) and Japanese titbits. Wine bars (see below) are good for French regional meats and cheeses, usually served with brown bread (*pain de campagne*).

For picnic and takeaway food, there's nothing to beat the charcuterie ready-made dishes – salads, meats and fully prepared main courses – also available at supermarket *charcuterie* counters. You buy by weight, or you can ask for *une tranche* (a slice), *une barquette* (a carton), or *une part* (a portion).

Alternatively, *salons de thé*, which open from mid-morning to late evening, serve brunches, salads, quiches, etc., as well as cake and ice cream and a wide selection of teas. They tend to be a good deal pricier than cafés or brasseries – you're paying for the chi-chi surroundings.

More serious business

There's no difference between restaurants (or *auberges* or *relais* as they sometimes call themselves) and brasseries in terms of quality or price range. The distinction is that brasseries, which resemble cafés, serve quicker meals at most hours of the day, while restaurants tend to stick to the traditional meal times of noon–2pm and 7–9.30 or 10.30pm. After 9pm or so, restaurants often serve only à la carte meals – invariably more expensive than eating the set *menu fixe*. For the more upmarket places it's wise to make reservations – easily done on the same day. In small towns in may be impossible to get anything other than a bar sandwich after 10pm; in major cities, town centre brasseries will serve until 11pm or midnight and one or two may stay open all night. When hunting, avoid places that are half empty at peak time and treat the business of sizing up different menus as an enjoyable appetizer in itself. Don't forget that hotel restaurants are open to non-residents – often very good value. On the road look out for the red and blue sign of the *Relais Routiers* – always reasonably priced and gastronomically sound.

Prices and what you get for them are posted outside. Normally there is a choice between one or more *menus fixes*, where the number of courses has already been determined. The choice is limited and the *carte* (menu) has everything listed. *Service compris* or *s.c.* means the service charge is included. *Service non compris, s.n.c.* or *servis en sus* means that it isn't and you need to calculate an additional 15%. Wine (*vin*) or a drink (*boisson*) may be included, though rarely on menus under 60F. When ordering wine, ask for *un quart* (¼), *un demi-litre* (½) or *une carafe* (a litre). You'll normally be given the house wine unless you specify otherwise; if you're worried about the cost ask for *vin ordinaire*.

In the French sequence of courses, any salad (sometimes vegetables, too) comes separate from the main dish, and cheese precedes a dessert. You will be offered coffee, which is always extra, to finish off the meal.

At the bottom of the price range, *menus fixes* revolve round standard dishes such as steak and chips (*steack frites*), chicken and chips (*poulet frites*), or various concoctions involving innards. Look for the *plat du jour* which may be a regional dish and more appealing.

Going *à la carte* offers much greater choice and, in the better restaurants, access to the chef's specialties. You pay for it, of course, though a simple and perfectly legitimate ploy is to have just one course instead of the expected three or four. You can share dishes or just have several starters – a useful strategy for vegetarians. There's no minimum charge.

The current gourmet trend in French cooking has abandoned rich, creamy sauces and bloating portions, concentrating instead on the intrinsic flavours of foods and on new combinations in which the mix of colours and textures complements the tastes. The courses are no more than a few mouthfuls, presented with oriental artistry and finely judged to leave you at the end well-fed but not weighed down. Known as *nouvelle cuisine*, this at its best can induce gastronomic ecstasy from an ungarnished leek or carrot. What it does to salmon, lobster, or a wild strawberry pastry elevates taste sensation to the power of sound and vision. But alas, since this magical method of cooking requires absolutely prime and fresh ingredients and precision skills in every department, *nouvelle cuisine* meals are usually horrendously expensive.

A LIST OF FOODS AND DISHES

These lists, though not comprehensive, should help you understand what you're ordering, both in French and ethnic restaurants. Most of the latter describe their dishes in French, and standard North African main courses of *couscous* (steamed cracked wheat with meat or vegetables) and *tagine* (spiced casserole) are part of French food language.

Soups *(Soupes)*

Bisque	Shellfish soup	*Pistou*	Parmesan, basil, and garlic paste sometimes added to soup
Bouillabaisse	Marseillais fish soup	*Potage*	Thick soup, usually vegetable
Bouillon	Broth or stock	*Rouille*	Red pepper, garlic, and saffron mayonnaise served with fish soup
Bourride	Thick fish soup	*Velouté*	Thick soup, usually fish or poultry
Consommé	Clear soup		

Starters *(Hors d'Oeuvres)*

Assiette anglaise	Plate of cold meats
Crudités	Raw vegetables with dressings
Hors d'oeuvres variés	Combination of the above plus smoked or marinated fish

Fish *(Poisson)*, Seafood *(Fruits de mer)* and Shellfish *(Crustacés* or *Coquillages)*

Aiglefin	Small haddock	*Homard*	Lobster
Anchois	Anchovies	*Huîtres*	Oysters
Anguilles	Eels	*Langouste*	Spiny lobster
Barbue	Brill	*Langoustines*	Dublin Bay Prawns
Bigourneau	Periwinkle	*Limande*	Lemon sole
Brème	Bream	*Lotte*	Burbot
Bulot	Whelk	*Lotte de mer*	Monkfish
Cabillaud	Fresh cod	*Loup de mer*	Sea bass
Calmar	Squid	*Louvine, loubine*	Similar to sea bass
Carrelet	Plaice	*Maquereau*	Mackerel
Claire	Type of oyster	*Merlan*	Whiting
Colin	Hake	*Morue*	Salt cod
Congre	Conger eel	*Moules (marinière)*	Mussels (with shallots in white wine sauce)
Coques	Cockles		
Coquilles St-Jacques	Scallops	*Oursin*	Sea urchin
Crabe	Crab	*Palourdes*	Clams
Crevettes grises	Shrimp	*Poulpe*	Octopus
Crevettes roses	Prawns	*Praires*	Small clams
Daurade	Sea bream	*Raie*	Skate
Ecrevisse	Freshwater crayfish	*Rascasse*	Scorpion fish
Eperlan	Smelt or whitebait	*Rouget*	Red mullet
Escargots	Snails	*Saumon*	Salmon
Flétan	Halibut	*Saint-Pierre*	John Dory
Friture	Assorted fried fish	*Sole*	Sole
Gambas	King prawns	*Telline*	Tiny clam
Grenouilles (cuisses de)	Frogs (legs)	*Thon*	Tuna
		Truite	Trout
Hareng	Herring	*Turbot*	Turbot

Terms: (Fish)

Aïoli	Garlic mayonnaise served with salt cod and other fish	*Fumé*	Smoked
Béarnaise	Sauce made with egg yolks, white wine, shallots, and vinegar	*Fumet*	Fish stock
Beignets	Fritters	*Gigot de Mer*	Large fish baked whole
Colbert	Fried in egg and breadcrumbs	*Grillé*	Grilled
Darne	Fillet or steak	*Hollandaise*	Butter and vinegar sauce.
La douzaine	A dozen	*A la meunière*	In a butter, lemon and parsley sauce
Frit	Fried	*Mousse/mousseline*	Mousse
Friture	Deep fried small fish	*Pané*	Breaded
		Quenelles	Light dumplings
		Tourte	Tart or pie

Meat *(Viande)* and Poultry *(Volaille)*

Agneau	Lamb	*Grillade*	Grilled meat
Agneau de pré-salé	Lamb grazed on salt marshes	*Hâchis*	Chopped meat or hamburger
Andouille, andouillette	Tripe sausage	*Langue*	Tongue
Boeuf	Beef	*Lapin, lapereau*	Rabbit, young rabbit
Bifteck	Steak	*Lard, lardons*	Bacon, diced bacon
Boudin blanc	Sausage of white meats	*Lièvre*	Hare
Boudin Noir	Black pudding	*Marcassin*	Young wild boar
Caille	Quail	*Merguez*	Spicy, red sausage
Canard	Duck	*Mouton*	Mutton
Caneton	Duckling	*Oie*	Goose
Cervelle	Brains	*Os*	Bone
Châteaubriand	Porterhouse steak	*Porc, pieds de porc*	Pork, pig's trotters
Cheval	Horse meat	*Poulet*	Chicken
Chevreau	Kid goat	*Poulette*	Young chicken
Contrefilet	Sirloin roast	*Poussin*	Baby chicken
Coquelet	Cockerel	*Ris*	Sweetbreads
Dinde, dindon, dindonneau	Turkey of different ages and genders	*Rognons*	Kidneys
Entrecôte	Ribsteak	*Rognons blancs*	Testicles
Faux filet	Sirloin steak	*Sanglier*	Wild boar
Foie	Liver	*Steack*	Steak
Foie gras	Fattened liver of duck or goose	*Toro*	Bull meat
Fraises de veau	Veal testicles	*Tortue*	Turtle
Fricadelles	Meatballs	*Tournedos*	Thick slices of fillet
Gibier	Game	*Travers de porc*	Spare ribs
Gigot (d'agneau)	Leg of lamb	*Tripes*	Tripe
Gigot de . . .	Leg of another meat	*Veau*	Veal
Graisse	Fat	*Tête de veau*	Calf's head
		Museau de veau	Calf's muzzle
		Venaison	Venison

Meat and Poultry – Dishes and Terms

Boeuf bourguignon	Beef stew with burgundy, onions, and mushrooms
Canard à l'orange	Roast duck with an orange-and-wine sauce
Canard périgourdin	Roast duck with prunes, pâté de foie gras, and truffles
Cassoulet	A casserole of beans and meat
Choucroute	Pickled cabbage with peppercorns, sausages, bacon, and salami
Coq au vin	Chicken cooked until it falls off the bone with wine, onions, and mushrooms
Steak au poivre (vert/rouge)	Steak in a black (green/red) peppercorn sauce
Steak tartare	Raw chopped beef usually accompanied by a raw egg yolk
Terms:	
Blanquette, daube, estouffade, hochepôt, navarin and ragoût	All are types of stews
Aile	Wing
A l'Americaine	In a white wine, Cognac and tomato sauce
A l'Arlésienne	With tomatoes, onions, aubergines, potatoes and rice
Auvergnat	With cabbage, sausage and bacon
Blanc	Breast or white meat
Bordelaise	In a red wine, shallots and bone marrow sauce
A la boulangère	Baked with potatoes and onions
A la bourgeoise	With carrots, onions, celery, bacon and braised lettuce
A la broche	Spit-roasted
Carré	Best end of neck, chop or cutlet
A la châtelaine	With artichoke hearts and chestnut purée
Civit	Game stew

Confit	Meat preserve
Côte	Chop, cutlet or rib
Cou	Neck
Cuisse	Thigh or leg
Epaule	Shoulder
Médaillon	Round piece
Pavé	Thick slice
En croûte	In pastry
Farci	Stuffed
Au feu de bois	Cooked over wood fire
Au four	Baked
Galantine	Cold dish of meat in aspic
Garni	With vegetables
Gésier	Gizzard
Grillé	Grilled
A la Hongroise	With paprika and cream
Jarret	Knuckle
Magret de canard	Duck breast
Marmite	Casserole
Mijoté	Stewed
Museau	Muzzle
A la Périgordine	In a truffle and foie gras sauce
Rôti	Roast
Sauté	Lightly cooked in butter
For steaks:	
Bleu	Almost raw
Saignant	Rare
A point	Medium
Bien cuit	Well done
Très bien cuit	Very well cooked
Brochette	Kebab
Garnishes and sauces:	
Beurre blanc	A sauce of white wine and shallots, thickened with butter
Chasseur	White wine, mushrooms, and shallots
Diable	Strong mustard seasoning
Forestière	With bacon and mushroom
Fricassée	Rich, creamy sauce
Mornay	Cheese sauce
Piquante	Gherkins or capers, vinegar, and shallots
Provençale	Tomatoes, garlic, olive oil, and herbs
Véronique	Grapes, wine, and cream

Vegetables *(légumes)*, herbs *(herbes)*, and side dishes spices *(epices)*, etc.

Ail	Garlic
Algue	Seaweed
Aneth	Dill
Anis	Aniseed
Artichaut	Artichoke
Asperges	Asparagus
Avocat	Avocado
Basilic	Basil (almost always fresh)
Betterave	Beetroot
Cannelle	Cinnamon
Carotte	Carrot
Céleri	Celery
Champignons	Mushrooms; types include: *de bois, de Paris, cèpes, chanterelles, girolles, grisets, mousserons*
Chicorée frisée	Curly chicory
Chou (rouge)	(Red) cabbage
Choufleur	Cauliflower
Ciboulettes	Chives
Citrouille	Pumpkin
Coeur de palmier	Palm tree shoots
Concombre	Cucumber
Cornichon	Gherkin
Courge	Squash
Cresson	Watercress
Echalotes	Shallots
Endive	Chicory
Epinards	Spinach
Epis de maïs	Corn on the cob
Estragon	Tarragon
Fenouil	Fennel
Fèves	Broad beans
Flageolet	White beans
Fleur de courgette	Cougette flower
Genièvre	Juniper
Gingembre	Ginger
Girofle	Clove
Haricots	Beans
Verts	String (French)
Rouges	Kidney
Blancs	White
Beurres	Butter
Laitue	Lettuce
Laurier	Bay leaf
Lentilles	Lentils
Maïs	Corn
Marjolaine	Marjoram
Menthe	Mint
Moutarde	Mustard
Navet	Turnip
Nouilles	Noodles
Oignon	Onion
Oseille	Sorrel
Panais	Parsnip
Pâte	Pasta or pastry
Persil	Parsley
Petits pois	Peas
Piment	Pimento
Pois chiche	Chick peas
Pois mange-tout	Snow peas
Pignons	Pine nuts
Pissenlits	Dandelion leaves
Pistou	Ground basil, olive oil and garlic
Poireau	Leek
Poivron (vert, rouge)	Sweet pepper (green, red)
Pommes (de terre)	Potatoes
Radis	Radishes
Raifort	Horseradish
Riz	Rice
Romarin	Rosemary
Safran	Saffron
Salade verte	Green salad
Sarrasin	Buckwheat
Seigle	Rye
Serpolet	Wild thyme
Tomates	Tomatoes
Truffes	Truffles

Some Dishes

Gratin dauphinois	Potatoes baked in cream and garlic
Pommes château, fondantes	Quartered potatoes sautéed in butter
Pommes lyonnaise	Fried onions and potatoes
Ratatouille	Mixture of aubergine, courgette, tomatoes, and garlic
Rémoulade	A mustard mayonnaise
Salade niçoise	Salad of tomatoes, radishes, cucumber, hard-boiled eggs, anchovies, onion, artichokes, green peppers, beans, basil, and garlic (rarely as comprehensive, even in Nice)

Further Vegetable-Connected Terms and Expressions in Common Usage

A l'anglaise	Boiled	*Parmentier*	With potatoes
Beignet	Fritter	*Primeurs*	Early vegetables
Farci	Stuffed	*Raclette*	Toasted cheese served with potatoes, gherkins and onions
Gratiné	Browned on top with cheese or butter		
A la Grecque	Cooked in oil and lemon	*Sauté*	Lightly fried in butter
Jardinière	With a mixture of diced vegetables	*A la vapeur*	Steamed
A la parisienne	Sautéed in butter (potatoes); with white wine, sauce, and shallots	*Je suis végétarien (ne). Il y a quelques plats sans viande?*	I'm a vegetarian. Are there any non-meat dishes?

Fruits *(Fruits)* and nuts *(Noix)*

Abricot	Apricot	*Mirabelles*	Greengages (type of plum)
Acajou	Cashew nut		
Amandes	Almonds	*Myrtilles*	Bilberries
Ananas	Pineapple	*Noisette*	Hazelnut
Banane	Banana	*Noix*	Nuts
Brugnon, nectarine	Nectarine	*Orange*	Orange
Cacahouète	Peanut	*Pamplemousse*	Grapefruit
Cantaloup	Cantaloupe	*Pastèque*	Watermelon
Cassis	Blackcurrants	*Pêche (blanche)*	(White) peach
Cérises	Cherries	*Pistache*	Pistachio
Citron	Lemon	*Poire*	Pear
Citron vert	Lime	*Pomme*	Apple
Citrouille	Pumpkin	*Prune*	Plum
Coing	Quince	*Pruneau*	Prune
Dattes	Dates	*Raisins*	Grapes
Figues	Figs	*Rhubarbe*	Rhubarb
Fraises	Strawberries		
Fraises de bois	Wild strawberries	**Terms**:	
Framboises	Raspberries	*Beignets*	Fritter
Fruit de la passion	Passion fruit	*Compôte de . . .*	Stewed . . .
Grenade	Pomegranate	*Corbeille de fruits*	Fruit basket
Groseilles	Redcurrants and gooseberries	*Coulis*	Sauce
		En feuilletage	In puff pastry
Mangue	Mango	*Flambé*	Set aflame in alcohol
Marrons	Chestnuts		
Melon	Melon	*Frappé*	Iced

Desserts *(Desserts* or *Entremets)* and Pastries *(Pâtisserie)*

Bombe	An ice cream dessert made in a round or conical mould	*Clafoutis*	Fruit tart, usually with berries
Bonbons	Sweets	*Crème Chantilly*	Vanilla-flavoured and sweetened whipped cream
Brioche	Sweet, high yeast breakfast roll		
Charlotte	Custard and fruit in lining of almond fingers	*Crème fraîche*	Sour cream

Desserts (Continued)

Crème pâtissière	Thick pastry-filling made with eggs	*Religieuse*	Coffee or chocolate-coated choux pastry puffs, supposedly in the shape of a nun
Crêpes suzettes	Thin pancakes with orange juice and liqueur	*Yaourt, yogourt*	Yoghurt
Fromage blanc	Cream cheese, more like strained yoghurt		and many, many more . . .
Glace	Ice cream		
Ile flottante/ oeufs à la neige	Soft meringues floating on custard	**Terms:**	
Macarons	Macaroons, not necessarily almond	*Barquette*	Small boat-shaped flan
Madeleine	Small, shell-shaped sponge cake	*Bavarois*	Refers to the mould, could be a mousse or custard
Marrons Mont Blanc	Chestnut purée and cream on a rum-soaked sponge cake	*Biscuit*	A kind of cake
Palmiers	Caramelised puff pastries	*Chausson*	Pastry turnover
Parfait	Frozen mousse, sometimes ice cream	*Coupe*	A serving of ice cream
Paris-Brest	Pastry cakes filled with crème pâtissière	*Crêpes*	Pancakes
Petit Suisse	A smooth mixture of cream and curds	*Galettes*	Biscuits or pancakes
Petits fours	Bite-sized cakes or pastries	*Gênoise*	Rich sponge cake
Poires Belle Hélène	Pears and ice cream in chocolate sauce	*Quatre quarts*	Pound cake
		Sablé	Shortbread biscuit
		Savarin	A filled, ring-shaped baba (cake)
		Tarte	Tart
		Tartelette	Small tart
		Truffes	Truffles, the chocolate or liqueur variety

Cheese *(Fromage)*

There are over 400 types of French cheese, most of them named after their place of origin. *Chèvre* is goat's cheese. Le *plateau de fromages* is the cheeseboard, and bread, but not butter, is served with it.
Some useful phrases: *une petite tranche de celui-ci* (a small piece of this one); *je peux le gouter?* (may I taste it?)

Basics

Pain	Bread	*Vinaigre*	Vinegar
Beurre	Butter	*Bouteille*	Bottle
Oeufs	Eggs	*Verre*	Glass
Lait	Milk	*Fourchette*	Fork
Huile	Oil	*Couteau*	Knife
Poivre	Pepper	*Cuillère*	Spoon
Sel	Salt	*Table*	Table
Sucre	Sugar	*L'addition*	Bill

And one final note: always call the waiter or waitress *Monsieur* or *Madame* (*Mademoiselle* if a young woman), never *garçon*, no matter what you've been taught in school.

DRINKING

Where you can eat you can invariably drink and vice versa. **Drinking** is done at a leisurely pace whether it's a prelude to food (*apéritif*), a sequel (*digestif*), or the accompaniment, and **cafés** are the standard places to do it.

Wine – *vin* – is drunk at just about every meal or social occasion. Red is *rouge*, white *blanc*, or there's *rosé*. *Vin de table* or *vin ordinaire* – table wine – is generally drinkable and always cheap. In wine-producing areas the **local table wine** can be very good indeed.

A.C. (*Appellation d'Origine Contrôlée*) wines are another matter. They can be an excellent value at the lower end of the price scale, where favourable French taxes keep prices down to £1 or so a bottle, but move much above it and you're soon paying serious prices for serious bottles.

Restaurant markups of *A.C.* wines can be outrageous. **Popular *A.C.* wines** found on most restaurant lists include *Côtes du Rhône* (from the Rhône valley), *St-Emilion* and *Médoc* (from Bordeaux), *Beaujolais* and very upmarket Burgundy.

The **basic terms** are *brut*, very dry; *sec*, dry; *demi-sec*, sweet; *doux*, very sweet; *mousseux*, sparkling; *méthode champenoise*, mature and sparkling. There are grape varieties as well but the complexities of the subject take up volumes.

A **glass of wine** is simply *un rouge* or *un blanc*. If it is an *A.C.* wine you may have the choice of *un ballon* (round glass) or a smaller glass (*un verre*). *Un pichet* (a pitcher) is normally a ¼ litre. If you buy at the vineyards, however (for which you'll find details in the guide), you can sample the wines first and pay very low prices for excellent stuff. It's best to make clear at the start how much you want to buy (if it's only one or two bottles) and you will not be popular if you drink several glasses offered by the *vigneron* (wine grower) and then leave without making a purchase. The most economical option is to buy *en vrac*, either at the vineyard or in some wine shops: taking an easily obtainable plastic five- or ten- litre container and getting it filled straight from the barrel. Outside the wine regions, supermarkets are the best places to buy your wine.

The familiar Belgian and German brands account for most of the **beer** you'll find, plus brands home-grown from Alsace. Draft (*à la pression*, usually *Kronenbourg*) is the cheapest drink you can have next to coffee and wine – ask for *un demi* (1/3 litre). For a wider choice of draughts and bottles you need to go to the special beer-drinking establishments, or English-style pubs found in many major cities, and in abundance in Paris.

Cocktails are served at most late-night bars, discos and music places, as well as at upmarket hotel bars.

Stronger alcohol is drunk from 5am as a pre-work fortifier, right through the day, though the national reputation for drunkenness has lost some of its truth. **Cognac** or **Armagnac** brandies and the dozens of *eaux de vie* (brandy distilled from fruit) and **liqueurs** are made with the same perfectionism as in the cultivation of vines. Among less familiar names, try *Poire William* (pear brandy), *marc* (a spiritdistilled from grape pulp), or just point to the bottle with the most attractive colour. Measures are generous, but they don't come cheap: the same applies for imported spirits like whisky, always called *Scotch*. *Pastis*, aniseed drinks such as *Pernod* or *Ricard*, are served diluted with water and ice (*glaçons*) – very refreshing and not expensive. Two drinks designed to stimulate the appetite are *Pineau*, cognac and grape juice and *Kir*, white wine with a dash of blackcurrant syrup – or champagne for a *Kir Royal*.

On the **soft drink** front, bottled fruit juices include apricot (*jus d'abricot*), blackcurrant (*cassis*) and so on. You can also get fresh orange and lemon juice (*orange/citron pressé*). Otherwise there's the standard canned lemonade, Coke (*coca*) and so forth. Bottles of **spring water** (*eau minérale*) – either sparkling (*pétillante*) or still (*eau plate*) – abound, from the best-seller *Perrier* to the obscurest spa product. But there's not much wrong with the tap water (*l'eau du robinet*).

COMMUNICATIONS – POST, PHONES AND MEDIA

The French term for a post office is either ***PTT*** or ***Bureau de Poste.*** You can have letters sent to any post office; they should be addressed (preferably with the surname underlined and in capitals) **Poste Restante**, followed by the name of the town. Post offices are generally open 8–noon and 2.30–7pm, Monday to Saturday morning. To collect your mail you need a passport or other convincing ID and there may be a small charge. You should ask for all your names to be checked, as filing systems are not brilliant. For sending letters remember that you can buy **stamps** (*timbres*) with less queuing from *Tabacs*.

You can make international phone calls from any box (or ***cabine***) and can receive calls where there's a blue logo of a ringing bell. A 50F **phone card**, obtainable from post offices and *PTT* boutiques can be convenient if you're likely to make a lot of calls. Otherwise put the money (½F, 1F, 5F, 10F pieces) in first, dial ☎19, wait for a tone, and then dial the country code (44 for Britain) and the number minus its initial 0. For calls within France – local or long distance – dial all 8 digits of the number (which includes the former area code – displayed in every *cabine*). The exceptions are that to call from Paris to anywhere else in France, you must first dial ☎16, or to call a Paris number from anywhere else, first dial ☎16–1. To save fiddling around with coins or phone cards, post offices often have metered booths from which you can make calls connected by a clerk; you pay afterwards.

British newspapers, and the ***International Herald Tribune,*** are on sale in most large cities and resorts. Of the **French daily papers** *Le Monde* is the most intellectual and respected, with no concessions to entertainment (such as pictures) but a correctly styled French that is probably the easiest to understand. *Libération* is moderately left-wing, independent and more colloquial with good, if choosy, coverage, while the best criticism of the French government from the left comes from *L'Humanité*, the Communist party paper. All the other nationals are firmly on the right. So too are the majority of the regional newspapers, which enjoy much higher circulation than the Paris nationals. The most important of these is the Rennes based *Ouest France* – though for travellers this, like the rest of the regionals, is mainly of interest for its listings. Weeklies of the *Newsweek/Time* model include the wide-ranging and socialist inclined *Le Nouvel Observateur* and its counterpoint *L'Express*, property of James Goldsmith, who sacked the editor for an anti-Giscard article before the 1982 presidential election. The best investigative journalism is in the weekly satirical paper *Le Canard Enchainé*, unfortunately unintelligible to non-native speakers. And the foulest rag of the lot is *Minute*, the *Front National*'s organ. 'Moral' censorship of the press is rare. As well as pornography of every shade you'll find on the newsstands covers featuring drugs, sex, blasphemy and bizarre forms of grossness alongside knitting patterns and DIY. French comics, which often indulge these interests, are wonderful. *Charlie-Hebdo* is one with political targets; and *A Suivre*, which wouldn't cause problems at British customs has amazing graphics.

French TV in contrast, is prudish and lacking in imagination. If you've got a radio, you can tune into English news on the BBC World Service on 463m or between 21m and 31m shortwave at intervals throughout the day and night.

BUSINESS HOURS AND HOLIDAYS

Almost everything in France – shops, museums, tourist offices, most banks – closes for a couple of hours at midday. There's some variation, and the lunchbreaks tend to be longer in the south, but the basic **working hours** are 8–noon and 2–6pm. Food shops often don't reopen till halfway through the afternoon, closing just before supper-time between 7.30 and 8pm. Sunday and Monday are the standard **closing days**, though you'll always find at least one *boulangerie* (baker's) open. The main thing to watch out for is getting picnic shopping done in time before the French shut their doors for lunch.

Museums open at round 10am and close between 5 and 6pm. Summer times may differ from winter times; if they do, both are indicated in the listings. Summer hours usually extend from mid-May or early June to mid-September, but sometimes they apply only during July and August, occasionally even from Palm Sunday to All Saints' Day. Don't forget closing days – usually Tuesday or Monday, sometimes both. Admission charges can be very off-putting, though most state-owned museums have one or two days of the week when they're free and you can get a big reduction at most places by showing a student card (or passport if you're under 18/over 60). Churches and cathedrals are almost always open all day, with charges only for the crypt, treasuries, or cloister and little fuss about how you're dressed. Where they are closed you may have to go during Mass to take a look, on Sunday morning or at other times which you'll see posted up on the door. In small towns and villages, however, getting the key is not difficult – ask anyone nearby or hunt out the priest, whose house is known as the *presbytère*.

One other factor can disrupt your plans. There are thirteen national holidays (*jours fériés*), when most shops and businesses, though not museums or restaurants, are closed. They are:

January 1
Easter Sunday
Easter Monday
Ascension Day (forty days after Easter)
Pentecost (seventh Sunday after Easter, plus the Monday)
May 1
May 8 (VE Day)
July 14 (Bastille Day)
August 15 (Assumption of the Virgin Mary)
November 1 (All Saints' Day)
Christmas Day

ENTERTAINMENTS

What follows is obviously a broad introduction. For specific outlets and listings, consult relevant sections of the text – and particularly Chapter 1 for all that's happening in Paris.

MUSIC

The best contemporary music you'll hear in France is likely to be distinctly un-French – salsa, calypso, reggae, Algerian Raï and African sounds from Zaire, Congo and Nigeria; every variety of Jazz and Celtic folk in Brittany.

Standard French rock deserves its miserable reputation. Prince is better known to French kids than any home-grown pin-up and what isn't American or British on the jukebox is crooning French schmaltz that makes Abba sound ultra-radical. With the possible exception of trashpop (see below), the Belgians have much better bands.

As far as mainstream culture is concerned, rock does not come under the heading of music, but rather on a blacklist that includes drugs, sex, riots and disorder. There's also the chauvinism that cannot bear to recognise an art so dominated by the English language. Up until now, any French rock'n'roller would sing in English – not just to make foreign gigs and recording contracts possible, but because French simply doesn't have the full throat vowels and consonant drive that rock requires, while English with a French accent is not much better.

Recently, however, French musicians have stopped their serious attempt to emulate the Americans and British, and something known as **Trashpop** has appeared. It's fun, funky, a bit punky, with splashes of be-bop, heavy metal and even Seventies as well as Eighties psychedelia, too. The videos are vital to the music, the clothes are over the top, and for all the mishmash of styles and influences, it's a genuinely French phenomenon. Names to look out for are **Les Rita Mitsouko**, with lead singer Catherine Ringer; **Niagra**, a duo of Muriel Moreno and Daniel Chevenz; and Etienne Daho, with four albums out to date.

Perplexing or infuriating, trashpop is at least fairly accessible, which is less likely to be the case with French **Rap**, though if hip-hop energy turns you on even without understanding the words, then follow the graffiti and listen in to DJ Dee-Nasty's weekly **Nova Radio Show**.

But the sounds dominating the popular music scene are still **Brazilian**. Everyone dances to salsa, and the divisions between Latin rhythms, jazz and African beats are progressively harmonised in mixed bands and mixed music outlets.

One variety of home-grown music that survives is the tradition of **popular songs** epitomised by Edith Piaf and George Brassens, although even here the Belgians have an equal contributor in Jacques Brel, the most famous post-war singer in the French language. Two of the best contemporary *chansonniers* are Alain Souchon and Serge Lama. Despite the emphasis on poetic lyrics, French folk songs can cross frontiers, as Françoise Hardy proved in the 1960s. But English audiences, permeated by rock, are likely to find most of this form unbearably vapid and wimpish.

Jazz is a different matter. in Paris most of all, where you could listen to a different band every night for weeks in the capital's clubs, from trad, through be-bop and free jazz, to highly contemporary experimental. And there are many excellent festivals, particularly in the south; Juan-les-Pins, Nîmes and Nice (all in July), Paris (Oct./Nov.), Nancy (every other year), and as part of general arts festivals in Billom (June/July) and Bordeaux (Nov.). If you hear of **Urban Sax** playing at any of these – or elsewhere – go along, if only for the drama of sixty-plus saxophonists performing together.

If your taste is for **classical music** and its descendants, you're also in for a treat. Pierre Boulez experiments with hi-tech sound beneath Beaubourg. Paris has now got a second opera house and in the provinces there are no less than twelve other companies (Strasbourg and Toulouse are said to be the best), and a further dozen orchestras. The places to check out for concerts are the *Maisons de la Culture* (in all the larger cities), churches (where chamber music is as much performed as sacred music, often for free), and festivals – of which there are hundreds, the most famous being at Aix in July.

FILM AND THEATRE

The French have treated **film** as an art form, deserving of state subsidy, ever since its origination with the Lumière brothers in 1895. The medium has only very recently been threatened by TV, the seat of judgement is still in Cannes, and Paris is the cinema capital of the world. True, the country's high street *Gaumonts* screen the annual Belmondo gangster movie and dubbed Sci-Fi trash from the States, but there are *ciné-clubs* in almost every city, censorship is very slight, students get discounts and foreign films are usually shown in their **original language** with subtitles (look for *version originale* or *v.o.* in the listings). Some British movie buffs actually go to Paris just for English-language films – classics and rarities are always playing.

The Cannes Film Festival where the prized *Palme d'Or* is handed out, is not, in any public sense, a festival. Those that are, where anyone can pay to see the films, happen at La Rochelle (*Rencontres Internationales d'Art Contemporain*, June–July), Sceaux (festival of women's films); La Ciotat (silent films; July); and Reims (thrillers, novels and films; Oct.–Nov.).

In **theatre**, directors not playwrights dominate. Scripts are there, if at all, to be shaken up or scrambled (Richard II in Japanese Noh style, for example). The earlier generation of Genet, Anouilh, Camus, joined by Beckett and Ionesco, hasn't really had successors. In the 1950s Roger Planchon set up a company in a suburb of Lyon, determined to play to working-class audiences and did so. It became the *Théâtre Nationale Populaire*, the number two state theatre after the *Comédie Française*, which does the classics with all due decorum. Another interesting group, *Théâtre de l'Action*, tours round the country staying in places before creating a show round local issues; while Ariane Mnouchkine organises militant improvisations with her workers' co-op in the *Cartoucherie* at Vincennes. Other big names come from novels and movies into drama (Marguerite Duras) or involve themselves with opera as well as theatre (Patrice Chéreau). Peter Brook now works almost exclusively in France and Jean-Louis Barrault (of *Baptiste* fame) and Madeleine Renaud (one of the great stage actresses) are still round producing theatrical events in huge, bizarre spaces.

In all this, theatrical moments rather than speech, and the theatrical light on the subject rather than realism, are tantamount. If you find one of these shows on, it might be quite an experience even with language difficulties. **Café-Théâtre**, though far from avant-garde, is probably less accessible: satire, chansons and dirty jokes are the standard ingredients. But you could look out for **mime**. Marcel Marceau still performs and new talent keeps appearing from the *Jacques Le Coq* school of mime in Paris. And finally, there are the classics and bourgeois favourites, staple fodder to keep municipal subsidies coming in.

For details of **Paris theatres** see Chapter one. In other cities the theatres are often part of the *Maisons de la Culture* or *Centres d'Animation Culturelle*; local SIs should have schedules. The two major theatre festivals are the *Festival Mondial du Théâtre* in Nancy (June) and the *Festival d'Avignon* (July–August).

FETES AND FOLK FESTIVALS

Catholicism is deeply ingrained in the culture of French rural areas, particularly in the West. As a result, religious feast days still bring people out in all their finery, ready to indulge once Mass has been said. These occasions, along with the celebrations around wine and food production, are usually pretty genuine affairs. Other festivals, based for example on historical events, folklore or literature, are often very obviously money and municipal prestige spinners – not something to go out of your way for.

One folk festival that is definitely worth attending is the **Inter-Celtic** event held at **Lorient** in Brittany every August. Another annual event with long historical roots is the great gypsy gathering at **Les-Saintes-Maries-de-la-Mer** in the Camargue. Though exploited for every last centime, and, in recent years, given a heavy police presence, it is a unique and exhilarating spectacle to be part of.

Bonfires are lit and fireworks set off for **Bastille Day** (July 14) and for the **Fête de St Jean** three days from the summer solstice on June 24. **May Day** is a public holiday and celebrated, by the left at least, with carnivals and parades. ***Mardi Gras*** – the last blow-out before Lent – is far less of an occasion than in other Catholic countries. But the towns on the Côte d'Azur put on a show, at great expense and in questionable taste.

More than any of these traditional jamborees, it is sporting events that really excite the populace. First and foremost, the ***Tour de France*** cycling race in July, closely followed by football matches and the Open tennis championship, held in early June at Roland Garros in Paris. ***Boules*** championships are major events throughout the country and particularly in the south. Crowds gather in the Basque country for the national ball game of ***pelota***, and in the Camargue for the bloodless Provençal style of bull-fighting.

TROUBLE AND THE POLICE

Petty theft is endemic along the Côte d'Azur and pretty bad in the crowded hangouts of most big cities. Take normal precautions: keep your wallet in your front pocket and your handbag under your elbow, and you won't have much to worry about. If you should get attacked, hand over the money and start dialling the cancellation numbers for your travellers' cheques and credit cards.

Drivers face greater problems, most notoriously break-ins. Vehicles are rarely stolen, but tape decks as well as luggage left in cars make tempting targets and foreign number plates are easy to spot. Good insurance is the only answer, but even so try not to leave any valuables in plain sight. If you have an accident while driving, you have officially to fill in and sign a *constat à* *l'aimable* (jointly agreed statement); car insurers are supposed to give you this with a policy, though in practice few seem to have heard of it.

For non-criminal **driving violations** such as speeding, the police can impose an on-the-spot fine. Should you be arrested on any charge, you have the right to contact your consulate (see 'Directory' below). Although the police are not always as cooperative as they might be, it *is* their duty to assist you – likewise in the case of losing your passport or all your money.

People caught smuggling or possessing **drugs**, even a few grammes of marijuana, are liable to find themselves in jail and consulates will not be sympathetic. This is not to say that hard-drug consumption isn't a visible activity: there are scores of kids dealing in *poudre* (heroin) in the big French cities and the authorities are unable to do much about it. As a rule, people are no more nor less paranoid about marijuana busts than they are in the U.K.

THE POLICE

There are two main types of French police (in popular argot, *les flics*): the **Police Nationale** and the **Gendarmeries Nationale**. For all practical purposes, they are indistinguishable; if you need to report a theft, or other incident, you can go to either.

A different proposition entirely are the **CRS** (*Compagnies Républicaines de Sécurité*), a mobile force of heavies, sporadically dressed in green combats and armed with riot equipment, whose brutality in the May 1968 battles turned public opinion to the side of the students. They still make demonstrations dangerous. Not quite in the same league, but with an ugly recent history, is the separate **Paris police force**. This bunch are prone to pulling the 'nonconforming' – often just ordinary teenagers – in off the streets for identity checks. You can in fact be stopped anywhere in France and asked to produce ID. If it happens to you, it's not worth being difficult or facetious.

Lastly, in the Álps or Pyrenees, you may come across specialised **mountaineering sections** of the police force. They are unfailingly helpful, friendly and approachable, providing rescue services and guidance.

SEXUAL AND RACIAL HARASSMENT

Women are bound to experience **sexual harassment** in France, where many people make a habit of looking you up and down and, more often than not, passing comment. Generally it is no worse than in the U.K., but problems arise in judging men without the familiar linguistic and cultural cues.

A '*Bonjour*' or '*Bonsoir*' on the street is almost always a pick-up line. If you so much as return the greeting, you've left yourself open to a persistent monologue and a difficult brush-off job. On the other hand, it's not unusual to be offered a drink in a bar if you're on your own and not to be pestered even if you accept. This is rarer in big cities than in the countryside, but don't assume that any overture by a Frenchman is a come-on.

Late-night métros in the big cities are nowhere near as unnerving as in London, simply because of greater passenger numbers and the fact that people are more inclined to intervene if nasty scenes develop. Hitchhiking is risky – as it is anywhere – and few French women do it except on the Côte d'Azur where public transport is minimal. If you want to hitch it's best to use the agencies and take the same precautions as you would at home.

If you need help, don't go to the police. The *mairie/hôtel de ville* will have addresses of women's organisations (*Femmes Battues, Femmes en Détresse* or *SOS Femmes*), though this won't be much help outside business hours. You'll find detailed listings for Paris in Chapter one. We've given contacts for other cities where possible, but there are very few permanent centres.

You may, as a woman, be warned about '*les Arabes*'. This is an instance of French **racism**. If you are Arab or even just look as if you are, your chances of avoiding unpleasantness are very slim. Empty hotels claiming to be full, police demanding your papers and abusive treatment from ordinary people is horribly commonplace. In addition, being black, of whatever ethnic origin, can make entering the country difficult and immigration officers can be obstructive and malicious to black holidaymakers.

WORK AND STUDY

Much the simplest way of finding a job in a **French language school** is to apply from Britain. Check the ads in the *Guardian's* 'Educational Extra' or in the Times Educational Supplement. Late summer is usually the best time. You don't need fluent French to get a post, but a TEFL (Teaching English as a Foreign Language) qualification is a distinct advantage.

If you apply from home most schools will fix up the necessary papers for you. EC nationals don't need a work permit, but getting a *carte de séjour* and social security can still be tricky when employers refuser to help. It's quite feasible to find a teaching job while you're **already in France** but you may have to accept semi-official status and no job security. For the addresses of schools, look under *Ecoles de Langues* in the Professions directory of the local phone book. Offering **private lessons** (via university notice boards or classified ads), you'll have lots of competition, and it's hard to reach the people who can afford it, but it's always worth a try.

For **temporary work**, there's no substitute for checking the papers, pounding the streets, and in Paris and other large cities, keeping an eye on the notice boards at the British and American churches. Other good sources include the *Offres d'Emploi* in *Le Monde, Le Figaro* and the *International Herald Tribune.*

Although working as an **au pair** is easily set up through any number of agencies (lists are available from the closest French embassy or consulate), this sort of work is really a last resort, even if you're just using it to learn the language. Conditions, pay, and treatment by your employers are likely to be the next worst thing to slavery. If you're determined to try, it's better to apply once in France, where you can at least meet the family first and check things out.

Another possibility, perhaps more remote, and definitely to be arranged before you leave, is to get a job as a **travel courier.** You'll need good French (German would also help) and should write to as many tour operators as you can, preferably in early Spring. Ads occasionally appear in the *Guardian*'s 'Creative and Media' pages.

Finally, it's worth noting that if you're a full-time student in France (see below), you can get a **work permit** for the following summer as long as your visa is still valid.

STUDYING IN FRANCE

It's relatively easy to be a **student** in France. Foreigners pay no more than French nationals (around 550F a year) to enrol for a course, and of course there's the cost of supporting yourself. Your *carte de séjour* and – for EC nationals – social security will be assured, and you'll be eligible for subsidised accommodation, meals, and all the student reductions. Few people want to do undergraduate degrees abroad, but for higher degrees or other diplomas, the range of options is enormous. Strict entry requirements, including an exam in French, apply only for undergraduate degrees. Generally, French universities are much less formal than British ones and many people perfect their fluency in the language while studying. For **full details and prospectuses**, go to the Cultural Service of any French embassy or consulate (see p.8 for the addresses).

Language courses are offered at a number of establishments in university towns. They are listed in the handout *'Cours de Français pour Etudiants Etrangers,'* also obtainable from embassy or consular cultural sections.

DIRECTORY

BEACHES are public property within 5m of the high tide mark, so you can kick sand past private villas and arrive on islands but, under a different law, you can't camp.

CONSULATES See Paris and Marseille listings.

CONTRACEPTIVES Condoms (*préservatifs*) have always been available at pharmacies, though contraception was only legalised in 1967. You can also get spermicidal cream and jelly (*dose contraceptive*), plus the suppositories (*ovules, suppositoires*) and (with a prescription) the pill (*la pillule*), a diaphragm or IUD (*le sterilet*).

CUSTOMS If you bring in more than 5000F worth of foreign cash, you need to sign a declaration at customs. There are also restrictions on taking francs out of the country, but the amounts are beyond the concern of most people. Tobacco and alcohol import limits are 400 cigarettes and two litres respectively.

DISABLED TRAVELLERS France has no special reputation for ease of access and facilities, but at least information is available. The tourist offices in most big towns have a free booklet *Touristes Quand Même* covering accommodation, transport, accessibility of public places and particular aids such as buzzer signals on pedestrian crossings. The *ATH* hotel reservation service in Paris (☎48.74.88.51) has details of wheelchair access for three- and four-star hotels. Useful guides in English include the *Access Guides* to Paris, Brittany and the Loire Valley, from the *Pauline Hephaistos Survey Project*, 39 Bradley Gdns, London W13.

ELECTRICITY is 200V out of double, round-pin wall sockets. In out of the way rural districts you may still find 110V.

FISHING You need to become a member of a fishing club to get rights – this is not difficult, any tourist office will give you a local address.

GAY AND LESBIAN LIFE France is more liberal than most other European countries on homosexuality. The legal age of consent is 15 and there are thriving gay communities in Paris and many of the towns in the south. Lesbian life is rather less upfront. Addresses are listed in the guide and you'll find details of groups and publications for the whole country in the Paris chapter.

KIDS/BABIES pose few travel problems. They're allowed in all bars and restaurants, most of whom will cook simpler food if you ask. Hotels charge by the room – there's a small supplement for an additional bed or cot – and family-run places will usually babysit while you go out. You'll have no difficulty finding disposable nappies, baby foods and milk powders. The *SNCF* charges half-fare on trains and buses for kids aged 4–12, nothing for under 4s. As far as entertainment goes, most local tourist offices detail specific children's activities (we've included some of the more exciting), and wherever you go there's generally a good reception.

LAUNDRY Launderettes used to be almost impossible to find. They have multiplied over the last few years but are still not the commonest sight along French main streets. We've given addresses for the major cities – elsewhere look in the phone book under *Laveries Automatiques*. It's a good idea to carry travel soap or cold water washing liquid so that you can wash your own.

LEFT LUGGAGE There are lockers at all train stations and *consigne* for bigger items or longer periods.

SWIMMING POOLS are well posted in all French towns and reasonably priced.

TAMPONS are available from all pharmacies, but are much cheaper in supermarkets.

TIME France isalways one hour ahead of Britain except between the end of September and the end of October, when it's the same.

TOILETS are usually to be found downstairs in bars, along with the phone, but they're often hole-in-the-ground squats and paper is rare.

PART TWO

THE GUIDE

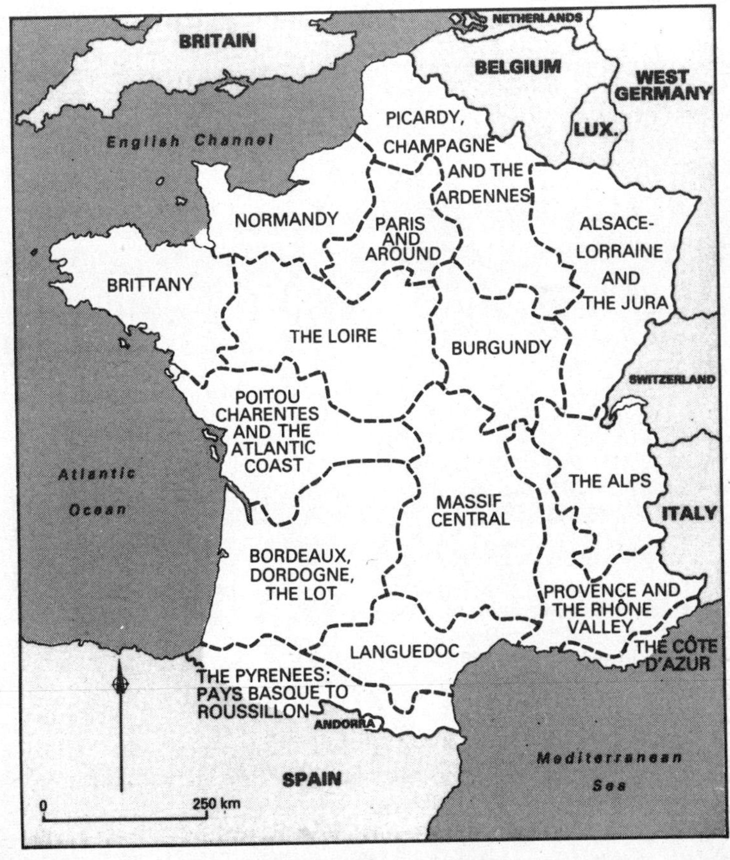

CHAPTER ONE

PARIS

PARIS is the paragon of style – perhaps the most glamorous and the most high-tech city in Europe. And yet it is also deeply traditional, a village-like and in parts dilapidated metropolis whose appeal to outsiders is tempered by what must be the rudest and most arrogant citizens on earth. While such contradictions and contrasts may be the reality of any city, they are the makings of Paris. Consider the village atmosphere of Montmartre against the cold hard lines of La Défense; the multiplicity of markets and small shops against the giant malls of Montparnasse and Les Halles; or the devotion to *l'informatique* – minitel link-ups for all phone subscribers, micro-computer route finders in métro stations, against the old ladies ironing sheets by hand in the laundries of Auteil.

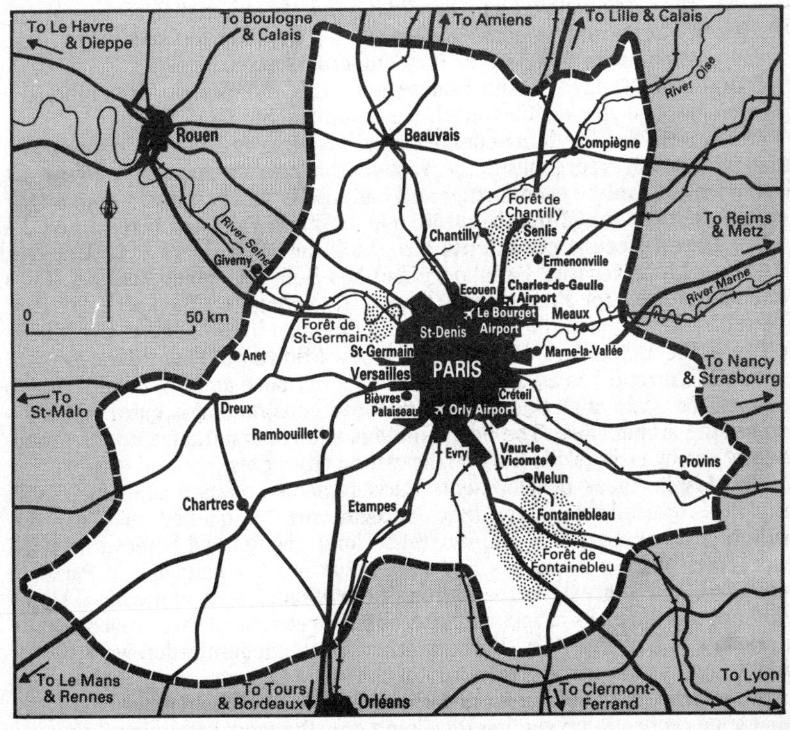

But Paris has long created its own myth. People and events – Sun King, Revolution, Commune, Resistance, May '68 – are invested with a peculiar glamour that elevates the city and its people to a legendary realm. And it is only in the last couple of decades that Paris has let slip its status as centre of movements in the west: whether artistic (spawning impressionism and surrealism), intellectual (existentialism, structuralism) or literary (from Sartre and Camus to Joyce and Beckett). Perhaps it is not surprising that, finding themselves at the supposed navel of the world, Parisians feel that they are superior to ordinary mortals.

Some history

History itself has conspired to create this sense of being apart. From a shaky start the kings of France, whose seat was Paris, gradually extended their control over their feudal rivals, centralising administrative, legal, financial and political power as they did so, until anyone seeking influence, publicity or credibility, in whatever field, had to be in Paris. **Louis XIV** consolidated this process. Supremely autocratic, considering himself the embodiment of the state – 'L'état, c'est moi' – he inaugurated the tradition of Paris as symbol: the glorious reflection of the pre-eminence of the State. The Cour Carrée of the Louvre, the Observatoire and Invalides, and the triumphal arches of the Portes St-Martin and St-Denis are his. It is a tradition his successors have been only too happy to follow, be they emperor or president.

Napoléon I added to the Louvre and built the Arc de Triomphe, the Madeleine, and Arc du Carrousel. He instituted the Grandes Ecoles, those super-universities for super-competent administrators, engineers and teachers (and totally reorganised the rest of the country too). **Napoléon III** extended the Louvre even further and had his Baron Haussmann redraw the rest of the city. The **Third Republic** had its World Fairs and bequeathed the Eiffel Tower. **Recent presidents** have built the skyscrapers at La Défense, the Tour Montparnasse, Beaubourg and Les Halles shopping precinct. They initiated projects for **President Mitterrand** to complete: the space age Parc de la Villette complex, the glass pyramid entrance to the Louvre, the Musée d'Orsay, the arch at La Défense, and the new Ministry of Finance quarters, to which Mitterrand has added the Bastille opera house and Institut du Monde Arabe. The scale of all this publicly financed construction is extraordinary – so too the architecture. The new buildings should, and do, feature as prominently on any visitors' itinerary as the classic city sights.

Yet despite these developments Paris remains compact and remarkably uniform, basically the city that **Haussmann** remodelled in the **mid-nineteenth century**. He laid out those long geometrical boulevards lined with rows of grey bourgeois residences that are the hallmark of Paris. In doing so, he cut great swathes through the stinking wen of medieval slums that housed the city's rebellious poor, already veterans of three revolutionary uprisings in half a century. If urban renewal and modernisation were part of the design, so too was the intention of controlling the masses by opening up more effective fields of fire for artillery and facilitating troop movements. Not that it succeeded in preventing the Commune, the most determined insurrection since 1789.

The **tradition of conflict** between the citizenry and its rulers dates back well into the Middle Ages. Although the nation prospered, and Paris acquired an ever-increasing number of monuments, nothing was ever done to alleviate the misery of the poor. Although the traditional barricade-builders have long since been booted into the suburban factory-land, or housed in depressing satellite towns, the old pattern still continues. Corporate business gets its way, the state invests in the monumental building, the housing shortage remains acute, large areas of the city, especially in the east and north, fall into a state of decay that only the underprivileged immigrant communities are prepared to tolerate while other working-class bastions are yuppified, and the unemployed beg on the streets in increasing numbers.

Ethnic diversity is an important, if volatile, element in the weft of the city's life. Long a haven and magnet for foreign refugees and artists, Paris in this century has sheltered Lenin and Ho Chi Minh, White Russians and Iranians (the Ayatollah as well as the Shah's son), dissidents from Eastern Europe, disillusioned writers from America and a host of other assorted expatriates. The newest settlers are immigrants from the former French colonies in South-East Asia, West Africa and North Africa; well-entrenched, if not assimilated, they have their own quartiers, shops, cafés and cultures.

And some highlights

The most tangible and immediate pleasures of Paris are to be found in its **streetlife**. Few cities can compete with the thousand-and-one cafés, bars and reastaurants – modern and trendy, local and traditional, humble and pretentious – that line every street and boulevard. And the city's compactness makes it easy to experience the individual feel of the different **quartiers**. You can move easily, even on foot, from the calm, almost small-town atmosphere of **Montmartre** and parts of the **Latin Quarter** to the busy commercial centres of the **Bourse** and **Opéra** or to the aristocratic mansions of the **Marais**. At **Les Halles** you can shop inside an ultra-modern mall, in **Belleville** at markets that resemble North African *souks*. The city's lack of open spaces is redeemed by unexpected spots of garden or churchyard like the **Mosque**, **Arènes de Lutèce** and the courtyard of the **Cluny museum**.

A grand and imposing backdrop to the streetlife is provided by monumental architecture such as the **Arc de Triomphe**, the **Eiffel Tower**, **Concorde** and the **bridges**. This century's contributions include the **Art Nouveau** and **Cubist** innovations in the *16e arrondissement*, and the current innovations from **Beaubourg** through to **La Villette**, the **Institut du Monde Arabe**, and the **Louvre pyramid**. But these contemporary innovations aside, Paris is less remarkable for its buildings than for its art. There are some glorious **museums** to see: the **d'Orsay**, modern art at **Beaubourg**, the **Cité des Sciences** at La Villette, **Marmottan**, **Picasso,** the **Orangerie** and **Cluny**.

As for entertainment, the city's strong points are in film and music. Paris is a real **cinema** capital, and although french rock is notoriously awful, the best Parisian **music** encompasses jazz, avante-garde, salsa and, currently, Europe's most vibrant African music scene.

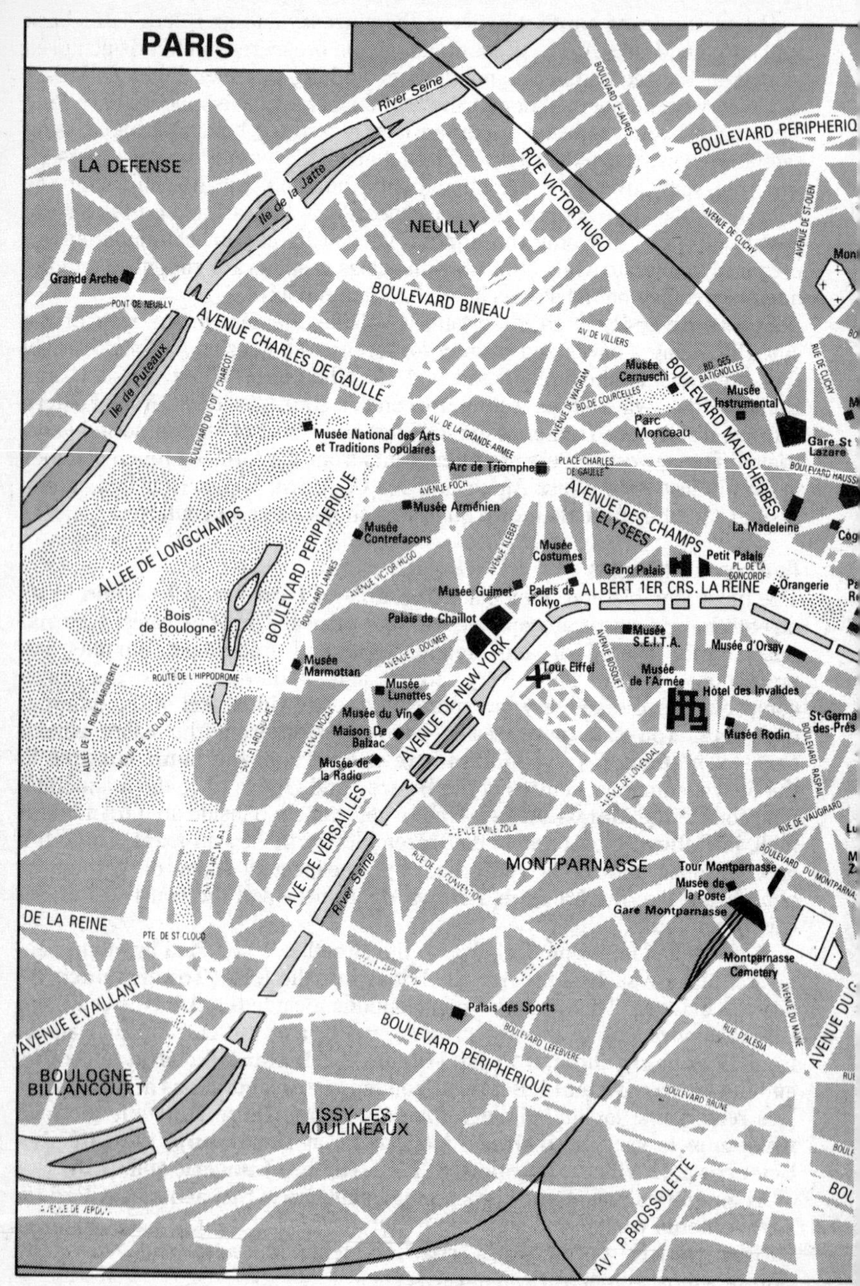
PARIS
River Seine
LA DEFENSE
Ile de la Jatte
NEUILLY
RUE VICTOR HUGO
BOULEVARD PERIPHERIQ
Grande Arche
PONT DE NEUILLY
BOULEVARD BINEAU
AVENUE CHARLES DE GAULLE
Ile de Puteaux
AV. DE VILLIERS
Musée Cernuschi
BOULEVARD MALESHERBES
Musée Instrumental
Parc Monceau
Gare St Lazare
Musée National des Arts et Traditions Populaires
AV. DE LA GRANDE ARMEE
Arc de Triomphe
PLACE CHARLES DE GAULLE
AVENUE FOCH
Musée Arménien
AVENUE DES CHAMPS ELYSEES
La Madeleine
ALLEE DE LONGCHAMPS
BOULEVARD PERIPHERIQUE
Musée Contrefacons
Musée Costumes
Petit Palais
Grand Palais
PL. DE LA CONCORDE
Orangerie
Musée Guimet
Palais de Tokyo
ALBERT 1ER CRS. LA REINE
Bois de Boulogne
Palais de Chaillot
Musée S.E.I.T.A.
Musée d'Orsay
Musée Marmottan
ROUTE DE L'HIPPODROME
Tour Eiffel
Musée de l'Armée
Hôtel des Invalides
Musée Lunettes
Musée du Vin
AVENUE DE NEW YORK
Maison De Balzac
Musée Rodin
Musée de la Radio
AVE. DE VERSAILLES
River Seine
AVENUE EMILE ZOLA
MONTPARNASSE
Tour Montparnasse
Musée de la Poste
Gare Montparnasse
DE LA REINE
PTE. DE ST CLOUD
Montparnasse Cemetery
AVENUE E. VAILLANT
Palais des Sports
BOULEVARD PERIPHERIQUE
BOULOGNE-BILLANCOURT
ISSY-LES-MOULINEAUX
AV. P. BROSSOLETTE

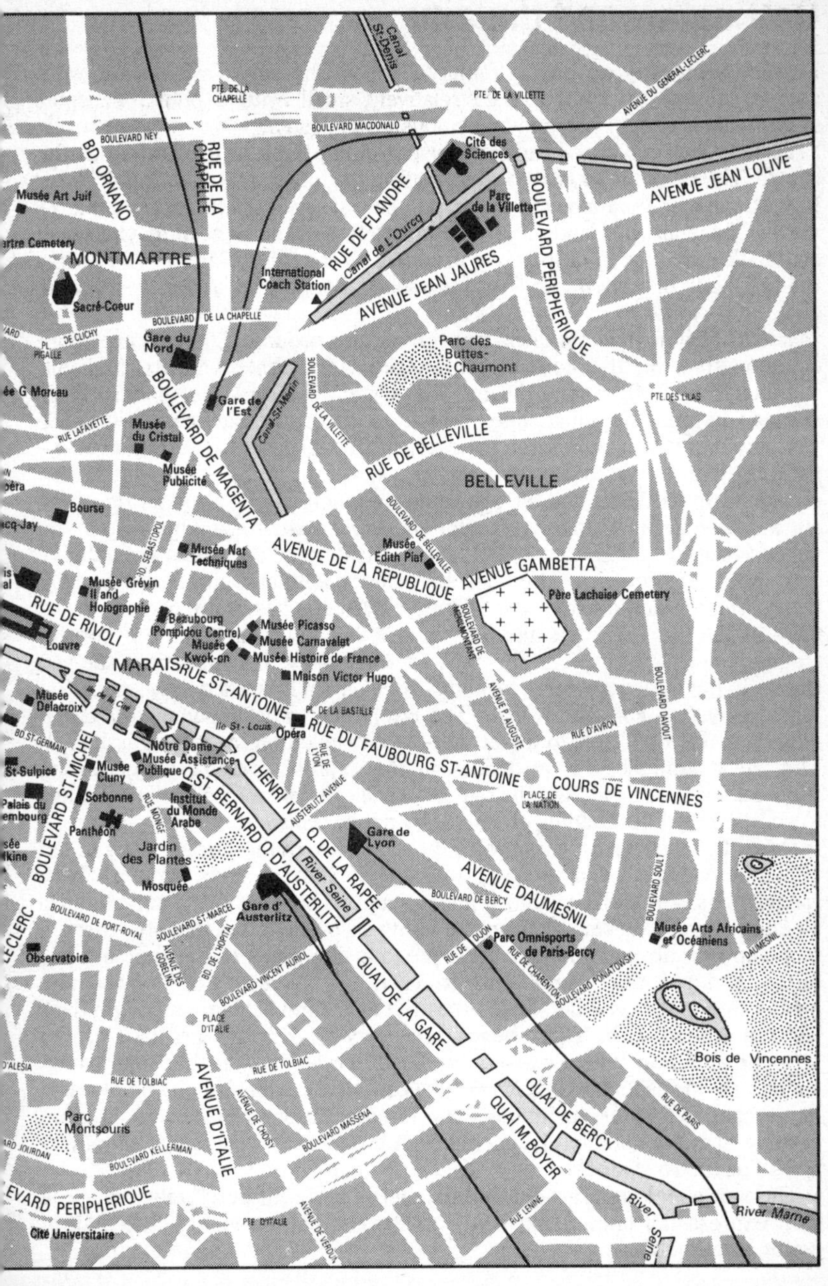
Canal St-Denis
PTE. DE LA CHAPELLE
PTE. DE LA VILLETTE
AVENUE DU GENERAL-LECLERC
BOULEVARD MACDONALD
BOULEVARD NEY
BD. ORNANO
RUE DE LA CHAPELLE
Cité des Sciences
Parc de la Villette
BOULEVARD PERIPHERIQUE
AVENUE JEAN LOLIVE
Musée Art Juif
RUE DE FLANDRE
Canal de L'Ourcq
MONTMARTRE
International Coach Station
AVENUE JEAN JAURES
Sacré-Coeur
BOULEVARD DE LA CHAPELLE
DE CLICHY
PL PIGALLE
Gare du Nord
Parc des Buttes-Chaumont
BOULEVARD DE LA VILLETTE
Canal St-Martin
PTE. DES LILAS
Gare de l'Est
RUE LAFAYETTE
Musée du Cristal
RUE DE BELLEVILLE
Musée Publicité
BELLEVILLE
BOULEVARD DE MAGENTA
Bourse
BOULEVARD DE BELLEVILLE
Musée Nat Techniques
AVENUE DE LA REPUBLIQUE
Musée Edith Piaf
AVENUE GAMBETTA
Père Lachaise Cemetery
Musée Grévin II and Holographie
RUE DE RIVOLI
Beaubourg (Pompidou Centre)
Musée Picasso
Musée Carnavalet
Musée Kwok-on
Musée Histoire de France
BOULEVARD DE MENILMONTANT
Louvre
MARAIS
RUE ST-ANTOINE
Maison Victor Hugo
BOULEVARD DAVOUT
AVENUE P. AUGUSTE
Musée Delacroix
Ile de la Cité
PL. DE LA BASTILLE
BD ST-GERMAIN
Ile St-Louis
Opéra
RUE DU FAUBOURG ST-ANTOINE
RUE D'AVRON
Notre Dame
Musée Assistance Publique
RUE DE LYON
St-Sulpice
Musée Cluny
Q. HENRI IV
Q. ST BERNARD
COURS DE VINCENNES
PLACE DE LA NATION
Sorbonne
Institut du Monde Arabe
AUSTERLITZ AVENUE
BOULEVARD ST. MICHEL
RUE MONGE
Panthéon
Gare de Lyon
Jardin des Plantes
Q. D'AUSTERLITZ
Q. DE LA RAPÉE
AVENUE DAUMESNIL
BOULEVARD SOULT
Mosquée
River Seine
BOULEVARD DE BERCY
Gare d'Austerlitz
Musée Arts Africains et Océaniens
BOULEVARD DE PORT ROYAL
BOULEVARD ST-MARCEL
Parc Omnisports de Paris-Bercy
RUE DE DIJON
Observatoire
AVENUE DES GOBELINS
BD. DE L'HOPITAL
RUE DE CHARENTON
BOULEVARD PONIATOWSKI
BOULEVARD VINCENT AURIOL
QUAI DE LA GARE
PLACE D'ITALIE
RUE DE TOLBIAC
Bois de Vincennes
AVENUE D'ITALIE
AVENUE DE CHOISY
QUAI DE BERCY
RUE DE PARIS
Parc Montsouris
BOULEVARD MASSENA
QUAI M. BOYER
BOULEVARD KELLERMAN
BOULEVARD PERIPHERIQUE
River Seine
River Marne
RUE LENINE
PTE. D'ITALIE
AVENUE DE VERDUN
Cité Universitaire

Getting around the city

Finding your way around is remarkably easy, because Paris proper, without its suburbs, is compact and relatively small, with a public transport system that is cheap, fast, and meticulously signposted.

To help you get your bearings above ground, think of the Louvre as the centre. The Seine flows east to west, cutting the city in two. The Eiffel Tower is west, the white pimples of the Sacré-Coeur on top of the hill of Montmartre north. These are the landmarks you most often catch sight of as you move about. The area north of the river is known as the Right Bank or *rive droite*; the Left Bank or *rive gauche* lies to the south. Roughly speaking, west is chic and east is scruffy.

The **métro** is the simplest way of getting around. Stations are more common than on the London Underground and the trains are frequent, running from 5.30am to 12.30am. The system includes the modern **RER** (Réseau Express Régional) lines, which go out to the suburbs. Within the city boundaries you can switch back and forth between RER and the métro – the only difference is you have to put your ticket through the turnstile as you change to an RER line, and the platforms are much bigger. **Free route maps** are available at most stations. In addition, every station has a big map of the network outside the entrance and several inside (station names are abbreviated: M° Concorde etc). The lines are colour-coded and numbered, in addition to being marked within the system with the names of the stations at the ends of the lines. For instance, if you're travelling from Gare du Nord to Odéon, you follow the sign *Direction Porte-d'Orléans* because that's the last station in the direction you're heading; from Gare d'Austerlitz to Grenelle you follow *Direction Pont-de-St-Cloud*. The numerous transfer points (*correspondances*) make it possible to travel over the city in a more or less straight line. The latest technology is evidenced in the express stations' computerised route-finders – at a touch of the button they'll give you four alternative routes to your selected destination, on foot or by public transport.

Don't, however, use the métro to the exclusion of the **buses**. They're not difficult to work out and of course you see much more above ground. There are **free route maps** available at métro stations, bus terminals, and the tourist office. Every bus stop displays the numbers of the buses that stop there, a map showing all the stops on the route, and the times of the first and last buses. And as if that weren't enough, each bus has a map of its own route inside. Generally speaking, buses start out at around 6.30am and begin their last run around 9pm. **Night buses** run every hour from place du Châtelet near the Hôtel de Ville. Service is reduced Sunday. For further information contact the transport board, *RATP* (☎43.46.14.14), which, incidentally, runs numerous excursions, including some to quite far-flung places, much more cheaply than the commercial operators. A brochure is available at all railway and some métro stations.

The **same tickets** are valid for bus, métro, and, within the city limits, the RER express rail lines. Long bus journeys can use up to two tickets; if in doubt, ask the driver.

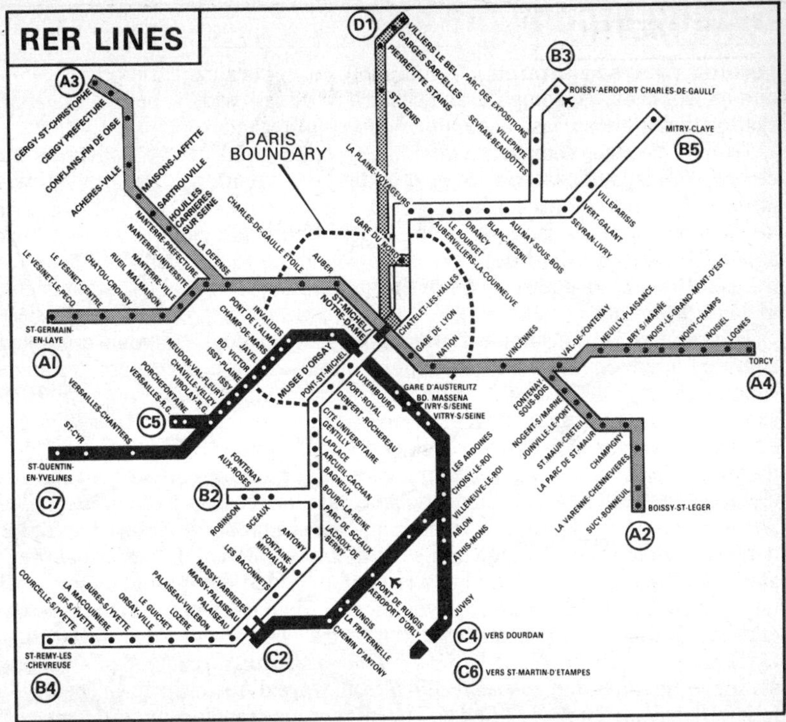

The most economical **ticket**, if you are staying more than a day or two, is the **Carte Orange**, obtainable at all métro stations (you need a passport photo), with a weekly (*hebdomadaire*; valid Mon.–Sun.) or monthly (*mensuel*) coupon. It entitles you to unlimited travel on the bus or métro. On the métro you put the coupon through the turnstile slot; make sure to return it to its plastic folder since it is reusable throughout the period of its validity. On a bus you show the whole *Carte* to the driver as you board – don't put it into the punching machine. There is also a tourist ticket, *billet de tourisme*, but it is overpriced. For a short stay in the city, **individual tickets** can be bought at a reduced price in *carnets* of ten (from any station). If you buy from the ticket touts who hang round the main stations, you'll pay inflated prices. All tickets are sold as first or second class (though class distinctions are only in force between 9am and 5pm; the second-class cars are nearly as nice as the first, in any case), and there's a **flat rate** within the city – one ticket per journey. Be sure to hang on to your ticket until the end of the trip; you'll be fined on the spot if you can't produce one.

If it's late at night or you feel like treating yourself, don't hesitate to use the **taxis**. Their rates are very reasonable. Three small lights on the roof indicate which fare rate the metre is switched on to: A (passenger side) is daytime, B

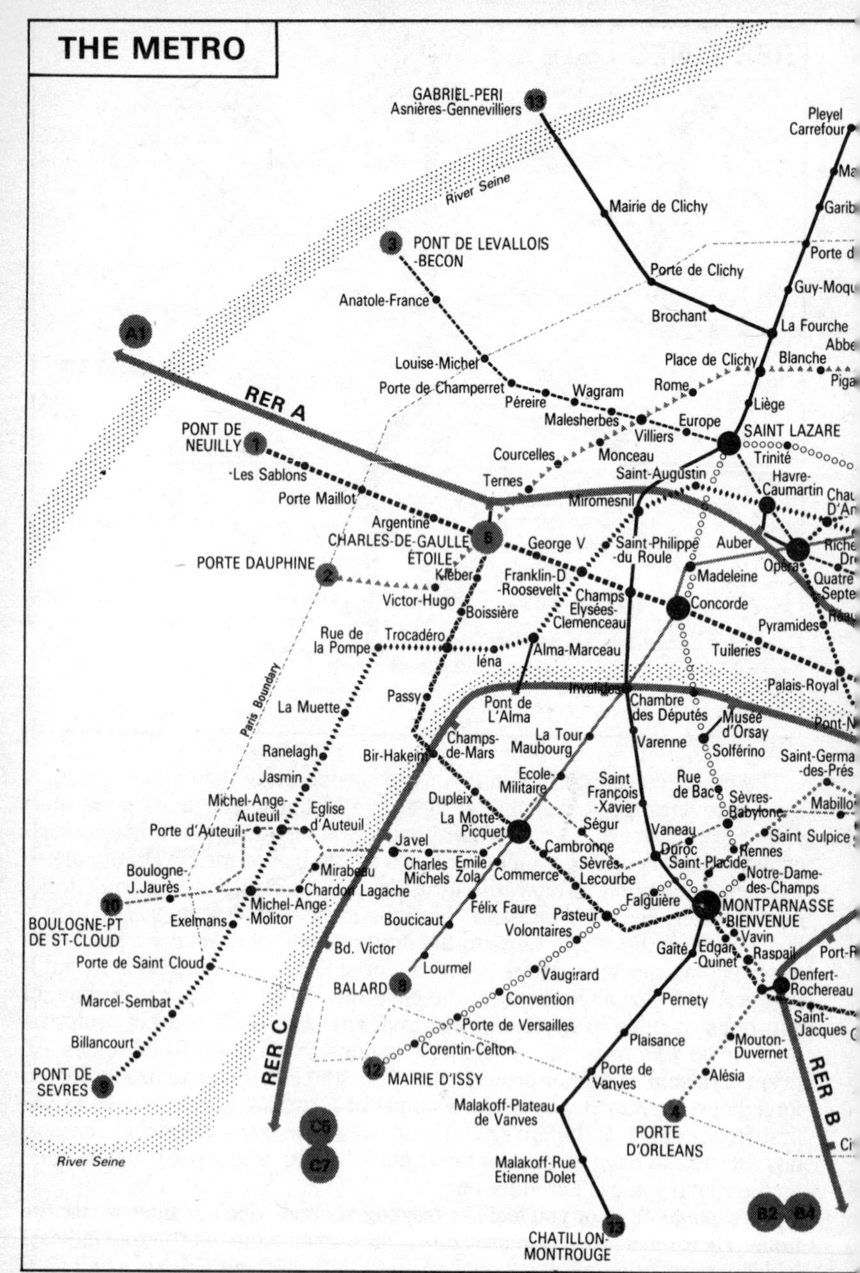
THE METRO
GABRIEL-PERI
Asnières-Gennevilliers
13
Pleyel
Carrefour
River Seine
Mairie de Clichy
3
PONT DE LEVALLOIS
-BECON
Porte de Clichy
Anatole-France
Brochant
La Fourche
A1
Louise-Michel
Place de Clichy
Blanche
RER A
Porte de Champerret
Péreire
Wagram
Rome
Liège
Malesherbes
Europe
PONT DE
NEUILLY
1
Villiers
SAINT LAZARE
Courcelles
Monceau
Trinité
Les Sablons
Saint-Augustin
Havre-
Caumartin
Ternes
Porte Maillot
Miromesnil
Argentine
6
CHARLES-DE-GAULLE
ÉTOILE
George V
Saint-Philippe
-du Roule
Auber
Opéra
PORTE DAUPHINE
2
Kléber
Franklin-D
-Roosevelt
Madeleine
Victor-Hugo
Champs
Elysées-
Clemenceau
Concorde
Boissière
Pyramides
Rue de
la Pompe
Trocadéro
Alma-Marceau
Tuileries
Iéna
Paris Boundary
Invalides
Palais-Royal
Passy
Pont de
L'Alma
Chambre
des Députés
Musée
d'Orsay
La Muette
La Tour
Maubourg
Varenne
Solférino
Ranelagh
Bir-Hakeim
Champs-
de-Mars
Ecole-
Militaire
Saint
François
-Xavier
Rue
de Bac
Jasmin
Dupleix
Sèvres-
Babylone
Michel-Ange-
Auteuil
Eglise
d'Auteuil
La Motte-
Picquet
Ségur
Porte d'Auteuil
Vaneau
Saint Sulpice
Javel
Cambronne
Duroc
Rennes
Charles
Michels
Emile
Zola
Sèvres-
Lecourbe
Saint-Placide
Boulogne-
J.Jaurès
Mirabeau
Commerce
Notre-Dame-
des-Champs
Chardon Lagache
Falguière
10
Michel-Ange
-Molitor
Félix Faure
MONTPARNASSE
BIENVENUE
BOULOGNE-PT
DE ST-CLOUD
Exelmans
Boucicaut
Pasteur
Vavin
Volontaires
Gaîté
Edgar
-Quinet
Raspail
Bd. Victor
Porte de Saint Cloud
Lourmel
Denfert-
Rochereau
Vaugirard
BALARD
8
Marcel-Sembat
Convention
Pernety
Saint-
Jacques
Porte de Versailles
Plaisance
RER C
Billancourt
Mouton-
Duvernet
Corentin-Celton
RER B
PONT DE
SEVRES
9
12
MAIRIE D'ISSY
Porte de
Vanves
Alésia
Malakoff-Plateau
de Vanves
4
PORTE
D'ORLEANS
C5
C7
River Seine
Malakoff-Rue
Etienne Dolet
B2
B4
13
CHATILLON-
MONTROUGE

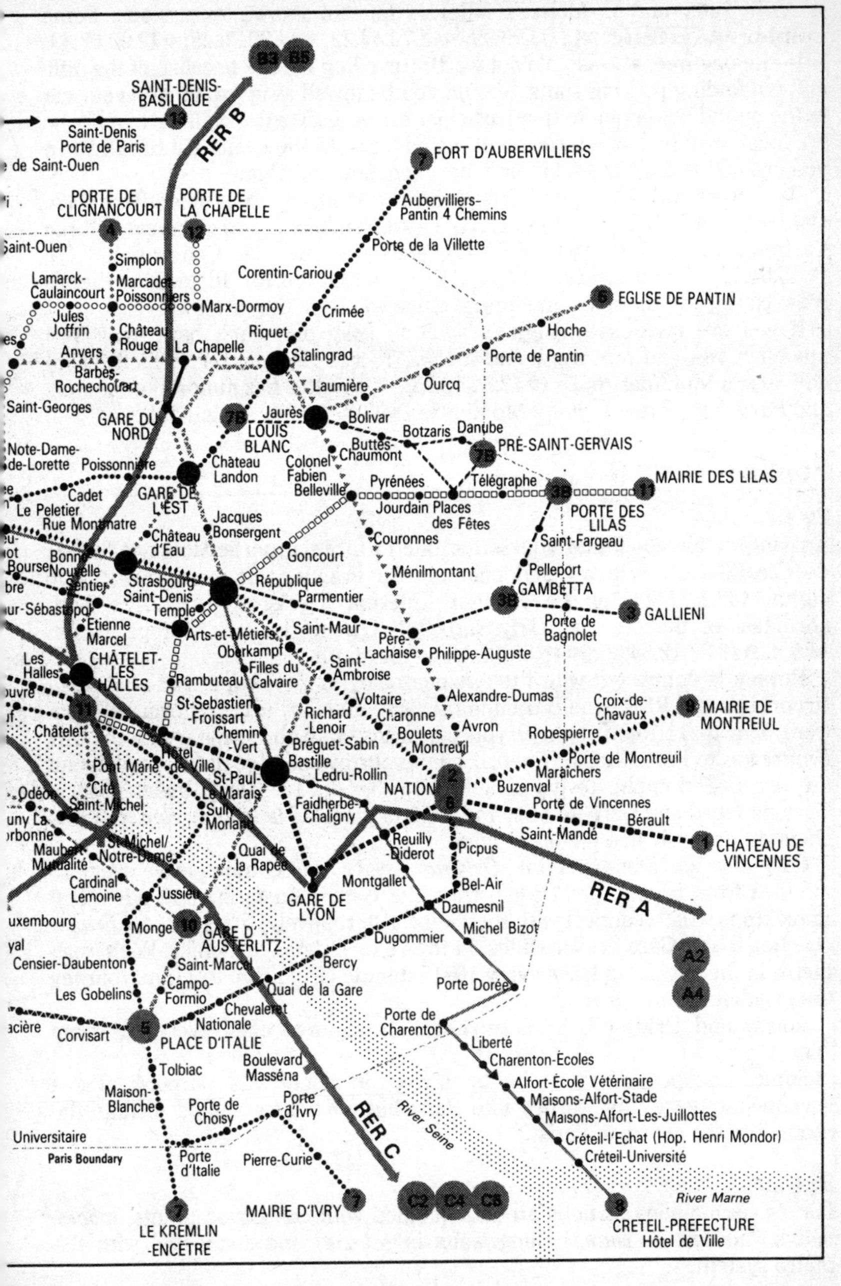
B3
B5
SAINT-DENIS-BASILIQUE
13
RER B
Saint-Denis Porte de Paris
de Saint-Ouen
7
FORT D'AUBERVILLIERS
PORTE DE CLIGNANCOURT
4
PORTE DE LA CHAPELLE
12
Aubervilliers-Pantin 4 Chemins
Saint-Ouen
Simplon
Porte de la Villette
Lamarck-Caulaincourt
Marcadet-Poissonniers
Corentin-Cariou
Marx-Dormoy
Crimée
6
EGLISE DE PANTIN
Jules Joffrin
Château Rouge
Riquet
Hoche
Anvers
La Chapelle
Stalingrad
Porte de Pantin
Barbès-Rochechouart
Laumière
Ourcq
Saint-Georges
GARE DU NORD
7B
Jaurès
Bolivar
LOUIS BLANC
Botzaris
Danube
Buttes-Chaumont
PRÉ-SAINT-GERVAIS
Note-Dame-de-Lorette
Poissonnière
Château Landon
Colonel Fabien
Pyrénées
Télégraphe
MAIRIE DES LILAS
11
Cadet
GARE DE L'EST
Belleville
3B
Le Peletier
Jourdain
Places des Fêtes
PORTE DES LILAS
Rue Montmatre
Jacques Bonsergent
Château d'Eau
Couronnes
Saint-Fargeau
Bonne Nouvelle
Goncourt
Pelleport
Bourse
Sentier
Strasbourg Saint-Denis
République
Ménilmontant
GAMBETTA
Parmentier
3
GALLIENI
Temple
Porte de Bagnolet
Étienne Marcel
Arts-et-Métiers
Saint-Maur
Père-Lachaise
Philippe-Auguste
Oberkampf
Les Halles
CHÂTELET-LES HALLES
Filles du Calvaire
Saint-Ambroise
Rambuteau
Alexandre-Dumas
Croix-de-Chavaux
9
MAIRIE DE MONTREIUL
St-Sebastien-Froissart
Voltaire
11
Richard-Lenoir
Charonne
Châtelet
Chemin-Vert
Boulets Montreuil
Avron
Robespierre
Hôtel de Ville
Bréguet-Sabin
Porte de Montreuil
Pont Marie
Bastille
Maraîchers
St-Paul-Le Marais
Ledru-Rollin
2
NATION
Buzenval
Odéon
Cité
Saint-Michel
6
Porte de Vincennes
Sully Morland
Faidherbe-Chaligny
Béraut
Saint-Mandé
Reuilly-Diderot
1
CHATEAU DE VINCENNES
St-Michel/Notre-Dame
Maubert-Mutualité
Quai de la Rapée
Picpus
Cardinal Lemoine
Montgallet
Bel-Air
RER A
Jussieu
GARE DE LYON
Daumesnil
uxembourg
Monge
10
GARE D' AUSTERLITZ
Michel Bizot
Dugommier
A2
Censier-Daubenton
Saint-Marcel
Bercy
Porte Dorée
A4
Les Gobelins
Campo-Formio
Quai de la Gare
Chevaleret
Porte de Charenton
Corvisart
5
Nationale
PLACE D'ITALIE
Liberté
Charenton-Écoles
Tolbiac
Boulevard Masséna
Alfort-École Vétérinaire
Maisons-Alfort-Stade
Maison-Blanche
Porte de Choisy
Porte d'Ivry
RER C
River Seine
Maisons-Alfort-Les-Juillottes
Universitaire
Créteil-l'Echat (Hop. Henri Mondor)
Paris Boundary
Porte d'Italie
Pierre-Curie
Créteil-Université
7
MAIRIE D'IVRY
C2
C4
C8
River Marne
8
7
LE KREMLIN-BICÊTRE
CRETEIL-PREFECTURE Hôtel de Ville

is night rate, and C (driver's side) is for out-of-town excursions. Some **numbers to call** are: ☎42.03.99.99; ☎42.70.44.22; ☎47.30.23.23; ☎42.00.67.89.

In the daytime, at least, it's not worth travelling **by car** because of the difficulty of finding parking spots. Should you be towed away, you'll find your car in the pound belonging to that particular *arrondissement*. You'll have to phone the local town hall or *mairie* to get the address. In the event of a **breakdown** you can call ☎42.57.33.44, but only between 7am and 10pm.

For **car rental**, some good French firms are: *Mattei*, 205 rue de Bercy, 12e (☎43.46.11.50), 102 rue Ordener, 18e (☎42.64.32.90), and *Autorent*, 11 rue Casimir-Périer, 11e (☎45.55.53.49), 98 rue de la Convention, 15e (☎45.54.22.45) and 196 rue St-Jacques, 5e (☎43.25.88.10). In addition there's Avis, Hertz, and the rest – the tourist office will have the rundown.

If you are reckless enough to want to **bike** and don't have your own machine, you can rent from: *Autothèque*, 16 rue Berger, 1er (☎42.36.39.36) and 80 rue Montmartre, 2e (☎42.36.50.93) – the latter has motorbikes as well; and *Paris-Vélo*, 2 rue du Fer-à-Moulin, 5e (☎43.37.59.22). Watch out!

Points of arrival

By air

Arriving by air you'll find yourself at one of three airports: **Roissy-Charles de Gaulle** (BA, British Caledonian and Air France, plus most transatlantic flights 48.62.22.80), or **Le Bouget** (internal flights; ☎48.62.12.12), both northeast of the city; or, **Orly-Sud/Orly-Ouest** (Eastern Europe, Spain, Africa; ☎48.87.12.34 and ☎48.53.12.34) to the south.

Roissy is connected with the city centre by: *Roissy-rail*, a combination of airport bus and RER ligne B train to the Gare du Nord (exit 6B; every 15 min. from 5am to 11.15pm), where you can transfer to the ordinary métro; *Air France bus* to Porte-Maillot (métro) on the northwest edge of the city beyond the Arc de Triomphe (every 15 min from 5.45am to 11pm); buses #350 to Gare du Nord and Gare de l'Est and #351 to place de la Nation. *Roissy Rail* is cheapest and quickest (about 35 min.).

Orly also has a bus–rail link, *Orly-rail*. RER Ligne C trains leave every 15 minutes from 5.30am to 11.30pm from the Gare d'Austerlitz and other Left Bank stops which connect with the métro. Alternatively, there are *Air France* coaches to the Gare des Invalides, in the 7e or *Orlybus* to Denfert-Rochereau métro in the 14e. Both leave every 10–15 minutes from 6am to 11pm. Journey time is about 35 minutes.

Roissy and Orly both have **bureaux de change** open every day from 7am–11pm.

Some cheaper charter flights arrive in **Beauvais** airport. It's a seventy-kilometre bus journey into Paris but air tickets should include the coach into the centre of Paris.

By train

Paris's six mainline stations are all equipped with cafés, restaurants, *tabacs*, banks, *bureaux de change* (long waits in season) and connected with the métro system.

The **Gare du Nord** (serving Boulogne, Calais, the UK, Belgium, Holland and Scandinavia; ☎42.80.03.03 for information, ☎42.06.49.38 for reservations) and Gare de l'Est (serving eastern France, Germany, Switzerland and Austria; ☎42.08.49.90 for information, ☎42.06.49.38 for reservations) are side by side in the northeast of the city, with the **Gare St-Lazare** (serving the UK, Dieppe and the Normandy coast; ☎43.38.52.29 information; ☎43.87.91.70 reservations) a little to the west of them.

Still on the right bank but towards the southwest corner is the **Gare de Lyon** serving the Alps, the south, Italy and Greece (☎43.45.92.22 information; ☎43.45.93.33 reservations), while **Gare Montparnasse** serves Versailles, Chartres, Brittany and the Atlantic coast (☎45.38.52.29).

By coach

Almost all coaches coming into Paris – whether international or domestic – use the main **gare routière** at Porte de la Villette; there's a métro station here to get into the centre.

By car

If you're **driving** in yourself, don't try to cross the city to your destination. Take the ring road – the *boulevard périphérique* – to the Porte nearest your destination: it's much quicker, except at rush hour, and easier to find your way. Once ensconced wherever you're staying, you'd be well advised to garage the car and use public transport. Parking is a big problem in the centre.

Finding a place to stay

The hotel situation in Paris is not promising at the best of times. The **worst periods** according to the hoteliers' own organisation are: January 9 to 13, February 2 to 13, March 4 to 8, April 5 to 8 and 17 to 22 , May 16 to 18 and 25 to 31, June 1 to 11, September 7 to 10 and 20 to 30, October 14 to 18, November 8 to 17. And in July and August you have to compete with all the other tourists. But there are various agencies to help, which we mention below.

Hotels

For independence and choice of location there's scope in the city's **hotels**, and a few of them work out cheaper than hostels for two or more people. Below is a list of places that we've checked out ourselves, divided into two broad categories – under 180F and between 180–300F a room. Some may have one or two cheaper rooms – but don't count on getting them. If you arrive late, or you don't feel like tramping the streets, head for one of the **bureaux d'accueil** operated by the tourist office, where they will find you a room for a fixed commission of about 10 percent of its price. This service is provided at the main office (127 Champs-Elysées, daily 9am–8pm) and at the principal railway stations: Austerlitz (Mon.–Sat. 9am–8pm); Est (Mon.–Sat.

8am–1pm, 5–8pm); Lyon (Mon.–Sat. 8am–1pm, 5–8pm); Nord (Mon.–Sat. 8am–8pm) and all extend their hours to 10pm in summer. If you don't like the room you get you can always move on after one night.

Under 180F

Hôtel de Bayonne, 41 rue d'Aboukir, 2e. M° Sentier (☎45.08.40.09). Very basic but lively location in the rag trade district.

Castex Hôtel, 5 rue Castex, 4e. M° Bastille, St-Paul (☎42.72.31.52). Foul decor made up for by the kindness of the management.

Hôtel du Centre Est, 4 rue Sibour, 10e. M° Gare-de-l'Est (☎46.07.20.74). A fantastic deal for which you'll need a reservation.

Hôtel Henri IV, 25 place Dauphine, 1er. M° Pont-Neuf, Cité (☎43.54.44.53). Beautifully situated on the Ile de la Cité. Very cheap and very booked up.

Idéal Hôtel, 3 rue des Trois-Frères, 18e. M° Abbesses (☎46.06.63.63). Very basic, but marvellous location. No reservations, so there is a good chance of finding space if you turn up before 11am.

Hôtel Lion d'Or, 5 rue de la Sourdière, 1er. M° Tuileries (☎42.60.79.04). Spartan, but clean, friendly and very central.

Hôtel Moderne, 3 rue Caron, 4e. M° St-Paul (☎48.87.97.05). Unprepossessing entrance but adequate rooms.

Hôtel Nesle 7 rue de Nesle, 6e. M° Odéon (☎43.54.62.41). Once a hippy haunt and still geared to gregarious Californians. No reservations and one of the cheapest.

Hôtel de l'Ouest, 144 rue St-Honoré, 1er. M° Louvre (☎42.60.79.04). Small and dilapidated rooms but close to the Louvre. Need to book two weeks ahead.

Hôtel de la Poste-Ouest, 80 rue de l'Ouest, 14e. M° Pernety (☎43.22.20.59). Very spartan, looks like a slum outside but is immaculately clean inside.

Hôtel Pratic, 9 rue d'Ormesson, 4e. M° St-Paul (☎48.87.80.47). The cheapest rooms go fast; basic but O.K.

Hôtel du Ranelagh, 56 rue de L'Assomption, 16e. M° Ranelagh (☎42.88.31.63). Very pleasant and accessible cheapie near the Bois de Boulogne.

Hôtel St-Michel, 17 rue Gît-le-Coeur, 6e. M° St-Michel (☎43.26.98.70). Very central – near place St-Michel.

Hôtel du Théâtre, 5 rue de Chéroy, 17e. M° Rome (☎43.87.21.48). Near St-Lazare station. No beauty.

180–300F

Hôtel André Gill, 4 rue André Gill, 18e – off rue des Martyrs. M° Abbesses, Pigalle (☎42.62.48.48). Cheap and friendly.

Hôtel des Batignolles, 26–28 rue des Batignolles, 17e. M° Rome, place Clichy (☎43.87.70.40). Villagey area close to Montmartre with lots of small shops and restaurants.

Hôtel California, 32 rue des Ecoles, 5e. M° Jussieu, Cardinal-Lemoine (☎46.34.12.90). A comfortable Latin Quarter base.

Hôtel des Carmes, 5 rue des Carmes, 5e. M° Maubert-Mutualité (☎43.29.78.40) Some much cheaper rooms.

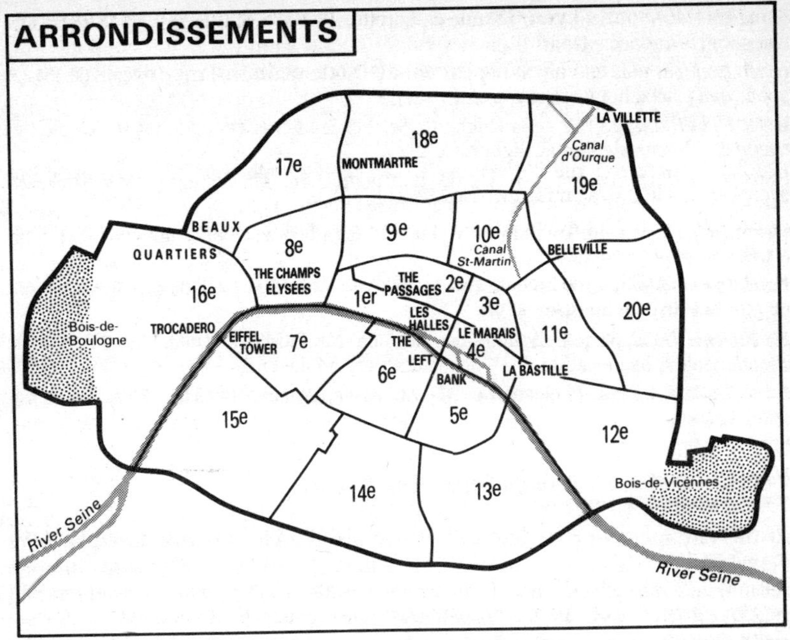

Hôtel Chopin, 46 passage Jouffroy, 9e. M° Montmartre (☎47.70.58.10.). Off one of the old-fashioned *passages*, near Chartier's.

Hôtel de la Cité Bergère, 4–6 Cité Bergère, 9e. M° Montmartre (☎47.70.52.98) One of many hotels in this mews near all the soft-porn shows.

Hôtel Esmeralda, 4 rue St-Julien-le-Pauvre, 5e. M° St-Michel, Maubert-Mutualité (☎43.54.19.20). Right on square Viviani with a superb view of Notre-Dame – cheaper rooms at the back.

Hôtel Gay-Lussac, 29 rue Gay-Lussac, 5e. M° Luxembourg (☎43.54.23.96). Book a week ahead if possible.

Grand Hôtel Lévèque, 29 rue Cler, 7e. M° Ecole-Militaire, Latour-Maubourg (☎47.05.49.15). Clean and decent; nice people. Good location smack in the middle of the rue Cler market Book a month in advance.

Grand Hôtel Jeanne d'Arc, 3 rue de Jarente, 4e. M° St-Paul (☎48.87.62.11). Clean, attractive but going upscale fast.

Institut Hôtel, 23 bd Pasteur, 15e. M° Pasteur (☎45.67.10.48). Clean and adequate, on a leafy, animated street.

Le Latania, 22 rue de la Parcheminerie, 5e. M° St-Michel (☎43.54.32.17). Unassuming outside, but adequate.

Lévis-Hôtel, 16 rue Lebouteux, 17e. M° Villiers (☎47.63.86.38). Only ten rooms, but very nice, on small street off the rue de Lévis market.

Hôtel de Madrid, 1 rue Geoffroy-Marie, 9e. M° Le Péletier, Cadet (☎47.70.85.87). Old-fashioned rooms with marble fireplaces and big, framed mirrors.

Mondial Hôtel, 21 rue Notre-Dame-de-Lorette, 9e. M° St-Georges (☎48.78.60.47). Unevocative but acceptable.

Hôtel Le Montana, 28 rue St-Benoît, 6e. M° St-Germain-des-Prés (☎45.48.62.15). A good, well-placed hotel at the top of the range.

Hôtel Mont-Blanc, 28 rue de la Huchette, 5e. M° St-Michel (☎43.54.49.44). Simple but adequate. Rooms are lighter higher up.

Hôtel du Palais Bourbon, 49 rue de Bourgogne, 7e. M° Varenne (☎45.51.63.32). Attractive eighteenth-century street near Musée Rodin.

Plessis-Hôtel, 25 rue du Grand-Prieuré, 11e. M° République, Oberkampf (☎47.00.13.38). A friendly, good-value hotel.

La Résidence Montmartre, 10 rue Burcq, 18e. M° Abbesses (☎46.06.45.28). Quiet and comfortable in Montmartre.

Ste-Eugénie Hôtel, 31 rue St-André-des-Arts, 6e. M° St-Michel (☎43.26.29.03). Rooms are adequate; great location.

Hôtel Tholozé, 24 rue Tholozé 18e. M° Abbesses, Blanche (☎46.06.74.83). Basic but good location.

Youth hostels, foyers and campsites

At the **cheapest end** of the scale there are the city's **youth hostels**, *Jules Ferry* (8 bd Jules-Ferry, 11e; M° République; ☎43.57.55.60; some double rooms); *D'Artagnan* (80 rue Vitruve, 20e; M° Porte de Bagnolet; ☎43.61.08.75); and *Y&H Hostel* (80 rue Mouffetard, 5e; M° Monge; ☎45.35.09.53; reception 8–11am and 5pm–1am). These should all be booked in advance – a couple of months ahead for the summer – but out of season it's worth giving them a call.

Slightly more expensive, but a better bet unless you've been super-efficient, are the **foyers** (hostel) run by **Accueil des Jeunes (AJF)**. They have offices in the Gare du Nord arrivals hall (Oct.–June, Mon.–Fri. 9.15am–6.15pm; June–Sept., 8am–10pm daily; ☎42.85.86.19); at 119 rue St-Martin, 4e, opposite the Centre Beaubourg (M° Châtelet-les-Halles; Mon.–Sat. 9.30am–7.30pm; ☎42.77.87.80); at 16 rue du Pont-Louis-Phillipe, 4e (M° Hôtel-de-Ville; Mon.–Fri. 9.30am–6.30pm; ☎42.78.04.82); and at 136 bd St-Michel, 5e, in the Quartier Latin (M° Pont-Royal; Mon.–Sat. 9.30am–7pm; ☎43.54.95.86). They guarantee finding you 'decent and low-cost lodging with immediate reservation'. Phone or call in when you arrive – there's no advance booking. The organisation runs five *foyers* of its own: *Fourcy*, 6 rue de Fourcy, 4e (☎42.74.23.45); *Le Fauconnier*, 11 rue du Fauconnier, 4e (☎42.74.23.45); *Maubuisson*, 12 rue des Barres, 4e (☎42.72.72.09); *François Miron*, 4e (☎42.72.72.09); – all four very central, in historic buildings in the Marais (M° St-Paul, Pont-Marie or Hôtel-de-Ville) – and *Résidence Bastille*, 151 av Ledru-Rollin, 1e (M° Ledru-Rollin; ☎43.79.53.86). Some of their *foyers* have double (or triple) rooms as well as dormitory beds.

Another organisation, the **Centre International de Paris (BVJ)**, has fractionally more expensive **foyers**, equally central if not more so. These are *Paris/Louvre*, 20 rue Jean-Jacques Rousseau, 1er (M° Louvre; ☎42.36.88.18); *Paris/Opéra*, 11 rue Thérèse, 1er (M° Pyramides; ☎42.60.77.23); *Paris/Les*

Halles, 5 rue du Pélican, 1er (M° Les Halles/Louvre; ☎42.60.92.45); *Paris/ Quartier Latin*, 44 rue des Bernadins, 5e (M° Maubert-Mutualité; ☎43.29.34.80). You can't book in advance so turn up early or phone as soon as you arrive.

CIDJ at 101 quai Branly, 15e, (M° Bir-Hakeim; ☎45.66.40.20; Mon.–Fri. 9am–7pm) can provide further lists of youth centres. Another possibility for longer stays is **France Monde Etudiants**, (14 rue du Regard, 6e; ☎45.44.47.52) who offer vacationing French students' rooms to foreigners from June to September. Try also the notice boards at the American and British churches (65 quai d'Orsay, 7e and 5 rue d'Aguesseau, 8e).

There is a **campsite** – usually crowded and in theory reserved for French camping club members – by the Seine in the Bois de Boulogne (allée du Bord-de-l'Eau, 16e; M° Porte-Maillot; ☎45.06.14.98) and two in Champigny-sur-Marne just east of the city: *Camping du Tremblay*, quai de Polangis (RER A2 to Joinville-le-Pont, bus #108; ☎42.83.38.24) and *Camping de Paris-Est*, bd des Alliés (RER A2 Joinville-le-Pont; ☎42.83.38.24). There's also one at Versailles: *Camping Municipal de Versailles*, 31 rue Berthelot (RER C5 to Porchefontaine; ☎49.51.23.61). Or, if you're desperate, you can camp at two of the **suburban hostels** at Choisy-le-Roi (125 av de Villeneuve-St-Georges; ☎48.90.92.30; RER C2/C4/C6 to Choisy-le-Roi, cross the the Seine, turn right and follow the signs – about a 20 min. walk) and at Chatenay-Malabry (3 voie du Loup-Pendu; ☎46.32.17.43; 3 nights minimum; RER B2 to Robinson, bus #198A to place Cyrano-de-Bergerac, *AJ* signed 200m).

THE CITY

There are obviously numerous ways of approaching a city as big as Paris – you don't have to start with the Eiffel Tower or Champs-Elysées. We've **structured** our account in chunks of territory that share a common identity. Though they do not correspond exactly to the boundaries of the twenty *arrondissements*, they are arranged in the same configuration, starting in the centre of town and working outwards, south and west, north and east. Apart from a couple of suggested walks – from the Parc Monceau to the edge of Montmartre and along the St-Denis canal – the descriptions that follow are designed for getting the most out of a neighbourhood, rather than as strict itineraires to be followed.

Some cafés, markets, shops and museum buildings are mentioned here in passing. For full details or listings see relevant chapters below.

The Champs-Elysées

La Voie Triomphale, or Triumphal Way, stretches in a straight line from the western end of the **Louvre** to the modern complex of skyscrapers at **La Défense**, 9km away, incorporating some of the world's most famous urban landmarks – the Champs-Elysées, Arc de Triomphe and the Louvre. Its monumental constructions have been erected over the centuries by kings and emperors, presidents and corporations, to propagate French power and prestige. The tradition dies hard. Further aggrandisement has been accomplished to coincide with the bicentennial celebrations of the 1789 Revolution: an enormous white marble arch at the head of La Défense commemorates the Declaration of the Rights of Man (women still invisible), and a glass pyramid entrance in the central courtyard of the much-expanded Louvre.

The best view of this grandiose and simple geometry of kings to capital is from the top of the **Arc de Triomphe**, Napoléon's homage to the armies of France and himself (10am–6pm in summer, 10am–5pm in winter; expensive). Your attention, however, will be somewhat distracted by the mesmerising traffic movements in **place de l'Etoile**, the world's oldest organised roundabout, directly below you. From here, the broad **avenue des Champs-Elysées** sweeps downhill to the east to end in the motorised maelstrom of **place de la Concorde**, where the same anarchic vehicles make crossing to the centre point a death-defying feat.

As it happens, some 1300 people did die here between 1793 and 1795, beneath the Revolutionary guillotine: Louis XVI, Marie-Antoinette, Danton and Robespierre among them. The centrepiece of the *place*, chosen like its name to make no comment on these events, is an **obelisk** from the temple of Luxor, offered as a favour-currying gesture by the viceroy of Egypt in 1829. It serves merely to pivot more geometry: the alignment of the French parliament, the **Chambre des Deputés**, on the far side of the Seine with the church of the **Madeleine** to the north. And the symmetry continues beyond the *place* in the **Tuileries gardens** where statues look down with equal indifference on prams pushed by nannies or backpackers sunbathing on the formal squares and circles that accentuate the axis running through to the Louvre.

Back to the west, between Concorde and the Rond-Point roundabout, the Champs-Elysées is bordered by chestnut trees and municipal flowerbeds, pleasant enough to stroll among but not sufficiently dense to muffle the

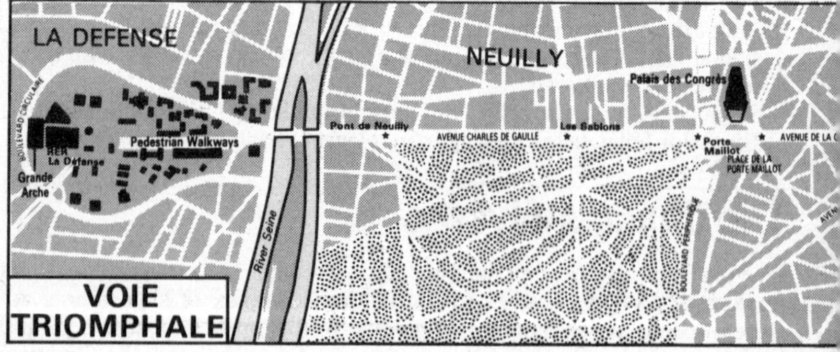

disconcerting squeal of accelerating vehicles. The two massive buildings rising above the greenery to the south are the **Grand** and **Petit Palais** with their overloaded neoclassical exteriors and railway station roofs. On the north side, combat police guard the high walls around the presidential **Elysée palace** and the line of ministries and embassies ending with the U.S. at the corner of place de la Concorde. On Sundays you can see a stranger manifestation of the self-images of states in the postage **stamp market** at the corner of avenues Gabriel and Marigny.

Though the glamour of the Champs-Elysées has long since been dissipated by airline and automobile head offices, it is still the setting for major jamborees. On December 31 it's the Paris equivalent of Trafalgar Square with everyone happily hooting the New Year in. On Bastille Day – July 14 – it turns into a parade ground for guns, tanks, missiles and President.

To reach **La Défense** at the extreme western end of the *Voie Triomphale,* go one stop on the RER from Etoile – there you follow the signs for *Parvis,* avoiding, at all costs, the snare of the *Quatre Temps* hypermarket. Once on the *parvis,* you have before you and above you a perfect monument to wastefulness and inhumanity of capital production. There is no formal pattern to the arrangement of towers. Apartment blocks, offices of ELF, Esso, IBM, banks and other businesses compete for size, dazzle of surface and ability to make you dizzy. Only the megalithic white hollow cube of the new **Tête Défense** (Mon–Sat 9–6pm, Sun 9.30–midnight) brings the whole conglomeration into line – the line of the Voie Triomphale. Mercifully, **bizarre art works** transform the nightmare into comic entertainment. Jean Miró's giant wobbly creatures despair at their misfit status beneath the biting edges and curveless heights of the buildings. Opposite, Alexander Calder's red iron offering is a *stabile* rather than a mobile and between them a black marble metronome shape without a beat releases a goal-less line across the *parvis.* A classic war memorial perches on a concrete plinth in front of a plastic coloured waterfall and, nearer the river, disembodied people clutch each other around endlessly repeated concrete flowerbeds.

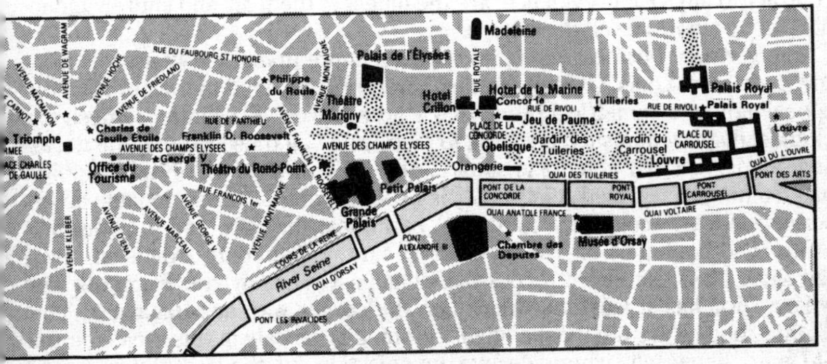

The *Passages*: Right Bank commerce

In the narrow streets of the 1er and 2e *arrondissements*, between the **Louvre and bd Montmartre**, the grand institutions of state are embedded in a welter of small business premises – the ragtrade, media, sex and old-fashioned shopping. The greatest contrast is provided by the crumbling and secretive **Passages**, shopping arcades with glass roofs, tiled floors and unobtrusive entrances, that predate the imposition of the major boulevards. Some are being done up and taken over by designer fashion, such as **Galerie Vivienne** (between rue Vivienne and rue des Petits-Champs) with flamboyant Grecian and marine motifs, and Jean-Paul Gaultier's shop. The neighbouring **Galerie Colbert**, lit by bunches of bulbous lamps, has become a showcase extension for the Bibliothèque Nationale.

North of rue St-Marc the decline of the *passages* from their nineteenth-century chic is more noticeable. The grid of half-abandoned arcades around **passage des Panoramas** has a typical combination of bric-à-brac shops, bars, stamp dealers, and an upper-crust printer, established 1867, with intricately carved shop-fittings of the same period. In **passage Jouffroy** across bd Montmartre, a Monsieur Segas sells walking canes and theatrical antiques opposite a North African and Asian carpet emporium. Further on, beyond the next street, you can hunt for old comics and cameras in **passage Verdeau.**

The best, stylistically, are the dilapidated three-story **passage du Grand-Cerf** (at the bottom of rue St-Denis) and **Galerie Véro-Dodat** (off rue Croix-des-Petits-Champs). This is the most homogenous and aristocratic, with painted ceilings and panelled shop-fronts divided by black marble columns. At no. 26, Monsieur Capia keeps a collection of antique dolls in a shop piled high with miscellaneous curios.

Place du Caire is the centre of the ragtrade district, where frenetic trading and deliveries of cloth, the food market on rue des Petits-Carreaux, and general to-ing and fro-ing make a lively change from the office-bound quarters further west. Beneath an extraordinary pseudo-Egyptian facade of grotesque Pharaonic heads (a celebration of Napoléon's conquest of Egypt), an archway opens onto a series of arcades, the **passage du Caire**. These, contrary to any visible evidence, are the oldest of them all, and entirely monopolised by wholesale clothes shops.

The garment business gets progressively more upmarket westwards from the trade area. Louis XIV's **place des Victoires**, adjoined to the north by the appealingly unsymmetrical **place des Petits-Pères**, is a centre for designer clothes, displayed in such a way as to discourage all those without the necessary funds. Another autocratic square, **place Vendôme**, with Napoléon high on a column of recycled Austro-Russian canons, offers the fashionable accessories for haute couture – jewellery, perfumes, the Ritz, and a Rothschild office. The boutiques on **rue St-Honoré** and its Faubourg extension reach the same class, paralleled across the Champs-Elysées by **rue François 1er** where **Dior** has at least four blocks on the corner with av Montaigne. After clothes, bodies are the most evident commodity on sale in this area – on rue St-Denis, above all, where despite unionisation by the prostitutes, pimps

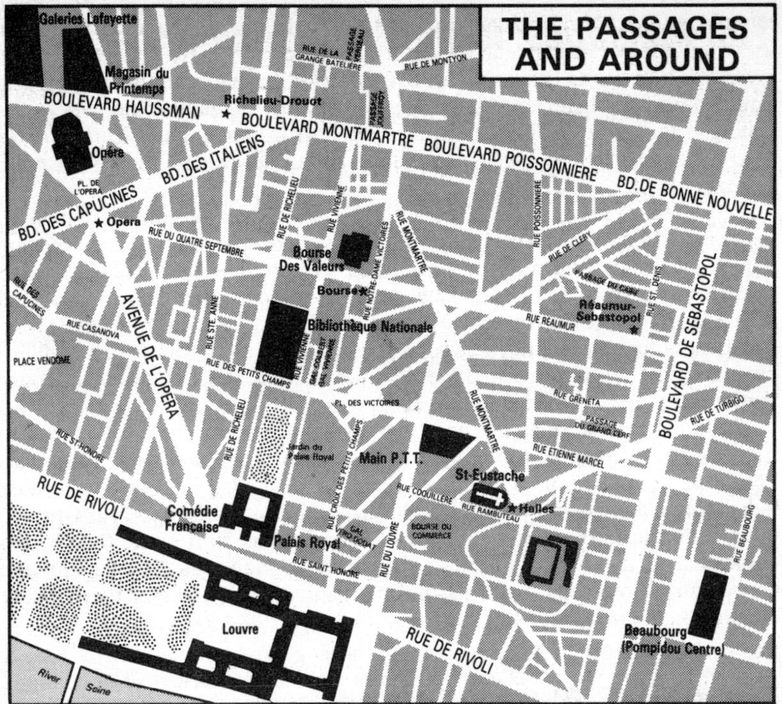

reign supreme. Rue Ste-Anne is considerably more discreet, and the prostitutes are gay, transvestite, and underage.

Nearby, the **Bourse** is the scene for dealing in stocks and shares, dollars and gold. The classical order of the facade utterly belies the scene within, which is like an unruly boys' public school, with creaking floors, tottering pigeon-holes and people scuttling about with bits of paper. They've only very recently latched on to microchips and the real financial sharks go elsewhere for their deals.

There is another obese building on the Greek temple model in the neighbouring *quartier*, the **church of the Madeleine**, which serves for society weddings and the perspective across place de la Concorde. There's a **flower market** every day except Monday along the east side of the church and a luxurious Art Nouveau loo by the métro at the junction of place and bd Madeleine. In the northeast corner of the *place* are two blocks of the best food display in Paris – at *Fauchon's*. If you want a cheap midday meal in this area, try rue des Capucines, off the boulevard half way between the Madeleine and the **Opéra**, the city's most preposterous building. Its architect, Charles Garnier, looks suitably foolish in a golden statue on the rue Auber side of his edifice that so perfectly suited the court of Napoléon III. Excessively ornate and covering three acres, it provided ample space for aristocratic preening, ceremonial pomp and the social intercourse of opera-goers, for whom the performance itself was a very secondary matter. Contemporary lovers of the art who can't afford a £15–30 ticket have to wait in line all night. You can visit the **interior** (11am–5pm), including the auditorium, where the ceiling is the work of Chagall. The classic horror movie, *The Phantom of the Opera*, was set, though never filmed, here and underground there is a stream to lend credence to the tale.

At the other end of av de l'Opéra, the **Palais Royal**, originally Richelieu's residence, then royal property, now houses various government and constitutional bodies and the **Comédie Française** – where the classics of the French theatre are performed. The palace **gardens** were once a café hotspot and arena for public entertainment overlooked by flats lived in by Cocteau and Colette among others. Folly has returned in the form of zebra pillars in different sizes, like sticks of rock standing amid flowing water in the main courtyard – the work of Daniel Buren in 1982.

These gardens are now no more than a useful shortcut from the Louvre to rue des Petits-Champs, though a certain charm lurks about rue Beaujolais bordering the northern end, with its corner café looking onto the Théâtre du Palais Royal and short arcades leading up to the main street. Across, just to the left, is the forbidding wall of the **Bibliothèque Nationale**, the French equivalent of the British Library. They have a public display of coins and ecclesiastical treasures (open 1–5pm), so you can at least enter the building should you feel so inclined.

Les Halles and Beaubourg

In 1969 the main food market was moved out to the suburbs after more than 800 years in the heart of the city. There was widespread opposition to the destruction of Victor Baltard's nineteenth-century pavilions and considerable disquiet at what renovation of the area would mean. The authorities' excuse was the RER and métro interchange they had to have below. Digging began in 1971 and the hole that remained unfilled for 15 years was one of the sore spots and jokes of Paris. In **Les Halles** now, no trace has survived of the working-class quarter with its night bars and bistros serving the market traders. Rents rival the 16e, and the all-night places serve and profit from the salaried and cocaine-sniffing classes.

From Châtelet-Les Halles RER, you surface only after ascending levels 4 to 0 of the **Forum des Halles** shopping centre. The aquarium-like arcades are enclosed by glass buttocks with white steel creases sliding down to an imprisoned patio. A cultural centre tops two sides of the Forum in a simple construction – except for the mirrors – that just manages to be out of sync with the curves and hollows below. Trees, lawns and fountains (above more underground commerce and culture) have finally flourished in the park that stretches from the forum to the rotunda of the **Bourse du Commerce** and the Gothic monkeys' rock of **St-Eustache** (where a woman spoke out for the abolition of marriage during the Commune of 1871).

If you get bored on a futile bargain-hunt in the Forum, the **Vidéothèque de Paris** (Porte St-Eustache, 2 Grande Galerie; Tues–Sun, 12.30–7.30pm, Fri 12.30–10pm) has four video projections a day (features and ducumentaries). It also boasts an impressive collection of documentaries, newsreels and commercials, all of which are either about Paris or have Paris as a backdrop. Pick up the users guide at the desk, sit down at one of the screens and key in a place name, a date, an actor's or a director's name, and a list of options will appear on the screen (costs 18F).

Or instead, join the throng around the **Fontaine des Innocents** and watch and listen to water cascading down perfect Renaissance proportions. There are hundreds of people all around the Forum, filling in time, hustling

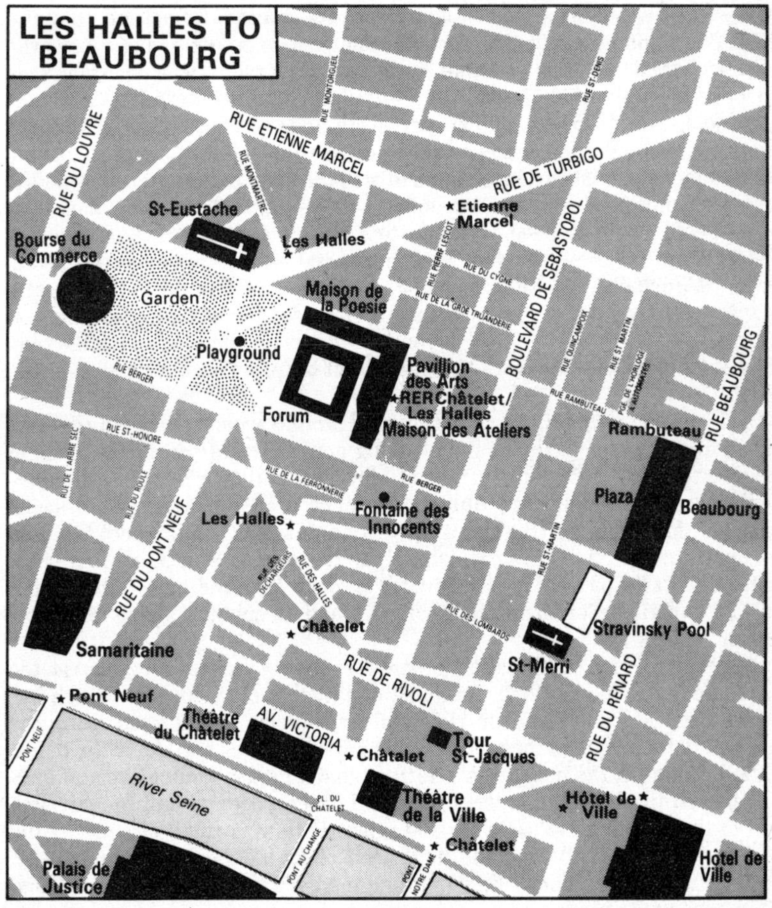

or just hanging around. Pick-pocketing and sexual harassment are pretty routine and it can be very tense at night, particularly when the police dogs arrive.

Retreating back towards the Louvre, streets like **de l'Arbre-Sec** and **du Roule** revive the attractions of window shopping, with displays of 1920s clothes, decorated shop fronts and secluded *salons de thé*. Or you can shop in the Art Nouveau gold, green, and glass decor of the **Samaritaine** department store on the waterfront. **To the east** the area between place du Châtelet and Les Halles teems with jazz bars, night clubs and restaurants and is more crowded at 2am than 2pm.

In the daytime the main flow of feet is to and from Les Halles and **Beaubourg**, the **Georges Pompidou National Art and Culture Centre**. At least this much-discussed building with its external frame and coloured pipes, ducts and escalator, and serious maintenance problems has a powerful presence. And no matter what is going on inside it is permanently surrounded by the mime, magic and fire of street performers. The centre is open, free, every day except Tuesday, from noon to 8pm and until 10pm at weekends; for galleries, cinema, kids, etc. see the relevant chapter. On the ground floor the postcard selection and art bookshop betters anything on the streets outside (and there are free toilets). The escalator is usually an endless line of people, but you have to ride up this glass intestine once. As the circles of spectators on the plaza recede, a horizontal skyline appears: the Sacré-Coeur, St-Eustache, the Eiffel Tower, Notre-Dame, the Panthéon, the Tour St-Jacques with its solitary gargoyle and La Défense, menacing in the distance. From the platform at the top you can look down on the château-style chimneys of the Hôtel de Ville with their flowerpot offspring sprouting all over the lower rooftops.

Back on the ground, **visual entertainments** around Beaubourg don't appeal to every taste. There's the clanking gold *Défenseur du Temps* clock in the Quartier de l'Horloge, courtesy of Mayor Chirac (see below); a *trompe-l'oeil* as you look along rue Aubry-le-Boucher from Beaubourg; and sculptures and fountains by Tinguely and Nicky de St-Phalle in the pool between the centre and Eglise St-Merri, which pay homage to Stravinsky and show scant respect for passersby. The locality is much favoured by small commercial art galleries, St-Martin, Quincampoix and Beaubourg being the most popular streets.

Rue Renard, the continuation of rue Beaubourg, meets the river at the **Hôtel de Ville**, the city hall. An illustrated history of the edifice, which has always been a prime target in riots and revolutions, is displayed along the platform of the Châtelet métro on the Neuilly-Vincennes line. After the defeat of the Commune, the bourgeoisie decided that a Parisian municipal authority was against the better interests of law and order, property and the suppression of the working class. So for 100 years, Paris was ruled directly by the ministry of the interior and the next head of an independent municipality, elected in 1977, was none other than the man who would be president, and failed – Jacques Chirac.

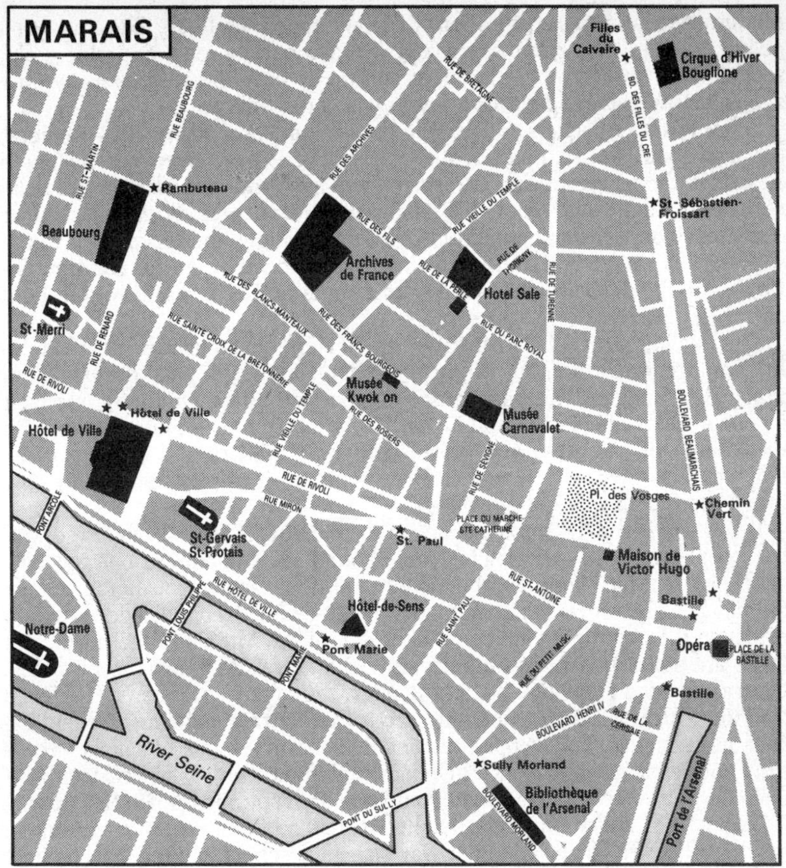

The Marais and the Ile St-Louis

Jack Kerouac translates **rue des Francs-Bourgeois** as 'street of the outspoken middle classes'. The original owners of the mansions that line its length would not have taken kindly to such a slight on their blue-bloodedness. The name's origin is medieval and it was not until the sixteenth and seventeenth centuries that the **Marais**, as the area between Beaubourg and the Bastille is known, became a fashionable aristocratric district. It was later abandoned to the masses, who, until some fifteen years ago, were living ten to a room on unserviced, squalid streets. Since then, gentrification has taken over and the middle classes are finally ensconced – not all outspoken, and mainly media, arty or gay. The renovated mansions, their grandeur mostly concealed by the narrow streets, have become museums, libraries, offices or trendy apartments. Though ringed by Haussmann's boulevards, the

Marais itself was spared the Baron's heavy touch, and very little has been pulled down in the recent upgrading. It is Paris at its most desirable – old, secluded, as unthreatening by night as it is by day, and with as many little shops, *salons de thé* and places to eat as you could wish for.

A few low-rent pockets still exist to the east and around **rue des Rosiers**, the traditional Jewish quarter of the city. There have been several bomb attacks in the last few years on synagogues here and on Goldenberg's deli/restaurant, and FN (Front National) spray cans periodically eject their obscenities on walls and shopfronts. Not surprisingly, the reception given to strangers is rather stiff, but you can shrug off hostility in the **Hamam St-Paul** or in the deep armchairs of **Le Loir dans la Théière** *salon de thé*, both on rue des Rosiers.

The peeling streets between **rues de Sévigné** and **Turenne** near rue St-Antoine are worth walking through just for contrast, if your destination is **place des Vosges**. This vast square of stone and brick symmetry was built for the majesty of Henri IV and Louis XIII, whose statue is hidden by trees in the middle of the grass and gravel gardens. Toddlers and octogenarians, lunch-time workers and school children come to sit or play here, in the only green space of any size in the Marais.

Below rue Rivoli/St-Antoine, many of the old houses have disappeared with the people in a post-war hatchet job. Around rue St-Paul are outrageously expensive antique shops and the modern upmarket apartments of the 'Village St-Paul'. Though seventeenth- and eighteenth-century magnificence is still in evidence it lacks the architectural cohesion of the Marais to the north. But there are still a few medieval leftovers – the **Hôtel de Sens** (now a public library) on rues Hôtel-de-Ville and Figuier, the tottering timbered dwellings on **rue François-Miron** and the *Acceuil de France* buildings behind St-Gervais-et-Protais. The stepped rue des Barres with its mix of smells – scent from gardens, incense from St-Gervais and food from a tiny restaurant – makes a tranquil passage down to Pont Louis-Philippe and the **Ile St-Louis**.

This island, unlike its larger neighbour, has no monuments or museums, just high houses on secluded one-way streets, a school, church and the best sorbets in the world chez *M Berthillon*. If you're the Pretender to the French throne or the Aga Khan, this is where you have your Paris home. If not, then you can still seek seclusion on the *quais*, tightly clutching a *Berthillon* triple scoop as you descend the steps or climb over the low gate on the right of the garden across bd Henri IV to reach the best sunbathing spot in Paris. Nothing can rival the taste of iced passion or kiwi fruit, guava, melon or whichever flavour – a sensation that ripe, fresh-picked fruit can only aspire to. Nevertheless the island does have its own considerable charm, even when Berthillon and his six concessionaries are closed.

Ile de la Cité

The **Ile de la Cité** is where Paris began. The earliest settlements were sited here, as was the small Gallic town of Lutetia overrun by Julius Caesar's troops in 52 B.C. A natural defensive site commanding a major east–west river trade route, it was an obvious candidate for a bright future. The Romans garrisoned it and laid out one of their standard military town plans, overlapping onto the Left Bank. While it never achieved any great political importance, they endowed it with an administrative centre which became the palace of the Merovingian kings in 508, then of the counts of Paris, who in 987 became kings of France.

Today the lure of the island lies in its tail-end – the **square du Vert-Galant** – its **quais**, **place Dauphine** and the **cathedral of Notre-Dame** itself. The central section has been dulled by heavy-handed nineteenth-century demolition that displaced 25000 people and replaced them by four vast edifices largely given over to housing the law. The litter-blown space in front of the cathedral was a by-product though that, at least, has the virtue of allowing a full-frontal view.

If you arrive by the **Pont-Neuf**, the city's oldest bridge, you'll see some steps behind the statue of Henri IV leading down to the *square*, a small tree-lined green enclosed within the triangular stern of the island. The prime spot to occupy is the extreme point beneath a weeping willow – haunt of lovers, sparrows and sunbathers.

On the other side of the bridge, across the street from king Henri, who incidentally commissioned the Pont-Neuf, the sanded, chestnut-shaded **place Dauphine** remains one of the city's most secluded and exclusive squares, with a couple of restaurants, a *salon de thé* and a much-sought-after cheap hotel, the *Henri IV*. Behind it the nondescript **Palais de Justice** has swallowed up the palace that was home to the Roman governors and then to the French kings until a bloody revolt in 1358 frightened them off to the greater security of the Louvre.

In a courtyard to the left of the Palais de Justice main gate (on bd du Palais), stands the **Sainte-Chapelle**, built by Louis IX to house a collection of holy relics he had bought at extortionate rates from the bankrupt empire of Byzantium. Though much restored, it remains one of the finest achievements

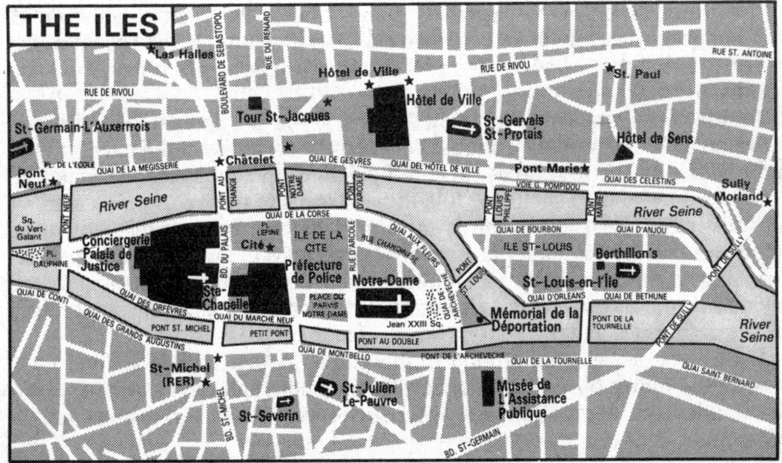

of French Gothic (consecrated in 1248). Very tall in relation to its length it looks like a cathedral choir lopped off and transformed into an independent building. Its most radical feature is its fragility: the reduction of structural masonry to a minimum to make way for a huge expanse of stunning **stained glass**. The impression inside is of being enclosed within the wings of a myriad of butterflies – the predominant colours blue and red, and, in the later rose window, grass-green and blue. It pays to get there as early as possible (open 10am–6pm summer, 10am–5pm winter, Oct–Mar; half-price Sun. and holidays). It is a terrible tourist trap, and expensive. The ticket includes entry to the **Conciergerie**, the old prison where Marie-Antoinette and, in their turn, the leading figures of the Revolution were incarcerated before execution. The chief interest of the Conciergerie is the enormous late Gothic *Salle des Gens d'Armes,* canteen and recreation room of the royal household staff. You are missing little in not seeing Marie-Antoinette's cell and various macabre mementoes of the guillotine's victims.

On the north side of the island by the Cité métro station there's a **flower and plant market** six days a week, with birds on Sunday. The *place* is named after one Lépine, the police boss who gave Paris *gendarmes* their white truncheons and whistles. The police headquarters is right behind.

The **Cathédrale de Notre-Dame** is photographed so much that even seeing it for the first time, you might find your response dulled by familiarity. Yet it is truly impressive, that great H-shaped west front, with its strong vertical divisions counterbalanced by the horizontal emphasis of gallery and frieze, all centred by the rose window. It demands to be seen as a whole, though that can scarcely have been possible when the medieval houses clustered around it. It is a solid, no-nonsense design, confessing its Romanesque ancestry. For the more fantastic kind of Gothic, look at the **north transept facade** with its gables and huge, fretted window space.

Notre-Dame was begun in 1160 under the auspices of Bishop de Sully and completed around 1245. In the nineteenth century, Viollet-le-Duc carried out extensive renovation work, including remaking most of the statuary – the entire frieze of kings, for instance – and adding the steeple and baleful-looking gargoyles, which you can see close-up if you brave the ascent of the towers (1–5.45pm in summer, 1–4.45pm in winter; half price Sun. and holidays).

Inside, the immediately striking feature, if you can ignore the noise and movement, is the dramatic contrast between the darkness of the nave and the light falling on the first great clustered pillars of the choir, emphasising the special nature of the sanctuary. It is the end walls of the transepts that admit all this light, nearly two-thirds glass, including two magnificent **rose windows** coloured in imperial purple. These, the vaulting, the soaring shafts reaching to the springs of the vaults, are all definite Gothic elements, yet, inside as out, there remains a strong sense of Romanesque in the stout round pillars of the nave and the general sense of four-squareness.

Before you leave, walk around to the public garden at the east end for a view of the **flying buttresses** supporting the choir, and then along the riverside under the south transept, where in spring the cherry trees are in blossom.

There is an interesting but expensive museum, the *Crypte Archéologique* (10am–6pm in summer, 10am–5pm in winter; half-price Sun.) under the place du Parvis where you can see the remains of walls, streets and houses of first millennium Paris.

The Left Bank

The term **Left Bank** (*rive gauche*) connotes Bohemian, dissident, intellectual – the radical student type, whether eighteen or eighty years old. As a topographical term it refers particularly to their traditional haunts – the warren of medieval lanes around the **boulevards St-Michel** and **St-Germain**, known as the **quartier Latin** because that was the language of the university located there right up until 1789. In modern times its reputation for turbulence and innovation has been renewed by the activities of such painters and writers as Picasso, Apollinaire, Breton, Henry Miller, Anaïs Nin and Hemingway after World War I, and Camus, Sartre, Juliette Greco and the Existentialists after World War II and the political turmoil of 1968, which escalated from student demonstrations and barricades to factory occupations, massive strikes and the near-overthrow of de Gaulle's presidency. This is not to say that all of Paris south of the Seine is the exclusive territory of revolutionaries and avant-gardists. The area does, however, have a different and distinct feel, and appearance, that you notice as soon as you cross the river.

St-Michel to rue Mouffetard

Bd St-Michel itself and the riverside streets to the east have become tawdry now and commercial, cashing in on the tourist appeal of the Latin Quarter. The narrow **rue de la Huchette**, once the mecca of avant-gardists, is, except for one theatre stuck in a 1950s timewarp, entirely given over to Greek restaurants of indifferent quality and inflated prices. At its further end is **rue St-Jacques**, aligned on the main street of Roman Paris, and in medieval times the road up which millions of pilgrims trudged at the start of their long march to St-Jacques-de-Compostelle in Spain. Just to the right, one block up from rue de la Huchette, the largely fifteenth-century **St-Séverin** is one of the more attractive Parisian churches with splendidly virtuoso chiselwork on the pillars of the Flamboyant choir (11am–1pm and 3.30–7.30pm).

Back toward the river on the other side of rue St-Jacques **square Viviani** provides the most flattering of all views of Notre-Dame. The mutilated little church of **St-Julien-le-Pauvre** in one corner is as old as the cathedral, though not much to look at. It once held university assemblies until some rumbustious students tore it apart in the 1500s. To the left on rue de la Bûcherie the English bookshop, **Shakespeare and Co**, is haunted by the shade of Joyce – and other great expatriate literati – though only by proxy, as Sylvia Beach, publisher of *Ulysses*, had her original shop on rue de l'Odéon. Despite their romantic reputation, the local *quais* hereabouts are not much fun to walk because of the traffic, unless you get right down by the water's edge.

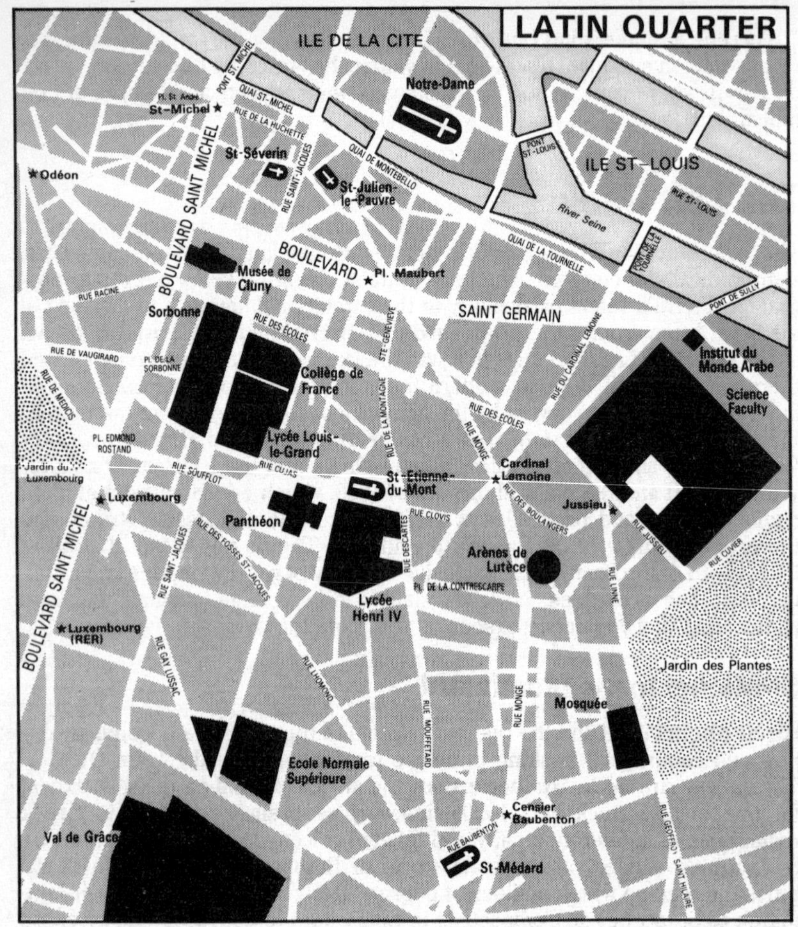

The best strolling area this side of bd St-Michel is around the slopes of the **Montagne Ste-Geneviève**, the hill on which the Panthéon stands. The best way in is either from **place Maubert** (good **market** Tues., Thurs. and Sat. am) or from the St-Germain/St-Michel intersection, where the walls of the third-century **Roman baths** are visible in the gardens of the **Hôtel de Cluny**. A sixteenth-century mansion resembling an Oxford or Cambridge college, the hôtel was built by the abbots of the powerful Cluny monastery as their Paris pied-à-terre. It now houses a very beautiful **museum** of medieval art. There is no charge for entry to the quiet shady courtyard.

The grim-looking buildings on the other side of rue des Ecoles are the **Sorbonne, Collège de France,** and **Lycée Louis-le-Grand**, all major constituents of the brilliant and mandarin world of French intellectual activity. You can put your nose in the Sorbonne courtyard without anyone objecting. The **Richelieu chapel**, dominating the uphill end, was the first Roman-influenced building in seventeenth-century Paris and set the trend for subsequent architectural developments. Nearby the traffic-free **place de la Sorbonne** with its lime trees, cafés and student habitués is a lovely place to sit.

Further up the hill the broad rue Soufflot provides an appropriately grand perspective on the domed and porticoed **Panthéon**, Louis XIV's thank-you to Sainte Geneviève, patron saint of Paris, for curing his illness. Imposing enough at a distance, it is cold and uninteresting close-up – not a friendly detail for the eye to rest on. The Revolution transformed it into a mausoleum for the great. It is deadly inside (10am–6pm in summer 10am–4pm in winter; closed Tues.). There are, however, several cafés to warm the heart's cockles down towards the Luxembourg gardens.

More diverting than the Panthéon is the mainly sixteenth-century church of **St-Etienne-du-Mont** on the corner of rue Clovis, with a facade combining Gothic, Renaissance and Baroque elements. The interior, if not exactly beautiful, is highly unexpected. The space is divided into three aisles by free-standing pillars connected by a narrow catwalk, and flooded with light by an exceptionally tall clerestory. Again unusually – for they mainly fell victim to the destructive anti-clericalism of the Revolution – the church still possesses its rood screen, a broad low arch supporting a gallery reached by twining spiral stairs. There is some good seventeenth-century glass in the cloister. Further down rue Clovis, a huge piece of king Phillippe Auguste's thirteenth-century city walls emerges from among the houses.

Just a step **south from place du Panthéon**, in the quiet rue des Fossés-St-Jacques, the curbside tables of the *Café de la Nouvelle Mairie* make an excellent lunchstop, while at the end of the street on rue St-Jacques there are several cheap restaurants, mainly Chinese. There is not much point in going further south on rue St-Jacques. The area is dull and lifeless once you're over the Gay-Lussac intersection, though Baroque enthusiasts might like to take a look at the seventeenth-century church of **Val-de-Grâce**, with its pedimented front and ornate cupola copied from St. Peter's in Rome. If you've got this far there's another big market and several brasseries around the corner on **bd Port-Royal.**

More enticing wandering is to be had in the villagey streets **east of the Panthéon. Rue de la Montagne-Ste-Geneviève** (a good restaurant street) climbs up from place Maubert across rue des Ecoles to the gates of the **Ecole Polytechnique,** one of the prestigious academies for entry to the top echelons of the state. It's now the Ministry of Research and Technology, the school having moved to the suburbs. There's a sunny little café outside the gates, and several cheap restaurants on rue de L'Ecole-Polytechnique, as well as *L'Harmottan*, a well-known publisher and bookshop specialising in Africa and the Third World.

From here rue Descartes leads into the medieval **rue Mouffetard**, a cobbled lane winding downhill to the church of **St-Médard**, once a country parish beside the now-covered river Bièvre. The bottom half of the street with its fruit and vegetable stands is still attractive. The upper half is all eating places, mostly Greek and not much better than those on rue de la

Huchette. Like any place devoted to entertaining tourists, it has lost its soul. The tiny **place de la Contrescarpe** halfway down was once an arty hangout; Hemingway wrote and George Brassens sang there. It is a dossers' rendezvous now.

A little **further east**, across rue Monge, however, are some of the city's most agreeable surprises. Down rue Daubenton, past a delightful Arab shop selling sweets, spices, and gaudy tea glasses you come to the crenellated walls of the Paris **mosque**, overtopped by greenery and a great square minaret. You can walk in the sunken garden and patios with their polychrome tiles and carved ceilings, but not into the prayer room (9am–noon and 2–6pm; closed Fri. and Muslim holidays). There is a **tea room** too, open to all, and a hamam.

Opposite the mosque is an entrance to the **Jardin des Plantes**, with a small, cramped, expensive zoo, botanical gardens, hothouses and museums of palaeontology and mineralogy – a pretty space of greenery to while away the middle of a day. By the rue Cuvier exit is a fine Cedar of Lebanon planted in 1734, raised from seed sent over from the Oxford Botanical Gardens, and a slice of an American sequoia more than 2000 years old with Christ's birth and other historical events marked on its rings. In the nearby physics labs Henri Becquerel discovered radioactivity in 1896, and two years later the Curies discovered radium – unwitting ancestors of the *force de frappe* (the French nuclear deterrent). Pierre Curie ended his days under the wheels of a brewer's cart on rue Dauphine.

Nearby, on the other side of the Science Faculty between the river and rue des Fossés-St-Bernard, is the **Institut du Monde Arabe**, one of the mammoth public projects initiated by Mitterrand. Almost all glass, with a central tower meant to resemble a pile of books, its most stunning aspect is the south side on which high-tech filters respond to the light like automatic lenses, contracting and expanding in a complex pattern of hexagons – a microchip age homage to Arab lattice walls.

A short distance away, with an entrance on rue de Navarre and another through a passage on rue Monge, is Paris's other Roman remain, the **Arènes de Lutèce**, an unexpected backwater, quite hidden from the street. It is a partly restored amphitheatre, with a *boules* field in the centre, benches, gardens and a kids' playground behind.

St-Germain

The northern half of the *6e arrondissement* centred on **place St-Germain-des-Prés** is the most physically attractive, lively and stimulating square kilometre in the entire city. The most dramatic approach is over the **Pont des Arts**, with the classic upstream view of the Ile de la Cité, the barges moored at the quai de Conti and the Tour St-Jacques and Hôtel de Ville breaking the Right Bank skyline. Downstream the eye is carried to the greenery of the Tuileries and the roofs of the Grand and Petit Palais. The dome and pediment at the end of the bridge belong to the **Institut de France**, seat of the Académie Française, an august body of writers and scholars whose mission is to safeguard the purity of the French language. This is the grandiose bit of

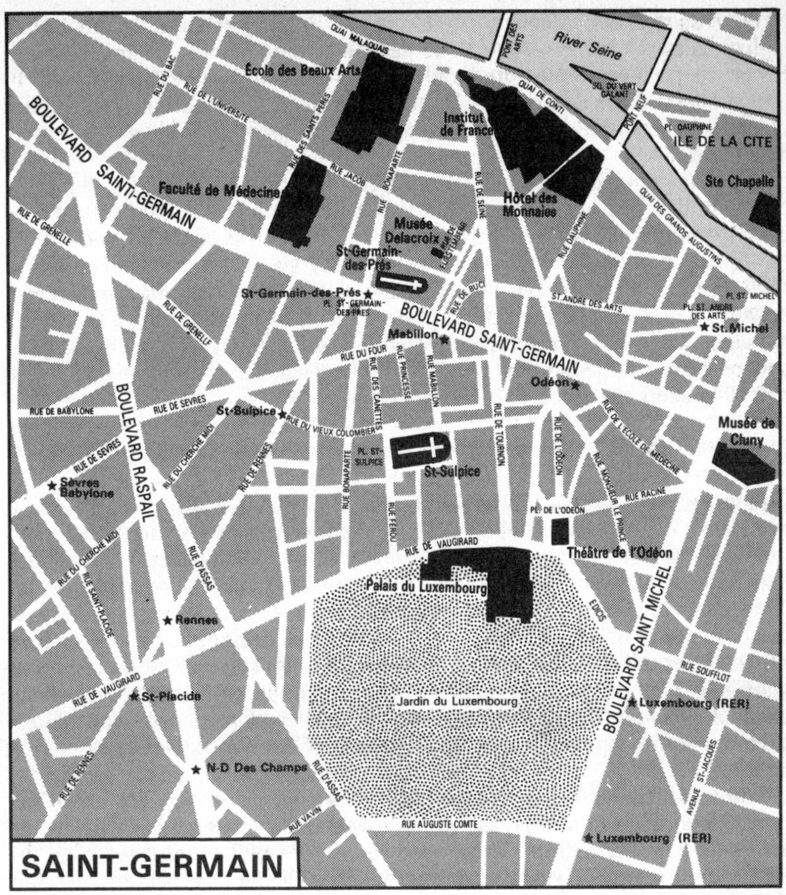

the Left Bank waterfront. To the left is the **Hôtel des Monnaies**, redesigned as the Mint in the late eighteenth century. To the right is the **Beaux-Arts**, the school of Fine Art, whose students throng the *quais* on sunny days, sketch pads on knee. Behind, the streets are full of smart little **art galleries,** some of them with extraordinary works for sale. You can wander in and have a look for nothing. Further down the river is the most elegant ex-railway station in existence – the **Museé d'Orsay.**

The **riverside quarter** is cut lengthwise by **rue St-André-des Arts** and **rue Jacob**. It is full of bookshops, galleries, antique shops, cafés and restaurants. Poke your nose into courtyards and sidestreets. The houses are four to six stories high, seventeenth- and eighteenth-century, some noble, some stiff, some bulging and tilted, all painted in infinite gradations of grey, pearl and off-white. Broadly speaking, the further west, the posher. Historical associations are legion. Picasso painted Guernica on rue des Grands-Augustins.

Molière started his career on rue Mazarine. Robespierre and Co. split ideological hairs at *Café Procope* on rue de l'Ancienne-Comédie. In rue Visconti, Racine died, Delacroix painted and Balzac's printing business went bust. In the parallel rue des Beaux Arts, Oscar Wilde died, Corot and Ampère – father of amps – lived, and the poet, Gérard de Nerval, went walking with a lobster on a leash.

If you're looking for lunch, **place** and **rue St-André** offer a tempting concentration of places – from Tunisian sandwich joints to seafood extravagance – and a brilliant **food market** on rue Buci up towards bd St-Germain (closed Mon.). Nearby rue Dauphine is pretty good, too. Before you get to Buci, there is an intriguing little passage on the left, **Cour du Commerce**, between a *crêperie* and the café, *Le Mazet*. Marat had his printing press in the passage, while Dr. Guillotin perfected his notorious machine by lopping sheeps' heads in the loft next door. A couple of smaller courtyards open off it, revealing another stretch of Phillippe Auguste's wall.

An alternative corner for midday food or quiet is around rue de l'Abbaye (vegetarian meals at *Guenmaï*) and the **place Furstemberg**, a tiny square where **Delacroix's old studio** has been converted to a museum (at no. 6). One street away are the square and church of **St-Germain-des-Prés**, with the *Deux Magots* café on the corner and *Flore* just down the street, both renowned for the number of philosophico-politico-poetico-literary backsides that have shined their seats. If you sit at the *Deux Magots' terrasse* you are more likely to be dragged into some street-clown's act than engaged in high-flown debate. The square tower across the *place* belongs to the **church of St-Germain**, all that remains of an enormous Benedictine monastery. The interior is best, its pure Romanesque lines still clear under the deforming paint of nineteenth-century frescoes. The oldest elements are the stubby columns in the arcade which have been re-used from a sixth-century church on the site.

South of bd St-Germain the streets around St-Sulpice are calm and classy. **Rue Mabillon** is pretty, with a row of old houses set back below the level of the modern street. There are two or three restaurants, including the old-fashioned *Aux Charpentiers*, property of the Guild of Carpenters, which is decorated with models of rafters and roof trees. On the left are the **halles St-Germain**, on the site of a fifteenth-century market.

Rue St-Sulpice, with a delicious *pâtisserie* and a shop called *L'Estrelle* specialising in teas, coffees and jams, leads through to the front of the enormous church of **St-Sulpice**. The *Café de la Mairie*, on the sunny north side of the eighteenth-century square, is popular with the student crowd. The church, erected around 1700, is austerely classical, with a Doric colonnade surmounted by an Ionic, Corinthian pilasters in the towers, only one of which is finished, and Delacroix frescoes (in the first chapel on the right). In the square outside, the chestnut trees and fountain work to create a peaceful and harmonious effect.

The adjoining rue Férou, where a gentleman called Pottier composed the Internationale in 1776, connects with **rue de Vaugirard**, Paris's longest street, going all the way out to Porte-de-Versailles, where the *Foires* (Ideal Home, Agricultural Show, etc.) take place. On the south side of the street are the **Luxembourg gardens** and **palace**, which Henri IV's widowed queen, Marie de Médicis, built to remind her of the Palazzo Pitti and Giardino Boboli of her native Florence. Today it is the seat of the French Senate. The gardens, with formal chestnut *allées*, sunken pond and some unlandscaped land over to the southwest, are the chief lung and recreation ground of the Left Bank. The shady corner by the **Fontaine de Médicis** close to rue de Médicis is an ideal place to relax on a hot summer's day. There are tennis courts, pony rides, a playground, a *boules* pitch, boats for hire on the pond, and in the southwest corner a miniature orchard of pear trees. To the south the treelined gardens of avenue de l'Observatoire stretch down to the **Observatory**. Just before you get to it, on the corner of bd Montparnasse, in front of the *Closerie des Lilas* café, is a **statue of Marshal Ney**, one of Napoleon's most dashing generals, on the spot where he faced the firing squad in 1815.

Rue de Médicis has some handsome **bookshops**, though not for bargain hunters. Albert Blanchard specialises in the very best antiquarian scientific books. No. 3 concentrates on the occult. *L'Impensé Radical* deals exclusively in games. At the Vaugirard end, the attractive café *Au Petit Suisse* is right next door to the back of the **Théâtre de l'Odéon**, whose pleasing Doric portico faces a semi-circular *place* and rue de l'Odéon, with more bookshops, leading back to bd St-Germain.

Montparnasse

Like other Left Bank *quartiers* **Montparnasse** still trades on its association with those responsible for the inter-war artistic and literary boom, habitués of the *Select, Coupole, Dôme and Rotonde* cafés, all still going strong on bd du Montparnasse east of the Gare. In the first years of the century it was also the stamping ground of outlawed Russian revolutionaries, so many of them that the Tsarist police ran a special Paris section to keep tabs. Trotsky and Lenin both lodged in the area, Trotsky on rue de la Gaîté, now a seedy street of sex shops, and cinemas showing blue films.

The boulevard teems with people, cinemas, restaurants, cafés, brasseries, and bookshops. **Rue de Rennes** opposite the station is a major shopping street. Though the café clientele is arty/bourgeois, the boulevard is far from smart. It is the frontier between the bourgeois streets to the north and the working-class, villagey, even slummy streets to the south, especially between av de Maine and the railway tracks which used to suck thousands of emigré Bretons into this part of the city. The station itself is the site of a huge modernistic redevelopment project, dominated by the **Tour de Montparnasse**, at 56 stories, one of Europe's tallest office buildings. You can go to the top more cheaply than the Tour Eiffel, but it certainly isn't worth it for the price, unless it's a very clear day (9.30am–11pm in summer, 10am–10pm in winter.)

On **bd Edgar-Quinet**, beyond the **street market**, is the main entrance to the **Montparnasse cemetery**, a gloomy city of the dead, with ranks of miniature temples, dreary and bizarre, and plenty of illustrious names, from Baudelaire to Sartre and André Citroën to Saint-Saens. Near the southwest

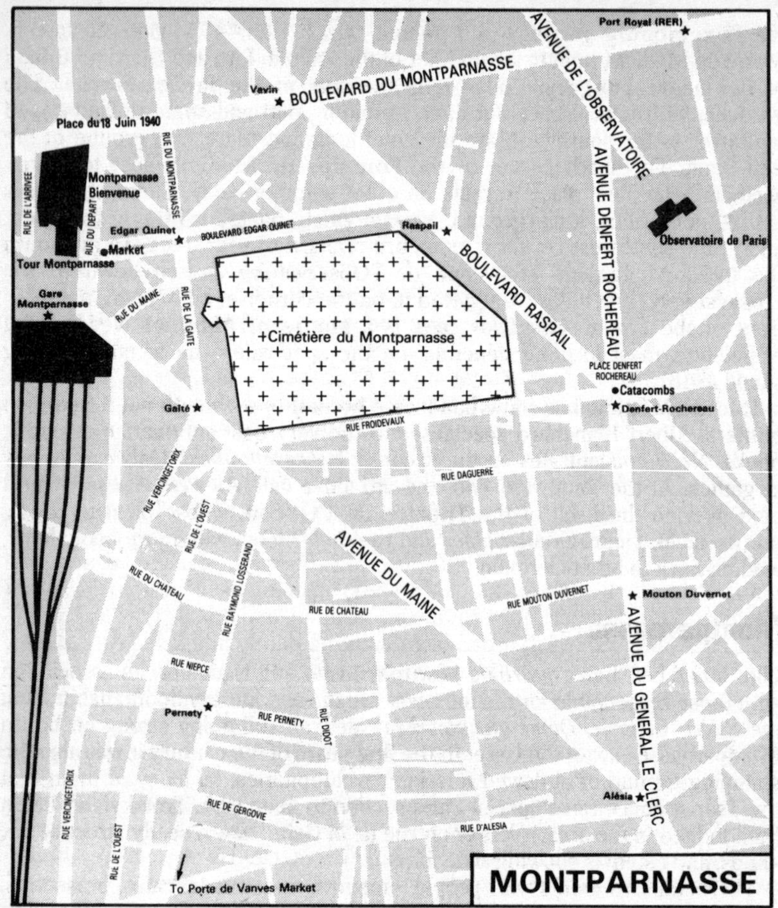

corner is an old windmill, one of the seventeenth-century taverns frequented by the carousing, versifying students who gave the district its name of Parnassus. If you are determined to spend your time among the dear departed, you can get down into the **catacombs** (Tues.–Fri. 2–6pm; Sat. and Sun. 9–11am and 2–4pm) from nearby place Denfert-Rochereau; they are abandoned quarries stacked with millions of bones cleared from over-crowded cemeteries in 1785 – claustrophobic in the extreme. Punks and art-radicals developed a taste for this as a party location – something the authorities soon put a stop to.

For an idea of an older, working class, almost provincial Paris, wander the back streets between here and **Porte-de-Vanves**. Rue Didot, for instance, will take you to the Porte where, on Saturday and Sunday in av Lafenestre and Marc-Sangnier, there is a **market** of old clothes, books, records and assorted bric-à-brac amid workers' housing developments.

The *15e arrondissement* to the west is of little interest, though there is a long **food market** on rue de la Convention, and off it, in passage de Dantzig, a curious polygonal building known as **La Rûche**, where Modigliani, Léger, and Chagall among others had their studios. It was designed by Eiffel as the wine pavilion for the 1900 trade fair.

Trocadero, Eiffel Tower and Les Invalides

The vistas are splendid: from the terrace of the **Palais de Chaillot** (place du Trocadéro) across the river to the Tour Eiffel and Ecole Militaire, from the ornate 1900 Pont Alexandre III along the grassy Esplanade to the Hôtel des Invalides.

The Palais de Chaillot, like a latter-day Pharaoh's mausoleum (1937), is, however, home to several interesting **museums** and a theatre used for diverse but usually radical productions. And the **Eiffel Tower**, though no beauty, is an amazing structure. When completed in 1889 it was the tallest building in the world at 300m. Its 7000 tons of steel, in terms of pressure, sit as lightly on the ground as a child in a chair. Reactions to it were violent. Outraged critics protested 'in the name of menaced French art and history' against this 'useless and monstrous' tower. 'Is Paris', they asked, 'going to be associated with the grotesque, mercantile imaginings of a constructor of machines?' Eiffel himself thought it was beautiful, and it stole the show at the 1889 Exposition for which it had been built. Its purely functional design was, and still is, a welcome and radical change from the stuffy monumentality of the buildings promoted by officialdom here and elsewhere in the world. Going to the top (10am–11pm in summer, 10.30am–11pm in winter) is expensive and there's no guarantee, even on a sunny day, that haze won't cloud the view.

Between the two bridges just downstream from the tower stretches a narrow artificial island with a walkway on top, known as the **Allée des Cygnes**, once a favourite walk of Samuel Beckett. By the further bridge stands the original Statue of Liberty; model for the larger New York version. Upstream, between Pont de l'Alma and Pont des Invalides on quai d'Orsay is the **American church**, which, with the American College in nearby av Bosquet (no 31), is a nodal point in the well-organised life of the large American community. The notice board is plastered with job offers, rooms to let, etc.

The other quayside attraction is the **sewers**, *les égouts* (entrance at the southeast corner of Pont de l'Alma; 2–5pm, Mon., Wed. and last Sat. of the month). Your nose will tell you, if not the cadaverous pallor of the superannuated sewermen who wait on you. It's usually billed as an outing for kids; I doubt it. The visit consists of an unilluminating film, a small museum and a very brief look at some tunnels with a lot of smelly water swirling around.

The **Esplanade des Invalides**, striking due south from **Pont Alexandre III,** is a more attractive and uncluttered vista than Chaillot-Ecole Militaire. The wide facade of the **Hôtel des Invalides**, overtopped by its distinctive dome, fills the entire far end of the Esplanade. It was built as a home for invalid soldiers on the orders of Louis XIV. Under the dome are two churches, one for the soldiers, the other intended as a mausoleum for the king but now containing the mortal remains of Napoléon. The Hôtel (*son et lumière* in English from April to Sept.) houses the vast **Musée de l'Armée**.

Both churches are cold and dreary inside. The **Eglise du Dôme**, in particular, is a supreme example of architectural pomposity. Corinthian columns and pilasters abound. The dome – pleasing enough from outside – is covered with paintings and flanked by four round chapels displaying the tombs of various luminaries. Napoléon himself lies below ground level in a cold, smooth sarcophagus of red porphyry, enclosed within a gallery decorated with friezes of execrable taste and grovelling piety, captioned with quotations of awesome conceit from the great man: 'Cooperate with the plans I have laid for the welfare of the people'; 'By its simplicity my code of law has done more good in France than all the laws which have preceded me'; 'Wherever the shadow of my rule has fallen, it has left lasting traces of its value'.

Immediately east of the Invalides is the **Musée Rodin**, on the corner of **rue de Varenne**, housed in a beautiful eighteenth-century mansion which the sculptor leased from the state in return for the gift of all his work at his death. The garden, planted with sculptures, is quite as pretty as the house, with a pond and flowering shrubs and superb view of the Invalides dome rising above the trees. The rest of the street, and the parallel **rue de Grenelle**, is full of aristocratic mansions, including the **Hôtel Matignon**, the Prime Minister's residence. At the further end the **rue du Bac** leads right, cutting across **rue de Babylone**, another of the *quartier's* livelier streets with the rich man's folly, **La Pagode** (now a cinema), down on the left beyond the barracks. Rue du Bac joins rue de Sèvres by the city's oldest department store, *Au Bon Marché*.

Beaux Quartiers and Bois de Boulogne

The **Beaux Quartiers** are most of the 16e and 17e *arrondissements*. The 16e is aristocratic and rich, the 17e, or at least the southern part of it, bourgeois and rich, embodying the staid, cautious values of the nineteenth-century manufacturing and trading classes.

The northern half of the 16e toward place Victor-Hugo and place de l'Etoile is leafy and distinctly metropolitan in feel. The southern part, around the old villages of **Auteuil** and **Passy**, has an almost provincial air, and is full of pleasant surprises for the walker. There are several interesting pieces of **twentieth-century architecture** scattered through the district, especially by Hector Guimard, designer of the swirly green Art Nouveau métro stations, Le Corbusier and Mallet-Stevens, architects of the first 'cubist' buildings. Also worth a visit is the the **Musée Marmottan** in av Raphael, with its depleted but still marvellous collection of late Monets.

A good place to start is the **Eglise-d'Auteuil** métro station with several **Guimard** buildings in the vicinity for aficionados: 34 rue Boileau, 8 av de la Villa-de-la-Réunion, 41 rue Chardon-Lagache, 192 av de Versailles and 39 bd

Exelmans. From the métro exit, **rue d'Auteuil**, with a lingering village high-street air, leads to **place Lorrain** with a Saturday market. More Guimard houses are to be found at the further end of rue La Fontaine, which begins here; no. 60 is perhaps the best in the city. On rue Poussin, just off the *place*, is the entrance to **Villa Montmorency**, a typical 16e villa, a sort of private village of leafy lanes and English-style gardens. Gide and the Goncourt brothers of *Prix* fame lived in this one. Behind it is rue Dr-Blanche where, in a cul-de-sac on the right, are **Le Corbusier**'s first private houses (1923), one of them now the *Fondation Le Corbusier* (10am–1pm and 2–6pm; closed weekends and Aug.). Built in strictly cubist style, very plain, with windows in bands, the only extravagance is the raising of one wing on piers and a curved frontage. They look commonplace enough now, but what a contrast to anything that had gone before. Further along rue Dr-Blanche, the tiny rue Mallet-Stevens was built entirely by **Mallet-Stevens** also in cubist style. If you go through from there to the almost rural cutting of the disused Petite Ceinture railway, turn to the right and under the subway, you'll come out by av Raphael with the *Musée Marmottan* on the corner of rue Boilly.

The **Bois de Boulogne**, running down the west side of the 16e, is supposedly modelled on Hyde Park, though it is a very French interpretation. It offers all sorts of facilities: the **Jardin d'Acclimatation** with lots of attractions for kids; the excellent **Musée National des Arts et Traditions Populaires**; the **Parc de Bagatelle**, with beautiful displays of tulips, hyacinths and daffodils in the first half of April, irises in May, waterlilies and roses at the end of June; a riding school; **bike rental** at the entrance to the Jardin d'Acclimatation; **boating** on the Lac Inférieur; **race courses** at Longchamp and Auteuil. The best, and wildest part for walking is towards the southwest corner. When it was opened to the public in the eighteenth century people said of it '*les mariages du Bois de Boulogne ne se font pas devant Monsieur le Curé*' – 'Unions cemented in the Bois de Boulogne do not take place in the presence of a priest'. Today's after-dark unions are no less disreputable – it's a sort of drive-in, open-air market catering for every sexual quirk. Close by this corner of the woods, across the Seine, the **Parc de St-Cloud** is better for fresh air and the visual order through pools and fountains down to the river and across to the city (M° Pont-de-Sèvres, Boulogne-Pont-de-St-Cloud, then walk across the river; or, take a train from St-Lazare to St-Cloud and head south).

The 17e *arrondissement* is most interesting in its eastern half. The classier western end is cold and soulless, cut by too many wide and uniform boulevards. A route that takes in the best of it would be from **place des Ternes** with its cafés and flower market, through the stately wrought iron gates of av Hoche into the small and formal **Parc Monceau**, surrounded by pompous residences, and on to the village of **Batignolles** on the wrong side of the St-Lazare railway tracks. By the av Velasquez exit from the park the **Musée Cernuschi** has a small collection of ancient Chinese art. From there, turn left on bd Malesherbes, then right along rue Legendre until you reach **place de Lévis**, already much more interesting than the sedate streets you left behind. **Rue de Lévis** has one of the city's most strident, colourful and appetising markets every day of the week except Monday. This is a good restaurant area, too, particularly up towards the railway around rue des Dames, rue Cheroy (try the Moroccan *Zerda*) and the bottom-line rue Dulong.

Across the tracks, **rue des Batignolles** is the heart of Batignolles 'village', now sufficiently self-conscious to have formed an association for the preservation of its '*caractère villageois*'. At the north end of the street is a semi-circular *place* with cafés and restaurants framing a small colonnaded church. Behind it is the tired and trampled greenery of square Batignolles, with the marshalling yards beyond. The long **rue des Moines** leads northeast towards Guy-Moquet. This is the working-class Paris of the movies, all small, animated, friendly shops, four- to five-story houses in shades of peeling grey, brown-stained bars where men drink standing at the 'zinc'. If you come back on av de St-Ouen, go through **rue du Capitaine-Madon**, a cobbled alley with washing strung at the windows, leading to the wall of the **Montmartre cemetery**, on the off-chance that the Hôtel Beau-Lieu still exists. Run by a ninety-year-old, who has just died, it has remained unchanged for sixty years. Ramshackle, peeling, on a tiny courtyard full of plants . . . it epitomizes the kind-hearted, no-nonsense, instinctively arty, sepia Paris that every romantic visitor secretly cherishes. Most of the guests have been there fifteen years or more. The new owner plans to refurbish it, so its days are probably numbered.

Montmartre and beyond

Montmartre lies in the middle of the largely petit-bourgeois and working class 18e *arrondissement*, respectable around the slopes of the *Butte* (hill), distinctly less so towards the **Gare du Nord** and **Gare de l'Est**. Beyond the tracks of the Gare de l'Est you're into the slums, rotting and depressed.

The Butte itself has a relaxed, sunny, countrified air. In **Pigalle** at the foot of the hill, things get seedier, as sex shops and peep shows are interspersed with tired-looking women in shop doorways. It hardly lives up to its romantic, Bohemian screen image, but then it probably never did.

The Butte

Everyone goes up via the rue de Steinkerque and the steps below the Sacré-Coeur. A quieter approach leads from the west or southwest via **rue Lepic, place des Abbesses** or the **cemetery** in a quiet hollow below rue Caulaincourt (graves of Berlioz, Degas, Stendhal, Zola . . .).

Place des Abbesses has one of the few complete surviving Guimard métro entrances: the glass porch railings, and the slightly obscene orange-tongued lanterns. There is a nice bookshop on rue Yvonne-Le-Tac, the street where St-Denis, the first bishop of Paris, had his head chopped off by the Romans circa 250. Legend has it that he carried his head until he dropped, 9 kilometres north of here, where the cathedral of St-Denis now stands. **Place Dullin**, a bit further over, is also a beauty.

The district of Montmartre was the centre of the **school of Paris** for thirty years until the first world war, when Picasso began an exodus to Montparnasse, on the Left Bank. Until then its cafés and bars were a forum for discussion for artists from all over Europe. They came to take advantage of the relative artistic freedom in Paris, newly-won by the Impressionists and Symbolists, which including unrivalled opportunities for exhibiting their works.

The appearance and spirit of those times is well preserved on canvas, its interiors in the works of Degas, Lautrec and Renoir, and its exteriors in those of Pisarro, Renoir and Utrillo. But while the *Moulin de la Galette*, portrayed in the works of the last two of these artists, has been restored as a music hall (on rue Lepic), and the cancan is still performed at the *Folies Bergéres,* little else remains by way of memorabilia on the streets of Montmartre to satisfy the tourists who flock there throughout the year. Once famous haunt of Toulouse-Lautrec, the *Moulin Rouge*, is now a tacky cinema. The Bateau-Lavoir studios no 13 pl Emile-Goudeau, where Picasso, Braque and Juan Gris invented Cubism, were destroyed by fire in 1970 and rebuilt in concrete. The **Musée de Montmartre** on rue Cortot just over the brow of the hill tries to recapture something of the feel of those pioneering days, but the exhibits are a disappointment. The house itself, rented at various times by Renoir, Dufy, Suzanne Valadon, and her alcoholic son Utrillo, is worth visiting for the view over the neat terraces of the **Montmartre vineyard** and the north side of the Butte. The entrance to the vineyard is on the steep rue des Saules. Harvest time is the beginning of October.

The heart of tourist Montmartre is **place du Tertre**, photogenic but totally bogus, jammed with overpriced restaurants and street artists doing quick portraits while you wait. Here, on March 18, 1871, Montmartre's most illustrious mayor, a future Prime Minister of France, Georges Clémenceau, flapped around trying to prevent the bloodshed that started that terrible and long-divisive civil war between the Commune and Thier's Third Republic, between the radical, Communist, urban, muddled Left and the frightened, unwilling or reactionary Rest.

France had provoked a disastrous war with Bismarck's Germany. The emperor, Napoléon III, had been captured and Paris surrounded. The Germans would not accept surrender from any but a properly elected government. A cautious and reactionary government under Thiers was duly elected and promptly capitulated, handing over Alsace and Lorraine. Frightened of Paris in arms, they tried to get hold of the artillery still in the hands of the National Guard. When, however, government troops went to fetch the guns parked at Montmartre, the people, fearing another restoration of empire or monarchy as after the 1848 revolution, persuaded them to take no action. Two of their generals were seized and shot against the wall on rue du Chevalier-de-la-Barre (behind the present site of the Sacré-Coeur), where, a few weeks later, Thiers' followers took revenge by shooting Eugène Varlin, founder member of the First International. The terrified government fled to Versailles, leaving the chaotic starving city that had been under Prussian siege for months to the Commune.

Divided among themselves and isolated from the rest of France, the *Communards* fought for their city street by street against government attack for one week between May 21 and May 28. No one knows how many died, certainly no fewer than 30,000 with another 10,000 executed or deported. A working-class revolt, as the particulars of those arrested clearly demonstrate, but it hardly had time to be socialist, as subsequent mythologising would have it. The terrible cost of repression had long-term effects on the French working-class movement, both psychologically and in terms of numbers lost.

The Basilica of the Sacré-Coeur was built in expiation of these events and the Franco-Prussian War, initiated privately by Catholics but decreed as a national votive offering in 1873. It is a graceless and vulgar pastiche, but its white pimply domes are an essential part of the Paris skyline. The best thing about it is the **view from the dome** (9.30am–12.30pm and 1–5.30pm). It costs next to nothing, is almost as high as the Eiffel Tower, and you can see across virtually the whole city.

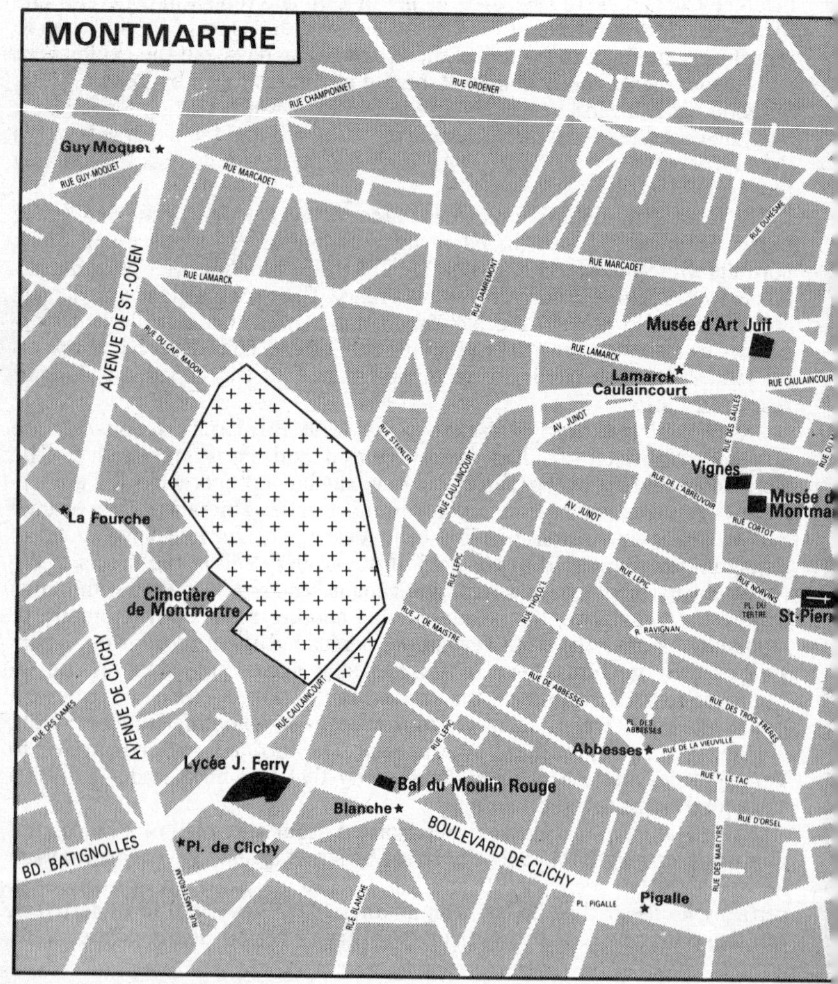

Between place du Tertre and the Sacré-Coeur is the old church of **St-Pierre**, all that remains of the Benedictine convent that occupied the Butte Montmartre from the twelfth century on. Though significantly altered, it still retains its Romanesque and early Gothic feel. In it are four ancient columns, two by the door, two in the choir, leftovers from a Roman shrine that stood on the hill – 'mons mercurii', Mercury's hill, as the Romans called it.

If you go down the north side off the Butte by the long **rue du Mont-Cenis**, where Berlioz lived, across the quiet and agreeable rue Caulaincourt, you come eventually to **Porte-de-Clignancourt**, where the main *marché aux puces*, or **flea-market**, is located under the *boulevard périphérique*. You won't

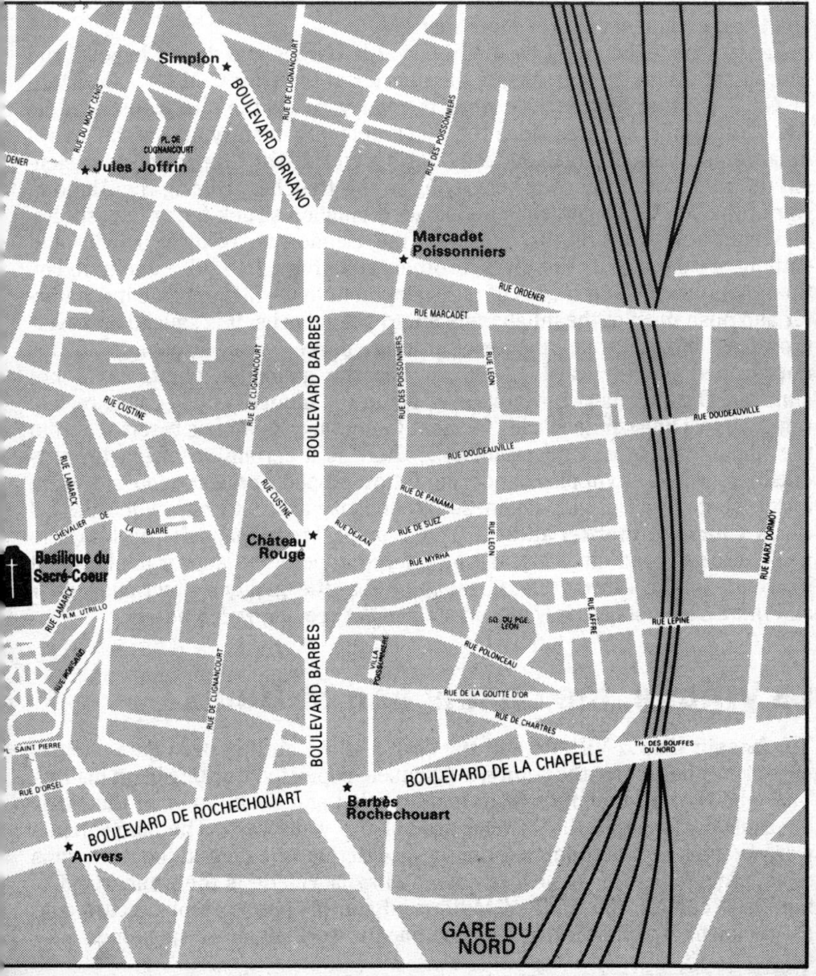

find many bargains, but it is an entertaining trip to wander around the stalls and shacks selling jeans, bags, shirts, leather jackets, furniture and assorted junk (Sat., Sun., and Mon., mornings mainly). *Chez Lisette*, a scruffy *restaurant-buvette* in the centre, was one of the venues frequented by the great gypsy jazz guitarist, Django Reinhardt, the first European jazz musician to influence the black American jazz scene. Just outside the market, at 126 av Michelet, *La Cigale*, a slightly seedy bar-restaurant serves a decent meal (with affordable mussels) to the wheeze of an old accordion.

The **eastern slopes** of the Butte drop steeply down to the renovated covered **Marché Saint-Pierre**, where African, Arab and French women jostle in colourful quest of some of the best fabric and textile bargains in town. Further downhill, towards bd Rochechouart and its junction with bd Barbès, where the métro clatters by on iron trellises, the crowds get thicker and the mingling of cultures more marked.

East of here, bounded by the boulevards Barbès and de la Chapelle, rue Myrha and the railway tracks, is the quarter of the **Goutte d'Or** – the Drop of Gold: a name that derives from the vineyard on the site in the Middle Ages. An immigrant area since the mid-nineteenth century, it saw the arrival of large numbers of North Africans during World War I, imported to replenish the ranks of French workers dying in the trenches. During the Algerian war of the late 1950s and early 1960s, its reputation struck terror in respectable middle-class hearts, as much for the clandestine political activity and settling of scores as its low dives, brothels and drugs. It is still a ghetto today, though in the opening throes of redevelopment that will annihilate its character and push most of the inhabitants out to the suburbs. It is squalid and overcrowded, but, despite the ever-lurking police vans swooping in for unprovoked identity card checks, it has the ambience of places in hot climates. Old men talk for hours over tea in the numerous tiny cafés; restaurants serve Tunisian delicacies for next to nothing; Rai music resonates from the upper balconies. Understandably, there is a certain suspicion towards outsiders, whether yuppies pondering future property prices or tourists wanting to photograph urban seediness. Wednesday and Saturday, when the **bd de la Chapelle market** attracts large crowds, are perhaps the best days to go. There's a good chance you'll be offered dope if you appear aimless and irresolute on the street – offers best ignored as the quality is notoriously poor and there's almost certainly a plain-clothes *flic* keeping watch nearby.

La Villette, the canals and St-Denis

The **bassin de La Villette** and the canals at the northeastern gate of Paris were, for generations, the centre of a densely populated working-class district. The jobs were in the city's main meat market and abattoirs or in the many interlinked industries that spread around the waterways. The amusements were skating or swimming, betting on cockfights or eating at the numerous restaurants famed for their fresh meat. Now la Villette is the wonderland of high-tech culture, the pride of Mitterrand and his predecessor Giscard, and the recipient of well over half-a-million pounds worth of public spending.

The number one extravagance has been the concrete hulk of the abandoned abattoirs metamorphosed into the **Science, Industry and Technology Museum** at the Porte de la Villette end of the site. It's cold, clinical, and complicated, three times the size of Beaubourg. Walls of glass hang beneath a dark blue lattice of steel. White rod walkways accelerate into the building which, despite its height, emerges reluctantly from the ground. But it creates its own looking-glass effect because in front of it balances the **Géode**, a bubble of reflecting steel dropped from an intergalactic *boules* game, landing there as if by fluke. Inside, half the sphere is a projection screen – the largest in existence – and half the space an arena for hologram and laser shows.

The largest of the market halls – an iron-frame structure designed by Baltard, the engineer of the vanished Les Halles pavillions – has become a vast and brilliant exhibition space, the **Grande Salle**. Close by it, near the Porte-de-Pantin métro, is a theatre and cinema, and the worksite of the future music conservatory. Away to the east, beyond the Grande Salle is the Zenith inflatable theatre for rock music. The surrounding recreation park is gradually taking shape, dominated by great, red, constructivist-style sheds by Tschumi, housing workshops, crêches, First Aid etc. Equally bizarre, though rather different is the **Dragon Slide** for children made from recycled drums and pipes on the slope west of the Géode. The Parc de la Villette information centre is on your right as you approach the Grande Salle from the Porte de Pantin métro.

The whole Villette complex stands at the junction of the **Ourcq** and **St-Denis canals**. The first was built by Napoléon to bring fresh water into the city. The second is an extension of the Canal St-Martin built as a shortcut to the great western loop of the Seine around Paris. If you like decaying industrial townscapes, both make interesting quayside walks.

The **Canal St-Martin** runs underground at the Bastille to surface again at the intersection of rue du Faubourg-du-Temple and bd Jules-Ferry. This part of the canal is the most attractive. Plane trees line the cobbled *quais* and elegant high-arched footbridges punctuate the spaces between locks. But gentrification and modernisation are on the way. An eighteen-floor tower with orange-tinted balconies has already elbowed in among the traditional four-to-six-storey, solid, mid-nineteenth-century bourgeois residences. The more drastic changes from the area's former leather trade and barge-tending identity have taken place north of rue des Recollets, with redevelopment mutilating both banks. You have to make a brief detour away from the canalside at the grubby, noisy **place de Stalingrad** (lots of socialist street names in working-class Paris and suburbs). In the middle of the *place*, up against the overhead métro line, is one of **Ledoux's** toll-houses in Louis XVI's tax wall, where taxes were levied on all goods coming into the city – a major bone of contention in the lead-up to the Revolution.

Beyond the *place* begins the now defunct **Bassin de la Villette** dock – Paris used to be the first port of France. Along the cobbled quay the remaining warehouses await demolition. The people you pass are anglers, dog-walkers, lonelyhearts and the occasional glue-sniffer. At the further end, the run-down **rue de Crimée** crosses a unique hydraulic bridge (1885), operated by the canal water. From here on, the *quartier* to your left is as decrepit as you could find, full of close, decaying houses with burrowing, smelly passages into courtyards held together by improvised repairs. The film *Diva* was shot around here. It is petty-crook, no-hope territory, both sides of **rue de Flandre**. And the high-rise estate on the west side of the street does not hold much promise of a brighter future either. Another immigrant ghetto, it is mainly North African this side of the rue de Tanger and place du Maroc, predominantly African around rue d'Aubervilliers.

From La Villette along the **St-Denis canal** to St-Denis itself is about a 1½-hour walk. You may prefer to take the métro to the town first and then see if you feel like walking back. St-Denis's chief claim to fame – apart from being staunchly Communist – is its magnificent **Cathedral,** close to the St-Denis-Basilique métro station. It was begun by Abbot Suger in the first half of the twelfth century and is generally regarded as the birthplace of the Gothic style.

Though its west front was the first ever to have a rose window, it is in the **choir** that you see the clear emergence of the new style, the slimness and lightness that comes with the use of the pointed arch, the ribbed vault and the long shafts of half-column rising from pillar to roof. It is a remarkably light church too, thanks to the clerestory's (ca.1230) being almost 100 per cent glass – another first for St-Denis. And the **rose windows** in the transepts are so big they occupy the entire end wall. Once the place where the kings of France were crowned, since A.D. 1000 the cathedral has been the burial place of all but three. Their very fine **tombs** and **effigies** are deployed about the transepts and ambulatory – though there is a shocking charge for entry to this part of the church.

Never a beauty, the centre **of St-Denis** still retains traces of its small-town origins amid the ready-built workers' flats. The thrice-weekly market still takes place around place de l'Hôtel-de-Ville and the covered *halles*. It is a truly multi-ethnic affair these days, and the quantity of offal on the butchers' stalls – ears, feet, tails and bladders – shows it is not the territory of the rich.

To return along the **canal**, go down rue de la République, past the church at the bottom and turn left when you hit the canal. There are stretches where it looks as if you shouldn't be walking. Just pay no attention and keep going. Not far from the start of the walk, past some peeling villas with unkempt gardens, you come to a cobbled ramp on your left where there is a cheap friendly restaurant called *La Péniche* (The Barge). Rue Raspail leads from there to a dusty square, where the town council has named a street for IRA hunger-striker Bobby Sands.

Continuing along the canal, you can't get lost. You pass patches of greenery, country-style cottages butting directly on to the towpath, empty lots where larks sing, slums and brightly painted improvised shacks, derelict factories and huge sheds where trundling gantries load bundles of steel rods onto Belgian barges. Barge traffic is regular and the life appears attractive to the outsider at least. The old steel hulks slide by, gunwhales down, a dog at the prow, lace curtains at the window, a potted plant, bike propped against the cabin side, a couple of kids . . .

But the keynote is decay. This is ground for the industrial archaeologist, not your go-getters of the electronic age.

East: from Belleville to Chinatown

The **eastern districts** are no longer revolutionary hotbeds but it's still the cheapest side of town to live and the least visited by tourists. Graced with the **Parc des Buttes-Chaumont**, the **Bois de Vincennes** and the hills of **Belleville**, it offers a different, less monumental Paris to explore.

Belleville and Père-Lachaise cemetery

At the northern end of the Belleville heights, a short walk from La Villette, is the **parc des Buttes-Chaumont** (M° Buttes-Chaumont or Botzaris) constructed under Haussmann in the 1860s to camouflage what until then had been a desolate warren of disused quarries and miserable shacks. The sculpted beak-shaped park stays open all night and, equally rarely for Paris, you're not cautioned off the grass. At its centre is a huge rock upholding a delicate Corinthian temple and surrounded by a lake which you cross via a suspension bridge or the shorter Pont des Suicides. Louis Aragon, the literary grand old man of the French Communist Party, wrote of this bridge that it claimed victims among passers-by who had no intention of dying, but found themselves suddenly tempted by the abyss. Feeble metal grills erected along its sides put an end to such impulses.

The route from Buttes-Chaumont to Père-Lachaise will take you through the one-time villages of **Belleville** and **Ménilmontant**, among the poorest quarters of the city. Each has large immigrant populations (and consequently a dangerous reputation as far as western Parisians are concerned) of Yugoslav, Portuguese, Chinese, Cambodian, Jewish, Arab, Armenian, Senegalese, Malian, and Chadian origins – the last three groups the least assimilated, poorest and most oppressed. Various municipal projects have been introduced to 'ameliorate' the area and around every corner the narrow streets are blocked by bulldozers and concrete mixers. There is presently an incredible number of 1960s and 70s tower blocks, and in all probability Belleville and Ménilmontant will end up looking more like the suburbs than Paris proper. To get an idea of how it all once was, take a look at *Villa Castel* off rue du Transvaal, *Villa Ermitage* off rue de l'Ermitage, passage de la Duée by 17 rue de la Duée, rue de la Mare and rue de la Voulze.

The first main street you cross coming down from Buttes-Chaumont, **rue de Belleville**, has become the new Chinatown of Paris. Vietnamese and Chinese shops and restaurants have proliferated over the last few years, adding considerable visual and gastronomic cheer to the area. African and oriental fruits, spices, music and fabrics can be bought at the **bd de Belleville market** on Tuesday and Friday. For French associations, Edith Piaf was dumped, a few hours old, on the steps of no. 72 rue de Belleville. Rue Ramponneau, just southeast of the crossroads with bd de Belleville, was where the last *Communard* on the last barricade held out alone for a final fifteen minutes.

From almost every street you get fantastic views down onto the city, but the best is from **rue de Ménilmontant**, just before it kinks above rue de l'Ermitage – the road appears to target the rooftops of Beaubourg. Just south,

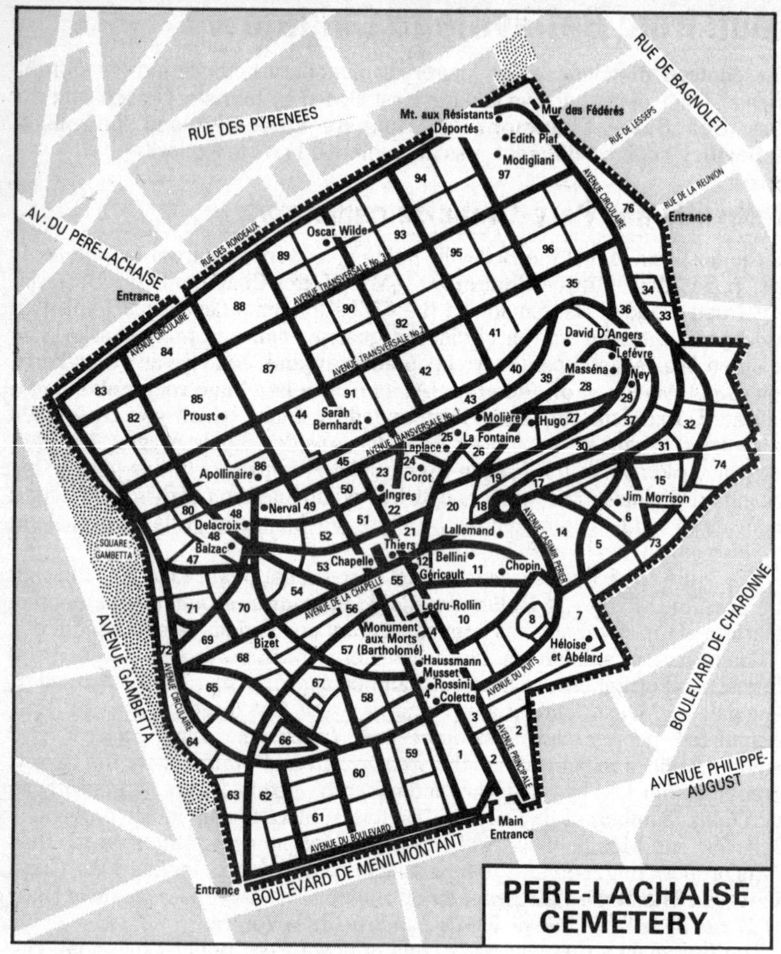

at 25 rue Boyer, is a beautiful building that may not be preserved for long, *La Bellevilloise*, built for the *PCF* in the 1920s in Soviet revolutionary style, now taken over by sweatshops. Further up rue Ménilmontant, at no. 150–154, is one of the best bakers in Paris, *Ganachaud*.

The **Père-Lachaise cemetery** (M° Père-Lachaise, Gambetta or Philippe-Auguste) is like a miniature city devasted by a neutron bomb, with a great number of dead, empty houses, and temples of every size, style and date, and exhausted survivors – congregating aimlessly or searching with persistence. The aimless can be seen around **Jim Morrison's tomb** (in division six), where French hippies roll joints against a backdrop of graffitied lyrics and love declarations in every western language on every stone in sight. The persistent are everywhere, looking for their favourite famous dead in an arrangement of numbered divisions that is neither entirely haphazard nor strictly systematic. A safe bet for a high score is to head for the southeastern corner (near M° Gambetta and the rue de la Réunion entrance and furthest from the main gate on bd de Ménilmontant). There you will find memorials to concentration camp victims and executed Resistance fighters of World War II, Communist Party general secretaries, Laura Marx and the **Mur des Fédérés**, where captured *Communards* were shot. Abélard and Héloise are side by side in prayer, still chastely separate (division seven). The cemetery is open from 7.30am to 6pm every day.

From the Bastille to Vincennes

The column with the 'Spirit of Liberty' on **place de la Bastille** was erected not to commemorate the surrender of the prison in 1789, but the July Revolution of 1830 which replaced the autocratic Charles X with the 'Citizen King', Louis-Philippe. When Louis-Philippe fled in the much more significant 1848 revolution, his throne was burned beside the column and a new inscription was added. The Liberal and Socialist provisional government that replaced the king introduced universal male suffrage, the right to free education and to work. Revolt had spread across all Europe but the victors of the 1789 French Revolution were not now going to make concessions to the working class. Reaction set in and, four months after the birth of the Second Republic, the workers took to the streets. All of eastern Paris was barricaded, with the fiercest fighting on rue du Faubourg-St-Antoine. The rebellion was quelled with the usual massacres and deportations of survivors, and it is still the 1789 Bastille Day that France celebrates.

The current ruler's project for meeting the demands of the populace is a new **opera house** that rears its ugly head at the Bastille between rues Charenton and de Lyon. It was originally planned to be even bigger with every sort of facility attached. But plans had to be scaled down to get it finished – and performing – in time for the 1989 bicentennial celebrations. A good deal of low-rent housing was lost to the site and neighboring blocks are changing hands, thus prices are going through the roof. The Bassin de l'Arsenal between the Seine and the Bastille has already become a marina. Ignored local protest centred around the nearby **place d'Aligre** – a daily market place and one of the best for bargains.

In the quieter backwaters to the north of rue Faubourg-St-Antoine, on **rue de Lappe**, there are remnants of a very Parisian tradition – the **bals musettes**, or music halls of 1930s 'gai Paris', between the wars, often visited by Piaf, Jean Gabin and Rita Hayworth. The most famous is *Balajo*, founded by one Jo de France, who introduced glitter and spectacle into what were then seedy gangster dives, and brought Parisians from the other side of the city to the rue de Lappe low-life.

On the waterfront, along quai de la Rapée, high office blocks conceal a classic nineteenth-century building behind them, the **Gare de Lyon**. At the upstream end of the *quai* the planned home of the Ministry of Finance strains to become a complete and suitably overbearing building. It already overshadows the not insubstantial **Palais des Omnisports de Bercy** with its lawn-clad sides one block beyond, home of opera, rock concerts and sporting events.

In the face of all these *grands projets*, it is not surprising that the planned cycle track from Bastille to the Bois de Vincennes along the disused railway track of the old Reuilly freight line has fallen by the wayside. But public transport is just as efficient this side of town and going over, rather than underground, is recommended. From Faubourg-St-Antoine various buses will take you out towards **Vincennes**. #86 crosses **place de la Nation**, another much barricaded junction, decorated with the bizarre ensemble of two medieval monarchs, looking very small and sheepish in pens on top of two high columns and below, in bronze, the Triumph of the Republic. Bus #46, with the same destination, passes the **Musée des Arts Africains et Océaniens** with its 1930s colonial facade of jungles, hard-working natives and the place names of the French Empire representing the 'overseas contribution to the capital'. The bus's next stop is the **Parc Zoologique**, which was one of the first zoos to replace cages with ditches, and give the animals a bit more room to roam. It's quite expensive and open from 9am to 6pm in summer; 5.30pm in winter.

In the **Bois de Vincennes** itself, you can spend an afternoon **boating** on Lac Daumesnil (near the zoo) or on Lac des Minimes across the other side of the wood. The fenced enclave on the southern side of Lac Daumesnil is a **Buddhist centre** with a Tibetan temple, Vietnamese chapel and international pagoda, all of which you can visit. The Bois gains some pastoral plausibility once you're east of av de St-Maurice, but the area is so overrun with roads that countryside sensations don't stand much of achance. The largest road-free space, between routes de la Tourelle and Dauphine, is fenced off for tree planting, following the demolition of the open **University of Vincennes**, a traditional centre of subversion razed to the ground in 1980 and incorporated in reduced form with Nanterre University on the other side of La Défense. Between this absence and the Lac des Minimes, the **Parc Floral** testifies to the French lack of imagination in landscape gardening, but there are some fun things for kids (bus #112 from Vincennes métro). On the eastern side of the garden is the **Cartoucherie de Vincennes**, an old ammunitions factory, now home of the radical *Théâtre du Soleil*. On the northern edge of the Bois, the **Château de Vincennes**, medieval royal residence, then state prison, porcelain factory, weapons dump and military training school, is still undergoing restoration work started by Napoléon III. A real behemoth of a building, no amount of stone scrubbing and removal of nineteenth-century gun positions is likely to beautify it.

Chinatown and the southeast

The southeast quarter of Paris, **the 13e** was not long ago a tightly-knit community around rue **Nationale** living for the most part in slum conditions. Paris was another place, rarely ventured into. But come the 1950s and 60s, the city planners, here as elsewhere, came up with their sense-defying solution to housing problems. A little west, between av d'Italie, rue Tolbiac and bd Masséna, is the **Chinatown** of Paris, (now rivalled by Belleville), with the same concrete eruptions and every variety of Far Eastern cuisine, movies, tapes and publications on sale. A **market** between av de Choisy and d'Ivry (every day except Monday) makes even the French look unimaginative in their choice of food.

Nearer to the city centre, above bd Vincent-Auriol, the buildings are ornate and bourgeois, dominated by the immense **Hôpital de la Salpêtrière**, built under Louis XIV to dispose of the dispossessed. It later became a psychiatric hospital, fulfilling the same function. Jean Charcot, who believed that susceptibility to hypnosis was proof of hysteria, staged his theatrical demonstrations here, with Freud a captive member of his audiences. If you ask very nicely in the *Bibliothèque Charcot* (block 6, red route), the librarian may show you a book of photographs of the poor female victims of these experiments. For a more positive statement on women, take a look at the building at 5 rue Jules-Breton which declares in large letters on its facade, 'In humanity, woman has the same duties as man. She must have the same rights in the family and in society.'

West of av d'Italie small houses with fancy brickwork or decorative timbers have remained intact and there's a rare taste of pre-highrise living. On **rue de la Butte aux Cailles** you'll find book and food shops, a community action centre, a worker's co-operative jazz bar (*La Merle Moqueur* at no 11), and bars and bistros open until midnight. And there's a food market nearby on bd Auguste-Blanqui. On the other side of the boulevard, rues Berbier-du-Mets and Croulebarbe run over the river Bièvre, covered over in 1910 as a health hazard. The main source of the pollution was the dyes from the **Gobelin tapestry workshops**, in operation here for some 400 years. Tapestries are still being made by the same methods on cartoons by contemporary painters – a painfully slow process which you can watch (Tues., Wed., and Thurs; 2–3.30pm; guided visit; 42 av des Gobelins).

In the *14e arrondissement*, to the southwest, several thousand students from over 100 different countries live in the curious array of buildings in the **Cité Universitaire** between bd Jourdan and the *périphérique*. The *Maisons* represent the unobvious selection of nations or peoples willing to subsidise foreign study. Armenia, Cuba, Indo-China and Monaco are neighbours at one end; Cambodia has been boarded up for years; Switzerland (designed by Le Corbusier in his stilts phase) and the U.S. are the most sought-after for their relatively luxurious rooms; an extradition debate closed Spain; and the Collège Franco-Britannique is a red brick monster. The atmosphere is far from internationalist but you can eat very cheaply in the **cafeterias** if you have a student card.

Parc Montsouris, across bd Jourdan, is a tempting place to collapse but you'll be up against more of the city's obsessionally whistling park police the moment you touch the grass. A beautiful reproduction of the Bardo palace in Tunis, built for the 1876 *Exposition Universelle*, is decaying. Lenin took strolls here in 1909 when he was living with Krupskaya, mother and sisters at **4 rue Marie-Rose** (now a small museum belonging to the Soviet Union – contact their embassy on ☎45.04.05.50 to visit). Later walkers in the park, no doubt, included Dali, Lurcat, Miller, Durrell and other artists who found homes in the tiny cobbled street of **Villa Seurat** off rue de la Tombe.

Due north of the park – past Ste-Anne's psychiatric hospital where one of the greatest living political philosophers, Louis Althusser, is committed – lies the **Observatoire de Paris**. From the 1660s, when it was constructed, until 1884, all French maps had the zero meridian through the middle of this building. After that date, they reluctantly agreed that 0° longitude should be redefined as running through Greenwich in London. Gaining entrance to view the old maps and instruments inside is a complicated procedure, but you can sit in the **garden** on summer afternoons and admire the dome (entrance on bd Arago).

THE MUSEUMS

While you may find sufficient visual stimulation just wandering around the streets of Paris, your appreciation of them can only be heightened by an exploration of **the museums**. The wealth of art in Parisian galleries, for example, does it justice as the birthplace of Impressionism, Fauvism, Cubism, Surrealism and Symbolism. If established art appeals at all, the Paris collections are not to be missed.

Among the city's other **technical, historical, social and applied arts museums** – of which there are many – the **Musée National des Arts et Traditions Populaires**, a more conventional equivalent to the Cité des Sciences, dealing with bygone technology, is good fun. Some of the smaller collections are dedicated to a single person – **Balzac, Hugo, Piaf** – and others to very particular subjects – **spectacles, counterfeits, tobacco,** even **bread**. We've detailed all we found interesting and some are mentioned in the description of the city. Full lists (with their ever-changing opening times, from any tourist office) will reveal others of appeal to the committed exhibit-gazer or the specialist.

Admission prices vary: some, like the Marmottan and the Cité des Sciences, are pretty expensive though all offer student reductions if you've got a card (preferably *ISIC*). If you intend to visit as many museums as possible, you may be better off buying the new *Carte Musées-Monuments* which gives free entry to sixty museums and monuments in and around Paris. You won't have to wait in line and you'll be able to go in and out of the same museum as many times as you like. You can buy the card at metro stations or at the museums and monuments, for 50F for one day, 100F for three days, or 150F for five days. We've indicated which museums are part of the deal in the lists that follow. The Louvre and other state-owned museums **close** on either Monday or Tuesday (as throughout France) and have **free days** usually Wednesday and/or Sunday, which are normally packed.

Finally, keep an eye out for **temporary exhibitions** – some of which match any of Paris's regular museums – held in Beaubourg and the Grand Palais; they are usually well advertised by posters or there are full details in *Pariscope* and the other listings magazines. The same goes for the numerous **commercial galleries**, heavily concentrated in the Beaubourg and St-Germain areas, which you can visit without charge.

The Big Four

Musée d'Orsay

1 rue de Bellechasse, 7e; M° Gare-d'Orsay, Solférino. Open Tues, Wed., Fri., and Sat. 10am–6pm, Thurs. 10am–9.45pm, Sun. 9am–6pm. Card entry through *groupes et adhérents* gate.

The disused Gare d'Orsay was no ordinary railway station when it was built in 1900, but a *Belle Epoque* marvel with vast arches of glass, which on the north side let in light reflected from the river. The roof-mounted statuary so beloved of that era, the no expense-spared detail – even of the station clocks – and its cast iron durability cried out to exemplify the art and design of the period, 1848–1914, of which it is part. To turn that into a reality has been an arduous undertaking, not least saving it from a hotel developer's bulldozer. Some may have shadowy memories of the building from the Orson Welles' film of Kafka's *The Trial*, in which the characters moved through terrifying narrow and confined corridors. Gae Aulenti, the Italian architect responsible for the conversion, has brought back and extended the light and space of the original. She has kept the station clocks, and some of the pattern of the rails, and the only problem is that the place is always packed, as if it's rush hour for commuter trains.

The general layout is as follows. On the **ground floor**, the mid-nineteenth-century sculptors, including Barye, caster of super-naturalistic bronze animals, occupy the central gallery. To the right, a few canvases by Ingres and Delacroix (the bulk of whose work is in the Louvre) serve to illustrate the transition from the early nineteenth century. Puvids de Chavannes, Gustave Moreau, the Symbolists and early Degas follow, while in the galleries to the left, Daumier, Corot, Millet and the realist school lead on to the first Impressionist works, including Manet's *Déjeuner sur l'Herbe*, which sent the critics into apoplexies of rage and disgust when it appeared in 1863. *Olympia* is here too, equally controversial at the time – for the colour contrasts and sensual surfaces, rather than the content (though the black cat was thought a touch bizarre).

To get the chronological continuation you have to go straight up to the top level, where numerous landscapes and outdoor scenes by Renoir, Sisley, Pissarro and Monet owe much of their brilliance to the novel practice of painting in the open air to catch a momentary light – a point emphasised by some Renoir canvases being displayed on easels. Monet's waterlilies are here in abundance, too, along with five of his Rouen cathedral series, each painted under different light conditions. *Le Berceau* (1872), by Morisot, the only woman in the early group of Impressionists, is one of the few to have a complex human emotion as its subject – perfectly synthesized with the movement's light-playing techniques. A very different touch, all shimmering light and wide brush strokes, is in Renoir's depiction of a good time being had by all at *Le Moulin de la Galette* in Montmartre.

The post-Impressionists are not as well treated as their predecessors, with the exception of van Gogh, whose blinding colours and disturbing rhythms are given perfect space. The others are, though, brilliantly represented, in particular Cézanne, whose *Still Life with Apples and Oranges* reveals his art, and differences to the Impressionists so well. Among a number of pointillist works by Seurat and others, is Signac's horrible *Entrée du Port de Marseille*. There's Gauguin, post- and pre-Tahiti, as well as some inticing derivatives like Georges Lacombe's carved wood panels; several superb Bonnards and Vuillards and lots of Toulouse-Lautrec at his nightclubbing best.

The **middle level** takes in Rodin and other late-nineteenth-century sculptors, and furniture and fittings of the period – one of the few sections with foreigners. There are William Morris panels, a Rennie Mackintosh bedroom suite, Frank Lloyd Wright seats, but, most of all, French Art Nouveau from mirror frames to métro entrances. Lastly, some Klimts and Matisses mark the transition to the moderns housed in the Beaubourg collection.

Beaubourg (The Pompidou Centre)

Centre Beaubourg, rue Beaubourg, 4e; M° Rambuteau/Hôtel-de-Ville. Open 12 noon–10pm, weekends 10am–10pm; closed Tues.; free Sun.; card entry.

The **Musée National d'Art Moderne** on the third and fourth floors of Beaubourg is in no way upstaged by the Musée d'Orsay. The art is exclusively twentieth-century and the collection constantly expanding. Contemporary movements and works dated the year before last find their place here, along with the late-Impressionists, Fauvists, Cubists, Figuratives, Abstractionists and the rest of this century's First World art trends.

Among highlights are Henri Rousseau's *Charmeuse de Serpent* (1907), an extraordinary idiosyncratic beginning. Picasso's *Femme Assise* of 1909 introduces the reduced colours of Cubism, represented in its developed style by Braque's *L'Homme à la Guitare* (1914) and, later, in the perfect balancing act of Léger's *Les Acrobats en Gris* (1942–44). Among Abstracts, there's the sensuous rhythm of colour in Sonia Delaunay's *Prismes Electriques* (1914) and a good collection of Kandinskys at their most harmonised and playful. In contrast, Dali disturbs, amuses or infuriates with *Hallucination Partielle, Six Images de Lénine sur un Piano* (1931) and there are more surrealist images by Magritte and de Chirico. Moving to the Expressionists, one of the most compulsive pictures – of 1920s female emancipation as viewed by a male contemporary – is the portrait of Sylvia von Harden by Otto Dix. The sex of the sleeping woman in *Le Rêve* by Matisse is not a focus – the subject is the human body at its most relaxed. Jumping forward, to Francis Bacon, you find tension and torment in the human body and mind.

There are temporary exhibitions of photographs, drawings, collages and prints in the **Salle d'Art Graphique** and **Salon photo**, part of the permanent collection of the museum, and **films** are projected several times daily, either as art history or as experimental art themselves. On the mezzanine floors (down the stairs to the right of the plaza doors) are the **Galeries Contemporaines** where the overspill of the museum's contemporary collection is rotated, and young artists get a viewing. The **Grande Galerie** right at the top of the building is where the big-time exhibitions are held, usually lasting for several months. Yet more temporary shows on equally diverse themes are to be seen in the basement **Centre de Création Industrielle**.

Entry to the Centre is free, but the museum and Galeries Contemporaines have admission charges (except on Sundays), as do the major exhibitions. Given the amount to see it may be worth getting a daypass (if you haven't invested in a *Carte Musées-Monuments*). Beaubourg also has an excellent cinema, a **reference library** including foreign newspapers, a **record library** where you can take a music break, a **snackbar** and **restaurant** (with seating on the roof), a **bookshop, contemporary music centre, dance** and **theatre** space and **kid's workshop.**

The Louvre

Palais du Louvre, 1er; M° Palais-Royal, Louvre. Thurs.–Sun. 9am–6pm, Mon. and Wed. 9am–9.45pm; free Sun.

> *'You walked for a quarter of a mile through works of fine art; the very floors echoed the sounds of immortality . . . It was the crowning and consecration of art . . . These works instead of being taken from their respective countries were given to the world and to the mind and heart of man from whence they sprung . . .'*

William Hazlitt, writing of the Louvre in 1802, goes on, in equally florid style, to claim for this museum the beginning of a new age when artistic masterpieces would be the inheritance of all, no longer the preserve of kings and nobility. Novel the Louvre certainly was. The palace, hung with the private collections of monarchs and their ministers, was first opened to the public in 1793, four years after the Revolution. Within a decade Napoléon had made it the largest art collection on earth with takings from his empire.

However inspiring it might have been then, the Louvre has been a bit of a nightmare over the last few decades, requiring heroic willpower and stamina to find one work of art that you want to see amongst the 300,000. But in 1984 a radical process of transformation was set in motion. The new *'Grand Louvre'*, finally inaugurated by President Mitterrand in the autumn of 1988, has solved many of the problems for visitors and provoked passionate responses of love and hate for its centrepiece, the 21-metre high glass pyramid created by the Chinese-American architect I.M. Pei in the *Cour Napoléon*. This is now the main entrance to the Louvre, a subterranean but day-lit concourse – the *Hall Napoléon* – with lifts and escalators leading directly into each section of the museum. Every high-tech facility is on hand to guide you to the treasures, many of which have never been on display before.

The removal of the Ministry of Finance from the north wing has greatly increased the available space. The third floor of the north and south wings and the *Cour Carré* house the paintings, in much enhanced lighting conditions. The Applied Arts now join up with the Musée des Arts Décoratifs collection on the second floor of the former Finance Ministry and the north wing of the Cour Carré. Finding your way around is simplified by ubiquitous ground plans and in each level in each wing you'll find a place to rest and have a cup of coffee.

A bonus of the building works has been the opportunity to excavate the remains of the medieval Louvre – Phillipe Auguste's twelfth-century fortress and Charles V's fourteenth-century palace conversion – under the *Cour Carré* and some houses and streets under the *Cour Napoléon*. These are now on view along with an exhibition on the history of the Louvre in three lots of antiquities, sculpture, painting, applied and graphic arts. **Oriental Antiquities** cover the Sumerian, Babylonian, Assyrian and Phoenician civilisations, plus the art of ancient Persia. **Egyptian Antiquities** contains jewellery, domestic objects, sandals, sarcophagi – a thousand marvellously decorative pieces. Some of the major exhibits are: the pink granite *Mastaba sphinx*, the *Kneeling Scribe* statue, a wooden statue of *Chancellor Nakhti*, the god *Amon*, protector of Tutankhamun, *Sehti I* and the *goddess Hathor*, a bust of *Amenophis IV*. The **Greek and Roman Antiquities** include the *Winged Victory of Samothrace* and the *Venus de Milo*, biggest crowd-pullers in the museum after the Mona Lisa. Venus, striking a classic model's pose, is one of the great sex-pots of all time. She dates from the late second century B.C. Her antecedents are all on display too, from the delightful *Dame d'Auxerre* of the seventh century B.C. to the fifth-century B.C. bronze *Apollo of Piombino*, still looking straight ahead in the archaic manner, the classical perfection of the *Athlete of Benevento*.. In the Roman section are some very lovely mosaics from Asia Minor and luminous frescoes from Pompeii and Herculanum, which already seem to foreshadow the decorative lightness of touch of a Botticelli still 1000 years and more away.

The **Applied Arts** collection is heavily weighted on the side of vulgar imperial opulence – beautifully crafted and monstrously expensive pieces of furniture, which arouse no aesthetic response at all. This applies just as much to the work of the renowned cabinet-maker, Boulle (active around 1700), recognisable by the heavy square shapes and lavish use of copper, bronze and pewter inlays and such ecologically catastrophic extravagance as entire doors of tortoise shell. There are also several acres of tapestry – all of the very best quality and workmanship, but a chore to look at. The **sculpture** section covers the entire development of the art in France from Romanesque to Rodin, including Michelangelo's *Slaves* commissioned for the tomb of Pope Julius II.

The largest and most indigestible section is the **paintings** – French from the earliest to mid-nineteenth-century, with Italians, Dutch, Germans, Flemish and Spanish represented too. Among them are many paintings so familiar from reproduction in advertisements and on chocolate boxes that it is a surprise to see them on a wall in a frame. And unless you are an art historian, the parade of mythological scenes, classical ruins, piteous piety, acrobatic saints and sheer dry academicism is hard to make much sense of. A portrait, a domestic scene, a still life, is a real relief. Walking by with eyes selectively shut is probably the best advice. The early Italians are the most interesting part of the collection, at least up to Leonardo and the sixteenth century. Giotto, Fra Angelico, Uccello's **Battle of San Romano**, Mantegna, Botticelli, Filippo Lippi, Raphael . . . all the big names are represented. It is partly their period, but there is still an innate classical restraint which is more appealing to modern taste than the exuberance and grandiloquence of the eighteenth and first half of the nineteenth century. If you want to get near the *Mona Lisa*, go first or last thing in the day. No one, incidentally, pays the slightest bit of attention to the other Leonardos right alongside, including the *Virgin of the Rocks*.

Access to the *Hall Napoléon* and its shops, information services, audovisual shows etc., is free. You can reach it through passage Richelieu, from rue de Rivoli, from the underground carpark or through the Tuileries, taking the spiral staircase down from the base of the pyramid.

Cité des Sciences et de l'Industrie

Porte-de-la-Villette, 18e; M° Porte de la Villette. Open Tues., Thurs. and Fri. 10am–6pm; Wed. noon–9pm; Sat., Sun. and holidays noon–8pm; closed Mon.; card entry.

The science museum, in fact. It would be worth visiting for the interior of the building alone: all glass and stainless steel, crowsnests and cantilevered platforms, suspended walkways and bridges, in a cross between a *2001* film set, a real life NASA work station, the Superbowl and a new métro train (those are its colours). What it isn't like is a museum.

The **permanent exhibition,** *Explora*, is arranged around a huge central space open to the full 40-metre height of the roof. Its themes are From Earth to the Universe, the Adventure of Life, Matter and Human Labour, and Languages and Communication. This is no conventional museum-repository of accumulated objects. The keynote is exploration and participation. But the chances of coming out any the wiser about the fundamental forces of nature, how black holes can be recognised, or how we're going to prevent the earth's ecosystems breaking down, are slim. It does, of course, mean to be extremely serious and educational but its appeal lies in its entertainment value, which is pretty high. You can play games, manipulate blips on screens, watch videos, listen to tapes, or if you've got the time you can witness two slabs of wall part company at the rate of 2cm a year. There are models of space stations and the Ariane rocket, working robots, an ongoing experiment in plant husbandry, salmon egg incubators, computer-generated fractals, satellite pictures . . . and bars where you can have a drink (and smoke) without leaving the exhibition space.

There is also a **resources centre** (*médiathèque*), **kids' activity centre** (*inventorium*), a changing exhibition of contemporary French **industrial achievements** (*la maison de l'industrie*) and a whole programme of **temporary exhibitions. Admission** is a bit steep but there is enough to keep anybody busy for days. English-language audio-guides are available that know where you are in the building and inform accordingly.

The rest of the art museums

The **Musée d'Orsay** is universally acclaimed as the new shining wonder of French public art. But other, smaller museums of the same pre-modern period – the **Orangerie** and **Marmottan** – hold their ground, and the modern art treasures housed in **Beaubourg**, the **Palais de Tokyo** and the **Musée Picasso**, taking up where the d'Orsay leaves off, are as enthralling as ever.

Musée de Cluny

6, place Paul-Painlevé. 5e (off rue des Ecoles); M° Odéon, St-Michel. Open 9.45am–12.30pm and 2–5.15pm; closed Tues.; card entry.

If you have always found tapestries boring, this treasure house of medieval art may well provide the flash of enlightenment. There are numerous beauties: a marvellous depiction of the grape harvest; a Resurrection embroidered in gold and silver thread, with sleeping guards in medieval armor; a room of sixteenth-century Dutch tapestries, full of flowers and birds, a woman spinning while a cats plays with the end of the thread, a lover making advances, a woman in her bath, which overflows into a duck pond. But the greatest wonder of all is *La Dame à la Licorne*, the Lady with the Unicorn: six enigmatic scenes featuring a beautiful woman flanked by a lion and a unicorn, late fifteenth-century, perhaps made in Brussels. Quite simply, it is the most stunning piece of art you are likely to see in many a long day. The ground of each panel is a delicate red worked with a thousand tiny flowers, birds and animals. In the centre is a green island, equally flowery, framed by stylised trees, and here the scene is enacted. The young woman plays a portable organ, takes a sweet from a proffered box, makes a necklace of carnations while a pet monkey, perched on the rim of a basket of flowers, holds one to his nose.

Musée Marmottan

2 rue Louis-Boilly, 16e (off av Raphael); M° La Muette. Open 10am–5.30pm; closed Mon.; expensive admission.

The star of the show here is the collection of **Monet paintings**, despite the theft in 1985 of nine pictures including *Impression, Soleil Levant*,which gave Impressionism its name. Most of the canvases date from Monet's last years at Giverny and these are the most startling: numerous *Nymphéas* (Water-lilies), *Le Pont Japonais, L'Allée des Rosiers, La Saule Pleureur* where rich colours are laid on in thick, excited whorls and lines. Marks on white canvas: form dissolves. To all intents and purposes, these are abstractions and far more 'advanced' than the work of, say, Renoir, Monet's exact contemporary. The missing paintings, stolen in broad daylight while the museum was open, were five Monets, a Morisot, Naruse and two Renoirs. They have been hunted for in Japan to no avail, and the museums' owners have given up hope, particularly over the Monets which they say will decay if not kept in stringent conditions. Police are now turning their attention back to the Paris region.

The Orangerie

Place de la Concorde, 1e; M° Concorde. Open 9.45am–5.15pm; closed Tues.; free Wed.; card entry.

The **Orangerie**, on the south side of the Tuileries terrace overlooking place de la Concorde, has two oval rooms arranged by **Monet** as panoramas for his largest water-lily paintings. In addition there are southern landscapes by Cézanne, massive Picasso nudes, portraits by Van Dongen, Utrillo and

Derain, Monet's *Argenteuil* and Sisley's *Le Chemin de Montbuisson*. Small, select, and spaciously laid out, this is one of the least visited and most enjoyable of the Paris art museums.

Palais de Tokyo

11 av du Président-Wilson, 16e; M° Iéna, Alma-Marceau. Musée d'Art Moderne de la Ville de Paris, open 10am–5:40pm (Wed. till 8.30pm); closed Mon; card entry. Centre National de la Photographie, open 9.45am–5.15pm; closed Tues.

In the east wing, the **Musée d'Art Moderne de la Ville de Paris** has a large permanent collection of works by Vlaminck, Zadkine, Picasso, Braque, Juan Gris, Matisse, Valadon, Utrillo, Dufy, both Delauneys, Chagall, Léger, Modigliani and many others, including contemporary artists. The most spactacular room is one devoted to four huge Robert Delaunays – great whirling wheels and cogs of rainbow colour – with the pale figures of Matisse's *La Dance* leaping off their long arcaded canvas across the end wall. Next door, Dufy's enormous mural, *La Fée Electricité* (done for the electricity board), illustrates the story of electricity from Aristotle to the then modern power station. And a little number worth checking out: the shop in the foyer, which, among other artists' designs, sells a set of Sonia Delaunay's playing cards.

The west wing of the Palais is dedicated to photography, past and present, in temporary exhibitions.

Institut du Monde Arabe

23 quai Saint-Bernard; M° Jussieu/Cardinal-Lemoine. Open 1–8pm; closed Mon.

The permanent collection includes glass, rugs, ceramics, illuminated manuscripts, woodcarving, metalwork and scientific instruments, much of it acquired from collections in the Louvre and Musée des Arts Décoratifs. The photosensitive filters of the southern facade ensure perfect lighting conditions for the displays, which cover five floors of this enormous building. The sense of spaciousness created may arouse the suspicion that the collection is less complete than might be expected, but it's a pleasant place to wander in. Permanent displays are: Arab-Islamic art and civilisation from the seventh to the nineteenth century, anthropology of Arab societies (with rather poor audio-visual aids) and an excellent collection of contemporary Arab art of the last fifty years.

Grand and Petit Palais

Av W-Churchill, 8e; M° Champs-Elysées, Clemenceau. Grand Palais open 10am–8pm (Wed. till 10pm); closed Tues. Petit Palais open 10am–5.40pm; closed Mon.; free on Sun.; card entry.

The **Grand Palais Galeries** hold major temporary art exhibitions, good ones obvious from the long lines of people down av Churchill. *Pariscope* and co. will have details and you'll probably see plenty of posters around.

In the **Petit Palais,** whose entrance hall is a brazenly extravagant painted dome, you'll find the *Beaux Arts* museum, which seems to be a collection of leftovers – from all periods – after the other main galleries had taken their pick. There's a certain interest in this – being able to compare the ugliness of an Art Nouveau dining room with the effete eighteenth-century furniture in the *Salles Tuck* – but this collection shouldn't be at the top of your list. Nor should the **Palais de la Découverte** at the back of the Grand Palais, in the same block – the city's old science museum, dull, traditional and a total anachronism given La Villette.

Musée des Arts Africains et Océaniens

293 av Daumesnil, 12e; M° Porte-Dorée. Open 9.45am–noon and 1.30– 5.20pm; closed Tues.; card entry.
This strange museum – one of the cheapest and least crowded in the city – has an African gold brooch of curled up sleeping crocodiles on one floor and, in the basement, five live crocodiles in a tiny pit surrounded by tanks of tropical fishes. Imperialism is evident in a gathering of culture and creatures from the old French colonies. Hardly any of the black African artefacts are dated – the collection predates European acknowledgment of the history of that continent – and the captions are a bit suspicious too. These masks and statues, furniture, adornments and tools should be exhibited with paintings by Expressionists, Cubists and Surrealists to show the extent to which the French school was influenced by African art. Picasso and his friends certainly came here often to study the patterns, shapes and materials.

Musée Picasso

5 rue de Thorigny, 3e; M° St-Paul/Filles-du-Calvaire. Open 9.45am–5.15pm; (Wed. till 10pm); closed Tues.; card entry.
The largest single collection of Picassos, beautifully arranged in the seventeenth-century mansion Hôtel Salé, became state property in lieu of tax after the artist's death. It includes all the different mediums he used, the paintings he bought or was given, his African masks and sculptures, photographs, letters and other personal memorabilia. You will leave with a definite sense of the man and his life in conjunction with his production, partly because these were the works he wanted to keep. The paintings of his wives, lovers and children are some of the gentlest and most endearing. There are portraits during the period of the Spanish Civil War when Picasso was going through his worst personal and political crises. He is at his best when emotion and passion play hardest on his painting, though for *Guernica* you have to go to Madrid. But taken as a whole, the Hôtel Salé does not represent his most enjoyable creations, and can't compare with the Barcelona gallery. Temporary exhibitions, however, enlarge on the periods least represented: the Pink, Cubism, the immediate post-war and the 1950s and 1960s.

Musée Guimet

6 place d'Iéna, 16e; M° Iéna. Open 9.45am–noon and 1.30–5.15pm; closed Tues.; card entry.

Little visited, this museum features a huge and beautifully displayed collection of Oriental art, from China, India, Japan, Tibet and southeast Asia. There is a particularly fine collection of Chinese porcelain on the top floor.

Musée Rodin

77 rue de Varenne, 7e (just to the east of the Invalides); M° Varenne. Open 10am–5pm (5.45pm in summer); closed Tues.; half-price Sun.; card entry.
This collection represents the whole of Rodin's work. Major projects like *Les Bourgeois de Calais, Le Penseur, Balzac, La Porte de l'Enfer, Ugolini et fils*, are exhibited in the garden – the latter forming the centrepiece of the ornamental pond. Indoors (very crowded) are works in marble like *Le Baiser, La Main de Dieu, La Cathédrale* – those two perfectly poised, almost sentient, hands. There is something particularly fascinating about the works, like *Romeo and Juliet* and *La Centauresse*, which are only half-created, not totally liberated from the raw block of stone.

Musée Jacquemart-André

158 bd Haussmann, 8e; M° Miromesnil, St-Phillipe-du-Roule. Open 1.30–5.30pm, closed Mon, Tues. and Aug.
The ceilings of the staircase and three of the rooms of this museum are decorated with **Tiepolo** frescoes. The works of his French contemporaries of the eighteenth century hang in the ground floor along with his fellow Venetian, Canaletto. The collection contains several Rembrandts and, best of all, fifteenth- and sixteenth-century Italian genius in the works of Botticelli, Donatello, Mantegna, Tintoretto, Titian and Uccello.

Musée Delacroix

6 place de Furstemberg, 6e; M° St-Germain-des-Prés. Open 9.45am– 5.15pm; closed Tues.; card entry.
Some attractive watercolours, illustrations from *Hamlet* and a couple of versions of a lion hunt hang in the painter's old studio, but there's nothing much in the way of major work.

Musée Zadkine

100 bis rue d'Assas, 6e; M° Vavin. Open 10am–5.40pm; closed Mon.
Studio, garden and works of the Cubist sculptor, Ossip Zadkine.

Musée Gustave Moreau

14 rue de la Rochefoucauld, 9e; M° Trinité. Open 10am–12.45pm and 2–4.45pm; closed Mon., Tues. and holidays; card entry.
An out-of-the-way, bizarre, overcrowded collection of cluttered, joyless paintings by the Symbolist, Gustave Moreau. If you know you like him, go ahead. Otherwise, skip it.

Applied art, fashion and miscellany

Musée des Arts Décoratifs

107 rue de Rivoli, 1e; M° Palais-Royal. Open 12.30–6.30pm; Sun. 11am–6pm, closed Mon. and Tues.; card entry.

This is an enormous museum, except by the standards of the building housing it – the Louvre – of which it takes up the end of the north wing. The contents are objects: beds, blankets, toys, tools and lampshades, in fact, almost anything that illustrates the decorative skills from the Middle Ages to the 1980s. The contemporary section is rather meagre given the availability, though there is a fabulous table by Totem, and the museum shop, with clothes and accessories, books, and cards, is very good.

Musée des Arts de la Mode

Pavillon de Marsan, 111 rue de Rivoli, 1er; M° Palais-Royal. Open Wed.–Sat. 12.30–6.30pm. Sun. 11am–6pm; closed Mon. and Tues.

The newest fashion museum of Paris is part of the *Arts Décoratifs* set-up in the north wing of the Louvre (but with a separate entrance and admission charge). The views from the circular roof windows are better than the displays inside, if recent exhibitions are anything to go by. The fixation is with pre-1940 and avoiding any treatment of the subject other than glitz. Like its partner, it has a shop of desirables.

Musée de la Publicité

18 rue du Paradis, 10e; Château-d'Eau. Open noon–6pm, closed Tues.

Publicity posters, ads and TV and radio commercials are presented in monthly exhibitions, concentrating either on the art, the product or the politics. There's an excellent selection of postcards for sale and very beautiful surroundings of Art Nouveau tiles and wrought iron.

Musée de l'Holographie

Niveau I, Forum des Halles, 1e; M° Les Halles. Open 10.30am–7pm; Sun. and Mon. 1–7pm.

Like most holography museums, this is less exciting than you expect, the fault lying with the state of the art. But there are a couple of holograms more inspired than women winking as you pass, and works where artists have combined holograms with painting. Most impressive technically are the reproductions of museum treasures which, just like the originals, you can't touch.

Musée des Lunettes et Lorgnettes de Jadis

2 av Mozart, 16e; M° La Muette. Open 9am–1pm and 2–7pm; closed Sun. and Mon.

An ordinary optician's shop hosts this huge collection of people's focussing aids: medieval lenses, Restoration monocles, lenses set in fans, twentieth-century fashion specs and those worn by the famous.

SEITA

12 rue Surcrouf, 7e; M° Invalides, Latour-Maubourg. Open 11am– 6pm; closed Sun.; free.
The state tobacco company has this small and delightful museum in its offices, presenting the pleasures of smoking with pipes and pouches from every continent – early Gauloise packets, painted *tabac* signs and, best of all, a slide show of tobacco in painting from the seventeenth century to now.

Historical, technical, scientific . . .

Musée National des Arts et Traditions Populaires

6 rte du Mahatma-Gandhi, Bois de Boulogne, 16e (beside main entrance to Jardin d'Acclimitation); M° Les Sablons, Porte-Maillot. Open 10am–5.15pm; closed Tues.; card entry.
If you have any interest in the beautiful and highly specialised skills, techniques, and artefacts developed in the long ages that preceded industrialisation, standardisation and mass-production, then you should find this museum fascinating. Boat-building, shepherding, farming, weaving, blacksmithing, pottery, stone-cutting, games, clairvoyance . . . all beautifully illustrated and displayed. Downstairs, there is a study section – cases and cases of implements of different kinds, with cubicles where you can watch explanatory slide shows.

Musée de l'Histoire de France

Archives Nationales, 60 rue des Francs-Bourgeois, 3e; M° Rambuteau. Open 2–5pm, closed Tues.; Wed. free.
The **Archives Nationales** have on show some of the authentic bits of paper that fill the vaults: edicts, wills and papal bulls; a medieval English monarch's challenge to his French counterpart to stake his kingdom on a duel; Henry VIII's RSVP to the Field of the Cloth of Gold invite; fragile cross-Channel treaties; Joan of Arc's trial proceedings with a doodled impression of her in the margin; and more recent legislation and constitutions. The Revolution section includes Marie-Antoinette's book of samples from which she chose her dress each morning and a Republican children's alphabet where J stands for Jean-Jacques Rousseau and L for labourer. No English translations.

Musée Carnavalet

23 rue de Sévigné. 3e; M° St-Paul, Chemin-Vert. Open 10am–5:40pm; closed Mon.; card entry.
A Renaissance mansion in the Marais presents the **history of Paris** as viewed and inhabited by royalty, aristocrats and the bourgeoisie – from François I to 1900. The rooms for 1789–95 are full of sacred mementoes: models of the Bastille, original Declarations of the Rights of Man and the Citizen, tricolours and liberty caps, sculpted allegories of Reason, crockery

with revolutionary slogans, glorious models of the guillotine and execution orders to make you shed a tear for the Royalists as well. In the rest of the gilded rooms, the display of paintings, maps, and models of Paris at different dates is too exhaustive to give you an overall picture of the city. A great pity.

Musée de l'Armée

Hôtel des Invalides, 7e; M° Invalides, Latour-Maubourg, Ecole-Militaire. Open 10am–5pm (6pm in summer); card entry.

France's national war museum is enormous. By far the largest part is devoted to the uniforms and weaponry of Napoléon's armies. There are numerous personal items of Napoléon's, including his campaign tent and bed, and even his dog – stuffed. Later French wars are illustrated, too, through paintings, maps and engravings. Sections on the two world wars are good, with deportation and resistance covered as well as battles. Some of the oddest exhibits are Secret Service sabotage devices, for instance a rat and a lump of coal stuffed with explosives.

Palais de Chaillot

Place du Trocadéro, 16; M° Trocadéro. Musée de l'Homme: open 9.45am–5.15pm; closed Tues. Musée de la Marine: 10am–6pm; closed Tues.; card entry. Musée des Monuments Français: 9.15am–12.30pm and 2– 5pm; closed Tues.; card entry.

A mixed bunch here. The first, the **Musée de l'Homme**, contains displays illustrating the way of life, costumes, characteristic occupations, etc. of numerous countries, and is beginning to look a little dilapidated. Next door, the **Musée de la Marine** has dozens of beautiful, large-scale models of French ships, ancient and modern, war-like and commercial. In the east wing of the Palais, the **Musée des Monuments Français** comprises full-scale reproductions of the most important church sculpture from Romanesque to Renaissance. Moissac, Saintes, Vézelay, Autun, Chartres, Strasbourg and Crusader castles are all represented. This is the place to come to familiarize yourself with the styles and periods of monumental sculpture in France. Also included are reproductions of all the major frescoes.

Jardin des Plantes

5e; M° Austerlitz, Jussieu. Open 1.30–5pm, Sun. 10.30am–5pm; closed Tues.

There are three museums in the *jardin*: paleontology, botany and mineralogy, of which the best is palaeontology with a great collection of fossils, pickled bits and pieces and things dinosaurian.

Musée National des Techniques

270 rue St-Martin, 3e; M° Réaumur-Sébastopol, Arts-et-Métiers. Open Tues.–Sat. 1–5.30pm; Sun. (free) 10am–5.15pm.

Utterly traditional and stuffy glass-case museum with thousands of technical things from fridges to flutes, clocks and trains. The only exceptional part is the entrance – an early Gothic church filled with engines, aeroplanes, cars and bikes.

Musée de la Contrefaçon

16 rue de la Faisanderie, 16e; M° Porte-Dauphine. Open 8.30am– 5pm; weekdays only.
One of the odder ones – examples of imitation products, labels and brand marks trying to pass as the 'genuine article'.

Musée Grévin I

10 bd Montmartre, 9e; M° Montmartre. Open 1–7pm, during school holidays 10am–7pm; no admissions after 6pm; very expensive.
The main Paris waxworks are not nearly as extensive as London's more famous collection, and only worth it if you are desperate to do something with the kids. The ticket includes a 10-minute conjuring act.

Musée Grévin II

Niveau I, Forum des Halles, 1e; M° Les Halles. Open 10.30am–7.30pm; equally expensive; no admissions after 6.45pm.
Preferable to the wax statue parade of the parent museum but typically didactic. It shows a series of wax model scenes of French brilliance at the turn of the century, with automatically opening and closing doors around each montage to prevent your skipping any part of the voice-over and animation.

Musée Arménien and Musée d'Ennery

59 av Foch, 16e; M° Porte-Dauphine. Open 2–5pm; Sun. and Thurs; card entry. Musée Arménien Sun. only; free.
On the ground floor artefacts, art and historical documents of the Armenian people from the Middle Ages to the genocide at the start of this century by the Turks. On the floors above, the personal acquisitions of a nineteenth-century popular novelist – Chinese and Japanese objects including thousands of painted and sculpted buttons.

Performing arts and literature

Maison de Balzac

47 rue Raynouard, 16e; M° Passy, La Muette. Open 10am–5.40pm; closed Mon.; free Sun.; card entry.
Contains several portraits and caricatures of the writer and a library of his works and those of his contemporaries and critics. Balzac lived here between 1840 and 1847, but literary grandees seem to share the common fate of not leaving ghosts.

Musée du Cinéma

Palais de Chaillot, place du Trocadéro, 16e; M° Trocadéro. Open for guided tours only at 10am, 11am, noon, 2pm 3pm and 4pm; closed Mon.
Costumes, sets, cameras, projectors etc., from the early days on.

Musée Edith Piaf

5 rue Crespin-du-Gast, 11e; M° Ménilmontant, St-Maur. Admission by appointment only (☎43.55.52.72). Mon.–Thurs., pm only; closed July; free.
Exhibits of the possessions – clothes, letters – and pictures of the great cabaret singer.

Musée Instrumental

14 rue de Madrid, 8e; M° Europe. open 2–6pm; closed Sun.–Tues.
The Paris Conservatory has on show several thousand musical instruments dating from the Renaissance onwards, many of which have been played by the classical greats.

Musée Kwok-On

41 rue des Francs-Bourgeois, 4e; M° Rambuteau, St-Paul. Open noon–5.30pm; weekdays only.
The exhibits here are all theatrical props and costumes from southern Asia: Peking opera outfits; masks from Japan; figures for shadow theatre from India, Cambodia and Indonesia; puppets and paintings of stage scenes – all fascinating and very beautiful.

Maison de Victor Hugo

6 place des Vosges, 4e; M° Bastille. Open 10am–5:40pm; closed Mon.; card entry.
This museum is saved by the fact that Hugo decorated and drew, as well as wrote. Many of his ink drawings are exhibited and there's an extraordinary Japanese dining room he put together for his lover's house. Otherwise the usual pictures, manuscripts and memorabilia shed sparse light on the man and his work.

THE FACTS

Cafés, bars and cultural centres detailed below should give you an idea of Paris's potential for entertainment. For exhaustive **listings of what's on** in the city, there are three weekly guides, published on a Wednesday: *Pariscope, L'Officiel des Spectacles* and *7 Jours à Paris. Pariscope* is probably the easiest to find your way around, but since all three are just listings, with a minimum of comment, there is not much difference between them. If you can read French, a worthwhile supplement is the left-wing monthly cultural paper, *Globe*. If you can't, three American free-distribution magazines have newly appeared in Paris: *Paris Traveler's Gazette* has articles on the lesser known sights in Paris and elsewhere in France; *Paris Free Voice* is a monthly arts and entertainment tabloid and *France USA Contacts* has articles on cultural events and practical information.

Café life and drinking

You'll be happy in Paris if you're addicted to sitting around watching other people go about their business. **Cafés, bars** and **brasseries** beckon at every turn. All serve coffee, alcohol, sandwiches, ice cream and other snacks. In the morning you can get breakfast, of croissants, a *tartine* (*baguette* and butter, with jam sometimes), even eggs in the right place. And for the price of a coffee you can sit undisturbed for hours. Costs, inevitably, escalate in the posher neighbourhoods (beware the Champs-Elysées and rue de Rivoli) and anything consumed seated will be twice the price of standing at the counter, and even more if you're on the *terrasse* (at the front by the windows or on the sidewalk). But prices are always posted outside, so there's no excuse for being ripped off.

The most enjoyable cafés are often ordinary, local places but there are **particular areas** which café-lizards head for. The most famous, perhaps is bd Montparnasse, where you'll find the *Select, Coupole, Dôme, Rotonde* and *Closeries des Lilas* – hangouts of Sartre and Apollinaire, Miller, Nin and Hemingway, and most other **literary-intellectual** figures of the last six decades. Most of them are still frequented by the big, though not yet legendary, names in the Parisian world of arts and letters, cinema, politics and thought, as well as by their hangers-on, and the sets have remained unchanged. *Flore* and *Deux Magots* on bd St-Germain are in similar vein. The location of other lively **Left Bank café concentrations** is determined by the geography of the university. Art students from the Beaux Arts school patronize the old-time *La Palette* on the corner of rue Jacques-Callot. Science students gravitate towards the cafés on rue Linne (opposite the rue Cuvier exit from the Jardin des Plantes). The Humanities gather on place de la Sorbonne and rue Soufflot. And all the world – especially non-Parisians – finds its way to place St-André-des-Arts and the downhill end of bd St-Michel.

The **Bastille** is another good area to tour – always lively at night, as is **Les Halles**, though the latter's trade is principally the transient out-of-towners up for the bright lights. The much-publicised *Café Costes* is here, Mecca of the self-conscious and committed trendies (*branchés* or *super-branchés* – 'plugged in' – as they're called in French).

As well as cafés and brasseries, there are **wine bars** where you can try out the country's best produce by the glass; bars specialising in **beer** or trying to imitate British pubs; New York-influenced bars with music, soft chairs and cocktails; and **salons de thé,** chic and comfortable places for snacks, light lunches, and tea. Remember, anywhere that serves drinks will serve food, and vice versa.

Around St-Germain and Montparnasse:

Les Deux Magots (170 bd St-Germain). Famed literary spot, over-run by tourists in summer, with street entertainers playing to the packed terrace.

Le Flore (172 bd St-Germain). Long-time rival of *Deux Magots*, with similar clientèle.

La Coupole (102 bd du Montparnasse). Still the haunt of the chic, with dancing in the afternoons and evenings.

Le Dôme (108 bd du Montparnasse). Another in the *Deux Magots* mould, though now more restaurant than café.

Le Select (99 bd du Montparnasse). Most traditional of the Montparnasse cafés, open till 3am.

La Rotonde (105 bd du Montparnasse). Another of the Montparnase *grandes dames*, with the names of the departed famous on the menu – Lenin, Trotsky, etc.

Café de la Mairie (place St-Sulpice). Relaxed literary-youthful spot.

La Chien qui Fume (19 bd du Montparnasse). Old, ordinary café, a refuge from its tourist-haunted famous neighbours.

Au Petit Suisse (place Claudel). Small café among antiquarian bookshops.

The Village Voice (6 rue Princesse). Combines English language bookshop and café; you can nibble and sip while you read.

L'Ecluse (15 quai des Grands-Augustines). Wine bar, expensive, but in the best tradition.

Pub St-Germain (17 rue de l'Ancienne Comédie). Beer on tap twenty-four hours a day, huge and crowded.

In the 5e Arrondissement

Café de la Nouvelle Mairie (19 rue des Fossés St-Jacques). Small sawdusted bar with literary-academic clientele, serving wines, *saucisson* and sandwiches.

Crocodile (6 rue Royer-Collard). Cosy old-fashioned late-night bar.

La Chope (place de la Contrescarpe). Old Hemingway haunt, much touristified but pleasant out of season.

Café de Cluny (corner of bds St-Michel and St-Germain). Very crowded though quiet upstairs, a good meeting-place.

Académie de la Bière (88 bis bd de Port-Royal). Beer from twenty-two countries.

Mayflower Pub (49 rue Descartes). More international brews, open all night with mainly student clientele.

Polly Magoo (11 rue St-Jacques). Scruffy and friendly all-nighter frequented by chess addicts.

Café de la Mosquée (39 rue Geoffroy-St-Hilaire). Mint tea in Islamic courtyard of Paris's main mosque.

Les Halles and Beaubourg

Conways (3 rue St-Denis). Trans-Atlantic set-up and very relaxed.

Tribulum (62 rue St-Denis). Cocktail bar for indulgers in mysticism and zodiacs.

Café Costes (4 rue Berger). A major posing station, this was the first big '80s designer bar – from its chairs to the (original and impractical) loos.

Café Beaubourg (45 rue St-Merri). Clone of Café Costes by a different designer.

La Pointe St-Eustache (1 rue Montorgueil). Outside the hype – an ordinary café-brasserie.

Guinness Tavern (31 rue des Lombards). Live folk, jazz and rock on Mon., Tues. and Thurs., and Guinness.

The Marais, Bastille, and Northwards

La Tartine (24 rue de Rivoli). Brilliant 1900s winebar.

Le Temps des Cérises (31 rue de la Cérisaie). Young, local, un-*branché*.

Bleue Nuit (9 rue des Virtus). Late-night bar, relaxed and affordable.

Hôtel Central (33 rue Vieille-du-Temple). Popular men's gay bar; women excluded.

Le Duplex (25 rue Michel-le-Comte). Gay and lesbian, young and arty.

H.L.M. (3 rue des Haudriettes). Ever-changing decor, videos and cocktails.

La Mousson (9 rue de la Bastille). Trendy, lounging colonial-style cocktail bar.

Le Swing (42 rue Vieille-du-Temple). 1950s style bar – fun and with a very mixed clientèle – gay, lesbian and straight.

Le Clown (114 rue Amelot). Rendezvous for professional circus artists.

Le Petit Lappe (20 rue de Lappe). Simple with beautifully painted exterior.

Le Taxi Jaune (13 rue Chapon). Late night unpretentious bar and restaurant.

Le Loir dans la Théière (rue des Rosiers). *Salon de thé* with Mad Hatter's mural.

Centre Culturel du Marais (20 rue des Francs-Bourgeois). Art bookshop with *salon de thé.*

Piccolo Teatro (6 rue des Ecouffes). Wonderful tiny vegetarian *salon de thé*-cum-restaurant.

Up Past the Louvre and Opéra to the Champs-Elysées

Café de la Paix (12 bd des Capucines). Pricey, glittery, Third Empire fittings to match the opera house across the square.

La Chope du Croissant (corner of rues Montmartre and du Croissant). Preserves the table where socialist leader Jean-Jaurès was assassinated for his anti-war activities in 1914.

Tigh Johnny (55 rue Montmartre). Mainly Irish clientel, impromptu Irish music a possibility.

Le Grand Café (40 bd des Capucines). Favourite all-nighter.

Kléber (place du Trocadéro). For watching the sun rising behind the Eiffel Tower.

La Champmeslé (4 rue Chabanais). Backroom for lesbians, not very friendly.

The Look (49 rue St-Honoré). Nice gay bar, women and straight men welcome.

Aux Bons Crus (7 rue des Petits-Champs). Pleasantly unchic wine bar.

Willi's (13 rue des Petits-Champs). British-run wine bar, stockbroker and lawyer clientele.

Au Général La Fayette (52 rue La Fayette). Lots of bottled beers and Belle Epoque decor.

A Priori Thé (35–37 Galerie Vivienne). Quiet, secluded *salon de thé.*

Angelina (226 rue de Rivoli). The original gilded tea room.

The 7e Arrondissement

Au Bon Accueil (15 rue Babylone). Cosy, characterful old-time café.

La Pagode (57 bis rue de Babylone). Tea room in the city's most beautiful pagoda-cinema.

Au Sauvignon (80 rue des Saints-Pères). Small Alsatian wine bar with excellent selection of wines to try.

Eating

Eating out in Paris can break most budgets with little difficulty – but it need not be an enormous extravagance. There are numerous **fixed price menus between 45F and 85F** providing simple but well-cooked fare. At *Casa Miguel*, a restaurant featuring in the record books as the cheapest in Western Europe, a big-hearted Spanish woman serves full meals for five francs. On the whole, paying around 100F gives you the chance to try out a greater range of dishes; for serious gourmet satisfaction you'll usually need to pay over 150F. The **ethnic cuisines** of just about the whole world can be tasted in Paris – we've listed them by country of origin. Don't consider them as second-best after French – there's just as great a range from the dull to the delicious, and in the price category (mentioned with each listing). We've also listed **vegetarian** and **late night** restaurants as separate categories.

Far too many Parisian restaurants trade on tourists, especially in the Latin Quarter and around Les Halles. Be selective – the more crowded the place is with locals, the better it's likely to be. If you want to eat a *menu fixe*, go early: in the evenings after 9.30pm it's often *à la carte* only and later than 10.30pm it can be difficult to get a meal at all except in a few specific late night places. We have given opening times where they are exceptional. Many restaurants close on Sunday and Monday or both, and quite a number close down for parts of July and August.

Snacks

Stands along most **boulevards** sell *crêpes, croques-monsieurs* (toasted ham and cheese sandwich), *frites* (fries) and *baguette* sandwiches at reasonable prices: there's a particular concentration around the junction of bd St-Michel and St-Germain. For variety, **Tunisian** snacks like the *brik à l'oeuf* (a pastry envelope with a fried egg inside, ready to splash over your face) are common, as are **Greek** *souvlaki* (kebabs) and the **North African** spicy sausage *merguez. La Roi Falafel*, at 34 rue des Rosiers, sells the classic **Egyptian** falafel and, at 163 rue de Rivoli, you can sample **Japanese**-style snacks. For more bloating fare, try some **pasta** at *La Table d'Italie* (69 rue de Seine; 6e).

Cafés will generally do you an omelette or fried eggs, as well as sandwiches, and menus at **salon de thés** can constitute whole meals – see the preceding section. There are **drugstores** – pricier but good for salads, ice cream and *plats du jour* till 2am. You will find them at 149 bd St-Germain (6e); 133 av des Champs-Elysées (8e); 1 av Matignon (8e).

The best **ice creams and sorbets** in France are made and sold by *Berthillon* on the Ile St-Louis (31 rue St-Louis-en-l'Ile; open 10am–8pm, Wed.–Sun., closed July–Aug.). Their products are also available at *Lady Jane* and *Le Flore-en l'Ile*, both on quai d'Orléans.

Meals between 45F and 85F

Note that this – and subsequent – price categories are based on the lowest available *menu fixe*. Going *à la carte* will cause the bill to sky-rocket at almost all of them, while anything more than the cheapest of house wines can add substantially to the cost. Restaurants are arranged in order of *arrondissement.*

Bistro de la Gare (30 rue St-Denis, 1er). Good quick standby from a limited French-Italian menu.

Aux Deux Saules (91 rue St-Denis, 1er). Very cheap omelettes, sausages, chips etc.

Le Petit Ramoneur (74 rue St-Denis, 1er; till 9.30pm; closed weekends and Aug.). Elbow-rubbing cheapie in good bistro tradition.

L'Atelier Bleu (7 rue des Prouvaires,1er). A bit touristy but good food for the price.

Monoprix (self-service on top floor of shop, 23 av de l'Opéra, 1er). A place to stuff yourself in not very congenial surroundings, but for very little money.

Drouot (103 rue de Richelieu, 2e). Admirably cheap and good food, served at frantic pace, in an Art Nouveau decor. Same management as the better known *Chartier* (in the 9e, see below).

Le Grand-Cerf (10–12 passage du Grand-Cerf, off rue St-Denis at no.145, 2e; till 10pm; closed Sun. and Aug.). Paella and other Spanish dishes as well as French.

L'Ebouillanté (rue des Barres, 4e; open noon–9pm, last order 8.30pm; closed Mon.). Small and unintimidating with tables outside and 'Parisian cuisine' of *Blinis, brics* and gooey dessert.

Aux Savoyards, Le Baptiste (14 and 11 rue des Boulangers, 5e; closed Sat. pm and Sun. am). Different establishments, both noisy, friendly and full of students.

La Ferme Ste-Geneviève (40 rue de la Montagne Ste-Geneviève, 5e; closed Mon. and Tues. am). Good for hors d'oeuvres – which you can eat as much of as you want.

Bistro de la Gare (59 bd de Montparnasse, 6e). Same style (and management) as the *gare* in the 1er.

Restaurant des Omelettes (29 rue St-André-des-Arts, 6e). A hundred varieties.

Restaurant des Beaux-Arts (11 rue Bonaparte, 6e; closed Mon. and Aug.). Generous portions, wide choice and often a long wait.

Restaurant des Arts (73 rue de Seine, 6e; closed Fri. pm, Sat., Sun. and Aug.). Simple, home-cooked fare in *sympa* surroundings.

Au Babylone (13 rue de Babylone, 7e; midday only; closed Sun.). Murky, with lots of old-fashioned charm.

Valentin (19 rue Marbeuf, 8e; open every day). A rare realistic option if you want to eat in the centre of monumental Paris.

Bistro de la Gare (38 bd des Italiens, 9e). Yet another one (see above).

Casa Miguel (48 rue St-Georges, 9e; till 8pm; closed Sun.pm). The five franc full meal – you'll have to wait in line.

Chartier (7 rue Faubourg-Montmartre, 9e; open till 9.30pm). Another traditional cheapie with manic service and frogs and snails on the menu. Not for lingering but not to be missed.

Bar des Sports (15 rue de la Buttes-aux-Cailles, 13e). A local bistro with unusual and unecological fare (crocodiles, sometimes turtles).

Bergamote (1, rue Niepce, 14e). Good Normandy cooking. Cider as well as wine.

Café-Restaurant à l'Observatoire (63 av Denfert-Rochereau, 14e; closed Sun.). A straightforward, fast-food place with *steack frites* at their most basic and best. Very crowded at lunchtime.

Le Commerce (51 rue de Commerce, 15e; till 9.30pm). Another in the Chartier/Drouot line (see above) but less touristy and rushed.

Le Bistrot Champêtre (107 rue St-Charles, 15e; open till 11pm). Unusually imaginative – and quality – *menu fixe*. Definitely recommended.

Palais de Tokyo (av du Président-Wilson, 16e). Snack bar between the museums – an excellent place for a midday meal.

Janot la Frite (place Clichy, 17e). No great excitement but edible and rock-bottom.

Au Petit Moulin (17, rue Tholozie, 18e; closed Wed.). Tiny restaurant in a picturesque old house; excellent *plats du jour* and changing menus.

Le Maquis (69 rue Caulaincourt; closed Sun.). Brilliant lunchtime food which in summer you can eat outside

Around 150F

La Petite Chaumière (41 rue des Blancs-Manteaux, 4e; open till 10pm; closed Sun. and Mon.). Tremendous seafood dishes. Relaxed place.

Brasserie Balzar (49 rue des Ecoles, 5e; open till 1.30am.; closed Tues.). Classic, well-fed feeding place, near the top of the range.

Polidor (41 rue Monsieur-le-Prince, 6e; till midnight; no plastic). Very busy and popular, for the food rather than the mythical celebrities who have eaten and washed dishes here.

Aux Charpentiers (10 rue Mabillon, 6e; till 11.30pm; closed Sun.). Friendly, old-fashioned place belonging to the Guild of Carpenters – appropriate decor.

La Maison de la Lozère (4 rue Hautefeuille, 6e; till 10pm; closed Sun., Mon. and Aug.). A scrubbed wood restaurant serving up the cuisine of the Lozère *département*.

Au Vieux Paris (2 rue de l'Abbaye, 6e; closed Mon.pm and Tues.). Good value for money in an attractive cock-eyed medieval house.

Brasserie Lipp (151 bd St-Germain, 6e; till 12.45am; closed Mon.). If you can gain the approval of the fastidious and unpredictable owner at the door, you can get away with a 130F meal in one of the most famous Paris brasseries.

L'Oeillade (10 rue de Saint-Simon, 7e; open till 9.45pm; closed Sun.). Home cooking in a very pleasant atmosphere; run by two women.

Pour Le Plaisir (257 rue du Faubourg-St-Antoine, 11e; till 1am). Not the most hygienic of places but excellent food and a piano for anyone feeling inclined to play.

La Coupole (102 bd du Montparnasse, 14e; till 1.45am; closed Sun. am and Aug.). Another famous brasserie/café, where if you choose carefully the bill won't be outrageous.

L'Eléphant Rose (7 rue Francis-de-Pressensé, 14e). A co-op restaurant/*salon de thé*, good at any time of day.

Au Bon Accueil (corner of rue Wilhelm and av de Versailles, 16e). Rare simple and pleasant *restaurant de quartier*.

Le Mouton Blanc (40 rue d'Auteuil, 16e). A haunt of Racine, Molière and La Fontaine several hundred years ago, it now serves the well-heeled locals with an appealing choice of dishes.

Natasha (35 rue Guersant, 17e; closed Sun.). A bit out of the way but excellent and not too expensive.

Les Chants du Piano (3 rue Steinlen, 17e; closed Sun. and Mon.) Wonderful, visually and orally, with awesome desserts.

A La Pomponnette (42 rue Lepic, 18e; closed Sun. pm, Mon. and Aug.). Regulars' diner-zinc counter, tobacco stains, and a friendly crowd feasting on culinary classics.

Ethnic restaurants

Paris's **ethnic restaurants** offer some of the best though not necessarily the least expensive food in the city: North African, 'French' West African, Chinese, Vietnamese, Arab, East European . . . The selections below scarcely scratch the surface of what's available. **North African** places are widely scattered throughout the city, with extra concentrations in the touristy rue Xavier-Privas in the Latin Quarter and in the 'Little Maghreb' district along bd de Belleville in the 20e. **Chinese** and **South-East Asian** eateries are equally ubiquitous with major congregations again in Belleville, and around the av de la Porte-de-Choisy in the 13e. The **Greeks** are corralled on rue de la Huchette, rue Xavier-Privas and along rue Mouffetard, all in the 5e – and frankly a rip-off. **Caribbean** restaurants are very common, but often lack their true fresh fish ingredients. **Russian** and **Lebanese** food is brilliantly represented but beyond most people's budgets.

West/Central African

Le Kinkeliba (5 rue des Déchargeurs, 1er). Gabonese with wonderful smoked fish and yassa chicken. Around 100F.

L'Ajoupa (8 place Ste-Opportune, 1er; closed Sun., and Mon. am). Cheap and spicy.

La Savane (17 rue Marie-Stuart, 2e). Panther milk cocktails, tropical, nut pâtés and other sun-soaked fare.

Kin Malebo (2 passage Louis-Philippe, 11e; till 2am). Zairean meals at around 70F.

Le Fouta Toro (3 rue du Nord, 18e; pm only; closed Sun.). Senegalese dishes for around 75F, including *thiep*, the national dish.

Le Port de Pidjiguiti (28 rue Etex, 18e; closed Mon.). Excellent food from Guinea-Bissau, run by the people from a village to whom the proceeds go; around 70F.

Arab/North African

Hassan (27 rue de Turbigo, 3e; till midnight, closed Mon.). Ace Moroccan restaurant – North African food at its best and most beautiful. Over 120F.

Le Liban à Mouff (18 rue Mouffetard, 5e). Very pleasant Lebanese fare. Unusually cheap.

Chez Nacef (26 rue de Bière, 5e). Above average Algerian restaurant and over 120F.

Chez Marcel (16–18 rue Lalande, 14e). Good deal *menu fixe* until 9pm, very friendly and couscous at all times. Around 70F.

Le Golestan de Perse (4 rue Sévero, 14e). Not Arab but Iranian with an excellent *menu fixe* around 70F.

Zerda (corner of rue Chéroy and rue des Dames, 17e). Good unpretenious Moroccan around 120F.

Oaj Djerba (110 rue de Belleville, 20e; midnight, closed Fri., and Sat. am). Basic Tunisian-Jewish food, around 70F.

El Karnak (13 rue Louvel-Tessier, 10e; till 12.30am). Very cheap Egyptian.

Bar Sassia (12 place de la Bastille, 11e; till 12.45am). Brilliant Moroccan *tagines*, First Empire mirrors and twentieth-century trees, with friendly service. Around 120F.

L'Oasis Tunisien (place St-André-des-Arts, 6e). Basic but edible Tunisian food served in a friendly fashion.

East European

Goldenberg's (7 rue des Rosiers, 4e; till 11pm). More central European than east – the best known Jewish restaurant in the capital, not just for the *Front National* attacks it has suffered, but for the brilliance of Jo Goldenberg's kitchen. Around 130F.

Bulgare Village (8 rue de Nevers, 6e). Ace Bulgarian specialities such as *Cirène au Four* (baked ewe's cheese with vegetables) and Gamza wine. Around 120F.

Kazatchok (7 rue Manuel, 9e; till 2am; closed Sun.). Most Parisian Russian restaurants are high-class establishments run by old aristos. This isn't: a small, friendly place with great smoked salmon blinis, kotlet kievski and other Slavic specials. Around 120F.

La Cracovia (10 rue Alexandre-Dumas, 11e). Good properly over-filling Polish bistro.

Tokaj (57 rue du Chemin-Vert,11e; till 11pm; closed Sun. and Mon.). Hungarian with a midday menu around 70F.

Chinese/South East Asian

L'Ermitage de Chine (274 bd Jean-Jaurès, Boulogne-Billancourt, near the river). Cheap, delicious and very agreeable Chinese restaurant to stop at if you're wandering the western docks.

L'Orient Express (rue des Gravilliers, 3e). Chinese and Vietnamese with no frills, but good and reasonably priced at around 120F.

L'Auberge des Temples (74 rue de Dunkerque, 10e; open till 10.30pm). Choice of Chinese, Vietnamese, Thai, Cambodian and Japanese concoctions all under the one roof. Around 120F.

Eléphant Blanc (33 rue des Trois-Frères, 18e). Best in Lao-Thai cuisine – rich in ginger, citronella and coconut milk. Around 120F.

Restaurant Lyly (rue Bosquet, 7e; till 10.30pm). Simple local Vietnamese around 65F.

Qua Nho (5 rue du Sommerard, 5e; till 10.30pm; closed Sat. pm and Sun.). A real cheap Vietnamese place in the Latin Quarter.

Yakatori (64 rue Montparnasse, 14e; till 11pm). Japanese: *brochettes* served with a variety of piquant sauces.

Lao-Thai (34 rue de Belleville, 20e; till 11.30pm; closed Wed). Cheap midday menu for authentic cuisine from Laos and Thailand.

Réunion/Antillean

La Créole (122 bd Montparnasse, 14e). A bit gaudy, unpredictable, but well located.

Ile de la Réunion (119 rue St-Honoré, 1er; closed Sat. am and Sun.). Tropical island cuisine from one of France's remaining colonies. Cheap lunchtime menu, pricier at night. There are also Antillean restaurants nearby in the 1er along rue de Montorgueil.

Irish

John Jameson (above Kitty O'Shea's, rue des Capucines, near place Vendôme, 1er). Good quality Irish food, the seafood flown from Galway. Expensive.

There are also Turkish restaurants, South American, Italian of course, Swiss, Scandinavian, Mexican, Portuguese, Spanish, Armenian, Korean, Austrian, and even Ethiopian.

Vegetarian/Macrobiotic

Tripti-Kulai (2 place du Marché-Ste-Cathérine, 4e; open noon–6pm; closed Sun.). Small, quiet – around 70F.

Piccolo Teatro (6 rue des Ecouffes, 4e; open till 12.30am; closed Tues.) – see salons de thé.

Aux Abeilles d'Or (12 rue Royer-Collard, 5e). Vegetarian *nouvelle cuisine.*

Mary's Restaurant (9 rue de Turenne, 9e; open till 10pm). The English one – gourmet flans and tarts. Around 70F.

Le Bol en Bois (35 rue Pascal, 13e; open till 9.30pm, closed Sun.). Rather austere macrobiotic restaurant, with *plats du jour* for under 65F and a veggie grocery next door.

Au Grain de Folie (24 rue La Vieuville, 18e; pm only till 10pm; closed Wed). Good unpretentious cheapie with generous helpings. Around 65F.

Naturalia (107 rue Caulaincourt, 18e; till 9.30pm; closed, weekends). Does serve meat but has a vegetarian menu at midday.

Le Grenier de Notre-Dame (18 rue de la Bûcherie, 5e; till 11pm). A place to avoid, despite the view of Notre-Dame – nothing, least of all French Gothic, goes with the 'protein plates' served here.

For the early hours

La Nouvelle Gare (49 bd Vincent-Auriol, 13e; 24 hr.; closed Sat. am and Sun.). For people coming off night shifts, lowest late night prices and great atmosphere.

Au Pied de Cochon (6 rue Coquillère, 1er; 24 hr.). The best known all-nighter with a *terrasse*, seafood specialities and cheaper eats at the bar. Coming close to 170F.

Pub Saint-Germain-des-Prés (17 rue de l'Ancienne-Comédie, 6e; 24 hr.). Seats 500 people and has an equally phenomenal range of beers. Food from omelette and *steack frites* to a full meal at unshocking prices.

La Corossol Doudou (1 rue de la Ferrière, 9e; open till 7am). Antillais restaurant.

La Verre Bouteille (85 av des Ternes, 17e; till 5am); more of a wine bar than a restaurant, but serves grills, salads etc, for around 130F.

La Boulangerie (6 rue de l'Ancienne Comédie, 6e). Not a restaurant but a bakery – bread, brioche and croissants from 1am to 6am.

Le Pigalle (22 bd de Clichy, 9e; 24 hr.). Bar, brasserie and *tabac.*

Music and nightlife

French rock has a – deservedly – miserable reputation, but in Paris there are plenty of musical alternatives. The **West African** link has spawned bands of its own in the city and brings others on tour; everyone dances to **salsa** and the divisions between **Latin and Caribbean** rhythms, jazz and **African** beats are progressively harmonised in mixed bands and mixed clubs. **Rai** music, though still mainly restricted to private functions in the Algerian communities, is being listened to (for concerts your best bet is to scour the posters in the Goutte d'Or *quartier*) and the French themselves take their **jazz** and **classical music** seriously.

Paris **clubs and discos** can be very pretentious affairs, with obnoxious admission procedures and wildly overpriced drinks; we've indicated which ones are not so. The 1930s *bals musettes* or music halls relive (a bit) one of the city's most mythical periods, and still offer you the chance to dance an afternoon away. **Gay and lesbian** clubs are listed separately.

Paris is indisputedly the **jazz** capital of Europe but the clubs – with the notable exception of *Le 28 Dunois* – are expensive, and whiling away every evening listening to jazz of every type and origin is unfortunately not possible on a tight budget.

Big shows, be they **rock concerts** by Springsteen, **opera**, **ballet**, or **performance art**, are staged at the **five locations:** *Bataclan* (50 bd Voltaire, 11e; M° Oberkampf) *Olympia* (28 bd des Capucines, 2e; M° Opéra), *Palais des Sports* (Porte de Versailles, 15e; M° Porte-de-Versailles), *Zenith* (Parc de la Villette, 19e; M° Porte-de-Pantin) or the *Palais Omnisports de Bercy* (Porte de Bercy, 12e; M° Bercy). You'll see posters advertising these shows throughout the city. The *FNAC* shops take reservations for most of them without charging a commission, though you can, with rather more hassle, buy directly from the place putting on the show.

Jazz clubs

Le Bilboquet (13 rue St-Benôit, 6e; M° St-Germain; 7pm–2.30am).
A bar/restaurant with mainly local instrumentalists, occasionally big names over for a few gigs. Food is very expensive.

Au Duc des Lombards (42 rue des Lombards, 1er; M° Châtelet; till 2am).
Recently enlarged, with good Black American pianists and singers.

L'Eustache (37 rue Berger, 1er; M° Châtelet-Les Halles; closed Sun.).
Cheap beers and good jazz by local musicians in this young and friendly Les Halles café.

Latitudes (7–11 rue St-Benoît, 6e; M° St-Germain-des-Prés; Thurs.–Sat.).
Unusually comfortable and rather outlandish surroundings for this new club where the likes of Roy Haynes, Kim Parker and Rashied Ali have played.

Le Montana (28 rue St-Benoît, 6e; M° S-Germain-des-Prés).
Yet another club on St-Benoît, this one predominately bebop.

Magnetic Terrace (2 Rue de la Cossonnerie, Tues.–Sat.)
A large soundproofed cave featuring the likes of Chico Hamilton and James Moody. Entrance fees unfortunately reflect this.

New Morning (7–9 rue des Petits-Ecuries, 10e; M° Château-d'Eau. 9e; till 1.30am – concerts start around 10pm).
This is the place where the big international names in all the American jazz variants come to play. Spacious, comfortable and uncluttered by clever-conscious decor, it's a treat, though not, unfortunately, a very cheap one.

Le Petit Journal (71 bd St-Michel, 5e; M° Luxembourg and 13 rue du Commandant-Mouchotte, 14e; M° Bienvenue; both 9pm–2am; closed Sun.).
The original St-Michel outfit is small and smoky with mainly mainstream sounds. The new branch under the Hôtel Montparnasse has less atmosphere, but a more adventurous and modern programmeme.

Le Petit Opportun (15 rue des Lavandières-Ste-Opportune, 1er; M° Châtelet; 11pm–3am)
It's worth arriving early to get a seat for the live music in this dungeon-like cellar where the acoustics play strange tricks when you can't see the musicians. Mainly traditional American and revival sounds with tapes in the bar upstairs and a crowd of genuine connoisseurs.

Slow Club (130 rue de Rivoli, 1er; M° Louvre/Pont-Neuf; 9.30pm– 2.30am; closed Sun. and Mon.).
A jazz club to be-bop the night away to the sounds of Claude Luter's sextet and visiting New Orleans trumpeters and saxophonists.

Utopia (1 rue Niepce, 14e; M° Pernéty; 8.30pm–dawn; closed Sun. and Mon.).
No genius here but good French blues singers interspersed with jazz and blues tapes, the people listening mostly young and studentish. No admission charge and cheap drinks. Generally very pleasant atmosphere.

Le 28 Dunois (28 rue Dunois, 13e; M° Chevaleret. Concerts Fri.–Mon. 8.30–11.30pm).
Modern European improvised jazz gets consistent support from this out-of-the-way warehouse which is large enough for very big bands. It's also cheap and entirely unsnobbish. When there aren't jazz concerts the space is used for musical theatre, video and shows for children.

Mainly Rock, Latin and African

Baiser Salé (58 rue des Lombards, 1er; M° Châtelet. 8.30pm–4am).
When the music's good – rhythm & blues, Latino-rock, reggae or Brazilian – then the cocktails and comfort are great. Otherwise it's not much more than videos in the bar and men on the make.

Centre Latino-Américain (1 rue Montmartre, 1er; M° Châtelet. 8.30pm onwards; closed Mon. and Tues.).
Excellent concerts in the sounds that have dominated the recent Paris music scene.

Chapelle des Lombards (19 rue de Lappe, 11e; M° Bastille. 10.30pm–dawn; bands Thurs.–Sat.; closed Sun. and Mon.)
An occasional waltz and tango but the music is mostly salsa, reggae, steel drums, gwo-kâ and the blues. The doormen aren't friendly but it's relatively cheap and once inside a good night is assured.

Discophage (11 passage du Clos-Bruneau, off 31–33 rue des Ecoles, 5e; M° Maubert-Mutualité; 9pm–3am; closed Sun. and Aug.).
A jam-packed, tiny and under-ventilated space but all such discomforts irrelevant for the best Brazilian sounds you can hear in Paris.

L'Ecume (99 rue de l'Ouest, 14e; M° Pernéty. till 3am).
Live Brazilian or Caribbean music on weekends in a dark, cramped smoky cellar – just as Paris dives are supposed to be. Space upstairs for chess, cards and chat.

L'Escale (15 rue Monsieur-le-Prince, 6e; M° Odéon; 11pm–4am).
More Latin American musicians must have passed through here than any other club. The dancing sounds, salsa mostly, are in the basement (disco on Wed.) while on the ground floor every variety of South American music is given an outlet.

La Falaise (rue Fontaine, 9e; M° Pigalle; till dawn).
Algerian cabaret with very expensive drinks and the possibility, if you turn up around 3am, of hearing Cheb Dany and Cheb Kada sing bitter-sweet Rai.

Gibus (18 rue du Faubourg-du-Temple, 11e; M° République. 11pm– 5am; closed Sun, Mon. and weekdays in Aug.).
Where up and coming English rock bands over the last twenty years have played their first Paris gig. Fourteen nights of dross will throw up one decent band but it's always hot, loud, energetic and relatively cheap.

Phil' One (Place de la Patinoire, 3e niveau, Parvis de la Défense; opposite CNIT building; RER La Défense. Thurs.–Sat., 10pm onwards.)

Brilliant sound system, no trendy decor, pit and gallery dance floor and tables, and quirky musical policy encompassing Antillais, African, a bit of jazz, English and French rock – one of the best.

Rex Club (3 bd Poissonnière, 2e; M° Montmartre. 8.30pm–5am.)
Rock concerts upstairs in the Rex Cinema, mainly French and U.S., otherwise a mixture of live music, transvestites' nights out and similar, with black bands most Friday nights.

Rock'n'Roll Circus (6 rue Caumartin, 9e; M° Havre-Caumartin).
A smallish place for top French rock bands.

Les Trottoirs de Buenos Aires (37 rue des Lombards, 1er; M° Châtelet. 9.30pm onwards; closed Mon.)
Argentinian tango is the only music performed. The drinks are very expensive, and the dancing is for professionals only – it's all part of the act. You'll either be fixated or very frustrated.

Nightclubs and discos

Les Bains (7 rue du Bourg-l'Abbé, 3e; M° Etienne-Marcel; 11.30pm–6am).
Trendy club in an old Turkish bath with tedious music and American bouncers who judge whether you're stylish enough to enter.

Balajo (9 rue de Lappe, 11e; M° Bastille. Fri., Sat. and Mon. 3pm–6pm and 10pm–4.30am.)
The old-style music hall of *gai* but straight Paris – extravagant thirties' decor, working class Parisians in their weekend best and the music everything to move to from mazurka, tango, waltz, cha-cha, twist, and the slurpy chansons of between the wars. Disco, modern hits and loss of atmosphere on Monday nights. Afternoon sessions a uniquely Parisian experience.

Blue Moon (160 bd St-Germain, 6e; M° St-Germain-des-Prés).
The best reggae disco.

La Boule Rouge (8 rue de Lappe, 11e; M° Bastille).
A similar venue to *Balajo* opposite but cheaper, scruffier and less tolerant of outsiders.

The Cellar (54/56 rue de Ponthieu, 8e; M° Franklin-Roosevelt; till 6am).
A different style of music every night, no entry charge but pricey drinks.

La Locomotive (96 bd de Clichy, 18e; M° Blanche)
New, and enormous high-tech nightclub.

La Main Jaune (Square de l'Amérique Latine, Porte de Champerret, 17e; M° Porte-de-Champerret; 10pm–5am; closed Mon. and Tues.).
Disco on a roller-skating rink to radio hits with some free nights – check with *Pariscope* and co.

Le Malibu (44 rue Tiquetonne, 2e; M° Etienne-Marcel. 8.30pm–5am.)
Music from all over West Africa and the West Indies in a crowded basement beneath a restaurant. No entrance problems here. Blacks outnumber whites, and everyone is under thirty.

Mambo Club (20 rue Cujas, 5e; M° St-Michel/Odéon).
More Afro-Cuban and Antillais music in a seedy dive with people of all ages and nationalities.

Memphis (3 Impasse Bonne-Nouvelle, 10e; M° Bonne-Nouvelle; 10.45pm–6am.)
Long-established, laid-back disco done out as the 'Mississippi Queen' with video screens and large dance floors, but unfortunately nothing very original coming out of the speakers.

L'Opéra Night (30 rue Gramont, 2e; M° Richelieu-Drouot. 11pm–5am.)
A cinema during the day transformed to Afro-funk space every evening after the last film. Renowned for the quality of the dancing to African and Caribbean funk, reggae and salsa.

Le Palace 999 (8 rue du Faubourg-Montmartre, 9e; M° Montmartre. 11pm–dawn. Closed. Mon. and Tues.).
The best and most exuberant bopping in town – everyone goes, everyone gets in. It's big and the music various.

La Piscine (32 rue de Tilsitt, 17e; M° Etoile. 10pm–dawn; closed Tues.)
A converted thirties' swimming bath where you dance on the tiles or in the drained main pool. Top of the league architecturally, passable music and usually a young and enthusiastic crowd.

La Plantation (45 rue de Montpensier, 1er; M° Palais-Royal).
Despite the reputation for welcoming everyone, the doormen are fussy, particularly if you're white. Inside, excellent Cuban, Angolan, Congolese and Antillais music awaits you.

Le Tchatch au Tango (13 rue au Maire, 3e; M° Arts-et-Métiers. 2.30–6.30pm and 11pm–5am; closed Sun.–Tues.).
The tango has been played here since the turn of the century and the decor looks as if it's retained layers from every decade since. Cheap entry and cheap drinks (obligatory cloakroom fee), people dancing in any old clothes, with anyone who agrees to join them, to the waltz, tango or cha-cha in the afternoon sessions, salsa, calypso or reggae in the evenings.

Le Village (7 rue Gozlin, across rue de Rennes from Le Drugstore).
Modern Jazz club run for young French jazz musicians by the non-profit making organisation Jazz Plus.

Lesbian and gay clubs

Women's

Chez Moune (54 rue Pigalle, 18e; M° Pigalle. 10pm–dawn).
In the red light heart of Paris, predominately women's cabaret and disco may shock or delight feminists, often involving as it does female strip-tease (any man causing the slightest disturbance or unease is kicked out). Sunday afternoons from 4.30–8pm are women only.

Le Katmandou (21 rue du Vieux-Colombier, 6e; M° St-Sulpice. 11pm– dawn).
The best known and most upmarket of the lesbian venues. Good music of the Afro-Latino varieties but not an easy place to meet people.

Le Garage (41 rue de Washington, 8e; M° George V; 11pm–dawn; inconsistent opening days).
Spacious disco, varied crowd, Wednesday nights gays too.

Le Morocco (9 rue Guisarde, 6e; M° Mabillon; 7pm–2am; closed Sun.).
Not exclusively female, but women predominate and the music is good.

Men's

Le BH (7 rue du Roule, 1er; M° Louvre/Châtelet-Halles; 10pm– 6am).
Bopping downstairs, drinks and chats upstairs. Very popular with all sorts and still cheap.

The Broad (3 rue de la Ferronerie, 1er; M° Châtelet-Halles; 10.30pm–dawn; closed Mon.).
Young, chic and perennially popular as is the Broad Side cocktail bar that keeps the same hours next door.

Haute Tension (87 rue St-Honoré, 1er; M° Châtelet; 11pm–dawn).
Discreet and rather subdued surroundings for a bar-disco that has become a favourite with all types and all ages.

Le Manhattan (8 rue des Anglais, 5e; M° Maubert-Mutualité; 11pm– 6am).
Men only with a good funky disco.

Le Piano Zinc (49 rue des Blancs-Manteaux, 4e; M° Rambuteau. 6pm– 2am; closed Mon.).
At 10pm, when the piano-playing starts, this bar becomes a happy riot of songs, music hall acts and dance which may be hard to appreciate if you don't follow French too well. Not exclusively gay but near enough and an easy place to make contact.

Scaramouche (44 rue Vivienne, 2e; M° Montmartre; 11pm–6am).
Young, trendy, gay hangout where women are welcome. Shows every Wednesday and Sunday evening.

Classical music

A strange but agreeable phenomenon for a big city: most of Paris's classical musical **concerts** are held in **churches** and are free or very cheap. Keep your eye out for posters around town – or check *Pariscope*, etc. or the magazine *Le Monde de la Musique*. There are scores of possibilities, especially during the summer, from Vivaldi to Stockhausen and the new Systems composers. Good bets include *St-Germain-des-Prés, St-Julien-le-Pauvre, les Invalildes, St-Séverin, St-Thomas-d'Aquin*. There are free organ recitals in *Notre-Dame* on Sundays at 5.45pm, and free concerts at *Radio-France* (166 av du Président-Kennedy, 16e; M° Passy; ☎45. 24.15.16).

The top **auditoriums** where you may find Barenboim (if he settles his lunch disputes) conducting the *Orchestre de Paris* are the *Salle Pleyel* (252 rue du Faubourg-St-Honoré, 8e; M° Place-des-Ternes), the *Théâtre Musical de Paris* (1 place du Châtelet, 1er; M° Châtelet); *Epicerie-Beaubourg* (12 rue du Renard, 4e; M° Hôtel-de-Ville); *Gaveau* (45 rue de la Boétie, 8e; M° Miromesnil); and the *Théâtre des Champs-Elysées* (15 av Montaigne, 8e; M° Richelieu-Drouet). **Opéra** is performed with all due pomp at the *Opéra* and with marginally less superfluous carrying-on at the *Epicerie-Beaubourg* (see above) and the *Opéra-Comique* (Salle Favard, 5 rue Favard, 2e; M° Richelieu-Drouot). When the Bastille opera house opens, there may be more chance of getting a seat, but whether it will be any less exorbitant is unlikely. The musical experiments enjoying the most state funds are **Pierre Boulez's** and others' researches into electronic, acoustics and resulting Systems compositions. Boulez's laboratory/concert hall is beneath Beaubourg (entrance beside the Stravinsky pool). There are frequent performances and you can listen to tapes of recent excerpts at the reception (during office hours).

Movies and theatre

There are over 350 **films** showing in Paris in any one week – all of them detailed in the listings magazines. Most cinemas have low prices on Monday and reductions for students Monday to Thursday, all are non-smoking and some still expect you to tip the ushers. Almost all of the huge selection of foreign films get original version showings (*v.o.* in the listings as opposed to *v.f.* which means it's dubbed).

Of all the capital's **cinemas,** the most beautiful is the *Pagode* (57 bis rue Babylone, 7e; M° François Xavier), originally transplanted from Japan at the turn of the century to be a rich Parisienne's party place. The wall panels of the *Grande Salle* are embroidered in silk. Golden dragons and elephants hold the lights and a battle between Japanese and Chinese warriors rages on the ceiling. If you don't want to see the films being shown you can still come here for tea and cakes. Equally outrageous, but in the kitsch line, is *Le Grand Rex* (1 bd Poissonnière, 2e; M° Bonne-Nouvelle) with 2800 seats, a ceiling of stars and city skylines, plus flying whales and dolphins, all as a frame for the largest cinema screen in Europe. It's the good old 1930s public movie-seeing experience, though unfortunately all its foreign films are dubbed. *Max Linder Panorama* opposite (24, bd Poissonnière; M° Bonne-Nouvelle) always show films in the original, has almost as big a screen, plus Art Deco decor.

Cinémathèques at Beaubourg and at the Palais de Chaillot show several different films daily from their library of international classics and obscurities, and seats are cheap. Several cinemas also run **festivals** so that you can pass an entire day or more watching your favourite actor/actress, director, genre or period. One such is *Le Studio 28* (10 rue de Tholozé, 18e; M° Blanche/Abbesses) which in its early days was done over by extreme right-wing Catholics who destroyed the screen and the paintings by Dali and Ernst in the foyer, after one of the first showings of Buñuel's *L'Age d'Or*. The cinema still shows avant-garde premières, followed occasionally by discussions with the directors. An **International Festival of Womens' Films** takes place in March at the suburb of Sceaux – details from the *Maison de Femmes* (8 Cité Prost, 11e; ☎43 48.29.91).

Alternatively you could while away several hours watching **videos** at the *Vidéothèque de Paris* (2 Grande Galerie, Porte St-Eustache, Forum des Halles; M° Châtelet-Les Halles). Programmes start at 2.30pm and run on till the early hours, showing work of all kinds and from all over, with the odd film mixed in as well. For a high-tech type of film – 70mm on the Omnimax system – but a pretty reactionary or very conventional content, you need to book a seat at *La Géode* in front of the *Cité des Sciences* at La Villette (☎46 42.13.13). It's expensive and often booked up weeks in advance, but if you can get in, the 180° projection is boggling whatever's on it. At the other end of the scale, viz the **TV** screen, the *Cinéma de Minuit* on the third channel puts on old movies, in the original – often Hollywood classics – every Sunday night at 8.30pm.

Parisian **theatre** – at least at the **avant-garde** end of the spectrum – can be amazing simply as a spectacle. A handful of directors (Antoine Vitez, Ariane

Mnouchkine, Peter Brook) have superstar status, and their productions are frequently epic. If you're interested, *Passion* magazine has regular coverage. Among their most promising locations are the *Théâtre du Soleil* (Mnouchkine's theatre, run as a workers' co-op at La Cartoucherie, Bois de Vincennes, M° Vincennes), the *Théâtre National de Chaillot,* (Palais de Chaillot, place du Trocadéro, 16e; M° Trocadéro); the *Bouffes du Nord* (Brook's theatre, 37 bis bd de la Chapelle, 10e; M° Chapelle) and the *Théâtre du Rond-Point* (av Franklin-Roosevelt, 16e; M° Franklin-Roosevelt) where Beckett is performed with brilliance. The *Escalier d'Or* theatre (18 rue d'Enghien, 10e; M° Strasbourg-St-Denis) often hosts political shows from abroad as well as radical French plays by young or little-known writers. The most likely location for such productions is the *Théâtre de la Bastille* (76 rue de la Roquette, 11e; M° Bastille) – also one of the best places for **mime** and **contemporary dance**. Shows at all these places will be listed in *Pariscope* etc.

Café-théâtre, which all hip guide-writers feel obliged to recommend, is usually hard or impossible to understand, relying heavily as it does on contemporary allusions, slang and humour. If you want to try, the *Café de la Gare* (41 rue de Temple, 4e; M° Hôtel-de-Ville), *Blancs-Manteaux* (15 rue des Blancs-Manteaux, 4e; M° Hôtel-de-Ville) and *Au Café d'Edgar* (58 bd Edgar-Quinet, 14e; M° Edgar-Quinet) are among the best known.

For serious straight theatre, check out the programmes of the **state-subsidised theatres**. The *Comédie Française* (2 rue de Richelieu, 1er; M° Palais-Royal) specialises in the seventeenth-century classics (left-over tickets sold off cheap on the night). More modern plays are performed at the *Théâtre de France* (at the Odéon, place Paul-Claudel, 6e; M° Odéon), and at smaller houses spread about the city; the *Cité Internationale, Théâtre du Marais, Montparnasse*, and *Présent* are all names to look for in the listings. The *Huchette* (23 rue de la Huchette, 5e; M° St-Michel) has been playing the Absurd equivalent of the *Mousetrap* – Ionesco's *La Cantatrice Chauve* – every night for more than twenty-five years.

Kids' Paris

The star attraction for young children is the **Jardin d'Acclimatation** (M° Porte-Maillot) in the Bois de Boulogne, open every day from 9am to 6.30pm with special attractions Wednesday, Saturday and Sunday and during school breaks. There are puppets, bumper cars, go carts, pony and camel rides, sea lions, a mini-train from Porte Maillot, a sort of magical mini-canal ride, and a superb collection of antique dolls at the *Grande Maison des Poupées*. For the older ones there is **mini-golf** and **bowling**, and, at the entrance, **bike hire** for roaming the park's cycle trails. Also, **boating** on the Lac Inférieur. The one drawback with the Jardin is that nearly every activity costs an additional fee.

Other places you can let kids off the lead are the **Jardin des Plantes** (M° Jussieu/Monge) with a small **zoo** (9am–5.30pm) and **Natural History Museum** (10am–5.30pm; closed Tues.). The **best zoo** – and both are expensive – is the **Bois de Vincennes** (9am–6pm; 5pm in winter; M° Porte-Dorée). The **parc Floral** on the other side of the wood (rte de la Pyramide;

RER Vincennes; 9.30am–8pm and until 10pm on Sat. in summer; 9.30–6pm in winter; free for under-sixes and a lot cheaper than the *Jardin d'Acclimatation*) has train tours of the gardens, clowns, puppets and magicians on summer weekends, and a children's theatre, the *Théâtre Astral*. Numbers of squares and small public gardens have play areas with sandpits and slides; square Viviani, for instance, opposite Notre-Dame could provide quick relief for a child with the screaming abdabs. As for kids too young to enjoy the **Cité des Sciences** at La Villette (which is a treat and a half), there's the **Dragon Slide** just outside. Back in the centre of town, the **Forum des Halles** grounds include a supervised play area. The **Parc Monceau** in the 17e has a roller-skating rink and the **Luxembourg gardens** have a larger playground, pony rides, toyboat rental on the pond, and puppets.

Other **puppet-shows** take place Wednesday, Saturday and Sunday at the Champs-Elysées Rond-Point and the Buttes-Chaumont park (M° Buttes-Chaumont). For these and the **circus**, check *Pariscope* and its peers. Carousels appear from time to time at the Forum des Halles or beneath the Tour St-Jacques at Châtelet, but amusement parks are not part of the Paris entertainment.

Potential mountaineers can practice breaking their necks – no charge – on the **kid's climbing wall** at *Au Vieux Campeur* climbing-camping shop, 2 rue de Latran, 5e (closed Sun.).

The **children's workshop**, Atelier des Enfants, at the **Centre Beaubourg** could be fun (Wed. 10–11.30am, Wed. and Sat. 2–3.30pm and 3.45–5pm; free for visitors to the centre). They organise games, painting, sculpture, etc. for the over-fives and there's no language problem as the *animateurs* – organisers – speak English.

You could also try some **museums**: the **aquariums** at the **Musée des Arts Africains et Océaniens** and beneath the Palais de Chaillot (Trocadéro, 16e; 10am–5.30pm); the waxworks, **Musée Grévin; Musée de L'Armée, de la Marine, de l'Homme** – see *Museums* for these – but avoid the **Musée des Enfants**, which purveys romantic sentimental images of childhood, not children's entertainment.

The ghoulish and horror-movie addicts should get a really satisfying shudder from the **Catacombs** (Tues.–Fri. 2–4pm; weekends 8–11am and 2–4pm) while the other pre-teen fixation might find fulfillment in the **sewers** – *Les Egouts* (boat tours Mon., Wed. and the last Sat. of the month, 2–5pm).

Boat tours on the surface might also appeal. If you look under *Promenades* in *Pariscope* you'll find details of the grotesque *Bateaux-Mouches* which blare their multi-lingual commentaries between the grand landmarks of the Left and Right Bank quaysides, and their various competitors. A much better deal is on the **canal rides**. You can go from the Musée d'Orsay (quai Anatole-France by the Deligny swimming pool car park; M° Solférino) to the Parc de la Villette (by the *Information Villette*; M° Porte-de-Pantin) from April 1 to November 3 at 9.30am or 2.30pm, and from La Villette to the Musée d'Orsay at 9.45am or 2.30pm. The journey takes three hours and you can reserve a seat with *Paris Canal* (☎48.74.75.30). Alternatively *Canauxrama* (☎46.07.13.13) has rides, also three hours, between the Port de l'Arsenal just south of the Bastille and La Villette (5 bis quai de la Loire; M° Jaurès).

Feminist Paris

With French feminism in its present doldrums, places are closing rather than starting up, and the longstanding *Carabosses* bookshop-café haven in the 11e has long since changed hands. Even the **Maison des Femmes** (8 Cité Prost, 11e; ☎43.48.24.91), the **feminist centre** for information, help, food, recreation and a meeting place for different organisations, can't guarantee its opening hours. They sporadically publish a bulletin, *Paris Féministes*, which, if you can get it, should help with other contacts.

Intellectual feminist life is still well provided for. The *Centre Audio-Visuel Simone de Beauvoir* (29 rue du Colisée, 18e; 42.25.17.75), named after its founder, is an **archive of audio-visual works** by or about women which you can peruse for a small fee. For **books and reviews**, try the *Librairie Anima* (3 rue Ravignan, 18e) and *La Brèche* (9 rue de Tunis, 12e). The most comprehensive **library** is the *Bibliothèque Marguerite Durand* (79 rue Nationale, 13e; 45.70.80.30). *Elles Tournent La Page* (8 impasse des Trois-Soeurs, 11e) has a library along with **dance, fitness** and **writing workshops**.

There are **courses and classes** from mime to plumbing organised by and for women, but what's lacking in Paris is more **eating and drinking places**. *Le Potiron* (see 'Restaurants') is the only feminist restaurant in town.

Harassment on the streets is worse, and more constant here than in the rest of France. If things get bad, you could turn to *SOS Femmes Alternatives* (54 av de Choisy, 13e; ☎45.85.11.37) or the *Foyer Flora Tristan* (7 rue du Landy, 92110, Clichy; ☎47.31.51.69). These organisations are primarily for battered women but since there's no rape crisis centre, they try to help all victims of male violence. If you feel that speaking on the phone would be too difficult, go to the nearest of the addresses above or to the Mairie of the *arrondissement* (and not to the police). In cases of sexual harassment at work, contact the *Association Contre les Violences au Travail des Femmes* (71 rue St Jacques, 5e).

Gay and lesbian Paris

Paris is very much the San Francisco of Europe for **gay men.** New bars, clubs, restaurants, saunas and shops open all the time and in Les Halles and the Marais every other address is gay. For a long time the emphasis has been on providing the requisites for a hedonistic life style, rather than political activism. During the Chirac government various gay cultural manifestations were suppressed, but discrimination and harassment are not routine, and the age of consent is still fifteen.

Things have changed, here as elsewhere, since the onset of AIDS (*SIDA* in French). The resulting homophobia has not been extreme, but has been enough to activate the community. A group of gay doctors, *Association des Médecins Gais* (45 rue Sedaine, 11e; ☎48.05.81.71), and the organisation *AIDES* (☎42.72.19.99, 7–11pm) have, along with the gay press, done an excellent job of spreading information and providing support. Otherwise gay activism, like most things in France, splits along party political lines with the

GPL (Gais pour les Libertés) on the left, and *MGL (Mouvement des Gais Libéraux)* on the right. The oldguard *CUARH (Comité d'Urgence Anti-Répression Homosexuelle*; 1 rue Keller, 11e; ☎48.06.09.39) is still the main meeting place for **both gays and lesbians** and organises social and other events. Another mixed cultural outfit that welcomes individuals dropping in is *L'Escargot* (40 rue Amelot, 11e; M° St-Sébastien; ring to enter, 1st floor of courtyard staircase). If you need **help** for any reason, try these two places, or phone the Gay Switchboard equivalent, *SOS Gaies* (Women: ☎42.26.61.07, Sat. 3pm–7pm; Men: ☎42.61.00.00 Wed. and Fri. 6pm–midnight).

Lesbian groups have always tended to be more politically active than gays, with separatists often dominating the Women's Movement. But it's still the case that many lesbians never come out and places they run don't publicise their orientation for fear of reprisals. The most active groups are **MIEL** (c/o *Maison des Femmes*), *Archives, Recherches et Cultures Lesbiennes* (☎48.05.25.89) and the collective that publishes *Lesbia* (see below) which has an open line (☎43.48.89.54, Mon. and Tues. evening every other week and every Wed. 3–10pm).

To find out what's going on, your best bet is to head for the main gay and lesbian **bookshop**, *Les Mots à la Bouche* (6 rue Ste-Croix-de-la-Bretonnerie, 4e; 11am–8pm; closed Sun.). There you should find the weekly *Gai Pied Hebdo* (predominately male); *Lesbia* – a monthly national lesbian magazine; the **international gay press** and the English gay guide to the city, *Weaver's Gay Paris*. If you're going to be travelling throughout France, buy the annual **Gai Pied Guide**, which gives gay and lesbian addresses for the whole country. *Gay Pied Hebdo* and *Lesbia* are also on sale at most newstands.

The gay and lesbian **radio station**, Fréquence Gaie, was cut during the major rearrangement of local radio but has now reappeared on the airwaves as **Future Génération** – 24 hours on 94.4 Mhz.

Lesbian and gay **clubs** and **bars** are listed under 'Nightlife'.

Consuming interests: markets and shops

Even if you don't plan – or can't afford – to spend any money, Parisian **shops** are a vital part of the cityscape. There is an amazing density of them, given even greater emphasis by the compactness and walkability of the *quartiers* and by the French knack of creating a dazzling illusion of glamour and gloss. Window-shopping, particularly for clothes, is a real joy (and the price tags a real joke). Bargains are few and far between, even at the flea markets. These selections cover the rare exceptions and the best places to gape or browse.

Most shops stay open until 7 or 8pm and take an hour or more's lunch between 1 and 3pm. Sunday and Monday are the normal closing days. The biggest **sales** are in January and August. For **late-night** shopping there's a 24-hour Monday to Saturday 'supermarket', *As Eco*, near Beaubourg at 11 rue Brantôme. For **mundane needs**, your best bets are the ordinary **local markets** for food, and for toiletries, underwear etc, the **supermarkets**, of which the cheapest chains are *Ed-Discount* and *Franprix*. **Drugstores** are pricey but good for basics and open until 1am.

Markets

Street markets provide one of the capital's more exacting tests of willpower. At the top of the scale, there are the satanic arrays in **rue de Lévis** (17e, closed Mon.) and **rue Cler** (7e; closed Mon.) in which most of the stands have become permanent shops. Of the markets for ordinary mortals, Number 1 is **rue de Buci/rue de Seine** (6e; closed Mon.). **Rue Mouffetard** (the southern end; daily), **place Maubert** and **place Monge** (Wed., Fri. and Sun.), all in the 5e, are almost as tempting. There are much bigger markets in **rue de la Convention**, 15e (Tues., Thurs., Sun.); **bd Port-Royal**, 5e (end of rue St-Jacques; Tues., Thurs., Sat.); and **bd Edgar-Quinet**, 14e (Wed. and Sat.). **Belleville** has a cosmopolitan market Tuesday and Friday (bd de Belleville, 20e), and, equally good for hot herbs and spices, there's the **Goutte d'Or** market (around Barbès-Rocherchouart métro; Wed. and Sat.). There are **covered markets** (every day except Mon. and Sun. pm) in **St-Germain**, rue Mabillon, 6e, on rue du Château-d'Eau, 10e and **av Secrétan**, 19e – the latter in a fine old iron-frame building.The most handsome of the nineteenth-century iron and glass *halles*, the renovated **Carreau du Temple** on rue Perrée, 3e (daily except Monday until noon, 1pm weekends) deals in mostly new clothes, but at wholesale prices.

The **flea markets**, or *Marchés aux Puces*, are at **Porte de Clignancourt**, 18e (Sat., Sun., Mon. 7am–7pm); **Porte de Vanves**, (av Georges-Lafenestre, on bridge over *périphérique*, 14e) (Sat., Sun. 7am–7pm); **place d'Aligre**, 12e (daily except Mon. until 1pm); and **Porte de Montreuil**, 20e (Sat., Sun., 7am–7pm, Mon. 7am–noon). Clignancourt is the biggest and also the most touristy, selling clothes, records, shoes, books, junk and expensive antiques – fun to visit despite its popularity and prices. Vanves (avenues Marc-Sangnier and Lefenestre) is best for bric-à-brac bargains, and artists show and sell their work: jewellery, painting and sculpture, in pl des Artistes. Porte de Montreuil has good rétro clothes, but get there early for bargains. The *Marché d'Aligre* occupies both a covered space and the surrounding streets, with clothes, books, prints, dishes and junk as well as food. Its prices are among the lowest in town.

Of the innumerable **flower markets** that once perfumed every other street, only three survive: **place des Ternes** (daily) and the **Madeleine** (closed Mon.), both in the 8e, and **place Lépine** on the Ile de la Cité, which becomes a **bird market** on Sunday.

Collectors markets are worth a visit; people with a passion are good entertainment value even if you're not among the initiated. For vintage stamps and postcards, or collectors thereof, try the **stamp market** at the junction of the avenues Marigny and Gabriel in the 8e (Thurs., Sat. and Sun.). **Postcards, stamps, coins** and **old letters** can be found at the corner of Gambetta and rue de Vautetard, (Métro Corentin-Celton) on Tuesdays and Thursdays; and there is a market of **second-hand** and **antiquarian books** (weekends 9.30am–6pm) in Parc Georges-Brassens, rue Brancion 15e.

Clothes

There's nothing to stop you from trying on fabulously expensive creations by famous **couturiers** on rue Faubourg-St-Honoré and av François 1er, apart from the intimidating scorn of the assistants. Likewise you can treat the **younger designers** around place des Victoires or Tina Turner's and Grace Jones' couturier Azzedine Alaia (showroom at 1 rue du Parc-Royal, 3e) as sightseeing. You can also find end-of-lines at *Mendés-St-Laurent* (65 rue Montmartre, 9e) or 50% discount on last year's designer stock at *Cacharel Stock* (114 rue d'Alésia, 14e, ☎45.42.53.04) or *Dorothy Bis Stock*, (76 rue d'Alésia, 14e, ☎45.42.40.68). The easiest, though not the most exciting way to check out designer fashions is to go to one of the main **department stores**. *Galeries Lafayette* (40 bd Haussmann, 9e; 9.30am–6.30pm; closed Sun.) is the best, with two whole floors devoted to the latest creations by leading designers. Prices are not bad but not cheap.

For **affordable clothes** in a more uniquely Parisian context, the best area is the 6e: around rues de Rennes and de Sévres, rue St-André-des-Arts, and rue St-Placide – the latter particularly good at the lower price range. Next best is **Les Halles** but beware of rip-offs. *Comme ça des Halles* (105 rue Berger, level-1 for women; 12 rue Basse, level-3 for men) has fashion from 50 European designers and *Bravo les Filles* (15 Grande Galerie, les Halles) specialises in the outrageous or bizarre. *Gaultier Junior* (7 rue du Jour, 1er) stocks the less expensive lines of the man himself, and *Elizabeth de Seneville*, (3 rue du Turbigo, 1er) stocks simple styles and zany fabrics. More individual boutiques are to be found in the **Marais** – rue du Temple, rue Quincampoix – and for modern designer clothes, there's *Popy Moreni*, (13 place des Vosges). This end of rue de Rivoli also has plenty of cheap chain stores, incuding a *Monoprix* supermarket for essentials, or you can get even better bargains on the boulevards between Richelieu-Drouot and République (*Tati* at 13 place de la République is the cheapest of the cheap) and in the **ragtrade district** around place du Caire.

Where Paris excels, aside from *haute couture*, is in the **secondhand gear**, from reject *fripe* to antique *rétro*. Some places to look for – or at – the latter are *Rag Time* (23 rue du Roule, 1er; afternoons only; 1900s to 1950s); *Hébé* (41 rue de l'Arbre-Sec, 1er; great hats and stockings); *Duo 29* (29 rue du Roi-de-Sicile, 4e; very precious 1920s and 1930s dresses, shirts and jackets from latterday East Europe); and *Anouchka* (27 rue de la Grande-Truanderie, 1er, 1950s speciality). For **more affordable** garments, try *Rétro Activité* (38 rue du Vertbois, 3e), *Réciproque* (95, 101, and 123 rue de la Pompe, 16e), *Mise en Troc* (63 rue Notre-Dame-des-Champs, 6e) and *Violence et Passion* (1 rue Keller, 11e). Or, do a round of the markets outlined above.

Books and records

With the size of the reading public in Paris you'd think **books** would be cheap. They're not, and that makes foreign publications extortionate. There are, however, a fair number of bookshops with English-language sections.

The largest Anglo-American bookshop is *Nouveau Quartier Latin* (78 bd de St-Michel, 6e). *Shakespeare and Co.* (37 rue de la Bûcherie, 5e) is a cosy literary haunt with the biggest selection of second-hand English books. Others include *Galignani's* (224 rue de Rivoli, 1er); *W. H. Smith* (248 rue de Rivoli, 1er); *Village Voice* (6 rue Princesse, 6e; with café and committed Californians); *Brentano's* (37 av de l'Opéra – good kids' section) and *Gilbert Jeune* (5 place St-Michel and 27 quai St-Michel, 5e; English section includes second-hand).

By far the most pleasant browsing, when the weather's good, is at the **quayside stalls** where you might come across anything. **Parallèles** (47 rue St-Honoré, 1er) is one place to go for **left-wing/eco/feminist** publications. Other alternative bookshops include *Autrement Dit* (73 bd St-Michel, 5e), *La Fourmi Ailée* (8 rue du Fouarre, 5e) and *Actualités* (38 rue Dauphine, 6e). An old-style haunt specialising in **French poetry** is *Le Pont Traversé* (64 rue de Vaugirard, 6e). For literature in French from **Africa, the Middle East** and **Antilles**, go to the excellent and very knowledgeable *L'Harmattan* (16 rue des Ecoles, 5e). For old **travel books** try *Ulysses* (35 rue St-Louis-en-Ile, 4e). And for **comics** take a look at *Virgule* (2 rue des Tournelles, 4e).

The most reliably comprehensive and up-to-date **French bookshop** is *Fnac* (Forum des Halles, level 2, 1er, 26 av de Wagram, 8e and 136 rue de Rennes, 6e), which also has large English selections and massive stocks of **tapes and records** of every persuasion. Other bookshops that have music are *Gilbert Jeune* and *Parallèles* (see above). **Second-hand records** have a big market: *Le Crocodisc* (42 rue des Ecoles, 5e; for rock, jazz, reggae, Brazilian); *Disques B* (17 rue de Lappe, 11e; New Wave and Afro-Samba); *Dreamstore* (4 place St-Michel, 6e; jazz, rock and folk). The city's main **jazz** specialist is *Les Mondes du Jazz* (2 rue de la Petite-Truanderie, 1er); for **classical** it's *Dave Music* (19 rue du Faubourg-du-Temple, 11e). And, finally, good arrays of **Arab music**, including Rai, are to be found at *Le Disque Arabe* (116 bis bd de la Chapelle, 18e and 125 bd de Ménilmontant, 11e).

Food

The street markets or their super/hyper replacements like place d'Italie's *Galaxie* (13e) are the most sensible places to buy food. But there are some **specials**. *Fauchon* (26 place de la Madeleine, 8e) is the Fortnum and Masons of Paris groceries with pâtisserie and coffee bar; across the *place* at no. 21 *Hédiard* is much smaller but even more upmarket; *Ladurée* (16 rue Royale, 8e) features more cakes at great expense, with chocolate and coffee macaroons out of this world, and, at the other end of the scale, there's the tiny chocolate shop *La Petite Fabrique* (19 rue Daval, 11e). The Jewish restaurant *Goldenberg's* (7 rue des Rosiers) has a fine deli at the front; *Elombo* (29 rue de la Terre-Neuve, 20e) is good for African specialities; and at *Androuet* (41 rue d'Amsterdam, 8e) you'll find a startling selection of cheeses, with expensive *dégustation* in the restaurant. For bread baked to a secret family recipe, there's *Poilâne* (8 rue du Cherche-Midi, 6e and 49 bd de Grenelle, 7e).

Wine

Supermarkets are your best bet for cheap wines and spirits, but if you want a more reliable service there are wine experts on hand to give advice at the following outlets.

Grands Millèsimes, (8 rue de l'Arcade, 8e. Mon–Sat 10am–8pm). Boasts a seventeenth-century humidity-controlled cellar.

Nicolas (31 pl de la Madeleine, 8e; 9am–9pm)One of a chain, with an impressive stock of regional wines.

Toys, trivia, and miscellany

The most entertaining and tempting Paris window-shopping is offered by those small cluttered shops that reflect the owner's particular interest, obsession or taste. Perhaps the strangest collections are in the *Passages* of the 2e *arrondissement* – sculpted canes in Passage Jouffroy, old comics in Passage Verdeau, pipes in Passages des Princes . . . but you'll find traders in offbeat merchandise all over the place.

Among the more wonderful are *Au Chat Dormant* (15 rue du Cherche-Midi, 6e) – for feline obsessives; *Carambol* (20 rue des Francs-Bourgeois, 4e)– wooden toys and kaleidoscopes; *Pierre Sieur* (3 rue de l'Université, 5e) – playing cards from all over the world; *L'Impensé Radical* (1 rue de Médicis, 6e) – games familiar and obscure plus reading matter; *Les Cousins d'Alice* (on the corner of rues Lalande and Daguerre, 14e) – Alice in Wonderland decorations and reasonably priced wooden toys; *A l'Image du Grenier sur l'Eau* (45 rue des Francs-Bourgeois, 4e) – 1900s postcards; *Jadis et Naguère* (57 rue Daguerre, 14e) – jewellery, clothes, gadgets, and silly souvenirs such as Eiffel Tower candles; *Atelier des Brikezolces* (21 rue Liancourt, 14e) – ceramics; *Chic et Choc* (by rue Rambuteau exit of Les Halles RER station) – the owner being the Paris transport authority – towels, wallets, lighters, etc. all with a métro ticket emblem.

Directory

Airlines *Air France* is at 2 rue Scribe 9e (☎42.66.90.20; 42.99.23.57); *Air-Inter* at 228 rue de Rivoli, 1er (☎45.39.25.25); full lists of the rest from any Tourist Office. For details of **transport to the airports**, see 'Points of Arrival'.

American Express 11 rue Scribe, 9e (☎42.66.09.99; M° Opéra). Banking service open Mon.–Fri. 9am–5pm. Office and post–restante, until 5.30pm.

Babysitting There are two main agencies. *Ababa Une Maman en Plus* (☎43.22.22.11, seven days a week; includes English speakers) and *Allo Maman Poule* (☎47.47.78.78). Apart from these, you could try the American College in Paris (103 bd de l'Hôpital, 13e; ☎45.86.19.42), or if you know someone with a phone, dial Babysitting on 'Elletel' via *minitel.*

Banks Standard banking hours are Mon.–Fri. 8.30am–5pm. Branches open on Sat. include *Crédit Commercial de France*, 115 Champs-Elysées, 8e – all day; *BNP* 49 av des Champs-Elysees and 2 place de l'Opéra, 2e – mornings;

and *UBP* at 125 av des Champs-Elysees, – open Sat. and Sun. 10.30am–1pm and 2–6pm. The **Bureaux de Change** at the railway stations are open all day until 9 or 10pm: at Gare de Lyon and Gare du Nord every day; St-Lazare and Austerlitz every day except Sunday. *Crédit Agricole* (for **credit-card** cash advances) have branches at 16 bis bd Sébastopol, 4e; 31 rue de Constantine, 7e; 14 rue de la Boétie, 8e; and 91/93 bd Pasteur, 15e. Most of the major British banks have Paris branches – check the phone book in a post office for your nearest one. **Bike hire** *Autothèque*, 16 rue Berger, 1er (☎42.36.39.36) and 80 rue Montmartre, 2e (☎42.36.50.93) – the latter has motorcycles as well; *Paris-Vélo*, 2 rue de Fer-à-Moulin, 5e; (☎43.37.59.22).

Car pound If you car is towed away, the *Mairie* of the *arrondissement* will give you the address of the local pound, or ask the police.

Car hire Good French firms include *Mattei*, 205 rue de Bercy, 12e (☎43.46.11.50), 102 rue Ordener, 18e (☎42.64.32.90) and *Autorent*, 11 rue Casimir-Perier, 11e (☎45.55.53.49), 98 rue de la Convention, 15e (☎45.54.22.45) and 196 rue St-Jacques, 5e (☎43.25.88.10). In addition there's Avis, Hertz and the rest – the tourist office will have all the info.

Car repairs ☎42.57.33.44 is the emergency number if you're stuck – but only between 7am–10pm.

Consulates/Embassies British – 16 rue d'Anjou, 8e (☎42.96.87.19; M° Madeleine); Irish – 12 av Foch, 16e (☎45.00.20.87; M° Etoile); American – 2 av Gabriel, 8e (☎42.96.12.02; M° Concorde); Austrialian – 4 rue Jean-Rey, 15e; (☎45.75.62.00; M° Bir-Hakeim); Canadian – 35 av Montaigne, 8e (☎47.23.01.01; M° Roosevelt); Dutch – 7–9 rue Eblé, 7e (☎43.06.61.88; M° St-Francois-Xavier); New Zealand – 7 rue Léonard-de-Vinci, 16e (☎45.00.24.11; M° Victor-Hugo); Swedish – 17 rue Barbet-de-Jouy, 7e (☎45.55.92.15; M° Varenne).

Dental treatment emergency service: *SOS-Dentaire*, 85–87 bd de Port-Royal, 14e (☎43.37.51.00; 8pm–noon).

Emergencies *SOS-Médecins* (☎47.07.77.77) for 24-hour medical help; ☎43.78.26.26 for **24-hour ambulance service**. American Hospital: 63 bd Victor-Hugo, Neuilly (☎47.47.53.00; M° Porte-Maillot, bus #82 to end of line).

Festivals There's not much in the carnival line, though kids armed with bags of flour and aiming to make a total fool of you appear on the streets during **Mardi Gras** (in Feb.). There are marching bands and street performers for the **Summer Solstice** (June 21) and **July 14** (Bastille Day) is celebrated with official pomp in parades of tanks down the Champs-Elysées, firework displays and concerts. If you're into the politics of the European Left, however, the French Communist Party hosts an annual **Fête de l' Humanité** in September at La Courneuve, just north of Paris, with representatives of just about every CP in the world and information tables, bands and eats that bring in Parisians of most political persuasions, and good times had by all.

Haircuts For free as long as you let the trainees do anything, at *Ecole de Coiffure* (7 rue Darboy, 11e; ☎43.57.18.80), *Co-ordination Coiffure* (120 rue la

Boétie, 8e; ☎42.56.10.16) or *Jean-Louis David* (50 bis rue Pierre Charron, 8e; ☎47.20.68.58).

Hamams Turkish baths – an unexpected Parisian delight. The *Hamam St-Paul* (4 rue des Rosiers, 4e; open 10am–10pm; women: Wed. and Fri.; men: Thurs. and Sat.) has sauna, massage, etc. – and a restaurant. At *Hamam de la Mosquée de Paris* (39 rue Geoffroy-St-Hilaire, 5e; open 10am–7pm; women: Mon., Thurs. and Sat.; men: Fri. and Sun.) you can take a steambath in the Mosque complex with mint tea to follow.

Hitching out of Paris can be a nightmare but for a small fee you can join *Allostop*, which will arrange a ride for you; you just make a small contribution towards petrol: 84 passage Brady, 10e (☎42.46.00.66; open Mon.–Fri. 9am–7.30pm, Sat. 9am–1pm and 2–6pm).

Language schools French lessons from the *Alliance Française* (101 bd Raspail, 6e) and numerous other establishments. A full list, *Cours de Français pour Etudiants Etrangers*, is obtainable from embassy cultural sections.

Launderettes Self-service places have multiplied in Paris over the last few years and you'll probably find one near where you're staying. Central locations include: 24 place Marchais-St-Honoré, 1er; 1 rue de la Montagne-Ste-Geneviève, 5e; 91 rue de Seine, 6e; 108 rue du Bac, 7e; 5 rue de la Tour-d'Auvergne, 9e; and 96 rue de la Roquette, 11e.

Left Luggage Lockers and longer term *consigne* at all the railway stations.

Libraries Foreign Cultural Institutes (Britain: 9 rue de Constantine, 7e; U.S.: 10 rue du Général Camou, 7e) have free access libraries, with newspapers etc. Interesting Parisian collections include the *BPI* at Beaubourg (vast – and with all the foreign press, too), *Forney* (books being a good excuse if you want to visit the medieval bishop's place at 1 rue du Figuier in the 4e), and the *Historique de la Ville de Paris*, a sixteenth-century mansion housing centuries of texts and picture books on the city (24 rue Pavée, 4e).

Lost property 36 rue des Morillons, 5e (M° Convention).

Pharmacies 24-hour service at *Dhery* (84 av des Champs-Elysées, 8e).

Police Dial ☎17 for emergencies. The main Préfécture, if you need to report a theft, is at 7 bd du Palais, 4e (☎42.60.33.22).

Post office Main office at 52 rue du Louvre, Paris 75001: open 24 hours for **telephones** and **poste restante**.

Swimming pools *Butte aux Cailles* (5 place Paul-Verlaine, 13e; municipal, therefore cheap, in bizarre brick building); *Pontoise* (19 rue de Pontoise, 5e; reserved for school children most of the time, but nude swimming two evenings a week – check *Pariscope*, etc.); *Déligny* (opposite 25 quai d'Anatole France, 7e; open-air, crowded and an amusing, if expensive, spectacle).

Telephones Card phones here, as elsewhere, in France are beginning to overtake the cash ones which nine times out of ten are defunct. The cards can be bought from the PTT and some *tabacs*.

Tourist information Main office at 127 av des Champs-Elysées, 8e (☎47.23.61.72); open 9am–10pm, Sun. 9am–8pm in summer; 9am–8pm, Sun.,

9am–6pm in winter. Other offices at the four main stations: Austerlitz, Nord, Lyon and Est. For info in English ☎47.20.88.98.

Train information see *Getting Around.*

Travel firms *USIT Voyages* (6 rue de Vaugirard, 15e; M° Odéon) is an excellent and dependable **student-youth agency** – good for buses to London, Dublin, Amsterdam, etc. as well as discount flights. *Nouvelles Frontières* (166 bd St-Michel, 6e) has some of the cheapest charters going, and **flights** just about anywhere in the world. For national and international **buses** you can get information and tickets at the main terminus in Porte de la Villette (☎42.05.12.10; M° Porte-de-la-Villette).

VD clinic *Institut Prophylactique* (36 rue d'Assas, 6e; ☎45.44.38.94; free).

Work Not easy: look for ads in *Libération, Le Figaro* or *Passion* magazine, or try the youth organisation *CIDJ* (101 quai Branly, 15e) or the French job agency *ANPE* (*Agence Nationale Pour l'Emploi*) – check the phone book for the nearest office.

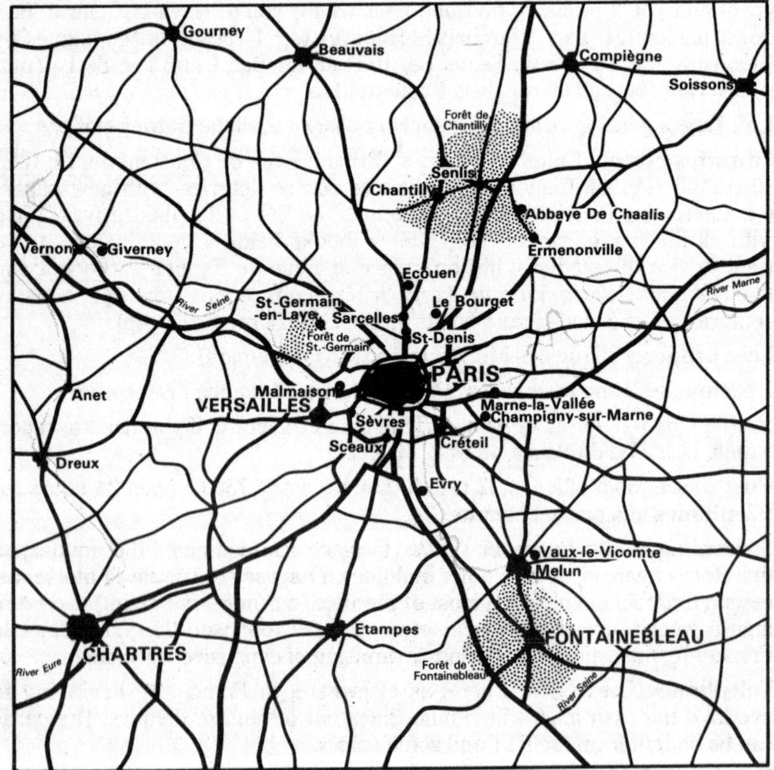

OUT FROM THE CITY

Given all there is to see, eat, do and experience in Paris itself, excursions outside the city don't have the highest priority. But if you're staying longer than a week you may well get fed up with traffic fumes, noise and general city stress. If you do, there are some very pleasant retreats in the area known as the **Ile de France**, or, more prosaically and colloquially, the *Région Parisienne*. Most are accessible by the RER or by short train rides. Some, a little further afield, such as Monet's garden in Giverny, are detailed in other chapters (Normandy in this case) but are still potential day trips from the capital.

The *Région Parisienne* and the borders of all neighbouring provinces are predictably studded with large-scale **châteaux**. Many were once royal or noble retreats for hunting and other leisured pursuits, some like **Versailles**, for more serious state business. The mansions and palaces themselves – and Versailles above all – can be extremely tedious. But **Vaux-le-Vicomte**, at least, is magnificent; **Fontainebleau** is pleasantly Italian; and at any of them you can get a taste of country air in the surrounding forests and parks, and get back to Paris comfortably in a day.

If you only intend one outing though, and even have only the slightest curiosity about church buildings, forget the châteaux and make for the **cathedral of Chartres** – it's all it's cracked up to be. From here too, you can easily return to Paris, or heading onwards you're well situated for Le Mans and Brittany. Other points to leave Paris by, detailed in this section, include **Anet** (a short detour on the road to western Normandy), and **Chantilly** and **Senlis** off the routes north to Lille and Calais. These are enjoyable enough stopovers if you're rambling out by car but don't really merit special excursions.

For a change from spiritual and temporal palaces there's the **air museum at Le Bourget** – a good one for kids – and the outrageous contemporary housing projects at **Marne-La-Vallée**. **Chatou**, **Sceaux** and the **Marne-side towns** all evoke the seemingly carefree days of the 1900s when the Impressionists et al took their easels out to what was then open countryside.

Chartres and Anet

The mysticisms of medieval thought on life, death and deity expressed materially in the masonry of the **Cathedral** at **CHARTRES**, should best be experienced on a cloud-free winter's day. The low sun transmits the stained glass colours to the interior stone, the quiet scattering of people leaves the acoustics unconfused, and the exterior is unmasked for miles around. The masterwork is flawed only by changes in Roman Catholic worship. The immense distance from the door to the altar, through mists of incense and drawn-out harmonies, emphasised the doctrine of priests as sole mediators of the distance betwen worshipped and worshippers. The current central altar, from a secular point of view, undermines the theatrical dogma of the building and puts cloth and boards where coloured light should play.

A less recent change, of allowing the congregation chairs, also covers up the **labyrinth** on the floor of the nave – an original thirteenth-century arrangement and a great rarity, as the authorities at other cathedrals had them pulled up as distracting frivolities. The Chartres labyrinth traces a path over 200m long enclosed within a diameter of 13m, the same size as the rose window above the main doors. The centre used to have a bronze relief of Theseus and the Minotaur, and the pattern of the maze was copied from classical texts, the idea of the path of life to eternity being fairly similar in Greek myth and medieval Catholicism. During pilgrimages the chairs are removed, so you may be lucky and see the full pattern.

But there are more than enough wonders to enthrall: the geometry of the building, unique in being almost entirely unaltered since its consecration in the thirteenth century; the details of the stonework – the western facade including the Portail Royal saved from the cathedral's predecessor that fire destroyed in 1194, the Renaissance choir screen and the hosts of sculpted figures above each transept door; and the shining circular symmetries of the transept windows. Among paying extras the *crypt* and *treasures* can be ignored without much loss but, crowds permitting, it's worth climbing the **north tower**. Admission hours for the main building are 7.30am–7.30pm in summer; 7pm in winter. There are gardens at the back from where you can contemplate the complexity of stress factors balanced by the flying buttresses. If, as you're wandering around, you hear a passionate and erudite Englishman giving guided tours, that is Malcolm Miller, almost an institution in himself and a world expert on Chartres cathedral. He does two tours daily from April to November – the SI (see below) can provide details.

The town

Though the cathedral is why you come here, **Chartres town** is not without appeal. The **Beaux Arts museum** in the former Episcopal palace just north of the cathedral has some beautiful tapestries, a room full of Vlaminck and Zurbaran's **Ste-Lucie**, as well as good temporary exhibitions (10am–noon and 2–5pm; closed Tues.). Behind it, rue Chantault leads past old townhouses to the **River Eure** and Pont des Massacres. You can follow this reedy river lined with ancient washhouses upstream via rue des Massacres on the right bank. The cathedral appears from time to time through the trees, and on the left bank is the Romanesque church of **St-André**, now used for art exhibitions, jazz concerts, etc. Crossing over at the end of rue de la Tannerie onto rue du Bourg takes you back to the cathedral through the medieval town, decorated with details such as the carved salmon on a house on place de la Poissonnerie. Further south, around **rue du Cygne** is the place to look for bars and restaurants. The **SI** is on the cathedral *parvis*, at 7 Cloître-Notre-Dame, and can supply **free maps** and help with **rooms** if you want to stay.

When you **arrive** at the **Gare SNCF** (frequent trains from Paris-Montparnasse in 50–65 min.), av J-de-Beauce leads straight up to place Châtelet. Past all the buses on the other side of the *place*, rue Ste-Mesme crosses place Jean-Moulin – the cathedral is down to the left. Rue d'Harleville goes to the right to bd de la Résistance, a section of the main beltway around the old town: the memorial on the corner of the street and the boulevard is to **Jean Moulin**, Prefect of Chartres until he was fired by the Vichy government

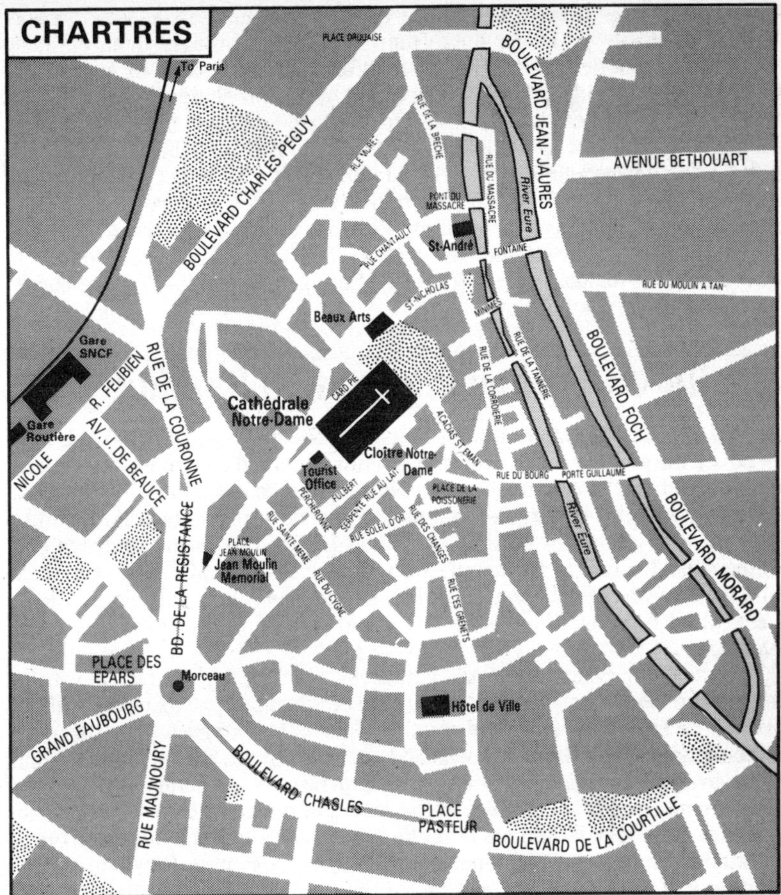

in 1942. When the Germans occupied Chartres in 1940, he had refused under torture to sign a document to the effect that Black soldiers in the French army were responsible for Nazi atrocities. He later became de Gaulle's number one man on the ground, coordinating the Resistance groups. He died at the hands of Klaus Barbie in 1943.

If you're heading up towards Rouen from Chartres or driving towards western Normandy from Paris, you might like to stop at **ANET**, 20km or so north of Dreux, and dominated by another semi-royal **château**. Diane de Poitiers, respected widower in the court of François I, and also wielding power as the lover of the king's son, Henri, decided that her marital home at Anet needed to be bigger and more comfortable. Work started with Philippe de l'Orme as architect in charge and the designs are as delicate and polished as the Renaissance could produce. Within a year Henri inherited the throne and immediately gave Diane the château of Chenonceau. But the Anet project continued, luckily for Diane since Henri's reign was brought to an untimely end and his wife demanded Chenonceau back. Diane retired to Anet where she died. Her grandson built a chapel for her tomb alongside the château, which has remained intact. The château would have been completely destroyed by the first owner after the Revolution had it not been for a protest riot by the townspeople that sent him packing. As it is, only the front entrance, one wing and the château chapel remain, now restored to its former glorification of hunting and feminine eroticism, with the swirling floor and domed ceiling of the chapel its climax. The château is open March to November 2.30–6.30pm except Tuesday; Sunday all year 10–11.30am and 2–6pm in summer, 5pm in winter.

The Ile-de-France museum at Sceaux

The **Musée de l'Ile-de-France** is housed in the **château of Sceaux**, a nineteenth-century replacement for the original (demolished post-Revolution), which matched the now-restored Le Nôtre grounds. As a park it's the usual classical geometry of terraces, water and woods – if you feel like taking a walk you can get off the RER at LA-CROIX-DE-BERNY at the southern end. Otherwise it's a five- to ten-minute walk from PARC DE SCEAUX station (15 min. from Denfert-Rochereau, RER line B): turn left, then right onto av R. de Launay and right again on av Le Nôtre and you'll find the château gates on your left.

The museum evokes the Paris countryside: of the *ancien régime* with its aristocratic and royal domains; the nineteenth-century expansion with its riverside scenes and eating and dancing places, the *guinguettes*, that inspired so many artists; and the new towns and transport of the current age. Exhibits range from the predictably dull to the very bizarre – a series of plates and figurines inspired by the arrival, in the 1830s, of the first giraffe in France, for example. Kids should find some of it amusing – it's free for them and cheap for adults. Hours are 10am–noon and 2–6pm in summer, 5pm in winter; Monday and Friday pm only; closed Tuesday.

Temporary exhibitions and a summer festival of classical chamber music are held in the Orangerie which, along with the Pavillon de l'Aurore (in the northeast corner of the park), survives from the original residence. The concerts take place on weekends, from July to October – details from the museum (☎46.61.06.71) or from the *Direction des Musées de France*, Palais du Louvre, Cours Visconti, 34 quai du Louvre, Paris, 1e.

Versailles

The **Palace of VERSAILLES** is foul from every aspect, a mutated building gene allowed to run for lengths no feet or eyes were made for, its decor a grotesque homage to two of the greatest of all self-propagandists – Louis XIV and Napoléon. The mirrors, in the famous Hall of, are smeared, scratched and not the originals – for these a Breton boy is currently serving fifteen years for breaking glass with explosives. In the park, a mere two and a half square miles, the fountains gush on selected days only. The rest of the time the statues on the empty pools look as bad as gargoyles taken down from cathedral walls.

It's hard to know why so many tourists come out here – in preference to all except the most obvious sights of Paris. Yet they do, and the **château** (9.45am–6pm in summer, 5pm in winter; closed Mon.; card entry) is always a crush of bodies. If you are curious, you have a choice of itineraries and whether to be guided or not, but either way you won't have much chance to take your time. If you just feel like taking a look, and a walk, **the park** (open dawn to dusk) is free and the scenery better the further you go from the palace – there are even informal groups of trees near the lesser outcrops of royal mania, the Grand and Petit Trianon. (The Grand Trianon is open the same hours as the château, the Petit Trianon 2–5pm; card entry for both). There is, too, a wonderfully snobbish place to have **tea** – the *Hôtel Palais Trianon* (near the park entrance at the end of bd de la Reine), much more worthwhile than shelling out for château admission, with trays of all-you-can-eat pastries about 60F. It also happens to be the place where the Treaty of Versailles was signed.

The style of the *Hôtel Palais Trianon* is very much that of the town in general. The dominant population is aristocratic with the pre-revolutionary titles disdainful of those dating merely from Napoléon. On Bastille day both groups show their colours with black ribbons and ties.

To get to Versailles, take the RER line C5 to VERSAILLES-RIVE-GAUCHE (40 min.), turn left out of the station and immediately right to approach the palace. Maps of the park are available at the SI on rue des Réservoirs to the right of the palace.

Malmaison, Chatou, St-Germain-en-Laye

Josephine Bonaparte's country house, an island in the Seine once frequented by the stars of Impressionism, and a museum of prehistoric, Celtic, and Roman France – all three places lie to the west of Paris on the RER A1 line. As Saint-Germain, the furthest, is only 20 minutes away, half a day is enough to visit any of them.

Malmaison

The **Château of MALMAISON** was the home of the Empress Josephine and, during the 1800–1804 Consulate, of Napoléon too. According to his secretary, 'it was the only place next to the battlefield where he was truly himself'. After their divorce, Josephine stayed on here, occasionally receiving visits from the Emperor, until her death in 1814. The **château** (10am–noon and 1.30–4.30pm; closed Tues.; card entry; guided tours only) is set in the beautiful grounds of the Bois-Préau. It's relatively small and surprisingly enjoyable. The visit includes private and official apartments, in part with original furnishings though complemented with pieces imported from other imperial residences. There are further Napoleonic bits and pieces in the **Bois-Préau museum** (same hours as above).

To get there take the RER to La Défense, then bus #158A to MALMAISON-CHATEAU. Alternatively, if you'd like a walk, take the RER to RUEIL-MALMAISON and follow GR11 from the Pont de Chatou along the left bank of the Seine and into the château park.

Ile de Chatou

A long narrow island in the Seine, the **ILE DE CHATOU** was once a rustic spot where Parisians came on the newly opened railway to row and dine and flirt at the riverside *guinguettes* (eating and dancing establishments). One of these survives, rather forlorn and abandoned, just below the Pont de Chatou road bridge. It is the **Maison Fournaise**, a favourite haunt of Renoir, Monet, Manet, Van Gogh, Seurat, Sisley, Courbet – half of them in love with the proprietor's daughter, Alphonsine. One of Renoir's best-known canvases, *Le Déjeuner des Canotiers*, shows his friends lunching on the balcony. Vlaminck and his fellow-Fauves, Dérain and Matisse, were also habitués. Restoration work is afoot – the elegant ironwork of the balcony has been renewed and there are plans to turn it into a restaurant again. It's certainly a great site, with a huge plane tree shading the riverbank and a view of the barges racing downstream on the current.

The downstream end of the island has been made into a **park**, which tapers away into a tree-lined tail hardly wider than the path. The upstream end is incredibly spooky. A track, black with oil and ooze and littered with assorted junk, bumps along past yellowed grass and bald poplar trees to a group of ruined houses stacked with beat-up cars. Beyond the railway bridge a chalet, guarded by louche-looking alsatians, stands beside the track. A concrete block saying No Entry in homemade lettering bars the way. If you're bold enough to ignore it, there's a view from the head of the island of the old market gardens on the right bank and the decaying industrial landscape of Nanterre on the left.

Access to the island is from the Reuil-Malmaison RER stop. Just walk straight ahead on to the Pont de Chatou. It could be fun to check out the twice-yearly ham and antique fair on the island (March and Sept.).

St-Germain

ST-GERMAIN is not especially interesting as a town, but if you've been to the prehistoric caves of the Dordogne or plan to go, you'll get a lot from the **Musée des Antiquités Nationales** (open 9.45am–noon and 1.30–5.15pm; closed Tues.; card entry). It is in the unattractively renovated château (opposite the RER station) which was one of the main residences of the French court before Versailles was built and the place where Louis XIV was born.

The presentation and lighting make the visit a real pleasure. The extensive Stone Age section includes a mock-up of the Lascaux caves and a profile of Abbé Breuil, the priest who made prehistoric art respectable, as well as a beautiful collection of decorative objects, tools and so forth. All ages from prehistory to the history of the Celts, Romans and Franks are covered; abundant evidence that the French have been a talented, arty lot for a very long time. The end piece is a room of comparative archaeology, with objects from cultures across the globe.

From right outside the château, a **terrace** – Le Nôtre arranging the landscape again – stretches for more than 2km above the Seine with a view over the whole of Paris. All behind it is the **forest of St-Germain**, a sizeable expanse of woodland, but criss-crossed by too many roads to be convincing as wilderness.

Le Bourget

The French were always adventurous, pioneering aviators and the name of **LE BOURGET** is closely connected with their earliest exploits. Lindbergh landed here after his epic trans-Atlantic flight – the first ever. From World War I to the development of Orly in the 1950s, it was Paris's principal airport. Today it is used only for internal flights, but some of the older buildings have been turned into a fascinating **museum of flying machines**.

To **get there** you can take the RER from Gare du Nord to DRANCY, where the Germans had a concentration camp for Jews en route to Auschwitz and where, among others, the poet Max Jacob died. Be sure to get a train that stops at Drancy. From the station follow av Francis-de-Pressensé as far as the main road. Turn left and, by a *tabac* on the left of the first intersection, get bus #152 to LE BOURGET/MUSEE DE L'AIR. Alternatively, bus #350 from Gare du Nord, Gare de l'Est, Porte de la Chapelle or #152 from Porte de la Villette.

The **Musée de l'Air et de l'Espace** (open 10am–6pm May – Oct., 10am–5pm Nov.–April; closed Mon.) consists of five adjacent hangars, the first devoted to **space**, with rockets, satellites, space capsules, etc. Some are mock-ups, some the real thing. Among the latter are a Lunar Roving Vehicle, the Apollo XIII command module in which James Lovell and his fellow-astronauts nearly came to grief, the Soyuz craft in which a French astronaut flew, and France's own first successful space rocket. Everything is accompanied by extremely good explanatory panels – in French only.

The remainder of the exhibition is arranged in chronological order, starting with hangar A (the furthest from the entrance), which covers the **period 1919–39**. Several record-breakers here, including the Bréguet XIX which made the first-ever crossing of the South Atlantic in 1927. Also, the corrugated iron job that was featured for so long on U.S. postage stamps: a Junkers F13, which the Germans were forbidden to produce after World War I. Hangar B shows a big collection of **World War II planes** (and photographic evidence of some of the damage they did), including a V1 flying bomb and the Nazis' last jet fighter, the largely wooden Heinkel 162A. Incredibly, the plans were completed as late in the war as September 24, 1944 and it flew on December 6.

Hangars C and D cover the years **1945 to the present day**, during which the French aviation industry, having lost 80 percent of its capacity in 1945, has recovered to a pre-eminent position in the world. Its hi-tech achievement is represented here by the super-sophisticated, best-selling Mirage fighters, the first Concorde prototype and – symbol of national vigour and virility – the Ariane space-launcher (the two latter are both parked on the tarmac outside). No warheads on site, as far as we know. Hangar E is light and sporty aircraft.

Chantilly, Senlis and Ecouen

CHANTILLY is the kind of place you go when you think it's time you did something for the weekend, like get out and get some culture and fresh air. It comprises a château, a park, and two museums, one of which is devoted to live horses; some 3000 thoroughbreds prance the forest rides every morning, and two of the season's classiest flat races are held here. Forty kilometres north of Paris the town is accessible **by train** from the Gare du Nord. The footpaths **GR11** and **12** pass through the park and forest, for a more peaceful and leisurely way of exploring this bit of the country.

The Chantilly estate used to belong to two of the most powerful clans in France, the Montmorencys, and, through marriage, the Condés. The present **château** (10.30am–6pm in summer, 5pm in winter, closed Tues.) was put up in the late nineteenth century, an imposing rather than beautiful structure, too heavy for grace, but it is well-positioned, surrounded by water and looking out in haughty manner over a formal arrangement of pools and pathways designed by the busy Le Nôtre.

The entrance to the château is across a moat past two realistic bronzes of hunting hounds. The visitable parts are all **museum**: mainly, an enormous collection of paintings and drawings. They are not well displayed and you quickly get visual indigestion from the massed ranks of good, bad and indifferent, deployed as if of equal value. Some highlights, however, are a collection of portraits of sixteenth- and seventeenth-century French monarchs and princes in the Galerie de Logis; interesting Greek and Roman bits in the tower room; a big series of sepia stained glass illustrating Apuleius's *Golden Ass* in the Galerie de Psyche, together with some very lively portrait drawings; and, in the so-called Santuario, some Raphaels, a Filippino Lippi and forty miniatures from a fifteenth-century *Book of Hours* attributed to the French artist Jean Fouquet.

The museum's single greatest treasure is in the library, the Cabinet des Livres, entered only in the presence of the guide. It is **Les Très Riches Heures du Duc du Berry**, the most celebrated of all *Books of Hours*. The illuminated pages illustrating the months of the year with representative scenes from contemporary (early 1400s) rural life – like harvesting and ploughing, sheepshearing and pruning – are richly-coloured and drawn with a delicate naturalism, as well as being sociologically interesting. Unfortunately, and understandably, only facsimiles are on display, but they give an excellent idea of the original. Sets of postcards, of middling fidelity, are on sale in the entrance. There are thousands of other fine books as well.

Five minutes' walk along the château drive is the colossal stable block, transformed into a Museum of the Horse, the **Musée Vivant du Cheval**.

The building was erected at the beginning of the eighteenth century by the incumbent Condé prince, who believed he would be reincarnated as a horse and wished to provide fitting accommodation for 240 of his future relatives.

In the main hall horses of different breeds from around the world are stabled, with a ring for demonstrations, followed by a series of life-size models illustrating the various activities horses are used for. In the rooms are collections of paintings, horseshoes, veterinary equipment, bridles and saddles, a mock-up of a blacksmith's, children's horse toys, including a chain-driven number with handles in its ears that belonged to Napoléon III, and a fanciful Sicilian cart painted with scenes of Crusader battles.

Opening hours are complicated: 10.30am–6pm April 1–October 31, with demonstrations at 11.45am, 3.15pm and 5.15pm; 1–5pm weekdays November 1–March 31, with demonstrations at 3pm and 5pm; 10.30am–5.30pm Sat., Sun. and holidays throughout the year, with demonstrations at 11.45am, 3pm and 5pm. Admission is pricey, with a slight reduction for children.

Senlis, Ermenonville and Ecouen

A picture-book old town 10km east of Chantilly, **SENLIS** (trains from Gare du Nord to Chantilly followed by 1 hr. busride) has a cathedral contemporary with Notre-Dame and all the trappings of medieval ramparts, Roman towers and royal palace remnants to entice hordes of visitors from the capital. Blood sports enthusiasts can see how the French do it at the **Musée de la Vénerie** (10am–noon and 2–6pm in summer, 5pm in winter; closed Tues. and Wed. am). Another dozen kilometres away is the eighteenth-century château and park of **ERMENONVILLE**, where **Rousseau** died and was buried on an island in the lake; shortly afterwards the Revolution moved him to the Panthéon.

ECOUEN lies to the south on the N16, the Chantilly–Paris road, just before the monstrous high-rise suburb of Sarcelles. Its **Renaissance château**, that belonged like Chantilly first to the Montmorencys, then to the Condés, has been converted into the **Musée National de la Renaissance** (9.45am–12.30pm and 2–5.15pm; closed Tues.; card entry). In addition to some of the original interior decoration, including frescoes and magnificent carved fireplaces, the rooms display a choice and manageable selection of Renaissance furniture, tapestries, woodcarvings, jewellery and so forth. But you need to know you have a definite interest in the period to make it worth the effort of getting there. (Porte-de-la-Chapelle métro, then #268C bus, or SNCF train from Gare du Nord to Ecouen-Ezanville followed by a short bus ride).

In the loops of the Marne

In the good old days of the nineteenth century people with time, spirit, and a few sous would leave the city for an evening meal and a dance at their favourite *guinguette*. These mini music halls-cum-restaurants were to be found on the banks of the Seine, the Marne, the Bièvre, – some of them feature in the Gare d'Orsay Impressionist collection. Most of them have disappeared along with their surroundings of meadows, poplar-lined paths and peasant villages. But the same combination of open-air eating, riverside views and live music can still be had in a *guinguette* established in the 1900s: *Chez Gégène*, 162bis, quai de Polangis, JOINVILLE-LE-PONT, open from March to October. **JOINVILLE-LE-PONT** is east of Paris, just across the Marne from the Bois de Vincennes (RER line A2, then buses #106 and #108 from rue J.-Mermoz or walk across the river). Quai de Polangis runs upstream (northwards at this point) and there are several places where you can rent canoes or pedaloes.

Downstream (or RER three stops then buses #208, #116 or bus #108A from Joinville) is **CHAMPIGNY-SUR-MARNE,** one of the few *banlieue* addresses that feels like a place in its own right. There are tiny terraced flats with wooden stairs and balconies beside the bridge; a gracefully sweet and ancient church, St-Saturnin, nestling on a cobbled square a block away from place Lénine and the central crossroads. Old and new co-exist and most of the streets bear revolutionary or resistance names. The defeat of 1940 is the subject of the **Musée de la Résistance Nationale** at 88, av Marx-Dormoy (bus #208 from the station or the centre; stop *Musée de la Résistance*). Only recently opened and exemplary in its high-tech design and facilities, it nevertheless lacks a clearly defined purpose. Since the fortieth anniversary of the liberation of France, Resistance museums are back in vogue. This one, to its credit, includes the immediate pre-war period and the *Front Populaire*, acknowledges the major role of the Communists in the Resistance and covers the Socialist reforms after the liberation. But it can't escape the need to rescue French glory nor can it relate the dignity it accords to this resistance with other clandestine revolts whether in the past or the present. The museum is open 10am–5pm; Sunday pm only; Friday closed noon to 2pm; closed all day Tuesday.

You can hire boats from the *Centre Nautique* in Champigny (near the railway bridge ¾km upstream from the road bridge) or you can wander down the path on the left bank to the Pont de Chennevières. There are some good **riverside restaurants** too, such as *L'Ecu de France,* 31 rue de Champigny before you reach the Chennevières bridge; *Le Pavillon Bleu,* a genuine *guinguette* at 66 promenade des Anglais, further on towards the Pont de Bonneuil on the right bank; and *La Bréteche,* 171 quai de Bonneuil, on the same side, past the Bonneuil bridge. The nearest RER station is La Varenne-Chennevières.

One other possible stop on these meanders of the Marne is **NOGENT-SUR-MARNE** back by the Bois de Vincennes north of Joinville. The one remaining pavilion of the **old market at Les Halles** has been resurrected here in a bizarre setting of ocean liner apartment buildings on one side and mismatched pre-war houses on the other. Baltard's construction, all gleaming glass and paint above the diamond patterned brickwork, is a pleasure to behold. In front of the entrance is a **'square of bygone Paris',** replete with Wallace fountain, theatre ticket kiosk, cobbles and twirly lamp post. But that is all there is to see since the hall is given over to private functions for most of the year, – fashion shows, International Police Association balls, weapons fairs and the like. There are cultural events open to all, but disseminating the programme is not a high priority. From Nogent-sur-Marne RER you exit onto av de Joinville, cross over and turn left past the SI (who can tell you if there is anything interesting on) and then first left onto av Victor-Hugo which brings you to the unmistakable building.

Much of Nogent's obvious prosperity comes from the rates the electricity board pays for its PWR (Pressurised Water Reactor) nuclear power station beside the town. Another reactor is being built alongside it, and, typically, much of the population seems unconcerned. Nor are the Parisians, despite the fact that 'Chernobyl-sur-Seine', as Nogent has been dubbed by one engineer-author, must represent the closest nuclear reactor to a major population centre of almost anywhere in the world. Sorry we mentioned it.

Vaux-le-Vicomte and Fontainebleau

VAUX-LE-VICOMTE, 46km southeast of Paris, is one of the great classical châteaux. Louis XIV's finance superintendent, Nicholas Fouquet, had it built at colossal expense using the top designers of the day – the royal architect Le Vau, the painter Le Brun and Le Nôtre, the landscape gardener. The result was magnificence and precision in perfect proportion and a bill that could only be paid by someone who occasionally confused the state's account with his own. The housewarming party to which the king was invited was more extravagant than any royal event – a comparison that other finance ministers ensured Louis took to heart. Within two months Fouquet was jailed for life on trumped-up charges and Louis carted Le Vau, Le Brun and Le Nôtre off to Versailles to work on a gaudy and gross piece of one-upmanship. The château is **open** April to October 10am–6pm in summer (winter: weekends afternoon only; and closed Jan.); **trains** from the Gare de Lyon leave for MELUN (25 min.) and there are direct **buses** from Melun SNCF to the château.

If you're energetic, you could spend the morning at Vaux-le-Vicomte and continue by train from MELUN to **FONTAINEBLEAU** – an instructive and remarkably pleasant exercise in rapid châteaux touring. A hunting lodge from as early as the twelfth century, the **château** here began its transformation into a palace under the sixteenth-century François I. A vast, rambling place, unpretentious despite its size, it owes its distinction to a colony of Italian artists imported for the decoration – above all Rosso Il Fiorentino, who completed the celebrated **Galerie François I**, vital to the evolution of French aristocratic art and design. The gardens are equally luscious but if you want to escape to the wilds, the surrounding **forest of Fontainebleau** is full of walking and cycling trails and its rocks are a favourite training ground of French climbers. Paths and tracks are all marked on Michelin map 196 (*Environs de Paris*).

The château, rarely overcrowded, is **open** from 9.30am to 12.30pm and from 2 to 5pm; closed Tuesday; card entry. **Trains** take around 45 min. from Gare de Lyon (25 min. from Melun) and there's a local bus to the gates from the SNCF.

The new towns and *grands ensembles*

Investigating life in the **suburbs** is hardly a prime holiday occupation but if you are interested in the question of housing, including architects'arrogance and the nose-length perspectives of planners, then the 'Greater Paris' new towns of the 1970s/80s and the 1950s/60s vast housing estates known as *Grands Ensembles* could be instructive.

The most depressing and notorious of the latter is **SARCELLES**, 12km north of the city. It gave a new word to the French language, *sarcellitis,* the social disease of delinquency and despair spread by horizons of interminable, identical, high-rise hutches. A few years after its creation, at the end of the sixties, the architect Emile Aillaud tried a very different approach in **LA GRANDE BORNE**, 25km south of Paris and directly overlooking the Autoroute du Sud. It was hardly a promising site. But for once, a scale was used that didn't belittle the inhabitants and the buildings were shaped by curves instead of corners. The facades are coloured with tiny glass and ceramic tiles, there is inlaid art – landscapes, animals, and portraits of Rimbaud and Kafka – and the whole ensemble is for pedestrians only. To get there by public transport can be quite a drag – train from the Gare de Lyon, direction Corbeil-Essones, to Grigny-Centre then bus or walk – but with wheels it's a quick flit down A6 from Porte d'Orléans; turn off it to the right on D13 and both the first and second right will take you into it.

Having come out this way, you could also take a look at **EVRY**, one of the five new towns in the Paris region (Evry-Courcouronnes SNCF two stops on from Grigny). French *villes nouvelles* were grafted on to existing towns – streets of tiny detached houses where old-time residents cower beneath buildings from another world. As with any new town there's the unsettling reversal that the people are there because of the town and not vice versa, and the towns seem to be there only because of the rail and RER lines.

If you follow the signs from Evry station to the *centre commercial* and keep going through it till you surface on a walkway bridging bd de l'Europe, you'll come to **Evry 1 housing project,** a multicoloured ensemble resembling a group of ransacked wardrobes and chest of drawers. The architects call it pyramidal and blather on about how the buildings and the urban landscape articulate each other. It's quite fun really even if the 'articulating' motifs on the facade overlooking the park are more like fossils than plants.

The New Town with the most to shock or amuse, or even please, is undoubtedly **MARNE-LA-VALLEE**, where Terry Gilliam's totalitarian fantasy *Brazil* was filmed and where the real life European Disneyland is going to be. It starts 10km east of Paris and hops for 20km from one new outcrop to the next with odd bits of wood and water in between. The RER stops from Bry-sur-Marne to the Torcy terminus are all in Marne-la-Vallée but **NOISY-LE-GRAND**, or MONT D'EST as the planners call it, is probably the best section to sample.

You surface at Noisy on the *Arcades*, a stony substitute for a town square and there you have the poetic panorama of a controlled community environment. Bright blue tubing and light blue tiling on split-level walkways and spaceless concrete fencing; powder-blue boxes growing plants on buildings beside grey-blue roofs of multi-angled leanings; walls of blue, walls of white, deep blue frames and tinted glass reflecting the water of a chopped up lake; islands linked by bridges with more blue railings – it goes on and on. The two acclaimed architectural pieces in this monolith have only one thing in their favour – neither is blue. They are both low cost housing units, both gigantic, quite unlike anything you're likely to have seen before and both unmitigatedly horrible. The **Arènes de Picasso** is in the group of buildings to the right of the RER line as you look at the lakes from the Arcades, about half a kilometre away. It's soon visible as you approach: two enormous circles like loud speakers facing each other across a space that would do nicely for a Roman stadium. At the other end of Mont d'Est, facing the capital, is the extraordinary semi-circle, arch and half square of *Le Théatre et Palacio d'Abraxas*, creation of Ricardo Boffil. Ghosts of ancient Greek designs haunt the facades but proportion there is none, whether classical or any other.

For those with wheels, further delights of Marne-la-Vallée include the mosaiced **'Totem' water tower** with clown and robot faces in the woods by **LE LUZARD**; another water tower, with plants growing through its grill cladding, at the head of bd Salvador Allende at **NOISEL-MAIRIE**; sympathetic small scale housing in **LE VAL-MAUBOUE** and, with easy access, the RER station on a lake, **LOGNES-LE-MANDINET. Maps and information** as well as models and photos on view are available from the *CIVN*, 2, place de l'Arche-Guédon, Torcy; bus #220 from Noisel RER, direction Torcy, stop *L'Arche-Guédon.*

travel details

Trains

From Gare du Nord through services to Britain via Calais and Boulogne (frequent) and Dunkerque (less so), and to Belgium, Holland and Amsterdam; also to Amiens (at least hourly; 1¾ hr.), Arras (1 hr. 40 min.) and Lille (2–2½ hr.).

From Gare de l'Est frequent trains to Nancy (2½–3 hr.), Reims (1½ hr.), Strasbourg (4 hr.), Besançon (3 hr.) and Metz (2½ hr.).

From Gare St-Lazare 2 to Dieppe (2¼ hr.); frequent service to Le Havre (2–2½ hr.), Cherbourg (3–3½ hr.), Rouen (1¼ hr.).

From Gare Montparnasse frequent service to Brest (5½–6 hr.), Nantes (3½ hr.) and Rennes (2½ hr.).

From Gare d'Austerlitz numerous trains to Tours (2 hr.), Poitiers (3 hr.) and Bordeaux (5 hr.); about 6 each to Bayonne (6–8 hr.) and Toulouse (7–8hr.).

From Gare de Lyon almost hourly TGVs to Dijon (1 hr. 40 min.) and Lyon (2½ hr.); 7 or 8 regular trains to Dijon (2½ hr.) and Lyon (5–6 hr.); almost hourly service to Grenoble, changing at Lyon (3 hr. 45 min. by TGV); 10 or more to Marseille (5 hr. by TGV) and Nice (10½ hr.).

Buses

Regular connection to just about all points in France – and Britain, Belgium, Holland, Scandinavia, Spain, Morocco, Italy, etc. – from the terminal at **Porte-de-la-Villette** (M° Porte-de-la-Villette).

Hitching

Hitching out of Paris isn't easy, especially in high summer when you are likely to face very long delays. It's much better to spend a few extra francs taking a train or bus 50km clear of the city down our planned route. If, however, you are determined to try, place yourself at one of these points:

Heading south: M° to Porte d'Italie, then walk 300m south to the motorway slip roads – A6 for Lyon, Marseille, Nice or Perpignan, A10 for Tours, Bordeaux and Le Mans.

Heading east: M° to Porte de Charent,on then walk 500m south to the A4 slip road (for Reims, Metz, Strasbourg, Nancy) just north of the Pont National.

Heading north: M° to St-Denis-Porte de Paris and look for the blue highway signs – N1 for Boulogne, Calais and Amiens, N14 for Rouen, Dieppe and Le Havre.

Alternatively, for a small fee, you can register with the hitching organisation Allostop; they will find you a ride and you just make a small contribution towards petrol (see Travel Firms, above, for their address and opening hours).

Flights

Inter-Air and *Air-France* connect Paris with all major **French cities.** For **International Flights** see Travel Firms, above.

Transport connections with the three Paris airports – Roissy-Charles de Gaulle, Le Bourget and Orly.

CHAPTER TWO

THE NORTHEAST: PICARDY TO CHAMPAGNE

When conjuring up exotic holiday locations, northeast France is unlikely to get a mention. Even among the French, the most enthusiastic tourists of their own country, it has few adherents. Picardy includes the most heavily industrial and most densely populated part of the country, while in the more sparsely populated Champagne a few drops of rain are all that is required for total gloom to descend.

It is likely, however, that you'll both arrive and leave France via this region, and there are curiosities within easy reach of the channel ports and main routes to Paris. Situated as it is on the obvious invaders' path into the country, from northern Europe as well as from Britain, the events that have taken place in Picardy have shaped much of French history. The most bitter battles were those of this century's wars, above all the Battle of the Somme in 1916. Throughout the region, but particularly around the villages of the Somme north of Amiens, there are powerful reminders, monuments and cemeteries of those devastating human episodes. At **Vimy Ridge** the First World War trenches have been preserved in perpetuity.

Three of France's finest cathedrals – at **Amiens, Reims** and **Laon** – are situated in Picardy. Other attractions include the *maisons,* vineyards and produce of the **Champagne** region; the bird sanctuary of **Marquenterre** at the mouth of the Somme estuary; the sinuous wooded wilderness of the **Meuse Valley**; industrial archaeology in the coal fields where Zola's *Germinal* was set; the great medieval castle of **Coucy-le-Château,** and the battle sites of the Middle Ages – **Agincourt, Crécy** – whose names are so familiar in the history of Anglo-French rivalry.

Though the past is not forgotten, the present life of the region does not feed on it. In the city centres of **Lille, Compiégne, St-Quentin,** and **Laon** you'll find your fill of food, culture and entertainment in the company of locals similarly hell-bent on having a good time; and in addition to the more obvious delights of the Champagne region there is the possibility of finding relatively lucrative **employment** during the harvest towards the end of September.

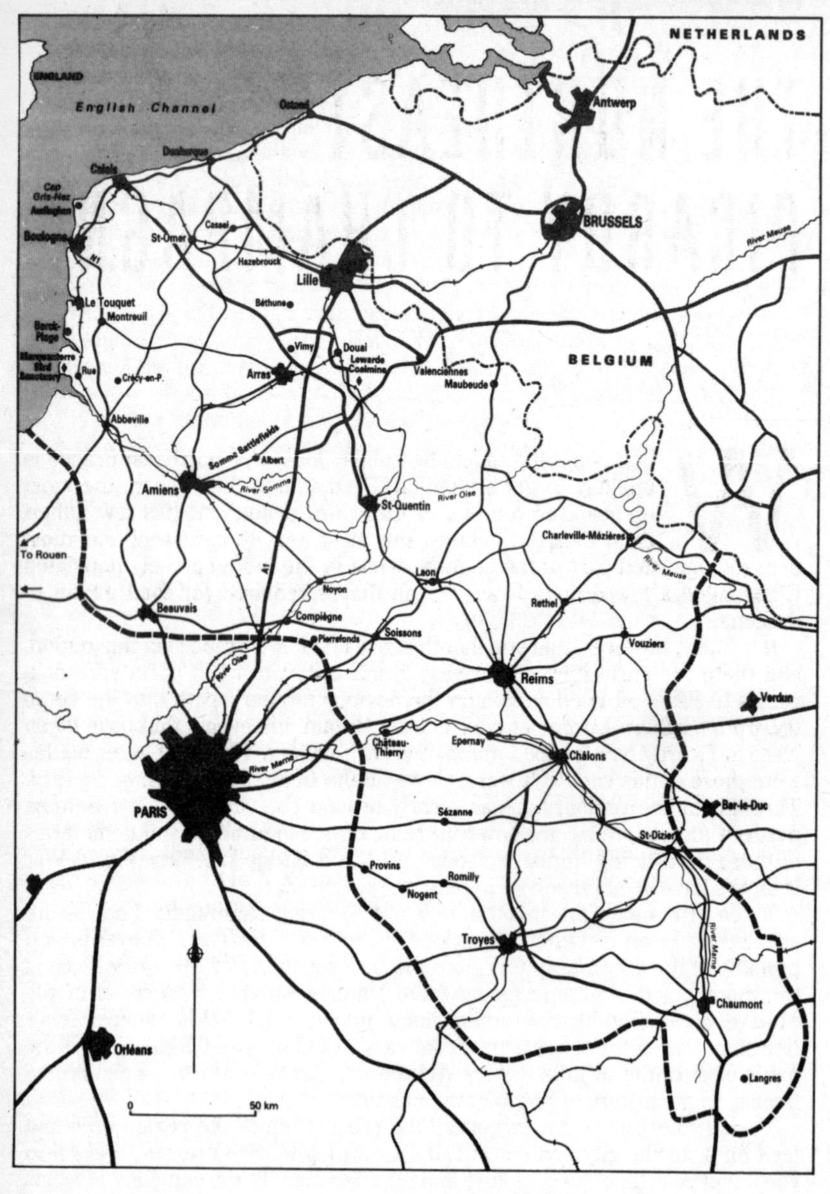
NETHERLANDS
ENGLAND
English Channel
Ostend
Antwerp
Dunkerque
Calais
Cap Gris-Nez
Boulogne
BRUSSELS
River Meuse
Cassel
St-Omer
Hazebrouck
N1
Lille
Béthune
Le Touquet
Montreuil
Vimy
Douai
Lewarde Coalmine
Rue
Arras
Valenciennes
BELGIUM
Crécy-en-P.
Maubeude
Abbeville
Somme Battlefields
Albert
Amiens
River Somme
St-Quentin
River Oise
Charleville-Mézières
To Rouen
A1
River Meuse
Laon
Noyon
Rethel
Beauvais
Compiègne
Pierrefonds
Soissons
Vouziers
River Oise
Reims
Verdun
Château-Thierry
Epernay
Châlons
River Marne
PARIS
Bar-le-Duc
Sézanne
St-Dizier
Provins
Romilly
Nogent
River Marne
Troyes
Chaumont
Orléans
Langres
0
50 km

THE CHANNEL PORTS AND ROUTES TO PARIS

Apart from their attraction for day-trippers after a sniff of something foreign and a shopping-bag full of exotic produce, the chief function of the **ports** in this section – **Boulogne**, **Calais** and **Dunkerque** – is to provide the cheapest and most efficient route between Britain and France. You'll find details of crossings in the *Travel Details* at the end of this chapter.

Moving on is just as easy. There are frequent **train** connections eastwards to **Lille** and beyond and south towards **Paris**. Of **road routes** your choice will depend on your priorities and your ultimate destination. The **A1 autoroute** with its A26 and A25 feeders from Calais and Dunkerque is quickest, but also dull and rather bleak. For a much more immediate immersion into Frenchness – little towns, different-looking farms, a comfortable verge to sleep off the first *baguette* and *rouge* – the old **N1** is infinitely preferable. There are also interesting things to see on or near the road: Amiens' cathedral, Montreuil, the Atlantic Wall, and Marquenterre bird sanctuary.

For scheduled trains and buses on all routes, again see the *Travel Details* at the end of the chapter.

Dunkerque (Dunkirk)

Frequently under a cloud of chemical smog and unstylishly resurrected from wartime devastation, **DUNKERQUE** is about as unappealing an introduction to France as could be imagined. It is the country's third largest port and a massive industrial centre in its own right, with oil refineries and steel works producing a quarter of total French output (railway bogeys and drilling shafts for oil exploration a speciality).

Save for the occasions when French fishermen rule *aux quais*, there seems little to detain you here. If you are stuck with time on your hands, however, the only sights are the unexpectedly brilliant **Musée d'art contemporain** (10am–7pm; closed Tues.) with works by Karel Appel, Vasarely, César and many other stars of the post-war era, housed in a suitably serious, pared-down, white ceramic building in a landscaped canalside sculpture park in av des Bains; and the **Musée des Beaux-Arts** (10am–noon, 2–6pm; closed Tues.), on place de Gaulle by the **Post Office**, with good collections of Flemish, Dutch and French painting, natural history and, inevitably, a display on the withdrawal of the 350,000 Allied soldiers from the beaches in May 1940 after the Nazis' lightning and crushing tank attack across the plains of northern France. Also, if you want a closer look at the mammoth port installations, steel works, dockyards and factories, there are **boat trips** from place du Minck, Bassin du Commerce, at the northern end of the continuation of rue Clemenceau (ask SI for times).

If you **arrive by car**, there are clinical rewards in the rapid and easy access to the autoroute system, with links to Belgium and Germany as well as

Paris. By **public transport** things are a little slower, with the ferry terminal some 15km from the town and SNCF station. There is, however, a **free shuttle service**, *Sally Lines* buses dropping you in the central **place Bollaert**, whence it is a short walk back to **place Jean-Bart** (named for Louis XIV's licensed pirate), then left up **rue Clemenceau** to the **SI** (☎28.66.79.21; Mon.–Sat. 9am–noon, 2–6.30pm; money exchange), in the base of a tall medieval brick **belfry** that is the town's chief landmark.

Believers in millenial catastrophe might like to take a trip to Vauban-walled **GRAVELINES** 15km west of Dunkerque for a firsthand assessment of what might happen to southeast England if a Chernobyl-style accident were happen to the massive nuclear power station there. To arrange a visit, phone ☎28.23.99.00.

Shopping

Short-stay **shoppers** should head for the main drag, bd Alexandre-III with its continuation, rue Clemenceau, and the cross-street, rue Poincaré. In addition to clothes, perfume, fancy tobacconists, and kitchenware shops, *Le Sanglier* stocks all manner of saliva-inducing edibles, including numerous take-out *plats*, while *Pimkie*, also on bd Alexandre-III, is a riotous press of style-conscious shoppers seeking fashion bargains. On place de la République just off the boulevard, the *Uniprix* department store stocks everything you can think of, including masses of food and booze. In rue Clemenceau *Le Don Miguel* newsstand is the place to head for your daily English-language fix. In rue Poincaré *Le Manoir* is for groceries, *Boulangerie Hossaert* and the *pâtisserie*, *Poulain*, for tarts, cakes, biscuits and the like. As everywhere on this coast, your well-defended crustaceans and shellfish are a tempting and bargain buy, but if you want to take them home, you need to be quick about it and preferably come armed with a cool bag.

If you have no time to wander from shop to shop, don't despair. *Sally Lines* (the only ferry operator into Dunkerque; ☎28.68.43.44) run a free bus service from the port to three giant everything-under-one-roof **hypermarkets**, *Auchan*, *Carrefour* and *Cora*.

Eating and staying

Train travellers could do a lot worse than eat at the station buffet, the *Richelieu*. It's not especially cheap but they accept some brands of plastic. A convenient place in town is the self-service *Cafétéria Forum* in the shopping centre of the same name on rue de l'Amiral-Ronarc'h. Other possibilities include the excellent pizzeria, *La Farigoule*, and the café, *Aux Halles*, both in the same street; *Auberge du Flamand*, 11 place Charles-Valentin (near the townhall), and *La Crêperie* on place Roger-Salengro.

Two further possibilities worth considering are the *Hôtel Hirondelle* (46–48 av Faidherbe; ☎28.63.17.65; closed Mon. and Sun. evening, and Aug. 15–Sept. 7) and *Au Bon Coin* (49 av Kléber; ☎28.5912.63), both in **MALO-LES-BAINS**, from whose vast sandy strand the Allied troops were embarked in 1940. The prices are very reasonable, and neither place is hard to reach, for Malo is merely the eastward extension of Dunkerque.

The *Hirondelle* also has moderately priced **rooms**. Otherwise the grubby place de la Gare in town is best for **inexpensive hotels**, the best being the moderately expensive *XIX Siècle* (☎28.66.79.28). As usual, nothing beats the **youth hostel** for the impecunious or fraternally-minded; it is at place Paul-Asseman, 2km east of the town centre (☎28.63.36.34; bus #3 to *Piscine*).

Calais

CALAIS is under 40 kilometres from England – the Channel's narrowest crossing – and comfortably established as the most popular, or at least the busiest, French passenger port. The port easily dominates the town, for there's not much else here. In the last war the British destroyed it to impede its use, fearing a German invasion.

Ironically, the French still refer to it as 'the most English town in France', an influence which began after the battle of Crécy in 1346, when Edward III seized it for use as a beach-head in the Hundred Years' War. It remained English until 1558, when its loss caused Mary Tudor to make her famous schoolroom history quote: 'When you open my heart, you will find the name of Calais engraved upon it'. The association, however, has been maintained across the centuries by Brits both desired and undesired back home: Lady Hamilton, Lord Nelson's ex; Oscar Wilde on his uppers; Nottingham lace-makers who set up business in the early nineteenth century; assorted **tunnellers** (their latest efforts can be inspected in a high-tech compound outside SANGATTE 9km south of town on the coast road); and, most notably today, 8 million British travellers per annum, plus 1 million daytrippers. A hypermarket trolley should be emblazoned on the city's coat of arms!

The town basically is divided into two. **Calais-Nord**, the old town rebuilt after the war with the **place d'Armes** as its focus, is separated by canals from **Calais-Sud** with its focus the **Hôtel de Ville** and the main shopping streets, **bd Jacquard** (named after the inventor of looms who mechanised Calais lacemaking) and **bd Lafayette**. Don't try to walk into town. There is a **free daytime bus service** from the ferries (**Calais-Maritime** station) to **place d'Armes** and the central **Calais-Ville** station in Calais-Sud.*

Once you've checked out the **shopping** on place d'Armes and adjacent **rue Royale**, with everything from clothes to chocolate to leather and dolls, Calais-Nord's charms wear thin. Collectors of oddities will find the only English Perpendicular church on the continent off rue de la Paix, while frill freaks can enjoy the unusual lacemaking exhibition in the **Musée des Beaux-Arts et de la Dentelle** (10am–noon, 2–5pm; closed Tues.) on rue Richelieu, opposite Parc Richelieu. The **SI** is at 12 bd Clemenceau; ☎21.96.62.40.

Calais-Sud is scarcely more significant. Just over the canal bridge where rue Royale becomes bd Jacquard, the town's landmark, its Flemish extrava-

* A word of warning: should you arrive at the port late at night without your own transport, you'll need to take a taxi into town – currently about 40F.

ganza of a **townhall**, rears its belfry 200-plus feet into the sky. Although of twentieth-century construction it is practically the only building, apart from the **medieval tower** on place d'Armes, to have survived wartime bombardment. For a record of Calais' other wartime travails you can consult the **Musée de la Guerre** (10.30am–5.30pm June–Sept. closed Tues.) installed in a former German blockhouse in the **Parc St-Pierre** across the street, while right outside the building **Rodin's** famous bronze **Burghers of Calais** records forever the tense and tortured self-sacrifice of these local dignitaries, who offered their lives to assuage the brutal lusts of the English conqueror, Edward III.

Less harmful appetites can be sated in the **shops** down bd Jacquard and into bd Lafayette. Again there are shoes, clothes, household goods, scents, wines and food. The *Prisunic* and *Printemps* stores face each other across the street, the former with a food and wine department, though you may prefer the more individual character of *Caves de France* for your wine or the charcuterie *Lablanche* with take-out *plats* and salads, or – better still – the **markets** off place d'Armes (Wed./Sat.) and bd Lafayette (pl Crêvecoeur; Thurs./Sat.). For seafood try *Huitrière Calaisienne* in bd Lafayette or *Sole Berckoise* in Jacquard. **Hypermarket** – *grands surfaces* – addicts with their own transport can trek out to the *Mammouth* (sic) complex on the Boulogne road or take bus #4 from the railway station to *Le Continent* (open daily 9am–9pm).

Eating, sleeping and other practicalities

Place d'Armes, is also a good area for **eating places**. Two that come highly recommended are *Le Touquet* (☎21.34.64.18) at no. 57 in the nearby rue Royale and the slightly more expensive *Le Channel* at 3 bd de la Résistance, overlooking the yacht basin (☎21.34.42.30; closed Wed. and Sun. eve, June 1–12 and Dec. 20–Jan. 15). *Café de Paris* (rue Royale) and the self-service *Le Templier* at the beach offer cheaper fare.

There is no youth hostel, but inexpensive hotels are plentiful, if you have to stay, and there is a **camping municipal** (26 av Poincaré; ☎21.97.99.00) by the beach beyond the end of rue Royale. Two good-value **hotels** are the *Folkestone* (28 rue Royale; ☎21.34.63.26) and *Boulogne* (41 quai du Rhin, near the station). Other possibilities are close to the parks. You could try *Hôtel du Cygne* (32 rue Jean-Jaurès; ☎21.34.55.18) off bd Jacquard behind the Hôtel de Ville and *Le Littoral* (71 rue Aristide-Briand; ☎21.34.47.28) beside Parc St-Pierre. Nicer and a bit more expensive are the *Richelieu* (rue Richelieu; ☎21.34.61.60) opposite the eponymous park and the *Bristol* (rue Duc-de-Guise; ☎21.34.53.24). Or you could use the **SI accommodation service** (12 bd Clemenceau), for which there is a small charge.

Hitching south to **Paris,** take bd Gambetta from the end of bd Jacquard; it leads to both the A26 autoroute and the old N1. The **bus station**, of limited use, is close to the intersection.

To phone the ferry companies, dial ☎21.96.67.10 for *Hoverspeed* or ☎21.34.55.00 for *Sealink SNCF*.

Inland and along the shore

The first stop inland for many visitors to France is **ST-OMER**, a rather cold little town, though one which establishes an immediately distinct and foreign character. The landscape seems to expand and the town itself has flights of Flemish magnificence, especially in the townhall and some of the mansions on rue Gambetta. There is a fine Gothic church in the **Basilique Notre-Dame** with some noteworthy statuary, and some handsome exhibits in the **Beaux-Arts** museum (10am–noon, 2–6pm Wed. and Sun.; Thurs. and Fri. am only), in particular, a glorious piece of medieval goldsmithing known as the *Pied de Croix de St-Bertin*.

Accommodation is satisfactory and cheap: a couple of options are *Hôtel du Commerce* (3 rue Ste-Adegonde) and *Hôtel de l'Industrie*, a nice place with an active bar in rue Louis-Martel (pedestrians only). There are pleasant public gardens and some very Flemish-seeming waterways cut between plots of land on reclaimed marsh just outside town along the river Aa, accessible by boat from *Taverne Flamande* at 60 route de Clairmarais.

More interesting perhaps than anything at St-Omer is **CASSEL**, 20km east on route D933, scene of a British rearguard action in the retreat to Dunkerque in the World War II. A tiny place, this has a very Flemish character: a fine Gothic church, a lovely broad Grand-Place, a public garden and a mill, and some magnificent old mansions, *hôtels* and stepped alleyways. Unless you're coming from Dunkerque by train (several daily), you'll need your own transport to justify the trip – worthwhile if you have it.

Another interesting excursion is to the forest of **EPERLECQUES** (3 or 4 trains daily from Calais to nearby WATTEN) 15km from St-Omer on the Dunkerque road. Here in 1944 the Germans, or rather 6000 half-starved slave labourers, built the largest ever concrete bunker from which to **launch V-2 rockets** against London. Luckily the RAF and the French Resistance prevented its ever being ready for use. (Open daily June 15–Sept. 15; April–June 15 and Sept. 15–Nov. 15 Wed., Sat. and Sun. am only).

The coast road to Boulogne

This is the *Côte d'Opale*, the Opal Coast, where sea and sky merge at some indefinable point into an oyster-grey to opalescent continuum and the air is tangy with salt. The long sandy beaches are exposed by huge tide flows and backed by high chalk cliffs and the road belongs to drivers or cyclists. Right on the outskirts of Calais, BLERIOT-PLAGE commemorates Blériot's epic **first cross-channel flight** in 1909. SANGATTE is the **Channel tunnel**; an earlier attempt – dating from 1877 – is clearly visible nearby. Thereafter, the road winds up on to grassy windswept heights between Cap Blanc-Nez and Cap Gris-Nez, studded with massive concrete bunkers, that were part of the German World War II defenses known as the **Atlantic Wall.** One of them, right beside the road at **AUDINGHEN**, equipped with a gun that could hit the English coast, has been converted into a rather rough and ready **museum** (open daily Easter–Oct. 9am–6pm) of the paraphernalia of war. Burrowing two or three floors below ground level, it has curiosity value rather than any great attractions. The best exhibits are British propaganda material, and a poster cautioning troops against the dangers of VD, (showing a German fraülein propositioning a portly officer, buttons popping with excitement: 'Come mit me!') Below, a road goes down to **WISSANT** and the enormous beach between the capes. There is a beautiful walk along the cliff tops.

Boulogne

BOULOGNE is quite distinct from Dunkerque and Calais: recommendation in itself. Rising above the port is a medieval centre, the **Haute Ville**, flanked by grassy ramparts and a grand black-domed cathedral. Below, amid the newer shopping streets of the **Ville Basse**, are some of the best *charcuteries* and *pâtisseries* in the north, and an impressive array of fish restaurants. Alone among the northeast Channel ports it is a place that might tempt you to stay.

It is also an important harbour – largest fishing base in Europe, so it is claimed – and long established. Julius Caesar crossed to conquer Britannia from here in 53 B.C. But for a last minute change of heart, Napoléon would have done the same in 1803. Just north of the town on N1 stands the **Colonne de la Grande Armée**, where the Emperor is said to have turned his troops east towards Austria. The column was originally capped by a bronze figure of Napoléon symbolically clad in Roman garb – though its head, equally symbolically, was shot off by the British navy in the last war. It is now displayed, along with items donated by a local born Egyptologist, including a good collection of Greek pots, in the château **museum** in the old fortified town (April–Oct. 10.30am–5.30pm; Nov.–March 11am–4pm; closed Mon.).

The **Cathédrale Notre-Dame**, dominating the town from its site in the Haute Ville, is worth making time for. It's an odd building, raised in the nineteenth century, without any architectural knowledge or advice, by the town's vicar. Against all the odds it seems to work. In the crypt (open 2–5pm; closed Mon.) you can see frescoed remains of the Romanesque building and relics of a Roman temple to Diana. Above, a curiosity is a white statue of the Virgin and Child on a boat-chariot, drawn here on its own wheels from Lourdes.

Practicalities and shopping

Ferries dock within a few minutes' walk of the town centre, **place Dalton**. (**Operators' telephones**: *Hoverspeed*, ☎21.30.27.26; *Sealink SNCF*, ☎21.30.25.11.) Arriving by hovercraft, a little further out, you'll be met by a free shuttle bus.

If you **intend to stay,** stop at the **SI** (☎21.31.68.38; over the bridge as you come out of the ferry terminal). They can supply a mass of information and advise on availability of rooms, which in summer fill early. Your best bet is probably the friendly and modern **youth hostel**, up by the old town walls on the east side, at 36 rue de la Porte-Gayole. It's a fair climb, so phone first to check for space: ☎21.31.48.22. Most of the other cheap **hotels** enclose the port area. The small *La Plage*, with a reasonably inexpensive restaurant, at 124 bd Ste-Beuve (continuation of quai Gambetta) towards the beach

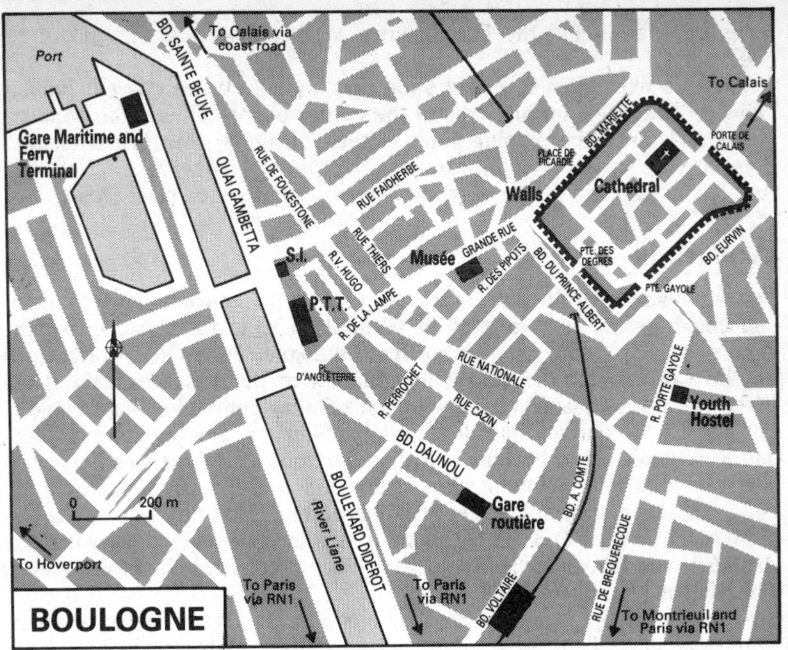

(☎21.31.34.78; closed Mon. and Sun. eve, and Dec. 19–Jan. 26) is worth a try, though not rock-bottom in price. Another, cheaper possibility is *Hôtel Hamiot*, 1 rue Faidherbe (☎21.31.44.20). Further along bd Ste-Beuve, on the way to the sandy strand of **Wimereux** (see below), is *Camping Moulin Wibert*, a 3-star place (10 minutes by bus).

For **eating**, there are dozens of possibilities around place Dalton and the cathedral, but bear in mind the day-tripper trade and be selective. The brasserie *Chez Jules*, on the *place*, is always a good bet, and serves food all day. The *Hamiot* (see above) right opposite the port is a basic alternative, or, for beer drinkers, *La Houblonnière* on rue Monsigny has a vast international selection of brews to wash down its *plats du jour*. For something a bit more refined, try *La Matelote* (85 bd Ste-Beuve) or the *Welsh Pub* (rue Boussemart), both specializing in fish and sea food. Vegetarians should head for *La Vie Claire* (20 place des Victoires). And for sheer convenience there is the cafeteria in the *Champion* supermarket on the pier.

For **shopping** head straight for the same establishment, unless you have your own transport, in which case head for the monstrous *Auchan* **hypermarket** 7km out on the St-Omer road. More fastidious guzzlers should cross the Pont de l'Entente-Cordiale into Grande-Rue, slip into *Derrien's* **charcuterie** and stuff their pockets with snails, sausages, *foie gras*, and pigs' trotters before sidling up the street to *Lugand's* **pâtisserie**, where the aforementioned trophies can be swallowed as appetisers to handfuls of chocolates, *tartes aux fraises* and the like. There's a **launderette** at the end of rue Nationale.

There is one other specialist shop that should not be missed: Philippe Olivier's **cheese shop** just around the corner on rue Thiers. But whatever you're after in the consuming line – clothes, furniture, sheets, hats, plates – these are the streets to find it: Grande-Rue, Thiers, Faidherbe and Nationale. And don't forget the Wednesday and Saturday **markets** on place Dalton.

Wimereux

Instead of spending the day calculating kilos to pounds and pence to francs, you could get away from it all in **WIMEREUX**, a traditional, turn-of-the-century seaside resort just 4km north of Boulogne. Once a kind of Blackpool on the Channel for the vacationing miners of the Pas de Calais, it still preserves a certain faded charm with mock Gothic and Tudor chalets holding out against the encroaching developers' bulldozers. Sale boards proliferate and it all looks set to become heavily gentrified. But the shore is pleasant sand and rock, with plenty of wind-surfing and, to the north, walks along the cliffs. The main shopping street has a cheap and good **hotel**, *Hôtel des Arts* (143 rue Carnot; #21.32.43.13), with a popular bar and restaurant. *Hôtel Aramis* (1 rue Romain; ☎21.32.40.15)) is more expensive and not as pleasant. The **SI** is on place du Roi-Albert.

Access from Boulogne is either by bus or train (every couple of hours) from Boulogne-Ville to Wimille, the village abutting Wimereux inland. A taxi will set you back less than a fiver.

Le Touquet and inland

Thirty-eight kilometres from Boulogne by road, through dunes planted with wind-flattened tamarisks and pines, **LE TOUQUET** is one of those peculiarly French northern resorts, once the height of fashion, now essentially suburban. In the 1920s and 1930s, and for a spell after World War II, the town, with its broad sands and leafy luxury villas, ranked with places on the Côte d'Azur. At one time, so it is said, it saw flights from Britain every 10 minutes. The opening up of long-distance air travel put an end to this, though not completely and forever. The new British rich, sniffing a fresh chance of elitism, are now back in some force, pouring water over each other's heads in smart restaurants in typically British fun. Their private aircraft are now the airport's only traffic.

It is an extraordinary set-up really and not advisable unless you're armed with a sense of humour and a camera. For anyone interested, though, **access** is quite simple. You take the train from Boulogne to ETAPLES and from there – where signs in English almost take over – a local bus. For somewhere reasonable to **spend the night** try *L'Union* (71 rue de Metz), *L'Auberge* (42 rue d'Etaples) or *Hôtel Armide* (56 rue Léon-Garet: room and board at a good price). There's also a campsite, on the waterfront of the Canche estuary, but this requires three nights minimum stay, which is almost certainly too long. If you've come here with strict **sociological intent**, take a glimpse at the *Hôtel Manoir*.

Heading inland: Montreuil

MONTREUIL-SUR-MER is a place with character. Once a port and now stranded far inland, it was the scene of much of the action in Victor Hugo's *Les Misérables*. Lawrence Sterne spent a night here on his *Sentimental Journey*, and Douglas Haig set up his First World War HQ here.

It is strikingly set on a sharp little hilltop, with a fortress enclosed by a ring of Vauban **walls**, rebuilt after the destructive sixteenth-century attentions of Charles V, Holy Roman Emperor. The 'new' town lies outside these, its mostly cobbled streets climbing up from the river Canche and the railway station (on a little country line to Arras and Lille). There are inexpensive **rooms** and meals at the *Hôtel Central* (7 rue du Change), but unless you're after privacy you might as well stay at the **youth hostel** (☎21.06.10.83) in the citadel itself. This option offers the additional advantage of gaining free access to the *enceinte*, which is otherwise open only from 9am–noon and 2–6pm, and for a small fee.

Entered through a gate between sturdy thirteenth-century towers, the **Citadelle**, like the walls, was reconstructed by Vauban. It is overgrown and after dark quite atmospheric. There are subterranean casemates and a fourteenth-century tower which records the coats of arms of the French noblemen killed at **Agincourt** in 1415. Ten thousand of them died in the bloodiest defeat ever of France's feudal knighthood. Forced by muddy conditions to fight on foot in their heavy armour they were sitting ducks to the lighter, mobile English archers. The battle took place near present-day AZINCOURT, about 40km away, north of HESDIN on D928. Just east of the village, by the crossroads of D104 with the lane to Maisoncelle, a copse and a cross mark the position of the original grave pits. The place's reputation was so grim it used to be called The Carrion. But it's hard not to smile thinking of Shakespeare's King Harry going incognito among his men at night and the braggart Pistol uttering bloodcurdling threats in the hopes of getting money out of a scared French soldier: 'O Signieur Dew, thou diest . . . Thou damned and luxurious mountain-goat, Offer'st me brass?'

Although the place is in the middle of nowhere it's not that difficult to reach. **Three or four trains** a day on the Boulogne-Arras line stop at BLANGY-SUR-TERNOISE (and a couple more at Hesdin), about 6km or a 1½ hour leisurely walk from the battlefield. And it's where the real King Harry spent the eve of the battle, not in fact exchanging quips with Fluellen and Gower and Co.

Oddly enough almost the same distance south of Hesdin, west of the Abbeville road, is the site of another of the great battles of the Middle Ages, **CRECY**, where Edward III had inflicted an earlier defeat on the king of France in 1346, thus beginning the Hundred Years' War. This was the first appearance of the new English weapon – the longbow – on the continent and the first use in European history of a primitive mortar. Again not a lot to see, just the knoll 1km north of the little town of Crécy-en-Ponthieu on D111 from where Edward watched the to-and-fro of the battle. Again, not that difficult of reach – 17km from the station at RUE (see below).

Marquenterre bird sanctuary

MARQUENTERRE – *Le parc ornithologique du Marquenterre,* to give it its full name – is one of only two bird sanctuaries in the whole of France. In terms of landscape, it is beautiful and strange, all dunes, tamarisks and pine forest, full of salty meres and ponds thick with water plants. It's 'new' land, formed by the erosion of the Normandy coast and the silting of the Somme estuary, where thousands of cattle are grazed today to give their flesh the much-prized flavour of the 'salt meadows'.

Bird connoisseurs of course need no persuasion. But, if you know next to nothing of birds, the sanctuary will be a revelation. Entry isn't cheap and you'll need to rent binoculars. There is no point in trying to manage without.

There are two itineraries, the longer being the more interesting. It takes you from resting area to resting area whence you can train your glasses on all manner of species – ducks, geese, oyster-catchers, terns, egrets, redshanks, greenshanks, spoonbills, herons, storks, godwits – some of them fat-cat residents, most taking a breather from their epic migratory flights to and from the ends of the earth. In April and May they head north, and they return from the end of August to October, so these are the best times to visit.

The Marquenterre sanctuary is a tiny outfit in an area which gives new meaning to the word 'sanctuary'. All around gunshot can be heard, day and night from the opening of the water-fowl season on – horrible irony – July 14th, Bastille Day. No species, however rare, is spared. Even the swallow gets shot.

Access to the sanctuary, at least as far as the attractive little town of **RUE** on the main Calais-Paris railway, is easy. From there it's a 7km walk, except in July and August, when a bus meanders between the now dry fishing hamlets, whose low-crouched cottages bespeak their former poverty. Some, such as LE CROTOY with enough sea still to attract the yachties, are enjoying the inevitable holiday and second-home boom, though they are not without charm for all that.

Amiens

Few travellers would stop at **AMIENS** unless they were visiting its cathedral. Badly scarred during both world wars, and with heavy traffic pounding along the through-roads built over the old city walls, it is not an immediately likeable place. Yet it is not uninteresting. There's a major university here, which makes its presence felt in the rundown medieval **quartier St-Leu** north of the cathedral, sandwiched between the canal and the Somme. Currently the city's hottest tourist property, the attractive canalside cottages are being renovated and gentrified.

It is, however, the **Cathédrale Notre-Dame** that provides the city's focus, whatever your interests. First, it dominates all else by sheer dint of size, and is, in fact, the biggest Gothic building in France. But its appeal lies mainly in its unusual uniformity of style. Begun in 1220 under the architect Robert de Luzarches, it was pretty well complete by the end of the century, with just the tops of the towers left to do, and thus escaped the influence of succeeding architectural fads that marred the 'purity ' of some of its slower sisters.

In need of a good scrub, the west front is best seen with early afternoon sun falling obliquely across it – not too easy given the climate – to give some good *chiaroscuro* effects and bring out the detail of the riot of sculpture adorning the three main porches. Ruskin thought the apse 'not only the best, but the very first thing done perfectly in its manner by northern Christendom'.

The interior is all straight up and no fuss: a light, calm and unaffected space. If there is any pretence, it's in the later embellishments, like the

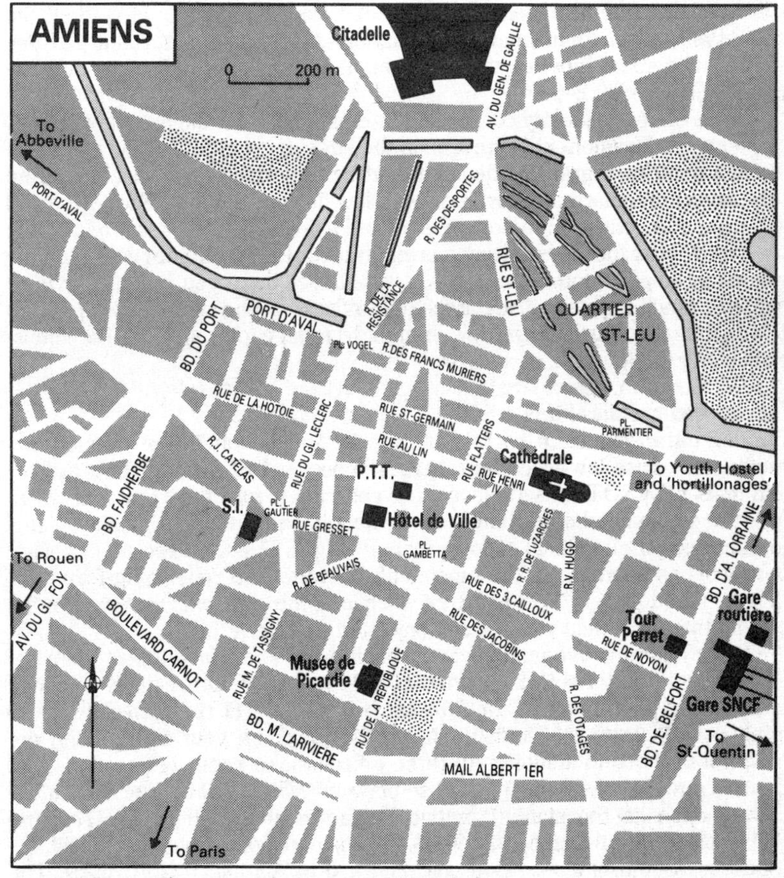

sixteenth-century **choir stalls** (guided tours only), but they are works of such breathtaking virtuosity you can forgive anyone who handles a chisel like that for wanting to show off. The same goes for the sculpted panels depicting the **life of St-Firmin,** Amiens' first bishop, on the right side of the choir screen. Anachronistically, the figures in the crowd scenes are shown in fifteenth-century costume, the men talking serious business among themselves, while their wives listen more credulously to the preacher's words.

If you're spending time in Picardy, you might take a look at Amiens' two **regional museums**. Close by the cathedral in the seventeenth-century **Hôtel de Berny** (10am–noon, 2–6pm; closed Mon.; Nov.–April open only Wed. and weekends) there are local history collections, while another mansion some five minutes' walk south of central place Gambetta houses the **Musée de Picardie** (10am–noon, 2–6pm; closed Mon.), whose star exhibit is a collection of rare sixteenth-century paintings on wood donated to the cathedral by what was in effect a local literary society, some of the pictures still in their original frames carved by the same craftsmen as worked the choir stalls. A third museum-cum-documentation centre is devoted to **Jules Verne**, who spent most of his life in this city. It's in his old house at 2 rue Dubois (Tues.–Sat. 2–6pm).

This, aside from strictly consuming interests, is about the extent of curiosities – except for the **hortillonages**, on the edge of town. These are a series of incredibly fertile market gardens intercut by tiny waterways, reclaimed from the marshy mush created by the very slow-flowing Somme. Farmers travel about them by black, high-prowed punt and a few still take their produce into the city by boat for the Saturday morning **market, Marché sur l'eau**, on the riverbank on place Parmentier. If you want to see them you can take an inexpensive **boat trip** from the riverside offices of the *Association pour la Sauvegarde des Hortillonages* (57 chemin de Halage; closed Mon.), or simply walk along the towpath, eastwards.

Arrival and practicalities

Coming out of the **train or bus station** in Amiens you'll find yourself in a rectangular square whose one otherwise open end is closed, like a magnet and its bar, by a tall miserable-looking concrete tower, the **Tour Perret**. In fact, the whole ensemble is the work of Perret, whose only originality seems to have been the espousal of concrete and height. The windows are as classic bourgeois as anything in the nineteenth century. The redeeming feature of this wretched place Fiquet is the excellence of the *croissants au beurre* in the café on the right (help yourself and pay later: expensive!).

The cathedral is five minutes away behind the Tour. In summer there are **SI** offices in front of both the cathedral and the station. Other times you need to go to the main office in the *Maison de la Culture* (1 rue Jean-Catelas) 15 minutes walk from the station, leaving the tower on your right, along rue Noyon and its continuations. All three offices make **room** reservations, but there is nowhere very cheap. Choose between *Hôtel Central* (rue Alexandre-Fatton: opposite the station) or two by the cathedral: *Hôtel Les Touristes* (22bis place Notre-Dame; ☎22.91.33.45) and *La Renaissance* your best bet (8bis rue St-André; closed Sun. and 2nd half of August; ☎22.91.70.23). The

youth hostel (one of the most unwelcoming I've seen) and **campsite** are a lot less pricey, but some 20 minutes slog on foot. Turn right out of the station along bd Alsace-Lorraine, over the Somme bridge, and take the first slip road on the left. They are side by side by a bleak-looking lake.

Good places to **eat** include a number of cheap brasseries and restaurants in front of Tour Perret and towards the centre of town round place Gambetta, a small square surrounded by snackbars and food shops. Other specific places worth seeking out are the slightly more expensive but extremely good *Le Vieil Amiens* on the canalside rue Belu right below the cathedral (fantastic view of same); *La Mangeoire* crêperie (3 rue des Sergents; closed Sun/ Mon.); *Valentin* (52 rue des Jacobins; closed Sat. pm/ Sun. and Aug.); and *Pizzeria Richard* (54 rue Jean-Jaurès; closed Mon.). For a fairly expensive splurge, you couldn't do better than *Les Marissons* just along the canal from the *Vieil Amiens*.

Finally, some details on **getting out**. For Paris and beyond, choose between train, bus or the ride-sharing agency *Allostop* (45 rue des Otages; Mon.–Fri. 9.30am–12.30pm and 1.30–6.30pm; Sat. am only). For St-Quentin or Beauvais you're best off by bus. Albert (at the heart of the battlefields region) is about 40 minutes by bus or train, either of which continues on to Arras and the Canadian memorial at nearby Vimy Ridge.

A little note of hope: On the west side of town, the former bd Thiers, named for the politician who swore to wipe socialism off the face of the earth in 1870, was renamed bd des Fédérés after the soldiers of the Revolution and the Commune, and then again, bd Salvatore Allende!

Beauvais

As you head south from Amiens towards Paris the countryside becomes broad and flat – agricultural, but not rustic. **BEAUVAIS** seems to fit into this landscape. Rebuilt, like Amiens, after the last world war, it's a drab, neutral place, redeemed for tourists only by its radiating Gothic **cathedral**. This rises crablike above the town, its roof unadorned by tower or spire and seeming squat for all its height. It is a building that perhaps more than any other in northern France demonstrates the religious materialism of the Middle Ages – its sole intention and function to be taller and larger than its rivals.

The **choir**, completed in 1272, was once in fact 5m higher than that of Amiens, though only briefly; it collapsed in 1284. Its replacement, only completed three centuries later, was raised by the sale of indulgences – a right granted to the local bishops by Pope Leo X. This too, however, fell within a few years and, the authorities having overreached themselves financially, the church remained unfinished, forlorn and mutilated. The appeal of the building, and its real beauty, is in its glass, its sculpted doorways, and the remnants of the so-called **Basse-Oeuvre**, a ninth-century Carolingian church incorporated into the structure. (Stained-glass lovers will find even more spectacular **Renaissance windows** in the church of St-Etienne a few blocks to the south on rue de Malherbe.)

Stopping at Beauvais to break the journey, you'll probably want to give the rest of the town no more than a passing look. If you're between buses, there's a **museum of tapestry**, for which Beauvais was once renowned (*Galerie nationale de la Tapisserie*; 9.30am–12.30pm and 1.30–5.30/6.30pm; closed Mon.), behind the cathedral and another, devoted to painting, local history and archaeology, in the sharp, black-towered building opposite (*Musée départemental;* 10am–12pm, 2–6pm; closed Tues.). The rousing statue in the central square is local heroine Jeanne Hachette, a fighter and inspiration in the defence of the town against Charles the Bold, Duke of Burgundy, in 1472. Just off the square, on place Clemenceau, the **SI** can provide exhaustive further information. If you want to stay, two moderately cheap **hotels** are *Bristol Hôtel* (58–60 rue de la Madeleine; ☎44.84.33.85) and *Le Brazza* (22 rue de la Madeleine; ☎44.45.03.86), and there's a **campsite** just out of town on the Paris road. The **gare SNCF**, however, is only an hour away from Paris: the station, a short walk from the centre and cathedral, is on bd de Gaulle.

THE BATTLEFIELDS AND THE INDUSTRIAL NORTH

Normandy, Picardy and Flanders are littered with the monuments, battlefields and cemeteries of the two World Wars, but nowhere as intensely as the region north of Amiens, around Albert and Arras. It was here, among the fields and villages of the **Somme**, that the main battlelines of the First World War were drawn. They can be visited most spectacularly at **Vimy Ridge**, just off the A26 north of Arras. Lesser sites, often more poignant, are dotted around the **Circuit de Souvenir**, signposted from Albert and detailed on a local tourist pamphlet, somewhat kitschily translated into English as 'Down Memory Lane'.

An equally unvisitable, though more enduring and more domestic presence in the life of northern France has been that of King Coal and all his heavy industrial works. The coalfields stretch from Béthune to Valenciennes, and at **Lewarde** at last you can visit a pit, while at **Lille**, the Coalville of the north, you can see what the masters did with the brass from the muck.

Albert and the Circuit de Souvenir

The church at **ALBERT** – now, with the rest of the town, completely rebuilt – was one of the minor landmarks of the First World War. Hit by German bombing, its tall tower suspended at a precarious angle a statue of the Madonna. The British, entrenched over three years in the region, came to know it as the leaning Virgin. Army superstition had it that when she fell the war would end, a myth inspiring frequent hopeful potshots by disgruntled troops.

As you arrive – by train from Amiens or Arras – the town's new tower is the first thing that catches the eye, capped now by an equally improbably posed statue. There is an **SI** close by on rue Gambetta (open June–mid-Sept only, 2–

5pm) and a couple of good inexpensive **hotels**: *Basilique*, in the same street, and *La Paix* on rue Victor-Hugo. Modern Albert does not, however, invite much of a stay unless you've a really strong battlefield interest, in which case you could spend weeks in the region.

Albert was in the middle of the British sector during the **battle of the Somme**, launched jointly with the French on July 1, 1916 to relieve pressure on the French army defending Verdun. The front ran roughly NW–SE 6km east of Albert across the valley of the Ancre and over the almost treeless high ground north of the Somme, huge hedgeless wheat fields now, their monotony relieved by an undulation as slow as the rhythm of a long sea swell.

The **circuit** conducts you from graveyard to mine crater, trench to memorial. But there is no need to follow it religiously; in fact, you could not without a car or bike – and the latter would be the ideal way of getting about, its pace appropriately solemn. For you are not really seeing anything very much: nothing at least that is going to satisfy any ghoulish appetite for shock-horror atrocities or amazing scenes of destruction. You are not even going to get much sense of a battle: tactics, or movement. But you'll find that even if you started out with the embarrassing feeling that your interest in war was somehow puerile or mawkish, you have in fact embarked on a sort of pilgrimage, in which each successive step becomes more harrowing and oppressive.

The **cemeteries** are the most moving aspect of the region. Beautiful cemeteries: the grass perfectly mown, an individual bed of flowers at the foot of every gravestone. And there are tens of thousands of them, all identical, with a man's name, if it is known (nearly half the British dead have never been found), his rank and regiment. Just reading the names of the regiments evokes a world and an experience quite different from today's: locally recruited regiments, young men from Welsh border farms, mill towns, and villages, who had never been abroad, wiped out in a morning. There were 57,000 British casualties on the first day, approximately 20,000 of them dead. These windy open hills had no intrinsic value – it was all for a gain of fifty metres of mud. Wilfred Owen's poem, *Futility*, suggests that concepts like victory and defeat were not foremost in the mind of at least one victim of trench warfare:

> Was it for this the clay grew tall?
> O what made fatuous sunbeams toil
> To break earth's sleep at all?

You'll see the cemeteries everywhere, if you cycle down the lanes between Albert and Bapaume, full of men from all corners of the Empire, at the angle of copses, in the middle of wheat fields. On the way to **BEAUCOURT-HAMEL**, for instance, (SNCF station: trains from Albert) there is one in the middle of a bluebell wood, moving and terrible in its simple beauty, while just across the river, at **THIEPVAL**, is **Lutyens'** colossal memorial to the 73,000 British troops missing at the Somme. Half an hour's hike from Hamel station, where the 51st Highland Division walked abreast to their deaths with their pipes playing, is the Newfoundlanders' memorial of **BEAUMONT-HAMEL**. Here, on the hilltop where most of them died, a stretch of trenches, grassed over and partly eroded, has been preserved, where German faced Canadian a few paces apart. It seems all so small-scale now – more appropriate to the antics of a party of school kids running around shooting each other with their fingers.

Back across the Albert-Bapaume road, at **LONGUEVAL**, a new **museum** has just opened, the *Musée 1914–1918* (open daily, 9.30am–6pm). Still unfinished, it consists mainly of a section of trench reconstructed in a café back garden and 'equipped' with genuine battlefield relics. It's a bit amateurish, but quite interesting if you're going through. The guide told me he had first collected objects from the battlefield as a boy, to sell for pocket money. Farmers apparently still turn up about 75 tons of shells every year – not really surprising when you think the British alone fired a million and a half in the last week of June 1916.

Arras and Vimy Ridge

ARRAS, birthplace of Robespierre – arguably the most important figure in French history – has been rebuilt perhaps more times than any other town in France. Its history of conflict dates from the early fifteenth-century – a temporary truce was signed here before Agincourt – and in addition to the destruction of this century it has seen capture and bombardment by the Austrians, Spanish, British and Germans.

Oddly enough it bears few obvious marks. Reconstruction here, particularly after the last war, has been careful and stylish, and two grand arcaded squares in the centre – **Grand'Place** and **Place des Héros** – preserve their historic character. Around both are restored Renaissance mansions, built in relatively restrained Flemish style, and on the latter a grand and ornate **town hall**, its entrance hall sheltering a pair of *géants* (festival giants) awaiting the city's next annual fete. By a slightly unsettling quirk of architectural development the town hall actually looks very like a cathedral, with its tremendous and flamboyant belfry, while the **cathedral** – originally seventeenth century – looks not unlike a town hall. More striking in itself, again in this historic centre, is the former Benedictine **abbey of St-Vaast**, revived from its ruins after wars in the eighteenth and present centuries. It now houses a city museum with unexciting collections of paintings, fragments of sculpture and local ceramics; hours are 10am–noon and 2–5.30pm (closed Tues.), if you need somewhere to escape the frequent rain.

The most fascinating sight in Arras, perhaps understandably in view of its history, is underground: **les souterrains** (or *les boves*), dark passageways and spacious vaults tunnelled beneath the centre of the city. Their entrance (Tues.–Sat. 2.30–6pm; Sun. 10.30am–12.30pm and 3–6.30pm; pricey) is actually inside the townhall. Once down you are escorted around an impressive physical area and given an interesting survey of local history. During World War I the rooms, which often have fine tiled floors and lovely pillars and stairways, were used as a British barracks and hospital.

Extending this memory, on the western edge of town next to the modern barracks housed in **Vauban's** old **fortress**, is another **Lutyens memorial**, this one a movingly elegaic classical colonnade of ivy-covered brick and stone, commemorating 36,000 more missing soldiers, the endless columns of their names inscribed on the walls. It's a long time ago now and the numbers of surviving relatives is obviously dwindling fast. There is little more poignant than the fading posies left with a card beneath a name, a shaky eighty-year-old hand reminding 'Dad' that she has not seen him since she was seven and it won't be long now.

Decidedly, this is a mournful corner of the town. Next door, down the lane and around the back of the old brick fortress, in an overgrown moat, is the **Mur des Fusillés**, where some 200 Resistance members were shot by firing squad in the last war, most of them of Polish descent, most of them miners, and most of them Communists.

If you are staying in the town – as you'll probably need to, visiting Vimy without your own transport – there's a newly modernized **youth hostel** at 59 Grand'Place (☎21.21.07.83), a **campsite** 1km out of town from the station on the Bapaume road, and two well-priced **hotels**: *Les Grandes Arcades* in Grand'Place (☎21.23.30.89), which, although it only has a couple of cheap rooms, is not as posh as it appears, and *Le Rallye* at 9 rue Gambetta (☎21.51.44.96) near the station. The *Arcades* also serves very good and not wildly expensive **food**, or there are several **crêperies** round place des Héros. Other Arras restaurants tend to be expensive, often featuring local speciality *andouillet* (tripe sausage – delicate palates beware!). The **SI**, who are worth consulting on transport to and tours of local battlefields, are at 7 place du Maréchal-Foch, opposite the station.

Vimy Ridge

Eight kilometres north of Arras on D49, VIMY RIDGE was the scene of some of the direst fighting of the first World War: almost two full years of battle, culminating in its capture by the Canadians in April 1917. It is a vast site, given in perpetuity to the Canadian people out of respect for their sacrifices, and has been preserved in part as it was during the conflict. Long worms of trenches meander over the now grassy ground, still clearly pitted and churned by shell bursts beneath the planted pines. There are underground clearings, hideous places, where men used to shelter during heavy bombardments and make-shift hospitals were set up. Beneath the ground there are still some 11,000 bodies unaccounted for and countless rounds of unexploded ammunition. Signs are still required to warn against straying from the directed paths.

On the brow of the ridge, facing north over a steep escarpment, a great white **monument** towers, like a giant funerary stele, rent down the middle by elemental force, with allegorical figures half-emerging from the stone towards the top. On its stepped and monumental plinth the names of 60,000 Canadians are inscribed. An unenviable task to design a fitting memorial to such slaughter, but this one, aided by its setting, succeeds with great drama.

Visits to the site (10am–6pm daily, April–Sept.) are supervised by Québecois students, who can fill you in on all the horrific details. In the woods behind, on the headstone of another exquisitely maintained cemetery, you can read the names of half the counties of rural England, while just visible to the west is Notre-Dame-de-la-Lorette, a memorial to the French, who also died in hecatombs on this ridge.

Two kilometres from Vimy across the A26 autoroute, at NEUVILLE-ST-VAAST (buses from Arras, direction LENS), the **Musée de la Targette** (open daily, 9am–7pm) contains a fascinating collection of World War I uniforms, weapons, and assorted objects. It is the private collection of David Bardiaux, assembled with passion and with meticulous attention to detail, under the inspiration of tales told by his grandfather, a veteran of Verdun. Its interest lies in the absolute exactness with which the 30-odd mannequins of British, French, Canadian and German soldiers are dressed and equipped, down to their sweet and tobacco tins and such rarities as a 1915 British-issue cap with earflaps, very comfortable for the troops, but withdrawn because the top brass thought it made their men look like yokels! All the exhibits have been under fire; some belonged to known individuals and are complete with stitched up tears of old wounds. Right opposite, the *Café Flambeau* serves well-priced food.

Douai And The Mining Country

Though not really worth an overnight stay, DOUAI is a surprisingly attractive and lively town, its streets of old houses cut by both river and canal. Centre of activity is the **place d'Armes**, overlooked by the massive Gothic belfry of the town hall on nearby rue de las Mairie. The **SI** is on the *place* facing the moderately-priced *Hotel de Paris* (☎27.88.95.63). (For an alternative, try the cheaper *Grand Cerf* at 46 rue St-Jacques; ☎27.88.79.60). To one side is the **post office,** where buses leave (*Ligne no. 1,* orange) for **LEWARDE.**

Lewarde: *Centre Minier Historique*

This visit is a must for admirers of Zola's *Germinal,* perhaps the most electrifying 'naturalistic' novel ever written. The bus from Douai heads east across the monotonously flat and featureless beet fields, down a road lined with poor brick dwellings that recall the company-owned housing of *Germinal,* intersected by streets named for Pablo Neruda, Jean-Jacques Rousseau, Georges Brassens, and other luminaries of the French and international left. This is the heart of France's coal mining country. always dispiriting and now depressed by closures. Even the distinctive landmarks of slag heap and winding gear are fast disappearing with demolition and landscaping.

The bus puts you down at the square in Lewarde, leaving a 15-minute walk fown the road towards ERCHIN. The Centre (open daily, 10am–5.30pm; office closed at 4pm) is on the left in the old Fosse Delloye, sited like so many pits in the midst of fields and woods.

Visits are unavoidably guided, helmeted and expensive. The guides are retired miners, some of whom are Polish. Polish labour was introduced in the 1920s, Italians after World War II, then Algerians and Moroccans. My guide went down the pit at 14 and at 38 was brought up with silicosis, which had also killed his father at 52. *'Ce n'est pas un métier'*, he said. 'It's not what you'd call a career'.

You can't yet go underground, but, in addition to watching film shows and visiting the surface installations – winding gear, machine shops, cages, sorting areas, etc. – the main part of the tour is through a surface reconstruction of the pit-bottom roadways and faces, variously modelled and equipped to show the evolution of mining from the earliest times to today.

These French pits were extremely deep and hot, with steeply inclined narrow seams that forced the miners to work on slopes of 55° and more, just as Zola's Etienne and the Maheu family do. Though a certain edge of excitement is missing through not being able to go underground, the whole thing is a salutary reminder that the wealth and culture of western Europe is built on poverty, suffering and even blood – for accidents were a regular occurence in the old days – of a large proportion of its population. In fact, these northern French pits seem to have had a particularly bad record in the last years of the nineteenth century. The very worst disaster occurred at Courrières in 1906, when 1100 men were killed. Incredibly, despite the fact that the owners made little effort to search for survivors, thirteen men suddenly emerged after twenty days of wandering in the gas-filled roads without food, water or light. The first comrade they met thought that they were ghosts and fainted in fright. More incredible still, a fourteenth man surfaced alone after another four days. To its credit the town of Biarritz offered them all a holiday to recuperate.

Lille

LILLE, by far the largest city in these northern regions, is the very symbol of French industry and working-class politics. Its mayor, Pierre Mauroy, was the first Socialist Prime Minister appointed by the newly elected President Mitterrand in 1981. The city spreads far into the countryside in every direction, a mass of suburbs and heavy industrial plant, and contains, on a significant scale, most of the problems and assets of contemporary France. There is some of the worst poverty and racial conflict in the country here, and a crime rate rivalled only in Paris and Marseille. There is regionalism: Lillois sprinkle their speech with a French-Flemish patois and to an extent assert a Flemish identity, holding joint anti-nuclear demonstrations with Belgian groups, for example. And there is classic French affluence. The city has a lovely central heart – **Vieux Lille** – vibrant and obviously prosperous commercial areas and modern residential squares, and it's a place that takes its culture and its restaurants very seriously.

All of which is to say that, though you may not consider Lille a prime destination, if you're travelling through this region, it's at least worth a night. **On arrival** the encroaching suburbs look pretty grim, but from the **gare SNCF** (or adjoining **gare routière**) you're only a few minutes' walk from Vieux Lille and the central pedestrianised area around it. The point to make for is **place Ribour**, an airy, modern-looking square with an old palace that now houses the **SI**. Vieux Lille begins immediately to the north. Off to the southeast stylish rue de Béthune leads into **place Béthune**, another fine square, with some excellent cafés, and beyond to the city's **Musée des Beaux Arts** on place de la République. The museum (open 9.30am–12.30pm and 2–6pm, closed Tues.; free Wed./Sat. pm) is like so many of those in major French cities in its studious collections of each art genre: paintings, ceramics, tapestries, etc. Here, the emphasis is very much on the Flemish painters, from 'primitives' like Dirk Bouts, through the Northern Renaissance to Ruisdael, De Hooch and seventeenth-century schools. It's an instructive display, helped by a small library of art books provided for browsing in the entrance hall, and boasts, too, an additional scattering of Impressionists, including works by Monet and Corot.

Vieux Lille

It's in **Vieux Lille**, though, that you're likely to spend most time. Just north of place Ribour, the old exchange building or **Bourse** is lavishly ornate, and as perfect a representative of its age as could be imagined. To the merchants of seventeenth-century Lille, as prominent then as now, all things Flemish were the very epitome of wealth and taste, and they were not men to stint on detail, here or on the imposing mansions around. The building today, long pre-empted, has been converted to an organised flea market, with stalls selling books, junk and flowers.

Turning the corner from the Bourse, you can see how the Flemish Renaissance architecture developed, becoming distinctly French, and combining brick with stone in grand flights of Baroque extravagance. The superlative example of this style, the **Théâtre de l'Opéra,** has a facade so strident it's almost ridiculous. It was built only at the turn of this century, along with the equally inflated Town Hall **belfry** and **Chamber of Commerce** opposite. Beyond, there's a similar fascination in many of the streets, added to by the fact that many of the buildings here still are used in almost the same way as they were originally. The **Hospice Comtesse,** for example, twelfth century in origin though much reconstructed in the eighteenth century, served as a hospital right through to World War II. Its old ward, the Salle des Malades, can be visited; it's more or less opposite the Cathedral on rue de la Monnaie. The **Cathedral** itself, built only in the last century, is undistinguished, particularly so in comparison with Lille's earlier principal church, Gothic **St-Maurice,** toward the station.

The **Citadelle,** towering above the old city, was constructed in familiar star-shaped fashion by Vauban. Still in military hands, it can be visited only on Sunday by guided tour (details from SI for enthusiasts). Wandering through the old city, however, it is interesting to walk up this way. Turning a corner at rue de la Monnaie onto rue d'Angleterre you enter a completely **Arab quarter** of town, a sudden and unexpected change from the refined neighbouring streets. Conditions here, as in most of the big city Arab districts, are poor and overcrowded; a straight reflection of French attitudes towards what many still regard as a 'migrant' work force.

Rooms and details

For a good room and a good location in Lille you'll need to pay . Most of the inexpensive **hotels** are gathered around the railway station and are pretty uninviting, especially since the quarter converts to a red-light district in the evenings. One of the best places is *Floréal* (21 rue Ste-Anne; ☎20.06.36.21;

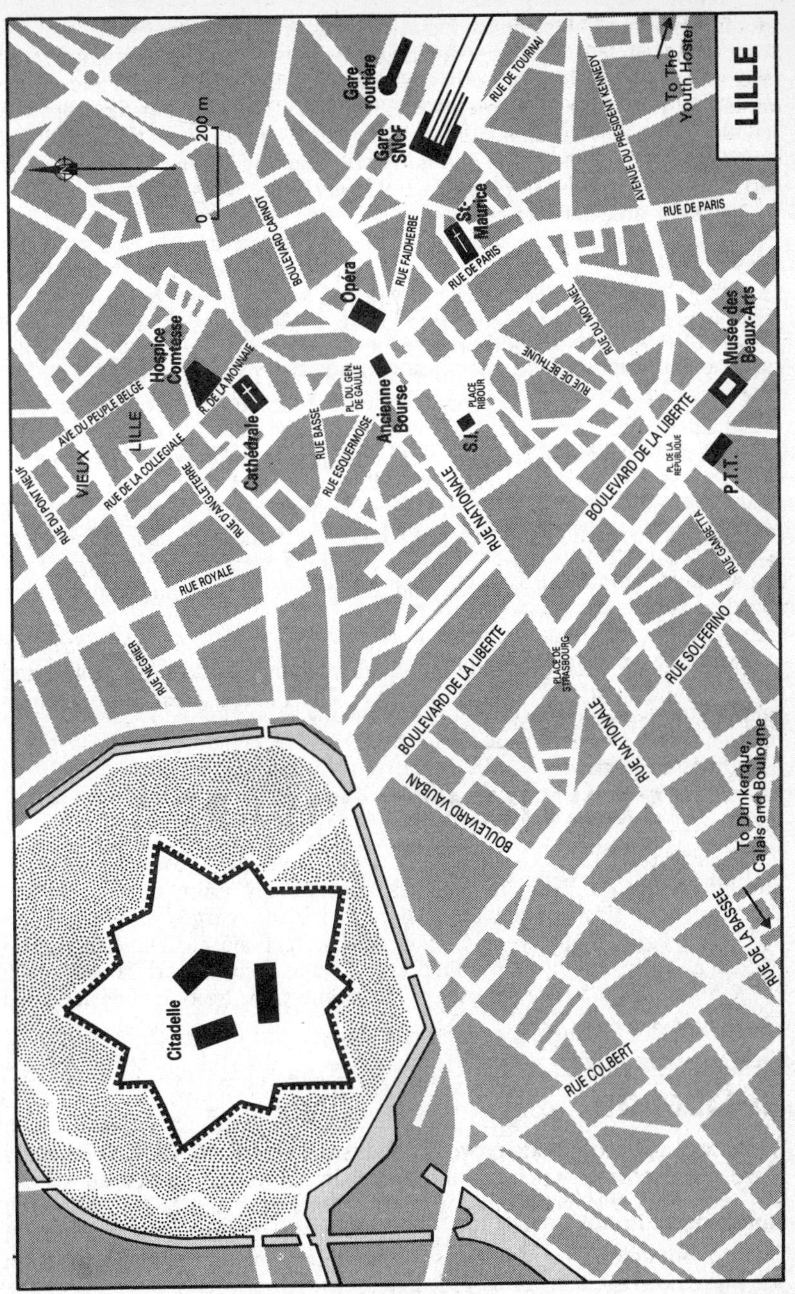
LILLE
To The Youth Hostel
Gare routière
Gare SNCF
0
200 m
RUE DE TOURNAI
AVENUE DU PRESIDENT KENNEDY
RUE DE PARIS
St-Maurice
RUE DE PARIS
BOULEVARD CARNOT
RUE FAIDHERBE
Opéra
Hospice Comtesse
AVE. DU PEUPLE BELGE
R. DE LA MONNAIE
Cathédrale
VIEUX LILLE
RUE DE LA COLLEGIALE
RUE DU PONT NEUF
RUE D'ANGLETERRE
RUE BASSE
PL. DU GEN. DE GAULLE
Ancienne Bourse
RUE ESQUERMOISE
PLACE RIBOUR
S.I.
RUE DE BETHUNE
RUE DU MOLINEL
RUE NATIONALE
BOULEVARD DE LA LIBERTE
Musée des Beaux-Arts
PL. DE LA REPUBLIQUE
P.T.T.
RUE GAMBETTA
RUE ROYALE
RUE NEGRIER
BOULEVARD DE LA LIBERTE
PLACE DE STRASBOURG
RUE NATIONALE
RUE SOLFERINO
BOULEVARD VAUBAN
To Dunkerque, Calais and Boulogne
RUE DE LA BASSEE
Citadelle
RUE COLBERT

one block from the station). Further away *Hôtel Constantin* (5 rue des Fosses; ☎20.54.32.26; in the pedestrianised centre) is a step upmarket in all respects. A good fallback, despite an unpromising approach, is the **youth hostel** at 1 av Julien-Destrée (☎20.52.76.02). This isn't too far from the station: to get there walk southeast along rue Tournal, cross the pedestrian underground walkway below the autoroute and you'll find it across the car park opposite the Foire Commerciale. It looks like a Swiss chalet.

The main area for **brasseries,** in all price categories, is around place Ribour and place Béthune. Rue St-Etienne, too, just across rue Nationale, has a good selection. Among more specific places to recommend, outside this area, there's ambitious and reasonably-priced food at *L'Idéal* (8 rue du Vieux-Faubourg), a nice crêperie at 4 place Louise-de-Bettignies (*La Galatière*) and an all-night brasserie (*Jean's*) on place du Théâtre. On rue Royale, below the **Citadelle**, you'll find a cluster of **ethnic** places: Tunisian, Cambodian and Vietnamese. But Arab restaurants around here tend to be overpriced, at least to outsiders. For **drinking**, Lille students with money hang around *Le Pubstore* at 44 rue de la Halle. A good bit cheaper is *La Petite Cour* (rue du Curé-St-Etienne: almost opposite rue St-Etienne across rue Esquermoise).

Art and music **events** are always worth checking up on, either at the SI (who publish a monthly guide called *Chtimi*) or in the local paper. The major **fair** of the year is the *Grande Braderie,* a vast marketplace filling miles of the city streets over the Whitsun weekend. A big street parade, and festival of the giants, is held at this time.

Getting around Lille you may want to make use of the city's métro, the totally automatic *VAL* (map and info at all stations). **Getting out**, trains and buses complement each other's services. The *Allostop* agency for hitchers shares an office with the SI.

SOUTHEAST PICARDY

As Picardy reaches to the southeast, away from the coast and the main through routes to Paris, it becomes considerably more inviting. In the *département* of Aisne, particularly, where the region merges with neighbouring Champagne, there are some very real attractions in their own right – handsome cathedral towns set amid lush, wooded hills. All are in easy reach of the main routes, with a network of bus connections from Amiens and good train and bus links to Paris.

St-Quentin

A pleasant and prosperous provincial industrial centre, **ST-QUENTIN** could make a convenient stopping point, especially for **youth hostellers**, on the way east from the battlefields or south from Douai and Lille. The **hostel** (☎23.62.68.66) is on bd Jean-Bouin, 2km from the station – bus #3 to rue H Dunant. But unless you have a passion for entomology (see below), the town will make no great demand on your time.

The centre of town is the **place de l'Hôtel de Ville,** reached, from the station, along rue Général-Leclerc, over the Somme, and up rue d'Isle. One side of it is dominated by a particularly good-looking late Gothic **town hall**, whose bells ring protracted, syncopated changes every quarter-hour; the **SI** (☎23.67.05.00) is in the left-hand end of it. From the other side, rue St-André leads to the town's skyscrapingly massive, but outwardly rather uninspiring Gothic **Basilica**.

Of much greater, if specialist interest is the big collection of locally-born **Quentin La Tour's** pastel portraits of the leading politicians, nobles, artists and socialites of eighteenth-century France, in the **Musée Antoine-Lécuyer**, on rue Lécuyer, at the end of rue Raspail, which starts by the Basilica (10am–12pm, 2–5pm; Sat. 10am–noon, 2–6pm and Sun. 2–6pm only; closed Tues.). The other unique collection, apparently one of the largest in the world, is the **butterflies and insects**, more than half a million of them, in the entomological museum. It could be the one thing to put St-Quentin on the map. Ask the SI for its whereabouts.

The SI will also recommend **accommodation**, which should not be a problem. You could try the bargain *Hôtel du Départ* on place du Monument-des-Morts (☎23.62.31.69; with brasserie), and there is a **campsite** by the river.

Laon

Looking out over the plains of Champagne from the spine of a high narrow ridge, girt still by its gated medieval walls, **LAON's** old town, the **Ville Haute**, is one of the gems of the region. Dominating it all, and visible for miles around, are the five great towers of one of the earliest and finest Gothic **cathedrals** in the country. This is the place to head for.

Arriving by train or road, you'll find yourself disappointingly in the lower town, or **Ville Basse**, by contrast shabby and characterless, though cheap **accommodation** may be easier to find. Try the unprepossessing but perfectly decent *Le Vauclair* (☎23.23.02.08), *Hôtel Welcome* (☎23.23.06.11) or *Le Nord-Est* (☎23.23.25.55), all in the short av Carnot straight in front of the **gare SNCF**. The *Vauclair* also has a good, no-frills **restaurant**. The **camping municipal** is on the south side of the Ville Basse, near the *stade municipal*, just off N44.

To get to the upper town you can either walk – a stiff climb up the steps at the end of av Carnot – or, pride and joy of Laon, you can now take the world's first cable-hauled, pilotless, rubber-tired aerial *métro*, the **Poma 2000**. You board next to the railway station and get out by the town hall on place Général-Leclerc; from there a left turn down rue Serurier brings you nose to nose with the magnificent **Notre-Dame**. Built in the second half of the twelfth century, it was a trend-setter in its day, elements of its design being borrowed at Chartres, Reims and Notre-Dame in Paris: the gabled porches, the imposing towers, and the gallery of arcades above the west front. Seen wrapped in thick mist, the towers seem quite otherworldly. What appear to be reckless mountain goats borrowed from some medieval bestiary are apparently craning from their uppermost ledges. In fact, the statues represent horned steers, reputedly carved in memory of the valiant beasts who lugged the cathedral's masonry up from the plains below. **Inside**, the effects are no less dramatic – the mitred bishop with beer can in hand not, I think, part of the original design. The high white nave is lit by the dense ruby, sapphire and emerald tones of the **stained glass,** which at close range reveals that appealing scratchy, smoky quality of medieval glass.

Crowding in the cathedral's lee are a web of quiet, grey eighteenth-century streets. One, rue Pourier, leads to the **Post Office** and on to the thirteenth-century **Porte d'Ardon** looking out over the southern part of the Ville Basse, while a left turn at the Post Office along rue Hermant brings you to the little twelfth-century octagonal **Chapelle des Templiers** – the Knights Templar – set in a secluded garden by the local **museum** (10am–noon, 2am–5pm winter, 2–6pm summer, closed Tues.).

The rest of the Ville Haute, which rambles off to the west of the cathedral into the *Bourg* quarter around Eglise St-Martin, is good to wander in, with universally grand views from the **ramparts**. The **SI**, which, temporarily at least, is in a mobile cabin by the cathedral, will provide information on the surrounding villages and possible walks, and will steer you to any **events** that are on. There's usually something at the *Maison des Arts* on place Aubrey, and a concentration during the *Heures Médiévales* festival in the second and third weeks of September. If you feel like trying *pétanque,* the town also has an impressive **sports centre** (in the Basse Ville) along with a tremendous heated **swimming pool** (8am–1pm and 3–8pm; closed Sun. pm/Mon. am).

For **accommodation in the Ville Haute**, the cheapest solution is the *Maison des Jeunes* (with cafeteria) next to the cathedral, 20 rue du Cloître (☎23.20.27.64). (Whatever you do, don't even try the listed youth hostel, at least without phoning – ☎23.23.06.81; it's 5km out on the Soissons road and so disorganised it doesn't even appear to know it's supposed to be a hostel.) As for **hotels,** *Hôtel de la Paix* (52 rue St-Jean; closed Aug.) is a good bet. *La Bannière de la France* (11 rue Roosevelt; ☎23.23.21.44) has some cheapish rooms, but is generally more expensive, as is *Les Chevaliers* on rue Serurier (no. 3; ☎23.23.43.78).

Going **on from Laon** keep in mind that last trains leave early: to Amiens around 7.30pm, to Paris, via Soissons, shortly after 8pm.

Around Laon

About 30km west of Laon, across the forest of St-Gobain and set in hilly countryside (a worthwhile cycling trip in itself) lie the straggling ruins of one of the greatest castles of the Middle Ages, **COUCY-LE-CHATEAU**. The power of its lords, the *sires de Coucy,* rivalled and often even exceeded that of the king. One of them, Enguerrand VII, who had a finger in all sorts of pies – he had powerful relatives among the English aristocracy – is the hero of Barbara Tuchman's brilliant account of the fourteenth century *A Distant Mirror* (see *Contexts*). Romantically, if uncomfortably, he ended his days in a Turkish jail.

The retreating Germans capped the destruction of World War I by blowing up the keep as they left in 1917. But enough remains, crowning a wooded spur, to be extremely evocative, especially if you know the book. The entire modern village is contained within the vast ring of walls, entered through the original gates, squeezed between powerful, round flanking towers. There is a *romauntic* footpath all around the outside, and the *Hôtel Bellevue* within (☎23.52.70.12), should you be hungry or benighted.

It's hard to get to without a car, though several Laon-Soissons **trains** stop at ANIZY-PINON, which cuts the hitching distance by about half, and there is an infrequent **bus** on to SOISSONS. If you continue into the forest, include **ST-GOBAIN** itself in your itinerary. It's the original eighteenth-century glassworks – the firm is now a vast conglomerate – hiding behind a classical facade, pretending it is nothing as vulgar as a manufacturing plant.

Soissons

Half an hour by train from Laon, **SOISSONS** can lay claim to a long and highly strategic history. Before the Romans arrived it was already a town, its kings controlling parts of Britain as well as Picardy. And in 486 it was here that the Romans suffered one of their most decisive defeats at the hands of Clovis the Frank, making Soissons one of the first real centres of the Frankish kingdom. Napoléon, too, considered it a crucial military base: a judgement perhaps borne out this century in extensive war damage.

The town is a useful and attractive place to stay if you're exploring this part of the country. There are several moderately-priced **hotels**: *de la Gare* (place de la Gare; ☎23.53.31.61; closed Mon. and Aug.), *du Nord* (☎23.53.12.55; take a left out from the station on rue de Belleu: a cheaper option) and *de la Marine* (2 rue St-Quentin in the centre; ☎23.53.31.94). Rooms are sometimes available as well at the two youth *foyers* (women at 8 rue de Bauton; men at 20 rue Malieu). Or again there's a **campsite** – 1km from the *gare* on av du Mail.

Soissons itself has a fine, if little sung, **cathedral**, thirteenth century with majestic glass and vaulting, but the ruined **Abbaye de St-Jean-des-Vignes** is the highlight. The facade of this tremendous Gothic building rises sheer and grand, impervious to the empty space behind it. The monastery, save for remnants of a cloister and refectory, was dismantled in 1804.

Soissons is relatively compact. From the **gare SNCF** (with good services to Laon and Paris) the town is a short walk away, along av de Gaulle. The **halte routière** is near the town hall in av du Mail; infrequent buses leave for Noyon and Compiègne as well as Laon.

Compiègne

COMPIEGNE'S reputation as a tourist centre rests on the presence of a vast royal palace, built at the edge of the forest, so generations of French kings could play at being 'peasants' – Louis XIV's word. Worth a visit certainly, but the town is not the mecca of the hype. It has that bland Sunday afternoon feel of places that have lived too long in the stifling orbit of Establishment power: a yawning mediocrity. Perhaps that is due, above all, to the last tenant, Napoléon III.

But for all that there is a certain fascination about the **interior of the palace**: the lavishness of Marie-Antoinette's rooms, the sheer, vulgar sumptuousness of the First and Second Empire. And Napoléon I moving back in within scarcely a dozen years of the Revolution. The guided tours (9.30–11.15am and 1.30–4.30pm; closed Tues.), however, are expensive and the Museums of Vehicles and the Second Empire included therein are not unmissable. The palace gardens – the **petit parc** – are probably enough. Serene and formal, with a long avenue extending away into the forest, they are open daily from 7.30am to 8pm summer, 7.30am to 6.30pm winter.

In the town the most striking building is, as so often in Picardy, the **Hôtel de Ville** – Louis XII Gothic with a riot of nineteenth-century statuary including, inevitably, Joan of Arc, captured in this town by the Burgundians before being handed over to the English. The **SI** has its offices here and will provide you with a plan of the town, an exhaustive visitors' route conveniently marked on. In good Michelin fashion they suggest half an hour to get around the whole thing which would really mean jogging. It's better to be more selective. If you've got an interest in Greek vases **Musée Vivenel** (rue d'Austerlitz; 9am–noon and 2–6pm summer 2–5pm winter) has one of the best collections around, especially a series illustrating the Panathenaic Games from Italy – a welcome dose of classical restraint and good taste after the excesses of the palace. There is also a section on the fauna and flora of the forest, including a wild boar the size of an armoured car.

Best of all, though, especially if you're here in spring or autumn, is to head out to the **forest** , whose sixty or more square miles of green glades and rides touch the edge of the town. Very ancient, and cut by a succession of hills, streams and valleys, this is grand rambling country – on foot (**GR12** goes through) or by car. The SI can again provide routes. There are a couple of villages right at the heart – VIEUX-MOULIN and ST-JEAN-AUX-BOIS and on farther at **PIERREFONDS** (9am–noon and 1.30–6pm summer; 10am–noon, and 1.30–4.30pm winter last visits 11.15am and 5.15pm; closed Tues.; 3 buses daily) a classic medieval romance castle.

Just east of Compiègne, some 8km into the forest, is a stranger sight: a green and sandy clearing guarded by cypress trees, known as the **Clairière de l'Armistice**. Here, in what was then a railway siding constructed for rail-mounted artillery, World War I was brought to an end on November 11, 1918. A plaque commemorates the deed: 'Here the criminal pride of the German empire was brought low, vanquished by the free peoples whom it had sought to enslave'. To avenge this humiliation, Hitler had the French sign their capitulation in 1940 in the very same railway car, on the same spot. The original car was carted off to Berlin and has since disappeared. Its replacement, housed in a small museum (open 8am–1.30pm and 2–6.30 summer) is similar and the objects within are the originals.

Compiègne can have a lot going on – with more non-mainstream events than its neighbours in Picardy – and there's no shortage either of **brasseries.** There are good prices at *Cafétéria Le Lys* (37 rue Solférino; closed Sun./Mon. and July/Aug.), *Crêperie l'Igloo* (31 rue de Paris) and *A la Dernière Minute* (on place de la Gare, with a few rooms, too). Slightly more expensive are *La Pizza* (10 rue des Boucheries) and an excellent Vietnamese place, *Le*

Phnom Penh (13 rue des Lombards). **Pâtisseries** are also rewarding, with liqueur-laced cream pastries, and there's a big all-day Saturday **market** in the square by place de l'Hôtel-de-Ville. As for **rooms**, the **youth hostel** is 1km from the station at 6 rue Pasteur (☎44.40.26.00; served by bus #3 to rue des Fosses), and there are lowish prices at the *Hôtel Biguet* (off place St-Clement on rue des Bouvines). Other possiblities are *Le Solférino* (4 rue Solférino; ☎44.23.33.18) and the *Lion d'Or* (4 rue du Général-Leclerc; ☎44.23.32.17). There is **camping** along av Royale, into the forest from the palace.

Bus and **railway stations (bike rental)** are adjacent. Coming into town, cross over the wide river Oise and walk up rue Solférino to place de l'Hôtel-de-Ville. Services are both a bit sketchy in this area, but they do complement each other, so you can usually get where you want.

Noyon

Rowing along the Oise on his *Inland Journey* of 1876, Robert Louis Stevenson stopped briefly at Compiègne and at neighbouring **NOYON**, which he described as 'a stack of brown roofs at the best, where I believe people live very respectably in a quiet way'. It *is* a bit like that, though the **Cathedral**, to which Stevenson warmed – 'my favourite kind of mountain scenery' – is impressive, at least in passing. Spacious and a little stark, it blends Romanesque and Gothic with easy success, and is flanked by the ruins of thirteenth-century cloisters and a strange, exquisitely shaped **Renaissance library**. Close by, signs direct you to **Musée Calvin**, ostensibly on the site of the reformer's birthplace. The house, though, is a reconstruction, hoping to raise the town's tourist potential. The respectable citizens of Noyon were never among their local boy's adherents and tore down the original long ago.

Hotels here are pricier than at Soissons. The cheapest, if you're stuck, are *Le Balto* on place de l'Hôtel-de-Ville and, for doubles, *Hôtel-Restaurant Le Grillon* (rue St-Eloi). The local **campsite** is 4km out of town along the Compiègne road, towards the roofless abbey of CHIRY-OURSCAMP. **Buses**, mainly for Compiègne, leave from outside the gare SNCF. **Bikes** are for rent there, too. Big days in Noyon are Saturday morning, when a colourful **market** spills out across place de l'Hôtel-de-Ville, and the first Tuesday of the month, which sees a cattle market taking over virtually the entire town centre.

CHAMPAGNE

Slothrop's head is a balloon, which rises not vertically but horizontally, constantly across the room, whilst staying in one place. Each brain cell has become a bubble: he's been transmuted to black Epernay grapes, cool shadows, noble cuvées.

Thomas Pynchon, *Gravity's Rainbow*

From summer through to the late September harvest – and afterwards when the leaves turn gold and amber – the **Champagne vines**, seen from a distance in evening sunlight, perhaps under a rainbow or two, have a strong affinity with the future of their fruit. From close up they're rather menacing, planted with the tightness and precision of armies, pacing down the slopes.

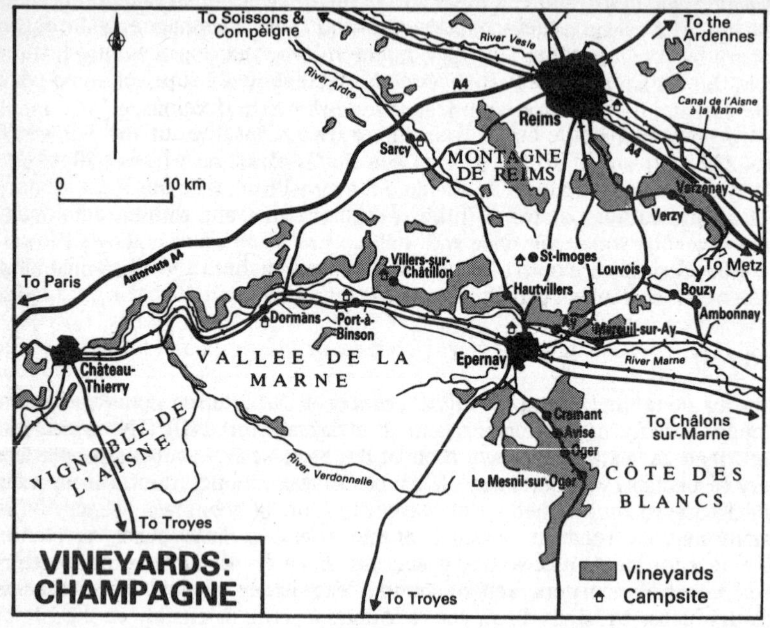

Nowhere else in France, let alone the rest of the world, are you allowed to make champagne. That is to say, you can blend wines from chalk soil vineyards, double ferment them, turn and tilt the bottles bit by bit to clear the sediment, add some vintage liqueur, store the result for years at the requisite constant temperature and produce a bubbling golden liquid, but you cannot call it champagne. An outrageous monopoly to keep the region's sparkling wines in the luxury class, perhaps, but the locals will tell you the difference comes from the squid fossils in the chalk, the lie of the land and its critical climate, the evolution of the grapes, the regulated pruning methods, the legally enforced quantity of juice pressed. All of which is really rather irrelevant – like relating the effect of cocaine to some Bolivian bug secretions in the soil the coca bush grew in. And the comparisons don't end there. In the promotional literature put out by the champagne industry – gloss, full colour, multilingual, extravagant praise – not one mention is made of why people really buy the stuff and love it so much: champagne is a powerful, exhilarating drug, the cocaine of alcohol if you like.

The vineyards are owned either by *maisons* who produce the *grande marque* champagne, or by small cultivators, *vignerons*, who sell the grapes to the *maisons*. The **vignerons** also make their own champagne and will happily offer you a glass and sell you a bottle at half the price of a *grande marque* (ask at any Champagne region SI or the CIVC – see below – for a list of addresses). The difference between the two comes down to capital. The *maisons* can afford to blend grapes from anything up to sixty different vineyards and to tie up their investment while their champagne matures for several years longer than the legal minimum (one year for nonvintage, three years vintage). So the wine they produce is undoubtedly superior – and not a lot cheaper here than in a good discount off-licence in Britain.

If you could visit the head offices of Cartier or Dior, the atmosphere would probably be similar to that in the champagne **maisons** whose palaces are divided between Epernay and Reims. All the visits are free but some require appointments: don't be put off – they'll speak English and with an individually arranged visit you're more likely to get a *dégustation*. Their audiovisuals and (cold) cellar tours are on the whole very informative, and don't just plug brand names. The professional body that regulates the industry is the *Comité Interprofessionel du Vin de Champagne* (*CIVC*, 5 rue Henri-Martin, Epernay). They can provide copious info and a full list of addresses and times for visits, as can the local SI's.

Though there are **campsites** and **places to stay** in the countryside – a youth hostel in VERZY (14 rue du Bassin; ☎26.97.90.10), or a good *gîte d'étape* in AY (c/o M. Brun, 1 Impasse St-Vincent) – the best **bases** are EPERNAY, for total champagne dedication, and REIMS, with an easy train link between them. If you want to work on the **harvest,** contact either the *maisons* direct (see below, or SI lists); the *Agence Nationale pour l'Emploi* (at 11 rue Jean-Moêt, EPERNAY; ☎26.51.01.33, or 57 rue Talleyrand, REIMS; ☎26.88.46.76); or try the Verzy youth hostel (where casual workers are often recruited, or work advertised).

Away from bubbly land, the Champagne region is not the most enthralling. There's charm and interest in the ancient cities of **TROYES**, **CHAUMONT** and **LANGRES** but it's a bit of a backwater culturally. The scenery is not amazing either – with the notable exception of the **ARDENNES** region round the valley of the Meuse. This is frontier land, and feels like it: walks, boat trips or even good old trains and buses along the meanders of the river, can give a sense of exploration.

Epernay

Though a pleasant enough town, the only real reason for coming to **EPERNAY** is to visit the **champagne maisons**, whose tours, should you decide to take them all, could keep you fully occupied for a couple of days. Largest, and probably the most famous, is **Moët et Chandon** (20 av de Champagne), who own Mercier, Ruinart and a variety of other concerns, including, incidentally, Dior perfumes. By its own reckoning, a Moët champagne cork pops somewhere in the world every two seconds. The cellars are adorned with mementoes of Napoléon, a good friend of the original M. Moët, and the vintage is named after the monastic hero of champagne history, Dom Perignon. It's open 9.30am to 12.30pm and 2 to 5.30pm, weekdays in summer, weekends only in winter; the visit ends with a glass.

Of other *maison* visits, the most rewarding are Mercier (up the road at no. 70) and Castellane. **Mercier's** glamour relic is a giant barrel that held

200,000 bottles worth when M. Mercier took it to the Paris Exposition of 1889, with the help of twenty-four oxen – only to be upstaged by the Eiffel Tower. Visits round the cellars here are by electric train. They are fun, and again climax in *dégustation*. Hours are Monday to Saturday 9.30am to noon and 2 to 5.30pm, Sunday till 4.30pm only. **Castellane**, over by the station at 57 rue de Verdun in a kind of neoclassical signal box, keeps similar hours, though only from 15 June to 15 September. If you go on a weekday, you'll see all the processes. The tour is much less gimmicky and chic than at Mercier's or Moët's and the *dégustation* a lot more generous.

Hotels do not come cheap in Epernay. Your best bet would be *de la Cloche* (5 place Thiers; ☎26.55.24.05) and *Le Progrès* (6 rue des Berceaux; ☎26.55.22.72) in the centre and *de la Terrasse* (7 quai de la Marne; ☎26.55.26.05) by the river. The **youth hostel** may have reopened – enquire at the **SI** in place Thiers, a short walk from the gare SNCF, or at the **MJC** (8 rue de Reims; ☎26.55.40.82), which also has accommodation. The **campsite** is 1½km to the north in the Parc des Sports, on the south bank of the Marne (route de Cumières). **Bikes**, if you feel like roaming around the *vignerons*, can be rented at the station or behind the church near the SI, c/o M. Buffet.

Reims

Walking the streets of REIMS in the knowledge that below your feet are millions upon millions of bottles of bubbly can be a depressing or cheering experience, depending on how you look at it. Above ground the action of 1914–18 saw the end of all but 200 buildings. The **Cathedral** was badly battered but survived to redeem a visit to this otherwise rather dreary city.

The cathedral's lure is threefold: kaleidoscopic patterns in the stained glass (Marc Chagall designs in the east chapel, champagne processes glorified in the south transept), a series of unusually lovely tapestries, and a joke, running inexplicably around the restored but still badly mutilated statuary on the west front. The giggling angels responsible for disseminating the prank, be it gossip about the prophets (who aren't amused), some hard-to-fathom glee about the earth, or the effects of a metaphysical champagne substitute, are a rare delight. Not all the figures are the originals – some have been removed to spare them further erosion by the elements; they're now at the former bishops' palace, the **Musée Tau** (10am–noon and 2–6pm summer, 2–5pm winter), next door. These oddities of sculpture, viewable from up close instead of from the distance of spire to ground, suggest an almost fractal understanding of perception on the part of the sculptors – the figures are equally expressive at short range as in their intended monumental positions on the cathedral. There are more grinning angels, friendly-looking gargoyles and a superb Eve, shiftily clutching the monster of sin. And as added narrative, embroidered tapestries of the *Song of Songs* line the walls.

The building also preserves, in a state of somewhat absurd veneration, the paraphernalia of the archreactionary Charles X's coronation in 1824 – right down to the Dauphin's hatbox. In being anointed here in purple pomp, after Revolution, Robespierre, and Napoléon had tried to achieve a new France,

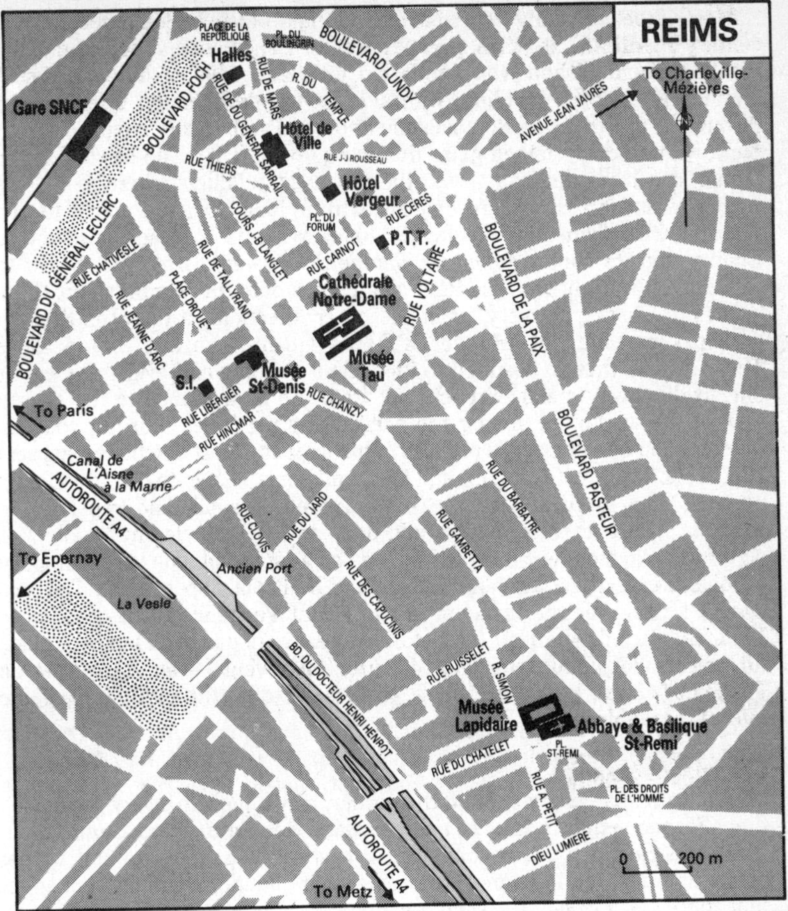

Louis XVI's brother clearly stated his intention to return the country to the *Ancien Régime*. As it happened, his attempt was short-lived, but the tradition he was calling upon dated back to A.D. 496 when Clovis, King of the Franks and of the first identifiable French post-Roman entity, was baptised in Reims. Reims cathedral was where Joan of Arc succeeded in getting the Dauphin crowned as Charles VII in 1429, an act of immense significance when France was more or less wiped off the map by the English and their allies. In all, 26 kings of France were crowned in the Gothic glory of this edifice. Between July and September the upper parts of the cathedral are open to the public so you can look down on its space and contemplate the vice and virtues of those who have made the procession down its nave.

Most of the early kings were buried in Reims' oldest building, the eleventh-century **Basilique St-Rémi**, part of a former Benedictine abbey named after the 22-year-old bishop who baptised Clovis and 3000 of his warriors. An immensely spacious building, with side naves wide enough to drive a bus through, it preserves its Romanesque choir and ambulatory chapels, some of them with modern stained glass that works beautifully. The basilica, on rue Simon, can be visited along with the monastic buildings where more stone sculpture and tapestries are displayed from 10am to noon and 2 to 6pm, Tuesday 2 to 6pm only, weekends 10am to 7pm. To reach it follow rue Chanzy and its continuation rue Gambetta eastwards from just below the cathedral, turn right onto rue Ruisselet and left onto rue Simon (about 1km).

On rue Chanzy not very far in the other direction (at no. 8) is the city's principal museum, the **Musée St-Denis** (10am–noon and 2–6pm, closed Tues.) which, though ill-suited to its ancient building and over diverse, does effectively cover (mainly French) art from the Renaissance to the present. Few of the works are among the particular artists' best, but the collection does contain one of David's replicas of his famous Marat death scene; a set of 27 Corots; two great Gauguin still-lifes; and some sixteenth-century German portraits that fascinate, for the power of observation, and repel for the subjects. There are also models and odds and ends, including an old *tabac* sign from nineteenth-century Reims, and as long as you don't feel compelled to look at everything, an hour or so could be happily spent here. The same cannot be said for the museum in the **Hôtel Vergeur** (10am–6pm; closed Mon.; 36 place du Forum). It's a stuffed treasure house of all kinds of beautiful objects, including two sets of Dürer engravings – an *Apocalypse* and *Passion of Christ*. But to see these you'll have to go through a long guided tour of the whole works.

Champagne tasting

Which, with champagne around the corner, may not seem a very good use of time. For the serious business, head to **place des Droits-des-Hommes** and **place St-Niçaise** (just beyond the Abbaye de St-Denis), around or near which are most of the Reims *maisons*. If you're limiting yourself to one – not that there's any need for such abstinence – the **Maison Veuve Cliquot-Ponsardin** (1 place des Droits-des-Hommes) is as good as they come. In the early growth days of capitalism, the widowed Mme. Cliquot took over her husband's business, and later bequeathed it not to her children but to her business manager – both rather radical breaks with tradition. In keeping with this past, the *maison* is one of the least pompous and its video is the best. The *caves*, with their horror-movie fungi, are old Gallo-Roman quarries. Visits are 9 to 11.15am and 2 to 5pm; weekends 2 to 5pm; November to April by appointment only.

Pommery, too, at 5 place du Général-Gouvard, has excavated Roman quarries for cellars (they claim – in good champagne one-upmanship – to have been the first to do so). And at **Tattingers** (9 place St-Niçaise) there are still more ancient *caves*, with doodles and carvings added by more recent workers, and statues of St-Vincent and St-Jean, patron saints respectively of *vigne-*

rons and cellar hands. Visits are 9 to 11am and 2 to 5pm at both – Pommery from March to November only.

Some practical details

The expressway running along the Marne canal and the horrendous two-lane highway around its centre make Reims feel much bigger than it is. Having crossed two of these boulevards just outside the station and bearing to your right you come straight to **place Drouet d'Erlon**, an avenue with bars, restaurants and most of the city's life, such as it is. At the end, the road veers sharply to the right and becomes rue Dubois, then rue des Capucins. The **SI**, 1 rue Jadart, is just off rue des Capucins after crossing rue Libergier, which goes straight up to the cathedral. Some **hotels** to try in the centre are *Thillois* (17 rue de Thillois; ☎26.40.65.65), *d'Alsace* (6 rue Général Sarrail; ☎26.47.44.08), *de l'Univers* (41 bd Foch; ☎26.88.68.08), *Welcome* (29–31 rue Buirette; ☎26.47.39.39), and *Libergier* (20 rue Libergier; ☎26.47.28.46). The **Camping municipal** is about 1½km further out from the *maisons* on av Hoche (bus Z, 4 stops after place des Droits des Hommes).

Troyes

Away from the vineyards, the **plains of Champagne** are not an inspiring sight. They grow more wheat and cabbages per hectare than any other region of France, yet this seems to bring no great benefit to the villages. Some look so rundown you feel the shutters would fall off if you so much as popped a paper bag – and few are much more than hamlets, with grocery vans doing the rounds once a week and not a *boulangerie* in sight. Neither Chalons, looming in the distance from Reims, nor the smaller towns that follow the Marne to its source, are sufficient inducement to cross the plains. After Reims and Epernay, the single major attraction of the region is the town of Troyes, off to the south.

The mayor of **TROYES** as housing minister under Giscard introduced measures to curb property developments in old town centres, not in order to limit speculation but because high-rise eyesores between historic buildings were not acceptable for the most aesthetic nation in the universe. His policies may have failed elsewhere, but the mayor could head back home and take comfort in the restored and preserved quarters of the ancient capital of Champagne. And there were certainly architectural glories to protect amid the high narrow city streets: an elegant Gothic cathedral, half-a-dozen superb lesser churches, and a couple of fistfuls of Renaissance mansions.

The old town walls, however, are gone – replaced by the usual circuit of boulevards, shaped, as the tourist pamphlets are at pains to point out, like a champagne cork. In fact they're more like a sock – eminently suitable since hosiery and knitted goods have been Troyes's most important industry since the end of the Middle Ages. In 1630 Louis XIII decreed that charitable houses had to be self-supporting, so the orphanage of the **Hôpital de la Trinité** set their charges to work making knitted stockings. Colbert introduced better machines, thanks to his spies in England, by the time the first generation of child labourers were experienced *bonnetiers*. Today the business accounts for more than half the town's employment. Some of the machines and products can be seen in a **Musée de la Bonneterie** in **Hôtel de Mauroy** at 7 rue de la Trinité. The *Hôtel*, beautifully restored, is an example to all 'crafts' museums – visually appealing and unsentimentally respectful of the traditions. It's open daily 9am to noon and 2 to 6pm.

The other outstanding museum in Troyes is the **Musée d'Art Moderne** housed in the old Bishops' Palace in the cathedral square (11am–6pm; closed Tues.). It shows part of an extraordinary private collection of art from Vlaminck and Dérain – and with other works by Degas, Courbet, Gauguin, Matisse (a tapestry and three canvases), Bonnard, Braque, Modigliani, Rodin, Robert Delaunay, and Ernst – none of them second bests.

The **Cathédrale St-Pierre et St-Paul** next door is hardly less gorgeous in colour and light: a pale Gothic nave stroked with reflections from wonderful stained-glass windows. It is open 8.30am to noon and 2 to 5pm. Other Troyes churches also have visiting hours and you're only allowed to peer into the sumptuous **St-Pantaléon**, opposite Hôtel de Vauluisant. In the **Eglise St-Jean**, now surrounded by a pedestrian precinct, Henry V married Catherine of France after being recognized as heir to the French throne in the 1420 Treaty of Troyes, his claim to the title being that he had successfully ravaged the already divided country – no doubt without a single one of the qualities attributed to him by Shakespeare.

Practicalities

Arriving at Troyes you should find yourself a short walk from the centre: the **gares SNCF** and **routière** are side by side, at the end of av Joffre off bd Carnot (one of the circuit). Not all buses use the main station, though, and if you're heading for the sticks it's best to check first with the SI around the corner from the *gares* at 16 bd Carnot. **Places to stay** around the station are plentiful: *de la Gare* (8 bd Carnot; ☎25.78.22.84), *Splendid* (44 bd Carnot; ☎25.73.08.52) and *de Paris* (54 rue Roger-Salengro; ☎25.73.36.32) are inexpensive. Others, more centrally located, include *Le Champenois* (15 rue Pierre-Gauthier; ☎25.76.16.05) and the *Poste* (35, av Emile-Zola; ☎25.73.05.05). Outside of university breaks, there may be rooms in the city's *foyers* – the SI will have details. The **youth hostel** is 6km out of town at 8 rue Jules-Ferry, Rosières (☎25.82.00.65; bus to the Chartreux terminus, then bus #11 to ROSIERES, stop *Liberté*). Opposite the sign saying 'Vielaines', a path leads down to the fourteenth-century priory – a youth hostel with a difference – where you can stay year round as well as camp in the grounds. The municipal **campsite** is 2km northeast of Troyes at PONT STE-MARIE (bus #1).

For **eats** there's considerable variety, with plenty of brasseries around the pedestrian precinct. *Le Provençal* at 18 rue Gen-Saussier with cheap and quick standard fare proves how unnecessary fast food is in France. On the same street there's a very good (though fairly expensive) Lebanese restaurant, *Tou-Feu-Tou-Flam*, which stays open late.

Towards Dijon: Chaumont and Langres

The Seine, Marne, and Aube and several other lesser rivers rise in the Plateau de Langres between Troyes and Dijon. Source hunting is a thankless task – there are no bubbling springs promising bigger things to come, and you're likely to be more conscious of undifferentiated water everywhere, rather than emanating from a particular spot. Main routes from Troyes to the Burgundian capital skirt this area, the eastern one, which the train follows, taking in CHAUMONT and LANGRES, two towns that could briefly delay you en route if you're in no hurry.

Between Troyes and Chaumont (1 hr. by train) there's one stop-off that might appeal for those with their own transport: the **Cristallerie de Champagne** below the church in Bayal, 7.5km southeast of Bar-sur-Aube on D396. The glassworks can be visited if you make an appointment (☎25.92.05.02; every day except Sun., 9.30am–5.30pm) or you can simply visit the shop (Mon.–Sat. 8.30am–12.30pm and 2.15–5.30pm, Sun. 2.30–5.30pm). Most of the exquisite crystal on display is very expensive but they also sell irregular and end-of-season items at greatly reduced prices.

In **CHAUMONT**, apart from honouring the birthplace of the French inventor of gas lamps (there's a statue of him in the garden at the end of rue Verdon), you can admire strange, bulging towers on the houses in which the shapes of wide spiral staircases show through. A twelfth-century keep of the old counts of Champagne's castle is unimpressive – the main building to go look at is the **Basilique St-Jean**. Built with the same unluminous grey stone of most Champagne churches, it has, nevertheless, a wonderful Renaissance addition to the Gothic transept of balconies and turreted stairway. The decoration includes a fifteenth-century polychrome *Mise en Tombeau* with muddy tears but very expressive faces, and an *Arbre de Jesse* of the early sixteenth-century Troyes school in which all the characters are sitting, properly dressed in the style of the day, in the tree. Not the most animated of places, Chaumont should come alive on June 24, 1991, the date of the next seven-yearly Pardon. Otherwise, try and go on Wednesday or Saturday, when a **market** is held on place des Halles.

LANGRES, 35km south of Chaumont, suffered far less war damage and retains its encirclement of gateways, towers and ramparts. Walking this circuit, with views east to the hills of Alsace and southwest across the Plateau de Langres, is the best thing to do if you're just stopping for an hour or so. Wandering inside the walls is not without rewards either – Renaissance houses and narrow streets give the feel of a place time left behind, hidden by the mists of south Champagne. The point people like to make about this town is that were Diderot, the eighteenth-century Enlightenment philosopher who spent the first sixteen years of his life here, to return, he'd have no trouble finding his way around. The **Musée de l'Hôtel du Breuil**, in one of the best of the sixteenth-century mansions (10am–noon and 2–6pm summer, 2–5pm winter; closed Tues.), dedicates a room to Diderot with the encyclopaedias, various other first editions of his works, and one of Van Loos's portraits of the savant. In addition, the museum contains a collection of beautiful ivory pieces, and sets of knives – of the cutlery kind – for which this area was famous for several centuries. Local faience is featured too, though these nicely crafted pieces are well upstaged by the sixteenth-century tiles from Rouen in one of the nave chapels of the **Cathédrale St-Mammès**. This grey stone edifice has not been improved by the eighteenth-century addition of a new facade, but, in addition to the tiles, there's a rather amusing sixteenth-century relief of the *Raising of Lazarus* with the apostles watching, totally blasé, while the locals look like kids at a good horror movie. For entertainment in the form of food and drink, head for the central place Diderot.

The Ardennes

The people of **the Ardennes** have suffered protracted last-ditch battles in war after war down the valley of the Meuse – which, once lost, gave invading armies a clear path to Paris. The hilly terrain and deep forests (that frightened even Julius Caesar's legionnaires) gave some advantage to the last war's Resistance fighters when Ardennes was annexed to Germany, but even peacetime living has never been easy. The main employment over the last century is coming to an end – the slateworks have all closed down and the ironworks are following suit. The only offering from Paris has been a nuclear power station in the loop of the Meuse at Chooz, to which one local comment

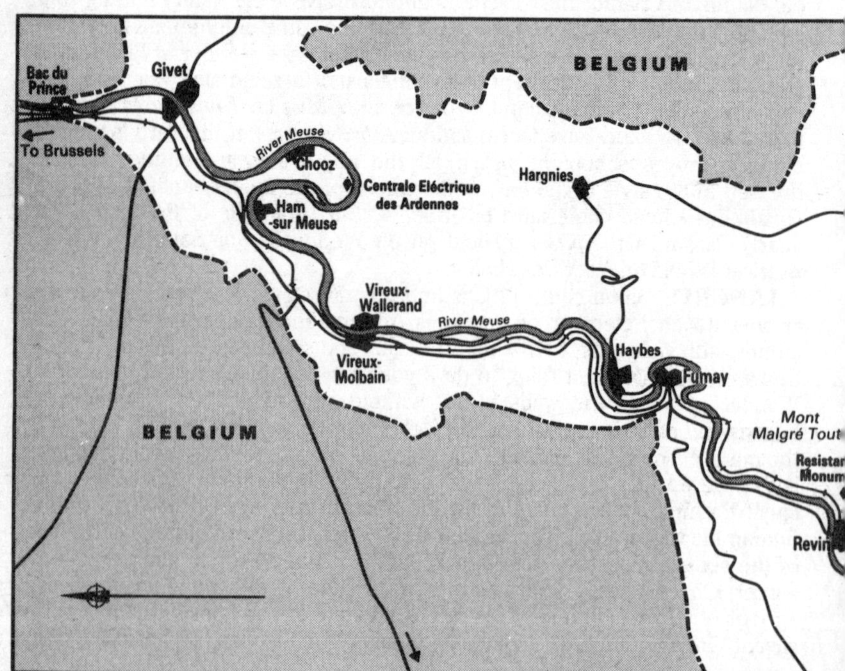

is to be seen etched high on a half-cut cliff of slate just downstream: 'Nuke the Elysée!'

The land is rugged and unarable and tourism is the main growth industry. As yet it's far from developed – but in fact that's its greatest attraction.

Charleville-Mézières

The usual starting point for exploring northwards is **CHARLEVILLE-MEZIERES** which spreads across the meandering Meuse before the valley closes in and the forests take over. It's a somber town that has only one native to honour, the poet Arthur Rimbaud (1854–91). He ran away from Charleville four times, the last time aged seventeen when he joined Verlaine in Paris, fought in the Commune, and, after twice surviving attempts by the elder poet on his life, gave up poetry for good and fled the country (aged nineteen). For a while he journeyed between Europe and the Far East before establishing himself as a successful trader in Ethiopia and Yemen. He only returned to France at the age of 37 for surgery in a Marseille hospital, which killed him. His body was brought back to his home town – probably the last place he would have wanted to be buried. The **Musée Arthur Rimbaud** in the *Vieux Moulin* on quai Arthur-Rimbaud contains a lot of pictures of this strange youth and those he hung out with as well as facsimiles of his writings and related documentation. It's open 9am to noon and 2 to 6pm every day

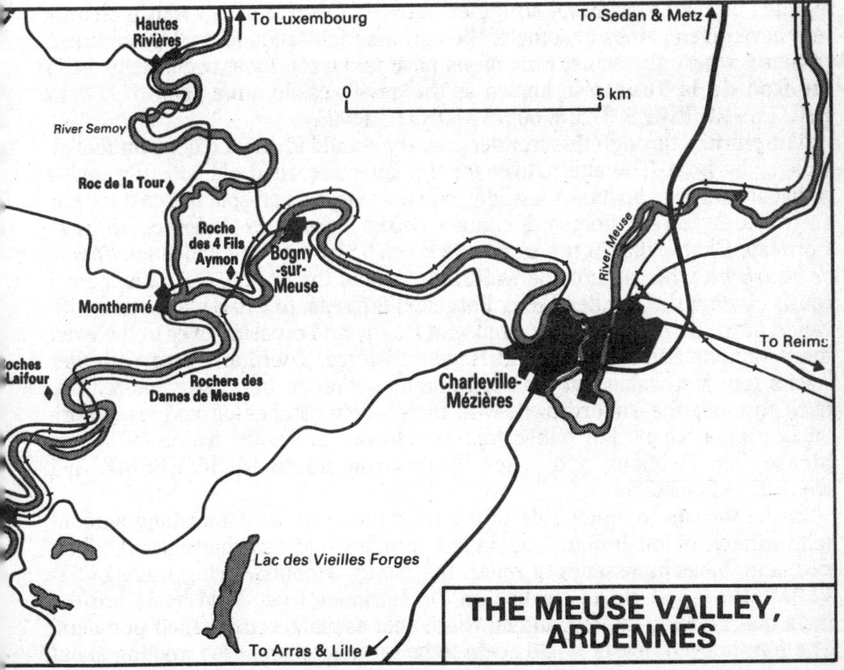

except Monday along with an ethnographical museum of the Ardennes in the same old windmill. A few steps down the quayside is the spot where Rimbaud's *Le Bateau Ivre* was composed.

The central square of Charleville, **place Ducale**, is the result of the seventeenth-century local duke's envy of the contemporary place des Vosges in Paris. The **SI** is just off it to the west at 2 rue Mantoue, and can provide information for the whole region. The **gare SNCF** is a five-minute bus ride away (take any of the buses going to the right as you come out, and ask someone to tell you when you reach place Nevers, just below place Ducale): the **gare routière** is a couple of blocks north of place Nevers, between rues du Daga and Noel. Three fairly central **hotels** to try are *de Paris* (24 av G-Corneau; ☎24.33.34.38), *Europe* (18 rue Porte-Lucas; ☎26.51.80.28) and *Pomme d'Or* (12 rue E. Mercier; ☎26.53.11.44); for the **youth hostel** (3 rue des Tambours; ☎24.57.44.36), take bus #9, direction La Brouette from the station or place Nevers (stop *Auberge de Jeunesse*). The town **campsite** is south of place Ducale, over the river past the Vieux Moulin and to the left.

Northern Ardennes – along the Meuse

George Sand wrote of the Ardennes stretch of the Meuse that 'its high wooded cliffs, strangely solid and compact, are like some inexorable destiny that encloses, pushes and twists the river without permitting it a single whim or any escape'. What all the tourist literature writes about, however, are the legends of macho medieval struggles between Good and Evil whose characters have given names to some of the curious rocks and crests. The grandest of these, where the schist formations have taken the most peculiar turns, is the **Roc de la Tour**, also known as the devil's castle, up a path off D31 to HAUTES RIVIERES, 3½km out of MONTHERME.

The journey through this frontier country should ideally be done on foot or skis, or by **boat**. The alternatives for the latter are good old *bateau-mouches* or live-in pleasure boats – not wildly expensive if you can split the cost four or six ways. If you're interested, contact *Loisirs Accueil en Ardennes*, 18 av G Corneau, Charleville. At the same office you'll also find the Ardennes *Comité de Tourisme*, who can provide **walking maps** of the region. **GR12** is a good route, circling the Lac des Vieux Forges (17km east of Charleville – and with canoe hire), then meeting the Meuse at Bogny and crossing over to the even more sinuous Semoy Valley and Hautes Rivières. There are plenty of other tracks too; just watch out for *chasse* signs – French hunting types tend to hack through the undergrowth with their safety catches off and are notoriously trigger-happy. For public transport from Charleville, **trains** follow the Meuse into Belgium, and a few **buses** run up to MONTHERME and HAUTES RIVIERES.

In the **forests** to either side of the river there are an astonishing amount (and variety) of mushrooms, and in late summer wild strawberries and bilberries, and, for connoisseurs of water, the faintly lemoned spring water of ST-VLADIMIR – just out of Haybes on the Hargnies road. Wild boars are the main quarry being hunted, and nowhere near as dangerous as their pursuers. The four-hooved beasts would seem to be more intelligent too, rooting about near the crosses of the Resistance memorial near REVIN while hunters stalk the forest at a respectful distance.

Campsites through the region are easily found and there are a few cheap **hotels** along the way: *Micass* in BOGNY-SUR-MEUSE (1 place de la République); *Terminus* in REVIN (44 av Danton); *Lion* in FUMAY (7 rue de la Gare); *Jeanne d'Arc* in HAYBES-SUR-MEUSE (32 Grande Rue); *Debette* (place de la Mairie; ☎24.41.64.72); and *Lido* (2 rue du Gen-de-Gaulle; ☎24.42.06.78) in GIVET, the last town before the border.

travel details

Trains

London to Paris through services run direct from the port stations at Calais or Boulogne, stopping en route only at Amiens.

From Calais-Ville 6 daily to Paris (3½ hr.), via Amiens (1¾ hr.); 9 or 10 daily to Boulogne-Ville (½hr.) and Etaple-Le Touquet (1 hr.); frequently to Lille and stops en route (1–1½hr.; some with change at Hazebrouck).

From Boulogne-Ville 8 daily to Paris (3 hr.), via Amiens (1¼ hr.); 9 or 10 to Calais-Ville (½hr.) and Etaple-Le Touquet (20 min.), Montreuil (½ hr.) and Arras (2 hr.).

From Dunkerque 7 or 8 daily to Paris (3 hr. 10 min.), via Arras (1 hr. 20 min.); 3 or 4 daily, not Sun., to Calais-Ville (1 hr.).

From Amiens very frequently to Paris (1¾–2hr.); several daily to Compiègne (1¼hr.) and Laon (2 hr.).

From Beauvais 6 or 7 daily to Paris (1 hr. 10 min.).

From St-Quentin frequent service (7am–midnight) to Paris (1¾hr.), some via Compiègne (50 min.), a few stopping at all stations including Noyon and Tergnier (change for Laon); additional stopping trains run between Compiègne and Tergnier, and 4 daily from Tergnier to Laon (25 min.).

From Laon erratic service (mornings/evenings) to Paris (2 hr. 20 min.), via Soissons (1 hr. 40 min.); more frequent between Laon and Soissons.

From Lille very frequently to Paris (2–2½hr.); **TGV** daily around 7am to Arras (40 min.), Longeau (1 hr. 10 min.) and Lyon (4 hr. 40 min.); regularly to Brussels (2 hr.).

From Reims frequently to Paris (2 hr.); to Epernay (25 min.); to Charleville-Mézières (55 min.).

From Troyes frequently to Paris (1 hr. 30 min.).

Buses

From Dunkerque several daily to Calais.

From Calais 5 daily to Boulogne (1 hr.) and Le Touquet (2 hr.).

From Boulogne 5 daily to Calais (1 hr.) and Le Touquet (1 hr.).

From Amiens buses in all directions, including Beauvais (1¾hr.), St-Quentin (2½hr.) and Albert (40 min.). South Picardy sporadic buses link most of the towns – Compiègne, Beauvais, Soissons, Chantilly, St-Quentin, Noyon – with each other and with Amiens and Paris.

From Reims 3 daily to Troyes (2 hr. 30 min.).

From Epernay 1 daily to Troyes, changing at Romilly (3 hr. 30 min.).

CHAPTER THREE

NORMANDY

To the French, at least, the essence of **Normandy** is its produce. This is the land of butter and cream cuisine, famous cheeses and seafood, cider, and calvados. There is also something unique about a French region where the lack of vineyards is almost a virtue. The province is not short on conventional sights either. There are churches here, at **Rouen, Caen** and **Bayeux,** as impressive as any in the country, and, of course, there's **Mont St-Michel**. It is remarkable how much has survived or been restored since the 1944 Battle of Normandy. You could spend months without exhausting the province's **Romanesque** and **Gothic architecture**, let alone all the châteaux and medieval manorhouses. And there are more recent creations too – **Monet's garden at Giverny** and, at **Le Havre**, a fabulous collection of paintings by **Dufy, Boudin** and other **Impressionists**.

Economically, the richness of the dairy pastures has been Normandy's downfall in recent years. EEC milk quotas have liquidated many small farms and stringent sanitary regulations have forced many small-scale traditional cheese factories to close. Parts of inland Normandy are now among the most depressed of the whole country, and in the forested areas to the south where life has never been easy, things have not improved. But in contrast with the coastal towns people tend to be friendlier with more time for you.

Politically, Normans have a reputation for being mistrustful, closed and conservative, with a love of taking each other to court. The rural population identifies with the age-old *pays* and tends to use the phrase 'gone east' with equal disapproval for a move of 10km away as for one to Alsace. None of this bodes well for the region's minuscule and somewhat bizarre separatist lobby, the **Normandy Nationalist Party**. These neo-Norse people use English as the next best language after Saxon and talk about Sinn Fein and the Duchess of Normandy (the Queen of England) in equally glowing terms. The only sentiment that they share with their compatriots is a hatred of the Parisians, who use the Seine valley for their country homes and the Côte Fleurie for their seaside weekends.

COTE D'ALBATRE

There's no doubt that Normandy's Channel ports, **Dieppe** and **Le Havre**, provide a better introduction to France than their counterparts to the north of Picardy. The white cliffs put on an impressive show, almost justifying the 'Alabaster coast' epithet. There are occasional surprises beyond the wind-swept and tide-chased walks – a wonderful Lutyens fantasy at **Varengeville**, the Hammer Horror Benedictine distillery at **Fécamp**. Otherwise there's still the **Beaux Arts** in **Le Havre,** although beyond this you may want to move

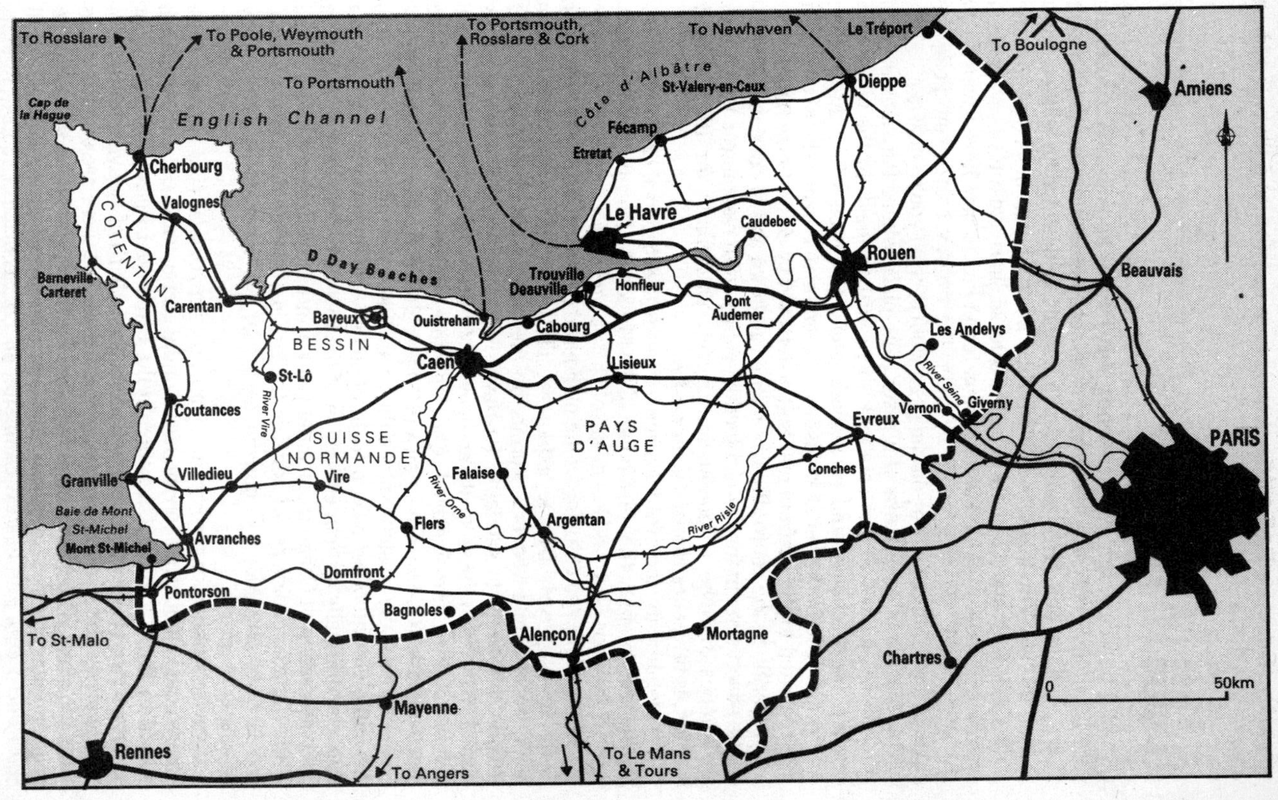
To Rosslare
To Poole, Weymouth & Portsmouth
To Portsmouth, Rosslare & Cork
To Newhaven
Le Tréport
To Boulogne
Amiens
To Portsmouth
Côte d'Albâtre
St-Valery-en-Caux
Dieppe
Cap de la Hague
English Channel
Fécamp
Etretat
Cherbourg
Valognes
Le Havre
Caudebec
Rouen
Beauvais
COTENTIN
Barneville-Carteret
D Day Beaches
Trouville
Deauville
Honfleur
Carentan
Pont Audemer
Bayeux
Ouistreham
Cabourg
Les Andelys
BESSIN
Caen
Lisieux
St-Lô
River Vire
River Seine
Coutances
Vernon
Giverny
PAYS D'AUGE
Evreux
PARIS
SUISSE NORMANDE
Conches
Falaise
Granville
Villedieu
Vire
River Orne
Flers
Argentan
River Risle
Baie de Mont St-Michel
Avranches
Mont St-Michel
Domfront
Pontorson
Bagnoles
To St-Malo
Alençon
Mortagne
Chartres
0
50km
Mayenne
Rennes
To Le Mans & Tours
To Angers

on swiftly. There are livelier, warmer coasts to the west, and it's only a short train or bus ride to Rouen.

Dieppe

Crowded between high cliff headlands, **DIEPPE** is an enjoyably small-scale port. It's industrious, with the commercial docks unloading half the bananas of the Antilles and forty percent of all shellfish destined to slither down French throats. The markets sell fish right off the boats, displayed with the usual Gallic flair, and it's likely to be the sole, scallops and turbots available in profusion at most of the restaurants that tempt you to stay here. Even if you are immediately heading south by train, the railway tracks run along the *quais* of the fishing port, so you can get a whiff of what you're missing.

The **town** was once more of a resort, the place where Parisians used to take the sea air before fast cars took them further afield. In the nineteenth century, the French would promenade along the front while the English colony indulged in the peculiar pastime of swimming – hence the extravagant space allotted to the seafront and 'salt water therapy centre' now hemmed in by car parks. In the centre the streets are run down and in continual shadow – little advertisement for the eighteenth-century town planning to which they are supposed to be a monument. Livelier, particularly for its **Saturday market**, is the pedestrianised **Grande-Rue**.

For monuments, the obvious place to start is the medieval **castle** overlooking the seafront from the west, home of the **Musée de Dieppe** and two showpiece collections. The first is a group of *Dieppe carved ivories* – virtuoso pieces of sawing, filing and chipping of the plundered riches of Africa, shipped back to the town by early Dieppe 'explorers'. The other permanent exhibition is made up of a hundred or so prints by the co-founder of cubism, *Georges Braque*, who went to school in Le Havre, spent summers in Dieppe and is buried just west of the town at Varangeville-sur-Mer (see below). Only a small number of prints are displayed at any one time but in theory you can see the rest if you ask. (Open 10am–noon and 2–6pm; closed Tues. out of season).

An exit from the western side of the castle takes you out on to a path up to the **cliffs**. On the other side, a flight of steps leads down to the **square du Canada**, originally a commemoration of the role played by Dieppe sailors in the colonisation of Canada. Since the last war it has dedicated a small plaque to the Canadian soldiers who died in the suicidal 1942 raid on Dieppe, justified later by the Allied Command as a trial run for the 1944 Normandy landings.

If you're looking for a **room** in Dieppe, try *Les Arcades* (1–3 Arcades de la Bourse, quai Duquesne – on the curve of the port towards the ferry terminal; ☎35.84.14.12), *Au Grand Duquesne* (in the centre at 15 place St-Jacques) or *La Providence* (157 av de la République in the suburb of Neuville to the west of the ports). The *Arcades* has a good restaurant and there are several others along the *quais*. The **youth hostel** (☎35.84.85.73) is 2km to the south, on rue Louis Fromager; take the *Janval* bus from the gare routière and get off at *Ecole Jules Ferry*. The nearest **campsite**, *du Pré St-Nicolas* (☎35.84.11.39), is

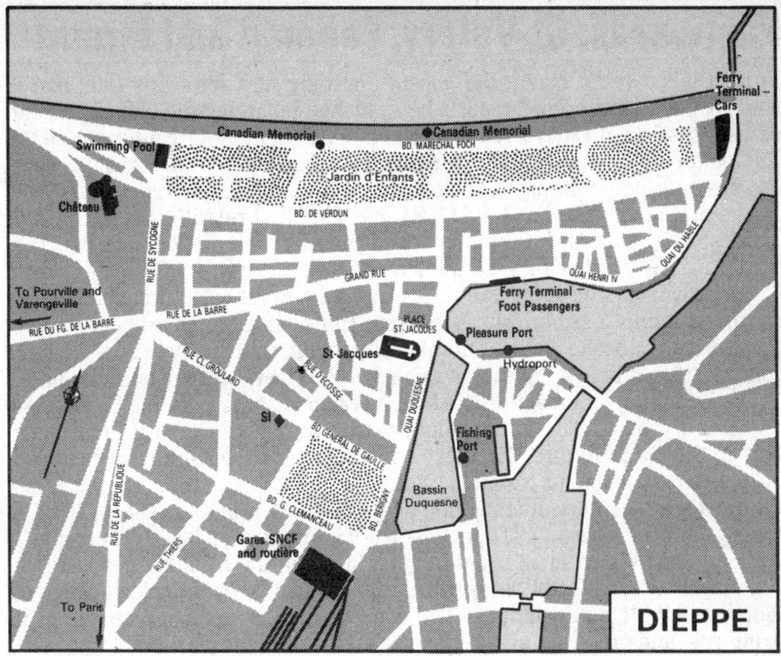

3km down the coastal road to Pourville. The **gares SNCF** and **routière** are about 150m south of the ferry terminal; the **SI**, in the modern Hôtel de Ville on bd Général de Gaulle, west from the fishing port, can supply maps and plans for the region.

Varengeville: Lutyens and Braque

Braque's grave is in the clifftop church of **VARENGEVILLE** (a 25-min. bus ride, #311, #312; afternoons only). The tombstone is monstrous and the view along the cliffs more appealing than the artist's stained-glass windows. But the main point of the excursion – something un-French in almost every respect – is the **Bois des Moutiers**, one of the architect Edwin Lutyens's first commissions. Back along the road from the church, you can visit its gardens from March 15 to November 15 (9am–noon and 2–7pm; closed Sat. am) and the house in July and August (closed Sun. am and Tues.). Admission is expensive but you'll be guided with genuine enthusiasm around the quirks and games as well as highly innovative engineering of the house. The colours of the Burne-Jones tapestry hanging in the stairwell were copied from Renaissance cloth in William Morris's studio; the rhododendrons were chosen from similar samples. Paths lead through vistas based on paintings by Poussin, Lorrain and other eighteenth-century artists; no modern roses are allowed to update the colours.

Eastwards: St-Valéry, Fécamp and Etretat

From Dieppe to Le Havre the coast is eroding at a ferocious rate, and it's conceivable that the small resorts here, tucked in among the cliffs at the ends of a succession of valleys, may not last more than another century or so. For the moment, however, they are quietly prospering, with casinos, sports centres and yacht marinas ensuring a modest but steady summer trade.

The first of any size is **ST-VALERY-EN-CAUX**, a rebuilt town which is the clearest reminder of the fighting – and massive destruction – of the Allied retreat of 1940. There's a monument on the western cliffs to the French cavalry division who faced Rommel's tanks on horseback, brandishing their sabres with hopeless heroism. Beside the ruins of a German artillery emplacement on the opposite cliffs is another monument, this time to a Scots division, rounded up while fighting their way back to Le Havre and the boats home.

Further along you reach **FECAMP**, a serious fishing port like Dieppe, with a seafront promenade. A compelling reason to pay a brief visit here is for a look at the **Benedictine Distillery** on rue Alexandre-le-Grand, in the narrow strip of streets running parallel to the ports towards the town centre. A taste for nineteenth-century operatic horror sets is more important than a liking for the liqueur in question. Tours lasting 45 minutes (9.30–11.30am and 2–5.30pm) start with a small **museum**, set firmly in the Middle Ages beneath a nightmarish mock-Gothic roof with props of manuscripts, locks, testaments, lamps and religious paintings. The first whiff of Benedictine comes in the grim rust-and-grey-coloured *Salle des Abbés*, and at this point the script abruptly changes – from mysterious monks to PR for an exclusive product. The boxes of ingredients are a rare treat for the nose (take it easy with the myrrh) and there's further theatricality in the old distillery where boxes of herbs are thrown with gusto into copper vats and alembics. (Commercial production has long since moved to an out-of-town site). Finally you are offered a *dégustation* in their bar across the road – neat, in a cocktail, or on crêpes; make sure you hold on to your ticket to qualify.

If your aesthetic sensibilities need soothing after this, the soaring medieval nave and Renaissance carved screens of the **Eglise de la Trinité,** up in the town centre, may do the trick. Alternatively, you could feast your eyes on a Renaissance chancel on a grass floor with the open sky above and an intact Gothic lady chapel: the remains of the **Abbaye de Valmont**, 11km east from the coast (bus #261, #311 from Fécamp). This is open 10am to noon and 2 to 6pm, except Wednesday (and, from Oct.–April, Sun.).

The **hotels** in Fécamp tend to be set back away from the sea on odd side streets. It's a popular place; you need to reserve a room at the *Hôtel de l'Univers* (5 place St-Etienne; ☎35.28.05.88) or the *Angleterre* (93 rue de la Plage; ☎35.28.01.60). The **youth hostel** (☎35.29.75.79; for reservations ☎35.29.36.35) is open from July to September 15; it's east of the port, along the route du Commandant Roquigny, on the Côte de la Vierge. A superb **campsite**, the *Camping de Renneville* (☎35.28.20.97), is a short walk away on the western cliffs. The **SI** is just behind the seafront where it meets the yacht harbour; the **gares SNCF** and **routière** between the port and the town centre on av Gambetta.

On to Etretat

The cliff formations of **ETRETAT** are splashed across most of the *département's* tourist brochures. Without the prior publicity, these could be quite thrilling as you first catch sight of the arches and needles from the beach or clifftop. You'll need transport though – Etretat is not on the bus and train routes – and to explore them you've got just three hours either side of low tide. The standard high vantage point on the eastern side has a lifesized aeroplane in concrete relief and an elongated arch inclining to the sky, a moving commemoration of two pilots last seen over Etretat attempting a Paris–New York flight in 1927.

Well sheltered from the elements, the town itself is a pleasant enough little resort and has a nice idiosyncrasy in the form of beached boats converted with thatched roofs into sheds, or these days, bars. If you want to stay, there's not much **accommodation** available. Try along av George V – either the *Windsor* (☎35.27.07.27) at no. 9, or *de la Poste* (☎35.27.01.34) at no. 6; or try the municipal **campsite** (☎35.27.07.67), 1km out on rue Guy-de-Maupassant. There is an **SI** on the central place de la Mairie.

Le Havre

Most ferry passengers move straight out from the port of **LE HAVRE** and most guidebooks dismiss the city as dismal, disastrous and gargantuan. While it is not the most picturesque or tranquil place in Normandy, it is not the soulless urban sprawl the warnings suggest. Conclusively destroyed during the last war, it was rebuilt along new lines from the plans of a single architect, Auguste Perret, between 1944 and 1964. As such, it is a rather rare entity – and much better than newer major developments around Paris. There is exciting use of public space, sensitive integration of the surviving churches and monuments, and few high-rises. Le Havre's city council has been Communist-led for decades and its two twin towns are Leningrad and Southampton. Thanks to the politics of the town hall, the museums are free or have a minimal token charge.

The port, the second largest in France after Marseille, takes up half the Seine estuary, extending far further than the town. Av Foch, the central street, runs east–west, looking on to the sea between the beach and the yacht harbour at one end, and at the other the **SI**, Hôtel de Ville and a kiosk where you can get a bus map. The **gares SNCF** and **routière** are 1km further east along rue Lecesne and the transport system includes a funicular and giant escalator to get up north. If you're looking for **accommodation**, try *Jeanne d'Arc* (91 rue Emile-Zola; ☎35.41.26.83), *Séjour Fleuri* (71 rue Emile-Zola; ☎35.41.33.81), *St-Michel* (36 rue d'Ingouville; ☎35.43.55.24), or the municipal **hostel** at 27 rue de la Mailleraye (contact via the SI, ☎33.21.22.88). The **campsite** is in the Fôret de Montgeon (bus #12 from Hôtel de Ville, direction Rouelles, stop *Hallates* and a walk through the woods).

The finest buildings in Le Havre surround the **Bassin de Commerce** with tinted glass at the eastern end, a slender white footbridge and, at the other

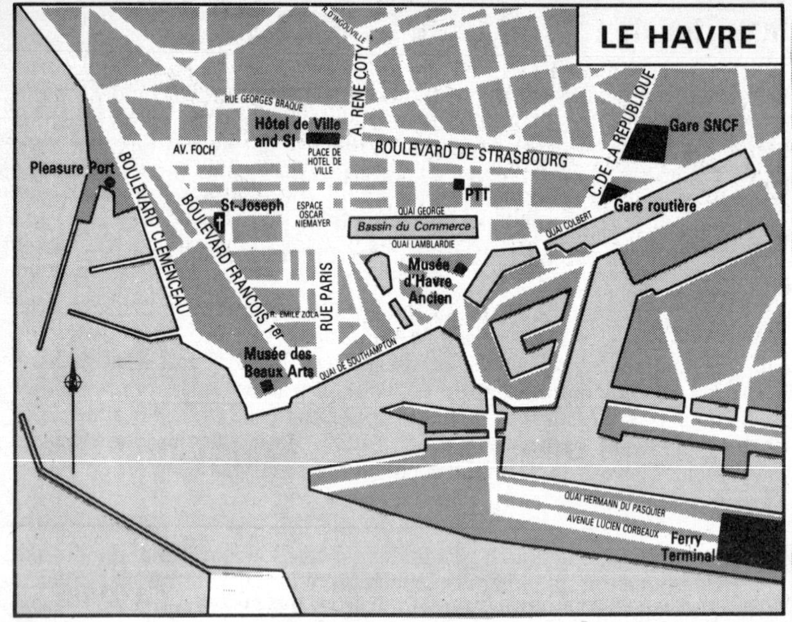

end, the equally gleaming truncated cooling tower of the **Espace Oscar Niemeyer.** Framed by the pier and St. Joseph's lighthouse-like belfry in the distance, the tower holds a theatre and cinema and has a steadfast socialist sentiment inscribed by the fountain at its base. A plaza for street performance and strolling slopes down to bars and shops as well as exhibition and concert space (what's on details from SI). This is all part of the town's multi-million pound cultural centre whose director is the exiled Chilean film director Raul Ruiz.

On bd J.-F.-Kennedy, overlooking the port entrance, is the **Beaux Arts**, one of the best designed art galleries in the country and with one of the loveliest collections of its nineteenth- and twentieth-century paintings – fifty canvases by Eugène Boudin and works by Corot, Courbet, Pissarro, Sisley, Gaugin, Léger, Braque and Lurçat. Raoul Dufy, a native of Le Havre (1877–1953), has a whole room for his drawings and paintings in which the windows at the base of the walls reveal waterlilies in a shallow moat outside. Waterlilies in oil appear along with Westminster and a sunrise snowscape by Monet. Even if you're determined to rush off, find time for a visit; it's open 10am–noon and 2–6pm, closed Tuesday. With more time to spare, you might like to see what the **old Havre** looked like in the pre-war days when Sartre wrote *La Nausée* here: there are pictures and mementoes gathered from the rubble in one of the very few buildings that escaped, the **Musée de l'Ancien Havre** at 1 rue Jérome-Bellarmato, south of the Bassin du Commerce (open 10–noon and 2–6pm, closed Mon. and Tues.).

THE SEINE VALLEY

The days of the **Seine's** tidal bore and treacherous sandbanks are over. Heavy ships serenely make their way up the looping river to the provincial capital of **Rouen**, the largest city of Normandy and the only one meriting a long stay. Further upstream, Monet's wonderful house and garden at **Giverny** and the English frontier stronghold, the **Château Gaillard** at **Les Andelys**, also justify taking a slow route into Paris. The immense **Tancarville** suspension bridge spans the opening of the estuary just beyond Le Havre, while at Caudebec the yellow stays of the Pont de Brotonne produce magical optical effects on your way across; for unhurried river crossings there are *bacs* (ferries: cheaper for cars than the bridge tolls). The Le Havre–Rouen buses (#191, #192) follow the north (right) bank, the best in terms of scenery.

Towards Rouen: Jumièges Abbey and the Brotonne Park

Le Havre and Rouen are such vast industrial conglomerates that the promise of the countryside around them isn't obvious. In fact, it's a surprisingly beautiful area, designated the **Parc Naturel Régional de Brotonne** with imaginative projects run by local people to preserve the environment and traditional activities. Its highlight, to outsiders, is the majestic **Abbaye de Jumièges** but if you have time there are less crowded attractions south of the river. **Details** on all aspects of the park can be obtained from the very helpful *Maison du Parc* (2 rond-point-Marbec, LE TRAIT). After the oil refineries of Le Havre, the *parc* comes as quite a shock. On the south bank Camargue horses and Scottish highland cattle graze in the Vernier marshes and upstream the scenery on both sides of the Seine is soft and lush like a sleeping, giant green cat. The first town of any size on the right bank is **CAUDEBEC-EN-CAUX**, with most traces of its long past destroyed by fire in the last war. The damage – and previous local history – is recorded in the thirteenth-century **Maison des Templiers**, one of the few spared buildings, now a museum. The town has one cheap **hotel**, the *Cheval Blanc* (☎35.96.21.66), (and even there the food is pricey), and a **campsite**, *Barre Y Va* (☎35.96.11.12). You can **hire bicycles** from M. Jaubert on rue de la Vicomte. A **market** has been held every Saturday since 1390 in the main square.

Upstream, just beyond the Pont de Brotonne, is the medieval **L'ABBAYE DE ST-WANDRILLE**, founded, so legend has it, by a seventh-century count who, with his wife, renounced all earthly pleasures on the day of their wedding. The abbey's buildings are an attractive if curious collection: part ruin, part restoration and, in the case of the main buildings, part transplant – a fifteenth-century barn brought in here just a few years ago from another Normandy village miles away. Monks will show you around every afternoon at 3 and 4pm, and at 11.30am on Sunday.

In the next loop of the Seine, 12km upstream, squats the more famous **Abbaye de Jumièges**, a haunting ruin whose main outline dates from the eleventh century; William the Conqueror himself attended its consecration in 1067. The towers, nearly 60m high, still stand. So too does part of the nave, roofless now and even more impressive because of it. (Unescorted visits from 9–noon and 2–6pm in summer, 10–noon and 2–4pm in winter). If you get off the Le Havre–Rouen bus at YAINVILLE or DUCLAIR you can pick up a connection (or hitch) down to Jumièges.

On the opposite side of the river near **HAUVILLE** (off the road to GUERANDE), you can look around a **windmill**, one of six owned by the Jumièges monks, who farmed and forested the entire area in the Middle Ages. Its outline – based on contemporary castle towers – looks just like a kid's drawing. Restored by the *parc*, it is open at weekends, from 2.30 to 7pm. If you have time, move on from here to the neighbouring village of **LA HAYE-DE-ROUTOT**. The churchyard is a novelty – a pair of millennia-old yew trees shaped into a chapel and grotto – but the feature for which the village is best known (at least in Normandy) is its annual **Fête de Ste-Claire**, held on her feast day, July 16. The centrepiece of this is a towering, conical bonfire, topped by a cross, which must survive to ensure a good year. The smouldering logs are taken home as protection against lightning. Should you miss the big day, a video recording of the events is shown in a reconstructed *boulangerie* (July–Aug. 2.30–6.30pm daily except Tues.; April–June and Sept.–Oct. weekends only).

For **accommodation** in the *Parc* south of the river, there's a *gîte d'étape* at ROUTOT (c/o M Verhaeghe, ☎32.57.31.09) and a few rooms available at the *Maison des Métiers* (☎32.57.40.41) in BOURNEVILLE which is also a beautifully presented **museum** of traditional farming and building techniques (open April–Dec. 2–7pm, closed Mon.). The most practical places to stay are on the north bank, either at Caudebec or in **DUCLAIR** with a couple of cheap hotels, *L'Aigle d'Or* (75 rue Jules Ferry; ☎35.37.50.38) and *Le Tartarin* (125 place du Général-de-Gaulle; ☎35.37.50.38).

Rouen

You could spend a day wandering around **ROUEN** without realising that the Seine runs through the city. The war destroyed all the bridges, the area between the cathedral and the *quais*, and much of the left bank industrial quarter. After repairing the damage, an enormous amount of money was spent on restoration to turn the centre into an idealised medieval city – it looks authentic and probably isn't in the slightest. Historians consulted on the project suggested that the houses would have been painted in bright, clashing colours – an idea not considered sufficiently evocative or picturesque by the city authorities. Still, the churches are extremely impressive and the whole place faintly seductive.

Outside the renovated quarters, things are rather different. The city spreads deep into the loop of the Seine to the south, and increasingly into the hills to the north, while the riverbank itself is lined with a fume-filled motor-

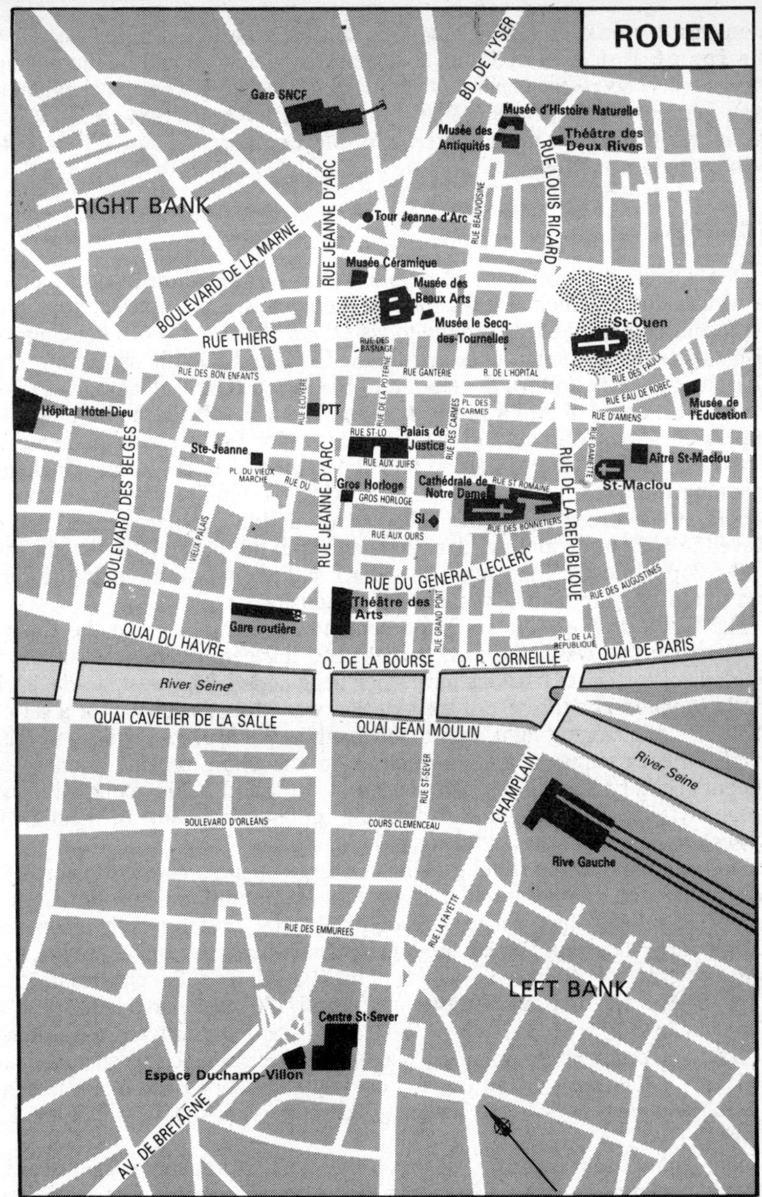

way. As the nearest point that large container ships can get to Paris, the port remains the country's fourth largest – albeit in decline. Rouen's docks and industries stretch endlessly away to the south. Many workers live outside the municipal boundaries, which might explain why the left is never elected to the Town Hall. However, a tour of Rouen's politicians would be interesting: the mayor is secretary-general of the UDF (the Giscard centrist conglomerate); Laurent Fabius, the Socialist Prime Minister from 1984 to 1986, is a *député* for the area; and the Director of the Communist daily, *L'Humanité*, belongs to Rouen PCF.

The town

Rouen spends a bigger slice of its budget on **monuments** than any other provincial town, which annoys many a Rouennais. As a tourist, your one complaint may be the lack of time to visit them all. The obvious buildings to visit as you stroll around the centre are the Cathedral (Gothic perfection), the church of St-Ouen (ditto), the church of St-Maclou (Gothic-Flamboyant near perfection), **Joan of Arc's modern memorial church** on the burning site at place du Vieux-Marché, and the Palais de Justice (Renaissance perfection). Between place du Vieux-Marché and the cathedral is the **Gros Horloge**, spanning the street named after it, and giving the time of day to the townspeople. It was originally on the belfry alongside but popular demand had it moved in 1529 to be more visible. You can climb the belfry (10am–noon and 2.30–5.30pm; closed Tues. and Oct.–Mar.) and see the surrounding towers and spires arraying themselves in startling density.

The **Cathédrale-de-Notre-Dame** somehow remains at heart the Gothic masterpiece that was built in the twelfth and thirteenth centuries, although all kinds of vertical extensions have since been added. The west facade, intricately sculpted like the rest of the exterior, was Monet's subject for a series of studies of changing light, which now hang in the Musée d'Orsay in Paris. Inside, the carvings of the misericords in the choir provide a study of fifteenth-century life – in secular scenes of work and habits along with the usual mythical beasts. Unfortunately the ambulatory, with its recumbent English royals, is only accessible on guided tours.

St-Ouen, next to the Hôtel de Ville in a large open square to the north, is larger than the cathedral and has far less decoration, so that the Gothic proportions have that instant impact rivalled by nothing built since the Middle Ages. The world which produced it, and nearer the end of the era, the light and grace of St-Maclou, was one of mass death from the plague; and the **Aître St-Maclou** (entrance between 184 and 186 rue Martainville) was a cemetery for the victims. It's now the tranquil garden courtyard of the Fine Arts school, but if you examine the one open lower storey of the surrounding buildings you'll discover the original deathly decorations and a mummified cat. In the square outside are several good antique bookshops, and a few art shops.

Then come the **museums**. Of these, the most interesting and unusual is the ironmongery museum, **Musée Le Secq des Tourelles**. Housed in the old and barely altered church of St-Laurent on rue Jacques-Villon, it is a brilliant collection of wrought iron objects of all dates and descriptions. The museum is right behind the **Beaux Arts**, and admission is by the same ticket, as is the Gros-Horloge belfry. The Beaux Arts itself is not very enthralling but it does include works by the Rouennais Géricault, Sisley and Monet in the Impressionist section, Dadaist pictures by Marcel Duchamp, and a collection of portraits by Jacques Emile Blanche (1861–1942) of his contemporaries – Cocteau, Stravinsky, Gide, Valéry, Mallarmé and others. Both museums are open 10am to noon and 2 to 6pm, closed all day Tuesday and Wednesday morning.

You can pick up a full list of museum times and addresses from the **SI,** 25 place de la Cathédrale. Others include **Antiquités**, way up north on rue Beauvoisine, which is particularly good on tapestries, and **Ceramics**, a speciality of Rouen, very near the Beaux Arts. On the corner of rue Eau-de-Robec and rue Ruissel there is, too, one of a new breed of intellectually self-conscious French museums – the **Musée de l'Education** (Tues.–Sat. 1–6pm), which covers the upbringing, education and general influences on children. If you're interested in conservative French ideology it's illuminating. If not, **rue Eau-de-Robec** is a good example of Rouen restoration: a pure, shallow stream makes aesthetic appearances between paved crossings to the front doors of neatly quaint houses, now inhabited by successful antique dealers. In an earlier age these were described by one of Flaubert's characters as a 'degraded little Venice'.

To understand more of Flaubert himself, and for an insight into the Rouen that he knew, the place to look is not the *Pavillon Flaubert* at Croisset-Canteleu, which like the other two literary museums – the two homes of Pierre Corneille – only prove the pointlessness of the genre. It is, rather, the **Musée Flaubert et de l'Histoire de la Médicine**, at the Hôtel Dieu Hospital. This stands on the corner of rue de Lecat and rue du Contrat-Social, walkable from the centre (or bus #2a) and it's infinitely more relevant to Flaubert's writings than the manuscript copies and personal mementoes in the Pavillon museum. Flaubert's father was chief surgeon and director of the medical school, living with his family in this house within the hospital. Even during the cholera epidemic when Gustave was 11, he and his sister were not stopped from running around the wards or climbing along the garden wall to look into the autopsy lab. Some of the medical exhibits would certainly have been familiar objects to him – a phrenology model, a childbirth demonstrator like a giant ragdoll, and the sets of encyclopedias. Hours are 10am to noon and 2 to 6pm; closed Monday; ring several times.

Practicalities

A five-minute bus ride (#12, #15, #20) from the **gare SNCF** will bring you to the centre. You can get off at the 3rd, 4th or 5th stop, the last being the *Théâtre des Arts* backing on to the river, one block east from the **gare routière**.

Cheap and central **hotel accommodation** is no problem: try the *Régent* (128 rue Beauvoisine; ☎35.71.86.03), *des Flandres* (5 rue des Bons Enfants; ☎35.71.56.88), *Saint Ouen* (43 rue des Faulx; ☎35.71.46.44) or *Moderne* (59 rue St-Nicolas; ☎35.71.14.41). The **youth hostel**, south of the river at 17 rue

Diderot (☎35.72.06.45) is ten minutes from the Théâtre des Arts on the bus lines to Grand Quevilly: stop *Diderot* on #5 or *Barcelone* on #6. The **campsites** are all out of town, the two closest being *L'Aubette* (☎35.56.78.70) at 23 rue du Vert Buisson, St-Léger-du-Bourg-St-Denis (bus #180 from gare routière, stop *Carville*); and *Le Cheval Rouge* (☎35.60.31.31) at Isneauville (buses #15, #150, #151 from gare routière, stop *Cheval Rouge*).

Rouen has a good **food** reputation, with its most famous dish being duckling (*caneton*). Like all specialities it doesn't come cheap but you won't be too ripped off trying it at *Pascaline* (5 rue de la Poterne). For good basic meals, the south side of place du Vieux-Marché and the north side of St-Maclou church are both lined with competing good-quality restaurants. Some specific recommendations are: the traditional *Le Vieux Carné* at 34 rue Ganterie; *Le Green Park*, 9 rue Grand-Pont, for a good cheap midday meal; for functional eating there's *Matussière* at 97 rue Ecuyère; or, for the best deal in town, *Cave Royale* at 48 rue Damiette near St-Maclou, which serves mountains of couscous and paella.

For wicked snacks, **pâtisserie** shops on almost every street make this the capital of the cream and butter province. A daily **food market** graces place du Vieux-Marché and the maze of streets north up to rue Thiers is full of Tunisian **take-aways, crêperies** and so forth, as well as loads of good **bars**.

For what it's worth, Rouen is said to be the capital of French **rock**. The place to check out bands is *Exo 7* (militaristic pun) on place Chartreux south of the river (buses #5, #170, #120) with live gigs at no. 44 and disco Friday and Saturday nights at no. 13. Closer to the river, tucked into the **St-Sever complex** the *Espace Duchamp Villon* is the place for (fairly) **alternative events** – theatre, films, dance and jazz (programmes from SI or newspapers). And for modern **visual arts**, there's the *Centre d'Art Contemporain* on the right bank (11 place du Général-de-Gaulle).

Most of the classier **shops** in Rouen are in the pedestrian streets close to, and slightly north of, the cathedral. But if you're looking for giant supermarkets and cheap clothes, St-Sever is the place to go. There's an outdoor **antiques and bric-à-brac market** nearby on place des Emmurées. Back to the north of the river, the *Dépôt Vente du Rouen* on rue des Augustins is a **junk shop** where you might find something good. Two shops with large stocks of English **books** are *L'Armitière* at 5 rue des Basnage, and *FNAC* on rue Ecuyère. If you're planning to stay for more than a week or so, the handbook sold in all the newsagents, *Le P'tit Normand*, is very helpful with addresses.

Upstream: Château Gaillard and Monet's Gardens

Upstream from Rouen, high cliffs on the north bank imitate the coast while looking down on waves of green and scattered islands in the Seine. But the most dramatic sight, high above **LES ANDELYS**, is Richard the Lionheart's **Château Gaillard**. Constructed in a position of indubitable power, it looked down over any movement on the river at the frontier of the English king's domains. It was built in less than a year (1196–97) and might have survived intact into this century if Henry IV hadn't ordered its destruction in 1603. As it is, the dominant outline remains and, for once, there's free access at all times. The best route up is the path off rue Richard Coeur-de-Lion in PETIT ANDELYS.

For a strange and complete shift of mood you could, with a car or a lucky hitch, leave the ancient fortifications and within half an hour be in **Monet's gardens** with the waterlily pond at **GIVERNY**. Monet lived in this house from 1883 till his death in 1926 and the gardens that he laid out were considered by many of his friends to be his masterpiece. Each month is reflected in a dominant colour, as are each of the rooms, hung as he left them with his Japanese print collection. May and June, when the rhododendrons flower around the lily pond and the wisteria winds over the Japanese bridge in bloom are the best times to visit. But any month, from spring to autumn, is overwhelmingly beautiful in this arrangement of living shades and shapes. You'll have to contend with crowds and cameras snapping up images of the waterlilies far removed from Monet's renderings – and it's expensive – but there's no place like it. The gardens are open 10am to 6pm; the house 10am to noon and 2 to 6pm; closed Monday and November to March. If you want to see the real painted lilies, the best collections are in Paris – the Marmottan, Orangerie and Musée d'Orsay.

Neither Giverny nor the Château Gaillard is easy to get to **by public transport**. Your best bet **for Giverny** from Rouen would be a train to VERNON and then a ten-minute ride on the rare *Gisor* bus from the station. For **Les Andelys** there's an equally infrequent bus from Rouen or, more expensive but scenic, a tourist boat from the POSES DAM (bus #130 from Rouen); the boat goes to Les Andelys and Vernon – ask at Rouen SI for details.

Accommodation is not much easier, with just one cheap hotel at Les Andelys, *Au Soleil Levant* (2 rue du Général-de-Gaulle; ☎32.54.23.55), and a youth hostel in Vernon (28 av de l'Ile-de-France; ☎32.21.20.51). In such agreeable countryside so close to the capital where large country estates abound – empty half the time – and where whole villages have turned into Parisian weekend colonies, it's assumed any visitor has, if not a residence, then at least a car.

BASSE NORMANDIE

Self-satisfied resorts for the capital's rich are followed by the beaches of the Allied armies' landings in 1944 and then the wilder, and in some places, deserted shore around the Cotentin peninsula to make up the coast of Lower Normandy. Getting to see the top two favourite sights – Mont St-Michel and the Bayeux tapestry – is easy. What's more difficult is exploring inland: the constantly changing countryside, its edibles and intoxicants – the most famous taking its name from the *département* of Calvados.

Eastern Calvados Coast: Honfleur to Cabourg

HONFLEUR, the best-preserved of the old ports of Normandy, is a near-perfect seaside town missing only the beach. It used to have one, but with the accumulation of silt from the Seine the sea has steadily withdrawn, leaving the eighteenth-century waterfront houses of bd Charles V stranded and a little surreal. The ancient port, however, still functions – the channel to the beautiful *Vieux Bassin* is kept open by regular dredging – and though only pleasure craft now use the moorings in the harbour basin, fishing boats tie up alongside the pier nearby. There is usually fish for sale either directly from the boats or from stands on the pier, still by right run by fishermen's wives. It's all highly picturesque, and very upmarket, but not altogether different to the town that had such appeal to artists in the second half of the nineteenth century.

Though the town has modern suburbs and developments, it's the old centre, around the **bassin**, to which you'll gravitate. At the *bassin*, slate-fronted houses, each of them one or two storeys higher than seems possible, harmonise despite their tottering and ill-matched forms, into a backdrop only rivalled by the **Lieutenance** – the King's Lieutenant's residence – at the harbour entrance. The church of **St-Stephen** nearby is now a **Musée Maritime**, which, with its accompanying ethnographic collection, is open for formal and lengthy guided tours in high season (10am–noon and 3–6pm; closed Fri.). Just behind it are two seventeenth-century salt stores where temporary art exhibitions are staged in summer.

Honfleur's artistic past – and its present concentration of galleries and painters – owes most to Eugène Boudin, forerunner of Impressionism. He was born and worked in the town, trained the fifteen-year-old Monet, and was joined for various periods by Pissarro, Renoir and Cézanne. At the same time, Baudelaire paid visits to the town, which was also home to the composer Erik Satie. There's a good selection of Boudin's works in the **Musée Eugène Boudin** – west of the port on place Erik-Satie — and they're quite appealing here in context, particularly the crayon seascapes. But it's the Dufys, Marquets, Frieszes and above all the Monets that are so impressive. The museum is open in summer 10am to noon and 2 to 6pm; winter 2.30 to 5pm (and 10am–noon on weekends); closed Tuesday and January to mid-Febuary.

Admission also gives you access to one of Monet's subjects featured in the museum, the detached belfry of **Ste-Cathérine**'s. The church and belfry are built almost entirely of wood – supposedly due to economic restraints after the Hundred Years War. It's a change from the great stone Norman churches and has the added peculiarity of being divided into twin naves, with one balcony running around both. From rue de l'Homme-de-Bois behind you can see yacht masts through the houses overlooking the *bassin* and in the distance, the huge industrial panorama of Le Havre's docks.

The most reasonable **restaurants**, and liveliest **bar**, are on rue Haute, on the way up to the Boudin museum. The bar, *des Amis* , is at no. 35; the restaurants, *Les Frères de la Côte* and *Au P'tit Marayeur*, at nos. 3 and 4; a speciality (mainly in Oct.–Nov.) is *crevettes grises*, tiny shrimp eaten with an unsalty Spanish-style bread, *pain brié*. Otherwise, meals do not come cheap – Bohemian life is no longer catered to in Honfleur and none of the **hotels** is very affordable either. The *des Pèlerins*, west from the centre at 6 rue des Capucins (☎31.89.19.61) is the best bet, or there's a **campsite** at the west end of bd Charles V on place Jean de Vienne. If you need help, the **SI** is near the **gare routière** at 33 cours des Fosses. The town is on the direct **bus** route #20 from CAEN to LE HAVRE, with eight buses per day in each direction; the nearest train station is at PONT-L'EVEQUE, connected by the Lisieux bus, #50 (about a 20-min. ride).

Trouville and Deauville

Heading **west along the corniche** from Honfleur, green fields and fruit trees lull the land's edge and cliffs rise from sandy beaches all the way to Trouville (15km). The **resorts** aren't exactly cheap but they're relatively undeveloped and if you want to stop along the coast this is the place to do it. The next stretch, from Trouville to Cabourg, is what you might call the **Riviera of Normandy** with Trouville as 'Nice' and 'Deauville' as Cannes, within a stone's throw of each other.

TROUVILLE retains some semblance of a real town, with a constant population and industries other than tourism. But it is still a resort – and has been ever since the imperial jackass, Napoléon III, started bringing his court here every summer in the 1860s. One of his dukes, looking across the river, saw, instead of marshlands, money and lots of it, in the form of a racetrack. His vision materialised and villas appeared between the racetrack and the sea to become **DEAUVILLE**. Now you can lose money on the horses, cross five streets and lose more in the casino, then lose yourself across 200m of sports and 'cure' facilities and private swimming huts before reaching the *planches*, ½km of boardwalk, beyond which rows of primary-coloured parasols obscure the view of the sea. French exclusiveness and self-esteem ooze from every suntanned pore and a visit to the **SI** on place de la Mairie in Deauville – or by the casino in Trouville – is repaid with some spectacularly revolting brochures (in English).

As you might have guessed, **hotels** are either luxurious or overpriced. If desperate, try *Le Lutrin* (48 rue Gambetta; ☎31.88.32.38) in Deauville, *La Paix* (4 place F-Moureaux; ☎31.88.35.15) and *Charmettes* (22 rue de la Chapelle; ☎31.88.11.67) in Trouville, or one of the three **campsites** (two in Trouville, one in Deauville). The **gares SNCF** and **routière** are between the two towns just south of the marina. A possible reason for staying could be the **American Film Festival** held in Deauville in the first week of September, with public admission to a wide selection of previews.

West to Cabourg

The smaller **resorts west towards Cabourg** are equally crowded and equally short on inexpensive hotels, but they're less snobbish, and there are plenty of campsites. With an eye on the tides you can also walk beneath the **Vaches Noires** cliffs from VILLERS to HOULGATE (4½km).

At **CABOURG**, the town centre fans out in perfect symmetry fronted by the straightest promenade in France. The resort, contemporary with Deauville, seems to be stuck in the nineteenth century, immobilized by Proust perhaps, who wrote for a while in the **Grand Hôtel** – one of an outrageous ensemble of buildings around the **Jardins du Casino**. There's an **SI** here with full details on **rooms** (try hotels *Le Crible* on place du 8-Mai, and *Le Rally* at 5 av Général-Leclerc). Arriving by **bus** you'll be dropped off at the gardens on av Pasteur. Walking through them and turning right on av de la Mer will take you down to the Jardins du Casino. By **train** you'll come in at Cabourg's much older neighbour, **DIVES**, which is across the river. It has nothing in common with the aristocratic resort except for its significance to Proust. The land's end church of Balbec in *Du Côté de Chez Swann* is Proust's dream version of **Notre Dame** in Dives. There's a reasonable **hotel** here, *de la Gare* (☎31.91.24.52), or a **campsite** in between Cabourg and Dives (and a couple of others off the Cabourg–Lisieux road). The town has a lively **Saturday market** around the ancient timbered *halles*; in early August it hosts a puppet festival.

The Bessin: Caen and Bayeux

CAEN, capital and largest city of Basse Normandie, is not a place where you're likely to spend much time. In the months of fighting in 1944, it was devastated. The central feature is a ring of ramparts that no longer have a castle to protect, and, though there are the scattered spires and buttresses of two abbeys and eight old churches, roads and roundabouts fill the wide spaces where pre-war houses stood. Approaches are along thunderous dual-carriageways through industrial suburbs – once an economic success story, currently hammered by unemployment. Caen University's latest toy, and one of the biggest recent constructions in the town, is a particle accelerator for militarily-orientated nuclear physics research – not something that helps to shorten the dole queues.

Nonetheless, Caen, favoured residence of William the Conqueror, is still impressive. The **château ramparts** are dramatically exposed, having been cleared of their attached medieval houses by aerial bombardment. Within are two museums (10am–noon and 2–6pm; closed Tues.), devoted to Norman history and Fine Arts. The former is unmemorable but the **Beaux Arts** is a treat. Amid comprehensive displays – from fifteenth-century Italian and Flemish primitives to contemporary French artists – it includes masterpieces by Poussin, Géricault, Monet and Bonnard, as well as an exceptional collection of engravings by Dürer and Rembrandt.

To the north of the château lie the buildings of the **University** , founded in 1432 by Henry VI of England. Below the ramparts to the south is the fourteenth-century church of **St-Pierre**, its facade reconstructed since the war, which spared the magnificent Renaissance stonework of the apse. To the west and east of the town stand the two great Romanesque constructions, the **Abbaye des Hommes** with its church of **St-Etienne**, and the **Abbaye des Dames** with **La Trinité** church. The first was founded by William the

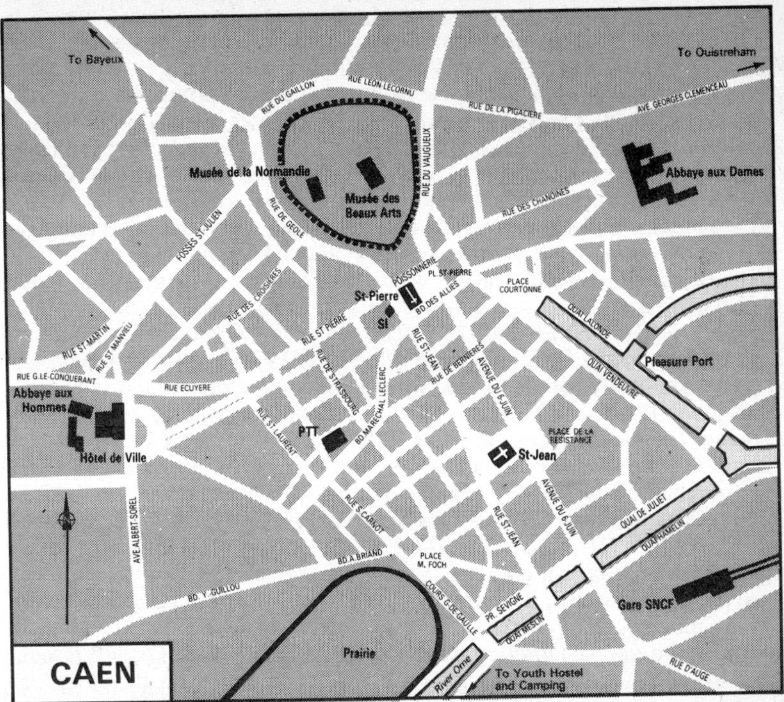

Conqueror and designed to hold his tomb; the other was commissioned by his wife, Queen Matilda. Hers is more starkly impressive, with a gloomy pillared crypt, wonderful stained glass behind the altar, and odd sculptural details like the fish curled up in the holy-water stoup. It stands at the end of rue des Chanoines. William's abbey, reached via rue St-Pierre, incorporates the town hall (visitable during office hours). The great church, where much of Caen's population took shelter during the 1944 bombardment, towers beside it.

Most of the centre of Caen is taken up with busy new shopping developments and pedestrian precincts, where the cafés are distinguished by names such as *Fast Food Glamour Vault*. Outlets of the big Parisian stores – and of the aristocrats' grocers, *Hédiard,* in the Cours des Halles – are here, along with good local rivals. The **market** takes place on Friday, spreading along both sides of Fosse St-Julien. The **pleasure port,** at the end of the canal which links Caen to the sea, is where most life goes on, at least in summer.

The port is also the area where most of the **hotels** are situated, including a number of good inexpensive ones like the *Weekend* (14 quai Vendeuvre; ☎31.86.39.95) and the *Bernières* (50 rue de Bernières; ☎31.86.01.26). The **youth hostel** (☎31.52.19.96) is a bit further out, southwest of the railway station in the *Foyer Robert-Remé* at 68 bis rue E-Restout. Close by the hostel is the town **campsite** – set beside the River Orne on route de Louvigny (bus #13, stop *Camping*).

For **restaurants**, rue de Geôle, running alongside the western ramparts to place St-Pierre is the most promising location. There are some good Vietnamese and Chinese places as well as French. Another area worth trying is around the Abbaye aux Hommes: for a large traditional meal here, go to *Le Boeuf Ferré* at 10 rue des Croisiers, or for lighter nouvelle cuisine, *La Mandarine* at 18 rue Froide. If you plan to do some cheese, cider and calvados tasting in the countryside, *Calvados Tourisme* on place du Canada (☎31.86.53.30) can provide addresses.

As to other practicalities, the **SI** is on the central place St-Pierre, and from here regular buses leave for the **gare SNCF** on the south side of the river. The **gare routière** is a few blocks west of the SNCF on rue des Bras. Buses to **Ouistreham**, the new *Brittany Ferries* terminal port, leave from (and arrive at) the gare SNCF and are timed to coincide with crossings. If you're driving to catch the boat, the 15km of new dual carriageway are quick but give yourself plenty of time to cope with Ouistreham's knotted traffic system.

North of Caen, at the end of av Marshal-Montgomery, a brand new museum, the **Caen Memorial**, stands on the plateau named after General Eisenhower which ends on a clifftop beneath which the Germans had their HQ in June and July 1944. Funds and material for it have come from the U.S., Britain, Canada, East and West Germany, Poland, Czechoslovakia, the USSR and France. It's a typically French high-tech, novel-architecture conception, and its idea is to be a museum of peace rather than war. One section deals with the rise of fascism in Germany, another with Resistance and collaboration in France. A third charts all the major battles of World War II and finally there's a film documentary on all the conflicts since 1945. Though a touch naive in its historical analysis, it is a great improvement on the older war-glorifying museums of Normandy. It is open June to August 9.30am to 10pm, last entry 8.30pm; winter 9.30am to 7.30pm, last entry 6pm. Admission is steep though there are reductions for students, the young and the over 65s, and it's free for World War II veterans. Bus #12 during the week or #14 on the weekend (from the *Tour le Roi* stop in the centre of town) go direct to the museum (about 20 min). By car the route is well-signposted – if you get lost ask for La Folie Couvrechef, the name of the area.

Bayeux – and the Tapestry

BAYEUX's perfectly preserved medieval ensemble, magnificent cathedral, and world-famous tapestry make it one of the high points of this part of Normandy. Only fifteen minutes by train from Caen, and a much smaller city, however, its charms can pall somewhat with the influx of summer tourists.

The Bayeux Tapestry is housed in the **Centre Guillaume le Conquérant**, clearly signposted on rue de Nesmond, open June–Sept. 8am–9pm; winter 8am–noon and 2–9pm Sundays 8.30am–12.30pm and 2.30pm–7pm). Visits are well planned and highly atmospheric, if somewhat exhausting. You start off with a projection of slides on swathes of canvas hung as sails, before moving on to an almost full-length reproduction of the original, complete with photographic extracts and detailed commentary. Upstairs in the plush theatre there's a film (French and English versions alternate) on the general context and craft of the piece – which you can skip if you feel you know the 1066 story well enough by now. Beyond this – and the souvenirs table – you finally approach the real thing, a 70m strip of linen embroidered with coloured wools nine centuries ago. By this stage, however tortuous the build-up, you can race along reading the tapestry as you would a cartoon strip, which is really what its style resembles. Look out for the incidental details of domestic and daily life, and the scenes from Aesop's fables, that run along the bottom as a counterpoint to the military scenes above.

From the centre it is a short and very obvious walk to the **Cathédrale Notre-Dame** for whose consecration in 1077 the tapestry was commissioned. Despite some eighteenth-century vandalism, like the monstrous fungoid baldachin that flanks the pulpit, the original Romanesque plan is still intact. The crypt, entirely unaltered, is a beauty, its columns graced with frescoes of angels playing trumpets and bagpipes, looking exhausted by their performance for eternity.

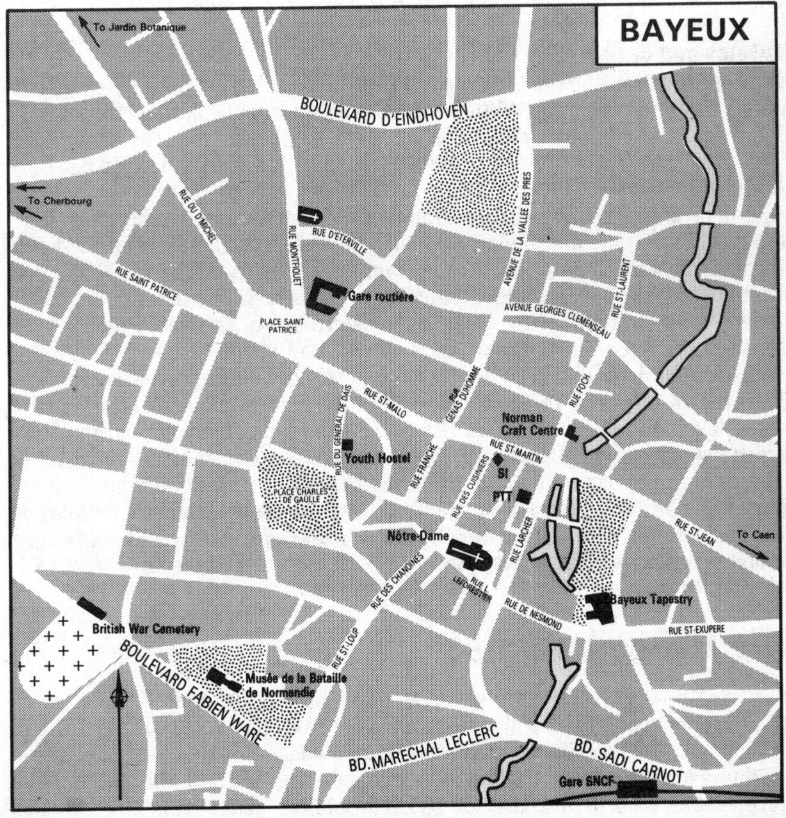

Bayeux's **Musée de la Bataille de Normandie** is a particularly offensive example of the genre which appears to consider its chief purpose to be crude Cold War propaganda. It's a sorry contrast with the tranquil dignity of the British war cemetery across the road.

Bayeux details

None of Bayeux's **hotels** is particularly cheap. *Notre-Dame* (44 rue des Cuisiniers; ☎31.92.87.24) and *de la Gare* (26 place de la Gare; ☎31.92.10.70) are the best deals; the *Argouges* (21 rue St-Patrice; ☎31.92.88.86) is pricier but old and stylish. Something that calls itself the *Family Home* at 39 rue Général-du-Dais (☎31.92.15.22), a little north of the cathedral, doubles up as the **youth hostel**; its prices are higher than usual. Final options are the two **municipal accommodation centres** run by the **SI** (whom you'll find at 1 rue des Cuisiniers; ☎31.92.16.26); phone for details.

As for food, most of the **restaurants** are in the pedestrianised rue St-Jean – *La Rapière* at no. 53 is the most popular. If they are all full, try the *Angevin* (open on Sunday evenings) on rue Genas-Duhomme. **Buses** leave from the central place St-Patrice; the **gare SNCF** is on the other side of town.

Balleroy and Cerisy

Heading **southwest from Bayeux**, towards ST-LO, you pass close to two remarkable buildings: the **Abbaye de Cerisy-la-Forêt** (5km north, midway along) and the **Château de Balleroy** (3km southeast from the same junction). Neither is easy to get to without transport but with a bike or car they shouldn't be missed.

Romanesque CERISY, with its triple tiers of windows and arches, laps light into its cream stone and makes you sigh in wonder at the skills of medieval Norman masons: it is open 9am to 6pm (free visit). At BALLEROY, you switch to an era when architects ruled over craftsmen. The main street of the village leads straight to the Château, masterpiece of the celebrated seventeenth-century architect, François Mansard, and standing like a faultlessly reasoned and dogmatic argument for the power of its owners and their class. The present owner is the American press magnate Malcolm Forbes, pal of Nixon, Ford and Nancy Reagan. His is the enlarged colour photograph sharing the stairwell with Dutch still lifes and he's made a mark on most other aspects of the house, too – only the *salon* has been left in its original state of glory, with brilliant portraits of the then royal family by Mignard. Admission (expensive) includes a **hot air balloon musuem,** one of Mr. Forbes's hobbies; hours are 9am to noon and 2 to 6pm, closed Wednesday.

The D-Day beaches

It is hard now to picture the scene at dawn on **D-Day**, June 6, 1944, when Allied troops landed along the Norman coast from the mouth of the Orne to Les Dunes de Varneville on the Cotentin peninsula. For the most part, these are innocuous beaches backed by gentle dunes, and yet this foothold in Europe was won at the cost of 100,000 soldiers' lives. That the invasion happened here, and not nearer to Germany, was partly due to the failure of the Canadian raid on Dieppe in 1942. The ensuing **Battle of Normandy** killed thousands of civilians and reduced nearly 600 towns and villages to rubble but, within a week of its conclusion, Paris was liberated.

The **beaches** are still often referred to by their wartime codenames: Sword, Juno, Gold, Omaha and Utah. Bits of shrapnel could still be found, and sold, along with packets of sand, in the junketings of the fortieth anniversary celebrations. But more substantial traces of the fighting are rare. The most remarkable are the remains of the prefab **Mulberry harbour**, built in Britain while 'doodlebugs' blitzed overhead. It now lies where it served its purpose on the seabed and beach at ARROMANCHES-LES-BAINS. At POINTE DU HOC on Omaha beach the cliff heights are still deeply pitted with German bunkers and shell holes. And the church at STE-MERE-EGLISE from which the U.S. paratrooper dangled during heavy fighting and survived, his parachute entangled in the roof, still stands.

Just about every coastal town has its **war museum**, tending as a rule to shy away from the unbearable reality of war in favour of Boy's Own style heroics. The wealth of incidental human detail can nonetheless be overpowering. There are also numerous cemeteries, each usually devoted to one specific country, and providing strong reflections of different national characteristics and experiences. The largest of the American cemeteries, at ST-LAURENT, is a disturbing place, with its clinical rows of impersonal crosses resembling nothing so much as a vast corporate balance sheet, and an air of martial exaltation – complete with maps and battle plans – that does little to inspire thoughts of peace; in comparison the German cemetery at ORGLANDES to the west is subdued, sombre, and heavy with futility, free of slogans or monuments.

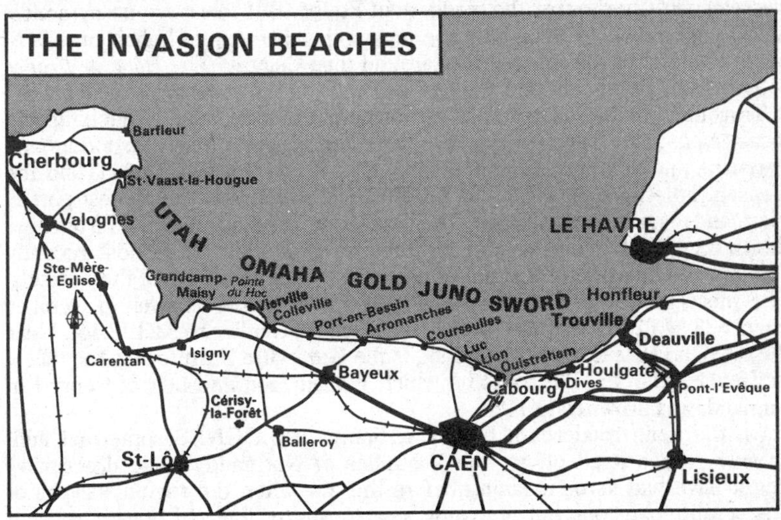

Along with the veterans and their descendants, visitors these days come to this stretch of coast for its **seaside**: sand and seafood (best oysters at Courseulles), plenty of campsites and no Deauville chic. It's good for **windsurfing** too. Reasonably priced **places to stay** include: at LUC-SUR-MER *Beau Rivage* (☎31.96.49.51); at ARROMANCHES, the *Normandie* (place du 6-Juin; ☎31.22.34.32); at PORT-EN-BESSIN, *de la Place* (quai Letourner); at GRANDCAMP-MAISY *du Guesclin* (4 quai Crampon; ☎31.22.64.22) and *Grandcopaise* (84 rue A-Briand; ☎31.22.63.44); at ISIGNY-SUR-MER, *du Commerce* (5 rue E.-Demagny; ☎31.22.01.44); and a **youth hostel** at VIERVILLE-SUR-MER (in the Stade Municipal; open June–Sept.; ☎31.22.00.33). From Bayeux the *coastal buses* are #74 to Arromanches and Courseulles; #70 for Port-en-Bessin and Vierville and #7, #30 for Isigny.

In theory there are **buses** running all along this coast. **From Bayeux**, #74 goes to Arromanches and Corseulles, #70 to Port-en-Bessin and Vierville, #7 to Isigny. **From Caen**, #30 runs inland to Isigny via Bayeux, #1 to Ouistreham and on to Luc. None of these services, however, except for those linking Caen with the Ouistreham ferries, is reliable – you're better off cycling, or at least trying to hitch while you wait for the bus.

Cherbourg and the Cotentin Peninsula

If the mucky metropolis of **CHERBOURG** is your port of arrival, head straight for the **gares SNCF** and **routière** on either side of av Millet – a five-minute walk from the ferry terminal behind the inner dock. The town itself is almost devoid of interest. Napoléon inaugurated the transformation of what had been a poor, but perfectly situated, natural harbour into a major transatlantic port. An equestrian statue commemorates his boast that he would 'recreate (in Cherbourg) the wonders of Egypt'. But there are no pyramids, and if you're waiting for a boat the most enjoyable way of killing time is to settle into one of the **restaurants** around quai Caligny. The *Hôtel de France* (41 rue Maréchal-Foch) and the *Café de Paris* (on the *quai*) are excellent.

Travelling by bus is not easy in northern Cotentin. Nor is hitching: the local *patois* has a special pejorative word for 'stranger' used for foreigners, Parisians and southern Cotentins alike. But if you head east you'll find the pleasant little harbour village of **BARFLEUR** which was the biggest port in Normandy seven centuries ago. The population has since dwindled from nine thousand to six hundred, and fortunes have diminished – most recently through the invasion of a strain of plankton which poisoned all the mussels. The more modest-priced **hotels** include the *du Phare* (Easter to October only; ☎33.54.02.07) and *Le Moderne* (1 place de Gaulle; ☎33.23.12.44). Near the town, about a thirty-minute walk, is the **Gatteville lighthouse**, the tallest in France, guarding the rocks on which William, son and heir of Henry I of England, was drowned in 1120.

On the main road south from Cherbourg, **VALOGNES** somewhat ludicrously passes itself off as 'the Versailles of Normandy'. The description might have had some meaning before the war when the region was full of aristocratic mansions but now only a scattering of fine old houses remain.

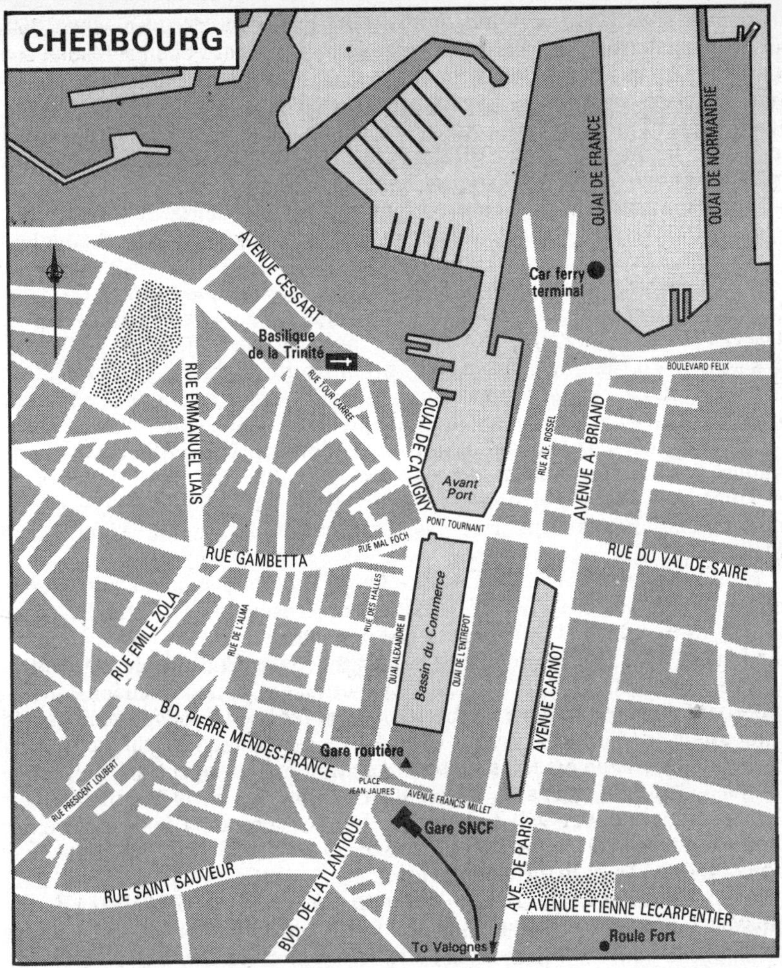

There's a cider museum, a little public garden, and a big empty square – activated only for the Friday **market**. But it's a quiet, convenient alternative to waiting around in Cherbourg: for the night try the *Hôtel de l'Agriculture* (16 rue L-Delisle; ☎33.40.00.21).

If you go west from Cherbourg to **LA HAGUE**, the northern tip of the peninsula, you'll find wild and isolated countryside where you can lean against the wind, watch waves smashing against rocks or sunbathe in a spring profusion of wild flowers. But the discharges of 'low-level' radioactive wastes from **Cap Hague nuclear re-processing plant** may discourage you from swimming. In 1980, the Greenpeace vessel, *Rainbow Warrior*, chased a ship bringing spent Japanese fuel into Cherbourg harbour. The *Rainbow*

Warrior's crew were arrested, but all charges were dropped when 3000 Cherbourg dockers threatened to strike in their support. Such anti-nuke solidarity is rare in France, one of the few remaining countries with an ambitious 'civil' nuclear programme. Even Chernobyl failed to dent confidence in the 'cathedrals of the twentieth century', which continue to be built at incredible expense. In the spring of 1985 the French secret service finally took their revenge on the *Rainbow Warrior*, killing a member of the crew.

From the cape, bracken-covered hills and narrow valleys run west to the cliffs of the Nez de Jobourg, claimed in wild local optimism to be the highest in Europe. On the other side, facing north, PORT RACINE proclaims itself more plausibly the smallest port in France. **Accommodation** is distinctly lacking in these half-tumbled-down villages. There are **campsites** at OMONVILLE-LA-ROGUE, VAUVILLE and further afield at URVILLE-NACQUERVILLE, which also has the **hotel** *Beaurivage* (☎33.03.52.40).

South of La Hague a great curve of sand – some of it military training ground – takes the land's edge to FLAMANVILLE and another nuclear installation. But the next two sweeps of beach down to CARTARET, with sand dunes like mini-mountain ranges, are probably the best beaches in Normandy if you've got transport and a desire for solitude. There are no resorts, no hotels and just two **campsites** – at LE ROZEL and SURTAINVILLE.

Bronzed poseurs with their turbo-charged status symbols conglomerate further south, at COUTAINVILLE, the nearest resort to **COUTANCES**. This old hill town, confined by its site to just one main street, has on its summit a landmark for all the surrounding countryside, the **Cathédrale de Notre-Dame**. Essentially Gothic, it is still very Norman in its unconventional blending of architectural traditions. The *sons et lumières*, on Sunday evenings and throughout the summer, are for once a true complement to the light stone building. Also illuminated on summer nights (and left open) are the formal fountained **public gardens**. If you want to stay, the **SI** in the modern *Les Unelles* cultural centre will be happy to find you a room. The best place, for food as well as beds, is the **hotel** *Relais du Viaduc* (☎33.45.02.68) at the junction of D7 and D971 to the south of town.

From Coutances, D971 runs down to the coast at **GRANVILLE**, the Norman equivalent to Brittany's St-Malo with a history of piracy and a severe citadel, the *haute ville*, guarding the approaches to the bay of Mont St-Michel. Though the most lively town and popular resort in the area, it can't quite match the appeal of its Breton rival. However, if you want to get to the Channel islands, or to the offshore Iles Chausey whose granite was quarried for the Mont St-Michel, this is where you embark. Most of the shops and hotels, including *Terminus* (☎33.50.02.05) and *de la Gare* (☎33.50.00.05), are in the new town towards the **gare SNCF**. **Bikes** can be hired from *Le Coulant* (av de la Libération) and there's a covered **market** opposite the Mairie on Saturday mornings.

South of Granville the crowded towns and small resorts all compete for views and proximity to Mont St-Michel. ST-JEAN-LE-THOMAS is the first point from which you can walk at low tide across the bay to the abbey. This is not a walk to take on drunken or any other impulse. The tide, as they say, comes up faster than galloping horses. A special phone line on ☎33.50.02.67 gives advice on timing.

Avranches

AVRANCHES is the nearest large town to Mont St-Michel and it has always had close connections with the abbey. The Mont's original church was founded by a bishop of Avranches, spurred on by St. Michael who supposedly became so impatient with the lack of progress that he prodded a hole in the bishop's skull (viewable in Avranches' St-Gervais basilica). Robert of Torigny, a subsequent abbot of St-Michel, played host in the town on several occasions to Henry II of England, the most memorable being when Henry was obliged, bare-footed and bare-headed, to do public penance for the murder of Thomas-à-Becket. The arena for this act of contrition was Avranches cathedral, designed, most inexpertly, by de Torigny himself: it swiftly 'crumbled and fell for want of proper support'. All that marks the site is a fenced-off platform. A more vivid evocation of the area's medieval splendours comes from the illuminated manuscripts from the Mont, on display in the town **museum** (open Easter–Sept., 9am–noon and 2–6pm; closed Tues.).

Though still some distance from the Mont, Avranches is not a bad place to base yourself. Reasonable **hotels** include *du Jardin des Plantes* (10 place Carnot; ☎33.58.03.68); *Le Central* (2–4 rue du Jardin-des-Plantes; ☎33.58.16.59) and *Bellevue* (2 place du Général-Patton; ☎33.58.01.10). **Market** day is Thursday, and piped disco music on the streets goes on all summer. The **gare SNCF** is far below the town centre, but the views make up for that.

Mont St-Michel

The island of **MONT ST-MICHEL** was once known as the Mount in Peril from the Sea. The Archangel Michael was its vigorous protector, the most militant spirit of the Church Militant, with a marked tendency for leaping from rock to rock in titanic struggles against Paganism and Evil.

The Mont is barely an island anymore – the causeway that now leads to it is never submerged, and is silting up on both sides. Although it was once a large community – a fortress town – there were never more than forty monks until its closure at the time of the Revolution. On its 1000th anniversary, in 1966, the Benedictines were invited to return; today, three nuns and three monks maintain a presence.

The Abbey church, long known as the *Merveille*, is visible from all around the bay, and it becomes more awe-inspiring the closer you get. In Maupassant's words:

> *'I reached the huge pile of rocks which bears the little city dominated by the great church. Climbing the steep narrow street, I entered the most wonderful Gothic dwelling ever made for God on this earth, a building as vast as a town, full of low rooms under oppressive ceilings and lofty galleries supported by frail pillars. I entered that gigantic granite jewel, which is as delicate as a piece of lacework, thronged with towers and slender belfries which thrust into the blue sky of day and*

the black sky of night their strange heads bristling with chimeras, devils, fantastic beasts and monstrous flowers, and which are linked together by carved arches of intricate design'.

The Mont's rock comes to a sharp point just below what is now the transept of **the church**. The Chausey granite was sculpted to match the exact contours of the hill and though space was always limited, the building has grown through the centuries in ever more ingenious uses of geometry. Not everything has lasted; the original church, choir, nave, and tower have all collapsed and been superseded. To visit, you must join a **tour**. These run between 9.30am and 5.30pm in summer; 10am and noon and 1.30 and 4pm in winter; a timetable at the entrance lists those in English. The visit lasts for about an hour, and the guides are experts, pointing out among much other useful information that the current unadorned state of the stone walls around you is a far cry from the way the medieval monastery would have looked, brightly painted and festooned with tapestries. There's a church service at 12.15pm every day, with a nursery provided below for children under eight years old.

The base of Mont St-Michel is a jumble of over-priced postcard and souvenir shops and restaurants, maintaining the great tradition of extorting money from pilgrims. The most famous **hotel**, *La Mère Poulard*, uses the time-honoured legend of its fluffy omelettes to justify extortionate charges. Higher up the one twisting street, however, prices fall to surprisingly realistic levels. The *Hôtel Croix Blanche* (☎33.60.14.04) has very inexpensive rooms and an exceptional restaurant.

The nearest **gare SNCF** is at **PONTORSON**, 6km south, where you can hire a bike from the station or take an expensive bus to the Mont. The best budget **hotel** is the *de France* (2 rue de Rennes; ☎33.60.29.17), next to the railway crossing; it has a late and youthful bar, with pool and a good jukebox. But otherwise Pontorson is eminently forgettable.

FROM THE SEINE TO THE BOCAGE: INLAND NORMANDY

It's hard to pin down specific highlights in **inland Normandy**. The pleasures lie in the feel of particular landscapes – the lush meadows and orchards, the classic half-timbered houses and farm buildings, and the rivers and forests of the Norman countryside. **Gastronomy** is of course another major motivation – the cheeses, creams, apple and pear brandies and ciders for which the region is famous. The **Pays d'Auge** country south of Lisieux and the **Vire Valley** to the west are the best for this. **Suisse Normande** is canoeing and rock-climbing country and there are endless good walks in the stretch along the southern border of the province designated as the **Parc Naturel Régional de Normandie-Maine**. Of the towns, **St-Lô** is the most interesting; **Conches** the most charming. **Falaise** has William the Conqueror as a constant fall-back attraction, and **Lisieux** has religious myths and a spectacularly revolting basilica to back them up.

South of the Seine

Heading south from the Seine you can follow the RISLE River from the estuary just east of Honfleur, or the EURE and its tributaries from upstream of Rouen. Between the two stretches the long featureless **Neubourg plain**.

The lowest major crossing point over the Risle is at **PONT-AUDEMER**, where medieval houses lean out at alarming angles over the criss-crossing roads, rivers, and canals. From here, perfect cycling roads lined with timbered farmhouses follow the river south. Just before you reach BRIONNE you come to the **ABBAYE DE BEC-HELLOUIN** whose size and tranquil ethos give a monastic feel to the whole valley. Bells echo across the water and white-robed monks go soberly about their business. From the eleventh century onwards, the abbey was one of the most important centres of intellectual learning in the Christian world; the philosopher Anselm was abbot here before becoming Archbishop of Canterbury in 1093. Due to the Revolution, most of the monastery buildings are recent – the monks only returned in 1948 – but there are some survivals and appealing clusters of stone ruins. The present Archbishop of Canterbury has maintained tradition by coming here on retreat. Tours are at 10am, 11am, 3pm, 3.45pm, 4.30pm, 5.15pm; Sunday and holidays at 9.30am, noon, 2.45pm, 3.30pm, 4.15pm and 6pm; closed Tues. In the rather cute adjacent town of **BEC-HELLOUIN** is a **vintage car museum** and a distinctly un-ascetic **restaurant**, the wonderful *Auberge de l'Abbaye*.

BRIONNE, which is on the Rouen–Lisieux rail line, is a small town with large regional **markets** on Thursday and Sunday. The fish hall is on the left bank, the rest by the church on the right bank. Above them both, with panoramic views, is a **donjon**. If you decide to **stay**, the *Auberge du Vieux Donjon* (☎32.44.80.62) on the marketplace is good, though very pricey; the *Routiers*, next door, more manageable.

The Charentonne River joins the Risle near SERQUIGNY. The town is also the meeting point of rail lines and main roads and the banks are clogged with fuming industrial conglomerations. But 7km upstream, at **BEAUMONT-LE-ROGER**, you are back in pastoral tranquillity. The ruins of a thirteenth-century priory church slowly crumble to the ground, the slow restoration of one or two arches unable to keep pace. In the village, little happens beyond the hammering of the church bell next door to the abbey by a nodding musketeer. Just across the Risle from here, on D25 near LE VAL-ST-MARTIN, huge stables are spread across an absurdly sylvan setting, and horses are available for rent.

The next riverside village, LA FERRIERE-SUR-RISLE, has an especially beautiful church and old covered market hall. Paddocks and meadows lead down to the river and two small and inviting **hotels**, the *Croissant* (☎32.30.70.13) and *Vieux Marché* (☎32.30.70.69). It is the wild and open woodland of the **Forêt de Conches** across which, 14km to the east, lies CONCHES itself, every Norman's favourite heartland town.

CONCHES-EN-OUCHE stands above the Rouloir River on an abrupt and narrow spur. At the highest point, in the middle of a row of medieval houses, is the church of **Ste-Foy**, its windows a stunning sequence of Renaissance stained glass. Behind are the gardens of the **Hôtel de Ville**, where a robust, if anatomically odd, stone boar gazes proudly out over a spectacular view. Next to that, you can scramble up the slippery steps of the ruined twelfth-century **castle**. What gives Conches the edge over other towns with equal lists of historic relics, are the pieces of modern sculpture that you run into around every other corner.

Across the main street from the castle is a long **park**, with parallel avenues of trees, a large ornamental lake and fountain, and the **hotel** the *Grand Mare* (☎32.30.23.30). This has cheap rooms and very pricey gastronomic dinners; the *Cygne* (☎32.30.20.60), at the north end of town, is more affordable; or there's a **municipal campsite** (☎32.30.22.49). On Thursday the whole town is taken up by a **market**.

If you're heading south to Conches from Rouen, you follow the Eure River, then its tributary the Iton, passing through **EVREUX**, capital of the Eure *département*. It's hardly an exciting place but an afternoon's wander in the vicinity of the cathedral – a minor classic with its flamboyant exterior decoration and original fourteenth-century windows – and the ramparts alongside the Iton riverbank is pleasant. Most of the cheaper hotels in the town tend to shut during August. An evening is better spent in Conches or at **PACY-SUR-EURE**, where the *Hôtel de l'Etape* (☎32.36.12.77) nestles at the water's edge.

Lisieux and the Pays D'Auge

LISIEUX, 35 minutes by train from Caen, is the main town of the Pays d'Auge, and a good place to get to know its cheeses and ciders, at the large **street market** on Wednesday and Saturday. Most people, however, come to Lisieux as a place of pilgrimage based around the cult of Sainte-Thérèse, the most popular French spiritual figure of the last hundred years. Passivity, self-effacement and masochism were her trademarks and she is honoured by the grotesquely gaudy and gigantic **Basilique de Ste-Thérèse**, completed in 1954 on a slope to the southwest of the town centre. Huge mosaics of her face decorate the nave and every night at 9.30pm as part of a stunningly tasteless (and expensive) laser show, her face is simultaneously projected on every column in the church. The faithful can ride on a white, flag-bedecked, fair-ground train around the holiest sites which include the infinitely restrained and sober **Cathédrale St-Pierre.**

The quantity of pilgrims means that Lisieux is full of reasonably-priced places to stay. Try the **hotels** *de la Terrasse* (25 av Ste-Thérèse; ☎31.62.17.65), *Condorcet* (26 rue Condorcet; ☎31.62.00.02) or *de l'Avenue* (4 av Ste-Thérèse; ☎31.62.08.37). There is also a large **campsite**, but campers would probably be better off somewhere more rural nearby, such as Livarot or Orbec. The **SI**, at 11 rue d'Alençon (left out of the station, then right), is the best place to gather information on the rural areas further inland.

South of Lisieux, the rolling hills and green twisting valleys of the **Pays d'Auge** are scattered with magnificent half-timbered manor houses. The pastures here are the lushest in the province, their produce the world-famous cheeses of Camembert, Livarot, and Pont L'Evêque. And beside them are acres of orchards, yielding the best of Norman ciders, both apple and pear (*poiré*), as well as Calvados apple brandy. For really good solid Norman cooking this is the perfect area to look out for *Fermes Auberges*, working farms which welcome paying visitors to share their meals. Local *Syndicats* can provide copious lists of these and of local producers from whom you can buy your cheese and booze. In addition a **Route de Fromage** and **Route du Cidre** are signposted – the manor houses of BEUVRON-EN-AUGE on the Cider route, and MONTPINCON and LISORES on the Cheese route, are well worth finding but you won't be missing out if you don't follow these itineraries.

There was little left after the war of the old **PONT-L'EVEQUE**, the northernmost of the Pays d'Auge towns. Since then it has become such a turmoil of major roads that it's no place to stay. **CORMEILLES** on the other hand is a tiny (Friday) market centre, with several half-timbered restaurants to its credit. **ORBEC** lies just a few miles along a pleasant valley from the source of its river, the Orbiquet. It consists of little more than the main road of classic Norman houses with patterned tiles and bricks between the beams, ending in the huge tower of Notre-Dame church.

The centre of the cheese country is the old town of **LIVAROT**, with the **hotel** and restaurant *du Vivier* (☎31.63.50.29) in its centre. The main attraction is the **Conservatoire du Fromage**, a small-scale working cheese factory. For a few francs, you can see Camembert, Pont L'Evêque and Livarot cheeses at every stage of their production.

At **ST-PIERRE-SUR-DIVES**, the medieval market hall has been converted into a slightly academic annexe to the Livarot cheese museum. It's an impressive building, though, almost rivalling the Gothic-Romanesque church (whose windows depict the history of the town). A large **market** still takes place every Monday in the adjacent square.

West of Livarot, just off D47 towards Orbec, you'll find some of the Pays d'Auge's rare budget **accommodation** – the unlikely-sounding *Happy's Holiday Homes*. These large luxury chalets are available at a cheap weekly rent from former racing cyclist Wally Happy – who also, naturally enough, hires out cycles. Contact him in advance on ☎31.32.35.96.

VIMOUTIERS, due south of Livarot, contains another **cheese museum**, this one specialising in labels – the cheeses underneath are mostly polystyrene. At the tiny village of **CAMEMBERT**, nearby, Marie Harel developed the original cheese early in the nineteenth century, skilfully promoting it, even sending free samples to Napoléon. The **hotels** *Soleil d'Or* (16 place Mackau; ☎33.39.07.15) and *Couronne* (9 rue du 8-Mai; ☎33.39.03.04) are good, economic places to stay, and there is also a **campsite**. Just outside the village is the **Escale du Vitou**, a lake, beautifully sited, with everything you need for windsurfing, swimming, and horseback riding.

Along the **valley of the Vie** south of Vimoutiers runs D26 – a route that takes in many of the best features of Normandy, lined along the way with old ramshackle barns and farm buildings. Faded orange clay crumbles out from between the weathered wooden beams of these flower-covered beauties. At the intersection with D13 is the **hotel-restaurant** *Relais St-Pierre*. For any sensible kid this should be a principal holiday target – mini 125cc motorcycles and three-wheelers are hired out to hurtle around a course of bales of hay. There's additional lodging available at a farm a little further north, and several further **hotels** at **GACE**.

South from Caen: The Suisse Normande and Falaise

The area known as the **'Suisse Normande'** lies along the gorge of the River Orne, between Thury-Harcourt and Putanges. The name is a little far-fetched – there are certainly no mountains – but it is quite distinctive with cliffs and crags and wooded hills at every turn. The energetic race along the Orne in canoes and kayaks, the less so are content with pedalos or a bizarre species of inflatable rubber tractor, while high above climbers dangle from thin ropes clawing at the sheer rockface. For mere walkers the Orne can be frustrating: footpaths along the river are few and far between and often entirely overgrown.

The Suisse Normande is usually approached from CAEN or FALAISE and contrasts dramatically with the prairie-like expanse of wheatfields en route. On wheels, the best access is via D235 from Caen, (signed to Falaise then right through Ifs). The *Bus Verts* #34 will take you to THURY HARCOURT or CLECY on its way to Flers and there are occasional special summer train excursions from Caen.

At **THURY-HARCOURT**, the **SI** on place St-Sauveur can suggest walks, rides and *gîtes d'étape* throughout the Suisse Normande; *SIVOM* at 15 rue de Condé hires canoes. Unfortunately there's no very affordable hotel in the town, but there are a couple of three-star **campsites** – *Vallée du Traspy* (☎31.79.61.80) and *Camping du Bord de l'Orne* (☎31.79.70.78; June–Sept. only). In summer, the public park allows access to the riverside.

CLECY is a slightly better bet for finding a room, although its visitors outnumber its residents in peak season. You'll probably need the **SI** – tucked behind the church in the village centre, which is about one kilometre above the river at PONT-DU-VEY. On the road down, in the Parc des Loisirs, is a **Musée du Chemin de Fer Miniature** (open June to mid-Sept. 10am–noon and 2–7pm), featuring a model railway which may appeal to children. At the bridge is a restored watermill, run as a restaurant and hotel. The riverbank continues in a brief splurge of restaurants, take-aways and snackbars as far as the 100-space **campsite**.

An alternative base could be **PONT-D'OUILLY**, at the point where the main road from VIRE to FALAISE crosses the river. It's a small town, with a few basic shops, an old covered market hall and a promenade (with bar) slightly upstream alongside the weir. As well as the riverside **campsite**, there's an attractive **hotel**, the *du Commerce* (rue de Falaise; ☎31.69.80.16), with cheap rooms and wonderful food. A short distance south of Pont-d'Ouilly is the **Roche d'Oëtre**, a high rock with a tremendous view, not over the Orne but into the deep and totally wooded gorge of the Rouvre. The river widens soon afterwards into the **Lac du Rabodanges**, formed by the many-arched Rabodanges Dam. It's a popular spot where people practise every watersport, and with a **campsite**, *Les Retours*, perfectly situated between the dam and the bridge on D121.

Falaise

The birthplace of William the Conqueror, or William the Bastard as he is more commonly known over here, is desperate to attract tourists. The population of **FALAISE** is dwindling, its factories are moving out and the agriculture of the surrounding plain is no longer bringing in much cash. So in 1987, on the 900th anniversary of William's death, an open-air theatrical extravaganza was instigated, to run nightly shows for three summers, based on his life. The story begins in Falaise castle where William was born in 1027, son of Duke Robert of Normandy and Arlette, the laundress whom Robert had fallen for at the washing place below the château. The local population plays the invading army of 1066; the professional playing the lead does not get crushed by his horse as William did in 1087. The show is called *Le Conquérant* – details from the **SI** (32 rue G-Clemenceau).

When Falaise is not celebrating the Bastard, it concentrates on D-Day anniversaries, and is spending money developing a local war museum. The struggle to close the 'Falaise Gap' in August 1944 was the climax of the Battle of Normandy, as the Allied armies sought to encircle the Germans and cut off their retreat. By the time the Canadians entered the town on August 17, they could no longer tell where the roads had been and had to bulldoze a new twelve-foot strip straight through the middle. The **castle keep**, and **Fontaine d'Arlette** on the riverside beneath it, still exist, though so heavily restored as to be scarcely worthy of the ten-minute tour. The few **hotels** are mostly situated along rue G-Clémenceau (the Argentan road) – all very noisy. The **campsite**, *Camping du Château* (☎31.90.16.55), next to Arlette's fountain and the municipal swimming pool, has a better location.

The Bocage: St-Lô and the Vire Valley

The term *bocage* refers to a cultivated countryside common in the west of France where fields are cut by tight hedgerows rooted into walls of earth at least four feet high. An effective form of smallhold farming, at least in pre-industrial days, it is also a perfect system of anti-tank barricades. When the Allied troops tried to advance through the region in 1944 it proved almost impenetrable – certainly bearing no resemblance to the East Anglian plains where they had trained. The war here was hand-to-hand, inch-by-inch slaughter; the destruction of villages often wholesale.

The city of **SAINT-LO** is still known as the 'Capital of the Ruins'. Memorial sites are everywhere and what is new speaks as tellingly of the destruction as the ruins that have been preserved. In the main square, the gate of the old prison commemorates Resistance members executed by the Nazis, people deported east to the concentration camps and soldiers killed in action; when the bombardment of Saint-Lô was at its fiercest, the Germans refused to take any measures to protect the prisoners and the gate was all that survived. Samuel Beckett was here during the battle and after, working for the Irish Red Cross as interpreter, driver and provision-seeker – for such things as rat poison for the maternity hospitals. He said he took away with him a 'time-honoured conception of humanity in ruins'.

All the trees in the city are the same height, all planted to replace the battle's mutilated stumps. But the most visible – and brilliant – reconstruction is the **Cathédrale de Notre-Dame**. Its main body, with a strange southward veering nave, has been conventionally repaired and rebuilt. But the shattered west front and the base of the collapsed north tower have been joined by a startling sheer wall of icy green stone that makes no attempt to mask the destruction.

In contrast to such memories, a lighthouse-like 1950s folly spirals to nowhere on the main square; should you feel the urge to climb its stairway, ask at the Mairie opposite. More compelling, around behind the Mairie, is a **Musée des Beaux Arts**. This is full of treasures: a Boudin sunset; a Lurçat tapestry of his dog Nadir and the Pirates; works by Corot, van Loo, Moreau; a Léger watercolour; a fine series of unfaded sixteenth-century Flemish tapestries on the lives of two peasants, and sad bombardment relics of the town. The museum is free, and open 10.30am to noon and 2.30 to 6pm in summer; till 5pm in winter, closed all day Tuesday and Sunday morning.

St-Lô makes an interesting pause but it's virtually abandoned at night. Most of the hotels, restaurants and bars are by the river and **gare SNCF**. The *Terminus* (3 av Briovère, ☎33.05.08.60), one of a row of modern, slightly expensive riverside hotels, has a good 50F menu. A better deal for rooms, if you get through the owners' eccentric selection process, is the *des Remparts* (3 rue des Prés; ☎33.57.08.06). The **SI** is just off the central square at 2 rue Havin. The **gare routière** is on the rue du 80e and 136e, which leads south from the SI.

Once St-Lô was taken in the Battle of Normandy, the armies speedily moved on for their next confrontation. The **Vire Valley**, trailing south from St-Lô, saw little action – and indeed its towns and villages have rarely been touched by any historic or cultural mainstream. The motivation in coming to this landscape of rolling hills and occasional gorges is essentially to consume the region's cider, calvados – much of it bootleg – fruit pastries and sausages made from pigs' intestines.

The best section of the valley is south of St-Lô through the Roches de Ham to TESSY-SUR-VIRE. The **Roches de Ham** are a pair of sheer rocky promontories high above the river. Though promoted as 'viewing tables', the pleasure lies as much in the walk up, through lanes lined with blackberries, hazelnuts and rich orchards. Downstream from the Roches, and a good place to stop for the night, is **LA CHAPELLE-SUR-VIRE**. Its church, towering majestically above the river, has been an object of pilgrimage since the twelfth century. Next to the bridge on the lower road is the *Auberge de la*

Chapelle (☎33.56.32.83), a good but rather expensive restaurant that has a few cheap **rooms**.

An alternative base for the Roches, over to the east, is **TORIGNY-SUR-VIRE**, which was the base of the Grimaldi family before they attained princeliness in Monaco. A spacious country town, it boasts a few grand buildings and an attractive **campsite**, *Camping du Lac* (☎33.56.91.74). At **TESSY-SUR-VIRE** there's little to see other than the river itself, though the town has a luxurious **campsite**, along with a couple of **hotels** and Wednesday **market**.

VIRE is worth visiting specifically for the food. The town is best known for its dreaded *andouille* sausages but you can gorge yourself instead on salmon trout fresh from the river, accompanied by local *poiré*. The biggest treats are to be found at the *Hôtel des Voyageurs* (☎31.68.01.16), at the bottom of av de la Gare, by the station. For around 60F you can have a sublime and almost interminable meal in opulent surroundings. Good **restaurants** are to be found, too, at the more central *Hôtel de France* (4 rue Aignaux, ☎31.68.00.35) and *Hôtel du Cheval Blanc* (2 place du 6-Juin-1944, ☎31.68.00.21). The only problem is what to do when you're not eating. The only action in Vire is at the Friday **market**, again obsessively dedicated to food.

For some exercise (and you'll need it), head 6km south along D76 to **Lac de la Dathée**. Set in open country, the lake is circled by footpaths or can be crossed by hired sailboat or wind-surfer (contact the *Maison des Jeunes et de la Culture*, 1 rue des Halles, Vire; ☎31.68.08.04).

West from Vire, VILLEDIEU-LES POELES – literally 'City of God the Frying Pans' – is a lively though touristy place. Copper souvenirs and kitchen utensils gleam from its rows of shops and the **SI** (on place des Costils) has lists of dozens of local *ateliers* for more direct purchases and details of the copperwork museum. All of which seems a bit over-enthusiastic though there is more authentic interest at the **Fonderie Cornille Havard** at 13 rue du Pont Chignon, one of the twelve remaining bell foundries in Europe. Work here is only part-time due to limited demand but it's always open to visits during the week (8am–noon and 2–6pm in summer; 1.30–5.30pm in winter) and you may find the forge lit. If you're charmed into staying, there's a **campsite** by the river and excellent basic food and accommodation at the *Hôtel de Paris* (☎33.61.00.66), on Route de Paris.

Southern Normandy: from Alençon westwards

ALENCON, a fair-sized and busy town, is known for its traditional – and now pretty much defunct – lace-making industry. The **Musée des Beaux Arts et de la Dentelle** (closed Mon.), is housed in a former Jesuit school and has all the best trappings of a modern museum. The highly informative history of lace-making, with examples of numerous different techniques can, however, be tedious for anyone not already fascinated by the subject. It also contains an unexpected collection of gruesome Cambodian artefacts, spears and lances, tiger skulls and elephants' feet, gathered by a 'militant socialist' French governor at the turn of the century. The paintings in the adjoining *Beaux Arts* section are nondescript, except for a few works by Courbet and Géricault. Wandering around the town might take you to Ste-Thérèse's birthplace on rue St-Blaise, just in front of the gare routière – if, that is, you haven't had a surfeit of the saint at Lisieux. The **Château des Ducs**, the old town castle close by the museum, looks impressive but doesn't encourage visitors. It is a prison and people in Alençon have nightmarish memories of its use by the Gestapo during the war.

If you want to stay – and the town has good shops and cafés – the main concentration of **hotels** is around the **SNCF** station on the northeast side of town. The two *logis*, *L'Industrie* (20 place Général-de-Gaulle, ☎33.29.06.51) and the *Grand Hôtel de la Gare* (50 av Wilson; ☎33.29.03.93) are very decent and have fixed-price menus for around 50 francs. There's a **youth hostel** out on D204 towards Colombiers, at 1 rue de la Paix, DAMIGNI (☎33.29.00.48). If you're interested in **horseback riding** – along the Orne – the *Association Départmentale de Tourisme Equestre et d'Equitation de Loisir de l'Orne* has its headquarters in Alençon at 60 Grand-Rue. They can also tell you about the various stud farms open to the public – another speciality of this area.

The **Forêt d'Ecouves**, north of Alençon and inaccessible by public transport, is a dense mixture of spruce, pine, oak and beech, unfortunately a favoured spot of the military – and in autumn of deerhunters, too. To avoid risking life and limb, check with the *Parc Regional Normandie-Maine* (see below). But you can usually ramble along the cool paths, happening on wild mushrooms and even the odd wild boar. The *gîte d'étape*, on D26 near LES RAGOTIERES on the edge nearest Alençon, is an ideal spot from which to explore the forest (contact the local *gîte* office at 60 rue St-Blaise in Alençon (☎33.32.09.00). Alternatively, at the western end of the woods, you could base yourself in **CARROUGES**, at the *Hôtel du Nord* (☎33.27.20.14) or *Saint-Pierre* (☎33.27.20.14).

Carrouges' **château** (10.30am–noon and 2–6.30pm), a castle, contains the offices of the *Parc Regional Normandie-Maine* (☎33.27.21.15) which covers an amorphous area stretching from Mortain in the west to within a few kilometres of Montagne-au-Perche in the east. The organisation is attempting to revitalise the region, encouraging small-scale agricultural producers – rabbit and bee farmers, cider-makers and the like. They also direct tourism in the region and can provide original information on footpaths and bird-watching trails. In the **Maison des Métiers**, the former castle chapel, local artisans sell their products.

West of Carrouges, the spa-town of **BAGNOLES-DE-L'ORNE** is quite unlike anywhere else in this part of the world. The monied sick and invalid come from all over France to its thermal baths. Business is so good they maintain a reservations office next to the Pompidou Centre in Paris. The layout is formal and spacious centring on a lake with gardens where horse-drawn calèches take the clients to an enormous Casino. And with so many visitors to keep entertained, and spending money, there are innumerable cultural events of a restrained and stressless nature. Whether you'd actually want to spend time in Bagnoles, though, depends on your disposable income as well as health. The innumerable **hotels** are expensive and sedate places, in which it's possible to be too late for dinner at 7pm and locked out altogether at 9pm, and the **campsite** is rather forlorn. You may do better at Bagnoles' less exclusive sister town of TESSE-LA-MADELEINE. **Restaurants**, in both towns, are reasonable; the *de la Terrasse* in Bagnoles is well-tried and popular.

Away from its main roads, the surrounding **Forêt des Andaines** is pleasant, with scattered and unspoiled villages such as JUVIGNY and ST-MICHEL. The road west through the forest from Bagnoles, D335 and then D908, climbs above the lush woodlands and progressively narrows to a hog's back before entering **DOMFRONT**. Less happens here than at Bagnoles, but it has the edge on countryside. A public park, near the **gare SNCF**, leads up to **castle ruins** on an isolated rock. Eleanor of Aquitaine was born in the castle in October 1162, and Thomas-à-Becket came to stay for Christmas 1166, saying mass in the nearby Notre-Dame-sur-l'Eau. The views from the gardens surrounding the mangled keep are spectacular, including a very graphic panorama of the ascent you've made. Domfront is a useful stopover, with several **hotels** around the railway station; beware though that the **campsite** has only ten spaces.

The **SI** at Domfront on rue Fossés-Plissons can provide details of the neighbouring forests, the **Forêt de Lande-Pourrie** and **Forêt de Mortain**. The eleventh-century vestiges of **LONLAY L'ABBAYE**, 9km out on D22 towards TINCHEBRAY, is one destination. Another is the **Fosse d'Arthur** to the west, a waterfall plunging into deep grottoes, and one of the many claimants to King Arthur's death scene. At the town of **MORTAIN** there are **waterfalls** and a tiny chapel on a high rock from which the neighbouring province of Maine spreads before you.

If you're heading down into Brittany, a last Norman stop, 7km southeast of ST-HILAIRE-DU-HARCOUET, is **ST-SYMPHORIEN-DES-MONTS**, where the park of the now nonexistent château is run as a **wildlife sanctuary**. Contented-looking beasts, like yaks and bisons and threatened domestic animals, graze in semi-liberty in fields and woods around a lake inhabited by swans and flamingos. In order to attract French visitors, there are wolves, too. Admission (mid-March to mid-Nov. only, 9am–8pm daily) is expensive but worth it.

travel details

Trains

Through services to Paris connect with all ferries at Dieppe, Le Havre and Cherbourg: if you're doing this it's easiest to buy a combined rail-ferry-rail ticket from your point of departure.

From Dieppe 5 daily to Rouen (3/4 hr.); 5 daily to Paris-St-Lazare (2 1/4 hr.).

From Le Havre at least hourly to Rouen (3/4 hr.) and Paris (2 hr.).

From Rouen 8 daily to Caen (2 1/4 hr.); at least hourly to Fécamp (1 hr.) and to Paris-St-Lazare (1 1/4 hr.).

From Caen at least hourly to Paris-St-Lazare (2 1/4 hr.); 2 daily to Rennes (2 hr.) via St-Lô (1 hr.), Coutances (1 1/4 hr.) and Mont St-Michel (1 1/2 hr.);

9 daily to Le Mans (2 hr.) and Tours (2½ hr.); hourly to Cherbourg (1–1½ hr.).

Buses

From Dieppe 5 daily to Paris (2¼ hr.; 1 daily to Fécamp (1½ hr.).

From Rouen hourly to Le Havre (2¾ hr.); 2 daily to Dieppe (1¾ hr.), Fécamp (2½ hr.) and Lisieux (2½ hr.).

From Caen 3 daily to Le Havre (3 hr.), via Cabourg, Deauville and Honfleur; 4 daily to Fécamp (1½ hr.).

From Lisieux 5 daily to Honfleur (¾ hr.).

Ferries

From Dieppe *Sealink* (☎35.21.36.50) to Newhaven (4 daily in 4 hr.).

From Le Havre *Townsend Thoresen* ☎35.21.36.50) to Portsmouth (2 daily in 5½ hr.). *Irish Continental Line* (☎35.26.57.26) daily to Cork (21 hr.) and to Rosslare (21 hr.).

From Cherbourg *Sealink* (☎33.96.70.70) to Portsmouth (1 daytime crossing; 4¾ hr.). *Townsend Thoresen* (☎33.44.20.13) to Portsmouth (3 daily; 4¾ hr.). *Irish Continental Line* (☎33.44.28.96) to Rosslare (17 hr.).

CHAPTER FOUR

BRITTANY

There's no one area – and certainly no one city – in **Brittany** that encapsulates the province's character. It lies in its people and in its geographical unity. For generations Bretons risked their lives fishing and trading on the violent seas or struggling with the arid soil of the interior. And this toughness and resilience is tinged with Celtic culture: mystical, musical, sometimes morbid and defeatist, sometimes vital and inspired.

The last independent ruler of Brittany, the Duchess Anne, succeeded in protecting Breton **autonomy** only through marriage to two consecutive French monarchs. After her death, in 1532, François I moved in, taking her daughter and lands, and sealing the union with an act supposedly enshrining certain privileges. These included a veto over taxes by the local *parlement* and the people's right to be tried, or conscripted to fight, only in their province. The successive violations of this treaty by Paris, and subsequent revolts, form the core of Breton history since the Middle Ages. Maintained often as a near colony, Bretons have seen their language steadily eradicated, and the interior severely depopulated through lack of centralised aid. Today, the people still tend to treat France as a separate country, even if few of them actively support Breton **nationalism** (which it's a criminal offence to advocate) much beyond putting **Breizh** (the Breton for Brittany) stickers on their cars. The recent economic resurgence, helped partly by summer tourism, has largely been due to local initiatives. Ignoring Paris pressures, **Brittany Ferries** has re-established an old trading link, carrying Breton produce as well as passengers across to Britain and Ireland. At the same time a Celtic artistic identity has consciously been revived. At local festivals, and above all the **Interceltic festival** at Lorient in August, traditional Breton music, poetry and dance are given great prominence and fellow Celts (Welsh-speakers will be understood) are treated as a comrades.

For most visitors to this province, though, it is **the Breton coast** that is the dominant feature. After the Côte d'Azur, this is now the most popular summer resort area in France – for both French and foreign tourists. The attractions are obvious: warm white sand beaches, towering cliffs, rock formations and offshore islands and islets, and everywhere the stone *dolmen* and *menhir* monuments of a prehistoric past. The most frequented areas are the **Côte d'Emêraude**, around **St-Malo**, and the **Morbihan coast** below **Auray** and **Vannes**. Accommodation and campsites here are plentiful, if pushed to their limits from mid-June to the end of August, and for all the crowds there are resorts as enticing as any in the country. Over in **southern Finistère** ('land's end') and along the **Côte de Granit Rose** in the north you may have to do more planning. This is true, too, if you come to Brittany out of season, when many of the coastal resorts close down completely.

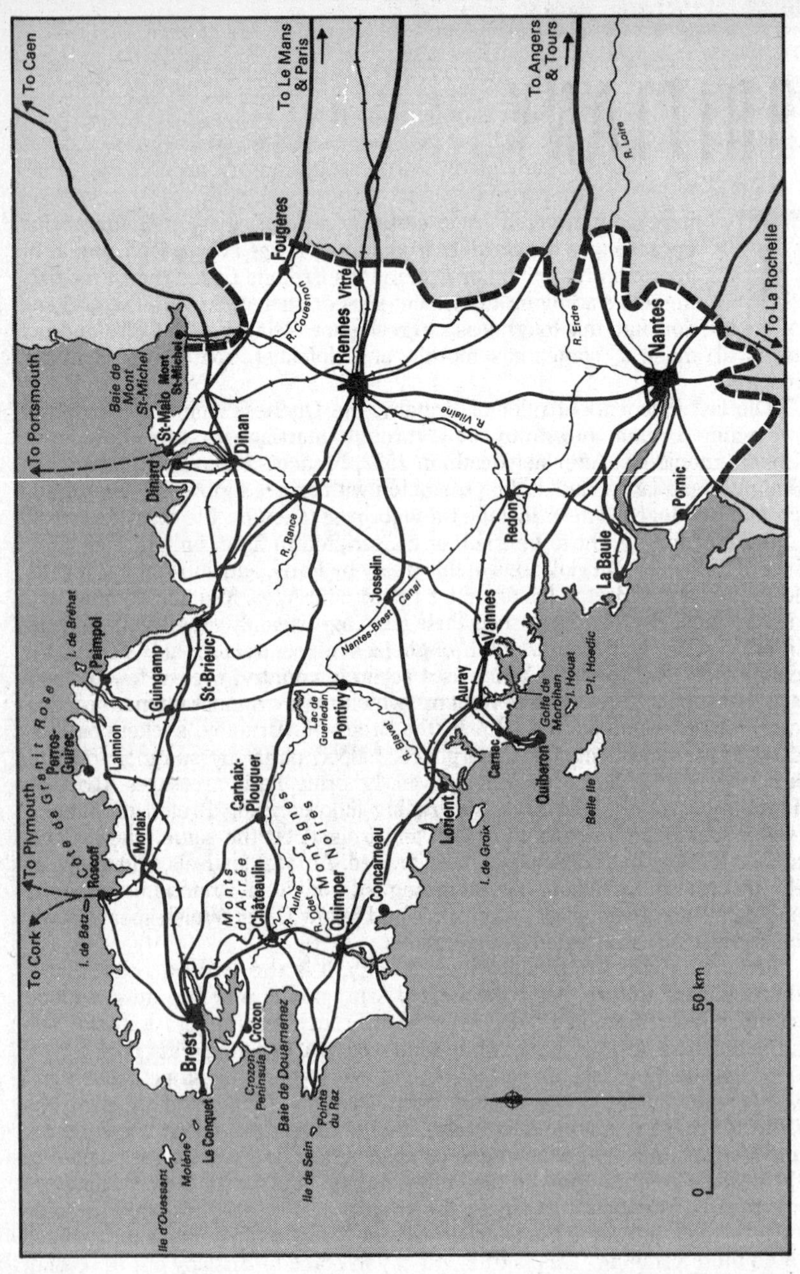
To Caen
To Le Mans & Paris
To Angers & Tours
R. Loire
Fougères
Vitré
R. Couesnon
Rennes
To La Rochelle
Nantes
R. Erdre
Baie de Mont St-Michel
Mont St-Michel
To Portsmouth
St-Malo
Dinard
Dinan
R. Vilaine
Redon
Pornic
La Baule
R. Rance
Josselin
Nantes-Brest Canal
Vannes
I. de Bréhat
Paimpol
Guingamp
St-Brieuc
Côte de Granit Rose
Perros-Guirec
Lannion
Pontivy
Lac de Guerlédan
Auray
Golfe de Morbihan
I. Houat
I. Hoedic
Carnac
Quiberon
Belle Ile
R. Blavet
Lorient
I. de Groix
Carhaix-Plouguer
Montagnes Noires
Monts d'Arrée
To Plymouth
Morlaix
Roscoff
To Cork
I. de Batz
Châteaulin
R. Aulne
R. Odet
Quimper
Concarneau
Brest
Crozon
Crozon Peninsula
Baie de Douarnenez
Pointe du Raz
Ile de Sein
Le Conquet
Molène
Ile d'Ouessant
0
50 km

But whenever you come, and wherever you're aiming for, don't leave Brittany without visiting at least one of its scores of **islands** (the **Ile de Bréhat** is one of the best and most accessible), or without taking in cities like **Quimper** or **Morlaix**, testimony (like the parish *enclos* of Finistère) to the riches of the medieval duchy. And take some time, too, to leave the coast and explore **the interior**, particularly the western country around the **Monts d'Arées**. Here you pay for the solitude with very sketchy transport and few hotels, but Brittany is one of the few areas of France where *camping sauvage* (not in campsites) is tolerated. There are sporadic *gîtes*, boats for hire on the **Nantes–Brest canal**, and hitching is very possible so long as you're happy to travel relatively small distances.

Finally, a note on the **Pardons**, pilgrimage-festivals commemorating local saints, which guidebooks (even local tourist offices) tend to promote as spectacles. They are not, unlike most French festivals, phoney affairs kept alive for the tourists, but instead deeply serious and rather gloomy religious occasions. If you're looking for traditional Breton fun, and you can't make the Lorient festival (or the smaller *Quinzaine Celtique* at Nantes in June/July), the events to look out for are gatherings organised by the numerous local **Celtic folklore groups** – *Circles* or *Bagadou*.

A BRETON GLOSSARY

Estimates of the number of Breton–speakers range between 400,000 and 800,000, but you are unlikely to encounter it spoken as a first, day-to-day language other than by the very old, or in the remoter parts of Finistère. Learning Breton is not really a viable prospect for visitors who do not already have a grounding in Welsh, Gaelic or some other Celtic language. However, as you travel through the province, it's interesting to note the roots of Breton place names, many of which have a simple meaning in the language. Below are some of the most common:

Aber	estuary	*Lann*	heath
Avel	wind	*Lech*	flat stone
Bihan	little	*Men*	stone
Bran	hill	*Menz*	mountain
Braz	big	*Mario*	dead
Creach	height	*Menhir*	long stone
Cromlech	stone circle	*Meur*	big
Dol	table	*Mor*	sea
Du	black	*Nevez*	new
Gavre	goat	*Parc*	field
Goat	forest	*Penn*	end, head
Goaz	stream	*Plou*	parish
Guen	white	*Pors*	port, farmyard
Hen	old	*Roch*	stone
Heol	sun	*Ster*	river
Hir	long	*Stivel*	fountain, spring
Inis	island	*Trez*	sand, beach
Ker	town or house	*Trou*	valley
Koz	old	*Ty*	house
Lan	church	*Wrach*	witch

THE NORTH COAST AND RENNES

Whether you approach across the Channel on the ferry from Plymouth, or along the coast from Mont St-Michel, the **Rance River**, guarded by **St-Malo** on its estuary, and **Dinan** 20km upstream, makes a spectacular introduction to Brittany. To the west stretches a varied coastline culminating in one of the most seductive of the islands, the **Ile de Bréhat**, and the colourful chaos of the **Côte de Granit Rose**. Inland all roads curl eventually to **Rennes**, the Breton capital, or out towards Normandy and Maine through **Dol** and the fortified frontier towns of **Fougères** and **Vitré**. South of Rennes you can encounter Celtic Brittany in the forest of **Brocéliande**, legendary location of the Arthurian tales.

The Rance Estuary: St-Malo, Dinard and Dinan

ST-MALO, walled and built with the same grey granite as the Mont St-Michel, presents its best face to the River Rance and the sea. If you're not planning to come here by ferry from Plymouth, it's still worth reaching it by boat – on the shuttle across the estuary from DINARD, or, more extravagantly, from DINAN (for details of both, see below). Otherwise, coming in by bus or train, you'll find the old city concealed by modern suburbs and dockside industry right until you're in it: the **buses**, however, do take you to the main city gate, the **Porte St-Vincent**; **trains** stop on the other side of the docks, a ten-minute walk away.

Once within the old ramparts, St-Malo can seem slightly grim and squat, and overrun by summer tourists – it is the most visited place in the province. But away from the popular thoroughfares of this tiny **citadelle**, with its high, late seventeenth-century stone houses, random exploration is fun and you can surface to the light on the ramparts or pass through them to the beaches. The prices on the open café terraces can be exorbitant, but with so many competing restaurants you'll find any number of mouth-watering **menus** to choose from; the *Etoile de Mer* (5 rue Jacques-Cartier) and the *Auberge Au Gai Bec* (see below) are particularly recommended. The *citadelle* is, however, not a good place for last-minute shopping if you're catching the ferry home. **Market days** are Tuesday and Friday.

The **town museum**, in the castle to the right as you enter Porte St-Vincent, glorifies, on several exhausting floors, St-Malo's sources of wealth and fame – colonialism, slave-trading and privateering among them. In the 1530s a St-Malo sea captain disembarked from the St. Lawrence River and declared Canada to be the possession of the King of France; the early free market economist, originator of the term *laissez-faire*, was a *Malouin* and the Argentinian (and most other people's) name for the Falklands, 'Las Malvinas', derives from the islands' first French colonists. The town's proud-

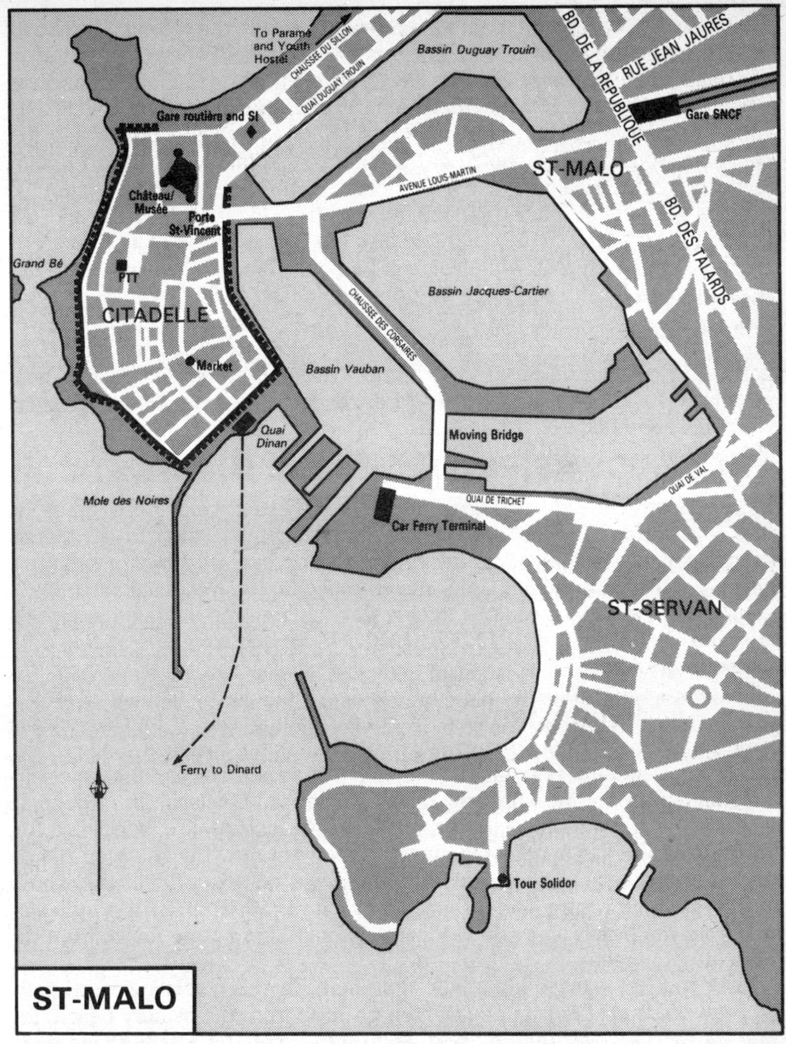

est boast, buried on the *Ile de Grand* (which you can walk to from the citadel at low tide) is the writer Chateaubriand. Chateaubriand gained his reputation, according to his contemporary, Marx:

> *'because he is the most classic incarnation of French vanité in every regard ... the false profundity, Byzantine exaggeration, emotional coquetry ... in form and content a never-before-seen mishmash of lies'.*

Suitably enough, he features heavily on all the tourist brochures as does his rather dull childhood mansion at nearby COMBOURG.

It's always more difficult to find **accommodation** in the old city, despite its extraordinary number of hotels; but this is very much where the action is, and rooms at the *Auberge Au Gai Bec* (corner of rue des Lauriers and rue Thévenard; ☎99.40.82.16), the *Moderne* (10 rue Corne-du-Cerf; ☎99.40.85.60), or the *Marguerite* (2 rue St-Benoît; ☎99.40.87.03) are well worth trying for. Otherwise, you have the choice of the rather staid family hotels in Paramé, the eastern suburb backing the main beach, or the array near the station on bd de la République, including the *Europe* (no. 44; ☎99.56.13.42) and the *Vauban* (no. 7; ☎99.56.09.39). Paramé also has a **youth hostel** at 37 av Père-Umbricht (☎99.56.15.32), while you can find out which of the various municipal **campsites** have free places by phoning ☎99.56.41.36. If you have problems, the **SI** is in front of the Porte St-Vincent. The **shuttle** to Dinard leaves from quai Dinan below the southern wall of the *citadelle* and takes ten minutes. **Bikes** can be hired from *Diazo Vélocation,* 3 bd des Talards near the railway station and **wind-surfing boards** from *Technic Plongée Comarin* (15 bd de la République).

Dinard

The road **from St-Malo to Dinard** crosses the estuary along the top of the world's first **tidal power dam** which, unfortunately, failed to set a non-nuclear example to the rest of the province. You can see how it works in a half-hour visit (8.30am–9pm) from the entrance on the west bank, just downstream from the lock. If you're catching the bus between St-Malo (St-Vincent gate) and Dinard, get off at LE RICHARDAIS for the dam, and at *Gallic* for the centre of Dinard.

The tastes of the affluent nineteenth-century English can be blamed for the metamorphosis of **DINARD** from a simple fishing village into something along the lines of a Côte d'Azur resort, with its casino, spacious shaded villas and social calendar of regattas and ballet. It's an expensive, and not especially welcoming place to stay – the only reasonably-priced hotels are *de l'Arrivée* (5 place de la Gare; ☎99.46.13.05) or *des Sables* (place Calvaire; ☎99.46.18.10). **Camping** is a better option: one site is to the west near the shore on rue du Sergent-Boulanger; another, *La Ville Maunay* (☎99.46.94.73) in the woods southwest of the centre, and a third, *Le Prieuré* (☎99.46.20.04) is a little way back from the beach on av de la Vicomte, about 2km up the Rance from the Pointe du Moulinet.

But if you just want to kill a little time here, there's a scenic coastal path, the *Promenade du Clair de Lune* which goes up from the estuary beach, the *plage du Prieuré*, over the tiny port, and up to Pointe du Moulinet for views over to St-Malo. You can continue around the point to another beach, by the casino, and on around more rocky outcrops to a secluded stretch at neighbouring ST-ENOGAT.

Dinan

You can buy **boat tickets** in Dinard at 27 av George V, either to St-Malo or, for a real pleasure trip, down the Rance to **DINAN.** The steep and cobbled street with fields and bramble thickets on either side that leads up to the 600-year-old ramparts partly hidden in the trees is certainly the best approach to Dinan. Its citadel has preserved, almost intact, the three-kilometre circuit of walls, inside which are street upon street of late medieval houses. It's a bit too good to be true, in brochure terms, but surprisingly not swamped by tourists. There are no very vital museums: the monument is the town itself, and time is easiest spent in rambling from crêperie to café, admiring the houses on the way. Unfortunately there's only one small stretch of the **ramparts** that you can walk along – from the gardens behind St-Sauveur to just short of the Tour Sillon – but you get a good general overview from the **Tour de l'Horloge** (open July–Aug. only, 10am–noon and 2–6pm; closed Sun.) on rue de l'Horloge or from the top of the keep guarding the town from the south. The latter keep, known as the **Château Duchesse Anne** is open 9am to noon and 2 to 7pm (earlier Tues. and out of season) and includes admission to the nearby **tour Coëtgen** where fifteenth-century stone nobles are gathered together as if in some medieval time capsule, about to depetrify at any moment. In the valley beyond the château there's an animal park and playground – good for kids bored with the Middle Ages.

St-Sauveur church, which seems an inevitable target of any Dinan wanderings, is a real mix-up of periods, with a Romanesque porch and eighteenth-century steeple. Even its nine Gothic chapels have numerous and asymmetrical vaulting; the most complex pair, in the centre, are wonderful. A cenotaph contains the heart of Bertrand du Guesclin, the fourteenth-century Breton warrior who defeated the English Knight, Thomas of Canterbury, in single combat in what is now place du Guesclin, to settle the siege of Dinan in 1364. Such chivalrous actions were rare for du Guesclin who favoured ambush, guerilla tactics and an organisation of armies far advanced for his day. He ended up in command of the French army that over the years managed to force the English back to Calais. North of the church rue du Jerzual leads down to the gate of the same name and on down (as rue du Petit Fort) to the port and a majestic old bridge over the Rance, lined with artisans' shops and restaurants.

Modern Dinan does exist, though rather gloomily, excluded from the *enclos*. In it you'll find the **gares SNCF** and **routière** a short walk away from place Duclos, and the Grande Rue entrance to the citadel (left along rue Carnot and right at place du Général-Leclerc). Two **hotels** near the station are *de France* (7 place du 11-Novembre; ☎96.39.22.56) and *de la Consigne* (40 rue Carnot). Within the walls there's *du Théâtre* (2 rue Ste-Claire; ☎96.39.06.91) and *La Duchesse Anne* (10 place du Guesclin; ☎96.39.09.43). The *Bar au Prélude* at 20 rue Haute-Voie is Dinan's liveliest late-night spot, with music and good basic food. The **SI** is opposite the Tour de l'Horloge in the Hôtel Kératry; the closest **campsite** is *La Nourais* (☎96.39.35.38) at 103 rue Chateaubriand which runs parallel to the western ramparts. Dinan's **youth hostel** (☎96.39.10.83) is very attractively set in the Moulin de Méen near the port at TADEN. Unfortunately it's not on any bus route, but if you follow the *quai* seawards from the promenade you'll see a small sign to the left after 2 km.

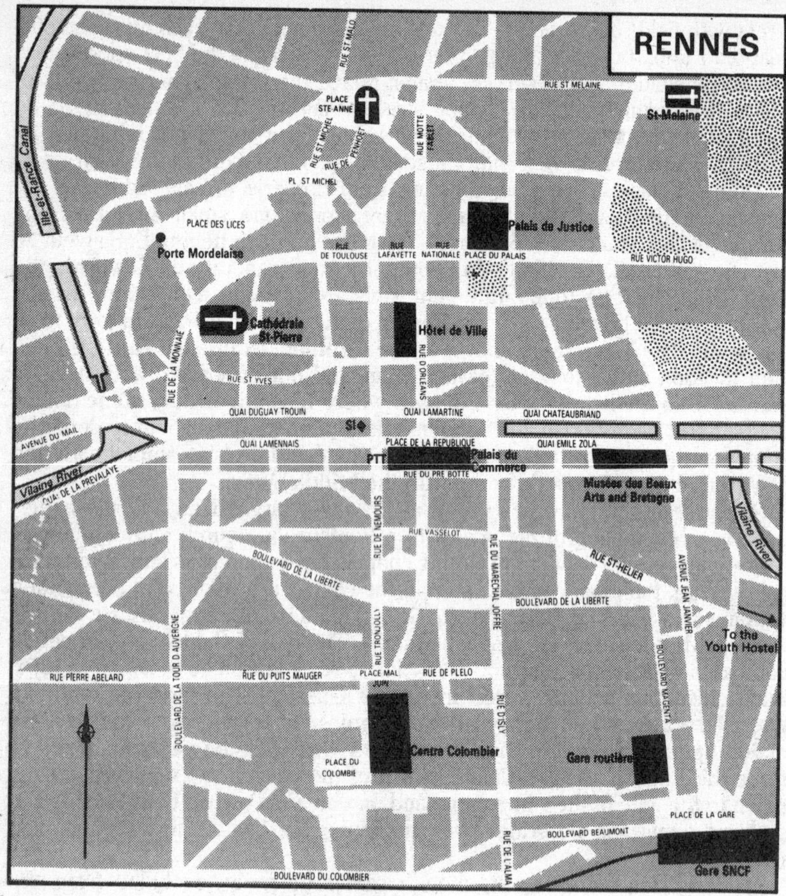

Rennes and Brocéliande

Capital and power centre of Brittany since the 1532 union with France, **RENNES** seems, outwardly at least, with its neoclassical layout and the pompous scale of its buildings, uncharacteristic of the province. It was razed in a fire of 1720 and the remodelling was handed out to Parisian architects – not in deference to the capital but to rival it.

Arriving here at the **gare SNCF/gare routière**, you may feel like moving straight on. But there's interest enough in and around the city if you're not exclusively committed to the picturesque. Buses #1/#20/#21/#22 will take you into the central **place de la République** (the 4th stop). Nearby, on the Pont du Nemours at the point where the Vilaine River goes underground, is the main **Tourist Office** for the province (Mon.–Sat. 9am–7.30pm; closed lunchtimes and Mon. out of season) where you can pick up full lists of Breton campsites, hostels and hotels. Further info on bikes, riding, hiking-routes, waterways and boats or canoes can be obtained at the **Association Bretonne** (*ABRI*) office at 3 rue des Portes-Mordelaise (Mon.–Sat. 9am–noon and 2–6pm), the last gatehouse left of the ramparts in the city's one surviving medieval quarter. **Hotels** are heavily concentrated around the place de la Gare in front of the station, with the *Bretagne* (no. 7; ☎99.31.48.48) and the *Brest* (no. 15; ☎99.30.35.83) both reliable. It's a long haul across town to find a good cheap alternative, although the Rocher de Cancale (10 rue Saint-Michel; ☎99.79.20.83) fits the bill to perfection, ideally situated in the medieval section. The **youth hostel** is 3km out at 10–12 Canal St-Martin (on bus route 22 towards St-Gregoire; stop Coetlogon; ☎99.33.22.33). Bus #3 takes you northeast to Gayeulles (direction St-Laurent) where there's a short walk down a lane to the city's **campsite**.

The city's one central building to survive the great fire was symbolically enough, the **Palais de Justice**, home of the old Rennes *parlement* – a mixture of high court and council with unelected members. You can see around this building where the *parlement* fought battles with the French governor from Louis XIV's reign up until the Revolution. Tours are at 9.45am, 10.30am, 11.15am, 2.15pm, 3pm, 4pm, 4.45pm daily in season, closed Tuesday, and start from the far right-hand corner of the courtyard. The seventeenth-century chambers are each more opulently gilded and adorned than the one before, culminating in the debating hall hung with Gobelin tapestries depicting scenes from the history of the duchy and the province. Every centimetre of the walls and ceiling is decorated – Sun-King-style, but on a relatively small scale.

The Vilaine flows through the centre of Rennes, miserably confined in a steep-sided channel and covered over in the very centre of town. On its south side, at 3 quai Emile-Zola, the **Musée de Bretagne** gives one of the best possible introductions to the culture and history of Brittany. Its presentation is impressively accessible, with a startling section dealing with the transition from the nineteenth to the present century – an ongoing process which you'll experience in peculiar jolts of time lag as you travel around Brittany. The **Musée des Beaux Arts**, in the same building, contains an outstanding collection of pictures, from Leonardo drawings to 1960s abstracts. One room is dedicated to Brittany with mythical scenes – the Ile d'Ys legend by Luminais – and scenes from real life – a woman waiting for the fishermen to come back through stormy seas. Both museums are open 10am to noon, 2 to 6pm, closed Tuesday, with a cheap combination ticket.

The surviving **medieval quarter**, bordered by the canal to the west and the river to the south, radiates from **Porte Mordelaise**, the old ceremonial entrance to the city. This is the liveliest part of town and stays up late, particularly in the vicinity of St-Aubin church. Good cheap **food** is to be had at *La Ship Shop*, 30 rue St-Malo; there's an excellent *crêperie* at 5 place Ste-Anne and around the back, through an archway off rue Motte-Fablet, you can get a wonderful view of medieval high-rise housing. More **restaurants** and an interesting selection of **bars** are congregated around place St-Michel, rue de Penhoet and rue St-Malo.

Rennes is seen at its best in the first ten days of July, when the **Festival des Tombées de la nuit** takes over the whole city to celebrate ongoing Breton culture with music, theatre, film, mime and poetry, in joyful rejection of the influences of both Paris and Hollywood. Lastly, a few **incidentals**: if you're interested in talking to nationalist Breton campaigners, the place to go is the *Centre Rennais d'Informations Bretonnes* (30 place des Lices). For cassettes of Breton-Celtic music, books, posters and postcards take a look at *Co-op Breizh* (17 rue Penhoet). The *L'Arvor* **cinema** (29 rue d'Antrain) shows *v.o.* (in the original language) films. And if you plan on long-distance **hitching**, the *Allostop* number is ☎99.30.98.87.

Brocéliande – the Forêt de Paimpont

Thirty kilometres to the west of Rennes, the **Forêt de Paimpont**, known also by its ancient name of **BROCELIANDE**, is Merlin's forest. Medieval Breton minstrels, like their Welsh counterparts from whom or with whom the stories originated, set the tales of King Arthur and the Holy Grail both in *Grande Bretagne* and here in *Petite Bretagne*. For all the magic of these shared legends, however, and a succession of likely sites, few people come out here. If you like the idea of roaming around for a day it isn't difficult. The bus from Rennes to Guer runs twice a day past the southern edge of the forest, stopping at FORGES-LES-PAIMPONT, and another, around the north corner, to **MAURON**.

Mauron is a good point to start. From the hamlet of **FOLLE-PENSEE**, just south of the village, it's a circuitous but enjoyable twenty-minute walk to **La Fontaine de Barenton** – Merlin's spring. The path leads off from the end of the road at Folle-Pensée, turning to the right, running through pines and gorse to a junction of forest tracks: here take the track straight ahead for about 100m, where an unobvious path to the left goes into the woods and turns back north to the spring – walled, and filled by the most delicious water imaginable, as you might expect from the elixir of eternal youth. After drinking, stroke the great stone slab beside the spring to call up a storm, roaring lions and a horseman in black armour. Here Merlin first set eyes on Vivianne who bound him willingly in a prison of air.

Another forest walk, more scenic but without a goal, is the **Val sans Retour** (the Valley of no Return), off the GR37 from TREHORENTEUC to La Guette. The path to follow leads out from D141 just south of Tréhorenteuc to a steep valley from which exits are barred by thickets of gorse and giant furze on the rocks above; at one point it skirts an overgrown table of rock, the *Rocher des Faux Amants*, from which the seducer Morgane le Fay enticed unwary boys.

If you feel like **staying** in these parts, **PAIMPONT** is the most enjoyable and easy place to base yourself. It's right in the centre of the woods and has two **campsites**, a **gîte d'étape** (c/o M. and Mme Grosset; ☎99.07.81.40), a **youth hostel** (☎97.22.76.75; a couple of kilometres out on the Concoret road) and the **hotel** *Relais de Brocéliande* (☎99.07.81.07). Next to the abbey on the edge of the lake is an **SI**. If you do head out to Concoret you'll find the **Etang du Comper**, overlooked by the château of the enchanter Vivianne.

There's another *gîte d'étape* at FORGES-LES-PAIMPONT which is on the GR37, south of Paimpont (c/o Mme Farcy; ☎97.06.93.46). Or, for two cheap **hotels**, the *Orée de la Forêt* (☎99.06.81.15) and the *Bruyères* (☎99.06.81.38), you could stop at **PLELAN-LE-GRAND**, east of the forest on the main Rennes road.

The frontier towns: Dol, Fougères and Vitré

If you're entering Brittany by road, from Normandy, Maine or Le Mans, you're likely to pass through Dol-de-Bretagne, Fougères, or close by to Vitré – all, at one time or another, heavily fortified strategic sites.

From Mont St-Michel, **DOL-DE-BRETAGNE** is the first Breton town. All approaches to it are guarded by the former island of **Mont Dol** – now eight rather marshy kilometres in from the sea. This abrupt granite outcrop, looking mountainous beyond its size on such a flat plain, was the legendary site of a battle between the Archangel Michael and the Devil. Various fancifully named indentations in the rock, such as 'the Devil's Claw', testify to the savagery of their encounter, which as usual the Devil lost. The site has been occupied since prehistoric times – flint implements have been unearthed alongside the bones of mammoths, sabre-toothed tigers, and even rhinoceri. Later on, it appears to have been used for worship by the Druids, before becoming, like Mont St-Michel, an island monastery, all traces of which have long vanished. A plaque proclaims that visiting the small chapel on top earns a Papal Indulgence. The climb is pleasant, too, a steep footpath winding up among the chestnuts and beeches to a solitary bar.

Close to the **cathedral**, with its strange squat and square tiled towers, is a **Musée d'Histoire et d'Art Populaire** (open Easter to the end of Sept., 9.30am–6pm daily). Though a bit full of posed waxworks it has two rooms of astonishing wooden bits and pieces rescued in assorted states of decay from churches, often equally rotting, all over Brittany. These carvings and statues, some still brightly polychromed with their crust of eggy paint, range from the thirteenth to the nineteenth centuries.

There is not a great deal more to Dol, for visitors anyway. The commercial part of town is lively without being too modern; the *Katédral* bar, between the church and museum, is worth some of your time. And there's one very reasonable **hotel**, the *Bretagne* (place Chateaubriand, ☎99.48.02.03).

Along the coast north of Dol the pinnacle of Mont St-Michel is clearly visible from every vantage point, of which the most spectacular is the **Pointe du Grouin**, a perilous and windy height which also overlooks the bird sanctuary of the **Iles des Landes** to the east.

Just south of the *pointe,* and less than 15km from St-Malo across the peninsula, is **CANCALE,** a place not to be missed by those who attribute magical qualities to **oysters**. In the old church of **St-Méen** at the top of the hill, a small **Musée des Arts et Traditions Populaires** (July–Aug. 10.30am–12.30pm and 3.30–7.30pm daily, closed Mon. am; rest of the year open Mon.–Sat. pm only) documents the town's obsession with meticulous precision.

Cancale oysters were found in the camps of Julius Caesar, taken daily to Versailles for Louis XIV, and even accompanied Napoléon on the march to Moscow.

From the rue des Parcs next to the jetty of the port, you can, at low tide, see the *parcs* where the oysters are grown. The rocks of the cliff behind are streaked and shiny like mother-of-pearl; underfoot the beach is littered with countless generations of empty shells. The port area is lined with upmarket glass-fronted hotels and restaurants – of the **hotels** the *Continentale* (☎99.89.60.16) and the *Emeraude* (☎99.89.61.76) on quai Thomas are among the more reasonable. The restaurants without exception specialise in every kind of seafood, but unfortunately oysters here are no less expensive than on a Paris boulevard.

FOUGERES lies on the main Caen–Rennes road and has a topography impossible to grasp from a map; streets that look a few metres long turn out to be precipitous plunges down the escarpments of its split-levelled site: lanes collapse into flights of steps. The **castle** is built well below the level of the main part of town, on a low spit of land that separates, and is towered over by, two mighty rock faces. Its massive and seemingly impregnable bulk is protected by great curtain walls growing out of the rock, and encircled by a hacked-out moat full of weirs and waterfalls – none of which prevented its repeated capture by such medieval adventurers as du Guesclin. It is, however, eighteenth-century Fougères that is always featured in the summer-night theatrical performances at the château, based on the book that immortalised the town, Balzac's *The Chouans*. It tells, in rampant best-seller vein, the story of the counter-revolutionary *Chouan* rebellion in Brittany during the early 1790s and makes great play of the strange layout of the town. Good reading while you're there.

Within the castle, the focus is more prosaic. Footwear, to this day the main industry of the town, is presented in a **museum** included in the **château tours** (on the hour from 9–11am and 2–6pm March–Oct., closed Tues. except in summer; weekends only in Nov.; Sun. only in Feb.). The best approach to the castle is from the **place des Arbres** beside St-Léonard's church off the main street of the old fortified town. The formal terraces give way to the water meadows of the River Nançon which you can cross beside medieval houses still standing on the riverbank. Alternatively, take the longer route down rue Nationale, where you'll pass, at no. 51, the **musée de La Villéon**, an Impressionist who painted numerous lovely Breton landscapes (open 9am–7pm daily in July and Aug.; at weekends April–June and Sept.).

The two *logis de France*, in old Fougères, are the best bet for **hotels**. The *du Commerce* (☎99.94.40.40) is in the large market-square near the station; the *Moderne* (☎99.99.00.24) at no. 15 rue du Tribunal, further up towards the town centre, has a good restaurant. There is a **youth hostel** at 11 rue Beaumanoir (☎99.99.22.06). The **SI** at 1 place Aristide-Briand provides copious information on all aspects of the town and local countryside.

Halfway between Fougères and Rennes, **St-Aubin-du-Cormier** has a sad tale to tell concerning English, French and Breton relations. A small monument in a field marks the battlesite where, in 1488, the forces of the Duke of

Brittany were defeated by the French army. Many of the Breton soldiers had dressed in the English colours, a black cross on white silk, to scare the French into believing that the Duke had extensive English reinforcements. The victorious French were told to spare all prisoners except the English; and so the hapless Bretons were massacred. St-Aubin's castle was then demolished – just one sheer wall survives, with a fireplace visible midway up. Should you wish to stop overnight there's a very cheap **hotel**, the *du Bretagne* (68 rue de l'Ecu, ☎99.39.10.22), a wonderful rambling old building serving very good food.

VITRE, just north of the Le Mans–Rennes motorway, rivals Dinan as the best-preserved medieval town in Brittany. Its walls are not quite complete, but what lies outside them has hardly changed. The **castle** has sharp-pointed towers with slate-grey roofs in best fairy-tale fashion though, unfortunately, the municipal offices and museum of shells, birds, bugs and local history inside are not exactly thrilling. Hours are 10am to 12.15pm and 1.30 to 6pm; closed Tuesday in winter.

Vitré is a market town rather than an industrial centre, with its principal **market** held on Mondays in the square in front of Notre-Dame church. The old city is full of twisting streets of half-timbered houses, a good proportion of which are bars. **Rue Beaudrairie** in particular has a fine selection. *Le Chaperon Rouge* at 12 bd des Jacobins is a vegetarian restaurant. An unusual visual treat, if you happen to be using the **post office**, is its modern stained-glass window behind the counter. Most of the **hotels** are around the station, where the ramparts have disappeared and the town imperceptibly blends into its newer sectors. This is a cheap as well as a pleasant place to stay; the *Petit-Billot* (place du Général-Leclerc; ☎99.75.02.10), *Chêne-Vert* (place de la Gare; ☎99.75.00.58) and *du Guesclin* (place du Général-Leclerc; ☎99.75.02.96) are all good deals.

The north coast from Dinard to Lannion

To the west of the Rance, beyond Dinard, begins the green of the **Côte d'Emeraude**. Though composed mainly of developed family resorts, it also offers wonderful camping, at its best, around the heather-backed beaches near **Cap Fréhel**. You can't camp within 5km of the headland itself, a high, warm expanse of heath and cliffs with views extending on good days as far as Jersey and the Ile de Bréhat. The **Fort la Latte**, to the east, is used regularly as a film set. Guided tours across its two drawbridges to the cannonball factory within its towers are from June–September 10am to 12.30pm and 2.30 to 6.30pm; rest of the year Sundays and holidays only, 2.30 to 5.30pm. The nearest places to stay are the ideal isolated **campsite** at PLEHEREL, and a summer-only **youth hostel** at PLEVENON (☎96.61.91.87).

Both **ERQUY** and **LE VAL-ANDRE** have superb crescent beaches, with long tides that recede beyond the rocky headlands. In Le Val-André the recently-refurbished *Hotel de la Mer* (63 rue A.-Charner, ☎96.72.20.44), as well as having good cheap rooms, serves food that is utterly magnificent, its *moules marinières* on a different plane to any you've ever tasted.

The major city by this coast, **ST-BRIEUC** is far too busy being the industrial centre of the north to concern itself with entertaining tourists. The predominant character is resolutely commercial and not at all inspiring. Every July, however, there is one concession to summer visitors in a **Festival of Breton Music**; if you're interested, the **SI** at 7 rue St-Goueno can supply all relevant information. The **gare routière** to get you out to the coast is close to the **SI** on rue Waldeck-Rousseau, which, from the **gare SNCF,** is at the end of bd Charner to your right as you come out of the station.

Moving northwest towards Paimpol, the coast becomes wilder and harsher and the seaside towns tend to be crammed into narrow rocky inlets or set well back in river estuaries. **BINIC** is a narrow port surrounded by meadows, with a thin strip of beach and a decent hotel, the *Galion* (☎96.73.61.30), while at the sedate family resort of **ST-QUAY-PORTRIEUX** just further on, the *Gerbot d'Avoine* (☎96.70.40.09) beside the beach is the best place to stay (despite the hideous decor of its rooms). After St-Quay, the coastal road shifts inland, through PLOUHA, the traditional boundary between French-speaking and Breton-speaking Brittany. It's a viable proposition to hitch to **KERMARIA-AN-ISQUIT** from here, signposted off D21 from Plouha. The point of this complex detour is to see the extraordinary medieval frescoes of a *Dance Macabre* in the **chapel** of the village. They show Ankou, who is death or death's assistant, leading representatives of every social class in a dance of death. An encounter between three living nobles out hunting and three philosophical corpses is also depicted and there's a statue of the infant Jesus refusing milk from Mary's proffered breast. To get into the chapel you'll need to get a key from Mme. Hervé Droniou in the house just up the road on the left.

To the north, back on the coast, **PAIMPOL**, though still an attractive town, has lost something in its transition from working fishing port to pleasure harbour. It was once the centre of a cod and whaling fleet that sailed for the fisheries of Iceland in February of each year, sent off with a ceremony marked by a famous *pardon*. From then until August or September, the town would be empty of all young men. A haunting glimpse of the way Paimpol used to look can be seen in the recently re-released silent film shot here in 1924 of Pierre Loti's book *Pêcheur d'Islande*. The **hotels** in the ugly new block that lines one side of the tiny harbour are reasonable enough, while of the restaurants the *Cotriade* to the right is much better value than the *du Port* to the left. On the whole, though Paimpol may be a very pleasant place to arrive by yacht, threading through the rocks, you'll probably prefer if you're landbound to continue to the spectacular **Pointe de l'Arcouest** and Bréhat – or to little **LOGUIVY**, a beautiful village where Lenin once briefly recuperated during his period in Paris.

The Ile de Bréhat

The **ILE DE BREHAT** – in reality two islands joined by a tiny bridge – gives the appearance of spanning great latitudes. On the north side are windswept meadows of hemlock and yarrow, sloping down to chaotic erosions of rock;

on the south, you're in the midst of palm trees, mimosa and eucalyptus. All around is a multitude of little islets – some accessible at low tide, others *propriété privée*, most just pink-orange rocks. Bréhat is connected regularly by **ferry** from POINTE DE L'ARCOUEST (hourly in high summer, slightly less otherwise, with the last boat back from Bréhat around 7pm). No cars are permitted on the island, and there's barely a road wide enough for its few light farm vehicles. You can walk from one end to the other in half an hour; but this has to be one of the most beautiful places in Brittany, or for that matter in all of France.

As you might expect, this island paradise has attracted Parisians and the like looking for holiday homes. Over half the houses now have temporary residents and young Bréhatins leave in ever-increasing numbers for lack of a place of their own, let alone a job. In winter the remaining 300 or so natives have the place to themselves, without even a *gendarme*; the summer sees two imported from the mainland, along with upwards of 3000 tourists. As a visitor, though, you should find the Bréhatins friendly enough – it's the holiday-home owners that they really resent.

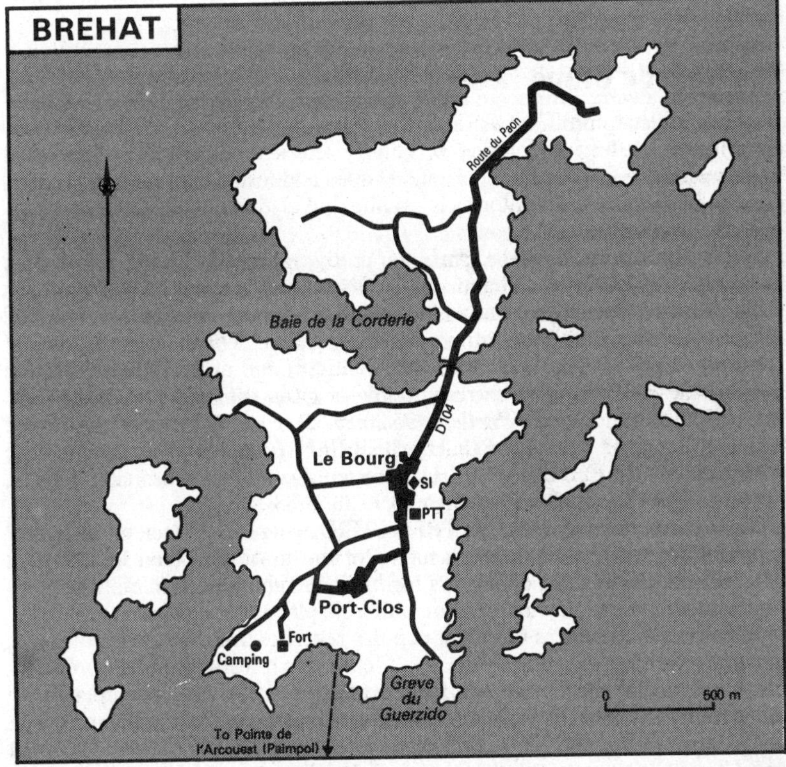

The island's three **hotels** are expensive and in any case permanently booked through the summer; in winter, only *Aux Pêcheurs* stays open. But for **campers**, Bréhat has a wonderful site in the woods high above the sea west of the port, and when that's closed you can pitch your tent almost anywhere. From the port the right-hand track leads past the island's only **bike hire** outlet and then turns north towards **Le Bourg** – Bréhat village – where the square is the centre of all activity. The **SI** is in the old Mairie on the right, and most days there's a small market; restaurants are neither numerous nor cheap, so picnic fare is the best bet.

The beach to swim from at low tide is the **Grève de Guerzido,** on the east side facing the mainland. Nearer the town the water is a bit murky, and the east coast generally is less accessible because of private property. But in the north, even when Le Bourg is blocked up with visitors, you can walk and laze about in near solitude. Bréhat no longer has a castle (blown up twice by the English), but it does have a lighthouse, and a nineteenth-century **fort** – in the woods before the campsite – with outer defences and an inner courtyard planted with azaleas, nasturtiums, potatoes and garlic by a dozen squatters who don't have to worry about eviction threats from the sympathetic island council.

The Côte de Granit Rose

Between Bréhat and TREGASTEL the shoreline is known as the **Côte de Granit Rose** after its pink-tinged, glittery and smooth granite which wind and waves have sculpted into curious shapes and forms. Not only the coastal chaos of rocks and promontories is granite, but also the houses, the breakwaters, the pavements, and so on.

Public transport in these parts is pretty marginal. There are **buses** between Paimpol, Trégastel and LANNION but that's about it. Walkers have GR34, which follows the coast a little inland. There are **campsites** dotted all along the coast but little other accommodation. **Youth hostels** are at Lannion (6 rue du 73e-Territorial; ☎96.37.91.28) and at TREBEURDEN (*Le Toeno;* ☎96.23.52.22). There are a couple of **gîtes d'étape**, at LOUANNEC (c/o Mme Kremer, *Villa Stelle*; ☎96.23.15.62) east of Perros-Guirec, and south of Treguier near LA ROCHE DERRIEN (*Château de la Roche Jagu*; ☎96.95.62.35). In PLOUMANAC'H, there are a couple of reasonable **hotels**, *Roch Hir* (☎96.23.23.24) and *du Parc* (☎96.23.24.88).

In passing, take a look at **TREGUIER**, where the ancient cathedral contains the tomb of St. Yves, a native of the town who died in 1303 and became the patron saint of lawyers for his incorruptibility. Attempts to bribe him continue to this day in the form of marble plaques and candles.

PERROS-GUIREC is the most popular resort of this coast, with the walk along the **Sentier des Douaniers** to Ploumanac'h leading past the region's most spectacular succession of bizarre granite outcrops – each complete with its own unlikely label as well. The **plage du Trestraou**, on the opposite side of the town to the port, is a good place to eat and drink – the *Homard Bleu* and *L'Excelsior* are particularly recommended. From here, boats sail on three-hour round trips to the bird sanctuary **Sept Iles** (June–Aug., usually at 2pm, sometimes also 9am; ticket office next door to the *Centre Nautique*, closed 11am–1.30pm). The strangest sight along this coast, however, outdoing anything the erosions can manage, is just south of TREGASTEL-BOURG, on the route de Calvaire, where an old stone saint, halfway up a high calvary, raises his arm to bless or harangue the gleaming white discs and dome of the Lannion telecommunications research centre.

Between Lannion and Morlaix, on the bus route, there's a good place to witness the traditional Breton death figure of Ankou in all his majesty (see also p.240). In the church at PLOUMILLAU he stands 1m high, a wooden skeleton with spade and scythe. He used to travel with every coffin to the cemetery, the familiarity of his presence perhaps making death less sinister.

Guingamp

If you skip the Pink Granite Coast and head directly west towards Finistère you'll pass through **GUINGAMP**. It's the only town of any size in the centre of this northern peninsula and an old weaving centre – its name possibly the source of the fabric 'gingham'. It's an attractive place, but there's not much to see beyond the main square, with its fountain bedecked in griffins and gargoyles, and the Black Virgin in the basilica. On the road out towards Morlaix is the 'mountain' of the **Ménéz Bré**, a spectacular height amid these plains. In the mid-nineteenth century, the local rector was often observed to climb to the mountain's peak on stormy nights, accompanied only by a donkey laden with books. For all his exemplary piety, his parishioners suspected him of sorcery and witchcraft; he was, it turned out, doing early research into natural electrical forces.

FINISTERE – THE LAND'S END

It's hard to resist the lure of the **Finistère coast** – with its ocean-fronting cliffs and headlands. Summer crowds may take away from the best brochure sights of parts of the **Crozon** peninsula and the **Pointe de Raz** but there are miles and miles of coast where you can enjoy near solitude. If you've transport, explore the semi-wilderness of the **northern stretches** beyond Brest and the little fishing village of **Le Conquet**, or the misty offshore islands, **Ouessant and Molène**. From the top of **Menez-Hom** you can admire the anarchic limits of western France, and in the two cities of **Morlaix** and **Quimper**, you'll witness distinctly Breton modern life as well as ancient splendours. Of these, the **parish closes** south of Morlaix reveal much of the mythology of the medieval past.

Roscoff, the Ile de Batz and St-Pol-de-Léon

The opening of the deep-water port at **ROSCOFF** in 1973 was part of a general attempt to revitalise the Breton economy. The ferry services to Plymouth and to Cork are intended not just to bring tourists, but also to revive the traditional trading links between the Celtic nations of Brittany, Ireland, and Southwest England – links which were suppressed for centuries as an act of French state policy after the union of Brittany with France in 1532.

Roscoff itself has, however, remained a small resort with almost all activity confined to **rue Gambetta** and the **old port** – the rest of the roads are residential back streets full of retirement homes and institutions. A factor in preserving its old character is that both the ferry port and the SNCF station are some way from the town centre. To **reach the town from the ferry**, turn right coming away from the terminal, and follow the signs that lead across a narrow promontory and down into the crescent of Roscoff's natural harbour. Later than 9pm it may be difficult to find a restaurant still serving, but **hotels** are used to clientele arriving on late sailings. The two most reasonable are both on rue Amiral-Réveillère: *des Arcades* (☎98.69.70.45) at no. 15, which has an unusually trendy bar and good cheap food; and the quieter, slightly more expensive *Les Chardons Bleus* (☎98.69.72.03) at no. 4.

Until the last couple of centuries, the town made most of its money from piracy – like so many other ports along the Breton coast. There are a few reminders of that wealth in the ornate stone houses, and the church with its sculpted ships and protruding stone cannons, all dating from the sixteenth century. A more unusual relic is the fig tree in the **Couvent des Capucines**, on rue des Capucines (left out of the station, then right). Planted in 1625, it now stands 25m wide, propped up by stone pillars and iron girders, and can still produce 400 kilos of fruit in a good year.

The Ile de Batz

In the summer there are several sailings each day to the **Ile de Batz** (pronounced Ba) – you can't actually get there along the pier that stretches several hundred tantalising metres towards it. The island is a somewhat windswept spot but well endowed with sandy beaches; for campers looking to have a stretch of coastline to themselves, it could be ideal. The **boats** arrive at the pier of the old island town. Walk uphill from here and you'll come to the **youth hostel** (98.61.77.69), at the picturesquely-named Creac'h ar Bolloc'h, and the **campsite**. Higher still, on the island's peak, is a lighthouse you can visit. And beyond that, it's just the sands and seaweed.

St-Pol-de-Léon

The main road **south from Roscoff** passes by fields of the famous Breton artichokes before arriving after 6km at **ST-POL-DE-LEON**. It's not an exciting place but – assuming you've got your own transport – it has two churches that at least merit a pause. The **Cathédrale**, in the main town square, was rebuilt towards the end of the thirteenth century along the lines of Coutances – a quiet classic of unified Norman architecture. The remains of Saint Pol are inside, alongside a large bell, rung over the heads of pilgrims during his *pardon* on March 12 in the unlikely hope of curing headaches and ear diseases. Just downhill is the original **Kreisker Chapel**, with access to the top of its sharp-pointed soaring granite belfry (now coated in yellow moss).

Morlaix and the Breton parish closes

MORLAIX, one of the great old Breton ports, thrived off trade with England in between wars during the 'Golden Period' of the late Middle Ages. Built up the slopes of a steep valley with sober stone houses, its present grandeur comes from the pink granite viaduct carrying trains from Paris to Brest way above the town centre. Coming by road from the north, the opening view is of shiny yacht masts paralleling the pillars of the viaduct. Orientation is quite straightforward. The central square, with the local **SI** and Hôtel de Ville, is **place des Otages**. To its south extends the **old town**, once a walled and moated *citadelle*, and still containing enough medieval houses to recall its existence. If you arrive at the **gare routière** you'll find yourself a couple of blocks from the main *place*, towards the port on **place Cornic**; from the **gare SNCF** the quickest route down to the centre is along the venelle de la Roche, which also brings you out at place Cornic.

Some **hotels** to try in the centre are *du Roy d'Ys* (8 rue de Jacobins, ☎98.88.61.19, closed Sun.), *des Halles* (23 rue du Mur, ☎98.88.03.86), *Ste-Mélaine* (77 rue Ange-de-Guernisac, ☎98.88.08.79), or *des Arcades* (11 place Cornic, ☎98.88.20.03); and nearer the station, *Calvez* (place Martin, ☎98.88.03.29). The **youth hostel** (3 route de Paris; ☎98.88.13.63) is 15-minutes' walk from the station, or you can take the KERNEGUES bus from the Hôtel de Ville as far as rue de Paris; the route de Paris is just beyond it if you turn left at place Traoulen. The same bus in the opposite direction takes you to LA VIERGE-NOIRE and its **campsite** (on the right about a 250-metre walk further north).

The streets between Eglise Ste-Melaine (above the SI) and place des Jacobins in the old town are the best **restaurant** hunting grounds. You can also get a inexpensive basic meal at the *Hôtel des Halles* (as above), on the south side of place des Halles. For late-evening **drinking**, *La Père Ubu* (37 rue de Callac, near the youth hostel) has good taped music, darts and boisterous Bretons till 1am (midnight in winter closed Sun. and Mon.) and occasional *café-théâtre* and live jazz.

Morlaix has recently acquired its own small brewery, set up to produce real ale similar to that its owners had enjoyed on visiting Britain. You should be able to find the resultant brew, *Coreff*, in local bars, or you can visit the brewery itself at 1 place de la Madeleine (groups of 10, Tues.–Thurs. by arrangement; ☎98.63.41.92). Apart from that, there's little to do in the daytime here, except to explore the stairways running up from places des Otages and Cornic and the almost rural paths around the viaduct. The town **museum**, in the place des Jacobins, has a reasonably entertaining assortment of Roman wine jars, bits that have fallen off medieval churches, cannons and kitchen utensils, and a few modern paintings (9am–noon and 2–6pm, closed Tues.). The only drawback is the powerful stench of fish that seeps up from the market held immediately below on the ground floor of this former church. But generally, Morlaix is a lot livelier than most Breton towns and a good base for visiting the parish closes (*enclos paroissiaux)*, in the countryside towards Brest.

The parish closes

Breton Catholicism has a very distinctive character, closer to the Celtic past than to Rome. There are hundreds of saints who've never been approved by the Vatican, but whose brightly painted wooden figures adorn every Breton church. Their stories merge imperceptibly with the tales of moving *menhirs*, ghosts and sorcery. Visions and miracles are still assumed; and death's workmate, Ankou, is a familiar figure, even if no one now would dread his manifestation.

Many of the churchyards in this part of Brittany have stone calvaries sculpted with detailed scenes of the Crucifixion above a crowd of saints, gospel stories, and legends. In the richer parishes a high stone arch leads into the churchyard adjoining an equally majestic ossuary where the old bones would be taken when the tiny cemeteries filled up. Most of them date from the two centuries on either side of the union with France in 1532 – Brittany's wealthiest period – and nothing is more telling of the decline in the province's fortunes. Everywhere you'll find magnificence in the *enclos paroissiaux*, walled churchyards which incorporate a trinity of further elements – cemetery, calvary and ossuary – in addition to the churches themselves. The interiors of the churches are often decorated as richly as the architectural ensemble without, while their villages are now often close to poverty.

The three most famous *enclos* are the neighbouring parishes of **GUIMILIAU, ST-THEGONNEC** and **LAMPAUL-GUIMILIAU**, off N12 between Morlaix and Landiviseau on a clearly signposted route served by the SNCF bus. At St-Thégonnec the entire east wall of the church is a carved and painted retable, with saints in niches and a hundred scenes depicted. The pulpit and the painted oak entombment in the crypt beneath the ossuary are the acknowledged masterpieces. At Lampoul-Guimiliau the painted wooden baptistery, the dragons on the beams and the suitably wicked faces of the robbers on the calvary are the key components. At Guimiliau poor **Katel Gollet** (Katherine the Damned) is depicted tormented in hell – for the crime of hedonism rather than manslaughter. In the legend she danced all her suitors to death until the reaper-figure **Ankou** stepped in to whirl her to eternal damnation. But at **LA ROCHE** (15km or so on towards Brest), where the ruined castle above the Elhorn estuary is said to have been her home, it is Ankou who appears on the ossuary with the inscription 'I kill you all'. If you've got transport, a 5km detour southeast of La Roche brings further variations at **LA MARTYRE** (where Ankou clutches his disembodied head) and its adjoining parish PLOUDIRY, the sculpting of its ossuary affirming the equality of social classes – in the eyes of Ankou.

If you have time and interest, **other calvaries** to take a look at include PLEYBEN, south of the Monts d'Arrée; LANRIVIAN, in the centre of Brittany; and GUEHENNO, southwest of Josselin. Another speciality to be seen in many Breton churches is the intricate carving and paintwork of **rood screens**: exceptional examples are the St-Fiacre chapel outside LE FAOUET (between Lorient and the Montagne Noire) and the chapel at KERFONS (south of Lannion), though both wonderful works of art are kept locked up except in July and August and for the annual *pardon*.

The Abers and the islands off Le Conquet

The coast west from Roscoff is some of the most dramatic in Brittany, a jagged series of *abers* – deep, narrow estuaries – in the midst of which are clustered small, isolated resorts. It's a little on the bracing side, especially if you're making use of the numerous **campsites**, but that just has to be counted as part of the appeal. In summer, at least, the temperatures are mild enough, and things get progressively more sheltered as you move around towards LE CONQUET and BREST.

If you're dependent on public transport, the only stop on the Roscoff–Brest bus before it turns inland is **PLOUESCAT**. Here you'll find **campsites** at each of its three adjacent beaches and the *Baie de Kernic* (☎98.69.63.41), best bet of the **hotels**. An old wooden market hall can provide picnic provisions and at the edge of the bay, about 1km out from the centre, the *Auberge Le Kersabiec* serves good food. **BRIGNOGAN-PLAGE**, on the next *aber*, has a small natural harbour, once the lair of wreckers, with beaches and weather-beaten rocks to either side, as well as its own menhir. The two high-season **campsites** are the *Keravezan* (☎98.83.41.65) and the *du Phare* (☎98.83.45.06), and there are schools for both sailing and riding. Further west, at **PLOUGERNEAU**, the **hotel/restaurant** *Les Abériades* (☎98.04.71.01) could make a good base.

The *aber* between Plougerneau and the yachting port of **ABER-WRAC'H** has a stepping-stone crossing just upstream from the bridge at LLANELLIS, built in Gallo-Roman times, and its long cut stones still cross the three channels of water (access off D28 signposted Rascol), and continue past farm buildings to the right to 'Pont du Diable'. For drivers and cyclists there's a beautiful corniche road west of TREMAZEN, whose ruined castle was the point of arrival in Brittany for Tristan and Iseult. Odd little chapels dot the route and the views of sea and rocks are unhindered before turning inland just before **LE CONQUET**.

Le Conquet is a wonderful place, scarcely developed, with a long beach of clean white sand, protected from the winds by the narrow spit of the Kermorvan peninsula. It is very much a working fishing village, the grey stone houses leading down to the stone jetties of a cramped harbour. It occasionally floods, by the way, causing great amusement to locals who watch the waves wash over cars left there by tourists taking the ferry out to Ouessant and Molène. There's a good walk 5km south which brings you to the lighthouse at **Pointe St-Mathieu**, looking out to the islands from its site among the ruins of a Benedictine abbey.

The *Hôtel du Bretagne*, 16 rue Lt-Jourden (☎98.89.00.02), has cheap **rooms** with a view across the grassy headland. Alternatives are the larger *Pointe Ste-Barbe* (☎98.89.00.26), or either of two well-equipped campsites, *Le Théven* (☎98.89.06.90) and *Les Sablons Blancs* (☎98.89.01.64).

The Iles d'Ouessant and Molène

The island of **Ouessant** lies 30km northwest of Le Conquet, its lighthouse marking the entrance to the English Channel. It's at the end of a chain of smaller islands, mostly uninhabited, and half-submerged granite rocks, but **Molène**, midway, has a village and can be visited. Not all boats from LE CONQUET (or from BREST), however, stop at both islands and it would be hard to visit more than one in a day.

You arrive on Ouessant at the new **harbour** in the ominous-sounding Baie du Stiff. There is a scattering of houses here, and dotted around the island, but the single town (with the only hotels and restaurants) is 4km away at LAMPAUL. Everybody from the boat heads there, either by the bus that meets each arriving ferry, or on bicycles hired from one of the many waiting entrepreneurs – a good idea, as the island is a bit too big to explore on foot. **LAMPAUL** has not a lot to it and quickly becomes very familiar. The best beaches are sprawled around its bay, and, in case you should forget the perils of the sea, the town cemetery's war memorial lists all the ships in which townsfolk were lost, alongside graves of unknown sailors washed ashore, and a chapel of wax '*proëlla crosses*' symbolising the many islanders who never returned. You can also visit the **Eco-Musée** – a reconstruction of a traditional island house – at nearby NIOU. The **Creac'h lighthouse**, closed to the public, is a good point from which to set out along the barren and exposed rocks of the north coast. The star-shaped formations of crumbling walls are not extra-terrestrial relics, but built so that the sheep – peculiarly tame here – can get shelter from the winds.

Staying overnight, you can camp almost anywhere on the island, making arrangements with the nearest farmhouse (which may well rent rooms, too). In Lampaul, the hotels *Océan* (☎98.48.80.03), *Roch ar Mor* (☎98.48.80.19) and *Fromveur* (☎98.48.81.30) are all reasonably priced, for a fairly minimal standard. There is, too, a small official campsite, the *Pen ar Bed* (☎98.48.84.65). **Restaurants** are not outrageously priced, but if you want to picnic, it's best to buy provisions on the mainland as the Lampaul shops have limited and rather pricey supplies.

MOLENE is quite well-populated for a sparse strip of sand. Its inhabitants make their money from seaweed collecting and drying – and to an extent from crabbing and crayfish, which they gather on foot, canoe and even tractor at low tide. The tides here are more than usually dramatic, halving or doubling the island's territory at a stroke. It's not called 'the bald isle' for nothing. Few people do more than look at Molène as an afternoon's excursion from Le Conquet, but it's quite possible to stay here and to enjoy it, too. There are rooms – very chilly in winter – at *Kastell en Doal* (☎98.84.19.11), an old house by the old port.

South from Brest: the Crozon Peninsula and down to Douarnanez

You may need to change buses in the monstrous port of **BREST** but there's little to entice you to stay, least of all the French Atlantic fleet that is based here and dominates the entire city. If by some chance you're stuck for a night, there's a reasonable **youth hostel** 3km to the east, set in woods at

MOULIN BLANC, near the beach at the mouth of the Elorn (☎98.41.90.41; take the *Bus Albatross* from the gare SNCF, and arrive 6pm–8pm to register) or the **hotels** *Siam* (8 rue du Couédic; ☎98.44.44.94), *de la Rade* (6 rue de Siam; ☎98.44.47.76), and *Pasteur* (29 rue Louis-Pasteur; ☎98.46.08.73). Otherwise head out fast, which you can do for a few francs by ferry across the bay to LE FRET on the **PRESQU'ILE DE CROZON** if you're on foot or bike. Cars with the same destination have to follow a circuitous route skirting this complex coast through **PLOUGASTEL-DAOULAS.** At the church here, the calvary shows more torment for Katel Gollet, in this case being raped by devils. The sculpting of Katel herself is more sympathetic than at Guimillau, but it is not difficult to imagine how such graphically portrayed myths have been used in gender politics.

The Crozon peninsula, a craggy outcrop of land shaped like a long-robed giant, arms outstretched to defend bay and roadstead, is the central feature of Finistère's torn chaos of estuaries and promontories. If you're approaching it by land and on wheels, head for the hill of **MENEZ HOM**, at the giant's feet, where you can climb up for a fabulous view of the land and water alternating out to the ocean. Getting down to the coastal headlands themselves can be a bit of a disappointment after this vision: CAP DE LA CHEVRE (the southern point), POINTE DU TOULINGUET (east of CAMARET) and the northern arm all have military installations, and the other extremities are too crowded. But it is the cliffs that tourists head for here and some of the **beaches**, like **LA PALUE** on the southern arm, are almost deserted. **Boat trips** around the headlands set off every quarter hour in high season from the dock at

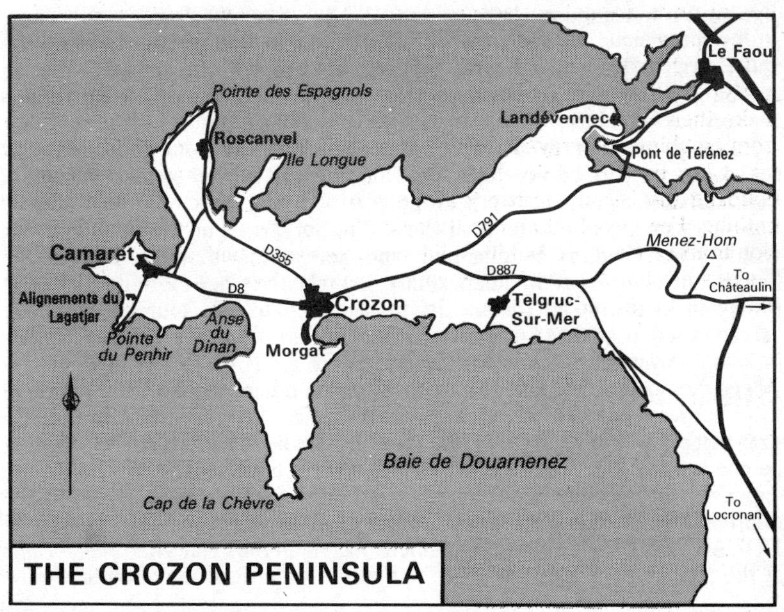

THE CROZON PENINSULA

MORGAT, one of the major resorts where you'll find the **SI** for the whole peninsula, at the start of the beach crescent on bd de France.

Hotels in Morgat, and in the other main resort of **CAMARET**, are all quite expensive. Best deals are the *Vauban* (☎98.27.91.36) and the *du Styvel* (☎98.27.92.74), both in Camaret. But there are **campsites** all around the peninsula and its hinterland, the best of the three-star sites being at *Plage de Goulien* (☎98.27.17.10) and *Plage de Trez-Rouz* (☎98.27.93.96). You can pick up a list of **gîte d'étapes** at Morgat SI or at the SI in the town of Crozon on place de l'Eglise. This latter is also the best place to go for **bike hire** addresses – don't, however, underestimate the winds you may have to battle against. There's a connecting **bus** from Le Fret to Crozon, Morgat and Camaret; three buses a day from LANDEVENNEC along the peninsula to CAMARET via CROZON and ROSCANVEL; and five from CHATEAULIN SNCF to PLOMODIERN, CROZON and CAMARET.

Back inland, a short way east of Menez-Hom on the intersection of the Argol–Dineault and Trégarven–Menez-Hom roads, is a **museum** that should fascinate anyone interested in how education can be used for subordination. The **Musée de l'Ecole Rurale** is housed in the village's old secondary school, closed down due to lack of numbers in 1974 and re-opened a decade later as a re-creation of a 1920's Breton classroom. At the time all the kids would have spoken Breton at home and been forbidden to speak it here. The teacher gave a little wooden cow to the first child to utter a word in the mother tongue, and they could get rid of the *vache* only by telling on the next offender. The lesson, to parents and pupils alike, was obvious enough: that Breton was backward and a handicap. It was taught, with considerable success, throughout the province, and only recently have things begun to change. Breton-language primary schools now exist; after battles with Paris, students are now allowed to write their exams in Breton, and recently the SNCF had to back down after refusing to accept a cheque made out in Breton. The museum is open from May to September from 2.30 to 7pm and is not accessible by bus.

Easier to reach on the road to Quimper a short way from from the sea at the southern end of the Baie de Douarnenez, is the fantasy village of **LOCRONAN**. Locronan has been popular with film directors, most notably Roman Polanski, who used it as the setting for *Tess*. For the filming, every visible porch had to be changed, and new windows were fitted to the Renaissance houses of the main square, to make the place more English. The town's main source of income is, in fact, high-budget tourists, who buy carved wooden statues by local artisans, pottery from the Midi or leather jackets, provenance unknown. Every sort of craft artefact is sold in this village, some of it produced in open **ateliers**, others through the hands of third parties whose sleek cars are parked beside the shops. One of the artisans suggested converting the loft above his studio to a *gîte d'étape* for young people but the idea was rejected by the powers that be. The two hotels are expensive and usually booked well in advance. A better place to stay is the unpretentious, though also rather unexciting, fishing port of **DOUARNENEZ**. The Port de Rosmeur has numerous cafés and restaurants at the pier and you can buy fresh fish at the waterfront. For **hotels** try the

Bretagne (23 rue Duguay-Trouin; ☎98.92.30.44) or *Voyageurs* (21 rue Duguay-Trouin; ☎98.92.01.48). There's a **boat** service between here and Morgat, and you can go on sea-fishing excursions. Swimming, however, despite the tempting look of the beaches, is dangerous.

Quimper and the Land's End *Pointes*

QUIMPER, capital of the ancient diocese, kingdom and later duchy of Cornouailles, is the oldest Breton city. According to the only source – legends – the original bishop of Quimper, St. Corentin came with the first Bretons across the channel to the place they named Little Britain, some time between the fourth and seventh centuries. He lived by eating a regenerating and immortal fish all his life, and was made bishop by one King Gradlon, whose life he later saved when the seabed city of Ys was destroyed. According to one version, Gradlon built Ys in the Baie de Douarnenez, protected from the water by gates and locks to which only he and his daughter had keys. She seems to have been very nice, giving pet dragons to all the citizens to run their errands for them, but St. Corentin saw decadence and suspected evil. He was proven right: the princess's keys unlocked the gates, the city flooded and Gradlon escaped only by obeying Corentin and throwing his daughter into the sea. Back on dry land and in need of a new capital, Gradlon founded Quimper.

Modern Quimper is very laid back, the sort of place you could wander solo from café to café without aggravation. And it's not bad-looking either, with old granite buildings, two rivers and the rising woods of Mont Frugy overlooking the centre of town. There's no pressure to rush around monuments

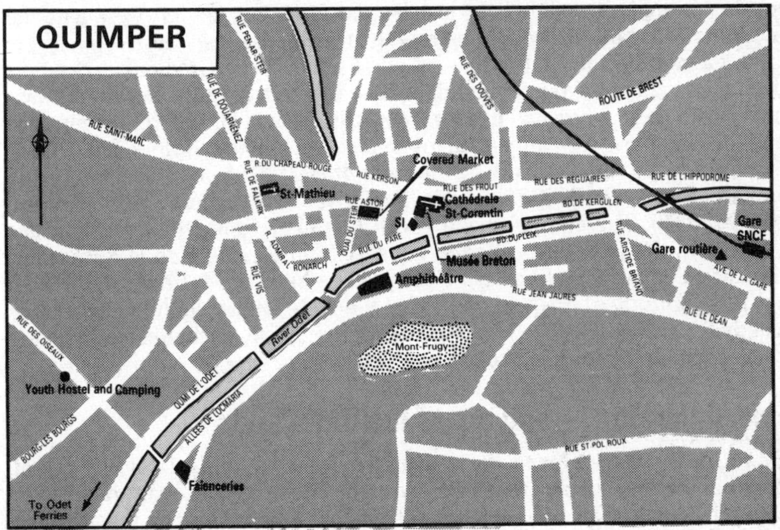

or museums and you can get to the sea in unhurried fashion on a boat down the Odet.

A short walk along the Odet brings you from the **gare SNCF** and main **gare routière** to the centre of the city around the enormous **Cathédrale St-Corentin**. There was a construction problem back in the fifteenth century when the nave was being added to the older chancel: the extension would either have hit existing buildings or the swampy edge of the then unchannelled river. The masons eventually hit on a solution, and placed the nave at a slight angle – a peculiarity which, once noticed, makes it hard to concentrate on the Gothic splendours within. The exterior, however, gives no hint of the deviation, with King Gradlon mounted in perfect symmetry between the spires. Alongside is the **Bishop's Palace**, also slightly quirky in its construction, with a wonderful spiral staircase.

The Bishop's Palace houses a small, very forgettable museum of Breton bits and pieces. Much more compelling is the **Beaux Arts** in the Hôtel de Ville (9.30–noon and 1.30–7pm in summer, 10am–noon and 2–6pm in winter; closed Tues.) with its amazing collections of drawings by Cocteau, Max Jacob and Gustave Doré (shown in rotation) and nineteenth- and twentieth-century paintings of the Pont-Aven school and Breton scenes by the likes of Eugène Boudin. If you're interested in seeing pottery made on an industrial scale, and an exhibition of the changing styles since the first Quimper *ateliers* of the late seventeenth century, the **Faïenceries de Quimper** is another worthwhile visit. It's on place Berardier, downstream from the centre on the south bank of the Odet (half-hour guided visits, Mon.–Fri. 9.30–11.30am and 1.30–5pm).

The liveliest corner of Quimper, with good crêpes and ice cream while you mull around in the cafés, is usually **place du Beurre**. Around the church of **St-Mathieu** can be fun, too, and across the river there are a couple of good **bars** on rue Ste-Catherine – Guinness is on tap at no. 15. The **covered market** is quite a delight, not just for the food, but for the view past the upturned boat rafters through the roof to the cathedral's spires.

As for **details** the **SI** (by the cathedral at no. 3 rue Gradlon) can supply lists of just about anything you might have in mind. If you're leaving **by bus** check with them where to head for – departure points for different companies and destinations are spread all over town. Economy **hotels** are the *de Cornouaille* (46 rue A-Briand, by the *gares*; ☎98.90.05.05), *de l'Odet* (83 rue de Douarnenez; ☎98.55.56.75) and *Sapinière* (286 route de Bénodet; ☎98.90.39.63). The **campsite** and **youth hostel** are downstream at 6 av des Oiseaux in the Bois du Seminaire (Bus #1 from the place de la Résistance, direction Penhar; stop *Chaptal*). **Bikes** can be hired at *M. Hénaff*, (107 av de Ty Bos). During the week preceding the last Sunday in July there's the **Festival Cornouailles**: a jamboree of Breton music, costumes and dances: every room in the town is booked.

Down the Odet – and out to the headlands

Boats down the Odet to the coast leave from the end of quai de l'Odet, opposite the Faïenceries; times vary with the tides so check with the SI (who also sell tickets). Once out of its city channel, the Odet takes on the anarchic shape of most Breton inlets, spreading out to lake proportions then turning narrow corners between gorges. The upmarket resort of **BENODET**, the boat's destination, has a long sheltered beach on the ocean side with lots of active amusements for children and beachside nurseries, too. **Hotels** are comparatively expensive – you could try the *Beau Rivage* (☎98.57.00.22) or *L'Hermitage* (☎98.57.05.37) – but there are several large **campsites**.

This bottom corner of Brittany, the **Pays de Bigouden**, is, with the exception of the 'land's end' points, the least touristed area of the province. Traditions have endured: it's the place you're most likely to see women wearing coiffes for non-promotional reasons. The local variety is fairly startling – 30cm-high tubes of lace that always stay on, defying gravity in the strong gusts of wind. World **windsurfing championships** are held at **POINTE DE LA TORCHE**, at the southern end of the Baie d'Audierne, and there are usually some aficionados twirling about with effortless ease. But warning signs about swimming should not be ignored. For safer seas framed by white sand beaches there's the coast from PENMARCH to LOCTUDY and beyond. It's about an hour on the bus from Quimper to this southern tip and it's one of the more frequent services.

An hour and a half's bus ride east of Quimper takes you to the land's end of France, the **POINTE DU RAZ**. As you approach, the vision of the ocean is blocked by a gaggle of souvenir shops, and then military installations, but once past these you reach plummeting fissures, filling and draining with deafening force, and you can walk on precarious paths above them (shoes that grip are a good idea). Two stops back on the bus back to **AUDIERNE**, the graffiti on walls and hoardings is the only reminder that this is **PLOGOFF** where ecologists, autonomists and, principally, the local people fought riot police and paratroopers for six weeks in 1980 to stop the opening move in a nuclear power station project. Mitterrand pledged to abandon the plans if elected, and did so.

Audierne is famous for its prawns and crayfish – the most affordable restaurant to try them is *Le Cornouaille*. From AUDIERNE-PLAGE, 3km from the town centre, there are boats to the **ILE DE SEIN** (three daily in July and Aug., one daily at 9.30am except Wed. the rest of the year: phone ☎98.70.02.38 for times; journey lasts 70 minutes). A misty, windy, treeless, dry spot, the island is reputed to have been the last refuge of the Druids in Brittany. A few hundred people still live on it, gathering rain water and fishing scallops, lobster and crayfish. There is one summer-only hotel, the *Armen* (June–Sept., ☎98.70.90.77).

Concarneau, Pont D'Aven and Quimperlé

The first major town east of Bénodet is **CONCARNEAU**, a fishing port doing a reasonable job of passing itself off as a holiday resort. Its greatest asset is its **Ville Clos**, the old walled city situated across a slender causeway on an irregular rocky island in the bay. It has been inhabited for at least 1000 years and was originally a priory founded by King Gradlon of Quimper. It has also been fortified for centuries – its current ramparts are as Vauban remodelled them in the seventeenth century. From Easter to the end of September (9am–7pm) you can walk along the top of them, admiring the climbing roses and clematis on the restaurants, snack bars, and gift shops below.

The **Musée de la Pêche**, immediately inside the Ville Clos, provides an insight into the traditional life Concarneau shared with so many other Breton ports. It details the history and practice of whaling, tuna fishing – with drag nets the size of central Paris – herring fishing and sardine processing; the building itself was a sardine cannery. The museum is open every day of the year, in July and August all day from 9.30am–8.30pm; the rest of the year it shuts for lunch and earlier in the evening.

The one thing the Ville Clos lacks completely is **hotels**. Those that there are in Concarneau skulk in the backstreets of the mainland, and tend to be full most of the time. The *Bonne Auberge* (Le Cabellou, ☎98.97.04.30) and the *Crêpe d'Or* (3 rue du Lin, ☎98.97.08.61) are worth trying, but the best bet in Concarneau is probably the **youth hostel** (☎98.97.03.47), for once very near the city centre. It's just around the tip of the headland on place de la Croix, with a good crêperie opposite. The town's main **market** is held in front of the Ville Clos on Friday, with a smaller one on Monday. For a cheap meal in the centre, *Ty Mad* near place du Guesclin features on its menu a Breton rarity – affordable scallops.

Gauguin and Pont-Aven

PONT-AVEN, 14km east at the tip of the Aven estuary, is a small port packed with tourists and art galleries. It was where Gauguin came to paint in the 1880s, before shuffling off to Tahiti. In his wake developed a 'Pont-Aven School' of painters, the best-known of whom was Emile Bernard. The so-called **Musée Gauguin** (Easter–Sept. 10am–12.30pm and 2–7pm) in the Mairie holds annual exhibitions of the many members of this school but, for all the local hype, the town does not possess a single work by Gauguin himself. Even without the master, the town is pleasant in its own right and the countless galleries can easily while away an afternoon. There is a small and neat port, with a watermill and, so it is said, leaping salmon; occasional cruises run down to the sea at Port-Manech. Upstream, a walk can take you into the **Bois d'Amour**, wooded gardens which have long provided inspiration to visiting painters – and a fair number of poets and musicians too. If you need to stay, be warned that the three **hotels** are expensive, and the nearest **campsite** is 4km away at ROZ PIN, on the road to Nevez.

Quimperlé

The final town of any size in Finistère, **QUIMPERLE** straddles a hill and two rivers, the Isole and the Elle, cut by a sequence of bridges. It's an atmospheric place, particularly in the medieval muddle of streets around **Ste-Croix** church. This was copied in plan from schema brought back by crusaders of the Church of the Holy Sepulchre in Jerusalem and is notable for its original Romanesque apse. There are some good bars nearby and, on Fridays, a market on the square higher up on the hill. The **hotels** *L'Europe* (☎98.96.00.02) and *Auberge de Toulfoen* (☎98.96.00.29) both have reasonable rooms.

INLAND BRITTANY: THE NANTES–BREST CANAL

The **Nantes–Brest canal** is a meandering chain of waterways from Finistère to the Loire, linking rivers with stretches of canal built at Napoléon's instigation to bypass the belligerent English fleets off the coast. Finally completed in 1836, it came into its own at the end of the century as a coal, slate and fertiliser route. The building of the dam at Lac Guerlédan in the 1920s chopped the canal in two, leaving a whole section unnavigable by barge. Road transport had already superseded water haulage; now tourism is breathing life back into the canal.

En route it passes through riverside towns, such as **Josselin** and **Malestroit**, that long pre-date its construction; commercial ports and junctions – **Pontivy**, most notably – that developed in the nineteenth century because of it; the old port of **Redon**, a patchwork of water, where the canal crosses the River Vilaine; and a sequence of scenic splendours, including the string of lakes around the **Barrage de Guerlédan** near Mur-de-Bretagne. As a focus for exploring **inland Brittany**, whether by barge, bike, foot or all three, the canal is ideal. Not every stretch is accessible but there are detours to be made away from it, such as the wild and desolate **Monts d'Arrée** to the north of the canal in Finistère.

The Finistère stretch

Before embarking on the Nantes–Brest canal, there is the region north of it, stretching from the base of the Crozon peninsula almost to Morlaix, of the **MONTS D'ARREE**. These hills, rising at their peaks to only 380m at the wild-looking ridge encircling the Lac de Brennilis, give the impression of being much higher than they are, due partly to the desolate infrequency of habitation, and partly to the lack of anything higher in the whole province.

They form part of the **Parc Naturel Régional d'Armorique**, an area, in theory at least, of conservation and rural regeneration along traditional lines. The administrative centre is at **MENEZ-MEUR**, off D342 near the Forêt de Cranou – just inland from the Brest–Quimper motorway. Menez is an official **animal reserve** with wild boar and deer roaming free (open June–Sept. every day 10.30am–7pm). At the reserve gate you can pick up a wealth of detail on the park and all its various activities (☎98.68.81.71).

To the north, at **SIZUN**, there's a research station, **aquarium** and fishing exhibition (open June 15–Oct. 15, 10.30am–7pm, and on public holidays for the rest of the year). East of here, 3km along D764 to COMMANA, is the abandoned hamlet of **MOULINS-DE-KEROUAT** (or MILIN KERROCH), which has recently been restored as an **Eco-Musée** (open March–Sept. 2–6pm, July–Aug. 11am–7pm, Sept.–Oct. weekends only). Kérouat's last inhabitant died in 1967 and, like many a place in the Breton interior, it might have crumbled into indiscernible ruins, but one of the hamlet's watermills has been restored to working order, and its houses have been repaired and refurnished. The largest belonged in the last century to the mayor of Commana, who also controlled the mills – its furnishings are those of a wealthy family.

The **ridge** around Brennilis is visible as a stark silhouette from the under-used **campsite** at **NESTAVEL-BRAZ** on the eastern shore of the lake. From this deceptively tranquil vantage point, the army's antennae near **Roc Trévezel** to the north are obscured, as are those of the navy at Menez-Meur to the west. Right behind you, however, is the BRENNILIS nuclear power station. In a rare manifestation of separatist terrorism, Breton nationalists attacked it in 1975 with a rocket launcher; it survived. In 1987, the SAS conducted an outrageously offensive exercise in this area, when they were invited by the French government to subdue a simulated Breton uprising, and in the process managed to run over a local inhabitant. Perhaps appropriately, across the lake where the tree-lined fields around the villages end, is **Yeun Elez**, one of the legendary 'holes to hell'. You can walk around the lake – gorse and brambles permitting; be very careful not to stray from the paths into the surrounding peat bogs. The ridge itself is followed most of the way by a road but in places it still feels like miles from any habitation.

Huelgoat

Up until October 1987, the **Forêt de Huelgoat** was one of the most beautiful places in Brittany, a too-good-to-be-true natural arrangement of rocks, waterfalls, grottoes and a gurgling stream. But the hurricane just about destroyed it, and it will take more than a lifetime to be restored. Though now a very depressing place **HUELGOAT** is still one of the best bases for this area, with accommodation at the *Hôtel l'Armorique* (1 place Aristide Briand; ☎98.99.71.24), the *du Lac* (☎98.99.71.14) on the lakeside, or the summer-only campsite (a short walk towards the lake along the Brest road). The **SI**, at 14 place Aristide Briand, or the Parc centre (see above) can provide details of the numerous campsites and **gites d'étapes** in the region. SIZUN has a reasonable **hotel**, the *des Voyageurs*, 2 rue de l'Argoat; ☎98.68.80.35. **Bikes** can be hired at Huelgoat (from the garage at 1 rue du Lac) and several of the other villages.

Along the canal

As late as the 1920s, there were steamers making their way across the Rade de Brest and down the Aulne River to CHATEAULIN, the first real town on the canal route. It's a quiet place, where the main reason to stay is the canal itself – or river as it is here. For its salmon and trout fishing, if you're interested, most bars (as well as fishing shops – some of which hire out tackle) sell permits. You should have little difficulty finding a room at the **hotel** *Le Christmas* (☎98.86.01.24) on rue des Ecoles, which climbs from the town centre towards Pleyben. Along **the riverbank**, there's a statue to Jean Moulin, the Resistance leader; the inscription reads *'mourir sans parler'* – to die without talking – which he did. He was *sous-préfet* in Châteaulin from 1930 to 1933. Within a couple of minutes' walk upstream from the statue and the town centre, you're on towpaths full of rabbits and squirrels and overhung by trees full of birds. If you're walking the canal seriously, PONT-COBLANT and PLEYBEN are just 10km away on the map, but be warned that the meanders make it a several-hour hike. Pick your side of the water, too; there are no bridges between Châteaulin and Pont-Coblant.

PONT-COBLANT is the first point at which you can **hire boats** – either canoes or houseboats (see the travel details at the end of this chapter). A small village, it also has a very basic (and cheap) forty-bed unofficial **youth hostel** (contact the *Moulin de Pont-Coblant*, 29190 Pleyben, ☎98.73.34.40 to reserve a bed) and a **campsite**.

PLEYBEN, 4km to the north, is renowned for its **parish close**. On its four sides the calvary traces the life of Jesus like a comic strip, with a naivety that is echoed by the hand-drawn and coloured exhibition in the repository of local customs, traditions, folktales and fountains. There's an **SI** in the adjacent place de Gaulle.

CHATEAUNEUF-DU-FAOU is similar to Châteaulin, sloping down to the tree-lined river. It's a little more developed, though, with a tourist complex, the *Penn ar Pont* (☎98.81.81.25), with swimming pool, *gîtes*, and camping as well as **cycle** and **boat hire**. The **canal proper** separates off from the Aulne a few kilometres to the east at PONT-TRIFFEN, staking its own path on past Carhaix, and out of Finistère. **CARHAIX**, an ancient road junction, has cafés and shops to replenish supplies, but not much to recommend it. Beyond it the canal – as far as PONTIVY – is navigable only by canoe.

The central stretch: Gouarec to Ploermel

Although the canal is limited to canoeists between CARHAIX and PONTIVY, it's worth some effort to follow on land, particularly for the scenery from GOUAREC to MUR-DE-BRETAGNE. At the centre is the trailing **Lac de Guerlédan**, created by the construction of a barrage near Mur, and backed, to the south, by the enticing **Forêt de Quénécan**. Approaching by road, the canal path is easiest joined at GOUAREC, covered by the five daily buses between Carhaix and Loudéac.

At **GOUAREC**, the River Blavet and the canal meet in a confusing swirl of water that shoots off, edged by footpaths, in the most unlikely directions. The old schist houses of the town are barely disturbed by traffic or development, nor are there great numbers of tourists. For a comfortable overnight stop, the 2-star **hotel**, *du Blavet* (☎96.24.90.03), is in an ideal waterside position; don't be put off by its extravagant menus – they have affordable meals as well. The municipal **campsite** (☎96.24.90.22) is next to the canal.

For the 15km between GOUAREC and MUR-DE-BRETAGNE, **N164** skirts the edge of **Quénécan Forest**, within which is the series of artificial lakes created when the Barrage of Guerlédan was completed in 1928. It's a beautiful stretch of river, a little overrun by campers and caravans but peaceful enough nonetheless. The best places to stay are just off the road, past the villages of **ST-GELVEN** and **CAUREL**. At the former, you can walk down to Lac Guerlédan and the **campsite** at KERMANEC. From just before Caurel, the brief loop of D111 leads to tiny, sandy beaches – a bit too tiny in season – with **campsites** *Les Pins* (☎96.28.52.22) and *Les Pommiers* (☎96.28.52.35). At the spot known as BEAU RIVAGE is a complex containing a campsite, hotel, restaurant, snackbar and mooring for a 140-seat glass-topped cruise-boat.

MUR-DE-BRETAGNE is set back from the eastern end of the lake, a lively place with a wide and colourful pedestrianised zone around its church. It's the nearest town to the barrage – just 2km distant – and has a **campsite**, the *Rond-Point du Lac* (☎96.26.01.90), with facilities for windsurfing and horseback riding. There's also a **youth hostel** a short way along N164 at **ST-GUEN** (☎96.28.54.34) – take the Loudéac bus and get off at *Bourg de St-Guen*.

Pontivy

You can again take **barges** – all the way to the Loire – from **PONTIVY**, the central junction of the Nantes–Brest canal, where the course of the canal breaks off once more from the Blavet. When the waterway opened, the small medieval centre of the town was expanded, redesigned, and given broad avenues to fit its new role. It was even renamed Napoléonville for a while, in honour of the instigator behind its new prosperity. These days it is a bright market town, its twisting old streets contrasting with the stately riverside promenades. At its northern end, occupying a commanding hillside site, is the **Château de Rohan**, built by the Lord of Josselin in the fifteenth century. Open to visitors, and used for low-key cultural events, the castle still belongs to the Josselin family, who are slowly restoring it. At the moment, one impressive facade, complete with deep moat and two forbidding towers, looks out over the river – behind that, the structure peters out.

Pontivy has several **hotels**, among them the low-priced *Martin* (☎97.25.02.04) and *Robic* (☎97.25.11.80), as well as a very spartan **youth hostel** (☎97.25.58.27), 2km from the **gare SNCF** on the Ile des Recollets. The **SI** is on rue de Gaulle.

Following the canal beyond Pontivy to ROHAN is difficult unless you're on it. Between Rohan and Josselin is the Cistercian **Abbaie de Timadeuc**, which you can enter only to attend mass. But it's beautiful from the outside, with its front walls and main gate covered in flowers at the end of an avenue of old pines. The abbey also provides an excuse to stay at nearby **BREHAN**, a quiet little village whose **hotel**, the *Cremaillère* (☎97.51.52.09), must be one of the best deals anywhere in the province, both for good rooms and excellent food at astonishingly low prices.

Josselin

A short way south from Timadeuc you come to the three Rapunzel towers embedded in a vast sheet of stone of the **château** of **JOSSELIN**. The family in possession of it used to own a third of Brittany, the present Duke contents himself with the position of local mayor. The pompous apartments of his residence are not very interesting, even if they do contain the table on which the Edict of Nantes was signed in 1598. But the Duchess's collection of **dolls**, housed in the *Musée des Poupées*, behind the castle, is something special. Hours for both are May to September 10am to noon and 2 to 6pm, closed Monday; rest of the year 2 to 6pm on Wednesday, weekends and holidays only. The **town** is full of medieval splendours, from the gargoyles of the

Basilica to the castle ramparts, and the half-timbered houses in between (of which one of the finest is the **SI** on place de la Congrégation). **Notre-Dame-du-Roncier** is built on the spot where in the ninth century a peasant supposedly found a statue of the Virgin under a bramble bush. The statue was burned during the Revolution but an important *pardon* is held each year on September 8.

If you want to **stay** at Josselin, there's a *gîte d'étape* right below the castle walls, where you can also hire **canoes**. Alternatively, the *Hôtel du Commerce* (rue Beaumanoir, ☎97.22.22.08) is reasonable.

One of the largest and best Breton calvaries is at **GUEHENNO**, south of Josselin on D123. Sculpted in 1550, the figures include the cock that crowed at Peter's denials, Mary Magdalene with the shroud, and a recumbent Christ in the crypt. Its appeal is enhanced by the naivety of its amateur restoration. After damage caused by Revolutionary soldiers in 1794 – who amused themselves by playing *boules* with the heads of the statues – all the sculptors approached for the work demanded exorbitant fees, so the parish priest and his assistant decided to undertake the task themselves.

Another unusual sculptural endeavour, this time contemporary, is taking place at the **Domaine de Kerguehennec**, which is marked a short way off D11 near ST JEAN-BREVELAY. This innovative **sculpture park** has plans to build up a permanent international collection and if the first pieces to be installed are anything to go by, it should be an increasingly compelling stop. Its setting is the lawns, woods and lake of an early eighteenth-century château. Over to the east, off D151, **LIZIO** has also set itself up as a centre for arts and crafts, with ceramic and weaving workshops its speciality. A *Festival Artisanal* takes place on the second Sunday in August, along with street theatre (and pancakes). There are several **gîtes** in the town and a **campsite**.

If you're travelling by rail, **PLOERMEL**, though a bit north of the canal, may be a useful base. It doesn't have anything special to offer other than a few Renaissance houses – it's no match for its old rival Josselin 12km east. The **hotels** *Saint Marc* (☎97.74.00.01) or *Cobh* (☎97.74.00.49) are reasonable and there's an **SI** on place Lamennais.

Towards Nantes: Malestroit and Redon

Not a lot happens in **MALESTROIT**, but that, along with the unexpected details of its ancient buildings and the serenity of the canal, is what gives it its charm. As you come in to the main square, **place du Bouffay** in front of the church, the houses are covered with unlikely carvings – an anxious bagpipe-playing hare looking over its shoulder at a dragon's head on one beam, while an oblivious sow in a blue-buckled belt threads her distaff on another. The **church** itself is decorated with drunkards and acrobats outside, demon torturers and erupting towers within; each night the display is completed by the sullen parade of metal-studded youth who weave in and out of the '*Vieille Auberge*' bar opposite. The only ancient walls without adornment are the ruins of the **Chapelle de la Madeleine**, where one of the many temporary truces of the Hundred Years War was signed.

Next to the grey canal, the matching grey slate tiles on the turreted rooftops bulge and dip, while on its central island overgrown houses stand next to the stern walls of an old mill. If you arrive by barge (this is a good stretch to travel), you'll moor very near the town centre, so you can lurch across to the only **hotel** and restaurant, the *Aigle d'Or* (1 rue des Ecoles; ☎97.75.20.10) where meals, if not rooms, are relatively cheap. The **gare routière**, served by buses from Vannes and Rennes, is on the main road, bd du Pont-Neuf; there's a **campsite** below the bridge that it crosses, and a **gîte d'étape** up at the canal lock (c/o M. Halier, ☎97.75.11.66). The **SI** is also on bd du Pont-Neuf, and has details of **canoe and boat hire**; **bikes** can be hired from the *Aigle d'Or.*

West of Malestroit about 2km (and with no bus connection), just past the village of **ST-MARCEL** off the Vannes road, the **Musée de la Résistance Bretonne** rests on the site of a June 1944 battle. Here the Breton *maquis*, joined by Free French Forces parachuted in from England, successfully diverted the local German troops from the main Normandy invasion movements. The museum's strongest feature is the presentation of the pressures that made the majority of French people collaborate: the reconstructed street corner from which all life has been drained by the occupiers; the big colourful propaganda posters offering work in Germany, announcing executions of *maquis*, equating resistance with aiding U.S. and British big business; and, to counter them, the low-budget, flimsily printed Resistance pamphlets. (Hours are June–Sept. 10am–7pm, otherwise 10am–noon and 2–6pm.)

Redon

Thirty-four kilometres east of Malestroit and at the junction of the Rivers Oust and Vilaine, the canal, railways to Rennes, Vannes and Nantes, and six major roads, **REDON** is not an easy place to avoid. And you shouldn't try to, either. A wonderful grouping of water and locks, the town has history, charm and life. It's probably the best stop along the whole course of the canal. Up until World War I, Redon was the seaport for Rennes. Its industrial docks – or what remains of them – are therefore on the Vilaine, while the canal, even in the very centre of town, is almost totally rural, its towpaths shaded avenues. Ship-owners' houses from the seventeenth and eighteenth centuries can be seen along quai Jean-Bart by the *bassin* and quai Duguay-Truin next to the river. A rusted wrought-iron workbridge, equipped with a gantry, still crosses the river, but the main users of the port now are cruise ships heading down the Vilaine to La Roche-Bernard.

Redon was once also a religious centre, its first abbey founded in 832 by Saint Conwoion. The most prominent church today is **St-Sauveur**, with its Gothic tower, entirely separated from the main building by a fire, and unique four-storeyed Romanesque belfry. The belfry is squat, almost obscured by later roofs and the high choir, and is best seen from the adjacent cloisters. Inside the church, you'll find the tomb of the judge who tried the legendary Bluebeard – Joan of Arc's friend, Gilles de Rais.

Most of the town's **hotels** are near the **gare SNCF**– and it's a small enough place for this to be no drawback. Good choices are the *de Bretagne* (place de la Gare; ☎99.77.00.42) and *de l'Ouest* (14 rue des Douves;

☎99.71.10.91), which also has a decent buffet. The *Hôtel de la Gare* (10 rue de la Gare; ☎99.71.02.04) has a reputation for gourmet **food,** there's a **vegetarian** restaurant, the *Lavomagic* (18 rue du Port, ☎99.72.21.08 – for some reason it's kitted out to look like a launderette), and a surprisingly dynamic **music bar**, *Le Trombone à Coulisse* (14 rue du Plessis). A large Monday **market** centres around the modern *halles*, where you can buy superb crêpes. The **SI** is based there too, offering information on hiring boats and gîtes; in summer it has an additional annexe in the port.

Nantes

NANTES, the former capital of Brittany, is no longer officially a part of the province. The city's medieval associations are dwarfed by the later dominance of its port and the wealth gained from colonial expeditions, slave trading and shipbuilding, and the recent, but now declining, industrial growth. Yet despite the tower-blocks masking the Loire and motorways tearing past the city, it remains to its inhabitants an integral part of Brittany; and its castle, the **Château des Ducs**, could never shed its historical associations with the province.

Though no longer on the waterfront, and subjected to a certain amount of damage over the centuries, the château still preserves the form in which it was built by two of the last rulers of independent Brittany, François II, and his daughter Duchess Anne, born here in 1477. The list of famous people who have been guests or prisoners, defenders or belligerents of the castle is impressive. It includes Bluebeard, publicly burnt to death in 1440; John Knox as a galley-slave in 1547–9; Bonnie Prince Charlie preparing for Culloden in 1745. The most significant act in the castle, from the point of view of European history, and the one for which the city is perhaps best known, was the signing of the Edict of Nantes by Henri IV in 1598. It ended the Wars of Religion and granted a certain degree of toleration to the Protestants, but had far more crucial consequences when it was revoked, by Louis XIV in 1685. To their credit the people of Nantes took no part in the subsequent general massacres of the Huguenots.

You can walk into the courtyard and up on to the low but solid ramparts for free; there are also three museums on the grounds, open 10am to noon and 2 to 6pm (closed Tues., except in July and Aug., and holidays). The first – housed in the old, well-graffitied prison of the Tour de la Boulangerie – is the **Musée des Arts Populaires**, a good introduction to Breton history and folklore, which is depicted in a series of murals and dioramas. The **Musée des Arts Décoratifs**, in the Governor's Palace, displays a refreshingly contemporary selection of textile work. The city's trading history is the subject of the **Musée des Salorges**, with numerous documents and objects connected with slavery, the 'ebony' trade as it was called, that brought in profits of as much as 200 percent per shipload. The abolition of slavery coincided with an increased use of domestic French sugar beet as opposed to Carribean sugar cane; the importance of the port began to wane, and heavy industry and wine-growing became more important.

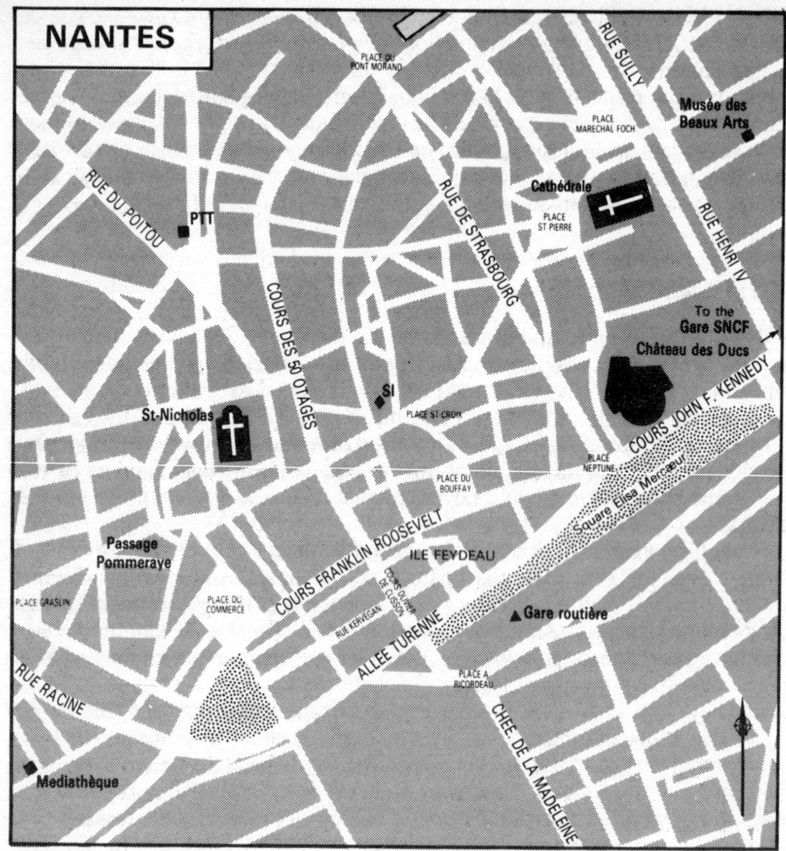

In 1800 the Spaniards Tower, the castle's arsenal, exploded, shattering the stained glass of the **Cathédrale de St-Pierre et St-Paul** over 200m away. This was just one of many disasters that have befallen the church. It was used as a barn during the Revolution; bombed during World War II; and damaged by a fire in 1971, just when things seemed in order again. Restored and finally reopened, its soaring height and lightness are emphasised by the clean white stone. It contains the tomb of François II and his wife, Margaret, the parents of Duchess Anne – with somewhat grating symbols of Power, Strength and Justice for him and Fidelity, Prudence and Temperance for her.

The **Musée des Beaux Arts** on rue Clemenceau has a respectable collection of paintings displayed in excellent new galleries – and is well worth checking for its temporary exhibitions. Not all its Renaissance and contemporary works are on view at any one time, but you should be able to take in works ranging from Italian miniatures to a gorgeous *David Triumphant* by Delaunay. It also contains the remarkable spectacle of two huge canvases by

Rubens dominating the damp and squalid basement bathrooms, and is open 9.15am to noon and 1 to 6pm, Sunday 11am to 5pm, closed Tuesday and holidays.

If you have time to kill, take the tram to the **Médiathêque** stop, where you'll find a superb modern library with bookstores and facilities to watch any of an eclectic selection of videos – *Sir Alf Ramsey* and the *Battle of Iwo Jima* side-by-side. From there, you can walk along quai de la Fosse to the point where the two remaining branches of the Loire meet up, with a good view of the port.

Very few medieval buildings survive in Nantes and, as ever, the best is now the **SI** – in **place du Change**. This area is largely pedestrian and contains several good **restaurants**, such as the *P'tit Bistrot* on rue de la Juiverie. Otherwise, the best restaurant area – try the *Salt and Pepper* – is among the former shipbuilders' houses on rue Kervegan on the **Ile Feydeau**. Jules Verne was born on the island and has a museum (10am–12.30pm and 2–5pm, closed Tues.) dedicated to him at 3 rue de l'Hermitage; it's more of an amusement for the fans of his stories than a source of any serious information, but the multitude of illustrated editions are rather nice. On place Graslin, behind the city theatre, are are a couple of large cinemas, together with a smattering of arty **cafés**. A spectacular nineteenth-century multi-level shopping centre, the **Passage Pommeraye**, is on nearby rue Crébillon.

The easiest way to **get around** in Nantes is on the rubber-wheeled trams that run along the old riverfront. These pass by both the **gare SNCF** and the **gare routière**, which are on the south side of the boulevard, a short way east of the castle. The flat fare you pay for the tram gives you a ticket valid for an hour rather than just one journey.

As for **places to stay**, try the *Centre Jean Macé* (90 rue du Préfet-Bonnefoy, ☎40.74.55.74), or the hotels *Ste-Reine* (1 rue Anatole-le-Braz, ☎40.74.35.61), *de l'Océan* (11 rue du Maréchal-de-Lattre-de-Tassigny, ☎40.69.73.51), *Fourcroy* (11 rue Fourcroy; ☎40.69.77.87) or *Grand Monarque* (36, rue du Maréchal-Joffre; ☎40.74.02.40). Of the three **youth hostels**, the summer-only one at 2 place de la Manu (☎40.20.57.25) is easiest to reach, by taking Tramway #1 towards Malachère and getting off at 'Manufacture'. The other two don't require youth hostel cards and are at 1 rue Porte-Neuve (☎40.20.00.80) and at 9 bd Vincent-Gache (☎40.47.91.64).

Within reach of Nantes

Immediately **upstream from Nantes** you are into the Loire wine-growing country that produces the two classic dry white wines, *Gros-Plant* and *Muscadet*. Any **vineyard** should be happy to give you a *dégustation*. Almost without exception the grapes are picked by machine so there's no opportunity for casual harvest work.

To explore the **last section of the Nantes–Brest canal**, you can take a river cruise from quai des Versailles at the end of cours des 50-Otages in the centre of Nantes. These cruises run up the Erdre to the point where it is joined by the canal coming from Redon. They thrive mainly because the Loire is not at present navigable by this sort of boat (although there are plans to change that) but the Erdre is itself beautiful and wide, with a fine selection of châteaux along its banks, chief among them **La Gâcherie**. At least two boats run every day in high season, one with a top-class restaurant on board – contact *Lebert-Buisson*, 24 quai des Versailles (☎40.20.24.50).

In summer Nantes empties, as everyone heads west to the beaches, either to the more upmarket resorts beyond St-Nazaire or **south of the Loire** to the almost unbroken line of holiday apartments, *pepsi* and *frites* stands of the **PAYS DE RETZ** coast. **PORNIC** is the one exception among these resorts, with a still-functional fishing port and one of Bluebeard Gilles de Retz's many castles. It is a small place: you can walk past the harbour and along the cliffs to a tiny beach where the rock walls glitter from the phosphorescent seawater. The **hotels** in town are not cheap; the *Relais Saint Gilles* (☎40.82.02.25), just down the road from the post office, is the most reasonable.

Between the coast and Nantes, the countryside is a series of marshes and mostly inaccessible lakes. The largest, the **Grand-Lieu**, contains two drowned villages, Murin and Langon. Along the **estuary** itself, the towns are depressed and depressing, their traditional industries struck hard by unemployment.

THE SOUTHERN COAST

Brittany's **southern coast** takes in the province's, and indeed Europe's, most famous prehistoric site, the **alignments of Carnac**, with the connected megaliths of the beautiful, island-studded **Golfe de Morbihan**. Though the beaches are not as spectacular as Finistère's, there are more safe places to swim and the water is warmer. Of the cities, **Lorient** has Brittany's most compelling **festival** and **Vannes** has one of the liveliest medieval town centres. Further east, **La Baule** does a good impression of a Breton St-Tropez, and there are the islands of **Belle Ile, Hoëdic**, and **Houat** to escape to. Inevitably it's popular, and in summer you can be hard-pressed to find a room, but if you're prepared to make reservations, or you're camping, there shouldn't be much problem.

Lorient and around

LORIENT, Brittany's fourth-largest city, is an immense natural harbour – protected from the ocean by the Ile de Groix and strategically located at the junction of the Rivers Scorff, Ter and Blavet. A functional, rather depressing port today, it was once a key base for French and English colonialism, and was founded in the mid-seventeenth century for trading operations by the *Compagnie des Indes*, an equivalent of the Dutch and English East India Companies. Apart from the name, little else remains to suggest the plundered wealth that once arrived here. During the last war, Lorient was a major target for the Allies; the Germans held out until May 1945, by which time the city was almost completely destroyed. The only substantial remains were the U-boat pens – subsequently greatly expanded by the French for their nuclear submarines.

Across the estuary in Port-Louis there's a museum of the *Compagnie des Indes*, a pretty dismal temple to imperialism. Time would be more enjoyably spent on a boat trip, either up the estuary towards Hennebont (see below) or out to the **Ile de Groix**. This 8km-long steep-sided rock is a short way out to sea and has no permanent population, though there is a summer-operated **youth hostel** (phone Lorient's hostel, see below, for details). The coast around Lorient itself is unenticing, and plagued with thick drifts of seaweed.

The overriding reason for coming to Lorient is for the **Inter-Celtic Festival**, held for ten days from the first Friday to the second Sunday in August. This is the biggest Celtic event in Brittany, or anywhere else for that matter, with representation from all seven Celtic countries. In a genuine popular celebration of cultural solidarity, with up to 250,000 people in attendance at over 150 different shows, five languages mingle and Scotch and Guinness flow with the French and Spanish wines and ciders. There is a certain competitive element, with championships in various categories, but the feeling of mutual enthusiasm and conviviality is paramount. Most of the activities – which embrace music, dance and literature – take place around the central place Jules Ferry, and this is where most people end up sleeping, too, as accommodation is pushed to the limits.

For the rest of the year, there is a huge choice of **hotels**. Among the best are the *Central* (1 rue de Cambry; ☎97.21.16.52), the *Saint-Christophe* (9 rue Beauvais; ☎97.21.18.70) and the *d'Arvor* (104 rue Lazare-Carnot; ☎97.21.07.55). The **youth hostel** is at 41 rue Victor-Schoelcher, 3km out on bus line C from the gare SNCF, next to the River Ter (☎97.37.11.65). For schedules of the festival, and further details of temporary accommodation, contact the *Office du Tourisme du Pays du Lorient*, place Jules-Ferry, 56100 LORIENT (☎97.21.07.84), bearing in mind that the festival schedule is not finalised before May. For certain specific events, you need to reserve tickets well in advance.

Hennebont

A few kilometres upstream from Lorient, at the point where the Blavet estuary narrows to river proportions, and a short hop from the port by train, is the old walled town of **HENNEBONT**. The fortifications, and especially the main gate, the Porte Broerec'h, are imposing, and from the top of the ramparts there are wide views of the river below. What you see of the old city within, however, is entirely residential – an assortment of clothes lines, budgies and garden sheds. All its public buildings were destroyed in the war and now not even a bar (or rented room) is to be found in the former centre.

The one time Hennebont comes alive is at the **Thursday market**, held below the ramparts and through the squares by the church. It's one of the largest in the region, with a heady mix of good fresh food, crêpes and Vietnamese delicacies alongside livestock, flowers, carpets and clothes. On other days, the only places you'll find any activity are along **place Maréchal-Foch** (in front of the Basilica) and **quai du Pont-Neuf**, beside the river. If you're **staying** – and few people do – the *Hôtel de France* at 17 av de la Libération (☎97.36.21.82) is a good proposition near the town centre. The town's **campsite**, the *St-Caradec* (☎97.36.20.14; June to Sept. only), has a prime site on the river bank opposite the fortifications. You can hire **bicycles** at 5 av de la République and 87 rue Maréchal-Joffre, and take **boat trips** either up the Blavet towards the Nantes–Brest canal or down the estuary to Lorient.

Lochrist

Just to the north, at **LOCHRIST,** the great chimneys of the Hennebont ironworks still stand, smokeless and silent, looking down on the Blavet. Strikes and demonstrations failed to prevent the closure of the foundry in 1966, and the only work since then has been to set up a museum, the **Musée Forges d'Hennebont**, which documents its 100-year history from the workers' point of view. Some of the men put out of work have contributed their memories and tools; for others the museum was a final bitter irony. It is excellent though, both in content and presentation, despite the sense of defeat after seeing the joyful pictures of successful strikes in the 1930s. If it's on your route it's worth a stop: the bus station is just opposite, on the other side of the river. (Tues.–Thurs. 9am–noon and 2–6pm, Fri. 9am–noon, weekends 2–6pm.)

Auray

There's something slightly dull about **AURAY**, and its quaint, over-restored old quarter – your most likely reason for coming here is that it's the main transport junction for the more compelling attractions of CARNAC, the Quiberon peninsula and the Golfe de Morbihan. Paris–Quimper **trains** make a stop here, with onward connections to Quiberon by train in July and August only, by bus at other times. You can hire **bikes** at the station – a good idea, as it's a mile from the centre, place de la République. Reasonable **hotels** to try are *Moderne* (in the *place*; ☎97.24.04.72), *L'Armoric* (rue St-Goustan; ☎97.24.10.36) and *Belvédère* (2 rue du Belvédère; ☎97.24.03.48). The **SI**, also in the *place*, has local maps; or if you're heading for the islands, you can pick up details at the *Iles du Ponant* Promotional Association at 11 place Joffre. The town's most remarkable building is near here, a vast Gothic church, dissolved by Louis XIV and now let out to clubs, with stray cats and the odd wrecked car keeping an eye on the gargoyles.

The showpiece of the town is the **St-Goustan quarter** – down through Promenade du Loch and across the highly picturesque bridge over the Auray river. Dolled up with expensive restaurants, it has a nice enough setting, but fails to be atmospheric or particularly entertaining. Its **quay**, downstream, is named after Benjamin Franklin – who landed here, blown off course from Nantes, on his way to negotiate the first alliance between the still-rebel U.S. colonies and France in 1776.

A short way north of Auray, on B768 to Baud, beyond the station on the left, is the grandiose **Abbaye de Chartreuse** housing a black-and-white marble mausoleum with sculpted reliefs by David d'Angers of the 1790s Royalist rebellion – viewable, bones and all, 10am to noon and 2 to 5.30pm. Another counter-revolutionary failure is recalled by the **Champs des Martyres**, nearby to the right of D120, where 350 *chouans* were executed. Two kilometres farther along D120, towards BRECH, you come to the **Ecomusée St-Degan** (July–mid-Sept. only, 2–6pm). This consists of a group of reconstructed farm buildings, representing the local peasant life at the beginning of this century. It's all a bit too rustically charming, but at least it does attempt to escape the glass cases and wax models of most folk museums.

Ste-Anne D'Auray

One of the largest of the Breton **pardons** takes place at **STE-ANNE D'AURAY** on July 26. Some 25,000 pilgrims gather for the occasion to hear mass in the church, mount the *scala sancta* on their knees, and buy trinkets from the street stalls. The origin of this *pardon*, typical of many, lies in the discovery in 1623 of a statue, of Ste-Anne by a local peasant, one Nicolazic. He claimed to have been directed to the spot by visionary appearances of the Saint (the Virgin's mother) and to have been instructed by her to build a church. Illiterate, speaking only Breton, and with no more than a subsistence livelihood, he managed to raise the necessary funds and construct his church (since destroyed, along with the statue during the Revolution). On his death-bed, twenty years later, the church authorities were still accusing him of making up his story and the debate continues today with the ongoing campaign to have Nicolazic canonised.

Ste-Anne's status as a pilgrimage centre led to its being chosen as the site for the vast **Monument aux Morts** erected to the memory of the 250,000 Breton dead of the Great War. Even the 200 metres of closely-inscribed wall which surrounds the monument is insufficient to list all the victims by name. All in all, Ste-Anne is a sad and solemn place, not really a place for stopping despite its plentiful hotels.

Carnac and the Presqu'Ile de Quiberon

According to local legend, the **alignments** at **CARNAC** – rows of 2000 or so menhirs stretching for over 4km to the north of the village – are Roman soldiers turned to stone by Pope St-Cornely. Another theory, with a certain amount of mathematical backing, says the giant menhir of Locmariaquer and the Carnac stones were an observatory for the motions of the moon. But history has seen them used as ready-quarried stone, and dug up and removed by peasants to protect their precious crops from academic visitors when prehistoric archaeology became fashionable. It's impossible to say how many have disappeared, nor really to prove anything from what's left; and in any case their actual arrangement may never have been particularly important, with their significance lying in some great annual ceremony as each one was erected.

They constitute, however, the most important prehistoric site in Europe, long predating Knossos, the Pyramids, Stonehenge, or the great Egyptian temples of the same name at Karnak. Aside from strolling in wonder among them, you can get a good deal of information, and entertainment too, from the **Musée de Préhistoire** on rue du Tumulus in Carnac-Ville. It combines

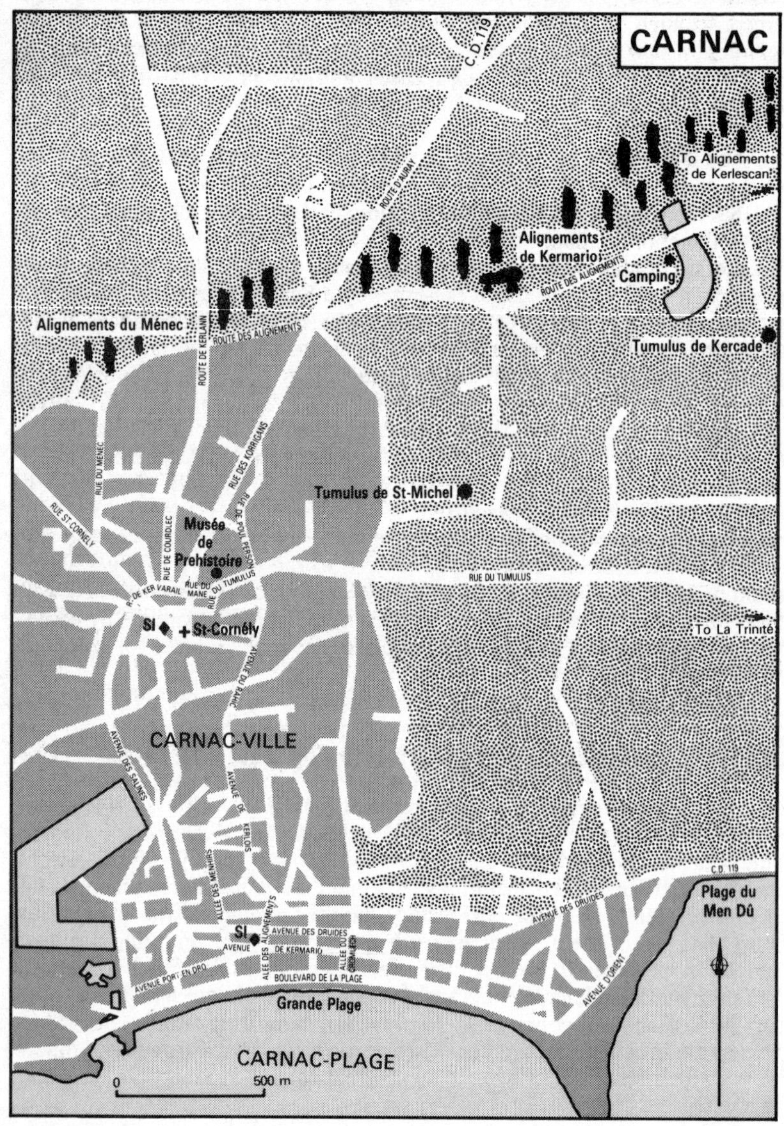

serious scholarship with large blowups of the French Asterix cartoons, and traces the history of the area from about 450,000 years ago up to and after the Romans. Hours are: July to mid-September, 10am to noon and 2 to 6.30pm daily; rest of the year, 10am to noon and 2 to 5pm, closed Tuesday.

Carnac, divided between the original Carnac-Ville and the seaside resort of Carnac-Plage, is extremely popular and crowded. The permanent **SI** is at 74 av des Druides in Carnac-Plage, but there's an annexe open in the church square of Carnac-Ville in summer. Among the innumerable **hotels**, the *Hoty* (15 av de Kermario; ☎97.52.11.12) is the best deal near the beach; in town, try *Chez Marylène* (27 rue St-Cornely; ☎97.52.06.22) or *Chez Nous* (2 rue Poul-Person, ☎97.52.07.28). The best of Carnac's many **beaches** is the smallest, the **Men Dû** on the road towards LA TRINITE. If you want to **camp** by the sea, go to *L'Océan* (☎97.52.02.71) or *Men Dû* (☎97.52.04.23) – otherwise, the best site is *La Grande Métairie* (☎97.55.71.47) on route des Alignements opposite the stones. **Market days** are Wednesday and Sunday.

For exploring the alignments other than on foot, you can hire **bicycles** at *Lorcy*, 6 rue de Cordiec, Carnac-Ville, at *Cyclo-Loisirs*, 62 av des Druides, Carnac-Plage, or at *BMX*, 20 av des Druides, Carnac-Plage. **Horses** are available from the *Centre Equestre des Menhirs*, which in summer is based at the *Grande Métairie* campsite (see above). Clearly, by far the best way to see the alignments would be from the air. If you split costs three or four ways, it's not much more costly than an extravagant meal. At the **Aérodrome de Quiberon**, near the tip of the Quiberon peninsula, two companies operate short flights over the peninsula and the Morbihan: the *Quiberon Air Club* (year round except Jan.), and *Thalass Air* (to the left of the Air Club building; July–Sept. with a reservation the same day ☎97.30.40.00).

The **Presqu'île de Quiberon** is well worth visiting on its own merits; **QUIBERON** is quite a lively port, and you can get boats out to the islands or walk the shores of this narrow peninsula. The ocean-facing shore, known as the **Côte Sauvage**, is a wild and highly unswimmable stretch, where the stormy seas look like flashing scenes of snowy mountain tops. The sheltered eastern side has safe and calm sandy beaches, and plenty of **campsites**.

Quiberon

The town of **QUIBERON** centres on a miniature golf course surrounded by bars, pizzerias and some surprisingly good clothes and antique shops. The cafés by the long bathing beach are the most enjoyable, along with the old-fashioned *Café du Marché* next to the PTT. **Port Maria**, the fishing harbour and **gare maritime** for the islands, is the most active part of town and has the best concentration of **hotels**. Try the *de l'Océan* (quai de l'Océan; ☎97.50.07.58) or *de la Mer* (quai de Houat; ☎97.50.09.05). The **youth hostel**, *Les Filets Bleus* (45 rue du Roch-Priol; ☎97.50.15.54), is set back from the sea but close to the **gare SNCF**. A vast array of **fish restaurants** lines the seafront of which the best, for its fish soup and *assiette de fruits de mer*, is *Au Bon Accueil* on quai de Houat. The **SI**, at 7 rue de Verdun, downhill and to the left from the train station, has timetables for boats to Belle-Ile and the smaller islands of Houat and Hoëdic.

Belle-Ile

BELLE-ILE, 45 minutes by ferry from Quiberon, has its own *Côte Sauvage* on its Atlantic coast, while the landward side is fertile, cultivated ground, interrupted by deep estuaries with tiny ports. To appreciate the island's contrasts, some form of transport is advisable – you can **hire bikes** at the port and main town of **LE PALAIS** and if you're in a small car the ferry fare is relatively low.

The island once belonged to the monks of Redon; then to the ambitious Nicholas Fouquet, Louis XIV's minister; later to the English, who in 1761 swapped it for Minorca in an unrepeatable bargain deal. Docking at Le Palais, the abrupt star-shaped fortifications of the *Citadelle* are the first thing you see. Built along stylish and ordered lines by the great fortress builder, Vauban, it is startling in size – filled with doorways leading to mysterious cellars and underground passages, endless sequences of rooms, dungeons, and deserted cells. It only ceased being a prison in 1961, having numbered a succession of state enemies and revolutionaries among its inmates, including Ben Bella of Algeria. Less involuntarily, painters such as Monet and Matisse, the writers Flaubert and Proust, and the actress Sarah Bernhardt all spent time on the island. And presumably Alexandre Dumas too, as Porthos's death, in *The Three Musketeers*, takes place here. A museum in the *citadelle* (open 9am–7pm) documents the island's history, in fiction as much as in fact.

Accommodation in Le Palais includes the reasonably priced *Hôtel du Commerce* (place Hôtel-de-Ville, ☎97.31.81.71), a **campsite** *Les Glacis* (☎97.31.41.76) or a **youth hostel** (reservations as for Quiberon, ☎97.50.15.54), a short way out of town along the clifftops from the *citadelle*, at Haute-Boulogne. Belle-Ile's second town, **SAUZON**, is set at the mouth of a long estuary 6km to the west. If you're staying any length of time, and you've got transport, it's probably a better place to base yourself. There's a good, cheap **hotel**, the *du Phare* (☎97.31.60.36), or two **campsites**, *Pen Prad* (☎97.31.62.79) and *Prad Stivell*. On the road towards these campsites is a **vegetarian restaurant**, *le Zénith*.

For exploring the island, a coastal footpath runs on bare soil the length of the **Côte Sauvage**. At the Sauzon end you'll find the **Grotte de l'Apothicairerie**, so called because it was once full of cormorants' nests, arranged like the jars on a pharmacist's shelves. It's reached by descending a slippery flight of steps cut into the rock. Be careful: most years someone falls and drowns. Inland, on D25 back towards Le Palais, you pass the two **menhirs**, Jean and Jeanne, said to be lovers petrified as punishment for wanting to meet before their marriage. Another larger menhir used to lie near these two; it was broken up to help construct the road that separates them.

Houat and Hoëdic

The islands of **HOUAT** and **HOEDIC** (boats from PORT MARIA, 90 min., daily except Tues.) are very much smaller versions of Belle-Ile. Both feel as though they've been left behind by the passing centuries, although the younger fishermen of Houat have revived the island's fortunes by establishing a successful co-operative. HOUAT, in particular, has excellent **beaches** –

as ever on its sheltered, eastern side – that fill up with campers in the summer. It also has the two isles' only (and very expensive) hotel, *La Sirène* (☎97.30.68.05).

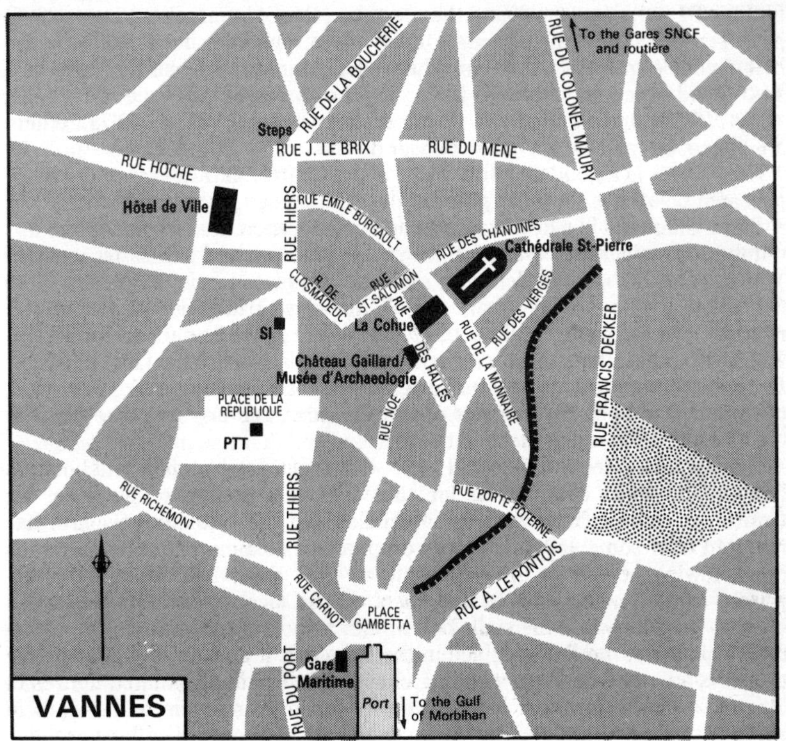

Vannes and the Golfe de Morbihan

It was from **VANNES** that the great Breton hero, Nominöe, set out to unify Brittany – giving the Franks a terrible beating and pushing the borders past Nantes and Rennes, where they remained up until the French Revolution nearly a millenium later. Here too the Breton *Etats* assembled to ratify the Act of Union in the building known as *La Cohue*. **Vieux Vannes**, the old centre of chaotic streets crammed around the cathedral and enclosed by ramparts and gardens and a tiny stream, has every reason to vaunt its historic charms.

It's about a ten-minute walk from the **gare SNCF** and main **gare routière** – to the right then left down rue Olivier de Clisson – to **place de la Répub-**

lique, the new town centre, shifted outside the medieval city in the nineteenth-century craze for urbanisation. The grandest of the public buildings here, guarded by a pair of sleek and dignified bronze lions, is the **Hôtel de Ville** at the top of rue Thiers. Walk a couple of blocks down from it and you'll find the **SI** (with free maps and the usual bundles of information) at no. 29. In peak season Vannes can become quite claustrophobic, but it still offers a better choice of **hotels** than anywhere else around the Golfe de Morbihan. Two good ones in the old town are *La Bretagne* (34 rue du Méne; ☎97.47.20.21) and *Le Moderne* (2 rue de la Boucherie; ☎97.47.40.78). There are cheaper places on rue Olivier-de-Clisson – the *Clisson* (no. 11; ☎97.54.13.94) is a good standby. The *Voile d'Or* (☎97.42.71.81) is in the lively port area below the southern gates of the ramparts on place Gambetta.

Place Gambetta is a key brasserie and café location, though you'll find any number of restaurants, *crêperies*, ice cream parlours and *pâtisseries* in *Vieux Vannes*. The *Bistrot des Halles* on place de la Poissonnerie serves excellent fish dinners with produce from the Wednesday, Friday and Saturday **fish market** in the covered hall on the *place*. A late night **bar** (open until 1am) with a friendly atmosphere and Irish folk bands worth checking out is *Le Pandemonium* on rue de la Boucherie. And if you're visiting in the first week of August, the open-air concerts of the **Vannes Jazz Festival** take place in the Théâtre de Verdure, close to the SI.

By day, the streets of the old city, with their overhanging, witch-hatted houses and busy commercial life, are the chief source of pleasure. **La Cohue**, stretching between rue des Halles and the Cathedral Square, has reverted after some 750 years to its original use as a marketplace (for crafts now), having served in the meantime as high court and assembly room, prison, revolutionary tribunal and theatre. The local *Beaux Arts* has taken over its top floor while the stalls below offer a short cut through to the cathedral. This is not the finest edifice in the town, but it does have one exquisite treasure, an early medieval wedding chest, with beautifully painted figures in enigmatic poses. It's kept in the *Sacristy* (open 10am–noon and 2–5pm in summer, closed Sun.). Nearby on rue Noë is the **Château Gaillard** archeology museum, its finds from 400,000 B.C. to the Roman occupation laid out with great and tedious precision. Around the corner in **Hôtel de Roscannec** (19 rue des Halles) there's an equally efficient display of stones, fossils, shells and stuffed birds. Both museums are open June to September 9.30am to noon and 2 to 6pm, though it seems a pity you can't just stumble onto their exhibits lying on the beaches or strewn around the dolmens and tumuli.

Morbihan – and its islands

It comes as rather a surprise to discover that Vannes is on the sea. Its harbour is a channelled inlet of the ragged-edged **Golfe de Morbihan**, which lets in the tides through a narrow gap between the peninsulas of **Rhys** and **Locmariaquer.** By popular tradition the **islands** scattered around this enclosure used to number the days of the year, though for centuries the waters have been rising and there are now less than one for each week. Of these, thirty are owned by film stars and the like, while two – the ILE AUX

MOINES and ILE D'ARZ – have regular populations and ferry services and end up being extremely crowded in summer. The rest are the best, and a **boat tour** around them, or at least a trip out to GAVRINIS near the mouth of the gulf, is a fairly compelling attraction. As the boats thread their way through the baffling muddle of channels you lose track of what is island and what is mainland; and everywhere there are megalithic ruins, stone circles disappearing beneath the water, and solitary menhirs on small hillocks.

In season, there are dozens of different **gulf tours** available, leaving from VANNES, PORT NAVALO, and LARMOR BADEN. Full details are available from the Vannes SI but briefly the options are these. **From Vannes**, there are SNCF-run *vedettes*, quite a deluxe service offering any combination of island and gulf visits, from the terminal next to the modern aquarium on promenade de la Rabbine; **from Port-Navalo** (four buses daily from Vannes) more basic and economic *TVCP* cruises (mid-March to mid-Sept.); **from Locmariaquer** (buses from Auray or Carnac) *TVCP* trips around the gulf, up the Auray River and intermittently to Gavrinis; **from Larmor-Baden** (one

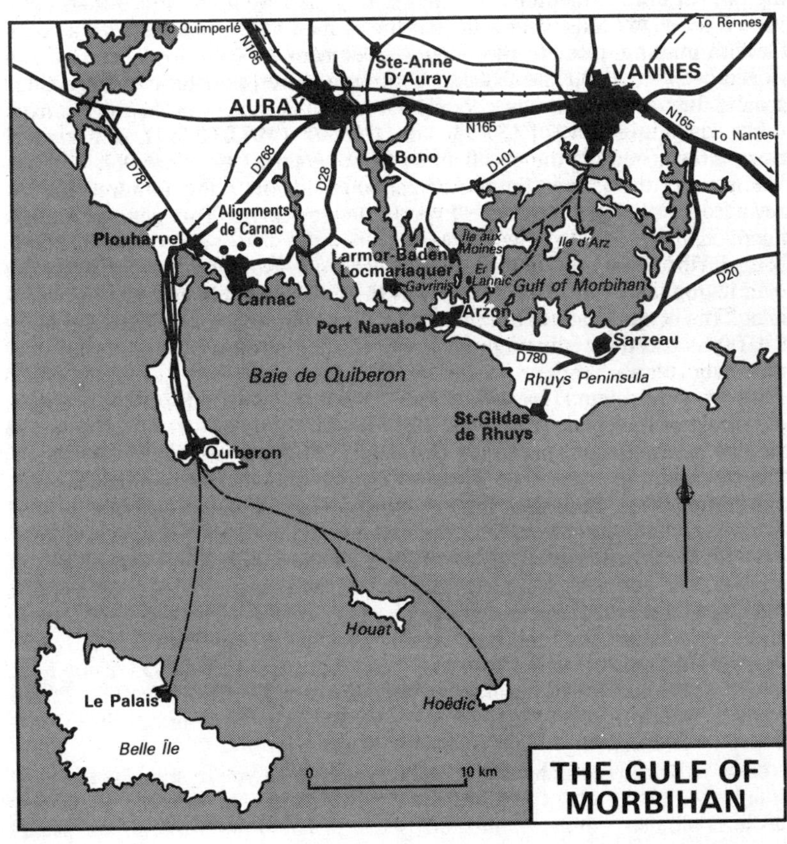

bus daily from Vannes) there's a regular run to Gavrinis only, leaving on the hour and returning on the half-hour (15min. crossing).

Gavrinis and Locmariaquer

A dramatic group of menhirs, arranged in a figure of eight, are to be seen on the tiny barren island of **Er Lannic** – though only at low tide when the water gives these smaller islets the appearance of stranded hovercraft skirted with mud. The best island for megalithic monuments is, however, **GAVRINIS.** It contains, almost consists of, a tumulus that has been partially uncovered to reveal a chamber in which all the slabs of stone are carved with curving lines like fingerprints, axeheads and spirals – purely decorative according to archaeologists. Thanks to the complex patterning, the stone of the roof has been identified as part of the same piece as the dolmen known as the **Table des Marchands** at **LOCMARIAQUER**. Locmariaquer also has the **Grand Menhir Brisé**, supposedly the crucial central point of the megalithic observatory of Carnac. Before being floored by an earthquake in 1722, it was by far the largest known menhir – 22 metres high and weighing more than a full Jumbo Jet at 347 tons. It now lies on the ground in four pieces, with a possible fifth missing, close to the *Table des Marchands*. Both are fenced off and closed between 12.30 and 2.30pm. There are more prehistoric constructions around the town, which has a couple of reasonable small **hotels**, the *Lautram* (place de l'Eglise, ☎97.57.31.32) and *L'Escale* (☎97.57.32.51), and several **campsites**, including the excellent *La Ferme Fleurie* (☎97.57.34.06).

The tip of the Presqu'Ile de Locmariaquer is only a few hundred metres away from Port Navalo and the **Presqu'île de Rhuys**. This peninsula has a micro-climate of its own, warm enough for pomegranates, figs, bougainvillaea, and the only Breton vineyards. Oysters are cultivated on the muddy gulf shores, but the currents of the gulf make this no place for swimming. The ocean beaches are the ones to head for: east from ST-GILDAS-DE-RHUYS is the most enticing and least crowded stretch with glittering gold and silver coloured rocks.

If you're spending any length of time on the peninsula, **ARZON** is probably the nicest of its towns; stay at the *Hôtel de Rhuys* (☎97.41.20.01) or either of the two big campsites, *Le Tindio* (☎97.41.25.59) or *Port Sable* (☎97.41.21.98). Near the tip of the peninsula, clearly visible to the north of the main road, is the **Tumulus de Thumiac**, from the top of which Julius Caesar is supposed to have watched the sea battle in which the Romans defeated the Veneti.

At **ST-GILDAS DE RHUYS**, Pierre Abelard, the theologian/lover of Héloïse, was abbot for a period from 1126, having been exiled from Paris. 'I live in a wild country where every day brings new perils', he wrote to Héloïse, eventually fleeing after his brother monks – hedonists unimpressed by his stern scholasticism – attempted to poison him. By the beaches around the village are a handful of **campsites**, among them *Le Menhir* (☎97.45.22.88) and *Les Govelins* (☎97.45.21.67); there's also an average-priced **hotel**, the *Giquel* (☎97.45.23.12).

Near SARZEAU, which also has accommodation if you're stuck, is the most impressive local sight, the **Château de Suscinio**. This fourteenth-century castle is almost completely moated, set in isolation amid marsh and sandy plain, and has a sagging but still vivid mosaic floor. You can take a precarious stroll around the high ramparts.

South to the Loire

South of the **Vilaine** River you leave the Morbihan *département* and technically you leave Brittany too. The roads veer firmly east and west – to Nantes or La Baule, avoiding the marshes of the **Grande-Brière**. For centuries these 20,000 acres of peat bog have been deemed to be the common property of all who lived in them. The scattered population, the *Brièrois*, made and make their living by fishing for eels in the streams, gathering reeds, and – on the nine days permitted each year – cutting the peat. Tourism has arrived only recently, and is resented. The touted attraction is hiring a punt which will get you lost for a few hours with your pole tangled in the rushes.

On the edge of the marshes, just before you come to the sea, is the walled town of **GUERANDE**. The moat around the thick ramparts, long filled, forms a spacious promenade around the old city, whose best feature is a market by the church. It's quite a metropolis by Brière standards, though not one likely to delay you for too long. There are more marshes between Guérande and the sea. This time, however, they are salt, a 'white country' of bizarre-looking *oeillets* – pens measuring 70 to 80 square metres, in which sea water, since Roman times, has been collected and evaporated.

There is something very surreal about emerging from the Brière to the coast at **LA BAULE.** This is Brittany's most upmarket pocket – an imposing, monied landscape where the dunes are no longer bonded together with scrub and pines, but with massive apartment buildings and luxury hotels. Around the crab-shaped bay, bronzed nymphettes and would-be Clint Eastwoods ride across the sands into the sunset against a backdrop of cruising lifeguards, horse-dung removers, and fantastically priced cocktails. It can be fun if you feel like a break from the more subdued Breton attractions – but expensive. What **campsites** there are charge what you'd normally pay for hotels, the **hotels** what you might pay for two weeks' accommodation. At the cheapest hotels – *Violettas* (44 av Georges-Clemenceau, ☎40.60.32.16) and the *Almadies* (☎40.60.79.05) – you're likely to find intense competition for rooms. Still, the resort's beach is undeniably impressive; there is a wonderful ice cream shop, *A. Manuel*, on the corner of the promenade; and, a little out of character, there's also an excellent bookshop, *Breizh* (at 9 av du Général-de-Gaulle), which specialises in Breton culture, language and politics.

Le Croisic

The small port of **LE CROISIC**, sheltered from the ocean around the corner of the headland, is probably a more realistic (and to many perceptions, more attractive) place to stay. These days it's basically a pleasure port, but fishing boats do still sail from its harbour and there's a modern **fish market**, near the long Tréhic jetty, where you can see the day's catch auctioned. The best **hotels** are *Les Nids* (83, bd Général-Leclerc, ☎40.23.00.63) or *Perthuy du Roy* (3 place Croix-de-Ville, ☎40.23.00.95).

Close by, all around the rocky sea coast known as the **Grande Côte**, is a whole range of **campsites**. Just outside Le Croisic itself is the *Océan* (☎40.23.07.69), and at BATZ there's the *Casse Cailloux* (☎40.23.91.71). For equally good beaches and a chance of cheaper **hotel** accommodation, you could go east from La Baule to **PORNICHET** (though preferably keeping away from the plush marina) or to the tiny **ST-MARC**, where in 1953 Jacques Tati filmed 'Monsieur Hulot's Holiday'.

The best sandy coves in the region are to be found on the western outskirts of **ST-NAZAIRE**, linked by wooded paths and almost deserted. But it's a gloomy city. It was bombed to extinction in World War II, and its shipyards, in more or less continuous operation since constructing Julius Caesar's fleet, are now closing. The one reason you might want to stay is the relative ease of finding inexpensive **hotel** space. Options include the *Normandy* (35 rue de la Paix), the *Touraine* (4 av de la République, ☎40.22.47.56), and the *Windsor* (53 av de la République); or the **hostel**, the *Foyer du Travailleur*, at 30 rue Soleil-Levant. Even if St-Nazaire is a familiarly depressing town in total industrial decline, it has one inspiring piece of engineering – the **Pont St-Nazaire**, a great elongated S-curved suspension bridge over the mouth of the Loire. Driving across it incurs a heavy toll, but bikes go over for free.

travel details

Transport in Brittany can be a tricky and time-consuming business. Most of the main towns have train links with Rennes and/or Nantes and there's a rough loop of the coast. Aside from these, getting between towns is often a matter of fitting in with a web of independent private bus lines – their services, especially inland, often geared to schools and markets. The timetables supplied at stations are a help – there's one for each of fourteen sectors detailing both buses and trains – but this is one part of France where you may find it more rewarding to pick a couple of main bases and hire a bike.

Trains

From Rennes frequently to Paris-Montparnasse (3¼ hr.) via Le Mans (2 hr.), to St-Malo (1 hr.), to Vannes/Lorient/Quimper (1 hr./1½ hr./2¼ hr.) and to Morlaix/Brest (2 hr./2¾ hr.); 5 daily to Roscoff (2¾ hr.; via Vannes – summer only and Mont St-Michel (¾ hr.).

From Roscoff 5 daily to Morlaix (½ hr.) and Rennes (2¾ hr).

From Brest 6 daily to Quimper (1½hr).

From Nantes very frequently to Paris-Montparnasse (3½ hr.); slightly less so to Angers (¾ hr.), La Baule/Croisic (1 hr./1¼hr.) and Vannes/Quimper (1¾ hr./3½ hr.).

Buses

From Rennes more or less hourly to Dinan (1¾ hr.); 8 daily to Dinard (1¾ hr.); 3 daily to Nantes (2½ hr.) and Josselin (1¼ hr.).

From Quimper 4 daily to Brest (1½ hr.); daily to Morlaix (1¾ hr.).

From Lannion 9 daily to St-Brieuc (1 hr.); 6 daily to Trégastel (1 hr.); daily to Morlaix 1¼ hr.).

From St-Brieuc 7 daily to Paimpol (1½ hr.); 4 daily to Dinan (1 hr.).

From Vannes daily to Malestroit (¾ hr.).

From Carnac 2 daily to Lorient (1¼ hr.).

Ferries

From St-Malo *Brittany Ferries* (St-Malo ☎99.56.68.40, Portsmouth ☎0705.827701) to Portsmouth: 9 hr. overnight crossing.

From Roscoff *Brittany Ferries* (☎98.69.76.22, Plymouth ☎0752.21321) to Plymouth (2 daily in 6 hr.) and to Cork (daily; 13½ to 17 hr.). Also to the Ile de Batz (several times daily in season, irregularly out; 15 min.).

From Dinan daily boat up the estuary to Dinard (2½ hr.) and to St-Malo (3 hr.); May–Sept. only.
Dinard-St-Malo Regular boats (10 min.).
From Pointe de l'Arcouest Regular ferry to the Ile de Bréhat (10 min.).
From Quimper Daily boat down the Odet to Benodet (1¼ hr.); May–Sept. only.
From Nantes boats can be hired for the Nantes–Brest canal. Also at Malestroit, Josselin, Quimper and elsewhere.
From Lorient regular summer ferry to the Ile de Groix (45 min.).
From Vannes/Port-Navalo/Lamor Baden (and other ports) ferries to Ile de Gavrines and boat trips to other islands in the gulf of Morbihan.
From Quiberon regular ferry to Belle Ile (1 hr.), less frequently to Houat and Hoëdic.

More details and ferry schedules for the Breton islands can be obtained from A.P.I.T. (11 place Joffre, Auray; ☎97.56.52.57) or principal tourist offices in the province, or Maison de la Bretagne, Centre Commercial, Maine-Montparnasse, 17 rue de l'Arrivée, 15e, Paris (☎45.38.73.15).

CHAPTER FIVE

THE LOIRE

Intimidated by the density of Châteaux – and all their great Renaissance intrigues and associations – people tend to make bad use of time spent in the Loire. Which is a pity, for if you pick your castles selectively, rid yourself of a sense of duty to the guided tours, and spend days on river banks supplied with cheese, fruit and white Loire wines, this can be one of the most enjoyable of all French regions.

The Loire's central *département* of **Touraine** – 'the heart of France' – has the best wines, the most scented flowers and delicious fruit, the top **châteaux (Chenonceaux, Azay-le-Rideau** and **Loches**), and the purest French accent in the land. It also takes in three of the Loire's most pleasurable tributaries – the **Cher, Vienne**, and **Indre** – each of which has its individual attractions, when you can gain access to their banks. If you have just a week to spare for the region, then these are the parts to spend it. **Orléanais**, along the northern stretches, does its best to compete but it is too close to Paris for comfort.

As for the **Loire** itself, its most salient features are whirlpools, banks of quicksand, vicious currents and a propensity to flood. No one swims in or boats on the Loire, no goods are carried along it – it's just there, the longest river in France. As well as the select handful of châteaux, the region has a few additional sights that live up to the pleasures of river picnics with a bottle of good wine: most unmissably the tapestries in **Angers**, the gardens at **Villandry** (outside Tours) and the Romanesque abbey at **St-Benoît-sur-Loire**. Of the cities, **Le Mans** is the least touristy, **Tours** can be tedious but is good for museums, **Orléans** has charm, **Saumur** is perfect for indolence but not hot on entertainment.

In general, this is a right-wing, laid-back region where air-conditioned cars and bus tours are the norm. For exploring on your own, it's a good idea to hire some means of **transport**, at least for occasional forays. Buses can be sparse (their schedules are not geared to outsiders), and trains are too limiting. But this is wonderful and easy **cycling** country, best of all on the flood-banks, or *levées* of the Loire.

Arriving at the northern channel ports, the only access on public transport is via Paris. If you wish to avoid this it's advisable to make for one of the ports either in Brittany, (change trains at Rennes), or Normandy, (change at Caen). See relevant *Travel Details* for further information.

ANJOU AND TOURAINE

This is the last – and best – stretch of the Loire, languidly floating by long islands of reed and willows before it enters the gorge down to Nantes and its estuary. Travelling upstream, or downstream if you approach from Paris and **Tours**, is reasonably straightforward with bus and train routes following the river for most of the way. The Anjou and Touraine **wines** can become addictive, and the **food markets** in this key region, which divides northern France from the South, are among the best in the country.

Angers

'Black' **ANGERS**, Anjou's capital, gained its epithet from the gloomy-coloured slate and stone that has been quarried here since the ninth century. It is a depressing town – not a place to spend a holiday – but worth visiting for a day. For Angers possesses two works of art more stirring and stunning than all the châteaux and their contents put together: both are **tapestries**, the fourteenth-century *Apocalypse* and the twentieth-century *Chant du Monde*.

The **Tapestry of the Apocalypse** is in **Angers Castle**, a formidable early medieval fortress with seventeen circular towers like elephants' legs gripping the rock below the kilometre-long curtain wall. Inside there are a few miscellaneous remains of the counts' royal lodgings and chapels, but the immediate and obvious focus is the tapestry, whose one-hundred-metre length (of an original 168m) is well displayed in a modern gallery. Woven between 1375 and 1378, it takes as its text **St. John's Vision of the Apocalypse**, as described in the Book of Revelations. If you happen to have a bible with you, so much the better since, though the French biblical quotations are given, the English 'translation' is just explanation. The vision is of the lead-up to the Day of Judgment signalled by seven angels blowing their trumpets after which . . .

> *'hail and fire mingled with blood . . . were cast upon the earth and the third part of trees was burned up and all green grass . . . and as it were a great mountain burning with fi.e was cast into the sea and the third part of the sea became blood . . .' (Rev. 8:7-8).*

A burning star poisons a third of the waters, locusts like scorpions are let loose from the bowels of the earth. The battle of Armageddon rages with Satan, 'the great red dragon', and his minions of composite animals marking their earthly followers. The holy forces retaliate by breaking the seven vials of plagues. The vision ends with the sacred city of the blessed, the heavenly Jerusalem, and Satan buried for a thousand years. The slightly flattened medieval perspective has a hallucinatory quality, extraordinarily beautiful and terrifying, and possessing an alarming power to evoke a sense of the end of the world either in accordance with the first-century text or as a secular holocaust.

If you can take anything else in, there are more tapestries, of a gentler nature, in the sporadically open **Royal Lodgings** and **Governor's Lodge**. The castle itself is open 9.30am to noon and 2 to 6.30pm in the summer; 10am to noon and 2 to 5.30pm in winter. The entrance fee is reasonable.

The city's modern tapestry, **Le Chant du Monde**, was designed, in response to the *Apocalypse*, by Jean Lurçat, who began the project in 1957 but died nine years later before its completion. The first four tapestries deal with

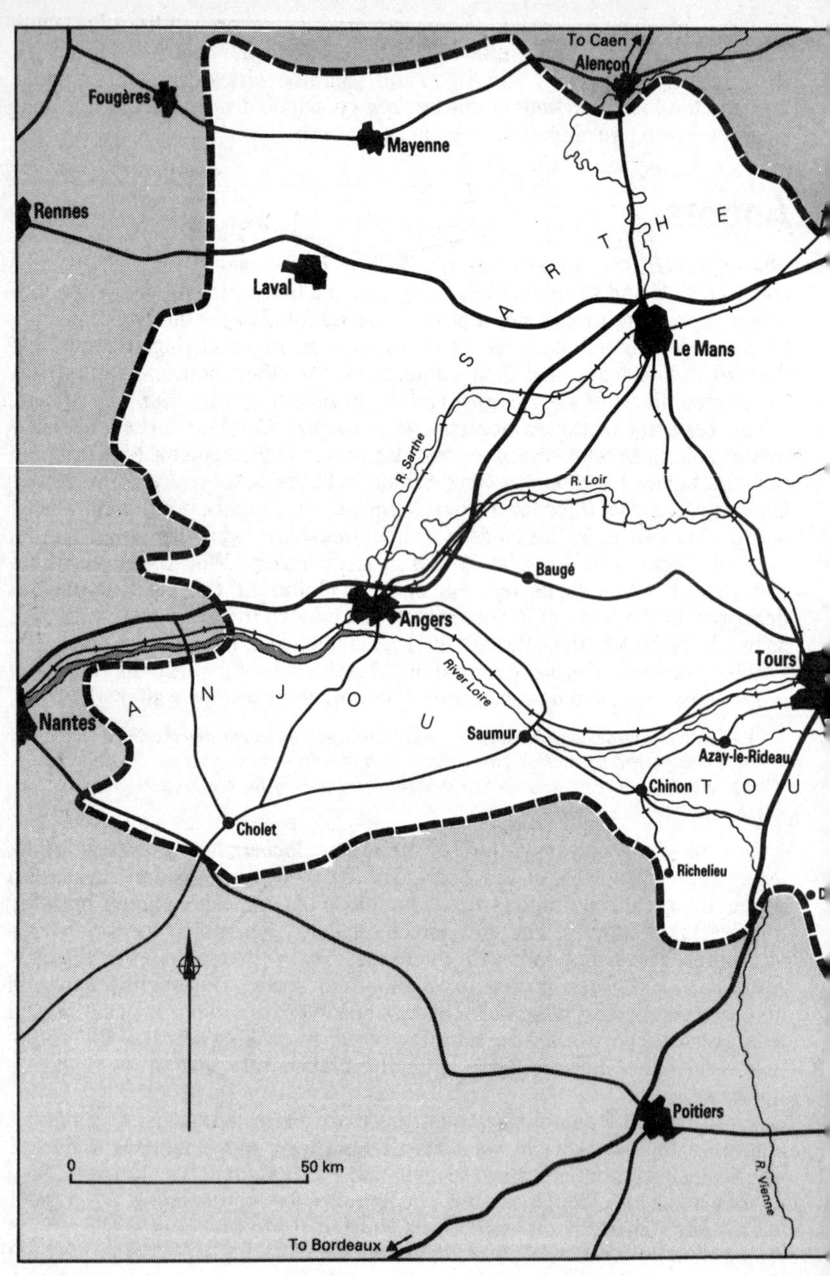
To Caen
Alençon
Fougères
Mayenne
Rennes
SARTHE
Laval
Le Mans
R. Sarthe
R. Loir
Baugé
Angers
River Loire
Tours
ANJOU
Nantes
Saumur
Azay-le-Rideau
Chinon
TOU
Cholet
Richelieu
Poitiers
0
50 km
R. Vienne
To Bordeaux

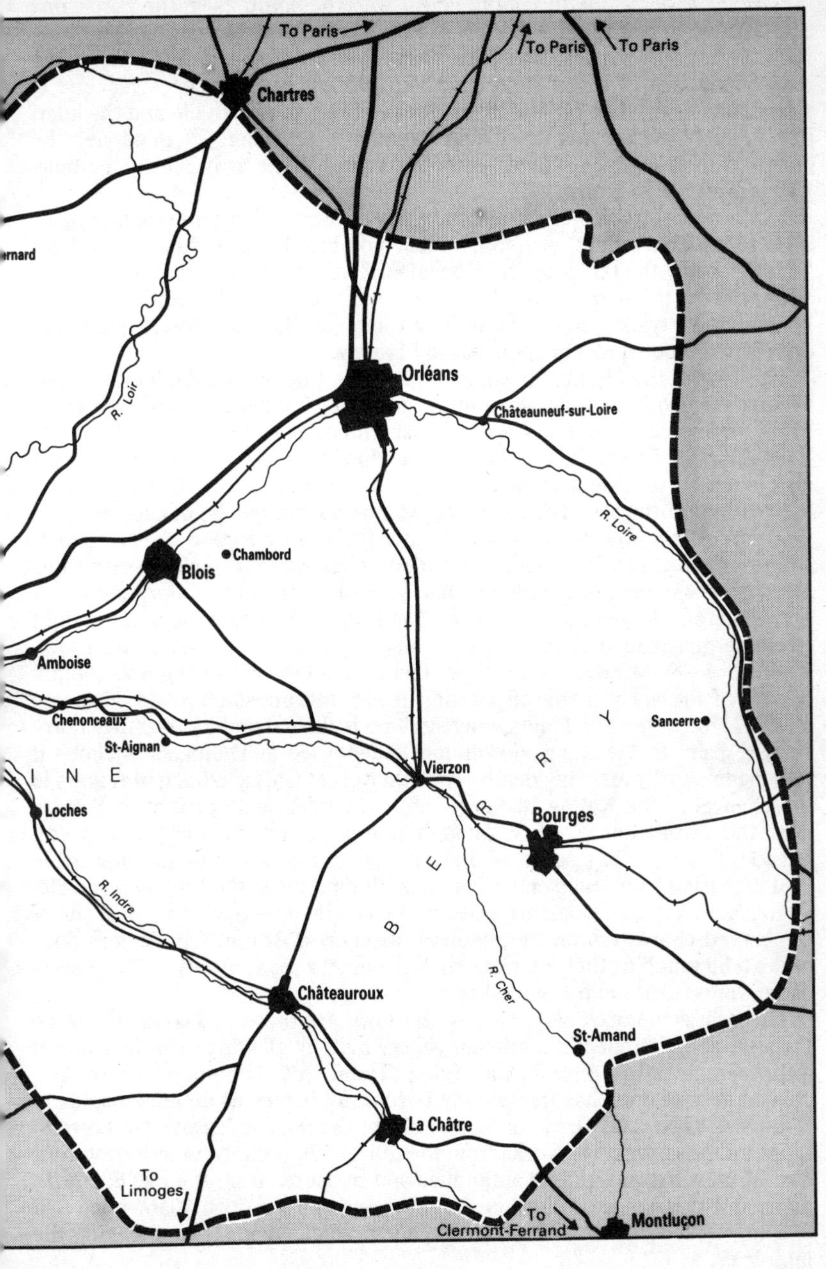
To Paris
To Paris
To Paris
Chartres
rnard
R. Loir
Orléans
Châteauneuf-sur-Loire
R. Loire
Chambord
Blois
Amboise
Chenonceaux
St-Aignan
Sancerre
Vierzon
I N E
B E R R Y
Loches
Bourges
R. Indre
R. Cher
Châteauroux
St-Amand
La Châtre
To
Limoges
To
Clermont-Ferrand
Montluçon

La Grande Menace, the threat of nuclear war: the bomb itself; the Hiroshima Man, flayed and burned with the broken symbols of belief dropping from him; the collective massacre of the *Great Charnel House*; and the last dying rose falling with the post-holocaust ash through black space – *the End of Everything*. From then on, the tapestries celebrate the joy of life and the interdependence of its myriad manifestations: fire, water, champagne, the conquest of space, poetry and symbolic language. The artist's own commentary is available in English.

Modern tapestry is an unfamiliar art, the colours are so bright and Lurçat's style so unlike anything else that initially you may be overwhelmed. If that's the case, enjoy the building, the Hôpital St-Jean, which from 1174 to 1854 was a hospital for the poor. It's on bd Arago, upstream from the castle – about a fifteen-minute walk – across Pont de la Haute Chaine and second left; hours are 10am to noon and 2 to 6pm; closed Monday.

This side of the Maine, known as **La Doutre** (the other side, literally), has several mansions and houses dating from the medieval period and later. From more recent times is a very odd slaughterhouse clock by the Pont de la Basse-Chaine. An official tour will get you into buildings you otherwise can't visit, such as the Romanesque galleries of the **Eglise de Ronceray**, with their beautiful murals. The abbey to which this church belonged, now the *Ecole des Arts et Métiers*, juts into the twelfth-century **Eglise de la Trinité**, where an exquisite Renaissance wooden spiral staircase fails to mask this bizarre piece of medieval building joinery. Apply to the SI for information.

If you cross the central Pont de Verdun back to the centre, just to the right after the quayside road, you'll see a long flight of steps leading up to the **Cathédrale St-Maurice** – the most inspiring approach, giving you the full benefit of the early medieval facade. Inside, the unusually wide, aisle-less nave with its dome-like Plantagenet vaulting is illuminated by twelfth-century stained glass. In the choir one window is dedicated to Thomas à Becket – it was made shortly after his death. The other great Gothic edifice in Angers is the chancel of the **Eglise St-Serge**, on av M-Talet, just north of the centre near the Jardin des Plantes. Though nothing much to look at from the outside, within, it has some of the most perfect and seemingly impossible vaulting rising from the slender columns. Behind the cathedral, on place Ste-Croix, is the town's favourite carpentry detail – the unlikely genitals of one of the carved characters on the medieval **Maison d'Adam**. Old Angers does not extend much further: on place du Ralliement a giant turkey made of aeroplane wings is the central sculpture.

The best sculptures elsewhere in the town are those of **David d'Angers** (1788–1856), exhibited in a brilliant gallery built by glassing-over the ruins of a thirteenth-century church, the **Eglise Toussaint**. The main **Beaux Arts** collection next door has delightfully purposeful babies as creative cupids in Boucher's *Génie des Arts*, the beautiful *La Femme au Masque* by Lorenzo Lippi and representative works from the thirteenth to the twentieth centuries. The **Musée Pince** exhibits antiquities and treasures from the Far East with an excellent Japanese collection. All the museums are open 10am–noon and 2–6pm (closed Mon.) and you can buy a single ticket that includes the tapestries.

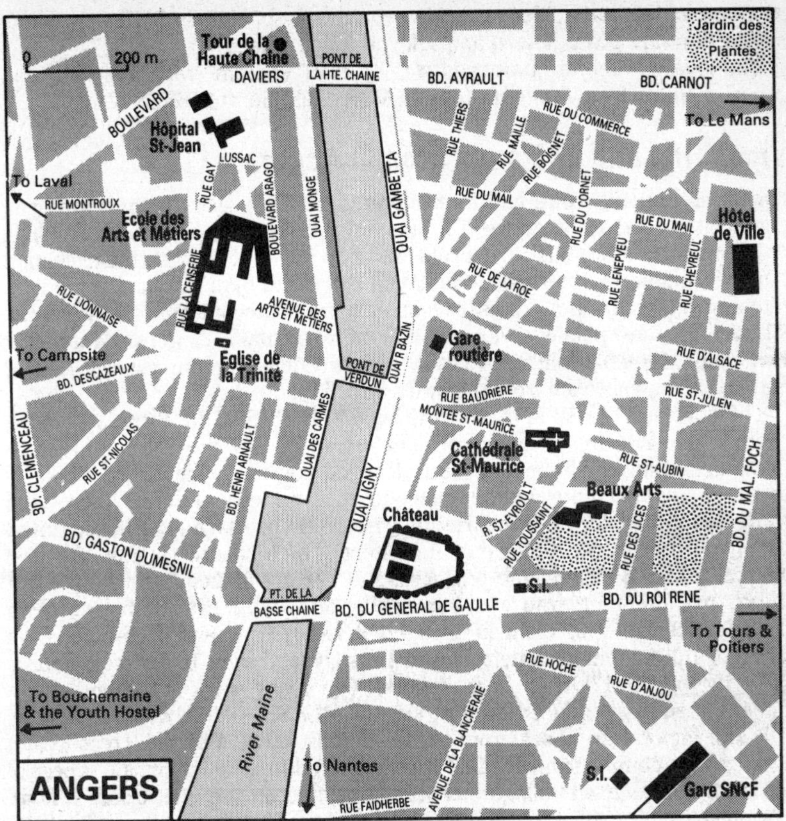

Some practical details

For a room, the two most central and affordable **hotels** are *Les Négociants* (2 rue de la Roë; ☎41.87.70.03) and *La Tour* (66 rue Baudrière; ☎41.87.72.71). There are cheap places around the **gare SNCF** such as *La Coupe d'Or* (5 rue de la Gare; ☎41.88.45.02). The station is south of the centre, about a five-minute walk from the castle; the **gare routière** is up by the Pont de Verdu, between place de la République and the river. The best **campsite** is north-east of the city at Parc de la Haye, AVRILLE: bus #3 to RONCEVAUX (change at Clinique from buses going to Avrillé); a **youth hostel**, open only in summer along with another campsite, is at the *Centre d'Accueil du Lac du Maine* (route du Pruniers; ☎41.48.57.01; bus #6 to Bouchemaine). You can **hire canoes** at the *Base Nautique* in the complex.

The streets around **place du Ralliement** and **place Romain** are the best for **restaurants** and there is a **market** every day on place Sainte-Croix. The **SI** (which runs an accommodation service) is on place Kennedy, facing the castle, with, just up the road, the *Conseil Interprofessionel des Vins d'Anjou et* *du Saumur* vineyards. They can give you details of vineyards to visit (some suggestions are given below) and sell you Anjou wines.

The *Allostop* phone number is ☎41.87.21.21 (5–7pm weekdays) and you can **hire bikes** from *Manceau* (rue du Maréchal-Juin; ☎41.66.28.17).

Vineyards and châteaux around Angers

Lazing around the Loire and its tributaries between visits to vineyards you could fill a good summer week around Angers, as long as you are mobile. Otherwise it is a two-bus-a-day problem, or no buses at all, with the exception of the Savonnières vineyards (which you can reach by train), and some easy hitching routes, such as Brissac-Quincé, 20km south of Angers (also on the #9 bus). The best plan is to **rent a bike**: there's rental in Angers, *Manceau*, at 8 rue du Maréchal-Juin, or various outlets (including the gare SNCF) at Saumur if you approach from the other direction.

The châteaux to visit in these parts include **BRISSAC** (at Brissac-Quincé), owned since 1502 by the same line of dukes, with a seventeenth-century addition outreaching the fifteenth-century fortified towers – which were supposed to have been pulled down in deference to the symmetry of the building – and some beautiful ceilings. It is a riot of aristocratic bad taste, but has an interesting portrait in the Gallery of Ancestors – of Madame Cliquot, the first woman to run a champagne business, and her grand-daughter, the present duke's grandmother, who was, apparently, one of the first women to get a driver's licence. The château is open 9.30–11.20am and 2.15–5.45pm in summer (till 4.15pm in winter), closed Tuesday, and from 16 Nov. to 6 Feb.

To the north (17km on from Angers), five years' work at the end of the fifteenth century produced the fortress **LE PLESSIS-BOURRE**, looking as if it still expects an attack from across its vast moat. But the Treasurer of France who commissioned it had it redecorated luxuriously inside – best of all are the secular and allegorical scenes painted on the guardroom ceiling. It's open from 10am–noon and 2–7pm in summer (till 5pm the rest of the year). It is closed on Wednesday and Thursday mornings except in July and August, and it is closed from 15 November to 15 December. It is, however, impossible to get to on public transport. For a more accessible glimpse of a real monster of a mansion, try the **CHATEAU SERRANT**, just outside ST-GEORGES-SUR-LOIRE on bus route #18 from ANGERS.

Nearby, along the north bank of the Loire, BOUCHEMAINE, SAVENNIERES and LA POSSONNIERE are the **communes** for the dry white *appellation Savennières* one of the few white wines that can mature for a century. The most famous is *Coulée de Serrant* to be tasted and bought at the **CHATEAU DE LA ROCHE-AUX-MOINES**, just upstream from Savennières. **ROCHEFORT-SUR-LOIRE**, on the south bank, is the first of the *appellation Côteaux du Layon-Villages,* a sweet golden wine. Following this wine along the River Layon, winding below vine-covered hills as far as FAYE-D'ANJOU is a hedonist's dream. The road is free of *Dégustation* signs but the *vignerons* are not hard to find. In the summer at **ST-AUBIN-DE-LUIGNE** (#6 bus after Rochefort) you can rent **rowing boats** at the SI, next to the **campsite**.

Saumur and around

Angers to Saumur is the loveliest stretch of the Loire. The land on the south, planted with vines and sunflowers, gradually rises away from the river with long-inactive windmills still standing and no vast châteaux eagling on rocks. Across the water cows graze in wooded pastures. For **transport** you can take the train or one of three buses – #5 along the south bank, #11 that crosses half-way, or #10 that stays north of the river.

Saumur

Unlike many small Loire towns, **SAUMUR** is not dominated by its castle. Nor is it dominated by the military – which it might well be as the home of the French Cavalry and its successor the Armoured Corps Academy since 1763. Even the local sparkling wines are based elsewhere – in the suburb of St-Hilaire-St-Florent. Saumur is simply peaceful and pretty, to the dismay of the Town Hall which busily strives to attract festivals and conferences. When they're successful, finding a room can be a problem, and even at the best of times, reservations are essential. But it's a good place to stay, with Angers, Chinon and plenty of vineyards within easy reach.

But before venturing further afield you should go dragon-hunting in the **Eglise St-Pierre**. There are at least seven, one in stone, one carved in wood, and more woven into the sixteenth-century tapestries that tell the legend of St-Florent, an early scourge of these beautiful beasts who symbolise sin. Medieval fantasy creatures would not be out of place romping around the ramparts of the **Castle**: you can visit its dungeons and watch-tower on your own, with relaxed guides taking over for the two museums. The **Musée des Arts Décoratifs** has a huge collection of European china, among other things, but it's the **Musée du Cheval** that's the real treat. Progressing from a horse skeleton, through the evolution of bridles and stirrups over the centuries, you finally reach an amazing collection of saddles from all over the world; the difference between the art of California and Iran, Japan and Tibet, the Sudan and China is as much in evidence in saddlery as it is in poetry or music. Both museums, and the castle are open: in July to August 9am to 6.30pm and 8.30 to 10pm, otherwise 9 to 11.30am and 2 to 6pm (closed Tues. and at 5pm Nov.–March).

By knocking at the guarded gate on av Maréchal-Foch, west of rue d'Orléans, you can also visit, escorted by a soldier, the **Musée de la Cavalerie** (2–5pm; Sun. 9–11.30am; closed Fri. and Aug.). Among the uniforms, weapons and battle scenes (including very recent engagements), there is one moving room, dedicated to the cavalry cadets who held the Loire bridges between Gennes and Montsoreau against the Germans for three days in 1940, after the French government had surrendered. The **Riding School**, demilitarised in 1972, has moved to St-Hilaire-St-Florent. Horse fanatics can apply to the SI for details of visits and displays of anachronistic battle manoeuvres by the crackshot *Cadre Noir*. The metal mounts of the twentieth century, if you like that sort of thing, can be seen at the **Musée des Blindés**, northeast of place du Chardonnet.

Lastly, the **Maison du Vin** next door to the SI, has information on local wines and addresses of wine growers. A good red is the *Saumur Champigny* from around the village of CHAMPIGNY. The *Caves Coopérative* s at ST-CYR-EN-BOURG (a short train hop south of Saumur and near the station) have miles of cellars, and you can taste different wines with no obligation to buy.

Practicalities

The best **hotel** by far is *Le Cristal* (10 place de la République; ☎41.51.09.54) with river views from most rooms and very friendly proprietors. Other options include *La Bascule*, 1 place Kléber; *Central*, 23 rue Daillé and *La Croix de Guerre*, 9 rue de la Petite-Bilange, all in the centre on the south bank, the *Bretagne* (55 rue St-Nicolas; ☎41.51.26.38) and the *de Volney* (1 rue Volney; ☎41.51.25.41). On the Ile d'Offard, connected by bridges to both banks of the town, there's also a good **youth hostel** (rue de Verdue, at the eastern end; ☎41.67.45.00; reception 8–10am and 5–10pm) with boat and bike rental, and a **campsite** next door. You can even swim, in the north stream.

Orientation is straightforward. Arrive at the **gare SNCF** and you'll find yourself on the north bank: turn right onto av-David-d'Angers and cross the bridge to the island. From the island the old **Pont Cessart** takes you to the main part of the town on the south bank. The **gare routière** is in the centre – a couple of blocks from the Pont Cessart by the church of St-Nicolas. Saumur's main street, **rue d'Orléans**, cuts back through the south bank sector: the **SI** is off to its right (coming from the river) along rue Beaurepaire (no. 25). The old quarter, around St-Pierre and the castle, is to the left. The best **eating** area is around **place St-Pierre**: *Auberge St-Pierre*, on the square, sometimes has *langoustines* on a fairly cheap menu, and there are good *crêperies* and other restaurants on the streets heading back to rue d'Orléans.

Baugé and Fontévraud

In **BAUGE**, north of Saumur on the railway to Le Mans, the nuns at the **Chapelle des Incurables** claim to have a cross made from the True Cross. The wood is certainly Palestinian, though its history prior to its donation to an Angevin crusader is dubious. But anyway, it's the double-armed cross that became the emblem of the Dukes of Anjou and Lorraine, and, in this century, of the Free French Forces. To see it, ring at no. 8 on rue de la Girouardière (10am–noon and 2.30–5pm; Sun. 3–4pm and 6–7pm). The **SI** in Baugé is worth visiting merely for the joy of walking freely into a fifteenth-century **castle**. And take a look, too, at the **Hospice St-Joseph** (east of the château up rue Anne-de-Melun) for its seventeenth-century pharmacy, with beautiful woodwork shelves, parquetry floor and sculpted ceiling, and the vials, flacons and contents as they were in 1874; it's open, for free, 10am–noon and 3–5.30pm in summer; till 4.30pm in winter; (Sun. 10.30am–noon) – the hospital receptionist will direct you. For those with an interest in ecclesiastical architecture, three parishes around Baugé have strange twisting towers – PONTIGNE, FONTAINE-GUERIN and VIEIL-BAUGE (the last leans as well).

The **ABBAYE DE FONTEVRAUD**, 13km southeast of Saumur (bus #16) is a seminal site in French and English history. It was founded in 1099 as both a nunnery and a monastery with an abbess in charge – a radical move even if the post was filled solely by queens and princesses. The premises had to be immense to house and separate not only the nuns and monks but also the sick, the lepers and repentant prostitutes – there were originally five separate complexes, of which three still gracefully stand in Romanesque solidity. A prison from the Revolution until 1963, its most famous inmate was the writer Jean Genet. But its chief significance is as the burial ground of the Plantagenet kings. Four tombstone effigies remain, of Henry II, Eleanor of Aquitaine, Richard the Lionheart and Isabelle of Angoulême (King John's wife). Recently, the Chirac government brought changes to the abbey which have horrified local inhabitants. After massive public funds had been spent on restoration, a multinational corporation was given a say in the cultural activities of the abbey, and control over the St-Lazare hostel; until then, the site had been the exclusive responsibility of the public organisation *Centre Culturel de l'Ouest (CCO)*. The villagers fear desecration of the sanctity of the place and its tombs, which have already been covered by 'viewing screens'. According to one local resident, what was happening was 'a profanity – an insult to the effigies of your kings of which we are all so justly proud'.

The guided tour around the site is long and pretty tiring, but it's quite a place and should be seen before privatisation has turned it into a 'Lion in Winter' theme park. Tours are from 9am–noon and 2–6.30pm (till 4pm Oct.–March); closed Tues., and the *CCO* may still be putting on some concerts, exhibitions etc. (details from Saumur SI).

Into Touraine: Chinon and Azay-Le-Rideau

A fortress of one kind or another existed at **CHINON** from the Stone Age up until the age of Louis XIV, the period of the most recent of its ruins. A favourite Plantagenet residence, it was, much later, one of the few places in which Charles VII could stay while Henry V of England held Paris and the title to the French throne. Charles' situation changed with the arrival here in 1429 of Joan of Arc who recognised him, disguised in a crowd of courtiers, and persuaded him to get his act together and give her an army. All that remains of the scene of this encounter, the *Grande Salle*, is a wall and first-floor fireplace. Visits to this and to the restored Royal Lodgings – both guided – are not wildly exciting. More interesting is the *Tour Coudray*, over to the west, covered with intricate thirteenth-century graffiti carved by imprisoned and doomed Templar knights; Joan is said to have stayed here too. Like the rest of the château complex, it is open 9am–7pm July to Sept. (9am–noon and 2–5pm the rest of the year); closed Dec., Jan. and Wed. from Oct. to mid-March.

Below, the town continues its celebration of the long dead, and in sterile fashion: medieval streets, a wine- and barrel-making museum with tacky, animated models and free tasting of the worst wine, very few **hotels** and everything closed up long before midnight. If you're looking for a room, the two cheapest alternatives are the *Point du Jour* (102 quai Jeanne-d'Arc; ☎47.93.07.20) and the *Jeanne d'Arc* (11 rue Voltaire; ☎47.93.02.85). There is a **youth hostel** (☎47.93.10.48 and 47.93.21.37) close to the **gare SNCF** on rue

Descartes (the continuation of quai Jeanne-d'Arc eastwards) and at the **campsite** (☎47.93.08.35), across the river at Ile-Auger, you can rent **canoes** during summer. The **SI** at 12 rue Voltaire has **bikes** for rent and so does the station. The **gare routière** is on place Jeanne-d'Arc. The most reasonable **restaurant** is *Le Panurge* on place de l'Hôtel-de-Ville.

The man who vies with Joan of Arc for snackbars, shops and streets named in his honour in Chinon is **Rabelais** (1494–1553), who wrote approvingly of wine, food and laughter in deeply serious and difficult humanist texts, and whose most famous creations are the giant son and father, Pantagruel and Gargantua. He was born at nearby **LA DEVINIERE** (requisite author's room on show). Another Touraine birthplace-plus-museum, its subject obvious enough, is over to the southwest at DESCARTES. The town of **RICHELIEU**, however, did not see the cardinal until he was grown up, had bought the place, had an enormous château built, and rearranged the village into an enclosed town of model classical planning. The château has disappeared without trace; the town survives to please those with a penchant for the right-angle.

If the château were removed from **AZAY-LE-RIDEAU**, you'd still have the serene setting of the island in the Indre, the old mill by the bridge, the Carolingian statues embedded in the facade of St-Symphorien church, and a quiet village. But the **Château** is one of the loveliest, pure Renaissance and required viewing – which you can do for free from the surrounding park. Guided tours of the interior, furnished in Renaissance style, don't add much to this experience, accompanied as they are by sexist jokes about the wife of the financier who had it built in the 1520s. The portrait gallery, however, has the whole sixteenth-century royal Loire crew – François I, Catherine de Médicis, the de Guises, etc. – and, the highlight, a semi-nude painting of Gabrielle d'Estrée, Henri IV's lover. If you're determined, hours are 9.15am–noon and 2–6.30pm April to September; till 5pm October to mid-November; 9.30am–noon and 2–4.45 mid-November to March. There is a large **campsite** (☎47.45.42.72) upstream from the château. Hotels in Azay-le-Rideau don't come cheap – check with the **SI** at 26 rue Gambetta if you're desperate. There are trains and buses to Chinon and Tours and you can rent **bikes** at the station or from *Le Provost* (13 rue Carnot).

For something rather strange and totally off the tourist track, make your way to **CHEILLE**, a small village 6km west of Azay and linked by some (not all) of the Chinon trains. In the church is a life-sized wooden crucifix that differs from almost every other representation of Christ – he has no beard. The effect is astounding: Christ no longer a hippy but someone whose face, though still inaccurately European, could belong to any period. It is the work of a very passionate artist, but who or when is not documented. If the church is locked, ask for the key at the house next door.

Tours

If you decide to stay in Tours it's likely to be for the museums – of wine, crafts, and an above-average *Beaux Arts* – and for the pleasures (and *dégustations*) of the vineyards. An English travel writer wrote in 1913:

'TOURS has an immense air of good breeding . . . you have visions of portentously dull entertainments in lofty gilded saloons where everything is rather icily magnificent.'

It is certainly a very bourgeouis city, and its culture and nightlife suffer through its near proximity to Paris. **Accommodation,** however, shouldn't be a problem. There's a **youth hostel** on av d'Arsonval in Parc de Grandmont (bus #6 or #2 to Chambray, stop *Auberge de Jeunesse*; ☎47.25.14.45; reception 5pm–midnight; closed Dec. and Jan.), and a **hostel** for under 25-year-olds *Le Foyer* (16 rue Bernard-Palissy; ☎47.05.38.81 – call first because they may be full. The municipal **campsite** (☎47.54.11.11) is on the north bank of the Loire (bus #6, stop *Ste-Radegonde*). The range of **hotels** is good. In the unpleasant area around the station you'll find the very cheap *L'Olympic*, (74 rue B-Palisy; ☎47.05.10.17) and *Family*, (2 rue Traversière; ☎47.05.25.63). Better located are the *Mon* (40 rue de la Préfecture; ☎47.05.67.53) towards the cathedral; *Le Sully* (7 rue Néricault-Destouches; ☎47.05.61.32) up by the old town, and the *Idéal* (11 rue de la Scellerie; ☎47.05.62.62). Not so central, but very pleasant is the *Gramont* (16 av de Gramont; ☎47.05.55.06).

At the head of **rue Nationale** – Tours' main street – statues of Descartes looking suitably doubtful and Rabelais gleefully certain, overlook the Loire. A short walk back from the river and you come to the church of St-Julien, and next door, two of the town's most compelling museums. In the **Musée de Compagnonnage** for once the people who built rather than ordered the châteaux and cathedrals are celebrated. As well as documents of the origins and militant activity of the 'guilds', there are masterpieces, in the original sense of the term, of various crafts from cake-making and carpentry to lock-smithery and brick-laying, the relevant tools exhibited alongside. The **Musée du Vin**, next door has some great quotations on the subject: Virgil on planting vines like arranging cohorts in battle; an anonymous Egyptian on the grape's being born from the blood of vanquished giants; Victor Hugo – 'God only created water; man made wine', and Colette, going over the top with 'the barren chalk weeps in wine tears of gold'. The exhibits make up a pretty comprehensive treatment of the history, mythology, related industries and production of the wondrous liquid, though there is nothing on recent technical innovations. Behind the museum, a Gallo-Roman wine press from Cheillé sits in the former cloisters of St-Julien's church. Both museums are open 9am–noon and 2–6pm (closed Tues.); admission is cheap.

Over towards the **Cathédrale St-Gatien** – with its crumbling, Flamboyant Gothic front – you'll find the city's third museum, the **Beaux Arts**, shadowed by a huge and aged Lebanon cedar. The museum has some beauties in its rambling collection: *Christ in the Garden of Olives* and the *Resurrection* by Mantegna; Franz Hals' portrait of Descartes; *Balzac* painted by Boulanger; prints of *The Five Senses* by the *Tourainais* Abraham Bosse; a somber Monet; and a cheering tapestry by Caldor. The museum's top treasure, Rembrandt's *Flight into Egypt*, is difficult to see through the security glass. Open 8am–12.45pm and 2–6pm.

Old Tours crowds around place St-Pierre-le-Puellier, over to the west of rue Nationale and past the *Hôtel Gouin* – a small archaeological museum with a Renaissance facade to stop you in your tracks. It is, however, the medieval

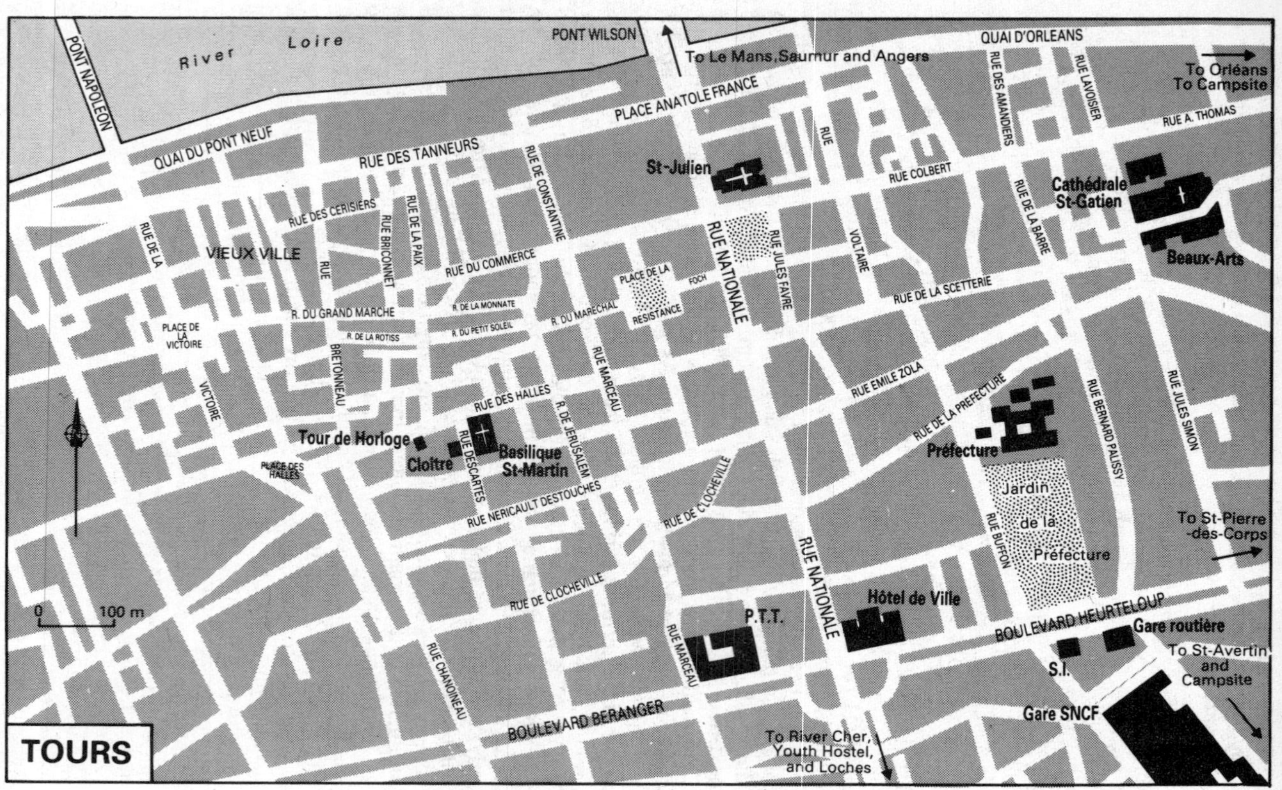
TOURS
0
100 m
River Loire
PONT NAPOLEON
PONT WILSON
To Le Mans, Saumur and Angers
QUAI D'ORLEANS
To Orléans
To Campsite
QUAI DU PONT NEUF
RUE DES TANNEURS
PLACE ANATOLE FRANCE
RUE A. THOMAS
RUE DES AMANDIERS
RUE LAVOISIER
RUE
RUE COLBERT
RUE DE LA BARRE
St-Julien
Cathédrale St-Gatien
Beaux-Arts
RUE DE LA
VIEUX VILLE
RUE DES CERISIERS
RUE BRICONNET
RUE DE LA PAIX
RUE DE CONSTANTINE
RUE DU COMMERCE
RUE NATIONALE
RUE JULES FAVRE
VOLTAIRE
PLACE DE LA RESISTANCE
FOCH
RUE DE LA SCETTERIE
R. DE LA MONNATE
R. DU GRAND MARCHE
R. DU MARECHAL
R. DU PETIT SOLEIL
R. DE LA ROTISS
PLACE DE LA VICTOIRE
BRETONNEAU
VICTOIRE
RUE MARCEAU
RUE EMILE ZOLA
RUE DE LA PREFECTURE
RUE BERNARD PALISSY
RUE JULES SIMON
RUE DES HALLES
R. DE JERUSALEM
Tour de Horloge
Cloître
RUE DESCARTES
Basilique St-Martin
PLACE DES HALLES
Préfecture
Jardin de la Préfecture
RUE BUFFON
RUE NERICAULT DESTOUCHES
RUE DE CLOCHEVILLE
To St-Pierre-des-Corps
Hôtel de Ville
P.T.T.
BOULEVARD HEURTELOUP
Gare routière
S.I.
To St-Avertin and Campsite
Gare SNCF
RUE CHANOINEAU
BOULEVARD BERANGER
To River Cher, Youth Hostel, and Loches

half-timbered houses and bulging stairway towers of the twelfth, thirteenth and fifteenth centuries (and 1970s' restoration) that are the city's showpiece. (Any landing tardis would be further confused by the excavated Gallo-Roman cemetery on place St-Pierre). The buildings look like cut-out models yet the Renaissance stone and brick constructions have a firmer grip on reality – particularly the **Ecoles des Langues Vivantes** on rue Briconnet with sculpted dogs, drunks, frogs and monsters. West of rue Bretonneau there are modern artisans' workshops between medieval dwellings. The pre-restoration inhabitants of the quarter were Portuguese (some of whom remain) and Algerians (whom the city council kicked out). But it's yuppies who dominate this surreal district now. Refreshingly downmarket, *Le Petit Faucheux* (23 rue des Cérisiers) has music and shows at weekends, and darts, cards and chess the rest of the week.

Rue du Grand-Marché and rue de la Rôtisserie, on the periphery of old Tours, and rue Colbert (which runs down to the cathedral), are the most promising **restaurant** streets; *Les Lionceaux* (at 17 rue Jules-Favre, off rue Colbert) has the cheapest *menu fixe*. The regional speciality is greasy potted pork *rillettes*, or pieces of cold pork – *rillons*. But for sugar and chocolate freaks, Tours also has some excellent **pâtisseries**: *La Marotte* (3 rue du Change), *La Chocolatière* (6 rue de la Scellerie) and others along rue Nationale. *Les Studios* on rue des Urselines shows eight good **films** a week (in the original) at reasonable cost. If you want to **rent bikes** try the station or *Au Col de Cygne*, at 46 rue du Dr-Fournier. If you have kids to entertain, there's a great, gleaming, and climbable SNCF **steam engine**, placed in a square by the intersection of boulevards des Deportés and Paul-Langevin in the suburb of St-Pierre-des-Corps (bus #3, stop *Deportés*).

Around Tours: gardens and vineyards

Forget any prejudices you might have about gardens being a middle-aged obsession and take time to get out to **VILLANDRY**. No ordinary patterns of opposing primary colours, this recreated Renaissance garden is more like a tapestry, but one that changes with the months and only fades in winter. Carrots, cabbages and aubergines are exalted to coloured threads woven beneath rose bowers. Herbs and ornamental box hedges are part of the same artwork, divided by vine-shaded paths. From a terrace above, you can see the Cher meeting the Loire and châteaux on the northern bank. The gardens are open from 9am until sunset; for an extra few francs you can see the Spanish paintings and medieval Moorish ceiling from Toledo in the château (guided tour, Palm Sunday–Nov 12, 9am–6pm). No buses go from Tours to Villandry, but the 13km bike ride along the Cher is particularly idyllic.

VOUVRAY, 10km east of Tours on the north bank, is the *appellation* for one of the most delicious white wines of the Loire. A good vintage lives to be 100, can be *sec, demi-sec* or *pétillant* (lightly sparkling) and is best from the grape of a single vineyard. The **SI** at the Hôtel de Ville can provide addresses of **vignerons** but all the roads leading up the steep valleys are lined with *caves*. The view of the vines from the top of the hill is an outrageous inducement to drunkenness. Vouvray has a **campsite** between the Loire and the

Cisse and bus #61 runs from place St-Vincent just south of the SI to place Jean-Jaurès in Tours.

To go with the wine, Touraine produces **chèvre** (goat cheese); the best of those cylindrical and speckled miniature building blocks you see at cheese stands come from around the small town of **STE-MAURE**. The SI here on rue du Château can provide addresses for *dégustations* and the medieval covered market will be well stocked. One producer is M. Raguin, by the Château d'Eau in NOYANT-DE-TOURAINE on the Chinon road. Ste-Maure is on the DESCARTES bus route from Tours.

Along the tributaries

The **Vienne, Indre** and **Cher** rivers share none of the Loire's dangerous habits, but they're difficult to get to unless you're prepared to hunt for the paths through the farmlands on their banks. Notices you see are more often about fishing restrictions than forbidding entry. Trains and roads follow the Cher from **Tours** and the Indre from **Loches**: for the Vienne it's better to **rent a canoe** at **Chinon**.

The Indre: Loches

The walled citadel of **LOCHES** is by far the most impressive of Loire valley fortresses with unbreached ramparts and Renaissance houses below still partly enclosed by the outer wall of the medieval town. It is an hour's train journey away from Tours and hotel accommodation is expensive, but there is a good **campsite** across the Indre. From the station av de la Gare leads to place de la Marne and the **SI**.

The southern end of the **Citadelle** is taken up by dungeons and a keep initiated by Foulques the Black, eleventh-century Count of Anjou, with cells and a torture chamber added in the fifteenth century. Climbing unescorted to the top of the keep is fun even if the surrounding countryside is no more exciting than the English home counties. There is not much left of the fifteenth-century extension, thanks to the people of Loches who destroyed most of the torture equipment in the Revolution. The very professional guides make up for the lack of exhibits with their spiel, but the English text can't capture the goriness.

At the other end are the **Royal Lodgings** of Charles VII and his three successors. The medieval half of the palace witnessed two women of some importance to Charles. Joan of Arc, victorious from Orléans, came here to give the defeatist Dauphin another pep talk about coronations. Some time after her death, *La Beauté* Agnès Sorel, Charles' lover, resided here. Even the Pope fancied her, which allowed Charles to be the first French king to have an officially recognised 'mistress'. Her tomb now lies in the fifteenth-century wing with her portrait by Fouquet and a painting of the Virgin in her likeness. Hours are 9am–6pm in July and August, otherwise 9am–noon and 2–6pm in summer (2–5pm in winter); closed Wednesday and December–January; guides are optional.

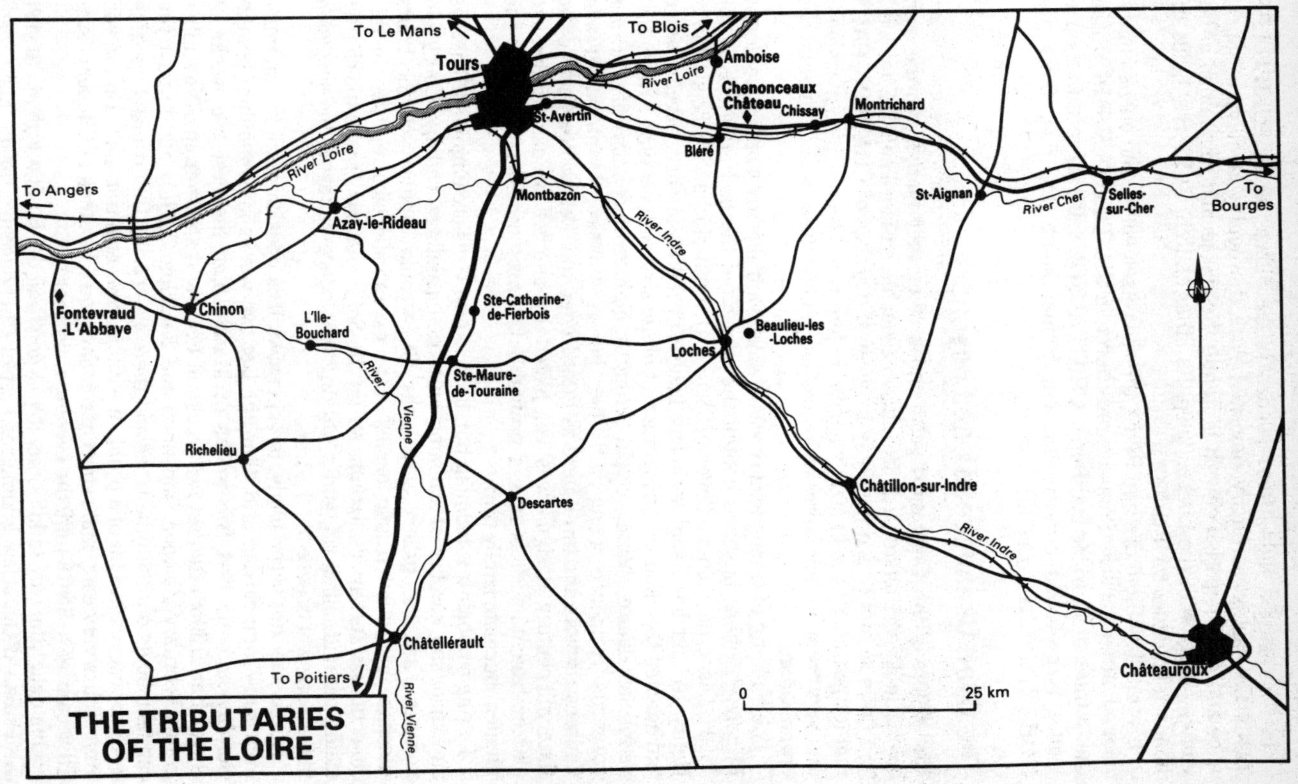
To Le Mans
To Blois
Tours
Amboise
River Loire
Chenonceaux Château
Chissay
Montrichard
St-Avertin
Bléré
River Loire
To Angers
Montbazon
St-Aignan
Selles-sur-Cher
River Cher
To Bourges
Azay-le-Rideau
River Indre
Fontevraud -L'Abbaye
Chinon
Ste-Catherine-de-Fierbois
L'Ile-Bouchard
Beaulieu-les -Loches
Loches
River
Ste-Maure-de-Touraine
Vienne
Richelieu
Châtillon-sur-Indre
Descartes
River Indre
Châtellérault
Châteauroux
To Poitiers
0
25 km
River Vienne
THE TRIBUTARIES OF THE LOIRE

Just across the Indre from Loches is the village of **BEAULIEU-LES-LOCHES** – an extraordinary, unvisited place, thoroughly medieval in appearance and with its parish church built into the spectacular ruins of an **abbey** contemporary with the Loches keep. Its other church, **St-Pierre**, holds the bones of Foulques the Black.

If you follow the Indre into Berry, the river itself will be the only source of interest, other than the Romanesque church in CHATILLON-SUR-INDRE on the borders of Touraine and Berry. CHATEAUROUX, the largest town on its banks, is grey and bureaucratic, but further south, the river flows past NOHANT and LA CHATRE.

The Cher: Chenonceaux and beyond

The waters of **the Cher** must get a shock when they merge with the main river. Unlike the anarchic Loire, this reasonable stream keeps to its depth and flows so slowly and passively between the arches of **CHENONCEAUX** that it's as though two châteaux appear before you. The reflected mansion is the very best of all Loire châteaux for architecture, site, contents and organisation.

The building of Chenonceaux was always controlled by women. Cathérine Briconnet, whose husband bought the site, hired the first architects in the 1520s. Diane de Poitiers (lover of Henry II), Catherine de Médicis (wife of Henry II) and her daughter-in-law Louise de Lorraine successively owned and adapted the château during the rest of the sixteenth century. After a long period of disuse, Mme. Dupin brought eighteenth-century life to this gorgeous residence along with her guests Voltaire, Montesquieu and Rousseau, whom she hired here as tutor to her son. Restoration back to the sixteenth-century designs was completed by another woman in the late ninteenth century. It is now a profitable business owned and run by the Menier chocolate family firm.

During summer it is teeming but, luxuriously, visits are unguided. There is an exhausting number of arresting tapestries, paintings, ceilings, floors and furniture, and the gallery across the Cher could capture you for hours (despite the potted plastic plants). One exceptional picture, even in this collection, is Zurbaran's *Archimedes* (in the *Salle François 1*) with his clothes inside out and falling off, and a working man's face betraying his suspicion that no one will believe his theories.

Admission, not surprisingly, is expensive. It is open through the summer from 9am–7pm; closing at 6.30pm the last two weeks in September, 6pm in October and the first two weeks of March, 5pm the first two weeks of November, 5.30pm the last two weeks of February; and from mid-November to mid-February it's open 9am–noon and 2–4.30pm. In July and August you can take boats out onto the Cher and there's a crèche. Unfortunately getting to Chenonceaux is a bit of a problem without your own transport. Unless you leave Tours very early and return at midday, you'll be stuck at Chenonceaux-Chisseaux gare SNCF until the evening train back.

One delightful way to kill time, if you don't mind a bit of a walk, is to visit the **Fraise d'Or**, a few kilometres east of Chenonceaux, on the main road.

It's an old-fashioned distillery, complete with shiny copper stills, which specialises in strawberry, raspberry and cherry liqueurs. The visit around the distillery includes a *dégustation* of three of their eighteen liqueurs and eaux-de-vie, of herb, spice, fruit, nut, and rose petal bases. (Open Easter–Sept., 9–11.30am and 2–6pm).

Practicalities

The best **places to stay** on the Cher are Montrichard, with its full complement of medieval houses and ruined castle, or the market town of St-Aignan, with no visitable château but a wonderful church. Two possibilities for rooms in **MONTRICHARD** are the **hotels** *du Courrier* (4 rte de Blois; ☎54.32.04.42) and *Gare* (20 av de la Gare; ☎54.32.04.36); there's an **SI** by the castle and a **campsite** on the river. At **ST-AIGNAN**, try the **hotel** *du Moulin* (7 rue Nouilliers; ☎54.75.15.54) or the riverside **campsite**; rent **boats** for an afternoon at the island; and treat yourself – the **food** market and shops are excellent. Not too expensive dishes using local wines are served at the *Relais de la Poste* (3 rue de l'Ormeau). In the **Eglise St-Aignan**, the capitals are adorned with mermaids, a multi-bodied snake biting its own necks, a man's head tunnelled by an eagle, doleful dragons and other wonders of twelfth-century imagination; in the crypt, if you can find the light switch, there are superb, brightly coloured medieval frescoes.

Amboise

Returning to the Loire, the **wine** of the **Touraine-Amboise appellation**, though not as famous as *Chinon* and *Vouvray*, is worth investigating for drivers at least. Take the road from Chenonceaux to Amboise and stop by the petrol station at the crossroads (4½km to Amboise) where M. Delecheneau sells his *sec* and *demi-sec* white and sublime *demi-sec rosé*, and will show you his barrels named after cows (Dauphine, Jolie, Violette, etc) and his grandfather's old press.

You will need some wine to deal with **AMBOISE**, a prissy little town trading on its long-gone splendours. It is the home power base of Michel Debré, de Gaulle's first Prime Minister, who keeps his master's flame alive and pure, and also one of Mick Jagger's favourite residences – no one recognises him there. There is a good **campsite** on the island across from the castle, the Ile d'Or, (☎47.57.23.37), but over-priced hotels and restaurants and nothing open after 10pm. The **Centre Charles Péguy** (☎47.57.06.36; reception 3–10pm; closed Mon. and Sun. in winter) on the west end of the Ile d'Or, has hostel-style rooms, and also hires **canoes**. The **hotels** worth trying are *Le Chaptal* (13 rue Chaptal; ☎47.57.14.46) and the *Plantanes* (rte de Nazelles; ☎47.57.08.60) behind the **gare SNCF** which is a fairly long walk from the centre on the north side of the river. For **bikes**, try either the station or the snackbar in the campsite; for information the **SI** is on the waterfront east of the bridge.

The best thing in Amboise is **Max Ernst's** prototype ET/toy bear and turtle **fountain**, with the Friday and Sunday **market** behind it on the riverside. What is left of the **Château** might qualify for second best if you could go around it slowly. The *Tour des Minimes*, the original entrance and fifteenth-century forerunner of the multi-storey carpark ramp, is architecturally the most exciting part. The Loire presents one of its best panoramas from the top. The hooks along the battlements were once smeared with the blood and guts of rebellious Huguenots. Caught plotting to get rid of the Catholic de Guise family, the power behind young François II, they were summarily tried in the *Salle des Conseils* and the whole town was hung with their corpses. The last French king, Louis-Philippe, stayed in this château, hence the abrupt switch from solid Gothic furnishings to 1830s post-First Empire style (open 9am–7pm in July and August; otherwise 9am–noon and 2–6.30pm, closing at sunset in winter).

One man, of far greater renown than any of the French kings, who died in Amboise in 1519 was **Leonardo da Vinci**, invited here by François I in order to bolster and encourage the French Renaissance. **Clos Lucé**, where he stayed, at the end of rue Victor-Hugo, does not contain a single original work, but it does have models of Leonardo's inventions, recently constructed according to his detailed plans. It is wonderful to see the mechanical manifestations of Da Vinci's technological achievements. But even the best model, the wooden tank, does not have the same effect as Leonardo's sketch, beetling along with manic velocity, kicking up a wake of dust. (Hours are June to mid-September 9am–7pm, otherwise 9am–noon and 2–7pm; admission is more expensive than it should be).

ORLEANAIS, BERRY AND SARTHE

Orléanais is in many ways a country suburb of Paris, and visiting its principal châteaux (detailed below), though entertaining, won't fill up an enormous amount of time. The city of **Orléans**, however, has enough in itself (and nearby) to merit a stop between Touraine and Paris.

To the south, **Berry**, centred on **Bourges**, has medieval links and more modern literary connections: an obvious route if you're heading towards the Massif Central and Roussillon. **Le Mans**, heart of the **Sarthe** region to the north of the Loire, is much less explored, except as a transit point en route from Brittany. But unpackaged and untouristed, it's an unexpected pleasure.

The monster châteaux

A mild climate, attractive setting and proximity to Paris have made the Loire an ideal location for the palaces and hunting lodges of the French ruling classes. After the Hundred Years War fortifications began to give way to more elegant facades. The influence of the Italian Renaissance, however imperfectly understood by French craftsmen, is in evidence, particularly in the detail of Blois and Chambord.

Chaumont and Blois

Catherine de Médicis forced Diane de Poitiers to hand over Chenonceaux in return for the château of **CHAUMONT**, upstream from Amboise towards Orléans. Diane got a very bad deal and so does any tourist who takes the guided tour: this is one to avoid unless you are a horse fanatic and like the idea of porcelain troughs and fancy stable-lighting.

Another of Catherine's residences, just to the north of the unwanted Chaumont, was the château at **BLOIS**, where she died in 1589. All six kings of the sixteenth century spent time here and in the early nineteenth century it was given to Louis XVIII's brother to keep him away from Paris. Hence the courtiers' mansions that fill the town, and, what with earlier non-regal ownerships, the **Château's** building montage of distinct, unmatching wings: feudal, Gothic, Renaissance and Classical. The Blois horror story is Henri III's murder of the Duc de Guise and his brother, the ones who had the Huguenots executed at Amboise. The King panicked after the *Etats-Généraux* assembled in the château's glossy medieval *Grande Salle* in 1588, with an overwhelming majority supporting de Guise, the stringing up of Protestants, and aristocratic rather than regal power. He did the deed himself and was then knocked off by a monk the following year. In a later century, revolutionaries were tried in this hall for conspiring to assassinate Napoléon III, a year before the Paris Commune. One good thing about Blois: you can go around without a guide (except in winter); it's open Easter and June–August 9am–6.30pm, the rest of the year 9am–noon and 2–6.30pm, closing at 5pm from October to mid-March. It also contains *Beaux Arts* and archaeological museums, but neither is very exciting.

Something in Blois that might be more appealing, is the **Poulain chocolate factory** – follow your nose from the train station. Tours are at 8.45am, 10am, 1.30pm, 2.45pm in summer; 10am and 2.45pm in winter; but be warned – even chocolate addicts have been deeply sickened by the experience.

Some inexpensive **hotels** in Blois are the *St-Nicolas* (2 rue du Sermon; ☎54.78.05.85), the *Etoile d'Or* (7–9 rue du Bourg-Neuf; ☎54.78.46.13), and *du Bellay* (12 rue des Minimes; ☎54.78.23.62). The **campsite** (☎54.74.22.78) with **bike** and **boat rental**, is across the river 2km from the centre on the Lac de Loire at Vineuil. There is one **youth hostel** at LES GROUETS, 5km downstream (18 rue de l'Hôtel-Pasquier; ☎54.78.27.21; open March to mid-November; closed daily 10am–6pm; bus #70, direction Les Grouets, stop *Eglise des Grouets*). Another is 10km upstream at MONTLIVAULT (levée de la Loire; c/o Beaugency youth hostel ☎38.44.61.31; open mid-June to mid-Sept.; Orléans bus, stop *Auberge de Jeunesse*). The Blois **SI** is at 3 av Jean-Laiguet which runs from place Victor-Hugo just behind the château, to the **gare SNCF**, which hires out **bikes**. Next to the **bus** office (at 6 place Victor-Hugo) there's a bar that stays open late, but this is not a town that guarantees excitement. By day, if you like your France eighteenth-century, it's a pleasant enough place to wander.

Cheverny and Beauregard

Seventeenth-century purists have their treat at the château of **CHEVERNY**, built between 1604 and 1634 and never altered. It belongs to a descendant of the original owner, whose entrance charges are the highest in the Loire. In winter he exercises his hounds and horses to the accompaniment of hunting horns and tourist buses.

Much more interesting, if you want to take in another château near Blois, is **BEAUREGARD** – closer, too, at a cyclable 9km. Highlight of the castle, most of it the same date as Cheverny, is a portrait gallery of 363 paintings of kings and their cohorts. Admission, at standard Loire rates, is 9.30am–noon and 2–6.30pm; closed at 5pm and all day Wednesday, October–March.

Chambord

CHAMBORD, François I's little 'hunting lodge', was one of the most extravagant commissions of the age. Its patron's principal object was to outdo the Holy Roman Emperor Charles V, and it would, he claimed, leave him renowned as 'one of the greatest builders in the universe'. It has its fans, though for many its pomp and mix of styles make it the single most ugly building in the Loire. Visits, at least, are unguided, and even if you loathe the château there's entertainment to be had from circling it on foot or by bike, and roaming around inside, up and down the spiral staircase, around the chimneys and through miles of mostly unfurnished rooms and corridors. Judge for yourself.

As for its architectural history, the design employed was that of the Italian architect Domenico de Cortona. It was begun in 1519, in another bid to introduce prestigious Italian Renaissance art forms to France, but the building work was executed by French masons, and the overall result is essentially French medieval. This is particularly evident in the massive round towers with their conical tops, and the forest of chimneys and turrets, which bring to mind Flamboyant Gothic. The details, however, are pure Italian, for example the double spiral **Great Staircase** (attributed by some to Da Vinci), panels of coloured marble, niches decorated with shell-like domes, and free-standing columns.

The château is open to visits daily from 9.30am–noon and 2–6pm (till 7 mid-June–Aug., till 5pm Nov.–March), and wandering through at leisure you can get a good feel for the contrasting architectural styles. There is free access to the extensive grounds. To get there on public transport you'll have to use the expensive château tour buses from Blois. Cycling is the best option – it's a flat and beautiful ride – but hitching should be possible too.

Orléans and upstream

Directly below the turned-up nose of the capital, poor **ORLEANS** feels compelled to recuperate its faded *gloire* from 1429, when Paris was infested by disease and the English, and the Loire valley was the capital of France. The city's deliverer on that date is honoured everywhere, though nothing contradicts the overriding feeling that Joan of Arc was and is a myth. In earlier times still, Orléans was Clovis's capital and in the days of Asterix it was one of the key Gallo-Roman cities. But now, not only do Orléanais go to Paris for their evenings out, they commute to work there as well.

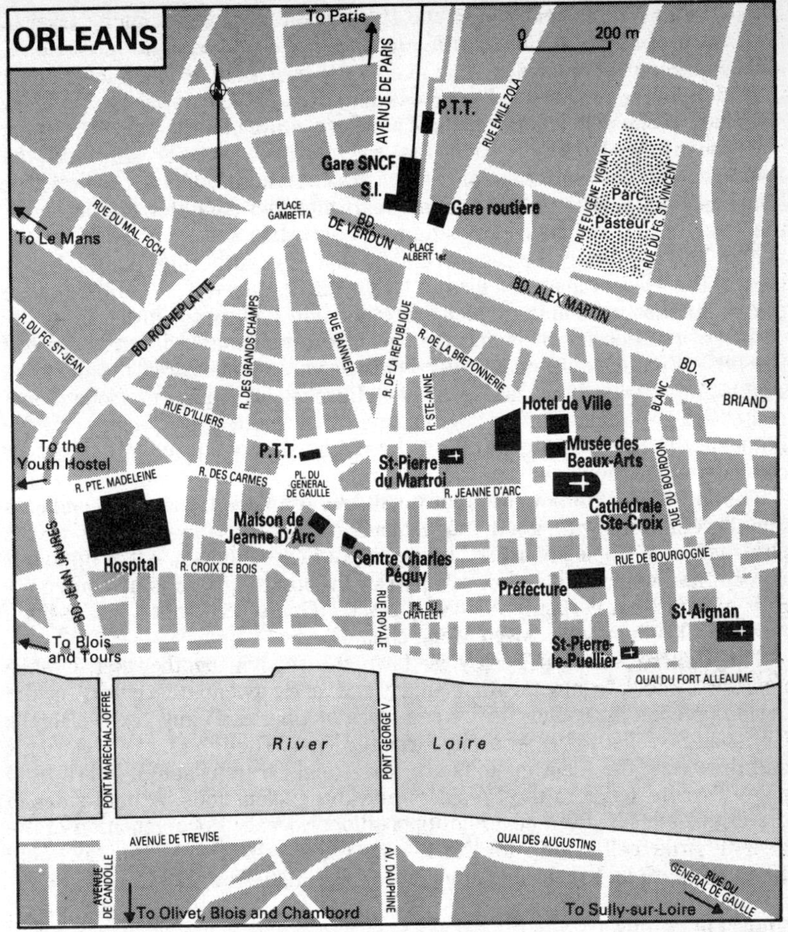

The **Cathédrale Ste-Croix**, battered for five-and-a-half centuries, is rather wonderful, and full of Joan, who celebrated her victory here. In the north transept, her pedestal is supported by two jagged and golden leopards (representing the English) on an altar carved with the battle scene. The late nineteenth-century stained glass windows in the nave tell the story of Joan's life (starting from the north transept) with caricatures of the snoutish, loutish Anglo-Saxons and snooty French nobles. She appears again in pensive mood, her skirt riddled with twentieth-century bullets outside the red brick Renaissance **Hôtel de Ville** across place d'Etape from the cathedral. The best escape from the Middle Ages is the modern art collection in the basement of the **Musée des Beaux Arts**, opposite the Hôtel de Ville, with canvasses by Picasso, Miró, Braque, Dufy, Renoir and Monet all, unfortunately, in horribly heavy frames. But if you want to go back much earlier in time, drop in at the modern **Préfecture** on rue de Bourgogne (door no. 9) and ask the receptionist if you can look in the basement, where a low budget reception room provides odd surroundings for an excavated first century dwelling, or bits of it, and the walls of a ninth-century church.

Between the Préfecture and the river, narrow streets surround the **Dassaux vinegar works**, an old establishment whose buildings encircle the house Isabelle Romée moved to a few years after her daughter was burned at the stake in Rouen. The factory's future is uncertain and such are the priorities of this culturally beleaguered city that the authorities have already bought the relevant part and plan to turn it into a museum. Down the road, a plaque marks the house of Joan's brother and companion-in-arms, on the corner of rue des Africains and **rue de la Folie**. Though deserted most of the time, this old quarter is a very pleasant area and spared the postcard stands and trendy shops and bars. Two churches are on the precious monuments list: the remains of **St-Aignan** and its eleventh-century crypt and the Romanesque **St-Pierre-le-Puellier**, the old university church, now used for concerts and exhibitions.

The inevitable **Maison de Jeanne d'Arc**, on place Général-de-Gaulle, is fun for children, with good models and displays of the breaking of the Orléans siege. Copies of artists' rendering of Ste-Jeanne show that the page-boy cut and demure little face are part of the myth – there is no contemporary portrait and certainly no death mask. (Open 10am–noon and 2–6pm, Nov.–April 2–6pm only; closed Mon.; cheap).

The **Centre Charles Péguy** is down the road in another Renaissance mansion. The late nineteenth century and early twentieth century is the period presented, around the life and work of Charles Péguy (1873–1914), a Christian Socialist writer who came from Orléans. Though there are cartoons and drawings, the main exhibits are texts (and no translation): Zola's front page *J'accuse'* letter to the President and the explanations by both sides in the Dreyfus affair; front covers of opposition journals; documentation of the general strike call in 1907 for the 40-hour week (which wasn't in effect until 1936) and various books and pamphlets. (Open 1.30–6pm, closed Sun.; free).

Practical details

The **gare SNCF** (with **bikes** for hire), **gare routière, urban bus office** and **SI** are grouped together at **place Albert I** on the semi-circle north of the town centre. Rue de la République leads down from here to the central **place du Martroi** and a nineteenth-century statue of the Maid. To the east and down to the river are the scattered vestiges of several older Orléans. Rue de Bourgogne, parallel to the river and erstwhile Gallo-Roman main street, has a good choice of **restaurants** of different ethnic origins. **Accommodation** is easy with the usual **cheap hotels** near the station and, in the centre, *des Carmes* (57 rue des Carmes; ☎38.53.39.60), the *Charles Sanglier* (8 rue Charles-Sanglier; ☎38.53.38.50) and, slightly more expensive, the *Saint-Jean* (19 rue Porte-St-Jean; ☎38.53.63.32). The **youth hostel** is at 14 rue du Faubourg-Madeleine across the road to the west of town (☎38.62.45.75; reception 7.15–9.30am and 5.30–10.30pm; open mid-Feb. to Nov.). The nearest **campsite** is at ST-JEAN-DE-LA-RUELLE, 2km out on the Blois road (rue de la Roche; ☎38.88.39.39; bus #B from place Albert I, stop *Roche aux Fées*). There's another, 7km south at OLIVET (rue du Pont-Bouchet; ☎38.63.53.94) between the Loiret River and the Loire.

Upstream – St-Benoît

Along the Loire **upstream from Orléans**, single lane roads run along the top of the flood banks, ideal for cycling. There are plenty of riverside campsites but the countryside is miserably dull, with the marsh-ridden Sologne to the south and the north bank gearing itself up for the treeless wheat plain to Paris. There is no more good wine either, until SANCERRE and POUILLY on the Burgundy border. The river looks incredibly calm here; a paddling pool on pramwheels could look more treacherous. In fact, it can swell within 24 hours and deluge the valley.

An afternoon's bike-ride crossing over to the north bank at Château-Neuf-sur-Loire would bring you to **ST-BENOIT-SUR-LOIRE** (and buses or hitching might take as long). In the **Abbaye de Flery** at this village, a marble mosaic of Roman origin covers the chancel floor of one of the most awe-inspiring Romanesque churches in France, built in pale yellow and cream-coloured stone between 1020 and 1218. The oldest part, the porch, illustrates the *Vision of the Apocalypse* by the fantastically sculpted capitals and by the layout that follows the description of the New Jerusalem in *Revelations*; four-square, with twelve foundations and three open gates on each side.

There are two more monster **châteaux** further down, at **Sully-sur-Loire** and **Gien**. The latter is a museum of hunting – the weapons, the victims in stuffed or skeletal forms, or just their antlers and horns, and paintings, pottery and tapestries venerating the sport. The château at Sully, however, does have its virtues. Rising massively out of its moat, it has all the picture-book requirements of pointed towers, machiolations and superb fourteenth-century carpentry holding the structure together from the inside. It's open 10–11.45am and 2–4.45pm; closed December to February. If you need a place to stay here, try the **hotel** *du Coq* (21 Faubourg St-Germain; ☎38.36.21.30) or there's a **campsite** by the river close to the castle (☎38.36.23.93). The **SI** is on place Général-de-Gaulle.

Bourges

There's a certain frustration to being in a city with a selection of the choicest of sights, which turns into a lifeless, provincial backwater come nightfall. Such is **BOURGES**. So, first things first – a fairly comprehensive list of **late night places**: *Le Guillotin*, bar, restaurant and café-théâtre upstairs (15 rue Edouard-Vaillant); *Crêperie des Jacobins*, bar and restaurant (rue des Armuriers); *Bar Mirabeau*, brasserie, comedian bartender, (59 rue Mirabeau). As for other practicalities, there is a **youth hostel** 2km out at 22 rue Henri-Sellier (☎48.24.58.09; closed Sat.; red bus #1 to Maison de la Culture, stop *Auberge de Jeunesse*), and a **campsite** across the stream from the hostel (bd de l'Industrie; ☎48.20.16.85; bus to JUSTICES from place Cujas, stop *Joffre* and walk down boulevard). Cheap **hotels** in the centre include the *de Tours* (3–5 rue Calvin; ☎48.24.22.78); *L'Etape* (4 rue Raphael-Casanova; ☎48.70.49.57); and *de l'Agriculture* (15 rue du Prinal; ☎48.70.40.84). The **SI** is by the cathedral on place E-Dolet. The **gare routière**, on place Parmentier, is halfway between the cathedral and the **gare SNCF**, ½km to the north. **Bikes** can be rented from *Loca Bourges*, rue Edouard-Vaillant.

From the outside, Bourges' **Cathédrale St-Etienne** looks like a failed medieval space programme. Encircled by stone rockets, the flying buttresses are all set to swing open, thereby releasing the vast coffin-like top story of the nave to be projected into space. But not long after the control towers were completed, a major technical hitch appeared in the form of a west front squatting on the launch pad, which, despite its depiction of some people ascending to the heavens and others being thrown into a gaping hole, was obviously not going to shift. This was followed by the collapse of the north tower. By the early sixteenth century, the rebuilding of the latter had grounded the cathedral for ever. All for the best no doubt, since Gothic purists love it, and the best feature of the interior, the stained glass windows, wouldn't have worked in outer space.

All the other old buildings and streets of Bourges are contained within a loop of roads northwest of the cathedral. On rue Jacques-Coeur stands the head office, stock exchange, dealing rooms, bank safes and home of Charles VII's finance minister, **Jacques Coeur** (1400–56). This medieval shipping magnate, moneylender and arms dealer dominates Bourges as Joan of Arc does Orléans – the 'King of Bourges' (Charles VII) doesn't get a look in. Jacques Coeur's career provides an early example of the profitability of war. Until just a few years before his death, the English were still in control above the Loire, yet his business interests stretched from Paris to Damascus. The visit to his palace is fun, starting with the fake windows from which very realistic sculpted figures look down. There are hardly any furnishings, but the decorations on the stonework (restored in the 19C), including numerous hearts and scallop shells (*coeurs* and *coquilles St-Jacques*), clearly show the mark of the man who had it built. It's also the only mansion where you are shown the original toilets. Guided visits are from 9–11.15am and 2.15–5.15pm May to October; 10–11.15am and 2–4.15pm the rest of the year.

The nearby pâtisserie, on the corner of rue d'Auron and rue des Armuriers, which claims to be Jacques Coeur's birthplace, isn't, but nevertheless, you can eat good cakes there in a partly medieval room. The SI will lovingly detail the city's **other mansions, ancient halls** and **museums** for you, but none of them match Jacques Coeur's palace and the cathedral.

Literary associations in Berry

Alain Fournier, author of *Le Grand Meaulnes*, was born near Bourges in 1886. Some scenes of the novel are set in the city, but the lost domaine of '*la fête étrange*' is somewhere near **EPINEUIL-LE-FLEURIAL** (the Ste-Agathe of the novel), 25km south of ST-ARMAND-MONTROND. Just before

Meaulnes first sees the château, the location is described: 'in the whole of the Sologne it would have been hard to find a more desolate spot than the region in which he now found himself'. Albicoco's film of the book was shot around Epineuil and is much more rewarding to see than searching for an actual château that fits all the details. Fournier spent his childhood in Epineuil and the elementary school described in the book can be visited outside class hours.

NOHANT, just north of La Châtre, is where **George Sand** (1808–76) spent half her life. After the publication of her novel *Valentine*, which was set locally and received considerable publicity, she wrote: 'this unknown *Vallée Noire*, this quiet and unpretentious landscape . . . All this had charms for me alone and did not deserve to be revealed to idle curiousity'. She went on to say that she was compelled to write and had not given a thought to potential notoriety. What the critics jumped on in this novel, and in the rest of her writings, were 'anti-matrimonial doctrines'. Her views on the matter were no more than that ill-matched couples should be able to separate. Simone de Beauvoir described Sand as a 'sentimental feminist' – she was certainly no activist except for the brief period of the 1848 revolution. But her male contemporaries called her a man-eater and she is too often referred to simply as Chopin's mistress. Though her literary output was enormous and the French recognize her as one of their great writers, her lasting reputation is based on her life – lived shockingly for her times, as she willed it and as she suffered it.

The **Château de Nohant** is open for quick guided tours (9–11.45am and 2–6pm, closed Tues. Apr.–Sept.; otherwise 10–11.45 and 2–4pm; closed Tues. and Wed.). You are shown the dining room, table all set for guests Flaubert, Turgenev, and Dumas. At the table also sat Delacroix, Balzac, and Liszt on many occasions. The piano that George Sand gave Chopin, her guest for ten years, sits in the living room with the family portraits. The writer's son Maurice built the puppet theatre with Chopin, and made the puppets with his mother.

In **LA CHATRE** itself, where every other place-name is connected with George Sand, the **Musée de la Vallée Noire** (71 rue Venose) dedicates one floor to the writer. There are plenty of pictures as well as words: George Sand's caricatures of her friends, a photograph of Chopin, drawings of other Nohant guests, Maurice's illustrations for his mother's work and the doodles on her manuscripts (open 9.30–11.30am and 2–5.30pm, closed Thurs. and Sun. am, March to mid-Oct.; otherwise Wed. and Sun.3–6pm).

If you're looking for a room here, try the **hotel** *La Boule d'Or* (1 rue Maurice-Sand; ☎54.48.33.58). There's a riverside **campsite** 2.5km along the Montgivray road, the *Château Solange Sand* (☎54.48.37.83). The **SI** in La Châtre is on the square George Sand.

Le Mans

Halfway between Normandy and the Loire, **LE MANS** is the capital of Sarthe, a department that contains more châteaux than both banks of the Loire put together. Most, however, are privately owned and closed to the public. The pastimes of wine-tasting, château-spying and water-gazing are best done on the Loir (as opposed to the Loire). Sarthe as a whole is France at its most gentle – a bit boring to some people, but less overrun by tourists than neighbouring regions.

Le Mans itself is taken over by car fanatics in the middle of June for the famous 24-hour race. The rest of the year it is still lively, with good public services and free museums (courtesy of the Communist Town Hall) and one of the most beautiful old quarters of any city in France. This, the **Vieille Ville**, floats on a hill above the Sarthe River, partly enclosed by third- to fourth-century Gallo-Roman walls and with the immense Gothic apse of **St-Julien's cathedral** ascending the hill from the southeast to its Romanesque nave on place du Château. According to Rodin, the now badly worn sculpted figures of the south porch were rivalled only in Chartres and Athens. Some of the stained glass windows here were in place when the first Plantagenet was buried in the church, but the brightest colours in the otherwise austere interior come from the tapestries.

Elsewhere in **the old town**, intricate Renaissance stonework, medieval half-timbering, sculpted pillars and beams and grand classical facades make up the scenery of the streets. In the 1850s a road was tunnelled under the quarter, then a slum, so there is a self-contained unity preserved above the modern town: steep, walled steps lead up from the river and longer flights descend the southern side using the old Gallo-Roman entrances. The new works well, too, and for once there's been resistance to simply anaesthetising the past into an upmarket mall. A recent council housing development manages not to clash with the third-century **Tour Madeleine** behind it; there are cafés and restaurants, a Friday/Saturday **market** on place du Château, a good cinema, *Ciné-Poche* at 97 Grande-rue, and theatre, *Les Treteaux du Perche* (21 bis rue des Fossées-St-Pierre), and a pleasant absence of souvenir shops. If you're intrigued you can see pictures, maps and plans of *Vieux Mans* plus examples of its ancient arts and crafts in the **Maison de la Reine Bérengère** (open 9am–noon and 2–6pm; closed Mon.), one of the Renaissance houses on rue de la Reine-Bérengère.

The road tunnel comes out on the south side – by an impressive monument to Wilbur Wright – into place des Jacobins, the vantage point for St-Julien's flying buttresses. From here, you can walk east through the park to the **Musée Tessé**, a mixed bunch of pictures and statues including George de la Tour's light at its most extraordinary in the *Extase de St-François* and copies of brilliant medieval populist murals in Sarthe churches (open 9am–noon and 2–6pm).

The modern centre of Le Mans is **place de la République**, lined by a mixture of Belle Epoque and Americana office blocks. The cafés and brasseries on the square stay open till late and restaurants are easy to find in the surrounding streets. The *charcuterie* on the *place*, *La Truie qui File* at no. 25, provides excellent picnic fodder, and if you want cake for afters, go to *Pasquier* at 33 rue Gambetta. The **SI** is on the north side of the *place* nearest the *Vieille Ville* (at no. 40) and below it is the city bus terminal in the underground shopping centre. Buses #16, #5, #31, #3 and #41 go between here and the the **gare SNCF** via av Général-Leclerc where the **gare routière** is

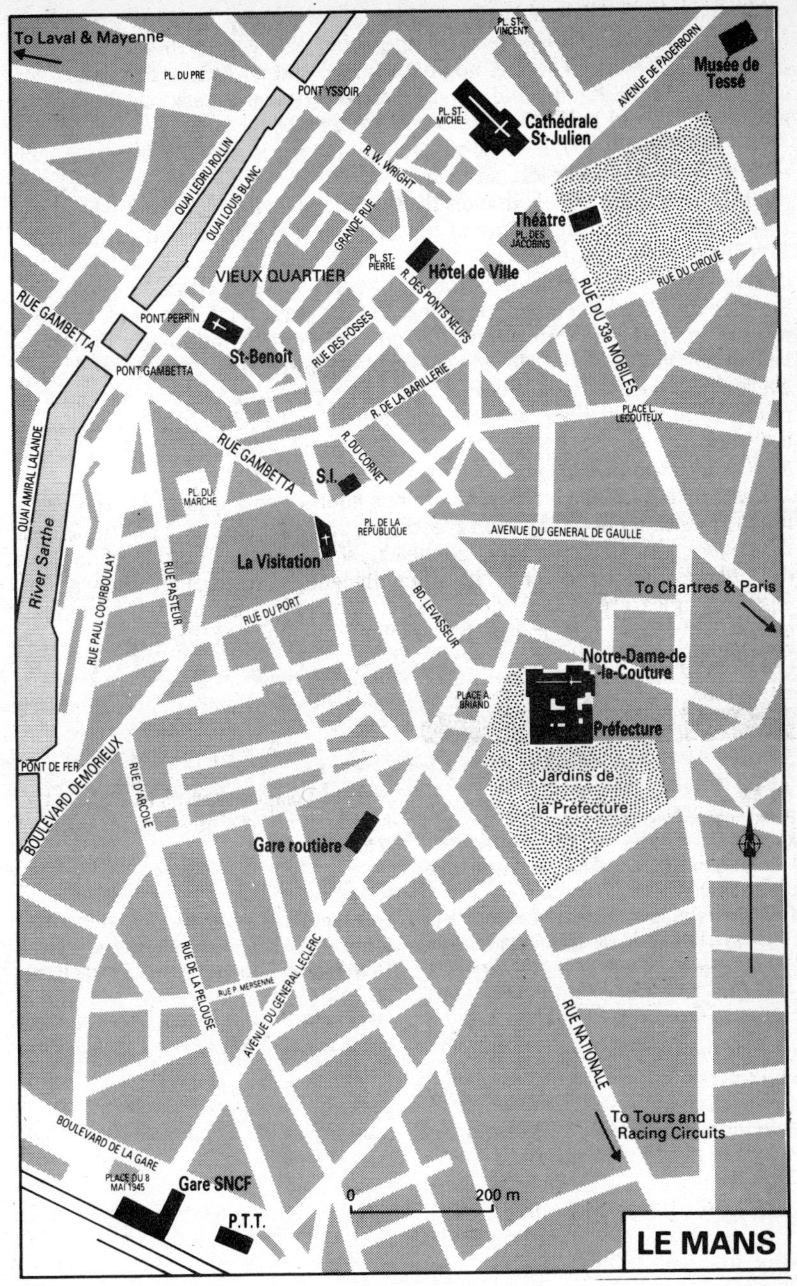
To Laval & Mayenne
PL. DU PRE
PL. ST-VINCENT
AVENUE DE PADERBORN
Musée de Tessé
PONT YSSOIR
PL. ST-MICHEL
Cathédrale St-Julien
QUAI LEDRU ROLLIN
QUAI LOUIS BLANC
R. W. WRIGHT
GRANDE RUE
Théâtre
PL. DES JACOBINS
PL. ST-PIERRE
Hôtel de Ville
VIEUX QUARTIER
R. DES PONTS NEUFS
RUE DU CIRQUE
RUE DU 33e MOBILES
RUE GAMBETTA
PONT PERRIN
St-Benoît
RUE DES FOSSES
PONT GAMBETTA
R. DE LA BARILLERIE
PLACE L. LECOUTEUX
QUAI AMIRAL LALANDE
RUE GAMBETTA
R. DU CORNET
S.I.
PL. DU MARCHE
PL. DE LA REPUBLIQUE
AVENUE DU GENERAL DE GAULLE
La Visitation
River Sarthe
RUE PAUL COURBOULAY
RUE PASTEUR
RUE DU PORT
BD. LEVASSEUR
To Chartres & Paris
Notre-Dame-de-la-Couture
PLACE A. BRIAND
Préfecture
Jardins de la Préfecture
PONT DE FER
BOULEVARD DEMORIEUX
RUE D'ARCOLE
Gare routière
RUE DE LA PELOUSE
RUE P. MERSENNE
AVENUE DU GENERAL LECLERC
RUE NATIONALE
To Tours and Racing Circuits
BOULEVARD DE LA GARE
PLACE DU 8 MAI 1945
Gare SNCF
0
200 m
P.T.T.
LE MANS

located. Off av Général-Leclerc, there are two cheap **hotels** on rue du P-Mersenne, *Au Vin d'Anjou* (no. 15) and *Select* (13) and at 15 bd de la Gare, *Hôtel de la Terrasse*. There is no youth hostel and no nearby campsites, but there are some *Foyers* and *Centres d'Hébergement* – ask at the SI for addresses. The **ALLOSTOP** number is ☎43.24.70.69.

In 1908, Wilbur Wright took off, alongside what is now the fastest stretch of the **24-hour racetrack**, and stayed in the air for a record-breaking one hour 31.5 minutes. The invitation to use the grounds came from two brothers, busy manufacturing some of the first internal combustion engine cars. The **Musée de l'Automobile**, in the middle of the Bugatti and 24-hours circuits, documents these early transport successes and has a superb collection of cars from 1885 to recent winners of the great race, almost all in working order. It is open 9am–noon, 2–7pm Easter to mid-October; otherwise 9am–noon and 2–6pm, closed Tuesday. Motorcycles, go-karts and even trucks race on the Bugatti circuit and some practising vehicle is bound to provide you with the appropriate soundtrack for the scene. Not surprisingly, the tracks are not on the bus routes – the nearest are the terminals of #6 and #7 (*Raineries* and *Guette-Loup*) – but you might get a fast ride.

If car racing holds no romance, there's another outing from Le Mans of a much quieter nature. The **Abbaye de l'Epau**, founded in 1229 by Queen Bérengère (wife of Richard the Lionheart), stands on the outskirts of the Bois de Changé, unaltered since its fifteenth-century restoration after a fire. Opening times are 9.30am–noon and 2–6pm, mid-April to mid-September; closed Thursday; and it can be reached by bus #14 from place de la République.

travel details

Trains

From Angers frequently to Paris (3¼ hr.) via Le Mans (1 hr.) to Nantes (¾ hr.) and to Tours (1½ hr.) via Saumur (¾ hr.); 8 daily to Savennières-Béhuard (¼ hr.).

From Tours at least hourly to Paris-Austerlitz (2½ hr.) via Blois (½ hr.) and Les Aubrais-Orléans (1¼ hr.); at least 10 daily to Angers (1½ hr.) via Saumur (¾ hr.) and to Le Mans (1¼ hr.); 8 daily to Azay-le-Rideau/Chinon (½ hr.–1 hr.); 6 daily to Loches (1 hr.); 5 daily to Chenonceaux-Chisseux/St-Aignan (½ hr.–1 hr.) and to Bourges (2 hr.).

From Orléans every 5 min. to Les Aubrais-Orléans (4 min.).

From Les Aubrais-Orléans 1 every half-hour to Paris (1¼ hr.); 4 daily to Bourges (1¼hr.).

From Le Mans frequently to Paris (1¾ hr.), to Nantes (1¾ hr.) via Angers (1 hr.) and to Rennes (2 hr.).

Buses

From Angers 6 daily to Saumur (1½ hr.); 2 daily to Rennes (1¾ hr.); 5 daily to Baugé (1¾ hr.).

From Saumur 3 daily to Fontévraud (½ hr.); daily to Chinon (¾ hr.).

From Tours 7 daily to Amboise (½ hr.); 4 daily to Loches (¾ hr.); 3 daily to Azay-le-Rideau/Chinon (½ hr.–1¼ hr.); 2 daily to Chenonceaux (1 hr.) and Ste-Maure (¾ hr.); daily to Montrichard (1¼hr.) and Richelieu (1½ hr.).

From Blois 4 daily to Orléans (1½ hr.); 1 or 2 daily to Cheverney.

CHAPTER SIX

POITOU-CHARENTES AND THE ATLANTIC COAST

Newsstands selling the *Sud-Ouest* paper announce that this is the beginning of the Southwest. Not the Mediterranean, certainly but in summer from here on, in the light, in the warm air, in the fields of sunflowers and the shuttered siesta-silent air of the farmhouses, you get the first exciting promise of the south.

The **coast**, on the other hand, remains distinctly Atlantic – dunes, pine forest, reclaimed marshland, and misty mud flats. It has great charm in places, particularly the islands of **Noirmoutier, Ré** and **Oléron** out of season. But it is family, camper caravanner seaside; it lacks the glamour and excitement of the Côte d'Azur. The sandy beaches are beautiful, though disappointing for enthusiastic swimmers, as the water is murky and often shallow for a long way out. The principal port, **La Rochelle**, however, is one of the prettiest and most distinctive towns in France.

Inland, the **valley of the Charente** river, slow and green, epitomises the blue-overalled, Gauloise-smoking, shrewd-eyed, bottom-fishing peasant France. The towpath is accessible for long stretches, on foot or mountain bike, and there are boat trips from Saintes and Cognac. The **Marais Poitevin** marshes, too, with their poplar groves and island fields reticulated by countless canals and ditches, are both unusual landscape and good, easy-going walking or cycling country.

But perhaps the most memorable aspect of the countryside – and indeed of towns like Poitiers too – is the exquisite **Romanesque churches**. This was a significant stretch on the medieval pilgrim routes across France and from Britain and northern Europe to the shrine of **Saint Jacques** (St. James, or Santiago as the Spanish know him) at Compostela in northwest Spain, and was well endowed by its followers. The finest of the churches, among the best in all of France, are to be found in the countryside around **Saintes** and **Poitiers**: informal, highly individual and so integrated with their landscape they often seem as rooted as the trees.

And lastly, of course, remember that this is a region of **seafood** – fresh and cheap in every market for miles inland, with oysters adding a touch of elegance to any picnic.

INLAND POITOU

Most of the old **province of Poitou** is a huge expanse of rolling wheatland, sunflower and maize plantations where the combines crawl and giant sprinklers shoot great arcs of white water over the fields in summertime. Villages are strung out along the valley bottoms. Heartland of the domains of Eleanor, Duchess of Aquitaine, whose marriage to King Henry II in 1152 brought the whole southwest of France under English control for 300 years, it is also the northern limit of the *langue d'oc*-speaking part of the country, whose **Occitan** dialect survives amongst old people even today.

Hitching is the easiest way of **moving around** within the area, though the main destinations are all directly accessible by train from Paris. POITIERS is just three hours away, with frequent connections on to LA ROCHELLE, BORDEAUX and the Atlantic coast.

Poitiers and around

Moving south from Tours on the Autoroute de l'Aquitaine, you'd hardly be tempted by the cluster of towers and office blocks rising from the plain, which is all you see of **POITIERS**. But go in close and things are very different. It is no seething metropolis, but a country town with a charm that comes from a long and sometimes influential history – as the seat of the Dukes of Aquitaine, for instance – discernible in the winding lines of the streets and the breadth of architectural fashions represented in its buildings.

Arrival and hotels

Arriving by train, you'll find yourself at the foot of the hill which forms the kernel of the town. It's a pretty unexciting neighbourhood, but if that does not bother you there are several **places to stay** right opposite the station. Try the *Cyrano* at 117 bd du Grand-Cerf (☎49.58.21.32); it's clean and unpretentious, with a cafeteria downstairs. For more entertaining surroundings it's only a short uphill walk – bd Solférino, then right up the steps – to the **town centre** on place du Maréchal-Leclerc. Here, on the north side of the square, you'll pay a bit more for the very much more attractive *Hôtel du Plat d'Etain* (7 rue du Plat d'Etain; ☎49.41.04.80). More downmarket alternatives include the *Alsace-Lorraine* (2 rue Alsace-Lorraine; ☎49.41.25.83); *Jules Ferry* (27 rue Jules-Ferry; ☎49.41.23.55); *Le Lion d'Or* (28 Faubourg du Pont-Neuf; ☎49.61.08.29); and the *Carnot* on rue Carnot (no. 40; ☎49.41.23.69) with a small, rather noisy restaurant underneath. There is also a **youth hostel** (☎49.58.03.05) at 17 rue de la Jeunesse (bus #9 from the gare SNCF to *Bellejouanne*: 3km) and **Camping municipal** on rue du Porteau, north of the town. If you have any difficulty with accommodation, ask the **SI**, whose principal office is at 8 rue des Grandes-Ecoles, with a summer annexe by the station.

Around the town

Tree-lined **place Leclerc,** and **place de Gaulle** a few streets north, are the two poles of communal life, the first with popular **cafés,** the second with a big

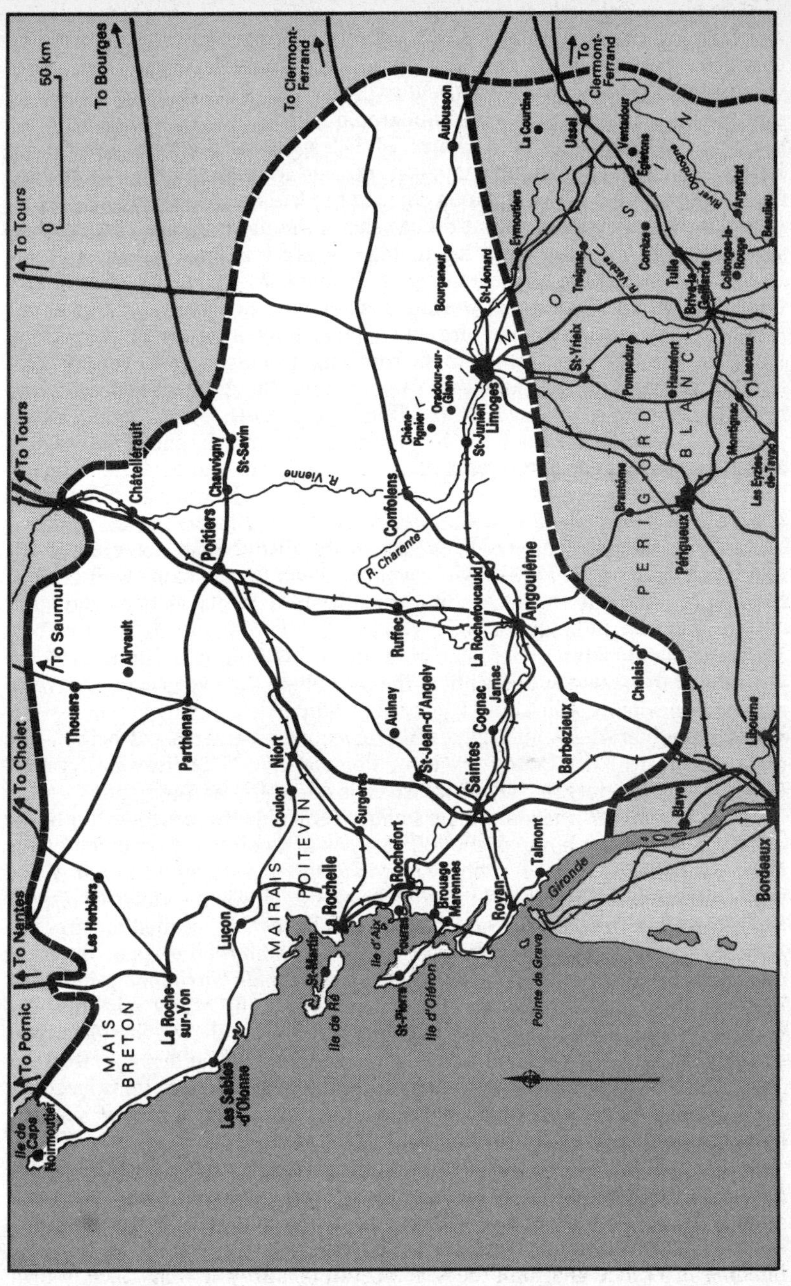
To Pornic
To Nantes
To Cholet
To Saumur
To Tours
To Tours
To Bourges
To Clermont-Ferrand
To Clermont-Ferrand
0
50 km
Ile de Noirmoutier
BRETON
Les Sables d'Olonne
La Roche-sur-Yon
Les Herbiers
Luçon
POITEVIN
Ile de Ré
St-Martin
La Rochelle
Ile d'Aix
Fouras
Rochefort
St-Pierre
Ile d'Oléron
Brouage
Marennes
Royan
Pointe de Grave
Talmont
Gironde
Bordeaux
Blaye
Libourne
Thouars
Airvault
Parthenay
Niort
Coulon
Surgères
Aulnay
St-Jean-d'Angely
Saintes
Cognac
Jarnac
Barbezieux
Chalais
Angoulême
La Rochefoucauld
Ruffec
Poitiers
Châtellérault
Chauvigny
St-Savin
R. Vienne
R. Charente
Confolens
St-Junien
Limoges
Oradour-sur-Glane
St-Léonard
Bourganeuf
Aubusson
Eymoutiers
La Courtine
Ussel
Egletons
Ventadour
Tulle
Corrèze
Treignac
St-Yrieix
Pompadour
Hautefort
Brive-la-Gaillarde
Collonges-la-Rouge
Argentat
Beaulieu
Lascaux
Montignac
Les Eyzies-de-Tayac
Brantôme
Périgueux
P E R I G O R D
B L A N C
L I M O U S I N

and bustling **market.** Between is a warren of prosperous streets, with rue Gambetta cutting north past the **Palais de Justice**, whose nineteenth-century façade hides the twelfth-century great hall of the dukes of Aquitaine, into rue de la Chaine, full of half-timbered medieval houses, and down to the river by the heavily restored church of St-Jean-de-Montierneuf. **Inside**, the Palais de Justice is a magnificent room nearly fifty metres long, where Jean, Duc de Berry held his sumptuous court in the late fourteenth century seated on the intricately carved daïs at the far end of the room. In one corner, stairs give access to the old **castle keep.** Joan of Arc was once put through her ideological paces here by a committee of bishops worried about endangering their own immortal souls and worldly positions by endorsing a charlatan or a heretic. They also had her virginity checked by a posse of respectable matrons. The stairs lead out on to the roof with a fantastic view over the town.

Right behind you, you look down upon one of the greatest and most idiosyncratic churches in France, **Notre-Dame-la-Grande**, begun in the reign of Eleanor. Access is via rue de la Régatterie or rue du Marché. The weirdest and most spectacular thing about it is the **west front.** You can't call it beautiful, at least not in a conventional sense. It is squat and loaded with detail to a degree that the modern eye finds fussy. And yet it is this **detail** which is enthralling, ranging from the domestic to the disturbingly anarchic. In the blind arch to the right of the door, a woman sits in the keystone with her hair blowing out from her head. In the frieze above, Mary places her hand familiarly on Elizabeth's pregnant belly. You see the newborn Jesus admired by a couple of daft-looking sheep and gurgling in his bath-tub. Higher still are portraits of the apostles, and right at the top, where the eye is carried deliberately and inevitably, Christ in Majesty in an almond-shaped inset. Such elaborate sculpted façades – and domes like pinecones on turret and belfry – are the hallmarks of the Poitou brand of Romanesque. The **interior,** crudely overlaid with nineteenth-century frescoes, is not nearly as interesting.

There is another unusual Poitiers church towards the southern tip of the old town, where the hump of the hill narrows to a point now occupied by the **Parc de Blossac**, a great spot to sit among the clipped limes and gravelled walks, to watch the *boules* and munch a baguette. This is the eleventh-century **St-Hilaire-le-Grand** on rue du Doyenné – unbelievably, pruned of part of its nave in the last century. Take the trouble to admire the **apse** from the outside; it has a particularly beautiful group of chapels surrounding it. Inside, there is the usual **ambulatory** to accommodate the many pilgrims who flocked in, one of whom perhaps caused the fire around 1100 that destroyed the original wooden roof and necessitated the improvised arrangement that makes St-Hilaire architecturally unique. Eight heavy domes introduced for the reroofing had to be supported somehow, hence the forest of auxiliary columns making three aisles either side of the nave.

And this is not the oddest or the oldest building in town. Literally in the middle of rue Jean-Jaurès, as you go down towards the river Clain, you come upon a chunky, square edifice with the air of a second-rate Roman temple. It is the mid-fourth-century **Baptistère St-Jean**, reputedly the oldest Christian building in France and until the seventeenth century the only place in town

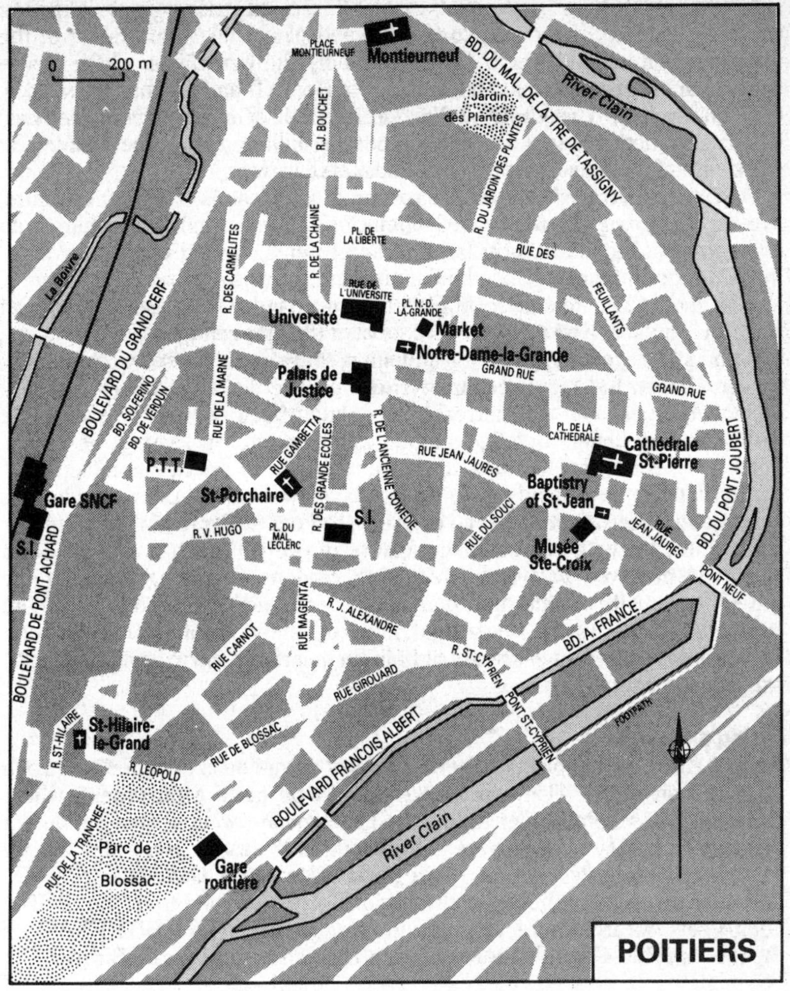

you could have a proper **baptism** (10.30am–12.30pm and 3–6pm; Oct.–March, 2–4pm). The 'font' was the octagonal pool sunk into the floor. The guide argues that the water pipes uncovered in the bottom show that the water could not have been more than 30 to 40cm deep, which casts doubt upon the popular belief that early Christian baptism was by total immersion. There are also some very ancient and faded **frescoes** on the walls, including the Emperor Constantine on horseback, and a collection of Merovingian sarcophagi.

Nearby is Poitiers' **cathedral of St-Pierre**, an enormous building on whose broad, pale façade pigeons roost and plants take root. Some of the **glass** dates from the twelfth century, notably the Crucifixion in the centre window of the apse, in which the features of Henry II and Eleanor are supposedly discernible. The **choir stalls**, too, are full of characteristic medieval detail: a coquettish Mary and child, a peasant killing a boar, the architect at work with his dividers, a baker with a basket of loaves.

Opposite, in the side street across rue J-Jaurès, is Poitiers' museum, **Musée Ste-Croix** (10–noon and 2–6pm; closed Tues.; free). Downstairs is an interesting collection of local farming implements, among them an *alambic ambulant* or itinerant still, of a kind in use until surprisingly recently. There is also a good Gallo-Roman section with some handsome glass, pottery and sculpture, notably a white marble Minerva of the first century.

If you still have an appetite for buildings, there's a seventh-century subterranean chapel, the **Hypogée martyrium**, on rue de la Pierre-Levée across the **Pont Neuf**, and the Pierre Levée dolmen itself, where Rabelais came with fellow-students to talk, carouse and scratch his name. Descartes, Poitiers University's other most illustrious student, was rather more serious.

Alternatively, you could take a more relaxed walk along the riverside path – on the right across Pont Neuf – upstream to Pont St-Cyprien. On the further bank, you can see a characteristic feature of every French provincial town: neat, well-manured *potagers* – vegetable gardens – coming down to the water's edge with a little mud quay at the end and a moored punt, where *monsieur* spends many a weekend hour patiently waiting for a fat carp. Sometimes you find such scenes right in the heart of a town: an atavistic refusal to become totally urban.

Eating and walking

As for **eating**, try the plain brasserie *Le Regal* on rue de la Régatterie, *Pizzeria Capucino* on rue de l'Université, *chez Pierrot* on place Montierneuf, where there are also several student-frequented bars, or the *salon de thé* – restaurant opposite Notre-Dame. If you are not too long in the tooth, you could also try wangling a university restaurant ticket; ask **CIJ** at 64 rue Gambetta.

Walkers can get a guide to the regional opportunities from the SI. The GR364 sets out from here, reaching the Vendée coast via PARTHENAY – if the idea appeals. **Gare routière** on place Thézard below Parc de Blossac.

St-Savin and Chauvigny

There is more Romanesque close by at ST-SAVIN and CHAUVIGNY, both with exceptionally fine churches and some great sculpture and frescoes. You need to get an early start if you are to do both in one day using public transport. The first bus leaves Poitiers at 6.15am, depositing you in St-Savin exactly one hour later. There is a bus back to Chauvigny at 10am. Then you have a choice of two buses to return to Poitiers. The timetable may seem brutal, but there is no other way of doing it unless you hitch. Alternatively, both places have two or three reasonable **hotels** and Chauvigny has a **camp-**

site. Try *Hôtel du Midi* (☎49.48.00.40) on route Nationale in St-Savin or *Le Chalet Fleuri* (☎49.46.31.12) by the river in Chauvigny.

St-Savin

In **ST-SAVIN**, which is scarcely more than a hamlet, the bus puts you down beside the abbey near the modern bridge over the poplar-lined River Gartempe. Walk downstream a little way to the **medieval bridge** for a perfect view of the **abbey church** – built in the eleventh century, possibly on the site of a church founded by Charlemagne – rising strong and severe above the gazebos and vegetable gardens and lichened tile roofs of the domestic dwellings at its feet. The soaring crocketed spire, which first catches the eye today, is a Gothic addition.

Inside (9am–12.30pm – closes 11am Sun. and holidays – and 2.30–7pm, closed 5pm from Oct.–June) steps descend to the narthex and thence to the floor of the nave, which stretches away from you to the raised choir: high, narrow, barrel-vaulted and flanked by bare, round columns, their capitals deeply carved with interlacing foliage. The whole of the vault is covered with **paintings**. The colours are few – red and yellow ochres, green mixed with white and black. Yet the paintings are full of light and grace, depicting scenes from the stories of Genesis and Exodus. Some are instantly recognisable: Noah's three-decked ark, Pharoah's horses rearing at the engulfing waves of the Red Sea, graceful workers constructing the Tower of Babel.

Chauvigny

CHAUVIGNY's pride, on the other hand, are the sculpted capitals of the **church of St-Pierre**. The place, by contrast with the sleepy nature of St-Savin, is a busy market town on the banks of the Vienne, its half-dozen porcelain factories and lumber mills providing work for the area. If you can manage it, the Saturday **market** gives an extra dimension to a visit. Held between the church of Notre-Dame and the river, it offers above all a mouth-watering selection of food – oysters, prawns, crayfish, cheeses galore, pâtés in pristine aspic, including the spectacular *amandes*, decorated with yellow segments of scallop flesh. The cafés are fun, too, bursting with noisy wine-flushed farmers combining business and society.

To get to the church you take rue du Château opposite Notre-Dame, winding up the spur on which the old town stands. Past the ruins of a castle that belonged to the Bishops of Poitiers and the better-preserved Château d'Harcourt, you come first to the attractive and unusual east end of **St-Pierre**. Once **inside**, it is damp, and in a poor state of repair.

The **choir capitals** are a visual treat. Each one is different, evoking a terrifying, nightmarish world. Graphically illustrated monsters – bearded, moustachioed, winged, scaled, human-headed with manes of flame – grab hapless mortals, naked, upside down and puny, and rip their bowels and crunch their heads. The only escape offered is in the naively serene events of Christ's birth. On the second capital on the south side of the choir, for instance, the angel Gabriel announces Christ's birth to the shepherds, their flock represented by four sheep that look like Pooh's companion Eeyore, while just around the corner the archangel Michael weighs souls in hand-held scales and a devil tries to grab one for his dinner. The oddest scene is on the north side: a Siamese-twin dancer grips the hindlegs of two horse-like monsters which are gnawing his upper arms. You get a strong feeling that here was an artist who came from the same peasant stock as his audience, prey to the same superstitions, the same fears of things that went bump in the night or lurked in the wet woods.

Parthenay and Niort

West of Poitiers the open landscape of the Poitou plain gradually gives way to *bocages* – small fields enclosed by hedges and trees. The local farmers' cooperative say the fashion for grubbing up woodland and creating vast windswept acreages in the name of efficiency and productivity is dying out. And not just for aesthetic reasons: wind erosion has left scarcely ten to fifteen centimetres of top soil.

Parthenay

On the edge of the plain, served by regular SNCF buses from Poitiers stands the small town of **PARTHENAY**, once an important staging point on the pilgrim routes to Compostela and now a major cattle market (Wed.). It's not a place to make a special detour for, but stop over if you're heading north for Brittany or west to the sea.

Finding your way around is easy. From the **gare SNCF, av de Gaulle** leads straight to the central square, with the **SI** on the righthand corner. The main part of town – essentially the medieval core, and fairly restricted in area at that – lies to the west, between here and the river Thouet. Rue Jean-Jaurès and rue de la Saunerie cut in through the largely pedestrian shopping precinct to the Gothic **Tour de l'Horloge**, the fortified gateway to the old citadel on a steep-sided neck of land projecting into a loop of the Thouet.

There is nothing very remarkable to see. On the right the *mairie* faces the attractively simple Romanesque church of Ste-Croix across a small garden with a view over the ramparts and the **gully of St-Jacques** with its medieval houses and vegetable plots climbing the opposite slope. Further along is a house where Cardinal Richelieu used to visit his grandfather, and then a handsome but badly damaged Romanesque door, all that remains of the castle chapel of **Notre-Dame-de-la-Couldre**. Of the castle itself practically nothing is left. From the tip of the spur where it once stood you look down on the twin-towered gateway and bridge of the **Pont St-Jacques**, dating back to the thirteenth century, through which the nightly flocks of pilgrims poured into the town for shelter and security. To reach it, turn left under the Tour de l'Horloge and down the **Vaux St-Jacques**, as this medieval lane is called. It is highly evocative of that period, with its crooked half-timbered dwellings crowding up to the bridge. They are only now beginning to be restored. Some look as if they have received little attention since the last pilgrim shuffled up the street.

If you're after shelter too, two reasonable **hotels** in bd Meilleraye by the main square are *Grand Hôtel* (no. 85; ☎49.64.00.16) and *Hôtel de la Meilleraye* (no. 93bis; ☎49.64.03.28). A third possibility is *Hôtel du Nord* at 86 av de Gaulle (☎49.64.00.14), while **campers** have to head out to LE TALLUD, about 3km west on D949.

There are three more beautiful Romanesque churches you might like to notch up within easy reach of Parthenay. One – with a sculpted façade depicting a mounted knight hawking – is only a twenty-minute walk on the Niort road, at PARTHENAY-LE-VIEUX. The others are at AIRVAULT, easily accessible on the Parthenay-Thouars SNCF bus route, and ST-JOUIN-DE-MARNES, 9km northeast (you'll have to hitch or walk that). Or, you could go on to THOUARS (cheap hotels and *Camping municipal*), and combine a visit to the sixteenth-century Château d'Oiron with St-Jouin – only 8½km.

Niort

NIORT, too, is a stop-over rather than a destination, most immediately and conveniently if your goal is the Marais Poitevin, the so-called *Green Venice*. If you're in a car, Niort is probably the best place to stay. If you're on foot, it's the last place before the marshes to get a really wide choice of provisions to stock up with. In itself it is a pleasant morning's stroll.

The **most interesting part** of the town is the mainly pedestrian area around **rue Victor-Hugo** and **rue St-Jean**, full of stone-fronted or half-timbered medieval houses. Coming from the **gare SNCF**, take rue de la Gare as far as av de Verdun with the **SI** and main **Post Office** on the corner. Turn right into **place de la Brèche**. Rue Ricard leaves the square on the left; rue Victor-Hugo is its continuation, following the line of the medieval market in a gully separating the two small hills on which Niort is built. Up to the right, opposite the end of rue St-Jean, is the old **town hall**, an odd-looking triangular building of the early sixteenth century with lantern, belfry, and ornamental machicolations, perhaps capable of repelling drunken revellers, but no match for catapult or sledgehammer.

At the end of the street is the river, the **Sèvre Niortaise**, not to be confused with the Sèvre Nantaise which flows northwards to join the Loire at Nantes. There are gardens and trees along the bank, and over the bridge the ruins of a glove factory, the last vestige of Niort's once thriving **leather industry.** At the time of the Revolution it kept more than thirty cavalry regiments in breeches. Today the biggest industry is **insurance**. The most bourgeois town in France, so it is said, because of the prosperity brought by the large number of major insurance companies making their headquarters here.

Just downstream, opposite a riverside car park, is the **market hall**, with a café doing a good cheap lunch, and beyond, vast and unmistakable on a slight rise, the **keep of a castle** begun by Henry II of England. Now a **museum** (9am–noon and 2–6pm in summer; till 5pm in winter; closed Tues.), it displays mainly **local furniture and costumes**, an extraordinary variety of which were still commonly worn in the villages right up until the beginning of this century. If you have decided to stay, there is the usual crop of **hotels** close to the station: *L'Univers* (22 rue Mazagran, place de la Gare;

☎49.24.41.70), *Terminus* (82 rue de la Gare; ☎49.24.00.38), and *Bordeaux*, the cheapest (117 rue de la Gare; ☎49.24.00.74). The **station** also has a convenient, if not particularly cheap, **restaurant.** The **camping municipal** is in the Parc des Expositions.

Bikes are for hire at the gare SNCF. The maximum period of rental is three days. If you found a trustworthy machine, you could hire it here and make a bike tour of the *marais* – the pleasantest way to see it. It is completely flat and small enough to be seen in two to three days. Before setting out, pick up the collection of walking itineraries available from the SI.

If you are using the buses, the **gare routière** is just off place de la Brèche on rue Viala.

The Marais

The **Marais Poitevin** is a strange, lazy landscape of fens and meadows, shielded by poplar trees and crossed by an elaborate system of canals, dykes and slow-flowing rivers. Recently declared a National Park, the French know it as *La Venise Verte* – the Green Venice – and a tourist industry of sorts has been developing around the villages. This, sadly, seems destined to be the region's future. But the marshes are not yet dead, or completely phoney, and the flat-bottomed punts remain the principal means of transport for many farmers – inevitably, for there is no dry land access to many of the fields. Be sure to avoid weekends, when the evidence of the coming transformation is all too clear.

Access is easiest at the village of **COULON**, on the river Sèvre, at the eastern edge of the marsh – just 10½km from NIORT, by bike or occasional bus. As you would expect in a marshland village, Coulon's houses are small, low and obviously poor. **Punts**, with or without a guide, can be hired here by the half day – touristy perhaps, but fun on a sunny day with a picnic. There are two **hotels** in the village: the *Central* (49.25.90.20; closed first half of Oct. and first half of Nov.) and the more expensive *Au Marais* (☎49.25.90.43; closed Dec. 22–Jan. 22), both likely to be full in season. A better bet if you're carrying a tent is the attractively sited *Camping Venise Verte* in a meadow about 2km or a 25-minute walk downstream .

For **getting around** the Marais as a whole, a **bike** would be ideal. However, if you **walk**, it's best to stick to the lanes since cross-country routes tend to end in fields surrounded by water and you're always having to backtrack. Once you're away from the riverside COULON-ARCAIS road there is practically no traffic, just meadows and cows.

At the seaward end of the marsh, **south of Luçon**, the landscape changes, all straight lines and open fields of wheat and sunflower. The villages cap low mounds that were once islands. Further north up the coast at LA DAVIAUD, in the **Marais Breton**, there is an **écomusée**, illustrating the social and environmental history of the marshes: the *Centre de Découverte du Marais Breton-Vendéen* (10.30am–12.30pm and 3–6pm; closed Mon.; Nov.–March weekends only).

LA ROCHELLE AND THE ISLANDS

This is a great stretch of coast for young families, especially the **islands**, with miles of safe sandy beaches and shallow water. But unless you're camping or have booked something in advance, accommodation will be a near-insuperable problem in August. Out of season you can't rely on sunny weather, but that should not deter you if you like the slightly melancholy romance of quiet misty seascapes and working fishing ports. **Nantes** in the north, **La Rochelle** and **Royan** in the south – all well served by trains – are the best bases. Away from these centres you'll have to take pot-luck with the rather quirky bus routes.

North: Les Sables and the Ile de Noirmoutier

The area around **LES SABLES-D'OLONNE** and northwards has been heavily developed with Costa-style apartment blocks. If you are passing through, there's a surprisingly good modern art section in the Musée de l'Abbaye Ste-Croix on rue Verdun (10.30–noon and 2.30–6.30pm), but there seems little reason **to stay**. If you need to, there's a **youth hostel** (July–Aug. only) on rue des Roses and a **campsite** on rue du Maréchal-Leclerc, both east of the centre and the railway and bus stations.

There are two possible attractions, however, which might make you want to linger in this part of the country. The Ile de Noirmoutier, one of the more desirable locations on this coast, can be reached in three hours by bus from LES SABLES: though an island, it's connected to the shore by a tollbridge. And inland, at the ruined **Château of Le Puy** in LES EPESSES, a remarkable **lakeside extravaganza** is enacted most nights from June to August. This is a weird affair: the enactment of the life of a local peasant from the Middle Ages to World War II, complete with fireworks, lasers, dances on the lake and *Comédie Française* voice-overs. The story, précised in a brief English text, is interesting but incidental – the spectacle is the thing. For details ask at the the **SI** in Les Sables (rue Leclerc) or, nearer to the event, at LES HERBIERS. To get to Les Epesses, you'll need to take a train to CHOLET and a bus from there; Puy de Fou itself is 2½km from Les Epesses, on D27 to CHAMBRETARD. There is one reasonably-priced **hotel** in Les Epesses (*Le Lion d'Or,* 2 rue de la Libération) and a wider choice (*Relais, Le Centre* or *Chez Camille*) at nearby Les Herbiers.

The Ile de Noirmoutier

The **ILE DE NOIRMOUTIER**, spared the high-rise development of its adjoining coast, was an early monastic settlement. It is now very much a tourist resort, and a relatively plush one: villas here are in great demand. But though this is the island's main economy, it doesn't dominate everything. Salt marshes here are still worked, spring potatoes sown and fishes fished.

The island town, **Noirmoutier-en-l'Ile**, boasts a twelfth-century castle (with a couple of museums), a church with a Romanesque crypt, an excellent market (Tues. and Fri.) and most of the life – piano bars which extend normal café hours. There are **campsites** dotted around the island – maps from the **SI** on the main road from the bridge at MARMATRE; **bike hire** from *Vel-hop* (55 av Joseph-Pineau) or *Fabre* (rue du Centre, Marmatre). Among **hotels** to try in the town are *Le Bois de la Chaize* (23 av de la Victoire), *La Marée* (2bis Grande-Rue), or at BARBATRE: *La Fosse* (57 rue de la Pointe) or *Le Marina* (1 route du Gois).

As for exploring **around the island**, the western coast resembles the mainland with great curves of sand, while the northern side dips in and out of little bays with rocky promontories between. Inland, were it not for the salt-water dykes, the horizon would suggest that you were miles from the sea. It is a strange place with only one hostile element apart from the storms in spring – a powerful community of mosquitoes. The more southerly resorts, though built up, have not been the main targets for the developers. In the village centres there are still the one-storey houses, whitewashed and ochre-tiled with decorative brickwork around the windows and S- or Z-shaped coloured bars on the shutters, that you see throughout La Vendée and southern Brittany.

La Rochelle and the Ile de Ré

LA ROCHELLE is the most attractive and unspoiled seaside town in France. Thanks to the foresight of Michel Crépeau, the left-wing 1970s mayor and subsequently Mitterrand's Minister for the Environment, its historic seventeenth- to eighteenth-century centre and waterfront were plucked from the clutches of the developers and its streets freed of traffic for the delectation of pedestrians. A real shock-horror revolutionary outrage at the time, the policy has become standard practice for preserving old town centres across the country – more successful than Crépeau's picturesque yellow bicycle plan, designed to relieve the traffic problem, and now somewhat watered down (see below).

La Rochelle has a long history, as you would expect of such a sheltered Atlantic port, and the inevitable English connection. Eleanor of Aquitaine gave it a charter in 1199, which released it from feudal obligations, and it rapidly became a port of major importance, trading in salt and wine, and skilfully exploiting the Anglo-French quarrels. After the disasters of the Wars of Religion it became the principal port for trade with the French colonies in the West Indies and Canada. Indeed, many of the settlers, especially in Canada, came from this part of France.

The Wars of Religion were particularly destructive for La Rochelle. It turned Protestant and because of its strategic importance drew the remorseless enmity of Cardinal Richelieu, who laid siege to it in 1627. To the dismay of the townspeople, who reasoned that no one could effectively blockade seasoned mariners like themselves, he succeeded in sealing the harbour approaches with a dyke. The English dispatched the Duke of Buckingham to their aid, but he was caught napping on the Ile de Ré and badly defeated. By the end of 1628 Richelieu had starved the city into submission. Out of the pre-siege population of 28,000 only 5000 survived. The walls were demolished and the city's privileges taken away.

Arrival and the town

From the visitor's point of view, **finding your way around** is absolutely straightforward. Everything you want to see is in the area behind the waterfront: in effect, between the **harbour** and the **place de Verdun**, about a ten-minute walk away. There is no need to bother about public transport, except for getting to the campsite or youth hostel. If you have arrived at the **gare SNCF**, take **av de Gaulle** opposite to reach the town centre. On the left as you hit the waterfront, quai du Carénage, is a **free municipal bike park**, heir to Michel Crépeau's original no-identity-check, no-restrictions, pick-up-and-leave scheme.

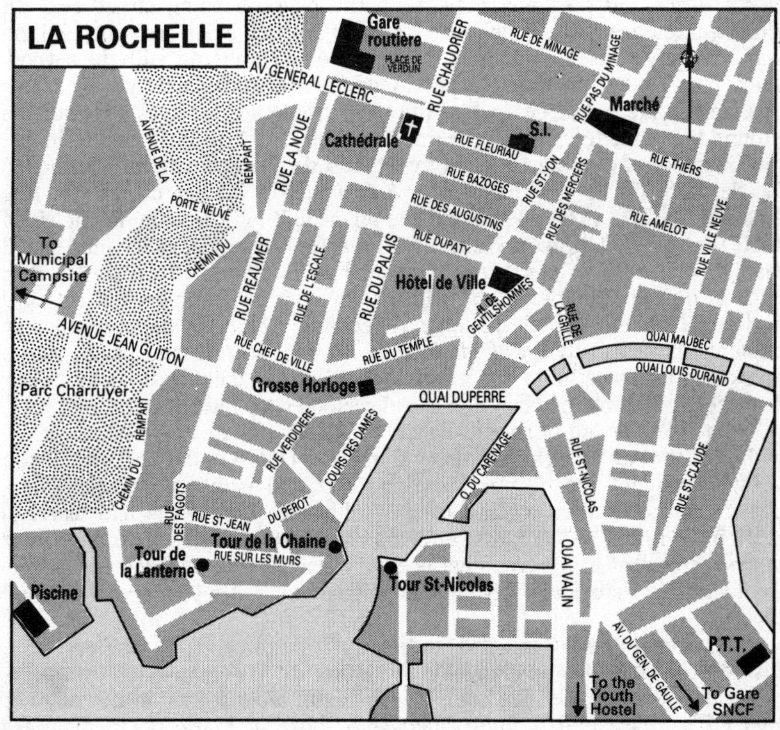

Ahead, dominating the inner harbour, the heavy Gothic gateway of the **Porte de la Grosse Horloge** straddles the entrance to the old town. The quays in front are too full of traffic to encourage loitering. For that, it's best to head out along tree-lined **cours des Dames** towards the fourteenth-century **Tour de la Chaine**, so-called because of the heavy chain that was slung from here across to the opposite tower, **Tour St-Nicolas**, to close the harbour at night. Today the only night-time intruders are likely to be yachties and yuppies from across the Channel. Their craft far outnumber the working boats – mainly garishly painted trawlers. Beyond the tower, steps climb up to **rue Sur-les-Murs**, which follows the top of the old sea wall to a third tower, the **Tour de la Lanterne** or Tour des Quatre Sergents, named after four sergeants imprisoned and executed for defying the Restoration monarchy in 1822 (April–Sept., 9.30–noon and 2–6.30pm; great views). From here there is a way up on to all that's left of the **city walls**, planted with unkempt greenery. Beyond is the **beach**, backed by casino, hot dog stands and amusement booths, and a belt of park, which continues up the western edge of the town centre.

But, for the real charm of the place turn in under the Grosse Horloge on to **place des Petits-Bancs**, where you are confronted with a statue of Eugène Fromentin, nineteenth-century Rochelais painter, writer, and traveller in North Africa and the Sahara. In front, the main shopping street, **rue du Palais**, stretches away to place de Verdun. On both sides are superb eighteenth-century houses, some grey stone, some half-timbered, with their woodwork protected from the weather in distinctive Rochelais style by slates overlapped like fish-scales, while the shop fronts are set back beneath the ground floor arcades. Among the finest are the **Hôtel de la Bourse** – in fact the Chamber of Commerce – and the **Palais de Justice** with its colonnaded façade, both on the left hand side. A few metres further on, in **rue des Augustins**, there is another grandiose affair built for a wealthy Rochelais in 1555, the so-called **Maison Henri II**, complete with loggia, gallery and slated turrets, where the regional tourist board has its offices. **Place de Verdun** itself is dull and characterless, with an uninspiring, humpbacked classical **cathedral** on the corner. Its only redeeming feature is the marvellously opulent Edwardian-style *Café de la Paix*, all mirrors, gilt and plush, where bourgeois ladies come to sip lemon tea and nibble daintily at sticky cakes. And there is a tempting charcuterie and seafood shop next door.

To the west or left of rue du Palais, especially in **rue de l'Escale**, paved with granite setts brought back from Canada as ballast in the Rochelais cargo vessels, you get the discreet residences of the eighteenth-century shipowners and chandlers, veiling their wealth with high walls and classical restraint. A rather less modest gentleman had installed himself on the corner of **rue Fromentin**: a seventeenth-century doctor who adorned his housefront with the statues of other famous medical men – Hippocrates, Galen and their ilk.

East of rue du Palais, and also starting out from place des Petits-Bancs, **rue du Temple** takes you up alongside the **Hôtel de Ville**, protected by a decorative but seriously fortified wall. It was begun around 1600 in the reign of Henri IV, whose initials intertwined with those of Marie de Médicis are carved on the ground floor gallery. It's a beautiful specimen of Frenchified Italian taste, adorned with niches and statues and coffered ceilings, all done in a stone the colour of ripe barley. And if you feel like quiet contemplation of these seemingly more gracious times, there's no better place for it than the terrace of the *Café de la Poste*, right next to the Post Office, in the small, traffic-free square outside. But for more relaxed, vernacular architecture nearly as ancient, keep on up **Grande-Rue-des-Merciers**, the other main shopping area, to the cramped and noisy **market** square

Some museums

Among a number of **museums**, the **Musée du Nouveau Monde** (Mon.–Sat. 10.30am–6pm; Sun. 3–6pm; closed Tues.), next to the **SI** on **rue Fleuriau**, is out of the ordinary. It occupies the former residence of the Fleuriau family, rich shipowners and traders, who, like many of their fellow-Rochelais, made fortunes out of the slave trade and West Indian sugar, spices and coffee. Its elegant, panelled interior, painted in a distinctively French grey, is pleasingly discreet. There is a fine collection of **prints, paintings and photos** of the old West Indian plantations; seventeenth- and eighteenth-century maps of America; photogravures of American Indians from around 1900, with incredible names like Piopio Maksmaks Wallawalla and Lawyer Nez Percé; and an interesting display of aquatint illustrations for Marmontel's novel *Les Incas*. They are an amazing mixture of sentimentality and coy salaciousness, permissible, no doubt, because of the exotic setting and 'primitive' native actors. The captions might have been lifted from Tintin: 'Alonzo dans le royaume de Tumbès', 'Naufrage de Telasco et d'Amazili'. Flimsily clad maidens abound.

Lesser museums include the **Musée d'Orbigny** (2 rue St-Côme; 10–noon and 2–6pm; closed Sun. am and Tues.) and a **Beaux Arts** museum (rue Gargoulleau; 2–6pm; closed Tues.); the former with a good collection of porcelain and pieces to do with the city's history, the latter not terribly exciting. There's also a wonderful **aquarium** as you head west on the south side of the harbour on rue du Cerf-Volant (10–noon and 2–5pm).

The facts

Staying in La Rochelle could be a bit of a problem in the summer season, particularly with the hotels. There's a **youth hostel** (☎46.44.43.11; in Port des Minimes to the west – left as you come out – of the gare SNCF; bus #10 from place de Verdun); and two **campsites** (*Soleil* by the hostel; *Municipal* on the northwestern side of town – bus #6 from Grosse Horloge, direction Pont-Neuf). The **hotels** have become more expensive, leaving only a handful of cheapies in the town centre, of which the best bets are: *Bordeaux* (43 rue St-Nicholas; ☎46.41.31.22), *Henri-IV* (31 rue des Gentilshommes; ☎46.41.25.79) and *Printania* (9 rue Brave-Rondeau; ☎46.41.22.86). Slightly more expensive, but worth trying if you're feeling flush, are the *François-1er* (15 rue Bazoges; ☎46.41.28.46) and the *Atlantic* at 23 rue Verdière behind the waterfront off cours des Dames.

For **eating**, try the rue du Port/rue St-Sauveur area just off the waterfront and rue St-Nicolas. *Pub Lutèce* on rue St-Sauveur is a reasonably priced brasserie. *Café-Resto à la Villette* behind the market has good *plats du jour*, as does *L'Ouvreboîte* on rue Verdière. For a slightly more expensive evening with live folk-singing, try *Le Coquelicot* at 2 rue du Collège (closed Sun.). The **seafood restaurants** on rue de la Chaine and rue St-Jean are excellent, but pricey.

As for other practicalities, there's **bike hire** at the gare SNCF and from **M Salaun**, 3 place de la Solette on the left bank of the canal – not forgetting the municipal bike pound on quai du Carénage (see above). **CDIJ** (14 rue des Gentilshommes) has an information service, including *Allostop*, for young people. For summer **boat trips** around La Rochelle and to neighbouring islands, ask at the SI. For **walkers**, the regional tourist board produce a pamphlet called *Promenades à Pied en Charente-Maritime*, covering the Ile de Ré, Ile d'Oléron, Brouage, Rochefort and Saintonge.

For **getting out** of town, the main **gare routière** is on place de Verdun, though for certain destinations you'll need to use to use other terminals. *Citram* (30 cours des Dames) run to Angoulême, Saintes, Cognac, St-Jean-d'Angeley and Rochefort; *Océcars* (44 cours des Dames) is more local, serving the coastal towns and villages.

The Ile de Ré and Ile d'Aix

Very close to La Rochelle, the **ILE DE RE** is a low, narrow island about 30km in length, surrounded by long sandy beaches. The northwest is salt marshes and oysterbeds, the central part small-scale cultivation of vines, asparagus and wheat. Out of season it has a slow, misty charm, life in its little ports revolving exclusively around the cultivation of oysters and mussels. In season, though, it is incredibly crowded, with upwards of 400,000 visitors passing through.

It is **easy to get to**, with or without your own transport: *Régie Départmentale d'Aunis et Saintonge* run **buses** from La Rochelle (SNCF, Grosse Horloge and place de Verdun). It is possible to juggle the timetable so you can spend time in, say ST-MARTIN and ARS-EN-RE or LES PORTES and still get back the same day. **Ferries** cross from LA PALLICE, La Rochelle's deep water port, to SABLONCEAUX every half hour (every 20 min. in season). **Hotels** and **campsites** are plentiful in all the island villages, though obviously packed to the gills through July and August.

LA PALLICE was a big commercial port with important shipyards. But, times have changed. The navy is based here, too. As you ride by in the bus, you notice some colossal weather-stained concrete sheds, submarine pens built by the Germans to service their Atlantic U-boat fleet during World War II. Too difficult to demolish, they are still in use.

ST-MARTIN, the island's capital, is an atmospheric fishing port with white-washed houses clustering around the stone quays of a well-protected harbour. Trawlers and flat-bottomed oyster boats, piled high with cage-like devices used for 'growing' oysters, slip out every morning on the muddy tide. The quayside *Café Boucquingam* (sic) recalls the military adventures of the said Duke.

To the east of the harbour, you can walk along the almost perfectly preserved **fortifications** – redesigned by Vauban, after Buckingham's attentions – to the citadel, long used as a prison. It was from here that the *bagnards* – prisoners sentenced to hard labour on Devil's Island in Guyana or New Caledonia – set out; most did not return. The notorious Papillon himself left from the harbour.

The Ile d'Aix

The tiny **ILE D'AIX**, just south of La Rochelle, where Napoléon spent his last days in Europe, is a good trip too. Less frequented than the bigger islands, it is small enough to be walked around in about three hours. **Access** is by *Océcars* bus to FOURAS (about 45 min. from La Rochelle), then to POINTE DE LA FUMEE for the ferry.

Rochefort to the Ile d'Oléron

With the exception of Rochefort, which has regular **train** connections with La Rochelle, you may find the simplest solution to travelling along this whole **section of coast** is **hitching**. Many of the towns, however, are also served by the Aunis and Saintonge **buses**. The Saintes-St-Denis-d'Oléron line serves all the towns of Oléron as well as Marennes, St-Sornin, and Balanza between one and three times a day. Other lines serve Marennes, Ronce-les-Baines, La Tremblade, Saugon and Royan. Check all these routes locally, because times and itineraries can vary on different days of the week.

Rochefort

ROCHEFORT dates from the seventeenth century. It was created by Colbert, Louis XIII's navy minister, as a naval base to protect the coast from English raids. It is a dull place: built on a grid plan with regular ranks of identical houses – a joy to the military mind. If, however, you have a taste for the bizarre, then there is one powerful reason for visiting – the house of the novelist Julien Viaud, alias **Pierre Loti**. Son of an impecunious town hall clerk, he joined the navy like many another Rochefort lad, and stayed forty years as an officer, writing numerous bestselling romances with exotic oriental settings and characters.

The **house** (April–Sept., 10–noon and 2–5pm; closed Sun. and Mon. am; Oct.–March, closed Tues. as well) is at 141 rue Pierre-Loti. It is part of a row of modestly proportioned grey stone houses, outwardly a model of petty-bourgeois conformity and respectability. Inside, surprise follows surprise: a medieval banqueting hall complete with Gothic fireplace and Gobelin tapestries, a monastery refectory with windows pinched from a ruined abbey, a Damascus mosque, where, in honour of guests, a man-servant was despatched to play the muezzin from a miniature minaret; a Turkish room, with kilim wall-hangings and a ceiling made from an Alhambra mould. To suit the mood of the place, Loti used to throw extravagant parties: a medieval banquet with swan's meat and hedgehog and a *fête chinoise* with the guests in costumes he had brought back from China where he took part in the suppression of the Boxer revolt.

Should you want to **stay**, the *Hippocampe* on rue Duvivier near place Colbert is about the cheapest, while the two-star *Hôtel de France* at 55 rue du Dr-Pelletier (☎46.99.34.00) also has some cheaper rooms. The **campsite** – *Camping municipal* – is a long haul if you've arrived at the **gare SNCF**. Take av du Président-Wilson and keep going straight, until you reach the bottom of rue Toufaire, where you turn right, then left – about half an hour all the way. For **eating**, the *Self-Service* by the Arsenal on rue Toufaire or *l'Etalon* on the same street are adequate and convenient. The **SI** and **gare routière**, if you need them, are both off rue du Dr-Pelletier.

Brouage, Marennes and the oysterbeds

Eighteen kilometres southwest, **BROUAGE** is another seventeenth-century military foundation, this time created by Richelieu after the siege of La Rochelle. From the map it appears to be sited in the sea. It is surrounded by salt marshes, now reclaimed and transformed into meadows grazed by white Charolais cows and intersected by dozens of reed-filled drainage ditches where herons watch and yellow flags bloom. It's a strangely beautiful landscape with huge skies specked with wheeling buzzards and kestrels.

To reach it, leave Rochefort by D733 ROYAN, which crosses the Charente river near the disused **Pont Transbordeur**, a great iron gantry with a raft-like platform suspended on hawsers, on which a dozen cars were loaded and floated across the river. In its time it was a technological wonder. There, either turn right for SOUBISE and MOEZE or go on to ST-AGNANT. Flat as a pancake, it is good country for cycling and walking.

The way into Brouage is through the **Porte Royale** in the north wall of the totally intact fortifications. Locked within its 400m square, it seems abandoned and somnolent. Even the sea has retreated and all that's left of the harbour are the partly fresh-water pools or *claires* where oysters are fattened in the last stage of their rearing.

Within the walls, the streets are laid out on a grid pattern, lined with low, two-storey houses. On the second cross street to the right is a memorial to **Samuel de Champlain,** the local boy who founded the French colony of Québec in 1608. In the same century Brouage also witnessed the last painful pangs of a **royal romance**. Here, Cardinal Mazarin, successor to Richelieu, locked up his daughter, **Marie Mancini,** to keep her from her youthful sweetheart, the Sun King, **Louis XIV.** Geopolitics of the time made the Infanta of Spain a more suitable consort for the king of France than his daughter – in his own judgment. Louis gave in, while Marie pined and sighed on the walls of Brouage. Returning from his marriage in St-Jean-de-Luz, Louis dodged his escort and stole away to see her. Finding her gone, he slept in her room and paced the walls in her footsteps.

Half a dozen kilometres south, on a narrow, drier spit of land, past the graceful eighteenth-century **Château de la Gataudière** built by the man who introduced rubber to France, you come to the village of **MARENNES**. It's the centre of **oyster production** for an area which supplies over 60 percent of France's supply. If you want to visit the oysterbeds, and see how the business works, you can do so here; just ask any of the local **SIs**. For

accommodation in the village, there's a **youth hostel** (☎46.85.22.78; open July and Aug. only) and the very agreeable and inexpensive *Hôtel du Commerce*, with a restaurant, on rue de la République (☎46.85.00.09)

Oysters

Marennes' speciality is fattening the oysters known as *creuses* – the other, tastier, type being the *plates*. It's a lucrative but precarious business, extremely vulnerable to storm damage, changes of temperature or salinity, the ravages of starfish and umpteen other improbable natural disasters.

Oysters begin life as minuscule larvae, which are 'born' about three times a year. When a 'birth' happens, a special radio service alerts the oystermen, who all rush out to place their 'collectors' – usually arrangements of roofing tiles – for the larvae to cling to. There they remain for eight or nine months, when they are scraped off and moved to *parcs* in the tidal waters of the sea, sometimes covered, sometimes uncovered. Their last move is to the *claires* – shallow rectangular pools where they are kept permanently covered by water less salty than regular sea water. Here they fatten up, and acquire the greenish colour the market expects. The whole cycle takes about two years with 'improved' modern oysters, as opposed to four or five with the old ones.

The Ile d'Oléron

The **ILE D'OLERON** is France's largest island after Corsica. It's up the road from Marennes, joined to the mainland by a toll bridge. Flat and more wooded than the Ile de Ré, with extensive pine woods at BOYARDVILLE and ST-TROJAN, it has miles of beautiful **sandy beaches**, the water rather shallow on the east coast facing the mainland. The little towns, inevitably, have been ruined by the development of hundreds of holiday homes – and it can be a real battle in the summer season to find a place to stay.

The **interior** is pretty and distinctive. Waterways wind right into the land, their gleaming muddy banks overhung by round fishing nets suspended from ranks of piers. There are so many oyster *claires* that, from above, the island must look like an Afghan mirrored cushion. With its pines, tamarisks, and woods of evergreen oak, the stretch from Boyardville to ST-PIERRE is the most attractive and St-Pierre is the best of the towns. Boyardville has no interest except for the ranks of *bouchots* – stakes for growing mussels – all along the shore. It's tempting to help yourself, but these are private property and you'll be in trouble if someone sees you.

Royan and the Gironde

Before World War II, **ROYAN** was a fashionable resort for the bourgeoisie. It is still popular, though no longer exclusive and the modern town has lost its elegance to the dreary rationalism of 1950s town planning: broad boulevards, car parks, shopping centres, planned greenery. Ironically, the occasion for this planners' romp was provided by Allied bombing, an attempt to dislodge a large contingent of German troops who had withdrawn into the area after the

D-Day landings. The **beaches**, however, are beautiful: fine pale sand, meticulously harrowed and raked near town, and wild, pine-backed and pounded by the Atlantic to the north.

There is also one sight worth seeing in Royan – the 1950s **cathedral** designed by Gillet and Hébrard, in a tatty square behind the main waterfront. Though the concrete has weathered badly, the overall effect is dramatic and surprising. Tall V-sectioned columns give the outside the appearance of massive fluting with a stepped roof-line rising dramatically to culminate in a 65m bell-tower like the prow of a giant vessel. The **interior** is even more striking. Using uncompromisingly modern materials and designs, the architects have succeeded in out-Gothicking Gothic. The **stained glass** panels, in each of which a different tone predominates, borrow their colours from the local seascapes – oyster, sea, mist and murk – before a sudden explosion of colour in the Christ-figure above the altar.

Accommodation in the town is expensive and, in season, short in supply. Your best bet would be to camp up the coast to the north or visit for the day from Saintes or Rochefort. The most interesting way to arrive is on foot: two days from Saintes on the **GR4**, via Brouage. The **SI** and **PTT** are close to the Rond-Point-de-la-Poste at the east end of the seafront; **gare routière** and **gare SNCF** in nearby cours de l'Europe. **Bike hire** from the SNCF or the bike shop in cours de l'Europe near the SI. Various **cruises** are also organised from Royan in season, including one to the **Cordouan lighthouse** commanding the entrance to the Gironde, first erected by the Black Prince. There's a twenty-minute **ferry** crossing to the Pointe de Grave, from where a **cycle trail** and the GR8 head down the coast to the bay of Arcachon .

Talmont

An ideal bike/picnic excursion – just over an hour's ride from Royan – is to **TALMONT** (on the GR360), 16km south on the shore of the Gironde. Apart from a few ups and downs through the woods outside Royan, it is all level. **Talmont church** (12C), clustered about its low-crouching village, stands at the edge of a cliff above the Gironde. Gabled transepts, a squat tower, an apse simply but elegantly decorated with blind arcading, the stone a tawny, warm colour, weathered and pocked like a sponge – in sun or cloud it stands magnificently against the forlorn brown or grey seascapes typical of the Gironde. Entrance is through the north transept, where the rings of carving in the arched doorway depict acrobats standing on each other's shoulders and, in the outer braid, two tug-of-war teams hauling roped lions up the arch. Inside is as simply beautiful as out.

THE CHARENTE

It is hard to believe that the peaceful fertile valley of the **river Charente**, which has given its name to the two modern *départements* that cover much of this chapter, was once a busy industrial waterway, bringing armaments from **Angoulême** to the naval shipyards at **Rochefort**. Low ochre-coloured farms crown the valley slopes, with green swathes of vineyard sweeping up to the walls. The turrets of minor châteaux poke from the woods, the properties of wealthy cognac-producers. The towns and villages may look old-fashioned, but the prosperous shops and classy new villas on the outskirts are proof that where the grape grows, money and modernity are not far behind.

The valley itself is easy to travel as the main road and railway to Limoges run this way. North and south, Poitiers, Périgueux (for the Dordogne) and Bordeaux are also easily reached by train. Otherwise, for cross-country journeys, you are heavily reliant on your own transport or patient hitching.

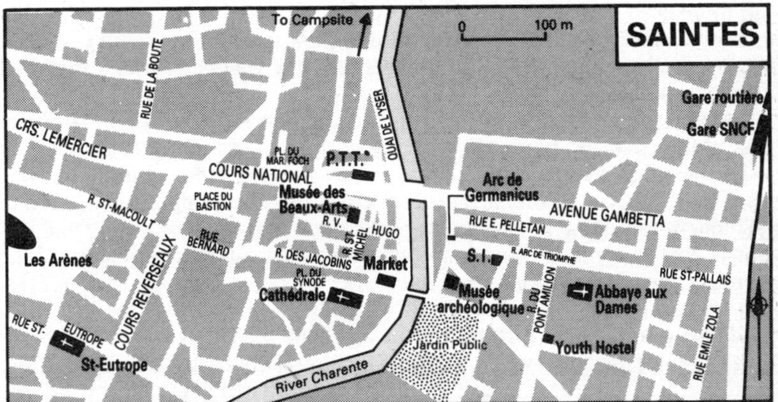

Saintes

SAINTES has been much more important than its present size suggests. Today a busy market for the surrounding region, it was capital of the old province of Saintonge and a major administrative and cultural centre in Roman times. It still sports some impressive remains from that period, as well as two beautiful Romanesque pilgrim churches and an attractive centre of narrow lanes and medieval houses. It also has the doubtful distinction of being the birthplace of Dr. Guillotin, who advocated execution by decapitation.

The modern town is bisected by av Gambetta and the cours National. Arriving by train you'll find yourself on av de la Marne at the east end of av Gambetta, with several cheap **hotels** in the vicinity. A right turn on av Gambetta will take you to the river Charente, where another right on the further bank leads to the riverside **Camping municipal** on rue de Courbiac. Other accommodation options are the **youth hostel** (6 rue Pont-Amilion; ☎46.92.14.82) and the *Hôtel St-Pallais* (place St-Pallais; ☎46.92.51.03), both to the left of av Gambetta near the abbey. The abbey church, the **Abbaye-aux-Dames**, is as quirky as Notre-Dame in Poitiers. It stands back from the street in a sanded courtyard behind the smaller Romanesque church of St-Pallais. An elaborately sculpted doorway masks a plain, broad interior space roofed with two big domes, evocative of a barefoot, vigorous faith. Its rarest feature is a tower, flanked with pinnacles and by turns square, octagonal and lantern-shaped, capped with the Poitou pinecone. It was built in the eleventh century.

From here rue Arc-de-Triomphe brings you out on the **riverbank** beside the **SI** and an imposing **Roman arch** that originally stood on the bridge until it was demolished in the nineteenth century to make way for the modern one. It is not in fact a triumphal arch, though it looks like one. It was dedicated to the emperor Tiberius, his son Drusus and nephew Germanicus in 19 A.D. And there is an **archeological museum** (10–noon and 2–6; winter Suns., 10–noon only; closed Tues.) next door with a great many more Roman bits and pieces, mostly rescued from the fifth-century city walls into which they had been incorporated.

A footbridge crosses from this point to the covered **market** on the west bank of the river and **place du Marché** at the foot of the rather uninspiring **cathedral of St-Pierre**, which began life as a Romanesque church, but was significantly altered in the aftermath of damage inflicted during the Wars of Religion, when Saintes, like La Rochelle, was a Huguenot stronghold. Its enormous, heavily buttressed tower, capped by a hat-like dome instead of the intended spire, is the town's chief landmark.

In front, the lime trees of **place du Synode** stretch away to the municipal buildings, with the old quarter up to the right and the Hôtel Martineau library in the rue des Jacobins with an exquisite central courtyard full of trees and shrubs. Back towards the bridge, a seventeenth-century mansion on rue Victor-Hugo houses the **Musée des Beaux-Arts** (10–noon and 2–6pm; closed Tues.), containing a collection of local pottery and some unexciting paintings.

If you continue along rue des Jacobins, past the library and up the hill to the Capitol, with an impressive view back over the cathedral tower, you eventually come to the broad **cours Reverseaux**. To the left the road dips downhill through an avenue of trees with a steep little valley on the right. Two signs advise you to see the concierge if you want to visit **Les Arènes**, the Roman arena, whose ruins you can see at the head of this valley. The conventional approach is from rue St-Eutrope, past the church and right on rue Lacurie. Much more interesting, but involving an illicit scramble over the fence, is straight down the path into the valley bottom.

The arena – in fact, an **amphitheatre** – is dug into the end of the valley. Dating from the early first century, it is one of the oldest surviving. Most of the seats are grassed over, but it is still evocative. You can easily imagine the echoes of the alien Latin mingling with some local Gaulish patois all those centuries ago, when Saintes had twice its present population.

On the way back from the amphitheatre, it's no extra trouble to take in the eleventh-century church of **St-Eutrope**. It is really two churches. The upper one, which lost its nave in 1803, has some brilliant **capital-carving** in the old choir – best seen from the gallery. But it's the **crypt** – entered from the street

– which is more atmospheric and primitive. Massive pillars carved with stylised vegetation support the vaulting in semi-darkness. There is a huge old font and the third-century tomb of Saintes' first bishop, Eutropius himself.

Practicalities

For **eating**, there are two good **restaurants** on riverside place Blair, a **crêperie** on rue Victor-Hugo and a couple more cheap places in the transverse rue St-Michel. Out of town, the *Restaurant de la Charente* (☎46.11.00.73), 10km away at CHANIERS and the Sunday haunt of prosperous locals, would make a more expensive but much more fulfilling gastronomic experience.

If your plan is to move on to COGNAC, you might consider getting there by river, on one of the SI's summer boat trips.

Aulnay and other churches

If you have a car there are several marvellous Romanesque churches within easy reach of Saintes, notably FENIOUX to the north towards St-Jean-d'Angely and RIOUX to the south. There is also the fine château of ROCHE-COURBON off the Rochefort road.

But car or no car, one place worth any amount of trouble to get to if you are into Romanesque is the twelfth-century pilgrim church of **St-Pierre** at **AULNAY**. Without your own transport, the simplest route there is by train from Saintes to ST-JEAN-D'ANGELY, a journey of 25 minutes. St-Jean has some pretty old houses, but is not worth a stop in its own right. Thereafter you have to hitch. After 3km on the Poitiers-Angoulême road, take the left fork for Aulnay on D950: St-Pierre is off to the right before you reach the town.

Aulnay church's **finest sculpture** is on the west front, south transept and apse. On the former, two blind arches flank the central portal. The tympanum of the right depicts Christ in Majesty; the left, St Peter crucified upside down with two extraordinarily lithe and graceful soldiers balancing on the arms of his cross to get a better swing at the nails in his feet. On the **south side**, the doorway is decorated with four bands of even more intricate carving. The **apse** too is a beauty, framed by five slender columns and lit by three perfectly arched windows, the centre one enclosed by figures wrapped in the finest twining foliage. **Inside** as well, there is extraordinary carving: capitals depicting Delilah cutting Samson's hair, devils pulling a man's beard, human-eared elephants, bearing the Latin inscription '*Hi sunt elephantes*', 'These are elephants' – presumably for the edification of the ignorant locals. **Outside**, in the cemetery, is a *croix hosannière*, so-called because on Palm Sunday the priest and congregation would re-enact Christ's entry into Jerusalem, with the priest reading the story while the congregation filed past laying branches by the cross and crying 'Hosanna'.

And if you are in a car, you might as well also visit one or all of NUAILLE-SUR-BOUTONNE, 9km west of Aulnay, or the even nearer ST-MANDE or SALLES-LES-AULNAY, with humbler but, in their way, equally charming churches of the same period.

Cognac

Anyone who does not already know what **COGNAC** is about will quickly nose its quintessential air as they stroll about the medieval lanes of the riverside quarter. For here is the greatest concentration of *chais* or warehouses, where the precious liquid is matured, its fumes blackening the walls with tiny fungi. Cognac is cognac, from the tractor-driver and pruning-knife-wielder to the manufacturer of corks, bottles and cardboard boxes. Untouched by recession (80 percent of production is exported), it will thrive as long as the world has sorrows to drown – a sunny, prosperous, respectable, self-satisfied little place.

The simplest way of **getting there** is by train – 20 minutes from Saintes, 45 minutes from Angoulême. From the **gare SNCF**, go down rue Mousnier, right on rue Bayard, past the **PTT**, up rue du 14-Juillet, with a good supermarket and the reasonably priced *Sens Unique* restaurant, to the central **place François Ier**, dominated by an equestrian statue of the king rising from a bed of begonias. There are a couple of **cafés** and a **brasserie** on the square. The **SI** is close by, where you can ask about visiting the various *chais*, the St-Gobain glass works (second biggest bottle-maker in Europe) and river trips – upstream through the locks to JARNAC is particularly beautiful.

From the north side of the square, **rue d'Angoulême** leads past shops specialising in those archetypal French frivolities – pastries and ladies' knickers – to the **market** square overlooked by the tower of St-Léger (entrance on rue Aristide-Briand). Straight on down, you come to **Grande-Rue** winding through the old quarter to the *chais*. On the right is all that remains of the château where King Francois Ier was born in 1494.

To the left are the *chais* and offices of the **Hennessy cognac** company. Like the other main **warehouses** they are open, free, from 9 to 11am and 2 to 5pm except weekends; only *Polignac* and *Otard* open on weekends, and then only in July and August. The consensus is that Hennessy are the best to visit – a seventh-generation family firm of Irish origin. The first Hennessy, an officer in the Irish brigade serving with the French army, hailed from Ballymacnoy in County Cork. He gave up soldiering in 1765 to set up a little business here.

The **Hennessy visit** begins with a film explaining what's what in the world of cognac. Only an *eau de vie* distilled from grapes grown in a strictly defined area can be called cognac and this stretches only from the coast at La Rochelle and Royan to Angoulême. It is all carefully graded according to soil properties: chalk essentially. The inner circle, from which the finest cognac comes – Grand Champagne and Petite Champagne (not to be confused with bubbly) – lies mainly south of the Charente River.

Hennessy alone keep 180,000 barrels in stock. All are regularly checked and various *coupages* or blendings made from barrel to barrel. Only the best is kept. And what is the best? That – and, in effect, the whole enterprise – depends on the tastebuds of the *maître du chais*. For six generations the job has been in the same family – an interesting genetic refinement for the Darwinian. The present heir apparent has already been sixteen years under his father's tutelage and is not yet fully qualified.

Upstream from the bridge, the oak woods of the **Parc François 1er**, where there's **swimming** in the river or a pool, stretch along the riverbank to the **Pont Chatenay** and the town **campsite**. As for **rooms**, the cheapest are *Tourist Hôtel* (166 av Victor-Hugo – the Angoulême road; ☎45.82.09.61) and *Le Cheval Blanc* (6–8 place Bayard; ☎45.82.09.55). For something a bit more expensive and more comfortable, try: *La Résidence* (25 av Victor-Hugo; ☎45.32.16.09) or *L'Etape*, a little further out on N141 at 2 av d'Angoulême (☎45.32.16.15).

Around Cognac

There are several attractive **walking possibilities** around Cognac. The best is the **towpath** or *chemin de hâlage* which follows the true left bank of the Charente upstream to **Pont de la Trâche**, then on along a track to BOURG-CHARENTE, with an excellent **restaurant** called *La Ribaudière* at the bridge and a Romanesque church – about three hours all in all. A byroad leads back to ST-BRICE on the other bank, past sleepy farms and acres of shoulder-high vines. From there another lane winds up the hill and over to the **ruined abbey** of CHATRES, abandoned amid brambles and fields about 3km away. Alternatively, at the hamlet of RICHEMONT, 5km northwest of Cognac, you can swim in the pools of the tiny **river Antenne** below an ancient church on a steep bluff lost in the woods.

Angoulême and the road to Limoges

The cathedral city of **ANGOULEME** turned Christian in the third century under the influence of Ausonius, a Gallo-Roman landed gent, poet and saint. It was heavily fought over in the Anglo-French squabbles and again in the Wars of Religion – another Protestant stronghold. After the revocation of the Edict of Nantes, a good proportion of its citizens – among them many of its skilled papermakers – emigrated to Holland, never to return. Marguerite de Valois, sister of François Ier, author, and one of the 'characters' of French royal history, was born here.

The **old town** occupies a steep-sided plateau overlooking a bend in the Charente. Its scruffy labyrinthine streets, only just beginning to undergo gentrification, fit every foreigner's stereotype of what a French working-class neighbourhood should look like. The papermills which employed the workers and made the city's prosperity are now almost completely defunct.

On the southern edge of the plateau stands the **cathedral**, whose west front, like Notre-Dame at Poitiers, is a fascinating display board for some very expressive and lively **medieval sculpture**, most of it twelfth-century and culminating, as ever, in a Risen Christ with angels and clouds about his head, framed in the habitual mandorla. The **frieze** beneath the tympanum to the right of the west door is interesting. It commemorates the recapture of Spanish Zaragoza from the the Moors and shows on the left a bishop transfixing a Moorish giant with his lance, and, on the right, Roland killing the Moorish king who, having invited Charlemagne to his aid, refused to let him into his city, thus forcing him to make the retreat that led to the massacre of his rearguard by the Basques above St-Jean-Pied-de-Port. Unfortunately much of the rest of the building has suffered from the attentions of the reviled Abadie and his desire to rediscover the pure Romanesque by destroying everything that followed it.

From the front of the cathedral, you can **walk** all around the **ramparts** encircling the plateau, with long views over the surrounding country, largely filled with urban sprawl now. There are **public gardens** below the parapet at the far end and a gravelly esplanade by the lycée where locals gather to play *boules*.

The facts

Angoulême is easily accessible **by train**: 45 minutes from Cognac, 50 minutes from Limoges and an hour from Poitiers. There is a branch office of the **SI** outside the **gare SNCF**, from which av Gambetta, with the **gare routière** and several cheap if unprepossessing **hotels**, leads uphill to the town centre through **place Pérot**. Try *Hôtel Le Crab* (27 rue Kléber; ☎45.95.51.80) or *Hôtel de la Paix* (place de l'Hôtel-de-Ville) among the cheapest rooms or – a little pricier – *Hôtel de la Bourse* (place Gérard-Pérot; ☎45.92.06.42) and *Hôtel du Palais* (4 place Francis-Louvel; ☎45.92.54.11).

Alternatively, there is a **youth hostel** (☎45.92.45.80; with canteen) on an island in the Charente. Turn right at the first lights on av Gambetta, cross the railway bridge and go right again down to the river. Cross by the footbridge and the hostel is on your left. **Camping municipal** is nearby, beyond the Pont de Bourgines.

For additional information consult the very friendly **SI** in the Hôtel de Ville. They will provide, among other things, route details for **walks** in the area: *circuits pédestres*. Angoulême **festivals** include a brief jazz blow at the beginning of June, and in February – unique and rather wonderful – the *Bande Dessinée*: a convention of comics from politics to pornography – high art in France.

Beyond Angoulême

There are two interesting places west of Angoulême on the way to Limoges – La Rochefoucauld and Confolens.

LA ROUCHEFOUCAULD (15km) is on bus and train routes. By road you pass through RUELLE, now an Exocet-missile-manufacturing centre, formerly a naval armaments foundry, specialising in casting gun-barrels, which were shipped down the Charente to the yards at Rochefort.

La Rochefoucauld itself is the site of a huge Renaissance **Château** on the banks of the river Tardoire, which still belongs to the family that gave its name to the town. It is only open in August, when there is a brigade-sized cast for the *son et lumière*. Unfortunately, you cannot quite see the courtyard, the château's best architectural feature, from outside. Two **hotels**, if you need them are: *Hôtel de France* (13 Grand-Rue; ☎45.63.02.29) and *Vieille Auberge* (Faubourg La Souche; ☎45.62.02.72). **Camping municipal** is on rue des Flots.

CONFOLENS is about 40km further (buses from Angoulême). Travelling by train, it's better to go to ST-JUNIEN on the Limoges line and hitch back. West of Angoulême the country becomes hillier and more wooded, with buttercup pastures grazed by liver-coloured Limousin cows. You enter the valley of the **river Vienne** and Confolens is on the left bank, a quiet town of ancient houses climbing a hill above the river (*Hôtel de Vienne*, 4 rue de la Ferrandie; ☎45.84.09.24; and *camping municipal*). Its chief claim to fame today is an **International Folklore Festival**, held every year in the second and third weeks of August.

LIMOGES AND THE LIMOUSIN

The **Limousin** – the country around Limoges – is hilly, wooded, wet and not overly fertile: ideal pasture for the famous Limousin breed of cattle and, higher up to the east, for sheep. Herdsman's country; whence, presumably, the widespread use of the shepherd's cape called a *limousine* gave its name to the big, wrap-around, covered twentieth-century car.

The only town of any consequence in the region is **Limoges** itself, whose turn-of-the-century reputation for revolutionary workers' politics struck terror in bourgeois hearts. While you're on an axis between Limoges and another significant town, transport presents no problem. Off such axes, however, you have to find your own solutions. An obvious and agreeable one is a bike, but be warned that in the beautiful eastern half of the province the climbs are long and steep towards the **Plateau de Millevaches**. A satisfying rural route would be to follow the course of the **river Vienne** – easier, of course, if you start from the source above **Eymoutiers** and move downstream.

Limoges

LIMOGES is not a city that strikes you as calling for a long stay. It is worth a look, however, for a magnificent railway station and the craft industries which made its name a household word: **enamel** in the Middle Ages and, since the eighteenth century, some of the finest **china** ever produced. If these appeal, then the city's unique museum collections – and its Gothic cathedral – will reward a visit. But it has to be said that the industry today seems a spent tradition. It has been hit hard by recession and changing tastes among the rich; also the local kaolin (china clay) mines are now exhausted. The workshops survive mainly on the tourist trade.

The best of the museums – with its showpiece collections of **enamel ware** from the twelfth century on – is the **Musée Municipal** (10–11.45pm and 2–6pm in summer, 5pm in winter; closed Tues. except in July and Aug.) in the old Bishop's Palace and gardens overlooking the Vienne. There's an interesting progression to be observed here, though to my taste the best stuff is the earliest, the *champlevé*. Done on copper plate, with the enamel filling hollowed-out designs, this is simple, sober and Byzantine in influence. The later work, especially the seventeenth and eighteenth centuries, is much

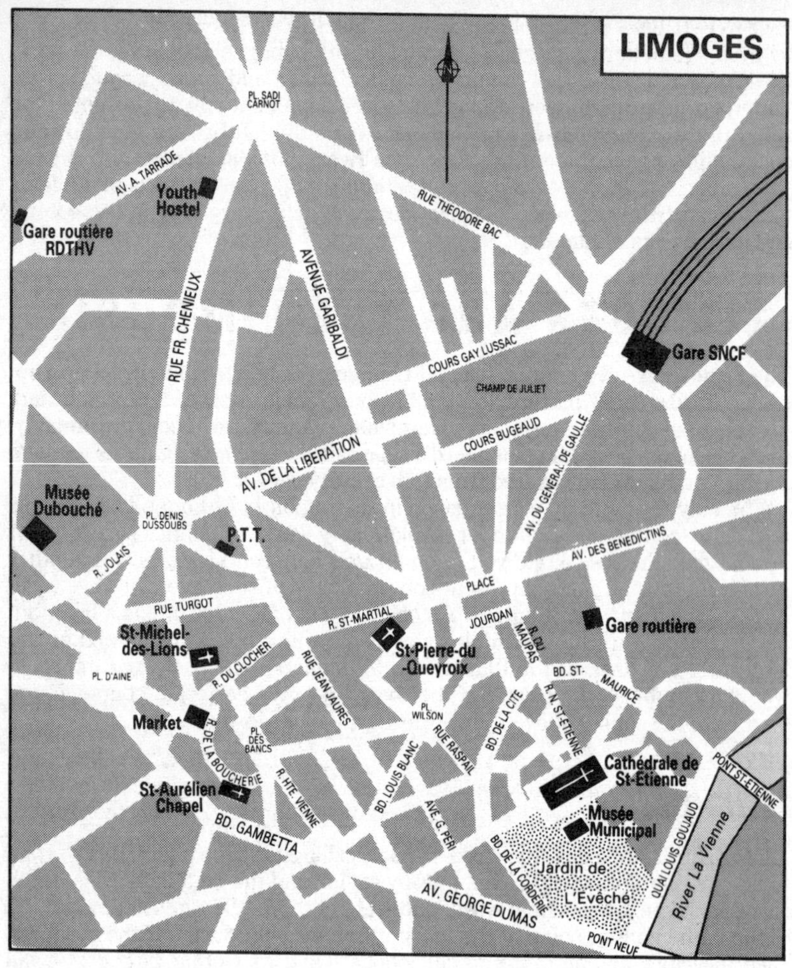

more exuberant, the range of colours far greater, the portraiture amazing. In the nineteenth century it seems to have lost all style, however, and though there are contemporary artisans in the city working in the medium, their work, too, judging from this display, is not much more successful.

For collections of the **porcelain**, along with extensive representative china displays from around the world, continue to the **Musée Adrien Dubouché** (10–noon and 1.30–5pm; closed Tues.), off place Winston-Churchill and close to **place Dussoubs**, the centre, such as it is, of café life and street activity. Various celebrity services are included: Napoléon, royalty, Charles and Di . . . The exhibits are well laid out, with explanatory panels describing the processes for making the different wares – much more interesting than you might expect. And if your interest is sufficiently aroused, the **SI** (bd de Fleurus) can arrange visits to a number of active workshops.

Opposite the municipal museum is the city's **cathedral** of St-Etienne. Begun in 1273, it was planned on the model of the cathedral of Amiens, though only the choir, completed in the early thirteenth century, is pure Gothic. The rest of the building was added in bits and pieces over the centuries, the western part of the nave not until 1876. The most striking external feature is the sixteenth-century **façade of the north transept**, built in full Flamboyant style with elongated arches, clusters of pinnacles and delicate tracery in window and gallery. The doors are carved with scenes from the lives of St-Etienne (St-Stephen) and St-Martial.

At the west end of the nave the **tower**, which was erected on a Romanesque base that had to be massively reinforced to bear the weight, has octagonal upper storeys, in common with most churches in the region. It once stood as a separate campanile and probably looked the better for it. **Inside**, the effects are much more pleasing. The rose stone looks warmer than on the weathered exterior. The sense of soaring height is accentuated by all the upward-reaching lines of the pillars, the net of vaulting ribs, the curling, flame-like lines repeated in the arcading of the side chapels and the rose window, and, above all, as you look down the nave, by the narrower and more pointed arches of the choir.

Over to the west of the cathedral is the **old quarter** of the town, partly renovated. Make your way through to **rue de la Boucherie**, for 1000 years the domain of the Butchers' Guild (with several good but pretty expensive restaurants). The dark, cluttered chapel of **St-Aurélien** with a fourteenth-century butter cross outside belongs to them. At the top of the street is the **market** in **place de la Motte** and to the right, partly hidden by adjoining houses, the church of **St-Michel-des-Lions** (fourteenth to fifteenth centuries), named after the two badly weathered Celtic lions guarding the south door. It's got one of the best towers and spires in the region. The **inside** is dark and atmospheric, with two beautiful densely-coloured fifteenth-century windows either side of the choir; one – in the south aisle – depicting the Tree of Jesse.

From place de la Motte, rue du Clocher leads to rue Jean-Jaurès, with the **Post Office** a couple of blocks up to the left. Straight across, **rue St-Martial** leads past the car park on place de la République, where the fourth-century crypt of the long-vanished **abbey of St-Martial** (July–Sept. 30 only, 9.30–noon and 2.30–5pm) was discovered during building operations in 1960 to the church of **St-Pierre-du-Queyroix**, whose belfry was the model for the cathedral and St-Michel. The interior, partly twelfth-century (the exterior was remodelled in the 16C), has a sombre strength from the massive round pillars which still support the roof. Like St-Etienne it has a slightly pink granite glow. There is a fine window at the end of the south aisle depicting the Dormition of the Virgin, signed by Jean Pénicault, one of the great enamel artists, in 1510.

Practicalities

Limoges has numerous **hotels** in the streets on both sides of Champs-de-Juillet in front of the railway station. There is a very clean and hospitable **youth hostel** in the *Foyer des Jeunes Travailleuses* (own room, and canteen; ☎55.77.63.97) on the tiny rue Encombe-Vineuse to the right off rue Chenieux south of **place Carnot**, with a useful **launderette** close by on av Labussière. Rue Chenieux has a couple of good brasseries.

The **gare SNCF** has rail connections to almost anywhere you might think of going. **Departmental buses** leave from **place des Charentes** on av Adrien-Tarrade (also off place Carnot); private buses from the **gare routière** on rue Gide near the railway station.

Around Limoges: Oradour and Limousin villages

The villages below are all within an easy day's reach of Limoges. Solignac can be reached on foot. And you'll need the walk from Oradour to the train station to recover from the macabre shock of the ruined village.

Oradour-sur-Glane

Twenty-five kilometres northwest of Limoges, the village of **ORADOUR-SUR-GLANE** stands just as the soldiers of the SS *das Reich* Division left it on June 10, 1944, after killing all the inhabitants in reprisal for attacks by French *maquisards*. It seems irreverent to approach it as a 'sight'; perhaps it should be seen more as a shrine.

There are **buses** from place des Charentes in Limoges, but the timetable is pretty inconvenient. The best thing is to take a **train** to ST-VICTURNIEN on the Angoulême line, about 25 minutes; you can get there and back in a day. Then walk the 7km to Oradour, in 1½ to 2 hours.

St-Victurnien is a tiny village on the Vienne, with a **hotel** and **campsite** (open only in season). Turn right out of the station, through the village and up a wooded hill past meadow and hedge to N141: 2km. Cross straight over and continue 5km through quiet, woody country with orchids and Lady's Smock in the verges, buttercups and asphodels in the pasture. You might get a lift, but there is very little traffic. Turn left at the next main road, and **Oradour** is in front of you, a modern village built beside the old, with a 1950s concrete church trying, but failing, to be impressive – and it would be difficult to devise an architectural space commensurate with the task of commemorating, forgiving and transcending that dreadful act.

A gate into **the old village** admonishes: '*Souviens-toi*. Remember'. The village street leads past roofless houses gutted by fire. Telephone poles, tram cables and gutters are fixed in tormented attitudes where the fire's heat left them. Pre-war cars rust in the garages. A yucca, grown into an enormous clump, still blooms in the notary's garden. Last year's grapes hang wizened on a vine whose trellis has long rotted away.

Behind the square is a **memorial garden**, a plain rectangle of lawn hedged with beech. A dolmen-like slab on a shallow plinth covers a crypt containing relics of the dead, and the awful list of names. Beyond, by the stream, stands the church where the women and children – five hundred of them – were burnt to death.

St-Léonard-de-Noblat

ST-LEONARD-DE-NOBLAT, 25 minutes by train from Limoges on a branch line, is a small market town of narrow streets and medieval houses with jutting eaves and corbelled turrets and a very lovely **church** (11–12C), whose six-storey tower looks out over the rising hills and woods where the river Vienne threads its course down from the heights of the Massif Central. The interior too is strong and simple: barrel vaults on big, square piles, a high dome on an octagonal drum, domed transepts – the whole in grey granite.

To **hitch** out of Limoges in this direction, take bus #1 from place Carnot, across Pont-Neuf to the last stop on the St-Léonard-Bourganeuf-Aubusson road.

Chalusset and Solignac

South of Limoges, infrequent trains down to Brive stop at the station of SOLIGNAC-LE-VIGET: closest point of access to the ruined castle of Chalusset and the abbey of Solignac, in the wooded valley of the Briance. This is perhaps the most attractive day excursion you could make from Limoges – and, if you're feeling energetic, you could even forget the trains and walk the whole way (13km to Solignac; 19km if you hike to Chalusset, too, and back). If you decide to do this, cross the Vienne in Limoges by the Pont St-Martial and take the back road to Solignac. If hitching, leave by Pont-Neuf on the Brive–Toulouse road. Turn right after a few hundred metres and continue uphill out of town. After 6km take the St-Yrieix turning on the right. It is 6km from there down into the green valley of the Briance at LE VIGET.

The twelfth-century **CHATEAU DE CHALUSSET**, which the English held during the Hundred Years War, is 4km on from here, up a lane to the left. At the highest point of the climb, about 40 minutes from Le Viget, an iron belvedere in the wood on the right of the road gives a dramatic view across the valley to where the ruined keep rises above the trees. To get there, turn downhill to the right for 1km until you cross the Briance. Opposite the end of the bridge a path climbs up to the castle. It's about an hour from Le Viget and an hour back.

SOLIGNAC is a 15-minute walk to the other side of Le Viget. You can see the **abbey** ahead of you with the tiled roofs of its octagonal apse and neat little brood of radiating chapels. The twelfth-century façade is plain with just a little sculpture; the granite of its construction of does not permit the intricate carving of limestone. Inside it is beautiful. A flight of steps leads down into the nave with a dramatic view the length of the church. There are no aisles, just a single space roofed with two big domes. No ambulatory either; an absolutely plain Latin cross in design. It is a simple, sturdy church, with the same feel of plain robust Christianity as the crypt of St-Eutrope in Saintes.

travel details

Trains

From Poitiers to Châtellérault (frequent; 20 min.); Paris-Austerlitz (frequent; 2 hr. 50 min.); Niort (frequent; 1 hr.), Surgères (frequent; 1 hr. 25 min.);La Rochelle (frequent; 1 hr. 45 min.); several daily to Angoulême (1 hr.), Bordeaux (2 hr. 10 min.), Dax (3½ hr.), Bayonne (4 hr.), Biarritz (4½ hr.), St-Jean-de-Luz (4 hr. 40 min.), Hendaye (4 hr. 55 min.) and Irun (5 hr. 5 min.) – all stops on the same line; Limoges (several; 2½ hr.).

From Les Sables-d'Olonne to Nantes (several; 1½ hr.) and Paris-Montparnasse (several; 4 hr. 45 min.).

From La Rochelle to Nantes (several; 1 hr. 50 min.); Bordeaux (several; 4 hr. – via Rochefort and Saintes).

From Royan to Angoulême (frequent; 2 hr.) via Saintes (40 min.) and Cognac (1 hr.).

From Angoulême to Limoges (4 daily; 1½–2 hr.).

From Limoges to Paris-Austerlitz (frequent; 3½–4 hr.); Poitiers (4 daily; 2–2¼ hr.); St-Léonard-de-Noblat (5; 25 min.); Eymoutiers (5; 50 min.); Meymac (3; 1 hr. 50 min.); Ussel (3; 2 hr.); Brive (frequent; 1 hr. 10 min.).

Buses

From Poitiers to Parthenay (several SNCF; 1–1½ hr.); Châteauroux (3 daily; 3½ hr.) via Chauvigny (35 min.), St-Savin (1 hr.), Le Blanc (1 hr. 25 min.); Ruffec (1 daily; 2½ hr.); Limoges (1 daily; 3 hr.).

From Parthenay to Thouars (several SNCF; 1 hr.) via Airvault (25 min.); Niort (several; 50 min.).

From Les Sables d'Olonne to Luçon (4 SNCF; 2 hr.); Nantes (4 SNCF; 5½ hr.) – both via the coast road.

From Saintes to St-Denis-d'Oléron (2 daily; 2 hr.).

CHAPTER SEVEN

BORDEAUX, DORDOGNE, THE LOT

This is the south without the aridity of the Mediterranean. Steamy and moist and green, it can feel like a kind of lower-latitude England – which is no doubt why it attracts so many urban Brits in search of the good life and that charming little farmhouse second home. In the Dordogne heartlands, the country is certainly beautiful, but the regional authorities are all too well aware of their assets, hyping up the landscape, caves, food, wine, churches, medieval towns as hard as they can go. The result is that the famous spots, especially in the Dordogne valley, are oppressively crowded in season. Nothing, however, should deter you from seeing the prehistoric cave paintings at **Les Eyzies** or the quieter **Pech-Merle** on the Lot. And the whole area, heavily contested by the English and French during the Hundred Years' War, is scattered with **ruinous castles** like **Bourdeilles**, **Beynac** and **Bonaguil**, and **bastides** – the small military settlements constructed by both sides to secure their respective patches. **Monpazier** is the best preserved, lying like the above-mentioned castles on the cross-country route of the **GR36**.

Several other **GRs** (marked footpaths) bisect the central and eastern parts of the region, and if you're into **walking**, these – or a **bike** – are the best way to get around. The **landscape** is small-scale and detailed, just right for slow travelling, and the hills are not too strenuous either, until you get up into the wilder foothills of the Massif Central to the northeast beyond Brive.

The **towns**, both the smaller ones like **Périgueux**, **Bergerac**, **Brive** and **Cahors** and even **Bordeaux** itself, are not really sufficiently interesting to hold your attention beyond a brief stay, though they are **useful as bases** to work out from in a region with notoriously bad **public transport**. If your interest is primarily in the region's **wine**, a car is virtually essential – though you can scratch the surface staying in Bordeaux and reaching the better-known vineyards on one or more of its SI tours. For those interested in ecclesiastical architecture, there is rich fare throughout the region, especially in the **Romanesque sculpture** at **La Sauve Majeure, Beaulieu, Souillac** and, above all, **Moissac.**

And talking of rich fare, the Dordogne has **the richest regional cuisine** in the country, thanks to the preference for goose fat over any other cooking medium and the widespread use of *confits* – preparations of cooked meats preserved in their own juices. But it is renowned too for its *foie gras*, truffles, *cèpes* or wild mushrooms, *cabécou* (goat cheese), *coq au vin*, stuffed poultry,

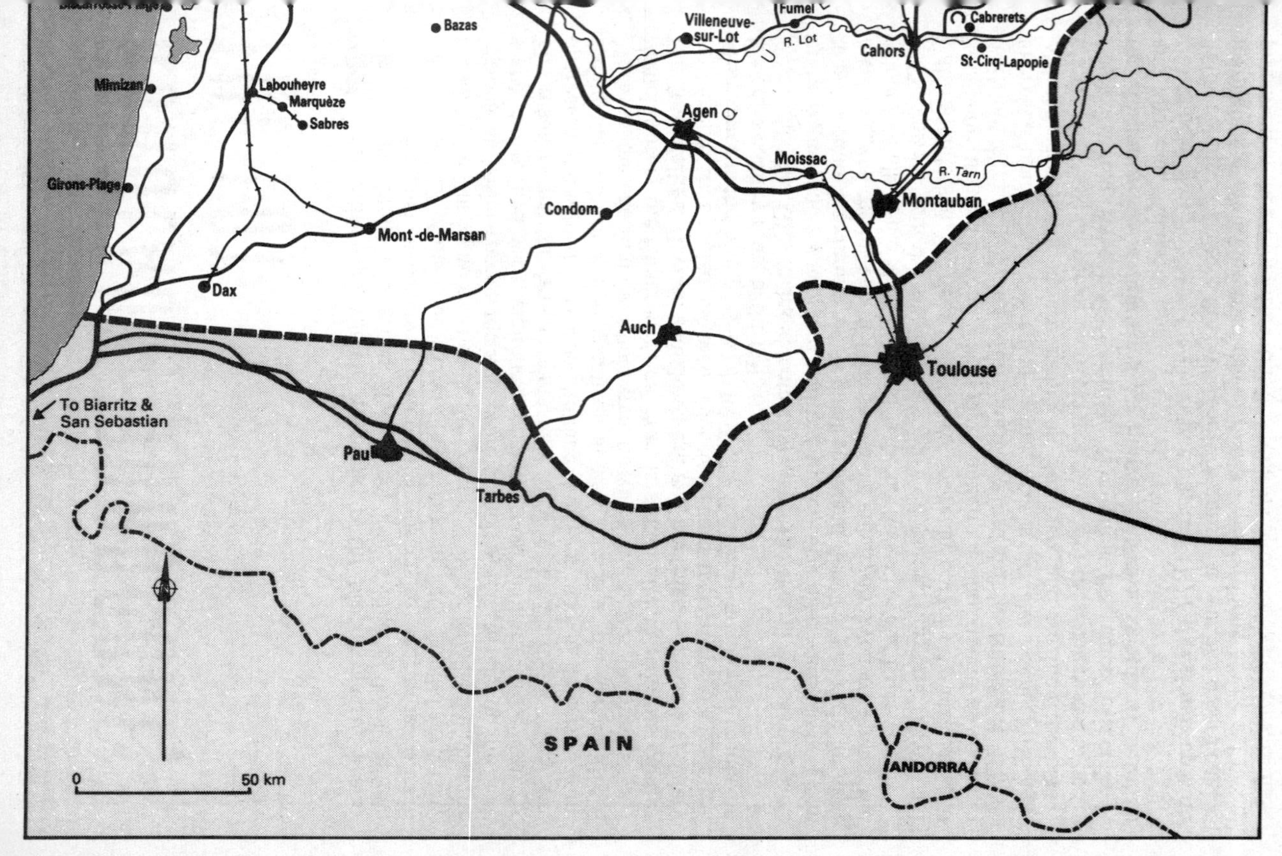

Bazas
Fumel
Villeneuve-sur-Lot
R. Lot
Cabrerets
Cahors
St-Cirq-Lapopie
Mimizan
Labouheyre
Marquèze
Sabres
Agen
Girons-Plage
Moissac
R. Tarn
Condom
Montauban
Mont-de-Marsan
Dax
Auch
Toulouse
To Biarritz & San Sebastian
Pau
Tarbes
SPAIN
ANDORRA
0
50 km

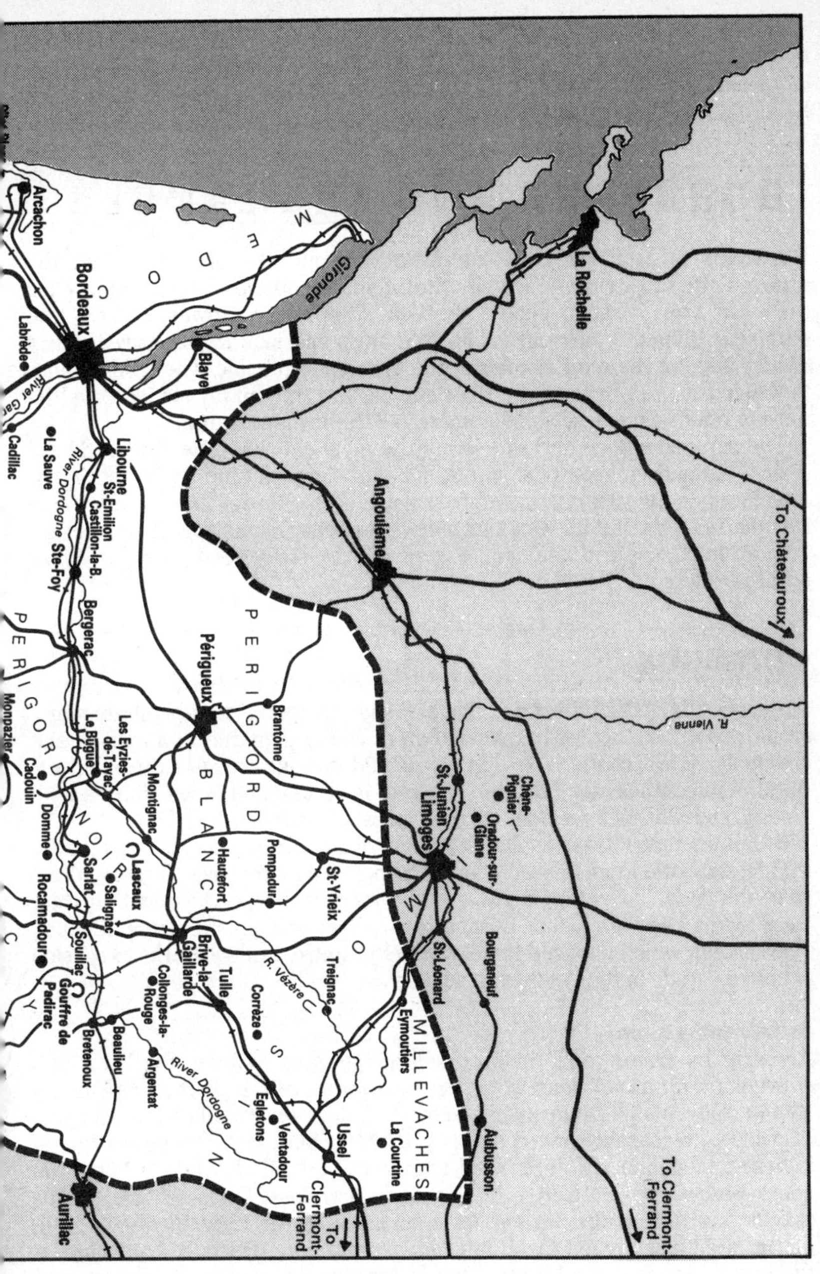

La Rochelle
To Châteauroux
R. Vienne
To Clermont-Ferrand
Arcachon
Bordeaux
Labrède
Cadillac
La Sauve
Blaye
Gironde
M E D O C
Libourne
St-Emilion
Castillon-la-B.
Ste-Foy
River Dordogne
Bergerac
Angoulême
Périgueux
Brantôme
P E R I G O R D B L A N C
P E R I G O R D N O I R
Le Bugue
Les Eyzies-de-Tayac
Montignac
Lascaux
Cadouin
Monpazier
Domme
Sarlat
Salignac
Souillac
Rocamadour
Gouffre de Padirac
Bretenoux
Beaulieu
Hautefort
Pompadur
St-Yrieix
Limoges
St-Junien
Chêne-Pignier
Oradour-sur-Glane
St-Léonard
Bourganeuf
Brive-la-Gaillarde
Collonges-la-Rouge
Tulle
Corrèze
R. Vézère
Treignac
Eymoutiers
Argentat
River Dordogne
Egletons
Ventadour
Ussel
La Courtine
Aubusson
MILLEVACHES
L I M O U S I N
Q U E R C Y
To Clermont-Ferrand
Aurillac

walnut oil, walnut salad, walnut preserves and the custom of *faire chabrol*, that is, pouring red wine into the remnants of your soup and slurping the delicious sludge directly from the bowl, formerly considered a low-class peasant habit but gaining ground among gourmets.

BORDEAUX AND THE LANDES

Bordeaux is probably most interesting if you have an entrée into the **student life** of its large university. But if you are just passing through – it's the main transportation centre between Paris and northwest Spain – the particular things to look out for are the city's spacious **eighteenth-century centre** and the **regional museum,** the Musée d'Aquitaine. The seedier quarters along the left bank of the river and around the railway station have the most to offer with markets and numerous **ethnic restaurants.**

The surrounding countryside is not the most enticing. The **vineyards** are mainly flat and monotonous: you go for the wines, not the landscape. More interesting is the vast pine-covered expanse of the **landes** and the huge wild Atlantic beaches. But it is not a landscape that charms. Its appeal, like desert, is more in its size and uniqueness. And you definitely need your own transport to explore it.

Bordeaux

The city of **BORDEAUX** is a puzzle and something of a disappointment for a casual visitor. It's big, with a population of nearly a quarter of a million, and obviously rich. Yet the only part you could call attractive is the relatively small eighteenth-century centre. The rest is scruffy and, even with its long history, contains far fewer 'sights' than many a lesser place.

In Roman times it was capital of the province of Aquitania Secunda. In the Middle Ages the English used it as the principal base for their three-hundred-year Aquitanian adventure and it was to their presence, and particularly their taste for its red wines, that Bordeaux owed its first great economic boom. The second, which financed the elegant city centre, came with the expansion of colonial trade in the eighteenth century.

Arrival and a room

Arriving by train, you'll find yourself at the **gare St-Jean**, the heart of a convenient if insalubrious area for **accommodation.** Right outside the station, rue Charles-Domecq and cours de la Marne are full of one- and two-star hotels, reasonably priced but no great treat to stay at. The **youth hostel** is here too, signposted *Foyer des Jeunes* to the left off cours de la Marne on cours Barbey (☎56.91.59.51); it's big and charmless. Further hostel rooms may be available at the *Maison des Etudiantes*, 50 rue Ligier (☎56.96.48.30), on the right just beyond the eighteenth-century arch, **Porte d'Aquitaine**, at the end of cours de la Marne. Mainly for women, it will also accept men during the summer. There are a lot of cheap **eating** places in the quarter too, as well as the **Marché des Capucins**. If, however, you prefer to stay in less seedy surroundings, you'll have to go into the town centre. There's a concentration of cheap hotels in rue du Temple: *Cazassus* (☎56.81.69.54) at no. 32, *Centre* (☎56.48.13.29) at no. 8, and *Trianon* (☎56.48.28.35) at no. 5. Other possibilities are the *Dauphin* (☎56.52.24.62) at 82 rue du Palais-Gallien and *La Boétie* (☎56.81.76.68) at 4 rue de la Boétie by the Beaux-Arts museum.

The town centre

Bus #7/8 links the *gare* to **place Gambetta**, a pivotal stop for museums, shops, cathedral. But, free of bags, it's more fun to walk, either north from Marché du Capuchins via rue Leyteire or rue de Mirail (good drinking places off to the left on place Augustine) or via the church of **St-Michel**, with its colossal 114-metre tower, nearer to the river and in the midst of a run-down ethnic area with **cheap eating.** Either way you'll come out on cours Victor-Hugo, in the middle of which is a heavy Gothic tower, the **Grosse Cloche**, originally part of the medieval townhall. A largely North African market sets up here on Sundays. Under the tower, rue St-James, with more cheap ethnic restaurants, goes down to cours Alsace-Lorraine. From here, just to the left, you get onto pedestrian **rue Ste-Catherine**, clean and modern and one of the main shopping streets.

This is the beginning of elegant – or at least once-elegant – Bordeaux, especially the streets to the right towards the river. Some have been done up, some are incongruously seedy, the haunts of alcoholics and prostitutes. Particularly pleasing is **place du Parlement** and the even more imposing **place de la Bourse** with the old customs house and stock exchange on the riverside. If you take a right on place du Parlement along rue du Parlement-St-Pierre and rue des Argentiers you come to the waterfront again at the fifteenth-century **Porte Cailhau**, so named for the stones – *caillou: cailhau* in the local dialect – unloaded on the neighbouring quay for ballast. Apart from a few sleazy bars the quays are nothing more than a lifeless stretch of road now. The **Pont de Pierre** just upstream – pink brick, in fact, and built at Napoléon's command during the Spanish campaigns, with seventeen arches in honour of his victories – and the eighteenth-century **Porte de Bourgogne** alone testify to a nobler past.

The real hub of the eighteenth-century city was the impeccably classical **Grand Théâtre** on **place de la Comédie** at the end of rue Ste-Catherine. Built in 1780 by the architect Victor Louis, it is faced with an immense colonnaded portico topped by Muses and Graces. From here, smart streets radiate out. Sanded and tree-lined **allées de Tourny** leads to a statue of Tourny, the eighteenth-century administrator who was prime mover of the city's Golden Age. **Cours du 30-juillet** (**SI** on the right) leads into the **Esplanade des Quinconces**, said to be Europe's largest municipal square, with an enormous memorial to the Girondins, the influential local deputies to the Revolutionary Assembly of 1789, purged by Robespierre as moderates and counter-revolutionaries. **Cours de l'Intendance** (Goya died at no. 57), full of chic shops, links up with **place Gambetta**.

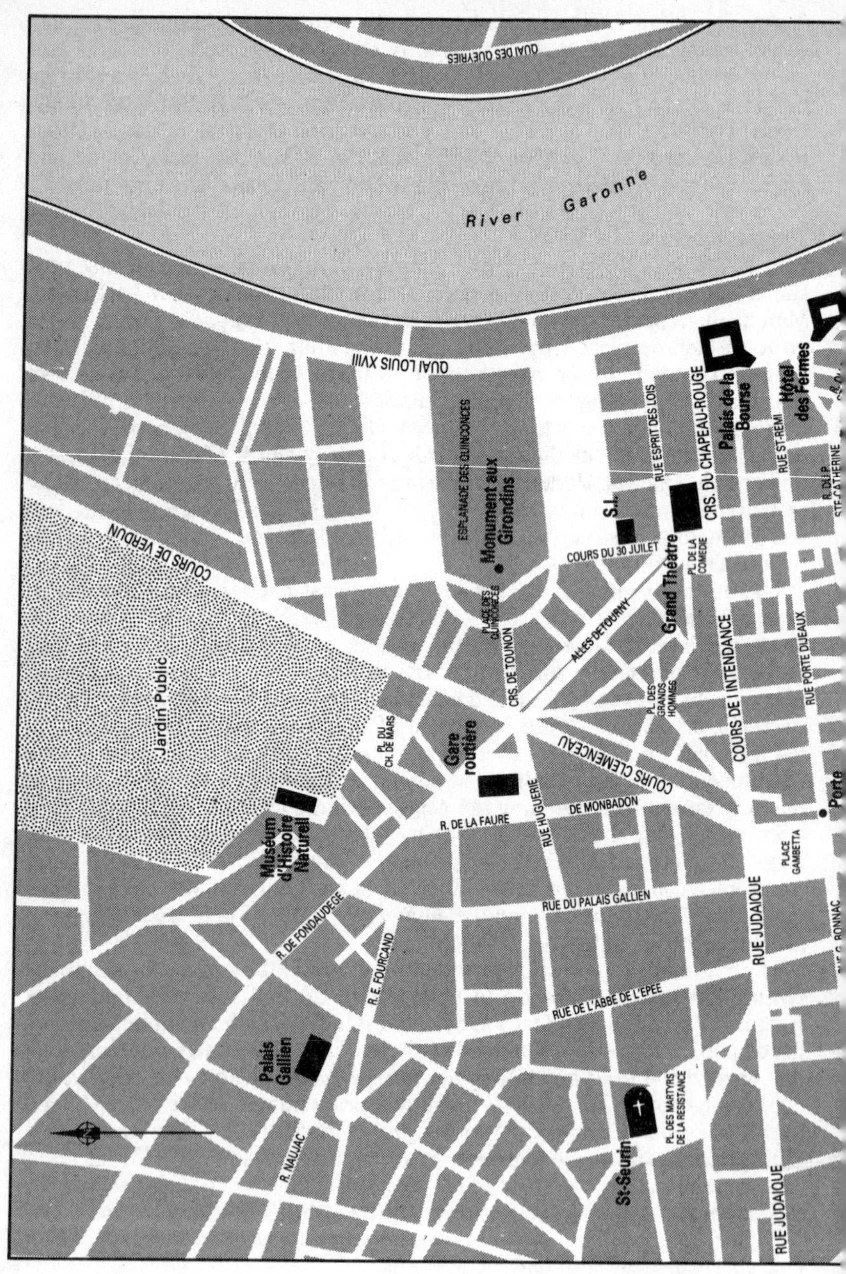
QUAI DES QUEYRIES
River Garonne
QUAI LOUIS XVIII
ESPLANADE DES QUINCONCES
Monument aux Girondins
PLACE DES QUINCONCES
S.I.
RUE ESPRIT DES LOIS
CRS. DU CHAPEAU-ROUGE
Palais de la Bourse
RUE ST-REMI
Hôtel des Fermes
R. DU P. STE-CATHERINE
COURS DU 30 JUILLET
PL. DE LA COMEDIE
Grand Théâtre
ALLES DE TOURNY
CRS. DE TOUNON
PL. DES GRANDS HOMMES
COURS DE l'INTENDANCE
RUE PORTE DIJEAUX
COURS DE VERDUN
Jardin Public
PL. DU CH. DE MARS
Gare routière
COURS CLEMENCEAU
RUE HUGUERIE
DE MONBADON
R. DE LA FAURE
Porte
PLACE GAMBETTA
Muséum d'Histoire Naturell
RUE DU PALAIS GALLIEN
R. DE FONDAUDEGE
R. E. FOURCAND
RUE JUDAIQUE
RUE DE L'ABBÉ DE L'EPEE
Palais Gallien
PL. DES MARTYRS DE LA RESISTANCE
St-Seurin
R. NAUJAC

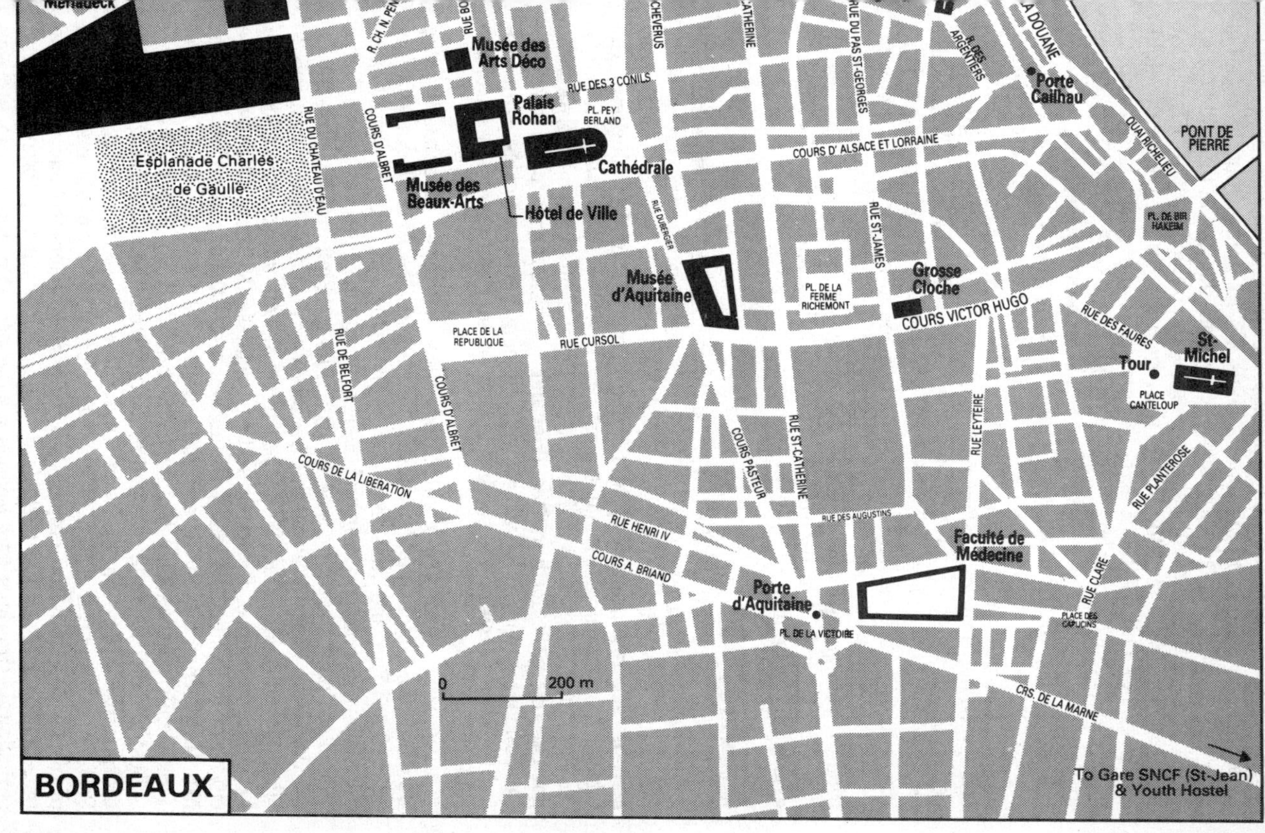
Meriadeck
Musée des Arts Déco
RUE BO
R. CH. N. PEN
RUE DES 3 CONILS
Palais Rohan
PL. PEY BERLAND
Esplanade Charles de Gaulle
RUE DU CHATEAU D'EAU
COURS D'ALBRET
Cathédrale
Musée des Beaux-Arts
Hôtel de Ville
CHEVERUS
CATHERINE
RUE DU PAS ST-GEORGES
R. DES ARGENTIERS
LA DOUANE
Porte Cailhau
QUAI RICHELIEU
PONT DE PIERRE
COURS D' ALSACE ET LORRAINE
PL. DE BIR HAKEIM
RUE DUBERGIER
RUE ST-JAMES
Grosse Cloche
Musée d'Aquitaine
PL. DE LA FERME RICHEMONT
COURS VICTOR HUGO
RUE DES FAURES
St-Michel
Tour
PLACE CANTELOUP
PLACE DE LA REPUBLIQUE
RUE CURSOL
RUE DE BELFORT
COURS D'ALBRET
RUE LEYTEIRE
COURS PASTEUR
RUE ST-CATHERINE
RUE PLANTEROSE
COURS DE LA LIBERATION
RUE DES AUGUSTINS
RUE HENRI IV
Faculté de Médecine
COURS A. BRIAND
RUE CLARE
Porte d'Aquitaine
PLACE DES CAPUCINS
PL. DE LA VICTOIRE
0
200 m
CRS. DE LA MARNE
BORDEAUX
To Gare SNCF (St-Jean) & Youth Hostel

Café-lined, the *place* is the city's pivot: a once majestic square, conceived as an architectural whole in the time of Louis XV. Its house fronts, arcaded at street level, are decorated with rows of carved masks, and in the middle a so-called English-style garden soaks up some of the traffic fumes. The guillotine lopped 300 heads here at the time of the revolution. In one corner the eighteenth-century arch of the **Porte Dijeau** spans the street, and at no. 32 there's an English bookshop, *Bradley's*, with a fair selection of English and French language textbooks, as well as a bulletin board for job ads.

Northwards, the broad **cours Clemenceau** – good for bookshops – takes you to the public gardens and left via rue Fondaudège to the broken down **amphitheatre**, Palais Gallien, all that remains of Aquitania's Roman capital. Southwest, down rue du Dr-Pénard, is Bordeaux's acknowledgement of twentieth-century architectural fashions, the **Centre Mériadeck**. Herald of a brighter future to some Bordelais, and a carbuncle to others, it hands its streets over to the car and elevates its humans to mid-air plazas and walkways. Despite some interesting shapes and textures, it's not very user-friendly; your most likely welcome will be an embrace around the legs by yesterday's windblown newspaper. The main **PTT** and **Poste Restante** is nearby on rue Bonnac.

Museums

South from the *place* are the city's main museums and the **cathedral** of St-André, whose most eye-catching feature is the great upward sweep of the twin steeples over the north transept, an effect that is heightened by the adjacent but separate campanile, the fifteenth-century **Tour Pey Berland.** The interior is not particularly interesting apart from the **choir**, which is one of the few complete examples of the Gothic Rayonnant style, and there's some fine **carving** in the north transept door and the Porte Royale to the right. The surrounding square is attractive with enticing pavement cafés – the old-fashioned *La Musée* on the south side, and another on the west by the classical Hôtel de Ville.

A similarly handsome eighteenth-century house in neighbouring rue Bouffard, the Hôtel Lalande, houses the **Musée des Arts Décoratifs** (pm only; closed Sun. and Tues.; free Wed.). The collections include some beautiful, mainly French, porcelain and faïence, furniture, glass, miniatures, Barye animal sculptures and prints of the city in its maritime heyday. Just around the corner on cours d'Albret, the **Beaux-Arts** museum (10am–noon and 2–6pm; closed Tues.; free Wed.) has a small and unexciting collection of Perugino, Veronese, Delacroix, Rubens, Matisse, Marquet (a native of the city). Smaller still is the Resistance museum and archive, the **Centre Jean-Moulin** (2–6pm; closed Sat. and Sun.), on the corner of rue Vital-Carles and Trois-Conils, one block north of the cathedral.

Best of the city's museums, and no further from the cathedral, the **Musée d'Aquitaine** (10am–6pm; closed Tues.; free Wed.) is now at 20 cours Pasteur. Imaginatively laid out with a stimulating variety of objects and types of display, the museum emphasises regional ethnography and covers the three main facets of the region's development: maritime, commercial and agricultural. Drawings and writings on the period enable you to see why eighteenth-century Bordeaux was so extolled by contemporary writers, who compared it to Paris. Take a look at the section on the wine trade before venturing off on a vineyard tour.

Some practicalities

Airlines *British Air*, galerie Frantel, Mériadeck (☎56.81.24.59); *Air France*, 29 rue Esprit-des-Lois (☎56.44.64.35). **Airport** Bordeaux-Mérignac, 10km west of the city (☎56.34.84.84): connected on weekdays by half-hourly shuttle to and from the SI (40 min.).

Bike hire from gare SNCF and *Cycles Pasteur*, 42 cours Pasteur.

Buses Tickets are available on the buses, but it's cheaper to buy packs of ten from a *tabac*. You must 'punch' your ticket on the bus; then it is valid for half an hour, even if you change bus and direction. The **gare routière** for out of town is on rue Fondaudège near place Tourny.

Consulates UK, 15 cours de Verdum (☎56.52.28.35; Mon.–Fri. 9–12.30pm and 2.30–5pm); Canada, Immeuble Croix-du-Mail, 8 rue Claude-Bonnier (☎56.96.15.61; Mon.–Fri., 9am–12.30pm and 1.30–4.45pm); USA, 22 cours du Maréchal-Foch (☎56.52.65.92; Mon.–Fri., 9am–noon and 2–6pm).

Food For delicatessen-type produce, as well as the usual fruit and vegetables, there is a marvellous round covered **market** near the church of Notre-Dame behind cours de l'Intendance. Or for a plain wholesome **meal** – and terrace drink – try the very popular *Café des Arts* on the corner of rue Ste-Catherine and cours Victor-Hugo. For something a bit different, there's French **Antillaise** cooking at *Le Balafon*, 15 rue des Bahutiers, and – rather cheaper – *Les Coralies*, 72 rue du Loup, with exotic salads, both greenery and fruit. There is French regional cooking at the nearby *La Tanière*, also on rue du Loup, and **vegetarian** fare at *Nyoti* on the corner of place du Parlement and rue du Parlement-St-Pierre, with *La Huitière* oyster bar next door. *Baud Millet Fromagerie*, 13 rue Huguerie near the gare routière, on the other hand, offer you as much of their 100-plus cheeses as you can manage, for 43F – not after 11pm, though.

Hitching For a prearranged ride, *Allostop* is at 59 rue des Ayres (☎56.81.24.59). Operating under your own steam, take the following buses to get clear of the city: for Bergerac, bus #5, from just across the Pont de Pierre to the corner of av Clemenceau; for Paris, #92, from Porte Cailhau to Ambares; for Toulouse, #B, from place de la Victoire to the terminus; for Bayonne-Biarritz, #G, from place de la Victoire to the terminus.

Listings For details of events in the city, consult the regional daily paper, *Sud-Ouest*.

Money exchange On weekends you can change money at the SI (9am–noon and 2–6pm).

Swimming pools *Olympique*, Grand Parc; *Judaique*, 166 rue Judaique.

Wine For tours of the vineyards, ask the SI at 12 cours du 30-juillet, and for general information the *Maison du Vin* on the opposite side of the same street. Also, see below.

Wines and vineyards

With Burgundy and Champagne, the wines of Bordeaux form the Holy Trinity of French viticulture. The reds in particular – known as claret to the English – have graced the tables of the discerning for many a century. The country that produces them stretches north, east and south of the city, and is the largest quality wine district in the world.

North along the west bank of the brown, island-spotted Gironde estuary is **Médoc** and **Haut-Médoc** whose wines have a full-bodied, smoky taste and a reputation for improving with age. Across the Gironde – seven or eight ferries a day from LAMARQUE to Vauban-fortified BLAYE – the green slopes behind the river, the *côtes* of **Bourg** and **Blaye** were home to wine production long before the Médoc was planted. The wine is a rather heavier, plummier red, and cheaper than anything found on the opposite side of the river.

South of the city is the domain of the great whites, the super-dry **Graves** (reds too) and the sweet dessert wines of **Sauternes**, which get their flavour from grapes left deliberately late to rot on the vine. East, on the other side of the River Garonne, are the **Premières Côtes de Bordeaux,** which form the first slopes of the **Entre-Deux-Mers**, (far the prettiest country in the Bordeaux wine region), whose wines are regarded as good, but less fine than the Médocs and Graves – less fine also than the superlative reds of **Pomerol**, **Fronsac** and **St-Emilion** just to the north of the River Dordogne.

The Bordeaux SI has a leaflet detailing all the châteaux that allow visits and wine-tasting. Since, however, getting to any of these places except St-Emilion without your own transport is hard work, the simplest thing is to take one of the SI's own **tours** (leave 1.45pm from June to mid-Oct.). They are quite expensive, but are generally interesting and informative (English translation for the commentary). Either take pot luck or choose according to your taste in wines.

If you are interested in **buying wines,** it is possible to find bargains at some of the châteaux, but bear in mind that anything pre-1987 is likely to be cheaper in Britain. The advantages of buying at source include the opportunity of tasting the wines before purchasing, and the possibility of receiving expert advice about vintages and flavours. In town the best place to go is *200 Crus de Bordeaux* next to the SI. If in recent years tales of machine oil and chemical additives have shaken your confidence in wine-drinking, you can be comforted by the growing fashion for organic methods and 'green' wines, already available on many good labels.

The Médoc

The landscape of the **MEDOC** is rather monotonous: its gravel plains rarely swell into anything resembling a hill, but paradoxically, this poor, gravelly soil is ideal for viticulture. Vines root more deeply if they don't find the sustenance they need in the topsoil: firmly rooted, they are less subject to drought and flooding; while the stable conditions required by the plant are further ensured by the insulating properties of the gravel.

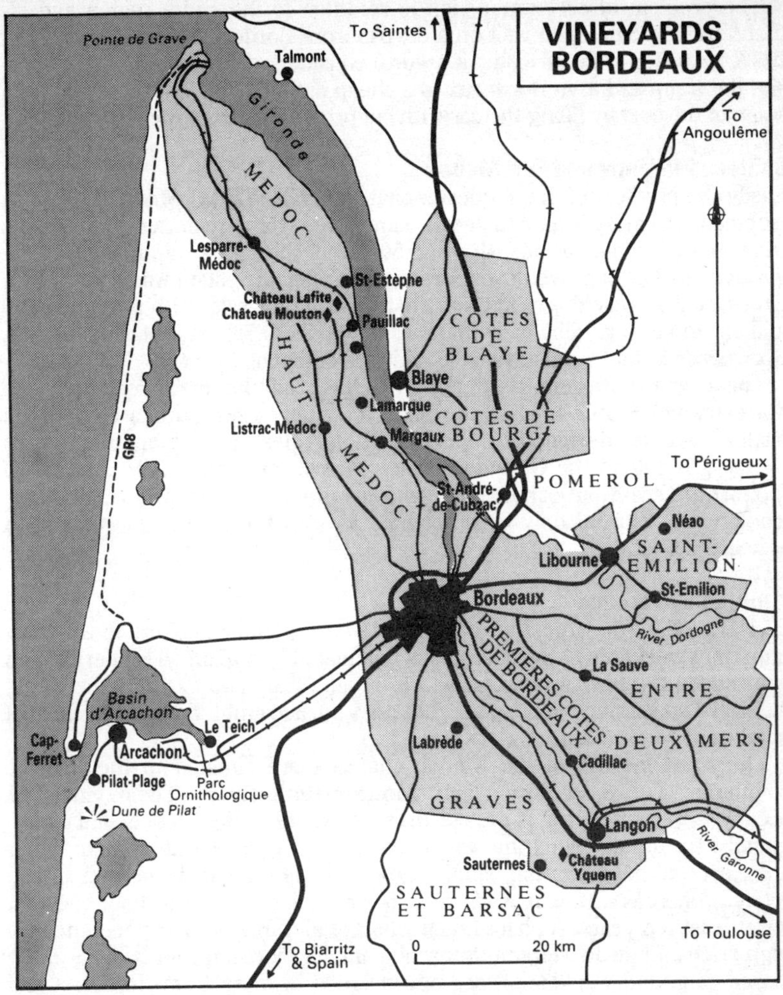

The wines of the Médoc châteaux were graded into five *crus*, or growths, in 1855. These were based on the prices the wines had fetched over the previous hundred years, and since then additional catagories have been added, for instance *Crus Bourgeouis Superieurs* or *Crus Paysans*. While a *Premièr Grand Cru Médoc* will always be an exceptional wine, the divisions between the five main *crus* tend to determine prices without necessarily reflecting quality and should not be taken too seriously.

The problem of accommodation is common to the entire region and it's therefore a good idea to visit on a daytrip from Bordeaux. There are regular *CITRAM* buses to Pouillac, but it's worth considering **car rental** (*Citer*, opposite the train station in Bordeaux is a cheap option). You will recoup at least some of the cost by filling the car with cut-price wines from the châteaux.

Château Margaux and Fort Médoc

Easily the prettiest of the Bordeaux châteaux, **CHATEAU MARGAUX** is an eighteenth century villa situated in extensive, sculpture-dotted gardens. Its wine, world famous in the 1940s and 50s, went through a rough patch in the 60s and 70s but improved over recent years after the estate was bought by a Greek family. Very discreetly, the château is up for sale, with a reputed £20 million price tag. Château Margaux (☎56.88.70.28) is not included in Bordeaux's SI tours and advance booking is essential.

The seventeenth-century **FORT MEDOC**, off the main road between Margaux and St Julien, is a good place to sample a few purchases between châteaux. It was designed by **Vauban**, the greatest military architect of his century, to defend the Gironde estuary against the British. The remains of the fort are scant but scramblable, and in summer its toytown aspect has a leafy charm, marred only by a splendid view of the nuclear power station across the river.

Pauillac and around

PAUILLAC is the largest town in the Médoc region and central to the most important vineyards of Bordeaux. It is dominated by a giant oil refinery which has caused the town's rapid growth in recent years and explains the bleak, industrial appearance of the place, but does not account for a severe dearth of hotels and good restaurants.

The most famous of the Médoc châteaux are situated in the Pauillac commune: **Lafite, Latour,** and **Mouton-Rothschild.** Their vineyards occupy larger single tracts of land than elsewhere in the Médoc, and consequently the qualities of the wines differ to a greater extent than other châteaux on neighbouring land: a good vintage *Lafite* is perfumed and refined, whereas a *Mouton-Rothschilde* is strong and dark, and should be kept for at least ten years. A shared distinction of all three is their phenomenally high prices. Château Mouton-Rothschild and its wine museum (☎56.59.22.22; closed Aug. and weekends), are not included in tours from Bordeaux and must be booked in advance.

Saint-Emilion

There are two distinct wine districts of St-Emilion: the **plateau** and the **Côtes de St-Emilion.** The product of the former are called Graves wines because of the gravelly soil in which they are grown. Côtes wines grow in alkaline soil which gives them added strength: they contain an average of 1% more alcohol than Médoc wines. The most famous wine of the region originates at **Château Ausone**, south of St-Emilion. The cellars (which can be visited) have been dug out of limestone directly beneath the vineyards.

The town

ST-EMILION itself is well worth a visit. Its old grey houses straggle down the south-hanging slope of a low hill, the green froth of vines pressing right to its walls and street ends. Many of the growers still keep up the old tradition of planting roses at the ends of the rows, which in pre-pesticide days served as an early warning system against infection, the idea being that the commonest bug, *oidium*, went for the roses first, thus giving you three days' notice of its intentions. If you are interested in seeing the vineyards, ask at the **Maison du Vin** at the top of the hill by the prominent belfry.

The belfry belongs to the rock-hewn **Eglise Monolithe** beneath it. Entry to the church is off a small square with a large locust tree in the middle, below the cliff on which the belfry stands. The visit starts in a dark hole in someone's back yard, supposedly the cave where Saint-Emilion lived a hermit's life in the eighth century. A rough-hewn ledge served as his bed and a carved seat as his chair, where, so you're told, barren women still come to sit in the hope of getting pregnant. Above is a half-ruinous Benedictine chapel that the Revolution converted into a barn. Fragments of frescoes include one of St-Valérie, patron saint of wine-growers. The church can only be visited in groups (tickets from the **SI** on place des Créneaux, also by the belfry. Tours operate from 9.45am to 12.30pm, and 1.45 to 6.30pm.)

On the other side of the yard, a passage tunnels beneath the belfry, where three chambers have been dug out of the soft limestone, used as ossuary and cemetery during the eighth to the eleventh century. In the innermost chamber, discovered by a neighbour enlarging his cellar some fifty years ago, a large tombstone bears the inscription: 'Aulius is buried between saints Valérie, Emilion and Avic'.

The **church** itself (9–12C) is an incredible place. Simple and huge, the entire structure, barrel-vaulting, great square piers and all, has been hacked out of the rock. The windows of Chartres cathedral were stored here for safekeeping during the war. The whole interior was painted once, but only faint traces survived the Revolution, when a gunpowder factory was installed in the church. These days, every June, the wine council – *La Jurade* – assembles here to evaluate the previous season's wine and decide whether each *viticulteur*'s produce deserves the '*appellation contrôlée*' accolade.

Behind the SI the town comes to an abrupt end with a grand view of the moat and old walls. To the right, is the Collegiate church of the Cordeliers with a handsome but badly mutilated doorway and a fourteenth-century cloister, which you have to consult the SI about visiting.

Entre-Deux-Mers

The landscape of **ENTRE-DEUX-MERS** or between-two-seas – so called because it is sandwiched between the tidal waters of the Dordogne and Garonne – is much more attractive than the other wine regions, with its gentle hills and scattered medieval villages. And it can be explored at least partly by public transport, should you feel like avoiding the SI tour.

The one place you should really try to get to is the **abbey of La Sauve Majeure** (usually one bus there and one back daily, but check carefully). You need about an hour and a half to do it justice. You can see the ruin as you approach. You will be dropped off in the middle of a tranquil valley of small vineyards and corn fields. Once it was all forest here, the abbey's name being a corruption of the Latin *silva major*, big wood. It was founded in 1079, and the treasure of what remains is the twelfth-century Romanesque apse and apsidal chapels and the outstanding **sculpted capitals** in the chancel. The finest are the historiated ones illustrating stories from the Old and New Testaments (Daniel in the lions' den, Delilah shearing Samson's hair etc), while others show fabulous beasts and decorative motifs. There is a **mini-museum** at the entrance (9am–noon and 2–6pm), with some excellent photos and keystones from the fallen roofs. But what makes the visit so worthwhile is not just the capitals themselves, but the remote, undisturbed nature of the site. If you had time, you could stroll over to the abbey's parish church, visible on the hill – just proceed up rue de l'Eglise.

If you're heading south from Entre-Deux-Mers, **ST-MACAIRE** and **LA REOLE** on the banks of the Garonne are good for a rest or food stop. St-Macaire still has its original gates and battlements; the Maison du Pays serves as *écomusée* and information centre on the region and its products.

Further south, the town of **BAZAS** has a laid-back, southern air. Its most attractive feature is the wide, arcaded cathedral square, **place de la Cathédrale**, overlooked by a lichenous grey **cathedral** that manages against all odds a harmonious blend of Romanesque, Gothic and Classical in its west front. Circling back towards Sauternes, you could pass through **UZESTE**, a quiet little place, where Pope Clement V – who controversially moved the Papacy to Avignon in the fourteenth century – erected the old church on the *place*; and then through neighbouring **VILLANDRAUT**, where Clement was born and built a colossal castle whose curtain walls and corner towers still stand beside the road.

The seaside and south

Summer weekends, the Bordelais escape en masse to **ARCACHON**, a seaside resort forty minutes' train ride across flat sandy forest. The beaches of white sand are magnificent, but crowded. The town, a sprawl of villas great and small, is expensive, though there are lots of **campsites**. If you're stuck, there's an **SI** to the left of the station on place Roosevelt. For the seafront, go straight ahead, past an **aquarium** run by Bordeaux University (9.30am–8pm June 1–Sept. 10; closed in winter).

Arcachon's chief curiosity is the **dune de Pilat**, at 114m the highest sand dune in Europe – a veritable mountain of wind-carved sand, about 8km down the coast. Buses leave from the **gare SNCF (bike hire)** every half hour in July and August – about five a day at other times. From the end of the line the road continues straight on uphill for about fifteen minutes. There is the inevitable group of stands selling ice cream, *galettes* and junk, and from the top a superb view of the bay of Arcachon and the forest of the *landes* stretching away to the south. There is also a great slide down to the sea – with a long haul back up.

At **LE TEICH** (gare SNCF), about 12km east of Arcachon in the southeast corner of the Bassin d'Arcachon, one of the most important expanses of wetlands remaining in France has been converted into a **bird sanctuary** (information from the *mairie* in Le Teich; admission normally 10am–6pm daily, March–Sept.).

The Landes

Travelling south from Bordeaux by road or rail, you pass for half a day through unremitting, flat, sandy pine forest. This is the **landes**. Until the nineteenth century it was a vast, infertile swamp, badly drained because of the impermeable layer of grit deposited by the glaciers of the quaternary age and steadily encroached upon by the shifting sand dunes of the coast. Today it supports over 2 million acres of trees.

At **MARQUEZE**, about 15km east of LABOUHEYRE on N10 from Bordeaux to Bayonne, the *Parc Naturel Régional des Landes de Gascogne* has created an *écomusée* (mid-June to mid-Sept., daily, 10.15am–5:40pm; offseason, Sat. 2.30–4.30pm and Sun. all day) to illustrate the traditional *landais* way of life, where shepherds clomped around the scrub on long stilts. A resuscitated steam train runs between Labouheyre and Sabres, stopping at the *écomusée* (June to Sept., several daily; check for other times of year). SNCF trains stop at Labouheyre on the Facture-Bayonne run; connections from Bordeaux to Facture.

PERIGORD BLANC

The northern half of the Dordogne *département*, the **Périgord Blanc** is named for the light, white colour of its rock outcrops. It is undulating, fertile, wooded country, rising in the north and east to the hills of **Limousin** and the edge of the **Massif Central**, which are also included in the section.

The regional capital is **Périgueux**, which because of its central position and relative ease of access makes the best base for the whole region. For the eastern periphery you are better off using **Brive**.

As throughout the region, the chief delights are off the main routes. The Dordogne is nothing if not rustic. So within the limitations of your means of transport, try to explore the lanes and villages. And it is worth trying to coordinate visits with **market days**, for then even places that otherwise seem dead – or dedicated to tourists – come to life with real people in from the farms to sell their produce.

Périgueux

PERIGUEUX is a busy and prosperous market for a province made rich by tourism and specialised farming – pleasant enough, but hardly compelling. If you arrive **by train**, you'll find there are a number of good cheap **hotels** right in front of the station: *Terminus* (☎53.53.48.19), *Midi* (☎53.53.41.06),

Voyageurs, and the one-star **Logis de France**, *Hôtel des Charentes* (☎53.53.37.10; closed mid-Dec. to mid-June), with an inexpensive restaurant. There's little to choose between them. Alternatively, there is **hostel accommodation** at the *Foyer des Jeunes Travailleurs* (☎53.53.52.05; canteen), *Résidence Lakanal*, bd Lakanal (follow the railway track to the right of the station to the far edge of town) and **camping** at *Barnabé-Plage* on the east bank of the River Isle and *l'Isle*, 3km out on the Brive road.

Old Périgeux

For the centre of town and the old quarter, which is still the only part really worth bothering with, head east and follow rues Mobiles-de-Coulmiers, then Président-Wilson with the **SI** in the transverse av d'Aquitaine – to **place Bugeaud.** Ahead of you, down rue Taillefer is the town's principal building, the **cathedral of St-Front**, its square, pineapple-capped belfry still surging far above the roofs of the surrounding medieval houses.

Unfortunately it's no beauty, having suffered, like Angoulême cathedral, from the zealous purist attentions of Abadie. The result is too white, too new, too regular, and the roof is spiked all over with ill-proportioned nipple-like projections serving no obvious purpose. 'A supreme example of how not to restore', Freda White tartly observed. Which is a pity, for it was one of the most distinctive Romanesque churches (1173) undertaken in France, modelled on St. Mark's in Venice and the Holy Apostles in Constantinople. Under the kitschy additions the Byzantine influence is still evident in the

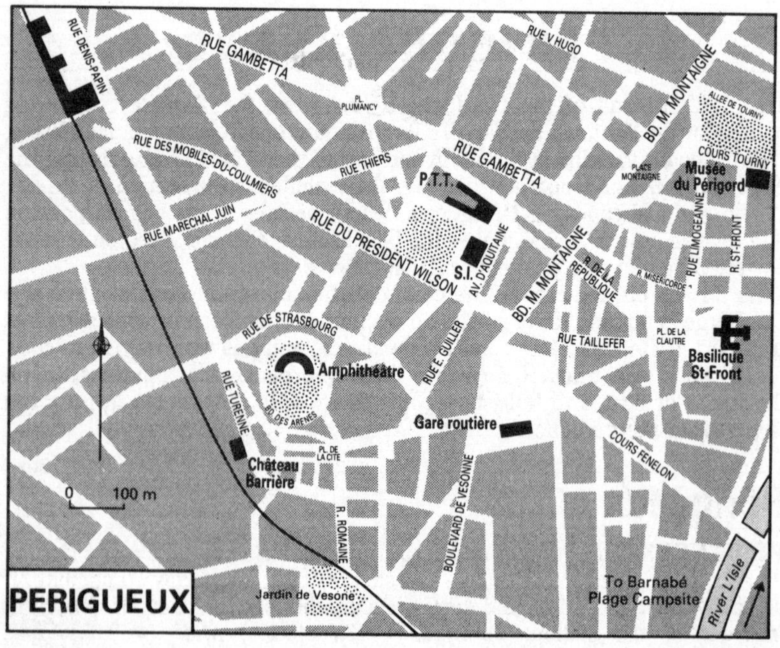

interior in the Greek-cross plan, most unusual in France, and in the massive clean curves of the domes and their supporting arches. The big Baroque **altarpiece** is worth a look too, depicting the Assumption of the Virgin, with a humorous little detail in the illustrative scenes from her life, of a puppy tugging the infant Jesus's sheets from his bed with its teeth.

At the west end of the cathedral in **place de la Claustre** beneath the blank facade of the original eleventh-century building there is a bi-weekly **market**, on Wednesday and Saturday. From the terrace below you look across to the wooded hills beyond the Isle, while north and south of the *place* crowd the renovated buildings of the **medieval quarter**. Limogeanne, St-Front, Eguillerie, Miséricorde, Constitution, Plantier: along these streets are scattered numbers of fine **Renaissance houses**, a particularly handsome one occupied by the Ministry of Culture at 3 rue de la Constitution, with the more sedate Hôtel de Crenoux next door. Another curious one is 17 rue de l'Eguillerie on the corner of the attractive place St-Louis, where a turretted watch-tower leans out over the street. There are other old houses down along the river by the Pont des Barris.

The **museum** (Musée du Périgord: 10am–noon and 2–5pm; closed Tues.) is in the area too, at the end of rue St-Front on the cours de Tourny, the limit of the old town. It has some very beautiful Gallo-Roman mosaics from local sites; under the name of Vesunna, Périgueux was a major provincial centre after the Roman conquest. There is an extensive but badly displayed prehistoric collection, again of local origin, and some exquisite Limoges enamels near the exit, especially portraits of the twelve Caesars.

For actual remains of the Roman heyday you have to go back to rue du Président-Wilson and take rue Duguesclin to the Jardin des Arènes, which conceals the ruins of an enormous **amphitheatre**, dismantled in the third century, while over by the railway at the end of rue Romaine a high brick tower, the **Tour de Vésone**, is the last vestige of a temple to the city's guardian goddess. More bits and pieces, chiefly jumbled masonry, are visible in the so-called Maison Romane and Porte Normande off rue Turenne, defensive works hastily cobbled together to keep the invading Visigoths at bay in the fourth century. The rather mutilated church – Huguenot anger – in this neighbourhood, on place de la Cité, is St-Etienne, the former cathedral.

Food and practicalities

There's no shortage of good **restaurants** in Périgueux, though they tend to the expensive. Exceptions, and good standbys, include *Lou Chabrol* (22 rue Eguillerie) and *Pizzeria Les Coupoles* (rue de la Clarté), both near the cathedral and both closed on Sunday and Monday. Also worth a try and nearby is the restaurant *Au Vieux Sarment*, through the courtyards between place Daumesnil and rue Limogeanne, at the further end of which *Le Point Chaud* is a good coffee/pastry stop.

Useful sources of information include the **CIJ** next to the SI in av d'Aquitaine and, if you're interested in **walking**, look in at the **GR office** at 15 av Lattre-de-Tassigny and ask for their booklet, *Randonnées Pédestres en Périgord*. Several GRs cross the area, among them: GR36, south to Les Eyzies and Biron, north towards Angoulême; GR461, the old packhorse trail from

Montignac to Terrasson (20km); GR36, a 68km haul from La Capelle-Biron to Monbazillac; GR6, Ste-Foy-la Grande to Souillac (75km), via Monbazillac, Trémolat, Sarlat and Carlux; and GR64, from Les Eyzies to Groléjac (65km). There are numerous shorter local walks as well.

Around Périgueux

This is one of the harder regions in France to explore without transport of your own. Buses are infrequent, trains almost non-existent, and hitching can be uncertain to say the least. If you're interested in the sights, it can be worth considering coach trips from Périgueux. The **Office Départemental de Tourisme**, on rue Wilson, organises trips from mid-June to mid-September.

Brantôme and Bourdeilles

BRANTÔME, 27km north of Périgueux on the Angoulême road, is lovely but touristy. It sits in a bend of the **Dronne,** whose still, water-lilied surface mirrors the limes and weeping-willows of the riverside gardens. To the left as you enter, beyond the park and the balustraded river banks, you glimpse the church and conventual buildings of the **abbey** that for centuries has been Brantôme's focus. Its stone facades, now masking the secular offices of the **Hôtel de Ville**, have that pallor and blank stare so characteristic of the self-denying institutional life, be it monastery, home, or school. Not that there was much of the flagellant about this monastery's most notorious abbot, **Pierre de Bourdeilles**, author of scurrilous tales of life at the royal court.

Take a look at the **church**, for the palm-frond vaulting of the chapterhouse and the font made from a carved and grounded pillar capital. There is a fine stone staircase too in this end of the Hôtel de Ville. But Brantôme's best architectural feature is the Limousin-style Romanesque **belfry** standing behind the church against the wooded and cave-riddled scarp that backs the village.

Getting to Brantôme can be problematic. Hitching is the simplest way; there are buses, but only for school and the Wednesday market. Hotels, be warned, are expensive, though there is a **campsite** to the right over the bridge on the Angoulême side of the village. Should you need the **SI** it is in a lime-shaded Renaissance pavilion on the river bank, with a beautifully-sited but rather fancy restaurant in the old mill below it.

And **BOURDEILLES**, being further, is that much harder to reach. 16km down the Dronne by a beautiful back road (8km if you turn left on D106 before Brantôme), it's a sleepy backwater, an ancient rural village clustering around its castle on a rocky spur above the river. The **castle** (9–11.30am and 2–6pm; closed Dec. 15–Feb.1, first week in Oct. and Tues. from Sept 15–June 15) consists of two buildings, one a thirteenth-century fortress, the other an elegant Renaissance residence begun by the lady of the house as a piece of unsuccessful favour-currying with Cathrine de Médicis. Unsuccessful, because Cathrine never came to stay and the château was left unfinished. Climb the octagonal keep to look down on the clustered roofs, the weir, and the boat-shaped mill parting the current, the cavernous shade of the Dronne's course, the cornfields and the manors hidden among the trees beyond.

The house is now home to an exceptional collection of **furniture** bequeathed to the state by its former owners. Among the more notable pieces are some splendid Spanish dowry chests; a sixteenth-century Rhenish Entombment with life-sized statues, the very image of the serious, self-satisfied medieval burgher; a fifteenth-century primitive Catalan triptych of an exorcism, with a bull-headed devil shooting skywards out of a kneeling princess; and, for pornographic tastes, an elaborately carved pair of buffets, the lock sliding between a maid's thighs.

Hautefort

From the same period, but much grander in scale and style is the castle of **HAUTEFORT** about 40km further east. It lies on D704 to Limoges. On Wednesdays and Saturdays there is a morning bus from Périgueux via CUBJAC, on other days only in the evenings. In either case it is impossible to get there and back in one day. You stand a fair chance hitching, or you could get a Brive train as far as LA BACHELLERIE near the turn-off for Hautefort. By car the most attractive route is along the river Auvézère via Cubjac and TOURTOIRAC, where Antoine-Orélie I, King of Araucania, died in 1878. This bizarre character was a Périgueux lawyer who, deciding he was born for higher things, borrowed money and set sail for Patagonia, where he proclaimed himself king of the Araucanian Indians.

The château (Palm Sun.–Nov. 1, 9.15–11.30am and 2.15–6.30pm; rest of year, Sun. only, 2–5pm), standing proud on the end of a wooded spur above its feudal village, has an elegance that is out of step with the usual rough stone fortresses of Périgord. You approach across a wide esplanade flanked by formal gardens, cross the moat by a drawbridge through the oldest part of the building and emerge into a stylish Renaissance courtyard backed by an arcaded gallery and enclosed by slated towers. Once the property of the troubadour Bertrans de Born, it passed into the hands of the Hautefort family in the seventeenth century and was extensively remodelled. It was the childhood home of Marie de Hautefort, the young beauty who so captivated Louis XIII.

Brive and the Upper Dordogne

BRIVE is a railway junction and the nearest thing to an industrial centre for miles around. Though it has no commanding sights, it makes an agreeable and convenient base for the upper reaches of the Dordogne river and the western periphery of the Massif Central.

Right in the middle of town is the much-restored church of St-Martin, with a number of turreted and towered houses, some dating back to the thirteenth century. The most impressive is the sixteenth-century **Hôtel de Labenche** on rue Blaise-Raynal, which now houses the town's museum.

Drawn tight around the nucleus of the old town is a ring of modern boulevards. Take a line southwest from St-Martin down rue de l'Hôtel-de-Ville, across the boulevard and down av Jean-Jaurès, and you come to the **gare SNCF** and several cheap **hotels**. A left turn on the boulevard – here, Maréchal-Lyautey – brings you to the attractive square Auboiroux, with the

PTT and **gare routière** nearby. The **SI** is north of the ring of boulevards on place 14-Juillet alongside a slick, Scandinavian-style timber-frame **market**. Youth-hostellers have the option of a clean new **hostel** at 56 av Maréchal-Bugeaud (☎55.24.34.00), with a **campsite** just across the river.

Close by and worth a patient hitch are two very beautiful villages, **TURENNE** and **COLLONGES-LA-ROUGE**. The first, a bare 15km south, was capital of the viscounty of Turenne whose most illustrious seigneur was Henri de la Tour d'Auvergne, the 'Grand Turenne', whom Napoléon rated the finest tactician of modern times.

The village today would not surprise him. The same mellow stone houses still crowd in the lee of the sharp bluff whose summit sprouts the towers of their castle. One forms part of someone's house. The other, known as **La Tour de César**, is visitable (mid-March to Oct., 9am–noon and 2–7pm; rest of the year Sun. only, 10am–noon and 2–5pm). One of the highest points for miles around, it's worth climbing for the views away over ridge and valley to the mountains of Cantal.

You might make Turenne by train. One southbound train a day makes a stop. **Collonges** is another matter. The easiest access is by D38 from Brive – about 23km. Or you could walk it from Turenne: most directly via NOILHAC on D150 – about 7km. The prettiest route is by the back lanes through meadow and walnut orchards to **SAILLAC**, whose Romanesque church sports an elaborately carved tympanum upheld by a column of spiralling animal motifs. It would take about three hours on foot.

You won't regret the effort, for Collonges is the epitome of rustic charm with its red-sandstone house, pepperpot towers and pink-candled chestnut trees. Though small-scale, there is a grandeur about the place, as if the Turennes' administrators who lived here were aping, within their means, the grandiloquent gestures of their superiors. On the *place* a twelfth-century church testifies to the imbecility of shedding blood over religious differences: here, side by side, Protestant and Catholic conducted their services simultaneously. Outside a covered market-hall still retains its old-fashioned baker's oven.

An additional reason for coming is the unpretentious **hôtel-restaurant**, the *Relais de St-Jacques*, whose beds are comfortable and food memorable. For cheaper **accommodation**, you have to head downhill a few minutes to the **campsite** at MEYSSAC or the **youth hostel** at BEAULIEU.

Uzerche and Pompadour

A half-hour train ride north of Brive along the course of the bubbling **river Vézère**, the town of **UZERCHE** is impressively located in a loop in the river's course. It's worth a passing visit as the town has several fine old buildings. The **SI** – behind the church – provides information on landmarks, but the place is so small you can easily find your own way around. Rues de la Justice, Pierre-Chaland, Furnestin and Jean-Genet are the most rewarding.

If you have arrived at the **gare SNCF**, there are cheap places to **eat** on the approach to the road tunnel into the town. Or you could try the *Hôtel Sagne* on the far side.

For a grand view of Uzerche, well worth the extra march, turn left onto rue du Champ-de-Foire as you come down from the station; pass the church and keep on to rue Ste-Eulalie, turning right at the end to cross the river on rue du Pont.

Roughly equidistant from Brive – forty minutes by train – is the **CHATEAU DE POMPADOUR**, presented by Louis XV to his mistress, Madame de Pompadour, in 1745, though she never actually visited it. Set in countryside reminiscent of parts of Ireland, the château is home to one of France's best known **stud farms** (*haras*), first created by Louis XV in 1761. For horse-lovers it's a must, and it is interesting even for the non-specialist. Its speciality is the Anglo-Arab breed, descendants of horses brought back from the Crusades. The stallions are kept at Puy Marmont (July 15–Feb. 21, weekdays only, Sun. am and pm; free guided tours every 40 min.), the mares 4km away at La Jumenterie de la Rivière (afternoons only). From May to October there are frequent race meetings and Open Days. In spring the fields are full of mums and foals, the best being kept for breeding, the rest sold worldwide as two-year-olds. Of the **castle** itself (**SI** in the foyer), only the terraces are visitable.

As you might expect, **eating** in this aristocratic village is expensive. The best bet is *Le Pompadour* at 5 av de la Gare on the other side of the railway tracks.

A little further north on the same railway line, **YRIEIX-LA-PERCHE** was the fount of Limoges' wealth, since kaolin was discovered here in 1765. There is a **porcelain museum** (9am–noon and 2–6pm; closed Sun. and Mon.) 2km out on the Limoges road, and an unusually well-endowed treasury in the otherwise unremarkable church.

East of Brive

As you climb eastwards towards the Massif Central, the country becomes progressively wilder and hillier, full of streams and woods of beech, birch, chestnut and conifer, good only for grazing sheep. Signs of human habitation are few and far between: isolated hamlets and grey stone farms peopled by weatherbeaten peasants inured to the hardships of upland life.

The main road and railway to CLERMONT-FERRAND run side by side through TULLE and USSEL. From the rather gloomy little town of EGLETONS a minor road (signposted Neuvic) runs past modest farms and springtime blossom to the romantic ruins of **VENTADOUR** castle perched on a precipitous ridge above the woods, where the troubadour, Bernard de Ventadour, was born, son of a castle servant. A path climbs up to the ruined walls and towers, with plummeting views into the valley below.

Thirty kilometres on, at **USSEL**, there is a **youth hostel** (on rue Pasteur, to the right in the centre of town; ☎55.96.13.17) and a **campsite**. It's a pleasant old place, with a folk art and crafts **museum** split between the Hôtel du Juge-Choriol on rue Michelet and the Chapelle des Pénitents-Blancs on rue Pasteur (July–Aug. 10am–noon and 3–7pm; same hours for both). Among the old houses is the Renaissance residence (behind the **market**) built by the Ventadours to replace their drafty and comfortless castle.

West of the Brive-Clermont road lies the starkly beautiful moorland of the Plateau de Milleuaches, with high ground up to 1000m – all bog, bracken and conifer plantations under wide skies. The easiest access is by train on the Limoges-Ussel line, which serves several small stations on the western edge of the plateau between EYMOUTIERS and MEYMAC (*Modern Hôtel*, in av Limousine; ☎55.95.10.19; closed Nov.1–Dec.8 and Sats. out of season). The principal walking centre is LA COURTINE on the east side (SNCF bus from Ussel).

If you're heading for the Massif Central, a beautiful route to take is from Ussel to BORT-LES-ORGUES and on to RIOM-ES-MONTAGNE. It takes you across the upper valley of the Dordogne and on to the high plateau of the Massif between the Puy de Saucy and the Central mountains. It's just about hitchable if you are not in a hurry.

PERIGORD NOIR

The **Périgord Noir** is the stretch of territory from Bergerac to Brive, said to be darker in aspect than the Blanc because of the preponderance of oak woods. **Sarlat** is its capital. This is the country people think of first when you say **Dordogne**: where the picture-book villages are, and the charabancs, where the cuisine is at its richest and the prices at their highest – where it is as well to be wary of restaurateurs who think their responsibilities end with having a Périgord address.

And here more than ever, it pays to slip away into the back country – by **GR** best of all.

Bergerac and the middle reaches

BERGERAC lies on the riverbank in the wide plain of the Dordogne. Once a flourishing port for the wine trade, it is still the main market centre for the surrounding maize, vine and tobacco farms. Devastated in the Wars of Religion, when most of its Protestant population fled overseas, it is essentially a modern town, yet it is still attractive. There is a cornucopia of a **market** in the covered *halles* on Wednesday and Saturday and, down by the river, to the right of rue Neuve-d'Argenson as you come from the **gare SNCF**, what is left of the old quarter has a lot of charm, with drinking fountains on the street corners and numerous late-medieval houses.

In rue de l'Ancien-Pont the seventeenth-century Maison Peyrarède houses a **tobacco museum** (10am–noon and 2–5pm in summer, till 6pm in winter; closed Sun. am and Mon.), detailing the history of the weed, with collections of pipes and tools of the trade. Bergerac is the mainstay of French tobacco-growing, somewhat in the doldrums today since the traditional *brune* – brown cigarette – is being superseded by the less harmful *blonde*, oven-cured and therefore less labour-intensive to make. There is also a small **wine and boat-**

ing museum (10am–noon and 2–5.30pm; closed Mon., Sun. and Sat. pm) on place de la Myrpe.

Half a dozen kilometres south of the town and best reached by **bike** (rental from 11 place Gambetta or 114 bd de l'Entrepôt), the small **Château de Montbazillac** stands on gently rising slopes among its long-famous vineyards. The wine – out of fashion for many years – is white, velvety and sweet, best drunk with desserts or chilled as an apéritif. Red Bergeracs, on the other hand, often produced by small growers on the slopes north of the river and for many years known only to local connoisseurs, are beginning to enjoy much greater popularity, at prices far more reasonable than the better known clarets of Bordeaux.

For **accommodation** in Bergerac, there are several small hotels in the back streets (a popular choice is the *Hôtel Pozzi*, 11 rue Pozzi; ☎53.57.24.90) and a **campsite** at *La Pelouse* (☎53.57.06.67). The **SI** is at 97 rue Neuve-d'Argenson.

Downstream

Downstream from Bergerac, past the riverside hamlet of LE FLEIX and the old Huguenot centre of **STE-FOY-LA GRANDE**, whose arcaded *place* recalls its *bastide* origins, committed fans of **Montaigne** can visit his tower-study. This is all that remains of the château, which was burned down in 1885. Getting there entails a train journey to CASTILLON-LA BATAILLE, (where a memorial commemorates the final defeat of the English in the Hundred Years' War in 1453), followed by an hour-long hike. A further complication is the need to telephone ahead for an appointment (☎53.58.69.74), which can only be arranged from Wednesday to Saturday, 9am–noon and 2–7pm.

Upstream or east from Bergerac, if you're travelling by car, you might stop at **BEAUMONT**, an English *bastide* of the thirteenth century. However, if you are relying on public transport (buses are infrequent), you would do better to save your energy for the better *bastides* of DOMME or MONPAZIER.

More rewarding – the effort here is a train ride to LE BUISSON and a 6km hike – is the twelfth-century Cistercian abbey of **CADOUIN**. Until 1935 it drew flocks of pilgrims to wonder at a piece of cloth thought to be part of Christ's shroud. Since that date, when the shroud was shown not to be authentic, the main attraction has been the flamboyant Gothic **cloister** with its fine sculpted capitals (July–Aug. 9am–noon and 2–7pm; April–June and mid-Sept. to mid-Oct. 9.30am–noon and 2–6pm; rest of year 10am–noon and 2–5pm; closed Tues., except in July and Aug.). Beside it is a Romanesque church (8.30am–7pm) with a stark, bold front and wooden belfry roofed with chestnut shingles. (Chestnut trees abound around here, the timber used in furniture-making and the nuts ground for flour in the once-frequent famines.) **Inside**, it is apparent that the nave is slightly out of alignment. This is thought to be deliberate, perhaps a vestige of pagan attachments; for the three windows are aligned so that at the winter and summer solstice the sun shines through all three in a single shaft.

The Vézère Valley: prehistoric caves

Half an hour or so by train from Périgueux lies **LES EYZIES**, centre of a luxuriant cliff-cut region riddled with caves and subterranean streams. It was here that skeletons of Cro-Magnon people – the first *Homo Sapiens*, tall and muscular with a large skull – were first unearthed in 1868 by labourers digging out the Périgueux-Agen railway line, and here too that an incredible wealth of archaeological and artistic evidence of the life of late Stone-Age people has since been found. The many cave paintings are remarkable not only for their great age, but also for their exquisite colouring and the skill with which they are drawn.

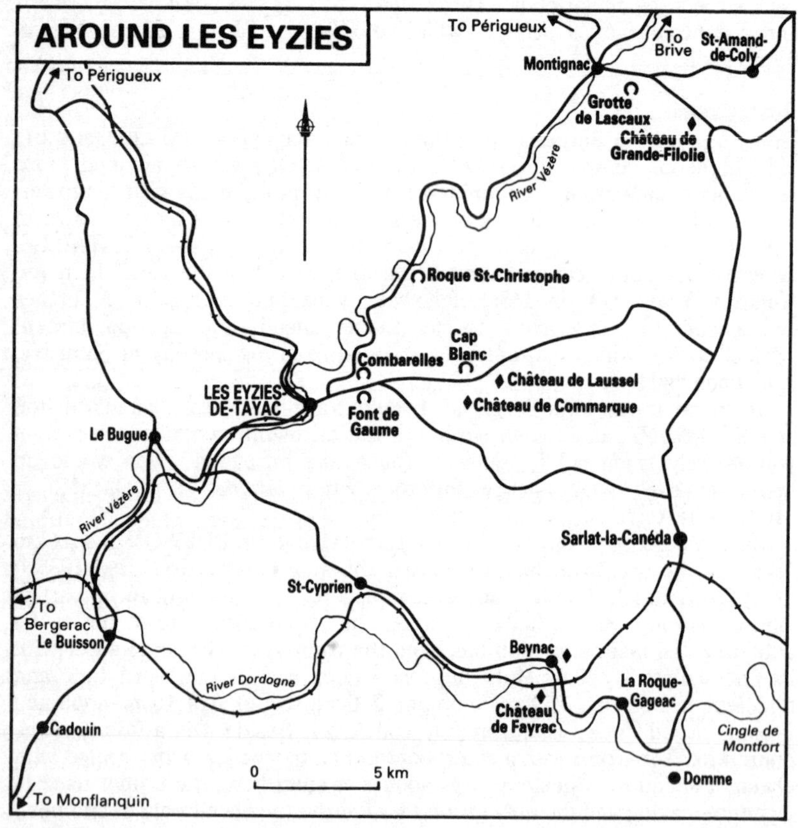

Les Eyzies

Les Eyzies itself is a rambling, unattractive little village completely dedicated to tourism. There's a riverside **campsite**, *La Rivière*, and a very attractive **gîte d'étape**, *La Ferme Eymaries* (☎53.06.94.73; kitchen, good food, books on the region; open Apr. to end of Oct.), ¾hour on foot from the village. To find it, cross the bridge on the Périgueux road, turn sharp left and continue to the railway track, where a signposted path turns right just before it. **Hotels** are pricey and likely to ask for *demi-pension*. Better to try **LE BUGUE**, 10km down the Vézère River, where there's an excellent and inexpensive **hotel-restaurant** by the station on the road into town. Four **trains** run daily to Les Eyzies from Périgueux, and the Périgueux SI issue a sheet detailing how to get there and back in the day. If you're coming from the other direction, there are two trains daily from Bordeaux to LE BUISSON, where you can either change or hitch. For getting around the area once you've arrived, Les Eyzies **SI** rent **bikes** by the day, half-day or week.

Also in Les Eyzies and worth a glance before or after visiting the caves is the **Musée National de Préhistoire** (9.30am–noon and 2–6pm in summer, till 5pm in winter; closed Tues.). It exhibits numerous prehistoric artefacts and art objects including copies of one of the most beautiful pieces of Stone Age art, two clay bison from the Tuc d'Audoubert cave in the Pyrenees, and the small bas-relief of an exaggeratedly female figure holding what looks like a slice of watermelon, known as *Vénus à la Corne* (Venus with the Horn of Plenty; the orginal is in the Musée d'Aquitaine, Bordeaux), found near Laussel (see below).

The most spectacular cave of all is at LASCAUX (see below), a little way up the Vézère near MONTIGNAC, the best base for this section of the valley (see "Up the Vézère Valley"). It was discovered in 1940 by four boys who were looking for their dog and fell into a deep cavern decorated with marvellously preserved animal paintings. Sadly, because of deterioration from the body heat and breath of visitors, the cave has been closed since 1963, and all you can see now is a tantalising replica. Other caves, however, are open.

Font de Gaume

Dozens of polychrome paintings have been discovered in this tunnel-like cave since 1901. The cave mouth is no more than a fissure from which a resurgent stream once flowed, situated off the D47 to Sarlat. Well concealed by rocks and trees, it now stands above a small lush valley, but when Stone Age people first settled here during the Ice Age – about 25,000 B.C. – the Dordogne was tundra, the domain of roaming bison, reindeer, and mammoth.

Inside, the cave is a narrow twisting passage of irregular height. There's no lighting, and you quickly lose your bearings in the dark. When the guide finally halts and focuses her torch, you see the first **paintings**, a frieze of bison, at about eye level: reddish-brown in colour, massive, full of movement, and very far from the primitive representations you might expect. Further on, in a side passage, two horses stand one behind the other, forelegs outstretched as if, as the guide suggests with some relish, to attempt *un début d'accouplement* ('the beginnings of copulation'). But the most miraculous of all is a frieze of five bison discovered in 1966 during cleaning operations. The colour, remarkably sharp and vivid, is preserved by a protective layer of calcite. Shading under the belly and down the thighs is used to give three-dimensionality with a sophistication that seems utterly modern.

Another panel consists of superimposed drawings, a fairly common phenomenon in cave painting, sometimes the result of work by succeeding generations, but here an obviously deliberate technique. A reindeer in the foreground shares legs with a large bison behind to indicate perspective.

Stocks of artists' materials have also been found: kilos of prepared pigments; palettes – stones stained with ground-up earth pigments; and wooden painting sticks. Clearly painting was a specialised, perhaps a professional act, reproduced in dozens and dozens of caves in the central Pyrenees and in northern Spain during the Upper Paleolithic era.

Font de Gaume is only 130m long, but many caves are far longer, with terrifyingly difficult access through twisting slippery passages, passable only on your belly. Cave people had just the most primitive lamps to light their way and paint by.

No-one ever lived in these caves, and there are various **theories** as to why these inaccessible spots were chosen. Most agree that the caves were sanctuaries: if not actually places of worship, they at least had religious significance. One theory is that making images of animals that were commonly hunted, like reindeer and bison, or feared, like bears and mammoths, was a kind of sympathetic magic intended to help men either catch or evade these animals. Another is that they were part of a fertility cult: sexual images of women with pendulous breasts and protuberant rumps are common, and it seems too that certain animals were associated with the feminine principle. Others argue, from parallels with the Australian aborigines who use similar images to teach their young vital survival information as well as about the history and mythological origins of their race, that these cave paintings served a similar purpose. But much remains unexplained, for instance, the abstract signs that appear in many caves and the arrows which clearly cannot be arrows, because Stone Age arrowheads looked totally different to ours.

Maximum group size for admission at one time is twenty and **tickets** sell out fast. To be sure of a ticket in season, especially on a Sunday when they're half-price, get to the ticket office as soon as possible – at least an hour before morning opening time, preferably earlier in July and August. It is best to be in the first group of the day; it's quieter then and you have a greater sense of discovery. (May–Sept., 9–11.15am and 2–5.15pm; rest of year 9–10.15am and 2–3.15pm; closed Tues.).

Grotte des Combarelles

The cave is 2km from Les Eyzies beyond Font de Gaume. Discovered in 1910 the innermost part is covered with **engravings** from the Magdalenian period, many superimposed, as they were drawn over a period of two thousand years. They include horses, reindeer, mammoths and crude human figures. Among the finest are the heads of a horse and of a lioness.

Hours are the same as Font de Gaume except that from April to September the last morning visit begins at 11am, and the afternoon visit at 5pm, and in winter the cave opens only at 10am. Unlike Font de Gaume you cannot buy afternoon **tickets** in the morning, so you have to arrive early for both sessions to be sure of a place.

Cap Blanc

Not a cave but a rock shelter, **Cap Blanc** is 7km from Les Eyzies. Turn left just past Les Combarelles; it's a steep but manageable bike ride. Hours are 9.30am–7pm in July and August, 10am–noon and 2–4.30pm outside peak season; in winter, contact the guide (☎53.59.21.74). No discounts because the site is privately owned.

The shelter contains a **sculpted frieze** of horses and bison dating from the Middle Magdalenian period, 14,000 years ago. The design is deliberate, with the sculptures polished and set off against a pock-marked background. But what makes this place extraordinary is not just the large scale, but the **high relief** of some of the sculptures. This was only possible in places where light reached in, which in turn brought the danger of destruction by exposure to the air. Of the ten surviving prehistoric sculptures in France this is the best.

Cro-Magnon people actually lived in this shelter, and a female skeleton has been found some two thousand years younger than the frieze.

Laussel and Commarque

Further up the primitive-looking and heavily wooded Beune Valley from Cap Blanc stands the **Château de Laussel** (closed to the public). Opposite is the **Château de Commarque**; it looks near but you need to know the terrain well to cross the valley. Alternatively, take the Sarlat road from Les Eyzies and follow the signs from Combarelles. If you want to **walk cross-country**, a GR will take you there: past Font de Gaume and on the right just after *Pizzeria Girouteaux*, take the path uphill (you can join up with it at Combarelles by following the path up through the woods at the back and turning left in the top clearing). Follow the red and white markers to Mazelée (two farmhouses), turn left down through the wood to the main road, go right and the path continues on the left up to SIREUIL. It's about another hour to the romantically **overgrown ruins** of the castle. Built in the thirteenth century, it played an important part in the Hundred Years' War. Substantial sections of the fortifications still stand.

Up the Vézère Valley

The first place of interest is an enormous prehistoric residential site, **La Roque St-Christophe** (Easter to mid-Nov. 9.30am–noon and 2–6pm; no lunchtime closing in July and Aug.). About one hundred caves on five levels have been hollowed out of a limestone cliff, 7–800 metres long and 80m high. The earliest traces of occupation go back over 50,000 years.

Another 15km bring you to **MONTIGNAC** (frequent buses to SARLAT), a more attractive place than Les Eyzies but short on even moderately priced accommodation. *Hôtel de la Grotte* (63 rue du 4-septembre; ☎53.51.82.99) has a couple of cheap rooms and a good cheap menu. Other possibilities are *Au Bon Accueil* in the same street and *Hôtel du Périgord* on place Tourny (☎53.51.80.38). There is also a three-star **campsite**. The **SI** (bike rental almost opposite) is on place Bertran de Born and the same building houses a **museum** of local crafts and trades, including a reconstruction of the household of Jacquou le Croquant, the poor peasant protagonist of Eugène le Roy's finest novel. He is the Dordogne's native novelist, who lived and died here in Montignac. His *L'Année Rustique en Périgord* is a good read for getting the feel of the region in the nineteenth century.

The cave of **Lascaux** is within walking distance, or takes about fifteen minutes by bike. What you see, since the closure of the original, is a facsimile (July and Aug. 9.30am–7pm, tickets from Montignac SI; low season 10am–noon and 2–5pm; closed Mon.; tickets on site; closed Jan., expensive admission; no reductions. Entry to the **Thot museum park**, with Disneyland-ish mock-ups of prehistoric scenes, is included in the ticket.) If you want to see the original you can put your name on the waiting list, but the quota is virtually taken up by specialists.

Lascaux II took eleven years to construct, using the same methods and materials as the original. Executed by Cro-Magnon people 17,000 years ago, the paintings are said to be the finest prehistoric paintings in existence. There are five or six identifiable styles and subjects include the bison, mammoth, and horse, plus the biggest known prehistoric drawing, of a five-and-a-half-metre bull with astonishingly expressive head and face. While Lascaux II does not offer the excitement of a real cave, the reconstruction has been extremely well done. The visit lasts forty minutes: commentary in French, with English translations if requested.

Sarlat and around

SARLAT, capital of the Périgord Noir, is held in a hollow between hills a few kilometres back from the Dordogne valley. As so often, one hardly notices the modern town, but the mainly sixteenth- to seventeenth-century core is alluring – busy in a friendly, rustic sort of way, mellow with time and warm with the honey colour of its stone.

Beneath its finest house, the one-time home of Montaigne's friend, La Béotie, a plaque pays tribute to de Gaulle's Minister of Culture, **André Malraux**, '. . . member of the Resistance, government minister and author of the law on the renovation of historic towns . . .' In one sense the renovation that has taken place in Sarlat since the passing of the *Loi Malraux* in '62 is a marvellous illustration of the success of that policy, yet it also exemplifies the negative side. In season, the town goes overboard, with caparisoned dames, jousting in the streets and other heritage junketing.

The old town, however, is an excellent example of medieval organic urban growth, violated only by the straight swathe of **rue de la République** cut through its middle. The west side alone remains un-chic and grubby. Turn onto the lanes through **Cour des Fontaines**, around the back of the large and unexciting cathedral, past the **Lanterne des Morts** on the bank behind, and onto place Peyrou, where **La Boétie's house** stands with its gabled tiers of windows and characteristic steep roof stacked with heavy stone tiles.

Beyond, in **place de la Liberté** where the **SI** lodges in the sixteenth-century **Hôtel de Maleville**. A big Saturday **market** spreads its stands of geese, flowers, *foie gras*, truffles and mushrooms in season. For a sense of the medieval town, the lanes to the north, especially **rue des Consuls**, and up the slopes to the east have some of the best of the old houses.

Though it will always be hard to find cheap accommodation in season, Sarlat has much to recommend it as a base. There is a **youth hostel** off the Périgueux road (15bis av de Selves; ☎53.59.47.59; May–Sept.), two four-star **campsites** – *Les Grottes de Roffy* and *Les Périères* – and the much simpler and prettily sited *Les Acacias* about 2km beyond the railway viaduct. **Hotels** to try include the *Marcel* with a good and reasonable restaurant (8 av de Selves; ☎53.5921.98; closed mid-Nov. to Dec.); *Lion d'Or* at 48 av Gambetta (☎53.59.00.83) at the north end of rue de la République and *Hôtel de la Mairie* on place de la Liberté (☎53.59.05.71; closed mid-Nov. to March). More important perhaps, if you have no transport of your own, a Sarlat-based organisation runs **mini-bus tours** from June to the end of October, taking in five or six different places, including some lesser sights, each day of the week. The cost is £8 and up, but you won't get to many places without this sort of help. Information from the SI or Gérard Dunoyer (☎53.28.10.04). **Bikes** can be rented from the hostel or 52 rue Gambetta, with recommendations for cycle trips from the SI or the author of their leaflet at the shoe shop, 3 rue de la République. For a place to **eat** that won't break the bank, try the *Restaurant du Commerce* close to the SI at 4 rue Albéric-Cahuet. Otherwise snack places are everywhere.

St-Amand-de-Coly

This supreme example of a **fortified Romanesque church** is part of the 'Our Origins' mini-bus tour from Sarlat (see above). Alternatively you could cover the 8km from Montignac to the village of LE BOUSQUET by bike.

Despite its bristling military architecture, the church – erected in the twelfth century – manages to combine great delicacy and spirituality. With its purity of line and simple decoration, it is at its most evocative in the low sun of late afternoon or early evening. Its defences, however, leave nothing to chance. A ditch runs all the way around and a passage once skirted the eaves, with numerous positions for archers to rain down arrows and blind stairways to fool and mislead attackers.

There is a guard on hand to give **guided tours**. Although not officially supposed to, he will usually agree to show you the roof and galleries, if you make a special request. If you don't mind heights, you'll be rewarded with a magnificent view down into the church and can climb secret stairs for a bird's-eye view of the roof. He also shows an informative and evocative thirty-minute film, but it is no substitute for discovering the church's secrets for yourself.

On the way back, if you're cycling, instead of retracing your route, turn left for Montignac, then right at the intersection and down to the bottom of a steep hill. When you reach the main road there, Montignac is to the right.

However, if you want to see an attractive **castle**, turn left and then right 100m on for the **Château de la Grande Filolie** (also included in trip from Sarlat). You can't go in, but the gardens are open and it's only a short detour. With a bigger detour you could take in **ST-GENIES** as well with another Romanesque church, also included in the 'Our Origins' trip. In fact, if you're feeling energetic, the whole area between here, SALIGNAC, Sarlat and SOUILLAC is very beautiful.

Riverside villages

Down on the Dordogne, particularly lovely here as it forms great loops (*cingles*) between rich fields and wooded hills, the village of **LA ROQUE-GAGEAC** is almost too perfect. Regular winner of France's prettiest village contest, it inevitably pulls in the coaches. It does have four **campsites**, should you want to stay, and a good, reasonably priced restaurant, *L'Ancre d'Or*, overlooking the Dordogne.

Opposite, high on the scarp overlooking the south bank of the river, **DOMME** is one of the best preserved of the *bastides*. Pedal-power is the best means of getting there, so do your renting in Sarlat and come up by the back road – about 45 minutes. Somewhat petrified by too careful grooming, Domme's attractions include three of the original thirteenth-century gateways and a section of wall. From the northern edge of the village – the *barre* – marked by a drop so precipitous fortifications were deemed unnecessary, you look out over a wide sweep of river country. Underneath the village are hundreds of metres of cave – entrance opposite the **SI** (closed lunchtime) – in which the townspeople took refuge in times of danger.

If you decide to **eat** here, you might as well succumb to the tourist blandishments and sample the sickly local walnut liqueur or the *eau de vie de prune* as a *digestif*. But it makes more sense to eat down at CENAC among the saggy, tea-cosy roofs and escape the worst of the crowds. While you're there, don't miss the round tile roof of the chapel or the modest but beautifully proportioned twelfth-century church on rue St-Cybranet. And have a dip in the Dordogne.

Beynac

Back on the north bank and downstream a little, another riverside eye-catcher is the village and castle of **BEYNAC**, built on an impregnable cliff edge in the days when the river was the only route open to traders and invaders. By road it is 3km to the **castle** (9.30am–noon and 2–7pm in summer; 10am–noon and 2.30–6pm in winter), but a steep lane leads up through the top of the village in fifteen minutes. It is protected on the landward side by a double wall; elsewhere, air does the job. The flat terrace at the base of the keep, which was added by the English, conceals the remains of the houses where the beleaguered villagers lived. One of the houses has been partly excavated. Richard the Lionheart held the place for a time, until a gangrenous wound received while besieging the castle of Châlus north of Périgueux ended his term of bloodletting.

Originally, to facilitate defence, the rooms inside the keep only communicated via a narrow spiral staircase – in stone, not wood, as in the reconstruction, because of the danger of fire. The division of domestic space into dining rooms and so forth only came about when the advent of artillery made these old *châteaux forts* militarily obsolete. From the roof, there is a stupendous – and vertiginous – view up-river to the châteaux of **MARQUEYSSAC, FAYRAC** and **CASTELNAUD**. Fayrac, all pepperpots and slated towers now, was an English forward position in the Hundred Years' War when the river marked the frontier between French- and English-held territory.

The upper reaches

As you head upstream, **SOUILLAC** is the last place reasonably accessible by public transport. Its only real point of interest – for Romanesque fans – are the wonderful **sculptures** decorating the back of the doorway of the twelfth-century domed **church of Ste-Marie** close to the river and the Sarlat road. The greatest piece is a bas-relief of **Isaiah**, fluid and supple, thought to be by one of the artists who worked at Moissac. Tucked away behind the **SI** on bd Louis-Jean Malvy is a good lunch place, full of hungry workers – its best advertisement. Called the *Hôtel-Restaurant du Beffroi* (6 place Martin; ☎65.37.80.33), it is also the cheapest **accommodation**, except for the large riverside **campsite**, *Les Ondines*.

South of the river the land climbs to the **Causse de Gramat**, one of the high limestone plateaux characteristic of the old province of Quercy, which begins around here. There is a distinct change of vegetation once you leave the valley behind. The soil is poor, the grass yellow, the ground littered with stones and patches of rock breaking through. Scrub oak and juniper abound; caves and underground rivers riddle the substrata. On it are two of the area's best known tourist traps, the pilgrim shrine of Rocamadour and the Goufre de Padirac cave. Neither is easy to get to without your own transport and unless you have a specific interest both could be avoided, especially since there are equally interesting sights within much easier reach, such as Castelnaud.

Rocamadour and Padirac

The village of **ROCAMADOUR** must have been beautiful once. Tucked under a cliff in the deep and abrupt canyon of the Alzou stream, and best seen from the hamlet of L'HOSPITALET up above, it has been visited for centuries for the shrine of its miracle-working **Black Madonna**. The devout drag themselves on their knees up the steps to the smoke-blackened and votive-packed **Chapelle Miraculeuse** where the statue resides. Nowadays they are outnumbered by coach-borne trippers, for whose delectation every house displays mountains of unmentionable junk. Brive-Capdenac **trains** stop at ROCAMADOUR-PADIRAC station about a forty-minute walk away.

PADIRAC – which, incidentally, is a good 2½-hour walk from the station – is an enormous limestone sink-hole, about 100m deep. There are some

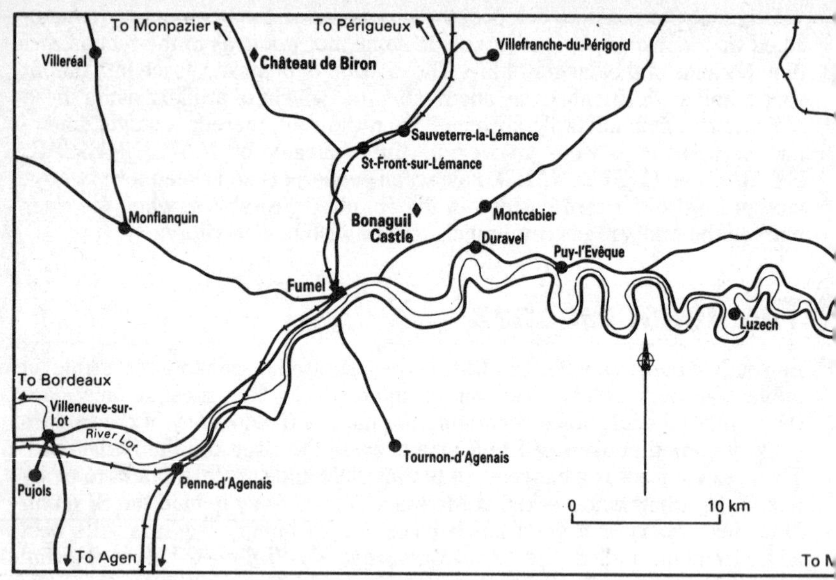

impressive formations of stalactites and waterfalls created by the accumulation of lime, but the naturalness of the place is spoiled by the lift apparatus and all the tourist paraphernalia. Visits are partly on foot, partly by boat. In wet weather you'll need a waterproof jacket. Open hours are 8am–noon and 2–7pm in summer; 9am–noon and 2–6pm in winter; and 8am to 7pm continuously in August.

Castelnaud

The sturdy towers and machicolated red-brown walls of the eleventh-century **Château de Castelnaud** (9–11.45am and 2–5.45 in summer: 10–11.45am and 2–4.45pm; closed Tues.) dominate a sharp knoll above the Dordogne, making a most harmonious whole with the village piled at its feet. Most of it has now been restored and refurnished. Below, on the banks of the River Cère, you come to the graceful little *bastide* of **BRETENOUX**, with two sides of its cobbled and arcaded square still intact. There's a grassy and shady **campsite** beside the river. A little further upriver is the château of **MILLANDES**, where Folies-Bergères star Josephine Baker set up a 'village of the world' for her adopted children.

Beaulieu-sur-Dordogne

Back on the Dordogne and just a little way to the north, **BEAULIEU-SUR-DORDOGNE** boasts another of the great masterpieces of Romanesque sculpture on the porch of the **church of St-Pierre**. This doorway is unusually deep-set, with a tympanum presided over by an

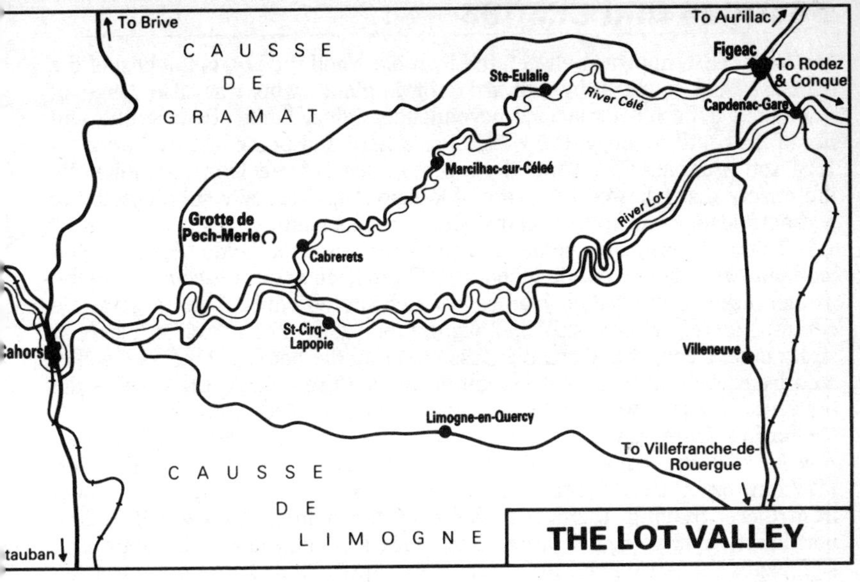

Oriental-looking Christ with one arm extended to welcome the chosen. All around him is a complicated pattern of angels and apostles, executed in characteristic 'dancing' style. The dead hopefully raise the lids of their coffins, while underneath a frieze of monsters crunches heads. Take the opportunity to go around into place des Pères for a view of the back of the church and some handsome **fourteenth-century houses** with sculpted facades. There's a **youth hostel**, if you want to stay, on place du Monturu (☎55.91.13.82), and SNCF **bus** connections from BIARS-BRETENOUX to ARGENTAT and TULLE.

THE VALLEY OF THE LOT

Travelling **south from the Dordogne** takes you into the drier, poorer and more sparsely populated province of **Haut Quercy,** through which the Lot river flows roughly parallel with the Dordogne. There aren't many facilities for tourists and, except in the Lot valley itself, not much help from public transport. So it's an ideal area to hike, bike and camp, and once you're away from the few sights you will have most of it to yourself. In addition to the GRs, some thoughtful authority has marked out a **circuit des bastides,** which makes an excellent **cycling** itinerary.

In the Cahors area, don't miss out on the local wine: heady, almost black in colour but dry to the taste, and not at all plummy like the Gironde wines from Blaye and Bourg which use the same Malbec grape.

Bastides and castles

MONPAZIER, midway between the Dordogne and the Lot, is the best of the *bastides*. Built in 1284 by Edward I of England, who was also Duke of Aquitaine, it hasn't spread far beyond its original limits. Picturesque and placid though it is today, the village has a hard and bitter history. Twice, in 1594 and again in 1637, it was the centre of peasant rebellions, provoked by the misery that followed the Wars of Religion* and brutally suppressed: the peasants' leader was broken on the wheel in the square.

It is now severely depopulated. At the street ends the fields begin and you look out over the surrounding country. There is an ancient *lavoir*, where the women used to wash their clothes, a much-altered church, and a gem of a central square – sunny, still, and slightly menacing, like a Sicilian piazza at siesta time. Deep, shady arcades pass under all the houses, which are separated from each other by a small gap to reduce fire risk. At the corners the buttresses are cut away to allow the passage of laden pack animals.

Coming from the north, there is a bus from Périgueux (*Transports Fauchier*, 2⁄ hr.; daily except Sun.), or you can take a train to BELVES (17½km) or LE GOT (13km) on the Périgueux-Agen line, and walk or hitch from there. **Staying**, there is a choice of **campsites**: the *municipal*, 2km northwest, or *camping à la ferme*, 5km along a country lane at Le Bouyssou, signposted as you enter Monpazier. It is a great spot. If there are not too many people, the old couple who run the farm let you camp under the pines by the house and provide meals. They still speak Occitan together, the old language of the south and west of France. It was, after all, their first language; they only learnt French when they went to school.

A short distance to the south the vast **CHATEAU DE BIRON** dominates the countryside for miles around. It is open for guided tours only (9–11.30am and 2.30–6pm in summer, 10–11.30am and 2.30–5pm in winter; closed Tues. for most of the year) and while they are in progress you are booted out unceremoniously even from the grassy courtyard within its walls, where there is a Renaissance chapel and guardhouse with tremendous views over the roofs of the feudal village below.

A single street runs through the **village**, past a covered market on timber supports iron-hard with age, and out under an arched **gateway.** Well-manured vegetable plots interspersed with iris, lily and Iceland poppies lie under the tumbledown walls. At the bottom of the hill, another group of houses stand on a small *place* with a broken well in front of a half-ruined **church,** its Romanesque origins covered by motley alterations, and with a massive home-made ladder leading to the belfry.

---

* Sully, the Protestant general, describes a rare moment of light relief in the terrible wars, when the men of the Catholic **bastide**, Villefranche-de-Périgord, planned to capture Monpazier on the same night as the men of Monpazier planned to capture Villefranche. By chance, both sides took different routes, met no resistance, looted to their hearts' content and returned home congratulating themselves on their luck and skill, only to find in the morning that things were rather different. The peace terms were that everyone should return everything to its proper place.

From here the road carries on south up hill and down dale, past a few poor farms and miles of oak woods to LACAPELLE-BIRON, where there is a monument to the wartime *déportés*, and on to ST-FRONT-SUR-LEMANCE, with a fortified church. St-Front is back on the railway line and the best point of access for **BONAGUIL** castle at the end of a wooden spur commanding two valleys, about 8km to the south-east. Built during the fifteenth to sixteenth century, with a double ring of walls, five huge towers and a narrow boat-shaped keep, it was the last of the really medieval castles to be constructed, albeit designed to resist artillery. The site is superb. Admission is expensive and only in guided groups (on the hour from 10am–noon and 3–6pm; out of season, Sun. only at 3pm).

Cahors

CAHORS, on the river Lot, was the capital of the old province of Quercy. In its time, Gallic settlement and Roman town; held briefly by the Moors; governed by the English; bastion of Catholicism in the Wars of Religion; sacked in consequence by Henri IV; 400 years host to a university; birthplace of Gambetta, after whom so many French streets are named . . . modern Cahors is a sunny southern backwater. Its two most interesting sights are the **cathedral** church of St-Etienne and the remarkable fourteenth-century **Pont Valentré**.

The **Pont**, with its three powerful towers, originally closed by portcullises and gates that turned it into an independent fortress, guards the river crossing on the west side of town. It is one of the most photographed monuments in France and rightly so, for it is one of the finest surviving bridges of its time. Just upstream a resurgent river flows from the valley-side, known as the **Fontaine des Chartreux**. The Roman town was named Divona Carducorum after it and it still supplies Cahors with drinking water.

The town is sited on a peninsula formed by a tight loop in the river. The layout is easily mastered. **Rue de la Barre** and **bd Gambetta** bisect it north to south from the old town walls that cut off the peninsula to the more modern bridge, Pont Louis-Philippe, with the ragged **Camping municipal** just to the right at the end. **Gare routière** and **gare SNCF** are at the end of av Jean-Jaurès off rue du Président-Wilson which leads to the Pont Valentré. For a map and further information on the area, make for the **SI** on the corner of bd Gambetta and allées Fénelon close to the cathedral. For **accommodation**, there's a **foyer** at 20 rue Frédéric-Suisse (☎65.34.64.71); turn right out of the station, second left, second right, first left – a twelve-minute walk. Alternatively, try the **hotels**: *Mon Auberge* in av Jean-Jaurès to the right of the station; *L'Escargot* at 5 bd Gambetta (☎65.35.07.66); or *Hôtel de la Paix* on place des Halles by the cathedral (☎65.35.03.40).

Consecrated in 1119 Cahor's **cathedral** is the oldest and simplest in plan of the Périgord-style churches. Like St-Etienne at Périgueux, it has a nave without aisles or transepts, roofed with two big domes. In the first are fourteenth-century frescoes of the stoning of St. Stephen. The Gothic choir and apse are extensively but crudely painted. To their right a door opens into a delicate

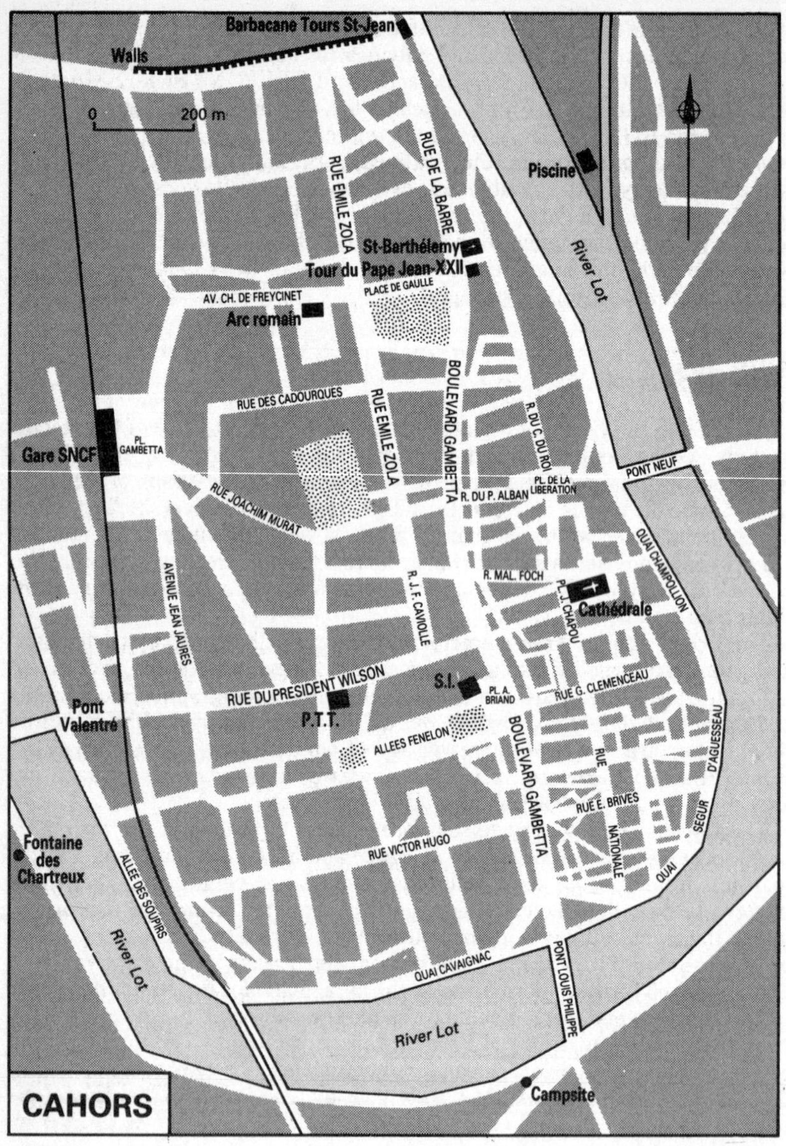

Flamboyant **cloister**, which, though damaged, still retains some intricate carving. On the northwest corner pillar a graceful girl with broad brow and ringlets to her waist serves as a model for the Virgin. In the northeast corner an arch opens on to a courtyard by the fine Renaissance **archdeacon's house.**

The **exterior** of the church is not exciting. A heavy square tower dominates the plain west front. The best feature is the elaborately decorated **portal** in the street on the north side, where a Christ in Majesty dominates the **tympanum**, surrounded by angels and apostles, while cherubim fly out of the clouds to relieve him of his halo. Side panels show scenes from the life of St. Stephen. On the outer ring of voussoirs a line of naked figures are being stabbed in the arse and hacked at with axes.

North and south of the cathedral, towards the river bank, there is a warren of narrow lanes and scruffy alleys. Many of the houses, turreted and built of flat, thin, southern brick, date from the fourteenth to sixteenth century. On the south side, the lime-bordered place Jean-Jacques Chapou commemorates a local trade-unionist and Resistance leader, killed in an ambush on July 17, 1944. Nearby are the *halles*, while for restaurant **food** you can try the convivial *La Brasserade* to the right on rue du Dr-Bergonniaux. A more commonplace alternative is the brasserie *Champ de Mars* at 17 bd Gambetta, while vegetarians should head for *Marie-Colline* at 173 rue Clemenceau opposite the SI.

Bike hire from *Ets Combes*, 117 bd Gambetta or the gare SNCF.

Upriver to Figeac

East of Cahors, SNCF buses follow the beautiful, deep-cut, twisting valley of the Lot to CONDUCHE (good value *Hôtel-Restaurant des Grottes*). From here it's a further 4½km up the tributary valley of the Célé to CABRERETS, then 1½km to the marvellous **prehistoric cave** of **Pech-Merle**. You'll need to hitch or walk – no hardship along this minor road through thick-wooded limestone hills. If you want to camp rough, there are numerous discreet sites between Cabrerets and Pech-Merle.

Pech-Merle

Pech-Merle is bigger and less accessible than Les Eyzies, and does not suffer from the same problems of overcrowding and consequent dangers of deterioration. Normally there should be no difficulty in getting **tickets** (Palm Sun.–Oct., 9am–noon and 2.30–6pm; out of season by arrangement – phone ☎65.31.23.33; expensive admission). The admission charge includes a film and excellent **museum**, where the history of prehistory is illustrated by colourful and intelligible charts, a selection of objects (rather than the usual 10,000 flints), and beautiful slides displayed in wall panels. It is interesting, too, to see the skulls of Neanderthals and Homo Sapiens side by side – the former's jaw muscles much cruder, to chomp chunks of raw meat and crush heads, like the cave bear illustrated alongside them.

The **cave** itself is far more beautiful than those at Padirac or Les Eyzies, with galleries full of the most spectacular stalactites and mites, structures tiered like wedding cakes, drapes, and shapes like whale baffles, discs and cave pearls. Yet the visit is less awe-inspiring than, say, Font de Gaume. The cave is wired for electric light and the guide, who talks like a recorded message, makes sure to rush you through in the scheduled time.

The first drawings you come to are in the so-called **Chapelle des Mammouths**. They are done on a white calcite panel that looks as if it had been specially prepared for the purpose. There are horses; bison charging head down, with tiny rumps and arched tails; tusked and whiskery mammoths. Then you pass into a vast, magical chamber where the glorious **horse panel** is visible on a lower level. Here is another remarkable example of the way in which the artist used the contour and relief of the rock to do the work: an utterly convincing mammoth is suggested by just two strokes of black. The cave ceiling is covered with finger marks, preserved in the soft clay. You pass the skeleton of a cave hyena that has been lying there for 20,000 years – wild animals used these caves for shelter and sometimes, unable to find their way out, starved to death in them. And finally, the most moving and spine-tingling experience at Pech-Merle – the **footprints** of a Stone Age adult and child preserved in a muddy pool.

St-Cirq

If you have your own transport you could easily make a side trip to the cliff-edge village of **ST-CIRQ-LAPOPIE** perched high above the south bank of the Lot. Though it is an irresistible draw for the tour buses with its cobbled lanes, half-timbered houses, gardens and fantastic site, it's still worth the trouble, especially if you visit early or late in the day. Public transport in the form of an **SNCF bus** will get you from Cahors to GARE ST-CIRQ in the valley bottom; thereafter, there's no alternative to legging it up the steep hill. For **accommodation** there is the *Hôtel du Causse* (☎65.31.24.16), and a **campsite** at LA TRUFFIERE 3km to the southeast and over the rim of the valley, while upstream, approximately ten and twenty kilometres respectively, there are **hostels/gîtes** at Calvignac (*La Ferme de Pars*; ☎65.40.64.54) and Cajarc (*gîte d'étape*; ☎65.40.65.20).

Figeac

FIGEAC, on the edge of the sombre country of the Auvergne, is a quietly busy little town, long a Protestant stronghold, with well-preserved and still inhabited medieval quarters. Its prosperity first grew out of its importance as a station on the pilgrim road from Conques to Compostella. In the thirteenth century it enjoyed the privilege of minting money and the original mint building, the **Hôtel de la Monnaie**, now housing the **SI**, survives on place de la Raison.

To reach the centre of town from the **gare SNCF** take the road to the left, then first right and down to the river and over the bridge. The **old section** of the town lies between the Mint and the two churches, with street signs directing you to the most interesting streets – place Carnot, rue Gambetta, rue Colomb, rue Boutaric – labelled bilingually in French and Occitan. The cobbled alley of rue Delzhem leads to the **Eglise Notre-Dame-du-Puy**, where you get a good view of the town. Just outside it are two thirteenth-century **obelisks**, thought to have marked the boundary of monastery lands.

There is an uninspiring **museum of old Figeac** above the SI, and a very different class of museum in the **Musée Champollion** (May–Sept., 10am–

noon and 2.30–6.30pm; closed Mon.), opened by President Mitterrand in 1986. It is dedicated to the life and work of native-born Champollion, the man who cracked Egyptian hieroglyphics by deciphering the triple text of the Rosetta Stone. Very well designed, with films and exhibits, it's an incredibly instructive and interesting place.

If you are **staying**, there is a **campsite** – *Camping des Carmes* – beyond the sports fields and a choice of reasonable **hotels**. *Hôtel de Toulouse* (4 rue de Toulouse; ☎65.34.11.40) is nearest to the station. *Hôtel de la Halle* (11 rue du Consulat; ☎65.34.04.28) is in the centre near the market place and the *Croix Blanche* (rue de la Croix-Blanche) also has a generous and fairly priced menu in its restaurant.

Transportation in the region is appalling. The only place you can get to with any ease is Brive on the main Toulouse-Limoges railway. For any other journeys you have to rely on your own resources.

Downriver to Villeneuve

As far as **FUMEL** the river winds generously between vine-grown banks dotted with small and ancient villages. An **SNCF bus** threads through them, and because there are six daily it's possible to get off, look around and pick up the next bus – not that any of the villages is worth more than a brief stay. **LUZECH** is the first, with Gaulish and Roman remains and the chapel of Notre-Dame-de-l'Ile dedicated to the boatmen who transported Cahors wines to Bordeaux. It stands in a huge river loop, overlooked by a thirteenth-century keep, with some picturesque alleys and dwellings in the quarter opposite place du Canal. Twenty minutes downstream, **PUY-L'EVEQUE** is probably the prettiest village around here, and an hour on the bus from Cahors is **DURAVEL**, with an eleventh-century church built on a tiny and even earlier **crypt.**

From Fumel on to **VILLENEUVE-SUR-LOT** the valley is ugly and industrial. Villeneuve itself, capital of the Lot-et-Garonne *département*, does not have a great deal to commend it, especially if you do not have a car, for there is no train station and bus links are poor – just Agen and Fumel/Cahors. If you do **stay over**, the centrally placed *Hôtel de l'Espoir* (5 place de la Marine; ☎53.70.71.63) is clean and welcoming, or you could try *Hôtel des Touristes* near the **gare routière**. Cheapest, but out of the way, is the *Terminus* on place de la Gare (☎53.70.30.87). For reasonable **eating** there is *Crêperie Kenavo* on rue Lakanal with a tempting range of *galettes*, salads and *crêpes* or the popular Italian *L'Intermezzo* at 18 rue Parmentier.

There are no very interesting sights: some attractive timbered houses in the streets around place Lafayette, a couple of towers which alone survive from the fortifications of this originally *bastide* town, a bridge resembling the Pont Valentré in Cahors, but devoid of towers and, rather unexpected, the **Musée Gaston Rapin** (2–7pm; closed Tues.) on bd Voltaire beyond the Tour Pujols, with sections on traditional crafts and local history, as well as some very good temporary exhibitions. For a pleasant **short walk** – about half an hour from the Tour de Pujols gate – you can climb south to the tiny walled village of **PUJOLS** with faded Romanesque frescoes in the church of Ste-Foy and great views over the surrounding country. Another side trip could be to the old fortress town of **PENNE** 8km back upstream on a steep hill also on the south bank – **by bus**, best to go to ST-SYLVESTRE on the north bank and walk. There are great views from the top, and excellent **home-cooking** to be enjoyed *Chez Madame Bonnet* on place Gambetta – rooms too (☎53.41.22.17). Otherwise, you'd have to stay in the lower town, where there is **camping** by the river and a **gîte d'étape** near the **gare SNCF** – Penne is on the Agen–Paris line.

This region is the **plum centre** of France, the plum said to have been brought back from Damascus during the Crusades. Most highly regarded are the ***prunes d'ente***, from the Old French *enter*, to graft, while star prunes come from Agen – ***pruneaux d'Agen***. You can buy or ogle them at the *Boutique des Pruneaux* next to the Porte de Paris in Villeneuve; they come straight or armoured with chocolate, Armagnac-soaked or *fourrés*, that is, stoned and stuffed with more prune flesh.

Moissac

MOISSAC, most easily accessible **by train** from Agen or Montauban (bus too, from Villeneuve; alternatively, part of SI-run tours from Cahors in high season) stands on the junction of the rivers Tarn and Garonne. And its claim to fame is the **cloister** of the abbey of St-Pierre, generally regarded as the finest achievement of Romanesque stone-carvers in the country. To find it from the **gare SNCF**, turn left and keep going straight until you see the sign for *cloître*. Built between 1059 and 1131 it has seventy-six delicate pointed arches supported on alternating single and double pillars, all of whose capitals are carved with animal or decorative motifs or anecdotal biblical scenes. Equally magnificent is the tympanum of the **south doorway** of the church. Dating from the early 1100s it illustrates a passage from the book of Revelations (iv.2-4): 24 old men, with marvellously expressive faces, strain their necks upwards to admire the **Christ in Majesty** – as we have to. To the side are **historiated scenes**, including the Flight into Egypt and a Jeremiah and St. Paul carved by the Souillac artist. The church itself is not very interesting, although inside there is a moving twelfth-century wooden sculpture of a suffering Christ on the cross. Behind the church is a **museum** of local arts and traditions, a bit shabby but with an atmospheric mock-up of a nineteenth-century Bas Quercy farm room. (**SI** next to the cloister.)

Auch

AUCH is an attractive old town on the River Gers, worth visiting primarily for the exceptionally beautiful stained glass and wood-carving (both sixteenth-century) of its cathedral church of Ste-Marie, and for its Armagnac brandy.

Auch and neighbouring Condom, are the main production centres of Armagnac. Distilled at a lower temperature than cognac, it has a stronger taste, and this is further enhanced by the black, sappy oak casks in which it is matured.

The **gare SNCF** is in the unprepossessing new town on the low ground by the river. For the **old town**, unmistakable on a high bluff across the water, go straight down rue Voltaire to the river, where there's a fine view of the east end of the cathedral as you cross the bridge. Then, turn left and climb the stone steps on the right to the tree-filled place Salinis abutting the south side of the cathedral. The fortified tower on your right is the fourteenth-century Tour d'Armagnac.

The **cathedral** is basically late Gothic, almost expiring Gothic in fact, with a classical west front. The wood-carving is in the **choir stalls**. Very similar to that at ST-BERTRAND-DE-COMMINGES (see below), it is believed to have been executed by the same craftsmen. Magnificent stuff, quite unsurpasssable. The **windows**, equally lovely and attributed to Arnaud de Moles, parallel the scenes and personages depicted in the stalls.

South of the cathedral, rue d'Espagne leads to the **Pousterles**, a number of scarcely shoulder-wide medieval stairs leading steeply downhill to rue Caumont. At the beginning of rue d'Espagne is the modest *Hôtel des Trois Mousquetaires* (this is d'Artagnan country), with a restaurant, and just beyond it the *Belle Epoque* restaurant, with good cheap *plats du jour*. On the opposite side of the cathedral square, the **SI** is located in a half-timbered fifteenth-century house on the corner of rue Dessolles (ask them for ideas and information about travelling in this backward and rarely visited corner of France). Beyond is place de la Libération, with cafés and restaurants, and off right, below the Allées d'Etigny, the **gare routière**.

Other hotels to try are: *Moderne*, opposite the station; *Le Relais de Gascogne* and *Hôtel de Paris*, both with restaurants, in av de la Marne, at the end of av de la Gare, which passes in front of the station. The **youth hostel** (☎62.05.34.80; *Foyer des Jeunes Travailleurs*; with a place to eat) is in a housing development at LE GARROS, about a 25-minute walk from the station; aim for rue Augusta and keep going until you reach the Nervol gas station, where you turn left, then right onto rue du Bourget. **Camping municipal** is also off the continuation of rue Augusta.

travel details

Trains

From Bordeaux: to Paris-Austerlitz (frequent; 4 to 5 hr.), stopping at Angoulême (1 hr.) and Poitiers (2 hr.); Bayonne-Biarritz (frequent; 1 hr. 40 min.); St-Jean-de-Luz (frequent; 2¼ hr.); Toulouse (frequent; 2 hr. 20 min.); Marseille (5 or 6 daily; 6–7 hr.); Nice (4 daily; 9–10 hr.); Périgueux (5 daily; 1 hr. 20 min.); Brive (5 daily; 2½ hr.); Bergerac (6 daily; 1½ hr.); Arcachon (frequent; ¾ hr.).

From Périgueux: to Le Buisson (5 daily; 50 min.); Bordeaux (5 daily; 1½–2 hr.); Brive (5 daily; 1–1¼ hr.); Les Eyzies (5 daily; ½ hr.); St-Front-sur-Lémance (3 daily; 1½ hr.); Agen (4 daily; 2½ hr.); Limoges (10 daily; 1–1½ hr.); for Paris-Austerlitz, change at Limoges.

From Le Buisson: to Sarlat (4 daily; ½ hr.); Bergerac (5 daily; 40 min.); Bordeaux (3 daily; 2 hr.).

From Bergerac: to Le Buisson (4 daily; ½ hr.); Sarlat (3 daily; 1½ hr.); Périgueux (1 daily; 1 hr. 50 min.); Bordeaux (6 or 7 daily; 1¼–3 hr.).

From Brive: to Pompadour (2 daily; 40 min.); St-Yrieix (2 daily; 1½ hr.); Uzerche (2 daily; ½ hr.);

Turenne (1 daily; ¼ hr., plus one morning train on Sundays); Souillac (4 daily; ½ hr.); Rocamadour-Padirac (3 daily; 40 min.); Cahors (10 daily; 1¼–1½ hr.); Figeac (5 daily; 1½ hr.); Toulouse (7 daily; 2½ hr.); Meymac (5 daily; 11/2 hr.); Ussel (3 daily; 1¾ hr.); Clermont-Ferrand (3 daily; 3 hr. 40 min.); Aurillac (6 daily; 1¾–2 hr.); Bordeaux (5 daily; 2½ hr.).

From Cahors: to Brive; Toulouse; Souillac; Montauban (4 daily; 1 hr. – with bus connection to Moissac in 20 min.).

From Agen: to Moissac (3 daily; 25 min., with bus connection from Villeneuve-sur-Lot to Agen).

Buses

From Bordeaux: to Blaye (frequent; 1¾ hr.); Pauillac (daily but infrequent; 1 hr.); Saint-Emilion (5 daily; 1¼ hr.).

From Brive: to Souillac (2 daily; 50 min.); Montignac (1 daily; ½ hr.).

From Cahors: to Figeac and Capdenac via Conduché and St-Cirq (infrequent; 2 hr.); Montsempron (6 daily; 1 hr. 20 min.) via Luzech (20 min.), Puy-l'Eveque (40 min.), Duravel (1 hr.).

From Sarlat: to Souillac (SNCF – 5 daily; ½ hr., connecting with trains to Brive and Cahors); Le Buisson (SNCF – 2 or 3 daily; 50 min.) via Beynac; Montignac (frequent).

CHAPTER EIGHT

THE PYRENEES: FROM THE ATLANTIC TO THE MEDITERRANEAN

Basque-speaking and wet in the west, craggy, snowy, patois-speaking in the middle, dry and Catalan in the east: **the Pyrenees** are physically beautiful, culturally varied and – so far – a great deal less developed than the Alps. The whole range is marvellous walkers' country, especially the central region around the **Parc National des Pyrénées**, with its 3000-metre peaks, streams, forests, flowers and wild-life. If you're a serious and committed hiker it's possible to go all the way across, from Atlantic to Mediterranean, along **GR10** or the more difficult **Haute Route des Pyrénées** (HRP). But there are numerous local (and low-key) walking centres as well – **Cauterets, Luz-St-Sauveur, Barèges, Ax,** for example. The **hiking season** is mid-June through to September; earlier in the year few refuges are open and you will run into snow even on parts of GR10. The routes don't need to be difficult or demanding, though they can be if that's what you're after. Whatever you intend, however, bear in mind that these are big mountains: treat them with respect. To cover any of the main walks you'll need hiking boots and, despite the southerly latitude, warm and wind-proof clothing.

As for more conventional tourist attractions, the **Basque coast** is lovely but very popular, suffering from seaside sprawl and a massive surfeit of camp-sites. **St-Jean-de-Luz** is by far the prettiest of the resorts; **Bayonne** the most attractive town (with an excellent Basque museum and art gallery); **Biarritz** the most over-rated. The foothill towns, on the whole, are dull, though **Pau** is worth a day or two, while **Lourdes** is such a monster of vulgarity, kitsch and B-movie sentimentality that it has to be seen.

The east – Catalan-speaking **Rousillon** – has beaches every bit as popular as those in the Basque country, and on the whole less inviting. But its interior is another matter: craggy landscapes split by spectacular canyons, a crop of fine Romanesque abbeys, of which **St-Martin-de-Canigou** and **Serrabonne** are the most dramatic, and a climate bathed in Mediterranean heat and light.

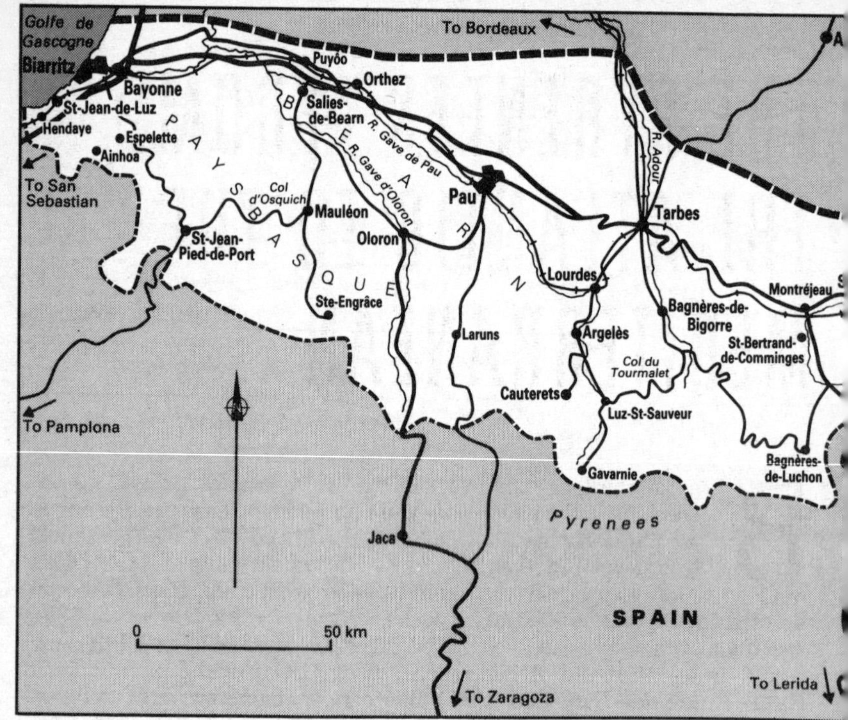

EUSKAL-HERRI: THE PAYS BASQUE

The three **Basque provinces** – Labourd, Basse-Navarre and Soule – share with their Spanish neighbours a common language, *Euskara*, and a strong sense of separate identity. The language is universally spoken, and Basques refer to their country as a land in itself, **Euskal-herri**, or, across the border in Spain, *Euskadi*. Unlike the Spanish, however, few French Basques favour an independent state or secession from France. There is no equivalent of ETA here, and there are signs that the old sympathy, which allowed refuge to Spanish Basques wanted on terrorist charges, is waning. It was Franco, dead now for a decade, who provided the political momentum.

Administratively, the three Basque provinces are organised together in a single *département* – the result of French centralising zeal after the Revolution, when the Basques' thousand-year-old *fors* (rights) were abolished. Ironically, this move has probably been responsible for preserving French Basque unity.

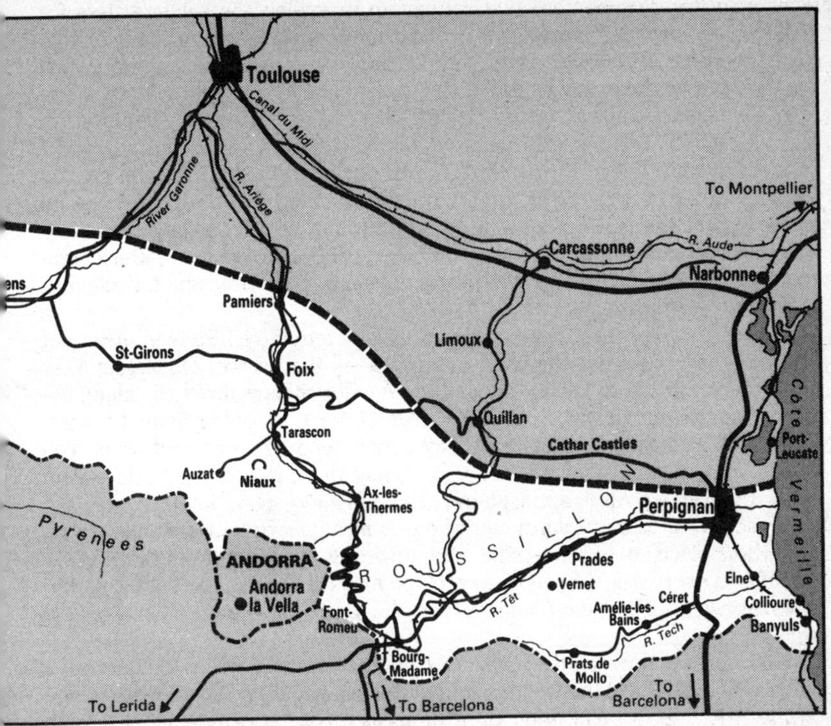

The Basque Hinterland: Orthez to St-Jean-Pied-de-Port

If you have a car and a tent – or a bike and a lot of energy – the Basque country offers a network of remote upland and valley lanes, beautiful country scattered with the distinctively built and coloured Basque villages. If you want to follow **GR65**, the pilgrim route to Compostela, the path crosses the main Pau road at ARAGNON about 8km east of Orthez.

The route from **ORTHEZ**, which has the remains of a towered medieval bridge spanning the rocky Gave (river) de Pau, starts on the main road, but from PUYOO to SALIES and beyond it is the kind of road where hitching seems a luxury: idling territory, which it would be a shame to pass through too quickly or easily. There are, though, SNCF **buses** over the whole stretch, and a **train connection** at Puyôo on the main BAYONNE–PAU road.

SALIES is a typical Béarnais village of winding lanes and flower-decked houses with brightly painted woodwork. The river Saleys, hardly more than a stream, runs through the middle separating the old village from the nineteenth-century development that sprang up to exploit the saline waters for which it has long been famous. It is a charming, if again unremarkable, little place, good for an overnight stop, with a **Camping municipal** and tiny **youth hostel**, both on the rugby field.

Going south again, D933 winds over hilly farming country to **SAUVETERRE-DE-BEARN**, another pretty country town beautifully sited on a scarp high above the Gave d'Oloron. From the terrace by the church you look down over the river and the remains of a fortified bridge. At the end of the terrace the ruins of a castle stand on top of the steep slope, its empty joist sockets making perfect pigeon-holes. The church itself, thirteenth-century with a square tower and tall apse, is attractive from the outside, but of little interest inside.

There are two or three reasonably priced and attractive **hotels** in the street past the church. Across the river (**campsite** by the bridge) D933 continues to an intersection with D936 – about 2km. A left turn here takes you along the flat bottom of the valley to **NAVARRENX** (18km), an old-fashioned market town, built as a *bastide* in 1316 and still surrounded by its ancient walls. You enter by the fortified Porte-St-Antoine. Again, there is nothing to do except enjoy the sleepy rural atmosphere. The mayor's office in the town hall dispenses what tourist information there is in a cheerful, unsystematic way. The whole place could have come off a movie set for a film about the French: it confirms every Anglo-Saxon's stereotype of rural France, the back country, or *arrière-pays. Hôtel du Commerce* by the Porte St-Antoine is reasonably priced.

GR65 passes through the town. You pick up the markers on the telephone poles in SUSMIOU at the western end of the bridge. Turn left over the bridge on the MAULEON road, then right on a back road shortly after. The path meanders westward following by-roads, farm tracks and footpaths to the vicinity of ST-PALAIS, where it turns southwest to follow the main St-Palais to ST-JEAN-PIED-DE-PORT road. To hitch to Mauléon, keep going to the intersection with the Sauveterre–Oloron road and go straight. It is wooded, hilly country all the way. It looks fertile, but there is little depth of soil and precious little level ground. You are now on Basque territory.

MAULEON was the ancient capital of the viscounty of Soule lying in the bottom of the flat hot valley of the River Saison. In the centre is the sombre Renaissance Hôtel d'Andurain, built around 1600 by a bishop of Oloron. The town claims fame as the world capital of espadrille manufacturing, but has certainly been superseded by that of China.

There is, however little to keep you here, though the surrounding areas have a lot of potential. One route follows the Saison river to STE-ENGRACE, with a very fine Romanesque church; it is one of the remotest corners of the Pays Basque and a major centre for sheep, cows, and *pottoks*, a breed of miniature horses raised for their meat. Nearby are the **Gorges de Kakouetta**, impressively deep and narrow but already something of a tourist trap. The trans-Pyrenean footpath, **GR10**, passes through.

On from Mauléon it is a twisty, hilly ride over the Col d'Osquich to the St-Palais/St-Jean-Pied-de-Port road (24km), then 16km southwest to St-Jean.

St-Jean-Pied-de-Port

The old capital of Basse Navarre, **ST-JEAN-PIED-DE-PORT** lies in a circle of hills at the foot of the Roncevaux pass into Spain. It owes its name to its position, 'at the foot of the *port*' – a Pyrenean word for pass. It has only been part of France since the Treaty of the Pyrenees in 1659. In the Middle Ages it was an important pilgrim centre, where numerous routes through Europe converged. It was the pilgrims' last stop before struggling over the pass to the Spanish monastery of Roncesvalles, where Roland, Charlemagne's general celebrated in medieval romance, wound his horn in vain and the pilgrims planted their palm-branch crosses so thick there were often thousands at a time.

The town lies on the river Nive, enclosed by walls of pinky-red sandstone. Above it rises a wooded hill crowned by the inevitable Vauban fortress, while to the east a further defensive system guards the road to Spain. The more recent overspill, pleasant but unremarkable, spreads down across the main road on to lower ground.

The **old town** consists of a single cobbled street, **rue de la Citadelle**, which runs downhill from the **Porte St-Jacques**, so named because it was the gate by which the pilgrims entered, to the **Porte d'Espagne** commanding the bridge over the Nive. A plain red church stands beside the Porte d'Espagne and, opposite, a short street leads through the **Porte de Navarre** to the modern road. From the Porte d'Espagne, with its view of balconied houses overlooking the stream, rue d'Espagne leads uphill to the so-called Route Napoléon. Off to the left is the town *fronton*, the pelota court which you'll find in just about every Basque town. Just beyond is the **Camping municipal**, the best bet if you want to stay, since St-Jean's quaintness brings in the tourists and its hotels are pricey and require half-board (two meals) in July and August.

Into the mountains

Numerous tracks lead from St-Jean up **into the mountains** towards the Spanish border. It is all sheep country, and if you are interested in getting an idea of what the old pastoral life was like, this is the place to do it. The **SI** (on the main road) can provide ideas for drivers. If you are a walker, the last leg of **GR65** starts from St-Jean and follows the line of the Roman road across to Spanish Asturia.

Go up rue d'Espagne and out through the city walls. The waymarks begin on the first telephone pole on the left. A little further on you turn up a lane to the right; GR10 and GR65 run together here. Follow the lane, between grassy banks, past fields and isolated farms. The farm houses have immensely broad roofs, one side short, the other long enough to cover space for stalls and tools; it's all very quiet and rural, with long views out across the valleys. The climb becomes steeper above a little group of houses known as HOUNTO. It is no good asking the way, even if you can find someone to ask: though everyone speaks French, the Basque names are impossible for a foreigner to pronounce. Above Hounto you come out on top of a grassy spur. GR65 turns left up what looks like an old drove road and rejoins the tarmac lane higher up by two small sheds at the edge of beech woods. It is about a two-hour brisk walk to these sheds. You get your first glimpse of the higher Pyrenean peaks to the east. Above the trees you come out on the bare grassy uplands dotted with sheepfolds. Where the lane bends around the head of a stream gully there is a sheepfold – *cayolar* – right beside the road; a shepherd lives there with his dog and flocks through the summer months, milking his sheep twice a day and making his cheese.

Much of the **grazing** throughout the mountains is owned in common by various communes, and from time immemorial they have made elaborate agreements to ensure a fair share-out of the best pasture and avoid disputes. One of the oldest of these *faceries*, as they are called, concluded by the inhabitants of Roncal and Baretous in 1375, is still in force, renewed each year on payment of three white heifers. A measure of the predominance of sheep in the Basque economy: *aberats* – the Basque for rich – means 'he who owns large flocks'.

The route continues along the track to a fork (3½hours) with a small white statue of the Virgin. Here, GR65 goes right towards Spain (another 1½ hours) and GR10 turns down left. The left fork is steep and bumpy but passable for cars. After a twisty descent it brings you out at the tiny hamlet of ESTERENCUBY, then down along the Nive and back to St-Jean.

The road to the sea: St-Jean-de-Luz

The main road to BAYONNE, D918, follows the twisting valley of the Nive to CAMBO, unfortunately bypassing the villages. Here, however, it turns sharply west for ST-JEAN-DE-LUZ, running along the way through a succession of small foothill communities.

ESPELETTE, the first, is a typical Basque village of gaily painted half-timbered houses. Take a look at the church with its heavy square tower and slated steeple. Stairs climb to the men's galleries, while you enter the body of the building through carved doors beneath. Inside is an aisleless nave with three tiers of galleries, the usual heavy gilt altarpiece and a painted wooden ceiling. In the churchyard are a number of the peculiarly Basque, disc-shaped gravestones.

About a fifteen-minute walk beyond Espelette, a minor road forks left to the delightful village of **AINHOA**, well preserved and undisturbed by any modern development. Most of the houses have their timbers painted red, in contrast to the dark blue *Hôtel Ohantzea*, a reasonably-priced two-star *Logis de France* patronised in the past by the Duke of Windsor. It would be a good place to give yourself a treat. The local church is of characteristic Basque design with a fine plain timber ceiling and altarpiece of gilded prophets and apostles with the air of modern bankers. **GR10** leaves the village just below the church.

The **Spanish frontier** is 3km away at DANCHERIA. There is a back road through the woods, ending at a stream crossed by a plank bridge with a *venta* on the Spanish side, selling booze, butter and numerous other French products much cheaper than in France. *Pernod*, for instance, is something like a quarter the price. Needless to say, they do a roaring trade. Hordes of French come to shop at these *ventas* all along the border on weekends. A certain amount of smuggling is tolerated, but you have to watch out for the *douane volante*, the flying customs, who lie in wait on back roads.

Frontier people always do a good line in illicit cross-border trading, but I was told that some sizeable fortunes had been made in Ainhöa, one gentleman managing to leave each of nine children £100,000. Wartime was particularly profitable, with an almost money-no-object trade in refugees. A nasty business: French fugitives were charged a 'reasonable' rate, while Jews had to pay £1000 a head whether they were alone or in a group. And then there was the Spanish Civil War and the Franco regime ... If it was not trading in people, it was blackmarket coffee or any other commodity in short supply one side of the border or the other.

Try GR10 for the AINHÖA-SARE stage – about 3 hours. From Sare there are **buses** to St-Jean-de-Luz on the sea.

St-Jean-de-Luz

ST-JEAN-DE-LUZ is by far the most attractive resort on the Basque coast. While it gets crowded, and its main seafront is undistinguished, it has a long curving beach of beautiful fine sand. It is still a thriving fishing port, the most important in France for catches of tuna and anchovy, and although the old houses around the harbour, both in St-Jean and across the water in Ciboure (effectively the same town) are very picturesque, they do not aspire to picture-postcard quaintness, despite the importance of tourist revenues. St-Jean is a small place, with a population of only about 12,000, but with a tough, resilient identity of its own.

As the only natural harbour on the coast between the Spanish frontier and Arcachon, it has been an important port for centuries. Whale and cod have been its special preoccupations. Local sailors voyaged as far away as Newfoundland, which the Basques claim to have discovered 100 years before Columbus reached America. In the seventeenth century, Dutch and English whalers, who had learned their trade from Basque harpooners, drove them from their traditional ports-of-call in Arctic waters, so an enterprising Basque devised a method of boiling down the blubber on board, enabling the ships to stay at sea much longer. In the eighteenth century, under the provisions of the Treaty of Utrecht, they lost their Newfoundland cod-fishing grounds and were only saved from ruin, like their brothers in Bayonne, by turning privateer and seizing other nations' shipping.

The major event in the school book history of St-Jean was the wedding of Louis XIV and Maria Teresa, Infanta of Castile. The couple were married in the church of St-Jean-Baptiste, and the door through which they left the church has been walled up ever since. The extravagance of the event defies belief. Cardinal Mazarin alone presented the queen with 12,000 pounds of pearls and diamonds, a gold dinner service and a pair of sumptuous carriages drawn by teams of six horses – all paid for by money made in the service of France.

The focus of life for visitors is **place Louis XIV** near the harbour, with its cafés, bandstand (free concerts) and plane trees. Leading to the beach is the short **rue de la République**, full of **restaurants**, with most price categories. The seventeenth-century house with turrets (10.30am–noon and 3–6pm, June 6–Sept. 15) on the harbour side of the *place* is where Louis XIV stayed at the time of his marriage. It was built by a shipowner, Lohobiague, in 1635 and still belongs to the same family. Maria Teresa lodged just along the quay in an Italianate mansion of faded pink brick. The corner house on rue Mazarin near the waterfront was Wellington's HQ during the 1813–14 winter campaign against Marshal Soult.

A short distance up **rue Gambetta** on the town side of the *place* you come to the church of **St-Jean-Baptiste**, the largest of the Basque churches. It is a plain fortress-like building from the outside. Inside, the barn-like nave is roofed in wood and lined on three sides with tiers of dark, oak galleries. These are a distinctive feature of Basque churches, and were reserved for the men, while the women sat in the floor of the nave. The walled-up door through which Louis and his bride passed is on the right of the main entrance. The ex-voto model of a paddle-steamer hanging from the ceiling is the Empress Eugénie's *Eagle*, which narrowly escaped wrecking on the rocks outside St-Jean in 1867.

The best view of old St-Jean is from the bridge to **Ciboure**, whose own waterfront, where Ravel was born, is even finer.

Accommodation

There are several reasonable **hotels** near the station: *Hôtel Toki-Ona*, rue Marian Garay; *Verdun*, opposite the station; *Continental* and *Hôtel de Paris*, both on the corner of rue Labrouche. *Camping de la Rade* is the nearest **campsite**, about a fifteen-minute walk from the **SI** in place du Maréchal-Foch (left of the station); go along Ciboure waterfront for about 300m and turn left on rue du Dr-Micé, then left again. The camp is on the flank of the hill. **Bikes** can be hired at the station or *ADO* on rue Labrouche. **Pelota** matches take place every Saturday at the *fronton* at the far end of rue Gambetta. You can arrange with the SI to visit the Irouléguy wine *caves*. Also there are buses up from the station to SARE for the **La Rhune railway**, 900m up and smack on the Spanish frontier.

Bayonne and Biarritz

Bayonne and Biarritz are virtual continuations of each other, filling in all available space behind the coast. Their characters, however, are entirely different: Bayonne, a clean, sunny, southern town, workaday and very Basque; Biarritz, sophisticated and prim, redeemed only by its waves – some of the best surfing territory anywhere in Europe.

Bayonne

BAYONNE stands back some 6km from the Atlantic: a position that's protected it from any real exploitation by tourism. This is fortunate, for, with its half-timbered houses, their shutters and woodwork painted in the pecu-

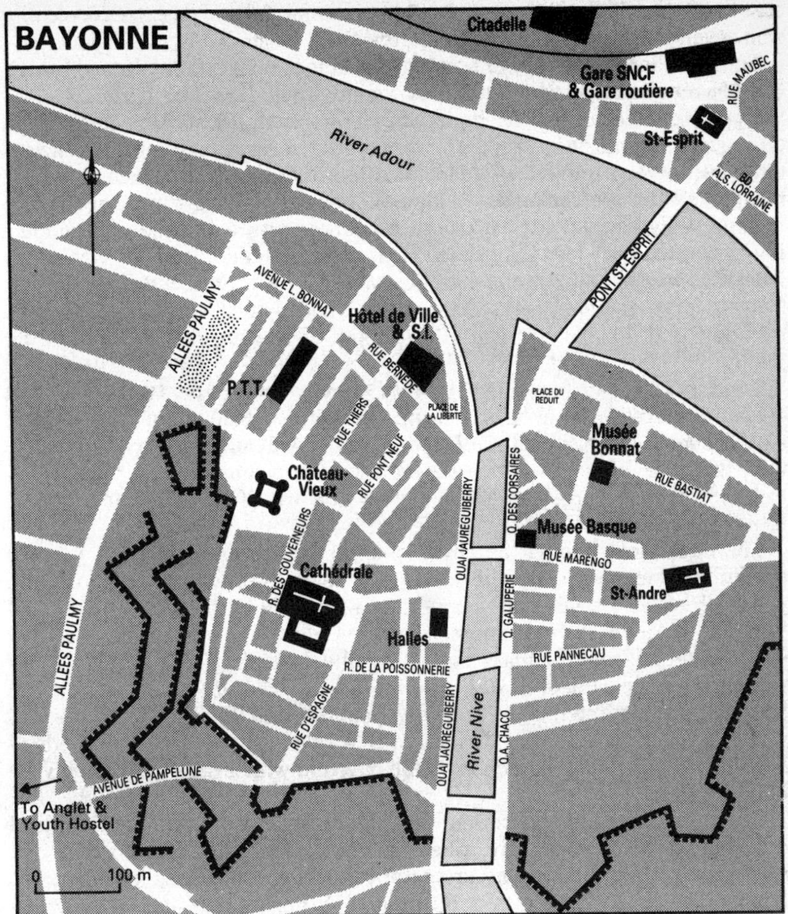

liarly Basque tones of green and red, it is one of the most distinctive and enjoyable towns in France. Most travellers treat it merely as a transit point between resorts, but if you want to spend time by the sea this is as good a base as any from which to make forays. And it is good for a while in its own right, too.

You arrive, by train or bus, at the **gare SNCF**, in the shabby quarter of **St-Esprit** on the bank of the Adour. Just upstream is a massive fortress built by Vauban in 1680 to defend the town against Spanish attack, though it did not see much action until the Napoleonic wars, the garrison here holding out against Wellington for four months in 1813. Immediately opposite the station, past the St-Esprit church, a long **bridge** spans the Adour to reach the old city centre, cut through by a second river, the Nive.

The **Nive quays** are fun to wander, and at the corner of the second bridge is a **Musée Basque**, which is worth visiting if you have any curiosity about the province and its people. Its exhibits are superb, illustrating Basque life through the centuries. There are reconstructed farm buildings and house interiors; various implements and tools like those used by pastoral people throughout Europe; *makhilas* – a kind of offensive walking-stick; a section on Basque seagoing activities (Columbus' skipper was a Basque and another Basque, Sebastian de Caro, made the first around-the-world voyage in 1519-22); *pelota*; and famous Basques, among them Simon Bolivar and de Lesseps of Suez canal fame. (Hours are 9.30am–noon and 2.30–6.30pm in summer, and 10am–noon and 2.30–5.30pm in winter; closed Sundays, all year).

The city's second museum, **Musée Bonnat** (June–Sept. 10am–noon and 4–8pm; otherwise weekdays 1–7pm, weekends 10am–noon and 3–7pm; closed Tues.), is nearby on rue Jacques-Lafitte, with another excellent collection, this time of works left to Bayonne by the painter. It's an unexpected treasury, and a refreshing change from the run-of-the-mill stuff of most provincial galleries.

The **cathedral**, across the Nive, looks its best from a distance, its twin towers and steeple rising with airy grace above the houses. Up close, the yellowish stone reveals bad weathering, with most of the decorative detail lost. The **interior** is more impressive thanks to the height of the nave and some sixteenth-century glass set off by the prevailing gloom. Like other southern Gothic cathedrals of the period (about 1260) it was based on more famous northern models, in this case Soissons and Rheims. On the south side is a fourteenth-century **cloister** with a lawn, cypress trees and beds of begonias: a quiet spot, hidden from the city, and with a rather flattering view of the church.

From the cathedral square, rue de la Monnaie and rue du Pont-Neuf lead downhill to the main square, **place de la Liberté**, full of *pâtisseries* and *confiseries* with a good strong aroma of chocolate, a business introduced to Bayonne by Jews expelled from Spain in 1611. For Biarritz and the **beaches** you can hop on a bus in the square, by the large Hôtel de Ville. The **SI** is inside here, and can give information about cruises on the Adour, visiting the Izarra liqueur distillery, and the various local **festivals**. Bayonne's own principal event is the *Fêtes traditionelles*, held with a *corrida* at the beginning of August.

There are several **cheap hotels** within sight of the station, as well as plenty of places to eat. The town's **campsite**, *la Chêneraie*, is in the St-Frédéric quarter on the north bank of the Adour, while the nearest **youth hostel** (☎59.63.86.49) is at ANGLET between Bayonne and Biarritz (*ligne bleue* bus, direction Biarrritz-La Négresse, from Hôtel de Ville to Cinq Cantons: there turn left down Promenade de la Barre, then fifth left along Promenade des Sables and finally right on to the Route des Vignes – about a 25-minute walk).

Biarritz

BIARRITZ developed as a watering place for the rich in the mid-nineteenth century, with the English, as on the Côte d'Azur, to the fore. The Empress Eugénie, wife of Napoléon III, spent her childhood summers here and in 1854 persuaded her husband to accompany her, which launched the place as a resort for Europe's aristocracy. The vast, barrack-like *Hôtel du Palais* above the Grande Plage was originally their holiday home. Queen Victoria visited once, and Edward VII and the Duke of Windsor were regulars. In season it is full of rich and not-so-rich people, yet it is an uptight place, and its pompous, ponderous architecture gives it an unfriendly air.

West of the **Grande Plage**, which is overlooked by two massive casinos, is a series of sea-girt rocks and promontories, and beyond, first, the sheltered **Plage du Port-Vieux**, then the immense **Plage de la Côte des Basques** backed by gray-white cliffs. The Atlantic weather of course is not as reliable as the Mediterranean. A clammy, though romantic, sea mist is not uncommon in the mornings. But if conditions are right, you can certainly get some marvellous swimming and surfing.

On the Plateau de l'Atalaye above the rocky promontory of the Rocher de la Vierge is a **Musée de la Mer** (July–Aug. 9am–7pm; rest of year 9am–noon and 2–7pm; expensive), hardly a must, but with interesting exhibits to do with the fishing industry, the region's birds, and an aquarium of North Atlantic fish.

Hotels are pricey and full in summer. Some cheaper ones are near the station in La Négresse. There are three city **campsites** *Splendid* (rue d'Harcet), *Biarritz* (28 rte d'Harcet), and *Municipal* (Bois de Boulogne) – and others dotted up and down the coast. But for a bed you'd do well to choose Bayonne or the Anglet youth hostel (*ligne bleue* bus, direction Bayonne, to Cinq Cantons from the Hôtel de Ville: then, see Bayonne, above, for directions).

THE CENTRAL PYRENEES

This is where the **high peaks** are, and the best part for anyone who likes the great outdoors. Getting there is simple enough, at least as far as the foothill towns – by train on the Bayonne–Toulouse line. It is inside the range that moving about is slow. The few buses, and most traffic, keep to the north–south valleys, which is frustrating when you want to switch from one valley system to the next without having to come all the way out of the mountains each time. **GR10** provides a good link if you are ready to walk all the way. Otherwise, it is possible to hitch. The main passes at **Col d'Aubisque** and **Col du Tourmalet** have spectacular scenery, though you will find you invariably get left on the top by drivers coming up for the view and going back the same way.

As for less hearty interests, there is a highly unusual fortified church at **Luz-St-Sauveur**, a place you are likely to be going through anyway. And at

St-Bernard-de-Comminges a bit further east, the whole package – village, church, surrounding countryside – definitely merits the short detour from the Luchon road.

For **ideas and information** (in French) about walking and other activities in the Pyrenees (canoeing, riding, cycling), contact *c.i.m.e.s.-pyrénées*, 3 square Balagué, 09200 Saint-Girons and ask for the booklet, *Randonnées Pyrénéennes*. The French walkers' guides are *Pyrénées Occidentales* by Ollivier; *Haute Randonnée Pyrénéenne* (the High Level Route, HRP) by Georges Veron, published by the Club Alpin Français (CAF); and the GR10 *Topo-guide*. An excellent **English guide** is Kev Reynolds' *Walks and Climbs in the Pyrenees* (Cicerone Press). There are also three small ones done by Arthur Battagel for West Col, which include the Spanish side of the range. The best **maps** are the IGN 1:25,000 series; nos. 273, 274 and 275 cover the Parc National.

Pau

Capital of the ancient viscounty of Béarn, **PAU** has had a more than usually turbulent history. In the sixteenth century it was at the centre of the Wars of Religion, provoked here by Béarn's tough Protestant ruler Jeanne d'Albret, whose activities led to equally ruthless reprisals by the Catholic King Charles X. Later, when Jeanne's son Henri himself became king of France, switching faiths in the process, he found it necessary to accommodate the regional sensibilities of his Béarnais subjects by announcing that he was giving France to Béarn rather than Béarn to France. Like the Basque and other Pyrenean provinces which came into existence as counties and viscounties in feudal times, it held on to its separatist leanings well into the seventeenth century. Even today many of the Béarnais still speak Occitan rather than French.

The town is good-looking and lively, with a university and, partly thanks to tourism, partly to the discovery of a gas field at nearby Lacq, a fairly buoyant prosperity. It occupies a grand natural site on a steep scarp overlooking the Gave de Pau and from its **boulevard des Pyrénées**, the promenade which runs along the rim of the scarp, there are superb views of the Pic du Midi d'Ossau, Vignemale and other high peaks. Not surprisingly, it has become the most popular starting point for the Parc National des Pyrénées, and it's well equipped for the purpose. The **SI** (at the end of place Royale) supplies all kinds of walking information and a useful pamphlet, *Randonnées Pyrénéennes*. More specialist knowledge can be gleaned from either the *Club Alpin Français* (rue René Fournets; ☎59.27.71.81.) or *Pyrénéa Sports* (12 rue des Bains; ☎59.27.23.11). There's an excellent climbing shop, *Romano-Sports*, knowledgeable, English-speaking and with good equipment for hire. And various organisations run guided hikes: among them *Randonneurs Pyrénéens* (9 rue Latapic; daily 6.45–7.45pm) and *Les Amis du PNP Occidentales* (24 rue Samonzet; ☎59.27.15.30).

As for its own sights, Pau's **château**, at the west end of bd des Pyrénées, was done up by Louis-Philippe in the nineteenth century after standing empty for 200 years, and then tinkered with by Napoléon III and Eugénie – it was another of their country places. Not much remains of its original appearance except the keep, but two museums are housed there. The *Musée National* (9–11.45am and 2–5.45pm in summer, and 9.30–11.45am and 2–4.45pm in winter) consists mainly of Napoléon III and Eugénies's pompous weekend apartments and Henri IV memorabilia (the sea-turtle's shell that served as his cradle, for example), while the **Musée Béarnais** (9.30am–12.30pm and 2.30–6.30pm), on the top floor, has a very good collection of costumes, Pyrenean animals, birds, butterflies and objects illustrative of the pastoral life.

Practicalities

Rooms are reasonably plentiful. There are two **youth hostels**, one at 30 rue Michel-Houneau (☎59.30.45.77; with canteen), the other in the Cité Universitaire at 3 av de Saragosse (☎59.02.88.46), as well as several reasonable **hotels** in and around rue du Maréchal-Joffre; **restaurants** too, especially towards the château. *Au Bon Coin* is a good local place, at the west end of place Forail, off rue Carnot; you eat watching TV in the back room of a café. Among more interesting **bars** are *La Poste* (along from the PTT on cours Basquet) and *Le Béarnais*, the latter a big student hangout at the east end of rue Emile-Guichenne. Two **campsites**: *municipal* on bd du Cami-Salie off av Sallenave towards the autoroute on the northern edge of town, and *Camping Le Coy* behind the **gare SNCF** at the Base Plein Air, Bizanos.

For people **arriving** at the **gare SNCF** down by the river, a free funicular shuttles you up to bd des Pyrénées. The **gare routière** (for non-SNCF buses) is near the youth hostel on rue Michel-Houneau. For long-distance **hiking**, check *Allostop* at ☎59.82.97.10. And lastly, but pretty essential if you're hitching around the region, you'll find a 24-hr service launderette at 11 rue Castelnau.

The Parc National des Pyrénées Occidentales

You really need to carry a **tent** to make the most of the park, unless you stick completely to the trails and hop from one refuge to the next for your accommodation – more expensive, of course, than camping. The hotels in the trailhead towns like Cauterets, Laruns, Gavarnie and Barèges tend to be booked from very early in the year.

As for the difficulty of **the walks** described here, there are not any which require special expertise. And none is beyond the capabilities of someone reasonably fit. The **Pic du Midi d'Ossau** is the most strenuous, and the best, because it is more off the beaten track.

This applies to good weather conditions. Obviously, if you see frozen snow and don't know how to cope with it, turn back. The Haute Route des Pyrénées and climbs to the **top** of many peaks are another matter. Basically, if you've never seen the likes of it before, don't do it.

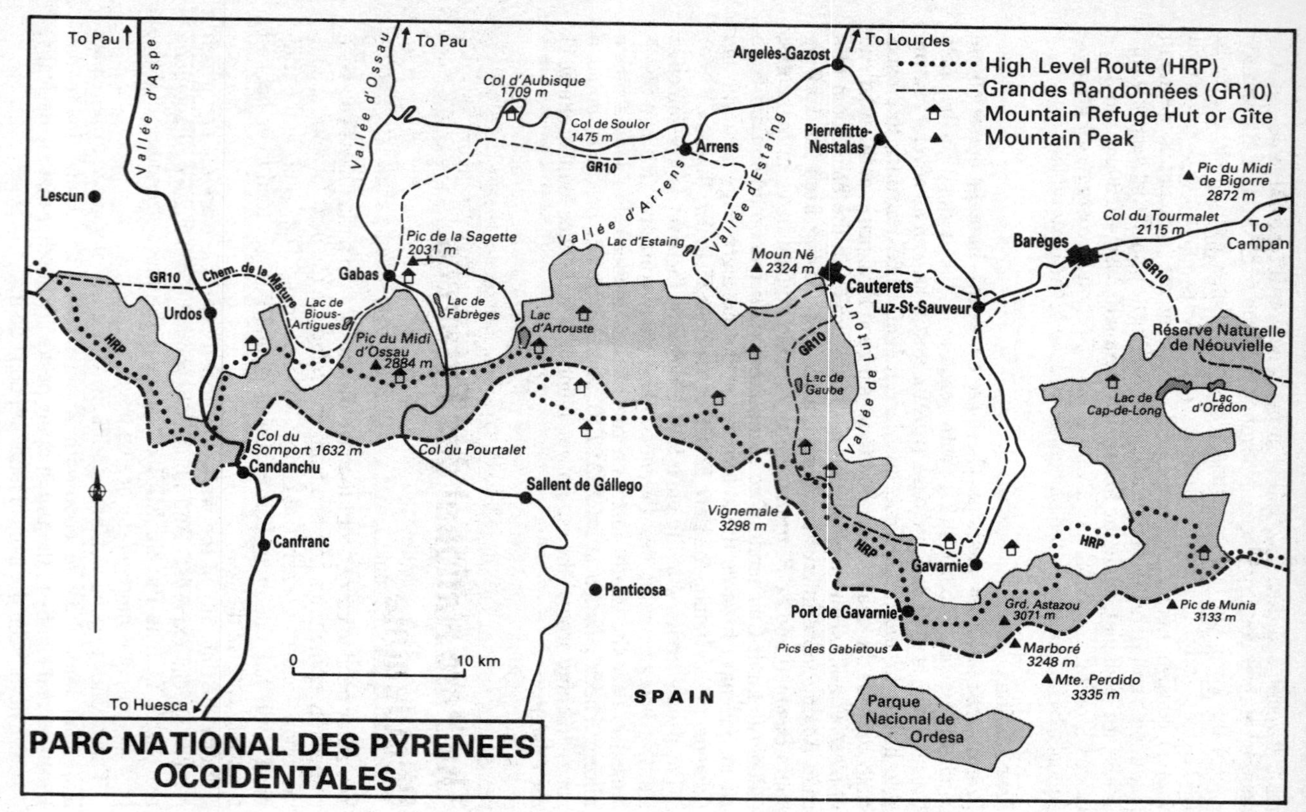

PARC NATIONAL DES PYRENEES OCCIDENTALES

Pau to Laruns and the Pic du Midi d'Ossau

Access to the trailhead for the **Pic du Midi** is not difficult. On Saturday and Sunday in summer an SNCF bus goes the whole way from PAU to GABAS and on to the start of the *téléférique* for the Artouste railway; it leaves at 9.50am and returns to Pau at 5.25pm. At other times there are *Citram* buses (from Palais des Pyrénées or the railway station in Pau) as far as LARUNS; or you can take a train as far as the station of BUZY and then an SNCF bus to LARUNS; or you could hitch – fellow hikers/climbers are always setting out.

The road runs due south up the valley of the Gave d'Ossau. If you're driving, be careful not to take the right fork for Oloron in Gan. **LARUNS** is enclosed in a narrow valley bottom, surrounded by steep grassy and wooded heights. There are some fine old houses in the back streets, especially down towards the river in the quarter known as Le Pont – old farms with mullioned windows and wide roofs spanning living quarters and farm space – and there are **hotels, restaurants** and an **SI** around the main square. Several **campsites**, too. If you are planning to hike or camp, it is best to stock up with provisions in Laruns. There is nothing in Gabas, though *Camping Bious-Oumettes*, close to the start of the Pic du Midi path, has a shop which opens around June 15.

To get to Gabas, take the right fork over the bridge south of Laruns, where the road winds steeply into the upper reaches of the Gave d'Ossau valley. It is 13km and there is not a lot of traffic, but you should get a lift without much difficulty from other walkers or employees of the various National Park installations, especially early in the morning.

From the old spa of EAUX-CHAUDES a tiny lane climbs the west flank of the valley to GOUST, a hamlet of two or three farms high on the valley side. It is a bit of a slog on foot, but good for an insight into what rural life in these remote parts must have been like. Just below the hamlet a path leads off left of the lane under the pylons to the **Pic de Bouerzy**, about 3½ hours. It is not very clear higher in the woods; you'd need the local guidebook, but there are fantastic views of the Pic du Midi from the summit.

GABAS is only a hamlet, with a CAF refuge, a National Park office and a minuscule ninth-century chapel by the road, now restored. The 'main' road continues left past the **Lac de Fabrèges** to the **Col du Pourtalet** on the Spanish frontier. From the lake a *téléférique* goes to Pic de la Sagette (2032m) above Gabas, where it connects with the **miniature railway** that runs for 10km through the mountains to the **Lac d'Artouste**. Built in the 1920s to service a hydroelectric project, it was later converted for tourist purposes. Weather permitting, the train normally starts operating in early June and keeps going until mid- or late September. It is a very beautiful and spectacular trip lasting about four hours, including time to walk down to the lake. The first train leaves at 10am, but you need to allow half an hour on the *téléférique*. Don't forget to take warm clothes, as you'll be at an altitude of 2000m.

The Pic du Midi

For the **PIC DU MIDI** take the lane to the right out of Gabas (it is also the route of **GR10**). It is a steep 4½km climb up a wooded ravine to the dammed-up **Lac de Bious-Artigues**, so named because it flooded the *artigue* – a Pyrenean word for mountain pasture – that formerly existed beside the infant *gave*. Just below the dam you pass the stony terraces of **Camping Bious-Oumettes**. Beside the lake at the end of the track is the **Refuge Pyrénéa Sports**, open to all (and serving meals): tended June 1 to October 31.

The twin-pointed summit of the Pic (2487m), sticking up out of the forest, is a landmark visible for miles in every direction. The round trip takes about seven hours, excluding the summit: it can be broken by a stay at the CAF *Refuge de Pombie* (tended June 15–Oct. 15) below the vast southern walls of the mountain.

From the Bious-Artigues lake, follow GR10 round, up the left bank of the *gave* and past the turning to **Lac d'Ayous** (another fine walk: *Refuge d'Ayous*, open June 15–Oct. 1). Cross the Pont de Bious and continue upstream across an expanse of flat wet meadow until you come to a sign to the left reading **Lac de Peyreget**. There follows a steepish zigzagging climb to the timber line and a long traverse right to the junction with the HRP path (1 hr. from *Pyrénéa Sports*). Keep left, with the ground falling away on your right. At the Lac de Peyreget, you can either follow the HRP steeply up left towards the **Col de Peyreget**, or alternatively keep right – due south – to the **Col d'Iou**. From the latter, traverse leftwards following the contour to the **Col de Soum**, where you turn first northwest, and then north to the **Refuge de Pombie** (about 4 hr.). From the refuge the path continues north beneath the Pic and the long Arête de Moundelhs back to *Pyrénéa Sports* (about 3 hr.).

There is a path **off the mountain** from the Col du Soum, and another from the Pombie refuge, which I took. The latter leads due east down the valley of the Pombie stream, through meadows full of flowers – daffodils, orchids, violets, fritillaries – where I saw a herd of izards. At the **Cabane de Puchéou**, a shepherd's hut, you cross to the left bank of the stream and carry on down to the next bridge. The HRP continues on the left bank past the Cabane d'Arrégatiou and comes out at the southern end of the Lac de Fabrèges. The right-hand path crosses the bridge and descends through the woods to a big expanse of meadow by the Gave de Brousset at **SOQUES** (about 2 hr. from Pombie), where you join the Col de Pourtalet road and can hitch back to Gabas.

I met a couple of young shepherds in the valley below Pombie, who told me that some young people were returning to the pastoral life. They had sheep, raised mainly for the milk for Roquefort cheese, and some horses which they sold for meat. They brought their flocks up to the mountains in May and took them down in late September before the first snow, in time for their ewes to lamb in October. They rented their pastures from the local communes.

The Col d'Aubisque, Cauterets and around

From Laruns there is one daily bus to the Col d'Aubisque. If you miss it, another couple go as far as EAUX-BONNES and one to GOURETTE, or you can hitch. Alternatively, GR10 runs from Gabas to Gourette over the Col de Tortes and on to the Col d'Aubisque and beyond, to ARRENS, and, via the Vallée d'Estaing, to CAUTERETS.

The only other approach to Cauterets is by bus from LOURDES (daily but infrequent service).

The Col d'Aubisque and the route to Cauterets

The **Col d'Aubisque** (1709m) is a grassy rounded ridge, an important grazing ground, with tremendous views over the valleys below and the rocky precipices of the Pic de Ger (2613m) to the south. Along the crest of the ridge are a number of shooting stands used in autumn for the massacre of the migrating ring-doves (*palombes*), a favourite sport along the Pyrenees. In choosing the low points of the cols to save labour, the poor birds present a sitting target. In some places they are caught in huge nets strung across their habitual routes. In others, the hunters construct wooden towers like forest fire-watch posts.

The Col is part of the *Tour de France*, an irresistible challenge to any French cyclist worth his salt. You see swarms of them toiling up, making it a matter of pride to find the breath for a cheery *bonjour*. There is a café at the top. If you're hitching, stay close to the café. The next possible stopping place is 18km away.

Down in the valley you pass through ARGELES, then PIERREFITTE-NESTALAS, where you fork left for **CAUTERETS**, which is a pleasant though unexciting little spa in a magnificent location, tightly enclosed by immense wooded hillsides and peaks. Its only interest is as a base for exploring the surrounding mountains. The **Parc National** has an office next to the **gare routière**, which looks as if it came off the set of a Swiss western. The **SI**, in the main square, houses a *Bureau des Guides* (July–Aug., 6am–7pm) ; services include organised walks and climbs, and a crèche in summertime – 8am to 12.30pm and 1.30 to 6pm, with meal provided. The cheapest **place to stay** is the *gîte d'étape, Le Cluquet* in av Dr-Donner (June 6–Sept. 9) past the *télésiège du Lys* and the tennis courts; you can put up your own tent or use one of the dormitories. The **hotels** – *Béarn* in av Général-Leclerc, *Bigorre* and *Centre-Poste* on rue de Belfort – aren't expensive, but are likely to require *demi-pension* (two meals) in summer. The nearest **campsite** is *Les Glères* at the entrance to Cauterets. For **eating**: the *crêperie* on rue Richelieu has a cheap four-course menu which includes wine; *Brasserie Le Centre*, at the corner of rue de Belfort and place Foch (by the SI), serves a *plat du jour* generously garnished with *frites* and salad – and quite interesting too: *agneau montagne*, quails, etc. *La Hutte Boyrie Sport*, a sports shop on place Foch, rents **hiking** and **climbing equipment**.

Hikes around Cauterets

The classic excursion from Cauterets is up the Val de Jéret to the **Pont d'Espagne**, where the Gave de Gaube and Gave du Marcadau hurtle together in a boiling spume of spray and go rushing down to Cauterets over a series of spectacular waterfalls. The best way to avoid the tourists is to take the **Parc National path** from LA RAILLERE, 3km from Cauterets (regular buses). It starts on the right by the bridge and runs all the way beside the stream through beautiful woods of beech and pine. It comes out by the café-bar at Pont d'Espagne: about 2 hours up and 1½ down.

From Pont d'Espagne you can fork right up the **Vallée du Marcadau** to the **Refuge Wallon** (about 5 hr. round trip) or left up into the hanging valley of the Gave de Gaube with the very lovely little **Lac de Gaube** backed by the high snowy wall and glaciers of **Vignemale** (3298m). There is even a *télésiège* to save you the first part of the ascent to the *lac*. Beyond, the path continues due south to the CAF **Refuge des Oulettes** below the north face of Vignemale (about 3 hr. from Pont d'Espagne). From here you can return to La Raillère via the beautiful and quieter **Vallée de Lutour** (about 2½hr.). The HRP and various Parc National paths crisscross the area, and any of the refuges can be used as a base for further day walks.

Another much less-frequented walk from Cauterets is to the **Lac d'Ilhéou along GR10**, which starts at the western edge of the town. To avoid the initial steep climb you can take the *télécabine du Lys*, near the Cauterets station, to the **gare intermédiaire de Cambasque**. Cross the stream and continue up the right bank to the end of the tarmac at the **Cabane de Courbet**. Then up a track, first on the left bank, then on the right. After a short distance – keep a good lookout – GR10 leaves the track and climbs up the slope to the left, steadily gaining height to cross a chute of boulders beside the long white thread of the **Cascade d'Ilhéou** waterfall. Over the rim of the chute you come to a small lake with the **Refuge d'Ilhéou** in sight ahead. A few more minutes on the track bring you to the refuge on the shore of the lake: very pretty in June with snow still on the surrounding peaks and ice floes drifting on its still surface (3–3½ hr.).

Luz and the Cirque de Gavarnie

The usual approach to Gavarnie, best known of the Pyrenean cirques, is via Luz-St-Sauveur, served by daily buses from Lourdes.

In addition to its convenience for the car-borne, with plentiful **hotels** and **campsites** around, **LUZ** boasts an interesting fortified church, built in the late twelfth century by the Knights of St. John and flanked by two stout towers. The entrance is beneath one of them, reached through an original doorway with a Christ in Majesty carved in fine-grained local stone. In the lanes around the church a regular market is held. On the uphill side is a good cheap *Logis de France*, the *Hôtel des Remparts*, and beyond it a **gîte d'étape**, **youth hostel** and **campsite** (*Les Cascades*). Another campsite, slightly nearer, is *Le Toy*, by the crossroads for Gavarnie, along with a helpful local **SI**.

GAVARNIE village is a further 20km up the ravine, with two daily bus connections from Luz. If you're really into hiking you could walk this, along a back road which follows GR10. The track leads through GEDRE (with two campsites and a fork, left, to the less touristed **Cirque de Troumousse**). The *Cirque de Gavarnie*, carved out by a glacier of which barely the roots of the tongue remain, is an awe-inspiring natural amphitheatre, nearly 1700m deep. It consists of three sheer bands of rock discoloured by the striations of seepage and waterfalls, and separated by sloping ledges covered with snow. To the east it is dominated by the jagged peaks of Astazou and Marbouré, both over 3000m. In the middle, a corniced ridge sweeps around almost level to Le Taillon, hidden behind the Pic des Sarradets which stands slightly forward of the rim of the cirque, obscuring the **Brèche de Roland**, a curious vertical slash, 100m deep and about 60m wide, said to have been hewn from the ridge by Roland's sword.

In sad contrast to these natural beauties, the village is an untidy straggle of souvenir shops, car parks and refreshment stands. And it stinks from the droppings of the dozens of mules, donkeys and horses used to ferry the idle and gullible up to the foot of the cirque – which is an easy fifty-minute walk.

The Cirque

Luckily, the scale of the cirque is sufficient to dwarf any number of tourists but it is best to go up before ten in the morning or after five o'clock when the grandeur and silence are almost alarming, and the dung less overpowering. The track ends at the *Hôtellerie du Cirque*, now a snack bar. To get to the foot of the cirque walls you have to clamber over slopes of frozen snow. Take care not to stand too close, especially in the afternoon, because of falling stones. To the left a 400m waterfall, the **Grande Cascade**, wavers and plumes down the rock faces. It is a fine sight in the morning when it appears to pour right out of the eye of the sun.

To the right of the first band of rock, a section of the **HRP** climbs steeply up behind the Pic des Sarradets to the CAF **Refuge des Sarradets**. An easier path goes up the Pouey Aspé valley and around the west side of the Pic (3–3½ hr.). Several 3000m peaks are easily accessible from the hut.

A good, not too demanding day's outing would be to visit the Cirque, then take the clear path from the Hôtellerie du Cirque up the east flank of the Gavarnie valley to the **Refuge des Espuguettes**. It is a beautiful path cut into steep rocky slopes. At the top you emerge into open meadows with the Cabane de Pailla in a hollow and the Refuge des Espuguettes on a grassy bluff about a 45-minute climb above you. The bare peak ahead is **Piméné** (2801m), an easy, if tedious, climb of about two hours, offering superb views of the Cirque, Monte Perdido and away into Spain. It is certainly worth climbing as far as the refuge. To return to Gavarnie, turn right at the signpost below the refuge.

Of **hotels in Gavarnie**, *Les Voyageurs* is the best bet with *L'Astazou* a poor second. A good place to **eat** is *La Ruade*, opposite the *Voyageurs*, very friendly and pretty cheap if two or more share a *raclette* or *fondue*. The *La Bergerie* **campsite** on the Cirque side of the village has the best view of the Cirque, and its bar provides breakfast; the other campsite, *Le Pain de Sucre*, is 2km north of the village. CAF's **refuge**, *Les Granges de Holle*, 1km up the track to the Port de Gavarnie, is open all year round. *La Cordée*, opposite *La Ruade*, rents axes and crampons. The CRS **mountain rescue post** opposite the *Bergerie* campsite provides the latest in weather reports, and snow conditions. And lastly, be warned that the village has just one *alimentation* and you'll need to get there early in the day to buy bread or fresh fruit.

East to Barèges and Bagnères de Bigorre

At the eastern edge of the Parc National, **BAREGES** is just 7km on from Luz (buses from Lourdes). It has been popular as a spa – its waters renowned for the treatment of gunshot wounds – since 1677, when it was visited by Mme de Maintenon with her infant charge, the seven-year-old Duc de Maine, son of Louis XIV. Today it is a skiing and mountaineering centre. **GR10** passes through and numerous other trails lead off into the **Néouvielle massif**, full of lakes and highly recommended as a walking area.

Above Barèges, the left side of the valley is a vast expanse of pasture completely denuded of trees, with clusters of stone *bergeries* dug into the slope, looking just as they do in nineteenth-century prints. The **Pic du Midi de Bigorre** (2872m) comes into view at the head of the valley. Jagged, precipitous ridges hang over the road to the right. The **Col du Tourmalet** itself, at 2115m the highest road pass in the Pyrenees, is a desolate windy spot with a track leading off left to the Pic.

Once over the col you drop down past the monstrously ugly ski resort of LA MONGIE into woods of spruce and pine which continue down to the broad green valley of **CAMPAN**, whose flowery meadows are dotted with farms. The village has an interesting sixteenth-century covered market, old houses and another curious-looking fortified church. School buses go from here to Bagnères.

BAGNERES DE BIGORRE, also a spa, and with a certain faded elegance, drew the attention of Hilaire Belloc in his book on the Pyrenees.

> *'The rule holds here as everywhere, that where rich people, especially cosmopolitans, colonials, nomads, and the rest, come into a little place, they destroy most things except the things that they themselves desire. And the things that they themselves desire are execrable to the rest of mankind'.*

This may be a little harsh as a description of Bagnères, but it is not a place to make a special stop. If you need to, there are reasonable rooms at the *Hôtel de Nice* and *Hôtel des Américains* in rue de l'Horloge, *Hôtel des Petites Vosges* (old-fashioned and quaint) and *Hôtel de France* in bd Carnot. **SNCF buses** leave for TARBES from the **gare SNCF** on av de Belgique just north of the town centre.

Lourdes

The raison d'être of **LOURDES** is clear the moment you arrive. Signs at the station direct the faithful: Secours Catholique, Accueil des Pèlerins, Sortie des Pèlerins, Trains de Pèlerinage. (A *pèlerin* is a pilgrim.)

Prior to 1858 Lourdes was nothing. In that year Bernadette Soubirous, the fourteen-year-old daughter of an ex-miller, had the first of eighteen visions of the Virgin Mary in a clammy rock overhang called the Grotte de Massabielle by the Gave de Pau. Since then, Lourdes (population 18,000) has become a Mecca for Catholics – over four million of them each year, many hoping for a miraculous cure for scientifically intractable ailments. All day every day the town is thronged with the disabled and their families, and yet there is no atmosphere of expectation: perhaps the pilgrimage is an end in itself.

The thing which strikes you first is the incredible concentration of cheap **hotels** – over 150 one-star hotels alone – and the equally startling number, and variety, of nuns. And after that it is hard to be charitable. Practically every shop is given over to the sale of indescribable religious kitsch: Bernadette in every shape and size, adorning barometers, thermometers, plastic tree trunks, key rings, perfume bottles, bottles, bellows, candles, candies, plastic grottoes illuminated by coloured lights; and the architecture of the **Cite Réligeuse** which has grown up around the Gave de Pau is scarcely any better. Woody Allen, who joked that he'd come here when he'd completed psychoanalysis, would be impressed.

The **Grotto** itself is a moisture-blackened overhang by the riverside with a statue of the Virgin in waxwork white and baby blue. Suspended in front are a row of rusting crutches, ex-votos offered by the putative cured.

Lourdes' only secular attraction is its **castle**, poised on a rocky bluff guarding the approaches to the valleys and passes of the central Pyrenees. Briefly an English stronghold in the late fourteenth century, it later became a state prison. Within, these days, is a surprisingly excellent **Musée Pyrénéen** (9–11am and 2–6pm; a little pricey – and go at opening time if you want to enjoy an hour of peace and quiet). Its collections include Pyrenean fauna, and all sorts of fascinating pastoral and farming gear. In the rock garden outside are some beautiful models of various Pyrenean styles of house, as well as of the churches of St-Bertrand-de-Comminges and Luz. There is also a section on the history of Pyrenean mountaineering.

The **SI** in **place du Champ-Commun** will help find a place to stay. The nearest **campsite** is on **rue de Langelle** off the principal north–south street. **Hostel-style** accommodation can be had at the *Centre Pax Christi* (route de la Forêt) and *Camp des Jeunes*, Ferme Milhas (av de Monseigneur-Rodhain), both on the western edge of town. The **gare routière** is on place Capdevielle.

Tarbes

TARBES, with its **youth hostel** on quai de l'Adour at the eastern edge of town (☎62.93.31.59; open daily July–Sept.; closed weekends the rest of the year) is useful as a base for visiting Lourdes (20 min. by train) or launching into the mountains to the south. Apart from that there is little to draw your attention except, if you've an interest in military history, the **Musée International des Hussards** (10am–noon and 2–6pm; closed Mon. and Tues.) in the very attractive **Jardin Massey** near the station. It houses an extensive collection of cavalry uniforms, principally nineteenth- and twentieth-century hussars, but including samples of other European and U.S. cavalry regiments. They are splendidly extravagant, the epitome of that old-fashioned quality of 'dash', which was supposed to make ladies' hearts ladies at glittering balls. (There is the usual crop of cheap **hotels** around the **gare SNCF** for non-hostellers.)

St-Bertrand and Bagnères-de-Luchon

If you are on your way south to walk at BAGNERES-DE-LUCHON, – Luchon, for short – there is a very attractive stop to be made en route, at the cathedral village of ST-BERTRAND-DE-COMMINGES, just a short distance from the railway station at MONTREJEAU, where there's a **youth hostel**.

To reach it, take an SNCF bus for Luchon from the station and get off in the hamlet of LABROQUERE by the bridge over the Garonne (about 5km). Turn right over the bridge: St-Bertrand is a pleasant 2km walk along a quiet country lane between fields of wheat, barley and hay, with the poplar-lined river on your right, and its cathedral on a neatly defined knoll commanding the plain, grey and fortress-like against the wooded slopes behind. Midway, you pass the village of **VALCABRERE** with rough stone barns and open lofts for hay-drying abutting the lane, and just off to the left, the exquisite eleventh-century Romanesque church of **St-Just-St-Pasteur**, long and low, with a square tower and a cemetery full of cypress trees. A little further is a crossroads with the foundations of various Roman buildings either side, the remains of **Lugdunum Conventarum**, founded in 72 B.C. It was once a town of some 60,000 inhabitants. The Jewish historian Josephus says it was the place of exile of Herod Antipas and his wife Herodias, who beheaded John the Baptist. It was destroyed by Vandals in the fifth century and again by the Burgundians in the sixth century, after which it remained deserted until Bishop Bertrand began to build his cathedral around 1120.

The village of **ST-BERTRAND**, many of its houses fifteenth- and sixteenth-century, clusters tightly around the church, protected by ramparts. The white-veined facade of the **cathedral** (closed for lunch; pricey admission) seems vaguely austere as you approach, elevated above a small square. Off to its right is a cloister, mostly Romanesque, open on the south side with a view over a narrow green valley to the hills beyond where a local *maquis* unit had its lair during the war.

In the aisleless **interior**, the small area at the west end reserved for the laity has a superbly carved sixteenth-century oak organ loft, a pulpit and spiral stair. But the church's great attraction – and if you are at all interested in Renaissance art this alone merits a visit – is its **choir**, built by Toulousain journeymen and installed in 1535. The elaborately carved stalls – sixty-six in all – are a feast of virtuosity, mingling piety, irony and malicious satire, each one the work of a different journeyman. It is in the misericords and partitions separating them that the ingenuity and humour of their creators is best seen. Each of the gangways dividing the sections of misericords has a representation of a cardinal sin on top of the end partition. In the middle gangway on the south side, for example, Envy is represented by two monks, faces contorted with hate, fighting over the abbott's baton of office, pushing against each other foot to foot in a furious tug-of-war. The armrest on the left of the rood-screen entrance depicts the abbot birching a monk. The Bishop's throne has a particularly lovely back panel in marquetry, depicting St-Bertrand himself and St. John. In the ambulatory a fifteenth-century shrine depicts scenes from St-Bertrand's life; the church and village are visible in the background of the top right panel.

Thirty-eight kilometres south of Montréjeau (and again on the SNCF bus routes), **BAGNERES-DE-LUCHON** is another excellent, though, in season, very crowded walking centre. The area to the south is particularly good: **Lac d'Oô, Lac d'Espingo, Lac Saussat** and the **Pic de Cécire** on GR10.

ROUSSILLON

The further you go to the east in the Pyrenees, the stronger the influence of the Mediterranean. The climate is the driest and sunniest in France. The landscape changes to heavily eroded limestone and Mediterranean scrub: goat country. The Spanish element is strong too, not only through the proximity of Spain, but because this is **Roussillon** – part of Catalonia until it was ceded to France in the seventeenth century. The region maintains its Catalan identity in language (most people are biligual in Catalan and French), though in contrast to their southern neighbours, there is little support nowadays for a political independence – nor for reunification with Spanish Catalonia. In fact the local people, especially in the remote mountain villages, were for a long time oblivious of the change from Spanish to French rule, and not until the outbreak of the First World War did it become common knowledge which country they actually belonged to.

The region's best feature is its countryside, with the valleys of the Ariège, Têt and Tech cutting into the hills. **Font-Romeu**, **Canigou** and the lateral gorges of the Tech provide some of the finest **walking**, and wild mountain **monasteries** will please those who like to walk with purpose. If **transport** is not that great, hitching is easy, and, in the Têt Valley, at least, there's always the open-air *Petit Train Jaune* to move you painlessly upwards.

The **coast**, though physically beautiful around **Collioure**, is a disappointment, with a lot of tacky development, as is the region's main town, **Perpignan**. However, before racing down to Spain in disgust, there is one **museum** you should turn off the main road for: the **modern art museum** at **Céret**, with superlative works by Picasso and contemporaries.

Note on Language: Catalan names abound in Rousillon and are an initial bar to pronunciation. X sounds as *sh*, CH as *k*, U as *oo*, and a final G as *tch*.

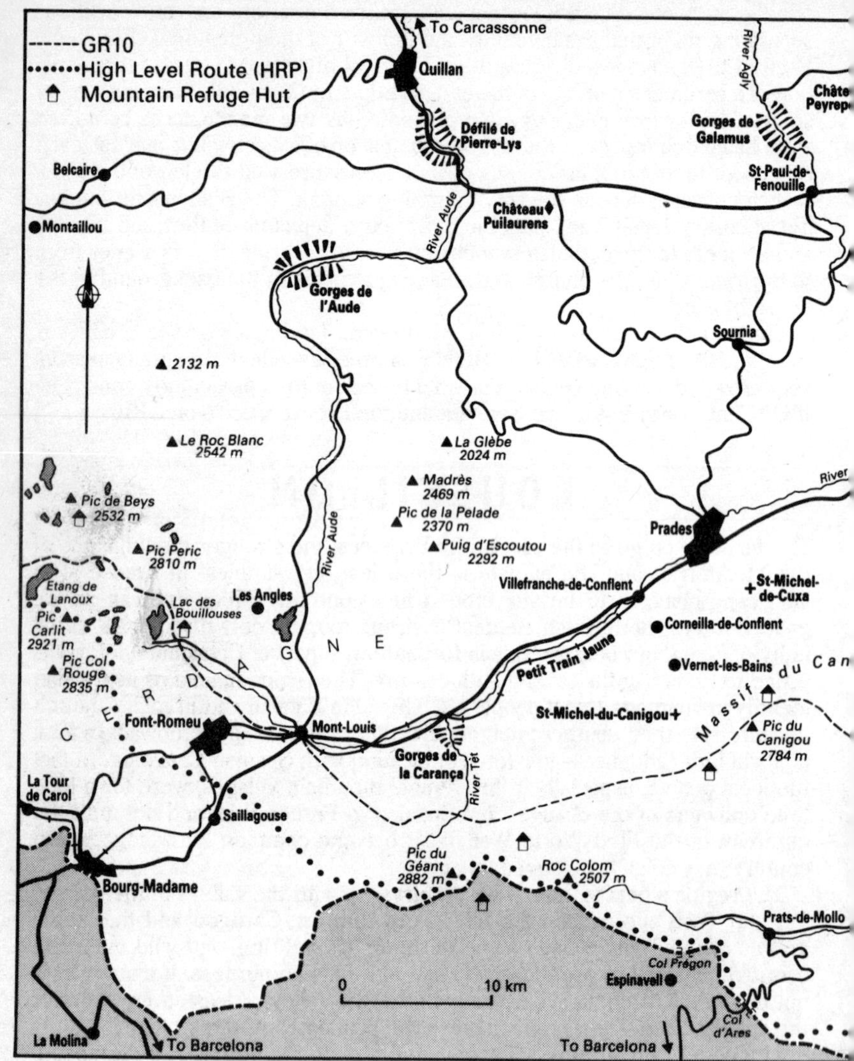

The Road to Andorra

As elsewhere in the Pyrenees, the principal lines of communication run north–south, following the river valleys: in this case, the Ariège. Toulouse is the communications centre, from which **buses and trains** run south through Foix and Ax-les-thermes. The road – N20 – is easily hitched too.

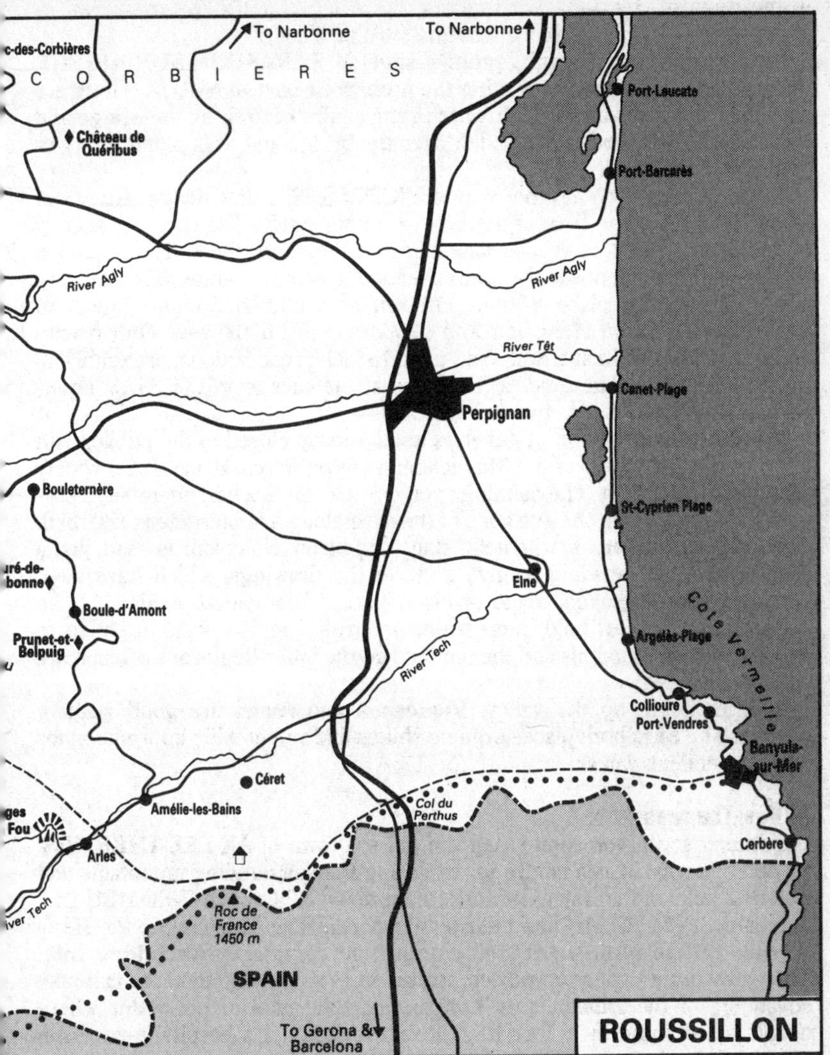

Prehistoric caves

FOIX, the first place of any consequence, is a small market town, tightly enclosed by steep hills and dominated by the three towers of its ruined castle. It looks well, but is not worth a special stop. Deeply embroiled in the Cathar struggles of the thirteenth century, in 1290 its counts married into the house of Béarn and moved their seat to Orthez. It became part of France only in the reign of Henri IV. For walkers, the Ariège *Comité Départemental de Randonnée Pédestre* is at 14 rue Lazéma (☎61.65.29.00).

Sixteen kilometres south, prettily situated **TARASCON-SUR-ARIEGE** makes a good stop-over for visiting the prehistoric cave at **NIAUX**. There are a number of **hotels** and **restaurants** in the centre of town by the bridge and a **campsite**, *Pré Lombard* (turn left over the bridge and walk along the river bank for about 10 min.).

Niaux is 5km away up the road to VICDESSOS, a tiny village strung out along the road at the base of a green mountain valley. The cave entrance is under an enormous rock overhang high on the south flank. The approach road is on the left opposite the church – about a twenty-minute walk, and very pretty. Visits take place 8.30 to 11.30am and 1.30 to 5.15pm, July 1 to September 30, and at 11am, 3pm and 4.30pm the rest of the year. Only twenty people are allowed in at a time. You need to make reservations, preferably 48 hours in advance. The guide's telephone at the cave is ☎61.05.85.10; otherwise, ring ☎61.05.88.37 between 7 and 8pm.

There are about 4½km of galleries in all, mostly closed to the public, with **prehistoric paintings** of the Magdalenian period (circa. 20,000 B.C.) widely scattered throughout. The paintings you can see are in a vast chamber, a slippery 800m walk from the entrance of the cave along a subterranean riverbed. The subjects are horses, wild goat, stags and bison. No colour is used, just a dark outline and shading to give body to the drawings, which have been executed with a 'crayon' made of bison fat and manganese oxide. It is an extraordinary mix of bold impressionistic strokes and delicate attention to detail: the nostrils, pupils and the tendons on the inner thighs of the bison are all drawn in.

Another 10km up the valley, **Vicdessos** and **Auzat** are good walking centres. The **SI** in both places organise hikes and will provide information for the independent walker.

Ax-les-Thermes

Continuing south you soon reach the old spa town of **AX-LES-THERMES**. Its chief interest is as a centre for exploring the surrounding mountains and watering-hole on the way to Andorra or on down N20 to FONT-ROMEU and, ultimately, PERPIGNAN and the Mediterranean. The **SI** is next to the Hôtel de Ville on the main street, and can provide comprehensive **hiking info**. They also run a variety of **guided walks**, for a price. The footsore can take advantage of the **Bassin des Ladres**, a public pool of hot water where people sit to bathe their feet; it is all that remains of a hospital founded in 1260 by St-Louis for soldiers wounded in the Crusades.

There are numerous **hotels**. *La Terrasse* on rue Marcaillou, over the bridge from the SI, is very cheap. *Hôtel des Pyrénées*, a one-star *Logis de France* with restaurant, opposite the SI, is very good value, and there is an attractive old café on the corner just uphill. *Terminus* opposite the **gare SNCF** on the way into the town is also reasonable and has a good restaurant. The nearest **campsite** is *Le Malazéou*, on the riverbank below the station. There is a *gîte d'étape* on GR10 at MERENS 8½km on the Andorra side of town.

Montaillou and beyond

Barely 20km northeast is the tiny village of **MONTAILLOU** (population: 10), subject of a learned and very readable study by the French historian, Le Roy Ladurie. The book covers the years around 1300 when the Inquisition was trying to extirpate the Cathar heresy from its last strongholds amongst the remote communities of the Pyrenees. Ladurie's research is based on Inquisition records of submissions under interrogation. What the locals revealed to their interrogators is incredible – details down to the most intimate minutiae of their lives. Much of the book reads like really good gossip: who is sleeping with who, where the sheep are being pastured this year, which paths you take to cross into Spain. A fascinating recreation of life in a medieval village.

There is not much traffic on the road, but it is possible to hitch. You take D613 from Ax over the steep Col de Chioula (1400m); **Montaillou** lies to the right of the road in the valley below the col. The whole area is very depopulated. Montaillou's inhabitants still bear the names of their Cathar ancestors; the churchyard is full of them. There is nothing left to see, but it is pretty and highly atmospheric, especially if you have read the book. A stump of tower remains of the castle, which was once 45m high to facilitate visual communication with **Montségur**, the noblest of the Cathar fortresses, about 11km northwest as the crow flies. You should be able to walk it in about five hours. There appears to be a track from COMUS just below Montaillou down the **Gorges de la Frau**. Otherwise, access has to be from LAVELANET on the Foix-Quillan road. There are buses that far. From there you'll certainly have to walk some of the 12km up the narrow hilly lane to the castle. Like its peers further east, Montségur balances giddily on top of sharp rock precipices, dominating the surrounding countryside. It's a good half-hour climb; if you suffer vertigo, don't get up on the battlements. Though not the last military engagement, the fall of impregnable Montségur after a ten-month siege in 1244 and the subsequent burning of 210 Cathars on a communal pyre in the field at the bottom has gone down in legend as the last desperate act in the Cathar tragedy.

On a happier note, BELCAIRE, 7km down the road from Montaillou, has an inexpensive and very good **restaurant** in the *Hôtel Bayle*.

Perpignan

This far south, not surprisingly, the influence of Spain is palpable. And **PERPIGNAN**, what's more, is capital of French Catalonia, with half its population of Spanish origin, refugees from the Civil War and their descendants. The only big city of the region, it's not, however, the most fascinating of places. Its heyday was really during the thirteenth and fourteenth centuries, when the kings of Majorca held their court here. For most of the Middle Ages its allegiance swung back and forth between France and Aragon, until finally it became part of the French state under Louis XIV in 1659.

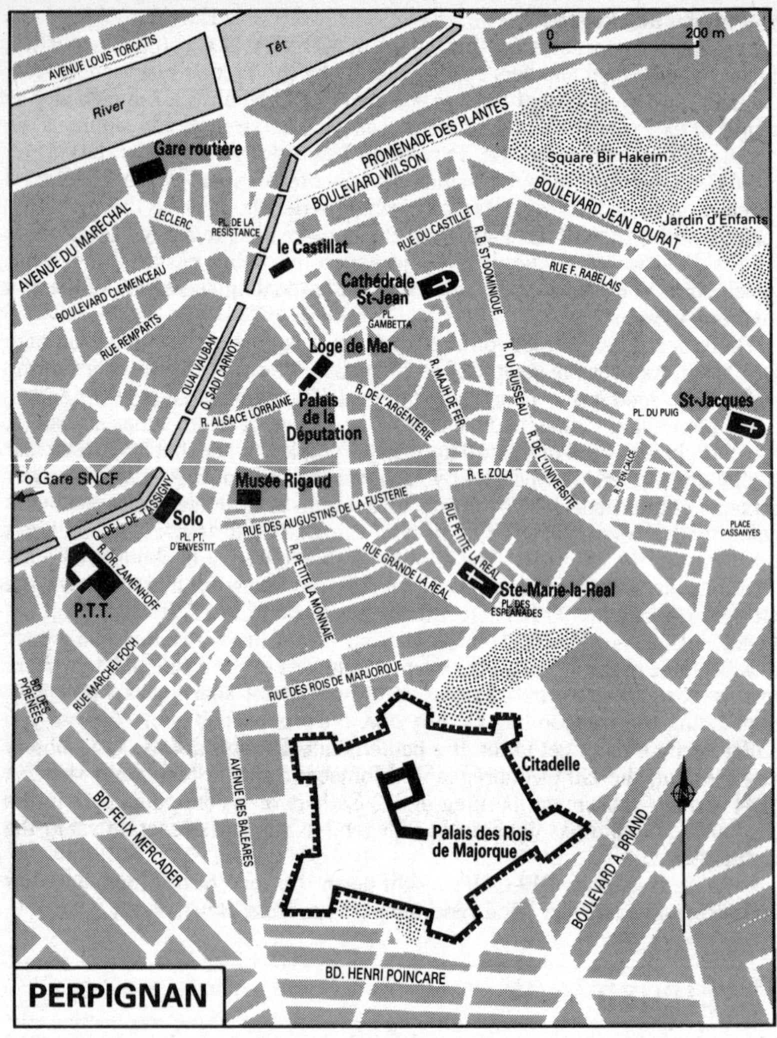

Arriving at the **gare SNCF**, you reach the centre by going straight up av Général-de-Gaulle to place de la Catalogne, right over the River Basse and left along the flower-lined quays to the palm trees and smart cafés of **place Arago**, which was named for the city's most famous native son, a scientist and member of the revolutionary government of 1848. The **old town** is in front of you. Rue Alsace-Lorraine and rue de la Loge take you past the Italianate fifteenth-century Palais de la Députation, once the parliament of

Roussillon, and the massive iron gates of the classical Hôtel de Ville, to **place de la Loge**.

This is the focus of the newly renovated and pedestrianised heart of the old town, and its most attractive quarter. Dwarfing the cafés opposite and beneath its colonnade, the **Loge de Mer**, a late fourteenth-century Gothic building, was designed to hold the city's stock exchange and a maritime court. In summer, two or three times a week, the *place* is the location for performances of the *Sardana*, a sober Catalan folk-dance accompanied by pipe and tambourine.

Northwards up rue Louis-Blanc you come to one of the city's few remaining fortifications, the crenellated fourteenth-century gate of **Le Castillet**, now home to the *Casa Pairal*, a fascinating **museum** of Roussillon's Catalan folk culture (9am–1pm and 2–7pm in summer; 10am–noon and 3–6pm in winter; closed Tues.; free). Beyond it a little bridge crosses the Basse to place de la Résistance and on to the River Têt, with the **gare routière** on av Général-Leclerc.

The fourteenth-century **Cathédrale St-Jean**, reached from place de la Loge down rue St-Jean and across place Gambetta, is most interesting for its elaborate Catalan altar-pieces, shadowy in the gloom of the ill-lit nave, and for a highly expressive, tortured, wooden crucifix known as the *Dévôt Christ* in a side chapel to the south. Dating from around 1400, it's of Rhenish, not local, origin and was probably brought back from the Low Countries by some travelling merchant.

Behind the cathedral, at the rear of the barracks on rue Rabelais, where a stretch of the old brick city wall survives, the **SI** can be found in the top corner of the shady garden of the Palais des Congrès. Alternatively, by following rue Rabelais around as far as **place du Puig**, you arrive in the centre of the poorest quarter of town, a section of grimy and run-down streets which accommodate an assortment of Spaniards, gypsies and North Africans.

On the hill above is the medieval church of **St-Jacques**, on the edge of the **Miranda** gardens. From here, on Good Friday, a very Spanish-looking procession of black- and scarlet-hooded penitents – the *Procession de la Sanch* (Catalan for blood) – sets out through the city streets bearing images of Christ's Passion.

About twenty minutes away, through place des Esplanades, crowning the hill which dominates the southern part of the old town, you come to the palace of the kings of Majorca, the **Palais des Rois de Majorque** (9am–noon and 2–6pm in summer; 9.30am–noon and 2–5pm in winter; closed Tues.). Vauban's walls surround it now, but the two-storey palace and its great arcaded courtyard date originally from the late thirteenth century. Thanks to the Spanish-Moorish influence, there's a sophistication and finesse about the architecture and detailing – for instance, in the beautiful marble porch to the lower of the two chapels – which you don't often find in the heavier, though still beautiful, styles of the north.

For **sleeping** and **eating**, the best place to look for cheapies is, as usual, around the gare SNCF. The **youth hostel** (☎68.34.63.32) is about 1km away in Parc de la Pépinière by the river (av Grande-Bretagne; turn left out of the station and right along the avenue). There are two **campsites**, *La Garrigole* on rue Maurice-Lévy and *Le Catalan* on route de Bompas, both signposted from the centre. A more attractive, though more expensive, area for **eating** is around place de la Loge, and there is always the inexpensive *Le Palmarium* on place Arago. Also near the *place*, the **Post Office** is on quai Lattre-de-Tassigny.

Around Perpignan

For a **swim**, the simplest thing is to take a 25-minute bus ride from Promenade des Platanes (two or three departures an hour) to **CANET-PLAGE**. There is nothing to recommend the place, except that the beach is wide and sandy and the sea is wet, which also goes for the other resorts around here: PORT-LEUCATE, PORT BACARES (complete with weathered Greek ferry beached to make a casino and nightclub) and ST-CYPRIEN. Apart from such beach-life, there is little to do around Perpignan except visit **ELNE**, just a ten-minute train ride to the southeast.

Elne, which was named after the Byzantine emperor Constantine's mother, Helena, and once had the honour of seeing Hannibal camp at its walls en route for Rome, used to be the capital of Roussillon. It was only overtaken by Perpignan when the latter became the seat of the kings of Majorca. Today, though little more than a village, it's worth a stop for its fortified, partially Romanesque **cathedral** and extremely beautiful **cloister** (9am–noon and 2–6pm). Though only one side of the cloister is Romanesque, immaculately carved with Romanesque motifs such as foliage, lions, goats and Biblical figures, the three later ones – fourteenth-century Gothic – have been made to harmonise perfectly. It's the best introduction to Roussillon Romanesque you could want, especially if you're planning to visit places like SERRABONNE and ST-MICHEL-DE-CUXA further west. There is also an interesting **museum** below the cloister exhibiting some of the finds from archaeological excavations here. Beyond the cathedral there are still a few streets of the old town left, twisting back down to the drab, flat and unremarkable modern development.

The Cerdagne and Canigou Massif

Heading west up the Têt Valley – the easiest way is by train – the first place to stop is **PRADES**, not so much for itself as for the abbey of **ST-MICHEL-DE-CUXA** (9.30–11am and 2.30–5pm) 3km up D27. Set magnificently at the edge of wooded slopes at the foot of the 2784m Pic de Canigou, its aged stone tower and Byzantine-looking apses rugged against the greenery, it is the only monastery in the area still occupied, by Benedictines. Mutilated, but still beautiful, it dates from the tenth century, though what survives of the cloister is twelfth-century; as at St-Guilhem-le-Désert, most of the capitals are in the Cloisters museum, New York. Concerts in the summer and the Pablo Casals **music festival** are held here; the cellist made Prades his home during his long exile from Franco's fascist Spain.

Next stop is **VILLEFRANCHE-DE-CONFLENT**: on the tourist itinerary, but a pleasant and interesting town, ringed by massive seventeenth-century fortifications put up by Vauban to defend the new border with Spain created by the annexation of Roussillon in 1659. A garrison was kept here right up until 1925. You can walk the walls, with good views over the old town (9am–noon and 1.30–6pm). And if you're inspired by military architecture, there's a **museum** near the main gate.

Continuing up the valley from here, a particularly nice way to travel, especially if you have children, is by **Le Petit Train Jaune**. An open-air rack-and-pinion job, it takes in all the little stops up to LA-TOUR-DE-CAROL on the frontier and allows you a walker's or cyclist's proximity to the scenery.

Canigou

But before you move on, Villefranche is the point to turn up D116 **towards Canigou**. Past **CORNEILLA-DE-CONFLENT**, with a pretty Romanesque church and eleventh-century tower and carved front (ask the guide at the house next door to let you in), you come to **VERNET-LES-BAINS**, a spa made fashionable by the English in the late nineteenth century. Surprisingly unspoiled by this function, its main attraction is as a base for **walking** in the Canigou massif. The **SI** provides a complete list of routes, all clearly waymarked and along fairly well-trodden paths. Even if you can't make it to the summit, it's still worth a few hours' walk for the amazing views.

As good a place to start is the dizzy tenth-century **abbey of St-Martin-de-Canigou**, crouched on a rocky terrace more than 1000m up on the northern flanks of the mountain. To reach it requires a stiff half-hour climb from the end of the Vernet road at CASTEIL. In fact, for the best view of its precarious perch among wooded pillars of rock, you should follow *Itinéraire 9* for about twenty minutes, until you can look down on it.

Inside (guided tours at 11am, 2, 3, 4, and 5pm), it is heavily, though faithfully, restored. It was abandoned after the Revolution, and the work did not begin until 1902. However, you can still get an idea of the atmosphere of the remote monastery in the lower chapel, with its dark interior, low ceiling, thick pillars and simple altar. It is now occupied by a group of young people, a warden and his family, and various Christian visitors, who live in a fairly similar style to the original monks: marooned on the mountainside away from the hedonists of Vernet, praying and eating communally. You can also **stay**, if you ask at the *Centre d'Accueil*, in a small hostel-like dormitory.

From the abbey it's 5½–6½ hours to the **top of Canigou**, and about an hour less to come down. Follow route 9 for about two hours up the mountain, then route 4 for about two hours almost level, and finally route 3 for the last 1½–2 hours to the summit. Remember to take plenty of water in summer. It's certainly well-worth the effort as the views on a clear day are amazing. Naturally enough, the mountain is an object of great Catalan pride, with separatist graffiti painted on the rocks, Catalan flags on the summit cross, and even a visitors' book in Catalan. An easier route involves driving to the Chalet des Cortalets and then walking – still about three hours, though. If you're feeling rich and lazy, you can get an expensive jeep ride up from Vernet.

On up the Têt

Higher up the Têt there's another superb walk up the **Gorges de la Carança**, an incredibly deep, wild, wooded canyon, where the old track follows the river over precariously suspended wooden ladders and bridges. It goes right up to the Spanish border, an old smugglers' route. It must be a good six hours to the border, maybe more.

Beyond, you come to the resort town of **FONT-ROMEU**, with a **campsite**, walking and skiing facilities and some pricey hotels. For cheaper accommodation, there's a **youth hostel** on the parallel N116 at SAILLAGOUSE. This is the territory of the **CERDAGNE**, whose once powerful counts controlled lands from Barcelona to Roussillon and endowed the monasteries of St-Michel-de-Cuxa, St-Martin-de-Canigou and Ripoll, now well inside Spain. It's an area that has never been sure whether it is Spanish or French. After the French annexation of Roussillon, it was partitioned, with Spain retaining – as it does today – the enclave of LLIVIA.

One of the region's most unexpected sights, at ODEILLO close to Font-Romeu, is an extraordinary experimental **solar furnace**, generating a thousand kilowatts by the use of mirrors, where you can look in on a fascinating inside exhibition, (9am–6pm; free). North towards **LES ANGLES** in the Lac des Bouillouses-Pic Carlit area, there is more good walking country. And the road back down the Aude Valley to QUILLAN is a beautiful route out of the region.

The Valley of the Tech

The first stop on D115 up towards the Spanish border at PRATS-DE-MOLLO is **CERET**, a delightful place which comes as a welcome relief after the heat, grime and hassle of Perpignan. It's friendly and bustling, with a wonderfully shady *vieille ville* dominated by huge plane trees. Towards the church, the streets are typically narrow and winding, opening on to small squares such as **place des Neuf-Jets**, so called because of the fountain in the middle. There's a large, varied and generally excellent Saturday **market** spilling out of place Pablo-Picasso into the main street, av d'Espagne. There are two remnants of the medieval walls: the fortified **Porte de France** on place de la République, and bits of the **Porte d'Espagne** on place Pablo-Picasso. In summer, Céret is also a big centre for *corridas* – to the death, of course; the arena is on the other side of town from the market, out towards the AMELIE-LES-BAINS road.

Céret's main sight, however, is the remarkable **Musée d'Art Moderne** just off bd Maréchal-Joffre near the SI (10am–noon and 2–6pm; closed Tues.). In the early twentieth century, Céret's charms, coupled with the presence here of the Catalan artist and sculptor, Manolo, drew a number of other avant-garde artists to the town, including Matisse and Picasso. Céret has even been dubbed the Mecca of Cubism. The museum, anyway, contains work by Matisse, Picasso, Chagall, Dali, Dufy and Manolo, among others, and is a fascinating collection. Both Picasso and Chagall actually dedicated some pictures specifically to the museum, scrawling '*pour le musée de Céret*' across the bottom of each work. The extensive Picasso section includes a marvellous series of ceramic bowls depicting bullfights, and a sketch of a local *sardana*, which he gave to the local branch of the PCF, who in turn donated it to the museum. Another ambitious and outrageously avant-garde project undertaken by the museum in summer 1986 was an earth-sculpture/ video exhibition, housed in the public wash-house next door. It took place while old women with huge baskets of laundry wandered in among the rows of video screens stuffed into the sinks.

If you want to stay, there's a good sprinkling of **hotels** and a couple of **campsites** on the road east towards LE BOULOU, one of which is a particularly nice *Camping municipal*. Cheap **food** is easy to find, many of the restaurants serving Catalan dishes; try *Le Pied dans le Plat* on place des Neuf-Jets or the *Pizzeria Quattrocento*. The bookshop on the *place*, *Le Cheval dans l'Arbre*, is worth a look too. The **SI** (9am–noon and 2–6pm; closed weekends) is on av Clemenceau.

To the Spanish frontier

Heading west from Céret, past the remarkable single-span fourteenth-century **Vieux Pont**, the view opens up northward towards the vast Canigou massif. The next place, **AMELIE-LES-BAINS**, is a health spa for the elderly and rheumatic.

A few kilometres further, **ARLES-SUR-TECH** has a beautiful Romanesque church and **cloister** (8am–noon and 2–6.30pm), whose pointed arches prefigure the Gothic, showing its relative lateness compared to other examples of Romanesque in the region, like SERRABONNE (see below). Nearby, just after Arles, is the turn to the long and spectacular **gorges de la Fou**. After that the road climbs on towards the border, to **PRATS-DE -MOLLO** and the spa of LA PRESTE.

Prats is the last French town before the border with Spain, and has a very Spanish atmosphere. Most of the population seems to sit around or play *pétanque* in El Firal, the main square (**SI**). It's surprisingly unspoilt for a border town, but the only notable attraction is the **Ville Haute**, with its steep cobbled streets, church and Plaça d'Amunt. Once the central square, this was the site of one of the major residences of the Counts of Besalù in the twelfth century, then rulers over the area. If you want to stay, there are a few cheap hotels and three campsites, including a **Camping municipal** about 1km towards La Preste.

From here it is only 13km to the border on the **Col d'Ares,** with the next place of any size on the other side being **Camprodòn**, a village about 18km away. Alternatively, if you're feeling especially energetic, you can bus or hitch the 8km to La Preste, and then walk over the **Col Prégon**. It's about an hour's steep climb to the top, followed by another hour's more gentle descent down to the small village of **Espinavell**. (Leave the road at the first turning on the right before you get into La Preste, and then take the path from La Forge.)

From Tech to Têt

The only practical route between the two valleys, especially if you're hitching, is D618 from Amélie-les-Bains to BOULETERNERE. It's an interesting mountain road with several good stops on the way.

About half way along is the ruined **Château de Belpuig**, some 25-minutes' walk from the road. There is not a lot there any more, though the views are glorious, across to Canigou, the Corbières and even the COTE VERMEILLE. Just below the castle, on the road, is the **Chapelle de la Trinité**, a tiny dark Romanesque church noted for a particularly finely carved twelfth-century crucifix. Then, a little further, through the pretty hamlet of BOULE D'AMONT with another minuscule Romanesque church, and off a turn up a series of hairpin bends, you come to the remarkable **Prieuré de Serrabonne** (9am–noon and 2–6pm; closed Tues.). Even without its carvings, Serrabonne would still be deeply impressive purely by virtue of its location: high up on the mountainside, with massive views out over the rocky Boulès valley and into the valley of the Têt. Yet it is also one of the finest – perhaps the finest – example of Roussillon Romanesque. The **interior** of the church is breathtakingly simple, making the beautiful **carvings** on the capitals of the pillars in the tribune even more striking: vividly carved lions, centaurs and griffons, all in the local pink marble. The altar is made of the same stone, as are the pillars and equally elaborate capitals of the cloister, which is set to one side of the church on a high terrace. Despite the rigours of monastic life here – all abandoned now – the settlement was relatively well developed, with the remains of terraced cultivation and irrigation systems still visible.

The Mediterranean coast

Known as the **Côte Vermeille**, the last few miles of shore before Spain, where the Pyrenees sweep down to the sea, once held a handful of attractive seaside villages. Tourism has put paid to that.

ARGELES, the first of the resorts, is lively and friendly, but packed with English. There's an interesting **Musée Catalan** in rue de l'Egalité (9am–noon and 3.30–6pm; closed Sat. pm and Sun.) with some good folk-life exhibits. **COLLIOURE**, set on its bay and once by far the prettiest of these places, inspiring Matisse and Derain in 1905 to embark on their explosive Fauvist colour experiments, is now overly quaint. Still, its seventeenth-century **church** on the harbour remains remarkable, with its belfry a former lighthouse and the best **beach** just beyond it, as does the **Château des Templiers** (2.30–7.30) on a rocky scarp above the sea. Dating from the twelfth to thirteenth century and added to at various later stages, the castle is a maze of rooms and halls, some with interesting permanent exhibitions, for example, on the 1848 revolution in Roussillon, roads in the area, wine-making, while under the central courtyard there's a labyrinth of passages built for defence in the seventeenth and eighteenth centuries.

PORT-VENDRES, next down the coast, is a functional sort of place. Although the harbour has never been as busy as it was in the nineteenth century with colonial trade and ferries from North Africa, it still lands more fish than any other on this stretch of coast. If you're interested, the boats come in between about 4.30 and 6pm every day, except Sunday. You can watch them unload and auction the catch on the dock at the far end of the harbour. Otherwise, there is not much to see here. Various places offer **wine-tasting**, since the town is in the *Banyuls* region. Try the *Cellier des Templiers* (Cave Violet) on rue Jules-Ferry. There's an **SI** on the harbour front, where, should you want to stay, you can ask about **accommodation**; there's plenty to choose from. **Campsites**: one just to the left of the station and one on the south side of the harbour, just up the hill.

Further south towards **BANYULS**, the road bends through attractive scenery with the Albères rising steeply on the landward side, with a small sandy cove at PAULLILES, accessible from the road. Banyuls itself, though a bit touristy, is more laid-back than Port-Vendres, with a broad sweep of pebble beach lined with palms and cafés. The **SI** is at the southern end of the beach, and, again, there are plenty of **hotels** and at least two **campsites**.

At **CERBERES**, last stop before the frontier, there is nothing but a handful of hotels, a scrubby little beach and a large and grubby international railway station. It's not worth getting off the train for.

travel details

Trains

From Bayonne several daily to Bordeaux (1 hr. 50 min.) via Dax; several to St-Jean-de-Luz (30 min.); several to Irun (1 hr.); 4 to St-Jean-Pied-de-Port (1 hr. 10 min.); 4 to Toulouse (4 hr.) via Puyôo (30 min.). Orthez (50 min.), Pau (1½ hr.), Lourdes (1 hr. 40 min.), Tarbes (2 hr.), Lannemazan (2 hr. 40 min.), Montréjeau (2 hr. 50 min.), St-Gaudens (3 hr.), Boussens (3¼hr.) – more frequent over short stretches of the route.

From Toulouse regular to Luchon (2¼hr.), and to Barcelona (7¼ hr.) via Pamiers (50 min.), Foix (1 hr. 5 min.), Tarascon (1 hr. 20 min.), Ax-les-Thermes (1 hr. 45 min.) and La-Tour-de-Carol (2 hr. 55 min.); several to Auch (1 hr.).

From Perpignan about 5 daily to Villefranche-de-Conflent (1 hr.) via Prades (45 min.); several to Narbonne (30–40 min.), Béziers (1 hr.), Montpellier (2 hr.), Nîmes (2½ hr.) and Avignon (3 hr.); 5 to Collioure (20 min.), Cerbère (30–50 min.) and Port-Bou (50 min.–1 hr. 20 min.); some continue into Spain.

Buses (SNCF)

From Puyôo 2 or 3 most days to Mauléon (1½hr.) via Salies-de-Béarn (¼ hr.) and Sauveterre (50 min.).

From Pau: 1 daily in summer to Artouste (1¼hr.) via Laruns and Gabas.

From Lourdes regular but infrequent to Cauterets (1 hr.) via Pierrefitte (35 min.) and to Barèges (1 hr. 25 min.) via Luz-St-Sauveur (1 hr. 5 min.).

From Tarbes regular to Bagnères-de-Bigorre (35 min.); some to Auch.

From Lannemazan regular but infrequent to St-Lary (1 hr.) via Arreau.

From Montréjeau regular but infrequent to Luchon (1 hr.) via Labroquère (5 min. – for St-Bertrand-de-Comminges).

From Boussens: regular but infrequent to St-Girons (45 min.).

Buses (private)

From St-Jean-de-Luz very frequent to Hendaye; 4 to San Sebastian; 6 to Sare-la-Rhune; also to

Espelette (35 min.), Cambo-les-Bains (45 min.) and Hasparren (1 hr. 5 min.).
From Bayonne 7 to Cambo-les-Bains; 2 to Mauléon; almost hourly to St-Jean-de-Luz; 4 to San Sebastian.
From Biarritz 4 to Hendaye; 3 to Pau (2 hr. 10 min.) via Orthez and 3 via Salies-de-Béarn (2½ hr.); very frequent to St-Jean-de-Luz.
From Pau to Lourdes (1½ hr.); Mauléon (1 hr. 50 min.); Orthez (1 hr.10 min.); 4 to Eaux-Bonnes (1 hr. 25 min.) via Laruns (1 hr.10 min.); 3 go on to La Gourette (1 hr. 45 min.) and 1 to Col d'Aubisque (2 hr.).
From Lourdes to Barèges (1 hr.) via Luz-St-Sauveur (45 min.); 2 to Gavarnie (1 hr. 25 min.) via Luz.
From Toulouse Several daily to Ax-les-Thermes (3 hr. 10 min.) via Pamiers (1 hr. 25 min.), Foix (2 hr.) and Tarascon (2 hr. 25 min.); also to Auch.
From Auch services to Tarbes, Lourdes, Montauban, Agen, Mont-de-Marsan and Lannermazan.
From Perpignan frequent to Canet and other coastal towns; a few to Collioure; a few along the Têt valley; 6 to Céret (40 min.).

CHAPTER NINE

LANGUEDOC

Languedoc is more an idea than a geographical entity. The modern region covers only a fraction of the lands where once **Occitan** or the *langue d'oc* – the language of *oc*, the southern Gallo-Latin word for *oui* – was spoken. These stretched south from Bordeaux and Lyon into Spain and north-west Italy. **Toulouse**, the cultural capital, though included in this chapter, lies outside the official region.

The heartland today is the **Bas Languedoc**, the coastal plain and dry stony vine-growing hills between **Carcassonne** and **Nîmes**. It is here that the **Occitan movement** has its power base. Its demands, separatist only on the lunatic fringe, are for greater independence and recognition of its linguistic and cultural distinctiveness. Its appeal derives from widespread resentment against subservience to the bureaucrats of remote and alien Paris. In recent times this has been focused on Parisian determination to drag the conservative province into the twentieth century with massive **tourist development** on the coast and drastic transformation of the **cheap wine industry**. But it is also mixed up in the collective folk-memory with the brutal repression of the Protestant **Camisards** around 1700, the thirteenth-century massacres of the **Cathars,** and the subsequent obliteration of the brilliant *langue d'oc* **troubadour civilisation**. And this same hostility has made an essentially rural and conservative population vote – paradoxically – massively **Left.**

It's a quirky, eccentric part of the world. And, though things are changing under the impact of a modernised economy, the sense of being Occitanian remains strong. Thousands of **students** take the language at school and follow courses at the universities of Montpellier and Toulouse. The **Cathars** have become a boom industry, and a number of writers use Occitan as their normal medium of expression, though none with the distinction of the poet **Frédéric Mistral**, who won a Nobel Prize in 1904 for his work in resuscitating Provençal (the same language as Occitan with different dialects).

High points for the visitor are numerous and various. There are great stretches of **dramatic landscape** and **river gorges**, from the Cévennes foothills in the east to the Montagne Noire and the Corbières hills in the west. There's **superb ecclesiastical architecture** in Toulouse, Albi, and St-Guilhem-le-Désert; **medieval towns** in Cordes and Carcassonne with the unforgettably romantic **Cathar castles** to the south; extensive **Roman remains** in Nîmes; and great swathes of **beach** where, away from the major resorts, you can still find a mile or two to yourself.

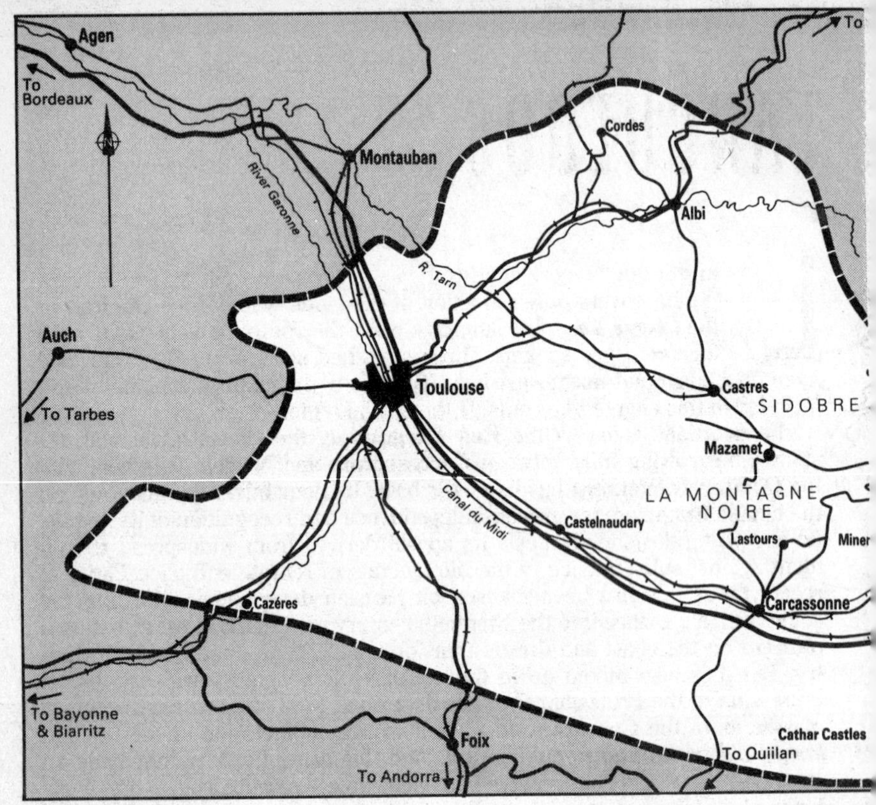

THE SEABOARD AND THE EAST

Heading south from Paris, via Lyon and the Rhône valley, you can go one of two ways: east to Provence and the Côte d'Azur, which is what most people do, or west to Nîmes, Montpellier and the comparatively untouched northern Languedoc coast. **Nîmes** itself, while not officially part of the modern Languedoc region, makes for a good introduction to the region, a hectic modern town impressive both for its Roman remains and some scattered attractions – the **Pont du Gard** for one – nearby. **Montpellier**, also, is worth a day or two, not so much for any historical attractions as for a heady vibrancy, proximity to **Sète** (much the best springboard for this part of the coast) and ease of access to the ancient villages, churches, and fine scenery of the upper **Hérault valley**.

This is the part of Languedoc most affected by the spread of **Protestantism** in the sixteenth century, an experience that has marked the

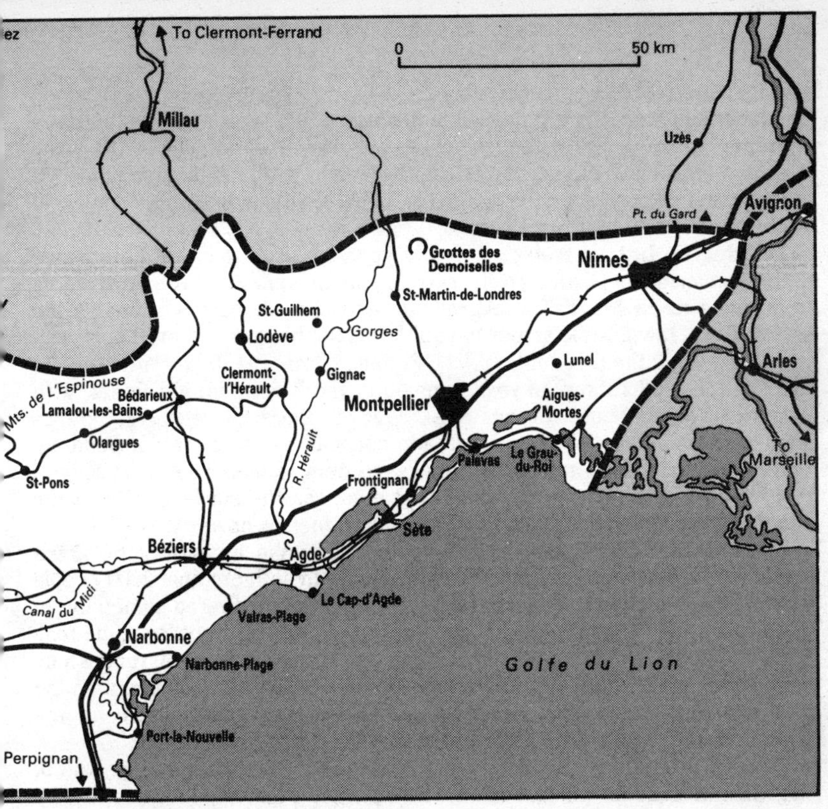

region's character more than any other. For the Protestants, with their attachment to rationality and self-improvement, espoused the cause of French over Occitan, supported the Revolution and the Republic, fought Napoléon III's coup against the 1848 revolution and adhered to the anti-clerical and socialist movement under the Third Republic. They dominated the local textile industry in the nineteenth century and, interestingly, were extremely active in the Resistance to the Nazis.

They also suffered a great deal for their cause, as did the whole region. After the Revocation of the Edict of Nantes – the treaty that had restored religious toleration at the end of the sixteenth century – in 1685, persecution drove their most committed supporters, especially in the Cévennes to the north, to form clandestine *assemblées du Désert* and finally, in 1702, to take up arms in the first guerrilla war of modern times, *la guerre des Camisards*. These conflicts are still very much present in the minds of both Huguenot and Catholic families.

Nîmes

The name of **NIMES** is inescapably linked to two things: denim and Rome. The latter's influence is highly visible in some of the most extensive **Roman remains** in Europe, while the former, equally visible on the backsides of the populace, was first manufactured in the city's textile mills (denim = *de Nîmes*), and exported to the southern USA in the nineteenth century to clothe the slaves. Come for the ruins.

Arriving by bus or train, you'll find yourself heading up **av Feuchères** to the Esplanade de Gaulle. To the right the main boulevards run northwards from **place de la Libération**. Ahead you have the tall, narrow streets of the oldest part of town, while across to your left is the biggest and most spectacular edifice of all: the first century A.D. Roman **arena**, *Les Arènes* (mid-June to mid-Sept., 8am–8pm; rest of year, 9am–noon and 2–6pm; **single ticket**, with half-price for students, for all sites). One of the best preserved arenas anywhere, its arcaded two-storey facade conceals massive interior vaulting, riddled with corridors and supporting raked tiers of seats with a capacity of more than 20,000 spectators. Blood and guts was the staple fare: feed the people pap and keep them quiet was the policy, then as now.

When Rome's sway was broken by the barbarian invasions, the arena became a fortress and eventually a slum, home to an incredible 2000 people when it was cleared in the early 1800s. Today it has recovered something of its former role. On summer Sundays the crowds still turn out for some real-life bloodletting, for Nîmes is the number-one European **bull-fighting** scene outside Spain, though it is also the location for gentler pursuits: opera on the grand scale, and Dizzy Gillespie going for the high notes in the **International Festival de Jazz**.

Going for the Roman angle: a short walk up bd Victor-Hugo brings you to the **Maison Carrée**, a neat, compact little temple, celebrated for its integrity and its almost Greek harmony of proportion. Built in 5 A.D., it is dedicated to the adopted sons of the emperor Augustus: all part of the business of blowing up the imperial personality cult. No surprise then that Napoléon, with his love of flummery and ennobling his cronies to boost his own legitimacy, should have taken it as the model for the church of the Madeleine in Paris.

It stands in its own small square opposite rue Auguste (**SI** at no. 6), where the Roman forum used to be. Around it are scattered pieces of Roman masonry, while inside is a **museum** with some good sculpture and a frieze of Nemausus, deity of the local spring, from whose name Nîmes is derived (mid-June to mid-Sept., 9am–7pm; rest of the year, 9am–noon and 2–5pm).

Though already a prosperous city on the *via Domitia*, the main road from Italy to Spain, Nîmes did especially well by Augustus. He gave it its walls, remnants of which surface here and there around the town, and its gates, as the inscription on the surviving **Porte d'Auguste** records, at the end of rue Nationale, the Roman main street. He also, indirectly, gave it the chained crocodile of its coat of arms. The device was copied from an Augustan coin struck to commemorate his defeat of Antony and Cleopatra. And he settled his veterans on the surrounding land.

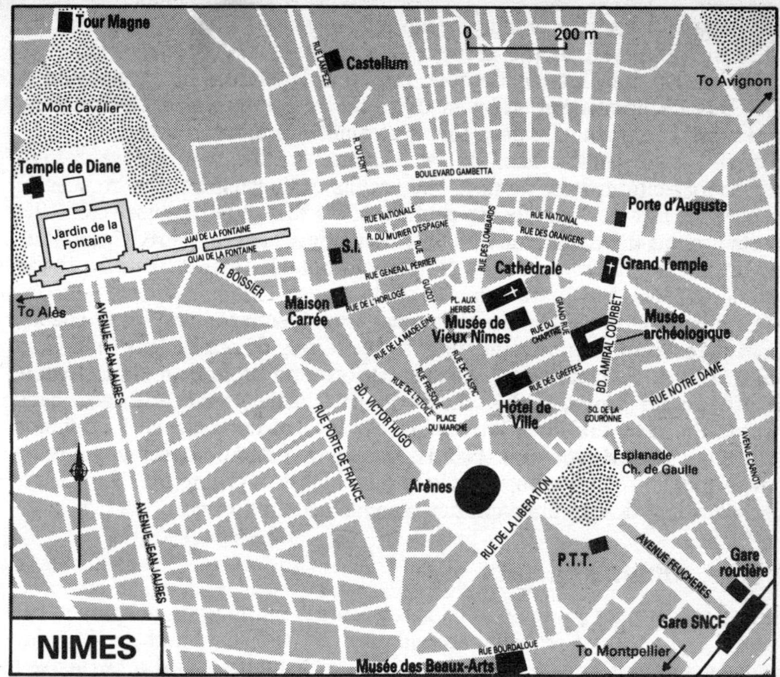

If you still have an appetite for things Roman, head for the very French and very eighteenth-century **Jardin de la Fontaine**, encircled by canals built to supplement the rather unsteady supply of water from the *fontaine*, the spring, whose presence in a dry, scrubby, limestone landscape gave Nîmes its existence. The crocodile appears on the entrance gates. Fountains and nymphs and formal trees enclose the so-called **Temple of Diana** (summer 9am–7pm; otherwise, same hours as other Romans), while behind, steps climb the steep slope to the **Tour Magne** (hours as above), a substantial watchtower from Augustus's walls, with a terrific view out over the surrounding country – as far as Mt. Canigou.

East from the gardens, classy quai de la Fontaine follows the canal to square Antonin. Ahead bd Gambetta joins bd Amiral-Courbet along the line of the old city walls. Just off to the left, with some rarity value, but still requiring real Roman commitment, the vestigial **castellum** on rue de la Lampèze (hours as above) houses the distribution device used by the Romans to channel water from the aqueduct to the various parts of the city.

Going right from square Antonin back towards the Maison Carrée, then left up rue de l'Horloge, you come to the **cathedral**, mutilated in the Wars of Religion and significantly altered in the last century. Alphonse Daudet was born in its shadow, as was Jean Nicot – a doctor, no less – who introduced tobacco into France from Portugal in 1560, and gave his name to the world's most popular drug. It is practically the only existing medieval building. The rest were destroyed in the turmoil that followed the *Michelade*, the St. Michael's Day massacre of Catholic clergy and notables by Protestants in 1567. Despite brutal repression in the wake of the *Camisard* insurrection, Nîmes was, and remains, a doggedly Protestant stronghold.

Banned from public office, the Protestants, like the Jews elsewhere, put their energy into making money. The results of their efforts can be seen in the seventeenth- and eighteenth-century *hôtels* they built themselves in the streets around the cathedral: rue de l'Aspic, du Chapitre, Doré, Grand'Rue, among others. Their church is the serious-looking **Grand Temple** on bd Amiral-Courbet.

Just along the boulevard, in a classical seventeenth-century Jesuit chapel, the **Musée archéologique** (in summer 9am–7pm; otherwise 9am–noon and 2–5pm; closed Sun. am) gives further background on Roman Nîmes, while the **Musée du Vieux Nîmes** (same hours), in the Bishop's Palace, back towards the cathedral, has interesting displays of Renaissance furnishings and décor. The **Musée des Beaux-Arts**, (rue Cité-Foulc; same hours as above) prides itself on a huge Gallo-Roman mosaic showing the *Marriage of Admetus*. Its contemporary work has recently been rehoused.

Events, rooms and eats

There's always a lot going on in Nîmes: a Sunday morning **fleamarket** at the eastern end of bd Gambetta around the St-Baudille church, a Monday **produce market** under the trees along the boulevard, and a permanent market at **Les Halles** on rue Général-Perrier near the Maison Carrée. From May to September dozens of other events take place: exhibitions, concerts, drama, **bullfights** and **festivals**. Particular bullfighting events to watch out for are the *corrida* of gypsy *torreros*, on September 7, and the *Feria des Vendanges* at the end of September. **Festivals** include the *Foire de Nîmes* in May, the brilliant big-name *Festival de Jazz* in the Arènes in mid-July, and the *Autumn Music Festival*, which runs from the end of September to the end of November – two months of great music, much of it to be heard at *Musique en Stock*, 28 rue Jean-Reboul, a club with plenty of blues, jazz, soul, funk and rock & roll. You can pick up information on these and other happenings at the **SI** on rue Auguste. It also changes money, if you're stuck.

For a room, middle-range **hotels** cluster around square de la Couronne at the beginning of bd Courbet. Try *La Couronne* at no. 4 (☎66.67.51.73) on the *square*, or the *Nouvel Hôtel* at 6 bd Amiral-Courbet (☎66.67.62.48), or there's the *Majestic* on rue Pradier just off av Feuchères. Around the arena is also a promising area to look. For the **youth hostel** (☎66.23.25.04; tent space) on chemin de la Cigale, take bus #6 from the **gare SNCF** to stop *La Cigale*. The last bus goes at 8pm. The main **campsite** is the *Domaine de la Bastide* on route de Générac 4km or so from the station (bus #4).

For **eating,** bd de la Libération and Amiral-Courbet harbour a stock of reasonably-priced **brasseries** and **pizzerias**, and the café scene is very lively along here. Bd Victor-Hugo also has several popular cafés and *La Feria* restaurant is worth a try. *A l'Escargot* and *Auberge Lou Gardianne* in the pedestrian zone on rue Fresque behind the arena do inexpensive menus.

Gare routière is on rue Ste-Félicité near the railway station. **Post offices** are in bd de Bruxelles at the top of av Feuchères and on the corner of bd Gambetta and rue de la Porte-d'Alès.

Around: the Pont du Gard and Uzès

Several **buses** a day head east from Nîmes' gare routière along the Avignon road to **UZES** via **PONT DU GARD**. Uzès – at the **source de l'Eure** – was the start of the 50km aqueduct built by the Romans in 19 A.D. to bring fresh water into Nîmes. With just 17 metres difference in altitude between start and finish, it was quite an achievement, running as it does up hill and down dale, through a tunnel, along the top of a wall, cut into trenches, over rivers. The greatest surviving stretch is the bridge that carries it over the river Gard, the **Pont du Gard**. Tourist trap it may be, but it's nonetheless a supreme piece of engineering, a brilliant combination of function and aesthetics. It made the impressionable Rousseau wish he'd been born Roman.

Three tiers of arches span the river, with the covered water conduit on the top, rendered with a special plaster waterproofed with a paint based on fig juice! Whatever the recipe, it's in need of a powerful descaler to remove the lime deposits of centuries. You can walk across, if the height does not bother you. The whole structure narrows as it rises and is slightly bowed on the upstream side for extra resistance to flooding. A visit was a must for French journeymen masons on their traditional tour of the country, and many of them have left their names and home towns carved on the stone work. You can also see markings of the this-side-up variety left on individual stones in the arches by the original builders: *FR S III – frons sinistra*, front side left no. 3, which seems to contract the span of the centuries rather fast.

Uzès is only another 17km, an attractive old town perched on a hill above the river Alzon, a bit of a backwater until renovation put it on the tourist circuit. Half a dozen medieval towers – the most fetching the windowed Pisa-like **Tour Fenestrelle**, tacked on to the much later cathedral – rise above its tiled roofs and narrow lanes of Renaissance and classical houses, the residences of the seventeenth- and eighteenth-century local bourgeoisie, grown rich like their Protestant co-religionists in Nîmes on textiles. From **Le Portalet**, with its view out over the valley, walk past the classical church of St-Etienne into the medieval **place aux Herbes** (Sunday am market: truffles in winter) and up the arcaded **rue de la République**. The Gide family used to live off the *place*, the young André spending summer vacations with his granny there. To the right of rue de la République the castle of **Le Duché** (9.30am–noon and 2.30/3.30–6.30 or dark), still inhabited by the same family a thousand years on, is dominated by its original keep, the Tour Bermonde. Opposite, the courtyard of the eighteenth-century Hôtel de Ville holds summer concerts. For details of these and other summer events, including more bull-running *corridas*, consult the **SI** in av de la Libération next to the **bus station** (**Post Office** opposite; **Camping municipal** off av Pascal).

Montpellier

A thousand years of trade and intellect have made **MONTPELLIER** a teeming, energetic city. Benjamin of Tudela, the tireless twelfth-century Jewish traveller, reported its streets crowded with traders, Christian and Saracen, Arabs from the Mahgreb, merchants from Lombardy, from the kingdom of Rome, from every corner of Egypt, Greece, Gaul, Spain, Genoa and Pisa. A few hiccups – like being sold to France in 1349, almost total destruction for its Protestantism in 1622, depression in the wine trade in the early years of this century – have done little more than dent this progress. The reputation of its university, founded in the thirteenth century, and especially its medical school, has shone untarnished. With its faculty and 46,000 students it still sets the intellectual and cultural tone of the city, which, since the repatriation of the *pieds noirs* from Algeria in the 1960s, has been the fastest-growing in France.

At its hub is **place de la Comèdie** – *L'Oeuf* to the initiated – a colossal oval square, paved with cream-coloured marble, with a fountain in the middle surrounded by cafés. At one end bulks the **Opéra**, an enormous, ornate nineteenth-century theatre. The other opens on to the **Esplanade**, a vast promenade about ½km long where the city's dodgy characters gather to do their deals under the lines of plane trees, and African musicians busk on summer nights. Off to the right is a typically French think-big urban development: the slightly tacky but comprehensive **Polygone** shopping complex, and behind it a whole new *quartier* designed by the Catalan architect, Ricardo Bofill, to house 10,000 people at moderate rents in colonnaded and painted concrete – the kind of project that gets compared to carbuncles.

To get to *L'Oeuf* from the **gare SNCF**, simply head up rue Maguelone more or less opposite as you come out. The main office of the **SI** is at no. 6, with an annexe in the station. Then continuing straight across the square in front of the theatre you penetrate the tangled, hilly lanes of Montpellier's **oldest quarter**. Practically no buildings survive from before the 1622 siege, but the city's busy bourgeoisie quickly made up for the loss, proclaiming their financial power in lots of austere seventeenth- and eighteenth-century mansions. Known as *Lou Clapas* (the rubble), the quarter is a curious mix of chic restoration and squalid disorder.

The first street you come to is the neat, pedestrians-only **Grand-Rue Jean-Moulin**. Moulin, hero of the Resistance, lived at no. 21. Back to your left, at no. 32, the present-day Chamber of Commerce is located in one of the fanciest eighteenth-century *hôtels*, originally built as a demonstration operating theatre for medical students, the **Hôtel St-Côme** (open daily, except weekends; free). On the opposite corner, rue de l'Argenterie forks up to **place Jean-Jaurès**. Through the Gothic doorway of no. 10 is the so-called palace of the kings of Aragon, who ruled Montpellier for a stretch in the thirteenth century. The *place* with its morning **market** and cafés is a nodal point in the city's commercial life. Next door is the **Halle Castellane**, Montpellier's answer to Paris' famous iron-framed *Halles*, and through it runs **rue de la Loge**, connecting at its northern end with **rue Foch,** the pair of them sliced through the city's heart in the 1880s in Montpellier's own Haussmannising spree.

A very short walk from the top side of the *place* the *Hôtel de Varennes* on place Pétrarque houses two local history museums of somewhat specialised interest: the **Musée du Vieux Montpellier** (10–11am and 1.30–5pm; closed weekends), concentrating on the city's history, and the more interesting, private **Musée du Fougau** (Wed. and Thurs. 3–7pm), dealing with the folk history of Languedoc and things Occitan. Off to the right you get into the lively little rue des Trésoriers-de-France with one of the best seventeenth-century houses, the *Hôtel Lunaret*, at no. 5.

Left from place Jaurès, on the hill at the end of rue Foch, from which the royal artillery bombarded the Protestants in 1622, you look out across the city and away to the rolling hills of the Cévennes from the formal gardens of the **Promenade du Peyrou**. At the farther end a swagged and pillared water-tower marks the end of an eighteenth-century aqueduct modelled on the Pont du Gard. Beneath its arches there is a huge Saturday **flea market**, which on Sundays moves to Nîmes. At the city end of the promenade a vain-

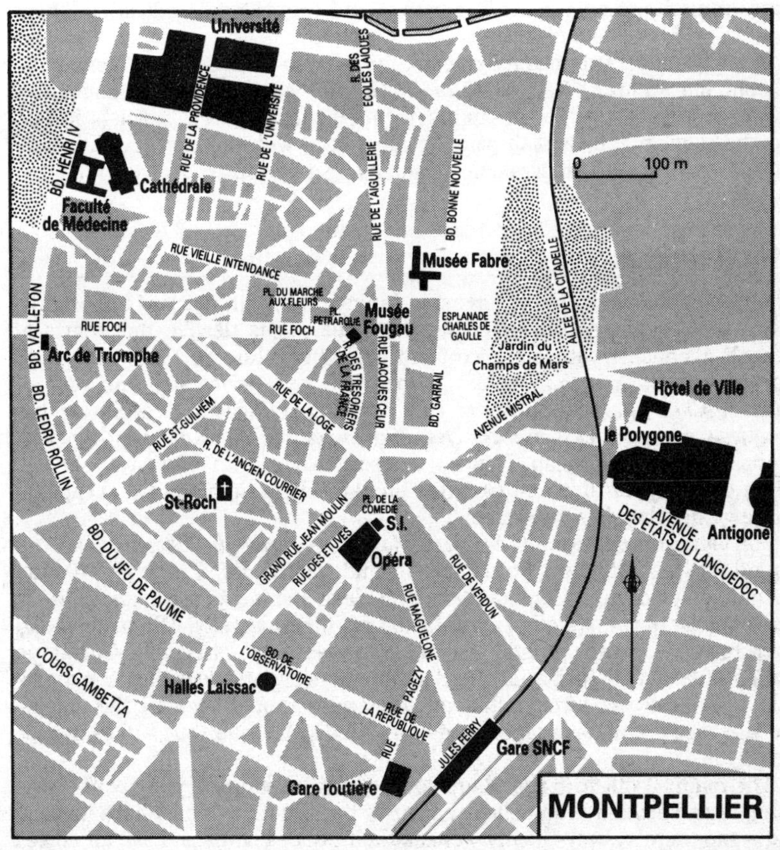

glorious **triumphal arch** shows Louis XIV-Hercules stomping on the Austrian eagle and the English lion, and tactlessly reminding the locals of his victory over their 'heresy'.

The **Jardin des Plantes** lower down the hill, with its alleys of exotic trees, is France's oldest botanical garden, where, in the poet Paul Valéry's words, 'the pensive, the careworn and talkers-to-themselves come towards evening'. Both this and the Promenade du Peyrou are great places for wandering aimlessly. Opposite, on the other side of bd Henri-IV, the university's prestigious medical school houses the **Musée Atger** (10am–6pm; closed weekends and university holidays) with a distinguished collection of French and Italian drawings and the macabre **Musée anatomique** (2–5pm; closed weekends). Behind is the long-suffering **cathedral**, a patchwork of styles from the fourteenth to nineteenth century. Inside is a memorial to the bishop of Montpellier who sided with the half-million destitute vinegrowers who came to demonstrate against their plight in 1907 and were fired on by government troops for their pains. Beyond it lies the old university quarter, with some good **bookshops** on rue de l'Université and the friendly, radical *Le Chant Général* on rue de l'Aiguillerie.

The city's most trumpeted museum, the **Musée Fabre** (9am–noon and 2–5.30pm; closed Mon.; free Wed.) on bd Sarrail by the Esplanade, contains a vast collection of seventeenth- to nineteenth-century French, Spanish, Italian, Dutch, Flemish and English painting most of it, with the exception of some Delacroix, Courbets, Impressionists and a few modernists, of academic interest only.

Practicalities

The Occitan movement is strongest in Montpellier, with many of the original Occitan street-names reinstated on the street signs despite the efforts of French nationalist enthusiasts to paint over them. Rue de l'Université – or *Carrieria de la Blancaria* – holds a number of inexpensive **cafés and restaurants** – *Chez Jules, La Saladière* and *Fac'Burger Caféteria*, – while on rue Jacques-Coeur are *Crêperie des Deux Provinces*, with 140 different types of crêpe, and a good cheap Chinese dim-sum place, with take-away service. More centrally, *Ya Bon* and *Le Yam's* on place de la Comédie are cheap and vibrant cafés that do simple meals.

For **accommodation**, the *Hôtel Majestic (4 rue du Cheval-Blanc,* off Grand-Rue-Jean-Moulin; ☎67.66.26.85) and *Hôtel des Touristes* (10 rue Baudin, off place de la Comédie) are both clean and inexpensive; and *Hôtel de Rouergue* at 18 rue JJ-Rousseau is handy for the university. The grubby and overcrowded **youth hostel** is at 2 impasse de la Petite-Corraterie (☎67.79.61.66). *CROUS*, at 11 rue Baudin, offers assistance with accommodation, specifically for foreign students. **Campers** should head for the municipal site 2km out of town to the east on route de Mauguio (bus #15 from gare SNCF).

The main **SI** office (6 rue Maguelone) has full listings of just about everything in and around Montpellier. For up-to-the-minute info on what's happening – and there's always plenty – check their notice-boards and ask for copies of *Le Mois à Montpellier* and *Montpellier Votre Ville*. Riotous **solstice fairs** take place all over town at midsummer (*Fêtes de St-Jean*); there's a superb month-long **dance festival** in June and July, and an international **Festival of music** (classical) from early July to the first week in August.

Montpellier has excellent bus (**gare routière** next to the railway station) and train connections; a free bus (#16, marked *Le Guilhem*) runs between the stations and the Promenade du Peyrou. The **airport** is about 8km away on the edge of Etang de Mauguio (☎67.65.60.65); *Air France* office, 6 rue Broussairolles (☎67.58.81.94).

There's an *Allostop* office at 9 rue du Plan-de-l'Olivier and a **discount travel service** in the gare SNCF. There, you can also hire a **bike**, or wait until you get into town and go to *Le Vélo*, 6 rue des Ecoles-Laïques. Should you need one, the main regional **hospital** is St-Charles, 300 rue Broussonet (☎67.63.91.64). The **Post Office** is on rue Rondelet.

For a **quick dip**, you can take the bus down to **PALAVAS**, more or less the town beach for Montpellier and very popular with the students. The sand is great, but it is often windy, and the beach is backed by an ugly concrete waterfront, packed with casinos and places to dance.

Heading inland

For getting out into the country of the Bas Languedoc, there are two good routes from Montpellier, both served by regular buses: D986 to **GANGES** and N109 to **LODEVE**.

The Ganges road weaves north across the plateau of the *garrigue*, a landscape of scrubby trees, thorns and hot-smelling herbs cut by torrent beds. The distance is dominated by the high limestone ridge of the **Pic St-Loup** until you reach the first worthwhile stopping place, **ST-MARTIN-DE-LONDRES**. The name derives from the Occitan word, *loundres* – otters. It's a lovely little place of arcaded houses and cobbled passageways, set around a triangular main square. Its pride is an exceptionally handsome early Romanesque church, the honey-coloured stone simply decorated with Lombard arcading, the plain rounded porch with a worn relief of St. Martin on horseback. There's a **campsite** just out on the SOMMIERES road.

Further north, almost to Ganges, through dramatic river gorges, you reach the **GROTTE DES DEMOISELLES** (April–Oct. 9am–noon and 2–6.30pm; rest of the year, 9.30–11.30am and 2–6.30pm), most spectacular of the region's many caves: a set of vast cathedral-like caverns hung with stalactites descending with millenial slowness to meet the limpid waters of eerily still pools. Deep inside the mountain, it is reached by funicular (regular departures).

GANGES itself is unremarkable, but pleasant enough with its small squares, tree-lined walks and vaulted alleys designed for defence in the Wars of Religion, for it too was a Protestant town, peopled by refugees from the plains. They made it famous for its silk stockings. And it was here too that the last-ditch revolt of the **Camisards** earned its name. The rebels sacked and pillaged a shirt factory and went off wearing the shirts – *chemises*.

The Gignac route

The other route runs west to the small wine town of **GIGNAC**, where a fine eighteenth-century bridge spans the Hérault. With its scatter of seventeenth- to eighteenth-century houses and churches, a small hotel and a campsite, it makes a viable stopover, especially if you're on your way to or from the glorious **abbey** and village of **ST-GUILHEM-LE-DESERT**.

Hitching, it's best to go through ANIANE (with the imposing classical church of St-Sauveur for enthusiasts) and across the eleventh-century **Pont du Diable**, supposedly the earliest medieval bridge in the country. **St-Guilhem** is in a side ravine of the Hérault gorge, here at its wildest and most spectacular. With a ruined castle spiking the ridge above, the ancient tiled houses of the village ramble down the banks of the rushing Verdus, everywhere channelled into carefully tended gardens. Grand focus is the tenth- to eleventh-century **abbey**, founded at the beginning of the ninth century by St-Guilhem, comrade-in-arms of Charlemagne and scourge of the Saracens. It is beautiful and atmospheric, though architecturally impoverished by the dismantling and sale of its cloister in the nineteenth century; it is now in the Cloisters Museum in New York. Sadly, tourism has hit the village in a big way, though out of season it still feels like a close religious community. There is another good cave, the **Grotte de Clamouse**, 3km back down the road.

Continuing west from Gignac you come to the bustling provincial town of **CLERMONT-L'HERAULT**, an important local centre with a big weekly market (Wed.), an impressive fortified church and a realistically priced hotel, the *Terminus*. Nearby, though not really worth the trouble without a car, is the cramped medieval village of **MOUREZE**, set in the weirdly eroded landscape of the **Cirque de Mourèze**.

Forging on to Lodève itself, the road hits country scarred by uranium mining, and threatened with further development. The fact that the area around the village of **ST-MARTIN-DU-BOSC** has soil with the highest concentration of radioactivity in the world gives some indication of just how much things are going to be changing here in the future. **LODEVE**, at the confluence of the Lergues and Soulondres Rivers, and almost in the shadow of Larzac, is a raucous sort of place with a huge Saturday market, another interesting fortified cathedral and, in the park alongside, a daring and unusual *Monument aux morts* by the self-taught local artist, Paul Dardé – more of whose work is on display in the unmemorable town museum in the Hôtel Fleury. If you're staying any length of time, the **SI** is at 7 place de la République, next door to the **gare routière**.

To the coast: , Sète, Agde and around

On the face of it **Languedoc beaches** aren't particularly enticing: bleak strands, often irritatingly windswept and cut off from their hinterland by marshy *étangs*. But what they do have is long hours of sunshine, 200km of sand still only sporadically populated, and relatively unpolluted water. This could change, as for the last couple of decades the French government has poured money into this area at an amazing rate, building seven new resorts in twice as many years. But for the moment, as long as you steer well clear of these new towns – ugly, soulless places for the most part, anyway – deserted beaches are still there for the walking.

First built of the new resorts, on the fringes of the Camargue, was **LA GRANDE-MOTTE**, an extravagant futuristic vision of concrete and glass pyramids and cones ranged around a broad sandy beach. In summer its seaside and streets are crowded with semi-naked bodies; in winter, it's a depressing, wind-battered place with few permanent residents. A little way east are **PORT-CAMARGUE** with a sparkling new marina and **GRAU-DU-ROI**, an older, and until recently slightly tattered fishing port, now moving into the twenty-first century. Inland a few kilometres lurks appealingly named **AIGUES-MORTES**, built by Louis IX in the thirteenth century and defended by massive walls and towers that remain virtually intact. Outside the walls, amid drab modern development, flat salt plains lend a certain other-worldly appeal, but inside all is geared to the tourist. If you visit, climb up the **Tour de Constance** on the northwest corner, where Camisard women were imprisoned (poor Marie Durand did 38 years) and walk the wall, gazing out over the weird mist-shrouded flats of the Parc de Camargue.

Sète

Further down the coast, perched around the steep and sudden slopes of the Mont St-Clair on the edge of the Bassin de Thau, **SETE** has been an important port for three hundred years. Intersected by waterways lined with tall terraces and seafood restaurants, it's a lively place, particularly during its intense summer *joutes nautiques*. As a base for exploring this part of the coast, or just a single night, it is hard to beat.

The pedestrian streets, crowded and vibrant, are scattered with café tables. Climb up from the *vieux port* to the **Cimetière marin**, the sailors' cemetery, where the poet Paul Valéry is buried. A native of the town, he called Sète his 'singular island', and the **Musée Valéry** above the cemetery has a room devoted to him, as well as a small but strong collection of modern French paintings. Georges Brassens has a room to himself too.

Singer-songwriter, associate of Sartre, and the radical voice of a whole generation in France, **Brassens** was also born and raised in Sète and is buried in the Cimetière le Py on the other side of the hill – despite his song, *'Plea to be buried on the beach at Sète'*.

'My family tomb
alas, is not that new.
To be blunt, it's chock-a-block.
If I wait for someone to move out,
It'll be too late; and I can't
Say to these good folk, 'Budge up a bit,
make way for the young'.

If you're feeling energetic, you should keep going up the hill through the pines to the top, for the view, if it isn't engulfed in sea mist.

Below the sailors' cemetery, couched neatly above the water, is Vauban's **Fort St-Pierre**, which hosts a *Festival of Open-air Theatre* in August and a film festival in June. And, on the subject of **festivals**, the aforementioned **joutes nautiques** are always spectacular: water jousting contests, and highly virile events, unchanged for three hundred years, in which young men in rival boats try to knock each other into the canal with three-metre-long lances to the accompaniment of music and lots of drinking. They take place throughout the summer, but especially on the Sundays near June 29 and July 14, the Monday near August 25, and the first Sunday in September. Another big festival is the *Fête de la Saint-Louis* at the end of August.

Practicalities

The **SI** has a central annexe on place Aristide-Briand, a summer desk at the gare SNCF and a main office way out on quai d'Alger, opposite the ferry port for **boats to Morocco and the Balearic islands**. The **gare routière** is even more awkwardly placed on quai de la République, and the **gare SNCF** further out still on quai Midi-Nord – though it is on the main bus route which circles Mont St-Clair (last bus about 7pm).

For **accommodation,** there is a new annexe to what used to be a filthy, smelly and overcrowded old **youth hostel** (☎67.53.46.68) high up in the town on rue Général-Revest. Otherwise the chances of a cheap room are not very good. But try *Hôtel Le Midi* (13 rue Sémard) or *Hôtel La Tramontane* (5 rue Mistral). For full details on the numerous **campsites** scattered about the Sète coast (they fill up too), phone the *Mairie Service des Campings* (☎67.74.88.30) or consult the SI. Two of the largest sites are *Les Régales* and *Le Pont-Levis*, both on the circular bus route (stops in town centre and at gare SNCF) and conveniently near a beach.

When leaving, keep in mind that **hitching out** is horribly difficult: you're better off taking a train or bus to the nearest town and trying from there.

Agde and nudism

At the other end of the Bassin de Thau, **AGDE**, where the Canal du Midi and the river Hérault reach the sea, is historically the most interesting of the coastal towns. Originally Greek, and maintained by the Romans, it thrived for centuries on trade with the Levant. Outrun as a seaport by Sète, it later degenerated into a sleazy fishing harbour. Today, however, it is a major tourist centre with few remains of its long history. Apart from the odd fragment of town wall there's precious little to see. The grim, heavily battlemented **cathedral** merits a brief stop: like the rest of the town it is built of the distinctive dark stone quarried from the nearby extinct volcano, Mont St-Loup.

Places to eat are numerous, but the quality is low, and the price high. **Hotel rooms** go for rip-off rates, and only a few offer reasonable prices for full or half board – *Chez Rosette* on rue Gohin is one. If you're **camping** there are around 25 sites in the vicinity, all vast, lavishly equipped and usually packed to the gills. Should none of this put you off Agde completely, and you want more information on the place, the **SI** is under the town hall arcade at the bottom of av de Vias.

Cap d'Agde

CAP D'AGDE, reachable by bus from Agde, lies to the south of Mont St-Loup. The largest and by far the most successful of the new resorts, it sprawls laterally from the large volcanic mound of the Cap in an excess of pseudo-traditional modern buildings that offer every type of facility and entertainment – all expensive. It is perhaps best known for its colossal **quartier naturiste**, one of the largest in France, with the best of the beaches, space for 20,000 visitors and its own (nude) restaurants, banks, post offices and shops. Access is possible, though expensive, if you're not actually staying there. But if you want to get inside for free, you can simply walk along the beach from neighbouring MARSEILLAN-PLAGE, and remove tell-tale fabrics en route. If you have time to fill, the unattractively named **Musée de la Clape** (April-Sept. 9am–noon and 2–7pm; in winter, 9am–noon and 3–6pm; closed Mon.) displays antiquities discovered locally, many of them from beneath the sea. It's worth a visit for the beautiful little Hellenistic bronze known as the **Ephèbe d'Agde**, until recently one of the treasures of the Louvre in Paris.

BEZIERS TO THE HILLS

The southern portion of Languedoc cuts a slender triangle west, its watery coastal flats rising to low undulating hills as you move inland. Though the coast is not generally noteworthy, **Narbonne** and **Béziers** are enjoyable diversions on the way to the more refreshing and spectacular upland delights of the **Monts de l'Espinouse** and the **Parc Regional du Haut Languedoc**. Transportation is difficult, but a patient hitch-hiker with an eye for scenery can get about without much hassle.

Béziers

Though no longer the rich city of its nineteenth-century heyday BEZIERS is still the capital of the Languedoc wine country, and a focus for the Occitan movement, whose *Centre International de Documentation Occitane* is at 7 rue Rouget-des-Villes-Marseillaises. The fortunes of the movement and the vine have long been closely linked, for Occitan activists have helped to organise the militant local vine-growers. There were ugly events during the mid-seventies, when blood was shed in violent confrontations with the authorities over the importation of cheap foreign wines and the low prices paid for the essentially poor-grade local product. Things are calmer now, as the conservatism of Languedoc farmers has given way to more modern attitudes in the face of public demand for something better than the traditional table wine. As a result some of the steam has also gone out of the movement; interest today is more in the culture than in anti-Paris separatist feelings.

The first view of the old town as you come in from CARCASSONNE and the west is spectacular. From the Pont-Neuf across the river Orb, you look upstream at the sturdy golden arches of the **Pont-Vieux**, with the **cathedral** crowning the steep-banked hill behind, more like a castle than a church. The surviving building is mainly Gothic, in the northern style, the original having been burnt in 1209, when most of the population was massacred for refusing to hand over about twenty Cathars. It's an atrocity Béziers has never forgotten or forgiven.

From the top of the cathedral's **tower,** there's a superb view out across the vine-dominated surrounding landscape. Next door, you can wander through the ancient cloister (9.30am–noon and 2–6pm) and out into the shady **bishop's garden** overlooking the river. In the adjacent place de la Révolution a **monument** commemorates the people who died resisting Napoléon III's *coup d'état* in 1851 and their leader, Mayor Casimir Péret, who was shipped off to Cayenne where he drowned in a Papillon-style escape attempt.

The narrow medieval streets make a pleasant stroll too, with their mixture of sunny southern elegance and dilapidation. In rue Massol, the **Musée du Vieux-Biterrois** (9am–noon and 2–6pm; closed Sun. am and Mon.; free) displays a variety of entertaining exhibits, ranging from Greek amphorae and nineteenth-century door-knockers to distilling manuals, clogs and wine-presses. The **Beaux-Arts**, however, (Hôtel Fabrégat, place de la Révolution; same hours) won't keep you long – a drossy provincial collection.

Centre of Béziers' life is the lively **allées Paul-Riquet**, a broad, leafy esplanade lined with cafés, bars and restaurants, and named for the seventeenth-century tax-collector who lost health and fortune in his obsession with building the **Canal du Midi** to join the Atlantic and the Mediterranean. Laid out in the last century, the *allées* run from an elaborate theatre in the north to the gorgeous little park of the **Plateau des Poètes**, designed in the so-called English manner by the man who created Paris' Bois de Boulogne.

If you arrive at the **gare SNCF**, the best way into town is through the Plateau opposite the station entrance and the *allées*. The **SI** is towards the top end, to the left, at 27 rue du 4-Septembre. There are a couple of **hotels** on place Jean-Jaurès (try the *Angleterre* at no. 22 ☎67.28.48.42), with others in av Gambetta (try the *Paris* at no. 70; ☎67.28.43.80) and across the allées Paul-Riquet. For **eating**, *L'Alhambra* on rue Solférino and *L'Aristo* on rue Fourier are dependable alternatives.

Bullfighting aficionados should come in August for the *feria* before the fifteenth, and **rugby** fans any time there's a game on, for Béziers is one of France's top teams.

The **gare routière** is located on place Jaurès.

Around Béziers: the Beaches and Pézenas

For a quick escape to the sea, just take a 20-minute bus ride. Buses for the old family resorts of **VALRAS** and **SERIGNAN** leave from place du Général-de-Gaulle, for **PORTIRAGUES-PLAGE** from just off place Jean-Jaurès.

For **PEZENAS**, you head inland back towards Montpellier on old N9. Market centre of the coastal plain, it looks across to rice fields and shallow lagoons, hazy with heat and dotted with pink flamingoes. Despite its smallness, local tourist pamphlets have dubbed it the Versailles of Languedoc –

reference to its long-standing political importance as the seat of the provincial *Etats-généraux* for Bas Languedoc. It has, however, perfectly retained the air of a gentrified resort, with its seventeenth-century centre, the **Vieille Ville**, carefully protected from development.

The town also plays up its association with **Molière**, who visited several times with his troupe in the mid-seventeenth century, when he enjoyed the protection of the local Conti lords. He put on his own plays at the **Hôtel Alphonse** on rue Conti, which now has an ice-cream parlour in its coach-house. When in town, he lodged at the Maison du Barbier-Gély in the unspoiled **place Gambetta**, today occupied by the **SI**. Although he figures prominently in the **Musée Vulliod St-Germain**, housed in an eighteenth-century palace just off the square, it does not fully convince with its recreated interiors and seventeenth- and eighteenth-century paintings. The SI sells a guide to all the town's eminent houses, but you can just as easily follow the explanatory plaques posted all over the centre. Not included in the route, (and with nothing very interesting to see), is the former Jewish ghetto on rue des Litanies and rue Juiverie.

Place de la République is the location of an enormous Saturday **market**, and it's also the place to take a bus to Montpellier, Béziers or Agde. The stop is outside *Café Alran*. For **brasseries**, **hotels** and the services of a **post office**, go to place du 14-Juillet, a five-minute walk away.

North from Béziers: The Parc Regional du Haut Languedoc

Buses and trains head north to **BEDARIEUX** across the wine country. Vines are everywhere. This is the area to look for **grape-picking work** during the *vendange*, especially in villages like PUIMISSON, ANTIGNAC and LAURENS. Picking starts around mid-September, depending on the weather; further north and higher, it's towards the end of the month. But you'd better go soon if you want the old-fashioned experience: machines are quickly taking over.

Bédarieux itself is right on the edge of the *parc*, a pleasant enough little town, good for a quick stop. The town **museum**, the Maison des Arts at 19 av Blanqui, has an odd, mixed collection of paintings, stuffed animals, folk articles and an incredibly corny 'Musée de l'Humeur' with such joke pieces as the Vénus de Milos' arms (daily 2–6pm). **SI** at 77 rue St-Alexandre; **market** on Monday next to place du Four-Vieil, where you'll also find the very reasonable *Hôtel Central*, if you decide to stay.

Continuing **westwards**, the road is an easy hitch through spectacular scenery, with the peaks of the **Monts de l'Espinouse** rising up to 1000m on your right. It is best to avoid the spa town of LAMALOU-LES-BAINS, but right after the village of COLOMBIERES a path leaves the road to take you down into the dramatic **Gorges d'Héric** (about a ¾hr. walk). Further yet, you reach the almost perfect medieval village of **OLARGUES** scrambling up the south bank of the Tour above its remarkable high, single-span stone bridge, the twelfth- to thirteenth-century Pont du Diable. The streets are steep, narrow and twisting, presumably almost unchanged since the bridge was built. It's an interesting and atmospheric little place, with a tiny **SI** on rue de la Place, a medium-priced **hotel** down near the old station, and a **campsite** out on the Colombières road.

ST-PONS-DE-THOMMIERES, further west, is a little larger and noisier. It boasts a small **cathedral** with some twelfth-century remains and a reasonably interesting **Museum of Prehistory** (10am–noon and 3–6pm in summer). If you need to stay, there's no camping nearby, but there are several cheap **hotels**: ask at the **SI** near the cathedral. North, towards the heart of the *Parc*, the scenery becomes ever more spectacular, lakes adding to its charms. The transport is worse, but it's never too hard to hitch.

Narbonne

Capital of Rome's first colony in Gaul, Gallia Narbonensis, **NARBONNE** was a thriving port and communications centre in classical times and again in the Middle Ages. Plague, war with the English and the silting-up of its harbour finished it off in the fourteenth century. Today, despite the ominous presence of the Malvesi nuclear power plant just 5km out of town, it's a pleasant provincial city of tree-lined walks and esplanades converging on graceful squares.

The only surviving legacy of Rome is the **horreum** at the north end of rue Rouget-de-Lisle (10–11.50am and 2–6pm in summer; till 5.15pm in winter; cheap admission to all museums and sites). An unusual site, consisting of two 'streets' lined with small shops, well preserved though now entirely underground, it was used to store grain and other produce. At the opposite end of the same street is Narbonne's other principal attraction, the enormous Gothic **cathedral** of St-Just and St-Sauveur, dominating the restored lanes of the old town. Despite its size it is actually only the choir of a much more ambitious church, whose construction was halted to avoid weakening the city walls. The interior has good **stained glass** and imposing Aubusson tapestries. The high north tower is open for a panoramic view of the surrounding vineyards.

The place de l'Hôtel-de-Ville next door is dominated by the great towers of St-Martial, the Madeleine and the donjon of Bishop Aycelin. From there the passage de l'Ancre leads through to the **Archbishop's palace**, housing a tedious **museum of art** (10am–11.50am and 2–6pm in summer; till 5.15pm in winter) but a good **archaeology museum** (10–11.50am and 2–6pm in summer; till 5pm in winter; closed Mon.) with interesting Roman remains, including some fine frescoes and mosaics.

If you're going across into the southern part of the town, beyond the bisecting **Canal de la Robine**, the small palaeo-Christian **crypt** of the church of St-Paul (10am–noon and 2–6pm) off rue de l'Hôtel-Dieu is worth a quick look, and perhaps the eerily empty deconsecrated church of Notre-Dame-de-la-Mourgié (10am–noon and 2–6pm in summer; till 5pm in winter), though the jumbled Roman stones of the Musée Lapidaire which it houses aren't very exciting.

The **SI** has a summer annexe by the canal along Cours de la République, and a more central office next to the cathedral on place Salengro. The **gare routière** is on quai Victor-Hugo. For **accommodation** it's best to walk north to the **gare SNCF** and av Pierre-Sémard, where you'll find most of the cheaper **hotels and restaurants**. *Hôtel de la Gare* (7 av Sémard; ☎68.32.10.54) is clean and reasonable. The closer you get to the sea, the more **campsites** you'll find. If you have a car or a bike (for hire, as usual, from the gare SNCF) and want to get **out of town** for an afternoon, head off to the strange moonscape hills of the **Montagne de la Clape**.

Narbonne-Plage

If you'd like to **swim**, the coast has broad deserted beaches with plenty of sunshine, but the truth is that most of them are windy, remote and shadeless, and what settlements there are, dull and run-down. Best bets, if you're determined, are probably **NARBONNE-PLAGE**, with several **campsites**, **cheap hotels** around place des Karentes and one good long beach, not entirely ruined by the flanking car parks; or **FLEURY-D'AUDE**, a new creation with major **naturist amenities**. Two to avoid are GRUISSAN, with its vast sand flats and a shoddy new resort area, and PORT-LA-NOUVELLE, the last of Languedoc's coastal towns, grouped about a grubby, unappealing harbour.

CARCASSONNE AND THE CASTLES OF THE CATHARS

Carcassonne couldn't be easier to reach, sited on the main Toulouse–Montpellier train link, and for anyone travelling through this region it is a must – one of the most dramatic (if also most visited) towns in the whole Languedoc. It is also a good historical introduction for the wild and ruinous **Cathar strongholds** to the north and south.

These castles and fortified villages were the ultimate refuges of the Cathars, a sect strong in this part of France, who were literally hounded to death, first in the **Albigensian Crusade**, promulgated by the Vatican and launched in 1208 under the leadership of the Abbot of Cîteaux, then by the notoriously cruel **Simon de Montfort** and finally by the king of France. The name derives from the Greek word for clean or pure, *katharos*, and the Cathars believed in the simple and humble Christianity of the Sermon on the Mount. They abhorred the materialism and worldly power of the established church. Their clergy or *parfaits* renounced the physical world as inherently evil. Though they saw themselves as good Christians, in the eyes of Rome they were abominable heretics – not least because among their adherents (probably never more than 10 per cent of the population) were many members of the nobility and the influential classes.

Cathars who were caught were burned in communal conflagrations, a hundred, two hundred at a time. Their lands were laid waste or seized by northern barons, de Montfort himself grabbing the properties of the Count of

Toulouse. The effect of this brutality was to unite Catholic and Cathar in southern solidarity against the barbarian north. Though military defeat became irreversible with the capitulation of Toulouse in 1229 and the fall of Montségur in 1244, it took the informers and torturers of the Holy Inquisition another seventy years and more to root them out completely.

Carcassonne

It is to these wars against the Cathars that **CARCASSONNE** owes its division into two separate 'towns', the Cité and Ville Basse. Following Simon de Montfort's capture of the town in 1209, its people tried to restore their traditional ruling family, the Trencavels, in 1240. In reprisal King Louis IX expelled them, only permitting their return on condition they built on the low ground by the river Aude.

Arriving by train, you'll find yourself here in the **Ville Basse**. Head for the centre of town past the Jardin Chénier into rue Clemenceau. To the right in rue du 4-Septembre is one of the churches Louis IX built for the new town, with its southern Gothic 'eyes' or *oculi* for windows, set high in the walls of the nave. The other, across the market square of place Carnot with its eighteenth-century fountain and right at the end of rue Courtejaire, is the heavily restored **cathedral** of St-Michel. The surrounding streets make for marvellous exploration.

But no matter how enticing the Ville Basse, the main attraction is the **Cité**, a double-walled and turretted fortress crowning the hill above the Aude. From a distance it's the epitome of the fairy-tale medieval town. Viollet-le-Duc rescued it from ruin in 1844, and his 'too-perfect' restoration has been furiously debated ever since. It is, as you would expect, a real tourist trap. Yet, in spite of the chintzy cafés, arty-crafty shops and the crowds, you have to be a very stiff-necked purist not to be moved at all.

Coming from the modern town, you enter the *enceinte* through the sturdy bastion of the **Porte d'Aude**. For a map, room, (see below) or details, the **SI** runs a summer annexe in the **Porte Narbonnaise**, the other main gateway, on the east side. There is no charge for admission to the main part of the city, or the grassy *lices* – lists – between the walls. However, to see the inner fortress of the **Château Comtal** and to walk the walls you have to join a guided tour. These are relatively expensive, and the hours are complicated – basically: mid-May to mid-September, 9am to 7 or 8pm continuously; for the rest of year, 9am to noon and 2 to 7pm. The tours – in French only – assume some knowledge of French history, pointing out the various phases in the construction of the fortifications, from Roman to Visigoth to Romanesque to the post-Cathar adaptations of the French kings.

In addition to wandering the narrow streets, you should not miss the beautiful church of **St-Nazaire** towards the southern corner of the Cité at the end of rue St-Louis. It's a serene combination of Romanesque nave with carved capitals and Gothic transepts and choir adorned with some of the loveliest stained glass. In the south transept is a tombstone believed to belong to Simon de Montfort.

Accommodation, as you would expect, is pricey, apart from the terminally overbooked **youth hostel** on rue Trencavel (☎68.25.23.16). Affordable **restaurants** are also rare, and other than the excellent *L'Ostal des Troubadours* at 5 rue Viollet-le-Duc you'd be better off back at the Ville Basse for both a meal and a bed. The **SI** here is at 15 bd Camille-Pelletan, with an annexe at the **gare SNCF**. This is also the main area for cheap **hotels**. Best is the *Bonnefoux*, 40 rue de la Liberté (☎68.25.01.45), with the *St-Joseph* (☎68.25.20.94) at no. 81 in the same street as an alternative. Otherwise, the *Centre International de Séjour* at 91 rue Aimé-Ramon has low-priced rooms and there's a cheap **Camping municipal** at the *Stade A. Domec*, off av Sarrail (coming from the station, turn left on bd Sarraut).

The **gare routière** is in bd de Varsovie. **Bike hire** is available from the station or *Bourrounet*, 12bis rue Auguste-Comte.

Out from Carcassonne

The village of **MINERVE** lies in the middle of the Minervois wine country, in a terrain of strange rock formations and magnificent views. Its location is superb, perched high at the head of the deep limestone gorge cut by the river Cesse, whose waters have formed two enormous tunnels in the rock known as the *Ponts naturels*. The village turned Cathar at the beginning of the thirteenth century, which made it a target for Simon de Montfort's crusade. On August 22, 1210, after a seven-week siege, he took the castle and promptly burned 140 *parfaits*. There is a memorial to them by the church and inside one of the most ancient altars in Gaul, dated 456. Nothing remains of the castle but the ruins of a tower. If you want to stay, **camping** is free: ask at the Mairie by the church. As for getting to Minerve, it's a manageable hitch from Carcassonne on D610, then D5, turning north at CABEZAC. Alternatively, the **bus route** between Narbonne and St-Pons (several daily) passes within 5km.

But the easiest, and by far the most impressive, local target from Carcassonne, is the **CHATEAUX DE LASTOURS** (buses), most northerly of the Cathar castles. As the name suggests, there is more than one castle – four, in fact, their ruined keeps jutting from a sharp scrub- and cypress-covered ridge that plunges to rivers on both sides. The two oldest, Cabaret (mid-11C) and Fleur d'Espine (1153), fell into de Montfort's hands in 1211, when their lords gave shelter to the Cathars. The other two, Tour Régine and Quertinheux, were added after 1240, when the site became royal property, and a garrison was maintained here as late as the Revolution. Today, despite their ruined state, they look as impregnable and beautiful as ever. There's a spectacular view from the belvedere on the hill opposite to the south, if you have time. For **cave** enthusiasts, there are the weirdly shaped rock and crystal formations of the **Grottes de Limousis** about 6km east of Lastours – hitchable, if you're lucky.

Northwards into the **Montagne Noire** the scenery is superlative, both by the main road from Carcassonne and, even more so, the road from Lastours along the Orbiel valley, though there are no stopping-places of any note. Mazamet, the first town of any size, is dull and industrial.

The Cathar Castles

The best way to head south into the Cathar country from Carcassonne, if you haven't got your own transport, is to take the train to **QUILLAN,** about 50km up the valley of the Aude. (By road you'll pass through LIMOUX, where you should be sure to sample the local sparkling wine, *Blanquette de Limoux.*) Quillan itself is a pleasant little town on the edge of the Pyrenean foothills: good for a stop-over, though there are no real sights. **Buses** run from here to PERPIGNAN along the main D117, close to the most interesting castles. It is also hitchable.

Puilaurens

To the south the road runs through the incredibly narrow **Defilé de Pierre-Lys** before swinging east to the village of LAPRADELLE and the first of the castles at **PUILAURENS** (July–Sept., 10am–6pm). You can either drive up, or there's a shorter and fairly gentle path from the hamlet of Puilaurens. From the entrance it's a steep climb up to the castle, perched on top of a high, wooded hill. There are fine crenellated walls built around the very top of the rock outcrops and a keep. Although the existence of a castle here dates from the tenth century, it seems more likely that it was fortified to something like its present extent in the early thirteenth century, when it passed from the king of France to the Count of Rousillon, and then to the king of Aragon. It sheltered many Cathars up to 1256, when Chabert de Barbera, effective controller of power in the region, was captured and forced to hand over his strongholds here and at QUERIBUS further east, to secure his release. The castle remained strategically important, being close to the Spanish border, until 1659, when France annexed Rousillon and the border was pushed away to the south. The **view** from the battlements, which you can just scramble up to at one point, is quite breathtaking; you are 700m up.

Queribus

QUERIBUS, another 30km east towards Perpignan, is even more spectacularly situated, balanced on a pillar of rock above a huge cliff, which formed the actual border with Spain before 1659 (Easter–Oct. 10am–6pm, until 8pm in winter). Because of the extreme, cramped topography of the rock, the keep and tower are on terraces. Inside, at the heart of the keep, is the remarkable **chapel** of St-Louis-de-Quéribus, surprisingly high and wide when you consider the keep's tortured position, and supported by a single pillar.

The history of Quéribus is similar to that of Puilaurens, though later, dating from the eleventh century. It was the target of the last Albigensian crusade in 1255. Although the crusades were unsuccessful, the luckless Chabert's capture the following year ended Quéribus' role as a sanctuary for the Cathars. You can see Canigou and the high Pyrenees to the south and the higher hills of the Corbières to the north. It's a pretty easy **hitch** from the village of MAURY on the main road.

Peyrepertuse

To reach neighbouring **PEYREPERTUSE** you can either hitch from Quéribus or, better, if you're coming directly from ST-PAUL-DE-FENOUILLET on the main road west of Maury, come through the **Gorges de Galamus**, as narrow and bristling as any nineteenth-century mountain engraving. The easiest approach to the castle is the track that winds up from the south, although if you like jungle ascents you can try the path marked 'Fontaine de la Jacquette' that leaves the road just outside the village of ROUFFIAC. It's a tough one-hour climb, and unless someone has been up recently with a billhook you could have problems getting through. But either way the effort is rewarded, for Peyrepertuse is one of the most awe-inspiring castles anywhere, clinging to the crest of a long, wickedly jagged spine of rock on the top of a mountain ridge, surrounded by sheer drops of two or three hundred metres. The castle is much larger than the others despite its precarious hold on the earth. There are extensive buildings inside the outer wall, culminating in a keep and tower on the highest point of the ridge, where such a pit of air opens at your feet that no man-made defence is necessary. Surprisingly, the castle was taken by the French without much difficulty in 1240, and it was after that that most of the existing fortifications were built. Whatever you do, don't go up in a thunderstorm. There can be some fierce ones in summertime, and the ridge brings down the lightning as sure as a high-tension cable. **Hours** are 9am to 7 or 8pm from Easter to October only.

TOULOUSE AND THE WEST

In addition to its own sunny, cosmopolitan charms, **Toulouse** is a very accessible kick-off point for any destination in the south and west of France. Of immediately adjacent places **Albi** is the number one priority, with its highly original cathedral and unique collection of Toulouse-Lautrec paintings. Once you've made it that far, it's worth the extra hop to the time-warped medieval town of **Cordes**. The southern **road to Andorra** and Spain may tempt you too, with more Cathar memories on the way. If it does you'll find this end of the Pyrenees very different from the west: drier, eroded and not as full of tourists.

Toulouse

TOULOUSE, with its beautiful historic centre, is one of the most vibrant and metropolitan provincial cities in France. This is a transformation that has come about since the war, under the guidance of the French state, which has poured in money to make Toulouse the think-tank of high-tech industry and a sort of premier trans-national Euroville. Always an **aviation centre**, – St-Exupéry and Mermoz flew out from here on their pioneering flights over Africa in the 1920s – Toulouse is now home to *Aérospatiale*, the driving force behind Concorde, Airbus and the Ariane space rocket. The national Space

Centre, the European shuttle programme, the leading aeronautical schools, the frontier-pushing electronics industry . . . it's all happening in Toulouse, whose 60,000 students make it second only to Paris as a university centre.

But it's to the old *ville rose* – pink only in its brickwork, no longer in its politics – that all these people go for their entertainment, not to the expanding suburbs of factories, labs, shopping and housing complexes.

This is not the first flush of pre-eminence for Toulouse. From the tenth to the thirteenth century the Counts of Toulouse controlled most of southern France. They maintained the most resplendent court in the land, renowned especially for its **troubadours**, the poets of Courtly Love, whose work influenced Petrarch, Dante and Chaucer and thus the whole course of European poetry. Until, that is, the arrival of the papal thugs in the Albigensian Crusade; in 1271 Toulouse became crown property.

The part of the city you'll want to see is a rough hexagon clamped around a bend in the wide, brown, river Garonne. If you **arrive** by bus or train, you'll find yourself about a fifteen-minute walk from the very heart of things at the **gare Matabiau** (☎61.62.50.50 for information). There's an **SI** annexe here, shower facilities, a **city bus terminal**, with the **gare routière** to the right, and, opposite, numerous **hotels**. *L'Europe, Le Perpignanais, Séverin* and *Toulouse* look the more salubrious. Be wary of the back streets towards place Belfort; the area is seedy and red-light. To get to the **youth hostel**, take bus #14 from the station to place Dupuy (not far: just across a canal bridge) and from there a #22 going back towards the canal and up av Jean-Rieux. The hostel – a bit pokey but very friendly – is at no. 125 (☎61.80.49.93). There are several cheap eating places around.

The simplest way into the centre is down the broad **allées Jean-Jaurès**, with numerous bars. At the bd Strasbourg intersection are several good **brasseries**, reasonably priced and with pavement tables. The quarter has a high proportion of West and North Africans, and a lot of big-city hustle, especially around **place Président-Wilson**. Turning due south down rue St-Antoine you reach the small and very attractive **place St-Georges**, focus of life for the fashion-conscious young, with its bars, cafés and street performers.

Nearby, on the corner of rue de Metz, is the first of the city's memorable sights, the **Musée des Augustins** (10am–noon and 2–6pm; closed Sun. am and Tues.), which incorporates the two surviving cloisters of an Augustinian priory. Its collections are outstanding **Romanesque** and **medieval sculpture**, much of it saved from the now-vanished churches of Toulouse's golden age. As always, regardless of the ostensible theme, what is interesting is the highly naturalistic representation of contemporary manners and fashions. Merchants with forked beards touch one anothers' arms in a gesture of familiarity and collusion that says, 'We understand each other. We're men of business. We belong to the same class'. *Notre-Dame-de-Grâce* represents the Virgin as a pretty, bored young mother looking away from her child, which strains to escape her hold. A headless Saint Barbara is characteristically posed with weight on one leg, hips and tummy thrust slightly forwards, slender-waisted, bodice framed by long tresses. A lot of beautiful work.

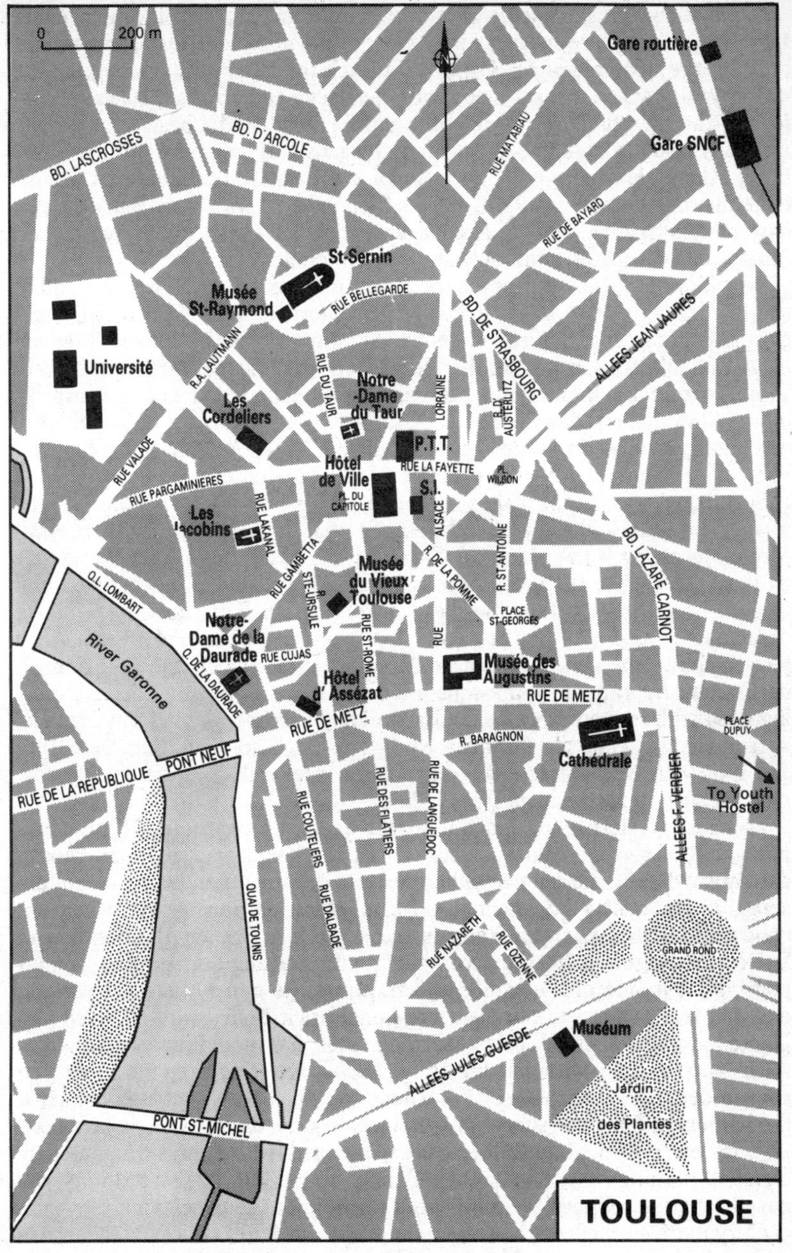
0
200 m
Gare routière
Gare SNCF
BD. LASCROSSES
BD. D'ARCOLE
RUE MATABIAU
RUE DE BAYARD
St-Sernin
Musée
St-Raymond
RUE BELLEGARDE
BD. DE STRASBOURG
ALLEES JEAN JAURES
Université
R.A. LAUTMANN
RUE DU TAUR
Notre
-Dame
du Taur
LORRAINE
B.D. AUSTERLITZ
Les
Cordeliers
P.T.T.
RUE VALADE
Hôtel
de Ville
RUE LA FAYETTE
PL. WILSON
RUE PARGAMINIERES
PL. DU CAPITOLE
S.I.
ALSACE
Les
Jacobins
RUE LAKANAL
RUE GAMBETTA
R. DE LA POMME
R. ST-ANTOINE
BD. LAZARE CARNOT
Q.L. LOMBART
Musée
du Vieux
Toulouse
STE-URSULE
PLACE
ST-GEORGES
River Garonne
Notre-
Dame de la
Daurade
RUE CUJAS
RUE ST-ROME
RUE
Q. DE LA DAURADE
Musée des
Augustins
Hôtel
d' Assézat
RUE DE METZ
RUE DE METZ
PLACE
DUPUY
R. BARAGNON
Cathédrale
PONT NEUF
RUE DE LA REPUBLIQUE
RUE DE LANGUEDOC
RUE DES FILATIERS
RUE COUTELIERS
ALLEES F. VERDIER
To Youth
Hostel
QUAI DE TOUNIS
RUE DALBADE
RUE NAZARETH
RUE OZENNE
GRAND ROND
Muséum
ALLEES JULES GUESDE
Jardin
des Plantes
PONT ST-MICHEL
TOULOUSE

Right outside the museum runs the main shopping street, **rue Alsace-Lorraine**. From here, west to the river, south to **place des Carmes** and north to the wide **place du Capitole**, stretch the labyrinthine streets of the **old city**, sunny and elegant, lined with the ornate and arrogant *hôtels particuliers* of the merchants who grew rich on the woad trade, basis of the city's economy in the sixteenth century, until the arrival of indigo from India wiped it out. Almost exclusive building material is the flat Toulousain brick, whose cheerful rosy colour gives the city its nickname of *ville rose*. But it is also extremely attractive, lending a small-scale, detailed finish to otherwise plain facades and setting off admirably any wood or stonework.

Best known of these palaces is the **Hôtel Assézat** towards the river end of rue de Metz, a vast brick extravaganza adorned with Doric, Ionic and Corinthian columns. Several others are to be found just to the south on rue de la Dalbade (where no. 25, the **Hôtel Clary**, is unusual for being built in stone), rue Pharaon, place des Carmes, rue du Languedoc; and northwards, on rue St-Rome, rue des Changes, rue de la Bourse, and rue du May with the unexciting **Musée du Vieux-Toulouse** in the Hôtel du May (June–Sept. 3–6pm; closed Sun.; March–May and Oct. Thurs. pm only).

Surprisingly, Toulouse makes nothing of its long waterfront on the river, as a walk around by the eighteenth-century church of **La Daurade** reveals. More interesting is the **place du Capitole**, site of the huge classical *capitole* or **town hall**, once the seat of the *capitouls*, the relatively independent city council, which dated from the days of the Counts. This form of primitive democracy, found in other Languedoc towns under the name of *consulat*, may have inspired the son of Simon de Montfort who created the first English parliament. Appropriately, the square today is a great meeting-place and talking-shop with numerous **cafés**, and a weekday **market**. Behind the Capitole, in a medieval keep, sits the main **SI** (Mon.–Sat. 9am–7pm; Sun. 9am–1pm and 2–5.30pm, May–Sept.; **money exchange** weekends in summer). Nearby, on rue Lafayette, is the main **Post Office**.

From its western end, and the corner of the *place*, rue du Taur heads north, full of second-hand bookshops, past the belfry wall of **Notre-Dame-du-Taur**, whose diamond-pointed arches and decorative motifs represent the acme of Toulousain bricklaying skills, to **place St-Sernin**. Here you are confronted with the largest Romanesque church in France, the **basilica of St-Sernin**. Begun in 1080 to accommodate the passing hordes of St-Jacques pilgrims, it is one of the loveliest examples of its genre. Its most striking external features are the brilliant octagonal brick **belfry** with rounded and pointed arches, diamond lozenges, colonnettes and mouldings picked out in stone, and the **apse** with nine radiating chapels. Entering from the south, you pass under the **Porte Miégeville**, whose twelfth-century carvings launched the influential Toulouse school of sculpture. **Inside**, the great high nave rests on brick piers, flanked by double aisles of diminishing height, surmounted by a gallery running right around the building. To get into the **ambulatory** you have to pay a small charge, but it's well worth it for the exceptional eleventh-century marble reliefs on the end wall of the choir. Right outside is the town's archaeological museum, **Musée St-Raymond** (10am–noon and 2–6pm;

closed Tues. and Sun. am) and on Sunday mornings an impressively shambolic flea market.

Back near place du Capitole, on rue Lakanal, the church of **Les Jacobins** is another ecclesiastical building you cannot miss in Toulouse. (The **cathedral** of St-Etienne, incidentally, at the end of the rue de Metz is an eminently missable hotch-potch of a building). Started in 1230 by Dominicans who had set up here in the wake of their founding father, St. Dominic, who himself had come to preach against the Cathars, the church is a huge fortress-like rectangle of unadorned brick, like Albi (see below), buttressed by plain brick piles – quite unlike the architecture you normally associate with Gothic. The **interior** is a single space divided by a central row of ultra-slim pillars from whose minimal capitals spring an elegant splay of vaulting ribs – twenty-two from the last in line, like the fronds of a palm. Beneath the altar lie the bones of the philosopher, St. Thomas Aquinas. On the north side you step out into the calming hush of a **cloister** with a formal array of box and cypress in the middle, and a superb view of the St-Sernin-like belfry.

Another good spot for city quiet is the **Jardin des Plantes** across the allées Jules-Guesde, but you can give its **Natural History Museum** a miss (afternoons; closed Mon.) – an enormous, but totally jumbled and moth-eaten collection of creatures. Other Toulouse museums aren't specially alluring either. The best of them is **Musée Paul-Dupuy** with collections of arts and crafts from the Middle Ages to today (13 rue de la Pleau; 10am–noon and 2–6pm; closed Tues.).

Practicalities

Lastly, a few **details**: the *CROUS* office at 7 rue des Salenques publishes a booklet on services for students; **Allostop** office at 2 rue Malbec (☎61.22.68.13; Tues.–Fri. 3.30–6.30pm; Sat. 10.30am–12.30pm); **airport** at Blagnac, 7km west (☎61.71.11.14 for info; *Air France*, ☎61.71.40.00 at airport and ☎61.62.84.04 in town – 2bd de Strasbourg); **camping** at Pont-de-Rupé, av des Etats-Unis, chemin du Pont-de-Rupé, on the Bordeaux road (☎61.70.07.35); **launderette** at 20 rue Cujas near La Daurade.

Albi

Though not itself an important centre of Catharism, **ALBI** gave its name to both the heresy and the crusade to suppress it. Today it is a small industrial town an hour's train ride northeast of Toulouse, with two unique sights: a museum containing the most comprehensive collection of **Toulouse-Lautrec's** work (Albi was his birthplace) and the most remarkable Gothic cathedral you'll ever see.

The **cathedral** is visible the moment you arrive at the train station, dwarfing the town like some vast bulk carrier run aground, the belfry its massive (13–14C) superstructure. If the comparison sounds unflattering, perhaps it is not amiss, for this is not a conventionally beautiful building; it's about size and boldness of conception. The sheer plainness of the exterior is impressive on this scale, and it is not without interest: arcading, buttressing, the contrast of stone against brick – every differentiation of detail becomes significant. Entrance is through the **south portal**, by contrast the most extravagant piece of Flamboyant sixteenth-century frippery. The **interior**, a hall-like nave of colossal proportions, is covered in richly colourful paintings of Italian workmanship (16C also). A good screen, delicate as lace, shuts off the choir: Adam makes a show of covering his privates, Eve strikes a flaunting model's pose beside the central doorway, and the rest of the screen is adorned with countless statuary.

Next to the cathedral, a powerful red-brick castle, the thirteenth-century Palais de la Berbie (**SI** in one corner), houses the **Musée Toulouse-Lautrec** (10am–noon and 2–6pm; closed Tues.), containing paintings, drawings, lithographs and posters from the earliest work to the very last – an absolute must for anyone interested in *Belle Epoque* seediness and, given the predominant Impressionism of the time, the rather offbeat painting style of its subject. The artist's house on rue Toulouse-Lautrec (July–Aug. 9am–noon and 3–7pm; expensive) is also open to the public.

Opposite the east end of the cathedral, rue Mariès leads into the shopping streets of the **old town**. The little square and covered passages by the church of St-Salvy on the right are interesting. If you keep going east you come to the broad **Lices Pompidou** leading down to the river and the road to CORDES. On the right is rue de la République, with a very scruffy **youth hostel** at no. 13. As for other places to stay: *Hôtel St-Clair* on rue St-Clair off rue Ste-Cécile is comfortable and central, or there are several **hotels** in **av Joffre** outside the railway station. **Camping** *Parc de Caussels* is about 2km east on D999. The **gare routière** is on place Jean-Jaurès*; bikes can be hired from *M Rey* at 41 bd Soult.

For **eats**, try *La Dariole* or *Auberge Saint-Loup*, both on rue Castelviel at the west end of the cathedral, or *La Crêperie* on rue Toulouse-Lautrec. The café on the cathedral square, *La Tartine*, does salads and desserts.

Cordes

Twenty-four kilometres northwest of Albi, an easy hitch or brief train ride (as far as Vindrac 3km away, with **bike hire** from the station), is the town of **CORDES**, founded in 1222 by Raymond VII, Count of Toulouse, and pretty much untouched, covering the top of a markedly conical hill. The ground beneath the town is riddled with tunnels, used for storage and refuge in time of trouble, for Cordes was a Cathar stronghold. It is worth seeing because it is such a perfect example of a medieval walled town, complete with thirteenth- and fourteenth-century houses climbing its steep cobbled lanes. It

*The Socialist leader and pacifist, Jean Jaurès was born in nearby Castres, and came to prominence as the leader of a glassworkers' strike in 1896. They set up a cooperative, the *Verrerie Ouvrière*, which still functions today, albeit automated and monitored by computer. The **Musée Jean-Jaurès** in av Dembourg (named for the Parisian woman who financed the first cooperative) contains documents to do with the strike and Jaurès' life – interesting if you can read French.

is also however, a major tourist attraction: medieval banners flutter in the streets and artisans practise their crafts – unfortunately, the kiss of death. The youth hostel, in considerable contrast, is in such a state of disrepair that it is unusable. There is, however, a **campsite** 1km down the GAILLAC road.

Castres

Though **CASTRES** is industrial it has some charm and is worth a stop for its **Jaurès museum**. The old houses overhanging the river are unusual and the centre is a bustling, businesslike sort of place, with a **market** from Wednesday to Saturday on place Jean-Jaurès.

The elegant **Hôtel de Ville**, whose adjoining gardens were laid out by Mansart and Le Nôtre – the team that designed Versailles and its grounds – is home to both the **Musée Jaurès** and the **Musée Goya** (9am–noon and 2–6pm in summer, till 5pm in winter; closed Mon.). The Goya museum is a bit of a misnomer: it's really a collection of mainly Spanish sixteenth- and seventeenth-century painting, with three Goyas, including a good self-portrait and the huge canvas of the Philippines junta, and a fair number of predictably macabre drawings. Jaurès gets one large room: a fascinating and well-displayed collection of memorabilia, cuttings and pamphlets, telling the story of his life from his birth in Castres to his assassination by a right-wing terrorist in 1914.

The **SI** is near the Hôtel de Ville. There is **camping** on av Lucien-Coudert. And for **hotels**, you could try *Le Terminus* at 135 av Albert-1er near the **gare SNCF**, or *Le Goya*, 16 place Soult, near the **gare routière**.

travel details

Trains

In summer, overnight sleepers link Languedoc with the Channel ports of Calais and Boulogne. Among other overnight trains is the occasional cheap summer special with a bar and disco on board, but no sleeping accommodation: one of these leaves Paris, Gare du Nord at midnight every Tuesday and arrives at Port-Bou on the Spanish frontier at 11.50 the following morning. The return trip leaves Cerbère at 17.27 on Wednesday, arriving in Paris at 5am.

From Nîmes 5–6 TGVs daily to Paris (4½ hr.); frequent to Avignon (½ hr.), Montpellier (½ hr.), Sète (1 hr.), Béziers (1½ hr.), Narbonne (1 hr. 50 min.), and Perpignan (2½ hr.) or Carcassonne (2½ hr.); 4 daily to Paris via Alès (40 min.), Cévennes villages, Clermont-Ferrand (5 hr.), and Vichy (6 hr.), including (June–Sept.) *Le Cévenol, a train touristique*, more frequent between Nîmes and Alès only; 3 to 4 daily to Arles (20 min.) and Marseille (1 hr.).

From Montpellier 5–6 TGVs daily to Paris (5 hr.); frequent to Lyon via Nîmes (½ hr.) and Avignon (1 hr.); and to Sète (½ hr.), Béziers (1 hr.), Narbonne (1 hr. 20 min.), Perpignan (2 hr.) or Carcassonne (2 hr.), and Toulouse (3¼ hr.); 3 to 4 daily to Arles (1 hr.) and Marseille (1 hr. 40 min.).

From Sète frequent to Montpellier (½ hr.), Nîmes (1 hr.), Avignon (1½ hr.); and to Béziers (½ hr.), Narbonne (50 min.), and Perpignan (1½ hr.) or Carcassonne (1½hr.): 3–4 daily to Marseille (2 hr. 10 min.) via Arles (1½ hr.).

From Béziers 4 daily to Bédarieux (40 min.), Millau (2 hr.), and into Massif Central; 3–4 daily to Marseille (2½ hr.) via Sète (½ hr.), Montpellier (1 hr.), Nîmes (1½hr.), Arles (2 hr.); more frequent continuing to Avignon (2 hr.) from Nîmes;

frequent to Narbonne (20 min.) and Perpignan (1 hr.) or Carcassonne (1 hr.).

From Narbonne frequent throughout day to Carcassonne (40 min.); 8 daily continue to Toulouse or Bordeaux; several daily to Perpignan (30–40 min.), Cerbère (1–1½ hr.), Port-Bou (1 hr. 20 min.–1 hr. 40 min.), and on into Spain; frequent to Béziers (20 min.), Sète (50 min.), Montpellier (1 hr. 20 min.), Nîmes (1 hr. 50 min.), Avignon (2 hr. 20 min.); 3–4 via Nîmes and Arles (2 hr.) to Marseille (2 hr. 40 min.).

From Carcassonne 8 daily to Toulouse (45 min.) or Bordeaux (3 hr. 20 min.); frequent to Narbonne (40 min.); several daily to Béziers (1 hr.), Sète (1½ hr.), Montpellier (2 hr.), Nîmes (2½ hr.), Avignon (3 hr.); 3–4 daily via Nîmes and Arles (3 hr. 20 min.) to Marseille (4 hr.); several daily to Quillan (1 hr.).

From Toulouse 8–10 daily to Bordeaux (2¾hr.) and Paris (8 hr.); 4 daily to Bayonne (4 hr.) via Tarbes (2 hr.), Lourdes (2 hr. 20 min.), Pau (2½ hr.); several to Auch (1 hr.), to Albi (1 hr.) and Castres (1½ hr.); several to Barcelona (7¼ hr.) via Pamiers (50 min.), Foix (1 hr. 5 min.), Tarascon (1 hr. 20 min.), Ax-les-Thermes (1 hr. 45 min.) and La-Tour-de-Carol (1 hr. 55 min.); 6 daily to Lyon (6 hr.) and 10 to 11 to Marseille (4½ hr.).

Buses

From Nîmes SNCF buses to Aigues-Mortes (6 daily; 50 min.) and Grau-du-Roi (1 hr.), 5 to La Grande-Motte (1¼hr.); 8 daily to Pont du Gard (½ hr.) and Uzès (55 min.); several to Avignon (1½hr.); hourly to Montpellier (1½hr.).

From Montpellier good network radiating out, with about 6 daily on N9 to Gignac (45 min.), Lodève (1¼hr.), Millau (2½ hr.); 4 to 5 to Clermont-l'Hérault (1 hr.) and Bédarieux (2 hr.); 5 to Ganges (1½ hr.); frequent to Palavas (20 min.), Aigues-Mortes (1½ hr.), La Grande-Motte (45 min.), Grau-du-Roi (1 hr.), Nîmes (1¾hr.) and Sète (1 hr.); 2 to 5 daily to Pézenas and Béziers; occasional to Sommières and Alès.

From Sète 6–11 daily to Montpellier (1 hr.).

From Béziers 2–5 daily to Montpellier, Agde, Bédarieux, Clermont-l'Hérault, Lodève.

From Bédarieux several daily to St-Pons-de-Thommières (1 hr.).

From Narbonne 4 or 5 daily to Béziers (40 min.); 1 to Perpignan (1 hr. 40 min.); 1 to Carcassonne (1 hr. 20 min.).

From Carcassonne 2 daily to Quillan, 3 to Toulouse (2½ hr.).

From Quillan 2 daily to Foix (1½ hr.), Perpignan (1½hr.); 1 daily in summer to Font-Romeu (2 hr.).

From Toulouse several daily to Ax-les-Thermes (3 hr. 10 min.) via Pamiers (1 hr. 25), Foix (2 hr.) and Tarascon (2 hr. 25 min.); several to Albi (1½ hr.); 2 to 3 to Castres (1½ hr.); also, to Auch (1½hr.).

From Castres 6 daily to Mazamet (½ hr.); 2 to Carcassonne; 2 to 3 to Toulouse (1½ hr.).

CHAPTER TEN

THE MASSIF CENTRAL

One of the loveliest spots on earth . . . a country without roads, without guides, without any facilities for locomotion, where every discovery must be conquered at the price of danger or fatigue . . . a soil cut up with deep ravines, crossed in every way by lofty walls of lava, and furrowed by numerous torrents.

So one of George Sand's characters described the Haute Loire, the central *département* of the Massif Central, and it's a description which could still be applied to most of the region. Thickly forested, and sliced by numerous rivers and lakes, these mountains are geologically the oldest part of France, and culturally one of the most firmly rooted in the past. Industry and tourism have made few inroads here, and the people remain rural and taciturn (they have a reputation, largely unfounded, for unfriendliness), with an enduring sense of regional identity.

The heart of the region is the **Auvergne**, a wild, inaccessible landscape dotted with extinct volcanic peaks known as *puys*, much of it now incorporated into the *Parc Naturel Régional des Volcans d'Auvergne*, France's largest regional park. Among the poorest regions in France, it is startlingly insular and staunchly religious, sheltering Romanesque churches in almost every village, and rigid, black sculptures of the Madonna and Child. To the southeast are the gentler wooded hills of the **Cévennes**, where Robert Louis Stevenson and his donkey made one of the more famous literary hikes in the late nineteenth century. They too are now part of a national park, the *Parc National des Cévennes*. The two together make for some of the **finest walking** in the land. Stop off at *CHAMINA* (the Occitan word for walking), at 5 rue Pierre-le-Vénérable in Clermont-Ferrand, for information on the paths, *gîtes d'étapes*, and anything else to do with the hills. The **information bureau** for the **Parc des Volcans** is at 28 rue St-Esprit.

The Massif Central takes up a huge portion of the centre of France, but only a handful of towns have gained a foothold in this rugged terrain. **Le Puy**, spiked with jagged pinnacles of lava and with a majestic cathedral, is the most compelling, but there is appeal, too, in the elegant spa city of **Vichy** and in the capital **Clermont-Ferrand**. Combined, they are a convenient basis for your explorations.

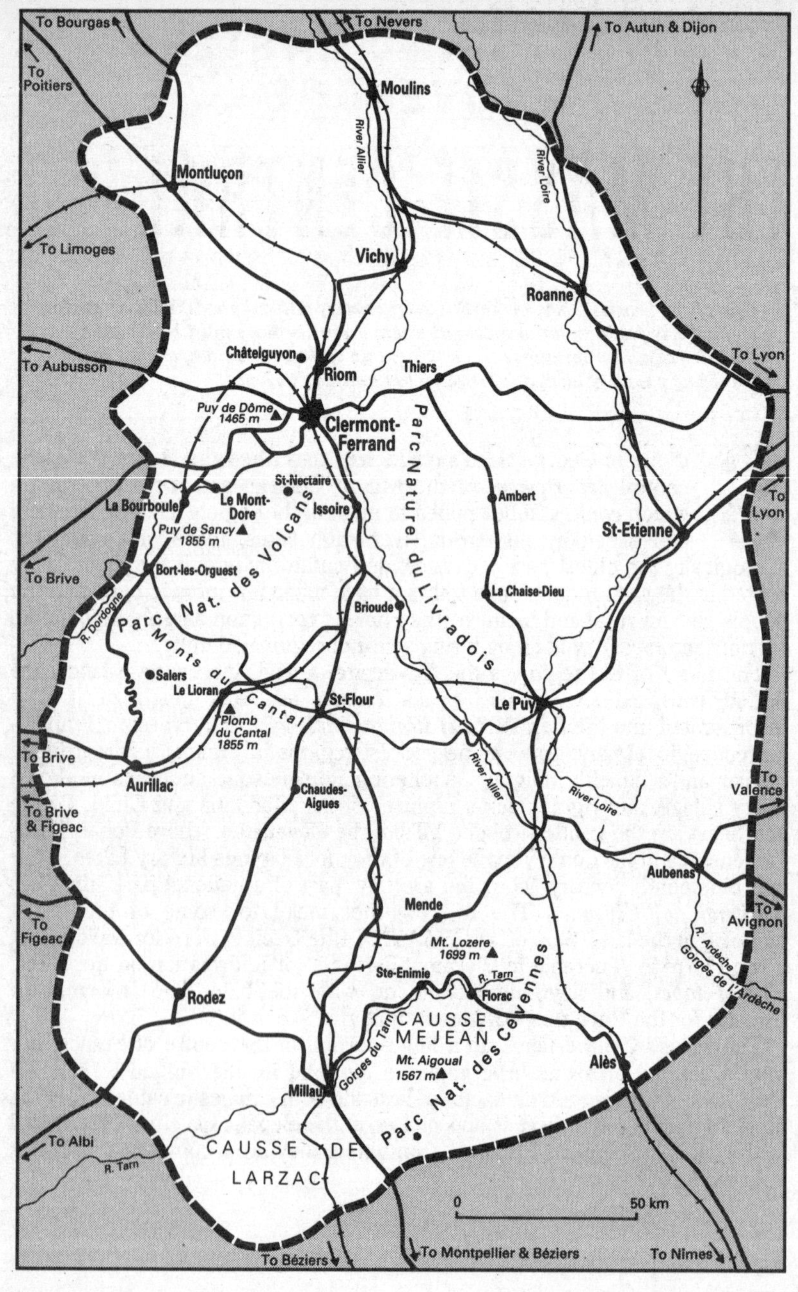

To Bourgas
To Nevers
To Autun & Dijon
To Poitiers
Moulins
River Allier
River Loire
Montluçon
To Limoges
Vichy
Roanne
To Lyon
Châtelguyon
To Aubusson
Riom
Thiers
Puy de Dôme 1465 m
Clermont-Ferrand
Parc Naturel du Livradois
St-Nectaire
La Bourboule
Le Mont-Dore
Issoire
Ambert
To Lyon
St-Etienne
Puy de Sancy 1855 m
Parc Nat. des Volcans
Bort-les-Orguest
To Brive
La Chaise-Dieu
Brioude
R. Dordogne
Parc Monts du Cantal
Salers
Le Lioran
St-Flour
Le Puy
Plomb du Cantal 1855 m
To Brive
Aurillac
River Allier
To Valence
Chaudes-Aigues
River Loire
To Brive & Figeac
Aubenas
Mende
To Avignon
To Figeac
Mt. Lozere 1699 m
R. Ardèche
Gorges de l'Ardèche
Ste-Enimie
R. Tarn
Florac
Rodez
CAUSSE MEJEAN
Parc Nat. des Cevennes
Gorges du Tarn
Mt. Aigoual 1567 m
Alès
Millau
To Albi
R. Tarn
CAUSSE DE LARZAC
0
50 km
To Béziers
To Montpellier & Béziers
To Nimes

NORTH AND EASTERN AUVERGNE

The north and eastern portions of Auvergne make up much the most densely populated part of the Massif Central, taking in Clermont-Ferrand, Vichy and Le Puy, and the industrial (and soccer) centre of St-Etienne. **Clermont** and **Vichy** both have good train links with Paris and make obvious jumping-off points – not just for parts in this section but for much of the vast National Park of the Auvergne, to the west. **Le Puy**, a slow haul through the central mountains, gives access to the Cévennes and Ardèche (both of which are discussed in the following section).

Clermont-Ferrand

Geographic and economic centre of the Massif Central, big, industrial **CLERMONT-FERRAND** is an incongruous capital for rustic Auvergne. It is a lively, youthful place, with a major university, and a manufacturing base that (with St-Etienne and Paris) has steadily been depopulating the villages of the province. As a base for this side of the Massif it's ideal, with a wide choice of rooms and some good restaurants and bars. And it is interesting in its own right too – a well preserved historic centre and the nearby spectacle of **Puy de Dôme** and of the **Parc des Volcans**.

Clermont and neighbouring Montferrand were united in 1631 to form a single city, but you're likely to spend most of your time in the former, since what is left of Vieux Montferrand stands out on a limb to the east. Both, despite long (and vaguely illustrious) pasts, were peacefully obscure by the time of their union. It took the arrival of one Mme Daubrée, niece of Charles Macintosh (of raincoat fame), to change things. She brought all the skills of her uncle to France with her, and made rubber into bouncing balls for her children, an idea taken up by her entrepreneurial husband when he opened a small factory in 1832 dedicated to making and marketing rubber goods. His partner's grandsons, Edouard and André **Michelin**, adapted the factory to the demands of the emerging pneumatic tyre industry and so the Michelin empire was forged – and with it the city's (continuing) industrial base.

Clermont

Clermont's *'ville-noire'* aspect – so-called after the local black volcanic rock used in the construction of many of its buildings – becomes immediately apparent on entering the remnants of pre-rubber Clermont. Dark and solid, it clusters untidily around the summit of a worn-away volcanic peak.

The main streets of this quarter are rue des Gras – where you'll find the **Musée Ranquet** (2–4pm; Sun. and Thurs. 10–noon, closed Mon.; free), one of the city's best museums with displays on local history back to Roman times – and, running roughly parallel, rue de la Boucherie, a fragrant bazaar

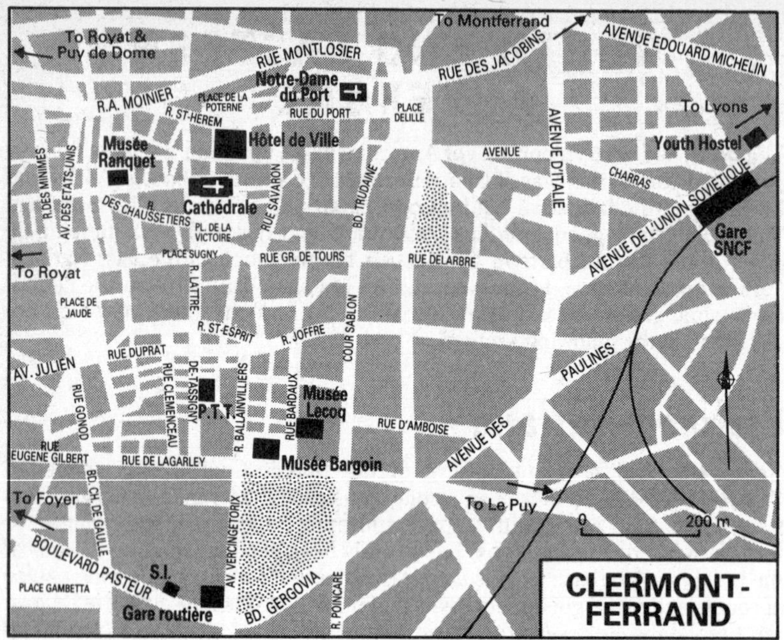

of tiny shops selling all kinds of food and spices. These streets gather up to the dark and soaring **Cathédrale Notre-Dame**, its black-grey volcanic stone evocatively and accurately described by Freda White as 'like the darkest shade of a pigeon's wing'. This stone, black lava brought from nearby Volvic, was first used in the thirteenth century (the cathedral dates from 1248 and until then tools were not strong enough to cut it), and its uncommon strength permitted a radical change in construction and design by making it possible to build vaults and pillars of unheard-of slenderness and height. Inside, the building is Gothic at its most movingly inspired, delicately aspiring heavenwards out of the gloom, despite its heavy nineteenth-century fixtures (the originals were destroyed in the revolution). Off the nave, there is access to the *Tour de la Bayette* (small charge) with extensive views across the city. From this vantage, too, you can understand why locals use the cathedral as a short cut – something the authorities have been trying to stop for years, though these days at least there aren't flocks of animals in tow.

A short step northeast of the cathedral stands Clermont's other great church, the **Basilique Notre-Dame du Port**. It is a century older and in almost total contrast, not only in style – it is Romanesque – but in substance, built from softer stone in pre-lava working days, and consequently corroding badly from exposure to Clermont's polluted air. For all that, it's a beautiful building, pure Auvergnat Romanesque with a Madonna and Child over the south door in the strangely stylised local form, both figures stiff and upright, the child more like a dwarf than an infant. Inside, it exudes the broody mysteriousness so often generated by Romanesque; put a franc in the slot and you can light up the intricately carved ensemble of leaves, knights and Biblical figures on the church's pillars and capitals. Outside the church, in **place Delille**, Pope Urban II preached the First Crusade in 1095, to a vast crowd who received his speech with the Occitan cry of 'Dios lo Volt' (God wills it), the phrase adopted by the crusaders in justification of all subsequent massacres.

On the edge of old Clermont, the huge and soulless **place de Jaude** is by day the noisome hub of the city centre and its main shopping area, and by night a desolate no-man's-land of drunks and glue-sniffers. In the centre stands a rousing statue of the Gallic chieftain Vercingétorix, who in 53 B.C. led his people to their only – and indecisive – victory over Julius Caesar, on the high windswept plateau of **Gergovie** about 12km south of town (buses from place de Jaude to ROMAGNAT, followed by a short walk, which could easily be extended through the villages of JUSSAT and CHANONAT to take in the medieval château of OPME).

North from place de Jaude, take a walk up to **place St-Pierre**, Clermont's principal marketplace, with a morning food **market** (Tues.–Sat.), at its liveliest on Saturday morning. South, just a few streets away on the busy boulevards that enclose the city centre, there are a couple of museums that may be interesting if you've got an hour or so to kill: **Musée Lecoq**, opposite a large park of the same name where you can't walk or even lie on the grass, has a fair natural history collection, while the almost adjoining **Musée Bargoin**, which forms the other half of the Musée Ranquet (see above), has exhibits of archaeology, religious sculpture and visual arts. Both museums keep the same hours as the Musée Ranquet.

The suburbs: Montferrand and Royat

Montferrand once greatly outshone its neighbour and rival but since the cities' union has gradually become enmeshed in suburbia, which is a pity – for what remains of the original town is elegant, and has recently been immaculately restored. For a break from the more frenetic atmosphere of Clermont, you can get out here easily enough on bus #7 from place de Jaude.

The other city suburb, **Royat**, to the west, began as a spa resort in the nineteenth century. Higher and breezier than Clermont, it is again an attractive hour or so's respite. There are few particular sights – the ruins of Roman baths in the park, a fortified Romanesque church – but the centre has a villagey feel about it, leading out to riverside walks along the valleys of the Tiretaine and the Charade. If you've got the energy to make the climb, there are fine views over the city and the surrounding country from the nearby *puys* of Montaudou and Chateix.

Puy de Dôme

For a longer and more directed walk, a couple of hours from Royat (or bus from Clermont) will bring you to Puy de Dôme, one of the tallest of the *puys*, with sweeping views back towards the town and over to Parc des Volcans, stretching away amid shreds of cloud. Close to the summit ruins survive of a Roman temple to Mercury, in its time considered one of the marvels of the Empire, fashioned from over fifty different kinds of marble and with an enormous bronze statue of Mercury where a TV antenna now stands.

Walking out to the Puy from Clermont, or Royat, allow a good half day – and take food. The restaurant on the top enjoys a monopoly and makes full use of it.

Some practical details

The main **SI office** in Clermont is at 69 bd Gergovia, with annexes at the railway station (Mon.–Sat. only), on place de Jaude (June–Sept.) and rue de la Rodade in Montferrand (June–Sept.). At any of these you should be able to pick up a copy of *Le Mois à Clermont*, which details everything that's happening in the city. Other sources of **information** include the *Centre d'Information Jeunesse* (8 place Regensburg) which concentrates on long-term accommodation and jobs; *Service d'Accueil des Etudiants Etrangers* and *CROUS*, both student offices on rue Etienne-Dollet, south of the main SI.

Cheap beds are easy to find. There's a *youth hostel* (55 av de l'URSS; ☎73.92.26.39) conveniently located just two minutes' walk from the **gare SNCF**; a *Foyer International des Jeunes*, at 12 place Regensburg (☎73.93.07.82), in the midst of a noisy housing development; and the *Maison St-Jean* (Foyer des Jeunes Travailleurs), 17 rue Gaultier-de-Biauzat (☎73.92.49.70), which has a bargain bed and breakfast. There are a range of **cheap hotels** in av de l'URSS right outside the station, of which the most reliable are *Le Bellevue* (1 av de l'URSS; ☎73.92.43.12) and the more expensive *Splendid Hôtel Terminus*. There are further possibilities in av Charras opposite: try the *Auvergne* at no. 67, the *Moderne* at no. 57 or *Hôtel de la Gare* at no. 76 (☎73.92.07.82). For something nearer the centre there's *Hôtel Foch* (22 rue Maréchal-Foch (☎73.93.48.40) and *Le Savoy* (22 rue de la Préfecture; ☎73.36.27.22), both close to place de Jaude. **For campers**, ROYAT has one- and four-star sites, and there's a three-star site a little farther out in CEYRAT.

For eating, four restaurants should be enough to cover most pockets, tastes and palates: the *Bungalow*, 30 rue Ballainvilliers, serves good fish and vegetarian dishes (the café next door is a popular punk-anarchist hangout); *La Couscousserie*, 20 rue Cadène, just off place de Jaude, is North African, and *Pied de Cochon*, at 4 rue Lamartine, again near place de Jaude, offers an amazingly cheap three-course menu. And if all of these are still too pricey, there's a *self-service restaurant* on rue Cheval-Blanc that costs even less. **Good places to drink** later on are *Le Clown*, 65 rue Anatole-France, which has nightly live jazz, and *Le Drop*, at bd Trudaine.

The focal point of the **city transport system** is place de Jaude: you can get just about anywhere in town from here, and there's an information and ticket booth to find out how. You can either buy a single ticket which lasts an hour, or, much cheaper, invest in a book of ten tickets or a daily *Carte de Jour*. There are frequent bus connections between the **gare routière**, next to the SI, and St-Etienne, Volvic, Riom, Le Puy and Vichy, and trains leave regularly for Paris via Riom and Vichy – the **gare SNCF** is on av de l'URSS. *Le Cévenol*, a stopping train **through the mountains to Nîmes**, is one of the most enchanting French rail journeys you can take – so much so that during the summer SNCF runs a *train touristique* with entertainment on board.

And finally, **bike rental** is available at *Mazerat* (5 bd Gergovia) and **Allostop** (hitching service) is at 22 av des Etats-Unis (☎73.36.72.33).

Riom

Just 15km north of Clermont, **RIOM** is sedate and provincial. One-time capital of the entire Auvergne, its Renaissance architecture now secures the town's status as a highlight of the northern Massif. You may not want to stay for more than a morning's wandering, but it provides a worthwhile stopover for lunch if you're on the way up to Vichy. It's an aloof, old-world kind of place, still Auvergne's judicial capital, with a nineteenth-century **Palais de Justice** that stands on the site of a grand palace built when the Dukes of Berry controlled this region in the fourteenth century. Of the palace, only the Ste-Chapelle survives, incorporated in the new buildings, with some fine stained glass and tapestries (guided visits, Mon.–Sat. 10–11.30am and 2–5.30pm). Not far away, on rue du Commerce, the **Eglise-Notre-Dame-du-Marthuret** holds Riom's most valued treasures, two statues of the Virgin and Child – one a Black Madonna, the other, the so-called *Vierge à l'Oiseau*, a touchingly realistic piece of carving that portrays the young Christ with a bird fluttering in his hands. A copy stands in the entrance hall of the church (its original site), where you can see it with the advantage of daylight.

Riom's **SI** is also on rue du Commerce and, if you decide to stay over, most of the **hotels** are near the junction of that street and bd Desaix. Cheapest are *Desaix* (☎73.38.20.36) and *Hôtel du Square* (☎73.38.46.52), both with their own restaurant and an inexpensive menu. Cheaper still is *Hôtel de Lyon* (☎73.38.07.66), a little further out at Faubourg de la Bade.

Trains from Riom run frequently to VICHY (and Clermont). Local buses – from the **gare SNCF** and various other points – also serve **MOZAC**, on the edge of town, with a twelfth-century **abbey church**, its Romanesque sculpture beautiful as ever, continuing on to the bourgeois spa-resort of **CHATEL-GUYON** (10–20 min.). With thirty different **hot springs**, great views over the surrounding countryside and *puys*, and a couple of well-equipped **campsites**, this is as good a place as any if you want to rest up for a night. And for an easy stroll, you can wander out along the leafy **valleys of the Sardon and Prades** to the château of Tournoël.

Vichy

VICHY is famous for two things: its World War II puppet government under **Marshal Pétain** and its curative **sulphurous springs**, which attract thousands of aging and ailing visitors – *curistes*, they're called – every year. And while there's nothing left to suggest that Vichy was once capital of a collaborationist Nazi state – the building that used to house the Pétain government has been anonymously turned into an anonymous building, and the **SI**, in the same building, is careful to make no reference at all to what once went on upstairs – the fact that it's one of France's foremost spa resorts colours everything you see here. The population is largely elderly, genteel and rich, and swells several-fold in summer; they come here to drink the water, wallow in it, inhale its steam or be sprayed with it, and the town is almost entirely devoted to catering to them.

All of which should make this a place to avoid. Yet it's hard to dislike. There's a real fin-de-siècle charm about the town, and a curious fascination in its continuing function. Vichy revolves around the **Parc des Sources**, a stately tree-shaded park that takes up most of its centre. At its north end stands the **Palais**, an enormous iron-framed greenhouse in which people sit around and chat or read newspapers, while from a large tiled stand in the middle the various waters emerge from their spouts. The *curistes* line up to get their prescribed cupful, and for a small fee you can join them. The *Célestin* is the only one of the springs that is bottled and widely drunk: if you're into a taste experience, try the remaining five. They are progressively more foul and sulphurous, with the *Source de l'Hôpital*, which has its own circular building at the far end of the park, an almost unbelievably nasty creation. Each of the springs is prescribed for a different ailment and the tradition is, conveniently enough for the local hotel and tourist business, that apart from the *Célestin* they must all be drunk on the spot to be efficacious: a dubious but effective way of drawing in the crowds.

Although all the springs technically belong to the nation, and treatment is partially funded by the state, they are in fact run privately for profit by the *Compagnie Fermière*, first created in the nineteenth century to prepare for a visit by the emperor Napoléon III. The Compagnie not only has a monopoly on selling the waters, but also runs the casino and numerous hotels, including Vichy's grandest, the *Pavillon Sévigné*. Even the chairs conveniently dotted around the Parc des Sources belong to the Compagnie. And Vichy never fails to make money: there are over 200 hotels in town – one reason that it was chosen for the wartime government. Marshal Pétain's own offices were at the *Pavillon*, while the Gestapo had their headquarters at the *Hôtel du Portugal*. There is absolutely nothing to commemorate either.

After the waters, Vichy's curiosities are limited. There is pleasant wooded riverside in Parc de l'Allier, created again for Napoléon III. And, not far from here, the old town boasts the strange **Eglise de St-Blaise**, actually two churches in one, with a 1930s Baroque number built onto the original Romanesque – an effect that sounds hideous but is rather imaginative. Inside, another Auvergne Black Virgin, *Notre-Dame-des-Malades*, stands surrounded by plaques offered by the grateful healed who stacked their odds with both her and the sulphur.

As for nightlife, Vichy, despite the *curistes*, can be surprisingly active. The area to head for, full of cafés and brasseries, is around the junction of rue Clemenceau, rue de Pans, rue Lucas and rue Jean-Jaurès, a corner known locally as *les quatre chemins*. Most of the places here serve cheap meals and snacks (*Vichyssoise*, inevitably, is available) and they're the obvious places to drink. If you want to move on from here, *Greenfields* – despite the name – is generally the most animated of the discos.

Inexpensive and adequate hotels can be found near the **gare SNCF**, along av des Célestins, or there's a **youth hostel** – invariably empty – across the river on rue du Stade (no. 19; ☎70.32.25.14). Local buses all stop at the **gare SNCF**, though the **gare routière** is on the corner of rue Doumier and rue Jardet, by the central place Charles-de-Gaulle.

South to Le Puy

The slowest and most beautiful route south from Vichy is along the *Sentier de la Loire*, **GR3**, starting at CHATEL-MONTAGNE, heading down the ridges of the Forez mountains east of Thiers, and through the Loire gorges to Le Puy. It's a serious commitment, requiring a ten-day to two-week walk.

Somewhat gentler, the parallel **D906** road winds through the forested valleys a short distance to the west. **THIERS**, the first town – on the banks of the fast, twisting Durolle river – is a pleasant surprise, its steep streets hiding some lovely fifteenth-century timbered houses and a couple of interesting Romanesque churches, as well as stupendous views over the surrounding mountains. Thiers is noted, in France at least, for its cutlery, and scores of shops sell fine quality knives and other implements. If you want to stay, **accommodation** is limited, but there's a **campsite** at nearby LE BREUIL and a reasonable **hotel** 6km west at PONT-DE-DORE on N89, *Hôtel de l'Aigle d'Or* (☎73.80.00.50). To the southwest, and only realistically accessible for drivers, are a scattering of medieval **castles: Aultéribe, Ravel** (Apr.–Nov. 10–noon and 2–7pm), **Mauzun and Martinanches** (mid–June to mid–Sept. 2–7pm), while to the southeast you can drive and hike up to the 1634m peak of **Pierre-sur-Haute**, the highest point of the eastern Auvergne. Climbing higher, the road winds on to AMBERT, the centre of a once thriving paper-milling district, with a mill still functioning at nearby **Richard-de-Bas**, well worth a visit (9am–noon and 2–6pm; July and Aug. 9am–8pm). Thirty kilometres on you reach **LA CHAISE-DIEU**, a hill village dominated by the sturdy square towers of an impressive medieval **abbey church**, one of the finest monastic buildings in the country and home to an eerily unfinished fresco of the *Dance of Death*, which shows the shadowy figure of Death plucking delicately at the coarse plump bodies of the living, who staunchly refuse to notice. 'It is yourself', says the fifteenth-century text below – as indeed it might have been in that age of the Black Death and Hundred Years War. Nearby, on place de l'Echo, the **Salle de l'Echo** is another product of the risk of contagion, if not from plague then from leprosy, for in this room, once used to take confession from the sick and dying, two people can turn their backs on each other and stand in opposite corners and have a perfectly audible conversation just by whispering. The **SI** is to the right of the church in the central **place de la Mairie**. A couple of **two-star hotels** (*Hôtel Terminus*, ☎71.00.00.73, closed Dec.–Feb. and *Hôtel Au Tremblant*, ☎71.00.01.85, closed mid-Nov. to mid-April) and a **campsite** offer a feasible chance of a bed for the night if you can't get down to LE PUY.

Clermont to Le Puy

An alternative route to Le Puy is to take the main N9 and N102 from Clermont-Ferrand. It's quicker but much less spectacular.

ISSOIRE is the only place of any note you pass, a small, rather drab industrial town, gathered into a tight centre within a wide circle of boulevards. A stronghold of Protestantism, it was decimated during the seventeenth-century Wars of Religion; a pillar erected in the *place* bears the simple legend, *Ici fut Issoire* (Here was Issoire). Just about the only thing to survive was the church – **St-Austremont** – Romanesque again, with marvellously carved capitals and a beautiful crypt. Otherwise there's not a great deal to see: Issoire is a popular spot for a stopover, but its hotels are not as cheap as they might be.

ST-ETIENNE, over to the east, lies on another possible approach to Le Puy. Its **Palais des Arts** at 8 place Louis-Comte, an unexpected mine of contemporary art, justifies a detour in itself. It houses a comprehensive group of work by Symbolist artists such as Meunier and Maurin, and a good modern American section, in which Andy Warhol and Frank Stella figure prominently. Look out, too, for the creations of Rodin, Matisse, Léger and Ernst, and rooms filled entirely with French art, all imaginatively laid out to exciting effect.

It would be a shame, though, if you were forced to stay here. *La ville où l'on fabrique de tout* (the town that makes everything), St-Etienne is otherwise unrelievedly industrial, a major armaments centre, and enclosed for miles around by grim mineworkings, factory chimneys and warehouses. One thing that redeems it for a visitor (and probably for most residents too) is the soccer team, *les Verts*, whose stickers you see on car windows all over the country. The centre is bland and characterless, the mood one of decline, after the recent closure of the coalfields. For the committed, or unfortunate, bus #10 runs into the centre of town (**SI** on the corner of place Jean-Jaurès) from the **railway station**. The cheapest **hotel** around is the *Splendid* (16 rue du Théâtre) near place du Peuple.

Le-Puy-En-Velay

A strange town in a strange setting, **LE-PUY-EN-VELAY** sprawls across a broad basin in the mountains, a muddle of red roofs barbed with tall poles of volcanic rock. Capital of the Haute Loire, it isn't easy to get to – from Clermont or Nîmes you have to change trains at St-Georges-d'Aurac – but it's well worth the effort. In medieval times it was the assembly point for **St-Jacques pilgrims** coming from the east of France and Germany* and amid the cobbled streets of the old town are some of the most richly endowed **churches** in the land. The strange surrounding countryside is an added attraction.

*The clearly marked GR65 follows their route all the way from here to ST-JEAN-PIED-DE-PORT in the Basque country and over the frontier into Spain.

Arrival and a room

Arriving by bus or train you'll find yourself on place du Maréchal-Leclerc, a ten-minute walk from **place de Breuil**, focus of the new town, and within easy striking distance of some reasonably-priced **hotels**.

Most are in the new town. Pride of place must go to the dirt cheap *Grand Hôtel Lafayette* (17–19 bd St-Louis; ☎71.09.32.85) in a quiet, leafy courtyard off the main traffic artery. Though sadly dilapidated – and due for metamorphosis into an old people's home – it is one of the sights of the town. Its once grand rooms still contain their period furniture and marble fireplaces; the dining room is Gothic with coffered ceiling and frescoed walls. Other possibilities include *Hôtel La Verveine* (☎71.02.00.77), in place Cadelade, with musical plumbing and a good restaurant; *Le Progrès*, in the same square, and *Les Cordeliers* – a little more expensive but a good deal, also hidden in its own courtyard down rue des Cordeliers, off rue Portail d'Avignon.

There are two **campsites**: *Bouthézard* (three-star), thirty minutes from the station along chemin de Roderie, and *Causans* (one-star) on bd Pte-Betrand. **Student foyers** are to be found in Faubourg St-Jean, at rue du Consulat (from place du Martouret: rue Courrerie, rue Pannessac and turn right) and in Roche-Arnaud, twenty minutes from the **gare SNCF** (left out of the station, left again before the park onto rue Rousseau, across rue Farigade to rue Lavastre, onto rue Reynaud and it's on the left). For information, the **SI** is in a large building between place Breuil and place Michelet, and has a **summer annex** on rue des Tables near the cathedral.

The old town.

Focussing the **old town**, and reached over the steep sequence of streets and steps that terrace the town's *puy* foundation, the **cathedral** is almost Byzantine in style, striped with alternate layers of light and dark stone and capped with a line of small cupolas. Oddly enough, you enter from below, the nave-level reached by clambering up yet more steps; on the way take a look at the *Fever Stone*, a curative shrine, named after the miracle of a woman's deliverance – restored to health having lain down upon it to die. Patchy gold frescoes pull you inside the church – dark and gloomy because of the volcanic rock of which it's built – and towards the city's own *Black Virgin*, copy of a revered original burnt during the Revolution, and still taken out, dusted, and paraded through the town every August 15. Other, lesser treasures are displayed at the back of the church in the sacristy, beyond which is the entrance to the twelfth-century cloister, disarmingly beautiful, and patterned with the same stripes as the cathedral facade. The surrounding ecclesiastical buildings – together with some splendid nineteenth-century stone mansions – form a small, independent *Ville Sainte*.

The cathedral is simply one of several strange and unique sights in this town, most of them stacked on wearisome heights. At the summit – visible from any street you might find yourself on – is the giant crimson statue of **Notre-Dame-de-France**, a fabulous monster fashioned from the metal of guns captured in the Crimean war.

The church of **St-Michel-d'Aiguilhe** (9am–dusk) sits precariously on the summit of the other, even steeper and pointed *puy*, the Rocher d'Aiguilhe, and the eleventh-century construction seems to grow out of the rock itself. It's a tough ascent, but one you should definitely make – a quirky little building decorated with mosaic, arabesques, and trefoil arches, its bizarre shape forced to follow that of the available flat ground.

Back down below, lacemakers – a traditional, though now commercialised industry – do a fine trade, doilies and lace shawls hanging enticingly outside shops for tourists. But it's surface only; deeper into Le Puy's maze of narrow streets the old lanes are uncluttered and wonderful. In the **new part of town**, beyond the squat **Tour Pannessac**, place de Breuil joins place Michelet and forms a social hub, with spacious public gardens. Busy bd Maréchal-Fayolle converges with place Cadelade, where lies another of Le Puy's crazier aspects: the extraordinary bulbous tower of the **Pages Verveine distillery**. The *verveine* (verbena) plant is normally used to make *tisane* (herb tea), but in this region produces a powerful digestive liqueur instead.

Food

Other local specialities are fat sausages, called *Jésus*, and green lentils, invariably cooked in pork fat or served with pork like most Haute Loire dishes; the *Salade auvergnat*, which features on most menus, is a substantial dish of green lentils cooked in lard, with chunks of ham, egg, potatoes and mayonnaise.

The least expensive **meals** in Le Puy are at the **self-service restaurant** in the same building as the SI. More interesting bars and restaurants are sprinkled around place Breuil and place Michelet. *Le Michelet*, a popular piano bar, can be lively, and in the old town, *Le Bistrot*, on place de la Halle, has live music and a connoisseur's choice of beers. Food **markets** take place on Wednesday and Saturday on place du Martouret, with a Saturday **flea market** on place du Clauzel.

Hiking and excursions

Committed walkers can tackle the **GR40** *Tour du Velay*, basically a high ridge walk encircling Le Puy and taking in an enormous variety of scenery from the 'lookouts' of the Devès overhanging the Allier gorges to the high pastures of the Mézenc, the volcanic plugs of the Meygal, and the woods and meadows of the Loire valley. Other good excursions include the ruins of the thirteenth-century château at POLIGNAC, the restored château of Lavoûte-Polignac (home of the Dukes of Polignac for forty generations) beyond the Peyredeyre gorges on the Loire, and, to the west, the spectacular **gorges of the Allier** between MONISTROL and ST-ARCONS.*

---

*Work is about to commence on a dam at Serre de la Fare, a spectacular gorge between Le Puy and Gerbier de Jonc (a volcanic rock at the source of the Loire). This will be the first of a series of ten dams proposed for the Loire and its tributaries, aimed at controlling floods and providing a regular flow of water in the summer. The village of Colempce, south of Le Puy, will be submerged in an artificial lake, and conservationists claim that the project poses a serious threat to the natural life of the river. They say that the floodplains of the Loire reduce the impact of severe floods while sheltering rare forms of wildlife. Additionally, the locals fear that in an area of volcanic activity, their lives will be put at risk by the huge volume of water contained by the dam. Public opinion is made evident by stickers and grafitti everywhere, stating 'non au barrage!'.

THE PARC DES VOLCANS AND SOUTHERN MASSIF

Much of Western Auvergne falls within the 350,000 hectares of the **Parc Naturel Régional des Volcans d'Auvergne** – the Auvergne Volcano park – a wild country of peaks, gorges, and lakes serrated by a phenomenal concentration of *puys*, most of them fragments of gigantic primaeval volcanoes that have been weathered away. The park is divided by three ranges: the Monts Dômes, the Monts Dores, and the Cantal mountains. Few people live here, and those mainly involved in sheep and cattle farming, and now, for better or worse, in tourism. Solitude is the order of the day. If you meet anyone on the great grassy expanses of pasture covering the lava plateaux, it's likely to be the occasional shepherd or forester.

Within all this are scattered traditional villages, a stylish handful of spa towns – **Le Mont-Dore** and **La Bourboule**, most notably – and a growing number of winter sports resorts. **GR footpaths** cross some of the most interesting and difficult terrain; for information on them or *gîtes d'étapes* and skiing in the park area, contact the *Centre d'Information* at 28 rue St-Esprit in Clermont-Ferrand.

Further south the cold, hard *causses* – plateaux – of the **southern Massif**, the quiet, wild hills of **the Cévennes,** and, to the east, the mountainous **Ardèche** are all arguably parts of the southern province of Languedoc, but have an identity shaped by the mountains, quite different from that of the Mediterranean provinces.

The Monts Dômes to the Monts Dore

The **Monts Dômes** range, west of Clermont-Ferrand, is the youngest in the region at 4000 years old, and includes 112 small volcanoes. The **Monts Dores**, slightly to the south had only three centres of volcanic activity but it was much more intense, leaving hundreds of jagged projections.

Orcival

Twenty kilometres southwest of Clermont, lush pastures and green hills punctuated by the abrupt eruptions of the *puys* enclose the village of **ORCIVAL (buses** from Clermont). A pretty but over-touristed little place dominated by the stunning Romanesque church of **Notre-Dame,** it makes a suitable base for hiking in the region. It was founded by the monks of La Chaise-Dieu in the twelfth century. Built of the same grey volcanic stone as the cathedral in Clermont, the exterior, topped with a spired octagonal tower and fanned with tiny chapels, is a treat, in happy contrast to the interior marred by Gregorian musak designed to encourage piety in the visitors, and an electronic alarm system sectioning off the choir. The purpose of the alarm is to protect another *Black Virgin*, this time enamelled and gilded, the object of pilgrimage since before the sixth century and still carried through the streets on Ascension Day. In the Middle Ages she was known as 'Our Lady of Iron and Chains', and was worshipped by former convicts who had survived imprisonment – ironic that today she is the one who is confined in high security. There's modest accommodation at the *Hôtel du Mont-Dore* (☎73.65.82.06; closed mid-Nov. to Dec.), a couple of **campsites** and a **gîte d'étape**, *La Fontchartoux*, 1km away on GR30/GR441, with meals available in the adjoining restaurant run by the *gîte* proprietor.

Along GR441 and other walks

GR441 continues right around the Monts Dômes on the hike known as the *Tour de la Chaine des Puys*. It's a seven-day outing, passing among more than forty extinct volcanoes – practicable only between May and October.

For something less drastic: an hour's walk away along a section of GR41, you can get to the **Château de Cordès**. A grand manor house rather than a castle, it dates from the thirteenth century with extensive alterations in the seventeenth century. Its elegant suites and gardens designed by Le Nôtre provide a worthy focus for those who seek a purpose to their strolls.

Other walking possibilities out of Orcival include trips to **Lac Servière** and **Lac de Guéry**, the first 2½ hours, the second 5½ hours to the south. For Lac Servière, follow GR4-GR30 through the woods above the valley of the Sioule. The lake is a beauty; it's 1200m up, with gently sloping shores surrounded by pasture and conifers. You can either head southeast to the **gîte d'étape** at PESSADE or continue on to the larger Lac de Guéry, lent a slightly eerie air by the black basaltic boulders strewn across the surrounding meadows. The town of MONT-DORE is only 9km further.

Saint-Nectaire

ST-NECTAIRE lies on the other – eastern – side of the Monts Dore from Orcival. It comprises the tiny spa of St-Nectaire-le-Bas with its main street lined with grand but fading *belle-époque* hotels (and a **gîte d'étape** just beyond) and the old village of St-Nectaire-le-Haut, overlooked by its magnificent **Romanesque church.** (It also gives its name to a great cheese, widely produced in the Puy-de-Dôme and Cantal *départements.*)

For a good aerial view of the local landscape take D150 out of the old village towards 919m **Puy de Mazeyres** and turn up a path to the right for the short final climb to the summit (1 hr.). An equally easy walk is along D966, following the valley of the Couze de Chambon to SAILLANT, where the stream cascades down a high lava rock face in the middle of the village. For a good view, cross the bridge and continue a short distance along D26E.

Stouter hearts can tackle a couple of longer hikes to local lakes. Particularly beautiful is the **Lac Chambon** (3 hr.), ringed with woodland and set with numerous islets. The waymarked GR30 will take you there, passing over lightly forested heath before reaching the vast medieval **castle of Murol** (June–Sept. 10am–noon and 2–7pm) perched on a basalt cone with commanding views over the lake to the mountains beyond. If you don't want to go back the way you came, there are **hotels** and **campsites** near the lake and a **gîte d'étape** on down GR30 at COURBANGES. Somewhat further off to the north – five hours – is the volcanic **Lac Aydat**, with **campsites** and a **gîte** in the nearby hamlet of PHIALEIX.

Le Mont-Dore and La Bourboule

Built along the banks of the young and shallow Dordogne, here hardly more than a trickle, **LE MONT-DORE** is an old-established spa resort in the best tradition – good food and drink, walks in pleasant countryside, and a hopefully bearable cure at the baths for some not-too-serious ailment. Altogether a wholesome and civilised sort of place. The **Etablissement Thermal** stands right in the town centre, and early every morning *curistes*, easily identifiable by tight-drawn scarves and overcoats, stream into the building, self-proclaimed 'world centre for the treatment of asthma'. Walkers frequent the town too, using it as a base for hikes out to the **Puy de Sancy** (see below) – 15km away, and, at 1885m, Auvergne's rooftop.

The town is brimming with **hotels**, so if you're planning on staying, there should be no problem finding a room – try *La Rûche* (☎73.65.05.93; closed Oct. to mid-May except at the weekend) or *Hôtel Terminus* (☎73.65.00.23; closed Oct.–Dec. and mid-April to mid-May). **Campsites**, too, are in good supply; the municipal *Les Crouzets* opposite the railway station is the nearest. And there's a big and comfortable **youth hostel** 3km out on Route de Sancy (☎73.65.03.53). For more general information, ask at the **SI** on the corner of av Leclerc for a copy of *La Semaine au Mont-Dore*, and also for their pamphlet on walks and drives in the area.

LA BOURBOULE is 7km down the road, an easy hitch. Known as the sister to Le Mont-Dore, it is another traditional spa – the 'capital of allergies' – but with a more open feel and, because of its lower altitude, weather a degree or two warmer. The big casino, the domed Grands Thermes baths and several other turn-of-the-century buildings, which used to house privately-run baths, are ornate, gilded and wonderfully vulgar, with a faded, permanently off-season look to them – as has the whole town.

Behind the townhall, the wooded **Parc Fenestre** turns out to be surprisingly large, a ***téléférique*** taking you right up to **Plateau de Charlannes** at 1300m, where it's possible to walk in the woods or ski in winter. All in all, it's a cool, tranquil place to unwind: as the SI's leaflet says, 'You will be able to put your vital node to rest in La Bourboule'. The SI (in the city hall on place de la République) also sells a booklet of local walks. **Hotels**, as at Le Mont-Dore, are plentiful, three good bargains being *Hôtel de la Poste* (☎73.81.09.66; closed Oct. to mid-May), *Le Pavillon* (☎73.81.01.42; closed Oct. to mid-May) and *Le Rocher* (☎73.65.54.82). There is also a good selection of **campsites**, for example at MURAT-LE-QUAIRE 4km away, and along the Mont-Dore road, while 2km east in the hamlet of LE PREGNOUX there's a **gîte d'étape**.

Some walks

Fit and serious walkers may want to conquer the **Puy de Sancy**, a six-hour hike south from La Bourboule on GR30-41, passing on the way the two fine waterfalls of the **Cascade de la Vernière** and **Plat à Barbe** after about two hours, and themselves a satisfying destination for a walk. From the summit of the Puy you can take the *téléférique* down to Le Mont-Dore. For a less strenuous outing you could take it up and walk down.

Another easier walk out of La Bourboule is to the 1500m summit of the **Banne d'Ordanche**. Pick up the GR path to the east of the town where it crosses the D130 road and the railway line, then take the signposted GR41 where it diverges from GR30.

In wintertime, both Le Mont-Dore and La Bourboule double as ski resorts – centres of a **ski-de-fond** (cross-country) network of circular pistes, some over 20km long. Skiable paths also connect La Bourboule to other ski villages in the locality – SANCY, BESSE, CHASTREIX, and PICHERANDE. Downhill skiing is possible too, on the Puy de Sancy.

South: to Aurillac and the Cantal Mountains

Just south of the Monts Dore the landscape is dotted with **volcanic lakes**, among them Pavin, Chauvet, and Montcineyre, with more to the west in the densely wooded country below the Plateau d'Artense. Apart from driving south on the EGLISENEUVE-D'ENTRAIGUES and CONDAT road (both good bases for exploring), the best way to see them is again **on foot**. **GR30**, *Tour des Lacs d'Auvergne*, takes in the Puy de Sancy, Orcival, and St-Nectaire as well as the lakes – about ten days: not passable in winter. Alternatively, a section of the Atlantic-to-the-Mediterranean **GR4** passes through, crossing the Puy de Dôme and the Monts Dore, over the pastures of the Plateau du Limon and up the ridges of the **Plomb du Cantal** to the high town of ST-FLOUR (10–14 days).

The Cantal mountains, geologists say, contained a three thousand metre-high volcano, which no longer exists, but has left a number of high crests. A relatively strenuous GR circuit encompasses the Cantal volcano – which with Etna is the largest, albeit extinct, volcano in Europe. Seventy kilometres in diameter, it is shaped like a wheel without a rim, the hub formed by its three spectacular conical peaks – Plomb du Cantal (1855m), Puy Mary (1787m), and Puy de Peyre-Arse (1686m) – and the spokes by deep valleys. The landscape is green and lush and devoted to sheep and dairy farming.

Convenient bases for exploring the massif are LE LIORAN (*Auberge du Tunnel*, ☎71.49.50.02 – open all year, but not particularly cheap; *gîte* in nearby Super-Lioran, June–Sept.) in the centre of the mountains; THIEZAC (*Hôtel du Commerce*, ☎71.47.01.67; campsite) – on the southern edge; and the pretty but touristy SALERS to the west (*Hôtel des Remparts*, ☎71.40.70.33, closed Nov. and Dec., and again not especially cheap; *Camping le Mouriol*, in summer only).

Aurillac

To the southwest lies the pleasant provincial capital of **AURILLAC**. From the **gare SNCF** it's a 15-minute walk into the centre, the vigorous **place du Square**, where you'll find the **SI**, which books hotel rooms and dispenses maps, including the invaluable *IGN Monts du Cantal*. Plenty of hotels have **cheap rooms** and **meals**. *Hôtel Damiens*, 20 rue des Carmes, *Hôtel du Palais*, 2 rue Beauclaire (☎71.48.24.86) and *Hôtel de Paris* next to the station are three good ones, and there's a municipal **campsite** just outside the town centre on av Veyre. Another option is the *Foyer des Jeunes Travailleurs* at 25 av de Tivoli (☎71.63.56.94). **Bikes** can be rented from *Malgouzou*, 22 rue Guy-de-Veyre, and **buses** leave daily from the main square for villages on the road to St-Flour and Conques.

The town itself can be toured fairly quickly. Apart from a couple of small **museums** concealed in the pedestrianised *vieille ville* – and a good one devoted to volcanoes in the Château St-Etienne (July and Aug., 10am–noon and 2–7pm; rest of year, 9am–noon and 2–6pm; closed Sun.) – there's not a lot to see or do. Wednesdays or Saturdays are the best times to be here, when peasants and farmers flock into town to sell their produce and livestock.

Aurillac and the Cantal generally are noted for a traditionally rustic cuisine, with dishes like *tripoux* – stuffed sheeps' feet wrapped in pieces of sheeps' stomach – seen on menus from here to St-Flour and down to Chaudes-Aigues on the southern edge of the Cantal. More enticing, perhaps is Cantal cheese – similar to cheddar, and one of the least expensive and most popular in France.

East from Aurillac

From **MURAT** on you begin to leave the Cantal mountains behind. 'A clambering little town', Freda White called it; industrial, but attractive nonetheless. The *puys* thin out and the country becomes high and flat all the way to **ST-FLOUR**, with an inviting old centre, worth the long haul uphill from the **gare SNCF** (catch a bus up to Allée Pompidou, on the old city's western fringe). There are numerous hotels: try *Hôtel du Nord* in the upper town (☎71.60.07.33) or *Hôtel du Commerce* in the lower (☎71.60.10.31; closed Nov.-March). There is hostel-type accommodation at *La Sanfloraine* in av de Besserette (☎71.60.13.60) and two **campsites**, one in the upper town, one down the hill near the station.

The focal point of the old city is the **place d'Armes**, made busy by a market on Saturday mornings and dominated by a severe fourteenth-century **Cathedral**, built of dull grey rock, squared-off in shape, and, outside at least, extremely plain. At first glance the interior seems equally austere. But it's big and beautifully vaulted with bare stone blocks, slight traces of frescoes and some elaborate woodcarving – most prominently, a fifteenth-century figure of a black Christ on the cross. Behind the cathedral, expansive vistas take in the lower town and its two rivers. Back on place d'Armes you'll find the **SI** and, in the Hôtel de Ville, a museum of local life, **Musée de Haute-Auvergne** (9am–noon and 2–6pm; closed Sat. and Sun. from Oct. to May).

Pushing on south, you reach a district in which the *Maquis* were very active: 15,000 Resistance fighters operated in this immediate locality, often having full-scale shootouts with the German army. A **monument** near the junction of D4 and N9 marks the site of a battle that left a thousand *maquisards* dead. (If you have your own transport, the D4 makes a slow but spectacular route to Le Puy, crossing the wooded heights of Mt Mouchet, with another Resistance memorial and the best of all views back west to the Cantral mountains.) Further on, the road winds below the **Garabit Viaduct**, an extraordinarily delicate tracery of steel, built by Eiffel of tower fame in 1884, to carry the railway over the River Truyère. This is wild, sparsely populated country whose grandeur and solitude not even the vast hydroelectric installations can mar. There are no towns of any size except CHAUDES-AIGUES, whose domestic hot water supply has been provided by natural springs since Roman times. It's hard to get to, but if you have an urge for the romantic, the ruins of the **Château d'Alleuze** about 20km south of St-Flour will satisfy it.

Larzac and the Causses

High plateaux, bleak, windswept, and sparsely populated with primitive villages, the **Causses** of the southern Massif – **Larzac, Noir, Méjean,** and **Sauveterre** – are rugged, independent countryside. All four are riddled with strange caves, rock formations, grottoes, and underground tunnels, in between deep and narrow gorges: between Larzac and Causse Noir cuts the Vallée de la Dourbie, between the Noir and Méjean the Gorges de la Jonte; and gashed between Méjean and Sauveterre lies the most spectacular valley of all, the Gorges du Tarn.

In recent years, the **CAUSSE DU LARZAC** has been in the headlines over sustained political resistance to the high-profile presence of the French military. Originally there was a small military camp at a village called LA CAVALERIE, long tolerated for the cash its soldiers brought in. But in the early 1970s, the army decided to expand the place and use it as a permanent strategic base. The result was explosive. A federation was formed – **Paysans du Larzac** – which gave its name (and impetus) to the local **separatist movement**; successful acts of sabotage were committed, and three huge peace festivals held here – in 1981, 1983, and again in 1985. The army has now moved out but you still find Larzac graffiti from here to Lyon, shorthand for opposition to the army, the state, and the Parisian central government, and in favour of self-determination and independence for the South.

Walking

The best way to immerse yourself in the empty, sometimes eerie atmosphere of Larzac is to walk – **GRs 7, 71**, and **74** cross the plateau – though you shouldn't attempt it without a *topo-guide*. The plateau's best-known village, **ROQUEFORT-SUR-SOULZON**, is home to Roquefort cheese, one of the most revered cheeses in France, sharp and creamy, blue-streaked and made from local ewes' milk. Its delicate maturity can only be reached in the caves here, and efforts to reproduce the conditions artificially elsewhere have failed. N9 (easy hitching) cuts all the way across the plain from here, through LA CAVALERIE to **L'HOSPITALET-DU-LARZAC**, a name recalling the days when Larzac was ruled by the Knights Templar and later the Knights Hospitaller. Farther on, **LA COUVERTOIRADE** lies 5km off the main road, an unrestored old Templar city within forbidding fortifications, and on the surface, hardly changed since the Middle Ages – until, that is, you get asked for money just to enter the place. South again is LE CAYLAR, a simple town in a wild rocky setting, and the **Pas de l'Escalette** (Ladder Pass), the dramatic twisting descent from Larzac to the Languedoc plain. The name dates from a time when the only way on to Larzac using this route was to climb ladders fixed to the 300 metre-high cliff-face.

Millau

At the foot of Causse Noir and Larzac, near where the Tarn and Dourbie meet, **MILLAU** is beautifully situated no matter how you approach it – a vivacious town, quite large, with broad streets arcaded by the branches of pollarded plane trees. There's not much to see, apart from the unusual octagonal belfry and fountain in the central square, but it has a good southern feel to it, and makes a wise overnight stop. The town has loads of **hotels**, though no amazing bargains, and two **campsites** just across the Pont de Cureplat. There's an **SI** on the corner of av Merle, and both the **gare SNCF** and the **gare routière** are a few hundred metres from the town centre on bd de la République.

The Gorges du Tarn

A narrow, difficult road, incongruously jammed with crawling traffic, follows the **Gorges du Tarn** all the way along its course – a dramatic ride, and at its most spectacular between LE ROZIER and the beautiful little town of **ST-ENIMIE**, full of cafés and places to rent bikes, or canoes for trips on the river. **Le Rozier** is a good walking centre and base for exploring some of the weird geological features of the *causses*: the caves at DARGILAN in the gorge of the River Jonte and ARMAND on the Causse Méjean, as well as the extraordinary rock formations around MONTPELLIER-LE-VIEUX to the south above the gorge of the Dourbie.

On to Mende

Continuing on from Ste-Enimie, the Tarn road runs to FLORAC and the Cévennes, while a minor route scurries up on to the **Causse de Sauveterre**, through the desolate village of SAUVETERRE to MENDE, capital of the Lozère, lounging comfortably in the valley of the Lot.

The old and twisting streets of **MENDE** enclose an immense, overbearing **Cathedral**, destroyed by Huguenots during the religious wars but conscientiously restored by a bishop of the town in 1600. Inside it is dark and powerful, the air heavy with the lingering odour of incense; when your eyes adjust, take a look at the Aubusson tapestries, impressively carved choir stalls, and stained glass. Just outside, in the dense network of medieval streets and Renaissance houses, is a **municipal museum** (Musée Ignon-Fabre, 10am–noon and 2–5pm; closed Sun), worth half an hour for its local and pre-history collections. **Foodwise**, Mende is blessed with an unusual number of good *pâtisseries* and *charcuteries*, but there isn't too much cheap **accommodation**. *Hôtel de Paris* on bd Soubeyran has a few moderately priced rooms; otherwise fall back on the **campsites**, one on either side of town on the N88. **Buses** leave from place du Foirail for Cévennes villages, and FLORAC, LE

PUY, and RODEZ; the **gare SNCF** is on the northern edge of town, across the Pont Berlière, and also has connections with villages in the Cévennes.

Florac and the Parc National des Cevennes

FLORAC lies at the centre of this, the second largest national park in France, and houses in its massive hilltop château the central information bureau of the park, with details about footpaths, *gîtes*, local history, and wildlife. The maps to get are IGN354 *Parc des Cévennes* and IGN265 *Mont Lozère*. *Grand Hôtel du Parc* is a reasonable place to stay and the popular *Restaurant des Fleurs* a good place to eat. There are buses on to Alès, Pont-de-Montvert, Genolhac, and Millau.

Hiking in the park

The principal hiking areas of the park are the **Mt. Aigoual** (1565m) massif to the south and the 1699m **Mont Lozère** just north of Florac. The latter is best reached from the little town of **Le Pont-de-Montvert**, where a seventeenth-century bridge crosses the Tarn by a stone tower that once served as a toll house. In this building in 1702 the Abbé Du Chayla, the priest appointed by the Crown to reconvert the Protestant Camisards in rebellion because of the revocation of the Edict of Nantes, set up a torture chamber to persuade the recalcitrant. Enraged at his brutality, a group of Protestants organised by the Camisard leader, Esprit Séguier, attacked and killed him on July 23. Reprisals were extreme; nearly 12,000 Camisards were executed.

From the town a lane climbs northwards to the tiny hamlet of FINIELS and from there up out of the trees and over the Col de Finiels. A path – GR7 – branches left from the hamlet to gain the 1699m summit. On the far side it drops down across alpine turf jewelled with rising springs, through the pine woods and into the village of LE BLEYMARD.

Robert Louis Stevenson followed this route with his donkey in 1878 on the way from Le Puy to ST-JEAN-DU-GARD* near ALES. If you should feel moved to do the same, there is no better companion than the biographer Richard Holmes' *Footsteps* (see 'Books' in *Contexts*), in the first part of which he recounts how he retraced Stevenson's journey in 1964.

The Ardèche

If you head east, the gentle hills of the Cévennes steepen into the mountains of **the Ardèche**, a craggy region cloaked with chestnut forests that produce delicious and much sought after *marrons glacés* and *purées*. It's savagely beautiful here, a popular area for activity holidays, with, at its dramatic heart,

*Near St-Jean-du-Gard, at the minuscule hamlet of **LE MAS-SOUBEYRAN**, the house of Roland, one of the Camisard leaders, has been converted into a museum and holy place of French Protestantism: the **Musée du Désert**, open 9.30am to noon and 2.30 to 6pm from March to November.

the gorge of the River Ardèche. Treacherously fast-flowing at times, until recently you could see it only by canoe, though now a road follows the ravine's rough northern clifftop. Travelling is difficult in the Ardèche – there are few towns and villages and even fewer buses and roads – but if you persevere you'll generally find the rewards more than repay the effort. **Canoes** can be hired at **VALLON-PONT-D'ARC**, a favoured tourist centre, though if you decide to do this, remember that the river froths with dangerous rapids, surges with an unpredictable current, and, in autumn, rises alarmingly fast (sometimes over 5m in a few hours).

travel details

Trains

From Clermont-Ferrand 4 daily to Paris (4 hr.) via Riom (12 min.), Vichy (38 min.), and St-Germaine des Fosses (46 min.); sleeper trains on this line at night, 11 daily just as far as St-Germaine, where you can change for Roanne (50 min.) and Lyon (2 hr. 10 min.); 3–6 daily to St-Etienne (2 hr. 40 min.) via Thiers; some night trains go to Nîmes (¼ hr.); in daytime, 2–3 daily to Nimes (4 hr. 50 min.) and Marseille (6 hr.), stopping at all stations including St-Georges d'Aurac, where change for Le Puy (2 hr.), 4 daily to Royat (6 min.), Laqueille (1 hr. 9 min.), La Bourboule (1 hr. 20 min.); le Mont Dore (1 hr. 30 min.); 4 others daily just to Laqueille, where connections for trains into the Dordogne; 4–5 daily to Toulouse (6 hr.) via Issoire (27 min.), Arvant (48 min.), Neussargues (1 hr. 33 min.), Le Lioran (1 hr. 57 min.), Vic-sur-Cère (2 hr. 14 min.), Aurillac (2½ hr.); some involve changing at Neussargues; also change there for St- Flour, Le Monastier (change for Mende), Millau, and into Languedoc.

From Riom 4 daily to Paris via Vichy (26 min.); very frequent to Clermont-Ferrand (12 min.).

From Vichy some night trains through to Nimes (7 hr.); 1 or 2 daytime stopping trains to Nimes (5½ hr.); 4 daily to Paris; frequent to Clermont-Ferrand (38 min.)

From Le Puy 3–4 daily to St-Etienne (1¾ hr.) and Lyon (3½ hr.); sporadic to St-Georges d'Aurac where change for Clermont-Ferrand (2 hr.) or Nîmes (4 hr.).

From St-Etienne 2 early morning trains daily to St-Germaine-des-Fosses (3 hr.); 3 TGV'S daily to Lyon (45 min.) and Paris (2 hr. 50 min.); 3–6 daily to Clermont-Ferrand (2 hr. 40 min.).

From Aurillac 4–5 daily to Vic-sur-Cère (15 min.), Le Lioran (½ hr.), Neussargues (1 hr.), Arvant (1¾ hr.), Issoire (2 hr.), Clermont-Ferrand (2½ hr.); 4–5 daily to Toulouse (4½ hr.).

From St-Flour 2–3 daily on line to Neussargues, Le Monastier (change for Mende), Millau, and on to Béziers.

Buses (slow)

From Clermont-Ferrand daily departures to St-Etienne, Volvic, Riom, Chatelguyon, Le Puy, Vichy.

From Le Puy daily SNCF bus to Chaise-Dieu, Thiers, Clermont (estimated 4 hr.); daily to local villages, including Le Monastier-sur-Gazeille.

CHAPTER ELEVEN

BURGUNDY

Peaceful, rural **Burgundy** is one of the most prosperous regions of modern France. For centuries its powerful dukes remained independent of the French crown, even siding with the English in the Hundred Years' War, when Philippe le Bon sold them the captured Joan of Arc. In the fifteenth century their power embraced all of Franche-Comté, Alsace and Lorraine, Belgium, Holland, Picardy, and Flanders. Their state was the best organised and richest in Europe, its revenues equalled only by Venice. It finally fell to the French kings when Charles le Téméraire was killed in battle in 1477.

Everywhere there is startling evidence of this former wealth and power, both secular and religious: at **Dijon**, the dukes' capital; in the great abbeys of **Vézelay** and **Fontenay**; in the ruins of the monastery of **Cluny**, whose influence was second only to the Pope's; in the châteaux of **Ancy** and **Tanlay**.

Because of its monastic foundations Burgundy became, with Poitou and Provence, one of the great **church-building** areas in the Middle Ages. Practically every village has its Romanesque church, especially in the country around Cluny and Paray-le-Monial. It is hard not to believe this had something to do with the reminders of its own illustrious Roman past so visible in the substantial Roman remains at **Autun**.

But Burgundy's historical range stretches even further. **Bibracte** on the atmospheric hill of **Mont-Beuvray** was an important **Gallic capital** and **Alésia** was the scene of Julius Caesar's epic victory over the Gauls in 52 B.C., while in modern times the rustic backwater of **Le Creusot** became a powerhouse of the industrial revolution.

Walkers can find a wide range of hikes, from the gentle to the relatively demanding, in the **Morvan Regional Park** and the **Côte d'Or**. There are several long-distance canal paths, which would also make great **bike** trips if you have a hardy bike. Aficionados rate most highly the **Canal de Bourgogne** and the **Canal du Nivernais**, both of which can be cruised by **rented barge**, though this is hardly a low-budget option.

Wine devotees, of course, head straight for the great Burgundy **vineyards**, whose produce has been a major money-maker for the local economy since Louis XIV's doctor prescribed the stuff as a palliative – perhaps an analgaesic – for the royal dyspepsia. If you lack the funds to indulge your taste for expensive drink, go in September or October when the *vignerons* are recruiting harvesters.

The trouble with good drink from the budget point of view is that it arouses the appetite for **good food**, which Burgundy's renowned cuisine can supply in abundance. Best known of the region's specialities are its snails, *escargots à la bourguignonne*, stuffed with garlic, shallots, parsley, and mush

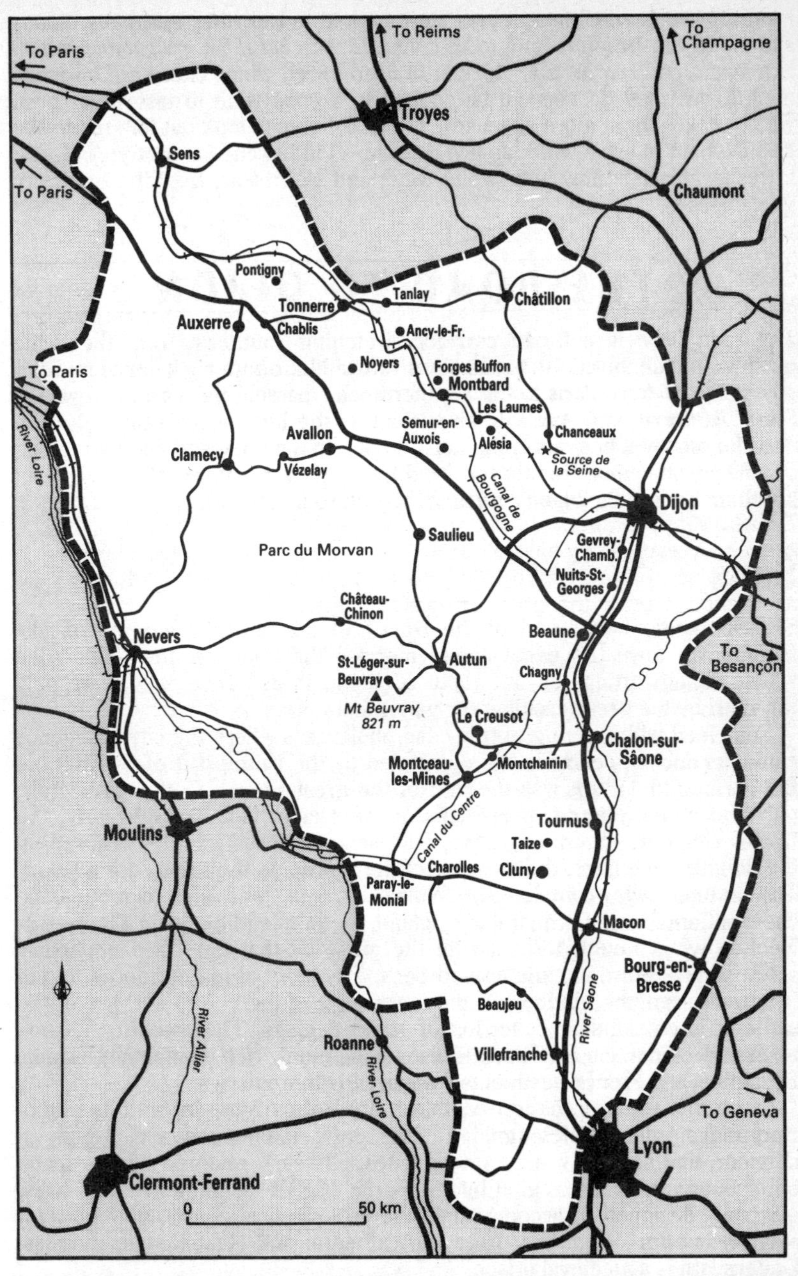
To Reims
To Champagne
To Paris
Troyes
Sens
To Paris
Chaumont
Pontigny
Tanlay
Châtillon
Tonnerre
Auxerre
Chablis
Ancy-le-Fr.
Noyers
Forges Buffon
To Paris
Montbard
Les Laumes
River Loire
Semur-en-Auxois
Alésia
Chanceaux
Avallon
Clamecy
Vézelay
Source de la Seine
Canal de Bourgogne
Dijon
Saulieu
Parc du Morvan
Gevrey-Chamb.
Nuits-St-Georges
Château-Chinon
Beaune
Nevers
Autun
To Besançon
St-Léger-sur-Beuvray
Chagny
Mt Beuvray 821 m
Le Creusot
Chalon-sur-Sâone
Montceau-les-Mines
Montchainin
Moulins
Tournus
Taize
Canal du Centre
Charolles
Cluny
Paray-le-Monial
Macon
Bourg-en-Bresse
River Saone
Beaujeu
River Allier
Roanne
River Loire
Villefranche
To Geneva
Lyon
Clermont-Ferrand
0
50 km

rooms; *boeuf bourguignon*, a beef stew cooked in red wine with baby onions and sliced mushrooms – not to be confused with *boeuf bourguignonne*, which is a *fondu*; and *coq au vin*, chicken braised in red wine. These are on many menus, but they do need to be cooked in a good wine to taste their best, which makes them more expensive. Other delights to look out for are *jambon persillé*, ham in aspic with parsley; *gougère*, a kind of cheese pastry; *pochouse*, a fresh-water-fish stew with white wine; and *chevrotons*, the little hard, dry goat cheeses.

THE ROAD TO DIJON

The road here is a broad corridor stretching southeast from the Seine outside Fontainebleau. Its backbone is **Route Nationale 6**, the once murderous old route from Paris to the Mediterranean, passing through the towns of **Sens**, **Auxerre**, and **Avallon**, as ancient as the history of France. But the corridor also reaches out to the north to pull in a motley and fascinating bag of abbeys, châteaux, ironmasters, and Celts. It's a lot more interesting than speeding around the bland curves of the Autoroute du Sud.

Sens

SENS, though never part of the Duchy of Burgundy, seems a typically Burgundian town. Its name commemorates the Senones, the Gallic tribe whose shaggy troops all but captured Rome in 390 B.C.; they were only thwarted by the geese cackling the garrison awake.

Contained within a ring of tree-lined boulevards where the city walls once stood, its ancient centre is still dominated by the **Cathedral of St-Etienne**. Begun around 1130 it was the first of the great French Gothic cathedrals; only the abbey church of St-Denis in Paris is earlier. Though early, the Gothic elements of airiness, space and weightlessness are fully realised, in the height of the nave, the arcading of the aisles and the great rose window. The architect who completed it, William of Sens, was later to rebuild the choir of Canterbury Cathedral in England, the missing link being **Thomas-à-Becket**, who, though ten years in the grave by that time, had previously spent several years in exile around Sens. The story of his murder is told in the twelfth-century windows in the north aisle of the choir, just part of the cathedral's outstanding collection of **stained glass**. The **treasury** (10am–noon and 2–5pm; closed Tues.) is also uncommonly rich, containing Islamic, Byzantine, and French vestments, jewels, and embroideries.

Just to the south is the thirteenth-century **Palais Synodal** with its roof of Burgundian glazed tiles (guided visits only, 10am–noon and 2–5pm in summer, and 6pm in winter; closed Tues. all year), restored like so many other buildings in this region by the 'purist' Viollet-le-Duc. Its vaulted halls, originally designed to accommodate the ecclesiastical courts, now house a small **museum** of statuary from the cathedral and Gallo-Roman mosaics. Underneath is a medieval prison.

Facing the cathedral across **place de la République** are fine wood and iron *halles*, where a **market** is held all day Monday, Friday, and Saturday mornings. The *place* stands right in the centre of town where the main streets, **rue de la République** and **Grande-Rue**, intersect. Lined with old houses now converted into shops, they are mainly reserved for pedestrians. There are a couple of particularly finely carved and timbered houses on the corner of rue Jean-Cousin, the **Maison d'Abraham**, and the **Maison du Pilier**, with **Maison Jean Cousin** on rue du Général-Alix.

At the far end of Grande Rue, the road crosses two broad arms of the **river Yonne**, with houseboats moored at the bank, and leads straight ahead to the **gare SNCF**, about ten minutes' walk from the cathedral. *Hôtel de la Gare* and *Hôtel Chemin de Fer* (☎86.65.10.27), both with cheap rooms, are opposite the station entrance. Try also *Hôtel du Centre*, 4–8 place de la République (☎86.65.15.92; closed mid-Sept. to mid-Oct., also Fri. and Sun. pm).

For **eating**, there is a cheap self-service place, *Brasserie le Senonais*, at 99 rue de la République, and a good *crêperie*, *Aux 4 Vents*, at 3 rue de Brennus. **Bike hire** from Nibel, rue V Guichard. The **SI** is at 3 bd Jean-Jaurès. The The **campsite**, *Entre-deux-Vannes*, is on rte de Lyon, just out of town (June–Sept. 15).

Auxerre

A pretty old town of narrow lanes and handsome squares, **AUXERRE** stands on a hill another 50km up the river Yonne. It looks its best seen from the riverside with its churches soaring dramatically above the surrounding roof-tops. The most interesting of them is the disused abbey church of **St-Germain** (9am–noon and 2–6pm, closed Tues.), at the opposite end of **rue Cauchois** from the cathedral. Partial demolition has left its belfry detached from the body of the building, but what gives it special interest is the **crypt**, one of the few surviving examples of **Carolingian** (9C and earlier) architecture, with its plain barrel vaults still resting on their thousand-year-old oak beams. Deep inside, the faded ochre frescoes of St. Stephen (St-Etienne) are among the most ancient in France (ca. 850).

The **Cathedral** itself, despite the fact that its construction was drawn out over more than three centuries (1215–1560), remains unfinished. The most southerly of the two west front towers was never completed. Compensation for this handicap is in the richly detailed **sculpture** of the porches and the glorious colours of the original thirteenth-century **glass**, that, despite the savagery of the Wars of Religion and the Revolution, still fills the windows of the choir. There has been a church on the site since about 400 A.D., though nothing visible survives earlier than the eleventh-century **crypt**. Among its **frescoes** is a unique depiction of a warrior Christ mounted on a white charger, accompanied by four mounted angels.

From the front of the Cathedral **rue Fourier** leads to **place du Marché** and off left to the Hôtel de Ville and the old city gateway known as the **Tour de l'Horloge** with its coloured clock face (15C).

The **SI** is down by the river at 2 quai de la République by the footbridge. There is a **Bureau d'Informations Jeunesse** at 70 rue du Pont with information on travel and leisure activities. The cheapest accommodation is in *foyers*: women, at 16 bd Vaulabelle; men, at 16 rue de la Résistance. Among **hotels**, you could try *Hôtel de la Porte de Paris* (5 rue St-Germain; ☎86.46.90.09; closed Sun.) and *Hôtel St-Martin* (9 rue Germain-Benard; ☎86.52.04.16; closed Sun). There is a **campsite** on rte de Vaux, open from April to October. Finding somewhere to **eat** is easy, as there are numerous reasonably priced restaurants, and a self-service place, the *Novéco*, at 9 place Charles-Surugue.

East of Auxerre

On or close to D965 and the Paris-Dijon railway, in the open, rolling country east of Auxerre, lie several minor attractions, ranging from **Greek treasures** to **Cistercian abbeys** and **Renaissance châteaux**.

Pontigny, Chablis, Noyers

The ravages of time – in particular the 1789 Revolution – destroyed most of the great monastic buildings of the Cistercians, whose rigorous insistence on simplicity and manual labour under their most influential twelfth-century leader, St. Bernard, was a revolutionary response to the worldliness and luxury of the Benedictine abbots of Cluny. Cîteaux and Clairvaux, the first Cistercian foundations, are unrecognisable today. The only places you can get an idea of how Cistercian ideas translated into bricks and mortar are **Pontigny** and **Fontenay**.

The beautifully preserved twelfth-century **abbey church of PONTIGNY** lies 18km northeast of Auxerre on the edge of Pontigny village, where its functional mass rises from the meadows. There is no tower, no stained glass, no statuary, no ornamentation at all to distract from its austere, harmonious lines and the interplay of light and shadow on the pale surfaces of its local stone. Surprisingly, **three Englishmen** played a major role in the abbey's early history, all of them Archbishops of Canterbury: Thomas-à-Becket took refuge in the abbey from Henry II in 1164, Stephen Langton similarly laid low here during an argument over his eligibility for the primacy, and Edmund Rich died here, his tomb in the church a goal of pilgrimages to this day.

A little way to the south and about the same distance from Auxerre is the small red-roofed town of **CHABLIS**, renowned for its light, **dry white wines**. It lies in the shallow, valley of the **river Serein** between the wide, and mainly treeless upland wheatfields typical of this corner of Burgundy.

The neatly-staked **vineyards**, originally planted by the monks of Pontigny, cover the sunny, well-drained, stony slopes on both sides of the valley. The grape is the *chardonnay*, which is to white wine what the *pinot noir* is to red: raw material of all the greatest Burgundies. If you want to **buy**, go for the ones with an *appellation*; the *grands crus*, from the northern slopes of the valley are the best, with the *premiers crus* next in line. You'll find plenty of producer-vendors advertising themselves in the meandering back streets of the town.

While wandering around you could take a look at the side door of **St-Martin's church**, bizarrely decorated with ancient horseshoes and other bits of rustic ironwork. Nearby, if you need to **spend the night**, *Hôtel de l'Etoile* in rue des Moulins (☎86.42.10.50; closed mid-Dec. to mid-Jan.) is reasonable; otherwise it is best to go on to TONNERRE.

Going south again a dozen miles – there's no alternative to hitching if you do not have your own transport – you come to the beautiful little town of **NOYERS**, locked from the modern world in a medieval time warp. Its half-timbered and arcaded houses, ornamented with rustic carvings, crowd around the Hôtel de Ville, corralled within a loop of the Serein and its own many-towered walls.

Tonnerre, Tanlay, and Ancy-le-Franc

Sited on the Paris-Sens-Dijon railway, **TONNERRE** is a useful starting point for exploring this corner of the region. A pleasant, if unremarkable town, its principal sight is a vast and well-conserved **medieval hospital** (guided tours June–Sept., 10am–noon and 2–5.30pm; closed Tues.) right on the main road in the middle of town. In the chapel is one of the best of those super-expressive and realistic pieces of Burgundian *tableau* statuary, an **Entombment** of Christ, in the style pioneered by Claus Sluter. The **SI** is directly opposite and in the same street, rue de l'Hôpital, at no. 65, the *Hôtel du Centre* (☎86.55.10.56) offers the cheapest **accommodation**. There is also a **campsite** (May–Sept.) between the **river Armançon** and the now more or less defunct **Canal de Bourgogne**.

A couple of blocks from the hospital, the Hôtel d'Uzès saw the birth of Tonnerre's quirkiest claim to fame, an eighteenth-century gentleman with the impossible handle of **Charles- Geneviève- Louise- Auguste- Andrée-Thimotée Eon de Beaumont**. He tickled his contemporaries' prurience by going about his important diplomatic missions for King Louis XV dressed in women's clothes. His act was so convincing that while in London bookies took bets on his real sex. Oddly enough, he was also a ferocious swordsman, though history does not relate what he wore to fight in. When he died the results of the autopsy were eagerly awaited by the Murdochs of the day.

Close to Tonnerre are two of the finest, though least known and therefore least visited **châteaux** in France, **TANLAY** and **ANCY-LE-FRANC**. The former has the edge for romantic appeal, the latter for architectural purity.

ANCY-LE-FRANC was built in the mid-sixteenth century for the brother-in-law of the notorious Diane de Poitiers, mistress of Henri II. More Italian than French, with its rather gloomily austere classical exterior, it is the only accepted work of the Italian, **Sebastiano Serlio**, one of the most important architectural theorists, who had been brought to France in 1540 by François I to work on his palace at Fontainebleau. The **inner courtyard** is more elaborate, and some of the **apartments** are sumptuous (guided tours only, Easter–Oct., 10am–noon and 2–6pm), decorated by the Italian artists, **Primaticcio** and **Niccolo dell'Abbate**, who also worked at Fontainebleau. The most impressive rooms are La Chambre des Arts with medallions by Primaticcio and La Galerie des Sacrifices with monumental battle scenes in monochrome by Abbate. Ancy has one small hotel, the one-star *Hôtel du Centre* (☎86.75.15.11; closed Jan.), with restaurant, at 34 Grande Rue.

TANLAY, by contrast, is much more French and full of *fantaisie*. It is only slightly later in date, about 1559, but those extra few years were enough for the purer Italian influences visible in Ancy to have become frenchified. It also feels much more feudal. The village crouches humbly at its gate. The approach road, a long straight tree-lined avenue, feels like a private drive, tying down the land on either side, proclaiming ownership.

Water-filled **moats** encircle the château. A wooded hill backs it. A grand lodge guards the entrance to a first grassy courtyard, from which you enter the château proper across a stone drawbridge. Domed and lanterned turrets terminate the wings of the *cour d'honneur*. Urns line the ridge of the roof, from whose slates project carved and pedimented dormers. The white stone and the round medieval towers, leftovers from the original fortress, add to the irregularity and charm.

The **interior** is visitable on guided tours only (April–Oct. 9.30, 10.30, 11.30am; pm every ¾ hr., 2.15–5.15pm; closed Tues.). The most remarkable, if overpowering room is the **Grande Galerie**, entirely covered by monochrome *trompe-l'oeil* frescoes.

Châtillon and the source of the Seine

If you are interested in pre-Roman France, as the French themselves are for obvious nationalistic reasons, there is one compelling reason for going to **CHATILLON-SUR-SEINE**, and that is the so-called **Treasure of Vix.** Housed in the town's **museum** (Maison Philandrier, rue du Bourg, close to the centre; June–Sept., 9am–noon and 2–6pm in summer, 7pm in winter, closed Mon.; Oct.–May, 10am–noon and 2–5pm, Wed., Sat., Sun.; pm only Tues., Thurs., Fri.), it consists of the finds from the **sixth-century B.C. tomb** of a Celtic princess buried in a four-wheeled chariot. In addition to pieces of the chariot, these include staggeringly beautiful jewellery, Greek vases, and Etruscan bowls. But the best on show is a gloriously simple **gold tiara**, actually found on the princess's head, and the largest **bronze vase** (*krater*) of Greek origin known to antiquity. It stands an incredible 1.64m high on triple tripod legs and around its rim is a superbly modelled **high-relief frieze** depicting naked hoplites and horse-drawn chariots, with Gorgons' heads for handles. How these magnificent objects found their way to such a remote place is something of a mystery. The village of **Vix** is the **highest navigable point** on the Seine and it is thought that the Celtic chieftains who controlled it received such gifts, possibly from traders in Cornish tin, which was shipped south from Britain by this route on its way to the Adriatic, and perhaps to the bronze workers of Bibracte, the capital of the Aedui.

On the rocky bluff overlooking the steep-pitched roofs of the old quarter are the ruins of a castle and the early Romanesque **church of St-Vorles**. At its foot in a luxuriantly verdant spot, a **resurgent spring** swells out of the rock to join the infant Seine.

The **SI** is off place Marmont, and there is a very welcoming **cheap hotel**, the *Jura* (☎80.91.26.96), on rue Docteur-Robert, and another, *Hôtel de la Montagne* (☎80.91.10.61), on place Joffre. Rooms at the *Hôtel de la Côte d'Or* (☎80.91.13.29), rue Charles-Ronot, are more expensive, but the restaurant is first class – not a cheapie, but it won't break the bank if you are careful.

To get to the **source of the Seine** you have to hitch about 30km down N71 to the hamlet of **Courceau** or, on foot, take **GR2**. From there, by road, take D103 through the upland hamlet of St-Germain, all crumbling stone farms and barns; or, better still, (because rides are unlikely), pick up the GR2 at the bridge in Courceau (2 hr.).

The **Seine**, no more than a trickle, rises in a tight little vale of beech woods. The spring is now covered by an artificial grotto complete with a languid nymph, Sequana, spirit of the Seine. In Celtic times it was a place of worship, as is clear from the numerous votive offerings discovered there, including a neat bronze of Sequana standing in a bird-shaped boat, now in the Dijon museum. Alone, it is a good place for rustic reverie; but if your arrival coincides with a coach load of Parisian Senior Citizens (the site belongs to the city of Paris) you'd be wise to retreat downstream. There is a **campsite** at Chanceaux (2km south to N71, then another 4km).

Fontenay, Montbard, Alesia

The abbey of **FONTENAY**, founded in 1118, is the only Burgundian monastery to survive intact, despite conversion to a paper mill in the early nineteenth century. It was restored earlier this century and is indeed one of the most complete monastic complexes anywhere, comprising caretaker's lodge, guest house and chapel, dormitory, hospital, prison, writing and warming rooms, bakery, kennels, dovecote, abbot's house and forge, as well as church, cloister, and chapter house. On top of that, its physical setting is superb, at the head of a quiet stream-filled valley enclosed by woods of pine, fir, sycamore and beech.

It is relatively **easy to get to**, 3km up a lane from D905, 6km altogether from MONTBARD (buses and trains). The best approach would be to walk it on **GR213**. The abbey is privately owned and visits are by guided tour only (45 min. duration, 9am–noon and on the hour, 2.30–6.30pm on the half hour).

There is a bucolic peacefulness about the place nowadays, but even so you still feel a slight chill, a *frisson* of unease, at the Spartan simplicity of Cistercian life. Not a scrap of decoration in the church, not one carved capital – the motherly statue of the Virgin arrived after St Bernard's death; no direct lighting in the nave, just an other-worldly glow from the square-ended apse, beautiful but daunting, and the perfect structural embodiment of St Bernard's hair-shirt principles.

There is not much to be seen in the **forge**, but it is interesting that there should have been such a large one here in the country where France's industrial ironmasters set up shop 500 years later.

Blessed with iron ore deposits, extensive forest for charcoal-burning, and water for hydraulic power, Burgundy became the Ironbridge of France (see also Le Creusot) in the eighteenth century. The earliest **foundries** were small-scale rural affairs, dependent on one man's knowledge. Production was minimal and costly despite the invention of the blast furnace (*haut fourneau*) and the use of water-power to drive hammers and bellows.

Just outside MONTBARD, 6km north on D905, beside the **river Armançon** and the **Canal de Bourgogne**, are the remains of one of the most influential eighteenth-century foundries, the **FORGES DE BUFFON** (June–Sept., 2.30–6pm; closed Tues.). It was built in 1768 by **Georges-Louis Buffon**, distinguished scientist, landowner, and lord of Montbard. Production was never more than 400 tons a year, but Buffon's main interest was experimental.

The site, now owned by an Englishman and being restored as part of the growing French interest in industrial archaeology, comprises **model dwellings** for 400 workers (woodmen, ox-drivers and miners along with 30 foundry workers) as well as the **foundry workshops**. These are situated on the banks of the river, designed in a most unindustrial **classical style**, with special viewing galleries for royal visitors and a grand staircase. There is not an enormous amount to see (some reproductions of machinery made by kids from the local school), but you get a unique insight into a pre-capitalist approach to industry. The foundry's most notable product was the railings of the Jardin des Plantes in Paris (still in place). The museum can provide information about other industrial sites in the area.

The best **approach** is a pleasant walk along the **canal path**, about an hour from Montbard (*Hôtel de la Gare*, by the **SNCF station**; **Camping municipal**). Montbard town has nothing to offer, but its predicament is typical of 1980s industrial Europe. Basically, a one-industry town – steel tubes – it is seeing the bottom drop out of its livelihood.

One train stop or three hours on the path brings you to **VENAREY-LES-LAUMES** (*Hôtel L'Esprit*, av de la Gare; ☎80.96.00.46), home to another ailing tube factory. Behind and above it, on the flat-topped hill of Mont Auxois **the Gauls**, united for once under the leadership of **Vercingétorix**, made their last stand against the military might of Rome at the **Battle of ALESIA** in 52 B.C. **Julius Caesar** himself commanded the Roman army. He surrounded the hill with a huge double ditch and earthworks and starved the Gauls out, bloodily defeating all attempts at a break-out. Vercingétorix surrendered to save his people, was imprisoned in Rome for six years until Caesar's formal triumph, and then strangled. Gaul remained under Roman rule for 400 years.

Towards the top of the hill the village of **ALISE-STE-REINE** has a small **museum** displaying finds from the Gallic town of Alésia and Caesar's earthworks (the line of them still clearly visible in aerial photographs). Directly above the village, steps climb up to a great bronze **statue of Vercingétorix**. Erected by **Napoléon III**, whose influence popularised the rediscovery of France's pre-Roman roots, the statue represents Vercingétorix as a romantic Celt, half virginal Christ, half long-haired 1970s matinée idol. **On the plinth** is inscribed a quotation from Vercingétorix's address to the Gauls as imagined by Julius Caesar: 'United and forming a single nation inspired by a single ideal, Gaul can defy the world'. Napoléon signs his dedication, 'Emperor of the French', obviously inspired by a vain desire to link his own name to a 'legendary' Celtic legitimacy.

The site of **Alésia the town** is back along the ridge, treeless and exposed, 3km from the village. It is extensive, but you can see little more than the layout. The interest of the whole area lies in such atmosphere as the imagination perceives rather than in anything concrete. Alésia was a 'great' battle: it marked the end of Gallic independence, but it also commemorates life in Europe before Greece and Rome.

Avallon and Vézelay

AVALLON stands high on a ridge above the wooded valley of the **river Cousin**, looking out over the hilly, sparsely populated country of the Morvan regional park. It is a small and ancient town of stone facades and cobbled, comatose streets, bisected wall to wall by the narrow **Grande-Rue-Aristide Briand**. Under the straddling arch of the **Tour de l'Horloge**, whose spire dominates the town, it brings you to the pilgrim church of **St-Lazare**, on whose battered **Romanesque facade** you can still decipher the graceful carvings of signs of the zodiac, labours of the months, and the old musicians of the Apocalypse. Almost opposite, in a house of the fifteenth century, is the **SI** with an uninspiring museum behind it. A couple of hundred metres further, past walled and shuttered houses, **Grande Rue** slips through the city walls and out on to the lime-shaded **Promenade de la Petite Porte**, with precipitous views across the plunging valley of the Cousin. You can **walk** from here around the outside of the walls.

Commercial activity today is concentrated in the new town north of the city walls, with a **Saturday market** in place des Odebert. From the **parc des Chaumes** on the east side of town there is a great **view** back to the old quarter, snug within its walls, with garden terraces descending on the slope beneath.

For cheap **accommodation** first try *Au Bon Acceuil* (4 rue de l'Hôpital; ☎86.34.09.33; closed Sun.), or *Hôtel du Parc*, (3 place de la Gare; ☎86.34.17.00), both with good cheap restaurants; but there are other possibilities in **rue de Lyon** and **rue de Paris**. There is an attractive **Camping municipal** 2km away off Route de Lormes. Reasonable **eating** at *Cheval Blanc*, 55 rue de Lyon, and other possibilities on Grande-Rue. **Bike hire** from the **gare SNCF**, a few minutes' walk from place des Odebert-place Vauban.

Vézelay

If you can get a reliable bike, **cycling** would be a pleasant way of covering the 15km to **VEZELAY**. Alternatively, there are infrequent **buses** from Avallon (*Cars de la Madeleine*; normally one a day) and **trains** to Sermizelles on the Auxerre-Avallon line with an SNCF bus link on to Vézelay. A hundred years ago the village of Vézelay was abandoned, although its **abbey church, La**

Madeleine, one of the seminal buildings of the Romanesque period, had already been saved from collapse by **Viollet-le-Duc** in 1840. Quintessentially picturesque and popular with the coach tours, it is still an undeniably attractive place.

As you emerge puffing from the climb (the lane is literally festooned with ice-blue wisteria blossom in May) into the rather desolate square in front of the church, the first·impression is disappointing: Viollet's reproduced west front does not look authentic. But veer to the right into the garden on the south side and you get an angle on the long buttressed nave and Romanesque tower that corrects the balance and sheds light on the nautical imagery of 'nave' – *navis*, ship or hull.

Once **inside** you find yourself in a colossal **narthex**, added to the nave around 1150 to accommodate the swelling numbers of pilgrims attracted by the supposed presence of the bones of Mary Magdalen. The abbey was one of the main assembly points for the pilgrimage to St-Jacques of Compostella. Your eye is first drawn to the superlative sculptures of the **central doorway**, on whose **tympanum** an ethereal Christ swathed in swirling drapery presides over a group of apostles and peoples, converted and unconverted, going about their business with cows, fish, crossbows, and so forth. Among the latter are giants, pygmies (one mounting his horse with a ladder), and dog-headed heathens. Somewhat better preserved, in the **outer arch**, are the charmingly small-scale medallions of the zodiac signs and labours of the months. In the **flanking portals** are depicted, on the right, nativity scenes and, on the left, Christ on the road to Emmaus after the resurrection.

From this great doorway you look down the long body of the church, vaulted by arches of alternating black and white stone, to a **choir** of pure early Gothic (completed in 1215), luminous with the delicacy of the inside of a shell by contrast with the heavier, more somber Romanesque nave. Its arches and arcades are edged with fretted mouldings, and the supporting pillars are crowned with finely cut **capitals**, 99 in all, depicting scenes from the bible, classical mythology, allegories and morality stories. The finest of all is **'The Mystic Mill'** at the end of the fourth bay on the right, showing Moses pouring grain (Old Testament Law) through a mill (Christ), the flour (New Testament) being gathered by St. Paul.

St Bernard preached the **Second Crusade** at Vézelay in 1146. Because the church was too small, he preached in the open below the hill. A commemorative cross marks the spot. Richard the Lionheart and Philippe Auguste, King of France, also made their rendezvous here before setting off on the **Third Crusade** in 1190. But the abbey's heyday came to an end in 1280 when it was discovered that the Magdalen's bones belonged to someone else. Its **decline** was hastened by Protestant vandalism in the sixteenth century and the whole establishment was disbanded during the Revolution.

The small **SI** is on the right in rue St-Pierre as you go up towards the abbey (Easter–Sept.; closed Wed. and Sun. pm). There are two **youth hostels**, both open July through August, one, on rue des Ecoles, the *Amis de Pax Christi*, the other about 1km along the road to L'ETANG (with camping space and also open for 3 weeks in April). SNCF **buses** for Sermizelles and buses for Avallon leave from Garage de la Madeleine on the main square.

Just at the foot of the Vézelay hill the village of **ST-PERE** boasts a lovely, if somewhat eccentric, Gothic church and a couple of kilometres out on D958 lie the archaeological remains of a Gallic sanctuary, Roman baths and salt springs.

Semur-en-Auxois

East of Avallon, the fortress town of **SEMUR-EN-AUXOIS** sits on a rocky bluff above the Armançon river. All roads here lead to **place Notre-Dame**, a handsome square dominated by the large thirteenth-century church of Notre-Dame, another Viollet-le-Duc restoration. The twin-towered west front has had many of its statues removed and the niches left bare. The best view is from the east in **place de l'Ancienne-Comédie**, past the finely sculpted north transept door (the life of Doubting Thomas), with a couple of Burgundy snails, symbol of Burgundy's culinary traditions, carved on the flanking columns. Inside, the windows of the first chapel on the left commemorate American soldiers of the First World War – a reminder that the battlefields were not far away. Also on the left are further fine **fifteenth-century windows** dedicated by the butchers' and drapers' guilds illustrating their trades, and a masterly Sluteresque painted **Entombment**.

Down the street in front of the church and off to the left you come to the four sturdy towers of Semur's once powerful **castle**, dismantled in 1602 because of its utility to enemies of the French crown. There is a dramatic view of it from the **Pont Joly** on the river below. Less specifically, the whole town is full of interesting buildings: there is scarcely a street without something to please the eye, and there is a pleasant shady **walk** around the fortifications.

The **SI** is on the small place Gaveau, at the junction of rues de l'Ancienne-Comédie, de la Liberté, and Buffon, where the medieval **Porte Sauvigny** and **Porte Guillier** combine to form a single long, covered gateway. Not far away on rue J-J-Collenot, the **library** (part of the **museum**: Wed. and Fri. 2.30–6.30pm, June 15–Sept.; library, every Wed. 2–6pm) has a fantastic collection of illuminated manuscripts and early printed books.

There is a **youth hostel** at 1 rue du Champ-de-Foire, to the left off rue de la Liberté, and a **campsite** at Lac du Pont, 3km south of town. *Hôtel des Gourmets* (4 rue de Varenne; ☎80.97.09.41; closed Tues.) has the cheapest **rooms** and an excellent, reasonably priced restaurant, as has *Hôtel de la Côte d'Or* (3 place Gaveau; ☎80.97.03.13; closed Wed. and Jan.–March), though its rooms are slightly more expensive. Both require at least *demi-pension* in the summer season.

Saulieu and the Parc du Morvan

SAULIEU, a thriving market town on the eastern edge of the park, renowned for its restaurants, is the best base for a visit to the park. Its principal sight is the twelfth-century **Basilique St-Andoche**, noted for its lovely **capitals**, probably carved by a disciple of **Gislebertus**, the master sculptor of Autun. The **museum** next door (10am–1pm and 2–7pm in summer, 6pm in winter; closed Tues.) is also surprisingly interesting, with good local **folklore displays** and a large collection of the works of the local nineteenth-century animal sculptor, **François Pompon**.

The town is not particularly easy to get to by public transport. **By train** from Dijon takes 3½ hours and involves two changes (as opposed to 40 minutes by car), and **bus** connections are not particularly helpful either: *Transco* has an evening run from Dijon, and also from Montbard and Semur, but not every day.

Coming from the station, walk up av de la Gare to the highway. Along to the right is the **SI** (out of season, go to the *mairie* in place de la République). Opposite is the reasonably priced *Hôtel Tour d'Auxois* and to the left the cheaper *Au Petit Marguery*, with a well-priced menu and brasserie. The **cheapest accommodation** is at the *Hôtel/Bar E. Belot,* in the main street, 23 rue de la Foire. There are also two *gîtes d'étape*, one almost opposite the SI off place de Gaulle, the other next to the riding centre 2km along N6 past the SI and right before the police station. The **campsite** is also off the Paris road.

Because of its gastronomic reputation you can spend a lot of money **eating** *à la carte* in Saulieu. It won't be money wasted, but if your budget can't stand that kind of extravagance, you can take heart from the fact that most hotel restaurants also offer fairly reasonable fixed-price menus.

Into the Parc du Morvan

If you are going into the **Park**, the best thing is to consult the SI in Saulieu. The **Maison du Parc**, the official information centre, is 13km away at ST-BRISSON and inaccessible without your own transport. One possibility would be **hiring a bike** (from SNCF for a regular bike; M. Pasquet, ☎ 80.64.09.63, for a mountain bike), but the thickly wooded country is hilly, often steep, so it requires some commitment. A **map**, *Saulieu Vélo Tout Terrain en Morvan*, marks cycling and walking routes. For the **walker** the most challenging trip is **GR13**, which crosses the park from Vézelay to MONT-BEUVRAY, taking in the major **lakes**, which are one of the park's most 'developed' attractions. There are **less strenuous possibilities**: for instance, a 4km walk to Lac Chamboux, leaving Saulieu by D26 and taking a track to the left (blue and yellow markers) after about ten minutes. For a starting point **deeper into the park**, there is a bus to MOUX near **Lac des Settons**, with a **campsite** and *gîte d'étape*.

The actual centre of the park is the medieval village of CHATEAU-CHINON, set in beautiful country (bus connection to Autun). **President Mitterrand** was a local council member here until as recently as 1983, and the town has been the home base of his political life for half a century. Thanks largely to him it boasts a major stocking factory and military printing works. In its **Musée du Septennat** you can see the extraordinary variety of gifts he has received as head of state. You could even **stay** at his preferred **hotel**, the *Vieux Morvan* (8 place Gudin; ☎86.85.05.01; closed mid-Nov. to mid-Jan.).

DIJON AND THE SOUTH

If calling Burgundy rural has conjured up for you an image of backward and ramshackle rustic charm, you'll have to do some adjusting when you encounter slick and prosperous Dijon, and the country to the south: it may be agricultural and look peaceful, but there is nothing medieval about the methods or the profits made in today's wine business. For the older traditions you have to head into the southwestern corner of the region.

Dijon

DIJON owes its origins to its strategic position in Celtic times on the tin merchants' route from Britain up the Seine and across the Alps to the Adriatic. But it was as capital of the dukes of Burgundy from 1000 A.D. that it knew its finest hour, its fortunes closely reflecting theirs. Its golden age occurred in the fourteenth and fifteenth centuries under the auspices of Dukes Philippe le Hardi (the Bold), who as a boy had fought the English at Poitiers and been taken prisoner, Jean sans Peur (the Fearless), Philippe le Bon (the Good), who sold Joan of Arc to the English, and Charles le Téméraire (the Rash). They used their tremendous wealth and power – they controlled Flanders, the industrial star of the day – to make Dijon one of the greatest centres of art, learning, and science in Europe. Though it lost its capital status with incorporation into the French kingdom in 1477, it has remained one of the pre-eminent provincial cities, especially since the railway and industrial boom in the mid-nineteenth century.

The city

You sense Dijon's former glory more in the lavish town houses of its rich burghers than in the former seat of the dukes, the **Palais des Ducs**. Though extensive in area, the palace is undistinguished from the outside. It has undergone so many alterations, especially in the sixteenth and seventeenth centuries when it became the Parliament of Burgundy, that the dukes themselves would scarcely recognise it. In fact, the only outward reminders of the older building are the fourteenth-century **Tour de Bar** above the east wing, which now houses the **Musée des Beaux-Arts** (see below), and the fifteenth-century **Tour Philippe-le-Bon** (9.30–11.30am and 2.30–5.30pm in summer; Wed. and Sun. pm only, Nov.–Easter), from whose terrace on the clearest of days they say you can see Mt. Blanc.

In front the palace, which still functions as the town hall, looks on to a spacious and gracious semicircular classical square, **place de la Libération**, bordered by houses of honey-coloured stone, designed like the similar place des Victoires in Paris by Jules **Hardouin-Mansart** in the late seventeenth century. Behind and to the west it leads to a tiny, enclosed square, **place des Ducs**, and a maze of lanes, especially **rue des Forges**, bordered by beautiful old houses. No. 34, the **Hôtel Chambellan** (1490), housing the **SI** and **Club**

Alpin, is a fine example. Go through into the courtyard where you can get a decent view of the building, with open galleries on the first and second floor, reached by a spiral staircase. There's a marvellous piece of stonemason's virtuosity at the top of the stairs: the vaulting of the roof springs from a basket held by the statue of a gardener. At the end of the street, with several other fine houses, you come to the attractive **place François-Rude** with its fountain graced by the bronze figure of a grape harvester. On sunny days it's a favourite hangout, with people crowding the café tables and sitting on the ground around the fountain. If you are interested in looking at more of the city's **mansions**, the tourist office issues a leaflet entitled *Maisons et Hôtels particuliers du XVe au XVIIIe siècle à Dijon*.

Parallel to rue des Forges, **rue de la Chouette**, with more splendid houses at nos. 8 and 10, passes the north side of the impressive thirteenth-century Gothic church of **Notre-Dame**. In the north wall is a small sculpted owl – *chouette* – which people touch for luck and which gives the street its name. The unusual **west front** consists of two galleries of arcades adorned with spectacular leaning **gargoyles.** The right-hand tower sports a Flemish **Jacquemart clock** with mechanical figures to strike the hours. The **interior** has some beautiful thirteenth-century windows, a black wooden Virgin of the

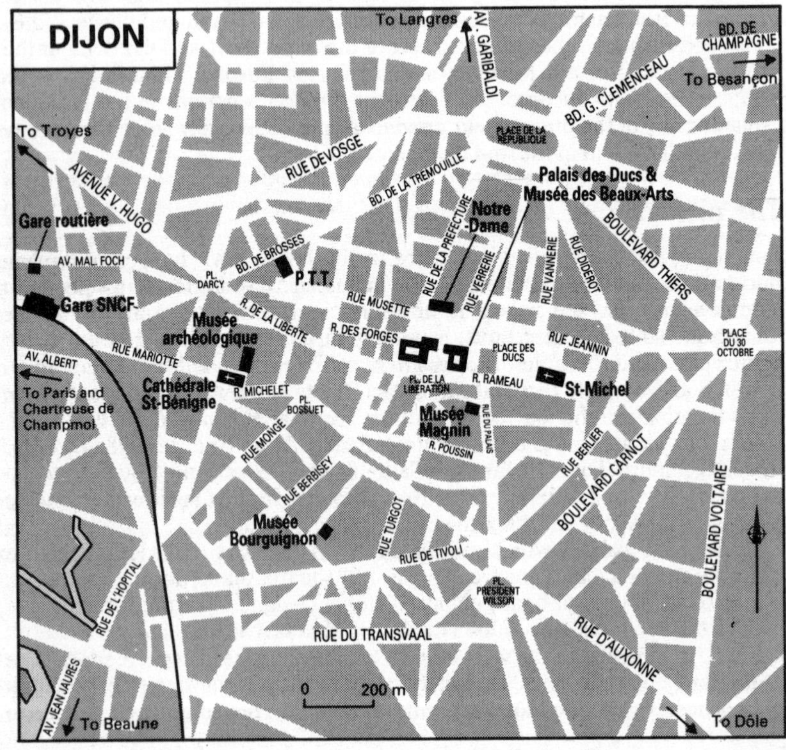

twelfth century (dear to the hearts of Dijon's citizens) and, in the north transept, a Gobelins tapestry commemorating the 1944 liberation from the Nazis.

The **Cathedral** church of **St-Bénigne**, of similar date to Notre-Dame, with the characteristic glazed-tile roof, lies just south of place François-Rude. Its circular **crypt** is the original tenth-century Romanesque church.

But among the greatest of Dijon's artistic monuments are the remains of the **Chartreuse de Champmol**, some 2km west of the city centre on av Albert-1er. Founded by Philippe le Hardi in 1383 as a suitably sumptuous burial place for the ducal family, it was practically destroyed in the Revolution and today is a psychiatric hospital. To adorn it, Philippe recruited a talented team of artists, foremost among them the Netherlander **Claus Sluter**, pioneer of realism in sculpture and founder of the Burgundian school. Most of the surviving works of art are in the city's museums, but the finest, the so-called **Well of Moses** featuring six highly realistic portrayals of Old Testament prophets, remains in situ, as does the **portal** of the chapel, both by **Sluter**.

The museums

Musée des Beaux-Arts

Palais des Ducs. 10am–6pm; closed Tues.

The collection of **paintings** represents many different schools and periods, from Titian, Rubens, and Schongauer to Monet, Manet and other Impressionists, with substantial numbers of Italian and Flemish works and quantities of religious artefacts, ivories, and tapestries. One of the most interesting exhibits is a small room devoted to the intricate woodcarving of the sixteenth-century designer and architect, **Hugues Sambin**, whose work appears throughout the old quarter of the city in the massive doors and facades of the aristocratic *hôtels*.

Visiting the museum also provides the opportunity to see the surviving portions of the original ducal palace, including the vast **kitchens** needed to service the dukes' gargantuan appetites and the magnificent **Salle des Gardes**, richly appointed with panelling, tapestries and a minstrels' gallery. Here are displayed the **tombs** from the Chartreuse de Champmol, of **Philippe le Hardi** and of **Jean sans Peur** and his wife, **Marguerite de Bavière**. Sluter and his nephew, Claus de Werve, worked on the former. Both follow the same pattern: painted effigies of the dead, attended by angels holding their helmets and heraldic shields and accompanied by a cortege of marvellously sculpted mourners. Also displayed in this room are two gilded retables from the Chartreuse with sculptures by **Jacques de Baerze** and paintings by **Melchior Broederlam** and a fine tapestry of the **siege of Dijon** by the Swiss in 1513.

Musée Magnin

4 rue des Bons-Enfants. 9am–noon and 2–6pm; closed Tues.; free Wed. and Sun.

The building is a seventeenth-century *hôtel particulier* complete with its original furnishings, more interesting than the exhibition of paintings by good but lesser-known artists, the personal collection of Maurice Magnin, donated to the state in 1938.

Musée Archéologique

5 rue Docteur-Maret. Open 10am–6pm, June–Sept.; 9am–noon and 2–6pm, Oct.–May; closed Tues. and Sun. morning in winter; free Sun. afternoon
Some extremely interesting finds from the Gallo-Roman period, especially **funerary bas-reliefs** depicting the perennial Gallic preoccupation with food and wine and a collection of ex-votos from the source of the Seine, among them the little bronze of the **goddess Sequana** (Seine) upright in her bird-prowed boat. Also on show is **Sluter's bust of Christ** from the Chartreuse.

Musée de la Vie Bourguignonne

17 rue Ste-Anne. Open 9am–noon and 2–6pm; closed Tues.; free guided visit Sun. 10am
Costumes, furniture, domestic industries like butter-, cheese-, and bread-making, a reconstructed kitchen: **Burgundian life in the nineteenth century** – this is what the museum, housed in a stark, well-designed modern setting within a former convent, is all about. Opening shortly, on the first floor, there will be a reconstruction of old Dijon streets and shop fronts.

Musée d'Art Sacré

In Ste-Anne chapel, next door to above. Open 9am–noon and 2–6pm.
An important collection of church treasures is kept here, including a seventeenth-century St. Paul, the first statue in the world to be treated with gamma-rays – carried out in Grenoble as part of the Nucle-art project. Formerly crumbling dust, it is now solid. There is a free guided visit that really perks up these special-interest exhibits.

Muséum d'Histoire Naturelle

Jardin de l'Arquebuse, av Albert-1er. Open 2–5pm; closed Tues.
In addition to just about every stuffed bird and animal you can think of, including the wild boar, the best thing is an exquisite collection of butterflies, and, for the morbid, a collection of animal mutants.

Living, eating, drinking

No need to satiate yourself on art and history alone in Dijon: it's a smart, modern, young city, with lots of students, in no way resting on its laurels.

The lean and hungry traveller is first struck by the inordinate number of **pâtisseries** full of high-quality, tempting confectionery, with marzipan and fruit featuring prominently. The more exotic ones also promote the *pain d'épices*, a sweet bread made with honey and spices eaten with butter or jam, and *cassissines* – blackcurrant candies, – while on rue de la Préfecture, down from the *pâtisserie* at no. 84, you can watch chocolate being made in a traditional workshop.

For loungers and those looking for a drink, the *Palais de la Gare* at the corner of rue Piron and rue Berbissey has charm and character and is good for a daytime or early **drink**, as are the two bars, popular with students, in front of the cathedral. Another youth-orientated hangout, good for sitting outside at lunchtime, is the *Bar Dauphine* behind the shopping centre between rue Dauphine and rue de la Liberté. For an **apéritif**, try *kir* – two parts dry white wine, traditionally *aligoté*, and one part *cassis*.

For more substantial fare, there is obviously no problem finding a good **restaurant** in this centre of *haute cuisine*, though locating cheaper places is harder. *Le Derly*, 17 rue de la Poste near Arc de Triomphe, – good for lunch or early supper (closes 10pm) – is a restaurant/*crêperie* with no menu but reasonable prices for light, interesting dishes and you can just have a *galette* or put together your own meal. Two popular **lunchtime places** are *Le Clair Castel* with good home cooking at 33 rue de la Verrerie and *Le Triskell*, a *crêperie* a couple of doors down. The *St-Jean* at 13 rue Monge has a regional menu at 75F (56F at lunchtime), including *escargots*, *jambon persillé* (ham with parsley in aspic), *coq au vin*, and *boeuf bourguignon*. Another cheap lunchtime possibility is *La Petite Flamande*, 9 rue des Bons-Enfants. To round the evening off there are many liqueurs to choose from, but Burgundy is particularly famous for its *marcs*, of which the best are matured for years in oak casks.

Apart from the cake shops and the food department in *Les Nouvelles Galeries*, there is nowhere to **buy food** in rue de la Liberté, the main street of stylish clothes and shoe stores. The best area is around the *halles centrales* (open Tues. and Fri. am and all day Sat.). *Le Panier Campagnard* (10 rue François-Rude) sells mountain sausages and very good, very expensive *jambon persillé* – cheaper elsewhere, but nowhere near as good. The legendary **Burgundy snail** comes in all guises and sizes, fresh, pre-cooked with garlic butter in the shell, or canned, at the speciality store at 14 rue Bannelier. And for **cheese** there is *Le Chalet Comtois* at 28 rue de la Musette, where the patient staff will explain, in French, what's what. This same area is also peppered with bars and cafés with cheap menus or sandwiches.

And you can hardly forget that Burgundy, and Dijon in particular, is also the high temple of **mustard** and **wine**. For the former there is the leading producer **Maille's** shop in rue de la Liberté selling a range from the mild to the cauterising. On the same block, at no. 11, there is *Bourgogne Tour* for **wine tasting** and, at 3 rue Jeannin behind the Palais des Ducs, *La Cour aux Vins*, with books on wine in the shop and English-language talks.

To consume these mouth-watering purchases *al fresco* there are several **green spaces** you can escape to. In or near the centre there's **place des Ducs** and **place Darcy**, or if you prefer something more spacious and private, there's the very attractive and meticulously labelled **botanical gardens**, Jardin de l'Arquebuse, behind the station, as well as **Parc Colombière** a ten-minute bus ride away (bus #3 from rue de la Liberté) by the **river Ouche**.

The city has a good summer **music season**, with classical concerts through June in its *Eté Musical* programme. **L'Estivade**, from June 20 to August 15, puts on endless music, dance, and street theatre performances. **Fête de la Vigne** at the beginning of September is a traditional costume/folklore jamboree, and the **Foire Gastronomique** in the first week of November is a pretext for a disgusting pig-out to see you through the lean months of winter.

Practicalities

The regional **SI** office in place Darcy has a **hotel reservation** service and **money-exchange**. The rue des Forges office (no. 34) is concerned just with Dijon and sells a cheap **all-in-one ticket** for the main museums and sights in the Côte d'Or department. You can also buy a cheap general **museum ticket** from any of the city's museums.

The **Club Alpin** in the rue des Forges SI produces a booklet, *Promenez-vous en Côte d'Or*, showing all the region's **marked paths**. **Agence Wasteels** at 20 av Maréchal-Foch near the station is a youth-orientated travel agent. **CIJ** has a helpful office at 22 rue Audra on the north side of the Darcy gardens. **Bike hire** is from *Rousseau*, 3 place Notre-Dame. The **university campus** is at the end of rue Mirande beyond bd Gabriel. **CROUS**, the student information service, is at 3 rue Maret near place Darcy.

Finding a **place to stay** is not difficult. *Foyer International d'Etudiants* on av Maréchal-Leclerc (☎80.71.51.01; bus #4, direction Grézille) is a cheap **student hostel**, while the **youth hostel** itself is in a modern complex with a diner at 1 bd Champollion (☎80.71.32.12; bus #6 from place Darcy) 4km from the centre.

As for **hotels**, there is the cheap and tacky *Hôtel de France* near the station at 16 rue des Perrières. *Hôtel Gare et Bossuet* (16 rue Mariotte, towards the cathedral; ☎80.30.46.61) is a bargain, though traffic noise is intrusive. Best is *Hôtel du Théâtre* (☎80.67.15.41) right in the Palais des Ducs quarter at 3 rue des Bons-Enfants – if there is room. Other good bets are *Miroir-Hôtel* (☎80.30.54.81) in a private alley at 7 rue Bossuet and *Hôtel Monge* (☎80.30.55.41), 20 rue Monge. The nearest **campsite** is by the lake off bd Kir.

There is a good city **bus** service, but distances are small enough to make walking easy. If you plan to use the bus a lot, it's worth getting a **pass** from *STRD*, in the middle of place Grangier. **Gare routière** for out-of-town journeys is next to **gare SNCF** at the end of av Maréchal-Foch, five minutes from place Darcy. **Hitching**: for **Paris**, go along av Albert-1er to Lac Kir; for **Beaune**, **Lyon**, etc., cross the canal from place 1er-mai and continue down av Jean-Jaurès.

Autun and around

A Gothic spire rising from the midst of red-brown lichenous roofs, against a backdrop of Morvan hills: even today **AUTUN** is scarcely bigger than the circumference of its medieval walls and they in turn followed the line of the earlier Roman fortifications.

The emperor Augustus founded it around 10 B.C. as part of his massive, and in the long term, highly successful campaign to pacify and Romanise the broody Celts of defeated Vercingétorix. **Augustodunum**, as it was called, was designed to eclipse by its splendour the memory of **BIBRACTE** (see below) the neighbouring capital of the powerful tribe of the Aedui. And it did become one of the leading cities of Roman Gaul.

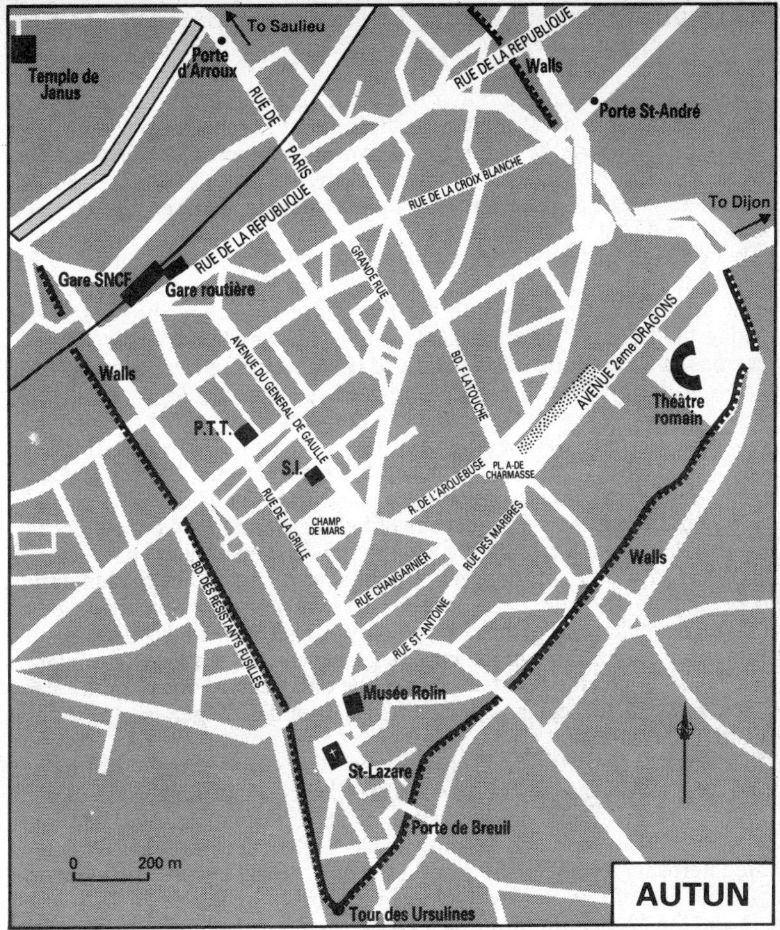

Traces of that period are surprisingly abundant. Two of the city's four **Roman gates** survive, **Porte St-André** spanning rue de la Croix-Blanche in the northeast and **Porte d'Arroux** in Faubourg d'Arroux in the northwest, while in a field just across the river Arroux stands the so-called **Temple of Janus**, a lofty section of brick wall that was probably part of the sanctuary of some Gallic deity. And a measure of Autun's importance at that time: off av du 2eme-Dragon are the few remains of the largest **Roman theatre** in Gaul, with a capacity of 15,000 seats. A cottage overlooking it has numerous pieces of Roman statuary incorporated into its walls.

Whether you arrive by **rail** or **road** you'll find yourself on av de la République by the **gare SNCF** (and **routière**). Opposite the station, *Hôtel de France* (☎85.52.14.00) and *Hôtel Commerce et Touring* (☎85.52.17.90; closed

Oct.) are both decent and cheap; the latter has a very acceptable, moderately priced **restaurant**. (There's a **campsite** just across the river beyond Porte d'Arroux.)

From here the broad and rather dull av de Gaulle (**SI** at no. 3) leads up to the square, Champ de Mars, where there are a number of **places to eat**, including the *Auberge de la Bourgogne* and the brasserie *Morvandiau*. Here begins the **old town** with its narrow streets (rue St-Saulge and rue Chauchien) converging towards the **Cathédrale de St-Lazare** in the most southerly and best fortified corner of Autun.

Though built in the twelfth century, the appearance of the cathedral has been significantly altered by the addition of the Flamboyant Gothic central tower, spire and side chapels in the fifteenth century and the twin towers flanking the front put up in the last century. But the church's unique importance lies in its **sculptures**, the work of **Gislebertus**, generally accepted to be one of the greatest, if not the greatest, of Romanesque sculptors. The **tympanum** of the Last Judgment above the west door bears his signature – *Gislebertus hoc fecit*; Gislebertus made this – beneath the feet of Christ. To the left and right of Christ are depicted the elect entering heaven, the apostles, the Archangel Michael disputing souls with Satan who tries to cheat by leaning on the scales, and the flames of hell licking at the damned. Luckily, during the eighteenth century the local clergy decided it was an inferior work and plastered it over, which saved it from almost certain destruction during the Revolution. The **interior**, whose pilasters and arcading were modelled on the Roman architecture of the city's gates, was also decorated by Gislebertus, who himself carved most of the **capitals**. Conveniently for anyone wanting a close look, some of the finest are now in the old chapter library, up the stairs on the right of the choir, among them a beautiful *Flight into Egypt* and *Adoration of the Magi*.

Just outside the cathedral, on rue des Bancs, the **Musée Rolin** in a Renaissance *hôtel* built by Nicolas Rolin, Chancellor of Philippe le Bon, is definitely worth a look (mid-March to Sept., 9.30am–noon and 2.30–7pm; Oct.–Mar., 10am–noon and 2–4pm; closed Tues. and Feb.). In addition to some interesting Gallo-Roman pieces, the star attractions are **Gislebertus**'s representation of **Eve** as – by medieval standards – an unashamedly sensual nude and the **Maître de Moulins'** brilliantly coloured *Nativity*. Also in preparation are some cases of exhibits from **Bibracte**.

Mont-Beuvray/Bibracte

Along N81, 23km west of Autun, then D61, past scattered farms amid coarse, marshy pastures and brown streams, between close, wooded hills, you come to the hamlet of ST-LEGER-SOUS-BEUVRAY (**youth hostel**). There is a morning and an afternoon bus; alternatively, you can tackle the seven-hour walk on **GR131** from the Croix de la Libération outside Autun. It is a further 1¾hours by the path or 8km by the road to **Bibracte** at the top of the *mont* (800m altitude) and if you're attempting to recapture a Celtic atmosphere it's worth doing this last stretch on foot. The path winds up through the woods, mostly beech at the top.

Great ceremonial rocks like the **Pierre de la Wivre** still exist close to the fortified earthwork which surrounds the site and which you can still follow through the trees. **BIBRACTE** was inhabited from 5000 B.C. Capital of the Aedui, all the Gallic nations assembled here in 52 B.C. to elect Vercingétorix their leader in one last desperate attempt to fight off Roman imperialism. Although it is two millenia since Bibracte was abandoned, probably on Roman orders, vague memories of its significance were preserved in the folk tales of the Morvan and a fair was held on the summit every May until the beginning of the First World War.

Le Creusot

LE CREUSOT means one thing to the French: the **Schneider iron and steel works**, maker of the first French railway engine in 1838, the first steam ship in 1839, the 75mm field gun, mainstay of the artillery in World War I, the iron work of the Pont Alexandre III and the Gare d'Austerlitz in Paris. Now **Creusot-Loire** manufactures specialised steels and boilers for the nuclear industry, and, like many steel works in Britain, employs far fewer people.

As you travel south through the wooded hills from Autun (30km; frequent buses because of the Montchanin **TGV** station), nothing prepares you for this former industrial powerhouse. You arrive suddenly to see, over the brow of a hill, spilling unattractively down the bottom of a valley, abandoned-looking factories and workers' apartments. Its interest – rather specialised, perhaps lies in the **Ecomusée de la communauté urbaine du Creusot-Montceau-les-Mines** (place Schneider; 10am–noon and 2–6pm; Sat. and Sun. 2–6pm; closed Mon.). The **exhibits** tell the story of heavy industry and agriculture in the area, with superb period photos, push-button models of the works, steam cranes, reconstructed workshops, models of locomotives, and a photo record of the great *Mistral* train's run from Paris to Marseilles. Also documented is the **life of the workers**, their living conditions, strikes and political struggles.

The **Schneiders**, who in 1836 took over the former **Royal Foundry**, in which Louis XVI was a shareholder before losing his head, were typically paternalistic employers. They provided housing, schools, and health care for their workers, but in return expected 'gratitude and obedience'. Thus the worker-mayor who proclaimed adherence to the Paris Commune in 1871 was sentenced to hard labour for life, while the army, as usual, moved in to quell the unrest. The local mine owners organised a private police force to keep an eye on workers' reading matter and church attendance and handed out building plots for 'good behaviour'.

A small street of rustic-looking workers' dwellings survives in the **Combes des Mineurs** across the valley from the château, while in place du 8-mai on the Montchanin road out of town a colossal 100-ton Schneider **drop-hammer** has been set up as a monument to past glories.

As the *écomusée* is still expanding, you should ask for information about other possible visits, to the **Canal du Centre** with its locks, the **coal mines** at Blanzy and Montceau, and a nineteenth-century industrial farm. In theory the modern Creusot-Loire works are visitable, but you are supposed to write to: Creusot-Loire, Services Relations Publiques, 60 rue Clemenceau, 71208 Le Creusot. The **SI** in rue Maréchal-Foch might be able to speed up the process.

If you need to stay overnight, *Hôtel des Voyageurs* (☎85.55.22.36) on place Schneider is cheap, though it probably makes more sense to go back to Autun or on to Chalon.

Cluny and nearby monasteries

The voice of **CLUNY**'s abbot once made monarchs tremble. His power in the Christian world was second only to that of the Pope, his intellectual influence arguably greater.

The monastery was founded in 910 in response to corruption of the existing church and a universal longing for some spiritual assurance at a time of great insecurity at the approach of the first millenium. All it took was a couple of vigorous early abbots to build the power of Cluny into a veritable empire. They established numerous subordinate houses, especially along the pilgrim routes of St-Jacques. Ironically, however, the growing wealth and secular involvement of the monastery led to the decline of its spiritual influence, which was superseded by the reforming zeal of St. Bernard and his Cistercians based at Cîteaux. In time Cluny became a royal gift – a convenient device for dressing the king's temporal machinations up in a little spiritual respectability. Both Richelieu and Mazarin did stints as abbot.

Now, apart from the very attractive village, practically nothing remains. The Revolution suppressed the monastery and **Hugues de Semur's** vast and influential **eleventh-century church**, the largest building in Christendom until St. Peter's in Rome, was dismantled in 1810. All you can see of it is an octagonal belfry, the south transept, and, in the impressive granary, the surviving capitals from its immense columns – disappointing, but evocative. From the top of the **Tour des Fromages** (entry inside the **SI**) you can reconstruct it in your imagination. The **Musée Ochier** (March–Sept., 9.30am–noon, 2–6.30pm; Oct.–Feb. 10am–noon and 2–6pm) in the fifteenth-century palace of the last abbot to be freely elected helps to flesh out the picture with reconstructions and fragments of sculpture, while the Romanesque belfry of the parish church of **St-Marcel** also recalls those that once adorned the abbey.

If you're planning to stay, a municipal **hostel**, *Cluny Accueil*, is the cheapest; it's in Chemin du Prado between rue Porte-de-Paris and the D980 bypass. The **campsite** is on rue des Griottons across Pont de la Levée on the right. *Hôtel de l'Abbaye* (☎85.59.11.14; closed Dec.–Feb. and Sun. pm), *Hôtel des Marroniers* and the *relais routier*, all on av de la Gare, have inexpensive rooms, as does the *Hôtel du Commerce* (8 place du Commerce; ☎85.59.03.09; closed Sun. pm in winter). The *Marroniers* has a reasonable **restaurant**; otherwise the cheapest bet is *crêperies* and cafés.

Paray-le-Monial

Architecture buffs can get a good idea of what Cluny must have looked like from the church of the **Sacré-Coeur** in the old town of **PARAY-LE-MONIAL** on the banks of the river Bourbince 50km to the west across the

Charolais countryside. The church was built on a smaller scale, but at the same time and in direct imitation of Cluny. It acquired its present name from the cult of the **Sacred Heart** which developed in the nineteenth century after the canonisation of a seventeenth-century nun from Paray, Marguerite-Marie Alacoque. It is now second only to Lourdes as a **pilgrim centre**. The first pilgrimage in 1873, encouraged as a means of fighting the socialist ideas espoused by the Commune, raised the money to construct that great white cheese on the hill of Montmartre in Paris.

For **accommodation** try *Hôtel Terminus* (☎85.88.84.45) or *Hôtel St-Roch*, both on av de la Gare. There is also a *Foyer des Jeunes Travailleurs* on rue Michel-Anguier, if you can get in. The **campsite** is by the river on bd Dauphin-Louis.

The **station** hires out **bikes**, which would be an excellent way of exploring the gentle **BRIONNAIS** country to the south, peppered with small villages and Romanesque churches, precursors or offspring of Cluny.

Taizé

A more powerful attraction for the converted might be the modern ecumenical community at **TAIZE**, 10km north of Cluny. Founded in 1940, its monks are drawn from both Protestant denominations and the Roman Catholic church. It is unashamedly populist in outlook, attracting hordes of youngsters who come to take part in discussion groups and camp out under canvas. If you are seriously interested – and it is not likely to be to the taste of the merely curious – you should write to Communauté de Taizé, 71250 Cluny.

Nevers

NEVERS is a large thriving city on the confluence of the **Loire** and the **Nièvre**. In France it is known for its *nougatine* candies and fine **porcelain**, a hallmark since the seventeenth century and well represented in the **municipal museum** in St-Genest (10am–noon and 2–6pm; closed Tues.). Movie connoisseurs might also know that Alain Resnais's *Hiroshima Mon Amour* was filmed here.

If you arrive at the **station**, av de Gaulle takes you due east to the central **place Carnot** by the city **park**, on the north side of which is the convent of St-Gildard, where **Bernadette of Lourdes** ended her days. On the south side of the *place* is the former **Palais ducal**, with octagonal turrets and an elegant central tower decorated with sculptures illustrating the family history of François de Clèves, the first duke in the mid-seventeenth century.

Hard at hand, opposite the **Hôtel de Ville**, is the **Cathédrale de St-Cyr**, a sort of wall display of every phase of French architectural style from the tenth to the sixteenth century. It even manages to have two opposite apses, one Gothic, the other Romanesque.

More interesting and aesthetically satisfying is the late eleventh-century church of **St-Etienne** on the east side of the town centre. Behind its plain exterior, it is one of the **prototype pilgrim churches**, with galleries above the aisles, ambulatory, and three radiating chapels around the apse.

North from here, up **rue du Commerce** into Nevers' main high street, **rue des Ardilliers**, you come to the eighteenth-century arch of the **Porte de Paris** straddling the street. It commemorates one of Europe's major conflicts, the battle of Fontenoy, fought out between Charlemagne's sons up towards Auxerre in 841 A.D.The stakes were Charlemagne's empire, and the outcome the division of his lands east and west of the Rhine, which formed the basis of modern France and Germany.

Down along the **riverbank** by place Mossé and the bridge over the Loire you pass a section of the old town walls and the **Tour Goguin**, part of which goes back to the eleventh century. If you turn in here to the right you come to the square machicolated tower of **Porte de Croux** with its barbican still intact in front and a small local **archaeology museum** inside. To your right again you get back to the **oldest quarter** of town around the cathedral – rue Morlon and rue de la Cathédrale, for instance – with its dilapidated half-timbered houses, alleys, and stairs extending down to the river.

Av de Gaulle is a good place to find inexpensive **restaurants** and **cafés**. Try *Gambrinus*, for example. There are several **hotels** in the area too, though it is on the noisy side: *Hôtel Villa du Parc*, 16 rue de Lourdes (☎86.61.09.48); *Hôtel Beauséjour* nearby at 5 rue St-Gildard, and *Hôtel Thermidor* on rue Tiller (first left in av de Gaulle). **Camping municipal** is on the other side of the Loire, just over the bridge.

SI is at 31 rue du Rempart near place Carnot. **Bike hire** is from Laroche, 28 rue St-Genest. **Gare routière** is on rue du Chemin-de-Fer.

The vineyards

Burgundy farmers have been growing grapes since Roman times, and their rulers, the dukes, frequently put their wines to effective use as a tool of diplomacy. Today they have never had it so good, which is why they are reticent about the quirks of soil and climate and tricks of pruning and spraying that make their wines so special. Vines are temperamental things. Frost on the wrong day, sun on the wrong day, too much water, poor drainage and they won't come up with the goods. And they like a slope, which is why so many wines are called *Côte* something.

The single most important factor determining the 'character' of wines is the soil. In the **COTE D'OR**, for instance, the relative mixture of chalk, flint, and clay varies over very short distances, making for an enormous variety of taste. Chalky soil makes a wine *virile* or *corsé*, i.e., heady; *il y a de la mâche*, they say – something to bite on. Clay makes it *féminin*, more *agréable*. These and other more extravagant judgements are made after the hallowed procedure of tasting: 'you introduce a draft of wine into your mouth, swill it across the tongue, roll it around the palate, churn it around emitting the gargling sound so beloved of tasters, which is produced by slowly inhaling air through the centre of your mouth, and finally eject it'.

Detailed in this section are the main wine-producing areas of Burgundy: **Côte d'Or, Mâcon, Beaujolais**, and the smaller **Chalonnais** region. All lie close to the main Dijon-Lyon roads: accessible and well visited. The fifth area, **Chablis**, is included with Auxerre.

The Côte d'Or

Burgundy's best wines come from a narrow strip of hillside called the **COTE D'OR** that runs southwest from Dijon to Santenay. It is divided into two regions: **Côte de Nuits** and **Côte de Beaune**. With few exceptions the reds of the Côte de Nuits are considered the best: they are richer, age better, and cost more. Côte de Beaune is known particularly for its whites, Meursault, Montrachet, and Puligny.

The countryside is attractive: the steep scarp of the *côte*, wooded along the top, is cut by deep little valleys called *combes*, where local rock climbers hone their skills (**GR7** and **76** run the whole length of the wine country as far as Lyon). Spring is a good time to come: you miss the crowds and the landscape is a dramatic symphony of browns – trees, earth, vines, with millions of bone-coloured stakes wheeling past you like crosses in a vast war cemetery.

The villages, strung along N74 through Beaune and beyond, (whose names – Gévry-Chambertin, Vougeot, Vosne-Romanée, Nuits-St-Georges, Pommard, Volnay, Meursault all sound like Pavlov's bell to the ears of wine buffs), are sleepy, dull, and exceedingly prosperous, full of houses inhabited by well-heeled *vignerons* in expensive suits and fat-cat cars. You make a very good living on a patch of ten to twelve acres, the average plot. The proof: none are ever up for sale.

There are numerous *caves* to taste and buy at, but as usual the former is meant to be a prelude to the latter. And there is no such thing as a cheap wine here, red or white, £7–9 being the minimum. The *Hautes Côtes* (Nuits and Beaune), from the top of the slope, are cheaper, but they don't have the connoisseur cachet of the big guys.

Château Clos-Vougeot

Though the whole French wine culture is fascinating, it is debatable whether making a special detour to see these vineyards is worth it. The only 'sight' perhaps worth seeing is the **château of CLOS-VOUGEOT** (between Gévry-Chambertin and Nuits-St-Georges on the N74; half-hour guided tours, 9–11.30am and 2–5.30pm), where you get to see the mammoth thirteenth-century wine presses installed by the Cistercian monks to whom these vine-yards once belonged. The château today is the home of a sort of phony chivalrous order, the **Confrèrie des Chevaliers du Tastevin**, whose principal reason for existence seems to be commerce and snobbery, though no doubt the food and wine are treated seriously at the trade's annual beanfeast, the so-called *Les Trois Glorieuses* on the third weekend in November.

Beaune

BEAUNE, the principal town of the region, has many charms, but it is totally devoted to *le Tourisme*. The chief attraction is the fifteenth-century hospital, the **Hôtel-Dieu** (guided tours, April–Nov. 9–11.30am and 2–6pm; Dec.–

March, 9–11am and 2–5pm), on the corner of place de la Halle opposite the **SI** (April–Oct., 9am–7pm; Nov.–March, 9–11.30am and 2–5.30pm; information and hype about every aspect of wine-related matters from tasting to touring). Once past the turnstile you find yourself in a cobbled courtyard surrounded by a wooden gallery overhung by a massive roof patterned with diamonds of gaudy tiles, green, burnt sienna, black, and yellow – ditto for the steep-pitched dormers and turrets. Inside is a vast paved hall with a painted timber roof, the **Grande Salle des Malades**, which until quite recently continued to serve its original purpose of accommodating the sick. The last item on the tour is the **Polyptych of the Last Judgment**, a splendid fifteenth-century altarpiece by Rogier van der Weyden, commissioned by millionaire Nicolas Rolin, who also founded the hospital. It is here that the Hospices de Beaune's wines are auctioned with much ado during the *Trois Glorieuses*, the prices paid setting the pattern for the season.

The private residence of the dukes of Burgundy on rue d'Enfer now contains the **Musée du Vin** (9am–noon and 2–5.45pm), with more giant wine presses and an interesting collection of tools of the trade. At the other end of rue d'Enfer the church of **Notre-Dame** is about the only thing free in town. Inside are five very special **tapestries** from the fifteenth century depicting the Life of the Virgin, these also commissioned by the Rolin family.

It is cheaper and pleasanter to use either Dijon or Chalon as a **base** for getting around in the area, as both are easily accessible by train and *Transco* buses, which service all the villages down N74. Beaune's **hotels** are pricey and likely to be full. A couple of possibilities, however, are *Hôtel St-Nicolas*, 69 rue du Faubourg-St-Nicolas, the Dijon road, (☎80.22.18.60) and *Hôtel Foch*, 24 bd Foch (☎80.22.04.29), both outside the town walls. There might also be room at the *Foyer des Jeunes Travailleurs* (☎80.22.21.83) opposite the hospital on rue Guigone-de-Salins. *Les Cent Vignes* **campsite** is about 1km out on rue Dubois off rue du Fbg-St-Nicolas.

Eating can also be expensive. The best places to look for something **cheaper** are rue Monge, place Carnot and rue de Lorraine. *La Jambe de Bois* on rue Carnot (no. 18) is a good cafeteria, and there is another on place du Beurre (closed 10pm). Other than the regular shops, there is a Saturday morning **market** in place Carnot for picnic food.

Coming in from **gare SNCF** you take a long walk up av du 8-Septembre, cross the big boulevard, and bear left onto rue des Tonneliers. **Bikes** can be hired from the station, or from M. Bouillot in rue du Fbg-St-Nicolas. **Buses** leave from right outside the walls at the end of rue Maufoux (times on SI display board).

Chalon, Mâcon and the Beaujolais

CHALON on the banks of the Saône has long been a thriving port and industrial centre, and its old riverside quarter has an easy charm. It is not a place you would want to stay very long, though there are numerous hotels and it is particularly convenient for **youth hostellers**, with an agreeably located riverbank hostel about a ten-minute walk north of the Pont St-Laurent, the last bridge upstream (coming from the station, go straight ahead into bd de la République as far as place de l'Obélisque, then work your way diagonally right until you hit the river).

The one thing you might want to see is the **Musée Nièpce** (9.30–11.30am and 2.30–5.30pm; closed Tues.) on the river quays just downstream from Pont St-Laurent. Local boy Nièpce is credited with inventing **photography** and the museum possesses a fascinating range of **cameras** from the first ever to the *Apollo* moon mission's, plus a number of 007-type spy's devices.

If you are staying at the **hostel**, the nearest and nicest place for cheap **eating** is on rue de Strasbourg on the **island** across Pont St-Laurent, where there are several establishments. There is also a cheap **hotel**, the *St-Laurent* at no. 37.

Mâcon

An **SNCF bus** goes south to MACON, passing through some of the **Chalonnais** wine villages, best known for their whites: **Mercurey, Givry, Buxy, Montagny**. **MACON** itself is a large, modern town where, again, you are not likely to want to do more than stop over. (**SI** at 187 rue Carnot. **Gares SNCF** and **routière** next to each other behind the busy intersection of rues Gambetta, V.-Hugo. and Bigonnet.)

The **Mâconnais wine-producing** country lies to the west. Its reds are good, but it is best known for the expensive white wines from the villages of **Pouilly, Fuissé, Vinzelles**, and **Prissé**. A curious phenomenon in the landscape is the 500m **Solutré** rock, which evidently puzzled prehistoric as well as modern visitors. An incredible quantity of horse, reindeer, bison, and mammoth bones have been found here covering an area of some 4000 square metres.

Beaujolais

Imperceptibly as you continue south, the Mâconnais becomes the **Beaujolais**, a larger area of terraced hills producing light, fruity red wines. The fashion now is to drink them too soon, and this is taken to ridiculous extremes in respect of **Beaujolais Nouveau.** The *vin de l'année* is transported to British winebars at breakneck speeds by drunken young tearaways during the **Beaujolais run** in November and should be polished off within six months (or preferably not at all).

The grape is the *Gamay*, which thrives on this granite soil. Of the **three categories** of Beaujolais, the superior ***crus***, including Morgon and Fleurie, come from the northern part of the region; **Beaujolais Villages**, which produces the best ***nouveau***, comes from the middle, and plain **Beaujolais** or **Beaujolais supérieur** comes from the vineyards southwest of VILLEFRANCHE.

The well-marked **route de Beaujolais** winds down through the wine villages to **VILLEFRANCHE**. Uninteresting in itself, it could be a useful starting-point if you are coming from Lyon. There are numerous cheap **hotels**, almost all near the station. A good one to try is the friendly and clean *La Colonne*, 6 place Carnot (☎74.65.06.42) with a popular, cheap **restaurant**, open every night, including Sunday when everything else is dead. Any of the cafés on **rue Nationale** are good for snacks or cheap menus too.

The **SI** at 290 rue de Thizy has all the information about *caves*, visits, and tours, though they're not overly helpful.

Tournus and Bourg-en-Bresse

TOURNUS is a small walled town on the banks of the **Saône,** just off the autoroute and N6 between Chalon and Mâcon. As you enter from the **station** through a narrow gateway flanked by medieval towers, it all seems a little too carefully preserved, especially around the old abbey church of **St-Philibert**, one of the earliest Romanesque buildings in Burgundy. Further into the town there are some lovely arcaded shopfronts and substantial hotels, and in **place de l'Hôtel-de-Ville** the remains of an arcaded pavement. From the **riverside quays**, you look out over the broad sweep of the river and its wide flat valley beneath the huge piling cloudscapes. If you walk in the riverside woods to the north of the town in springtime, you'll find colonies of the now rare Snake's Head fritillary, a beautiful flower whose high-shouldered bells are chequered with squares of rose- or rusty-brown.

Prosperous today from its agriculture and light industry, Tournus owed its first flowering to the growth of the monastic community around 900 A.D. **St-Philibert** bears witness to that wealth and importance. It has the mass and clean, pared-down lines associated more with a fortress than a church. It is equally strong inside, not to say primitive, with its massive round pillars and rough-looking stonework in the narthex. The **nave** is something of an architectural rarity in that the vaults of its ceiling run side to side instead of down the axis of the church; an ingenious idea, because it made it possible to have windows in the ends of the vaults opening directly into the nave – very unusual given the state of the art.

Beside the church, **Musée Perrin de Puycousin** (April–Oct. 9am–noon and 2–6pm; closed Tues.) is a moderately interesting museum of local life and costumes, while **Musée Greuze** nearby at 4 rue du Collège (April–Oct., 9.30am–noon and 2–6.30pm; closed Tues. and Sun. am) displays the eighteenth-century paintings of Tournus' native son, Greuze.

If you are **planning to stay**, *Hôtel Le Terminus* near the station in av Gambetta is a good deal. In the centre, a popular bar, *La Petite Auberge* in place Lacretelle, has simple rooms, while the *Hôtel de Bourgogne* has more expensive accommodation but good food. *Café de la Poste* on the corner of rue Jean-Jaurès has cheap snacks and meals. **Camping** *Le Pas-Fleury* is by the river just south of the town.

Bourg-en-Bresse and Brou

BOURG-EN-BRESSE, a few kilometres east of Mâcon means three things in France: chickens, Peugeot trucks, and **BROU**. Poultry-raising is the speciality of the flat farmland surrounding the town, trucks are made in the town, and **Brou** is an uninteresting suburban village about 1km away which happens to have a **church** which traditionally sends guidebook writers into raptures. Aldous Huxley, on the other hand, found it 'a horrible little architectural nightmare', its monuments 'positively and piercingly vulgar'.

The church is a very rich woman's very expensive folly, crammed with virtuoso craftsmanship from the dying moments of the Gothic style. It is interesting to see, but soulless, without a trace of vision or inspiration. It was undertaken in the early sixteenth century by Margaret of Austria after the death of her husband, Philibert, Duke of Savoy, and is in effect a mausoleum for the two of them and her mother-in-law. If you are heading east to Geneva or the Alps, take a look, but don't lose a lift or miss a train for it.

From Bourg **station** bus #2 goes to the town centre and #1 to Brou. The **SI** is in Centre Albert-Camus, 6 av Alsace-Lorraine. In summer there is an annex by Brou church. Wednesday is **market day** in place Carriat and on the first and third Wednesdays of each month there is a livestock market as well. There are three reasonable **hotels** in av Baudin, about a two-minute walk from the station: *Hôtel de Genève*, *Paris et Lyon*, and *Hôtel des Bains*. The last two have inexpensive restaurants. **Camping municipal** is on av des Sports.

travel details

Trains

From Sens frequent to Paris (50 min.–1½ hr.); 7 daily to Dijon (2 hr. 10 min.), via Laroche-Migennes junction (30 min.) and Tonnerre (55 min.); 3–5 daily to Auxerre (¾ hr.) and Avallon (2 hr.), a few continue to Autun (4 hr.). **From Auxerre** 7 or 8 daily to Paris (1¾hr.), some changing at Laroche-Migennes; 4 to 5 daily to Avallon (1 hr. 5 min.) and Autun (about 3 hr.).

From Avallon 2 or 3 weekly direct to Paris; 4 to 5 daily to Auxerre (1 hr. 5 min.); 4 to 5 daily to Autun (about 2 hr.).

From Tonnerre 6 daily on Paris (1¾ hr.)–Dijon (1¼hr.) line.

From Dijon 9 direct TGVs daily to Paris (1 hr. 40 min.); 6 stopping trains to Paris (3 hr.) via Les Laumes (½ hr.), Montbard (¾ hr.), Tonnerre (1¼hr.). Laroche-Migennes (1 hr. 40 min.), Sens (2 hr. 10 min.); several late at night and early morning only non-stop to Lyon (1 hr. 40 min.); about 14 others daily to Lyon (1¾ hr.) stopping variously at Nuits-St-Georges (20 min.), Beaune (25 min.), Chalon (40 min.), Tournus (1 hr.), Mâcon (1 hr.–1 hr. 20 min.), Villefranche (1 hr. 40 min.) – journey times vary.

From Beaune 2 TGVs daily to Paris (2 hr.); about 7 daily on Dijon (20 min.)–Lyon (2 hr.) line, some stopping everywhere, others only at Chalon and Mâcon.

From Mâcon 5 direct TGVs to Paris daily (1 hr. 40 min.); 4 TGVs daily to Bourg (20 min.) and Geneva (1 hr. 50 min.); note TGVs leave from Mâcon-Loché station 6km out of town. Several other trains/SNCF buses daily to Bourg; around 14 daily to Dijon (1 hr. 10 min.) and Lyon (40 min.).

From Bourg-en-Bresse 4 TGVs daily to Paris (2 hr.) via Mâcon (20 min.); 4 TGVs daily to Geneva (1½ hr.); 2 daily direct to Dijon (1¾–2½ hr.); 8 daily to Mâcon (½ hr.); 14 daily to Lyon (about 1 hr.).

From Autun 4 to 5 daily to Auxerre (3 hr.), Avallon (2 hr.), Sens (4 hr.).

From Nevers about 5 daily non-stop to Paris (2 hr.); several stopping trains daily to Paris (3 hr.); 5 daily to Clermont-Ferrand (1 hr. 50 min.).

Buses

From Sens 4 daily to Auxerre (very slow); 4 to 5 daily to Troyes (1¾ hr.).

From Auxerre 4 daily to Sens; other sporadic village buses, including to Chablis and Tonnerre.

From Avallon 1 daily (in early am) to Vézelay (½ hr.); 1 daily to Dijon (2½–3 hr.) via Semur.

From Semur SNCF buses to Les Laumes (on Paris–Dijon line), Saulieu and Montbard; 1 daily to Auxerre.

From Dijon daily services through villages to Avallon; Beaune; Nuits and other wine villages; Autun.

From Mâcon 7 SNCF buses daily to Chalon (2¼hr.) via Cluny (¾ hr.); 2 to 5 daily to Paray-le-Monial, Charolles, Cluny, and everywhere on N79.

From Bourg-en-Bresse 1 SNCF bus daily to Lyon (1 hr. 40 min.).

From Nevers several daily to La Charité, Cosne and Moulins on N7.

From Cluny 7 SNCF buses daily to Chalon (1 hr. 20 min.) and Mâcon (¾hr.); 2 to 5 daily to Charolles and Paray.

From Autun several SNCF buses daily to Montchanin TGV station (1 hr.) via Le Creusot (½ hr.); 1 daily to Château-Chinon (1 hr.); 2 to 3 daily to St-Léger-sous-Beuvray (1¼ hr.); to Chalon (1 hr. 20 min.); 1 daily to Beaune and Dijon.

From Paray-le-Monial 2 to 5 daily to Digoin, Charolles, Cluny, Mâcon.

From Montbard SNCF buses to Châtillon-sur-Seine and Chaumont; *Cars CDA* to Châtillon and Langres.

CHAPTER TWELVE

ALSACE-LORRAINE AND THE JURA

France's eastern frontier provinces, **Alsace**, **Lorraine,** and **Franche-Comté** – the province that covers the **Jura** mountains along the Swiss border – have had a complex and troubled history. For a thousand years they have been a battleground: disputed through the Middle Ages by independent dukes and bishops whose allegiance was endlessly contested by the kings of France and the princes of the Holy Roman Empire, and scene in this century of some of the worst fighting of both World Wars.

The democratically-minded burghers of **Alsace** created a plethora of well-heeled semi-autonomous towns for themselves centuries before their eighteenth-century incorporation into the French state. Sharing the Germans' taste for Hansel-and-Gretel decoration, they adorned their buildings with all manner of of fanciful frills – oriel windows, carved timberwork and Toytown gables – and with equally Teutonic orderliness they still maintain them, festooned with flowers and in mint condition.

Not that you should ever accuse an Alsatian of being German. They speak a Germanic dialect but their neighbours across the Rhine have behaved in decidedly unneighbourly fashion twice in the last hundred years, annexing them along with Lorraine from 1870-1918 and again under Hitler. Not an experience they found congenial: they remain fiercely and proudly Alsatian and French, in that order.

The combination of influences makes for a culture and atmosphere as distinctive as any in France. It is seen at its most vivid in the numerous little wine towns that punctuate the **Route du Vin** along the eastern margin of the wet and woody Vosges mountains, at **Colmar** and in the great cathedral city – and now European Community capital – of **Strasbourg**. Nor is the province just a quaint little Pixieland: it's also an industrial powerhouse, making cars, railway engines, textiles, machine tools, telephones – you name it – as well as half the beer in France.

By comparison **Lorraine**, though it has suffered much the same vicissitudes, is rather wan. Apart from the elegant eighteenth-century provincial capital of **Nancy** and the depressing if thought-provoking World War I battle site of **Verdun**, there is little to hold the attention. More impressive and dramatic are the wooded plateaux, pastures and valleys of the **Jura** further

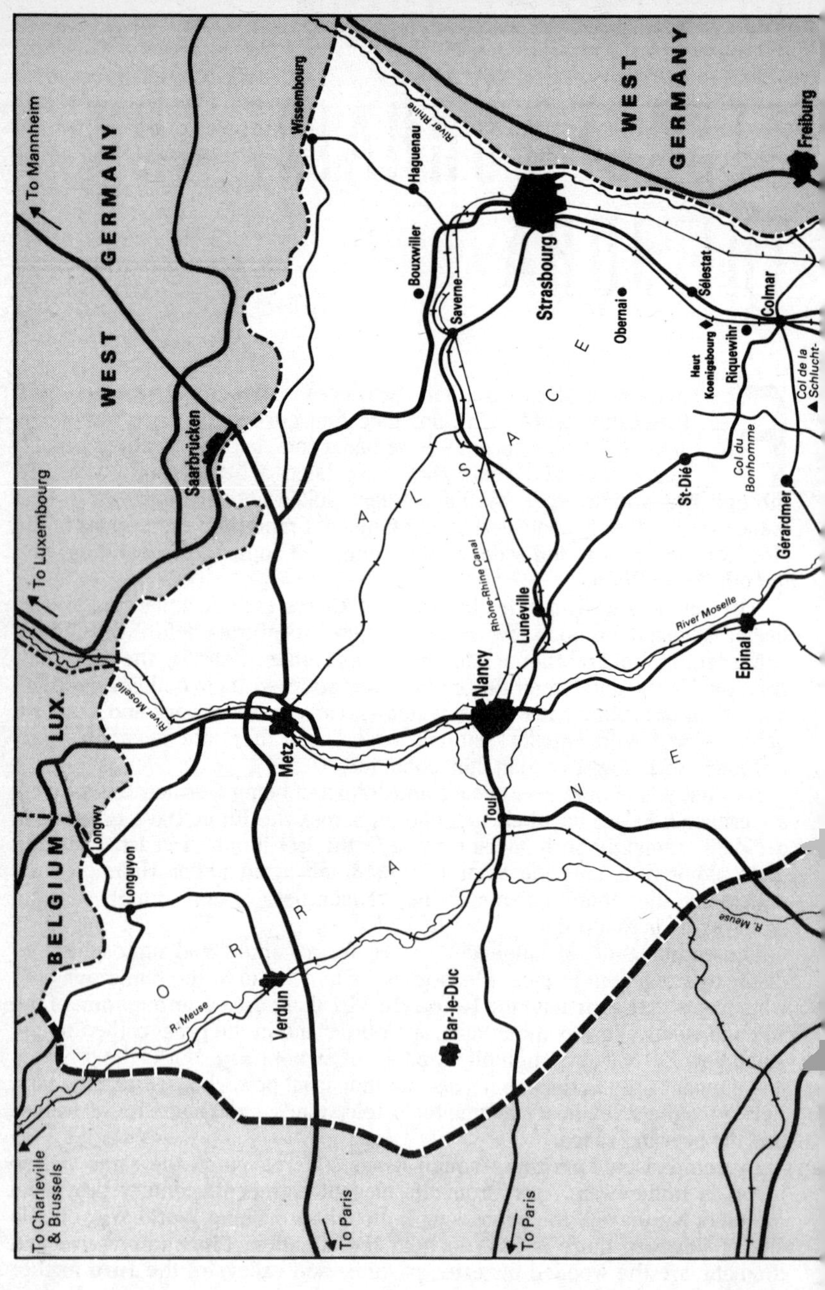
To Mannheim
WEST GERMANY
To Luxembourg
Saarbrücken
Wissembourg
Haguenau
River Rhine
Bouxwiller
Saverne
Strasbourg
WEST GERMANY
Freiburg
Obernai
Sélestat
Colmar
Haut Koenigsbourg
Riquewihr
Col de la Schlucht
Col du Bonhomme
St-Dié
Gérardmer
ALSACE
Rhône-Rhine Canal
Lunéville
River Moselle
Epinal
Nancy
LUX.
River Moselle
Metz
LORRAINE
Toul
Longwy
Longuyon
BELGIUM
R. Meuse
Verdun
Bar-le-Duc
R. Meuse
To Charleville & Brussels
To Paris
To Paris

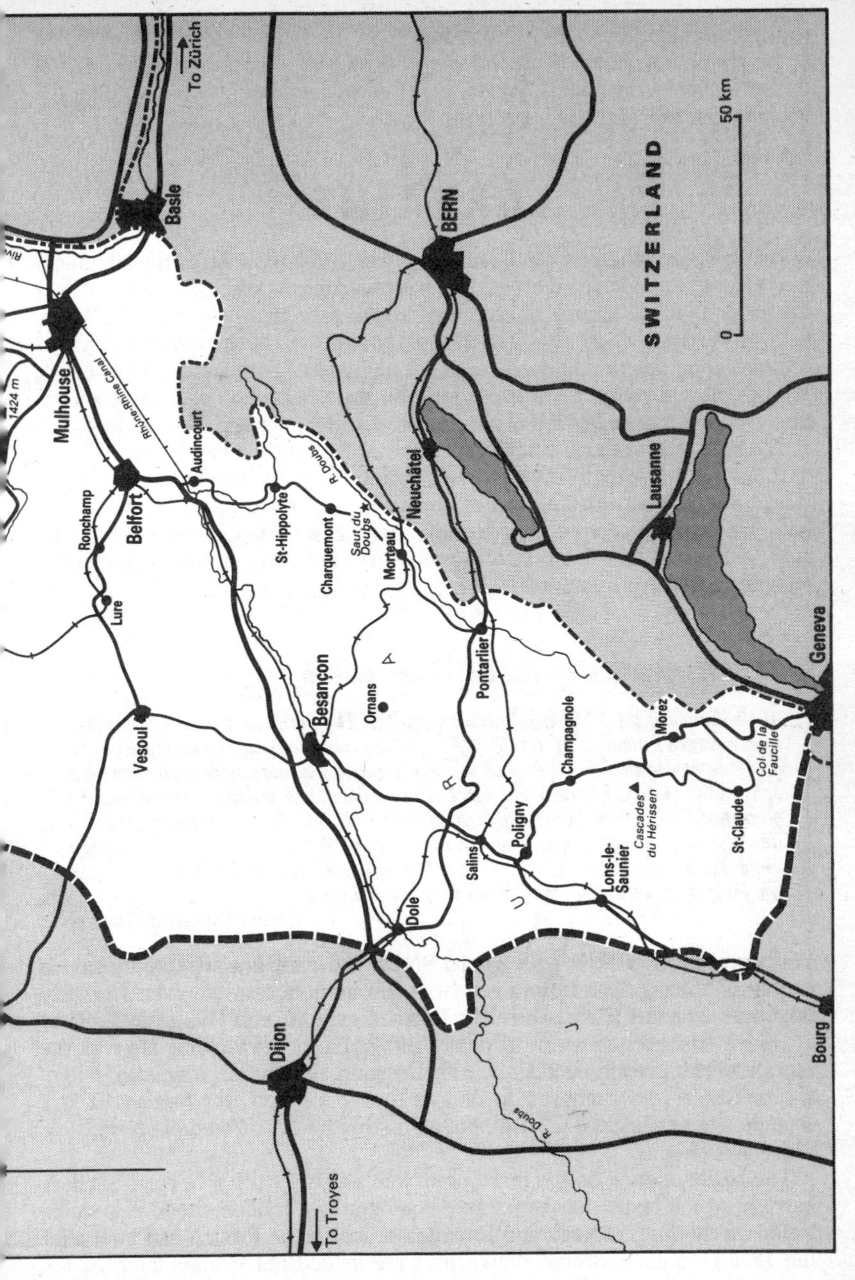

To Zürich
Basle
BERN
SWITZERLAND
50 km
0
Mulhouse
1424 m
Rhine-Rhône Canal
Audincourt
Belfort
Ronchamp
Lure
St-Hippolyte
R. Doubs
Charquemont
Saut du Doubs
Morteau
Neuchâtel
Lausanne
Pontarlier
Besançon
Ornans
Vesoul
Champagnole
Morez
Col de la Faucille
Geneva
Cascades du Hérissen
St-Claude
Poligny
Salins
Lons-le-Saunier
Dole
J
U
R
A
Dijon
Bourg
R. Doubs
To Troyes

south, middling-mountainous, rural and poor, but finding some compensation in the attentions of the leisure industry. *Ski de fond* – cross-country skiing – is the speciality; and it's ideal terrain. It's good walking country too, without the grinding ascents of the neighbouring Alps.

LORRAINE

In the last war, when de Gaulle and the Free French chose as their emblem **Lorraine's** double-barred cross they were making a powerful point. For it is this region, above all others, that the French associate with war. The battle field of **Verdun**, where the French army fought one of the most bloody and protracted battles of all time, is a site of national pilgrimage in all but name. The SNCF still lay on extra trains here for the celebration of Armistice Day, though there can be few left alive who knew and mourn the 700,000 dead.

The rest of Lorraine – rolling farmland in the south, ailing heavy industry in the north – seems to stand in the shadows, if you pause at Verdun or the World War II **Maginot line** fort of **Fermont**. And in truth there's not a lot to hold you here, except perhaps **Nancy**, the region's capital – an elegant city, lighter in tone than the rest of its province, and with a quietly wonderful museum of Art Nouveau.

Verdun and the Maginot Line

> *At Verdun even the pretence of rationality failed. The slaughter was so hideous that even a trench system could not survive . . . In the town, tourists inspect the memorials. One monument shows French soldiers forming a human wall of comradeship against the enemy. In another, France is personified as a medieval knight; resting on a sword, he dominates a steep flight of steps built into the old ramparts. There is another view of reality. Near the railway station, Rodin's statue shows a winged Victory as neither calm nor triumphant, but demented by rage and horror. Her legs are tangled in a dead soldier and she shrieks for survival.*
>
> Horne: *The Great Museum*

You arrive in **VERDUN** – the **gares SNCF** and **routière** are side by side, a couple of cheap, clean **hotels** nearby – and immediately the events of 1916 take over. For this place, which the German general, von Falkenhayn, chose 'to bleed the French army to death and strike a devastating blow at the morale of the French people', is, with Dresden, Stalingrad, Nagasaki, one of the names we have chosen to denote the concept of war forever. It is a strange site to pass into tourism, but an instructive one. You don't forget – or regret – seeing it.

The battle opened on the morning of February 21, with a German artillery barrage which lasted ten hours and expended two million shells. It concentrated on the forts of Vaux and Douaumont which the French had built after the 1870 German invasion. When the battle ended ten months later, its toll was approaching a million, and nine villages had been pounded to nothing –

not even their sites are detectable in aerial photos of the time and the land today still follows the curves of shell craters. It is said that the heavy artillery shells ploughed the ground to a depth of eight metres, and though much of it is now reforested there are parts that steadfastly refuse all but the coarsest vegetation.

From May 1 to September 15 the **Verdun SI** (across the river from the old tower) run minibus **tours of the battlefield**. They begin at 2pm, last four hours, and are expensive. But the guides are interesting and the expense is not one that you are likely to repeat. The tour covers the forts of Vaux and Douaumont, the Douaumont ossuary and a museum on the site of the vanished village of Fleury.

Douaumont commands the highest point of a ridge. Completed in 1912 it was the strongest of 38 forts built to defend Verdun. But by one of those characteristic aberrations of military top brass, the armament of these forts was greatly reduced in 1915. When the Germans attacked in 1916 twenty men were enough to overrun the garrison of 57 French territorials. The fort is built on three levels, two of them underground. Its claustrophobic, damp, dungeon-like galleries are hung with stalactites. The Germans, who held it for eight months, had 3,000 men housed in its cramped quarters, under siege continuously, with no toilets, the ventilation ducts blocked for protection against gas, infested with vermin, plagued by rats which attacked the sleeping and the dead indiscriminately. In one night, when their ammunition exploded, 1300 men died in the blast.

When the French retook the fort, it was with Moroccan troops in the vanguard. General Mangin, revered by officialdom as the heroic victor of the battle, was known to his troops as 'the butcher' for his practice of shoving colonial troops into the front line as cannon fodder. As the film shown in the projection room of the museum at Fleury observes, men who had no desire to kill were forced on pain of the firing squad to slaughter their fellow human beings. Official history accords little attention to their spontaneous and scarcely organised mutinies and refusals. By 1918 the ground around Verdun was completely devoid of vegetation and covered in fragments of corpses. 120,000 French bodies were identified, just a third of the total.

Close to the fort is a cemetery containing the graves of 15,000 men, the Christians commemorated by rows of identical crosses, the Moroccans with gravestones facing the direction of Mecca. In the centre of the battlefield nearby is a vast ossuary, one of the most moving war memorials of all time. At its inauguration in 1932 the President of the Ossuary Committee observed: 'Douaumont, rempart contre l'envahisseur, est devenu le rempart contre l'oubli'. ('Originally a rampart against invasion, Douaumont has become a rampart against forgetfulness'.) Beneath each of the eighteen alcoves inside, and at either end of the building are vast sepulchral vaults filled with the bones of unidentified corpses. The inlaid floor represents the different military orders and the names of the dead are inscribed all over the walls.

The events which necessitated such a horrifying monument are all graphically documented in the **museum at Fleury**. Contemporary newsreels and photos present the stark truth. In the well of the museum, a section of the shell-torn terrain has been reconstructed as the battle left it.

The tour's last call is at the fort of **Vaux**, where after six days' hand-to-hand combat in the confined, gas-filled galleries, the French garrison, reduced to drinking their own urine, were left with no alternative but surrender. On the exterior wall of the fort a plaque commemorates the last messenger pigeon sent to the command post in Verdun vainly asking for reinforcements. Having safely delivered its message, the pigeon expired as a result of flying through the gas-filled air above the battlefield.

The Maginot Line

About 50km north of Verdun, near the small town of LONGUYON, you can see how little was learned from the battle. For here – open daily 1.30–5pm in summer, 4pm in winter, weekends only in October – you can visit the underground fort of **FERMONT**, which, with a series of others, and various other defences above ground, formed the **Maginot line**, first grand failure of World War II.

Constructed between 1930 and 1940 **the Line** was the brain-child of the Minister of War (1929–31), André Maginot. It was incredibly expensive, spanned the entire French-German border and, when put to the test in 1940, proved totally useless: the Germans simply entered via Belgium. **FERMONT** was one of the largest forts, with nine fire points, served by 6km of underground tunnels and a garrison of 600. The entrance is hidden in woodland. Nothing shows above ground but the scarcely noticeable domes of the gun turrets. Below, the tunnels are equipped with electric trains, monorails, elevators, power plants and all the other technological paraphernalia necessary to support such a lunatic enterprise. The place has the feel of a nuclear bunker.

There are **trains** to LONGUYON from METZ and CONFLANS. From Verdun you have to change at Conflans. It is possible, though not easy, to hitch across country via DAMVILLERS and MARVILLE. It is 8km from Longuyon to Fermont and you'll probably have to walk it. Coming back the best thing is to hijack a fellow-visitor in the car park. In Longuyon *Hôtel de Lorraine* by the station is an attractive place to stay.

Metz

Very much a northern town, **METZ** seems solid, and confident of hard-headed business values. The **gare SNCF** sets the tone, a vast granite building of 1900 in Rhenish Romanesque, matched by the **Post Office** opposite. It's not a place to plan on staying, but there are several **hotels** and **eating** places in front of the station, and a **youth hostel** and **camping** on the banks of the Moselle by Pont Thionville.

To reach the centre take rue Gambetta, rue Harelle (**SI** by the reconstructed Porte Serpenoise) and turn right along av Schuman to **place de la République**, a big square with shops and cafés and the formal gardens of the Esplanade overlooking the Moselle. On the right of the Esplanade is a handsome classical Palais de Justice in yellow stone. To the left a gravel walk leads to **St-Pierre-aux-Nonnains**, not much to look at, but one of the oldest churches in the land – fourth-century, at least in places. Behind it, on the other side of the Ecole des Beaux Arts, rue de la Citadelle leads to an unusual octagonal chapel built by the Templars (13C) and on to the leafy square Giraud, with the splendidly gabled and ivy-covered Gothic mansion of the Governor of Metz.

From the north side of place de la République, **rue des Clercs** leads through the principal shopping area to the fine classical **place d'Armes** (18C) flanked by a pedimented and colonnaded **Hôtel de Ville**. All rather dwarfed by the short-in-length but very tall **Cathédrale de St-Etienne** (13C), its nave the highest in France after Beauvais and Amiens. The best feature – as at Reims – is the glass, both medieval and modern, and again including windows by Chagall.

Nancy

NANCY, capital of Lorraine, is lighter and more southern in feel than Metz. The central area, little affected by modern redevelopment, remains more eighteenth- than nineteenth-century. For this the city can thank the last of the independent dukes of Lorraine, Stanislas Leczinski, and dethroned King of Poland, father-in-law of Louis XV. During the twenty-odd years of his office in the middle of the eighteenth century he ordered some of the most successful urban redevelopment of the period in all France.

Pride of place goes to **place Stanislas**. From the **gare SNCF**, go under the Doric **Porte Stanislas** and all the way down **rue Stanislas** to the bottom. The middle of the wide square belongs to the solitary statue of the portly Stanislas himself. The south side is taken up by the **Hôtel de Ville**, its roof-line topped by a balustrade ornamented with florid urns and *amorini*. From its walls lozenge-shaped lanterns dangle from the beaks of gilded cocks. The other buildings are similar, though not as big. The entrances to the square are closed by superb wrought iron gates, but the best work of all is in the railings which close the northeastern and northwestern corners, framing gloriously extravagant fountains with lead statues of Neptune and Amphitrite.

The **SI, PTT,** and **Beaux-Arts** museum are all on the square: the latter (10am–noon and 2–6pm; closed Mon. am and Tues.) boasts Dufys and Matisses, but nothing outstanding. Time in museums here is better spent at the **Musée de Zoologie** (rue Ste-Cathérine, which leads off place Stanislas; 2–6pm, closed Tues.); upstairs is a colossal jumble of stuffed animals and birds, appallingly displayed and labelled, while downstairs is a startling **aquarium** of exotic fish whose colours surpass even the daring of Matisse.

Alternatively, make your way to the **Musée de l'Ecole de Nancy** (38 rue Sergent-Blandan; 10am–noon and 2–6pm in summer; till 5pm in winter; closed Tues.) in a 1909 villa built for the Corbin family, founders of the big *Magasins Réunis* chain of department stores. Even if you are not into Art Nouveau, this collection is exciting. Although not all the collection belonged to the Corbins the museum is arranged as if it were a private house. The furniture is outstanding – swirling curvilinear forms, whether the object is mantlepiece or sofa, buffet or piano. And the standards of workmanship are incredibly high. Nancy was the centre of the movement founded by Emile Gallé, manufacturer of glass and ceramics, prominent here, of course. A fourth museum – the **Musée Lorrain** (10am–noon and 2–6pm in winter; till 5pm in summer) – is devoted to the history of Lorraine. It contains a room full of superb etchings of the seventeenth-century artist, Jacques Callot, whose concern with social issues evidenced in series such as 'The Miseries of War' and 'Les Gueux' presaged much nineteenth- and twentieth-century art. The collection is housed in the old ducal palace, entered through an extravagant doorway surmounted by an equestrian statue of one of the dukes.

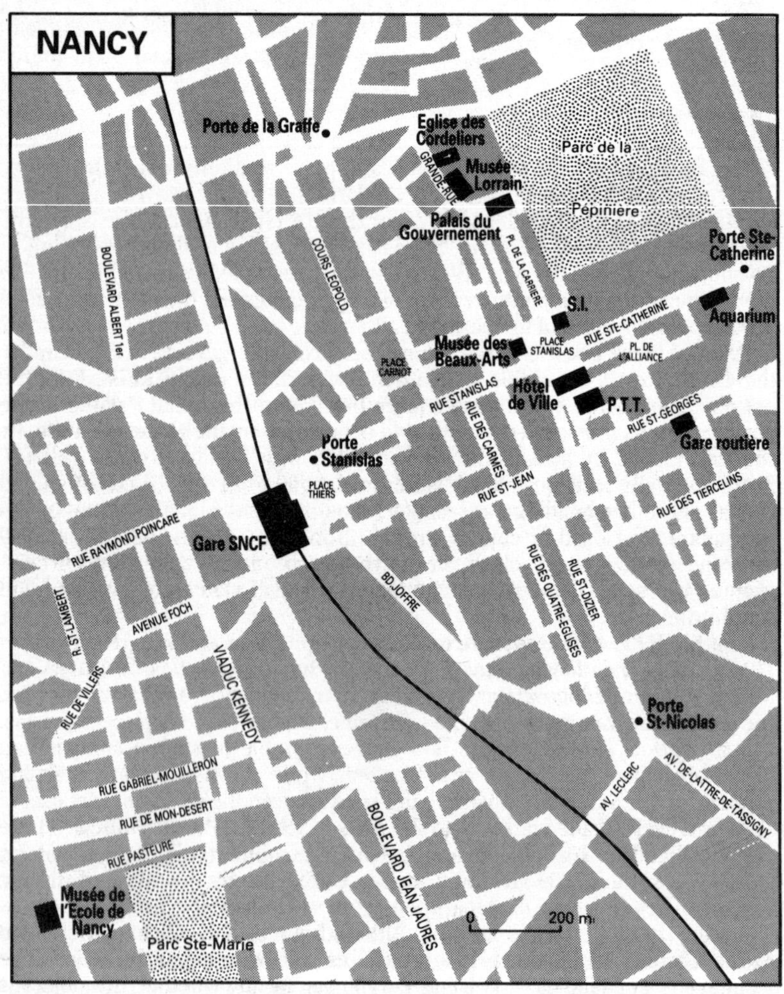

Accommodation

Looking for a cheap **place to stay**, it's best to try first in the rue Stanislas-rue des Carmes area. Try the *Académie* at 7 rue Michottes or *Choley*, 28 rue Gustave-Simon, both off rue Stanislas about halfway down. For **food**, rue Grande-rue Maréchaux is also good for restaurants. The **youth hostel** is out at the *Centre d'Accueil*, Château de Rémicourt, VILLERS-LES-NANCY (☎83.27.73.67): a fifteen-minute bus ride plus a fifteen-minute walk (no sign-posts). To find it take bus #6 on rue des Carmes, direction *Vandoeuvre*, and get off at the *Mangin* stop, immediately after a left turn by a housing development called Les Jonquilles; then go back to the main road, turn left and go straight across the first major intersection, leaving the Ecole d'Architecture at the edge of a park on your left; take the next left, a small road running uphill beside the park – a gate on the left leads to the château. *Camping de Brabois* is nearby.

Lunéville

Lunéville, twenty-minutes' train ride from Nancy, was renowned for the *faïence* works set up by Stanislas. There is a collection of it in a dusty museum (9am–noon and 2–6pm; closed Tues.) in the immense eighteenth-century **château**, but it is too small to merit a detour unless you're a specialist. The rest of the museum is occupied by cavalry uniforms and weaponry, Lunéville being a garrison town.

What is worth a detour is M Chapleur's private **motorcycle museum**, directly opposite the gates of the château, the *Musée de la moto et du vélo* (9am–noon and 2–6pm; closed Mon.). Monsieur Chapleur started collecting in the 1930s when he was a mechanic at Citroën's. He has over 200 models of different nationalities on display, all overhauled and in working order when they go into the museum. And they are beauties, works of art in copper, brass, chrome and steel. Some of the bicycles go back to 1865. The motorbikes are mostly 1900–40. Several of the older bikes are probably unique; one certainly is – a 1906 René Gillet 4½hp belt-driven tandem. Many look like flying bombs and must have been incredibly dangerous to ride: bits of meccano with a couple of hefty cylinders welded on and capable of 100kph in 1900.

To get to the museum and château from the **gare SNCF**, take rue Carnot (**hotels**), place Léopold, rue Général-Leclerc, rue de la Charité, and turn right in front of the vast red Baroque church of St-Jacques.

ALSACE

There's no denying **Alsace's** attractiveness, with its old stone and half-timbered towns set amid thickly wooded hills, but it's a quaintness that has also firmly been turned into a commodity. **Strasbourg**, the capital, escapes the tweeness of its smaller neighbours and should definitely be seen. Elsewhere you may want to direct your travels around some of the province's unusually good **museums**: Grünewald's amazing **Isenheim altarpiece** at **Colmar**, and the **car, railway,** and **printed fabrics** museums at **Mulhouse**.

Saverne and the Northern Vosges

SAVERNE, fifty minutes from Lunéville, is the first Alsatian town you come to on the Paris–Strasbourg line. It is not as picturesque as some, but has the region's characteristic steep-pitched roofs, dormer windows and window-boxes full of geraniums. It has always been strategically important because it commands the only easy route across the Vosges, at a point where the hills are pinched to a narrow waist.

As such, it is a good base for exploring the **Parc Naturel Régional des Vosges du Nord** and for day-hikes. There is a clean, friendly **youth hostel** (☎88.91.14.84) in the vast red sandstone château just over the canal bridge on Grand' Rue. A pretty and easy walk (about 2 hours there and back) is to the ruined castle of **Haut Barr**. Take rue Poincaré opposite the château, turn right on rue de Paris and immediately left onto rue du Haut-Barr along the canal. Keep going to the end, past leafy suburban villas. A wood begins at the end of the road with a signboard indicating various walks. Take the path marked Haut-Barr through woods of chestnut, beech and larch. The castle stands dramatically on a narrow sandstone ridge with fearsome drops on both sides and views across the wooded hills and eastward over the plain towards Strasbourg. MARMOUTIER – 6km from Saverne and easily walkable – has a fine church with an unusual front. Ask the **SI** (in *Hôtel de Ville*) for other hiking possibilities.

The obvious route on from here is to STRASBOURG, but if you're curious about this pocket of the country, SNCF buses wind through the villages and apple orchards along the German border. **WISSEMBOURG**, at the northern end of the Vosges, is one of the more interesting towns, and unspoiled despite its popularity with German weekenders. A considerable section of its walls survive, built like the stonework of the houses in the local red sandstone. Branches of the river meander through the town and around the thirteenth-century church creating an atmosphere of placidity and changelessness. The townspeople have one curious linguistic anomaly; they speaks a very ancient dialect derived from Frankish, unlike their fellow-Alsatians whose language is similar to that spoken on the German bank of the Rhine.

Should you wish to stay, the best **hotels** to try are *Hôtel de la Gare* and *Hôtel de l'Europe* by the **gare SNCF**; more luxurious but right in the centre and with one very nice inexpensive double, is the *Hôtel du Cygne*, by the townhall on the central place de la République.

OBERSEEBACH, HUNSPACH and the CHATEAU DE FLECKENSTEIN in the woods on the frontier make good local excursions.

Strasbourg

STRASBOURG is prosperous, beautiful and modern: big enough with a quarter of a million people to have a metropolitan air, but without being overwhelming. It has one of the loveliest cathedrals in France; one of the oldest and most active universities; and, ancient commercial crossroads that it is, is current seat of the Council of Europe and part-time base of the European

Parliament. You may not be planning time in eastern France, but if travelling through or near the region this is the one city worth a special detour.

The old town

It is not difficult to **find your way around**. The city is concentrated on a small island encircled by the River Ill. From the **gare SNCF** take rue du Maire-Kuss, cross the river onto rue du 22-Novembre and its continuation, rue des Bourgeois, where a left turn on rue Gutenberg brings you to **place Gutenberg**. From the city centre, **rue du 22-Novembre** takes you to **place Kléber**, the commercial centre, where all the bus routes converge.

A more picturesque approach to the old city centre is along **quai Turckheim** with the first of four square towers guarding the so-called **Ponts Couverts** over a series of canals. They are part of the fourteenth-century city fortifications. Just upstream is a dam built by Vauban to protect the city from waterborne assault. Known as **La Petite France**, the whole area is extremely attractive with winding streets bordered by sixteenth- and seventeenth-century houses with carved woodwork and decked with flowers, but predictably it is a tourist hot spot, with a horrid little *Petit Train* honking its twee way through the lanes.

The central **place Gutenberg** is named for the printer, pioneer of type, whose statue occupies the middle of the square; he lived in Strasbourg in the early fifteenth century. The west side of the square is taken up by the sixteenth-century *Hôtel de Commerce* (**SI** on ground floor), where the writer Arthur Young, fascinated, watched the night-time destruction of the magistrates' records during the Revolution. But all this is distraction. The one thing you are constantly aware of the **Cathédrale de Notre-Dame** (daily April–Sept. 10am–noon and 2–6pm; winter weekdays 2–6pm, Sun. 10am–noon and 2–6pm, closed Tues.), all in pinky sandstone, soaring out of the close huddle of medieval houses at its feet, with a spire of such delicate, flaky lightness it seems the work of confectioners rather than masons. Inside, too, it is magnificent, the high nave a model of proportion and enhanced by a glorious sequence of **stained glass** windows. The finest are those in the south aisle next to the door, depicting the life of Christ and the Creation. But all are beautiful, including the modern glass in the apse designed in 1956 by Max Ingrand to commemorate the first European institutions in the city.

On the left of the nave the late fifteenth-century **pulpit** is another masterpiece of intricacy in stone, while nearby in the south transept are two of the cathedral's most popular sights. One is the slender triple-tiered thirteenth-century column known as the *Pilier des Anges* decorated with some of the most graceful and expressive statuary of its age. The other is an enormous, and enormously complicated, **astrological clock** built by Schwilgué of Strasbourg in 1838: just the sort of curio that warms the cockles of wonder-seeking tourists and their organisers. They roll up in droves to witness the clock's crowning performance of the day, striking the hour of noon, which it does, with unerring accuracy, at 12.31, that being 12 o'clock Strasbourg mean time. Death strikes the chimes. The Apostles parade in front of Christ, who occupies the highest story of the clock; as each one passes he receives

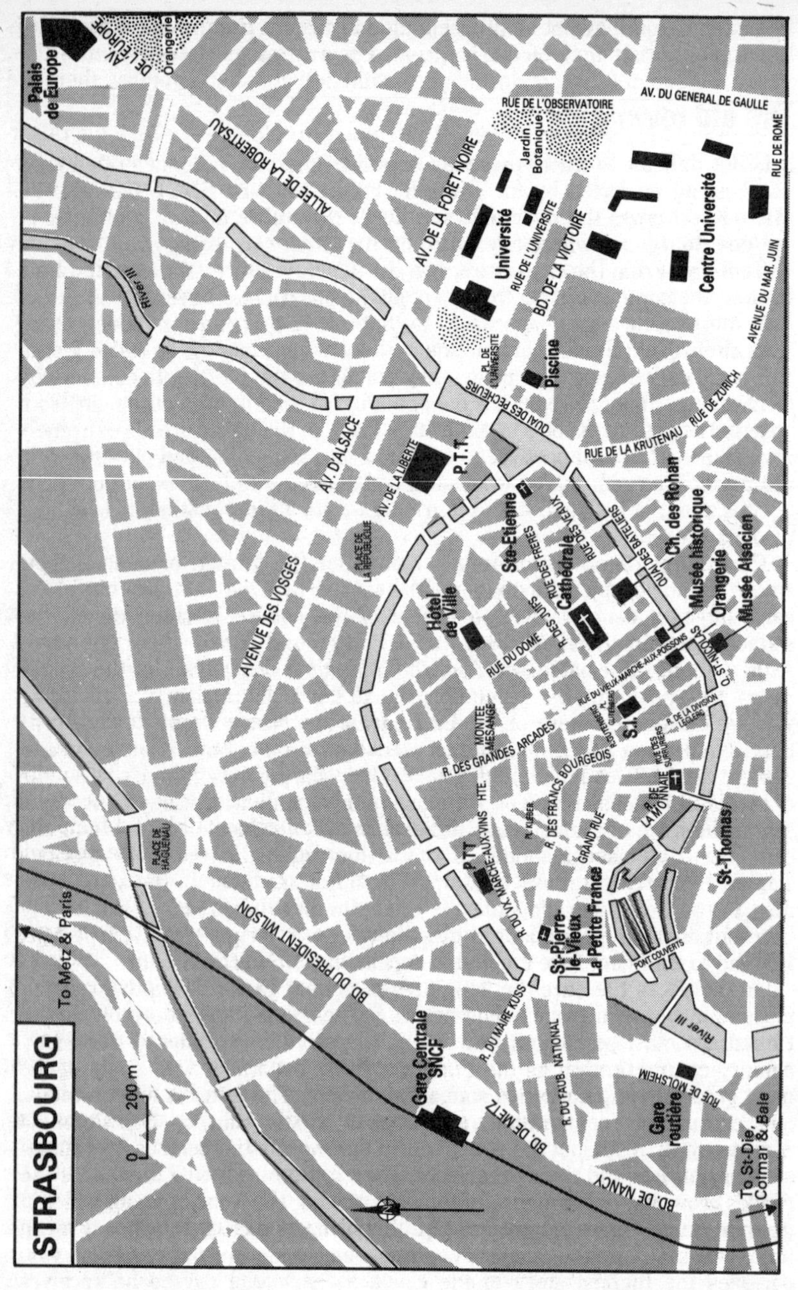
STRASBOURG
0
200 m
To Metz & Paris
To St-Dié, Colmar & Bâle
Palais de Europe
AV. DE L'EUROPE
Orangerie
AV. DU GENERAL DE GAULLE
RUE DE L'OBSERVATOIRE
Jardin Botanique
ALLEE DE LA ROBERTSAU
AV. DE LA FORET-NOIRE
Université
RUE DE L'UNIVERSITE
BD. DE LA VICTOIRE
Centre Université
RUE DE ROME
AVENUE DU MAR. JUIN
River Ill
PL. DE L'UNIVERSITE
Piscine
QUAI DES PECHEURS
RUE DE ZURICH
RUE DE LA KRUTENAU
AV. D'ALSACE
AV. DE LA LIBERTE
P.T.T.
Ste-Etienne
PLACE DE LA REPUBLIQUE
RUE DES VEAUX
RUE DES FRERES
Cathédrale
Ch. des Rohan
QUAI DES BATELIERS
Musée historique
Orangerie
Musée Alsacien
AVENUE DES VOSGES
Hôtel de Ville
RUE DU DOME
R. DES JUIFS
RUE DU VIEUX MARCHE AUX POISSONS
Q. ST-NICOLAS
S.I.
R. DE LA DIVISION LECLERC
MONTEE MESANGE
R. DES GRANDES ARCADES
R. DES FRANCS BOURGEOIS
RUE DES SERRURIERS
R. DE LA MONNAIE
HTE.
PL. KLEBER
GRAND'RUE
St-Thomas
PLACE DE HAGUENAU
P.T.T.
R. DU VX. MARCHE-AUX-VINS
St-Pierre-le-Vieux
La Petite France
PONT COUVERTS
BD. DU PRESIDENT WILSON
R. DU MAIRE KUSS
R. DU FAUB. NATIONAL
River Ill
Gare Centrale SNCF
BD. DE METZ
RUE DE MOLSHEIM
Gare routière
BD. DE NANCY
N

Christ's blessing. As the fourth, eighth and twelfth pass, a cock crows. It is entertaining, but the chief advantage of paying your 3F admission is that, since it is the only way of entering the cathedral at this time of day, there are fewer people about than at other times.

South of the cathedral, the tree-lined **place du Château**, where the ridiculous *Petit Train* starts its journey, is enclosed by the Lycée Fustel and the Château des Rohans, both eighteenth-century buildings, the latter designed for the immensely powerful Rohan family who for several generations in a row cornered the market in cardinals' hats. Next door the **Musée de l'Oeuvre Notre-Dame** (April–Sept., 10am–noon and 2–6pm; closed Tues.; rest of year Sun. and weekday mornings; closed Tues. – **same hours for all museums**) houses the original sculptures from the cathedral exterior, damaged in the Revolution and replaced today by copies. Both sets are worth seeing. And there are other treasures here: glass from the city's original Romanesque cathedral; the eleventh-century Wissembourg Christ, said to be the oldest representation of a human figure in stained glass; the architect's original parchment drawings for the statuary, done in fascinating detail down to the different expressions on each figure's face.

There are three other museums in the **Château des Rohans** itself: **Arts Décoratifs**, **Beaux-Arts** and **Archéologique** (same hours as above). The rooms of the château are not especially interesting: vast, opulent and ostentatious. Of the three collections only the Art Deco stands out – and that of slightly specialist interest – with its eighteenth-century faïence crafted in the city by Paul Hannong.

If you feel museum-oriented, though, there's another trio close by, around place du Marché-aux-Cochons-de-Lait (sucking-pig market). The **Musée Historique** in the old Grande Boucherie is mainly concerned with the city, though it also has an odd-ball collection of mechanical toys upstairs. Opposite, the **Musée d'Art Moderne** has an impressive permanent collection featuring such artists as Monet, Klimt, Ernst, Klee and Jean Arp, though it has an irritating habit of putting them away whenever there's a temporary exhibition on. And last but not least, there's the **Musée Alsacien** with painted furniture and other local artefacts in a traditional house just across the Pont du Corbeau. Upstream is **quai des Bateliers**, part of the old business quarter. Take a look at the fourteenth-century **Cour du Courbeau** off place du Corbeau. Two bridges downstream is Pont St-Thomas, leading to the church of **St-Thomas**, with a Romanesque facade and Gothic towers. Since 1549 it has been the principal Protestant church. Strasbourg was a bastion of the Reformation, and one of its leaders, Martin Bucer, preached in this church. The amazing piece of sculpture behind the altar is the tomb of the Maréchal de Saxe by the eighteenth-century sculptor, Pigalle.

The area east of the cathedral is good for a stroll too, rue des Frères leading to place St-Etienne and rue des Juifs. **Place du Marché-Gayot** behind the cathedral is very pretty with an unpretentious student-type café on one side. From the north side of the cathedral rue du Dôme leads to the eighteenth-century **place Broglie** with the Hôtel de Ville and *préfet's* residence and some imposing eighteenth-century bourgeois mansions around. It was at no. 4 place Broglie that Rouget de Lisle first sang the *Marseillaise* for the mayor of Strasbourg (1712), who had challenged him at dinner the night before to compose a rousing song for the troops of the army of the Rhine.

Across the river here, **place de la République** is surrounded by vast German-Gothic edifices erected during the Imperial Prussian occupation post-1870. The **Post Office** building down av de la Liberté is one such. If you cross the River Aar by Pont de l'Université (Goethe studied here), and turn left along Alleé de la Robertsau, flanked by confident turn-of-the-century bourgeois residences, you come to the **Orangerie park** and, opposite, the **Palais de l'Europe**, an imposing and adventurous piece of contemporary architecture (1977). It is suitably vast, in matt silver, pinky-bronze glass and red concrete, with the contemporary equivalent of a turret jutting from one corner. The interior, or at least the part you can visit, is surprisingly poky and cheaply finished, with the exception of the European Parliament's debating chamber.

The facts

There are several two-star **hotels** in the not especially salubrious station area; possibilities are the *Royale, Victoria, Grillon* or *Colmar*, all along rue du Maire-Kuss which leads to Pont Kuss over the Ill. But the best deal is the modern **youth hostel** (rue de l'Auberge-de-Jeunesse; ☎88.30.26.46) with a bar and excellent canteen. To get there, take a #3, #13 or #23 bus by the next bridge upstream from Pont Kuss and ask for *Auberge de Jeunesse*. And it could be worth checking with *CROUS* to see if there's any university accommodation going (1 quai du Maire-Dietrich; ☎88.36.16.91)

Strasbourg usually has lots **going on**. If you're here during term time, check noticeboards at the university. In summer, pick up the *Saison d'Eté* listings leaflet from the SI. Regular events include **free concerts** in the Orangerie and Contades parks, an international **music festival** (mid-June), independent European cinema in the autumn and **mime** and **clowning** in November.

For **food**, beware the more touristy places, and if you're hard-up go for Germanic Alsace snacks – *wurst, sauerkraut,* and the like. The *FEC* **student restaurant** on place St-Etienne has rock-bottom prices and good meals too: ask a student to buy you a ticket.

As for other practicalities, **bikes** can be hired from the SNCF; **buses** leave from place des Halles and place des Anciens-Abbatoirs; the *Club Vosgien* (4 rue de la Douane) have **hiking information**; the *CIJ* are at 7 rue des Ecrivains (☎88.37.33.33); and there's a launderette on Grand' Rue.

Hitching out towards the German frontier, take Pont du Corbeau, Pont d'Austerlitz and then route du Rhin. For *Allostop* call ☎88/37.13.13 or look in at the office at 5 rue Général-Zimmer.

Sélestat and the Route du Vin

From MARLENHEIM west of Strasbourg to THANN opposite MULHOUSE, the so-called **Route du Vin** winds southwards along the first slopes of the Vosges terraced with vineyards producing the region's famous fruity white wines, *Riesling*, *Sylvaner* and *Gewurztraminer*. Set in this sea of vines are dozens of flowery and typically quaint Alsatian villages, dominated from the heights above by an extraordinary number of ancient castles, testimony to its turbulent past. Hilly work on a bike – but it's definitely easier to get around with your own transport, otherwise you will be dependent on expensive coach tours (see the various SIs).

SELESTAT, midway on the Strasbourg–Colmar railway, is a good place to start. A delightful old town, it has a couple of interesting **churches** in the Romanesque Ste-Foy and the Gothic St-Georges (the latter with spectacularly multi-coloured roof tiles) and streets full of old houses. Just off rue de l'Eglise by St-Georges the **Bibliothèque humaniste** (9am–noon and 2–5pm; closed Sat. am and Sun.) is worth more than a glance for bibliophiles, with some unusual and very rare books and manuscripts from as far back as the seventh century.

Within easy range of the town there are three good groups of castles. **DAMBACH-LA-VILLE**, just 7km away, with its walls and three fortified gates is one of the highlights of the *route*. More formidable, however, is the castle of **BERNSTEIN**, a thirty-minute climb from the village. Alsace was culturally more German than French in the Middle Ages and this is a typically German mountain keep, tall and narrow, with few openings and little use for everyday living. Around it are residential buildings, enclosed within an outer wall, the masonry cut into protruding knobs, which gives it a curious pimpled texture.

From SCHERWILLER, another attractive village even closer to Sélestat, you can reach **ORTENBOURG** castle. It's steep but the way is marked. Like Bernstein, it has a lofty refuge-tower with courtyards outside, in a good state of preservation, protected by a rock-cut ditch. A few hundred metres off **RAMSTEIN** castle was originally built in 1293 to protect besiegers of Ortenbourg.

South to Colmar

The best pairing of castles, however, is at KOENIGSBOURG southwest of Sélestat, where **Oudenbourg** castle, with a sizeable hall preserved among the trees, is dwarfed by the massive **HAUT-KOENIGSBOURG** (9am–noon and 1–4, 5, or 6pm according to season), one of the biggest and – astride its 757-metre bluff – by far the highest castle in Alsace. (Without your own transport it's a good idea to take one of the many tour buses; ask at the **SI** in av Leclerc in Sélestat). Ruined after an assault in 1633, it was heavily restored in the early years of this century for Kaiser Bill of World War I fame. It's easy to criticise some of the detail of the restoration, but it's an enjoyable experience and a remarkably convincing re-creation of a castle-palace of the age of Dürer. There are guided tours, but it's best to avoid them. The views all around are fantastic. On the way down, stop off at **KINTZHEIM**, a smaller but still luxurious castle built around a cylindrical refuge-tower; it's used as an aviary – *Volerie des Aigles* – for birds of prey, with magnificent displays of aerial prowess by eagles and vultures (2–6pm in summer, 5.30pm in winter). If you have a yen to watch Atlas mountain macaques at play in the Vosgian jungle, you can do just that a couple of kilometres further on at the *Montagne des Singes* (mid-March to mid-Nov., 10am–noon and 2–6pm).

Continuing south towards COLMAR, **BERGHEIM** and **RIBEAU-VILLE** are two more little towns worth visiting. Bergheim has still got a goodly part of its old fortifications left, with three towers still intact. Ribeauvillé has only one, with storks nesting on its roof. There are more fortresses in the vicinity for the energetic: **ST-ULRICH**, an hour's haul up a marked path, and the smaller **GIRSBERG**, balanced on a pinnacle which somehow provides room for a bailey, two towers and other buildings. Again within walking range of Ribeauvillé, **HUNAWIHR** is another charmer, with a walled church standing out amid the green vines.

RIQUEWIHR, **KAYSERBERG** and **AMMERSCHWIHR** have the advantage for cyclists of being on flat land. All are exceptionally pretty, though the first two play host to more than their share of tour buses. Kayserberg, birthplace of Nobel prizewinner Albert Schweitzer, boasts a fortified bridge and a handsome sixteenth-century wooden altarpiece in its church; it also has a small lepers' colony outside its walls. Riquewihr has some splendid half-timbered houses lining its main street, while in Ammerschwihr's **Tour des Fripons** with its oddly-shaped embrasures you can see a good example of Alsatian architects' passion for modifying buildings to hold cannon.

Along the Rhine frontier: Colmar to Mulhouse

COLMAR, a fifty-minute train ride south of Strasbourg, has sprawled unattractively both sides of its railway tracks, but the old centre remains typically and picturesquely Alsatian, with crooked houses, half-timbered and painted, on crooked lanes: extremely pretty and very touristy. This is the chief problem with Alsace. Left to its own devices, it stays on the right side of Disneyland, but under the impact of tourism and the desire to make money it comes close to caricaturing itself.

But Colmar is also the proud possessor of some very remarkable paintings, housed in its **Musée d'Unterlinden**, above all, the altarpiece for St Anthony's monastery at Isenheim (1513-15), painted by Mathias Grünewald at the beginning of the sixteenth century, one of the last and most extraordinary of all medieval Gothic paintings. To reach the museum from the **gare SNCF**, go straight ahead and turn left onto av de la République (**hotels**; *L'Europe, La Chaumière, Rhin et Danube*; **PTT** on the left and a **cafeteria** which, though plastic in décor, sells good food at good prices). The museum is just beyond the intersection at the end of av de la République in a former Dominican convent (9am–noon and 2–6pm in summer, till 5pm in winter; closed Tues.).

Although displayed 'exploded', the **Isenheim altarpiece** was designed to make a single piece. On the front was the Crucifixion, almost luridly expressive: a tortured Christ with stretched bony rib-cage and outsize hands turned upward and fingers splayed in pain, flanked by his pale fainting mother, St John, and Mary Magdalene. Then it unfolded, respective to its function on feast days, Sundays and weekdays, to reveal an Annunciation, Resurrection,

Virgin and Child, and finally a sculpted panel depicting the saints Anthony, Augustine and Jerome. Completed in 1515, the painting is affected by Renaissance innovations in light and perspective but still rooted in the medieval spirit, with an intense mysticism and shifts of mood in its subject matter. Other works in the museum are, inevitably, secondary but there's a surprisingly interesting collection of modern paintings in the basement.

A little to the south, reached by rue des Têtes and rue des Boulangers, the **Dominican church** (9.30am–6.30pm; small charge) has some fine glass and, above all, a radiantly beautiful altarpiece by Schongauer (who is also represented in the Unterlinden), painted in 1473, known as *The Virgin in a bower of roses*. Down rue des Serruriers you come to the church of **St-Martin** on a square with numerous cafés. Parallel, rue des Marchands leads past the painted **Maison Pfister** and on towards the archly picturesque **Quartier de Krutenau**, with its houses backing on to the river.

If you plan to stay in Colmar, there's a reasonable **youth hostel**: from the station turn left over the railway bridge along av de la Liberté, then right at the second lights into rue Albert-Schweitzer. The hostel is behind the shops on the left: about a twenty-minute walk. The **SI** by the museum sells *Club Vosgien* maps and a booklet of day **walks** in the hills behind the town. From the gare SNCF, **buses** leave for most towns around here, including LE BONHOMME and mountain destinations.

Mulhouse

Twenty minutes down the line from Colmar, **MULHOUSE** is a large sprawling industrial city that got rich around 1800, on printed cotton fabrics and allied trades. Not having much of a centre it is no city for strollers but it does have three unusual **museums**. Closest to the **gare SNCF** just along the canal to the right, is the **Musée de l'Impression sur Etoffes** (10am–noon and 2–6pm; closed Tues.). It is expensive but excellent, a vast collection of the most beautiful fabrics imaginable – eighteenth-century Indian and Persian imports which revolutionised the European ready-to-wear market in their time; silks from Turkestan; batiks from Java, Senegalese materials, some superb kimonos from Japan, and a unique display of scarves from France, Britain and the U.S.

The other two museums are trickier to get to. For the railway museum, **Musée Français du Chemin de Fer** (10am–5pm; pricey), you'll need to take bus #1 to the end of the line, near the suburb of Dornach, then follow the signs. Rolling stock on display includes Napoléon III's ADCs' drawing-room, decorated by Viollet-le-Duc in 1856, and a luxuriously appointed 1926 diner from the *Golden Arrow*. There are cranes, stations, signals and other railway artefacts, but the stars of the show are the big locomotives with their brightly painted boilers, gleaming wheels and pistons, and tangles of brass and copper piping. Cold steel they may be, but you could be forgiven for thinking they had life in them. Real craftsmen's work.

As, too, are most of the 600 cars on exhibit in the **Musée National de l'Automobile** (10am–6pm; closed Tues.; also pricey), which you can reach by taking bus #2 or #7 from **place de l'Europe**. They range from the earliest attempts at powered vehicles, like the extraordinary wooden-wheeled Jacquot steam 'car' of 1878, to 1968 Porsche racing cars, and contemporary factory prototypes. The largest group are the locally made Bugattis: dozens of glorious racing cars, coupés and limousines, the pride of them the Bugatti Royales, with two of the seven made on show – one Ettore Bugatti's own, with bodywork designed by his son.

Mulhouse is not a place I'd choose to stay in. There are a couple of reasonable **hotels** by the railway station, but if these are full the **youth hostel** (☎89.42.63.28) is about your only bet. Again it's a little way out. Take bus #4 or #6 from place de l'Europe in the city centre to the *Salle des Sports* on rue de l'Illberg.

THE JURA MOUNTAINS

The mountains – gentle in the west, precipitous in the east, with wide, high forested plateaux in between – cover most of the old county of Franche-Comté, once part of the realms of the Grand Dukes of Burgundy, French proper only since the late 1600s.

With the exception of the city of **Besançon** what there is to see is countryside – acres of woodland, lake, and pasture: hard to get around without a car, but really best travelled on foot. There are several **GRs** in the area, including the marathon GR5. A winter mode of transport for the hardy could be **cross-country skiing** – very big in the Jura – down the long-distance, marked, *Grande Traversée du Jura*. For my money, I'd go for the Haut-Doubs, the northeast corner of this area, or the heights overlooking Lake Geneva.

Besançon and around

BESANCON, capital of Franche-Comté, is an ancient and attractive town enclosed in a loop of the River Doubs at the northern edge of the Jura mountains, precursors to the Alps. It was the birthplace of rayon, in 1890, and a major centre of clock-making in France, until the western Pacific started getting its act together – one of the reasons for the closure of the Lip works in the early seventies and the ill-fated attempt of its workers to carry on as a cooperative. Wooded hills enclose it tightly and it is the best place to begin a walking tour of the area. This constriction and the sober grey stone of its facades give it a slightly mournful air.

There is no youth hostel proper, but the **Centre International de Séjour** in the new town at 19 rue Martin-du-Gard (☎81.50.07.54; bus #8 from the station to L'Epitaphe) fulfils the same function, though slightly more expensively. Alternatively, there are two *foyers* and a university residence which will take passers-through when they have spare room: *Foyer des Jeunes Filles*, 18 rue de la Cassotte (☎81.80.90.01); *Foyer Mixte des Jeunes Travailleurs*, 48 rue des Cras (☎81.88.43.11); *Résidence Universitaire de la Bouloie*, 38 av de l'Observatoire (☎81.50.26.88). Or there are **hotels:** *Alsace-Lorraine* and *Florel* opposite the **gare SNCF** are cheap; also try *Regina* at 91 Grande Rue in the

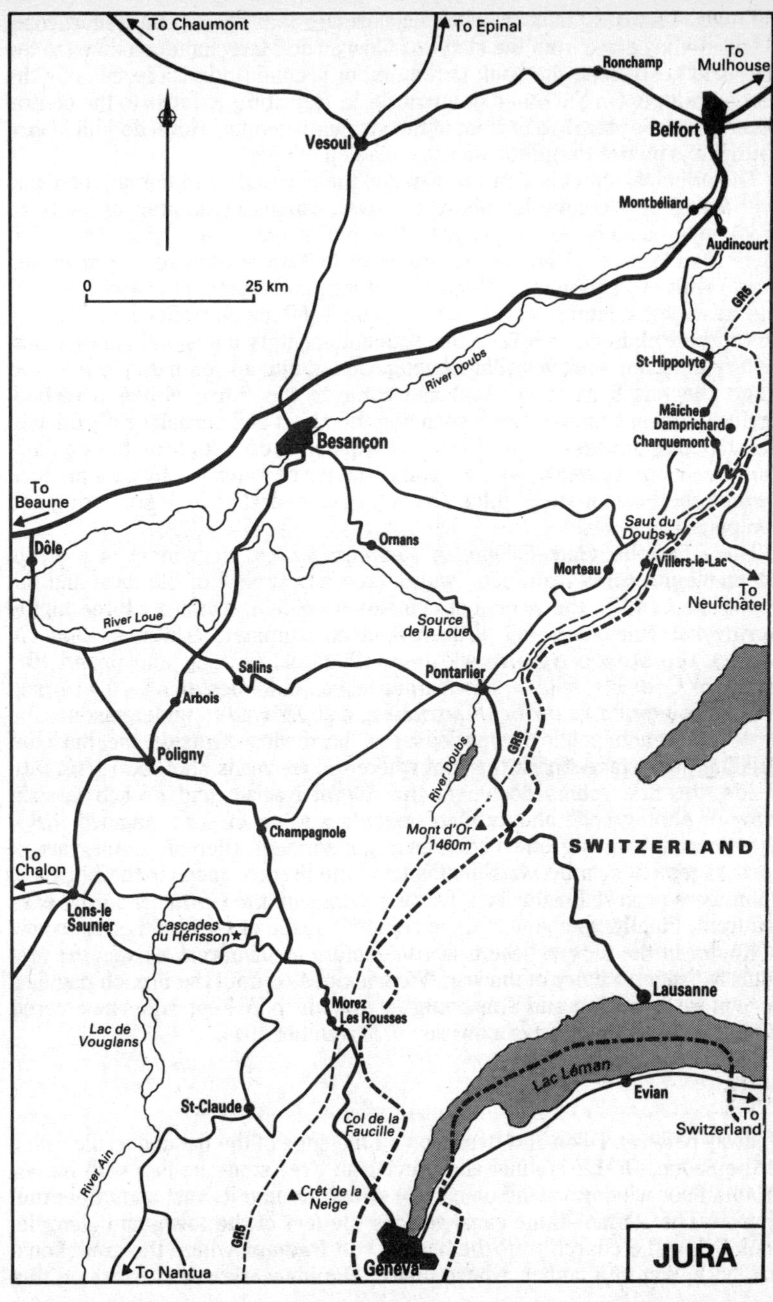
To Chaumont
To Epinal
Ronchamp
To Mulhouse
Belfort
Vesoul
Montbéliard
Audincourt
0
25 km
GR5
St-Hippolyte
River Doubs
Maîche
Damprichard
Besançon
Charquemont
To Beaune
Saut du Doubs
Ornans
Dôle
Morteau
Villers-le-Lac
To Neufchâtel
River Loue
Source de la Loue
Salins
Pontarlier
Arbois
Poligny
GR5
River Doubs
Champagnole
Mont d'Or 1460m
SWITZERLAND
To Chalon
Lons-le Saunier
Cascades du Hérisson
Lausanne
Morez
Les Rousses
Lac de Vouglans
Lac Léman
Evian
St-Claude
To Switzerland
Col de la Faucille
River Ain
Crêt de la Neige
GR5
To Nantua
Geneva
JURA

old town. **Camping** is at Plage de Chalezuele, 5km out on the Belfort road. To reach the centre from the station, follow av du Maréchal-Foch down to the river and keep along the bank to the first or second bridge. The **SI** is by the second bridge. On the other side **rue de la République** leads to the central **place du 8-Septembre** in front of the sixteenth-century Hôtel de Ville. **Gare routière** is on rue Proudhon off rue de la République.

The principal street is **Grande Rue**, on the line of the old Roman road, and overlooked by a craggy hill above the river, capped by another of Vauban's prodigious citadels. At its top end (the livelier part with shops and cafés) there is an excellent **Beaux-Arts museum** (9.30am–noon and 2–6pm; closed Tues.) with two magnificent Bonnards, other good representative nineteenth- and twentieth-century works, and a wonderful clock collection. Midway down, the **Palais Granvelle**, a fine sixteenth-century mansion houses a local history museum – not very illuminating. Continuing up you pass place Victor-Hugo (he was born at no. 140) and come to the **Porte Noire**, a second-century Roman triumphal arch spanning the street and partially embedded in the adjoining houses. In the shady little **square archéologique** beside it are the remains of a *nymphaeum*, a small reservoir of water fed by an aqueduct. Beyond the Porte is the eighteenth-century cathedral of **St-Jean**, boring and pompous.

The **Citadelle** (9am–6.30pm in summer; 5.30pm in winter) is a steep, fifteen-minute climb from here, with a crow's nest view of the town and the noose-like bend in the river that contains it. Within, it houses three highly worthwhile museums (all 9.15am–6pm in summer; 9.30am–5.15pm in winter): the **Musée Agraire** with marvellous old farming implements; the **Folklore Comtois**, with pottery, furniture, etc; but – best of all – the **Musée de la Résistance et de la Déportation**, a superb aid to understanding the post-war French political consciousness, harrowing. Outside the museum building, four stakes mark the spot where the Germans shot local *résistants*. Inside, the first rooms document the rise of Nazism and French fascism through photographs and exhibits, including a bar of soap stamped *RIF* – pure Jew fat. Moving on to the Vichy government, there is a telegram of encouragement sent by Marshall Pétain to the French troops of the Legion of Volunteers against Bolshevism, fighting alongside the Germans on the eastern front. Finally, as counterbalance much is made of General Leclerc's vow at Koufra in the Libyan desert, whose capture in January 1941 was the first entirely French victory of the war: 'We will not stop until the French flag flies once more over Metz and Strasbourg', a vow which he kept, when he entered the latter city at the head of a division in November 1944.

Dôle

Halfway between Dijon and Besançon on the edge of the flat and fertile valley of the Saône, **DOLE** is quiet and provincial. Grey stone houses with barred ground floor windows stand on narrow streets around its vast and rather dull church. The Rhône–Rhine canal washes the feet of the town, and along its bank below the church runs the narrow **rue Pasteur** where the great Louis was born, son of a tanner, whose house, like his workmates', backs on to a pretty waterside walkway leading to a semi-island. Whatever happens in Dôle, – eating, shopping, and other things – happens between **Grande Rue** leading up from the bridge and **place Grévy** (**SI** at no. 6). It's a place to stay overnight, or rest: attractive, but in a very subdued way.

The cheapest rooms are at the **youth hostel**, in fact a mixed *foyer*, on place St-Jean XXIII (☎84.82.0036). There are some reasonable **hotels** too: the *Moderne* opposite the **gare SNCF** at 40 av Aristide-Briand (☎84.72.27.04), *Le Grand Cerf* (☎84.72.11.68; with restaurant) at 6 rue Arney near place Grévy, and *Auberge du Père Guy* across the river on av Maréchal-Juin (no. 40; ☎87.72.40.32; with restaurant). Apart from pizzerias and crêperies, you should try the station's *Buffet de la Gare*, which has a good local reputation.

Gare routière is next to the train station.

Ornans and the Loue valley

ORNANS, 25km southeast of Besançon on D67, is the archetypal picturesque village. The Loue valley here is an abrupt trench, and Ornans lies in the bottom with the river actually washing the foundations of its ancient balconied houses. The painter and *communard* Gustave Courbet was born here and his house is now a museum (daily April–Nov. 10am–noon and 2–6pm; wintertime, closed Tues.).

It's only about 20km from the village to the source of the Loue, where the river issues from an enormous rock mouth beneath a tiered cliff, in winter entirely fringed with icicles. The best way would be by **GR595** up the valley from Ornans. By road you have to go around by OUHANS (occasional buses from Pontarlier) on D41 and just before the village take a lane down to the right, then walk a short distance.

There is **camping** in Ornans, VUILLAFANS, LODS, MOUTHIER and **gîtes d'étapes** in all except Lods.

Belfort and up the Doubs

Sitting in the gap between the bottom of the Vosges and the top of the Jura mountains – the one natural chink in France's eastern geological armour, and therefore the obvious route for invaders (usually the Germans) – **BELFORT** is assured of a place in French hearts for its deeds of military daring. Its name is particularly linked with the 1870 Prussian War, when its long resistance to siege spared it the humiliating annexation to Germany suffered by neighbouring Alsace and Lorraine. And its CO, Colonel Denfert-Rochereau, earned himself the honour of numerous street names as well as a Parisian métro station.

There are, however, few other reasons to give it much attention, though the train connections are good. Apart from that, it's a nondescript town, surrounded by heavy industry. If you are interested, the massive red **Vauban fortress** on the heights above can be visited (May–Sept. 9am–noon and 2–7pm; otherwise, 10am–noon and 2–5pm; closed Tues.). The gigantic red sandstone lion on the way up commemorates the 1870 siege. The **SI** is on place Dr-Corbis by the river, as is the **gare routière**; the **gare SNCF** is at the end of Faubourg de France.

But before you take to the hills, there is one trip worth undertaking: to **RONCHAMP**, **La Chapelle Notre-Dame-du-Haut**, one of Le Corbusier's enduring masterpieces. Twenty kilometres west on N19, with two trains and two buses a day from Belfort, it stands above the village on the top of a wooded hill, outrider of the Vosges. In leafless winter – I was lucky to see it in snow – it stood white and light-reflecting, visible from miles away, with its aerodynamic tower and wave-curved roof cutting into the black weather behind. All in concrete: **inside**, the rough-textured walls are pierced with unequal embrasures, several closed by patterns of primary glass, whose reds, blues, and yellows stain the dipping floor. Simplicity itself, with pared down crucifix and steel altar rail, it's highly atmospheric. Ronchamp reportedly now has a **mining museum** (May–Sept. 3–6pm).

If it's getting late and you're worried about a **place to stay**, hostellers can take another twenty-minute train ride to VESOUL, where the **youth hostel** is at 1 rue Paul-Petitclerc. Otherwise, you'll have to beat a retreat to Belfort, where there are cheap **hotels** by the station and on Faubourg de France.

Up the Doubs

The Doubs runs a course like a hairpin. It joins the Saône near Chalon and rises at MOUTHE near PONTARLIER, pinching the Juras in between. **AUDINCOURT**, south of Belfort, is where it doubles back on itself, the town where Peugeot bikes are made and the modern church of the Sacré-Coeur has windows and a tapestry by **Fernand Léger**.

From here, southwards and upstream, D437 follows the river, winding and climbing steadily between steep wooded banks, to **ST-HIPPOLYTE**, where the river loops into Switzerland before turning south again to mark the frontier. Without a car you'd have to hitch all this – manageable, but slow. But it's beautiful country. Above St-Hippolyte the land levels out into a wide **plateau** around 800–900m altitude, with grassy cow pastures encompassed by fir-clad ridges and dotted with broad-roofed farms and barns.

East of the main road, a network of lanes cross the plateau before corkscrewing down into the deep trench of the Doubs, through the villages of **FESSEVILLERS, DAMPRICHARD** and **CHARQUEMONT**, some continuing into Switzerland. Once on to the plateau, **biking** would be easy. Alternatively, a lovely stretch of **GR5** passes through St-Hippolyte and follows the riverbank up to the plunging waterfall of the **Saut du Doubs** outside **VILLERS-LE-LAC**, near MORTEAU (buses to MAICHE and TREVILLERS on the plateau). To reach the fall from Villers, it's a 4km walk from the last houses above the north end of the lake along a track through the woods.

For **accommodation** in the area, there are **hotels** in the bigger villages, but their prices are at least fifty percent higher than places less dependent on seasonal tourism. A well-heated, cosy shelter when the icicles hang from the eaves is *Hôtel de la Poste* opposite the church in Charquemont (☎81.44.00.20), with an unpretentious and good restaurant.

There are, however, numerous cheaper, if more primitive, alternatives. There are **campsites** in St-Hippolyte (May–Sept.), Maîche, Goumois (Point Accueil Jeunes), Le Russey, and Villers-le-Lac (April–Oct.); **gîtes** (or similar) in Maîche (☎81.64.12.58), Trévillers (☎81.44.43.73), Fessevillers (☎81.44.43.07), Damprichard (Chalet du Ski Club; ☎81.44.23.10), Villers-le-Lac (*La Petite Ferme*, rte de Morteau; ☎81.68.08.33; and the more expensive CAF-run *Les Tavaillons* at Le Chauffaud; ☎81.68.12.55), and Morteau (rue des Moulinots; ☎81.67.48.72).

Pontarlier

Thirty kilometres southwest of Morteau lies **PONTARLIER**, one of the bigger Jura towns, not very interesting except as a base and transit point. There are trains and buses to Besançon, trains to FRASNE to pick up the TGV from VALLORBE and Lausanne to Dijon and Paris, and local buses to **Mouthe**, where the Doubs emerges from an underground cavern, and to **Lac St-Point**, where you can pick up GR5 again to make the ascent of **Mont d'Or** overlooking Lake Geneva and the Alps.

There's a **youth hostel** (2 rue Jouffroy, near the **gare SNCF**; ☎81.39.06.57) and two **gîtes** (*Le Gounefay*, rte du Grand-Taureau; ☎81.39.05.99; and the Chalet-Refuge du Larmont; ☎81.46.44.03). Also close to the station are two or three cheap **hotels**; try the *Hôtel de France* at 8 rue de la Gare. The **gare routière** is nearby; the **SI** is in the Hôtel de Ville on the main street, rue de la République, along with places to **eat** (try *Brasserie de la Poste*). There is **camping** at *Les Gentianes*, av Paul-Robbe.

The road to Geneva

As elsewhere in the Jura, it's scenery rather than special places that enlivens the route to Geneva – mostly the old N5 from Dijon. Most of the journey can be covered by train from Besançon. As far as POLIGNY, where you join up with N5, you can travel direct on the Besançon–Lons–Lyon line, but for places beyond Poligny you have to change at MOUCHARD.

SALINS-LES-BAINS, 8km east of Mouchard, is worth a detour for industrial archaeology fans. Confined in the bottom of a narrow valley, guarded by two lofty forts, Salins has been a salt-mining town for most of the last thousand years, and the **salt works** with its ancient machinery is the town's only real attraction (9am–noon and 2–6pm). For any further information, the **SI** is next to the eighteenth-century Hôtel de Ville on the central place des Alliés. Accommodation options include **camping** , available from mid-June to mid-September, av Général-de-Gaulle; a **gîte d'étape** in Hameau de Baud (☎81.53.69.44); and **Point Acceuil Jeunes** (camping), on rte de Genève (☎84/37.90.98). More interesting from the architectural-historical point of view are the salt works at **ARC-ET-SENANS** 7km the other side of Mouchard; they were to have been the centrepiece of a utopian model city dreamed up by the revolutionary architect Ledoux (May–Sept., 9am–7pm; rest of year 9am– noon and 2–5pm).

ARBOIS, a dozen kilometres to the south and on the railway, is prettier and gentler, the centre of Jura wine-making. The **SI** (in the Hôtel de Ville by the river) will direct you to various *caves* for *dégustation*. The most distinctive local wines are the 'yellow' *Château-Chalon*, with a much stronger aftertaste than most wines, and the powerful but scarce *vin de paille*, so called because it's made from grapes dried on beds of straw. The town was also the principal boyhood home of **Louis Pasteur** and his house on av Pasteur is open to the public (April–Oct. 9 or 10am–noon and 2–6pm; closed Tues.). There is **camping** from June to September, on av Général-Leclerc.

Through CHAMPAGNOLE (train; **camping** on rue Georges-Vallerey June–Sept. 15; *Accueil Jeunes*, Base de la Roche-sur-Ain; ☎84.52.07.76), on the edge of the Forêt de la Joux and a remote upland plateau (difficult hitching), and on south about 20km through progressively wilder country, you reach **ST-LAURENT** (train; **camping** June–Sept./Nov.–April). A short distance west on N78 brings you to the hamlet of **ILAY**, where a 3½km path leads down through the woods to a spectacular series of waterfalls, the **Cascades du Hérisson**. Touristy in summer, you can have it to yourself in spring, with the bonus of much more water and wild daffodils growing in the oak woods on the sides of the gorge. Don't try to stay in the simple-looking hotel in Ilay; it's astronomically expensive.

Next stop on the way to the frontier is **MOREZ**, watch and spectacle king – another claustrophobic town squeezed out along the bottom of a slit of a valley. The **SI** is in central place Jaurès, with the **gare routière**, where buses leave for ST-CLAUDE and LES ROUSSES-LA CURE. From here there are trains down to NYON on Lake Geneva and on to GENEVA itself. It's not a place to linger, and neither is St-Claude, though the country in between is wonderful.

ST-CLAUDE, squeezed even more claustrophobically by even higher mountains than Morez, is scruffy and industrial: it makes pipes (the smokers' kind). Should you find yourself there, the *Hôtel La Poyat* at 7 rue de la Poyat off the main rue du Pré is a better bet than the dreary *Hôtel Jura* opposite the **gare SNCF**. **Camping** is at Le Martinet, 3km from town off the Col de la Faucille road. For **eating**, *Le Bayard* in the central place du Pré is convenient, wholesome and inexpensive. You could also try *Le P'tit Machon* on rue Voltaire behind, if it's still functioning.

Towards Geneva

What gives purpose to the rest of the route on from Morez is the superb country, with the road running close to the crest of the great fir-clad ridge that contains Lake Geneva on the west side, crossing it at the 1320m **Col de la Faucille**. **LES ROUSSES**, the first place you come to, exists purely for skiing, downhill and, especially, cross-country, but just before it a lane to the right goes down to a very attractive **youth hostel** at BIEF DE LA CHAILLE (2km), in an old red-shuttered farmhouse by a stream (Dec. to mid-April, mid-June to mid-Sept.; ☎84.60.02.80; phone in advance). There's also a **gîte d'étape** at Prémanon nearby (mid-Dec.–April, July–Aug.; ☎84.60.54.82), since **GR9** passes through, beginning a magnificent section all along the crest of the ridge to the Col de la Faucille and beyond.

If it's clear, the **view** is unbelievably dramatic, from the Col or GR, with the whole range of the western Alps stretched out before you, dominated by Mont Blanc, with the steely, cusp-shaped Lake Geneva or Lac Léman laid at your feet. Of course, if it's not clear, after all that hitching or walking, you're going to be disappointed. But it is **downhill** all the way to **GENEVA** and a couple of revitalising bars of Swiss chocolate.

travel details

Trains

From Verdun 1 to 4 trains daily to Paris-Est (3 hr.), changing at Chalons-sur-Marne (1 hr. 20 min.); 1 to 3 trains to Metz (1¼hr.), changing at Conflans (½ hr.).

From Metz 2 to Longuyon (1½ hr.); 3 or 4 to Paris-Est (3 hr.); 2 or 3 to Strasbourg (2½ hr.) – some go on to Colmar and Mulhouse: several to Nancy (1¼hr.).

From Nancy frequent service to Paris-Est (3½ hr.); several to Lunéville (40 min.); 2 or 3 to Saverne (1 hr.); 2 to Strasbourg (1 hr. 20 min.).

From Strasbourg frequent to Paris-Est (4 hr.); 1 to 3 to Wissembourg (1 hr.); several to Basel (1½–2 hr.), via Sélestat (20 min.), Colmar (50 min.) and Mulhouse (1 hr. 20 min.) – not all stop at Sélestat and Colmar.

From Mulhouse several to Belfort (30–45 min.).

From Belfort 2 to Epinal (1½ hr.) and on to Paris-Est (5¼hr.); 2 to Ronchamp (15 min.).

From Besançon several to Belfort (1–1½hr.); 5 to 6 to Paris-Lyon (2½ hr.) – more frequent if you change at Dijon (1 hr.); several to Dôle (½ hr.); 4 or 5 to Bourg-en-Bresse (2½ hr.); several to Lons (1–1½ hr.), some via Mouchard (½ hr.), Arbois (¾ hr.), Poligny (1 hr. 5 min.); 4 to St-Claude (2½–3 hr.), via Champagnole (1 hr. 40–1½ hr.), St-Laurent (1 hr. 40–2 hr.), Morez (2 hr. 10–2½ hr.); 3 to Morteau (1–1¾hr.).

From Dôle several to Dijon (½ hr.) and Paris-Lyon (4 hr.); 3 to Pontarlier (1 hr. 20 min.).

From St-Claude 4 or 5 to Bourg (1 hr. 40 min.–2 hr.), connecting with TGV to Paris.

Buses

From Colmar regularly to Mulhouse (1 hr.), Sélestat (1 hr.) and to destinations in Germany.

From Belfort 1 daily to Ronchamp (¾hr.).

From Besançon 3 or 4 to Ornans and Pontarlier (1½ hr.); occasional to Salins (1 hr.).

From Pontarlier regular to Frasne (SNCF); infrequent to Vallorbe, Mouthe, Ouhans.

From Morteau to Besançon, Pontarlier, Villers-le-Lac.

From Morez 3 weekly to St-Claude (1 hr.); 1 most days to Lons (1¾ hr.); to Les Rousses Thurs. and Fri.

From St-Claude 1 to Lyon (3 hr. 40 min.).

CHAPTER THIRTEEN

THE ALPS

Rousseau wrote in his *Confessions,* 'I need torrents, rocks, pine trees, dark forests, mountains, rugged paths to go up and down, precipices at my elbow to give me a good fright'. I would add wild flowers – best seen in the first half of July – but these are certainly the principal joys of **the Alps**. The best, though not the only, way to appreciate them is on foot.

There are four national or **regional parks** in the area covered by this chapter: Vanoise, Ecrins, Queyras and Vercors, all with round-the-park trails, requiring one to two weeks' walking. The **Tour of Mont Blanc** path is of similar length. Then there are two transalpine routes: the **Grande Traversée des Alpes**, which crosses all the major massifs from St-Gingolph on Lake Geneva to Nice, and **Le Balcon des Alpes**, a gentler, village-to-village itinerary through the western foothills.

All these **routes** are clearly marked, equipped with refuge huts and *gîtes d'étape*, and described in *Topo-guides*. The *CIMES* office in Grenoble (see below) will provide detailed information on all GR paths. In addition, local tourist offices often produce detailed maps of walks in their own areas (Chamonix and Sixt, for example). You should not however, undertake any **high-level, long-distance hikes** unless you are an experienced hillwalker. If you are not, and like the sound of some of these trails, first, before making any plans, or simply limit your sights to more **local targets**. You can find plenty of day-walks to do from a base in or close to any of the parks; and there are some satisfying road routes, too. A tent will give you greatest flexibility, since hotels are seasonal and their prices inflated. The **Vercors, Chartreuse, Aravis** (east of Annecy), **Faucigny** and **Chablais** (Morzine, Sixt) areas are the gentlest, and quietest, introductions.

The Alps get very crowded in season. Mountain holidays are in vogue, and walking is big business. Unfortunately, you are more or less obliged to go in **season** if you want to walk; apart from unreliable weather, anywhere above 2000m will be snowbound until the beginning of July. The Chamonix-Mont Blanc area is far the worst for overcrowding – best avoided, unless you are going to get out on the mountain where other people cannot go. The **Parc du Queyras** is perhaps the least touristy, and sunniest of the high parks. Together with parts of **Haute Tarentaise** it still has a few 'genuine' Alpine villages – a species that has become more or less extinct since the Alps have been turned into one great resort.

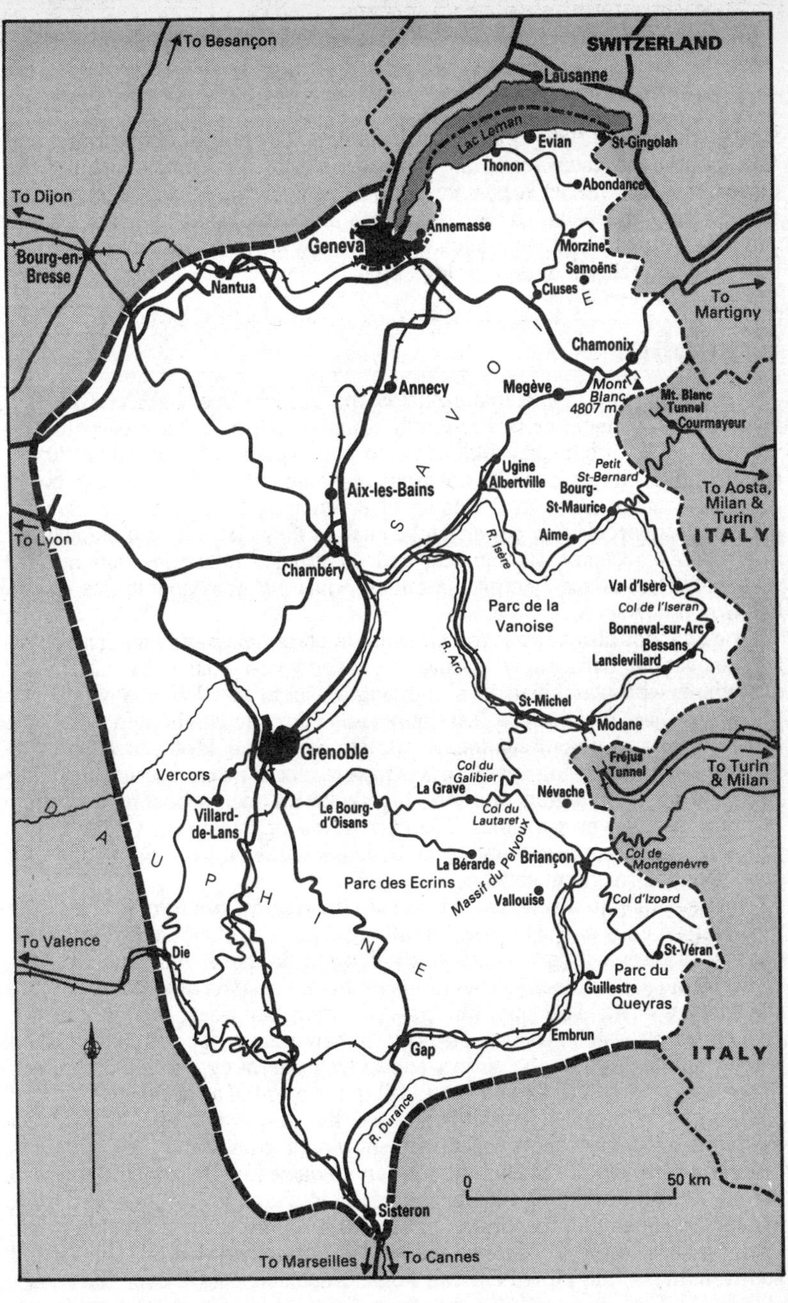
To Besançon
SWITZERLAND
Lausanne
Lac Leman
Evian
St-Gingolah
Thonon
Abondance
To Dijon
Geneva
Annemasse
Bourg-en-Bresse
Nantua
Morzine
Samoëns
Cluses
To Martigny
Chamonix
Mont Blanc 4807 m
Mt. Blanc Tunnel
Courmayeur
Annecy
Megève
S A V O I E
Ugine
Albertville
Petit St-Bernard
Bourg-St-Maurice
To Aosta, Milan & Turin
Aix-les-Bains
To Lyon
Aime
ITALY
R. Isère
Chambéry
Val d'Isère
Col de l'Iseran
Parc de la Vanoise
Bonneval-sur-Arc
Bessans
Lanslevillard
R. Arc
St-Michel
Modane
Grenoble
Fréjus Tunnel
To Turin & Milan
Vercors
Col du Galibier
La Grave
Névache
Villard-de-Lans
Le Bourg-d'Oisans
Col du Lautaret
La Bérarde
Briançon
Col de Montgenèvre
Massif du Pelvoux
Parc des Ecrins
Vallouise
Col d'Izoard
D A U P H I N E
To Valence
Die
St-Véran
Parc du Queyras
Guillestre
Embrun
Gap
ITALY
R. Durance
0
50 km
Sisteron
To Marseilles
To Cannes

THE FOOTHILL TOWNS AND VERCORS MASSIF

Strung in a line along their western edge, **Grenoble, Chambéry** and **Annecy** are the gateways to the highest parts of the French Alps. Of the three Grenoble, with its large university, is the liveliest, but all are interesting enough for a short stay. (There is a fourth town, Aix-les-Bains, but it's a dull and elderly spa.) You can't really avoid them anyway, as nearly all Alpine traffic – road and rail – is routed through them.

Grenoble

The economic and intellectual capital of the French Alps, **GRENOBLE** is a lively, thriving, modern city, beautifully situated on the Drac and Isère Rivers, surrounded by mountains and home to a university of more than 30,000 students. The city's prosperity was originally founded on glove-making, but in the nineteenth century its economy diversified to include mining, cement, papermills, hydroelectric power (white coal, as they called it) and metallurgy. Today, it is a centre of chemical and electronics industries and nuclear research. The Atomic Energy Commission has big new laboratories on the banks of the Drac.

Grenoble has also been at the forefront of social, environmental and cultural innovation, particularly during the twenty-year mayoralty of Hubert Dubedout, who was killed in a climbing accident in 1986. His Villeneuve housing project (between av Jean-Jaurès and cours de la Libération), though rather tatty and off-putting today, started out as an idealistic attempt to provide integrated living space for a complete mix of social classes, including Arab and other immigrant workers, together with open schooling and other community-based programmes. The current mayor, previously Chirac's environment minister, revived one of Dubedout's ideas in the construction of a new, pollution-free tram network.

The best thing to do on arrival is to take the **téléférique** from the riverside quai Stéphane-Jay to **Fort de la Bastille** on the steep slopes above the north bank of the Isère. It may be a touristy thing to do, but if you snub all *téléfériques* in the Alps – there are hundreds of them – you will miss out on a lot of spectacular views. This one, like most of them, is pricey, though you can economise by walking down. The ride is hair-raising, for you are whisked steeply and swiftly into the air in a sort of transparent egg, which allows you to see very clearly how far you would fall in the event of an accident.

Though the fort itself is of little interest, the view is fantastic. At your feet the Isère, milky-grey and swollen with snow-melt tears at the piles of the old bridges which join the St-Laurent quarter, colonised by Italian immigrants in the nineteenth century, to the nucleus of the medieval town, whose red roofs cluster tightly around the church of St-André. To the east, snowfields gleam in the gullies of the Belledonne massif (2978m). Southeast is Taillefer and south-southeast the dip where the Route Napoléon passes over the moun-

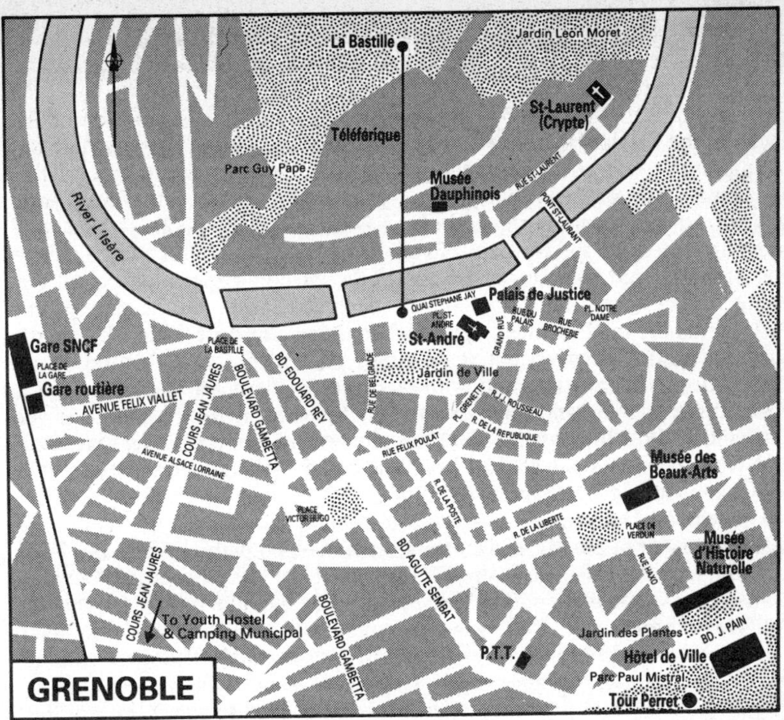

tains to Sisteron and the Mediterranean. This is the road Napoléon took after his escape from Elba in March 1815 on his way to rally his forces for the campaign that led to his final defeat at Waterloo. To the west are the steep white cliffs of the Vercors massif; the highest peak, dominating the city, is Moucherotte (1901m). The jagged peaks at your back are the outworks of the Chartreuse massif. Northeast on a clear day you can see the white peaks of Mont Blanc up the deep glacial valley of the Isère, known as La Grésivaudan. It was in this valley that the first French hydroelectric project went into action in 1869.

Upstream from the *téléférique* station is the sixteenth-century **Palais de Justice** (open to the public) with **place St-André** and the church of St-André behind. Built in the thirteenth century and heavily restored, the church is of little architectural interest, but the narrow streets leading back towards places Grenette, Vaucanson and Verdun take you through the liveliest and most colourful quarter of the city, the focus of life for shoppers and strollers alike. **Place Grenette** is the favourite resort of café loungers.

Nearby at 14 rue J-J-Rousseau is a small **museum** dedicated to the French Resistance (3–6pm, Mon. and Wed.; 3–7pm Sat.), who were particularly active in the Vercors massif. Stendhal was born in the house, though the city's museum of Stendhaliana is itself in a corner of the public gardens just behind the St-André church. Also close to place Grenette, at 14 rue de la République, are the offices of the **SI** and **CIMES**, the walkers' organisation for the Alpine region.

If you go to the **Musée des Beaux Arts** (1–7pm; closed Tues. and holidays) on the handsome nineteenth-century place de Verdun – worthwhile for its impressive collection of contemporary and representative works by the big names in twentieth-century art – you should continue to **Parc Paul Mistral**. On the corner at the end of rue Haxo is a pretty public garden with some fine trees and the **Natural History Museum**, which has a huge collection of fossils and rocks, animals and birds, including specimens of all the Alpine birds of prey, unfortunately very badly displayed. On the edge of the park stands the modern steel, glass and concrete **Hôtel de Ville**: all straight lines and square corners, but refreshingly contemporary. Its central courtyard and interior are adorned with works of modern art and in the park behind is an earlier and more frivolous structure, an 87m concrete tower designed in 1925 by Perret, one of the pioneers of modern French architecture. The concrete looks shabby now. You could not call it attractive, but it is bold and unapologetically modern.

The **Musée Dauphinois** (9–noon and 2–6pm; closed Tues.), occupies the former convent of Ste-Marie-d'en-Haut, up a cobbled path opposite the Isère footbridge by the Palais de Justice. Imaginatively laid out, it is largely devoted to the history, arts and crafts of the province of Dauphiné (unlike neighbouring Savoie, which with Nice was only relinquished by the Italians in 1860, Dauphiné has been French since the fourteenth century). There are exhibits on the life of the mountain people, *'les gens de là-haut'*, the people from up there, who like most poor mountaineers were obliged to travel the world as peddlers and knife-grinders. Many, too, were involved in smuggling, and there is a fascinating collection of body-hugging flasks used for contraband liquor. The most unusual section is the so-called *Roman des Grenoblois*, the story of the people of Grenoble told in an excellent audio-visual presentation through the lives of various members of a representative selection of families, ranging from immigrant workers to wealthy industrialists. France's first trade union was established in Grenoble in 1803 by the glove-makers.

There are numerous **hotels** in the railway station area: *Suisse et Bordeaux* (☎76.47.55.87) on the corner of av Viallet; *l'Université*, on rue Denfert-Rochereau; *Colbert* (☎76.46.46.65) at 1 rue Colbert. The *Bellevue* (☎76.46.39.64) has a better location, as its name suggests, on the corner of quai Stéphane-Jay and rue Belgrade near the *téléférique*, though the nicest of the cheapies I investigated was *Hôtel de la Poste* (☎76.46.67.25) at 25 rue de la Poste off place Vaucanson – the entrance is grubby and wicked-looking, but the hotel itself is spotless and friendly. Alternatively, there's a modern **youth hostel** (☎76.09.33.52; excellent canteen) at ECHIROLLES, a ten-minute bus ride south (#8 from cours Jean-Jaurès) to stop *La Quinzaine*, by a large Casino supermarket. The supermarket has an excellent *charcuterie* with take-out dishes and salads, and a cafeteria serving good, reasonably-priced meals. The hostel is 150m down av Grésivaudan, well placed if you are hitching south: just keep on down cours Jean-Jaurès. There is a large **Camping**

municipal between rue Albert Reynier and av Beaumarchais, which the #8 bus runs past on its way to the hostel. Beware, however, that buses stop running early in Grenoble, around 8pm.

Other **practical details: Allostop** at rue Barginet; **Information Jeunesse**, 1 passage du Palais-de-Justice; **bike rental** from M. Strippoli, 62 quai Perrière or M. Rollo, 1 av Jeanne d'Arc; **launderettes** at 65 place St-Bruno (on the way to Pont du Drac) and 27 av Jean-Perrot near the park. **Gare routière** is next door to **gare SNCF**. The main **PTT/Poste Restante** is miles away near the park, on bd Lyautey. **Club Alpin Français** at 32 av F-Viallet. **CIMES** (Maison du Tourisme, 14 rue de la République, 38027 Grenoble-Cedex) is *the* place for hiking information.

Around Grenoble: the Vercors and Chartreuse massifs

Both massifs, but particularly Vercors, are very close to Grenoble. They are relatively gentle too, so if you're starting your Alpine ventures here, you can use them to break your feet in. The Grenoble CIMES office publishes route descriptions with extracts from the IGN 1:25,000 map.

The Vercors massif

Simplest and most accessible of the CIMES walks is no. 4: a **4 hour round trip to St-Nizier**, just over the rim of the Vercors mountains. Start by taking bus #5 from place Victor-Hugo and get off in SEYSSINET village by the school. For most of the way you follow **GR9** with its red and white waymarks. The path starts about 200m uphill from the school on the right. It is not difficult, but the path does cross D106 a few times, and the continuation is not always obvious after the road sections, so you should get the leaflet. It is about 2½ hours to St-Nizier (return the same way) – a beautiful path through thick woods with long views back over Grenoble to the mountains beyond. The lovely purplish Martagon lily blooms in the woods in early July. ST-NIZIER has **hotels** and a small **campsite**. It is a further 3½hours (there and back) to the top of **Moucherotte** on GR91.

Two other good, though more strenuous, walks are described in leaflets 6 and 11. **6** is **from Villard-de-Lans** in the Vercors massif down to CLAIX, not far from Grenoble – a descent of 1700m: about 7 hours. **11** follows a long (9 hr.) and a shorter (6½ hr.) **circuit of Mont Aiguille**, starting from the railway station in Clelles (1 hr. by train south of Grenoble). Both are highly recommended, and by all accounts rightly so, by the CIMES office.

The best way to explore the Vercors would be to **base yourself**, say, in VILLARD-DE-LANS (**camping** and **hotels**) and backpack around.

If you just want **to travel through** – it is very pretty and undeveloped – you will have to hitch, which is perfectly possible. I got from Grenoble down the length of the plateau to Die and back to Grenoble over the Col de Grimone in a day. To get started, take the #11/14 trolley just off place Victor-Hugo to Sassenage Air Liquide and get off at *La Rollandière,* one stop before the terminus. Start hitching on the road to LANS-EN-VERCORS more or less opposite the stop. The road winds up through a steep wooded gorge to come out in a wide valley full of hay meadows towards LANS and VILLARD. Turn right at Villard on the Pont-en-Royans road into the **Gorges de la Bourne**. The gorge becomes rapidly deeper and narrower with the road cut right in under the rocks, the river running far below, with tree-hung cliffs almost shutting out the sky above. Take a left fork here and you climb up to a lovely green valley before descending to ST-MARTIN and LA CHAPELLE (*gîtes d'étape, Nouvel Hôtel, Hôtel des Sports*); thence the road climbs again to the wide dry **plateau of Vassieux** bordered to the east by a rocky ridge rising from thick pine forest and to the west by low hills covered with scrubby vegetation.

It was here around the village of **Vassieux** that the fighters of the Vercors *maquis* suffered a bloody and bitter defeat at the hands of the SS in July 1944. From 1942–3 they had been gradually turning the Vercors into a Resistance stronghold, to the annoyance of the Germans who finally, in June 1944, decided to wipe them out. They encircled and attacked the *maquisards* with vastly superior forces and parachuted an SS division on to Vassieux. The French appealed in vain for Allied support and were very bitter about the lack of response. The Germans took vicious reprisals, and despite their attempts to disperse into the woods, 700 *maquisards* and civilians were killed and several villages razed. The Germans' most ferocious act was to murder the wounded, along with their nurses and doctors, in **Grotte de la Liure**, a cave off the La Chapelle-Col de Rousset road, now a sort of national shrine.

Vassieux, a dull little village now rebuilt (*gîte d'étape*: Mme Chapays), has a memorial cemetery and small **museum** (9–6pm, April 1–Nov. 1; free) with documents, photos and other memorabilia to do with the *maquis* and the battle. In the field outside are the remains of two gliders used by the German paratroops.

From Vassieux, I followed the **Col de Rousset** road through woods of pine and fir and down the steep twisting descent to **DIE**, with terrific views of the white crags and pinnacles of the southeast end of the massif. Die (**Camping municipal** and **hotels**) is a pretty and hot little place, with sections of its third-century ramparts still visible to the northeast: as you go out of town on the Gap road there is a Roman triumphal arch built into the medieval city walls on the left. Its most alluring feature, though, is the bubbly white wine it produces, *Clairette de Die*.

South along the river Drôme you come to the **Pont de Quart** and fork left for Châtillon: not a bad place to wait on a hot day, for you can swim in the river below the bridge. **Châtillon** is a lovely village in a narrowing valley bottom surrounded by apple and peach orchards, vineyards, walnut trees and fields of lavender (two **hotels** and a **Camping municipal**). From here on, the road enters the narrow sunless trench of the **Gorges des Gas**, winding up between sheer rock walls to **Grimone**, a mountain hamlet on the flanks of a grassy valley with fir trees darkening the higher slopes. The Col de Grimone is visible above the village. If you have to walk it, a path cuts across

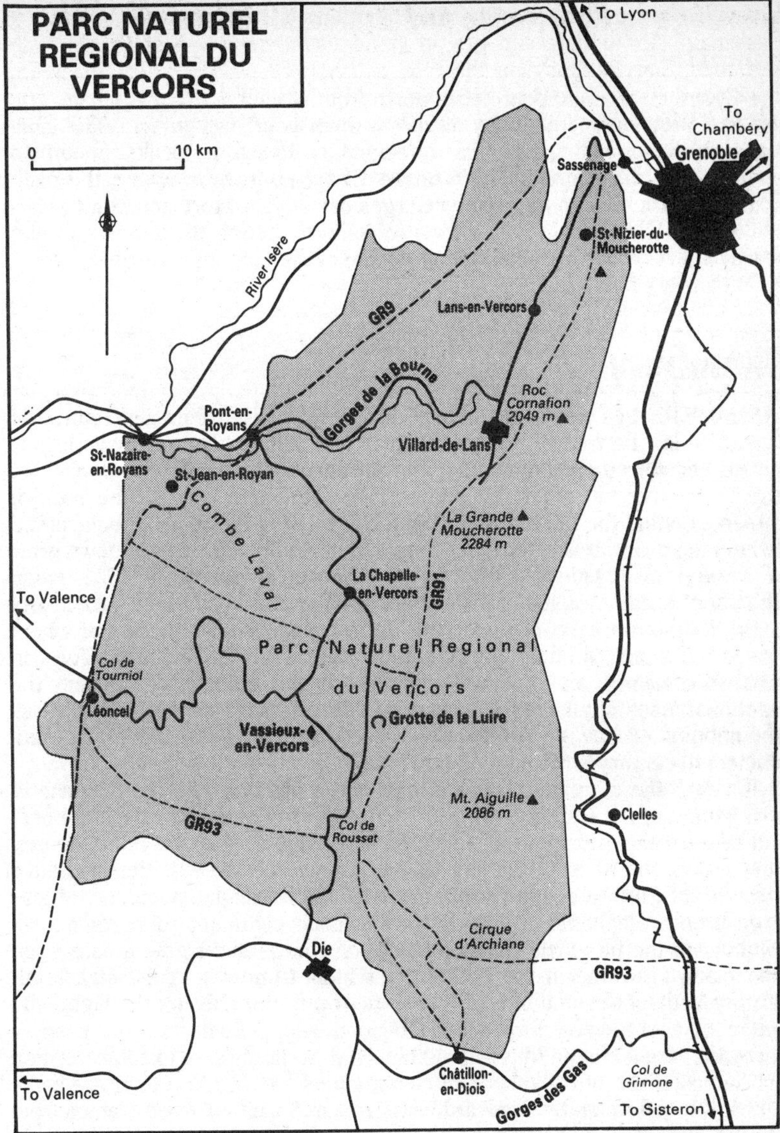

the valley directly to the col. From the col it must be about 7km down to the main Grenoble road, a tarmac trudge alleviated by the view eastwards to the mountains. If you are fed up with hitching you can get the train back to Grenoble.

Massif de la Chartreuse and Grande Chartreuse Monastery

The **Chartreuse massif** stretches north from Grenoble towards Chambéry, and like Vercors it is not easy to visit without your own vehicle. The landscape, however, is spectacular: precipitous limestone peaks, mountain pastures and thick forest. The **Grande Chartreuse monastery**, the main local landmark, lies up the narrow Gorges des Guiers Mort, southeast of ST-LAURENT-DU-PORT. It is not open to visitors, though there is a museum nearby at LA CORRERIE illustrating the life of the Carthusian order to which the monastery belongs.

Chambéry

CHAMBERY lies just south of Lac du Bourget in a valley separating the Massif de la Chartreuse from the Bauges mountains: historically, an important strategic position commanding the entrance to the big Alpine valleys that lead to the passes into Italy. The earliest settlement was on the rock of Lemenc, behind the railway station (the church of St-Pierre-de-Lemenc off bd de Lemenc has a sixth-century baptistery in its crypt). The present town grew up around the castle built by Count Thomas of Savoie in 1232, when Chambéry became capital of the ancient province, and flourished particularly in the fourteenth century under the three Amadeuses – the last of whom served ten years as anti-Pope. Although superseded as capital by Turin in 1563, it remained an important commercial and cultural centre and the emotional focus of all French Savoyards: 'the winter residence of almost all the nobility of Savoy', Arthur Young reported in 1789, before its mid-nineteenth-century incorporation into France.

As usual, the most interesting district is the **old city centre**. To reach it, turn left out of the station down rue Sommeiller to the crossroads at the end, and take another left into the tree-lined bd de la Colonne, where all the **city buses** stop; the **SI** is on the left. Half-way down the street is the splendidly extravagant **Fontaine des Eléphants**, with the heads and shoulders of four large bronze elephants projecting from a stone pediment supporting a tall column, on top of which stands a statue of Comte de Boigne, a native son who made a fortune in the French East India Company in the eighteenth century and spent some of it on his home town. Past this, on the right, and you're at the **Musée Savoisien** (10–noon and 2–6pm; closed Tues.), a Savoyard parallel to the Musée Dauphinois at Grenoble and, like it, recording the lost rural life of the mountain communities. On the first floor are some very lovely paintings by Savoyard primitives and painted wood statues from various churches in the region; up above, are tools, carts, hay-sledges, old photos, and some very fine furniture from a house in Bessans, including a fascinating kitchen range made of wood and lined with *lauzes* (slabs of schist). Well worth a visit.

Next to the museum, in the hot and enclosed little place Métropole, is the **Cathedral,** which has a handsome, though much restored, Flamboyant facade. The inside is painted in elaborate nineteenth-century *trompe-l'oeil*, imitating the twisting shapes and whorls of the Flamboyant style. During the Revolution it became the seat of the National Assembly of the Allobroges in a revolutionary attempt to revive pre-Roman tribal identity. A passage leads from the *place* to rue de la Croix-d'Or, with numerous restaurants, and to the right, the long rectangular **place St-Léger** with a fountain and cafés, hub of the city's social life (Rousseau and Mme de Warens lived at no. 54 in 1735). Street musicians and players perform here on summer evenings. Towards the further end of the *place*, the town's smartest street, **rue de Boigne**, leads back to the Elephant Fountain. Past this intersection, on the left, a narrow medieval lane, rue Basse-du-Château, brings you out beneath the elegant apse of the **Sainte-Chapelle**, the castle chapel (dating from the early fifteenth century).

The entrance to the Château itself (guided tours only, 10.30am and 2–5pm, June 15–Sept. 15; closed Sun. am) is on your left. I mistimed my visit and didn't get to see the inside. It is a massive and imposing structure, home of the Dukes of Savoie until they transferred to Turin, but I suspect the only part worth seeing is the Sainte Chapelle, whose lancet windows and star-vaulting look elegant and pleasing from photographs. It was built to house the Holy Shroud, that much-venerated and today highly controversial piece of linen brought back from the Crusades and reputed to be Christ's winding sheet. The Dukes took it with them to Turin where it still lies in the cathedral.

For **hotels**, try *du Château*, rue J-P Veyrat; *Home Savoyard*, 15 place St-Léger; *Perriat*, 20 place St-Léger; *Revard*, place de la Gare; or *Voyageurs*, 3 rue Doppet. The **Maison des Jeunes et de la Culture** at 311 Faubourg Montmélian (☎75.75.13.23) is another possibility. The nearest **campsites** are at BASSENS and ST-ALBAN: bus *ligne C*, direction Albertville, from the SI. **Bike hire**: *D Brouard*, 28 av de Turin. **Gare routière** is on place de la Gare (SNCF). **PTT** on av Général Leclerc, opposite the station.

Annecy

Sited at the edge of a turquoise lake, and bounded to the east by the eroded peaks of La Tournette (2351m) and to the west by the long wooded ridge of Le Semnoz (1699m), **ANNECY** is very much a transit point for hikers. It offers good access to the Mont Blanc area and on to Lake Geneva and the northern Prealps. Historically, it enjoyed a brief flurry of importance in the early sixteenth century, when Geneva opted for the Reformation and the fugitive Catholic bishop decamped here with a train of ecclesiastics and a prosperous, cultivated, bourgeois élite.

The most interesting core of the city lies at the foot of the castle mound. It is a warren of lanes, passages and arcaded houses below and between which flow branches of the **Canal du Thiou**, which drains the lake into the river Fier. The houses, canal-side railings and numerous restaurants and cafés are stacked with displays of geraniums and petunias. It is picture-book pretty and, inevitably, full of tourists.

If you are coming from the station, go straight ahead to rue Royale and turn left. Rue Royale becomes the arcaded rue Paquier, with the seventeenth-century **Hôtel de Sales** at no. 12, once a residence of the kings of Sardinia. Opposite the end of the street is the **Centre Bonlieu**, a modern shopping precinct which also houses the **SI**. Ask them, if you are having trouble finding a place to stay.

Beyond Bonlieu, the treelined avenue d'Albigny leads west past the lakeside lawns of the Champ de Mars, joined by a bridge to the shady public gardens at the back of the Hôtel de Ville. Opposite is the fifteenth-century chuch of **St-Maurice**, originally built for a Dominican convent. (Numerous Savoyard churches are dedicated to St-Maurice. He was the commander of a Theban legion sent to put down a rebellion in the late third century. Converted to Christianity, he and his soldiers refused to sacrifice to the pagan gods of Rome and were put to death for their pains.) Inside, the apse, with attractive Flamboyant windows, is badly distorted, the walls leaning outwards to an alarming degree; on the left of the choir is a fine fresco dated 1438, all in tones of grey.

Opposite the church door, rue Grenette leads into **rue Jean-Jacques Rousseau**. Just past the uninteresting Gothic cathedral where Rousseau sang as a chorister is an eighteenth-century bishop's palace, now the police commissariat, built on the site of the house where Mme de Warens, Rousseau's lover, lived. Converted from Protestantism, she was paid by the Catholic authorities to save other lost souls. The 16-year-old Rousseau, on the run from his miserable engraver's apprenticeship in Geneva, came to lodge with her on Palm Sunday 1728. She was 28. Their first meeting took place on the steps of the church, Rousseau recording 'in a moment I was hers, and

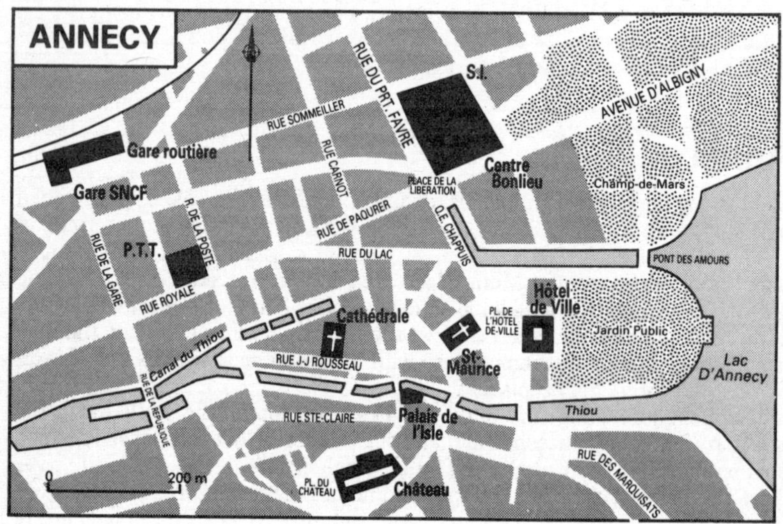

certain that a faith preached by such missionaries would not fail to lead to paradise . . .' His admirers have placed his bust in the courtyard of the commissariat. Continuing across the canal bridge, with a view of the grand old **Palais de l'Isle** (prison, mint, courtrooms in its time), you come to rue de l'Isle and **rue Ste-Claire**, the main street of the old town, with arcaded shops and houses. No. 18 is the Hôtel Favre, where in 1606 Antoine Favre, an eminent lawyer, and François de Sales founded the literary-intellectual Académie Florimontane 'because the Muses thrive in the mountains of Savoie'. At the end of the street is its original medieval gateway.

From rue de l'Isle the narrow Rampe du Château leads up to the **Castle**, former home of the Counts of Genevois and the Dukes of Nemours, a junior branch of the house of Savoy. There has been a castle on the site from the eleventh century. The Nemours, finding the old fortress too rough and unpolished for their taste, added living quarters in the sixteenth century, which now house the miscellaneous collections of the **Musée du Château** (10–noon and 2–6pm; closed Tues.): archeological finds from Boutae; Bronze and Iron Age metallurgy with comparative photos of similar still-surviving skills like scythe- and axe-making; Savoyard popular art, furniture and wood-carving, and, on the top floor, an excellent display illustrating the geology of the Alps.

Places to stay and other practicalities

The **youth hostel** (☎50.45.33.19) is a good 45-minute walk from the old town: cross the main canal bridge along rue des Marquisats, and turn right at the lights into av de Trésum, then left on bd de la Corniche, which loops up into the woods of Le Semnoz, becoming the Route de Semnoz; the hostel stands in a clearing by a small zoo (there is a shortcut through the woods but for the first time, at least, it is best to stick to the road). **Other good hostel-type accommodation** is available at: *Centre International de Séjour* on rue des Marquisats (☎50.45.08.80) by the lake (canteen); *Foyer d'Evire*, Montée de Novel, off rue des Martyres de la Déportation (bus #4 to Evire terminal); and, for women only, the *Maison de la Jeune Fille*, 1 av du Rhône (☎50.45.34.81). **Camping municipal** is off bd de la Corniche – turn right up a lane opposite Chemin du Tillier, it's round on the left past Hôtel du Belvédère. The best bet for **hotels** are *des Alpes* on rue de la Poste (☎50.45.04.56), *Nouvel* at 37 rue Vaugelas (☎.50.45.05.78) and *Rives du Lac* in rue des Marquisats.

As to **other practicalities**, there's **bike hire** from the gare SNCF and *Loca Sport* (37 av de Loverchy), and round-the-lake **boat trips**, at a reasonable price, from *Compagnie des Bateaux* by the mouth of the Thiou canal. The annual **Festival de la Vieille Ville** takes place in the first two weeks of July, with lots of music (pop, rock, classical), mostly free; a festival of **Italian cinema** at the end of September. You'll find a useful **launderette** in the *Nouvelles Galleries* shopping complex at 25 av du Parmelan; the **PTT** on rue de la Poste, near the stations (the gares routière and SNCF are side by side). The SI sells a 1:50,000 **map of the Annecy area** with **walking trails** marked. The best and longest hike is the **tour du Lac**, taking in Le Semnoz and La Tournette (path connects with GR96). There are also loops and shorter bits suitable for day walks.

THE NATIONAL PARKS

The trouble with designating an area as a **national park** is that it draws attention, i.e. loads of people, to it. These parks are beautiful and, luckily, the scale of the mountains is big enough to absorb considerable numbers of visitors. But you won't have the paths to yourself after about 10am in July and August – which are the only **times of year** when hiking is really practicable. As for **accommodation**, you can **camp** freely on the fringes of the parks, but once inside you are supposed to pitch a tent only in an emergency and move on after one night. **Gîtes** and **refuges** are probably the best solution – saves weight, too. Hotels are out – overpriced and overbooked.

For **guides**, there are the GR *Topo-guides* and CIMES' *La Grande Traversée des Alpes* in French; the Mountaineers/Cordée *100 Hikes in the Alps* and Cicerone Press's *GR5* by Colin Turner in English.

Access to **Vanoise** park is easiest from CHAMBERY (with frequent trains to MODANE). For **Queyras** and **Ecrins** it's best to set out from GRENOBLE: either by bus via LE BOURG-D'OISANS to BRIANCON (starting off point for the Ecrins), or by train via GAP to MONT-DAUPHIN (for Queyras) and on beyond to BRIANÇON. If you hitch – not hard if you look a hiker – you could follow any of these routes.

Parc Régional du Queyras

The **railway** from **GRENOBLE-GAP** seems an obvious approach to Queyras. It follows the **route Napoléon**, taken by the Emperor in 1815. It runs through the town of VIZILLE, where there's a vast château, meeting place in 1788 of the Estates of Grenoble, whose demand for liberty for all Frenchmen and the suspension of parliament is often thought of as the catalyst for the French Revolution. And then it veers off, climbing steeply, to the village of LAFFREY, where Napoléon, finding his way barred by troops from Grenoble, made his great melodramatic gesture of throwing open his coat, challenging: 'Soldiers, I am your Emperor! If anyone among you wishes to kill me, here I am!' The commanding officer ordered his soldiers to fire, but instead of shooting there were cries of *'Vive l'Empéreur!'* His own party augmented by these soldiers, Napoléon entered Grenoble in triumph. He wrote in his memoirs: 'As far as Grenoble, I was merely an adventurer. At Grenoble, I became a prince'.

From **GAP** (numerous **hotels** and three **campsites**, and good train links to Paris and Marseille) the railway and D64 strike east towards **EMBRUN**, the landscape becoming very Mediterranean, low scrub covering the mountainsides, poor shallow soil, and white friable rock. Embrun stands on a rock overlooking the huge man-made lake of **Serre-Ponçon**, which is rapidly being developed as a summer resort with campsites and wind-surfing schools etc. It has been a fortress town for centuries. Hadrian made it the capital of the Maritime Alps and from the third century to the Revolution it was the seat of an important archbishopric. The **SI**, in a former chapel of the Cordeliers, has a bureau for **mountain guides** (5–7pm, July–Aug.) and **accompagnateurs** who organise a daily programme of walks in the surrounding mountains. Embrun's chief sight is its twelfth-century **Cathedral**, with a porch in alternating courses of black and white marble in the Italian Lombard style, its roof supported on columns of pink marble resting on lions' backs – an arrangement that inspired numerous imitators throughout the region.

Eighteen kilometres up the road you come to **MONT-DAUPHIN**, where **buses** leave for Ceillac, Ville-Vieille and St-Véran in the Queyras national park. They meet the Paris-Briançon trains: the 7.45am bus going all the way

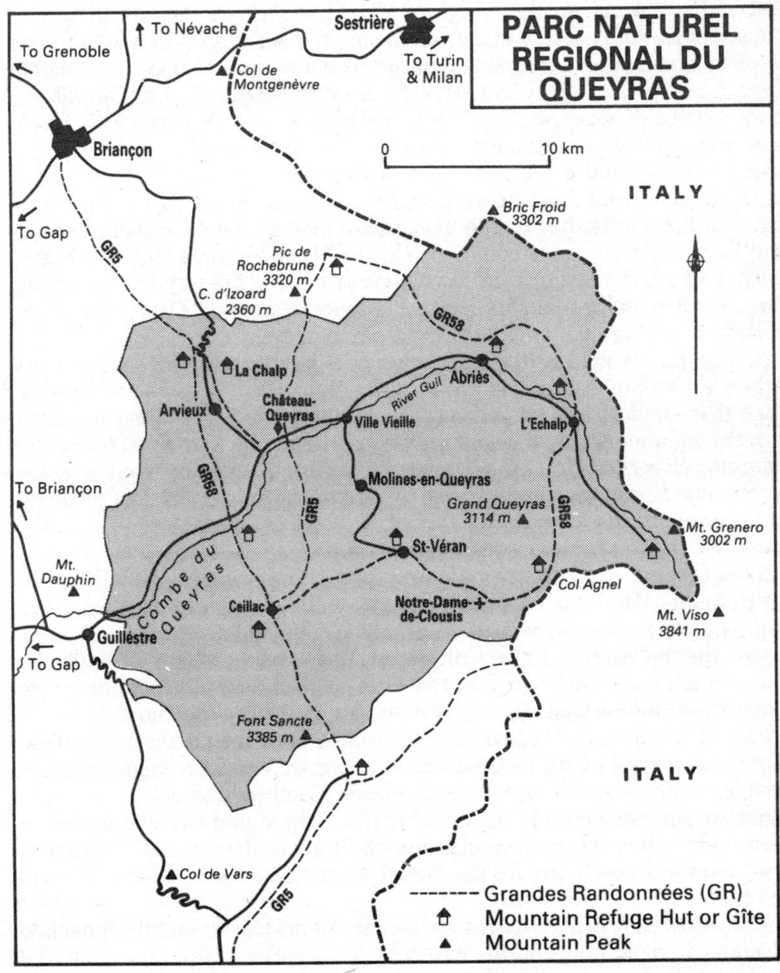

to ST-VERAN (arriving 9.10am, every day except Sun. throughout the year), others only as far as VILLE-VIEILLE (the 4.55pm operates only in the summer season). It is, however, easy to get a lift in these parts; there are always climbers and hikers with transport. Mont-Dauphin itself is just a station, with – opposite – an abandoned but formidably bastioned village – one of many Alpine fortifications designed by Vauban in the seventeenth century commanding the entrance to the valley of the Guil.

The park

The road into the Queyras park follows the river Guil from MONT-DAUPHIN, through to the village of **GUILLESTRE**, its houses in typical Queyras-style with open granaries on the upper floors, its church with a lion-porch emulating the cathedral at Embrun. You may want to stop here a night: there are several **hotels, campsites** and a **youth hostel**. Beyond the village, in the Combe du Queyras, the river gorge narrows to a claustrophobic crack with walls up to 400m high. Far below the road, the stream, incredibly clear, boils down over red and green rocks. It was only in this century that road-building techniques became sufficiently sophisticated to cope with these narrows. Previously they had to be circumvented by a detour over the adjacent heights. At the upper end of the Combe, the valley broadens briefly and ahead you see the fort of **Château-Queyras** barring the way so completely that there is scarcely room for the road to squeeze around its base. Vauban at work again, though the original fortress was medieval.

Just beyond is **VILLE-VIEILLE**, where the road for ST-VERAN branches right over the Guil and up the ravine of the Aigue Blanche torrent. A smaller place than Guillestre, it has only a few old houses still intact, and a church with the square tower and octagonal steeple flanked by four short triangular pinnacles characteristic of this corner of the Alps. A Latin inscription in the porch says the church was destroyed in 1574 by the 'impiety of the Calvinists' and restored by the 'piety' of the Catholics. There is a painted sundial on the tower, which is also characteristic of the region.

Straight on, the road follows the Guil through the villages of AIGUILLES, ABRIES, LA MONTA (all with *gîtes d'étape*), to the **Belvédère du Viso**, close to the Italian border and **Monte Viso**, at 3841m the highest peak in the area. Above the Belvédère is the **Col de la Traversette**, where in 1480 the Marquis of Saluces drove a 70m tunnel through the mountain. It has been reopened at various times through history, but is finally closed now.

East of L'ECHALP a variant of GR58, which does the circuit of the park, climbs up to the **Col de la Croix**, used in former times by Italian peasants bringing their produce to market in Abriès. South of the village the path climbs to the pastures of **Alpe de Médille**, where you can see across to Monte Viso, then on past the **lakes** of Egourgéou, Bariche and Foréant to **Col Vieux** and west to the **Refuge Agnel**, from where you can continue on to St-Véran.

At 2040m **ST-VERAN** claims to be the highest permanently inhabited village in Europe. It lies on the east side of the valley of the Aigue Blanche torrent, backed by acres of steep lush mountain pasture. Opposite, rock walls and slopes of scree rise to snowy ridges. In the valley bottom and on any treeless patch of ground, no matter how steep, you can see the remains of abandoned terraces. They were in use up until World War II, though as with most high Alpine villages, traditional farming activity has practically died out. Only one Provençal shepherd still brings his flocks to the village pastures in summertime. Today the principal economic activity is entertaining tourists. Though still pretty, it has lost its soul and looks rather uncared-for.

The houses are part-stone, part-timber. The upper storeys, usually timber, consist of long granaries with two or three tiers of rickety wooden balconies tacked on to the front for drying hay or firewood and ripening crops. The roofs are pine planks or huge slabs of schist – *lauzes* – arranged in diamond patterns. There are several refurbished old drinking-fountains, made entirely of wood. The stone church stands prettily on the higher of the two 'streets', its white tower silhouetted against the bare crags across the valley, as a mountain church should. It too has a porch whose columns rest on crudely carved lions, one holding a man in its paws. The interior is surprisingly rich, with Baroque altars and retables.

Just south of the village, past a triple cross adorned with the instruments of Christ's Passion and an inscription urging the passer-by to choose between the saintly, conventional or rebellious life (*'l'homme révolté qui n'est jamais content'*). **GR58**, waymarked and easy to follow, turns right down to the river, beside which there are some good places to camp. The path continues up the left bank through woods of pine and larch as far as the chapel of Notre-Dame-de-Clausis. There, above the timberline, it crosses to the right bank of the stream and winds up damp grassy slopes to the **Col de Chamoussière**, about 3½ hours from St-Véran. The ridge to the right of the col marks the frontier with Italy. In the valley below you see the **Refuge Agnel**, about an hour away, with the Pain de Sucre (3208m) behind it. From there you can continue on to **L'ECHALP**. In early July there are glorious flowers in the meadows leading up to the col: violets, potentilla, Black Vanilla Orchids, jovibarb, dianthus, silene acaulis, hypericum, anemones, trollius europaeus, Mountain Buttercup, gentians, soldanella and campanulas.

For a **base in these parts**, you're really best off camping. Rooms are expensive, though there's one reasonable hotel at ST-VERAN, the *Coste Belle* at the south end of the upper street, and a *gîte d'étape* by the hairpin bend at the north end, belonging to M. Brunet who keeps the *Hôtel Etoile de Neige*. The *Neige* also does meals. If you are feeding yourself, there are only two small shops and they have a tendency to run out of bread, fruit and vegetables.

Hiking down to VILLE-VIEILLE takes about 2½hours from ST-VERAN, all road (save for an initial short cut to MOLINES), but downhill and pretty. MOLINES and its neighbors, LA RUA and PONTGILLARDE, seem to have preserved their traditional rural character better than St-Véran. The houses are better kept, the hay meadows still mown – there is nothing prettier than these little patches of Alpine meadow, always steep and irregular in shape, full of wild flowers and neatly scythed by hand.

Queyras to Briançon

Running over the 2360m **Col d'Izoard**, the direct route from Queyras to Briançon is a beautiful trip and saves backtracking to MONT-DAUPHIN. There are no buses but it's reasonably promising hitching.

The road turns up right just west of CHATEAU-QUEYRAS along a wooded ravine to the village of **ARVIEUX** lying in a high valley surrounded by fields and meadows. A church with the characteristic tower and steeple stands guard at the entrance to the village. GR5 passes through. *Hôtel Casse Déserte* has dormitory accommodation. Further up the valley at LA CHALP and BRUNISSARD are *gîtes d'étape*.

Going up to **the col**, above the timberline, you cross the **Casse Déserte**, a wild, desolate region with huge screes running down off the peaks and weirdly eroded orangy rocks. From the top you look out over miles and miles of mountain landscape. The road loops down the other side through thick forest to LE LAUS, a cluster of half-a-dozen old stone houses with long, sloping, wooden roofs set in meadows beside the stream, then CERVIERES, and west into the deep valley of the Durance at BRIANÇON, dominated by the vast **Massif des Ecrins**.

Briançon and the Parc National des Ecrins

Imposing and fortified, built on a rocky height overlooking the valleys of the Durance and Guisane, **BRIANÇON** guards the road to the desolate and windswept **Col de Montgenèvre**, one of the oldest and most important passes into Italy, marked by a column commemorating Napoléon's construction of the road. Originally a Gallic settlement, the town was fortified by the Romans to guard their *Mons Matrona* road from Milan to Vienne. In the Middle Ages it was the capital of the '*république des escartons*', a federation of mountain communities grouped together for mutual defence and the preservation of their liberties and privileges.

The **old town**, mainly eighteenth-century, is enclosed within another set of Vauban's walls. If you come in a car the best thing is to stop at the **Champ de Mars** at the top of the hill and look around from there; otherwise you will have to struggle up from the unprepossessing modern town that has grown up on the more accessible ground at the foot of the hill. You enter the walls by the **Porte Pignerol**. In front of you the narrow main street, bordered by ancient houses, tips steeply downhill. It is known as the *grande gargouille* because of the stream running down the middle. To your right is the sturdy, plain **church of Notre-Dame**, designed by Vauban, again with an eye to defence. Beyond it there is a fantastic **view** from the walls, especially on a clear starry night, when the snows on the surrounding barrier of mountains give off an icy, silvery glow. Vauban's **citadel** above the Porte Pignerol, the highest point of the fortifications, can be visited, but only as part of an organized tour (ask the **SI**, on the right by the Porte). In marked contrast to the relatively untouristy Queyras, Briançon and all the other towns and villages on this side of the Ecrins park are crawling with people in summer.

For **places to stay**, try *Hôtel aux Trois Chamois* (☎92.21.02.29) in the Champs de Mars, still reasonably priced with the obligatory *demi-pension* (full board in July and Aug.) – and the food is good. Alternatives in the old town are *Hôtel de la Paix* at 3 rue Porte-Méane to the right of Grande-Rue, up for sale in 1988, so its future may be uncertain; and *Le Rustique* on rue Pont-d'Asfeld to the left of Grande-Rue. A bit more expensive, but perhaps a better bet than the latter two is the *Edelweiss* at 32 av de la République (☎92.21.02.94), the main road down to the new town – though it will certainly be full in July and August. In the lower town try *Hôtel de la Chaussée* at 4 rue Centrale (☎92.21.10.37) opposite the **SI** (which includes a **mountain guides'** desk). **Camping le Schappe** is further down the same street, to the left after the bridge on the Durance. There is also a *gîte d'étape* at LE FONTENIL 2km along the Montgenèvre road.

As for **eating** options, if you are not eating in a hotel, try one of the *crêperies* at the top of Grande-Gargouille or the *Café du Centre* on place du Temple by the church or the nearby *Entrecôte* in Porte Gargouille.

Névache

For a really beautiful day excursion from Briançon, head for the valley of the **river Clarée**. Without your own transport, you'll have to hitch or walk, but that should be no hardship because the scenery is truly magnificent.

Leave Briançon by the Montgenèvre road and take the left fork after 2km. A lane follows the wooded riverbank in the bottom of a narrow ravine parallel to the Italian frontier. On foot you could follow **GR5**, which passes through the main villages. If you are thinking of spending a night up here, the half-ruined hamlet of PLAMPINET has both hotel- and hostel-type **accommodation** in a vast renovated farm, *La Cleida* (☎92.21.32.48), as well as at the *Auberge de la Clarée* by the bridge. And there is more at **NEVACHE**, where the valley widens and there's already been a good deal of holiday development, though the old village nucleus of wide-roofed houses still huddles self-protectively around the church, which is, incidentally, worth a look for its carving, Baroque altarpiece, and a few items in the treasury, including some venerable, spiked eleventh-century doors. In addition to hotels and pensions, there are three **gîtes**: *Le Creux des Souches*, *Le Pontée*, and *Paschalet*.

The finest country is beyond Névache towards the head of the valley, where in May the meadows are running with snow-melt and carpeted with crocuses, and fat marmots whistle from the rocks. Six kilometres after the village, there are two refuges by the first bridge – *Fontcouverte* and *La Fruitière*, – another at the end of the road, as well as a *CAF* refuge on the slopes of Mt Thabor, none of which are open for much more than the summer season.

Into the park: towards Mont-Pelvoux

The usual **approach to the Parc des Ecrins**, with some very serious climbing goals at its end, is from the train station at ARGENTIERES-LA-BESSEE, a scruffy, depressed little place with a recently closed aluminum works, south towards MONT-DAUPHIN. From here a small road cuts into the valley towards VALLOUISE, the ice-capped monster of **Mont-Pelvoux** (3946m) rearing in front of you all the way.

On the right by the first village you come to, LA BATIE, are the remains of the so-called **Mur des Vaudois**. Despite the name, the origins of the wall are uncertain. It was probably built either to keep out companies of marauding soldiers-turned-bandits, or to control the spread of plague in the fourteenth century. These Vaudois (Waldensians in English) are not to be confused with the inhabitants of the Swiss canton of Vaud. They were members of a religious sect, sort of precursors of Protestantism, founded in the late twelfth century by Pierre Valdo, a merchant from Lyon, who preached against worldly wealth and the corruption of the clergy. Practising as he preached, he gave his wealth to the poor. Excommunicated in 1186 the Vaudois came more and more to deny the authority of the church. Persecuted, they sought refuge in the remote mountain valleys of Pelvoux, especially in the area around Vallouise and Argentières. Their numbers were also probably augmented by refugees from the Inquisition's persecutions of the Cathars in Languedoc.

There was a crop of executions for sorcery in the early fifteenth century, and many of the victims were probably Vaudois, burnt to death in wooden cabins built for this purpose. In 1488, Charles VIII launched a full-scale crusade against them. There is a spot west of Ailefroide known as Baume Chapelue where they were smoked out by the military and butchered. They were finally exterminated in the eighteenth century after the revocation of the Edict of Nantes, when 8000 troops went on the rampage, creating total desolation and 'leaving neither people nor animals'.

On the right beyond La Batie, the village of **LES VIGNEAUX** (with a *gîte d'étape*) shrugs off such a past: a lovely place, surrounded by apple orchards and backed by the fierce crags of Montbrison. The **church** has a fine old door and lock under a vaulted porch. Beside it on the exterior wall of the church are two bands of paintings depicting the Seven Deadly Sins. In the upper band the sins are naive representations of men and women riding various beasts (lion, hound, monkey) and chained by the neck. A man carrying a leg of mutton and drinking wine from a flask represents gluttony; a woman with rouged cheeks, green stockings and displaying an enticing expanse of thigh, represents lust. In the lower band they are all getting their comeuppance, writhing in the agonies of Hell fire.

VALLOUISE lies under a steep wooded spur at the junction of two valleys, the Gyrond (or Gyr, as it is called upstream of Vallouise) and the Gérendoine. The great glaciered peaks visible up the latter valley are Les Bans, up in front still is Mont-Pelvoux. The nucleus of the old village – narrow lanes between somber stone chalets – is again its **church**, fifteenth-century with characteristic tower and steeple and a sixteenth-century porch on pink marble pillars. A fresco of the Adoration of the Magi adorns the tympanum above the door, itself magnificent with carved Gothic panels along the top and an ancient lock-and-bolt with a chimera's head at one end. Remains of an enormously long-legged figure, partially painted over, cover the end wall of the apse. Inside, as at Les Vigneaux, are more frescoes, including at the back of the church six naive statues on painted wood.

There is a **campsite, gîte d'étape** and several **hotels** (open from Dec.–April and July–Sept./Oct). The *Edelweiss* is cheapest, but all rooms in the village are likely to be full in July and August.

GR54, which does the circuit of the Ecrins park, passes through Vallouise and the stage on from here to LE MONETIER – **Lac de l'Echauda** is one of the best. Another good walk is to the hamlet of PUY AILLAUD high on the west flank of the Gyr valley. The path starts just to the right of the church and zigzags up the steep slope behind it with almost aerial views of the valley beneath. The Vallouise *Maison du Parc des Ecrins* provides **hiking information.** There is a **minibus** service as far as AILEFROIDE in summer, starting from the bar next to the *Edelweiss* hotel; to walk takes 2 hours or so.

AILEFROIDE, under the last slopes of Pelvoux (three **campsites**), is also a major centre for climbers and walkers. There is a **Bureau des Guides**. A path follows the road on up the valley as far as the so-called **Pré de Madame Carle** by the old *refuge Cézanne* (1½hr.). In fact, it is not a 'pré' or meadow at all, but a jumble of rocks brought down by the torrent from which you can see the **Barre des Ecrins** towering above the Glacier Noir. At 4102m, it is also the highest peak in the massif – and one of the major Alpine climbs. From the bridge another path runs north, up to the **Refuge du glacier Blanc** on the edge of the glacier at 2550m (about 2½hr.). Anywhere beyond this on the **Pelvoux massif** is snow and ice – experienced climbers' territory.

From the North: La Grave, Lautaret and Le Casset

Coming in to the mountains from GRENOBLE along **N91**, you have various alternative approaches to the **Parc des Ecrins** – and the possibility of a substantial two-day circuit between LA GRAVE and LE CASSET. The road itself, though, is grand enough, twisting through the precipitous valley of the Romanche and up and over the 2058m **Col du Lautaret**, which is kept open all year round and served regularly by the GRENOBLE-BRIANCON bus.

For LA BERARDE right in the midst of the park's mightiest peaks, which the *Rough Guide* hasn't yet got to (contributions welcome), you leave the road just after **BOURG-L'OISANS**. Of no great interest in itself, it's a good place to catch your breath and pick up information from the **SI** (quai Girard, close to the main road in the middle of town) and the **park information centre** on av Gambetta. There are also numerous **places to stay**, although they will be crowded in summer: **Camping municipal** on rue Humbert near the town centre and a concentration of sites across the river on the ALPE D'HUEZ road. Among the cheaper **hotels** to try are *Beau Rivage* (☎76.80.03.19), *Le Reghaia* (☎76.80.03.31) and *Le Rocher* (☎76.80.01.53), all next to each other on the main street. If you like the idea of cycling in sharp mountain air, **bikes** can be rented from *Cycles d'Oisans* on rue Viennois – not such a crazy undertaking as you might think, for if you keep to the valley bottoms, the gradients aren't too fearsome.

LA GRAVE, 26km on, at the foot of the Col du Lautaret, faces the majestic glaciers of La Meije (3983m). It's a good base for walking. **GR54** climbs up to Le Chazelet on the slopes north-west of the village and continues to the

Plateau de Paris and the **Lac Noir**, which numerous walkers recommend for its breathtaking views of La Meije. And it is only 11km to the top of the Col, with the still higher Col du Galibier just beyond. There is no public transport up Galibier – which is closed by snow from mid-October to mid-June – but in season you should be able to hitch up, and back to LA GRAVE or on to LE CASSET in a day.

The **Col du Lautaret** has been in use for centuries. The Roman road from Milan to Vienne crossed it. In fact its name comes from the small temple (*altaretum*) the Romans built to placate the deity of the mountains. They called it '*collis de altareto*'. Around the col is a huge expanse of meadow long known to botanists for its glorious variety of Alpine flowers, seen at their best in mid-July. There is a **Jardin Alpin**, maintained by the University of Grenoble (8–noon and 2–6pm, July 1–Sept. 15), which includes plants from mountain ranges throughout the world. It is a great spot for picnicking or lounging waiting for a ride, for you look straight into the glaciers hanging off La Meije and the sight is intoxicating. On a clear sunny day the dazzling luminosity of the ice and the burning intensity of the sky above it is such that you can hardly bear to look.

The **Col du Galibier** is less frequented – a tremendous haul up to 2556m, utterly bare and wild, with the huge red-veined peak of the Grand Galibier rearing up on the right and a fearsome spiny ridge blocking the horizon beyond. To the north you can see Mont Blanc. The pass used to mark the frontier between France and Savoie. A monument on the south side of the col commemorates Henri Desgranges, founder of the Tour de France cycle race. Crossing the col is one of the most gruelling stages in the race. The long ascent is brutal, and the breakneck speed of descent terrifying. The road loops down in hairpin after hairpin, through VALLOIRE, a sizeable ski resort, whose church is reputedly one of the most richly decorated in Savoy, over the Col du Télégraphe at 1570m and steeply down into the deep wooded valley of the Arc, known as la Maurienne, with the Massif de la Vanoise rising abruptly behind.

LE CASSET, back on D28, just before MONETIER-LES-BAINS, is a hamlet of dilapidated old houses clustered around a church with a bulbous dome. The site is superb: streams and meadows everywhere, reaching to the foot of the larch-covered mountainsides, the Glacier du Casset imminent, white and dazzling above the green of the larches. There is a **campsite** and *gîte d'étape* near the church. But provided you choose a spot where the hay has already been mown it seems you can camp anywhere. There is a café and grocery store in the village, which in season is overcrowded.

GR54 goes through the village. A good day's walk is to follow it as far as the **Col d'Arsine**, about 3 hours, from which point you can either turn back or go on down to **La Grave** on the north side of the park, making an overnight stop at the *Refuge de l'Alpe* below the col.

The path crosses the Guisane near the *gîte* and follows a track through the woods, first on the left, and later on the right bank of the Petit Tabuc stream. From the end of the track you cross some grassy clearings before entering the trees again and climbing up to a milky-looking lakelet, the **Lac de la Douche**, at the foot of the Glacier du Casset. From here a clear path zigzags up a very steep slope coming out in a long valley, and eventually leading to the Col d'Arsine. Masses of ground-hugging red rhododendrons grow along the banks of the stream. About half-way up are some tumbledown huts, the **Chalets d'Arsine**, by a series of blue-grey tarns. Up on the left are a whole series of **glaciers**. The biggest is the Glacier d'Arsine, hanging from the walls of the long jagged ridge suspended between the Montagne des Agneaux, and the Pic de Neige Cordier to the west. Early in the morning there are colonies of marmots playing above the banks of the stream.

Parc National de la Vanoise

The park occupies the eastern end of the **Vanoise massif**, the area contained between the upper valleys of the Isère and Arc Rivers. It is extremely popular, with over 500km of marked paths, crossings of **GR5, GR55** and **GTA** (Grande Traversée des Alpes), and numerous refuges along the trails. For information on the spot, the **SIs** in **Modane, Val d'Isère, Bourg-St-Maurice** are helpful. The *Maison du Parc* in CHAMBERY (135 rue St-Julian) also gives advice and sell maps.

Modane and the Haute-Maurienne

MODANE is a dreary little place, destroyed by Allied bombing in 1943 and now little more than a railway junction. Nonetheless it is a good kicking-off point for walkers on the south side of the park – easily accessible by train and with a well-sited grassy **Camping municipal** just up the road to the Fréjus tunnel (which leads to Bardonecchia in Italy). The *Hôtel de l'Europe*, just beyond the Fréjus turn on the street parallel to the main road, is a friendly place if you want a room – and serves good home-cooked meals designed for the roadweary.

GR5 sets out from the northern edge of the transpontine section of Modane and leads up to the **Refuge de l'Orgère**, where a path joins up with **GR55** leading north to PRALOGNAN, over the **Col de la Vanoise** and right across the park to Val Claret on the Lac de Tignes – a tremendous walk. GR5 itself keeps east of La Dent Parrachée, describing a great loop through the Refuge d'Entre-Deux-Eaux before continuing up the north flank of the Arc valley and over the Col de l'Iseran to Val d'Isère.

The **Arc valley**, dark and enclosed below Modane, widens and lightens above it, with meadows and patches of cultivation in the valley bottom and the lighter foliage of larches gracing the mountainsides. It is hardly a joyous landscape, especially under a stormy sky. Bare crags hang above the steep meadows on the north flanks, glaciers threaten to the south and east. The villages, though attractive to the modern eye, are poor and humble places, the houses squat and built of rough grey stone, the homes of people who have had to struggle to wring a living from harsh weather and unyielding soil. It is surprising at first to find such a wealth of exuberant **Baroque art** in the outwardly simple **churches**. But probably it is precisely because of the harshness and poverty of their lives that these mountain people sought to express their piety with such colourful vitality. Schools of local artists flourished, particularly in the seventeenth and eighteenth centuries, inspired and influenced by itinerant Italian artists who came and went across the adjacent frontier. *Haute Maurienne Information* in LANSLEBOURG organize tours of the churches in AVRIEUX, BRAMANS (where Horace Walpole's dog Toby was eaten by a wolf), TERMIGNON, LANSLEVILLARD and BESSANS. **LANSLEBOURG** is also the start of the climb to the **Mont Cenis pass** over to Susa in Italy, another ancient trans-Alpine route. Last stop before the perils of the trek, it was once a prosperous and thriving town. Relief at finishing the climb from the French side was tempered by an alarming descent *en ramasse*, a sort of crude sledge, which shot downhill at breakneck speed much to the alarm of travellers. 'So fast you lose all sense and understanding', a terrified merchant from Douai recounted in 1518.

BESSANS, further up the valley, retains its village character better than most. Its low, squat dwellings are built of rough stone with tiny window openings and roofed with heavy slabs to withstand the long hard winters. Most have south-facing balconies to make the most of the sun and galleries under deep eaves for drying *grebons*, the bricks of cow-dung and straw used locally for fuel. The **church** has a collection of seventeenth-century painted wooden statues and a retable, signed by Clappier. The Clappiers were a local family who produced several generations of artists. On the other side of the small cemetery, where old women in black tend the graves, the **chapel of St-Antoine** has exterior murals of the Virtues and Deadly Sins and fine sixteenth-century frescoes; ask the priest to unlock the chapel – his house is on the right of the road leading east from the village square. Two kilometres up the road you pass the chapel of Notre-Dame-des-Grâces on the right, with another ex-voto by Jean Clappier. On the opposite side of the river the hamlet of LE VILLARON has a *gîte d'étape*.

BONNEVAL-SUR-ARC (1835m), 10km upstream, lies at the foot of the **Col de l'Iseran** in a rather bleaker setting close to the timberline. At the head of the Arc valley to the east you can see the huge glaciers of the *Sources de l'Arc*. Better preserved and more obviously picturesque than Bessans, Bonneval stops a lot of tourists on their way to and from the col. It is in danger of becoming twee.

Nonetheless, like all these Haute-Maurienne villages, Bonneval has a highly individual identity – quite different to Bessans. Its houses cluster tightly around the church, with only the narrowest of lanes between them. You feel the need for mutual protection and warmth being even stronger here, and sense how very isolated these places were until only a few years ago, cut off for months by heavy snow, forced in upon their own resources. Life was dangerous too, even for experienced locals. Several graves in the churchyard record deaths by avalanche.

Alternative bases to Modane and Bessans in Haute-Maurienne include the **campsites** at TERMIGNON, LANSLEBOURG and LANSLEVILLARD; *gîtes d étape* at TERMIGNON, SARDIERES, BRAMANS, and LE VILLARON; or the **youth hostel** at LANSLEBOURG. **Hotels** are also numerous, but expensive and hard to find space in summer.

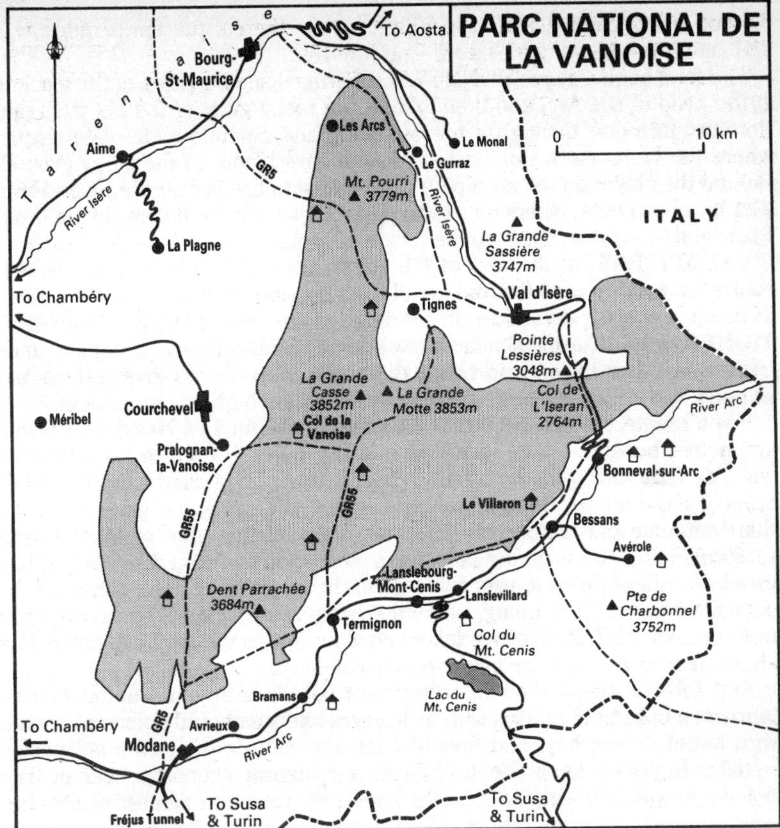

The Col de l'Iseran and Haute Tarentaise

As with all the other high Alpine passes the **Col de l'Iseran** has been used for centuries by local people. Despite the dangers of weather and the arduous climb, it was far the quickest route between the remote **upper valleys** of the **Arc** and **Isère**. The volume of traffic was too small to disturb the nature of the tiny communities that eked out an existence on the approaches. But twentieth-century roads and the development of winter sports have changed all that. VAL D'ISERE, for instance, once a tiny mountain village, has become a hideous agglomeration of cafés, supermarkets and apartments for skiers.

From October to June **the pass** is usually blocked by snow. But in summer, being the highest pass in the Alps at 2770m, it is one of the 'sights' that motorised tourists feel they must see; consequently it's relatively easy to hitch. A word of warning, though: if you do try, don't do it in light summer clothing, especially on a cool cloudy day. My lift put me down at the chalet on the col. It had been drizzling in Bonneval. On the col the temperature was 2°C, and it was blowing a blizzard – on July 18.

The road begins above BONNEVAL, offering splendid views of the glaciers at the head of the Arc, and then follows the rocky gully of the Lenta stream (lots of marmots) through a narrow defile and out into a desolate cirque, where the Lenta rises and masses of anemones bloom in the stony ground. Behind the chalet on the col a path climbs west to the **Pointe des Lessières** (2½ hr. round trip), where on a clear day you can see the Italian side of Mont Blanc and the whole of the frontier chain of peaks.

VAL D'ISERE, at the foot of the col on the north side, is a convenient centre for walking (details from the SI), but no place to stay. Should you need to camp, there's a **campsite** on the edge of the resort at LE LAISINANT. **TIGNES**, with its artificial lake, a few kilometres down river, is equally unattractive, another major resort. But thereafter the valley is lovely, deep and wooded, with villages perched on grassy shoulders high on either flank.

If you're interested in exploring the valley, make for **Les Brevières**. Seven kilometres beyond, a lane turns left into the valley bottom to LA SAVINAZ and LA GURRAZ, whose creamy church tower is a landmark for miles around. High above, though looking dangerously close, the green ice cliffs that terminate the Glacier de la Gurraz hang off the edge of Mont Pourri (3799m). From the turn, the lane veers steeply down through trees and hay meadows full of flowers, past ruined houses, to the river. The climb up the opposite bank is hard going, past impossibly steep fields. You take a right fork for LA GURRAZ across a rickety plank bridge in the jaws of a defile. It is about an hour's walk, once you're on the lane.

And **LA GURRAZ** shouldn't disappoint you. It is tiny and untouched by tourism: a dozen old houses with wide eaves and weathered balconies spread with sweet drying hay, and firewood stacked outside. Only the old people remain, but they keep the traditional agricultural economy ticking. The houses are all sited in the lee of a knoll for protection against avalanches which come thundering off the glacier above the village, thousands of tons of snow and rock, almost sheer down into a cwm behind. If you are unlucky enough to be out of doors when one occurs, the blast knocks you off your feet, and can even suffocate you. There are no provisions available, so bring your own. I camped 200m beyond the village overlooking the valley, with a tongue of glacier poised on the brow of a cliff not far above me. Other hamlets on the opposite flank of the valley look just as interesting. The prettiest is LE MONAL, in the mouth of a small hanging valley, also accessible by car from La Thuile further along the Bourg-St-Maurice road.

From La Gurraz a signposted path climbs to **Refuge de la Martin** in 1½ hours. It zigzags up the slope behind LA SAVINAZ, on to a spur by a ruined chalet, where a right-hand path goes up the rocks overhead to the edge of the glacier. The refuge path continues left along the side of a deep gully, whose flanks are thick with the white St. Bruno's Lily. It crosses a ferocious torrent by a plank bridge and follows a mule track up to the *alpage* by the refuge, where cows and sheep graze. The **Mont Pourri glaciers** are directly above. Opposite is the big **Glacier de la Sassière** and up to your right VAL D'ISERE with the Col de l'Iseran behind.

Continuing down the valley, **BOURG-ST-MAURICE** is the mid-point of the Tarentaise. Again, of little interest itself, it can be a useful place to stop. The big purpose-built ski resorts of LES ARCS and LA PLAGNE are nearby and the classic pass into the Italian Val d'Aosta, the **Col du Petit St-Bernard**, right behind. With its Swiss twin, the Grand St-Bernard, it was the only route around the Mont Blanc massif until the tunnel was opened in 1965. It's a rather spooky crossing, reaching 2188m, with a couple of barrack-like buildings and a row of statues of St-Bernard. It's at its most dramatic when you're coming over from the Italian side in evening, right into the eye of the setting sun. (There is one daily bus crossing in July and August.) If you do come over at that time of day and are worrying about a place for the night, stop off at the *Hôtel Belvédère* (☎79.07.02.04) just below the treeline about 8km above Bourg-St-Maurice. It's a marvellously old-fashioned establishment, with a good restaurant, which has been in the same family since 1903, when it used to be a posting stop for the *diligence*, the stage coach.

There are no very appealing **places to stay** in the town. It's best to look on Grande Rue, the old main street, where you could try the *Hôtel de Tignes* (☎79.07.04.80), *Hôtel du Centre* (☎79.07.05.13) or the slightly more expensive *Vallée de l'Arc* (☎79.07.04.12). There are other places on the dreary main road, av Leclerc, where you'll also find the **gare SNCF** and **routière**, with the **SI** almost opposite. The **campsite** is in route des Arcs on the right just past the sports ground on the Val d'Isère road.

Heading west towards Chambéry, there are a couple of places worth a brief stop. The first is **AIME**, whose Grande-Rue recalls what an Alpine village would once have looked like. Its principal sight, however, is the rough stone **church of St-Martin**, whose origins go back to a first-century Roman temple, swept away by the Isère in spate in the third century – an indication of how dangerous these mountain rivers could be in the days before flood control. What survives today is basically early Romanesque.

The other place that rewards a brief detour is **CONFLANS**, a small medieval town on a spur overlooking grim modern ALBERTVILLE, rather too cutely revived for its own good. From the public garden by the Tour Sarrazine, you can contemplate the contrast in town planning styles: spreading below are rectangular blocks of flats separated by rushing highways, against a steep backdrop of green slopes and terraces of vine and hay meadow.

MONT BLANC AND LAKE GENEVA

Mont Blanc is the biggest tourist draw in the Alps, but so spectacular it's worth seeing. Besides, if you're going to walk in the area, you soon get away from the worst of the crowds.

ANNECY is the easiest place to get to it from, and of the two road routes the one via the old ski resort of MEGEVE is the most interesting – though, from Ugine onwards, the hardest to hitch. The alternative route goes through CLUSES.

Mont Blanc

The two **approaches** to the 'Blonk' – as English climbers insist on calling the mountain – come together at LE FAYET, where the **tramway du Mont-Blanc** begins its 1 hour 15 minute haul to the **Nid d'Aigle**, a vantage point on the northwest slope. Unless you're doing a full photographic survey I'd say skip that. There's much more exciting access from CHAMONIX-MONT BLANC, just 30km further on.

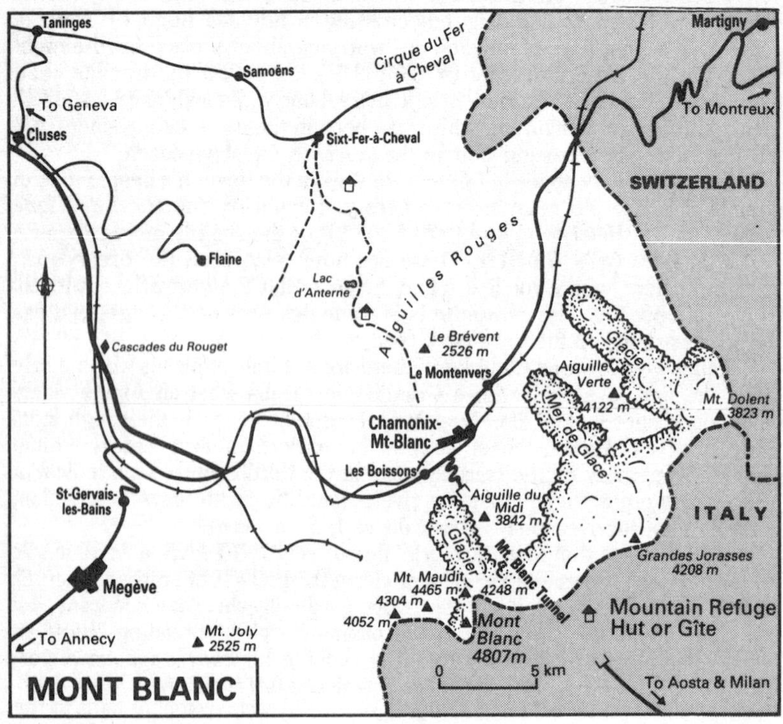

Chamonix-Mont Blanc

If Mont Blanc was anything less than outstanding there would be no point in going to **CHAMONIX**. Its village identity has been submerged in a sprawl of development; it's extremely expensive, and always crawling with tourists. The **Musée Alpin** (2–7pm, June–Sept.) will interest mountain freaks, though it is not as exciting as you would expect; among various bits of equipment, documents and letters is Jacques Balmat's account of his first ascent of the 'Blonk' written in almost phonetically spelled French. And **finding a bed** for the night can be a big problem. There is no such thing as a cheap hotel. The best bet is the comfortable, largely modernized and very welcoming **youth hostel** at LES PELERINS, just west of Chamonix proper (bus to les Houches and get off at *Pèlerins Ecole*: the hostel, signposted, is at 103 Montée Jacques-Balmat; ☎50.53.14.52; meals, if you book). Arriving by car or on foot from the west, it's very easy to miss the turn: look out for the Pèlerins-d'En-Bas sign on your left not long after the Bossons glacier – the hostel road is opposite, on your right. For other sporadic dormitory accommodation, ask the **SI** near the church. **Campsites**, however, are numerous, even if there is only room for a small tent. Two convenient ones are *Les Molliases* on the left of the main road going west from Chamonix towards the Mont Blanc tunnel entrance and *Les Arolles* on the opposite side of the road – about a fifteen minute walk from the station.

There are various touristy things to do that in other circumstances you might baulk at. But if you don't do them there is not much else, unless you are an experienced walker or climber. The first is to take the **track railway** from the Gare du Montenvers to the vast glacier known as the **Mer de Glace**, a favourite with Victorian travellers. The second, best of all, is the very expensive *téléférique* to the **Aiguille du Midi** (3842m): if mountains excite you, you won't regret the outlay, and penny-pinching by buying a ticket only as far as the Plan du Midi is a waste of money – you won't see anything. You must, however, go before 9am; first, because the summits usually cloud over toward midday and, second, because any later there will be huge crowds and you may have to wait for hours. And take warm clothes: even on a summer day it will be well below zero on the top. You need a steady head too, for the drop beneath your little bubble of steel and glass is truly appalling.

The Aiguille is a terrifying granite pinnacle on which the *téléférique* dock and a restaurant are precariously balanced. The view is incredible. At your feet is the snowy plateau of the **Col du Midi**, with the glaciers of the Vallée Blanche and Géant crawling off left at their millennial pace. To the right a steep snowfield leads to the 'easy' ridge route to the summit with its cap of ice (4807m).

Away to the front, rank upon rank of snow-and-ice-capped monsters recede into the distance. Most impressive of all, closing the horizon to your left, from the east to south, is a mind-blowing cirque of needle-sharp peaks and precipitous couloirs: the Aiguille Verte, Triollet, the Jorasses, with the Matterhorn and Monte Rosa visible in the far distance across a glorious landscape of rock, snow and cloud-filled valleys – the lethal testing-ground of all truly crazed climbers. And there are plenty of them still at it, swapping tales in the valley campsites of difficult pitches, rockfalls and other people's accidents, so casually you'd think the whole thing was a picnic.

The mountain was first climbed in 1786 by Dr. Paccard and Jacques Balmat, both natives of Chamonix, inspired by de Saussure, a Genevese naturalist's offer of a reward. The first woman to climb the mountain was Marie Paradis, who ran a tea-shop in Chamonix. Alpine exploration and climbing developed quickly in the nineteenth century. Early technique was primitive and extremely dangerous. Even when guides began to use rope at all, they did not bother to rope themselves to their parties. When Edward Whymper, one of the most renowned early alpinists, made the first successful ascent of the Matterhorn in 1865, his party lost four members because the old worn piece of rope they casually attached themselves to simply snapped.

Chamonix Valley: some possible hikes

Opposite Mont Blanc, the north side of Chamonix valley is enclosed by the lower but nonetheless impressive **Aiguilles Rouges**, with another *téléférique* to Le Brévent, the 2525m peak directly above the town. I didn't visit this side at all, but there are numerous walks along the massif; in particular, the **Grand** and **Petit Balcon Sud** trails give spectacular views of Mont Blanc and present no problems to the walker. A highly recommended **two-day hike** is the **GR5** stage north from Le Brévent to the village of SIXT via **Lac d'Anterne**, with a night at the Refuge d'Anterne. The classic **long-distance route** is the two-week **Tour du Mont Blanc** (TMB), described in a *Topo-Guide* and Andrew Harvey's *Tour of Mont Blanc* (Cicerone Press).

For up-to-the minute **walking and climbing information**, consult the SI or the **Maison de la Montagne**, both near the church in Chamonix. The Maison de la Montagne houses the *Bureau des Guides*, *Office de Haute Montagne* and a meteorological service. The SI publishes a large-scale **map of summer walks** in the area. The guides run rock and ice-climbing schools. If you are determined to conquer Europe's highest summit, a guide will cost you around £200 for the *voie normale*.

Northern pre-Alps: the Cirque du Fer-à-Cheval

The **Northern pre-Alps**, climbing back from the shore of Lake Geneva, are cooler, softer and greener country. They are less well known than the mightier ranges further south but they're also a lot less crowded. For walkers, there's considerable potential – the only real problem is access off the main routes. To get into the **Giffre valley**, with its **Fer-à-Cheval** hikers' circuit, you need to hitch or bus over to TANINGES, to SAMOENS and SIXT.

SAMOENS, at the foot of the Aiguille de Criou and with the tall peak of Le Buet in the distance, is an attractive village with an unusual church – very late Gothic with a doorway of crouching lions like those in Queyras. It was built in the sixteenth century well behind the times, given that the Renaissance was in full swing elsewhere though a pattern you find (and expect) in these remote Alpine valleys. Traditionally, Samoëns' chief product has been stonemasons. Up to World War I, the men of the village set out each spring, tools on their backs, to seek work in the cities of France and Switzerland. Their guild, *les frahans*, evolved its own peculiar dialect, *le mourne*, so they could communicate secretly among themselves.

East of Samoëns the valley narrows into the Gorge des Tines before opening out again at **SIXT**, another pretty village on the confluence of two branches of the Giffre, the Giffre-Haut which comes down from Salvagny, and the Giffre-Bas which rises in the Cirque du Fer-à-Cheval.

The Cirque begins about 6km from Sixt – there is a footpath along the left bank of the Giffre-Bas. It is a vast semicircle of rock walls up to 700m in height and 4 to 5km long, blue with haze on a summer's day and striated with long, tumbling chains of white water from the waterfalls. The left end of the cirque is dominated by a huge spike of rock known as the Goat's Horn, *La Corne du Chamois*. At its foot the valley of the Giffre bends sharply north to its source in the glaciers above the Fond de la Combe. The bowl of the cirque is thickly wooded except for a circular meadow in the middle where the road ends.

There is an **SI** and a **park office** here, though nowhere to buy provisions. The park office produce a folder of walks in the region – useful and well illustrated. They recommend, in particular, the walk to the **Refuge du Lac de la Vogeale** (3½hr.), the **Chalets de Sales** via the spectacular Cascade du Rouge waterfalls on GR5 and GR96, and the GR5 stage to the **Lac d'Anterne** and on to LE BREVENT and CHAMONIX. My 1902 *Baedeker*, which seems to have done every conceivable Alpine route, describes a 'fatiguing but interesting' 12–13 hour route over the Buet to CHAMONIX.

SIXT, SAMOENS and TANINGES are all equipped with **campsites**. SIXT also has a **gîte d'étape**.

Evian and Lake Geneva

The nicest way to reach EVIAN or any of the **lakeside towns** is by boat from GENEVA (3 hr. to Evian). 72km long, 13km wide and an amazing 310m deep, the lake – **Lac Léman** to the French – is fed and drained by the Rhône. It is a real inland sea, subject to violent storms, as Byron and Shelley discovered to their discomfort in 1816. On a calm day, though, sailing slowly across its silk-smooth surface is a serene experience. The boat calls first at a series of flower-decked villages on the Swiss shore with the long level ridge of the Jura mountains in the background. The first stop on the French side is the walled village of **YVOIRES**, its houses packed on a low rise behind the shore, guarded by a massive fourteenth-century castle. Mont Blanc and a host of other peaks appear shining in the distance. Next you call at THONON-LES-BAINS, flanked, just outside the town, by the fifteenth-century **Château de Ripaille,** built by Duke Amadeus VIII and used by him as a retreat before and after his stint as anti-Pope. '*Faire la ripaille*' has come to mean 'have a really riotous time' in French, which is apparently rather unfair to the Duke, who led a much quieter life than popular imagination wanted to believe. Thonon was also the place from which St-François de Sales set out on his donkey to reclaim the erring Protestants of Chablais for Rome.

Why visit **EVIAN**? Well, unless you are a well-heeled invalid or gambler, there probably isn't much point, except as the end of a pleasant, leisurely trip on the lake. The famous water is now bottled at Amphion, but the **Source Cachat** still bubbles away behind the Evian company's beautiful nineteenth-century offices, all wood, coloured glass, cupolas and patterned tiles – the best building in town. Anyone can go along and help themselves to spring water. The waterfront is elegantly laid out with squares of billiard-table grass, brilliant flowerbeds and rare trees. It is pretty, restful and not very exciting, like most spa towns. If you stay, there are several **hotels** that would make a large hole in your budget, and one or two that would wipe it out completely.

Near the port, at the east end of rue Nationale, the main shopping street, the hotels *Léman* and *Regina* are reasonable. There are numerous **campsites**, out of town. The **SI** and **gare routière** are both on the waterfront by the Casino.

travel details

Trains

From Grenoble to Paris-Lyon (2 or 3 daily; 7¼ hr.); Lyon (very frequent; 1½ hr.–1 hr. 45 min.); Gap (2 daily; 2½ hr.) and Briançon (4 hr.), changing at Veynes-Dévoluy.

From Annecy to St-Gervais (10 daily; 1¼–2 hr.).

From St-Gervais to Chamonix (7 daily; 35 min.).

From Chambéry to Modane (frequent; 40 min.–1 hr. 20 min.); Bourg-St-Maurice (5 daily; 2 hr.); Lyon (very frequent; 1½–2½ hr.).

From Briançon to Marseille (3 daily; 4½ hr.).

From Annemasse to Evian (very frequent; 35 min.); Annecy, changing at La-Roche-sur-Foron (4 or 5 daily; 1¼ hr.) – 1 through train daily only; 1 through train to Paris-Lyon (8 hr.).

From Geneva Paris-Lyon (4 daily; 3 hr. 45 min.).

Buses

From Chamonix 3 to Annecy via La-Roche-sur-Foron (3 hr.); 1 to Annecy via Megève (3 hr.); 1 to Geneva (2½ hr.); 1 to Grenoble (3½ hr.).

From Bourg-St-Maurice to Val d'Isère (1 or 2 daily; 50 min.–1 hr. 20 min.); Aosta (1 daily in July and Aug.; 2½ hr.).

From Grenoble to Briançon (1 daily; 3 hr.) via Bourg-d'Oisans (1 hr.), La Grave (1 hr. 40 min.), Col du Lautaret (2 hr.), Monetier-les-Bains (2 hr. 25 min.); Bourg-d'Oisans (5 daily; 1 hr. 20 min.); Gap (1 daily; 2¾ hr.).

Ferries

From Geneva several daily down the lake.

CHAPTER FOURTEEN

PROVENCE AND THE RHONE VALLEY

Of all the areas of France, Provence is the most irresistible. Geographically it ranges from the high mountains of the **southern Alps to** the wild plains of the **Camargue**; and has the greatest European canyon, the **Gorge du Verdon**. Fortresses like **Sisteron** and **Tarascon** guard its erstwhile borders and countless citadels perch defensively at strategic heights. The sensual inducements of Provence include warmth, even in winter, food and wine, and the perfumes of Mediterranean vegetation. Along with its coast (see the following chapter) it has attracted the rich and famous, the artistic and reclusive, and nameless numbers who have found themselves unable to conceive of life lived elsewhere.

In appearance, despite the throngs of foreigners and French from other regions, inland Provence remains remarkably unscathed. The history of its earliest known natives, of the Greeks, then Romans that squeezed them out, of raiding Saracens, schismatic popes, and shifting allegiances to different counts and princes, is still in evidence. The complete integration into France dates only from the nineteenth century, and though the Provençal language is rarely heard, the common accent is distinctive even to a foreign ear, and in the east the intonation is Italian.

Unless you're going to stay for months the main problem with Provence is choosing where to go. On the Rhône Valley side are the Roman cities, **Orange**, **Vaison-la-Romaine**, **Carpentras**, **Arles** and the papal city of **Avignon** with its brilliant summer festival. Aix is the mini-Paris of Provence, and home to Cézanne for whom the **Mont St-Victoire** was an enduring subject. Vasarely's works are on show in Aix and **Gordes**, Van Gogh's links are with St-Rémy and Arles. The Verdon gorge, the **Parc de Mercantor** along the Italian border, **Mont Ventoux** northeast of Carpentras, and the flamingo-filled lagoons of the Camargue are only some of the landscapes that should not be missed.

But before you reach Provence there are the **vineyards of the Rhône Valley** and before them, the French centre of gastronomy and the second largest city of the country, **Lyon**. With its choice of restaurants, clubs, culture and all the accoutrements of an affluent and vital Western city, it may be just the contrast you need to set against the medieval hilltop villages of Provence.

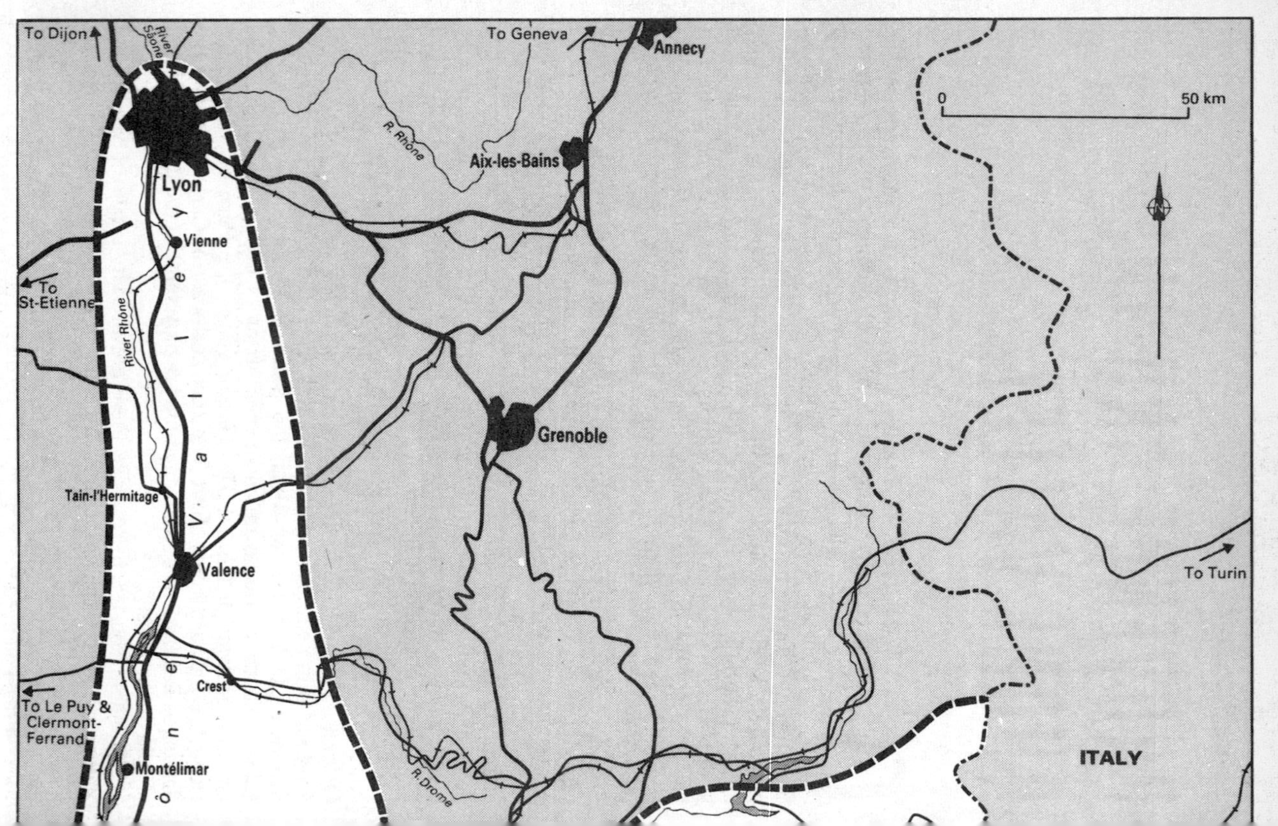
To Dijon
River Saône
To Geneva
Annecy
0
50 km
R. Rhône
Aix-les-Bains
Lyon
Vienne
To St-Etienne
River Rhône
Grenoble
Tain-l'Hermitage
Valence
To Turin
Crest
To Le Puy & Clermont-Ferrand
Montélimar
R. Drome
ITALY
V a l l e y
R h o n e

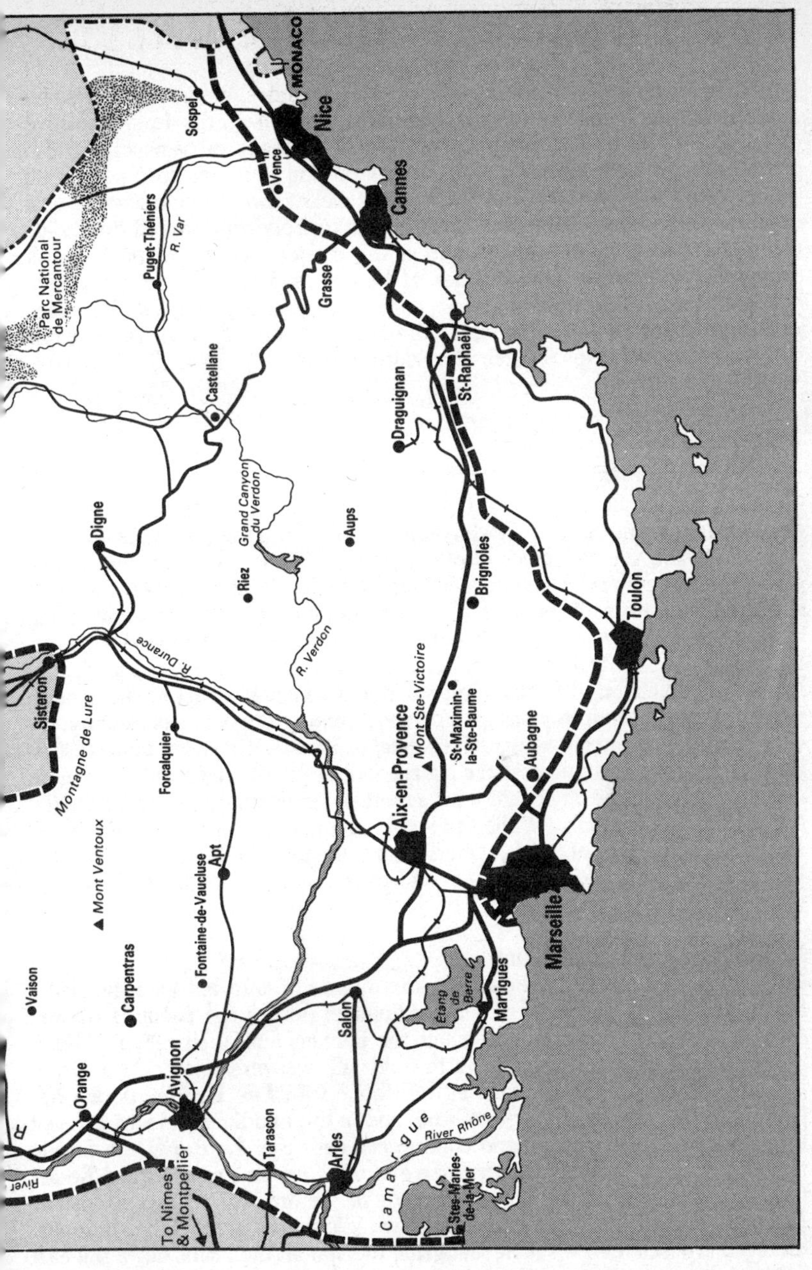
MONACO
Nice
Sospel
Vence
Cannes
Parc National
de Mercantour
Puget-Théniers
R. Var
Grasse
St-Raphaël
Castellane
Draguignan
Grand Canyon
du Verdon
Digne
Aups
Riez
Brignoles
Toulon
R. Durance
R. Verdon
Sisteron
Montagne de Lure
Forcalquier
Aix-en-Provence
Mont Ste-Victoire
St-Maximin-
la-Ste-Baume
Aubagne
Mont Ventoux
Apt
Fontaine-de-Vaucluse
Marseille
Carpentras
Vaison
Martigues
Etang
de
Berre
Salon
Orange
Avignon
Tarascon
Arles
River Rhône
Camargue
Stes-Maries-
de-la-Mer
To Nimes
& Montpellier
River

LYON AND THE RHONE VALLEY

The Rhône valley, North–South route of ancient armies, medieval traders and modern rail and road, is nowadays as industrialised as the least attractive parts of the North. Though the river is still a means of transport, it also provides, on a fairly massive scale, irrigation and hydro-electric power. Its waters cool the reactors of the Marcoule nuclear power station and act as a dustbin for the heavy industries along its banks. Following **the Rhône** holds few attractions, with the exceptions of the stretch of **vineyards** and fruit orchards between the Roman cities of **Vienne** and the distinctly southern city of **Valence**. And then of course there's **Lyon**, everything that big cities get bright lights for – good food, hundreds of bars, music, movies and people without provincial chips on their shoulders.

Lyon

LYON is physically the second biggest city in France, a consequence of its uncontrolled urban sprawl. Viewed at high speed from the *Autoroute du Soleil* the impression the city gives is of a major confluence of rivers and roads, around which only petro-chemical industries thrive. In fact, silk was the city's main industry from the sixteenth century right up until the present dominance of metallurgy, chemicals and lorries. But what has stamped its character most on the city is the commerce and banking that grew up with its industrial expansion. It is staid and stolid and somewhat austere, very bourgeois but not without its charms. Foremost among these is gastronomy, for which Lyon is, for many people, the capital of France. There are more restaurants per Gothic and Renaissance square foot of the old town than anywhere else on earth and the city could form a football team with its superstars of the international chef circuit. While the textile museum is the second reason for stopping here, the nightlife, cinema and theatre, including the famous Lyonnais puppets, antique markets and music festivals might tempt you to stay a few days.

Arrival, orientation and rooms

The centre of Lyon is the *Presqu'île*, the tongue of land between the rivers Saône and Rhône just before their confluence. Across the Saône is the old town at the foot of **Fourvière** on which the Romans built their capital of Gaul. To the north of the Presqu'île is the old silk weavers' district, **La Croix Rousse**. Modern Lyon lies east of the Rhône with **Les Brotteaux** *quartier* leading to the suburb of **Villeurbanne**, and in the middle the city at its most self-assertive in the cultural and commercial centre of **La Part-Dieu** beside the *TGV* station. Ordinary **trains** arrive at the *Gare de Perrache*, and **buses** too, on what was the tip of the Presqu'île before 1770 when Monsieur Perrache shifted the confluence some two kilometres south. The *Autoroute du Soleil* crosses the Presqu'île alongside the station then runs down the east bank of this extension past such attractive structures as St-Paul's prison and the wholesale market before recrossing the Saône just before the current merging of the rivers. Perrache is the exit to take from this manic highway. The **international airport, Satolas,** is off the Grenoble autoroute, with a 45-minute bus link to Perrache, or thirty minutes to La Part-Dieu. If you're in the intercity flying league and coming from Paris, be aware that it's quicker to go by *grande vitesse* rail than by plane.

There's an **SI** in the *Centre Perrache* in front of the station where you can pick up a **métro, bus, tram** and **funicular** map (also available at Perrache métro station) or just hop two stops on the métro to **place Bellecour** where the central **SI** is on the southeast corner. You can buy tickets in *carnets* of six or a *billet de tourisme* valid for 48 hours or 72 hours. The ordinary tickets are flat-rate within an hour's duration and limited to three changes using any combination of means of transport.

Hotel rooms should not be too much of a problem to find. If you don't want to stray far from Perrache, try the *Lux* (44 rue Duhamel) off place Carnot or *Vaubecour* (28 rue Vaubecour; ☎78.37.44.91) one block back from the Saône quays. Near place Bellecour *Des Célestins* (4 rue des Archers; ☎78.37.63.32) is worth a try. *Hôtel Select Home des Terreaux* (22 rue des Capucines; ☎78.28.26.92) is pretty basic but very cheap. *St-Vincent* (9 rue Pareille; ☎78.28.67.97) is in a good position just above the footbridge to *Vieux Lyon*. There's a **youth hostel** 4km southeast of the centre in Vénissieux (51 rue Roger-Salengro; ☎78.76.39.23; reception 8.30am–noon and 5–11pm; buses #53, #80 from Perrache or #36 from Part-Dieu, stop Etats-Unis-Viviani or Viviani Joliot-Curie). Not far away and a lot more expensive, though at least out of earshot of the main ring road, is the *Centre International de Séjour de Lyon* (48 rue Commandant-Pégoud; ☎78.01.23.45; bus #53 from Perrache or #36 from Part-Dieu, stop Etats-Unis-Beauvisage). If you have time, stop by the *Centre Régional d'Information Jeunesse* (9 quai des Célestins) close to place Bellecour on the Saône and they may be able to fix you up in student lodgings or residences closer to the centre.

The Presqu'île

If you're walking, two roads link the pleasant greenery of place Carnot in front of the Centre Perrache with the gravelly acres of place Bellecour, where even Louis XIV in the guise of Roman Emperor looks small. Rue Auguste-Comte is full of antique shops selling heavily framed eighteenth-century artworks. Rue Victor-Hugo is a pedestrian precinct, a welcome state of affairs that continues north of place Bellecour on rue de la République all the way up to the back of the Hôtel de Ville below La Croix Rousse.

Three blocks north from place Carnot on rue de la Charité, running parallel to rue A-Comte on the Rhône side, is the **Musée Historique des Tissus** (open 10am–noon and 2–5.30pm; closed Mon.; ticket also covers *Musée des Arts Décoratifs* next door). The museum doesn't live up to its claim to cover the history of decorative cloth through the ages. What it does have is brilliant collections from certain periods, most notably third-century Greek-influenced and sixth-century Coptic tapestries, woven silk and painted linen from Egypt.

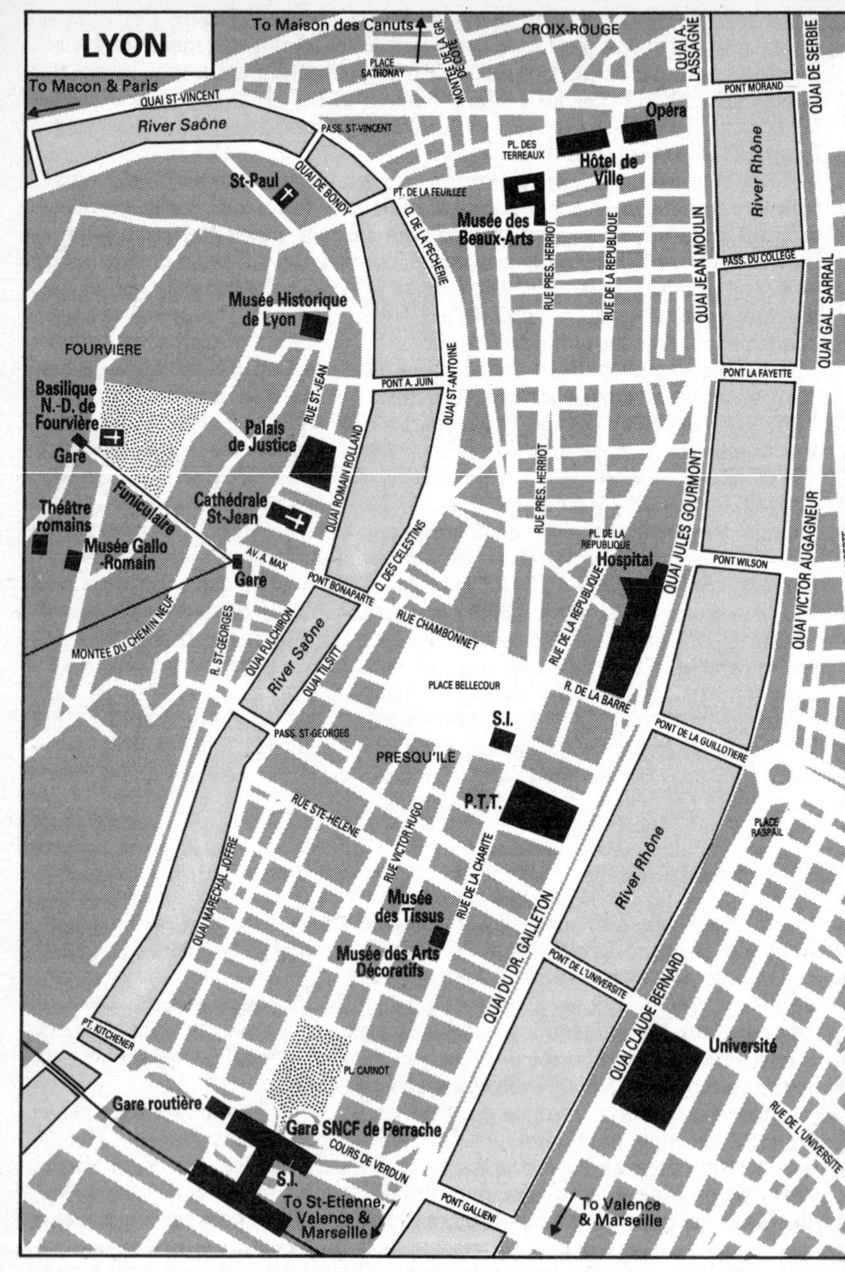
LYON
To Maison des Canuts
CROIX-ROUGE
To Macon & Paris
QUAI ST-VINCENT
River Saône
PLACE SATHONAY
MONTEE DE LA GR. DE COTE
QUAI A. LASSAGNE
QUAI DE SERBIE
PONT MORAND
Opéra
PASS. ST-VINCENT
PL. DES TERREAUX
Hôtel de Ville
River Rhône
St-Paul
QUAI DE BONDY
PT. DE LA FEUILLEE
Q. DE LA PECHERIE
Musée des Beaux-Arts
RUE PRES. HERRIOT
RUE DE LA REPUBLIQUE
QUAI JEAN MOULIN
PASS. DU COLLEGE
QUAI GAL. SARRAIL
Musée Historique de Lyon
FOURVIERE
PONT A. JUIN
QUAI ST-ANTOINE
PONT LA FAYETTE
Basilique N.-D. de Fourvière
Gare
RUE ST-JEAN
Palais de Justice
QUAI ROMAIN ROLLAND
QUAI JULES GOURMONT
QUAI VICTOR AUGAGNEUR
Funiculaire
Théâtre romains
Cathédrale St-Jean
Q. DES CELESTINS
Musée Gallo-Romain
AV. A. MAX
Gare
PL. DE LA REPUBLIQUE
Hospital
PONT WILSON
PONT BONAPARTE
RUE CHAMBONNET
MONTEE DU CHEMIN NEUF
R. ST-GEORGES
QUAI FULCHIRON
River Saône
QUAI TILSITT
PLACE BELLECOUR
R. DE LA BARRE
S.I.
PONT DE LA GUILLOTIERE
PASS. ST-GEORGES
PRESQU'ILE
RUE STE-HELENE
P.T.T.
PLACE RASPAIL
RUE VICTOR HUGO
RUE DE LA CHARITE
QUAI MARECHAL JOFFRE
Musée des Tissus
Musée des Arts Décoratifs
QUAI DU DR. GAILLETON
River Rhône
PONT DE L'UNIVERSITE
QUAI CLAUDE BERNARD
Université
PT. KITCHENER
PL. CARNOT
Gare routière
Gare SNCF de Perrache
COURS DE VERDUN
RUE DE L'UNIVERSITE
S.I.
To St-Etienne, Valence & Marseille
PONT GALLIENI
To Valence & Marseille

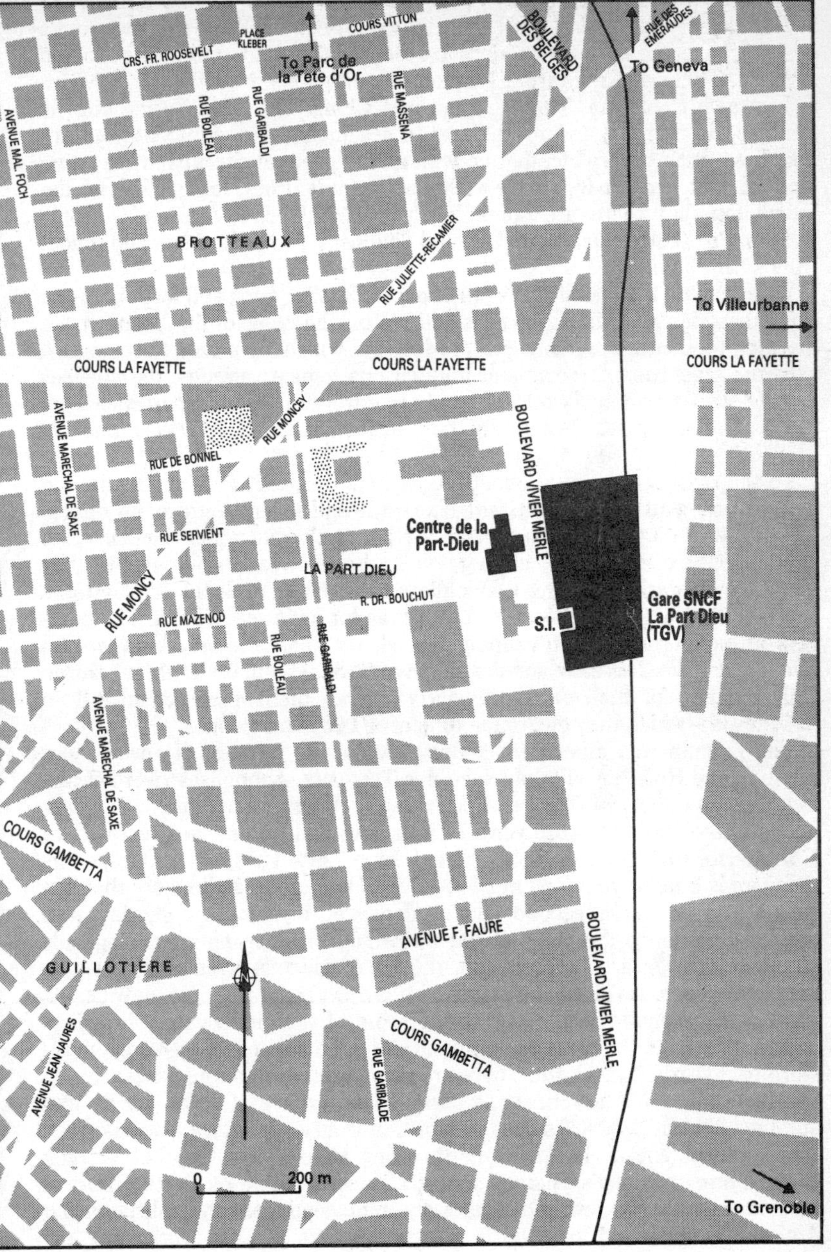
CRS. FR. ROOSEVELT
PLACE KLEBER
To Parc de la Tete d'Or
COURS VITTON
BOULEVARD DES BELGES
RUE DES EMERAUDES
To Geneva
AVENUE MAL. FOCH
RUE BOILEAU
RUE GARIBALDI
RUE MASSENA
BROTTEAUX
RUE JULIETTE-RECAMIER
To Villeurbanne
COURS LA FAYETTE
COURS LA FAYETTE
COURS LA FAYETTE
AVENUE MARECHAL DE SAXE
RUE MONCEY
RUE DE BONNEL
BOULEVARD VIVIER MERLE
Centre de la Part-Dieu
RUE SERVIENT
LA PART DIEU
R. DR. BOUCHUT
RUE MONCY
RUE MAZENOD
RUE BOILEAU
RUE GARIBALDI
S.I.
Gare SNCF La Part Dieu (TGV)
AVENUE MARECHAL DE SAXE
COURS GAMBETTA
AVENUE F. FAURE
BOULEVARD VIVIER MERLE
GUILLOTIERE
COURS GAMBETTA
AVENUE JEAN JAURES
RUE GARIBALDE
0
200 m
To Grenoble

The fragment of woven wool *aux poissons* (2–3C) has an artistry unmatched in European work until at least the eighteenth century. Some of the Coptic designs have the style of modern cartoons, others are more like Roman mosaics. There are silks from Bagdad contemporary with the *1001 Nights* and carpets from Iran, Turkey, India and China. The most boring stuff is produced in this very town – the sort of seventeenth- to eighteenth-century hangings, chair covers etc. that go with all the pastoral cherubs in the paintings of that era. Sadly, there's almost nothing from the period of the Revolution, but there are some lovely twentieth-century pieces – Sonia Delaunay's *Tissus Simultanés*, Michel Dubost's *L'Oiseau Bleu* and Raoul Dufy's *Les Coquillages*.

While rue de la République is full of people jostling back and forth between café-brasseries and shops, quai St-Antoine on the bank of the Saône has a morning **food market** (daily except Mon.), in which, by a very close contest with the mushrooms, meats and multifarious lettuce varieties, the cheeses are the star attraction. Two local numbers – from the Isère *département* – of the sort that squash beautifully into a *baguette* are *St-Félicien* and *St-Marcellin*.

To the right at the top of quai St-Antoine is the *quartier Mercière*, the old commercial centre of the town with sixteenth- and seventeenth-century financial houses lining rue Mercière, and St-Nizier's church, whose bells used to announce the closing of the city's gates. In the silk-weavers' uprising of 1831 (see below), workers fleeing the soldiers took refuge in St-Nizier only to be massacred, with more respect for profit than for hallowed ground. The bourgeoisie had certainly been running scared, with only the area between the rivers, place des Terreaux and just north of St-Nizier still under their control. Unfortunately for the *canuts* (the silk workers), their bosses could call on outside aid – which they did, to the tune of 30,000 extra troops.

The monumental nineteenth-century fountain in front of the even more monumental Hôtel de Ville on place des Terreaux, symbolises rivers straining to reach the ocean. The building taking up the southern side of the *place* is one of the four wings of Lyon's **Beaux Arts** and **Musée St-Pierre d'Art Contemporain** (10.30am–6pm; closed Mon. and Tues.). Thankfully this museum is free, so you don't need to worry if you can't handle more than ten rooms at a time. The second floor is dedicated to paintings, starting with medieval works to the right of the stairs and progressing chronologically counter-clockwise around the wings, the last of which is given over to temporary exhibitions. If you've started off with the Lyonnais paintings downstairs, you'll find a stairway leading up to the room of twentieth-century drawings and sketches and the most contemporary of the main collection – so you can work backwards if you want. There are some pretty wonderful works among the moderns: Gino Severini's *La Famille du Peintre* of 1939; spring and summer light in Bonnard's canvases beside wintry port scenes by Marquet; Van Dongens and de la Fresnayes throwing amused looks at their women friends; one of Monet's Thames series; *La Petite Niçoise* by Berthe Morisot just to mention a few. Of the early nineteenth-century collection *La Maraichère* attributed to David is outstanding, and you can work your way through Rubens, Zurbaran, El Greco, Tintoretto, and a hundred others back to the Middle Ages. Downstairs are numerous objects lifted around the turn of the century from Egypt, Iran and elsewhere, some ancient, some fourteenth- and fifteenth-century. The museum of contemporary art devotes three huge spaces to one or more artists to do with them as they wish for six weeks or so.

La Croix-Rousse

The old silk weavers' district is still a working-class area but only twenty or so people work on the modern high-speed computerised looms that are kept in business by the restoration and maintenance of the palaces and châteaux. You can watch the traditional looms in action at **La Maison des Canuts** at 10–12 rue d'Ivry, one block north of place de la Croix-Rousse (métro Croix-Rousse; Mon.–Fri. 8.30am–noon and 2–6.30pm, Sat. 9am–noon and 2–6pm; closed first two weeks and Mon. in Aug.).

The modern machines are no different in principle from the Jacquard loom of 1804 which made it possible for one person to produce 25 centimetres in a day instead of four people in four days. This was not the undoing of the *canuts*. Both masters and apprentices, and especially women and children workers, were badly paid whatever their output. And over the three decades following the introduction of the Jacquard the price paid for a length of silk was reduced by over fifty percent. Attempts to regulate the price were ignored by the dealers, even though hundreds of skilled workers were languishing in debtors' jails. On November 21, 1831 the *canuts* called an all-out strike. As they processed down the Montée de la Grande Côte with their black flags and the slogan 'Live working or die fighting', they were shot at and three people died. After a rapid retreat uphill they built barricades, assisted by half the National Guard who refused to fire canons at their 'comrades of Croix-Rousse'. For three days, until the reinforcements were brought in (see above) the battle raged on all four banks. Six hundred people were killed or wounded and in the end the silk industrialists were free to pay whatever pitiful fee they chose. But the uprising was, and is remembered as, one of the first instances of organised labour taking to the streets during the most revolutionary fifty years of French history. In 1834 Lyonnais workers again built barricades, this time with overtly political demands and were repressed with even greater ferocity.

The streets running down from bd de la Croix-Rousse, and many across the river in *Vieux Lyon*, are intercut with alleyways and tunnelled passages known as *traboules*. Their exits and entrances are sometimes visible; others have doors like any street door that often lead to an upstairs apartment and the *traboule*. You can get a map of them at the **SI,** but as an example try going up past the right of St-Polycarpe on rue Réné Leynaud above place Terreaux. Then take the *traboule* opposite 36 rue Burdeau, to the right around place Chardonnet, through 55 rue des Tables-Cludiennes, opposite 29 rue Imber-Colomés, up the stairs into 14bis, across and up three more courtyards, and you should come out at place Colbert.

Vieux Lyon

The streets pressed close together beneath the hill of Fourvière on the right bank of the Saône form an operatic set of Renaissance facades, bright nighttime illumination and a swelling chorus of well-dressed Lyonnais in search of supper or a midday splurge. One of the most impressive buildings at the northern end is the *Hôtel Paterin* at 4–6 rue Juiverie, best viewed from the bottom of Montée des Carmes-Déchaussés just up from place St-Paul. A short way south the **Musée Historique de Lyon** (place du Petit-Collège; 10.45am–6pm; closed Tues.; admission free) has a good collection of Nevers ceramics, but the **Musée de la Marionette** on the first floor of this fifteenth-century mansion (same hours) is a lot more entertaining. As well as the eighteenth-century Lyonnais creations, *Guignol* and *Madelon* (the French Punch and Judy equivalents), there are glove puppets, shadow puppets and every type of rod-and-string-propelled toy actors, from Europe and the Far East. If you want to see puppets in action, check out the times of performances at the **Nouveau Théâtre de Guignol** in the conservatory on rue Louis-Carrand by quai de Bondy (☎78.37.31.79; 10am–noon and ☎78.28.92.57 2–6pm).

The central and pedestrian street rue St-Jean ends at the **Cathédrale St-Jean**, a twelfth- to fifteenth-century construction. The damage of religious wars and revolutions to the most recent part, the West facade, is slowly being repaired but the thirteenth-century stained glass above the altar and in the rose windows of the transepts is in perfect condition. In the northern transept is a fourteenth-century clock rivalling modern digital watches for superlative functions: you can compute religious feast days till the year 2019. On the strike of noon, 1pm, 2pm, and 3pm (most days), figures of the Annunciation go through an automated set-piece.

Just beyond the cathedral, opposite Av Adolphe-Max and Pont Bonaparte is the **funicular station** from which you ascend either to the **Roman remains** (direction St-Just; stop *Minimes*) or to **Notre-Dame de Fourvière** (*Fourvière* terminus). The former consists of two theatres (entrance at 6 rue de l'Antiquaille; 9am to sunset) and an underground museum of Lyonnais life from prehistoric times to 7AD. A mosaic illustrates the circus and various Roman games; bronze inscriptions detail ecomomic, legal and bureacratic matters; there's a Gaulois lunar calendar and models aid the imagination in reconstructing the theatres outside. The **Musée Gallo-Romain** (9.30am–noon and 2–6pm; closed Mon. and Tues.; admission free) is at 17 rue Cléberg. From there it's a very short walk to the late nineteenth-century creation of **Basilique de Notre-Dame**, a sickening miasma of multi-coloured marble and mosaic. As a visual antidote make your way to the belvedere behind and you'll probably find Lyon and its curving rivers the epitomy of beauty by comparison.

Modern Lyon

On the skyline you may notice a gleaming cylinder with a pointed top with other Manhattanish protuberances around it. This is **La Part-Dieu**, a business-culture-commerce conglomerate including one of the biggest public libraries outside Paris, a mammoth concert hall and a shopping centre said to be the largest in Europe (métro Part-Dieu). On the corner of rue Garibaldi and Cours Lafayette in front of these homely structures are the main **market halls** of Lyon. For a break from city buildings head north to the **Parc de la Tête d'Or** (trolley #4 from Part-Dieu, métro Foch or Perrache). There are ponds and rose gardens, and, just when you thought things were beginning to relax, the international headquarters of Interpol just beside the river. The park and the university to the east are divided by bd de Stalingrad where there's another **antique market** around nos. 113–5 on Thursday and weekends.

Way down to the south, at 25 rue du Premier-Film (bus #9; direction Bron Libération; stop *Frères Lumières*) are the **Fondation Nationale de la Photographie** and the **Institut Lumière** (2–6pm; closed Mon.; free except for special exhibitions). The building was the home of Antoine Lumière, father of Auguste and Louis who made the first ever films, and the exhibits range from magic lanterns to the cameras used by the brothers, and various art photographs (the temporary exhibitions are more exciting – enquire at the SI). The *Institut* also hosts various **film festivals**. Another **cinema** where you'll find offbeat, undubbed films is *Sully 129* (129 rue Sully; métro Masséna) between Part-Dieu and the park. This side of the Rhône is also the best for **theatre** of which Roger Planchon's *TNP* (8 place Lazare-Goujon, Villeurbanne; métro Gratte-Ciel; ☎78.84.70.74) is the most famous. Programme details and bookings are available from the SI.

Food and nightlife

Lyon is not a vegetarian's dream. The specialities revolve around different things you can do with animals' heads, feet, balls and innards and even the *salade Lyonnais* is a combination of eggs, bacon, and fried bread on top of lettuce and tomatoes. There is one dish that comes in all different flavours and sauces, including non-meaty ones – *quenelles*, dumpling sort of things that might be solid béchamel sauce. However, this being a great gastronomic centre you'll find specialities from every region of France and elsewhere. And one very major plus – local wines are affordable. *Vieux Lyon* is the area with the greatest concentration of eateries, though you'll find cheaper and less busy ones between place des Jacobins and place Sathonay at the top of the Presqu'île.

Vieux Lyon Le Vieux Fourneau (19 rue de la Bombarde) has a good four course menu at a decent price and a lively atmosphere. At *Le Sain-Bel* (2 place St Paul) you can eat *raclette, fondue* or *spaghetti alla carbonara* and have *quenelles* as veggies. *Le Vieux St-Georges* (7 rue Mourguet) serves Lyonnais and general classics of French cuisine to the accompaniment, weekend nights, of live jazz and blues. *L'Amphitryon* (33 rue St-Jean) is open till midnight every night, packed with people shoulder to shoulder. The possibilities are endless, though on weekends you'll see a lot of hotel-style *complet* signs.

Vieux Lyon is also the place for **clubbing** though the price of entry and drinks is stiff. *L'Amnesia* (1 place de la Trinité) with a **disco** every Friday night from 10.30pm to dawn is not too bad, or there's *Madness* (18 quai R-

Rolland; 10pm–3am; closed Monday). *Taboo Club* (56 rue St-Georges; open 6pm–1am) has *café théâtre* some nights, other nights **jazz** or performance art and at least the beer is affordable. Other jazz clubs in town are *Bec de Jazz* (9 quai de Bondy) and *Via Colomés* (22 rue Imbert-Colomés). There are various 'Anglo-saxon pubs' such as *Albion Public House* (12 rue Ste-Catherine) where you can play darts and listen to jazz on Saturday nights; or the *Cocon D'Or* (19 rue Alsace-Lorraine) where the live music is sometimes Irish folk. For African and Carribean music the place is *Nuit Blanche* (2 rue de la Monnaie; open 6pm–1am; closed Monday). An exclusively **lesbian** club with a very friendly atmosphere, *Damière,* is at 8 rue St-Georges, with late nights Wednesday, Friday and Saturday, and shows, songs and cabaret acts. Or there's *Tchin-Tchin* at 17 rue Sergent-Blondon near place des Terreaux. **Gay** clubs include *Chez Swann* (13 rue Terme) and *Petite Taverne* (12 rue R-Leynaud; Fri.–Sun. from 10.30pm).

Listings

Airport information ☎78.71.92.21

Bike rental *Motobécane François* (139 av Maréchal-de-Saxe)

Boat Trips *Bateaux-Mouches* from quai des Célestins up the Saône (2pm and 5pm) or down to the confluence (3pm and 6pm) daily April to Nov.

Trips down the Rhône to Valence and Avignon on the *Calabrun*, weekends only; reservations from *Société Naviginter* (3 rue de l'Arbre-Sec; ☎78.27.78.02).

Books English bookshop, *Eton* (1 rue du Plat) near place des Terreaux.

Consulates U.S.: 7 quai Général Sarrail, 6e; ☎78.24.68.49.

Festivals

Sept: *Festival de la Marionnette;*

Oct: *Festival des Arts Contemporains;*

Nov: *Festival Lumière (Cinéma Jeune Public)*

The following are biannual:

Biennale du Théâtre; June 1991, 1993 etc.,

Festival International de la Musique Mécanique; June 1990, 1992 etc.,

Festival Berlioz; September 1989, 1991 etc.,

Biennale de la Danse. September 1990, 1992 etc.

The SI is the best source of information for these and many more.

Hitching *Allostop* (8 rue de la Bombarde) and *Lyon-Stop* (29 rue Pasteur).

Hospital *Hôtel-Dieu* (1 place de l'Hôtel-Dieu, 2e; ☎78.42.70.80); *Hôpital Edouard-Herriot* (place d'Arsonval, 3e; ☎78.53.81.11).

Post Office *PTT* place Antonin-Poncet, 1e.

Rape Crisis *Info-Victims* (4 rue St-Georges; ☎78.42.90.02; Mon., Tues., Thurs. 2–5pm).

What's On *Lyon-Poche* out every Wednesday and available from any newsagent.

Women's info *Les Dames* bookshop on place Célestines.

Vienne and onwards

Upon leaving Lyon, there seems little point in doing anything other than heading quickly down the Rhône, whether on the motorway, N7 or the train, and reaching the sun and the smells of Provence as fast as possible. The first stretch between Lyon and **VIENNE** is unlikely to distract you from this goal. There is absolutely nothing but oil refineries, steel, chemical and paper works, cement, fertiliser and textile factories, all sending up grey and orange plumes of pollution into the air and water.

Vienne is still a bit too close to all this for comfort, which is only partly compensated for by the remnants of its ancient history as a major seat of Roman power in Gaul. The colonnaded **temple**, the **theatre**, **portico** and excavated **Gallo-Roman quarter** are all suitably impressive, but not a match for the Roman cities in Provence. The centre of life in Vienne, the cours Brillier, runs at right angles to the river, with the the **SI** at no. 3 near quai Jean-Jaurès (where the main road comes in), and the **gare SNCF** at the other end. Halfway along the *cours*, rue Bosun leads up to the gothic **Cathédrale St-Maurice** – with various treasures including some superb stained glass. The Roman remains are in close proximity to the cathedral except for the **Cité Gallo-Romaine** on the right bank of the river. If you plan to stay over, some **hotels** to try are *Poste* (47 cours Romestang; ☎76.85.02.04) between the station and the central place de Miremont; *de la Gare* (37 cours Brillier; ☎76.85.38.10); *Union* (5 place St-Louis; ☎76.85.63.15) off quai Jean-Jaurès at the northern end of town.

Between Vienne and **VALENCE** things begin to cheer up with some of the oldest, and best, **vineyards** in France. The Romans planted vines around Ampius just south of Vienne – now the *appellation Côte Rôtie* – and around **TAIN-L'HERMITAGE** – the renowned *Hermitage* and *Crozes-Hermitage appellations*. Just south of Ampius, on the right bank, is the tiny area producing one of the most exquisite French white wines – *Condrieu*, and close by one of the most exclusive – *Château-Grillat* – an *appellation* covering just this single château. From mid-September to December the different wine-producing villages celebrate their cellars with drunken *Fêtes des Vins*. The SI's in Valence or Vienne can give you lists of addresses if you want to buy a few bottles, or take N86 along the right bank and follow the *dégustation* signs, crossing back over between Serrières and Chanas. At Tain-l'Hermitage you can sample a good selection of *Hermitage* and *Crozes-Hermitage* at the *Cave Coopérative des Vins Fins* (22 route de Larnage; ☎75.08.20.87). The **SI** at Tain is at 70 av Jean-Jaurès.

In spring you're more likely to be conscious of orchards everywhere rather than vines. Cherries, pears, apples, peaches and apricots, as well as bilberries and strawberries, are cultivated in abundance. Between St-Vallier and Tain even the Rhône becomes quite scenic, and after Tain you can see the Alps beyond the blossom. You may even conclude that it's worth slowing down. If you can choose your route, then head east towards Beaurepaire, and follow D538 down. At **HAUTERIVES** is one of the main reasons for taking this route – to view the mania of a postman by the name of Ferdinand Cheval, (1836–1912). His tombstone is bizarre enough but nothing compared to his **Palais Idéal** which took him thirty years to carve. Various surrealists have paid homage to it, no doubt psychoanalysts have given it their all, but it defies all classification (open daily 8am–7pm in summer, 8am–8pm in winter; closed Jan.). Tuesday is market day; there's a campsite, and one **hotel**, *Le Relais* (☎75.68.81.12).

South of Hauterives 28 kilometres and 15 kilometres from the Rhône at Tain, is **ROMANS-SUR-ISERE**, not the most pleasant of towns but with an interesting museum about shoemaking, the industry that has kept it going for the last five centuries. The *Musée de la Chaussure et d'Ethnographie Régionale* is in the former Convent of the Visitation on rue Ste-Marthe (Mon. and Wed.–Sat. 9–11.45am and 2–5.45pm; Sun. 2.30–6pm). The toes curl in horror at the extent to which women have been immobilised by their footwear from ancient times to the present – and on every continent – while at the same time you can't help but admire the craziness of some of the shoes. If you need information there's an **SI** on place Jules Nadi.

By Valence, to return to the Rhône again, an invisible sensual border has been crossed. The quality of light is different, the temperature is higher bringing with it the scent of eucalyptus and pine. The colours and contours are worlds apart from those of the cold northern land of Lyon and beyond. If you want to celebrate your arrival in the *Midi* – the French term for the South – there are plenty of bars and restaurants in the old town of Valence, around the **Cathédrale-St-Apollinaire**. Or, you could take a bottle or two to Parc Jouvet (straight up av P-Sémard from the **gare SNCF** and across place A-Briand). On an evening around sunset, or even better at dawn, this is definitely the best place to be in the city. If you'd prefer to be in a **hotel** room, there's *Lyon* (23 av P-Sémard; ☎75.41.44.66); *Angleterre* (11 av Félix-Faure; ☎75.43.00.35; turn right from the station down rue Papin); *Splendid* (20 av P-Sémard; ☎75.44.09.18); or *Oasis* (91 av Sadi-Carnot; ☎75.43.10.12; the continuation of av F-Faure).

South from Valence, the Rhône starts to subdivide in a strictly regulated manner, preparing itself for various power provision and industry servicing, not least the cooling of the nuclear reactor at Pierrelatte just before the regional border. The only city of any consequence before you reach Provence is MONTELIMAR, and that's no big deal aside from its seductive name. There are nougat shops everywhere but better places to buy it further south. Half-way between Valence and Montélimar the river Drôme joins the Rhône. Following it upstream by road or rail (trains from Valence SNCF) is one of the dramatic ways of entering eastern Provence – at Sisteron by rail or, by road only, at Barcelonette in the Alps. From Romans-sur-Isère if you keep going south on D538 you meet the Drôme at **CREST** beneath a massive ruin of a medieval castle. Snow-capped peaks lie east across an open rocky plain of pumpkin and sunflower fields, grazing goats, and vines for the speciality of **DIE** – the next town on the Drôme – the sweet white wine *Clairette de Die*.

WESTERN PROVENCE

The richest area of Provence, the Côte apart, is the west. Most of the large scale production of fruits, vegetables and wine is based here in the low-lying plains beside the Rhône and the Durance rivers. The only heights are the rocky outbreaks of the **Dentelles** and the **Alpilles**, and the narrow east–west ridges of Mont Ventoux, the Lubéron and the **Montagne St-Victoire**. Communications have always been relatively easy – the number of major Roman cities stands testimony to this. The two dominant cities of inland Provence, **Avignon** and **Aix**, both have rich histories and contemporary fame in their **festivals of art**. Around the Rhône delta, the **Camargue** is a unique self-contained region, as different from the rest of Provence as it is from anywhere else in France.

Orange

Days off in **ORANGE** circa 5 B.C. were most entertainingly spent from dawn to dusk at the **theatre**, watching farce, clownish improvisations, song and dance, and occasionally, for the sake of a visiting dignitary, a bit of heavy Greek tragedy (in Latin). The acoustics allowed a full audience of 10,000 to hear every word. The hill of St-Eutrope into which the seats were built, and a vast awning from the top of the stage wall protected the spectators from the weather. If they got bored with the play, according to rival archaeologists' theories, they either slipped out by the west door to the baths and gym with three 180m running tracks, or had a chat and a drink at the Forum. There is no question, however, about the Roman theatre. It is the best preserved example in existence, and the only one with the stage wall still standing. And stand it does, across 103m to a height of 36m, and completely plain like some monstrous prison wall when you see it from outside. The interior, though missing much of its original decoration, has its central over-lifesize statue of Augustus, and the columned niches for other lesser statues. (April–Sept. 9am–6.30pm; Oct.–March 9am–noon and 2–5pm; combined ticket with the municipal museum.)

The best view of the theatre in its entirety, (for which you don't have to pay), is from St-Eutrope hill. If you go past the Forum or gymnasium remains, across place Sylvian and take montée de Chalon to the left off rue de Tourre, you can follow a path up the hill until you are looking directly down onto the stage. The ruins around your feet are those of the short-lived seventeenth-century castle of the princes of Orange. Louis XIV had it destroyed and the principality annexed to France – a small price to pay for the ruler of the Netherlands who was also to become king of England. The **municipal museum**, across the road from the theatre entrance (9am–noon and 2–5pm in summer, 2–6.30pm in winter), has various unilluminating documents concerning the Orange dynasty, and for classical historians at least, a much more interesting property register and land survey of the city from 77AD. In the best traditions of provincial town museums there's also the extremely unlikely collection of works by one Frank Brangwyn, a Welsh painter with no connections with Orange, who learned his craft with William Morris and whose commissioned designs for the House of Lords were rejected as being better suited to a nightclub. The pictures here are stark portrayals of British workers early this century.

If you've arrived by road from the north you will have passed the town's second major monument, the **Arc de Triomphe**, whose intricate friezing and relief celebrates imperial victories against the Gauls. The **gare SNCF** is about one and a half kilometres east of the centre with the nearest bus stop at the bottom of rue Jean-Reboul on your left as you walk away from the station. Bus #2, direction Nogent, takes you to *Théâtre Antique* and the next stop *Gasparin* for the **SI** on cours Aristide-Briand. The **gare routière** is on cours Pourtoules, one stop before the theatre.

Le Paris (78 av Foch; ☎90.34.02.48) is a cheap **hotel** south of cours Pourtoules. Others to try are *St-Florent* (4 rue de Mazeau; ☎90.34.18.53), *Arcotel* (8 place aux Herbes) and *Freau* (13 rue Ancien-Collège; ☎90.34.06.26) all in the centre. For **food**, cheap chips with *plats du jour* to eat there or take away can be had at *La Fringale* on rue de Tourre (closed Wed.). *Le Yacca* (24 place Silvian) gives a generous choice of dishes in an old vaulted chamber. If it's full, try the neighbouring *Le Gallois*, or *Au Bec Fin* at 14 rue Segond-Weber. The *Café des Thermes* on rue des Vieux-Fossés is a billiards **bar** with youngish clientele. For a standard drinking place the square opposite the *mairie* has *Les Négociants* and the less chic *Le Commerce* (with a much better juke box).

In July and August, Orange is packed with opera fanatics for the *Chorégies* or **choral festival** performed in the Roman theatre. Regrettably it has turned away from productions of the spoken classics which actors such as Sarah Bernhardt performed here at the turn of the century, but if you're interested, and prepared to make a reservation well in advance, details can be had from the *Maison du Théâtre* (place des Frères-Mounet, 84100 Orange; ☎90.34.15.52).

Serignan

The village of **SERIGNAN-DU-COMTAT** is just a short drive northeast of Orange. This was the final home of **Jean-Henri Fabre**, a remarkable self-taught scientist famous for his insect studies, who composed poetry, wrote songs and painted his specimens with artistic brilliance as well as scientific accuracy. In the 1860s he had to resign from his teaching post at Avignon because parents and priests thought his lectures on the fertilisation of flowering plants to be licentious, if not downright pornographic. It was his friend John Stuart Mill who bailed him out with a loan, allowing Fabre to settle in Orange. Darwin was also a friend though Fabre was no evolutionist. In his house, which he named the **Harmas**, (9–11.30am and 2–4pm in summer, 2–6pm in winter; closed Tues.), you can see his jungle garden, the study with his complete classification of the herbs of France and Corsica, and, on the ground floor, a selection of Fabre's extraordinary watercolours of the fungi of the Vaucluse. At the crossroads in the centre of the town (the Harmas is on N976 towards Orange) there's a very sympathetic statue of Fabre in front of the red-shuttered buildings of the church and *mairie*.

Châteauneuf-du-Pape

For those heading down to Avignon, the slower route through **CHATEAUNEUF-DU-PAPE** (also taken by four buses daily) has the obvious attraction of good wine. The rather miserable ruins of the fourteenth-century Avignon popes' summer residence overlook the village with the heavily industrialised Rhône in the distance. The streets between the *Château des Papes* and place du Portail, the hub of the village, have no particular claim to picturesqueness. Only the vineyards have magic, their grapes warmed at night by the large pebbles that cover the ground and soak up the sun's heat during the day. The rich, ruby-red wine is the most renowned but the white too is exquisite. It does not come cheap however and there's no one place where you can taste a good selection from the scores of *domaines*. The **SI** on place du Portail can provide a complete list or you can visit an *Association de Vignerons* such as *Prestige et Tradition* on rue de la République that bottles the wine of ten producers. The *Cave Père Anselme* on av BX-Pierre-de-Luxembourg has a **Musée des Outils de Vigneron** (9am–noon and 2–6pm) plus free tasting of its own and other Rhône wines to attract visitors. On the first weekend of August you'll find *dégustation* stalls throughout the village celebrating the reddening of the grapes in the *Fête de la Véraison*.

Vaison-La-Romaine

For all its attractions as a medieval town with a ruined castle perched on a rock above the River Ouvèze and, on the opposite bank across a Roman bridge, a cloistered former cathedral and the remarkable remnants of a Roman settlement, **VAISON-LA-ROMAINE** is surprisingly uncommercialised.

There's not a great choice of **hotels** and few bargains though one of the nicer ones, the *Hotel du Théâtre Romain* (place Chanoine-Sautel; ☎90.36.05.87; closed mid-Nov. to mid-Feb.) has some low-priced rooms for which you need to book in advance. The *Burrhus* hotel on place Montfort (☎90.36.00.11) is more expensive and characterless but has the possible advantage of being amid all the bars with wide *terrasses* that stay open late. *Les Vaconces* (☎90.36.00.94) is also on place Montfort and a cheaper option. On the route de St-Marcellin, one kilometre east of town down av Geoffroy from the bridge you'll find the *Centre Culturel à Coeur Joie* with hostel-style rooms, and next door, the terrific **campsite**, *Le Moulin de César,* which in summer should also be phoned first (☎90.36.00.78).

For really **stylish lodgings**, the *Haute Ville* across the bridge is the best locality. Rue du Pont climbs upwards towards place des Poids and the fourteenth-century gateway to the town. More steep zigzags take you past the Gothic gate and overhanging portcullis of the belfry and into the heart of this sedately quiet, uncommercialised and rich *quartier*. A sixteenth-century residence on rue de l'Evéché is Vaison's best hotel and restaurant, *Le Beffroi* (☎90.36.04.71). One other stylish restaurant and the *crêperie* and pizzeria on place des Poids make up the sum of the *Haute Ville*'s public life.

Back on Grand Rue, the Indonesian eaterie *Java* at no. 19 serves wonderful multiple dishes of satés, gorings, etc. More standard fare is to be had at the brasseries on place Montfort, along with Whitbread pale ale at the *Café du Commerce*, and there are more menus to consider on cours Taulignan and place de la Poste. Place Montfort is the obvious drinking place to gravitate towards but if you want to be in a more 'local' ambiance try *Vasio Bar* on cours Taulignan.

Buses to and from Carpentras, Orange and Avignon stop at the **gare routière** on av des Choralies near the junction with av Victor Hugo. The **SI** shares a building with the *Maison des Vins* on place Chanoine-Sautel at the far end of Grande-Rue from the bridge. It's directly between the two excavated residential districts of Roman Vaison, **Puymin** on the right and **Villasse** on the left. The *fouilles de Puymin* contain the theatre, several mansions and houses thought to be for rent, a colonnade known as the *portique de Pompée* and the museum for all the discovered bits and pieces. The *fouilles de la Villasse* reveal a street with sidewalks and gutters with the layout of a parallel row of arcaded shops, more patrician houses, some with mosaics still intact, a basilica and the baths. The houses require a certain amount of imagination but the street plan of La Villasse, the colonnade with its statues in every recess, and the theatre which still seats 7000 people during the July festival, do allow you the vision of a comfortable, well-serviced town for the Roman ruling class.

Most of the detail and decoration of the buildings is displayed in the **museum**. Tiny fragments of painted plaster have been jigsawed together with convincing reconstructions of how whole painted walls would have looked. There are mirrors of silvered bronze, lead water pipes, taps shaped as griffins' feet, dolphin door knobs, weights and measures, plus impressive busts and statues.

The *fouilles* are open June to September 9am to 7pm; March to May, October and November 9am to 6pm; December to February 9am to 5pm; tickets can be bought at the Puymin entrance just by the SI or at the **cloisters** of the former **Cathédrale Notre-Dame** reached via Chemin Couradou on the south side of La Villasse, and included on the same ticket. The apse of the cathedral is a confusing overlay of sixth-, tenth-, and thirteenth-century construction, some of it using pieces quarried from the Roman ruins. The cloisters are fairly typical of early medieval workmanship: pretty enough but not wildly exciting. The only surprising feature is the large inscription visible on the north wall of the cathedral, a convoluted precept for the monks.

The Dentelles

The **DENTELLES**, a row of jagged limestone pinnacles, run across an arid, windswept, and near-deserted upland area, the Massif Montmirail-St-Amand just south of Vaison-La-Romaine. On the western and southern slopes lie the wine-producing villages of **GIGONDAS**, **BEAUMES-DE-VENISE**,

SABLET, **SEGURET**, **VACQUEYRAS** and, across the Ouzère river, **RASTEAU.** Each one carries the distinction of having its own individual *appellation controllée* within the *Côtes du Rhône* or *Côtes du Rhône Villages* areas. In other words their wines are pretty good.

Besides *dégustation* and bottle-buying, you can go for long walks in the Dentelles, stumbling upon mysterious ruins or photogenic panoramas of Mont Ventoux and the Rhône valley. The pinnacles are favourite scaling faces for apprentice rock-climbers and their wind-eroded patterns can be appreciated just as well without the ropes and crampons.

Though possible to get to Beaumes, Vacqueyras, Gigondas, Séguret and Sablet by **public transport** (there are two buses daily from Vaison and Carpentras) hitching may be easier. There are **campsites** in Sablet, Beaumes, Vacqueyras and a **youth hostel** at Séguret (route de Sablet;☎90.36.93.31), a village super-conscious of its Provençal beauty image. The *Auberge St-Roch* (☎90.62.94.29) and *Le Relais des Dentelles* (☎90.62.95.27) in Beaumes (past the old village and over the river) are quiet, old-fashioned **hotels** and middle of the range (both closed Mon.). Out of season you may be able to get one of the six rooms at *L'Oustalet* in Gigondas (place du Portail; ☎90.65.85.30).

Places to stop for a **drink** or **food** are few and far between once you leave the main villages – basically one café in Suzette and a restaurant in Lafare. In Sablet the *Café des Sports* on the last spiral of the dome-shaped village feeds you for fifty francs with no fooling around with menus. For a real treat, and not too expensive, *Lou Brasero* on the rte de Lafare to Malucène, one and a half kilometres from Beaumes, serves beautiful home-made pizzas preceded by local specialities such as hot goat cheese with salad.

The most reputed **wine** in this locality is Gigondas, almost always red, and quite strong with a flavour of spice or nuts. You can taste the produce from forty different *domaines* and buy *en vrac* (a real bargain for this wine) at the *Caveau des Vignerons* (closed Wed.) on place de la Mairie in the village. If the art and science of wine and the whole business of wine-tasting is a mystery to you, then take a visit to the **Musée du Vigneron** between Rasteau and Roaix on D975 (open April-Oct. 9.30am–12.30pm and 1.30–6pm; winter weekdays 1.30–5.30pm, weekends as in summer; closed Tues. all year). A *dégustation* is offered and there's no obligation to buy. The most distinctive wine, and elixir for those who like it sweet, is the pale amber-coloured Beaumes-de-Venise muscat which you can buy from the *Cave des Vignerons* (8.30am–noon and 2–6pm; closed Sun.) on D7 just outside Beaumes.

The tourist offices in Gigondas (place du Portail) and the *Cave des Vignerons* or Mairie in Beaumes can provide lists of particular *domaines* or *caves* grouping several *vignerons* for the other villages. The place to go for **walking** and **climbing** information and maps is the *Club Alpin* (Café de la Poste, Gigondas).

Twenty kilometres east of Vaison rises **MONT VENTOUX**, whose outline repeatedly appears upon the horizon from the Rhône or the Durance valleys. White with snow, black with storm cloud shadow or reflecting the myriad shades of blue, the barren pebbles of the final three hundred or so metres are like a colour weather-vane for all of western Provence. Winds can accelerate to 250 kilometres an hour around the meteorological, TV and military masts and dishes on the summit, but if you can stand still for a moment the view in all directions is unbelievable. A road, D974, climbs all the way to the top; no buses take it. If you want to make the ascent on foot, the best path is from Les Colombets or Les Fébriers, hamlets off D974 east of Bédoin whose **SI** (Portail-Olivier; ☎90.30.14.43) can give details. Bédoin has five **campsites** and over a dozen **gîtes ruraux** for anyone considering spending a week or more in the area.

Carpentras

With a population approaching 30,000 **CARPENTRAS** is a substantial city for this part of the world. It is also a very old city, its known history starting in 5 B. C. as capital to a Celtic tribe. The Greeks of Marseille came to Carpentras to buy honey, wheat, goats and skins, and the Romans had a base here. For a brief period in the fourteenth century it became the papal headquarters and gave protection to Jews expelled from France. Yet Carpentras, for all its ancient remains, seems incapable of working up an atmosphere to charge the present with its past.

Its local history museum is dark and dour. The **synagogue** on place de la Juiverie, the oldest in France (though rebuilt in 17C), is only worth seeing if you've never been into one. The erotic fantasies of a seventeenth-century cardinal frescoed by Nicolas Mignard on what is now the **Palais de Justice** in the centre of town were effaced by a later incumbent. The *Palais* is attached to the **Cathédrale St-Siffren** and behind, almost hidden in the corner, stands the Roman *Arc de Triomphe* inscribed with happy imperial scenes of prisoners in chains. Fifteen hundred years after its erection, Jews, coerced, bribed or otherwise persuaded, entered the cathedral in chains to be unshackled as converted Christians. The door they passed through is on the southern side and bears strange symbolism of rats encircling and devouring a globe. Apart from the *Porte Juive* the cathedral is exceedingly dull, as is the space around it.

By bus (the trains are freight only) you'll arrive at place Aristide-Briand, one of the two main centres for bars, brasseries and hotels. Rue de la République leads up to the cathedral past which rue d'Inguimbert turns right towards the synagogue and Mairie – another good drinking and eating area. If you want or need to stay, the **hotel/restaurant** *Mont Ventoux* (place de la Mairie; ☎90.63.04.89) is the pauper's option. For substantial **eats** *La Bagatelle* (88 rue Porte-de-Mazan) serves classic French dishes in huge proportions and, a short distance away, at 17 rue Calade, there's a *crêperie* with music, *La Blizribop*, that stays open till 1am Tuesday to Sunday. If you're searching for young, non-yuppie company with loud music, go play dice at *Le Petit Montmartre* on rue David-Guillabert. Friday is **market day** and one of the best reasons for being in Carpentras. The **SI** at 170 allées Jean-Jaurès dishes out pretty useless free maps. During **festival** time (July 15–Aug. 8) information on all events can be had from the *Bureau du Festival* on place d'Inguimbert.

Avignon

Outside festival time **AVIGNON**, great city of the popes and for centuries one of the major artistic centres of France, can leave you feeling rather cold. There is a daunting list of monuments and museums that can't be missed (without bringing on a bad attack of tourist conscience). And there is no particularly cosy area of knotted medieval streets for café-lounging. Parts of streets are good to wander down, a great many buildings have impressive decoration, there are the churches and chapels and convents. But it's easy to feel like an outsider, unless you're there during the **Festival d'Art Dramatique et de Danse** from mid-July to mid-August.

Central Avignon is enclosed by medieval walls, built by one of the nine popes that based themselves here throughout most of the fourteenth century, away from the anarchic feuding, or, in the case of the last two, away from the rival popes, in Rome. Benoit XII (1334–42) turned the episcopal palace into an austere fortress and his successor, Clement VI, added a new palace to it, a much more luxurious affair with distinctly worldly trimmings. He also managed to buy the town from Queen Jeanne of Naples and Provence, apparently in return for absolution for any possible involvement she might have had in the assassination of her first husband. Avignon was a pretty lively place while the papacy had its headquarters here. Every vice and crime flourished in the overcrowded, plague-ridden rats' bag of papal entourage and hangers-on, natives and visiting dignitaries with their retinues. According to Petrach it was 'a sewer where all the filth of the universe has gathered'. In 1403 the Antipope Benoit, who had built the walls in a fit of justified paranoia during the shifting alliances of the Great Schism, was ousted and the city had to content itself with mere cardinals.

The city

The **walls** today do not look very convincing as a city defence. When they were restored in the nineteenth century the moat could not be excavated, hence their original height is concealed. All the gates and towers are in place, however, and it's not difficult to know in which direction to go from the **gare SNCF** or **gare routière**. Both are beside porte de la République on bd St-Roch. Cours Jean-Jaurès on the other side of the gate, with the **SI** at no. 41, turns into rue de la République and runs straight up to the central café-lined square of **place de l'Horloge.** You can take bus #A from the main **PTT** on av du Prés.-Kennedy to the left just as you come through porte de la République from the station. Beyond place de l'Horloge is the **Palais des Papes,** the **cathedral,** the **Petit Palais** and **St-Bénézet's bridge**.

This is the famous **pont d'Avignon** of the song, which according to one theory says 'Under the bridge', not 'On the bridge', and refers to the thief and trickster clientele of a tavern on the Ile de la Barthelasse (which the bridge would have crossed) dancing with glee at the arrival of more victims. Repairing the bridge from the ravages of the Rhône was finally abandoned in 1660, three and a half centuries after it was built, and only four of the original

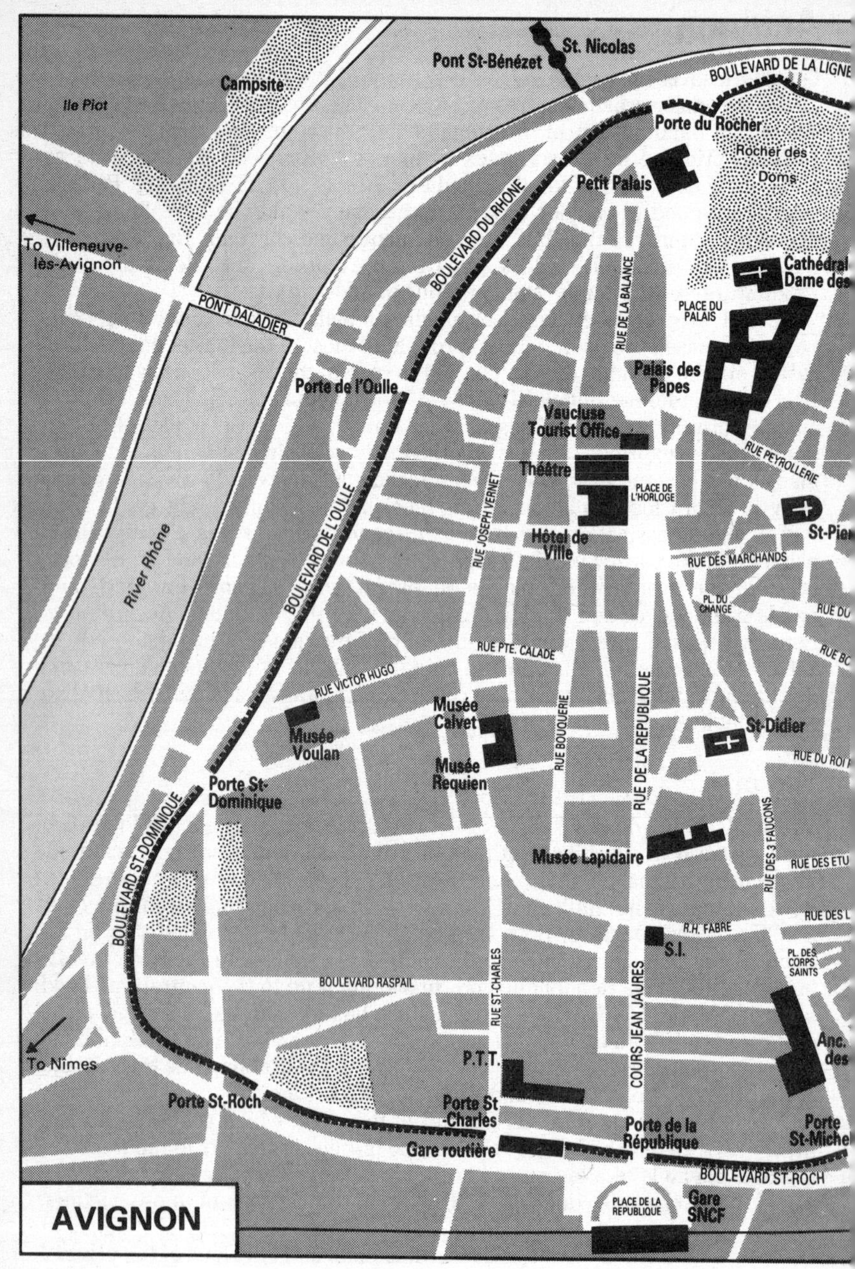
AVIGNON
St. Nicolas
Pont St-Bénézet
Campsite
Ile Piot
BOULEVARD DE LA LIGNE
Porte du Rocher
Rocher des Doms
Petit Palais
To Villeneuve-lès-Avignon
BOULEVARD DU RHONE
RUE DE LA BALANCE
Cathédral Dame des
PLACE DU PALAIS
PONT DALADIER
Palais des Papes
Porte de l'Oulle
Vaucluse Tourist Office
Théâtre
RUE PEYROLLERIE
PLACE DE L'HORLOGE
RUE JOSEPH VERNET
BOULEVARD DE L'OULLE
River Rhône
Hôtel de Ville
St-Pie
RUE DES MARCHANDS
PL. DU CHANGE
RUE DU
RUE PTE. CALADE
RUE BC
RUE VICTOR HUGO
Musée Calvet
RUE DE LA REPUBLIQUE
RUE BOUQUERIE
St-Didier
Musée Voulan
RUE DU ROI
Musée Requien
Porte St-Dominique
RUE DES 3 FAUCONS
Musée Lapidaire
RUE DES ETU
BOULEVARD ST-DOMINIQUE
RUE DES L
R.H. FABRE
S.I.
PL. DES CORPS SAINTS
BOULEVARD RASPAIL
RUE ST-CHARLES
COURS JEAN JAURES
To Nîmes
P.T.T.
Anc. des
Porte St-Roch
Porte St -Charles
Porte de la République
Porte St-Michel
Gare routière
BOULEVARD ST-ROCH
PLACE DE LA REPUBLIQUE
Gare SNCF

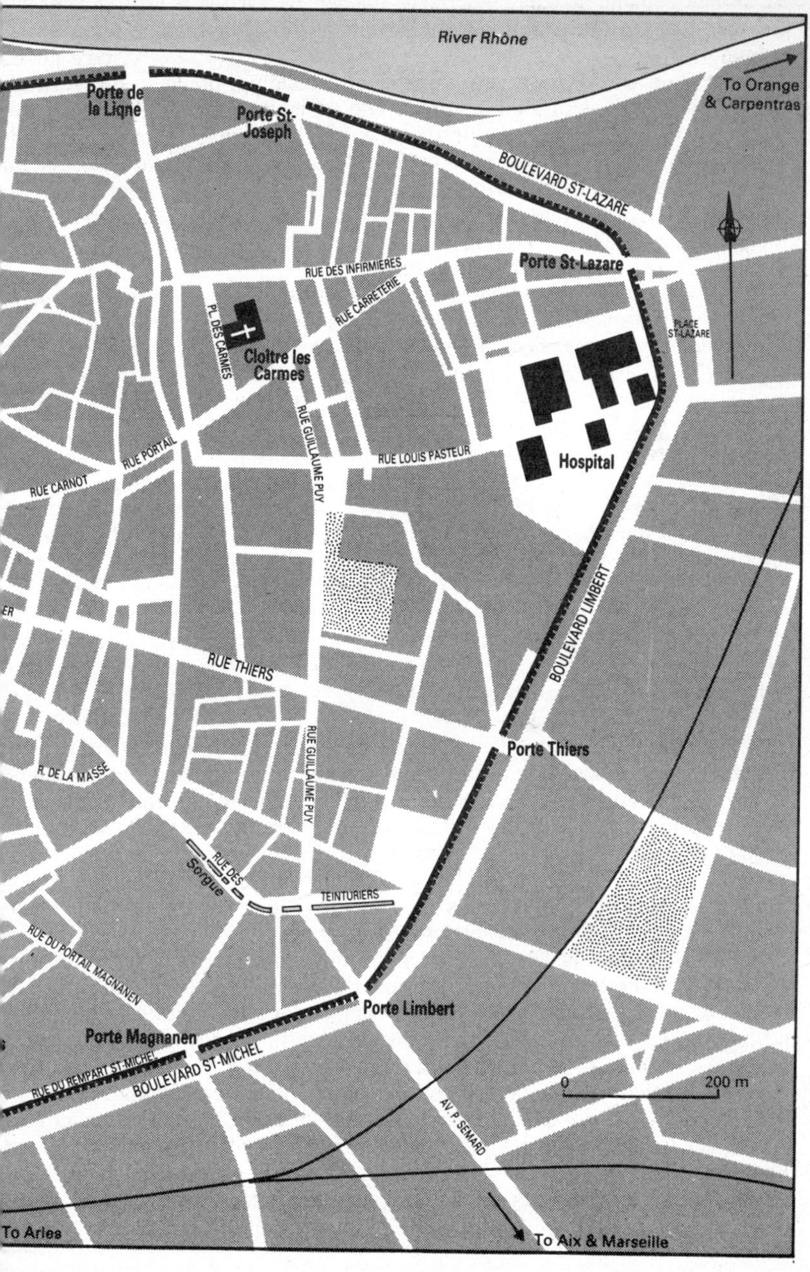
River Rhône
To Orange & Carpentras
Porte de la Ligne
Porte St-Joseph
BOULEVARD ST-LAZARE
RUE DES INFIRMIERES
Porte St-Lazare
RUE CARRETERIE
PLACE ST-LAZARE
PL. DES CARMES
Cloître les Carmes
RUE GUILLAUME PUY
RUE LOUIS PASTEUR
Hospital
RUE PORTAIL
RUE CARNOT
BOULEVARD LIMBERT
RUE THIERS
Porte Thiers
R. DE LA MASSE
RUE DES TEINTURIERS
Sorgue
RUE DU PORTAIL MAGNANEN
Porte Limbert
Porte Magnanen
RUE DU REMPART ST-MICHEL
BOULEVARD ST-MICHEL
0
200 m
AV. P. SEMARD
To Arles
To Aix & Marseille

22 arches remain. It can be walked, danced or sat upon from Easter to October 10am to 1pm and 2 to 6pm; November to Easter 10am to noon and 1 to 5pm.

The **Palais des Papes** is a monster of a building, doing to the vertical what Versailles does to the horizontal. The areas you can visit, however, are restricted to the ground and first floors, which are quite enough. Guided tours, in French, are obligatory only from October to March (at 9am, 10am, 11am, 2pm, 3pm and 4pm). For the rest of the year the Palais is open April to June 9.15 to 11.15am and 2.15 to 5.15pm; July to September, 9am–6pm, with English tours available. During the summer the central courtyard or *cour d'honneur* is taken over by a festival stage.

In the *Consistoire,* where sovereigns and ambassadors were received, is a nineteenth-century line-up of the popes, all looking very similar thanks to the one model the painter used. Of medieval artistry there is the *chapelle St-Jean* off the *Consistoire* and the *chapelle St-Martial* on the floor above, decorated by a Siennese artist, Matteo Giovannetti. He was commissioned by Clement VI who demanded the maximum amount of blue, the most expensive pigment, derived from lapis lazuli. The frescoes suffered at the hands of soldiers when the palace was a barracks in the nineteenth century but this allows you to see some of the technique – the outline drawn on the stone which would have been covered up bit by bit with the plaster to be painted on. Clement VI's secular concerns are further evident in the wonderful food-oriented murals and painted ceilings of his bedroom and study. With the study, or *Chambre du Cerf* you are into the New Palace of Clement VI, in which the *Grande Chapelle* has the proportions of a cathedral. The *Grande Audience,* its twin in terms of volume on the floor above, is used for concerts, exhibitions and, like most of the building, is closed off to the public for conferences and business meetings.

The **Cathédrale Notre-Dame-des-Doms** just north of the *Palais des Papes* might once have been a luminous Romanesque structure, but the interior has had a bad attack of Baroque. In addition, nineteenth-century maniacs mounted an enormous gilded Virgin on the belfry, which would look silly enough anywhere, but dwarfed by the fifty-metre towers of the popes' pile, is absurd. You could ignore it and go for a wander around the *Rocher des Doms* **park.** As well as ducks and swans and views over the river and beyond, it has a sundial for which your own shadow tells the time.

The **Petit Palais** just below the Dom rock is in some ways even more of an effort than the *Palais des Papes.* Unlike the basically bare and empty papal residence, this episcopal palace contains just under a thousand paintings and sculptures, most of them Italian of the thirteenth, fourteenth and fifteenth centuries. It's easy to get stuck, with more than a dozen rooms to go, on the mastery of colour and facial expressions, and hopeless background perspective of Simone Martini or Fabriano; or to pass out from a surfeit of Madonnas and Childs before you've got to Louis Brea's or Botticelli's. If you get as far as Room 15 you'll get a break from religious imagery with four scenes from Greek mythology. There is still an ecclesiastical connection: the labyrinth of the Minotaur is identical to the one sketched out on the floor of Chartres.

The *Petit Palais* is open winter 9.15 to 11.50am and 2 to 6pm; in summer 9.30 to 11:50am and 2 to 6.15pm; closed Tuesday.

The next major museum to tackle is the **Musée Calvet** (65 rue Joseph-Vernet; open 10am–noon and 2–6pm; closed Tues.). This has everything, from an Egyptian mummy of a five year-old boy to a Vaserély tapestry, taking in Renaissance armchairs, Géricault action/adventure tableaux, Utrillos, Laurençons, Sautines and Dufys; seventeenth-century Dutch still lifes, Gallo-Roman pots, sixteenth-century clocks, masses of wrought iron, and an anonymous sixteenth-century portrait of Henry VII of England. It's easier to traverse than the *Petit Palais.*

Rue Joseph-Vernet is where you'll find the most expensive shops of chocolate, haute couture and baubles, with restaurants to match. For chic furniture, both super-modern and antique, there's place Crillon just behind. This side of rue de la République and around the major monument conglomeration are the most desirable Avignon addresses. The sombre hotels with heavy wooden doors and highly sculptured lintels of **rue Banasterie** and its tributaries behind the *Palais des Papes* bear the name-plates of lawyers, psychiatrists and the like. The most spectacular doorway, which like the others is firmly closed, is the Renaissance creation of the *Eglise St-Pierre* on place St-Pierre. More Renaissance art is on show in the *Eglise St-Didier* (which can be entered except on Sun. pm), chiefly the altarpiece in which the realism of Mary's pain has prompted the somewhat uncomfortable name of *Notre-Dame du Spasme.* There are also some fourteenth-century frescoes in the left-hand chapel.

Between *St-Pierre* and *St-Didier* are the pedestrian precincts of **rue des Marchands** and **rue du Vieux-Sextier,** with their complement of chapels and late-medieval mansions, in particular the *Hôtel des Rascas* on the corner of rues des Marchands and Fourbisseurs, and the *Hôtel de Belli* on the corner of rues Fourbisseurs and Vieux-Sextier. One block south, rue de la Bonneterie runs east past the hideous **market hall** on place Pie (open every morning except Monday) into **rue des Teinturiers,** the most vaunted atmospheric street in Avignon. Its name refers to the eighteenth-and nineteenth-century business of calico printing. The cloth was washed in the Sorgue which still runs alongside the street turning the wheels of long gone mills. Following rue des Lices at the top of rue des Teinturiers brings you to **place des Corps-Saints (**near the SI), the alternative centre of the city's life to place de l'Horloge.

Food, fun and practicalities

Outside Festival time **finding a room** in Avignon should not be too difficult. Rue Perdiguier off cours Jean-Jaurès between the station and the SI has three cheap hotels: *Le Parc* at no 18 bis (☎90.82.71.55); *Splendid* at no. 17 (☎90.86.14.46) and *Pacific* at no. 7 (☎90.81.22.53) – although the latter has an unpleasant reputation. *Innova* (100 rue Joseph-Vernet; ☎90.82.54.10) and *La Bourse* (6 rue Portail-Boquier; ☎90.82.34.43) are also worth trying. The SI can provide travellers with a complete list of **hostels** and **foyers** and make reservations. For women, the best bet is *Foyer des Jeunes Comtadines* (75 rue

Joseph-Vernet; ☎90.86.10.52). There's a *Centre d'Hébergement* at 32, bd Limbert (☎90.85.27.78; bus #1, #3 direction place Pie or #2 direction Pont des Deux Eaux, from the PTT to *Thiers* stop). *Foyer Bagatelle* (☎90.86.30.39) is on the Ile de la Barthelasse along with four **campsites** – take bus #10 from the PTT, stop *La Barthelasse.* Single **bus tickets** or '*une planche de 10 voyages*' can be bought from the driver or from the TCRA kiosks at porte de la République and place Pie. You can **hire bikes** from *Cycles Peugeot* (19 rue Florence), *Dopieralski* (84 rue G-Puy) or at the *gare SNCF* (c/o *Services Bagages*).

Bargain midday **meals** are two a penny in Avignon and eating well in the evening shouldn't break the bank. The best areas to look are place de l'Horloge, around place du Change and rue des Teinturiers. *La Ciboulette* (1 bis rue Portail-Magnanen; closed Mon. and midday weekends), and, on rue des Teinturiers, *La Bonne Croûte* (evenings only; closed Sun.) and *Le Maquis* (Corsican cuisine) should provide a satisfactory level of gourmandise. For a sun-lounging midday meal try the *Grand Café du Commerce* (21 rue St-Jean-le-Vieux) and for snacks the *Côté Jardin* (7 rue des Trois-Carreaux) or *La Belle salon de thé* (19 rue du Vieux-Sextier). For **vegetarians** the place to go is *Le Pain Bis* (6 rue Armand-de-Pontmartin; closed weekends) near St-Pierre, and there's also an **organic market** around porte Magnanen on Saturday.

At no. 22 rue des Teinturiers is *La Tache d'Encre* (☎90.85.46.03), a restaurant with **live music** every Friday and Saturday night and sometimes during the week too. The food is not brilliant but the musicians, of jazz, rock, *chansons*, Afrofunk or salsa, usually are. Booking is advisable. An exclusively **jazz** club (without food) is the *AJMI Jazz club* at 8 rue Ste-Catherine, home of *Le Chêne Noir* one of Avignon's best **theatre** companies, which may have mime, a musical or Molière offer. *Herakles* (19 rue du Four de la Terre) off rue Thiers, a **gay** video club/bar is open every night from 10.30pm on. Straight **bars** or **cafés** with a reputation for hipness include *La Grand Siecle, Les Célestins* and *Le Bar des Quatre Coins,* all on place des Corps-Saints.

The festival

Unlike most provincial festivals of international renown, Avignon's is dominated by **theatre** and **film** rather than classical music, though there is plenty of that. The *Théâtre National Populaire,* one of the leading French companies, founded and directed for its first twelve years by Jean Vilar, comes to the *Palais des Papes* for the festival every year. In a dozen other locations the whole gamut of theatrical expression can be witnessed and every cinema in the city shows half a dozen different movies daily. The streets are taken over by the fringe, 'le off' as opposed to the mainstream 'in' – and by 250,000 non-native spectators; getting around or doing anything normal becomes virtually impossible. The headquarters of the festival is the *Maison Jean Vilar* in the *Hôtel de Crochans,* 8 rue de Mons (☎90.86.59.64/ 90.82.67.08). As well as providing programmes and **information** they show free videos and have a collection of festival memorabilia dating back to its inception in 1947.

Villeneuve-lès-Avignon

Avignon's neighbour, with monuments just as colossal and impressive, would do better on the tourist circuit stakes if it were further away. As it is, bus #10 from the PTT takes you to place Charles-David in Villeneuve in less than ten minutes (buses run every half hour or so – make sure you get the one going to Villeneuve first, not Les Angles). At place Charles-David you'll find the **SI** and, on Thursday mornings, a Provençal **market** of food, clothes and bric-a-brac. **Accommodation** may be easier to find here. There's a *UCJG-YMCA* **foyer** at 7 bis Chemin de la Justice (☎90.25.46.20) overlooking the river by pont Daladier (bus #10 stop *pont d'Avignon* or *Gal Leclerc,* if it's going to Les Angles). Just after Chemin de la Justice is a cheap but noisy **hotel** *Le Florence* (☎90.25.55.00). The *Midi* (place St-Pons; ☎90.25.44.24) is centrally located by the Mairie.

Between pont Daladier and the centre of Villeneuve you pass the **Tour Philippe-le-Bel**, once the end of pont St-Bénézet and hence a fortified border point for France. Even more indicative of French distrust of its neighbours is the enormous **Fort St-André**. Its bulbous double-towered gateway and vast white walls can almost be mistaken for storm clouds gathering on the horizon over Villeneuve. Inside is not a hint of a postcard stand or souvenir shop – just tumble-down houses and the former abbey, whose gardens of olive trees, ruined chapels, lilyponds, dovecotes and an amazing view across the river, can be explored. The fort is open from April to October (10am–noon and 2–6pm) and closed Tuesday except in July and August.

Almost at the top of rue de la République, on the right, allée des Muriers leads from place des Chartreux to the entrance of **La Chartreuse du Val de Bénédiction** (open April–June, Aug. and Sept. 9am–noon and 2–6.30pm; July 9am–6.30pm; Oct.–March 10am–noon and 2–5pm). This Charterhouse, one of the largest in France, was founded by the sixth of the Avignon popes, Innocent VI, whose sharp profile is well outlined on his tomb in the church. The buildings, sold off after the Revolution and gradually restored this century, are totally unembellished and plain. You come away with a strong impression of the austerity of the Carthusian order – only one hour of conversation a week and public confessions. During **festival time**, however, this site becomes one of the venues along with the fourteenth-century *Eglise Collégiale Notre-Dame* and its cloister.

Still on religious themes, the **municipal museum** on rue de l'Hôpital below place St.-Marc (open April–Sept. 10am–12.30pm and 3–7.30pm; Nov.–March 10am–noon and 2–5pm) contains various works that belonged to the Chartreuse. Of these, the altarpiece, *Le Couronnement de la Vierge,* certainly merits the room, with settees allocated solely to it. It's one of those medieval numbers with the social hierachy strictly defined, with exquisite minute detail and wonderful reds and incendiary devils. Many of the other paintings are too obviously PR work for patrons – putting the pope, lord or bishop beside the Madonna or Christ. But it's a beautifully laid out and spacious museum with lots of information with every picture.

The Alpilles

The roads south of Avignon lead through the watery and intensely cultivated plain of La Petite Crau, skirting the little ridge of La Montagnette that runs parallel to the Rhône. After eighteen kilometres or so the scenery abruptly changes with the eruption of the **CHAINE DES ALPILLES** whose peaks look like the surf of a wave about to engulf the plain.

St-Rémy-de-Provence

First casualty would be **ST-REMY-DE-PROVENCE**, a dreamy and rather sleepy town at the southern limit of La Petite Crau (daily buses from Avignon).

In 1889 Vincent Van Gogh, who was living in Arles, requested that he be committed to a hospital for several months. The hospital chosen by his friends was in the old monastery **St-Paul de Mausole** in St-Rémy, which remains a psychiatric clinic today. He was allowed to wander out around the Alpilles, and painted prolifically during his twelve-month stay. The *Champs d'oliviers, Le Faucher, Le Champ Clôturé* and *La Nuit Etoilée* are among the 150 canvases of this period. The driveway (with a statue of the artist), the church and cloisters can be visited 9am to noon and 2 to 6pm (no charge; follow avs Pasteur or Durand-Maillane out of the town centre, then av Vincent Van-Gogh from which av Edgar-Leroy leads left to the clinic; go past the main entrance and into the gateway on the left at the end of the wall). A permanent Van Gogh centre may by now be open in the Hôtel d'Estrine.

The **SI** is between avs Pasteur and Durand-Maillane on place Jean-Jaurès, and can provide maps for **cycling** and **walks** in and around the Alpilles. On the road up into the hills, a short way past the turning for the clinic, you pass a **Roman arch** and **mausoleum** in remarkably good condition – they were protected from quarrying from an early date. Having noted how unaesthetic Roman proportions are, you can head a short way onwards to **Glanum**, the dug out remains of an initially Gallo-Grecian, then Gallo-Roman town spanning five centuries from 200 B.C. (open 9am–noon and 2–6pm in summer, 2–5pm in winter – hefty admission charge).

The best time to visit St-Rémy is for the *Fête de la Transhumance* on Whit Monday, when the sheep do a tour of the town before being packed off to the Alps for the summer, and for the *Carretto Ramado* on August 15, a harvest thanksgiving procession in which the religious or secular symbolism of the floats reveals the colours of the various village councils. These festivities (among others) are genuine local manifestations with a long history, documented in the **Musée des Alpilles** housed in the Hôtel Mistral de Mondragon (10am–noon and 2–5pm; closed Jan.–March; combined ticket with the neighbouring *Musée Archéologique* and Glanum).

Le Monocle **restaurant** (48 rue Carnot) has an ace midday menu and delicious salads and desserts. If you prefer picnicking, shop at the Wednesday market. There are four **campsites** in St-Rémy, but **hotels** tend to be expensive – see if you can get a cheaper room in *Les Arts-La Palette* (30 bd Victor-Hugo; ☎90.92.08.50) or *Le Provence* (36 bd Victor-Hugo; ☎ 90.92.06.27).

Les Baux

At the top of the Alpilles ridge southwest of St-Rémy, is the unbelievable fortified village of **LES BAUX**. Unbelievable partly because the ruins of the eleventh-century citadel are hard to distinguish from the rock, which is both foundation and part of their structure, but also because the *ville morte* and a vast area of the plateau around it is accessible only via a turnstile, and payment, at the lapidary **museum** in the *village vivant*. The 'profiting village' might be a better term for the oh-so-perfect collection of sixteenth- and seventeenth-century churches, chapels and mansions whose residents blatantly live off tourism or businesses elsewhere. Once upon a time Les Baux lived off the power and widespread possessions in Provence of its medieval lords, who owed allegiance to no one. When the dynasty died out at the end of the fourteenth century the town, which had once numbered 6000 inhabitants, passed to the Counts of Provence and then the Kings of France, who eventually, in 1632, turned the feudal citadel into a 'dead city'.

It's almost a pity that people came back, though it has to be conceded that the lower village has some very beautiful buildings, and the view beside the statue of Mistral near the edge of the plateau is superb. If you're a good tourist you'll spend at least a whole day here, but don't expect any cheap accommodation. Whatever you do, don't miss the **Cathédrale des Images** in the quarries just north of Les Baux (signed right down the hill from the village car park). Created in the vast rectangular caverns which Jean Cocteau used for his last film, *Le Testament d'Orphée*, the *Cathédrale des Images* is a unique audio-visual experience. You are englobed by images that take up the whole floor, the ceilings and the walls, and music that resonates strangely in this captured space. For 1989 the show will be entitled *Les Droits des Hommes*. The projection is continuous, so you don't have to hang around outside. It's open March 20–November 11 10am–7pm; October 10am–6pm and closed Tuesday.

If you have yet to get your fill of medieval military installations, there are two major castles to be seen in the two cities that face each other across the Rhône, **TARASCON** and **BEAUCAIRE**. Neither are particularly attractive towns, but their castles are classics. Beaucaire's is thirteenth-century and French and not a lot remains of it; Tarascon's is fifteenth-century, Provençal and determinedly defensive to this day. At Beaucaire you're free to wander round the ruins on your own during daylight hours. At the *Château du Roy René* across the water, tours are guided (at 10am, 11am, 2pm, 3pm and 4pm; additional tours at 9am and 5pm in July and Aug.; closed Tues.) and culminate on the roof, from which revolutionaries and counter-revolutionaries were thrown in the 1790s, and which now is cursed by wafting fumes from the local paper factory.

One of the most famous carnivals of Provence, involving an amphibious monster known as the *Tarasque*, takes place at Tarascon on the last Sunday of June. There's a **youth hostel** at 31 bd Gambetta (☎90.91.04.08) open from March to December, and **train** connections to Arles, Avignon, St Rémy and Beaucaire.

Arles

An engraving of **ARLES** dated 1686 shows a snug spiral of buildings working its way around and within the oval surround of the **Roman arena**. There were three churches and 212 houses in all, including many in the two-story arches built 1500 years before this print was made. In 1830 the whole bunch was cleared and the *arènes* once again became a place of entertainment. The huddled, hapless *quartier* of seventeenth-century Arles could not be more radically different from the smug, conservative and French establishment town *par excellence* that Arles is today.

From the **gare SNCF** av Talabot takes you past place Lamartine, where the *Alcazar* bar is the *Café de Nuit* of Van Gogh's painting. The 'Yellow House' nearby, where the artist shared rooms with Gauguin, was destroyed in the war along with most of the waterfront, once busy with barges, and bars and bistros, where weary workers drank and danced away their woes.

What you are required to look at if you're going to do this properly, is stones – Gothic, Romanesque, funereal, early Christian and pagan – an awful lot of them. The obvious place to start is the central square, place de la République, between rue Jean-Jaurès and rue Hôtel-de-Ville which feels like a French equivalent of an Oxbridge College courtyard. Having greeted the lions around the obelisk, position yourself in front of the door of the **cathédrale St-Trophime**, one of the most famous bits of twelfth-century Provençal stone carving. It depicts the Last Judgement, trumpeted by angels playing with the enthusiasm of jazz musicians. Inside, the **d'Aubisson tapestries** on the high nave also have their lighter side – one shows mischievous dogs, a cat and a child in the scene of Mary Magdalene bathing Christ's feet. There is more Romanesque and Gothic stone carving, this time with New Testament scenes enlivened with other myths such as St. Marthe leading away the tamed Tarasque, in the **cloisters** (accessible from rue du Cloître alongside the cathedral). The cream-white vaulted galleries above the cloisters are given over to the **Musée Necropole** which displays, very beautifully, objects of everyday Roman life as well as coffins and urns.

On the other side of the square a deconsecrated seventeenth-century church holds the collection of the **Musée Lapidaire Paien**, or pagan art. Despite the resemblance to an amputation ward, there are some wonderful mosaics – of Zeus carrying off Europa, of Orpheus charming the animals – and a bust of Augustus dated post-Christianisation of the Roman Empire, suggesting that the cult of emperor-worship continued secretly. A headless bas-relief from a first-century triumphal arch (the only standard Roman structure missing from Arles) bears an extraordinary likeness to one of Botticelli's Graces. To see yet more fallen, chipped and time-eroded stones, cut through the ground floor of the Hôtel de Ville on the north side of the square and turn left into rue Blaze. The **Musée Lapidaire Chrétien** is almost all sarcophagi – once the Romans had been converted, they gave up their old and much more practical habit of cremation. From a flight of stairs in the museum you can descend to the **Cryptoporticus**, a huge, dark and dank underground gallery built by the Romans as a granary.

Roman Arles not only provided grain for most of the western empire, it was also one of the most important ports and ship-building yards, and, under Constantine, became the capital of Gaul, Britain and Spain. While being on the key road and river routes it was also, once the empire crumbled, isolated between the Rhône, the Alpilles and the marshlands of the Camargue, and so preserved its vestiges of an arrogant past. The **Roman baths** stand at the bottom of rue Hôtel-de-Ville; the **Roman theatre** is just south of the amphitheatre; **place du Forum** is still the centre of life; and **Les Alyscamps** is preserved as the burial place of Arlesians from 4 A.D. to the thirteenth century. The shaded walk, whose tree trunks are azure blue in Van Gogh's rendering, starts at the end of av des Alyscamps which joins the east end of bd des Lices. Going the other way from av des Alyscamps, bd Emile Combes skirts the medieval ramparts above the arena within which are the remnants of the Roman aqueduct, and if you're desperate to see it all, there's the remains of the Roman bridge on the other side of the river opposite rue Marius-Jouveau.

In case you feel that life stopped in Arles, if not after the Romans, then at least after the Middle Ages, you will be reassured in the **Musée Arlaten** on rue de la République. The museum was set up by Frédéric Mistral, the poet responsible for the turn-of-the-century revival of all things Provençal, who won the Nobel prize for Literature – a feat no other writer of a minority language has ever achieved. His statue stands on place du Forum, and in the museum a pleading notice instructs you to piously salute the great man's cradle. That apart, the collections of costumes, documents, tools, pictures and paraphernalia of Provençal life is alternately tedious and intriguing. The museum is not included on the 'global' ticket and the hours are April to September 9am to noon and 2 to 7pm; October to March, 9am to noon and 2 to 6pm.

In the **Musée Réattu**, opposite the Roman baths, you can finally return to the twentieth century, assuming you ignore the rigid eighteenth-century classicism of Réattu's work and that of his contemporaries. Of the moderns, Picasso is the best represented, with the sculpture, *Woman with Violin,* and 57 ink and crayon sketches which he donated to the museum. Among the split faces, clowns, and hilarious Tarasque is a beautifully simple portrait of his mother. There are contemporary works and, from time to time, exhibitions of photography.

Some practical details

From the Gare SNCF, Porte de la Cavalerie brings you into the northern section of old Arles and the best area for low-priced **accommodation**. In quick succession you can check out *Lamartine* (rue Marius Jouveau; ☎90.96.13.83) – a trifle gloomy; *Regence*, on the same street (☎90.96.39.85); *Mirador* (3 rue Voltaire; ☎90.96.28.05); *Voltaire* (place Voltaire; ☎90.96.13.58) – with hideous decor; *Le Rhône*, also on place Voltaire and with a bit more character (☎90.96.43.70); *Petit Hôtel de l'Arlesienne* (75 rue Amédée-Pichot; ☎90.96.11.36) – one of the better ones along with *Diderot* on place de la Bastille (☎90.96.10.30). If you want to stay right in the centre try *Moderne* on place du Forum (☎90.96.08.21) or *Musée* (11 rue du Grand-Prieuré; 90.96.04.49). There's a **youth hostel** at 20, av Foch (☎90.96.18.25; open all year; reception 7.30–10am and 5–11.30pm; 11.30pm curfew; bus from place Lamartine to *Foch*). There are six **campsites** in the vicinity of Arles, of which the nicest is *La Bienheureuse*, with a restaurant and very friendly *patronne* seven kilometres out on N453 at Raphèles-les-Arles (☎90.98.35.64; open all year). Closer, and on the Crau bus route is *Camping City* (67 route de Crau; ☎90.93.08.86; open April–Sept.).

The **gare routière** is opposite the *gare SNCF* though some buses, including those for the Crau, Aix and Marseille leave from 22 bd G Clemenceau. You can rent **bikes** at the train station or *Ets Montuori* on rue du 4 Septembre. The **SI** is on the other side of town from the station opposite rue Jean Jaurès on bd des Lices, the main promenading and market street. Rue Jean-Jaurès, with its continuation rue Hôtel-de-Ville, is the central axis of old Arles. The SI runs a hotel booking service for a small fee and you can also get a 'global' ticket for the **monuments** and **museums**. Their opening times are more or less standard – January, February, and November 9am to noon and 2 to 5pm; March and April 8.30am to noon and 2 to 6pm; May to September 8.30am to 7pm; October 8.30am to noon and 2 to 5.30pm; December 9am to noon and 2 to 4.30pm.

Place du Forum is a regular meeting place – *Bar Le Paris* being one lively place. Place de la République is more of a collapsing ground for exhausted tourists. *Le Gallion* on rue de l'Hôtel-de-Ville is a good, old-fashioned, friendly *bar-tabac* but for the big *café-brasseries* you need to wander down bd des Lices. For a special treat the place to **eat** is the *Hostellerie des Arènes* (62 rue du Refuge). Otherwise you'll find plenty of reasonable *menus* if you stroll between place Voltaire and place du Forum along rue du 4 Septembre. On quai Max Dormoy you can dine, borrow books from the library, and watch a show or a movie at *La Passage* (☎90.49.67.28). **Market** days are Wednesday and Saturday, the latter taking over most of the town around bd des Lices.

Arles, inevitably, has its calendar of **festivals** of which the most worthwhile are the *Rencontres Internationales de la Photographie* and the dance-orientated *Festival d'Arles* in July. For the locals, the key events are the crowning of the *Reine d'Arles*, once every three years, and the annual opening of the bull-fighting season on the first of May.

The Camargue

The **CAMARGUE** is where the bulls are bred, along with horses that their *gardiens* or herdsmen ride. These horses, symbol of the Camargue, are black or brown before they reach the age of four. Neither they nor the bulls are wild, though they run in semi-liberty. The true wildlife of the Camargue is something else – flamingos, migrating birds, marsh birds, seabirds, geese, ducks, birds of prey and a rich flora of reeds, wild irises, tamarisk, wild rosemary and juniper trees. There is water everywhere and total flatness. It is one of those geographically enclosed areas that are separate, and unique, in every sense.

BULLFIGHTING IN ARLES AND THE CAMARGUE

Contrary to some popular conception, bullfighting in Arles and the Camargue is not usually the Spanish-style *mise à mort*. Although the bulls probably don't enjoy their appearances very much, it is the bullfighters, or *razeteurs*, who get hurt, not the bull. It's a passion with the populace, and while the champion *razeteurs* are treated like football stars the bulls are also feted and adored, and before retirement are given a final tour around the arena while people weep and throw flowers. The shows involve various feats of daring but the most common form is where the bull has a cockade at the base of its horns and ribbons tied between them. Using blunt razor-combs (a recent regulation) the *razeteurs* have to cut the ribbons and get the cockades. There's no betting, but people add to the prize money as the fight progresses. The drama and grace of the spectacle is in the stylish way the men leap over the barrier away from the bull. You are much closer to the scene than with other dangerous sports and there are occasional casualties. For some shows involving horsemen, arrows are shot at the bull, though these don't go in deep enough to make the animal bleed. All this may leave you feeling cold, or sick, but it's the best way of experiencing the parallels with the Roman arena. The SI, local papers and publicity around the arena will give you the details – be sure to check that it's not a *mise à mort*.

Another aspect of the wildlife is a major problem though: namely the insects. Between March and November, if you have the sort of skin that attracts mosquitoes, you can't stay here unless you're by the sea. They are ferocious little devils and there are lots of them. They have been known to hospitalise foolhardy campers. Forget about cycling too, despite the perfection of the terrain – if it's not mosquitoes, other insects will blind you, or winds blow you off. Another problem, for those in cars, is organised gangs of thieves. Don't leave anything in the vehicle for a minute.

If you're interested in bird-watching, fishing or walking the *digues* that run around the lagoons, your first stop should be *La Capelière* **information centre** on the eastern side of the Etang du Vaccarès on the small road leading south off D37 from Villeneuve (9am–noon and 2–5pm). Large areas of the lagoons have restricted access as nature reserves; the centre can give you all the details. The **Musée Carmarguais**, halfway between Gimeaux and Albaron on D570, documents the traditions and livelihoods of the Camarguais people using self-consciously modern museum techniques (April–June and Sept. 9am–6pm; July and Aug. 9am–7pm; Oct.–March 10am–5pm, closed Tues.). After World War II the marshes in the north of the Camargue were drained and re-irrigated with fresh water to grow rice. The production of the Camargue paddy fields was so great, that until very recently France imported no rice at all. The other major produce of the region is salt, some 800,000 tons annually. You can view the lunar landscape of the salt piles from D36d running parallel to the Grand Rhône south of **SALIN-DE-GIRAUD**, the salt workers' town.

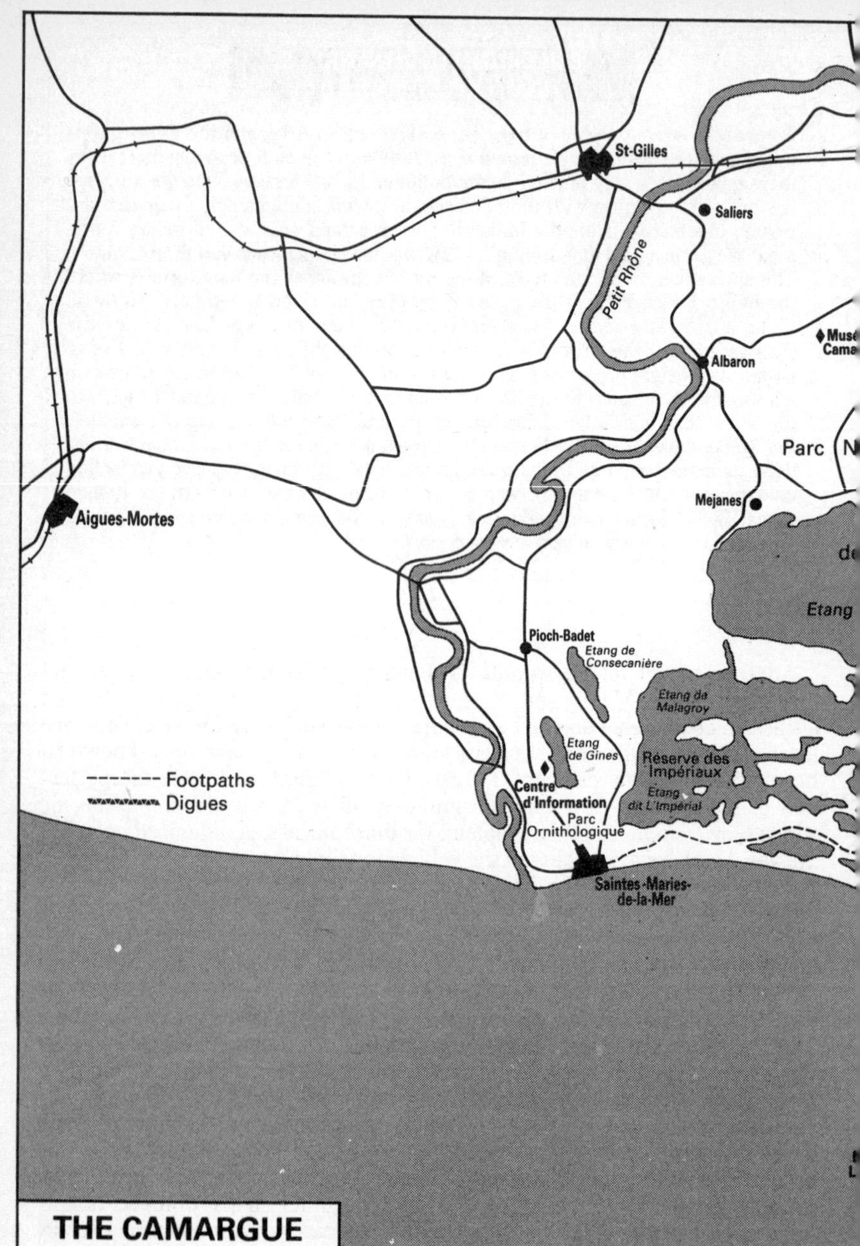
St-Gilles
Saliers
Petit Rhône
Albaron
Parc
Mejanes
Aigues-Mortes
Etang
Pioch-Badet
Etang de Consecanière
Etang da Malagroy
Etang de Gines
Réserve des Impériaux
Etang dit L'Impérial
Centre d'Information
Parc Ornithologique
Saintes-Maries-de-la-Mer
Footpaths
Digues
THE CAMARGUE

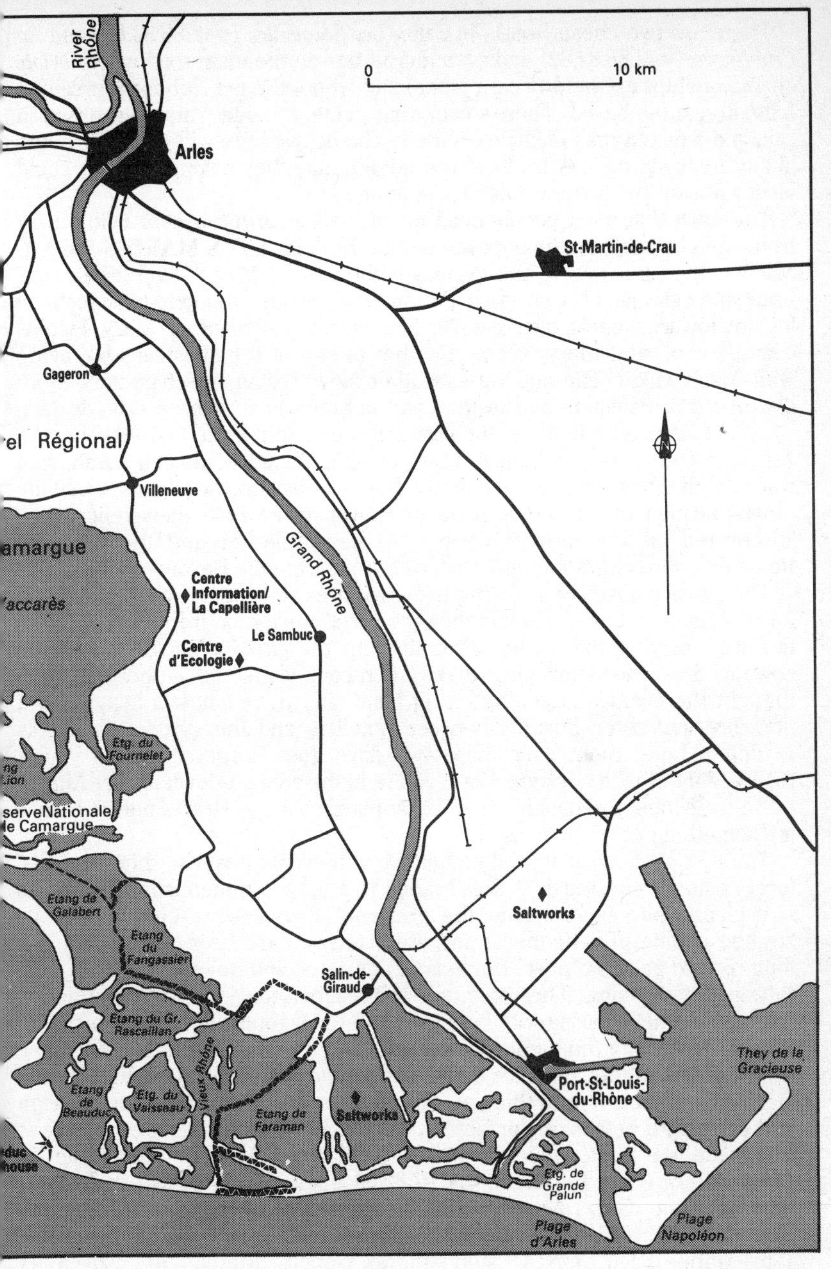
River Rhône
0
10 km
Arles
St-Martin-de-Crau
Gageron
rel Régional
Villeneuve
amarque
Centre Information/ La Capellière
'accarès
Grand Rhône
Le Sambuc
Centre d'Ecologie
Etg. du Fournelet
serveNationale de Camargue
Etang de Galabert
Etang du Fangassier
Saltworks
Salin-de-Giraud
Etang du Gr. Rascaillan
Vieux Rhône
Etang de Beauduc
Etg. du Vaisseau
Etang de Faraman
Saltworks
They de la Gracieuse
Port-St-Louis-du-Rhône
Etg. de Grande Palun
Plage d'Arles
Plage Napoléon

There are two cheap **hotels** in Salin: *Les Saladelles* (☎42.86.83.87) and *La Camargue* (☎42.86.82.82) and a wonderful **bar** on the main road where *belote* championships are held (a card game) and where the fan club for Marseille's football team is based. There's every bar game, a model ship crystallised in salt, and a mixed male/female clientele. The people here will go on for hours about the bastards in Arles to whose municipality they belong – if they could elect a mayor, he or she would be Communist.

The town that most people head for in the Camargue is over 60km away from Salin by road, on the opposite side of the delta. **STES-MARIES-DE-LA-MER** is the place where the gypsies gather, every May 24 and 25, to celebrate and ask favours from their Patron Saint, Sarah, who demands absolute loyalty towards one's own people. She was the servant of Mary Jacobé, Christ's aunt, and Mary Salomé, mother of two of the apostles who, along with Mary Magdalene and various other New Testament characters, were driven out of Palestine by the Jews and put on a boat with no sails or oars. The boat drifts effortlessly to the island in the mouth of the Rhône where the Egyptian god Ra is worshipped. Mary Jacobé, Mary Salomé and Sarah, who was herself Egyptian, remained on the island to convert the pagans, while the others headed off for other parts of Provence. In 1448 their relics were 'discovered' in the fortress church of Stes-Maries around the time the Romanies were migrating into western Europe from the Balkans.

The gypsies have been coming to Stes-Maries since that time. It's the time for weddings and baptisms and then the great procession from the church to the sea, carrying the statue of Sarah, with the *gardiens* in full Camargue cowboy dress accompanying them. In recent years the authorities have thought the event was getting out of hand, and there's now a heavy police presence and some hostility between hoteliers and the gypsies. As far as getting a hotel room over these two days goes, forget it unless you've reserved months in advance. But if you're in the area go down to Stes-Maries – the festivities, the dancing and guitar-playing in the streets and the cafés are something not to be missed.

The rest of the year is well inundated with events involving horses, bulls, local costume and music – Stes-Maries is a very commercialised town. Its streets of white houses, and the grey-gold Romanesque church with its strange outline of battlements and watch-tower, have been turned into one long picture postcard pose. But apart from peace and quiet you're not going to want for anything. There are miles of beaches (on which camping is not tolerated); a new marina with boat trips into the lagoons; horses (or bikes) to ride; an arena for bullfights, cavalcades and general entertainment; thousands of restaurants, bars, ice cream parlors etc; watersports, nightclubs and anything else you care to think of. The **SI** on av Van Gogh will happily weigh you down with details. As for **hotels,** the two low-priced ones are *Hôtel de la Plage* (bd de la République; ☎90.97.84.77; open May to Sept.) and *Le Mediterranée* (4 rue F Mistral; ☎90.97.82.09; open Feb. 14–Nov. 11). *La Brise de Mer* (31 av G Leroy; ☎90.97.80.21; open March–Nov.) is slightly more expensive. There's a **youth hostel** at Pioch-Badet 10km along the Arles road (Stes-Maries-Arles buses stop there), open March to November (☎90.97.91.72).

East of Avignon to the Luberon

From Avignon the roads to southern Provence and the coast run southeast past CAVAILLON and SALON, the latter the training ground for the French Air Force pilots who disturb the air for miles around. **CAVAILLON** is a major market town distinguished only by its production of Charentais melons (in season May–Sept.). Avignon trains and some buses veer east first to **ISLE-SUR-LA-SORGUE**, ten kilometres north of Cavaillon. The same stream that runs alongside rue des Teinturiers in Avignon splits here into five branches which meander their way through this strangely dilapidated town, turning huge blackened wheels that once powered a flourishing silk industry. If it grabs your interest you shouldn't have much problem finding a room here (the **SI** is beside the west door of the church), and there's a beautiful **campsite** near an expensive hotel, at **Partage-des-Eaux**, 'where the waters part', one and a half kilometres upstream from the junction of av de Gaulle and cours Salviati.

The **source of the Sorgue** is only a few kilometres further east at **FONTAINE-DE-VAUCLUSE**. At the top of the gorge above the village is a mysterious tapering fissure deeper than the sheer 230-metre cliffs that barricade its opening. This is where the waters of the Sorgue appear, sometimes in spectacular fashion bursting down the gorge (in March and April normally), other times seeping stealthily through subterranean channels to meet the riverbed further down. This being something of a phenomenon, tourists are attracted to Fontaine by the million, and with inevitable results. If you're intrigued by the source, and can follow French, visit the *Norbert Casteret Musée de Spéléologie* (10am–noon and 2–6.30pm; closed Nov.–Jan., and Mon. and Tues. except June–Aug.) in the underground commercial centre barring the path to the source. At the upper end of the centre you'll find a re-creation of the medieval method of pulping rags to paper – using river power – with a vast array of printed matter on the product for sale. Fontaine's hotels are overpriced and overbooked, but there's a **youth hostel** on Chemin de la Vignasse (☎90.20.31.65; open Feb.–Nov.).

Gordes

Further east **GORDES,** a village of country residences for Parisian media personalities, film directors, establishment artists and the like, is so full of itself that it's almost unbearable to go there. But it does have, in its castle stronghold, the **Didactic Museum** of the Hungarian artist that establishment critics deride as the inventor of op-art, **Victor Vasarély**. The upper floor charts the complex evolution of Vasarély's creative development. It's fascinating to see the training he gave himself in every aspect of the visual experience. On the first floor are gorgeous tapestries of cubes turning into spheres and colours chasing their way through squares, circles and diamonds. The museum is open 10am–noon and 2–6pm every day in July and August; closed Tuesday the rest of the year.

Just north of Gordes, among fields of lavender in a hollow of the hills stands the twelfth-century Cistercian **monastery of Sénanque**. Monks have very recently returned, after a twenty-year break, to re-establish its former use. It may, therefore, be closed to the public (Gordes **SI**, opposite the castle, will know). The other stone construction of note in the vicinity of Gordes (signed off the Cavaillon road) is the **Village des Bories** – strange dry stone dwellings lived in from the Middle Ages to the nineteenth century, despite their prehistoric appearance (9am–sunset). Quarries, for ochre pigment rather than stone, were the *raison d'être* for several villages between Gordes and Apt, including **ROUSSILON** and **RUSTREL**. Walks through the quarries rival Vasarely's works for colour sensation – details from Apt SI.

After its descent from the Alps the Durance river makes a wide southern curve before joining the Rhône, skirting the fold of rock known as the **LUBERON** that runs for fifty kilometres between Manosque and Cavaillon. The northern face is humid, more alpine in character and extremely cold in winter, whereas the southern slopes are Mediterranean in scent and feel. It's almost all wooded, except for the summer sheep pastures at the top and there is only one main route across it, through the Combe de Loumarin. On the north side, tiny villages cling stubbornly to the foothills, some abandoned like Oppède-le-Vieux, others basking in renovated glory like Lacoste and Ménerbes. The best town base for exploring the Luberon is APT, the confectionery capital of France.

Apt

APT is not much of a town for sightseeing, nor is it renowned for the charm and friendliness of its people. Its largest factory spews mucky froth into a concrete channelled stream, and in early Spring when mimosa is blossoming on the coast, the temperature around Apt can drop to well below freezing. It cheers up, however, every Saturday when cars are barred from the town centre to allow artisans and market gardeners from all the surrounding countryside to set up stands. As well as featuring every imaginable Provençal edible, the market is accompanied by barrel organ, jazz musicians, stand-up comics, aged hippies and assorted freaks. Apt is also the centre for the **Parc Naturel Regional du Lubéron**, source of information for walks, fauna and flora, pony rides, *gîtes* etc; (*Maison du Parc*, 1 place Jean-Jaurès; open Mon.–Sat. 8.30am–noon and 2–7pm).

If you're heading for Aix from Apt, you'll pass close to another ancient Cistercian abbey contemporary with Sénanque – **Silvacane**. Again isolated from its surrounding villages, on the banks of the Durance, its architecture has hardly changed at all over the last 700 years. The stark pale-stoned splendour of the church, its cloisters and surrounding buildings can be visited 10am–noon and 2–6pm in summer, 2–5pm in winter every day except Tuesday and holidays.

Food and practicalities

There's a good choice of **hotels** and **restaurants** in Apt, unlike the more scenic hilltop villages where all rooms are reserved months before the summer season. Arriving by bus you're most likely to be dropped at place de la Bouquerie, the main square lined with cafés and restaurants and with the **SI** at 2 av Philippe-de-Girard just up to your left as you face the river. At the opposite end of the town from place de la Bouquerie is the hotel *Aptois* (6–8 cours Lauze de Perret; ☎90.74.02.02) with some cheap rooms. A *Logis de France* establishment, *Le Ventoux* (67 av Victor-Hugo; ☎90.74.07.58) is flanked by petrol stations, but pleasant once you're inside and with a reasonably priced restaurant. The lowest priced rooms are in the centre at *Le Palais* (12 place Gabriel-Péri; ☎90.74.23.54) above a pizzeria.

Campers, for once, are treated to a ground within easy walking distance of the town – *Les Cèdres,* (rte de Viton; ☎90.74.14.61; open all year), across the bridge from place St. Pierre. Two **gîte d'étapes** an easy bike ride from Apt are the *Bardons* at Castellet to the southeast (☎90.75.20.87) and the *Relais de Roquefure* (☎90.74.22.80) off RN100 in the Avignon direction very close to the triple-arched Roman bridge dating from the days when Apt was Apta Julia. Be warned: most of the local buses are one-a-day jobs. Two **bike hire** places are D. Devoncoux, (17 quai Général-Leclerc), and Garage Maretto a few doors down. There are special **cycle paths**, courtesy of the *Parc*, from Apt to Cavaillon (40km), from Apt to La Begude (12km) and to Volx, all signposted in brown.

If you haven't stuffed yourself with candied fruit (Apt's speciality), by far the pleasantest place to **eat** is *Le Platane*, place Jules-Ferry (closed Mon.). For the cheapest of the cheap and an extremely edible four-course meal, go to *Le Bremondy* on place St-Pierre. *La Caleche* (4, rue Cély) is similarly priced but not quite as *sympa*. Argentinian specialities are available at 12 quai Général-Leclerc, with live music weekend nights. Anyone who likes jazz, mime and *café-théâtre* should go for a Friday or Saturday night meal at *L'Artifact* at 10, Cours Lauze-de-Perret.

Aix-en-Provence

AIX is the dominant city of central Provence, or would be were it not for the great metropolis on the coast only 25 kilometres away. Aix is everything that Marseille is not, and if you take a liking to one of these cities, you are bound to hate the other. Aix is bourgeois, its riches based on land-owning and the liberal professions. It was the capital of Provence from the twelfth century until the Revolution. In its days as an independent fiefdom, its most mythically beloved ruler, King Réné of Anjou, held a brilliant court renowned for its patronage of the arts and popular festivities. Réné introduced the muscat grape to the region and today he stands in stone in picture-book medieval fashion, a bunch of grapes in his left hand, looking down the majestic seventeenth-century avenue, the **cours Mirabeau**.

The cours is the central axis to the town, running from the multi-fountained place Général-de-Gaulle, or *La Rotonde*, at its west end. The **gare SNCF** is on av V-Hugo, the avenue leading south from the *place*, (bus #6, #9, or minibus #1 or #2, to *Rotonde/Jeanne d'Arc* or *Office de Tourisme*, but easily walkable); the **gare routière** is between the two western avenues, des

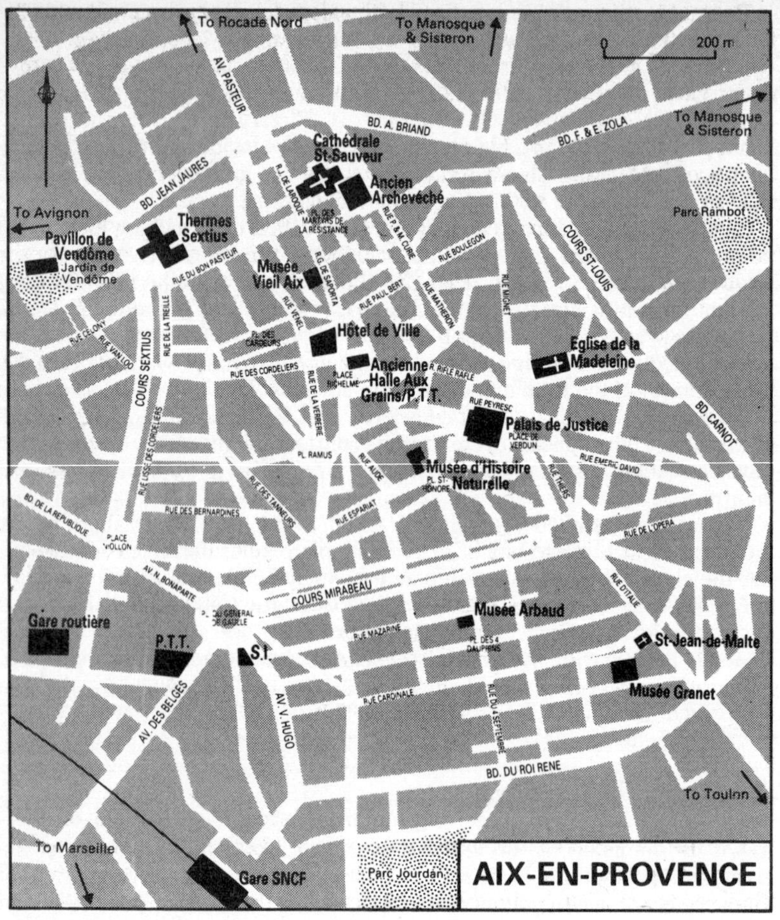

Belges and Bonaparte, on rue Lapierre (minibus #1 or #2 to *Rotonde/Jeanne d'Arc*; again nor very far). The **SI** or *Office de Tourisme* is at 2 place de Gaulle between av des Belges and av V-Hugo. The principal **post office** is also close by at 2 rue Lapierre.

As a preliminary introduction to *Aixois* life and lifeforms, a café-stopping stroll beneath the gigantic plane trees that shade the cours Mirabeau is mandatory. The north side is one long line of cafés; the south side banks and offices, all lodging in seventeenth- and eighteenth-century mansions of a uniform hue of weathered stone, with ornate wrought iron balconies and Baroque decorations. Of the cafés, *Les Deux Garçons* is the intellectuals' haunt, done up in the faded style of the *Orient Express*. The other cafés have a changing hierarchy of snob value, and all are pricey, though very tempting. The youth of Aix are immaculately dressed as if they'd just walked out of a Benetton ad. And what is most striking is the number of Americans, speaking fluent French and acting as if this were home. Indeed it is, for thousands of them, studying at the university.

To explore the heart of Aix, wander north from cours Mirabeau and then anywhere within the ring of cours and boulevards. The layout of *vieil* Aix is not designed to assist your sense of direction but who cares, when every street is busy with people, bars and shops with a backdrop of architectural treats from the sixteenth and seventeenth century, and every fifty yards or so, a fountained *place* in which to rest. Right in the middle, on place Richelme, you'll find a daily morning **market** of local exotica in the fruit and vegetable line. The **markets** of Aix are said to be the best in Provence, and there are plenty of them. Every Tuesday, Thursday and Saturday morning, place de la Madeleine, place des Prêcheurs, and place Richelme become a vast open-air market selling every edible from the region, with fish stands spreading down rue des Marseillais and flowers filling place de l'Hôtel-de-Ville. Place du Verdon has a flea market with bric-à-brac and everything from rabbit hats to plastic earrings, and the streets around the *Palais de Justice* have nothing but clothes.

To turn to the things you can't buy, the **Eglise de la Madeleine** on place des Prêcheurs has for decoration paintings by Van Loo and Rubens, and a three-panel medieval *Annonciation* in which Gabriel's wings are owl feathers and a monkey is positioned so its head is just below the deity's ray of light. The **town hall** on place de l'Hôtel-de-Ville has perfect classical proportions and an embroidery in wrought iron above the door. Beside it stands a clock tower which you can use to tell the season as well as the time. On the south side of the square, a delicate though fairly massive foot hangs over the architrave of the old corn exchange, now the post office. It belongs to the goddess Cybele dallying with the river Rhône.

Rue Gaston-de-Saporta takes you up from place Hôtel-de-Ville to the **Cathédrale St-Sauveur**, a conglomerate of fifth- to sixteenth-century building works and full of medieval art treasures. The best of these is a painting commissioned by King René in 1475, *Le Buisson Ardent*. The two side panels showing the king and his second wife are usually closed over the main picture. A notice in the south nave gives the times (Tues. and Sun. excluded) when the sacristan will open the picture and talk about it, at length, and very interestingly if you can follow. Mary and babe sit in the burning bush with castles, possibly Tarascon and Avignon, in the receding distance, and Moses surprised by an angel in the foreground. Every detail from the Virgin's mirror and the angel's medallion, to the dog's collar and the snail right at the bottom is steeped in theological significance. While you're still hunting for the snail the sacristan will close the painting up again and unlock the panels covering the west doors.

Just down from the cathedral, through place des Martyrs-de-la-Résistance, is the **former bishops' palace**, setting for part of the grandiose **music festival** each July, and housing the **Musée des Tapisseries** (9.30am–noon and

2.30–6pm in summer, 2.30–5.30pm in winter; closed Tues.). The tapestries are all wonderful and not the standard château type, hung to stop the draught. There's a contemporary section as well. The **Musée du Vieil Aix** at 17 rue Gaston-de-Saporta (10am–noon and 2.30–6pm in summer, 2–5pm in winter; closed Mon.) is worth a look while you're in this part of town. It has a set of religious marionettes, and a huge collection of *santons* (Provençal crib figures) but you won't be losing out that much if you miss it.

Museums

Aix's most substantial **museum** is in the *Quartier Mazarin* south of the cours Mirabeau, on place St-Jean-de-Malte. The ground floor of the **Musée Granet** exhibits the finds from the site of the original settlement of Aix, the *Oppidum d'Entremont* a couple of kilometres north of the city. Alongside are the remains of the Romans who routed this Celtic-Ligurian township in 90 B.C. and established their city of Aquae Sextiae – which evolved into Aix – around the thermal springs they found in the vicinity and around which there is still a spa. Upstairs are the paintings, a very mixed bag, Italian, Dutch, French, mostly nineteenth-century, appallingly badly hung and lit. The portraits of Diane de Poiters by Jean Capassin and Marie Mancini by Nicolas Mignard are an interesting contrast and there is also a self-portrait by Rembrandt. But the rows upon rows of eighteenth- and early nineteenth-century French paintings, including the massive *Jupiter and Thetis* by Ingres, make it only too clear why the country needed its revolutions. At the top of the stairs on the right, you do finally reach one wall dedicated to the most famous Aixois painter, **Paul Cézanne,** who studied on the ground floor of the building, then the art school. Two of his student drawings are here as well as a handful of minor canvases such as *Bethsabée, Les Baigneuses* and *Portrait de Madame*. Opening times are 10am to noon and 2 to 6pm; closed Tuesday.

One of Cézanne's many studios in Aix is at what is now 9, av Paul-Cézanne, overlooking the city from the north. The **atélier** is exactly as it was at the time of his death in 1906; coat, hat, wine glass and easel, the objects he liked to paint, his pipe, a few letters and drawings. . . everything save the man himself, who would probably have been horrified at the thought of its being public. The *Atélier Cézanne* is open 10am to noon and 2 to 6pm in summer, 2.30 to 5pm in winter; closed Tuesday; bus #1, stop terminus *Beisson,* or Coutheron/Puyricard bus, stop *Cézanne*.

For a totally different experience, both visually and conceptually, you can escape the cloying grandeur of seventeenth-century Aix by visiting the **Vasarely Foundation** (9.30am–12.30pm and 2–5.30pm; closed Tues.) on av Marcel-Pagnol, Jas de Bouffan (bus #8 or #12, stop *Fondation Vasarely*). There could be no mistaking the building, itself a black and white Vasarely creation. As at Gordes there are innumerable sliding showcases, showing images related to all the themes of Vasarely's work, including his 'plastic alphabet' and designs for apartment buildings. Downstairs, however, the seven high hexagonal spaces, each hung with six huge colour-wonder dimension-doubling designs, is where you'll get the immediate impact of this extraordinary man's work. He believed 'creation was, is, and will be collective: without Leonardo da Vinci there would have been no Cézanne, without Cézanne there would have been no Mondrian. . . and so forth. In short, the aim of any human work – whether its gestation be conscious or unconscious – cannot be other than social.'

Rooms, food and fun

From mid-July to mid-August, festival time, your chances of finding an unbooked **hotel room** are pretty slim – you need to reserve a couple of months in advance at least. Rents and rates in central Aix are very high and reflected in the prices of hotels, shops and restaurants. *Paul* (10 av Pasteur; ☎42.23.23.89), and next door *Le Pasteur* (14 av Pasteur; ☎42.21.11.76) are outside the boulevard ring but within easy reach and comfortable. *Pax* (29 rue Espariat; ☎42.26.24.79) has a few rooms that are the cheapest in the centre. For olde worlde charm (but breakfast compulsory) there's *Des Quatre Dauphins* (54 rue Roux-Alphéran; ☎42.38.16.39) in the *quartier Mazarin*. *Sully* (69 bd Carnot; ☎42.33.11.77) is a bit noisy but very welcoming. You can't make a reservation so turn up early. The **youth hostel** (3 av Marcel-Pagnol, ☎42.20.15.99; bus #8 or #12, direction Jas de Bouffan, stop *Vasarély*; reception 7.30am–noon and 5.30–10pm; closed Dec. 20–Feb. 1; no cooking facilities; restaurant April–Oct.) is excessive about its regulations (e.g. you can't use your own sleeping bag). If there are two or more of you you'd be better off in a hotel. *CROUS* (Cité Universitaire des Gazelles, 38 av Jules-Ferry; ☎42.26.33.75; bus #5, direction Gambetta, stop *Pierre-Puget*) can sometimes find rooms for you on the university campus during July and August. **Camping** is not a brilliant option: places in the suburbs are extremely expensive, and *Le Félibrige* (5km from Aix off RN7 to Puyricard at La Calade; ☎42.92.12.11; Puyricard bus from cours Sextius) is a bother to get to, though you can **hire bikes** once you are there.

For **eats** your best bet is to go ethnic. The excellent selection of different cuisines includes Italian, *Amalfi* (5 rue d'Entrecasteaux; ☎42.38.30.01; closed Sun.); Spanish, *La Bodéga* (8 rue Campra; ☎42.96.05.85; closed Sun. and Wed. noon) with live flamenco and rumba on Friday and Saturday night (reservations required); Tunisian, *Djerba* (8 bis rue Rifle-Rafle; ☎42.21.52.41; closed weekends); Egyptian, *Kéops* (28 rue de la Verriere; ☎42.96.59.05) – falafel, stuffed pigeon, and terrific milk-based desserts; and Iranian, *Le Jasmin* (6 rue de la Fonderie; ☎42.38.05.89;closed Sun. and Wed. pm). For local food place des Cardeurs is a good area to look – *Le Forum* at no. 20 has an excellent midday *menu*. For **vegetarians** there's *Le Blé en Herbe* (7 rue Mignet; closed Sun.–Tues. and Wed. pm) if you manage to find it open. *La Nouvelle Boulangerie* (rue Tournefort) is a bakery that's open 8760 hours a year, selling pizzas, pastries, and other snacks as well as bread. The region's best chocolates and the local almond paste speciality, *coulissons*, made by *Puyricard* can be bought at 7 rue Rifle-Rafle.

Monday evenings in late summer Aix can be dead around 10pm. During the **Festival of Music** however, the alternative scene of street theatre, rock concerts and impromptu gatherings liven up the town unrecognisably. The festival's mainstream musical events are extremely expensive. If you want to try to get tickets apply to the *Comité Officiel des Fêtes* at Complexe Forbin, cours Gambetta (☎42.63.06.75). They also deal with bookings for the **Dance Festival** in the first two weeks of July, the **Rock Festival** in June and numerous other propagations of Aix's reputation as a city of art.

For the rest of the year there's *Hot Brass* (rte d'Eguilles-Célony; ☎42.21.05.57), the best **jazz club** in Aix, and *Le Cousin Germain* (15 rue d'Italie; ☎42.38.14.05; Thurs.–Sat.) with Brazilian and New Orleans jazz and blues in an otherwise ordinary café. You can disco in a bowling alley at *Exagone* (23 bd Charrier), or see a golden oldie (usually undubbed) at *L'Eventail Cinema* (24 cours Sextius). *La Chimère* (Montée d'Avignon, on the northern by-pass towards Sisteron; ☎42.23.36.28) is a **gay** bar and disco.

Listings

Bike hire *Cycles Nadeo* (Montée d'Avignon; ☎42.21.06.93).

Condoms dispenser on rue d'Italie, on corner with rue Maréchal-Joffre.

Hospital av Pasteur; ☎42.23.96.00 or chemin de Tamaris; ☎42.23.98.00.

Language courses French lit and lang at university during the summer: 29 av Robert-Schuman; ☎42.59.22.71; apply to *Comité d'Acceuil*, BP 313, 21, rue St.-Fargeau, 75089, Paris CEDEX 20; ☎1.43.58.95.39.

Launderette 60, rue Boulegan; rue de la Fonderie; corner of rue Bernadines and rue de la Fontaine.

Political contacts *SOS Racisme* (27 rue Félibre-Gaut; ☎42.26.46.89); *Mouvement Contre Le Racisme, L'Antisémitisme et Pour la Paix* (Bourse du Travail, bd Jean-Jaurès; ☎ 42.23.29.76).

Telephones Just about every Aix phone box takes cards, not coins.

Travel agents *Gazelles Voyages Transalpino* (3 rue Lieutard; ☎42.27.93.83); *Nouvelles Frontières* (13 rue Aumône-Vielle; ☎42.26.47.22).

Women Contacts and information from *CIDF Informations Femmes* (24 rue Mignet; ☎42.20.69.82).

East from Aix

The **Montagne Ste-Victoire** lies east of Aix, a rough pyramid whose apex has been pulled off centre. Ringed at its base by the dark green and orange-brown of pine woods and cultivated soil, the limestone rock reflects light, turning blue, grey, pink, or orange. In the last years of his life Cézanne painted and drew Ste-Victoire more than fifty times. Part of his childhood landscape, it came to embody the incarnation of life within nature. Two of the greatest canvases, *La Montagne Sainte-Victoire* (1896–98, The Hermitage, Leningrad) and *Paysage d'Aix (La Montagne Sainte-Victoire)* (1905, Pushkin Museum, Moscow), are intricately colour-sculpted representations of solid physical nature – not the play of light or tricks of perception of the Impressionists.

You may, however, be more interested in climbing the Ste-Victoire and the view from it. The southern face has a sheer five-hundred-metre drop, but from the north the two-hour walk requires nothing more than determination. The path, GR9 or the *Chemin des Venturiers,* leaves D10 just before Vauvenargues (3 buses daily from Aix), by a small car park. After reaching the 945-metre summit, marked by a monumental cross that doesn't figure in any of Cézanne's pictures, you can follow the path east along the ridge and descend southwards to Puyloubier (about 15km from the summit).

In Vauvenargues a perfect weather-beaten, red-shuttered fourteenth-century **château** stands just outside the village with nothing between it and the slopes of Ste-Victoire. **Picasso** bought the château in 1958 and lived there till his death. He is buried in the gardens, his grave adorned with his sculpture *Woman with a vase.* Unfortunately the château can't be visited.

EASTERN PROVENCE

In Eastern Provence it is the landscapes not the cities that dominate. The foothills of the Alps gradually close in and up, until heights of over three thousand metres are reached in the far northeastern corner around **Barcelonette**. This is winter skiing and summer hard walking country. The **Parc National du Mercantour** is the best area for experiencing this mountainous terrain where many of the people still earn their livings by traditional peasant means. But the most dramatic geographical feature is the **Gorge du Verdon** – Europe's answer to the American Grand canyon – in the very centre of Provence.

St-Maximin-de-la-Ste-Baume

Back on the main road and rail routes running east is **ST-MAXIMIN-DE-LA-STE-BAUME**, whose name and existence relates to the story of the holy boat trip that wound up at Stes-Maries-de-la-Mer. St-Maximin was one of those on board. He was martyred at Aix and buried where the **basilica** stands, along with Mary Magdalene who had lived out her Provençal life in a cave in the **Massif de la Ste-Baume** to the south. Their remains were supposedly hidden during the Saracen invasions and rediscovered by the Count of Provence in 1279. He started the construction of the basilica and a monastery to guard it which were more or less completed 250 years later. Since that time, decoration of stone, wood, gold, silk and oil paint has been lavishly added, particularly during the reign of Louis XIV – one of many French kings to make a pilgrimage here. There is plenty to look at, from the beautifully detailed wood panelling in the choir to the utterly grotesque skull in a golden-haired and -necked glass helmet in the crypt. There are guided tours of the monastery (9–11.30am and 2.30–6pm from April to Oct.) which is now a cultural centre hosting classical concerts (for details: ☎94.78.01.93).

The medieval streets of St-Maximin with their uniform tiled roofs at anything but uniform heights have considerable charm, and there's a reasonable choice of restaurants and shops with local artisanal produce. The **SI** is in the Hôtel de Ville next to the basilica. If you walk west along rue de Gaulle you'll find a **hotel**, *Plaisance*, at 2 place Malherbe (☎94.78.16.74). Continuing in the same direction there's *de France* on av Albert Ier (☎94.78.00.14) near the *gare routière*. 3km along the Marseille road is the **camping** *Provençal* (chemin de Mazaugues; ☎94.78.16.97; open April–mid Oct.).

Mary Magdalene's *grotte*, where she was dumped by angels for a 33-year spell before being flown to St-Maximin for final confession, wouldn't really persuade you to suspend disbelief. But the ridge itself and the surrounding countryside is brilliant. The woods, flowers and wildlife of the northern face have a profusion rare in these hot latitudes, and the distance from the sea is just enough to limit widespread development. The whole area north to St-Maximin and south to SIGNES is protected. You are not allowed to camp in the woods or light fires and a royal edict forbids picking orchids. The forested plateau running parallel north of the ridge is, once you've got there, excellent cycling terrain. At **PLAN D'AUPS**, a tiny village 4km west of the *grotte*, you'll find a small **hotel** *Lou Pèbre d'Ai* (☎94.04.50.42) with some low-priced rooms and a restaurant. The **SI** in the *Maison de Pays* operates in summer.

Brignoles to Draguignan

If the mythology of St-Maximin is too much to take, you can head for the larger and less sleepy **BRIGNOLES**, where unemployment, particularly among immigrants has risen sharply recently due to the winding down of the bauxite quarries. But tensions aside, it's not a bad place to spend a night. The medieval quarter winds itself around the thirteenth-century summer residence of the counts of Provence, now the *Musée du Pays Brignolais*, and there are plenty of eating and drinking stops. The **hotel** *St.-Ursule* on rue St.-Ursule has the cheapest rooms (☎94.69.10.64). Other possibilities are *L'Universe* (11 place Carami; ☎94.69.11.08); *Farbre de Piffard* (27 rue Jules-Ferry; ☎94.69.00.29) which demands a key deposit; and the slightly more upmarket *Le Paris* (29 av Dréo; ☎94.69.01.00). The **municipal campsite** is one kilometre down the rte de Nice (☎94.69.20.10) and the **gare routière** is opposite the **SI** on place St-Louis.

Between Brignoles and Draguignan is the last of the three great Cistercian monasteries of Provence. Even more so than Silvacane and Sénanque, **LE THORONET** has been unscathed by the vicissitudes of time, and during the revolution was kept intact as a 'remarkable monument of history and art'. As with the other two there's not so much to see. It's the spaces, here delineated by walls of pale rose-coloured stone, that are to be experienced. The *abbaye* is not easy to reach without your own transport – it's on D79, 4½ kilometres from the village of the same name on D17. Opening hours are 10am to noon and 2 to 5pm; closed Tuesday, one hour earlier November to February and one hour later May to September.

If you can avoid **DRAGUIGNAN**, so much the better. It is the base for numerous army barracks and artillery schools (they practice in the Camp de

Canjuers to the north) and the town revolves around little else. It went bankrupt a few years ago after a manic right-wing mayor privatised everything. He resigned, but the right remained in office. It does, however, have one really beautifully displayed museum of the old industries of the Var *département* – silk, honey, cork, olive oil, and tile-making, along with local customs and festivities. The **Musée des Arts et Traditions de Moyenne Provence** is at 15 rue de la Motte, a couple of streets away from place du Marché, the centre of the old town. It's open 9am to noon and 2.30 to 6pm; closed Monday and Sunday morning. The **SI** is at 9 bd Clemenceau, the main street running south of the old town. The **gare routière** and **gare SNCF** (a terminus connecting Draguignan with the main line at Les Arcs) are at the bottom of bd Gabriel-Péri which joins the extension of bd Clemenceau, av Lazare-Carnot, from the south. Reasonably priced **rooms** and **eats** are not difficult to find in and around the old town.

Le Grand Canyon du Verdon

The vast area of the *Camp de Canjuers* blocks any approach from the south to the **GRAND CANYON OF VERDON**. The road north from Draguignan to Comps-sur-Autuby is one of the few public roads through the military terrain. From Comps, the road runs eastwards through sixteen kilometres of end-of-the-earth heath, hills and horizons of further heights. When you reach the canyon, it is as if a silent earthquake had taken place during your journey. Not only has the world opened up but a vertical dislocation takes place in which you cannot judge what is height and what is depth.

From this vantage point, known as the *Balcons de la Mescla*, you are at the base of the 21 kilometres V-shaped gorge made by the Verdon through limestone rock and natural fissures. The river is quite clear about the slopes and slants of this stretch of its course – it dives and tumbles headlong from Rougon and by the exit to the Lac de Ste-Croix is flowing fast still but steadily and deep. From the 'Mescla balconies', the *corniche sublime* follows the canyon high on the west: a road consciously built to give the most breathtaking and hair-raising views. On the north side, the *Route des Crêtes* does the same, at some points looking down a sheer 800 metres to the sliver of water below. The entire circuit is 130 kilometres, and it's not cycling country. For drivers it's a must, though the hidden bends, hairpin turns and ever-waiting precipices are hard work; so too is the July and August traffic, and petrol stations are few and far between.

However, it's far better, if your legs are strong enough, to discover this grand canyon in its depths. To follow the river from Rougon to Mayreste on the **Sentier Martel** takes two days and is not always possible depending on what the French Electricity Board – who control the volume of water of the Verdon – are up to. Anyway, it must be done in a group with a guide (crossing the torrent by rope is no simple matter on your own). Or, you can do the half between Rougon and Les Malines – get details of the route and advice on weather conditions before you start, and take drinking water, a torch (some of the way is through tunnels), and something to keep you warm in the cold shadows of the corridors of rock. Always stick to the path and don't cross the river (the Electricity Board may be opening dams upstream).

The best place **to stay** and to get **information** is **LA PALUD-SUR-VERDON** on the north side of the canyon from where the Route des Crêtes loops out. The **youth hostel** has **camping** in its grounds, is half a kilometre below the village (☎92.74.68.72; open March–Dec) and can help fix up guides, horses and canoes (the latter only for experts in the gorge). The most detailed information – maps, books and so forth – is available from the *Cabanon Verdon* on the main street. For **rock-climbers** *Le Perroquet Vert* sells equipment and the *Club Alpin* is based in the *Chalet-Hôtel de la Maline*; (☎92.74.68.05) at Les Malines on the Route des Crêtes. The centre of life in La Palud is *Lou Cafetié's* bar-restaurant. There are a couple of other places to eat, a market on Wednesday morning around the church and a municipal **campsite** just west of the village (☎92.74.68.13). For **hotels** there's *Les Gorges du Verdon* (☎92.74.68.26) below the youth hostel, and *L'Auberge des Crêtes* one kilometre east (☎92.74.68.47). The same management runs the *Auberge du Point Sublime* in Rougon (☎92.83.60.35) which lives up to its name and is not wildly expensive.

Public transport is not brilliant. There's just one bus between Aix, Moustiers, La Palud, Rougon and Castellane on Monday, Wednesday and Saturday from July to mid-September; the rest of the year just Saturday; and one bus daily except Sunday between La Palud, Rougon and Castellane in July and August.

During high summer the road from the gorge through MOUSTIERS is one long traffic jam. There's a glut of hotels, restaurants, souvenir stands and a veritable surfeit of *ateliers* making glazed pottery – Moustiers' speciality. It's pastel and pretty and you'd find it on sale in Regent's street, but if you want to lug plates home with you, here's your chance. All in all, Moustiers is a bit of a sham. The town closest to the other end of the gorge, CASTELLANE, is not a lot better.

Riez

Much more pleasant than either, though with very little accommodation, is **RIEZ**, fifteen kilometres west of Moustiers. There are a couple of pottery workshops here but the main business is derived from the lavender fields that cover this corner of Provence. Just over the river on the road south is a lavender distillery making essence for the perfume industry. At the other end of the town, off the road to Digne, is the **Maison de l'Abeille** or 'House of the Bee'. It's a research and visitors' centre, showing you the historical development of bee-keeping, plus the modern techniques. Different honeys and hydromel, the honey alchohol of antiquity, are on sale and you can be sure of an enthusiastic welcome any day from 9am to 7pm (no admission charge).

In size, Riez is more village than town but it soon becomes clear that at some point it was more influential than it is now. Some of the houses on Grande-Rue and rue du Marché, the two streets above the main through road, have rich Renaissance facades and the Hôtel de Ville on place

Quinquonces is a former episcopal palace. The cathedral disappeared 400 years ago, its remnants were excavated just across the river from allées Louis-Gardiol. Beside it is a baptistry, restored in the nineteenth century, but originally constructed, like the cathedral, around 600AD (key from the Hôtel de Ville). If you recross the river and follow it downstream you'll find the even older, and much more startling, relics of four Roman columns standing in a field. If you head for the clock tower above Grande-Rue and take the path past the cemetery and on upwards (leaving the cemetery to your left) you reach a cedar-shaded platform at the top of the hill where the pre-Roman Riezians and medieval generations lived. The only building now is the eighteenth-century *chapelle St-Maxime* with a gaudy or gorgeous, depending on your taste, patterned interior.

Riez is in danger of losing its out-of-the-way charm. Pedestrian precincts have been introduced in the last couple of years and the musty old *Hôtel des Alpes* on the allées Louis-Gardiol where you used to get rooms for 55F has been sold. A new **hotel**, the *Carina*, may be open by now, otherwise it's the **campsite** over the river on D11 before the distillery. There's no SI as such – the Hôtel de Ville (☎92.74.51.81/50.74) or the *Atelier Sol* (46 rue du Marché; ☎92.74.47.28) can provide information. Hopefully one place that won't have changed is the **restaurant** *Les Abeilles* on allées Louis-Gradiol, a Provençal variation on the greasy spoon, with the difference that the dishes are regional specialities like *aioli*, served with boiled carrots and potatoes and ketchup on request.

Farther away from the canyon, to the south, is another off-the-beaten-tracks town which would make a good base for both the gorge and the little villages of central Var if you have your own transport. Though not swamped by tourists, **AUPS** has several British and American residents. The church, designed by an English architect 400 years ago, has recently had its doors restored by two British carpenters. But fear not, Aups is a true agricultural Provençal town specializing in truffles (the root, not the chocolate variety). Whether you're coming from Brignoles or Draguignan you enter Aups along av Clemenceau which ends with place Mistral and place Martin-Bidoué, with the church to the right, the **SI** to the left (place de la Mairie), the old town in front of you and, on Wednesday and Saturday morning, a **market** all around you.

There is a monument on place Martin-Bidoué commemorating a period of republican resistance that is very rarely honoured in France. It says 'To the memory of citizens who died in 1851 defending the republic and its laws'. 1851 was the year Louis-Napoléon carried out his coup-d'état (crowning himself emperor the following year). Peasant and artisan resistance to yet another lost republic was strongest in Provence, and when the insurgents – both men and women, flying the red flag because the tricolour belonged to the usurper – were defeated, yet another White Terror had its blood, including a massacre at Aups.

One other surprising, though less impassioned feature of Aups is a **museum of modern art**, the *Musée Simon Segal et l'Ecole de Paris* in the former chapel of a convent on av Albert-1er (open mid-June to mid-Sept.

10.30am–noon and 3–6pm). The best works are those by the post-Expressionist Simon Segal but there are interesting scenes, many of them local, in the other paintings, such as the Roman bridge at Aiguines now beneath the artificial lake of Ste-Croix. One other work of art, recently restored, is the stained glass window in the church.

The **hotel** *Le Provençal* on place Martin-Bidoué (☎94.70.00.24) is the cheapest option. There are two **campsites**, half a kilometre down av Roziers (towards Fox Amphoux) and to the right off allée Charles-Boyer (towards Tourtour) past the canal. Good **eats** are available at *Framboise* (place Maréchal-Foch; closed Mon.) and at the pizzeria/crêperie on place Général-Girard. Close by, at the bottom of rue Maréchal-Foch you can buy wine in bulk, and there's a launderette and a shop selling natural products on the same street. If you're in Aups on a Thursday between November and February you can witness the **truffle market**.

The Route Napoléon: Grasse to Sisteron

When Napoléon was taken under armed escort to the island of Elba he was mocked and jeered from Avignon to Aix. Only around the coast at Fréjus was he among friends. On 1 March, 1815, in pursuit of the most audacious recapture of power in French history, he landed at Golfe-Juan. With many of his emmissaries taken prisoner in Cannes and Antibes, the old emperor bypassed Grasse and headed up through Haute Provence towards Digne-les-Bains and Sisteron along mule paths still deep with winter snow. By 6 March, he was in Dauphiné. On 19 March, he was back in the Tuileries Palace in the capital. One hundred days later, he lost the battle of Waterloo, and was finally and absolutely incarcerated on St. Helena. In typical French fashion the road known as the **ROUTE NAPOLEON** was built in the thirties specifically to commemorate their greatest leader's journey – though it does serve a useful communication service too.

You could follow Bonaparte's example and bypass **GRASSE** too, unless you think an overdose of perfume and an armful of lies about its manufacture are worth investigating. It is the world capital of *parfumiers* and has been for almost 300 years. It likes to promote its image as a chic eighteenth-century village with its medieval heart surrounded by fields of roses, jasmin, lavender, lemons and mimosa. Making perfumes is presented as a mysterious process, an alchemy, turning the soul of the flower into a liquid of luxury and desire. By the time you leave, you'll probably never want to smell another drop of the stuff in your life.

There are thirty factories in and around Grasse, most of them making, not perfume, but the essence which is then sold to Dior, Lancôme, Estée Lauder etc. They tell you that one litre of jasmin essence costs 90,000F. Perfume contains 20% essence (eau de toilette and eau de Cologne considerably less) and the bottles, if you recall, are extremely small. The major cost to this multi-billion dollar business is marketing, and the grand Parisian couturiers – for whom the clothes promote the perfume – go to inordinate lengths, spending over £10 million a year on advertising alone. No prizes for guessing the rates of pay the women picking the flowers receive. The charade you're invited to here is very low key in comparison, but you're still seen as a potential buyer. The **Parfumerie Fragonard** has two locations – in the centre of town at 20 bd Fragonard, and two kilometres towards Cannes at Les Quatre Chemins. The first shows traditional methods of extracting essence (using pork and beef fat in some cases) and has a collection of bejewelled *flagons*. The one outside town is far more informative and admits to modernisation of the processes. A map shows the worldwide sources for the ingredients – some of which may shock you, being taken from whales, beavers, cats, and Tibetan goats. Other *parfumeries* to tour include Galimard (73 rte de Cannes) and Molinard (60 bd V-Hugo). All are free, all have shops and frequent tours in English daily (Molinard is closed Sun.).

A museum you might like to take a quick flit through is the **Musée d'Art et d'Histoire de Provence** (2 rue Mirabeau; open 10am–noon and 2–5.30 in summer, 2–6pm in winter; closed Sat., the 2nd and 3rd Sunday of the month, and Nov.). The collection includes Louis XV furniture, wonderful eighteenth- and nineteenth-century faïence from Apt and Le Castellet, Mirabeau's death mask, a tin bidet, and six prehistoric bronze anklets.

The **old town** of Grasse is, surprisingly, a working class enclave obviously denied municipal attention. The inhabitants say it has very much a village atmosphere and everyone knows each other, while the rich live in the neighbouring villages like Mougins. **Bars** and **restaurants** are cheap; *Le Vieux Bistrot* (5 rue des Moulinets) is brilliant but closes very early. Rues Fontettes and Fabreries (with the *Crêperie Bretonne*) are good places to look and you'll find plenty of bars on place aux Aires. At the *Maison Venturini* (1 rue Marcel-Journet) you can buy fabulous savoury *fougasses* or sweet *fougassettes*, a sort of five-fingered unleavened bread, flavoured with olives, lemon or rose water. Two possible **hotels** are the *Napoléon* (6 av Thiers; ☎93.36.06.37), close to the **SI** on place de la Foux, and the *Sainte Thérèse* (39 bd Baudoin; ☎93.36.10.29) to the west of the old town and uphill. The **gare routière** is a short way downhill from the SI at the *Parking Notre-Dames-des-Fleurs*.

Grasse is itself on a pretty steep incline – after a few miles along the Route Napoléon you get fantastic views of the coast. There are plenty of **campsites** along the way. Roadside stands sell honey and perfume; each little hamlet has a petrol station and one hotel-restaurant and every so often you see a commemorative plaque carved with Napoléon's winged eagle. LA GARDE has a **gîte d'étape** (*La Galoche;* ☎92.83.62.26) and a tiny chapel by the road a short way before the dramatic descent alongside the Verdon River into Castellane.

Castellane

Being the nearest town to the start of the Gorges du Verdon, **CASTELLANE** is not short on **accommodation** – *Hostellerie du Roc* (place de l'Eglise; ☎92.83.62.65), *Le Verdon* (bd de la République; ☎92.83.62.02) are good deals and there are at least sixteen **campsites**. The town squats at the foot of an implausible rock on which stands, inevitably, a chapel to Our Lady of the

Rock. Since there's not much to do here you might as well climb up to it (M. le Curé at 35 rue de la Merci has the key to the chapel). It's assumed that you're in Castellane to visit the Verdon canyon (the **SI** at the top of rue Nationale will have all the info). Mountain bikes can be hired on the rte de Draguignan opposite the *gendarmerie* – routes north beside the lac de Castillon aren't too difficult.

Not a lot happens between Castellane and Digne except that at **BARREME** you can catch one of the great regular **train rides** of the South of France that runs from Digne along the Asse, Verdon, Vaire and heavily gorged Var vallies to Nice. There are bus connections between Castellane and Annot, four stops down from Barrème, and in summer the stretch between Annot and Puget-Théniers can be done by steam-train. Timetables are available from Castellane SI, Barrème *gare SNCF*, and Digne SI or *gare SNCF*.

Digne-les-bains

DIGNE-LES-BAINS is a depressing place. Despite its status as chief town of the Alpes-de-Haute-Provence *département*, it has nothing going for it except for those who need to take the cure for rheumatism and respiratory disorders. The baths, two kilometres along the *Torrent des Eaux Chaudes*, and the administrative offices of the *Préfecture* are the only new buildings; the rest is peeling and cracking into different shades of grey. The **Cathédrale St-Jerome** below its Gothic stained glass windows has a sad list of endless works for which financial contributions are requested. The roads and houses around it are in just as dire need of maintenance. The Route Napoléon enters Digne along the left bank of the Bléone arriving at the Rond-Point du 11 Novembre 1918 on which you'll find the **SI**. The **gare routière** is directly behind. The **gare SNCF** is across the bridge, left down av de Verdun and on Rond Point du 4 Septembre.

From Digne, the Route Napoléon turns west to Malijai before veering north again to follow the Durance upstream. If you have your own transport there are hundreds of miles of roads through the semi-deserted Pré-Alpes de Haute Provence north of Digne, and there are daily buses to Allos and Barcelonette.

Sisteron

Sticking to Bonaparte's boot tracks, however, you reach the most important mountain gateway to Provence, **SISTERON**. If you have the choice, take D4 on the left bank, as Napoléon did, and you will appreciate why he was so worried by this city. The site had been fortified since time immemorial and even now, half destroyed by the Anglo-American bombardment of 1944, it stands as a colossal and fearsome sentinel over the city and the Durance.

The **Citadel** (open mid-March to mid-Nov. 9am–7pm daily) could easily take a whole morning or afternoon to go around. There are no guides, just tape-recordings in French attempting to recreate historic moments, such as Napoléon's visit of course, and the imprisonment of Janus Kasimir, the future

King of Poland in 1639. Much of the extant defences are Vauban's work, when it was a front-line fort against neighbouring Savoy – the eleventh-century castle was destroyed in the mid-thirteenth century during a pogrom against the Jews of Sisteron. From the top, looking across the Durance at the vertical folds of rock running away into the distance like a dinosaur's back, you can see why this is such a strategic site. It's a romantic ruin and should definitely appeal to kids. In July and August, the **festival** known as *Nuits de la Citadelle* has open air perfomances of music, drama and, dance in the citadel and there are art exhibitions in the sixteenth-century chapel, restored and given rather beautiful modern stained glass windows in the seventies.

Arriving by train at Sisteron, turn right out of the station along av de la Libération until you reach place de la République. Here you'll find the **SI**, the **PTT** and the **gare routière**. Looking towards the river you'll see the three chimney- like towers built in 1370 as part of the ramparts around the growing town. To their left is the **Cathédrale Notre-Dame-des-Pommiers**, almost as decrepit as Digne's. Rue Deleuze past the cathedral brings you to place de l'Horloge where the Wednesday and Saturday **market** is held. For **rooms,** the most economical option is the *Centre de Hébergement* in the cultural centre on place du Tivoli (along rue de Provence from the SI; ☎92.61.27.49). The *Hostellerie Provençale* (av J-Moulin; ☎92.61.02.42) is almost as cheap and equally central. *Hôtel de la Citadelle* (rue Saunerie; ☎92.61.13.52) is only expensive for rooms with views down the valley. There are other reasonable hotels and plenty of affordable **restaurants**, though none that you'd write home about. *Le Mondial* **bar** at the top of rue Droite stays open late and so does *Le Primrose* on place de l'Horloge. The **campsite** is across the river and one kilometre along D951 to the left (open May–Sept.; ☎92.61.19.69). A **youth hostel**, ten kilometres north of Sisteron in the tiny village of Vaumeilh (through Valernes off D951; ☎92.61.43.78; open mid-June to mid-Sept.) is linked to a glider school. Learning to fly is expensive but you can just take a ride.

The Northeast and the Parc National du Mercantour

The northeastern corner of Provence is two different worlds depending on the season, but in either case there's no let up to the mountain barricades that range from 1000 to over 3000 metres. In winter the sheep and shepherds have gone to warmer pastures, leaving the snowy heights to antlered moufflons and chamois, and the perfectly camouflaged ermine. The villages, where the shepherds came to summer markets, are hatched down for the long cold haul. Other villages, or rather gatherings of Swiss-style chalets, sports shops and discotheques, come to life, with a ski lift instead of a church or market place as the focal point. In spring melting waters swell the Vésubie, the Tinée and the Roya, sometimes flooding villages and carrying whole streets away. The fruit trees in the narrow valley orchards blossom. In

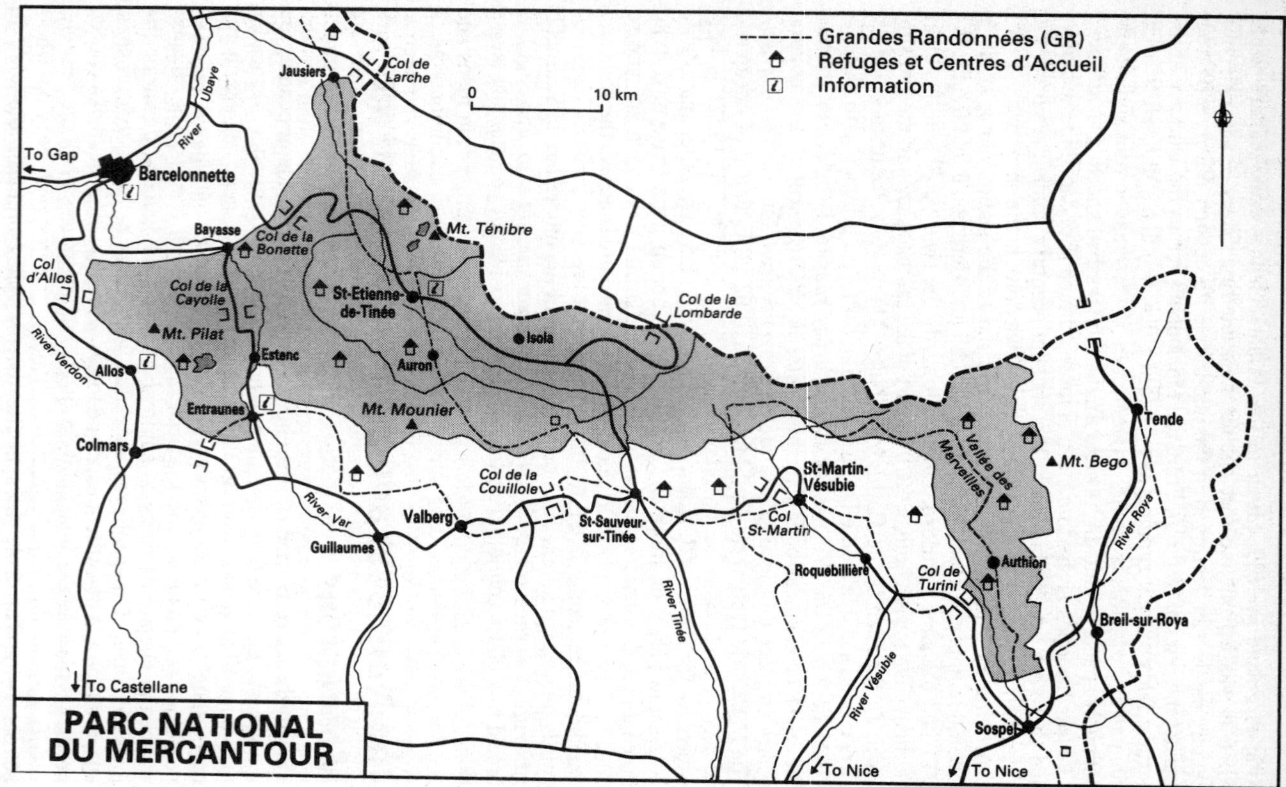
Grandes Randonnées (GR)
Refuges et Centres d'Accueil
Information
0
10 km
Jausiers
Col de Larche
River Ubaye
To Gap
Barcelonnette
Bayasse
Col de la Bonette
Mt. Ténibre
Col d'Allos
Col de la Cayolle
St-Etienne-de-Tinée
Col de la Lombarde
Mt. Pilat
Isola
River Verdon
Estenc
Auron
Allos
Entraunes
Mt. Mounier
Colmars
Tende
Vallée des Merveilles
Mt. Bego
Col de la Couillole
St-Martin-Vésubie
River Var
Valberg
Col St-Martin
Guillaumes
St-Sauveur-sur-Tinée
River Roya
Roquebillière
Authion
Col de Turini
River Tinée
Breil-sur-Roya
River Vésubie
To Castellane
Sospel
To Nice
To Nice
PARC NATIONAL
DU MERCANTOUR

summer and early autumn the ski resorts are ghostly and from the valleys to the peaks sunlight is filtered through chestnut and olive trees and then pine forests edged with wild raspberries, up to rocks with eagles' nests, moors and sheep pastures where wild rhododendrons and gentians grow.

A long narrow band of this region, stretching almost down to Sospel, has been designated the **PARC NATIONAL DU MERCANTOUR** with organised walks, mountain shelters and information centres. **Transport** other than by foot is a problem. Apart from the Turin–Nice railway line down the Roya valley close to the Italian border, there are regular **bus** connections going out from Barcelonette or from Sospel but not meeting, and infrequent buses between villages on market days.

From Gap in the Hautes Alpes, the closest roads into Provence bring you to Barcelonette, a place of immaculate charm in which snowcapped mountains are visible at the end of each short boulevard. It is not very big, and a more ideal spot for doing nothing would be hard to find. The central square, place Manuel, has café tables from which to gaze at the blue sky and the white clock tower on which the centenary of the 1848 revolution is commemorated. Overlooking the *place* at no. 4 is the *Hôtel des Alpes* (☎92.81.00.02), an old-fashioned affair with creaky linoleum and a few cheap rooms at the back. Or you could try the *Cheval Blanc*, just down the road at 12 rue Grenelle (☎92.81.00.19) or the *Provençal* (30 rue Manuel; ☎92.81.03.39). Pizzas and midday *plats du jour* are cheap on the corner of place St-Pierre and rue Bellon. And at 6 rue Bellon *Ubayoglace* serves incredible homemade ice cream and sorbet made of every imaginable fruit. The local specialities for serious eating are game and mutton, and for digestives, liqueurs made from alpine plants. The **SI** is on place Manuel along with an **information centre** for the Mercantour Park.

The other *Maisons du Parc* are at **ST-ETIENNE-DE-TINEE** (Quartier de l'Ardon) and at VALBERG (Maison Valberganne) where there's also a winter **youth hostel**, the *Relais International de la Jeunesse Neige et Soleil* (☎93.02.52.81; open Dec. 23 to April 1). The *maisons* can provide maps and accommodation details, and advise on footpaths, weather conditions etc. If you're starting off from Nice you can pick up all the information you need at 23 rue d'Italie, 06000 Nice; ☎93.87.86.10. **Camping** is not allowed in the park but there are plenty of sites outside its limits, never that far away. There are *gîtes d'étape* in many of the villages, and rather more basic *refuges* or mountain huts, accessible only by foot and rather expensive (more than a youth hostel). These tend to be on GR5 and 52 (signed red on white) which run through sections of the park. One of the few roads that cross the area – from Barcelonette – claims to be the highest in Europe, reaching 2800m at the Cime de la Bonette pass. You may have to brake for a marmot (a two-foot-long furry creature), or for an army truck, as the military are rather fond of this deserted spot. At St-Etienne-de-Tinée you can recover from vertigo and maybe see the sheep market held every three weeks. Down the valley, silvery crickets hold their own against the waters' roar and the villages have needle belfries and old women crocheting on sunlit benches.

GR5 climbs up the valley past the ski-resort of AURON, then up a further 800 metres until it joins the valley again at ST-SAVEUR-SUR-TINEE. From there roads and paths go east towards **ST-MARTIN-VESUBIE**, a lovely place but with just four expensive **hotels** and an overpriced **campsite** and *gîte*, the *du Touron* (open all year; ☎93.03.21.32), on the Nice road a short way out. If you can, treat yourself to a terrific pizza at *Chez Vidoni* (70 rue Cagnoli). The **restaurant** is on the main street of the old village – cobbled, no more than an arm's length wide with a stream of channelled water running down the middle, and overhung by roofs and balconies. The **SI** on place Félix-Faure can provide details on paths and *gîtes/refuges* in the vicinity.

GR52 loops north into the Mecantour before St-Martin and continues east along the peaks, turning south for the **VALLEE DES MERVEILLES**. The first person to stumble upon this high valley of lakes and tumbled rocks was a fifteenth-century traveller who had lost his way. He described it as 'an infernal place with figures of the devil and thousands of demons scratched on the rocks'. A pretty accurate description, except that some of the carvings are of animals, tools, people working, and symbols that could mean anything. There are 100,000 of them, dated some time in the second millenium B.C., and that's about all that's known about them. The shortest route to them takes between five and six hours there and back, excluding time spent looking at (and for) them. The path, marked in green and yellow, starts at *Les Mesces Refuge* on D91 west of ST-DALMAS-DE-TENDE (*gare SNCF* on the Turin-Nice line). When you're nearly there you'll find the *Refuge des Merveilles* where you can get sustenance, and shelter if need be. Never underestimate these mountains' ability to turn blue skies and sun into violent hailstorms and lightning.

Accommodation possibilities in the upper Roya Valley include, at St-Dalmas the *Hôtel Terminus* (rue Martyres-de-la-Résistance; ☎93.04.60.10); at **TENDE** further north, where French has a distinctly Italian accent, *Hôtel du Centre* (av du 16 Septembre; ☎93.04.62.19) or *Miramonti* (5-7 av Vassalo; ☎93.04.61.82 – close to the **gare SNCF** and opposite the **SI** at the back of the *Mairie*); and in **LA BRIGUE** *Fleurs des Alpes* (place St-Martin; ☎93.04.61.05). At around the same time the waylaid traveller was freaking out about the devils and demons of the *Merveilles*, one Giovanni Canavesio was carrying out a commission to paint just those things in the **Chapelle Notre-Dame-des-Fontaines** a few kilometres east of La Brigue. The frescoes, which cover the entire building, are the sort of thing that wouldn't be shown on television. The ultimate gore is a devil taking Judas' soul out of his disembowelled innards. The chapel is open all year: for exact times check with the *mairie* or any of the restaurants in La Brigue.

The road and railway down the Roya Valley meet the road from the Vésubie valley on the other side of the Mercantour at **SOSPEL**, a dreamy Italianate town spanning the gentle river Bévéra. You may find it so tranquil that it's fast asleep, but after storming the mountains or the Côte d'Azur, it's a pleasant break. From the **gare SNCF** turn left along av A Borriglione/des Martyres-de-la-Résistance then right to place St.-Pierre which is at the east end of the old town. Alternatively, head straight for the *Hôtel de la Gare* (☎93.04.00.73) as it's the only cheap **hotel**. The *Auberge Provençale* (rte de Menton; ☎93.04.00.31) is much nicer, not too expensive but one and a half kilometres uphill from the town. There are four **campsites**, the two closest along the road to Moulinet following the river upstream.

If you're unencumbered by the time you reach place St-Pierre, wander down rue St-Pierre. It's a gloomy, deeply shadowed street with equally uninviting alleyways running off it until suddenly it opens into place St-Michel. Before you is one of the most beautiful series of peaches and cream baroque facades in all Provence, made up of the **Cathédrale St-Michel**, two chapels and arcaded houses. The road behind the cathedral, rue de l'Abbaye, or the steps between the chapels, lead up to an ivy-covered castle ruin from which you get a good view of the town. Even better is from the **Fort St-Roch**, part of the ignominious inter-war Maginot Line (along chemin de St-Roch; open 9.30am–12.30pm and 4–6pm; closed Mon.).

Down below, place de la Cabrailla is the liveliest area, with the main **bus stop** and a petrol station. From the *place* av Aristide-Briand follows the river with various eating places including *Chez Freddy's* takeaway pizzas. The **SI** is in the tower on the central bridge – a tenth-century structure and kingpin to the picturesque quality of the town. (Out of season go to the *mairie* for information). Still on the right bank, just beyond the third bridge, tucked behind the public toilets, is the *Maison des Jeunes* where young folks occasionally gather for pool games and other low key entertainment. Sospel's **restaurants** are, on the whole, very overpriced – *L'Escargot d'Or* (3 rue de Verdun), just across the river on the third bridge is probably your best bet.

travel details

Trains and SNCF buses

TGV from Lyon 11–21 daily from Lyon-Perrache to Lyon-Part-Dieu (10 min.) and Paris (2 hr. 10 min.); 3 daily from Lyon-Part-Dieu to Lyon-Perrache (10 min.) and St. Etienne (47 min.); 2 or 3 daily from Lyon-Part-Dieu to Grenoble (1¼ hr.).

From Avignon 5–8 daily to Nîmes (30 min.) and Montpellier (55 min.); 10–13 daily to Valence (55 min.) and Paris (3¾–4 hr.); 9–11 daily to Marseille (55–60 min.), 2 continuing to Toulon (1 hr. 40 min.).

Other trains heading north from Lyon lots of sleepers late in the evening; 3 or 4 trains daily stopping at most stations on the way to Dijon (2 hr.) and Paris (5 hr.); 6 or 7 daily to Mâcon (40 min.), Chalon (1 hr. 10 min.), Dijon (1 hr. 44 min.).

East and West from Lyon frequent to Roanne (1½ hr.) and St-Etienne (approx. 1 hr.); 8–10 daily to Grenoble (1¼–1¾hr.); 5–6 daily to Bourg-en-Bresse (1 hr. 50 min.).

Rhône valley Numerous trains go up and down this line day and night - they don't all stop at every one of these places, but most do. Many others only cover part of the route. Journey times approx. from Lyon to Vienne (20 min.), Valence (55 min.), Montélimar (1 hr 20 min.–2 hr.), Orange (1hr. 50 min.–2½ hr.), Avignon (2–3 hr.), continue from Avignon to Arles (20–30 min.) and Marseille (about 1 hr.), about 6 daily.

From Digne 8 SNCF buses daily to St-Auban (about 35 min.), continue by SNCF bus or train to Veynes-Devoluy (another 1–1¼ hr.), and change at Veynes for train to Valence (2 hr.), or Grenoble (2 hr.). *Chemins de Fer de Provence*, a private railway company, goes from Digne station via 15 small stations to Nice; (3 hr. 20 min.), 4 daily, SNCF tickets not valid except France Vacances, or where Alpazur specified. Alpazur is a *train touristique* (1 July–9 Sept. only) running from Lyon via Grenoble to Digne, where change on to CFP to continue to Nice (8½ hr.); St Auban (SNCF bus, 35 min.); continuing by train to Manosque (25 min. from St-Auban); Aix-en-Provence (1 hr. 10 min.); Marseille (1 hr. 45 min.), 6 daily.

Eastern Provence From Nice via many small villages to Breuil-sur-Roya (1 hr. 10 min.), 6 daily, and Tende (2 hr.), 3 daily.

Buses

There's a good town-to-town service along **N7** all the way from Lyon to the Côte d'Azur. Two buses daily go all the way from Grenoble to Nice and back along N85, stopping at Grasse (2 hr. from Nice, via Cannes), Castellane (3 hr.; midday bus stops here 1 hr. for lunch break), Digne (1¼ hr. from Castellane), Sisteron (40 min. from Digne). Several buses between Grasse and Cannes only (45 min.). Avignon is the focus of a network of local and long-distance buses.

CHAPTER FIFTEEN

THE COTE D'AZUR

The **Côte d'Azur** has to be the most built-up, overpopulated, over-eulogised, and expensive stretch of coast anywhere in the world. There are only two industries to speak of – tourism and building, plus the related services of estate agents, yacht traffic wardens, and Rolls Royce valets. Le Pen posters go undefaced and construction companies pick their labourers from lines of North African immigrants just as galley owners chose their slaves. Meanwhile a hotel serves tender meat morsels to its clients' pets in a restaurant for dogs.

On the other hand, in every gap between the monstrous habitations – in the **Esterel**, the **St-Tropez** peninsula, the **islands** off Cannes and Hyères, the **Massif des Maures** – the remarkable beauty of the hills and land's edge, the scent of the plant life, the February mimosa blossom and the strange synthesis of the Mediterranean pollutants that make the water so translucent, devastate the senses. The chance to see the works of innumerable **artists** seduced by the land and light also justifies the trip. See, for example, **Cocteau** in Menton and Villefranche, **Matisse** and **Chagall** in Nice, **Picasso** in Antibes and Vallauris and collections of **Fauvists** and **Impressionists** at St-Tropez, Nice and Hauts-de-Cagnes. And it must be said that places like **Monaco** and **Cannes**, the star excrescences of the coast, have a twisted entertainment value.

The **months to avoid** absolutely are July and August, when the overflowing campsites become health hazards, all hotels are booked up, the people overworked, and the vegetation at its most barren.

NICE AND THE RIVIERA

Between Nice and the Italian border, the **Riviera** mountains break their fall for just a few precious metres levelling off to the shore. Before foreign aristocrats took a fancy to this coast – a phenomenon of the last century – there were just medieval hilltop villages and fishing ports. Now it is nonstop urbanisation and resorts, excessively luxurious. Only **Nice** has real substance – a major city far enough away from Paris to preserve a distinctive character.

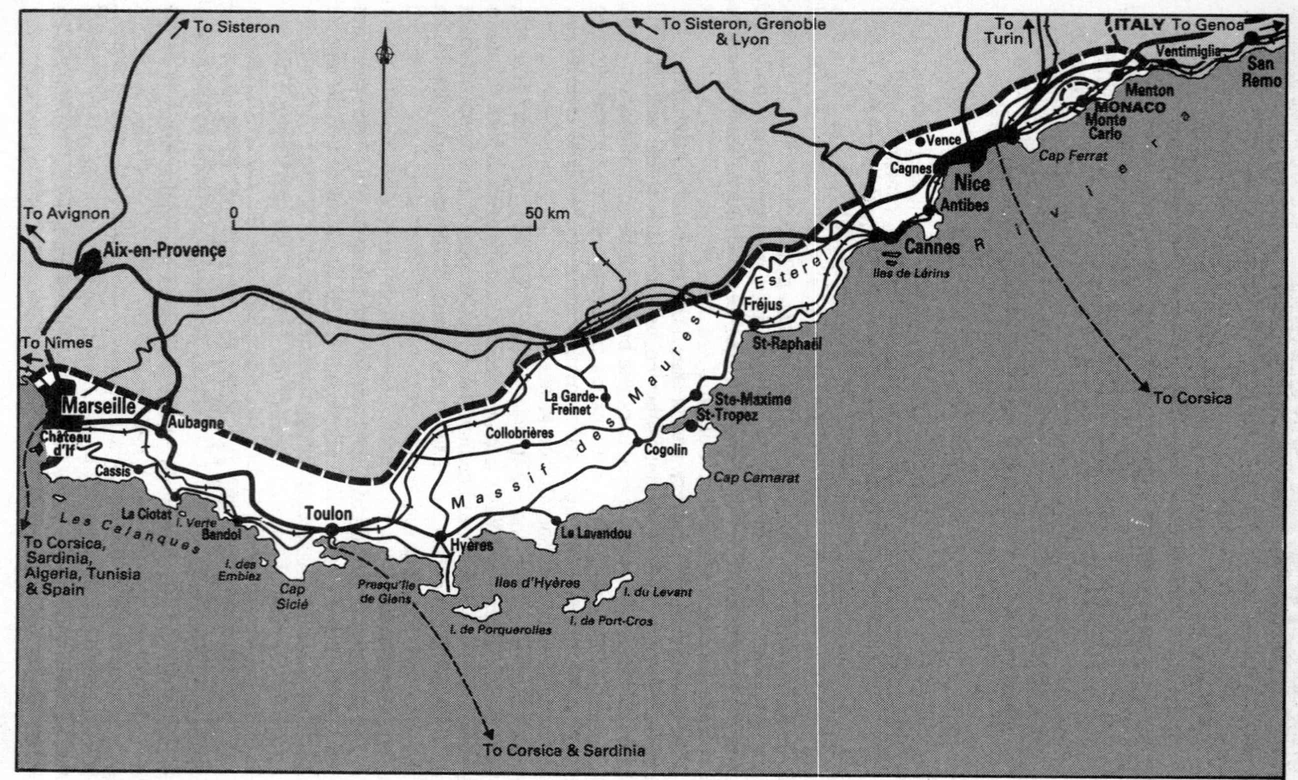
To Sisteron
To Sisteron, Grenoble & Lyon
To Turin
ITALY To Genoa
Ventimiglia
San Remo
Menton
MONACO
Monte Carlo
Cap Ferrat
Riviera
Vence
Cagnes
Nice
Antibes
Cannes
Iles de Lérins
To Corsica
To Avignon
0
50 km
Aix-en-Provençe
Esterel
Fréjus
St-Raphaël
To Nîmes
Marseille
Aubagne
Château d'If
Cassis
La Garde-Freinet
Collobrières
Massif des Maures
Ste-Maxime
St-Tropez
Cogolin
Cap Camarat
La Ciotat
I. Verte
Les Calanques
Bandol
Toulon
Hyères
Le Lavandou
To Corsica, Sardinia, Algeria, Tunisia & Spain
I. des Embiez
Cap Sicié
Presqu'île de Giens
Iles d'Hyères
I. du Levant
I. de Porquerolles
I. de Port-Cros
To Corsica & Sardinia

Nice

The capital of the Riviera and fifth largest town of France should be a loathsome place. It's twin-towned with Cape Town, South Africa, and it's been run for decades by a right-wing clique, subject of Graham Greene's *J'Accuse*, the accusation being outright corruption. Living off inflated property values and fat business accounts, **NICE**'s ruling class has not evolved much since the eighteenth-century Russian and English aristocrats first built their mansions here. The *rentiers* and retired of select nationalities now reside here with their pensions and incomes ensuring the startlingly high inverse ratio of individual income to economic activity. There are more vandalised phone boxes in Nice than in any other French town and it can't even boast a sandy beach. And yet it is delightful: the sun, sea and affable Niçois cover a multitude of sins. The city also makes the best base for visiting the 30km of the Riviera coast to the border, and west as far as Cannes.

Orientation and a room

It doesn't take long to get a feel for the **layout** of Nice. Shadowed by mountains that curve down to the sea east of its port, it still breaks up into old and new. The **Vieille Ville** groups about the hill of Le Château, its limits, once marked by the River Paillon, now **bd Jean-Jaurès**, built along its course. Along the seafront, the **promenade des Anglais** runs a cool 5km, until forced to curve inland by the sea-projecting runways of the airport. The central square, **place Masséna**, is at the bottom of the main street, av Jean Médecin, – the name of the present mayor though in fact named after his father, the previous incumbent. Off to the north is the exclusive hillside suburb of **Cimiez**.

Arriving is straightforward. The main **gare SNCF** (*Nice Ville*) is a relatively short step from all this, off a couple of blocks to the left from the top of av Jean-Médecin. The **gare routière** for once is closer in, on the promenade du Paillon on the corner of bd Jean-Jaurès and Traverse Emile-Zola, in the shadow of the old town.

In season, at least, the **SI's hotel reservation service** at the train station is worth taking advantage of. There are lots of cheap hotels close by, including *Les Orangers* (10 bis av Durante; ☎93.87.51.41) which is where all American students head and always recommend. But around the station is really not the most pleasant of areas. More centrally, **in the Vieille Ville**, the liveliest quarter day and night, you might try the *de Tende* (7 place St-François), *Saint-François* (3 rue St-François: ☎93.85.76.58) and *Cresp* (8 rue St-François-de-Paule; ☎93.85.91.76). Or **in the modern town**, to the east of av Jean-Medécin, there's the *Montreuil* (18 bis rue Biscarra; ☎93.85.95.90), and to the west, *du Centre* (2 rue de Suisse; ☎93.84.83.85) and the *Notre-Dame* (22 rue de Russie; ☎93.88.70.44). The *Félix* (41 rue Masséna; ☎93.88.18.05) is a bit finer but a very good deal. For a really central location, with expensive seaview rooms and out-of-season cheapies as well, try *des Anges* (1 place Masséna; ☎93.82.12.28).

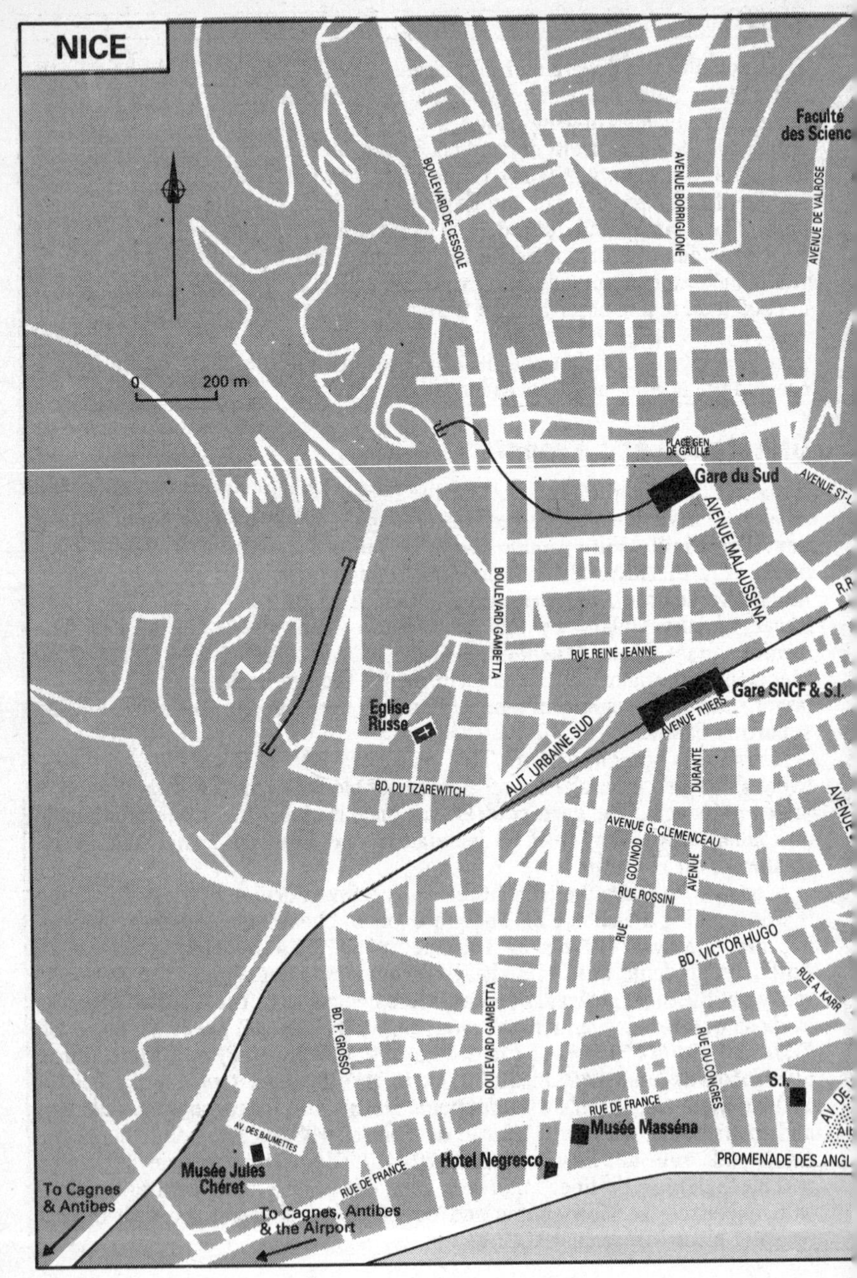
NICE
0
200 m
Faculté des Scienc
BOULEVARD DE CESSOLE
AVENUE BORRIGLIONE
AVENUE DE VALROSE
PLACE GEN. DE GAULLE
Gare du Sud
AVENUE ST-L
AVENUE MALAUSSENA
R.R
BOULEVARD GAMBETTA
RUE REINE JEANNE
Gare SNCF & S.I.
AVENUE THIERS
Eglise Russe
AUT. URBAINE SUD
DURANTE
BD. DU TZAREWITCH
AVENUE
AVENUE G. CLEMENCEAU
GOUNOD
AVENUE
RUE ROSSINI
RUE
BD. VICTOR HUGO
RUE A. KARR
BD. F. GROSSO
BOULEVARD GAMBETTA
RUE DU CONGRES
S.I.
RUE DE FRANCE
Musée Masséna
AV. DES BAUMETTES
Hotel Negresco
PROMENADE DES ANGL
Musée Jules Chéret
RUE DE FRANCE
To Cagnes & Antibes
To Cagnes, Antibes & the Airport

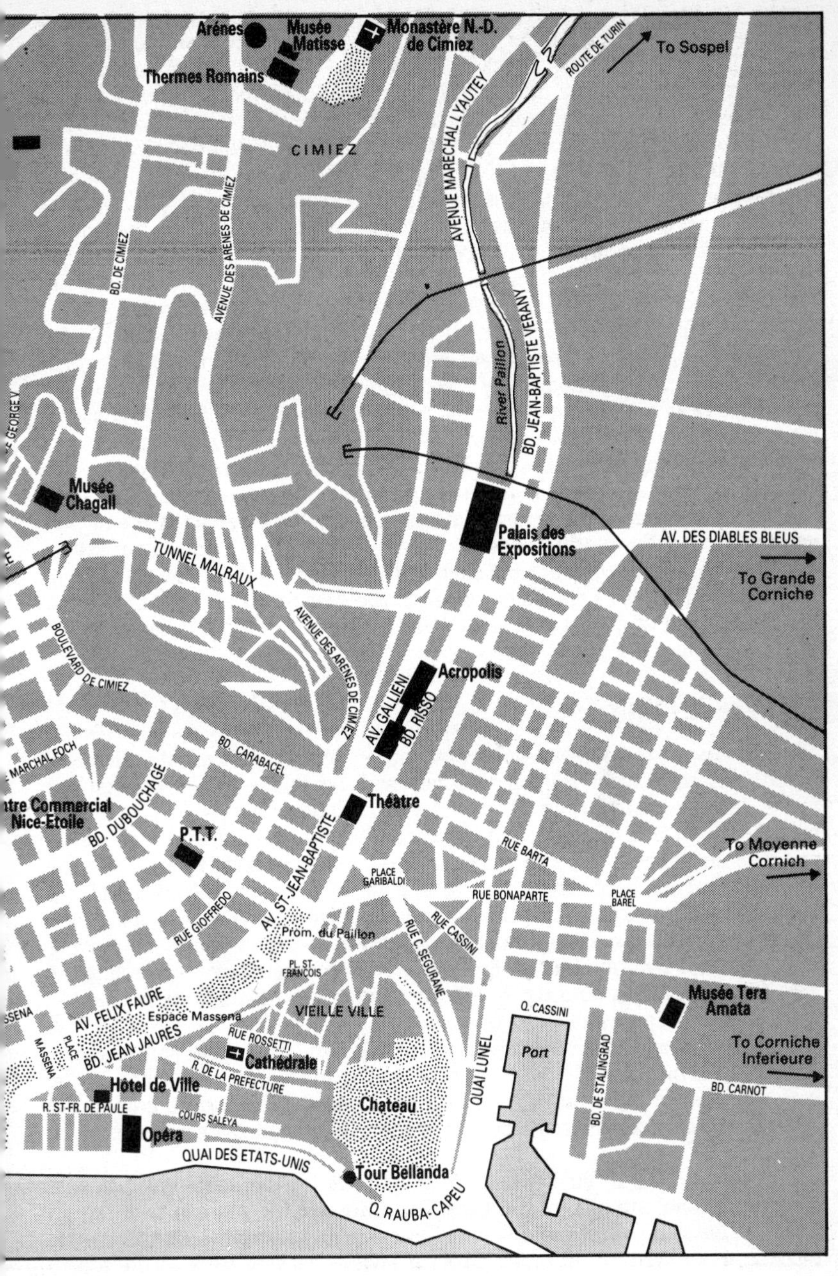
Arénes
Musée Matisse
Monastère N.-D. de Cimiez
Thermes Romains
To Sospel
ROUTE DE TURIN
CIMIEZ
AVENUE MARECHAL LYAUTEY
BD. DE CIMIEZ
AVENUE DES ARENES DE CIMIEZ
River Paillon
BD. JEAN-BAPTISTE VERANY
Musée Chagall
Palais des Expositions
AV. DES DIABLES BLEUS
To Grande Corniche
TUNNEL MALRAUX
BOULEVARD DE CIMIEZ
AVENUE DES ARENES DE CIMIEZ
Acropolis
AV. GALLIENI
BD. RISSO
MARCHAL FOCH
BD. CARABACEL
BD. DUBOUCHAGE
Théatre
P.T.T.
AV. ST.-JEAN-BAPTISTE
RUE BARTA
To Moyenne Cornich
PLACE GARIBALDI
RUE BONAPARTE
PLACE BAREL
RUE GIOFFREDO
RUE CASSINI
Prom. du Paillon
RUE C. SEGURANE
PL. ST-FRANCOIS
Musée Tera Amata
AV. FELIX FAURE
Espace Massena
VIEILLE VILLE
Q. CASSINI
PLACE MASSENA
BD. JEAN JAURES
RUE ROSSETTI
Cathédrale
Port
To Corniche Inferieure
R. DE LA PREFECTURE
QUAI LUNEL
Hôtel de Ville
BD. DE STALINGRAD
BD. CARNOT
R. ST-FR. DE PAULE
Chateau
COURS SALEYA
Opéra
QUAI DES ETATS-UNIS
Tour Bellanda
Q. RAUBA-CAPEU

The **youth hostel** is quite a way out of town and, for two people, more expensive than sharing a hotel room. It's on route Forestière on the slopes of Mont Alban (☎93.89.23.64; check-in 7–10am and 6–11pm; bus #14 from place Masséna, direction *place du Mont-Boron*, stop *L'Auberge*). Slightly cheaper but equally distant and with a 10.30pm curfew is *Clairvallon Relais International de la Jeunesse* north of Cimiez at 26 av Scudéri (☎93.81.27.63; check-in till 6pm; bus #15 or #15A, stop *Scudéri*). Much closer to the centre there's the *Résidence Les Collinettes* at 3 av R-Schuman (☎93.37.24.30; open July and Aug. only, 4–10pm; bus #17 from gare SNCF or #14 from the centre, direction *Parc Impérial*, stop *Chateâuneuf* and walk down av Schuman to the law faculty complex). Another possibility close by on the south side of the urban highway is the *MJC Magnan* (31 rue Louis-de-Coppet; ☎93.86.28.75; rooms available June to mid-Sept.) If you're lucky there may be space in the *International House for Young People* (22 rue Portinax; ☎93.62.02.79), which is very close to the station off av J-Medécin to the east. The only **campsite** anywhere near Nice is the very small *Camping Terry* (☎93.08.11.58; route de Grenoble, Lingostière, 6½km north of the airport on N202 and not on any bus route). In summer you'll find lots of people camping on the beach – it's the only stretch where it's tolerated on the whole Côte.

There's an **SI** near the seafront at 5 av Gustav V as well as at the airport and the station. For **getting around** the city, you can buy a one-day or seven-day bus pass, or a *carnet* of ten tickets with a reduction if you have a student card, from *TN*, 10 av Félix-Fauré, close to the *gare routière*. Ordinary *carnets* can be brought at kiosks and *tabacs*, and single tickets on the bus. The *TN* office will give you a free bus map.

The Vieille Ville

The **old town** used to have the reputation – part fact, part racist fiction – of being an area of drug-pushing muggers and car thieves. Over the last few years, the process of renovation and gentrification have been accelerated with the Town Hall using every means at its disposal to control who moves in and who gets shifted out. There are still unyuppified pockets where you'll still find little corner hardware stores selling brooms and bottled gas and see lines of washing strung high across the narrow streets. The inhabitants are much more scared of rising rents than they ever were of crime and most of their erstwhile neighbours now live in high-rise concrete boxes encircling the city. It's still wise as a tourist to take precautions, particularly if you have a vehicle, but that's true all along this coast.

The central and largest space is **place Rosetti**, where the soft coloured Baroque **Cathédrale de St-Réparate** just manages to be visible in the concatenation of eight narrow, crammed streets. Most wanders around the quarter will inevitably surface here to the awaiting shaded- or sunlit-terraced cafés.

Rue Rosetti or rue du Château, to either side of the cathedral turn into steps up to one entrance of the **Parc du Château** (or you can take the lift from the eastern end of rue des Ponchettes). The park, in which there is no château, is decked out in mock Grecian style – harking back to the fourth century B.C., and the original Greek settlement of *Nikea*. The point of the climb, apart from the very pleasant perfumed greenery, is the view stretching westwards and, nearer, the muddle of the *Vieille Ville*'s rooftops with the Niçois speciality of mosaiced green, red and yellow glazed tiles gleaming from the cathedral clock tower. Right at the top a viewing table points you in the useful direction of St. Petersburg and other, actual, places.

Below rue de la Préfecture, although still *Vieux Nice*, the atmosphere changes abruptly with wider streets meeting at right angles alongside grandiloquent municipal buildings. The **Cours Saleya** and **place Pierre Gautier**, once wholesale flower* and vegetable markets, still have enticing displays of flowers and edibles every day, along with bric-à-brac (on Monday) and arts and crafts (Sunday and Wednesday). The *cours* provides stylish backdrops for some of the best daytime eating and drinking. Over on place St-François, north from place Rosetti, the *Vieille Ville*'s fish market is firmly entrenched, its odours persisting till late at night when all the old streets are hosed down with enough water to wade in.

Cimiez and elsewhere

CIMIEZ has always been a posh place. Its principal streets – av des Arènes de Cimiez and bd de Cimiez – rise between plush, high-walled villas to what was the social centre of the town's elite some seventeen centuries ago, when the city was capital of the Roman province of *Alps-Maritimae*. Excavations of **Roman baths** have revealed enough detail to distinguish the sumptuous and elaborate facilities for the top tax official and his cronies, the plainer public baths and a separate complex for women. The accompanying archaeological finds have a brand new museum alongside, entrance on rue Monte-Croce (May–Sept. 10am–noon and 2.30–6.30pm; Oct.–April 10–noon and 2–5pm; closed Mon., Sun. am and Nov.;. free). The building overlooking the baths, the **Villa des Arènes** takes you worlds away from the military ancients into the joyous lines and light of **Matisse**, displayed in the same light as their creation, for it was in Nice that he spent most of his life. The collection covers every period and includes the studies for *La Dance*, the huge blue and pink mural in the Palais de Chaillot in Paris, models for the chapel he designed in Vence, and a nearly complete set of the bronze sculptures. Among the paintings are the 1905 portrait of Madame Matisse, *A Tempest in Nice* (1919–20), and the 1947 *Still Life with Pomegranates*.

At the foot of the hill, just off bd Cimiez on av du Docteur-Menard, **Chagall's Biblical Message** is housed in a perfect museum built specially for the work and opened by the artist in 1972. The rooms are light and white and cool, with windows allowing you to see the greenery of the garden beyond the indescribable shades between pink and red of the *Song of Songs* canvases. The seventeen paintings are all based on the Old Testament and

* The wholesale flower market has been moved miles away to bd Georges Pompidou in St-Augustin, near the airport (bus #9, #10, stop *Marché gare*). If you want an unparallelled seduction of two senses in the early hours of the morning – 8am at the very latest – a small sum paid to the guards at the gate will get you in.

complemented with etchings and engravings. To the building itself, Chagall contributed a mosaic and stained glass windows. It's open 10am–7pm July–September; otherwise 10am–noon and 2–5.30pm; closed Tuesday and free on Wednesday.

Bus #15, #15A from the centre of Nice (place Masséna) runs past the Chagall museum and up to bd Arènes. Alternatives for Cimiez, but not for the Chagall, are buses #17, #20 and #22.

Other museums

Other **Nice museums** have more limited appeal. For paintings the **Beaux Arts** (33 av des Baumettes, 10am–noon and 3–6pm, July–Sept.; 10am–noon and 2–5pm the rest of the year; closed Mon.; bus #38, stop *Chéret*) can't compare with the Matisses and Chagalls, and has too many whimsical canvases by Jules Chéret, who died in Nice in 1932, and far too much of G.A. Mossa, a recently deceased Nice establishment figure, whose lurid symbolist paintings reek of misogyny. But there are modern works that come as unexpected delights, a Rodin bust of Victor Hugo, a whole room full of Dufy and some very amusing Van Dongens such as the *Archangel's Tango*. Monet, Sisley and Degas also grace the walls.

Temporary exhibitions of **contemporary art** are shown at 59 and 77 quai des Etats Unis (10.30am–noon and 2–6pm except Mon. and Sun. am) and in the **Acropolis**. This gargantuan crouching hulk of concrete over the Paillon's course four blocks up from the *gare routière* is the municipal flagship for inveigling even more money into the city, from conferences, institutes etc. As well as vast exhibition spaces and auditoriums, it contains a *cinémathèque* and a bowling alley (open 11am–2am).

Elsewhere in Nice there's interest – and occasional surprises – in the older **architecture of money**: eighteenth- to nineteenth-century Italian Baroque and Neoclassical, florid Belle Epoque, and unclassifiable exotic aristo fantasy. One such building, exceptional even by Niçois standards, is the **Russian Orthodox Cathedral**, still practising and charging entry to the non-faithful. You'll see its gleaming domes off bd de Tsarevitch at the end of av Nicolas II (bus #14, #17, stop *Tsarewitch*). And finally there's the **Promenade des Anglais** itself, originally laid out by nineteenth-century English residents for their afternoon sea-breeze stroll, now full of screeching tyres, fumes and ever-tolerant, if rather frayed, palm trees. Below it is the **beach**, where people sunbathe from February to November.

Food, fun and practicalities

The old town stays up the latest and is full of **restaurants** from the very cheap to the over-priced. On Cours Saleya, *Le Safari* (at no. 1) serves good Niçois cuisine not too expensively, and there are takeaways (*not* fast food) for the Niçois speciality of tuna and salad-stuffed *pan beignat*. Rue de l'Abbaye, near the cathedral, has several new and good restaurants but the best blow-out for the least money has to be take-away *René Socca* (5 rue Miralhetti; closed Mon.) where you can try out all the classic local dishes including *socca*, an incredibly buttery crumbly pancake. *Le Papier Mâché* on rue Benoît-

Bunico, that used to be a leftist co-op, has changed hands and shows rock videos where there used to be political posters, but the food's still good. *Le Taverne* on rue St-François does extra large *socca*'s.

The port is another scenic spot for stuffing yourself, particularly on just one course of very filling fish soup which can be cheaper and more satisfying than a *menu fixe*. Or for a real cheapie try *Le Kentia* at 32, rue Trachel, north of the station. Just up the street at no. 50 *Chez Nino* is a **beer** emporium and a friendly place to drink. **Vegetarians** should try *Le Moulin Vert* (5 rue de Moulin) which does complete veggie dinners, or *Le Papier Maché* (see above) that usually serves several non-meat dishes, or they should just gorge themselves on *socca* and salads. The pedestrian precinct around rue Masséna is very touristy, with rip-off restaurants, fast food, sex shops and so forth, but places tend to be open on Sunday unlike the rest of Nice. *Le Bistingo*, the restaurant at 2 rue Masséna, stays open all night. Just to the north *Chez Davia* (11 bis rue Grimaldi) is a good back up if you don't want to eat in the old town.

At 1 rue de la Loge, in the old town, *Le Tube* has live reggae Thursday to Saturday nights and French piano and *chansons* the rest of the week (ring to enter, no admission charge, one-price drinks). For jazz piano and more expensive drinks, there's *L'Ascot* on the descente Crotti. Among **gay and lesbian** places, *Le Bentleys* (rue de la Tour, closed Sun.) is a women-only disco; *Blue Boy* (9 rue Spinetta; open from 11pm) is mixed and has shows on Wednesday nights; *Le Rusca* (2 rue Rusca; open 5pm–2.30am) is a relaxed gay bar. And in summer you may well find rock concerts – often British bands – on at the *Théâtre Verdure* tent in the Jardin Albert I; hear them for free outside, or pay if you want to go in.

Nice **festivals** include Italian films in December, jazz in mid-July – which, if you can take the heat and crowds, is fabulous – dance in August, and the unspeakably commercialised carnival in February. For information on official culture, you can get an info-sheet from the municipal office at 2 place Masséna.

Listings

And lastly, since Nice is the centre of the Riviera, a few practical listings:

Airport ☎93.72.30.30

Bike hire from the *Nicea Location* (4 rue Grimaldi) rents out mopeds too which may be a better option for exploring on the corniches eastwards.

Books *The Riviera Bookshop* (10 rue Chauvaiu).

Pharmacy – night time 7 rue Masséna; open 7.30pm–8.30am.

Doctor phone ☎93.83.01.01 for emergencies; *Hôpital de St-Roch*, rue Delille; ☎93.13.33.00.

Late night shopping *Mobil* petrol station, 123 bd Gambetta, west of the station.

Language Courses *Alliance Française* (1 rue Vernier; ☎93.87.42.11)

Launderette *Taxi-Lav* (7am–8pm) 24 av St-Augustine, or 22 rue Pertinax.

Poste Restante PTT, place Wilson, 06000 Nice.

Showers at the station.

Youth information *CIJ*, Esplanade des Victoires; ☎93.80.93.93.

The Corniches

The **corniche roads** – three of them – run east from NICE to MONACO and to MENTON, the last town of the French Riviera. They are each classic routes, switchbacking above the sea, and all on **bus routes**. In addition, the **train** line follows the lower road, the *Corniche Inférieure*. Staying in a **hotel** anywhere between Nice and Menton is going to be exorbitant. There's a not particularly cheap **campsite**, *Les Romarins* (☎93.01.81.64; above EZE on the *Grande Corniche*; open mid-April to Sept.) or there are two **youth accommodation** centres by the sea in CAP D'AIL. They are the *Centre Méditerranéen* (Chemin des Oliviers; ☎93.78.21.59; open all year) and the *Relais Internationale de la Jeunesse 'Thalassa'* (bd de la Mer; ☎93.78.18.58; open May–Sept.). But it makes more sense to base yourself in Nice and treat these routes as pleasure-rides.

The Moyenne Corniche

Of the three, the **Moyenne Corniche** is the most photogenic, a real cliff-hanging car chase road. Eleven kilometres from Nice, the medieval village of **EZE** clings to its rock just below the corniche, infested with antique dealers, pseudo artisans and other caterers to the rich tourists. As with the even more picturesque citadel of **ROQUEBRUNE**, above the Grande Corniche near Menton, it's hard to recall that the labyrinth of tiny vaulted passages and stairways was designed not for charm but from fear of attack. The ultimate defence, the castle, no longer exists in Eze itself: a cactus garden takes its place, providing the only escape from the commerce below and views of the far horizon from where the invaders used to appear. From Eze you can reach the shore through open countryside, via the **sentier Frédéric Nietzsche***, which descends from place du Centenaire at the foot of the rock to the Corniche Inférieure at the eastern limit of EZE-SUR-MER (signposted to *La Village*).

The characteristic **Côte d'Azur mansions** representing unrestrained fantasies of the original owners and the stylistic incompatability of same, parade along the **Corniche Inférieure** or lurk screened from view on the promontories of Cap Ferrat and Cap Martin with gardens full of man-eating cacti and piranha ponds – if the plethora of *'Défense d'entrer – Danger de Mort'* signs are anything to go by. A few have become museums such as the **Villa Kerylos** on av Gustav-Eiffel, just east of the casino in BEAULIEU (open July

* The philosopher is said to have conceived part of *Thus Spoke Zarathustra*, his shaggy dog story against believing answers to ultimate questions, on this path – which is not quite as hard going as the book.

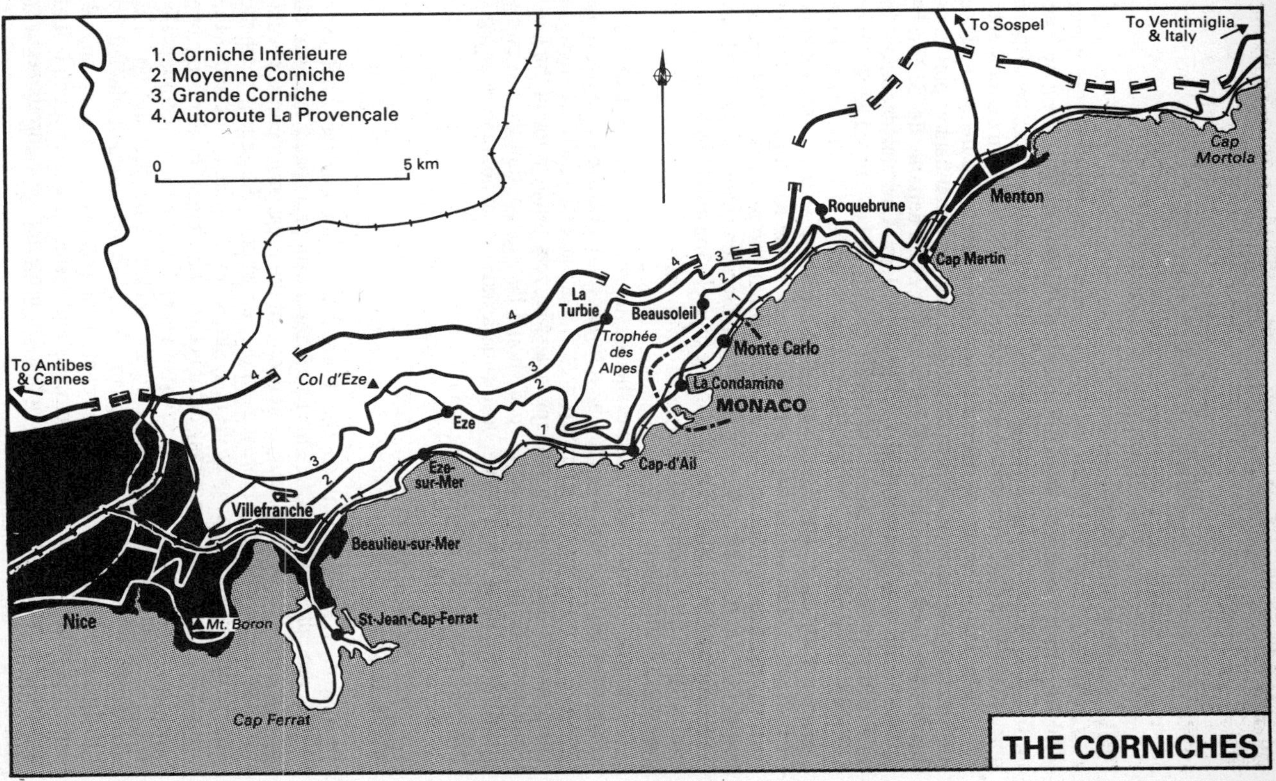
THE CORNICHES
1. Corniche Inferieure
2. Moyenne Corniche
3. Grande Corniche
4. Autoroute La Provençale
0
5 km
To Sospel
To Ventimiglia & Italy
Cap Mortola
Menton
Roquebrune
Cap Martin
La Turbie
Beausoleil
Trophée des Alpes
Monte Carlo
La Condamine
MONACO
To Antibes & Cannes
Col d'Eze
Eze
Cap-d'Ail
Eze-sur-Mer
Villefranche
Beaulieu-sur-Mer
Nice
Mt. Boron
St-Jean-Cap-Ferrat
Cap Ferrat

and Aug. 3–7pm; otherwise 2–6pm; closed Mon. and Nov.). The man responsible for this near-perfect reproduction of an ancient Greek villa used to eat, dress and behave as an Athenian citizen, taking social baths with his male friends and assigning separate suites to women. It's a visual knockout, however perverse.

The Lower Corniche: Villefranche

VILLEFRANCHE-SUR-MER, the resort closest to Nice on the lower corniche, has been spared architectural eyesores only to be marred by lurking U.S. and French warships attracted by the deep waters of the bay. But as long as your visit doesn't coincide with shore leave the old town on the waterfront feels almost like the genuine article – an illusion which the price of the quayside restaurants should quickly dispel. But the small fishing port does still operate, and it is overlooked by the medieval **chapelle de St-Pierre** (9.30am–noon and 2–6pm; closed Fri.) which **Jean Cocteau** decorated in 1957 in shades he described as 'ghosts of colours'. Above the altar St. Peter walks on water supported by an angel to the outrage of the fishes and the amusement of Christ. The fishermen's eyes are drawn as fishes; the ceramic eyes on either side of the door are the flames of the apocalypse and other eyes with no lids to blink appear amid the symmetric patterns on the pillars and arches. On June 29 each year the local fishermen celebrate the feast day of St. Peter and St. Paul with a mass in the chapel – the only time it's used.

The Grand Corniche

And finally, if you just want a view of the sea, there is the **Grande Corniche**, on the crest of the mountains. You pass through LA TURBIE en route, close by which is the **Trophie des Alpes** – a monumental plinth left here to commemorate Augustus Caesar's route, and his total subjugation of the local peoples. The sight of it from the road should be enough, though like everything in these parts it has been fenced and has admission hours for viewing – 9am to noon and 2 to 5.30pm.

Monaco

Monstrosities are common on the Côte d'Azur, but nowhere, not even Cannes, can outdo **MONACO**. This tiny independent principality has lived off gambling and class for a century and is one of the greatest property speculation sites in the world – Manhattan-on-the-sea without the saving aesthetic grace of the skyscrapers rising from a single level. Finding out about the workings of the regime is not easy but it is clear that Prince Rainier is the one autocratic ruler left in Europe. A copy of every French law is automatically sent to Monaco, reworded, and put to the prince. If he likes the law it is passed, if not, not. There is a parliament of limited function elected by *Monagesque* nationals – about 16 per cent of the population – and no opposition to the ruling family. What the citizens and residents like so much is that they pay no income tax and their riches are protected by rigorous security forces.

Arrival – and staying

The 3km-long state consists of the old town of **Monaco-Ville** around the palace on a high promontory, the new suburb and marina of **Fontveille** in its western shadow, **La Condamine** behind the harbour on the other side of the rock, **Larvotto**, the swimming resort with artificial beaches of imported sand to the east, and **Monte Carlo** in the middle. The **gares SNCF** and **routière** are at place d'Armes below the palace rock in La Condamine. If you must stay more than one day in Monaco this is the best area for **hotels**. But they're expensive. You could try *Cosmopolite* (4 rue de la Turbie; ☎93.30.16.95) near the station, or *de la Poste* (☎93.30.70.56) and *l'Etoile* (☎93.30.73.92) at no. 5 and no. 4 rue des Oliviers between Monte Carlo and Larvotto. If you arrive early enough you may be able to get a dormitory style bed at the *Centre de Jeunesse Princess Stéphanie* (near the station on av Prince-Pierre; ☎93.50.75.05; open 7–10am and 2pm–1am).

La Condamine and the old town are the places to look for **restaurants** but good food and reasonable prices don't exactly match. You should be able to fill yourself up at the *African King* (4 rue Langlé, off rue Princess-Caroline; closed Sun. and March); *Le Versailles* (6 av Prince-Pierre; closed Sun. pm) or *La Siesta* (25 rue Comte Félix Gastaldi). In Monte Carlo try *Ramon* (2 rue du Portier; closed Sat.), or the more snackish *La Scala* (1 av Henry Dunant; closed Sun.) and *Regina* (13/15 bd des Moulins). The standard fare at almost all the cheap eateries is pizzas and pasta.

Monaco has no campsite, caravans are illegal in the state – as are swim suits, bare feet and chests once you step off the beach. There are no border formalities, French currency is valid, and bus and museum charges are considerably higher. The one good free public service is the lifts (marked on the SI map), incredibly clean, un-graffitied and efficient, for north–south journeys. **Bikes** can be hire from *Auto-Motos* garage, 7 rue de la Colle, to the left off av Prince Pierre from place d'Armes. Bus #4 takes you from the station to the *Casino-Tourism* stop with the **SI** at 2a bd des Moulins and place du Casino to the south.

The casino and other amusements

The **casino** is a must. Entrance is restricted to those over twenty-one and you may have to show your passport. Shorts and teeshirts are frowned on and for the more interesting sections, skirts, jackets, ties and so forth are more or less obligatory; any coats or large bags mean cloakroom fees.

In the first gambling hall, the *American Room*, slot machines surround the American roulette, craps and blackjack tables, the managers are Las Vegas trained, the lights low and the air oppressively smoky. Above this slice of Nevada, the walls and ceilings are turn-of-the-century Rococco extravagance, and in the adjoining *Pink Salon* bar female nudes smoking cigarettes adorn the ceilings. But the heart of the place is the *European Gaming Rooms*, through the American Room and Salles Touzet. You have to pay to get in (around 50F) and you must lock like a gambler not a tourist (no cameras, for example). More richly decorated than the American Room and much bigger, the atmosphere, early afternoon or out of season, is that of a cathedral. No flashing lights or clinking coins, just quiet voiced croupiers and sliding chips.

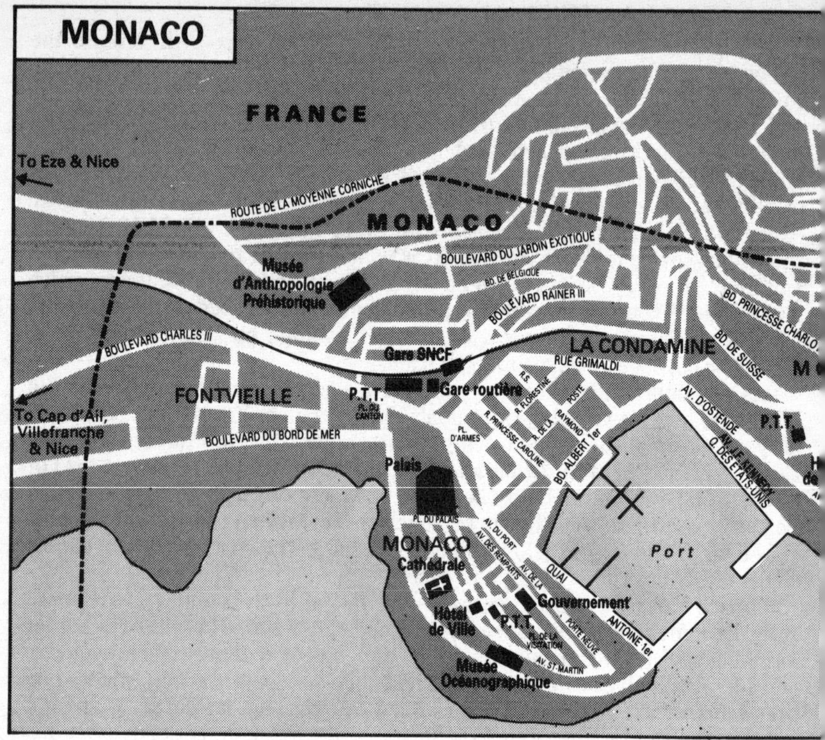

Elderly gamblers pace silently, fingering 500F notes (the minimum unnegotiated stake here is 500,000F), close circuit TV cameras above the chandeliers watch the gamblers watching the tables and no one drinks. On midsummer evenings the place is packed and it loses its sacred and exclusive touch.

Around the Casino are more casinos and the city's palace-hotels and *grands cafés* – all held by the same monopoly. The *American bar* of the **Hôtel de Paris** is, according to its publicity, the place where 'the world's most elite society' meets. As long as you dress up and are ready to be outraged (in English) if asked why you haven't ordered a £15 drink, you can entertain yourself, free of charge, watching tedious humans with fascinating bank accounts against the background of *belle epoque* decadence.

Other amusements such as the toy **palace** and assorted **museums** of the glacé icing **old town**, where every other shop sells Prince Rainier mugs and other assorted junk, are less rewarding. The possible exception is the aquarium in the basement of the **Musée Océanographique** (9am-9pm July and Aug.; otherwise 9.30am–7pm; bus #1, #2, *Monaco-Ville*) where the fishy beings outdo the weirdest Kandinsky, Hieronymous Bosch or Zandra Rhodes creations. Less exceptional but still peculiar cacti equivalents can be viewed

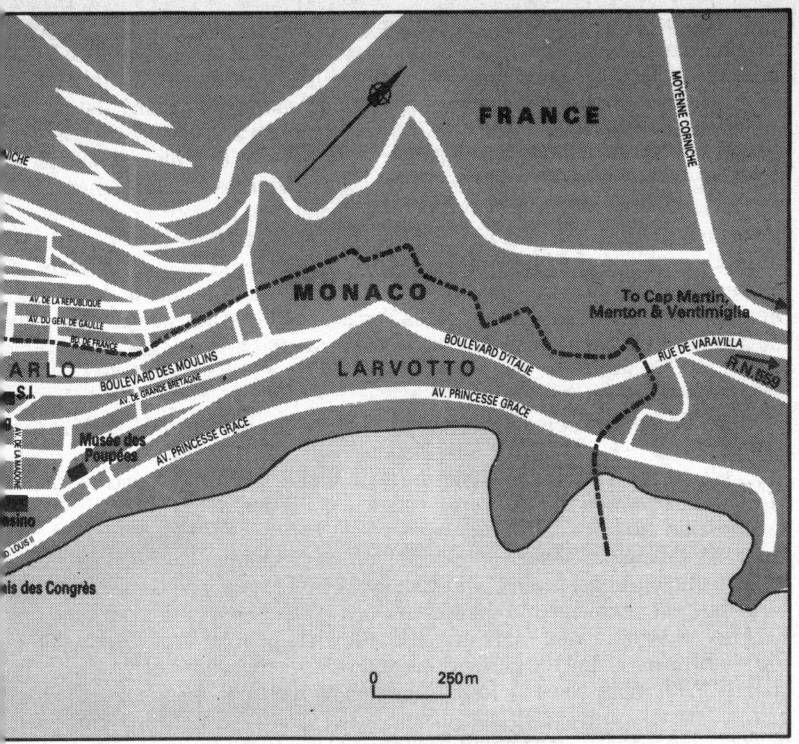

in the **Jardin Exotique** high above Fontvielle (9am–7pm May–Sept.; otherwise 9am–6pm).

One particular **time to avoid** Monaco is around the start of June (Ascension Day to the following Sunday) when racing cars burn around the port and Casino for the Formula 1 **Grand Prix**, and every space in sight of the circuit is inaccessible without a ticket. One way to **escape from Monaco** is to make your way through some of the world's highest-rent high-rises in Fontveille to the coastal path that leads out of the principality to Cap d'Ail.

Menton

MENTON, the easternmost town on the French coast, is even more of a rich retirement haven than Nice. No trace here now of its revolutionary 1848 days when, with Roquebrune, it broke away from Monaco to be an independent republic before Paris sucked it in twelve years later. The pride and joy of this town is its lemon crop which it celebrates in a citrus fruit extravaganza every February. But a *citron pressé* (pure lemon juice) served in a Menton bar still costs far more than an imported Belgian beer.

Its real speciality should be weddings, for this is the place to come to get a French marriage certificate. The **Salles des Mariages** in the **Hôtel de Ville** (on central place Ardoiono) was decorated by Jean Cocteau in his inimitable style and can be visited without matrimonial intentions by asking the receptionist by the main door (Mon.–Fri. 8.30am–12.30pm and 1.30–5pm). On the wall above the official desk a couple face each other with strange topological connections between the sun, her *Mentonaise* headdress and his fisherman's cap. A Saracen wedding party on the right hand wall reveals a disapproving bride's mother, the spurned girlfriend of the groom and her armed revengeful brother among the cheerful guests. On the left-hand wall is the story of Orpheus and Eurydice at the moment when Orpheus has just looked back. Meanwhile on the ceiling Poetry rides Pegasus, tattered Science juggles with the planets and Love, open-eyed, waits with bow and arrow at the ready. For further confusion the carpet is mock panther skin and lamps of bronze eucalyptus leaves line the hall.

There are other **Cocteau works** in the **museum** he set up himself in the little orange brick bastion by quai Napoléon III south of the old port. Open from Wednesday to Sunday 10am to noon and 3 to 6pm, it contains more *Mentonaise* lovers in the *Inamorati* series, a collection of delightful *Animaux Fantastiques* and the powerful tapestry of *Judith and Holopherne* simultaneously telling the sequence of seduction, assassination and escape. There are also photographs, poems, a portrait by friend Picasso, and ceramics.

As the *quai* bends around the western end of the Baie de Garavan from the Cocteau museum a long flight of black and white pebbled steps leads to the **Parvis St-Michel** and the perfect pink and yellow proportions of St. Michael's church. With more steps up to another square, a chapel of apricot and white marble, pastel campanales and disappearing stairways between long-lived houses, this is the Italianate and beautiful facade of the **Vieille Ville**. Just to the south the winding steps, tunnelled alleys and overhanging houses are the poorest part of the town and certain, soon, to face the speculators' gaze.

East of the old town overlooking the bay are the exclusive gardened villas of the Garavan district. *Les Colombières* with statues, a frescoed swimming pool and soaring views through the cypresses and olive trees out to sea, is one of a handful that are open to the public (4 bd de Garavan; open 9am–noon and 2–6pm; closed Oct.–Dec.; bus #7, direction bd de Garavan, stop *Colombières*).

The modern town and practicalities

To the west is the modern town arranged around three main streets parallel to the promenade. The **gare SNCF** is on the top one, bd Albert I, from which a short walk to the left as you come out brings you to the north–south avenues de Verdun and Boyer divided by the **Jardins Biovès**, central location for citrus sculptures during February's **Fête du Citron**. The **SI** is at 8 av Boyer in the **Palais de l'Europe** which has given up being a casino and, along with various cultural activities, hosts annual **contemporary art exhibitions** and an **international art biennale**. The **gare routière** and the **urban bus office** are between the continuation of the two avenues north of the railway line on the Esplanade de Carei.

Some **hotels** worth trying are the *Beauregard* (10 rue Albert 1er; ☎93.35.74.08; closed Nov. to mid-Dec.); the *Belgique* (1 av de la Gare; ☎93.35.72.66; closed Dec.) and the *Mondial* (12 rue Partouneaux; ☎93.28.30.30; closed mid-Nov. to mid-Dec.) – all three very central. For the overpriced **youth hostel** on Plateau St-Michel (☎93.35.93.14), take bus #6 from the gare routière, direction *Ciappes de Castellar* and get off at *Camping St-Michel*. As well as the **campsite** here (☎93.35.81.23; open March–Nov.) there are two more on the route de Gorbio to the west, *Fleur de Mai* (no. 67; ☎93.57.22.36) and St-Maurice (no. 49; ☎93.35.79.84), both at premium Côte prices.

Menton has a **food market** every day near the gare routière and in the covered *halles* on quai de Monléon below rue St-Michel, with bric-à-brac stands spreading up to the old town on Friday. Rue St-Michel and its continuation westwards, av Félix Faure, are pretty tacky and touristy but with plenty of cheap crêpes, pizzas, and midday meals to be had. For a real fish supper, try *Chez Gemaine* (46 promenade Maréchal-Leclerc) near the gare routière. You'll find cheaper menus at *Chez Maurice* (17 promenade de la Mer) and *L'Orchidée* (2 rue Masséna). Chocolate addicts can go salivate in front of the windows of *Godiva* (8 av Félix-Faure) or *Léonadas* (17 av de Verdun).

If you're heading east across the border, fill up with petrol in France, and with food, but not booze as even French brands are cheaper in Italy.

Art and artists: along the Baie des Anges and in the hills above

West of Nice airport the **baie des Anges** laps at twentieth-century resorts with two fine examples of concrete corpulence, the giant petrified sails with viciously pointed corners of the Villeneuve-Loubet-Plage marina, and an apartment complex 1km long and sixteen storeys high barricading the stony beach. The old towns and softer visual stimulation lie inland.

Renoir: Cagnes

At **CAGNES-SUR-MER**, which is north of the motorway not on the sea, the house where **Renoir** spent the last eleven years of his life, **Les Collettes**, has become a memorial museum (open 10am–1pm and 2–6pm in summer; 5pm in winter; closed Tues.). His atelier, north-facing to catch the late afternoon light, is arranged as if he had just popped out. In the rest of the house there are works by Renoir's friends – Dufy, Albert André, Bonnard and others and two of the artist's own bronzes, *La Maternité* and a medallion of his son Coco. You are free to wander around the olive and orange groves surrounding the house. Coming from Nice, you can get off the Cannes bus at the *Béal-Les Collettes* stop.

On the other side of the town, and to the north, is the ancient village of **HAUT-DE-CAGNES**, where the crenellated feudal **castle** houses museums of local history, fishing, the cultivation of olives, the **Musée d'Art Moderne Méditerranéen** with changing exhibitions of the painters who have worked on the coast in the last 100 years, and the **Donation Suzy Solidor** – wonderfully diverse portraits of the cabaret star from the 1920s to the 1960s by all the great painters. In addition, if you're here between July and September, you can see the entries from 40-odd countries for the **Festival International de la Peinture**. Opening times are 10am to noon and 2 to 5pm; closed Tues.; admission is cheap and includes all the collections. To get up here, other than by hefty heart exercise, there's a minibus service from the **gare SNCF** and from the centre of town, place de Gaulle, every 45 minutes.

Modernists: Vence

The next artistic treat, and one of the best in the whole region is the **Maeght Foundation** in **St-Paul-de-Vence**. The Nice–Vence bus stops at place de Gaulle in Cagnes-sur-Mer, and in St-Paul-de-Vence where you need to get off at the second stop and follow the signs up to the *Fondation*. It's open July to September 10am to 7pm; otherwise 10am to 12.30pm and 2.30 to 6pm. Admission includes the permanent collections, temporary exhibitions, bookshop, library and cinema, and is expensive but worth every last centime. Giacometti's Cat stalking along the edge of the grass; Miró's Egg smiling above a pond and his totemed Fork outlined against the sky; a Calder mobile swinging over watery tiles; on a sun-lit rough stone wall Léger's flowers, birds and a bench; metallic forms by Zadkine and Arp between the pine trunks; a clanking tubular fountain by Pol Bury . . . and that's just the outside of a building whose inside resolutely refuses any fixed barrier with the exterior light and space.

There's not much point hanging around in St-Paul, despite it's being an almost perfect *village perché*, unless you've got hold of someone else's plastic: **VENCE**, a short way north, is a real town with affordable places **to stay** and **eat**. Arriving here at the **gare routière** you'll find yourself on place du Grand Jardin, with **bike hire** (*Vence Motocycles*), the **SI** and, just beyond it, the main gate into the **old town**. For **hotels**, the cheapest option is *des Alpes* (2 av Général-Leclerc; ☎93.58.13.30) on the other side of the old town. Otherwise *La Closerie des Genets* (23 av M-Maurel; ☎93.58.33.25) on the south side, and *La Lubiane* (10 av Joffre; ☎93.58.01.10) to the west up av Henri-Isnard and av des Poilus, both have some low-priced rooms. There's a **campsite** 3km west on the road to TOURETTES-SUR-LOUP, *La Bergerie* (☎93.58.09.36; open March–Oct.). For a special meal, try *La Fariguoule* (15 av Henri-Isnard). On the same street there's *La Vieille Douve* at half the price, and the old town can't be beaten for snacks of every kind, and drinking (*Henry's Bar* on place du Peyra is young and noisy).

Vieux Vence may be blessed with numerous ancient houses, gateways, fountains, chapels and a cathedral, but the building which people come to Vence to see was built between 1949 and 1951, under the exclusive design and direction of Henri Matisse. The **Chapelle du Rosaire** was his last work, consciously so, and not, as some believe, a religious conversion. But self-abnegation was involved. He painted the black outline figures on plain matt tiles with a brush fixed to a six-foot bamboo pole specifically to remove his own signature from the lines. Colour comes from the light diffused through green, blue and yellow stained glass windows, changing throughout the day and the seasons. For some, the result is magic, for others a grating disappointment. The chapel is at 466 av Henri-Matisse, on the road to La Gaude from the Carrefour J-Moulin at the top of av des Poilus, and open Tuesday and Thursday only, 10 to 11.30am and 2.30 to 5.30pm.

Léger and Picasso: Biot, Antibes and Vallauris

Back towards the coast, between Cagnes and Antibes, is the village of **BIOT** where Fernand Léger spent a few years at the end of his life. A brilliant collection of his works can be seen in and on the **Musée Fernand Léger**, just southeast of the village (10am–noon and 2.30–6.30pm in summer; otherwise 10am–noon and 2–5pm; closed Tues.; bus from Antibes). His fellow pioneer of Cubism, **Pablo Picasso**, was offered, when he returned to the Mediterranean after the war, the dusty museum in **ANTIBES** castle as a studio. He spent an extremely prolific few months there and when he moved to Vallauris left his output to what is now the **Musée Picasso** (10am–noon and 3–7pm in summer; otherwise 10am–noon and 2–6pm; closed Tues. and Nov.) adding other works later on. There are numerous ceramics; still lifes of sea urchins; the wonderful *Ulysses et ses Sirènes* – a great round head against a mast which the ship, sea and sirens labyrinth around; goats and fauns in cubist undisguise; and a whole room full of drawings. Picasso is also the subject here of other painters and photographers, including Man Ray and Bill Brandt and there are works by contemporaries, among them **Léger's tapestry of construction workers**. This was a favourite subject of Léger's later years, on which there are several canvases at Biot. He described seeing a factory being built and men like fleas balancing on the steel beams. 'This is what I wanted to depict: the contrast between man and his creations, between the worker and this whole architecture of metal'. Though the Antibes museum does not represent anywhere near all of Picasso's periods, the contrast between these two contemporaries, colleagues and comrades is telling – Léger's commitment to collective working-class life never wavered; Picasso waved at it while trying to embrace the whole world.

Picasso stayed ten years in **VALLAURIS**, where he first began to use clay, thereby reviving one of the traditional crafts of this little town in the hills above Golfe Juan. Today the main street, av George-Clemenceau, sells nothing but pottery – much of it the garishly glazed bowls and figurines that could feature in souvenir shops anywhere. The **Madoura** pottery, where Picasso worked, is off rue 19 mars 1962, to the right as you come down av Clemenceau. It has the sole rights on reproducing his designs, which are for sale, at a price, in the shop (open weekdays only). At the top of the main street Picasso's bronze *Man with a Sheep* stands in the market place, opposite the castle courtyard, where an early medieval **chapel** with the architectural simplicity of an air raid shelter was painted by the artist as **La Guerre et la Paix** in 1952. At first glance it's easy to be unimpressed (as many critics still are). It looks mucky and slapdash with paint runs on the unyielding plywood panel surface. But stay a while and the passion of this violently drawn pacifism slowly emerges: a music score trampled by hooves and about to be engulfed in flames, a fighter's lance holding the scales of justice and a shield – symbol of peace. Recent 'just wars' and 'peace operations' come to mind. The chapel is open daily (except Tues.) 10am to noon and 2 to 6pm. Buses from CANNES and GOLFE JUAN SNCF arrive close to the castle.

Only a 20-minute train ride from NICE it is not worth hunting for rooms in **ANTIBES** (the SI is in the central place Général de Gaulle if you need details) or at neighbouring **JUAN-LES-PINS**, a summer St-Moritz. Antibes' daily **market** on Cours Masséna near the castle could provide a good picnic – then you can search for a public space to eat it among the well-screened cages on **CAP D'ANTIBES** where the rich and famed retreat to.

CENTRAL RESORTS AND ISLANDS

In which the **Côte d'Azur myth – St-Tropez** – turns out to be for real. Other resorts, with the honourable exceptions of **Hyères**, to the west, and the **islands**, fare less well . . .

Cannes and the Lerin Islands

Fishing village turned millionaires' residence, **CANNES'** main source of income is business junketing – in an ever multiplying calendar of festivals, conferences, tournaments and trade shows. The main locale for these events is the **Palais des Festivals**, an orange concrete mega-bunker, on the prime seaside spot beside the old port. The seafront promenade, **la Croisette**, and the **Vieux Port** form the focus of other Cannes life. The fine sand **beach** looks like an industrial production line for parasols with neat rows extending the length of the shore, changing colour with each change of concession for this privately exploited stretch. The 1km length of La Croisette is magnified, to little aesthetic effect, by the size of the apartment blocks and by the nineteenth-century palace-hotels like the *Carlton* and *Majestic*, survivors of a fast-disappearing breed. Halfway along is the tacky **Palais Croisette**, home of the film festival – which is strictly a credentials-only event.

As nowhere else along the *Côte*, except St-Tropez, the millionaires here choose to eat their meals served by white-clad crew on their yacht decks, feigning oblivion of landborne spectators a crumb's throw away. Behind this dubious entertainment of watching *langoustines* disappear down overfed mouths, you can buy your own food in the **covered market** two blocks back from the Mairie, and wander through the day's flower shipments along from the Allées de la Liberté opposite the port. The old town, **Le Suquet**, on the steep hill overlooking the bay, masks its miserable passageways, where those who don't benefit from the town's economy live, with quaint cosmetic streets. Beyond Le Suquet there's more beach and better chance of not having to pay for it.

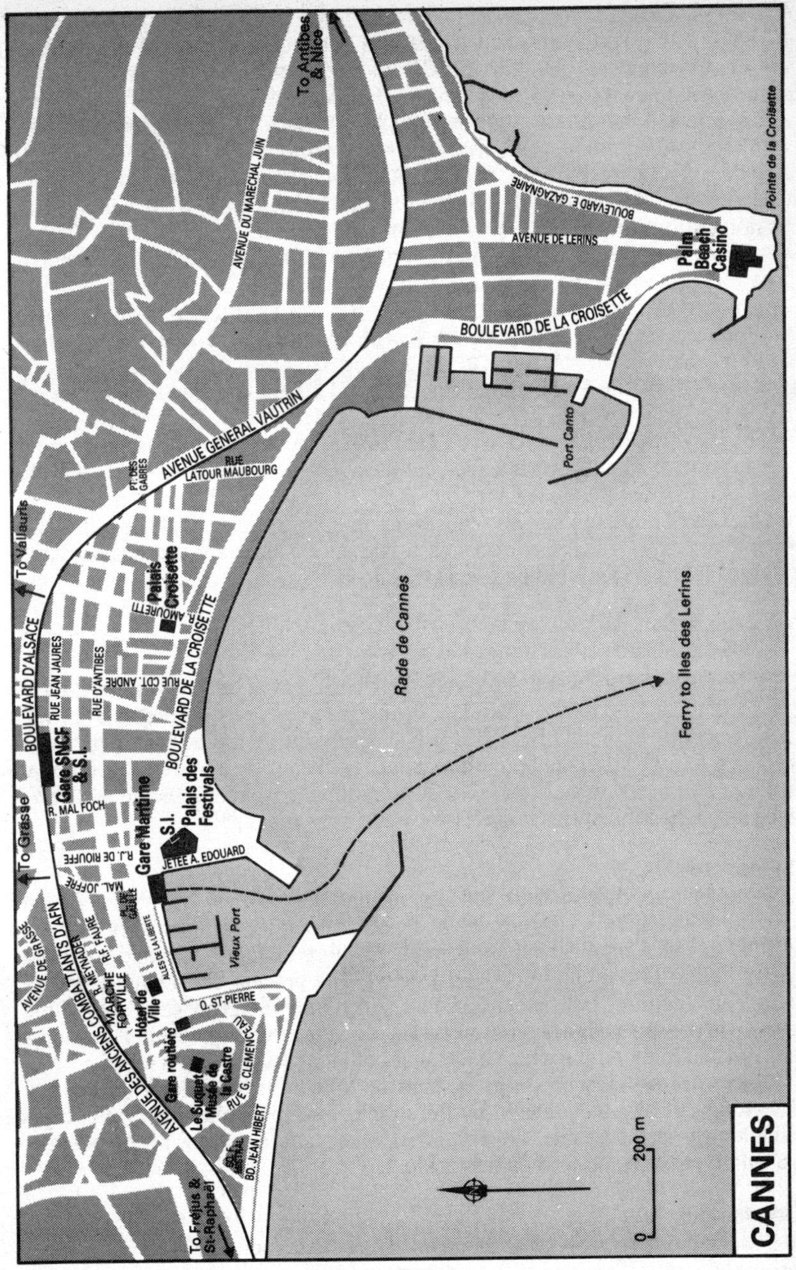
CANNES
0
200 m
To Fréjus & St-Raphaël
To Grasse
To Vallauris
To Antibes & Nice
AVENUE DES ANCIENS COMBATTANTS D'AFN
AVENUE DE GRASSE
R. MEYNADER
R.F. FAURE
MARCHE FORVILLE
Hôtel de Ville
ALLEES DE LA LIBERTE
Q. ST-PIERRE
Gare routière
Le Suquet
Musée de la Castre
RUE G. CLEMENCEAU
BD. JEAN HIBERT
MAL. JOFFRE
R.J. DE RIOUFFE
Gare Maritime
JETÉE A. EDOUARD
Vieux Port
S.I.
Palais des Festivals
R. MAL FOCH
Gare SNCF & S.I.
BOULEVARD D'ALSACE
RUE JEAN JAURES
RUE D'ANTIBES
RUE CDT. ANDRE
BOULEVARD DE LA CROISETTE
R. AMOURETTI
Palais Croisette
PT. DES GABRES
RUE LATOUR MAUBOURG
AVENUE GENERAL VAUTRIN
AVENUE DU MARECHAL JUIN
BOULEVARD DE LA CROISETTE
AVENUE DE LERINS
BOULEVARD E. GAZAGNAIRE
Palm Beach Casino
Pointe de la Croisette
Port Canto
Rade de Cannes
Ferry to Iles des Lerins

Existing in Cannes

If you're compelled to stay in Cannes, the best concentration of **hotels** is in the centre, between the **gare SNCF** on rue Jean-Jaurès and La Croisette, around the main street of rues Antibes/Felix-Fauré. Possibilities include the *Bourgogne* (13 rue de 24 Août; ☎93.38.36.73), *Azur* (15 rue Jean-de-Riouffe; ☎93.39.52.14), *National* (8 rue du Commandant-André; ☎93.39.24.82), *Chanteclair* (12 rue Fortville; ☎93.39.67.88) and *Les Roches Fleuries* (92 rue G Clemenceau; ☎93.39.28.78) below Le Suquet. Inevitably there's no youth hostel and not much in the way of reasonably priced camping either. There are **SI's** at the gare SNCF and in the Palais des Festivals. Le Suquet is full of **restaurants**, which get cheaper as you reach the top. Three good ones in the centre are *Au Bec Fin* at the hotel *Cybelle-Bec Fin* (12 rue du 24-Août; closed Sat. pm and Sun.) with superb traditional cooking, *La Croisette* (15 rue du Commandant-André; closed Tues.) serving excellent grilled fish, and *Le Bouchon* (10 rue de Constantine; closed Mon.) where you can drink green tea if you don't fancy wine.

The **gare routière** is next to the gare SNCF, except for the coastal bus and all seven of the town buses which leave from the Hôtel de Ville by the old port. A minibus shuttles along the seafront from square Frédéric-Mistral, west of Le Suquet, to Palm Beach Casino on Pointe Croisette at the other end of the bay. You can **hire bikes** at 5 rue Allieis near the station, and the *Allostop* number, for hitching out, is ☎93.38.60.88.

Iles de Lérins

The **Iles de Lérins** would be lovely anywhere, but at only 15 minutes' ferry ride from Cannes, they're paradise facing purgatory. **Boats** leave from the *gare maritime* in the old port, (7.30am–3.30pm summer; nine crossings daily; reduced to five, last at 2.45pm off-season. Last boats back leave St-Honorat at 4.45pm and Ste-Marguerite at 6 or 7pm summer). Taking a picnic is a good idea as the handful of restaurants have a lucrative monopoly.

St-Honorat

The smaller southern island, St-Honarat, has been owned by monks almost continuously since its namesake and patron founded a monastery here in 410AD. It was a famous bishops' seminary, where St. Patrick trained for seven years before setting out to convert Ireland. The present **abbey** buildings are nineteenth-century, with older cloisters which only men can visit. But behind them, on the sea's edge, stands an earlier, eleventh-century, fortified version – the only building on the whole coast that both looks and really is old.

There are no cars or shops or bars or hotels on St-Honorat: just vines, lavender and olives cultivated by the monks, and pine and eucalyptus trees shading the paths beside the white rock shore and mixing with the scent of rosemary, thyme and wild honeysuckle.

Ste-Marguerite

Ste-Marguerite is a bit of a let down by comparison. The water is sludgy around the port, the pond at the western end is stagnant and the aleppo pines and evergreen oak woods are so thick that most of the paths are in semi-darkness. The western end is the most accessible, and the best points to swim are the rocky inlets across the island from the port.

Fort Ste-Marguerite – the site – was built by the Spanish when they occupied both islands. Later Vauban rounded, or rather starred, it off, presumably for Louis XIV's *gloire* since the strategic value of an immense fort facing your own mainland would be strictly zilch. There are cells to see and a *Musée de la Mer* (9.30am–noon in summer; 10:20am–noon in winter and 2pm till the last boat) of local finds, mostly Roman but including remnants of a tenth-century Arab ship. But you may find it just as rewarding to laze around (for free) on the grassy ramparts of this vast construction.

Down the coast

Down the coast from Cannes an arc of brilliant red volcanic rock tumbles down to the sea from harsh crags. From the Corniche (on N98) minor roads lead up into this wild terrain, the **Massif d'Esterel**. The shoreline, a mass of little **beaches**, cut by rocky promontories, is the least inhabited stretch of the Côte. Some of the beaches are pebbles, some sand, and if you're after relatively uncrowded swimming they're a good choice for a couple of days.

The Cannes–St-Raphaël **train** follows the coast almost all the way and there are **buses** too. **Accommodation** is not so easy. There's a **youth hostel** that may well be full at LE TRAYAS, the *Villa Solange* (9 av de la Véronèse; ☎93.75.40.23; 2km signed from *Auberge Blanche* stop on Cannes–St-Raphaël bus route, same distance from Le Trayas gare SNCF), and another, next door to BOULOURIS gare SNCF on the outskirts of St-Raphaël, the *Centre International du Manoir* (☎94.95.20.58; open mid-June to Oct.). If you're prepared to pay a bit more than you would in a city for a **hotel room**, try *La Calanque* (bd Henri-Clews; ☎93.49.95.11) in LA NAPOULE; *Adrienne* (2 av Charles-Dahon; ☎93.49.96.06) in THEOULE-SUR-MER: *Robinson Crusoe* (Quartier de la Baumette; ☎94.44.81.09; closed Dec.–March) and *de la Plage* (Camp-Long; ☎94.82.00.77; closed Oct.–March) in AGAY, or *La Poste et des Terrasses* (☎94.44.14.13; closed Oct.–Jan.) in Le Trayas. **Camping** shouldn't be a problem – there are sites in La Napoule, ANTHEOR, Agay (with at least seven), LE DRAMONT and Boulouris. In summer, pick up lists and phone numbers from any of the Côte SIs and try to make reservations.

St-Raphaël and Fréjus

The familiar Côte scene of yachts and long parasoled beaches reasserts itself, after 40km or so, at **ST-RAPHAEL**, now more or less one conurbation with the town of **FREJUS**, 3km inland and linked with it by fast and frequent trains.

Both were established by the Romans – Fréjus as a naval base under Octavius, St-Raphaël as a resort for its veterans – and various remnants of this past lie scattered around the towns. Most of any significance are at Fréjus, whose population was far larger in Roman times. They include an **amphitheatre** (rue Henri-Vardon), used in its damaged state for bullfights and rock concerts, a **theatre** (av du XV-Corps-d'Armées), also pressed into service for shows, and, to its east, a few arches of the old **aqueduct**.

Perhaps more interesting, though, are the legacies of medieval Fréjus and of the early twentieth century. For the former, make for the **cathedral close** on place Formige, with superb twelfth-century Romanesque cloisters and a late medieval fantasy ceiling, and a small museum with a complete Roman mosaic of a leopard; guided tours only, daily except Tues., 9.30am to noon and 2 to 6pm in summer; 2 to 4.30pm in winter. The more recent past comes in the shape of a **Vietnamese pagoda** and an abandoned **Sudanese mosque** – both built by French Colonial troops. The pagoda, still maintained as a Buddhist temple, is at the intersection of RN7 to Cannes and D100, about 2km out of Fréjus; it is open daily 3 to 6pm. You may have to hitch to the mosque which is on the left off D4 to Bagnols, in the middle of an army camp 2km from the RN7 junction. A strange, guava-coloured and fort-like building, it is decorated inside with fading murals of desert journeys gracefully sketched in white on the dark pink walls.

Two possible **hotels** in FREJUS are *Les Glycines* (22 bd Sévérin-Décuers; ☎94.51.59.17) south of the centre, and *La Riviera* (90 rue Grisolle; ☎94.51.31.46), close to the station), or there's a **youth hostel** (Domaine de Bellevue, rte de Cannes; ☎94.52.18.75; bus from Fréjus or St-Raphaël station to *rue Grisole* then a 1km walk). **Campsites** are ubiquitous, with at least four on the Bagnols road and one close to the youth hostel. For further details there's the **SI** on place Calvini and another at 325 rue Jean-Jaurès. And for somewhere good **to eat**, *Les Potiers* (135 rue des Potiers; closed Wed. and midday in summer), has a menu of fresh seasonal ingredients for under 100F.

ST-RAPHAEL has more **hotels** but a bigger clientele. Try *des Templiers* (place de la République; ☎94.95.38.93) and the *Suisse* (6 av de Valescure; ☎94.95.25.00) in the old town north of the station; or *Le Grand Levant* (22 rue Thiers; ☎94.95.07.54) just back from the port – or the Boulouris youth hostel (see above). The **SI** is on place de la Gare along with the **gare SNCF** and **gare routière**. And between here and the seafront, with a second, truly tacky marina, you'll have no trouble finding **restaurants**.

If you want to head **straight to St-Tropez**, you can get a boat from the port (tickets and times from the St-Raphaël *gare maritime*; 3 to 4 per day in summer, otherwise 1 or 2; 50-min. journey), and it's hardly more expensive than a bus.

The Côte de Maures and St-Tropez

Where the Esterel gives out, the **Massif des Maures** takes over – providing a backdrop of cork, pine and chestnut-covered hills dropping into bowls of cultivated fields and vineyards alongside villages of medieval confinement. With the single, spectacular exception of St-Tropez, the tangle of resorts from the Golfe de Fréjus westwards are all smaller or lesser clones of a single resort, Ste-Maxime.

STE-MAXIME is the perfect Côte stereotype: palmed corniche and pleasure-boat harbour, casino, golden beaches with well-heeled windsurfers and waterskiers. It is beginning to sprawl a little too much, like many of its neighbours, but the seduction of the water's edge and the roads designed for topless speeding in convertibles is hard to deny.

The problem, inevitably, is one of money and space. All the resorts between St-Raphaël and Hyères are expensive and summer sees their **hotels and campsites** (which are spaced at intervals the whole way) severely overstretched. Before starting out it's essential to pick up full SI lists for the region and phone around. The only **youth hostel** is at LA GARDE FREINET, inland from St-Tropez, a one-time Saracen stronghold and now favoured retirement home of Oxford and Cambridge professors (rte de St-Tropez; ☎94.43.60.05; open mid-March to Sept.; bus from Toulon and Grimaud or St-Tropez and Cogolin). **Camping at farms** can be a good fallback: ask the SI for lists and numbers but check the price before pitching.

Travel along this strip of the Côte is done by boat or by car: either your own or someone else's. The trains are all inland, while buses, except for the direct route between St-Raphaël–Ste-Maxime–Hyères, are infrequent. An attractive and viable option, bypassing Ste-Maxime et al., is to take a boat from St-Raphaël straight to St-Tropez (see above).

The St-Tropez peninsula

ST-TROPEZ stands quite apart from its neighbours: a little village, gathered around a port founded by the ancient Greeks and which until recently was only easily accessible by boat. The road from Le Foux now has summer traffic jams as bad as Nice or Marseille – but you wouldn't guess by the look of the place. In fact it still looks pretty much as it did in the movies. An enduring and in some ways rather wonderful fantasy.

Its emergence to present chic and financial cachet parallelled the development of those other Mediterranean clichés – Ibiza, Mykonos, Hammammet. In the late nineteenth century, when only fishing boats moored here and strangers were virtually unknown, the painter **Paul Signac** turned up and stayed, soon followed by, among others, **Matisse, Bonnard** and **Marquet** – Bohemians hanging out in the sun away from the respectable convalescents of Cannes or Nice. And then in 1956 Roger Vadim arrived, with crew, to film **Brigitte Bardot** in *Et Dieu Créa La Femme*. The cult took off, the 1960s took place, and the resort has been big money mainstream ever since. Bardot still owns a house here (as do Elton John, Mick Jagger and Herbert von Karajan), but the yachts – bigger than anywhere else in Europe, in their restricted harbour space – are owned more often by City or Manhattan banks these days. If you can save your visit for a rainy winter's day (they happen now and again even here), you'll be able to separate the myth from the hype, and probably find a room and a place to eat, too. In July and August, come in your yacht or not at all.

The road into St-Tropez from LE FOUX splits in two as it enters the village, with the **gare routière** between them and, a short distance beyond on rue de la Nouvelle-Poste, the **Musée de l'Annonciade** (10am–noon and 3–7pm in

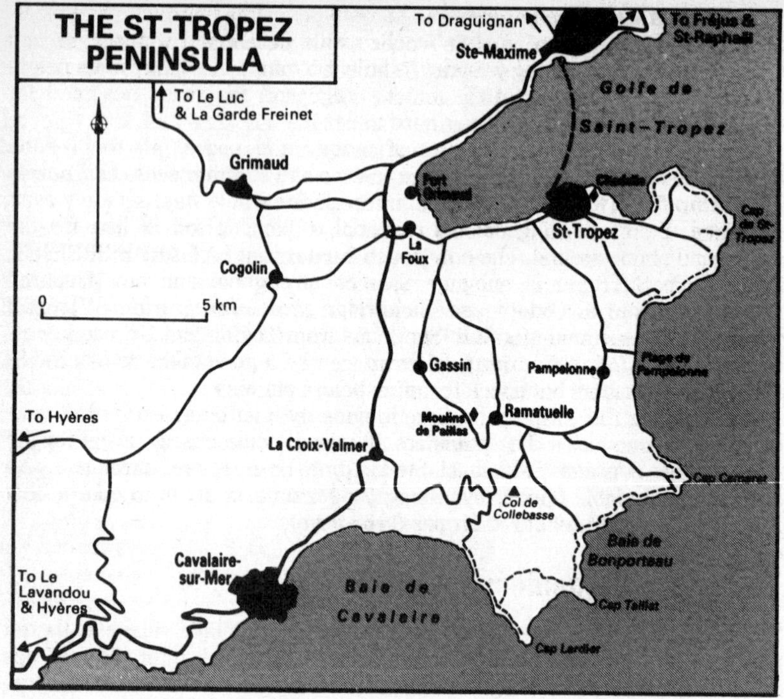

summer; 2–6pm in winter; closed Tues. and Nov.), a reason, if you have no other, for coming here. Within are representative works by Matisse and most of the other artists who worked here: grey, grim, northern scenes of Paris, Boulogne and Westminster, and then local, brilliantly sunlit scenes by the same brush. A real delight, and one of the top collections of 1890–1940 French art outside Paris.

Keep going, beyond the museum, and you will hit the **Vieux Port**. And here you have it, the *St-Tropez* experience of the late twentieth century: the dockside café clientele *face à face* with the yacht deck martini sippers, the latest fashions parading in between, defining the French word *frimer* (derived from sham) which means exactly this – to stroll vainly in places like St-Tropez.

Up from the port, at the end of quai Jean-Jaurès, rue de la Mairie passes the town hall, with a street to the left leading down to the rocky **Baie de la Glaye**. Further up, along rue de la Ponche, you reach the **fishing port** with a tiny beach. Both these spots are miraculously free from commercialisation. Beyond the fishing port, roads lead up to the sixteenth-century **Citadelle**. Its maritime museum is not much fun but the walk around the ramparts on an overgrown path has the best views of the gulf and the back of the town – views that have not changed since their translations in oil on to canvas in the *Annonciade*.

Accommodation and restaurants

The shops and restaurants of St-Tropez would be equally at home, serving the same clientele, in Bond Street, Madison Avenue or Paris's own rue de Faubourg St-Honoré. Absolutely nothing is cheap in this town.

Of **hotels**, the only two vaguely affordable are *Les Lauriers* (rue du Temple; ☎94.97.04.88; open April–Sept.) and *Les Chimères* (Quartier du Pilon; ☎94.97.02.90), a short way back from the gare routière towards La Foux on the left. Both are likely to be booked for the summer.

Camping on the peninsula poses similar problems. There are two sites on the plage du Pampelonne (see below), which, though closest to St-Tropez, cost a fortune and in high summer resemble an orgy with no sex. Within a 3 to 4km radius of Ramatuelle (see below) are *Les Tournels* (rte de Camarat; ☎94.79.80.54); *La Croix du Sud* (rte de St-Tropez; ☎94.79.80.84; open May–Sept.); and *La Cigale* (rte de l'Escalet off rte de Croix-Valmer; ☎94.79.22.53). The **SI** at St-Tropez, on quai Jean-Jaurès, can help with reservations and the **bike hire** place, *Vespa* (5 rue Quaranta) with getting there.

As for **eating**, forget the dockside – though the nougat at *Sénéquier*, which you can buy from the snotty shop at the back, is sensational. *La Patate* snackerie on rue G Clemenceau has omelettes, pasta, *pain beignats* and so forth – nothing special but it may save you from starvation. If you're prepared to go over 100F, there's still no great choice, but *Lou Revelen* near the fishing port at 4 rue des Remparts, will serve a very decent meal without treating you like poor foreign tourist scum.

The southern bay

The southern bay of **the St-Tropez peninsula** – CAVALAIRE – has long stretches of sheltered sandy beaches and slopes above sprouting second residences like a cabbage patch gone to seed. Around St-Tropez and east to the POINTE DE RABIOU, the same reproduction goes on, only with more luxurious villas and wider spaces between them. And then, amazingly, or rather because of government intervention and complex ownerships, the land in between is almost uninhabited.

The best view of this richly green and flowering countryside is from the hilltop village of **GASSIN**, its lower neighbour **RAMATUELLE**, or the tiny road between them, where three ruined windmills could once catch the wind from every direction. Gassin is the shape and size of a small ship perched on a summit, once a Moorish stronghold now, of course, highly chic. It's an excellent place for a blow-out dinner, sitting outside by the village wall with a spectacular panorama east over the peninsula. Of the handful of restaurants, *Bello Visto*, though no gourmet dream, is the least outrageously priced.

PAMPELONNE is the most famous of the beaches and credited with the first French topless bathing. Four kilometres long, shallow for 50m or so and exposed to the wind, it's sometimes scourged by dried sea vegetation but spotless glitter comes from the unending line of beach bars and restaurants with patios and sofas serving cocktails and gluttonous ice cream.

At the head of the Golfe de St-Tropez, **PORT GRIMAUD** is the ultimate Côte d'Azur property development and should, as such, unquestionably be visited. This is not just another private estate but a private lakeside pleasure city with waterways for roads and yachts parked at the bottom of every yard. Built in the 1960s, all the houses are in exquisitely tasteful old Provençal style, even if their owners, Joan Collins for example, are not. In a way it's surprising that the whole enclave isn't wired off and patrolled by Alsatians. The idea must be to generate enough envy to justify the prices.

Hyères and the Iles d'Or

Walled and medieval, old **HYERES** lies on the slopes of Casteou hill, 5km from the sea with a ruined **castle** on the summit. From the top of the keep and the ivy-clad towers that outreach the oak and lotus trees, you can see the modern expansion of the town with its proliferation of palm trees and, beyond, the peculiar Presqu'île de Giens, leashed to the mainland by a narrow isthmus and parallel sand bar enclosing salt marshes in between. Out to sea, east of Giens, the three **Iles d'Or** (or Iles d'Hyères) are visible.

Lacking a central seafront, Hyères lost out on snob-appeal when the Côte clientele switched from winter convalescents to dockside strutters. Consequently it's very appealing: the casino is used for cinema and youth clubs, the old town is neither a tourist trap nor a slum, and the land around is covered with strawberry fields, vines, and peach orchards rather than stacked up tourist hotels. The only blight on all this is the presence of a French air force base just north of the main port, from which test pilots play with the latest fiendish multi-million franc exports up and down the coast.

The **gare SNCF** is 1½km southwest of the centre at the end of av Edith Cavell, with frequent buses to the **gare routière** on place Clemenceau from which a medieval gatehouse opens onto rue Maissillon and the **Vieille Ville**. For **hotels**, apart from the *Globe* (10 cours de Strasbourg; ☎94.65.05.55) in the old town, you have the choice of the modern centre – try *Les Orangers* (64 av des Iles-d'Or; ☎94.65.07.01) or *de la Poste* (7 av Lyautey; ☎94.65.02.00) – or by the sea – *La Méditerranée* (av de la Méditerranée; ☎94.58.03.89) at HYERES-PLAGE, or *La Reine Jeanne* (☎94.66.32.64) at the Port de l'AYGUADE. There's no youth hostel but plenty of **campsites** on the coast: in LES SALINS, due east of Hyères and at L'Ayguade and LE CEINTURON further south where the beach gets rather stony and the air base too close (bus #66), several on GIENS and one at L'ALMANARRE west of the town. The **SI** is on the rotunda off av de Belgique, two blocks south of place Clemenceau, and **bikes** which you might need, can be rented at 59 av Alphonse-Denis or 33 av Gambetta.

For eating and drinking, there are the terraced **cafés** and **morning market** in the spacious square at the top of rue Maissillon; **restaurants** are all around this corner of the *Vieille Ville* as well as east along the street that divides the old and the new towns, as it becomes rue Alphonse-Denis. For a scenic wander, go up from the tower on the square and head through the oldest parts of the *Vieille Ville* to Parc St-Bernard. From these gardens, full of nearly every Mediterranean flower, you can continue up to the castle.

The Iles d'Or

A haven from tempests in ancient times, then peaceful habitat of monks and farmers, the **ILES D'OR** became a base for coastal attacks by an endless succession of assorted aggressors. They are covered in forts, half-destroyed, rebuilt, abandoned, from the sixteenth century when François I started a trend of underfunded fort building, to the twentieth century when the German gun positions on Port-Cros and Levant were put out of action by the Americans. Porquerolles and Levant are still not free of garrisons thanks to the knack of the French armed forces for getting prime beauty sites for bases.

Porquerolles

PORQUEROLLES, the largest and most easily accessible island, has a proper village around the port with a market, *boules* playing and plenty of cafés; there are also a few **hotels** and restaurants, though none of them particularly cheap. This is the only cultivated island and it has its own wine, *appellation Côtes des Iles*. The landscapes are beautiful and it's big enough to find yourself alone, and get lost. The southern shoreline is all cliffs with scary paths meandering close to the edge through heather and exuberant Provençal growth. The sandy beaches are on either side of the village and the *terrain militaire* is up on the northern tip. If you want to hire a **bike**, try at the top of the main square just to the left.

Port-Cros

The dense vegetation and mini mountains make **PORT-CROS** harder going though it's less than half the size of Porquerolles. It takes a couple of hours to walk from the port to the nearest beach, **plage de la Palu**; a similar amount of time to cross the island via **Vallon de la Solitude** or **Vallon de la Fausse-Monnaie**. The entire island is a protected zone (no smoking outside the port area, no picking of flowers) for it has the richest fauna and flora of all Provence. Kestrels, eagles and sparrow-hawks nest here, and there are shrubs that flower and bear fruit at the same time. More common species like broom, lavender, rosemary and heather flourish in abundance. The leaflet provided by the National Park organisation based at the port, will reveal all the species to be seen, watched and smelled. Come armed with a botanical dictionary. One thing, however, that is a complete waste of money, is the glass-bottomed boat offering submarine viewing. The sole island hotel is prohibitively expensive, as are the few restaurants around the port, though you should be able to get a snack.

Ile de Levant

On the **ILE DE LEVANT**, where it is almost always humid and sunny, cultivated plant life goes wild – giant geraniums and nasturtiums climb three-meter hedges overhung by gigantic eucalyptus trees. The tiny bit of the island spared by the military is a **nudist colony**, set up in the village of **Heliopolis** in the early 1930s. About sixty people live here year round, joined by thousands who come just for the summer, and tens of thousands of day visitors. The residents' preferred street dress is '*les plus petits costumes en Europe*', on sale as you get off the boat, and they are a lot more friendly to people who stay, even a few days, than to the voyeuristic two-hour visitors. Unfortunately, this option is only open to **campers** (*Le Colombero*; ☎94.05.90.29) or the rich and extravagant.

Access to the islands

You can **get to the islands** from LA TOUR FONDUE on the southeast tip of the Presqu'île de Giens (☎94.58.21.81; bus #66 from the Port d'Hyères), to all three in summer, otherwise just Porquerolles; from the PORT D'HYERES (☎94.57.44.07) to Port-Cros and Levant; from TOULON (quai Stalingrad; ☎94.92.96.82) to all three; from LE LAVANDOU (15 quai Gabriel-Péri; ☎94.71.01.02) to all three; from CAVALAIRE (☎94.64.08.04) to all three in summer and from ST-TROPEZ to all three and Toulon, mid-July and August. If you want to visit just one, Le Lavandou is the nearest port for Port-Cros (35 min.) and Levant (35 min.); La Tour Fondue for Porquerolles (20 min.).

NOT THE COTE: TOWARDS MARSEILLE

From the squalid naval base of **Toulon** to the vast and rather wonderful seediness of **Marseille**, this stretch of the Mediterranean is definitely not the Côte d'Azur. There is no continuous corniche, few villas in the Grand Style, and work is geared to an annual rather than summer cycle. **Cassis** is the exception, but Marseille the overriding attraction – a city that couldn't be confused with any other, no matter where you were dropped in it.

Toulon

Viewed from the distant heights of Mont Caume, Notre-Dame du Mai or the Fort de Six-Fours, the port of **TOULON** is a breath-taking sight. Home base to the French Mediterranean fleet and its arsenal, and until recently a major ship-building centre, Toulon's associations are with either military activities or inhumane punishment. Up until the eighteenth century, slaves and convicts were still powering the kings galleys. After the Revolution convicts were sent to Toulon with iron collars around their necks for sentences of hard labour – their crimes often no more than stealing a loaf of bread. After 1854 convicts were deported to the colonies in whose conquest ships from Toulon played a major part. The town was half destroyed in World War II and neither the history of the city nor its current status – which includes having voted in the one and only *Front National député* – offers much joy. But since it is a major nexus you may well find yourself there and it does have the one advantage of being cheap for this coast.

The town

The main street in the town centre is bd de Strasbourg becoming av Maréchal-Leclerc to the west and av George-Clemenceau to the east. The old town, much besieged by bulldozers and planners intent on its gentrification, crams in between bd de Strasbourg and quai de Stalingrad on the old port. The **gare SNCF** and **gare routière** are on place Albert 1er. If you turn left out of the station and follow bd de Tessé three blocks, av Colbert with the **SI** on your right at no. 8, leads down to bd de Strasbourg and the old town. One of the cheapest and nicest **hotels** is *Les Trois Dauphins* (9 place des 3 Dauphins; ☎94.92.65.79) looking out onto the eighteenth-century fountain of three endearing dolphins that are almost completely hidden by the organic growth from the porous stone base. Close by is *Little Palace* (6 rue Berthelot; ☎94.92.26.62), also a bargain and pleasant. *Prémar* (19 and 21 place Monsenergue; ☎94.92.27.42) is on the dockside, a bit seedy and rock-bottom cheap. The **youth hostel** operates only in July and August: it's on rue Ernst-Renan, Quartier Mourillon (☎94.31.59.11; open 6–11pm; bus #3 from av Leclerc, *direction Mourillon*, stop *Lamalgue* and walk up rue Castel). You could also try the *Foyer de la Jeunesse* (11–12 place d'Armes; ☎94.93.05.55) which will rent rooms (women only).

Dust and construction apart, the old town is pleasant during the day. It's full of fountains, (usually dolphins); an excellent market fills rue Landrin and cours Lafayette every day and there's a covered fish market on place de la Poissonerie. Wandering around the part of the old town closest to the docks, you'll find every other door leads to a cheap restaurant, bar, jazz dive, night-club or sex shop. As night falls men outnumber women ten to one on the streets and most of the women are working. A less paranoia-provoking area is the Mourillon quartier to the east (bus #3), where the beaches face the open sea and trendy nightlife glitters down the Littoral Frédéric-Mistral.

Museums

Toulon's **museums** are not particularly intriguing unless you are obsessed with military history and model ships. The *Musée d'Art* (113 bd Maréchal Leclerc; open 10am–noon and 2–6pm) has a very good collection of paintings and sculpture but not the space to show them all at once. The exhibitions are arranged around themes and the artists whose works you may or may not see include Breughel, Carracci, Puget and the Van Loos, among the moderns Vlaminck, Friez, Ziem and Rodin, and of contemporaries, Francis Bacon, Christo, Gilbert and George, and Sol Le Witt. The most impressive public artwork in the city is Pierre Puget's *Atlantes* which hold up all that is left of the old town hall on quai de Stalingrad. It's thought that Puget, working in 1657, modelled these immensely strong and tragic figures on the galley slaves.

Mont Faron

The best way to pass an afternoon in Toulon is to leave the town 542m below you on the summit of **Mont Faron.** Take bus #40, stop Téléphérique on bd Amiral Vence, Super Toulon and you'll find a funicular (operating 9.15am–noon and 2.15–6pm; closed Mon. am and all day in winter). It's a little expensive but a treat. At the top there's a **memorial museum** to the Allied landings in Provence of August, 1944 (open summer 9am–7pm; winter 9–11.30am and 2–5.30pm) with screenings of live film footage. In the surrounding park are two restaurants, and a little further up to the right, a zoo specialising in big cats. Beyond the zoo you can walk up the hillside to an abandoned fort and revel in the clean air, the smell of the flowers and the distance from the ugly city below.

Boat tours

Alternatively, you could pass the time in closeup with the port doing a boat tour. Several companies offer trips with commentary around the *grande* and *petit rade*, including *Service Maritime Touristique Varois* and *S.N.R.T.M* from quai Stalingrad; and *Vedette Alain* from quai de la Sinse. A much cheaper option, which also spares you the unintelligible or otherwise guide, is to take the public transport boats from quai Stalingrad to La Seyne, Les Sablettes, and Saint-Mandrier. La Seyne, a town inseparable from the naval shipyards, had a Communist city council for forty years, and it now has a mayor who has busied himself privatising once-public services, firing public employees, and contributing to an unemployment rate of 22%. St-Mandrier-sur-Mer is sandwiched between the high walls of *terrain militaire* that covers most of the peninsula. Only the bay of Lazaret just before you reach Les Sablettes is free of battleships, with rickety wooden jetties and fishing huts and a surreal Islamic building on the shore past Tamaris.

La Ciotat and Cassis

The shipbuilding town of **LA CIOTAT**, halfway towards Marseille, is a more inspiring prospect than the naval port of Toulon. It is the only small working-class town left on the coast – and one of the few places where socialists get more votes than Le Pen – though the yards have been laying off employees at an ever inceasing rate. But the harbour remains charming, sitting below a golden-stoned old town, sheltering the fishing fleet, the massive cranes and derricks of the shipyards and, since this is the south of France, the odd yacht or two. Pavement cafés and restaurants, fishermen mending nets and the industrial proleteriat changing shifts are an integral part of the same dock-side scene. La Ciotat was also the place where the very first movie was made, in 1895, by the Lumière brothers.

If you want to stop before Marseille, there are a string of **campsites** – the closest seaside one to the centre being *St-Jean* (30 av St-Jean; ☎42.83.09.68; open April–Oct.; bus #4, stop *St-Jean Village*). **Hotels** are expensive. *La Marine*, (1 av F-Gassion; ☎42.08.35.11) is probably the best bet. But the **beach** is excellent and there are **boat trips** out to the Ile Verte and nearby *calanques*, the mini fjords that cut into this stretch of the coastline. The strangest sight in La Ciotat itself are the rock formations of the promontory beyond the shipyards in the **Parc National du Mugel** (7am–8pm in summer; 7am–6pm in winter, free). A path leads up from the entrance through overgrown vegetation and then past scooped vertical hollows to a narrow terrace overlooking the sea. The cliff face looks like the habitat of some gravity-defying, burrowing beast – in reality the erosions by wind and sea on this chalk free matter.

Arriving **by train** you'll see a plaque commemorating the station's star appearance in a Lumière film. But don't loiter for long, as a bus meets every train for the 20–35-minute shuttle to the old town. The **SI** is at 2 quai Ganteaume on the *Vieux Port* and if you're here in the second week of July, they can provide details of the **Festival du Cinéma**.

Cassis

CASSIS, its old fishing port hemmed in by cliffs and with toytown development behind, could probably apply for a transfer to the Côte des Maures and go for a good price. It's a self-consciously cutesy place, with inflated Côte prices (not a cheap room to be had). It is dominated, as are all good southern resorts, by a medieval castle – though this one is not a sight to be visited, but the refitted residence of M. Michelin, of tyre and guide fame.

Portside strutting and drinking aside, the favoured tourist pastimes are **boat trips** to the **calanques** – at their most spectacular around here. Several companies operate from the port but find out if they let you off or just tour in and out – and be prepared for rough seas. Or, if you're feeling energetic, you can take the well-marked footpath from the route des Calanques behind the western beach. It's about a 1½-hour walk to the best, **En Vau**, where you can climb down rocks to the shore. Intrepid pines find root holds, and sunbathers find ledges on the chaotic white gnawed cliffs. Swimming in the deep water of the creeks beneath these heights is an experience not to be missed.

If you're **camping** don't go into town first. The campsite, *Les Cigales* (☎42.01.07.34), is just off D559 from Marseille before av de la Marne turns down into Cassis; it's about 1km from the port, but don't forget the angle. There's a gorgeously scenic but very inaccessible **youth hostel**, *La Fontasse* (☎42.01.02.72; open 8–10am and 5–11pm year round) in the hills above the *calanques* west of Cassis. From D559 (bus stop *Les Calanques*) a road leads down towards the Col de la Gardiole. When it becomes a track, take the left fork and after 2km at another fork you'll find the hostel. Rain water, beds and electricity are the only modern conveniences, but if you want to explore this wild uninhabited stretch of limestone heights the people running it will enthuse and advise you. To get to Cassis you can descend to the *calanques* and walk along the coast (about 1 hr.).

Marseille

The most renowned and populated city after Paris, **MARSEILLE** has, like the capital, prospered and been ransacked over the centuries. It has lost its privileges to French kings and foreign armies, refound its fortunes, suffered plagues, religious bigotry, republican and royalist terror and had its own Commune and Bastille storming. It was the presence of so many Marseillaise revolutionaries marching from the Rhine to Paris in 1792, which gave the name to the *Hymn of the Army of the Rhine* that became the national anthem.

Palais de Longchamp
BOULEVARD LONGCHAMP
BD. DE LA LIBERATION
4er
C'S F. ROOSEVELT
BD. CHAVE
5er
BOULEVARD BAILLE
AVENUE DE TOULON
PL. JEAN JAURES
Gare SNCF St-Charles
SQUARE STALINGRAD
COURS LIEUTAUD
RUE DE ROME
1er
BD. VOLTAIRE
R. DE LA PALUD
Musée Cantini
To the Airport & Aix
3er
PL. V. HUGO
RUE LONGUE DES CAPUCINS
LA CANEBIERE
RUE DE ROME
RUE S. FERREOL
6er
RUE PARADIS
RUE BRETEUIL
BD. C. NEDELEC
RUE D'AIX
COURS BELSUNCE
RUE PARADIS
S.I.
RUE GRIGNAN
COURS PIERRE PUGET
Centre Bourse
C. PELLETAN
R. COLBERT
P.T.T.
REPUBLIQUE
BD. NOTRE DAME
BD. DES DAMES
QUAI DE RIVE NEUVE
Jardin Puget
BD. ANDRE AUNE
2er
RUE DE LA
Hotel de Ville
QUAI DU PORT
BD. DE LA CORDERIE
To Martigues
La Vieille Charité
RUE DU PANIER
Vieux Port
AV. SCHUMAN
Cathédrale
Maison Diamantée
St-Victor
Fort St-Nicolas
QUAI DE LA TOURETTE
AV. DE LA CORSE
Fort St-Jean
Bassin de la Grande Joliette
AVENUE PASTEUR
Palais du Pharo
Jardin du Pharo
RUE DES CATALANS
Plage des Catalans
RTE DU VALLON DES AUFFES
Anse des Auffes

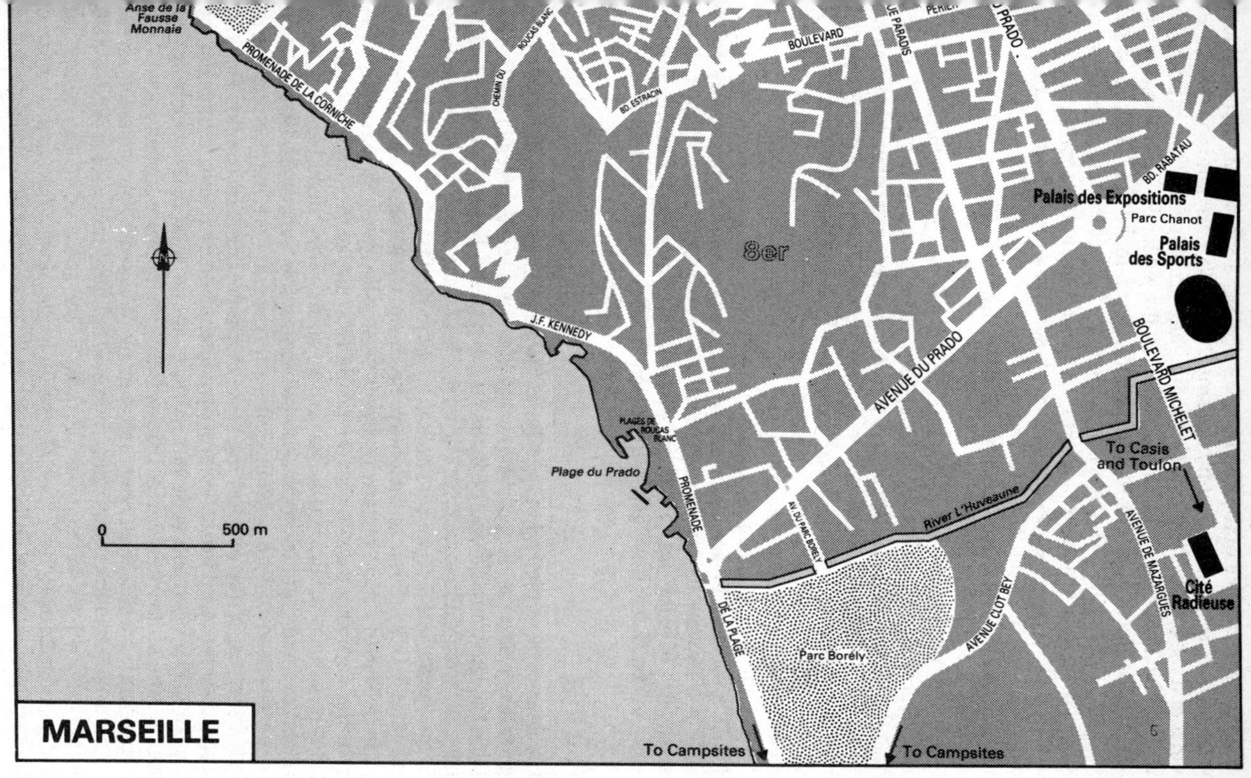
MARSEILLE
Anse de la Fausse Monnaie
PROMENADE DE LA CORNICHE
CHEMIN DU ROUCAS BLANC
BD. ESTRACIN
BOULEVARD
8er
BD. RABATAU
Palais des Expositions
Parc Chanot
Palais des Sports
J.F. KENNEDY
AVENUE DU PRADO
BOULEVARD MICHELET
PLAGES DE ROUCAS BLANC
Plage du Prado
PROMENADE
AV. DU PARC BORELY
River L'Huveaune
To Casis and Toulon
AVENUE DE MAZARGUES
Cité Radieuse
DE LA PLAGE
Parc Borély
AVENUE CLOT BEY
0
500 m
To Campsites
To Campsites

In the present state of the *Patrie*, Marseille has every social, economic and political conflict of the country at large, alongside its notorious vices of protection rackets, bribery, heroin trading and prostitution. One explanation of why the lawlessness never explodes is the endemic corruption in the police department and city hall. Marseille used to be the fiefdom of the Socialist Minister and Mayor, Gaston Deferre. His widow has now inherited control of the city's main newspapers, *Le Meridional* and *Le Provençal* and it's said that Deferre's successor was her personal choice. But at least Le Pen and his fellow fascists failed to win any seats in the 1987 presidential and parliamentary elections, and came nowhere near to winning the municipal elections in 1989.

Still, the ultra-conservative National Front has not lost its massive grass-roots following here. The dominating fear and violence in the city is racial. With the worst housing, lowest paid jobs and highest level of unemployment, the Arabs, mostly Algerian, live daily with assault, abuse and discrimination from their neighbours and the law. The lay-offs at the port and the decline of all Marseille's heavy industries have affected French and Arab workers alike, while adding grist to the racist mill.

Marseille is not a glamorous city and you might not choose to live there. But it's a wonderful place to visit – a real port city with a trading history going back over two and half thousand years. It's as cosmopolitan as Paris with the advantages of being nearly 800km farther south, having much more down-to-earth, informal, and unstylish natives, and avoiding the tourist trap label.

The city

The cafés around the end of the **Vieux Port** encourage you to indulge in the sedentary pleasures of observing street life, despite the fumes of traffic and fish – the latter straight off the boats on the quai des Belges – and the lack of any quay front claim to beauty. The clientele of Cannes and St-Tropez and, no doubt, the ancient Greeks who built the port in the first place, would find it all unbearably tacky. But it is, and always has been, the life centre of the city.

Up until 1943 a mass of narrow streets twisted their way up to rue Caisserie from the northern quay. It was the *vieille ville*, site of the original Massalia, densely populated, and anathema to the Nazis. They deported the 20,000 inhabitants and then, taking care to preserve a few 'superior' buildings such as the seventeenth-century Hôtel de Ville on quai du Port, the Germans dynamited the rest of the *quartier du Vieux Port* out of existence. After the war, archeologists reaped the benefits of this destruction by finding remains of the Roman docks equipped with vast storage jars for food stuffs which can be seen in situ at the **Musée des Docks Romains** on place Vivaux (open daily 10am–5pm). More recent mementos of old Marseille – a modelled street scene of nineteenth-century insurrectional fighting, recipes for plague antidotes, pre-1943 photographs of the area – are gathered in the wonderful hodge-podge **Musée de Vieux Marseille** in the *Maison Diamantée* – spared the dynamite – on rue de la Prison (open 10am–noon and 2–6.30pm; closed Tues., and Wed. am).

From rue Caisserie stepped passages and streets lead up into the surviving remnants of the old town, known as **Le Panier**. On the top of the hill to the west, best approached by rue des Petits-Puits and almost hidden by the high tenement buildings around it, stands the **Hospice de la Vieille Charité**, a seventeenth-century workhouse with a gorgeous Baroque chapel surrounded by columned arcades in pink stone, all recently restored. Only the tiny grilled exterior windows hint of its original use. It is now a cultural centre – hosting major, and usually brilliant, temporary exhibitions and sheltering the city's main **archaeological museum** – and perhaps the prettiest building in Marseille. But people in the local cafés will tell you that it was '*beaucoup plus jolie*' when a hundred local families, all with at least ten children, lived in the Hospice before it was renovated. They scoff at the idea of Le Panier's being gentrified and crack jokes about how the bourgeois are going to get to the concerts and exhibitions without passing through this 80 percent Arab quarter. There isn't much tension here between the working-class French and the immigrants, and none of them want to be moved out to high-rise low-income housing projects on the city's perimeter.

For the bourgeois French **the Canebière** is the alarmingly central *cordon sanitaire* with the Algerians. They see themselves as being driven by the Arabs southwards – into the most salubrious and chic parts of town. The area north of the Canabière, between St-Charles, bd d'Aix and cours Belsunce, is the first place the French will cite as the Algerian frontline. This triangle is a highly active and unofficial trading ground for Arabs in Europe and from the Arab world. Stereos, suits and jeans from France and Germany are traded with spices, cloth and metalware from across the Mediterranean on flattened cardboard boxes on the streets. No French middlemen are involved, hence the Gallic horror and disgust.

A suitable contrast is provided by the **Centre Bourse**, a standard fiendish giant mall of noise, air-conditioning and white light – but useful for mainstream shopping. Behind it is the **Jardin des Vestiges** which was where the ancient port extended to, curving northwards from the present quai des Belges. Excavations have revealed a stretch of the Greek port and bits of the city wall with the base of three square towers and a gateway, dated to the second or third century B.C. A museum in the Bourse complex, the **Musée d'Histoire de Marseille** (open 10am–7pm; closed Sun. and Mon.) presents the rest of the finds, including a third-century wreck of a Roman trading vessel.

The expansion of Marseille's present docks started in the first half of the nineteenth century, paid for, like the new cathedral overlooking quai de la Joliette and Marseille's own *Arc de Triomphe*, the **Porte d'Aix** at the top of Cours Belsunce/rue d'Aix, with the profits of military enterprise, most significantly, the conquest of Algeria in 1830. The Third Empire was the next boom time for Marseillais traders with the opening of the Suez Canal in 1869 giving the city a crucial advantage over other French ports. In the same year the **Palais de Longchamp**, 2km east of the *Vieux Port*, was completed, the grandiose conclusion of an aqueduct (no longer in existence) bringing water from the Durance to the city. Water is still pumped into the centre of the colonnade connecting the two palatial wings of the building. Below an enormous statue looks as if it's honouring some great feminist victory – three well-muscled women above four bulls wallowing passively in a pool from which a cascade drops four or five stories to ground level.

The palace's north wing is the city's **Beaux Arts**, hot, a little stuffy, but with a fair share of goodies – most notably three beautiful paintings by Françoise Duparc (1726–76), (whose first name has consistently been masculinised in French and British catalogues), and a room of political cartoons by the nineteenth-century satirist from Marseille, Honoré Daumier. Plans for the city, sculptures, and the famous profile of Louis XIV by the Marseillais Pierre Puget are on display along with contemporary graphic canvases of the plague that decimated the city in 1720. The museum is open along with the **Musée d'Histoire Naturelle** in the other wing, from 10am to noon and 2 to 6.30pm (closed Tues., and Wed. am) and accessible via buses #80 and #41 or métro Cinq Avenues-Longchamp. Marseille's main collection of twentieth-century and contemporary art is the **Musée Cantini** (19 rue Grignan, 6e; open daily noon–7pm). You'll find works by artists as diverse as Dufy, Léger, Balthus, Bacon, Vasarely and César, but the overdose of recent acquisitions means that the contents have to rotate. Between the Musée Cantini and the Canebière are the main shopping streets, rue de Rome and rue de Paradis. Sex is a visible commodity day and night, and Marseillais prostitutes are uniquely friendly to other women passing by.

Marseille's oldest church, the **Eglise St-Victor** stands above the Bassin de Carénage on the south side of the *Vieux Port*. Part of a monastery founded in 5 A.D. on the burial site of various third-century martyrs, the church was built, enlarged and fortified – a vital requirement given its position outside the city walls – over two centuries from the middle of the tenth century. It looks and feels like a fortress – the walls of the choir are almost 3m thick – and it's no ecclesiastical beauty. For a small fee you can visit (10–11.15am and 3–6pm; closed Sun. am) and descend to the crypt and catacombs, a warren of chapels and passages, where the weight of stone and age, not to mention the photographs of dug up skeletons, create an appropriate atmosphere in which to recall the horrors of early Christianity. St-Victor himself, a Roman soldier, was slowly ground to death between two millstones.

The striped Neo-Byzantine **Cathédrale La Major** across the port overshadows its predecessor, the Romanesque **Mayor Ancienne** standing, quite diminished, alongside. Both can be visited every day except Monday; tours of the old cathedral are guided, 9am to noon and 2.30 to 6pm, May to September; 9am to noon and 2 to 5pm the rest of the year.

Two fortresses guard the entrance of the *Vieux Port*. The enlargement of **St-Jean** on the north side and the construction of **St-Nicolas** on the south was part of Louis XIV's strategy to squash Marseille's independence. He sent in an army, suppressed the City's council, fined it, arrested all opposition, and, in an early example of rate-capping, set ludicrously low limits on Marseille's subsequent expenditure and borrowing.

On the headland beyond Fort Nicolas, the **Palais de Pharo** and its surrounding park is a prime place to hear rock music and gives the best view of the *Vieux Port*. To the west, the military monopolises the coast until the overcrowded and small **Catalans beach**. From there the long-winded **Promenade de la Corniche du Président J. F. Kennedy** follows the cliffs past the dramatic statue and arch that frames the setting sun of the **Monument aux Morts d'Orient**, to the heavily landscaped **Plage du Prado**, best of the local beaches – and with remarkably clean water due to recent anti-pollution projects.

South of the Monument aux Morts, steps lead down to an inlet, the **Anse des Auffes**, which is the nearest Marseille gets to being picturesque. Small fishing boats are beached on the rocks, the dominant sound is the sea, and narrow stairways and lanes lead nowhere. Back from here the route du Vallon des Auffes circuitously links up with a network of tiny streets high above the Anse, the quarter of **Endoume**. South, where the corniche cuts inland, **Malmousque** is another tranquil labyrinth. The end of the promontory is *terrain militaire* but an accessible path follows the coast eastwards with steps down to tiny bays and beaches – perfect for swimming when the Mistral wind is not inciting the waves. You can see along the coast as far as Cap Croisette and, out to sea, the abandoned monastery on the Iles d'Endoume and the **Château d'If.**

For **buses** along the corniche take #83 to av du Prado from the old port, #80 from the Estrangin-Préfecture métro to half way between Malmousque and the plage du Prado, #19 from av du Prado to MADRAGUE and #20 on out to Cap Croissette.

Boats and Dumas

Boats leave from the quai des Belges for this evil island fortress for which the required reading is Dumas' great adventure story, *The Count of Monte Cristo*. Apart from this fictional hero, no one ever escaped. Most prisoners, incarcerated for political or religious reasons, went insane or died (and usually both) before they reached the end of their sentences. The rich and blue-blooded tended to survive, having the less-fetid upper cells, like Mirabeau, in for debt, and one de Niozelles who was given six years for failing to take his hat off in the presence of Louis XIV. The château's opening hours are scheduled to the boat timetable – basically every hour, on the hour, from dawn to dusk (journey takes 15 min. one-way).

Food and action

Marseille is **gastronomically** significant – home base for the sea fish speciality *bouillabaisse*, a saffron and garlic flavoured fish soup with bits of fish, croutons and *rouille* to throw in and conflicting theories about which fish is used and where and how it must be caught. The vicious-faced rock-lurking rascasse has been scourged by pollution in the Med – one reason for the great expense of this peasant dish. But it's a meal in itself and known to be good at *La Samaritaine* (43 quai du Port) and perfect at the more expensive *Chez Michel* (63 rue des Catalans).

The pedestrian area around place Thiars, south of the port, is full of **seafood restaurants**, their offerings displayed on pavement stands. In **Le Panier**, the restaurant at 43 rue Lorette, with no name, no written menu and full of noisy parties and large families, is fun, has excellent food and doesn't have to be too expensive. *Chez Angèle* (50 rue Caisserie) has a good *menu fixe* of standard French fare. The **Anse des Auffes** restaurants are very tempting but not cheap. Best low-priced meals in the centre will be found around Cours Julien and place Jean-Jaurès. On this *place* you can sample Syrian, Senegalese, Madagascan, Vietnamese, French and Italian cuisines, and at *La Garga* (17 rue André Poggioli) excellent Provençal food. Brilliant and cheap Tunisian food is to be found on rue Pavillon off place G. de Gaulle. The *Auberge 'In'* on rue du Cheval Roze in Le Panier is a **vegetarian** restaurant. Two **all-nighters** are *Le Mas* (4 rue Lulli, 1er) and *O'Stop* (place de l'Opéra, 1er).

Takeaway food is excellent in this city. Along the main boulevards, and particularly Cours Belsunce, are stands where, for a couple of quid you can get a half-baguette filled with steak, or kebabs, omelettes, veal and mushrooms, fishcakes, or a hundred other proper dishes, with french fries thrown in. If it's picnic food you're after, the local **markets** will supply you with all you need and more. The biggest are the Cours d'Estienne d'Orves, place Bernard Cadanet in the 3e, place Sébastopol near the Palais Longchamp, place Jean Jaurès, and av du Prado by métro Castellane – all operating every morning except Sunday. A **flower market** takes place on the Canebière by métro Réformés on Tuesday and Saturday. Other markets include **stamps** on place G.-de-Gaulle near the *Vieux Port* on Sunday morning; **old books** and **records** all day, every day on place Auguste-Carli (métro Noailles); **clothes, new and old** all day, every day at 16 rue B Dubois (métro Colbert/Guesde); and the main **flea market**, Sunday morning, on rue Frédéric Sauvage in the 14e (métro Bourgainville, then bus #29, #30 to *Capitaine Geze*).

The book and record shop *FNAC* in the Centre Bourse, is the best place for **information** on concerts, theatre, free films and whatever cultural events are going on. And they can sell you tickets. Otherwise check the listings of the best daily paper, *La Marseillaise*, or pick up a copy from the SI of the free weekly *Marseille Poche* which comes out on Wednesday.

A handful of cinemas show foreign films in the original language (*v.o.* in the listings) and English shows are sometimes put on at the *Théâtre du Merlan* (av Raimu, 14e), part of a cultural centre which contains a police commissariat on the ground floor; in one of the worst concrete suburbs. *L'Avant-Scene* (59 Cours Julien, 6e; ☎91.42.19.29) is a theatre-cum-restaurant-cum-exhibition space which often puts on special events for **kids**. The *Espace Julien* just up the road at 33 Cours Julien (☎91.47.09.64) is another mixed cultural art centre, with theatre, jazz, dance and exhibitions. *Café-théâtre* alternates with country **music**, rock'n'roll and R'n'B at *La Maison Hantée* (10 rue Vian, 6e; ☎91.92.09.49; closed Mon.). *L'Arsenal des Galleries* (24 quai de Rive-Neuve) shelters a **jazz club** and a place for **rock, fashion, theatre** and **dance**. Near place Jean-Jaurès *Les Nuits des Thés* (21 rue Poggioli; ☎91.48.34.34) has live music, jazz mostly, Wednesday to Saturday till 1/1.30am and snacks to eat.

Unfortunately, nights out for the young and energetic without much cash are difficult in Marseille. The **clubs** around Cours d'Estienne-d'Orves – again mainly jazz, some Caribbean – are for trendy kids from the upper-crust *arron-*

dissements. If you're determined to bop, the *Rose Bonbon* (7 rue Venture, 1er, off rue Paradis) is probably the least rip-off and the pleasantest of the **discos**.

Gay Bars include *Chez Clairette* (7 rue Curiol, 1er; 4pm–2am; closed Mon. and Sept.) and *Le Kempson* (22 rue Beauvau, 1er; 5.30pm–2am; closed Thurs.). The main meeting place for **gay and lesbian activists** is *Le Bateau Ivre* (15 rue Fongate, 6er; ☎91.48.36.19 and 91.54.09.32; 7pm–midnight; closed Wed. and Sun.) with snacks, full meals on Friday night, and various exhibitions, discussions, etc.

Listings

Airlines: *TWA* (41 La Canebière, 1er; ☎91.91.66.44). *British Airways* (41 La Canebière, 1er; ☎91.90.77.10); *Air France* (14 La Canebière, 1er; ☎91.54.92.92); *Air Inter* (8 rue des Fabres, 1er; ☎91.91.90.90).

Airport: *Aéroport de Marignane* (☎42.78.21.00), bus every quarter hour from outside Gare St-Charles 6.15am–8pm and 1 hr. 20 min. before each night departure time.

Bike hire: *Ulysses* (av du Parc Borely, 8e) – very expensive and not really a good idea given the traffic, distances, and excellent public transport system.

Money exchange: *Thomas Cook* (Gare St-Charles; open Mon. to Fri. 6am–8pm, weekends and holidays 6am–6pm).

Pharmacy: Gare St-Charles Monday to Friday 7am–10pm, Saturday 7am–8pm.

Consulates: *USA* (9 rue Armény, 6e; ☎91.54.92.00); *Canada* (24 av du Prado, 6e; ☎91.37.19.37); *UK* (24 av du Prado, 6e; ☎91.53.43.32); *Eire* (148 rue Sainte, 1er; ☎91.54.92.29).

Disabled: *Office Municipal pour Handicappés* (128 av du Prado, 8e; ☎91.81.58.80) – information on access, facilities, etc.. Also operates a transport system.

Emergencies: Police ☎17; Fire ☎18; Ambulance *SAMU* ☎91.49.91.91; Hospital: *Hôtel-Dieu* 6 place Daviel, Le Panier, 2e, ☎91.90.61.14; Doctors: *SOS Médecins* ☎91.52.84.85; Poisoning: *Centre Anti-Poisons* ☎91.75.25.25; Dentist: *SOS Dentistes* ☎91.25.84.85; Drug problems: *Accueil* ☎91.50.56.99; Crisis line: *SOS Amitié* ☎91.76.10.10.

Hitchhiking: *Allo-stop* (1 place Gabriel-Péri, 1er; ☎91.56.50.51; open Mon. to Fri. 3.30–6.30pm, Sat. 10am–noon).

Launderettes: *Washmatic* (77 rue d'Aubagne, 1er); *Renov'Express* (62 rue Breteuil, 6e); *La Savonnière* (rue Rey, 6e).

Poste Restante: 1 place de l'Hôtel-des-Postes, 13001, Marseille.

Rape Crisis: ☎91.91.38.50.

Showers: (and baths) Gare St-Charles *Relais Toilettes* 5.30am–8.30pm.

Students: *CROUS* (38 rue du 141e R.I.A., 3e; ☎91.95.90.06) for information on work, lodgings and travel.

Travel agencies: *Nouvelle Frontières* (83 rue Sainte, 7e; ☎91.54.18.48); *Atoll Voyages* for *BIGE* tickets (103 La Canabière, 1er; ☎91.50.53.03).

Women's movement: based at 95 rue Benoît Malon, 5e, with people around on Tuesday and Thursday 6.30–10.30pm; *CODIF* runs a library and information centre at 81 rue Senac, 1er; ☎91.47.14.05.

Youth information: *CIJ*, (Stade Vallier, 4 rue de la Visitation, 4e; ☎91.49.91.55).

travel details

Trains

The **Ventimiglia line** follows the coast more or less all the way from Marseille to Menton, running inland only over the stretch between Fréjus and Toulon. Major stops are at Monaco, Nice, Antibes, Cannes, St-Raphaël and Toulon. The full journey takes between 2¾–3½ hr..

From Nice 8 daily to Menton (35–40 min.); 6 daily to St-Raphaël (1 hr.–1 hr. 25 min.); 20 daily to Marseille (2¼–2½ hr.) and 7 daily to Paris-Gare de Lyon (10 hr. 40 min.–12 hr.).

Cannes to Menton 18 daily (1 hr. 25 min.).

From Marseille 15 daily to Cassis (25–30 min.); 18 daily to La Ciotat (30–40 min.); 2 daily to Hyères (1 hr. 15 min.); 9 daily to Paris-Gare de Lyon (5 hr.–7 hr. 40 min.).

From St-Raphaël 7 daily to Paris-Gare de Lyon (9–9½ hr.).

Buses

For most journeys along the Côte, buses are much slower, more expensive and less frequent than trains.

Hyères to Toulon SNCF 10 daily (½ hr.); 5 daily to La Foux (1¼–1½ hr.).

Boats

From Marseille (Bassin de la Joliette) to Corsica, Sardinia, Algiers, Tunis and Majorca.

From Nice to Corsica (summer day excursions operated by SNCM, 3 av Gustav V, depart quai de la Commerce; also car ferry service).

From St-Raphaël to St-Tropez, Port Grimaud and the Iles de Lérins (summer excursions again operated by MMG, quai Nomy).

From St-Tropez to Ste-Maxime (MMG, quai Jean-Jaurès).

From Juan-les-Pins to the Iles de Lérins (embarcadère Coubet).

PART THREE

THE CONTEXTS

HISTORICAL FRAMEWORK

EARLY CIVILISATIONS

Traces of human existence are rare in France before about 50,000 B.C. Thereafter, beginning with the Mousterian civilisation, they become more and more numerous, with a particularly heavy concentration of continuously occupied sites in the Périgord region of the Dordogne. It was here, near the village of Les Eyzies, that the Late Stone Age 'Cro-Magnon' people were discovered. Flourishing from around 25,000 B.C., they were cave-dwelling hunters who developed a remarkably sophisticated culture, the evidence of which is preserved in the beautiful paintings and engravings on the walls of the region's caves.

By 10,000 B.C. human communities had spread out widely across the whole of France. The ice cap receded; the climate became warmer and wetter, and by about 7000 B.C. farming and pastoral communities had begun to develop. By 4500 B.C. the first **dolmens** showed up in **Brittany**; around 2000 B.C. copper made its appearance; and by 1800 B.C. the **Bronze Age** had arrived, particularly strong in the east and southeast of the country, and there is evidence of trade with Spain, central Europe and Wessex in Britain. Around 1200 B.C. the **Champs d'Urnes people**, who buried their dead in sunken urns, began to make incursions from the east. By 900 B.C. the **Halstatt people** brought iron – their settlements concentrated in Burgundy, Alsace and Franche-Comté near the principal deposits of iron ore – joined around 450 B.C. by Celts.

PRE-ROMAN GAUL

There were about 15 million people living in **Gaul**, as the Romans called what we call France (and parts of Belgium), when Julius Caesar arrived in 58 B.C. to complete the Roman conquest. The southern part – modern **Provence** mostly – had been a colony since 118 B.C. and exposed to the civilising influences of Italy and Greece for much longer. Greek colonists had founded Marseille/Massalia as far back as 600 B.C. But even the inhabitants of the rest of the country, what the Romans called 'long-haired Gaul', were far from shaggy barbarians. Though the economy was basically rural, they had established large **hilltop towns** by 100 B.C., notably at Bibracte near Autun, where archaeologists have identified separate merchants' quarters and so on. The Gauls had invented the barrel and soap and were skillful manufacturers. By 500 B.C. they were capable of making metal-wheeled carts, as was proved by the 'chariot tombs' of **Vix**, where a young woman was found buried seated in a cart with its wheels pushed against the wall. She was wearing rich gold jewellery and lying next to Greek vases and Black Figure pottery, dating the burial at round 500 B.C. and revealing the extent of commercial relations. Interestingly, too, the Gauls' money was based on the gold *staters* minted by Philip of Macedon, father of Alexander the Great.

CONQUEST AND ROMANISATION

Gallic **tribal rivalries** made the Romans' job very much easier. And even when at last they were able to unite under Vercingetorix in 52 B.C., the occasion was their total and final defeat by **Julius Caesar** at the battle of Alésia. This long-past event was one of the major turning points in the history of the country. **Roman victory** fixed the frontier between Gaul and the Germanic peoples at the Rhine. It saved Gaul from disintegrating because of internal dissension and made it a Latin province. During the five centuries of peace that followed, the Gauls farmed, manufactured and traded, became urbanised, embourgeoisied, and educated – and learned Latin. In other words, Roman victory at Alésia laid the foundations of modern French culture, and laid them firmly enough to survive the centuries of chaos and destruction that followed the collapse of Roman power.

Augustus and **Claudius** were the emperors who set the process of **Romanisation** going. Lyon/Lugdunum was founded as the capital of Roman Gaul as early as 43 B.C. Augustus initiated numerous other cities, like Autun, Limoges and Bayeux, built roads, settled Roman colonists on the land and reorganised the entire administration. Gauls were incorporated into the Roman army and given citizenship; Claudius made it possible for them to hold high office and become members of the Roman Senate, blurring the distinction and resentment between coloniser and colonised. Vespasian secured the frontiers beyond the Rhine, thus assuring a couple of hundred years of peace and economic expansion.

Serious **disruptions** of the Pax Romana only began in the third century A.D. Oppressive aristocratic rule and an economic crisis turned the destitute peasantry into gangs of marauding brigands – precursors of the medieval *jacquerie*. But most devastating of all, there began a series of incursions across the Rhine frontier by various restless **Germanic tribes**, the Alemanni and Franks first, who pushed down as far as Spain, ravaging farmland and destroying towns.

In the fourth century the reforms of the emperor **Diocletian** secured some decades of respite from both internal and external pressures. Towns were rebuilt and fortified, an interesting development that foreshadowed feudalism and the independent power of the nobles since, due to the uncertainty of the times, big landed estates or *villae* tended to become more and more self-sufficient – economically, administratively and militarily. By the fifth century the Germanic invaders were back, **Alans, Vandals** and **Suevi**, with **Franks** and **Burgundians** in their wake. While the Roman administration assimilated them as far as possible, granting them land in return for military duties, many Gauls, by now thoroughly Latinised, entered the service of the Burgundian court of Lyon or of the Visigoth kings of Toulouse as skilled administrators and advisors.

THE FRANKS AND CHARLEMAGNE

By 55 A.D. the **Franks**, who gave their name to modern France, had become the dominant invading power. Their most celebrated king, **Clovis**, consolidated his hold on northern France and drove the Visigoths out of the southwest into Spain. In 507 he made the until-then insignificant little trading town of Paris his capital and became a Christian, which inevitably hastened the **Christianisation** of the Frankish society. Under succeeding **Merovingian** – as the dynasty was called – rulers, the kingdom began to disintegrate until in the eighth century the Pepin family, who were the Merovingians' chancellors, began to take effective control. In 732 one of their most dynamic scions, **Charles Martel**, reunited the kingdom and saved western Christendom from the northward expansion of Islam by defeating the Spanish Moors at the **battle of Poitiers**. In 754 Charles's son, Pepin, had himself crowned king by the Pope, thus inaugurating the **Carolingian dynasty** and establishing for the first time the principle of the divine right of kings. His son was **Charlemagne**, who extended Frankish control over the whole of what had been Roman Gaul and far beyond. On Christmas Day 800 he was crowned emperor of the Holy Roman Empire, though again, following his death, the kingdom fell apart in his grandsons' squabbles over who was to inherit various parts of his empire. At the Treaty of Verdun in 843 they agreed on a division of territory that corresponded roughly with the extent of contemporary France and Germany.

Charlemagne's administrative system had involved the royal appointment of counts and bishops to govern the various provinces of the empire. Under the destabilising attacks of Normans/Norsemen/Vikings during the ninth century, Carolingian kings were obliged to delegate more power and autonomy to these **provincial governors**, whose lands, like **Aquitaine** and **Burgundy**, already had separate regional identities as a result of earlier invasions – the Visigoths in Aquitaine, the Burgundians in Burgundy, for example. Gradually the power of these princes overshadowed that of the king, whose lands were confined to the Ile-de-France. When the last Carolingian died in 987, it was only natural that they should elect one of their own number to take his place. This was Hugues Capet, founder of a dynasty that lasted until 1328.

THE RISE OF THE FRENCH KINGS

The years 1000 to 1500 A.D. saw the gradual extension and consolidation of the power of the **French kings**, accompanied by the growth of a centralised administrative system and bureaucracy. These objectives also determined their foreign policy, which was chiefly concerned with restricting papal interference in French affairs and checking the English kings' continuing involvement in French territory. While progress toward these goals was remarkably steady and single-minded, there were setbacks, principally in the seesawing fortunes of the conflict with the English.

Surrounded by vassals much stronger than themselves, **Hugues Capet** and his successors remained weak throughout the eleventh century, though they made the most of their feudal rights. As dukes of the French, counts of Paris and anointed kings, they enjoyed a prestige that their vassals dared not offend – not least because that would have set a dangerous precedent of disobedience for their own lesser vassals.

At the beginning of the twelfth century, having successfully tamed his own vassals in the Ile-de-France, Louis VI had a stroke of luck. **Eleanor**, daughter of the powerful Duke of Aquitaine, was left in his care on her father's death, so he promptly married her off to his son, the future Louis VII. Unfortunately, the marriage ended in divorce and Eleanor immediately – in 1152 – remarried, to Henry of Normandy, shortly to become **Henry II** of England. Thus the English gained control of a huge chunk of French territory, stretching from the Channel to the Pyrenees. Though their fortunes fluctuated over the ensuing 300 years, the English rulers remained a perpetual thorn in the side of the French kings and a dangerous source of alliances for any rebellious French vassals.

Philippe Auguste (1180–1223) made considerable headway in undermining English rule by exploiting the bitter relations between Henry II and his three sons, one of whom was Richard Coeur-de-Lion. But he fell out with Richard when they took part in the Third Crusade together. Luckily Richard died before he was able to claw back Philippe's gains and by the end of his reign, Philippe had recovered all of Normandy and the English possessions north of the Loire. For the first time, the royal lands were greater than those of any other French lord. The foundations of a systematic administration and civil service had been established in **Paris**, and Philippe had firmly and quietly marked his independence from the papacy by refusing to take any interest in the crusade against the heretic Cathars of Languedoc. When Languedoc and Poitou came under royal control in the reign of his son, Louis VIII, France was by far the greatest power in western Europe.

THE HUNDRED YEARS WAR

In 1328 the Capetian monarchy had its first succession problems, which led directly to the ruinous **Hundred Years War** with the English. Charles IV, last of the line, had only daughters, and when it was decided that France could not be ruled by a queen, the English king, **Edward III**, whose mother was Charles's sister, claimed the throne of France for himself. The French chose **Philippe, Count of Valois**, instead, and Edward acquiesced for a time. But when Philippe began whittling away at his possessions in Aquitaine, Edward renewed his claim and embarked on war. Though, with its population of about 12 million, France was a far richer and more powerful country, its army was no match for the superior organisation and tactics of the English. Edward won a total victory at **Crécy** in 1346 and seized the port of Calais as a permanent bridgehead. Ten years later, his son, the Black Prince, actually took the French king, Jean le Bon, prisoner at the battle of Poitiers.

Although by 1375 French military fortunes had improved to the point where the English had been forced back on Calais and the Gascon coast, the strains of war, administrative abuses, and the madness of Charles VI caused other kinds of damage. In 1358 there were **insurrections** among the Picardy peasantry (the *Jacquerie*) and among the townspeople of Paris under the leadership of Etienne Marcel – both brutally repressed, as were subsequent risings in Paris in 1382 and 1412.

The consequences of the king's madness led to the formation of two rival factions in the aftermath of the murder of the king's brother, the Duke of Orléans, by the Duke of Burgundy. The **Armagnacs** gathered round the young Orléans, and the other faction round the **Burgundys**. Both factions called in the English to help them.

In 1415 Henry V of England inflicted another crushing defeat on the French army at **Agincourt**. The Burgundians seized Paris, took the royal family prisoner, and recognised Henry as heir to the French throne. When Charles VI died in 1422, Henry's brother, the Duke of Bedford, took over the government of the whole of France north of the Loire, while the young king Charles VII rather ineffectually governed the south from his refugee capital at Bourges.

At this point **Joan of Arc** arrived on the scene. In 1429 she raised the English siege of the crucial town of Orléans and had Charles properly crowned at Reims. Although she fell into the hands of the Burgundians who sold her to the English, and was tried and burnt as a heretic, her dynamism and martyrdom raised French morale and tipped the scales against the English. Except for a toehold at Calais, they were finally driven from France altogether in 1453.

By the end of the century, **Dauphiné, Burgundy, Franche-Comté** and **Provence** were under royal control, and an effective standing army had been created. The taxation system had been overhauled, and France had emerged from the Middle Ages a rich, powerful state, firmly under the centralised authority of an absolute monarch.

THE WARS OF RELIGION

After half a century of self-confident but inconclusive seeking after military *gloire* in Italy, brought to an end by the Treaty of Cateau-Cambresis in 1559, France was plunged into another period of devastating internal conflict. The **Protestant** ideas of Luther and Calvin had gained widespread adherence among the poor, artisan, bourgeois and noble classes of society, despite sporadic brutal attempts by François I and Henri II to stamp them out. When Catherine de Médicis, acting as Regent for Henri III, implemented a more tolerant policy, she provoked violent reaction from the ultra-Catholic faction led by the Guise family. Their massacre of a Protestant congregation coming out of church in March 1562 began a civil **war of religions** that, interspersed with ineffective truces and accords, lasted for the next thirty years. Well-organised and well-led by the Prince de Condé and Admiral Coligny, the **Huguenots**, as the French Protestants were called, kept their end up very successfully, until Condé was killed at the battle of Jarnac, near Cognac, in 1569. The year 1572 saw one of the blackest events in the memory of French Protestants, even today: the **massacre of St. Bartholomew's Day**. Coligny and three thousand Protestants who were gathered in Paris for the wedding of Marguerite, the king's sister, to the Protestant Henri of Navarre, were slaughtered at the instigation of the Guises – a bloodbath that was copied across France, especially in the south and west where the Protestants were strongest.

In 1584 the king's son died, leaving his brother-in-law, **Henri of Navarre,** heir to the throne, to the fury of the Guises and their Catholic league who seized Paris and drove out the king. In retaliation Henri III murdered the Duc de Guise, and found himself forced into alliance with Henri of Navarre, whom the Pope had excommunicated. In 1589 Henri III was himself assassinated, leaving Henri of Navarre to become Henri IV of France. But it took another four years of fighting and the abjuration of his faith for the new king to be recognised. 'Paris is worth a mass', he is reputed to have said.

Once on the throne Henri IV set about reconstructing and reconciliating the nation. By the **Edict of Nantes** of 1598 the Huguenots were accorded freedom of conscience, freedom of worship in certain places, the right to attend the same schools and hold the same offices as Catholics, their own courts and the possession of a number of fortresses as a guarantee against renewed attack, the most important being La Rochelle and Montpellier.

KINGS, CARDINALS AND ABSOLUTE POWER

The main themes of the seventeenth century, when France was ruled by just two kings, **Louis XIII** (1610–43) and **Louis XIV** (1643–1715), are, on the domestic front, the strengthening of the centralised state embodied in the person of the king; and in external affairs, the securing of frontiers in the Pyrenees, on the Rhine and in the north, coupled with the attempt to prevent the unification of the territories of the Habsburg kings of Spain and Austria. Both kings had the good fortune to be served by capable, hard-working ministers dedicated to these objectives. Louis XIII had **Cardinal Richelieu** and Louis XIV had **Cardinal Mazarin** and **Colbert**. Both reigns were perturbed in their early years by the inevitable aristocratic attempts at a coup d'état.

Having crushed revolts by Louis XIII's brother, Gaston, Duke of Orléans, **Richelieu's** commitment to extending royal absolutism brought him into renewed conflict with the Protestants. Believing that their retention of separate fortresses within the kingdom was a threat to security, he attacked and took La Rochelle in 1627. Although he was unable to extirpate their religion altogether, Protestants were never again to present a military threat.

The other important facet of his domestic policy was the promotion of economic self-sufficiency – **mercantilism**. To this end, he encouraged the growth of the luxury craft industries, especially textiles, in which France was to excel right up to the Revolution. He built up the navy and granted privileges to companies involved in establishing colonies in North America, Africa and the West Indies.

In pursuing his foreign policy objectives he adroitly kept France out of actual military involvement by paying substantial sums of money to the great Swedish king and general, Gustavus Adolphus, to encourage him to continue his wars against the Habsburgs in Germany. When in 1635 he was finally obliged to commit French troops, they made significant gains against the Spanish in the Netherlands, Alsace and Lorraine and won Roussillon for France. He died just a few months before Louis XIII in 1642.

As Louis XIV was still an infant, his mother, Anne of Austria, acted as Regent, served by Richelieu's protegé, **Cardinal Mazarin**, who was hated just as much as his predecessor by the traditional aristocracy and the *parlements** who were protective of their privileges and angry that an upstart should receive such preferment over themselves. Spurred by these grievances, which were in any case exacerbated by the ruinous cost of the Spanish wars, various groups in French society combined in a series of revolts, known as the **Frondes**.

The first was the Fronde of 1648, led by the *parlement* of Paris, which took up the cause of the hereditary provincial tax-collecting officials who resented the supervisory role of the *intendants*, appointed directly by the central royal bureaucracy to keep an eye on them. Paris rose in revolt but capitulated at the advance of royal troops. This was quickly followed by an aristocratic Fronde, supported by various peasant risings round the country. These revolts were suppressed easily enough, and were not really revolutionary movements but, rather, the attempts of various reactionary groups to preserve their privileges in the face of growing state power.

Financial pressure was relieved when in 1659 Mazarin successfully brought the Spanish wars to an end with the **Treaty of the Pyrenees**, cemented by the marriage of Louis XIV and the daughter of Philip IV of Spain. On reaching the age of majority in 1661, **Louis** declared that he was going to be his own man and do without a first minister like Mazarin. He proceeded to appoint a number of able ministers of his own, with whose aid he embarked on a long struggle to modernise the administration in the face of opposition from a thoroughly reactionary society.

Le Tellier and his son Louvois provided him with a well-equipped and well-trained professional army that could muster some 400,000 men by 1670. But the principal reforms were carried out by **Colbert**, who set about streamlining the state's finances and tackling bureaucratic corruption. Although he was never able to overcome the opposition completely, he did manage to produce a surplus in state revenue.

*The French *parlements* were unelected bodies, with the function of high courts and administrative councils.

Attempting to compensate for deficiencies in the taxation system by stimulating trade, he set up a free trade area in northern and central France, continued Richelieu's mercantilist economic policies, established the French East India Company, and built up the navy and merchant fleets with a view to challenging the world commercial supremacy of the Dutch.

These were all policies that the hard-working king was involved in and approved of. But in addition to his love of an extravagant court life at Versailles, which earned him the title of the **Sun King**, he had another obsession more ruinous to the state – the love of a prestigious military victory. There were sound political reasons for the **campaigns** he embarked on, but they did not help balance the budget.

Using his wife's Spanish connection, he demanded the cession of certain Spanish provinces in the Low Countries, and then embarked on a war against the Dutch in 1672. Forced to make peace at the **Treaty of Nijmegen** in 1678 by his arch-enemy, the Protestant William of Orange (later king of England), he nonetheless came out of the war with the addition to French territory of Franche-Comté, plus a number of northern towns. In 1681 he simply grabbed Strasbourg, and got away with it.

In 1685, under the influence of his very Catholic mistress, Madame de Maintenon, he removed all privileges from the Huguenots by revoking the Edict of Nantes. This incensed the Protestant powers, who formed the League of Augsburg against him. Another long and exhausting war followed, ending, most unfavourably to the French, in the **Peace of Rijswik** (1697). No sooner was this concluded when Louis became embroiled in the question of who was to succeed the moribund Charles II of Spain.

Both Louis and Leopold Habsburg, Holy Roman Emperor, had married sisters of Charles. The prospect of Leopold acquiring the Spanish Habsburgs' possessions in addition to his own vast lands was not welcome to Louis or any other European power. When Charles died and it was discovered that he had named Louis' grandson, Philippe, as his heir, there again was a shift in the balance of power that the English, Dutch and Austrians were not prepared to tolerate. William of Orange, now king of England as well as ruler of the Dutch United Provinces, organised a Grand Alliance against Louis. The so-called **War of Spanish Succession** broke out and it went badly for the French, largely thanks to the brilliant generalship of the Duke of Marlborough. A severe winter in 1709 compounded the hardships with famine and bread riots at home, causing Louis to seek negotiations. The terms were too harsh for him and the war dragged on until 1713, leaving the country totally impoverished. The Sun King went out with scarcely a whimper.

LOUIS XV TO THE REVOLUTION

While France remained in many ways a prosperous and powerful state, largely thanks to colonial trade, the tensions between central government and traditional vested interests proved too great to be reconciled. As the *parlement* of Paris became more and more the focus of opposition to the royal will, bringing the country to a state of virtual ungovernability in the reign of **Louis XVI**, so the diversity of mutually irreconcilable interests sheltering behind that parliamentary umbrella came more and more to the fore, bringing the country to a climax of tension which would only be resolved in the turmoil of **Revolution**.

Louis XV was two when his great-grandfather died. During the Regency, the traditional aristocracy and the *parlements*, who for different reasons hated Louis XIV's advisors, scrabbled – successfully – to recover a lot of their lost power and prestige. An experiment with government by aristocratic councils failed, and attempts to absorb the immense national debt by selling shares in an overseas trading company ended in a huge collapse. When the prudent and reasonable Cardinal Fleury came to prominence upon the Regent's death in 1726, the nation's lot began to improve. The Atlantic seaboard towns grew rich on trade with the American and Caribbean colonies, though industrial production did not improve much and the disparity in wealth between the countryside and the growing towns continued to grow.

In the mid-century there followed more disastrous military ventures, the **War of Austrian Succession** and the **Seven Years War**, both of which were in effect contests with England for control of the colonial territories in America and India, contests that France lost. The need to finance the war led to the introduction of a new tax, the Twentieth, which was to be levied on everyone. The **parlement**, which had successfully opposed earlier taxation and fought the Crown over its religious policies, dug its heels in again. This led to renewed conflict over Louis' pro-Jesuit religious policy. The Paris *parlement* staged a strike, was exiled from Paris, then inevitably reinstated. Disputes about its role continued until the *parlement* of Paris was actually abolished in 1771, to the outrage of the privileged groups in society which considered it the defender of their special interests.

The division between the *parlements* and the king and his ministers continued to sharpen during the reign of Louis XVI, which began in 1774. Attempts by the enlightened finance minister Turgot to cooperate with the *parlements* and introduce reforms to alleviate the tax burden on the poor produced only short-term results. The national debt trebled between 1774 and 1787. Ironically, the one radical attempt to introduce an effective and equitable tax system led directly to the Revolution. Calonne, finance minister in 1786, tried to get his proposed tax approved by an **Assembly of Notables**, a device that had not been employed for more than a hundred years. His purpose was to bypass the *parlement*, which could be relied on to oppose any radical proposal. The attempt backfired. He lost his position, and the *parlement* ended up demanding a meeting of the **Estates-General**, representing the nobles, the clergy and the bourgeoisie, as being the only body competent to discuss such matters. The town responded by exiling and then recalling the *parlement* of Paris several times. As law and order began to break down, it gave in and agreed to summon the Estates-General on May 17, 1789.

REVOLUTION

Against a background of deepening economic crisis and general misery exacerbated by the catastrophic harvest of 1788, controversy focused on how the **Estates-General** should be constituted. Should they meet separately as on the last occasion – in 1614? This was the solution favoured by the *parlement* of Paris, a measure of its reactionary nature: separate meetings would make it easy for the privileged, i.e., the clergy and nobility, to outvote the Third Estate, the bourgeoisie. The king ruled that they should hold a joint meeting with the Third Estate represented by as many deputies as the other two Estates combined, but no decisions were made about the order of voting.

On June 17, 1789, the **Third Estate** seized the initiative and declared itself the National Assembly. Some of the lower clergy and liberal nobility joined them. The king appeared to accept the situation, and on July 9 the Assembly declared itself the National Constituent Assembly. The king then tried to intimidate it by calling in troops, which unleashed the anger of the people of Paris, the *sans-culottes* (literally, 'without trousers'). On July 14 they stormed the fortress of **the Bastille**, symbol of the oppressive nature of the *ancien régime*. Similar insurrections occurred throughout the country, accompanied by widespread peasant attacks on landowners' châteaux, the destruction of records of debt and other symbols of their oppression. On the night of August 4 the Assembly abolished the feudal rights and privileges of the nobility – a momentous shift of gear in the **revolutionary process**, although in reality it did little to alter the situation. Later that month they adopted the Declaration of the **Rights of Man**. In December church lands were nationalised, and the Pope retaliated by declaring the principles of the Revolution impious.

Bourgeois elements in the Assembly tried to bring about a compromise with the nobility with a view to establishing a constitutional monarchy, but these overtures were rebuffed. Emigré aristocrats were already working to bring about foreign invasion to overthrow the Revolution. In June 1791 the king was arrested trying to escape from Paris. The Assembly, following an initiative of the wealthier bourgeois **Girondin** faction, decided to go to war to protect the Revolution. But the ill-prepared Revolutionary army met with numerous setbacks.

On August 10, 1792, the *sans-culottes* set up a **revolutionary Commune** in Paris and imprisoned the king. The Revolution was taking a radical turn. A new National Convention was elected and met on the day the Revolutionary armies finally halted the Prussian invasion at Valmy. A major rift developed between the

Girondins and the **Jacobins** and *sans-culottes* over the abolition of the monarchy. The radicals carried the day. In January 1793 Louis XVI was executed. By June the Girondins had been ousted.

Counter-revolutionary forces were gathering in the provinces and abroad. A Committee of Public Safety was set up as chief organ of the government. Left-wing popular pressure brought laws on general conscription and price controls, and a deliberate policy of de-Christianisation. Robespierre was pressed onto the Committee as the best man to contain the pressure from the streets.

The Terror began. In addition to ordering the death of the hated Marie-Antoinette, Robespierre felt strong enough to guillotine his opponents to both right and left. But the effect of so many rolling heads was to cool people's faith in the Revolution. By mid-1794 Robespierre himself was arrested and executed, and his fall marked the end of radicalism. More conservative forces gained control of the government, decontrolled the economy, repressed popular risings, limited the suffrage, and established a five-man executive Directory (1795).

THE RISE OF NAPOLEON

In 1799 a **General Bonaparte**, who had made a name for himself as commander of the Revolutionary armies in Italy and Egypt, returned to France and took power in a coup d'état. He was appointed First Consul with power to choose officials, initiate legislation, etc. He redesigned the tax system and created the Bank of France, replaced the power of local institutions by a corps of *prefets* answerable to himself, made judges into state functionaries – in short, laid the foundations of the modern French administrative system.

Though he upheld the fundamental reforms of the Revolution, the retrograde nature of his regime became more and more apparent with the proscription of the Jacobins, granting of amnesty to the émigrés and restoration of their unsold property, reintroduction of slavery in the colonies, recognition of the church and so on. Although alarmingly revolutionary in the eyes of the rest of Europe, his Civil Code worked essentially to the advantage of the bourgeoisie. In 1804 he crowned himself **Emperor** in the presence of the Pope. After 1808 the revolt of Spain, aided by the British, signaled a turning of the tide in the long series of dazzling military successes. The nation began to grow weary of the burden of unceasing war. In 1812 Napoleon threw himself into the **Russian campaign**, hoping to complete his European conquests. He reached Moscow but the long retreat in terrible winter conditions annihilated his veteran *Grande Armée*. By 1814 he was forced to abdicate by a coalition of European powers, who installed Louis XVIII, brother of the decapitated Louis XVI, as king. In a last effort to recapture power, Napoleon escaped from exile in Elba and reorganised his armies, only to meet final defeat at **Waterloo** on June 18, 1815. Louis XVIII was restored to power.

THE RESTORATION AND 1830 REVOLUTION

The years following Napoleon's downfall were marked by a determined campaign, including a **White Terror**, on the part of those reactionary elements who wanted to wipe out all trace of the Revolution and restore the *ancien regime*. **Louis XVIII** resisted these moves and was able to appoint a moderate royalist minister, Decazes, under whose leadership the liberal faction that wished to preserve the Revolutionary reforms made steady gains. This process was wrecked by the assassination of the Duc de Berry in an attempt to wipe out the Bourbon family. In response to reactionary outrage, the king dismissed Decazes. An attempted liberal insurrection was crushed and the four Sergeants of La Rochelle were shot by firing squad. Censorship became more rigid and education was once more subjected to the authority of the church.

In 1824 Louis was succeeded by the thoroughly reactionary **Charles X**, who pushed through a law indemnifying émigré aristocrats for property lost during the Revolution. When the growing opposition won a majority in the elections of 1830, the king dissolved the Chamber and restricted the already narrow suffrage.

Barricades went up in the streets of Paris. Charles X abdicated and parliament was persuaded to accept **Louis-Philippe**, Duc d'Orléans, as king. On the face of it, divine right had been superceded by popular sovreignty as the basis of political legitimacy. The **1814 Charter**, which upheld Revolutionary and Napoleonic reforms, was retained, censorship abolished, the tricolour restored as the national flag and suffrage widened.

However, the **Citizen King**, as he was called, had somewhat more absolutist notions about being a monarch. In the 1830s his regime survived repeated challenges both from attempted coups by reactionaries and some serious labour unrest in Lyon and Paris. The 1840s were calmer under the ministry of Guizot, the first Protestant to hold high office in the state. It was at this time that Algeria was first colonised.

Guizot, however, was not popular. He resisted attempts to extend the vote to include the middle ranks of the bourgeoisie. In 1846 economic crisis brought bankruptcies, unemployment and food shortages. Conditions were appalling for the growing urban working class, whose hopes of a juster future received a more and more convincing theoretical basis in the **socialist writings** and activities of Blanqui, Fourier, Louis Blanc and Proudhon, among others.

When the government banned an opposition 'banquet', the only permissible form of political meeting, in February 1848, workers and students took to the streets. When the army fired on a demonstration and killed forty people, civil war appeared imminent. The Citizen King fled to England.

1848 AND THE SECOND REPUBLIC

A provisional government was set up, incorporating four radical Republican leaders, including the Socialist Louis Blanc and one Parisian worker. A **republic** was proclaimed. The government issued a right-to-work declaration and set up national workshops to relieve unemployment. The vote was extended to all adult males – an unprecedented move for its time. By the time elections were held in April a new tax designed to ameliorate the financial crisis had antagonised the conservative countryside. A massive conservative majority was reelected, to the dismay of the radicals. Three days of bloody street fighting at the barricades followed, when General Cavaignac, who had distinguished himself in the suppression of Algerian resistance, turned the artillery on the workers. More than 1500 were killed and 12,000 arrested and exiled.

A reasonably democratic constitution was drawn up and elections called to choose a president. To everyone's surprise, Louis-Napoleon, nephew of the Emperor, romped home. In spite of his liberal reputation, he restricted the vote again, censored the press, and pandered to the Catholic church. In 1852, following a coup and further street fighting, he had himself proclaimed Emperor Napoleon III.

THE SECOND EMPIRE 1852–70

Through the 1850s **Napoleon III** ran an authoritarian regime whose most notable achievement was a rapid growth in industrial and economic power. Foreign trade trebled, the railway system grew enormously, the first investment banks were established, and so on. In 1858, in the aftermath of an attempt on his life by an Italian patriot, the Emperor suddenly embarked on a policy of **liberalisation**, first of the economy, which alienated much of the business class. Additional reforms included the right to form trade unions and to strike, an extension of public education, lifting of censorship, and the granting of ministerial 'responsibility' under a government headed by the liberal opposition.

Disaster, however, was approaching on the diplomatic front. Involved in a conflict with Bismarck and the rising power of Germany, Napoleon declared war. The French army was quickly defeated and the Emperor himself taken prisoner in 1870. The result at home was a universal demand for the proclamation of a republic. The German armistice agreement insisted on the election of a national assembly to negotiate a proper peace treaty. France lost Alsace and Lorraine, and was obliged to pay hefty war reparations.

Outraged by the monarchist majority reelected to the new Assembly and by the attempt of its chief minister, Thiers, to disarm the National Guard, the people of Paris created their own municipal government known as **the Commune** (see *Paris* chapter).

THE THIRD REPUBLIC

Ironically, although **Thiers**'s ruthless repression of the Commune decapitated the working-class movement for several years to come, it also strengthened support for the Republic, by reassuring the conservative countryside that Republicanism did not mean subversion. By 1875, having eluded various attempts to restore the monarchy, the Republic began to look as if it were there to stay. The conservative forces predominated through the 1870s. One of their premiers, Jules Ferry, was responsible for creating a free, secular, compulsory public education system and – less laudably – the basis of the French colonial empire in southeast Asia, Tunisia and Madagascar.

In 1889 the collapse of a company set up to build the Panama Canal involved several members of the government in a corruption scandal, which was one factor in the dramatic **Socialist gains** in the elections of 1893. More importantly, the urban working class were becoming more class-conscious under the influence of the ideas of Karl Marx. The strength of the movement, however, was undermined by divisions, the chief one being Jules Guesde's Marxian Party. Among the independent Socialists was **Jean Jaurès**, who joined with Guesde in 1905 to found the **Parti Socialiste**, Section Française de l'Internationale Ouvrière (SFIO). The trade union movement, unified in 1895 as the **Confédération Générale du Travail** (CGT), remained aloof in its anarcho-syndicalist preference for direct action.

THE DREYFUS AFFAIR

In 1894 **Captain Dreyfus**, a Jewish army officer, was convicted by courtmartial of spying for the Germans and shipped off to the penal colony of Devil's Island for life. It soon became clear that he had been framed – by the army itself, yet they refused to reconsider his case. The affair immediately became an issue between the Catholic right wing and the Republican left, with Jaurès, Emile Zola and Clémenceau coming out in favour of Dreyfus. Charles Maurras, founder of the racist and facist *Action Française* – precursor of Europe's Blackshirts and Le Pen's *Front National* – took the part of the army. Though Dreyfus was officially rehabilitated in 1904 (his health ruined by penal servitude in the tropics), the issue is still considered sufficiently sensitive in the traditionalist, aristocratic ranks of the officer class for the Mitterrand government to have changed its plans to site a specially commissioned statue.

In the wake of the affair the more radical element in the Republican movement dominated the administration, bringing the army under closer civilian control and dissolving most of the religious orders.

Although the country enjoyed a period of renewed prosperity in the years preceding World War I, there remained serious unresolved conflicts in the political fabric of French society. On the right were Maurras's lunatic fringe with its strong-arm *Camelots du Roi*, and on the left, the far bigger constituency of the working class was simply not represented in government. Although most workers now voted for it, the Socialist Party was not permitted to participate in bourgeois governments under the constitution of the Second International, to which it belonged. Anyway, the government had given clear signs of its unwillingness to accommodate working-class interests in the brutal repression of several major strikes.

WORLD WAR I

When the time came the hitherto anti-militarist trade union and Socialist leaders (Jaurès was assassinated in 1914) rallied to the flag. The cost of **the war** was even greater for France than for the other participants because it was fought out on French soil. Over a quarter of the eight million men called up were either killed or crippled; industrial production fell to 60% of the pre-war level. This – along with memories of the Franco-Prussian war of 1870 — was the reason that the French were more aggressive than either the British or the Americans in seeking war reparations from the Germans.

In the **post-war struggle for recovery** the interests of the urban working class were again passed over, with the exception of Clémenceau's eight-hour day legislation in 1919. An attempted general strike in 1920 came to nothing, and the workers' strength was again weakened by the formation of new Catholic and Communist unions, and most of all by the irremediable split in the Socialist Party at the 1920 Congress of Tours. The pro-Lenin majority formed the **French Communist Party**, while the minority faction, under the leadership of Léon Blum, retained the old SFIO title. The bitterness caused by this split has bedevilled the French left ever since. Both parties resolutely stayed away from government.

As the **Depression** deepened in the 1930s and Nazi power across the Rhine became more menacing, fascist thuggery and anti-parliamentary activity increased in France, culminating in a pitched battle outside the Chamber of Deputies in February 1934. (Léon Blum was only saved from being lynched by a funeral cortege through the intervention of some building workers who happened to notice what was going on in the street below.) The effect of this fascist activism was to unite the left, including the Communists led by the Stalinist Maurice Thorez, in the **Front Populaire**. When they won the 1936 elections with a handsome majority in the Chamber, there followed a wave of strikes and factory sit-ins – a spontaneous expression of working-class determination to get their just desserts after a century and a half of frustration. Frightened by the apparently revolutionary situation, the major employers signed the Matignon Agreement with Blum, which provided for wage increases, nationalisation of the armaments industry and partial nationalisation of the Bank of France, a forty-hour week, paid annual leave, and collective bargaining on wages. These **reforms** were pushed thorugh parliament, but when Blum tried to introduce exchange controls to check the flight of capital, the Senate threw the proposal out and he resigned. The left remained out of power with the exception of coalition governments until 1981. Most of the *Front Populaire* 's reforms were promptly undone.

WORLD WAR II

The agonies of World War II were compounded for France by the additional traumas of occupation, collaboration and Resistance – in effect, a covert civil war. After the 1940 defeat of the Anglo-French forces, Marshal Pétain, a cautious and conservative veteran of World War I, emerged from retirement to sign an armistice with Hitler and head the collaborationist **Vichy government**, which ostensibly governed the southern part of the country, while the Germans occupied the strategic north and the Atlantic coast. Pétain's Prime Minister, Laval, believed it his duty to adapt France to the new authoritarian age heralded by the Nazi conquest of Europe.

There has been endless controversy over who collaborated, how much and how far it was necessary in order to save France from even worse sufferings. One thing at least is clear: Nazi occupation provided a good opportunity for the Maurras breed of out-and-out French fascist to go on the rampage, tracking down Communists, Jews, Resistance fighters, Freemasons – indeed all those who, in their demonology, were considered 'alien' bodies in French society.

While some Communists were involved in **the Resistance** right from the start, Hitler's attack on the Soviet Union in 1941 freed the remainder from ideological inhibitions and brought them into the movement on a large scale. Resistance numbers were further increased by young men taking to the hills to escape conscription as labour in Nazi industry. Général de Gaulle's radio appeal from London on June 18, 1940, rallied the French opposed to right-wing defeatism, and resulted in the *Conseil National de la Résistance*, unifying the different Resistance groups in May 1943. The man to whom this task had been entrusted was Jean Moulin, shortly to be captured by the Gestapo and tortured to death by Klaus Barbie, who was recently convicted for his war crimes.

Although British and American governments found him irksome, **de Gaulle** was able to impose himself as the unchallenged spokesman of the Free French, leader of a government in exile, and to insist that the voice of France be heard as an equal in the Allied councils of war. Even the Communists accepted his leadership, though he was far from representing the kind of political interests with which they could sympathise.

Thanks, however, to his persistence, representatives of his provisional government moved into liberated areas of France behind the Allied advance after D-Day, thereby saving the country from what would certainly have been at least localised outbreaks of civil war. It was also thanks to his insistence that Free French units, notably General Leclerc's 2nd Armoured Division, were allowed to perform the psychologically vital role of being the first Allied troops to enter Paris, Strasbourg and other emotionally important towns in France. Symbolic acts, perhaps, but nonetheless important for that.

THE AFTERMATH OF WAR

France emerged from the war demoralised, bankrupt and bomb-wrecked. The only possible provisional government in the circumstances was de Gaulle's **Free French** and the *Conseil National de la Résistance*, which meant a coalition of left and right. As an opening move to deal with the shambles, coal mines, air transport and Renault cars were nationalised. But a new constitution was required and **elections**, in which French women voted for the first time, resulted in a large left majority in the new Constituent Assembly – which, however, soon fell to squabbling over the form of the new constitution. De Gaulle resigned in disgust. If he was hoping for a wave of popular sympathy, he didn't get it and retired to the country to sulk.

The constitution finally agreed on, with little enthusiasm in the country, was not much different from the discredited Third Republic. And the new **Fourth Republic** appropriately began its life with a series of short-lived coalitions. In the early days the foundations for welfare were laid, banks nationalised and trade union rights extended. With the exclusion of the Communists from the government in 1947, however, thanks to the Cold War and the carrot of American aid under the Marshall Plan, France found itself once more dominated by the right.

If the post-Liberation desire for political reform was quickly frustrated, the spirit that inspired it did bear fruit in other spheres. From being still a rather backward and largely agricultural economy pre-war, France in the 1950s achieved enormous industrial **modernisation and expansion**, its growth rate even rivalling that of West Germany at times. In foreign policy France opted to remain in the U.S. fold, but at the same time took the initiative in promoting closer **European integration**, first through the European Coal and Steel community and then, in 1957, through membership of the European Community, (EC).

In its **colonial policy**, on the other hand, the Fourth Republic seemed firmly committed to antiquated imperialist attitudes. The vaguely cosmetic reform of renaming the Empire the French Union brought little result. In 1945, on the surrender of Japan to the Allies, the northern half of the French **Indochina** colony came under the control of Ho Chi Minh and his Communist Vietminh. Attempts to negotiate were bungled and there began an eight-year armed struggle which ended with French defeat at Dien Bien Phu and partition of the country at the Geneva Conference in 1954 – at which point the Americans took over in the south with well-known consequences.

And 1954 was also the year in which the government decided to create an **independent nuclear arsenal** and got embroiled in the horrendous **Algerian war of liberation**. If you want to take a charitable view, you can say that the situation was complicated from the French viewpoint by the legal fiction that Algeria was a *département*, an integral part of France, that there were a million or so settlers or *pieds noirs* claiming to be French – and the fact that there was oil in the south. But by 1958 half-a-million troops, most of them conscripts, had been committed to the war, with all the attendant horrors of torture, massacre of civilian populations and so forth. When it began to seem in 1958 that the government would take a more liberal line, the hard-line rightists among the settlers and in the army staged a putsch on May 13 and threatened to declare war on France. Général de Gaulle, waiting in the wings to resume his mission to save France, let it be known that in its hour of need and with certain conditions – i.e. stronger powers for the President – the country might call upon his help. Thus, on June 1, 1958, the National Assembly voted him full powers for six months and the Fourth Republic came to an end.

DE GAULLE FOR PRESIDENT

As Prime Minister, then President of the **Fifth Republic** – with powers as much strengthened as he had wished – **de Gaulle** wheeled and dealed with the *pieds noirs* and Algerian rebels, while the war continued. In 1961 a General Salan staged a military revolt and set up the OAS (secret army) organisation to prevent a settlement. When his coup failed, his organisation made several attempts on de Gaulle's life – thereby strengthening the feeling on the mainland that it was time to be done with Algeria. Eventually in 1962 a referendum gave an overwhelming yes to Algerian independence and *pieds noirs* refugees flooded into France, evoking new waves of fascist and racist activity. Most of the rest of the French colonial empire had achieved independence by this time also.

De Gaulle's style of leadership was haughty and autocratic, more concerned with *gloire* and grandeur than the everyday problems of ordinary lives. His quirky strutting on the world stage greatly irritated France's partners. He blocked British entry to the EC, cultivated the friendship of the Germans, rebuked the U.S. for its imperialist policies in Vietnam, withdrew from NATO, refused to sign a nuclear test ban treaty, and called for a 'free Quebec'. If this projection of French influence pleased some, the very narrowly won presidential election of 1965 (in which Mitterrand was his opponent) showed that a good half of French voters would not be sorry to see the last of the General.

But notwithstanding a certain domestic discontent, the sudden explosion of **May 1968** took everyone by surprise. Beginning with protests against the paternalistic nature of the education system by students at the University of Nanterre, the movement of revolt rapidly spread to the Sorbonne and out into factories and offices. On the night of May 10 barricades went up in the streets of the Quartier Latin in Paris and the CRS (riot police) responded by wading into everyone, including bystanders and Red Cross volunteers, with unbelievable ferocity. A general strike followed, and within a week more than a million people were out, with numerous factory occupations and professionals joining in with journalists striking for freedom of expression, doctors setting up new radically organised practices and so forth. *Autogestion* – workers' participation – was the dominant slogan. More than specific demands for reform, there was a general feeling that all French institutions needed overhauling: they were too rigid, too hierarchical, too elitist.

De Gaulle seemed to lose his nerve and on May 27 he vanished from the scene. It turned out he had gone to assure himself of the support of the commander of the French army of the Rhine. On his return he appealed to the nation to elect him as the only effective barrier against left-wing dictatorship and dissolved parliament. The frightened silent majority voted massively Gaullist.

Although there were few short-term radical changes (except in education), the shockwaves of May 1968 continue to be felt. Women's Liberation, ecology groups, a gradual relaxing of the formality of French society, a lessening of authoritarianism – all these can be traced to the heady days of May.

Having petulantly staked his presidency on the outcome of yet another referendum on a couple of constitutional amendments and lost, de Gaulle once more took himself sulkily off to his country estate and retirement.

AFTER DE GAULLE

De Gaulle was succeeded as President by his business-oriented former Prime Minister, **Pompidou**, who thought that wealth, property and competition would solve all the ills of society. In 1972 the much dreamed of and never credible Union de la Gauche came into being – a radical joint manifesto by Communists and Socialists. But Mitterrand did not use it for the Presidential election of 1974 after Pompidou's sudden death, and lost by a narrow margin to Pompidou's finance minister **Valéry Giscard d'Estaing**.

Having announced that his aim was to make France 'an advanced liberal society', Giscard opened his term of office with some spectacular media coups, like inviting Parisian trash collectors to breakfast and visiting prisons in Lyon. But aside from reducing the voting age to 18 and liberalising divorce laws, the advanced liberal society did not make a lot of progress. In the wake of the 1974 oil crisis the government introduced economic austerity measures. Giscard fell out with his ambitious prime minister, **Jacques Chirac**, who set out to challenge the leadership with his own RPR Gaullist party. And in addition to his superior, monarchical style, Giscard further compromised his popularity by accepting diamonds from the (literally) child-eating emperor of Central Africa, Bokassa and by involvement in various other scandals.

The left seemed well placed to win the coming 1978 elections, when the fragile Union cracked, as the Communists began to fear that the Socialists's rising popularity would turn them into the coalition's junior partners. The result was a right-wing victory, with Giscard able to form a new government, with the grudging support of the RPR. Law and order and immigrant controls were the dominant features of Giscard's second term.

THE POLITICAL PRESENT

THE PARTIES IN POWER

In May 1981, people danced in the streets of Paris to celebrate the end of 23 years of right-wing rule – and the victory of François Mitterrand's Socialist Party. Five years later, the Socialists conclusively lost their majority in the National Assembly while Le Pen's ultra-right *Front National* won a horrifying 35 seats. The Communist vote fell and the centre-right made inroads into traditionally left-wing constituencies. The new prime minister after this realignment – ominously, for anyone who had witnessed his autocratic methods and law-and-order campaigns on the domestic front – was the Paris mayor, **Jacques Chirac***.

The Socialist government had certainly recognised the omens, and the dramatic change that was in store. In their five years in power they had shifted from partnership with the Communists to somewhere very near the centre under Laurent Fabius's premiership. Their attempts to reform the education system were defeated by mass protests in the streets; ministers were implicated in cover-ups and corruption; unemployment continued to rise. Any idea of peaceful and pro-ecological intent was dashed, as far as international opinion was concerned, by the French Secret Service's murder of the Greenpeace photographer on the *Rainbow Warrior* in New Zealand. There were sporadic achievements in labour laws and women's rights, notably – but there was no cohesive and consistent socialist line. Their 1986 election slogan was 'Help – the Right is coming back!', a bizarrely self-fulfilling tactic that they defended on the grounds of humour.

For the unemployed and the low paid, for immigrants and their families, for women wanting the choice of whether to have children, for the young, the old and all those attached to certain civil liberties, the return of the right was no laughing matter.

Throughout 1987 the chances of Mitterrand's winning the presidential election in 1988 seemed very slim. But Chirac's economic policies had failed to deliver. Millions of first-time investors in 'popular capitalism' lost all their money on Black Monday. Terrorists planted bombs in Paris and took French hostages in the Lebanon. Unemployment continued to rise, and Chirac made the fatal mistake of flirting with the extreme right. Leading politicians of the centre-right, including Simone Weil, a concentration-camp survivor, denounced Chirac's concessions to Le Pen, and a new alignment of the centre started to emerge. Mitterrand, the grand old man with decades of experience, played off all the groupings of the right in an all-but-flawless campaign, and won another seven-year mandate.

His party, however, did not fare so well in the parliamentary elections called soon afterwards. The Socialists failed to achieve an absolute majority, leaving them dependent on either the Communist block or the centre. Mitterrand's new prime minister, Michel Rocard, has gone for the centrist coalition, causing friction in the party grassroots who see the Communists as the natural partners. The traditional Socialist supporters in the public-service sector have not been happy with Rocard's austerity measures. Wage increases have been restricted to two percent, and nurses, civil servants, teachers and the like have been quick to take industrial action. Though Chirac's programmes have been halted, they have not been reversed, and no alternative vision has been given to the populace.

The best news of those elections was the collapse, electorally, of the *Front National*. Le Pen failed to win a seat, only one *député* was re-elected (for the Invalides constituency), and she has since become an Independent. However, this optimistic trend received a setback in the election for the European Parliament in June 1989, when the fascists regained their highest level of electoral support, at 11%.

* Because of the different terms of tenure, **Mitterrand**, leader of the Socialist Party, remained president even though the government (which he technically controls) was superseded by the right-wing Gaullist-Giscardian coalition headed by **Jacques Chirac**.

THE UNDERLYING PATTERN

France is a highly secretive state. More so, if anything, than the U.K., whose political TV documentaries would not find air time across the Channel. And, as in the U.K., the truth about such things as nuclear accidents and agreements with foreign powers is often not revealed by the government. That the radioactive cloud from Chernobyl passed over areas of France was admitted very, very belatedly (and no advice given) when too many people had figured out the implausibility of the cloud being deflected by the French-German border. As regards their own **nuclear industry**, the biggest in the world in proportion to their energy needs, almost every French citizen believes that there has never been an accident. A halt to nuclear plant construction and increased investment in renewable sources promised by the Socialists in 1981 was immediately dropped. Like Britain, France has a nuclear reprocessing plant – on the Cotentin peninsula in Normandy – that discharges its waste into the sea. Cotentin also provided some air space for the American bombing raid on Libya in 1986 despite smug protestations that it had been denied.

In all these things it makes little difference whether power resides with the right or the so-called left, except in **relations with the superpowers**. Contrary to what you might expect, negotiation and trade with the Soviet Union always benefits by a Gaullist goverment, while Mitterrand was as beloved of Reagan as Margaret Thatcher. The taste for truculence on the right towards American desires goes back to de Gaulle and represents not anti-Americanism but pro-Frenchness. The independent nuclear arsenal and non-membership of NATO (for which there has long been cross-party consensus) is one of the major sources of French pride, French glory and French chauvinism. But the Communist Party has recently responded to Soviet initiatives, and, for the first time, called for the total abolition of nuclear weapons by the year 2000.

When it comes to **France's overseas territories**, there has been until very recently a similar consensus on 'No' to independence claims, with slight cosmetic differences. When the Kanaks of Nouvelle Calédonie (New Caledonia, an island near New Zealand) began to rebel against the direct, unelected rule by Paris, Mitterrand granted them compensation for their appropriated lands. Chirac reversed this. Mitterrand's 'autonomy' measures for the island were not a problem since they kept defense, foreign affairs, control of the television, law and order, and education firmly in the French governor's hands. A massacre of indigenous tribesmen in October 1986 by white settlers was deemed 'self defence' and appeals against the judgement prohibited by Paris. Eventually, however, the situation proved to be too much of a headache, and a referendum in November 1988 has committed France to granting independence to New Caledonia in ten years. Both the New Zealand and Australian governments have been warned to desist from their support for the island's independence – to stop meddling in French internal affairs as Paris sees it. Both countries take strong stands against the nuclear tests at Muroroa (with the concomitant suppression of information and strong-arm tactics against protestors). The two secret agents responsible for blowing up the *Rainbow Warrior* had been given ten-year sentences in New Zealand jails. French pressure resulted in a U.N.-sponsored compromise of a three-year confinement to the French island of Hao. On highly spurious medical grounds, both have found their way back to Paris – leaving New Zealand furious but impotent and French public opinion unperturbed. Meanwhile the subjugation of the Polynesian people to French interests, with slum dwellers surviving on subsistence while imported French goods decimate local economies, goes on, and will no doubt continue, whether independence becomes a reality or not.

On the **law and order** front, opinion polls suggested that Chirac hit a chord in most Frenchmen and Frenchwomen's hearts even before the Lebanese-inspired bombing campaign in the capital. The death sentence was not reintroduced – the message seems to have got through that 'civilised' European nations don't do that sort of thing. But maximum penalties of thirty years' imprisonment without parole were put on the statute books along with no juries for terrorist offenses, more incentives for turning king's evidence, detention without charge increased to a maximum of four days, and police powers of arrest extended. While French jails have become absurdly overcrowded, the response to 'state-terrorism' is always to wheel and deal. Understandably, the Parisian population reacts to a spate of random and densely-targetted bombing campaigns with heightened paranoia. After each attack the normal lingering street-life vanishes, leaving the city as if it were at war. But people retreat to their homes and personal security rather than putting pressure on the government.

The practice of **demanding ID papers** more or less randomly (e.g., from people who are young, black, not wearing suits, etc.) was enshrined in law soon after the right's return to power in 1986. If a policeman doesn't like the look of your passport or ID card, he can take you off to the station, photograph and fingerprint you, refuse you access to a lawyer, and charge you with non-cooperation if you vociferate. There has been some bad publicity on this, with children as young as thirteen and foreign tourists getting the treatment, but on the whole Chirac's government was as successful as the British Tory party in stuffing crime statistics and images of riotous Blacks and youth down the throats of the populace.

The record of the **police** when it comes to '*bavures*' ('blunders', usually resulting in the death or injury of an innocent person) is becoming alarming to say the least. After one such incident, which took place a week after the shooting of a policeman in the south, Chirac's Interior Minister made clear his view (shared by the police federation) that the one exempted the other, and in no event was an individual police officer to blame. The atmosphere in big cities is noticeably changed, with agents of the law arrogantly acting out their fantasies of power. The current government is conscious of the general support Chirac whipped up for the authoritarian approach and has yet to repeal most of the measures. Instead it contents itself with leaving the law as it stands but dissuading the police and courts from enforcing it.

Unemployment still has a way to go before it becomes a key issue. When Chirac came to power in 1986 the official figures stood at 2.4 million. During the election, the comedian Coluche set up thousands of '*restaurants du coeur*' (restaurants of the heart) to hand out soup and food parcels to those living below the poverty line, many of them the long-term unemployed. The money was raised through TV appeals. But if Coluche hoped to bring a point home rather than simply to mock the politicians, he failed. Falling outside the riddled net of the social security system is only too easy, and such luxuries as rent are certainly not covered. What this means can be seen at a glance. The numbers and the ages of people begging has drastically changed: the signs they hold almost all say, '*Je suis chomeur/chomeuse*' ('I'm unemployed'). Chirac mouthed concern for youth unemployment and money was allocated to businesses to take youngsters on. But jobs were lost in the mines, shipyards, transportation industry and in the denationalised industries.

Chirac's **privatisation programme** went much further than reversing the preceding Socialists' nationalisations – banks that de Gaulle took into the public sector after 1945 were sold off along with Dassault, the aircraft manufacturer and Elf-Aquitaine, the biggest French oil company. As in the U.S., monopoly corporatism is having a field day with mergers and takeovers ever decreasing the number of independent businesses. The contradiction for French national consciousness is that this process opens up French firms to Italian, German, British, or other EC members' ownership. That the Americans are kept at bay makes little difference to Gallic pride.

No further privatisations will take place under the present government, but Rocard has ruled out re-nationalisation. Public spending has been increased, but not enough to compensate for all the jobs lost in the preceding government's manic sell-offs. Where Chirac and his Interior Minister Charles Pasqua (who publically stated in May 1988 that the aims of the Gaullists and the *Front National* were the same) came down heavily on trade unionists, the Socialists have at least offered amnesty to some of those who were prosecuted. The most famous defendants to benefit have been those in the Renault Ten case, who were accused of conspiring to organise a strike in the car firm's Boulogne Billancourt works. The shock of Chirac's Thatcherite approach to the unions, which in France are mostly organised along political lines rather than by profession, galvanised the usually irreconcilably divided Communist CGT, Socialist CFDT and Catholic FO unions into finding a common cause. Rocard's centrist programme provoked a wave of strikes in the summer and autumn of 1988.

The most popular minister of the 1981–86 Socialist government, Jack Lang, is back as minister of culture, after the destructive period of Chirac's appointee, Francois Léotard, who suppressed all ventures tainted by feminism, gay rights, socialism, etc. Luckily Lang's work during his first term was so popular, even with conservative museum curators, that it could not be dismantled at a stroke.

In the culture and politics of the oppressed, **feminism and anti-racism** have begun to take stands together. The racism of the French establishment was trumpeted under the Gaullists. Birth control measures and the position of immigrants' wives and daughters have brought French feminists into the battle. The strength of the **Front National** after the 1986 election under proportional representation shocked a broad range of French into recognising the urgency of taking on and defeating racism. The pedigrees of the *Front National* deputies were almost ludicrously extreme. They included members of the Moonies, publishers of Hitler's speeches, a defector from the Gaullists (who thought they were too soft in the *Rainbow Warrior* affair), an 86-year-old who as a Paris city council member in 1943 voted for full powers for Marshall Pétain's Vichy regime, and the party leader **Jean-Marie Le Pen**. The fact that they are no longer represented in the parliament (proportional representation having been scrapped) does not mean that their grass-roots support is not still a threat.

The history of **immigrants** in France is a familiar one. From the mid-1950s to the mid-1970s a labour shortage led to massive recruitment campaigns in North Africa, Portugal, Spain, Italy and Greece. People were promised housing, free medical care, trips home and well-paid jobs. When they arrived in France they found themselves paid half of what their French co-workers earned, accommodated in prison-style hostels and sometimes poorer than they were at home. They had no vote, no automatic permit renewal, were threatened with deportation at the slightest provocation, were subject to constant racial abuse and assault and, until 1981, were forbidden to form their own associations. The Socialist government lifted this ban, gave a ten-year automatic renewal for permits, and even spoke about voting rights. Able to organise for the first time, immigrant workers immediately took on their employers at several car factories on the issue of racism in the selection of workers being laid off. Meanwhile in Paris, Chirac, as mayor of the city, was extending maternity leave to French women who were having a third child, while ensuring that no foreigner would receive the benefit. His line on population growth (a long-standing French obsession with no basis whatsoever in the new technological age) was that unless French women were encouraged to reproduce, nothing would stop the hordes south of the Mediterranean from taking over the north. In the context of newly-won abortion rights, many women, whether they were concerned with racism or not, began to worry.

Chirac's **anti-terrorism and immigration laws** provoked unprecendented alliances. The Archbishop of Lyon and the head of the Muslim Institute in Paris together condemned the injustice of their introduction, with the Catholic leader giving his blessing to a hunger-strike protest. Human rights groups, churches and trade unions joined immigrants' groups in saying France was on its way to becoming a **police state**. No idle rhetoric: the measures included the right of the police to expel immigrants without the interference of any courts or any other ministry except their own, i.e., Mr. Pasqua's; the annulment of the right to automatic citizenship for people born in France; the reintroduction of visas for visitors from North Africa, Turkey and the Middle East, and immediate deportation for any criminal offense. Since the 1986 bomb attacks, visa requirements have also been in force for all non-EC nationals – prompting outraged demands for exemption from Switzerland and Sweden.

The Socialists have always played electoral games with the immigration issue and have yet to prove that they are committed to combating racism. The popular anti-racist movement, supported by the Communist Party, some sections of the Socialists and the liberal centre, is meanwhile gaining ground, constituting one of the most hopeful developments in French politics. The problem with the government in power is not just that it needs to prove its commitment to crucial issues such as this, but, more generally, to prove its commitment to socialism, or at least to that nineteenth-century formulation: liberty, fraternity and equality.

THE ENVIRONMENT

Environmentalists in France defend the largest and most diverse country in western Europe, with the largest number of mammal species (113), and of amphibious species (29); and the second highest number of bird species (342). But most amphibians, half the mammals and one-third of the bird species are considered 'threatened'. Those threats include agriculture, and especially wetland drainage, acid and other forms of pollution, tourism and, ultimately, the world's largest nuclear power programme outside of the United States.

POLITICS

Despite its excellent showing in the 1989 European elections, the Green movement and its leaders, everywhere, have agonised over whether they should work inside or outside conventional politics. It's an academic debate in many countries but the French have some practical experience, through ***l'affaire Lalonde***. In 1981, Brice Lalonde polled one million votes in the presidential election as a Green and as an outspoken critic of **French nuclear testing** on **Mururoa** in Polynesia. In the summer of 1988 Prime Minister Michel Rocard made him Environment Minister. What happened next, according to the Green movement, was the proof of the old adage that 'power corrupts'. In July, just two months after his appointment, Lalonde visited Australia and announced that he no longer considered French nuclear tests a danger to the environment. 'The situation on the Muraroa test site', he told the local press, 'has considerably improved'. The official Communist paper *L'Humanité* was 'speechless' while nongovernmental Greens were astonished at the 'miracle' of suddenly inoffensive nuclear tests. As for Lalonde, he professed himself 'irritated at the attacks' on him.

According to the Independent Commission on International Humanitarian Issues, of which the French member is Simone Weil, France has conducted more than 130 atomic tests on Mururoa in the last twenty years. Fifty of them, prior to 1975, were above ground. The ICIHI reports an increase in leukemia, thyroid cancer and birth defects in the area. Lalonde is one of the few Greens in government anywhere in the world but there is the suspicion that he is a Green who has gone a bit mouldy.

NUCLEAR POWER

The stubborn French pride in things nuclear has muted environmentalists in what, post-Chernobyl, should be a deeply worried country. France has the second largest **nuclear power programme** in the world, with some fifty reactors in operation and a dozen more under construction. Two are fast breeders, the type experts admit could create a nuclear bomb-like explosion. Four are gas cooled reactors (GCRs) and the rest are pressurised water reactors (PWRs). Even ignoring the nuclear explosions and the very real possibility of a major accident, even a meltdown, leading to serious radiation leakage, there is still the problem of **waste**. According to the International Atomic Energy Agency (IAEA), French reactors now working or under construction will have produced some 44,000 metric tons of spent fuel and 687,500 cubic metres of low- and intermediate-level waste by the end of their lives. Reprocessing will have resulted in some 5,000 cubic metres of high-level waste, for which the French disposal plan is interim storage in solidified form.

WETLANDS

In its disregard for wetlands, France is no different from any other country, but, at 140,000 hectares a year, the rate of **field-drainage** is the highest in Europe. The World Wide Fund for Nature in France (formerly the World Wildlife Fund) has been running a public awareness campain and blaming Common Agricultural Policy (CAP) grants for the damage.

Wetlands are something of an acquired taste but not only are they often deliciously wild, they are also one of the most productive ecosystems in the world. According to wetlands expert Dr. Eric Maltby, their loss will have a serious impact on the food chain and on fisheries and will completely destroy the potential of aquaculture. Almost all European reptiles and amphibians and 47 percent of all endangered and vulnerable European bird species are threatened by the destruction of wetlands. By the end of the 1970s France had lost ten percent of its wetlands, including the Marais des Echets near Lyons. The *Office de la Chasse* (Hunters' Organisation) now asseses the total damage at 25 wetlands of national importance seriously affected; eighty percent of the *Landes* marshes and forty percent of the coastal wetlands of Brittany are lost. A further 600,000 hectares are at risk from drainage schemes due for immediate implementation. In addition, ten dams proposed for the Loire and its tributaries in the Massif Central pose a serious threat to rare forms of wildlife which thrive on its floodplains, as well as to the natural life of the river.

At least some of the wetlands now, thankfully, have protection. The remnants near Lyon are in the **Villars Les Dombes Nature Reserve**, a mere 23 hectares created in 1970 but better than nothing. This is a breeding ground for several rare species, including the black-necked grebe, whiskered tern and little egret. Just to the east, the **Marais du Bout du Lac d'Annecy Nature Reserve**, at the southern tip of the lake, is important for corncrake, water rail, garganey, teal, curlew and little bittern. Brittany, meanwhile, has the **Armorique Regional Park**, notable for a small colony of beavers, transported from the Rhône to a tributary of the River Aulne.

Moving south, other important protected wetlands include the **Golfe du Morbihan Nature Reserve**; the **Briere Regional Park** (one of the largest areas of marsh and lagoon in inland France, totalling 7,000 hectares); the **Baie de Bourgneuf**, like Morbihan very important for brent geese; the **St-Denis-du-Payre**, between Nantes and La Rochelle; the **Pointe d'Arcay**; and the **Baie de l'Aiguillon**, where vast numbers of wildfowl stay over the winter, among them one of Europe's largest concentrations of avocet.

As for the **Camargue**, with over 300 bird species recorded, only the Doñana of Spain and the Danube in Romania can rival it in Europe. Situated between the Petit and Grand Rhône, the marshes and lakes are under increasing threat, not merely from drainage but also from runoff of agricultural land. The Camargue is not exclusively for rare birds such as the gorgeous greater flamingo, bee-eaters and great spotted cuckoos, or for the bitterns, purple herons and egrets of the freshwater marshes, but also for the cultivation of rice, corn, wheat and the rearing of the famous Camargue bulls and semi-wild white horses.

France does not have the protected area that it should in respect of its land area. It may be more than 16,000 square kilometres, as opposed to only 621 square kilometres in 1950, but that comes out to a mere 30 protected hectares per 1000 inhabitants. It's better than some countries, but when you consider that Norway manages 1138.3 hectares per 1000 inhabitants, it's hardly enough. Considering the state of French seawater, and the role wetlands play in filtering out pollutants, conservation is vital.

SEA BATHING

The 1975 directive of the European Community requires designated bathing beaches to be tested every other week during the bathing season and sets a faecal coliform standard of 2,000 per 100 millilitres of water for 95 percent of samples. (The faecal coliform is a bacteria found in the human gastro-intestinal tract and therefore an indicator of the level of **sewage pollution**.) Many European beaches, including some in France (and the majority in Britain) were still failing this test in 1988. To put that into perspective, the U.S. Environmental Protection Agency sets a standard ten times more stringent, and Canada is 20 times more strict. To be within the EC standard is hardly an endorsement for safe bathing and to exceed it is disgusting. A study in Brittany in 1983 concluded that swimmers were more likely to suffer skin infections, nausea and conjuctivitis than people who did not swim.

The good news is that the French **situation is improving** in at least some respects. Back in 1979, the 930 coastal communes had sewerage for seven million people but a summer population, including six million tourists, almost double that. In 1980, more than a third of seawater samples were failing to reach the EC standard. Since then, increased investment, particularly in tourist sites with preinstalled sewerage facilities, had put some 84 percent of samples into the two top EC categories by 1985. The bad news is that many of the holiday-developments, though well provided with sewerage facilities, affect the environment in other ways, particularly, once again, by land drainage, as with the new resorts of Languedoc-Roussillon.

MOUNTAINS

Parallel to this shameful tourist destruction of the coast, the winter damage in the mountains by skiers and ski development has been equally severe. The ugliness of many 'third-generation' **ski resorts** has repelled even the holidaymakers themselves and created a 'fourth-generation' attempt to capture the charm of traditional mountain villages married to the mechanical excellence of high-technology lift systems. The notion that every French person should be able to enjoy a winter holiday in France has resulted in six million French skiers, all of whom seem to be either on the piste on peak weekends or jamming the roads that lead to them. The planners say that only a crash programme of resort construction could have fed the extensive lift network of the Tarentaise that has become the attraction for foreign skiers. Environmentalists argue that over-rapid development has upset the natural water level in lakes and streams, damaged **wildlife** through noise, pollution and habitat destruction, and increased the likelihood of avalanches and mudslides because of tree clearance.

The **tétras-lyre** or black grouse has been one of the species most affected, while the larger capercaillie is already extinct in the French Alps. The problem for the black grouse is that, in winter, it favours the same north-facing slopes, at 2,000 metres, as the skiers. The black grouse lookouts are also prime locations for mountain restaurants and lift stations, while birds not driven to death through exposure are frequently decapitated in mist by the ski-lift cables. Even breeding is affected, since predators attracted by ski station rubbish often turn their attention to black grouse eggs – as studies at Les Arcs have proved. Jacques Perrier, a *garde-moniteur* in the Parc National de la Vanoise, which the ski terrain of Les Arcs adjoins, describes the tétras-lyre as an indicator. 'When the tétras-lyre is gone', he says, 'people, too, will be finished'. If present trends continue, the black grouse, unfortunately for us, does not have long.

A bird that could make a tentative comeback in the Alps is the gypaete-barbu or **lammergeier**. A pair of these magnificent vultures, with their distinctive pinky-gold chest feathers and wedge-shaped tails, was reintroduced in Haute Savoie in 1987. Wiped out by hunting in the French Alps, the lammergeier retained a foothold in the Pyrenees where eight pairs are known to breed in and round the *Parc National des Pyrénées*. The relative remoteness of the Pyrenees has also allowed some 45 pairs of *vautours fauves* or griffon vultures to survive there.

The **hunting** that wiped out vast numbers of these spectacular but now protected species continues to decimate many smaller, lower-profile species. The hunting lobby in France is well-organised and represents around two million people. According to the Royal Society For the Protection of Birds, about one in seven migrant birds passing the Mediterranean are killed every year, by shooting, netting, trapping and bird liming as well as by natural hazards. That amounts to 900 million migrants and the French play their part with their key passes over the Alps and, as at Col d'Orgambideska, in the Pyrenees. It was there that a group of conservationists, including Tanguy Le Gac, rented the pass to keep the shooters out. Main victim in the Pyrenees is the pigeon, which crosses the range in October – up to 20,000 of them falling victim to traps each year.

Despite the claims hunters make for their role in preserving species (so that they can continue to hunt them), it was undeniably hunting that severely reduced numbers of chamois, almost caused the extinction of *bouqetin* (ibex) and so depleted brown bear in the Pyrenees that its extinction there is almost inevitable.

The creation of the national parks has saved the **chamois**, which became a source of food for the Resistance during World War II, but the appearance of the eye disease *kératoconjonctivite*, especially among the closely related *isards* of the Pyrenees, is a new source of concern. The much larger **bouquetin**, with its imposing ridged and back-curved horns, was reduced to just 60 individuals through hunting and had to be reintroduced into France, and particularly into the Vanoise, from the Gran Paradiso National Park in Italy. *Bouquetin* now number some 700 in the Vanoise and chamois round 4000. A policy of re-introduction has also helped the **castor** (beaver), down to less than 100 in the Rhône Valley at the end of the last century, but now numbered in the thousands. Sadly, re-introduction is unlikely to prove either acceptable or practical in the case of **l'ours brun**. Estimates are that only between 15 and 20 brown bears survive in the Pyrenees, scarcely a viable population. The French outdoor magazine *AlpiRando* suggests that the distribution could be nine to eleven bears on the slopes of the Aspe and Ossau valleys, three to five round the cirque of Lescun, three to five in Haut-Luchonnais near Andorra and perhaps one to three in Ariége and the Pyrénées-Orientales. In 1982 President Mitterrand announced that the bear must be saved but his funds have not been sufficient to hold back the logging and the ski station construction that is destroying the remaining habitat.

ACID RAIN

France's **upland forests** are also taking the brunt of the acid rain attack. The country has 13.6 million hectares (33.6 million acres) of forest but remained complacent until 1984, when the realisation that at least one third of deposition came from foreign sources, and that the damage was real and costly, caused an about face. The monitoring programme set up in 1983 in the Vosges discovered that 35,000 hectares (86,000 acres) were affected, of which 5000 hectares (12,000 acres) were rated serious. By early 1985 one in five conifers were damaged.

Defoliation is now also reported in the forests of Alsace, the Jura, Alps, Massif Central and Pyrenees.

Paul Jenner and Christine Smith

ART AND ARCHITECTURE

These are necessarily the briefest of introductions to the subjects, intended as working references to the country's innumerable galleries, collections and monuments.

PAINTING

From the Middle Ages to the twentieth century, France has held – with occasional gaps – a leading position in the history of European painting, with Paris, above all, attracting artists from the whole continent. The story of French painting is one of richness and complexity, partly due to this influx of foreign painters and partly due to the capital's stability as an artistic centre.

BEGINNINGS

In the late Middle Ages, the itinerant life of the nobles led them to prefer small and transportable works of art; splendidly **illuminated manuscripts** were much praised and the best painters, usually trained in Paris, continued to work on a small scale until the fifteenth century. In spite of the size of the illuminated image, painters made startling steps towards a realistic interpretation of the world, and in the exploration of new subject matters. Many of these illuminators were also panel painters, foremost of whom was **Jean Fouquet** (c.1420–c.1481), born in Tours in the Loire valley and the central artistic personality of fifteenth-century France. Court painter to Charles VIII, Fouquet drew from both Flemish and Italian sources, utilising the new, fluid oil technique that had been perfected in Flanders, and concerning himself with the problem of representing space convincingly, much like his Italian contemporaries. Through this he molded a distinct personal style, combining richness of surface with broad, generalised forms and, in his feeling for volume and ordered, geometric shapes, laying down principles that became intrinsic to French art for centuries to come, from Poussin to Seurat and Cézanne.

Two other fifteenth-century French artists deserve brief mention here, principally for the broad range of artistic expression they embody. **Emguerrand Quarton** (c.1410–c.1466) was the most famous Provençal painter of the time; his art, profoundly religious in subject as well as feeling, already shows the impact of the Mediterranean sun in the strong light that pervades his paintings. His *Pietà* in the Louvre is both stark and intensely poignant, while the *Coronation of the Virgin* that hangs at Villeneuve-Lès-Avignon is a vast panoramic vision not only of heaven but also of a very real earth, in what ranks as one of the first city/landscapes in the history of French painting: Avignon itself is faithfully depicted and the Mont Ste-Victoire, later to be made famous by Cézanne, is clearly recognisable in the distance. The **Master of Moulins**, active in the 1480s and 1490s, was noticeably more northern in temperament, painting both religious altarpieces and portraits commissioned by members of the royal family or the fast-increasing bourgeoisie.

MANNERISM & ITALIAN INFLUENCE

At the end of the fifteenth and the beginning of the sixteenth century, the French invasion of Italy brought both artists and patrons into closer contact with the Italian Renaissance. The most famous of the artists who were lured to France was **Leonardo da Vinci**, spending the last three years of his life (1516–19) at the court of François I. From the Loire valley, which until then had been his favourite residence, the French king moved nearer to Paris, where he had several palaces decorated. Italian artists were once again called upon and two of them, **Rosso** and **Primaticcio**, who arrived in France in 1530 and 1532, were to shape the artistic scene in France for the rest of the sixteenth century. Both artists introduced to France the latest Italian style, **Mannerism**, a sometimes anarchic derivation of the High Renaissance of Michelangelo and Raphael. Mannerism, with its emphasis on the fantastic, the luxurious and the large-scale decorative was eminently compatible with the taste of the court, and it was first put to the test in the revamping of the old castle of Fountainebleau. There, a horde of French painters headed by the two Italians came to form what was subsequently called the **School of Fontainebleau**. Most French artists worked at Fontainebleau at some point in their career, or were influenced by its homogeneous style, but none stand out as personalities of any stature, and for the most part the painting of the time was dull and fanciful in the extreme. **Antoine Caron** (c.1520–c.1600), who often worked for Catherine de Médicis, the widow of Henry II, contrived complicated allegorical paintings in which elongated figures are arranged within wide, theatre-like scenery packed with ancient monuments and Roman statues. Even the Wars of Religion, raging in the 1550s and 1560s, failed to rouse French artists' sense of drama, and representations of the many massacres then going on were detached and fussy in tone.

Portraiture tended to be more inventive. The portraits of **Jean Clouet** (c.1485–1541) and his son **François** (c.1510–72), both official painters to François I, combined sensitivity in the rendering of the sitter's features with a keen sense of abstract design in the arrangement of the figure, conveying with great clarity social status and giving clues to the sitter's profession. Though influenced by sixteeth-century Italian and Flemish portraits, their work remains nonetheless very French in its general sobriety.

THE SEVENTEENTH CENTURY

In the seventeenth century Italy continued to be a source of inspiration for French artists, most of whom were drawn to Rome, at that time the most exciting artistic centre in Europe. There, two Italian artists especially dominated the scene in the first decade of the century: Michelangelo Merisi da Caravaggio and Annibale Carracci. **Caravaggio** (d. 1610) often chose low-life subjects and treated them with remarkable realism, a realism that he extended to traditional religious subject matter and that he enhanced by using a strong, harsh lighting technique. Although he had to flee Rome in great haste under sentence of murder in 1606, Caravaggio had already had a profound effect on the art of the age, both in terms of subjects and in his uncompromising use of realism. Some French painters like **Moise Valentin** (c.1594–1632) worked in Rome and were directly influenced by Caravaggio; others, such as the great painter from Lorraine, **Georges de la Tour** (1593–1652), benefitted from his innovations at one remove, gaining inspiration from the Utrecht *Caravaggisti* who were active at the time in Holland. Starting with a descriptive realism in which naturalistic detail made for a varied painted surface, La Tour gradually simplified both forms and surfaces, producing deeply felt religious paintings in which figures appear to be carved out of the surrounding gloom by the magical light of a candle. Sadly, his output was very small – just some forty or so works in all. Low-life subjects and attention to naturalistic detail were also important aspects of the work of the **Le Nain Brothers**, especially **Louis** (1593–1648), who depicted with great sympathy, but never with sentimentality, the condition of the peasantry. He chose moments of inactivity or repose within the lives of the peasants and his paintings achieve timelessness and monumentality by their very stillness.

The other Italian artist of influence, the Bolognese **Annibale Carracci** (d. 1609), impressed French painters not only with his skill as a decorator but, more tellingly, with his ordered, balanced landscapes, which were to prove of prime importance for the development of the classical landscape in general, and in particular for those painted by **Claude Lorrain** (1600–82). Claude, who started life as a pastry cook, was born in Lorraine, near Nancy. He left France for Italy to practice his trade and worked in the household of a landscape painter in Rome, somehow persuading his master, who painted landscapes in the classical manner of Carracci, to let him abandon pastry for painting. Later he travelled to Naples, where the beauty of the harbour and bay made a lasting impression on him, the golden light of the southern port, and of Rome and its surrounding countryside, providing him with endless subjects of study which he drew, sketched and painted for the rest of his life. Claude's landscapes are airy compositions in which religious or mythological figures are lost within an idealised, Arcadian nature, bathed in a luminous, transparent light that, golden or silvery, lends a tranquil mood.

Landscapes, harsher and even more ordered, but also recalling the Arcadian mood of antiquity, were painted by the other French painter who elected to make Rome his home, **Nicolas Poussin** (1593–1665). Like Claude, Poussin selected his themes from the rich sources of Greek, Roman and Christian myths and stories, but unlike Claude, his figures are not subdued by nature but rather dominate it, in the tradition of the masters of the High Renaissance, such as Raphaël and Titian, whom he greatly admired. During the working out of a painting Poussin would make small models, arrange them on an improvised stage and then sketch the puppet scene – which may explain why his figures often have a still, frozen quality. Poussin only briefly returned to Paris, called by the king, Louis XIII, to undertake some large decorative works quite unsuited to his style or character. Back in Rome he refined a style that became increasingly classical and severe. Many other artists visited Italy but most returned to France, the luckiest to be employed at the court to boost the royal images of Louis XIII and XIV and the egos of their respective ministers, Richelieu and Colbert. **Simon Vouet** (1590–1649), **Charles Le Brun** (1619–90) and **Pierre Mignard** (1612–95) all performed that task with skill, often using ancient history and mythology to suggest flattering comparisons with the reigning monarch. The official aspect of their works was parallelled by the creation of the new **Academy of Painting and Sculpture** in 1648, an institution that dominated the arts in France for the next few hundred years, if only by the way artists reacted against it. Only **Philippe de Champaigne** (1602–74), a painter of Flemish origin, stands out at the time as remotely different, removed from the intrigues and pleasures of the court and instead strongly influenced by the teaching and moral code of Jansenism, a purist and severe form of the Catholic faith. The apparent simplicity and starkness of his portraits hides an unusually perceptive understanding of his sitters' personalities. But it was the more courtly, fun-loving portraits and paintings by such artists as Mignard which were to influence most of the art of the following century.

THE EARLY EIGHTEENTH CENTURY

The semi-official art encouraged by the foundation of the Academy became more frivolous and lighthearted in the eighteenth century. The court at Versailles lost its attractions and many patrons now were to be found in the hedonistic bourgeoisie and aristocracy living in Paris. History painting, as opposed to genre scenes or portraiture, retained its position of prestige, but at the same time the various categories began to merge and many artists tried their hands at landscape, genre, history, or decorative works, bringing aspects of one type into another. **Salons**, at which painters exhibited their works, were held with increasing frequency and bred a new, and some would say dangerous, phenomenon in the art world, the art critic. The philosopher **Diderot** was one of the first of these arbiters of taste, doers and undoers of reputations.

Possibly the most complex personality of the eighteenth century was **Jean-Antoine Watteau** (1684–1721). Primarily a superb draftsman, Watteau's use of soft and yet rich, light colours showed how much he was struck by the great seventeenth-century Flemish painter, Rubens. The open air scenes of flirtatious love painted by Rubens and by the eighteenth-century Venetian, Giorgione, provided Watteau with precedents for his own subtle depictions of dreamy couples (sometimes depictions from characters from the Italian Comedy) strolling in delicate, mythical landscapes. In some of these *Fêtes Galantes* and in pictures of solitary musicians or actors (*Gilles*), Watteau conveyed a mood of melancholy, loneliness and poignancy that was largely lacking in the works of his many imitators and followers (Nicolas Lancret, J. B. Pater). The work of **François Boucher** (1703–70) was probably more representative of the eighteenth century: the pleasure-seeking court of Louis XV found the lightness of morals and colours in his paintings immensely congenial. Boucher's virtuosity is seen at its best in his paintings of women, always rosy, young and fantasy-erotic. **Jean-Honoré Fragonard** (1732–1806) continued this exploration of licentious themes but with an exuberance, a richness of colour and a vitality (*The Swing*) that was a feast for the eyes and raised the subject to a glorification of love. Far more restrained were the paintings of **Jean-Baptiste-Siméon Chardin** (1699–1779), who specialised in homey genre scenes and still lifes, painted with a simplicity that belied a complex use of colours, shapes and space to promote a mood of stillness and tranquility. **Jean-Baptiste Greuze** (1725–1805) chose stories that anticipated reaction against the laxity of the times; the moral and sometimes sentimental character of his paintings was all-pervasive, reinforced by a stage-like composition well suited to cautionary tales.

NEOCLASSICISM

This new seriousness became more severe with the rise of **neoclassicism**, a movement for which purity and simplicity were essential components of the systematic depiction of edifying stories from the classical authors. Roman history and legends were the most popular subjects, and though **Jacques-Louis David** (1748–1825), a pupil of an earlier exponent of neoclassicism, J. M. Vien, conformed to that to a certain extent, he was different in that he was also keenly sensitive to the changing mood and philosophies of his time, and to the reaction against frivolity and self-indulgence. Many of his paintings are reflections of Republican ideals and of contemporary history, from the *Death of Marat* to events from the life of Napoléon who was his patron. For the Emperor and his family, David painted some of his most successful portraits – *Madame Recamier* is not only an exquisite example of David's controlled use of shapes and space and his debt to antique Rome, but can also be seen as a paradigm of neoclassicism. Two painters, **Jean-Antoine Gros** (1771–1835) and **Baron Gérard** (1770–1837), followed David closely in style and in themes (portraits, Napoleonic history and legend) but often with a touch of softness and heroic poetry that pointed the way to Romanticism.

Jean-August-Dominique Ingres (1780–1867) was a pupil of David; he also studied in Rome before coming back to Paris to develop the purity of line that was the essential and characteristic element of his art. His effective use of it to build up forms and bind compositions can be admired in conjunction with his recurrent theme of female nudes bathing, or in his magnificent and stately portraits that depict with subtle accuracy the nuances of social status.

ROMANTICISM

Completely opposed to the stress on drawing advocated by Ingres, two artists created, through their emphasis on colour, form and composition, pictures that look forward to the later part of the nineteenth century and the Impressionists. **Théodore Géricault** (1791–1824), whose short life was still dominated by the heroic vision of the Napoleonic era, explored with feeling dramatic themes of human suffering in such paintings as *The Raft of Medusa*, while his close contemporary, **Eugène Delacroix** (1798–1863), epitomised the **Romantic movement**, its search for emotions and its love of nature, power and change. Delacroix was deeply aware of tradition, and his art was influenced, visually and conceptually, by the great masters of the Renaissance and the seventeenth and eighteenth centuries. In many ways he may be regarded as the last great religious and decorative French painter, but through his technical virtuosity, freedom of brushwork and richness of colours, he can also be seen as the essential forerunner of the Impressionists. For Delacroix there was no conflict between colour and design: David and Ingres saw these elements as separate aspects of creation, but Delacroix used colours as the basis and structure of his designs. His technical freedom was partly due to his admiration for two English painters, John Constable and his close friend, Richard Parkes Bonington, with whom he shared a studio for a few months. Bonington especially had a freshness of approach to colour and a free handling of paint, both of which had a strong impact on Delacroix. His numerous themes ranged from intimate female nudes, often with mysterious and erotic Middle Eastern overtones, to studies of animals and hunting scenes. Ancient and contemporary history supplied him with some of his most harrowing and dramatic paintings: *The Massacre at Chios* was based on an event that took place during the Greek War of Independence from the Turks, and *Liberty Guiding the People* was painted to commemorate the Revolution of 1830. Both paintings were his personal response to contemporary events and the human tragedies they entailed.

Other painters working in the Romantic tradition were still haunted by the Napoleonic legends, as well as by North Africa (Algeria) and the Middle East, which had become better known to artists and patrons alike during the Napoleonic wars. These were the subjects of many paintings by **Horace Vernet** (1789–1863), **Jean-Louis-Ernest Meissonier** (1815–91), and **Théodore Chassériau** (1819–56). Among their contemporaries was **Honoré Daumier** (1808–79): very much an isolated figure, influenced by the boldness of approach of caricaturists, he was content to depict everyday subjects such as a laundress or a third class railway car – caustic commentaries on professions and politics that work as brilliant observations of the times.

THE NINETEENTH CENTURY

But some painters of the first part of the nineteenth century were fascinated by other themes. Nature, in its true state, unadorned by conventions, became a subject for study and running parallel to this was the realisation that painting could be the visual externalisation of the artist's own emotions and feelings. These two aspects, which until this time had only been very tentatively touched upon, were now more fully explored and led directly to the innovations of the Impressionists and later painters. **Jean-Baptiste-Camille Corot** (1796–1875) started to paint landscapes that were fresh, direct and influenced as much by the unpretentious and realistic country scenes of seventeenth-century Holland as by the balanced compositions of Claude. His loving and attentive studies of nature were much admired by later artists, including Monet.

At the same time a whole group of painters developed similar attitudes to landscape and nature. Helped greatly by the practical improvement of being able to buy oil paint in tubes rather than as unmixed pigments, they – known as the **Barbizon School** after the village on the outskirts of Paris round which they painted – soon discovered the joy and excitement of *plein-air* (open-air) painting. **Théodore Rousseau** (1812–67) was their nominal leader, his paintings of forest undergrowth and forest clearings displaying an intimacy that come from the immediacy of the image. **Charles-François Daubigny** (1817–78), like Rousseau, often infused a sense of drama into his landscapes. **Jean-François Millet** is perhaps the best-known associate of the Barbizon group, though he was more interested in the human figure than simple nature. Landscapes, however, were essential settings for his figures; indeed, his most famous pictures are those exploring the place of people in nature and their struggle to survive. *The Sower*, for instance, was a typical Millet theme, suggesting the heroic working life of the peasant. As is so often the case for painters touching on new themes or on ideas that are uncomfortable to the rich and powerful, Millet enjoyed little success during his lifetime, and his art was only widely recognised after his death.

The moralistic and romantic undertone in Millet's work was something that **Gustave Courbet** (1819–77) strove to avoid. Courbet was a socialist and his frank, outspoken attitude led to his being accused of taking part in the destruction of the column in place Vendôme in Paris after the outbreak of the Commune and, eventually, to his exile. After an initial resounding success in the Salon exhibition of 1849, he endured constant criticism from the academic world and patrons alike: scenes of ordinary life, such as the *Funeral at Orléans*, which he often chose to depict, were regarded as unsavoury and deliberately ugly. But Courbet had a deep admiration for the old masters, especially for Rembrandt and the Spanish painters of the seventeenth and eighteenth centuries, and his link with tradition was probably one of the underlying themes of his large masterpiece, *The Studio*, which was emphatically rejected by the jury of the 1855 Exposition Universelle, and in which Courbet portrayed himself, surrounded by his model, his friends, colleagues and admirers, among them the poet Baudelaire. Courbet subsequently decided to hold a private exhibition of some forty of his works, writing at the same time a manifesto explaining his intentions of being true to his vision of the world and of creating 'living art'. By writing the word **Realism** in large letters on the door leading to the exhibition he stated his intentions and gave a label to his art.

IMPRESSIONISM

Like Courbet, **Edouard Manet** (1832–83) was strongly influenced by Spanish painters, whose works had become more easily available to artists when a large collection belonging to the Orléans family was confiscated by the state in 1848. Unlike Courbet, though, he never saw himself as a socialist or indeed as a rebel or avant-garde painter, yet his technique and interpretation of themes was quite new and shocked as many people as it inspired. Manet used bold contrasts of light and very dark colours, giving his paintings a forcefulness that critics often took for a lack of sophistication. And his detractors saw much to decry in his reworking of an old subject originally treated by the sixteenth-century Venetian painter, Giorgione, *Le Déjeuner sur l'Herbe*. Manet's version was shocking because he placed naked and dressed figures together, and because the men were dressed in the costume of the day, implying a pleasure party too specifically contemporary to be 'respectable'.

Manet was not interested in painting moral lessons, however, and some of his most successful pictures are reflections of ordinary life in bars and public places, where respectability, as understood by the late-nineteenth-century bourgeoisie, was certainly lacking. To Manet, painting was to be enjoyed for its own sake and not as a tool for moral instruction – in itself an outlook on the role of art that was quite new, not to say revolutionary, and marked a definite break with the paintings of the past. With Manet the basis of our present expectations and understanding of modern art was set down.

Although it is doubtful whether Manet either wanted or expected to assume the role of leader, **Claude Monet** (1840–1926) looked to the older artist as the painter in whose works the principles of **Impressionism** were first formulated. Born in Le Havre, Monet came in contact with **Eugène Boudin** (1824–98) whose colourful beach scenes anticipated the way the Impressionists approached colour. He then went to Paris to study under Charles Gleyre, a respected teacher in whose studio he met many of the people with whom he formulated his ideas. Monet soon discovered that, for him, light and the way in which it builds up forms and creates an infinity of colours was the element that governed all representations. Under the impact of Manet's bright hues and his unconventional attitude, 'art for art's sake', Monet soon began using pure colours side by side, blended together to create areas of brightness and shade.

In 1874, a group of some thirty artists exhibited together for the first time. Among them were some of the best-known names of this period of French art: Dégas, Monet, Renoir, Pissarro. One of Monet's paintings was entitled *Impression: Sun Rising*, a title that was singled out by the critics to ridicule the colourful, loose, and unacademic style of these young artists. Overnight they became, derisively, the 'Impressionists'. **Camille Pissarro** (1830–1903) was slightly older than most of them and seems to have played the part of an encouraging father-figure, always keenly aware of any new development or new talent. Not a great innovator himself, Pissarro was a very gifted artist whose use of Impressionist technique was supplemented by a lyrical feeling for nature and its seasonal changes. But it was really with **Monet** that Impressionist theory ran its full course: he studied endlessly the impact of light on objects and the way in which it reveals colours. To understand this phenomenon better, Monet painted the same motif again and again under different conditions of light, at different times of the day, and in different seasons, producing whole series of paintings such as *Hay Stacks, Poplars*, and, much later, his *Waterlilies*. In the late 1870s and the early 1880s many other artists helped formulate the new style, but few remained true to its principles for very long. **Auguste Renoir** (1841–1919), who started life as a painter of porcelain, was swept away by Monet's ideas for a while, but soon felt the need to look again at the old masters and to emphasise the importance of drawing to the detriment of colour. Renoir regarded the representation of the female nude as the most taxing and rewarding subject that an artist could tackle. Like Boucher in the eighteenth century, Renoir's nudes are luscious, but they are rarely, if ever, erotic. They have a healthy, uncomplicated quality that was, in his later paintings, to become cloyingly, almost overpoweringly, sickly and sweet. Better were his portraits of women fully clothed, both for their obvious and innate sympathy and for their keen sense of design.

Edgar Degas (1834–1917) was yet another artist who, although he exhibited with the Impresssionists, did not follow their precepts very closely. The son of a rich banker, he was trained in the tradition of Ingres: design and drawing were an integral part of his art, and whereas Monet was fascinated mainly by light, Degas wanted to express movement in all its forms. His pictures are vivid expressions of the body in action, usually straining under fairly exacting circumstances – dancers and circus *artistes* were among his favourite subjects, as well as more mundane depictions of laundresses and other working women. Like so many artists of the day, Degas had his imagination fired by the discovery of **Japanese prints**, which could for the first time be seen in quantity. These provided him with new ideas of composition, not least in their asymmetry of design and the use of large areas of unbroken colour. **Photography**, too, had an impact on artists, if only because it liberated them finally from the task of producing accurate, exacting descriptions of the world.

Degas's extraordinary gift as a draftsman was matched only by that of the Provençal aristocrat **Henri de Toulouse-Lautrec** (1864–1901). Toulouse-Lautrec, who had broken both his legs as a child, was unusually small, a physical deformity that made him particularly sensitive to free and vivacious movements. A great admirer of Degas, he chose similar themes: people in cafés and theatres, working women and variety dancers all figured large in his work. But unlike Degas, Toulouse-Lautrec looked at more than the body, and his work is scattered with social comment, sometimes sardonic and bitter. In his portrayal of Paris prostitutes, there is sympathy and kindness, and to study them better he lived in a brothel for some time, revealing in his paintings the weariness and sometimes gentleness of these women rather than the squalor that might have been expected.

POST-IMPRESSIONISM

Though a rather vague term, as it's difficult to date exactly when the backlash against Impressionism took place, **Post-Impressionism** represents in many ways a return to more formal concepts of painting – in composition, in attitudes to subject, and in drawing. **Paul Cézanne** (1839–1906), for one, associated only very briefly with the Impressionists and spent most of his working life in relative isolation, obsessed with rendering, as objectively as possible, the essence of form. He saw objects as basic shapes – cylinders, cones, etc. – and tried to give the painting a unity of texture that would force the spectator to view it not so much as representation of the world but rather as an entity in its own right, as an object as real and dense as the objects surrounding it. It was this striving for pictorial unity that led him to cover the entire surface of the picture with small, equal brushstrokes which made no distinction between the textures of a tree, a house, or the sky. The detached, unemotional way in which Cézanne painted was not unlike that of the seventeenth-century artist, Poussin, and he found a contemporary parallel in the work of **Georges Seurat**. Seurat (1859–91) was fascinated by current theories on light and colour, and he attempted to apply them in a systematic way, creating different shades and tones by placing tiny spots of pure colour side by side, which the eye could in turn fuse together to see the colours mixed out of their various components. This **pointillist** technique also had the effect of giving monumentality to everyday scenes of contemporary life.

While Cézanne, Seurat, and, for that matter, the Impressionists, sought to represent the outside world objectively, several other artists – the **Symbolists** – were seeking a different kind of truth, through the subjective experience of fantasy and dreams. **Gustav Moreau** (1840–98) represented, in complex paintings, the intricate worlds of the romantic fairy tale, his visions expressed in a wealth of naturalistic details. The style of **Puvis de Chavannes** (1824–98) was more restrained and more obviously concerned with design and the decorative. And a third artist, **Odilon Redon** (1840–1916), produced some weird and visionary graphic work that especially intrigued Symbolist writers; his less frequent works in colour belong to the later part of his life.

The subjectivity of the Symbolists was of great importance to the art of **Paul Gauguin** (1843–1903). He started life as a stockbroker who collected Impressionist paintings, a Sunday artist who gave up his job in 1883 to dedicate himself to painting. During his stay in Pont-Aven in Brittany, he worked with a number of artists who called themselves **the Nabis, Paul Serusier** and **Emile Bernard** among them; he began exploring ways of expressing concepts and emotions by means of large areas of colour and powerful forms, and developing a unique style that was heavily indebted to his knowledge of Japanese prints and of the tapestries and stained glass of medieval art. His search for the primitive expression of primitive emotions took him eventually to the South Sea islands and Tahiti, where he found some of his most inspiring subjects and painted some of his best known canvases. A similar derivation from Symbolist art and a wish to exteriorise emotions and ideas by means of strong colours, lines, and shapes underlies the work of **Vincent Van Gogh** (1853–1890), a Dutch painter who came to live in France. Like Gauguin, with whom he had an admiring but stormy friendship, Van Gogh started painting relatively late in life, lightening his palette in Paris under the influence of the Impressionists, and then heading south to Arles where, struck by the harshness of the Mediterranean light, he turned out such frantic, expressionistic pieces as *The Reaper* and *Wheatfield with Crows*. In all his later pictures the paint is thickly laid on in increasingly abstract patterns that follow the shapes and tortuous paths of his deep inner melancholy.

Both Gauguin and Van Gogh saw objects and colours as means of representing ideas and subjective feelings. **Edouard Vuillard** (1868–1940) and **Pierre Bonnard** (1867–1947) combined this with Cézanne's insistence on unifying the surface and texture of the picture. The result was, in both cases, paintings of often intimate scenes in which figures and objects are blended together in a series of complicated patterns. In some of Vuillard's works especially, people dressed in checked material, for example, seem to merge into the flowered wallpaper behind them, and in the paintings of Bonnard, the glowing design of the canvas itself is as important as what it's trying to represent.

THE TWENTIETH CENTURY

The twentieth century kicked off to a colourful start with the **Fauvist** exhibition of 1905, an appropriately anarchic beginning to a century which, in France more than anywhere, was to see radical changes in attitudes towards painting. The painters who took part in the exhibition included, most influentially, **Henri Matisse** (1869–1954), **André Derain** (1880–1954), **Georges Rouault** (1871–1958) and **Albert Marquet** (1875–1947), and they were quickly nicknamed the Fauves (Wild Beasts) for their use of bright, wild colours that often bore no relation whatsoever to the reality of the object depicted. Skies were just as likely green as blue since, for the Fauves, colour was a way of composing, of structuring a picture, and not necessarily a reflection of real life.

But Fauvism was just the beginning: the first decades of the twentieth century were times of intense excitement and artistic activity in Paris, and painters and sculptors from all over Europe flocked to the capital to take part in the liberation from conventional art that individuals and groups were gradually instigating. **Pablo Picasso** (1881–1973) was one of the first, arriving here in 1900 from Spain and soon thereafter starting work on his first *Blue Period* paintings, which describe the sad and squalid life of intinerant actors in tones of blue. Later, while Matisse was experimenting with colours and their decorative potential, Picasso came under the sway of Cézanne and his organisation of forms into geometrical shapes. He also learned from 'primitive', and especially African, sculpture and out of these studies came a painting that heralded a definite new direction, not only for Picasso's own style, but for the whole of modern art – *Les Demoiselles d'Avignon*. Executed in 1907, this painting combined Cézanne's analysis of forms with the visual impact of African masks, and it was from this semi-abstract picture that Picasso went on to develop the theory of **Cubism**, inspiring artists such as **Georges Braque** (1882–1963) and **Juan Gris** (1887–1927), another Spaniard, and formulating a whole new movement. The Cubists' aim was to depict objects not so much as they saw them but rather as they knew them to be: a bottle, a guitar were shown from the front, from the side, and from the back as if the eye could take in all at once every facet and plane of the object. Braque and Picasso first analyzed forms into these facets (analytical Cubism), then gradually reduced them to series of colours and shapes (synthetic Cubism), among which a few recognisable symbols such as letters, fragments of newspaper, and numbers appeared. The complexity of different planes overlapping one another made the deciphering of Cubist paintings sometimes difficult, and the very last phase of Cubism tended increasingly towards abstraction.

Spin-offs of Cubism were many: such movements as **Orphism**, headed by **Robert Delaunay** (1885–1941), who experimented not with objects but with the colours of the spectrum; and **Futurism**, which evolved first in Italy, then in Paris, and explored movement and the bright new technOlogy of the industrial age. **Fernand Léger** (1881–1955), one of the main exponents of the so-called School of Paris, had also become acquainted with modern machinery during World War I, and he exploited his fascination for its smoothness and power to create geometric and monumental compositions of technical imagery that were indebted to both Cézanne and Cubism. The war meanwhile had affected many artists: in Switzerland **Dada** was born out of the scorn artists felt for the petty bourgeois and nationalistic values that had led to the bloodshed, a nihilistic movement that sought to knock down all traditionally accepted ideas. It was best exemplified in the work of the Frenchman **Marcel Duchamp** (1887–1968), who selected ready-made, everyday objects and elevated them, without modification, to the rank of works of art by pulling them out of their ordinary context, or defaced such sacred cows as the Mona Lisa by decorating her with a moustache and an obscene caption.

Dada was also a literary movement, and through one of its main poets, André Breton, it led to the inception of **Surrealism**. It was the unconscious and its dark unchartered territories that interested the Surrealists: they derived much of their imagery from Freud and even experimented in words and images with free-association techniques. Strangely enough, most of the 'French' Surrealists were foreigners, primarily the German **Max Ernst** (1891–1976) and the Spaniards **Yves Tanguy** (1900–55) and **Salvador Dali** (1904-89). Mournful landscapes of weird, often terrifying images evoked the landscape of nightmares in often very precise details and with an anguish that went on to influence artists for years to come. Picasso, for instance, shocked by the massacre of the Spanish town of *Guernica* in 1936, drew greatly from Surrealism to produce the disquieting figures of his painting of the same name.

World War II put an end to the prominence of Paris as the artistic melting pot of Europe. Painters had rushed there at the beginning of the twentieth century and after World War I, contributing by their individuality, originality and different nationalities to the richness and constant renewal of artistic endeavour, but at the beginning of World War II they emigrated to the United States. And although many have since drifted back, artistic leadership has remained in New York. Still, desertion of Paris should not obscure the fact that over a span of some six centuries, French painters or painters trained in France produced some of the most significant monuments of European painting.

Ann Rook

ARCHITECTURE

In common with all former provinces of Rome, it is to that city's model of organised authority that France's official architecture has returned most readily. A number of substantial Roman building works survive. In Nîmes you can see the Maison Carrée and the Temple of Diana, one of four vaulted Roman temples in Europe. Gateways remain at Autun and Reims, and amphitheatres can be seen at Nîmes and Arles. The Pont du Gard aqueduct at Nîmes is still a magnificent and ageless monument of civil engineering.

CAROLINGIAN AND ROMANESQUE

The **Carolingian** dynasty of Charlemagne attempted a revival of the symbols of civilised authority by recourse to Roman or 'Romanesque' models. Of this era, practically nothing remains visible, though the motifs of arch and vault are carried on in their simplest forms; and the semicircular apse and the basilican plan of nave and aisles persists as the basis of the succeeding phases of Christian architecture. An interesting anomaly is the plan of the church of **St-Front** at Périgueux, a copy of St. Mark's in Venice, brought by trading influence west along the Garonne in the early twelfth century.

Elsewhere development may be divided roughly north–south of the Loire. Southern **Romanesque** is naturally more Roman, with stone barrel vaults, aisleless naves and domes. **St-Trophime at Arles** (1150) has a porch directly derived from Roman models and, with the church at St-Gilles nearby, exhibits a delight in carved ornament peculiar to the south at this time. The **cathedral at Angoulême** typifies the use of all these elements.

The south, too, was the readiest route for the introduction of new cultural developments and it is here that the pointed arch and vault first appear – from Saracen sources – in churches such as **Notre-Dame at Avignon**, **Autun cathedral,** and **Ste-Madeleine at Vézelay** (1089–1206), which contains the earliest pointed cross vault in France.

In the northern region the nave with aisles is more usual, together with the development of twin western towers to mask the end of the aisles. The **Abbaye-aux-Hommes** at Caen (1066–77) is typical. It contains the elements later developed as 'Gothic', in piers, pillars, buttresses, arcades, ribbed vaults and spires. The best examples may be found in Normandy, and it is from here, with the introduction of the pointed arch from the south, that the Gothic style developed.

GOTHIC

The reasons behind the development of the **Gothic style** lie in the pursuit of sensations of the sublime; to achieve great height without apparently great weight would seem to imitate religious ambition. Its development in the north is partly due to the availability of good building stone and soft stone for carving, but perhaps more to the growth of royal aspiration and power based in the Ile de France, which, allied with the papacy, stimulated the building of the great **cathedrals of Paris, Bourges, Chartres, Laon, Le Mans, Reims and Amiens** in the late twelfth and thirteenth centuries. The Gothic phase began with the building of the choir of the **abbey of St-Denis** near Paris in 1140 to run through to the end of the fifteenth century. Architecturally, it encompasses the development of wider, traceried windows of coloured glass, filling the wall spaces liberated by the refinement of vertical structure; the 'rose' or wheel is an early and especially French feature in window tracery. The glass at Chartres shows better than anywhere the concerted architectural effect of these developments. Another distinctive element is the flying buttress outside the walls to resist the outward push of the vaulting.

In the south, as at Albi and Angers, the great churches are generally broader and simpler in plan and external appearance, with aisles often almost as high as the nave. Many secular buildings survive – some of the most notable the work of Viollet-le-Duc, the preeminent nineteenth-century restorer – and even whole towns, for example **Carcassone** and **Aigues Mortes; Avignon** has the **bridge** and the **papal palace.** Castles, of necessity, lent themselves less to the disappearing walls of the Gothic style. The **Château de Pierrefonds**, as restored by Viollet, may be taken as typical. The walls of many others disappeared by force, not whim, as gunpowder made them obsolete and a more settled and subjugated order led to the development of château-palaces, such as **Châteaudun** (1441) and **Blois**. The **Château de Josselin** in Brittany is a marvellous example of the smaller fortresses that became common towards the end of the Gothic period. A series of colonial settlements, the ***bastides*** of the English occupation, remain in the Dordogne region and are a refreshing antidote to triumphal French bombast.

RENAISSANCE

Quite early in the sixteenth century the influence of the new style of the Italian Renaissance began to appear. Coupled with the persistence of Gothic traditions and the necessity of steep roofs and tall chimneys in a

French climate, it appears immediately 'Frenchified' rather than in its pure imported form. The châteaux of kings and courtiers round Paris and in the Loire valley, such as **Blois, Chambord, Chenonceau and Fontainebleau**, exemplify this style. There is a wholly un-Italian concentration of interest on the skyline and an elaboration of detail in the facades at the expense of the clear modelling of form. With the passing of time, however, the style became more purely classical.

The Louvre in Paris and the Château de Blois are notable examples of the developing **classicism**. The wing of the **Château de Blois** containing the famous staircase designed for François I in 1515 shows the beginning of an emphasis on horizontal lines and an overlay of Italian motifs on a basically Gothic form. The elevations, designed by **Mansart** in 1635, though distinctively French, are just as typically classical.

The **Louvre** even more embodies the whole history of the classical style in France, having been worked over by all the grand names of French architecture from Lescot in the early sixteenth century, via François Mansart and Claude Perrault in the seventeenth, to the later years of the nineteenth century. A recent turning point is the controversial work of **I. M. Pei** to break the bonds of Rome with the power of his pyramid extension.

It is unfortunate that the Renaissance style in France is chiefly seen in such structures as the Louvre and Versailles, which because of their scale can scarcely be experienced as buildings. That this is the case is largely due to the developing despotism and concentration of power under Louis XIII and XIV. But there was a lighter side to this. François Mansart, at **Blois** and **Maisons Lafitte** (1640), shows a certain suavity and elegance, which appears again in the eighteenth century in the townhouses of the **Rococo** period, the generally reticent exteriors of which bely the vivacity and charm of the private life within.

On the other hand, **Claude Perrault** (1613–88), who designed the great colonnaded east front of the Louvre, gives an austere face to the official architecture of despotism, magnificent but far too imperial to be much enjoyed by common mortals. The high-pitched roofs, which had been almost universal until then, are replaced here by the classical balustrade and pediment, the style grand but cold and supremely secular. Art and architecture were at the time organised by boards and academies, and in the latter style and employment were strictly controlled by royal direction. Between 1643 and 1774 France was governed by two monarchs, who both ruled by the same maxim – absolute power. With such a limitation of ideas at the source of patronage, it is hardly surprising that there was a certain dullness to the era, at least in the acknowledged monuments of French architecture.

BAROQUE AND ROCOCO

In a similar way to the preceding century, the churches of the **seventeenth and eighteenth centuries** have a coldness quite different from the German and Flemish Baroque or the Italian. When the Renaissance style first appeared in the early sixteenth century there was no great need for new church building, the country being so well endowed from the Gothic centuries. **St-Etienne-du-Mont** (1517–1620) and **St-Eustache** (1532–89), both in Paris, show how old forms persisted with only an overlay of the new style. It is with the Jesuits in the seventeenth century that the church embraced the new style to combat the forces of rational disbelief. In Paris the churches of the **Sorbonne** (1653) and **Val-de-Grâce** (1645) exemplify this, as do a good number of other grandiose churches in the **Baroque** style, through **Les Invalides** at the end of the seventeenth century to the **Panthéon** of the late eighteenth century. Here is the church triumphant rather than the state, but no more beguiling.

The architect of Les Invalides was **Jules Hardouin Mansart**, a product of the academy, who also greatly extended the palace of **Versailles** and so created the cinemascope view of France with that seemingly endless horizon of royalty. As an antidote to this pomposity, the **Petit Trianon at** Versailles is as refreshing now as it was to Louis XV, who had it built in 1762 as a place of escape for his mistress. And even more so this is true of that other pearl formed of the grit of boredom in the enclosed world of Versailles – **La Petite Ferme,** where Marie-Antoinette played at being a milkmaid, which epitomises the Arcadian and 'picturesque' fantasy of the painters Boucher and Fragonard.

The lightness and charm that was undermining official grandeur with Arcadian fancies and rococo decoration was, however, snuffed out by the Revolution. There is no real Revolutionary architecture, as the necessity of order and authority soon asserted itself and an autocracy every bit as absolute returned with Napoléon, drawing on the old grand manner but with a stronger trace of the stern old Roman. One architect, **Claude Ledoux**, was highly original and influential, both in England and Germany. And the visionary millennialist **Boullée** could also be said to be a child of revolutionary times, though it is likely that such men were inspired as much by the rediscovered plainness of the Greek Doric order as by radical politics. In Paris it was not the democratic Doric but the imperial Corinthian order that re-emerged triumphant in the church of the **Madeleine** (1806) and, with the **Arc de Triomphe** like some colossal paperweight, reimposed the authority of academic architecture, in contrast to the fancy dress architecture of contemporary Regency England.

THE NINETEENTH CENTURY

The restoration of legitimate monarchy after the **fall of Napoléon** stimulated a revival of interest in older Gothic and early Renaissance styles, which offered a symbol of dynastic reassurance not only to the state but also to the newly rich. So in the private and commercial architecture of the nineteenth century these earlier styles predominate – in mine-owners' villas and bankers' headquarters. By the time we arrive at the mid-nineteenth century, a neo-Baroque strain had established itself, a style exemplified by Charles Garnier's **Opéra** in Paris (1861–74), which, under the heading of Second Empire and with its associations of voluptuous good living, seductive painting and general 'ooh-la-la', provides probably the most persistent image of France among the non-French – though you should avoid being blinded by Puritan distaste to the splendid spatial and decorative sensations that the style can arouse. Nineteenth-century French buildings are due for a reassessment and keener appreciation.

In addition to the correct, official classicism and the robust, exuberant and commercial Baroque, there is a third strand running through the nineteenth century that was ultimately more fruitful. The rational engineering approach, embodied in the official **School of Roads and Bridges** and invigorated by the teaching of Viollet-le-Duc who reinterpreted Gothic style as pure structure, led to the development of new structural techniques out of which 'modern' architectural style was born. Iron was the first significant new material, often used in imitation of Gothic forms and destined to be developed as an individual architectural style in America. In the **Eiffel Tower** (1889) France set up a potent symbol of things to come.

A more significantly French development was in the use of reinforced concrete towards the end of the century, most notably by **Auguste Perret** whose 1903 apartment house at 25 rue Franklin, Paris 16e, turns the concrete structure into a visible virtue and breaks with conventional facades. Changes in the patterns of work and travel were making the need for new urban planning very acute in such cities as Paris. Perret and other **modernists** were all for the high-rise buildings that were going to better the haphazard layouts in America by a rational integration to new street systems. Some of their designs for gigantic skyscraper avenues and suburban rings now look like totalitarian horror movie sets. But it was tradition, not charity, that blocked their projects at the time.

THE TWENTIETH CENTURY

The greatest proponent of the super New York scale, who also had genuine, if mistaken, concern for how people lived, was **Le Corbusier**, the most famous twentieth-century French architect. His stature may now appear diminished by the ascendancy of a blander style in concrete boxing, as well as by the significant technical and social failures of his buildings and his total disregard for historic streets and monuments. But while his manifesto, *'Vers une architecture moderne'*, sounds like a call to arms for a new and revolutionary movement, Le Corbusier would be perhaps more fairly assessed as the original, inimitable and highly individual artist he undoubtedly was. You should try to see some of his work – there's the **Cité Radieuse** in Marseille and plenty in Paris – to make up your own mind about the man largely responsible for changing the face and form of buildings throughout the world.

One respect in which Paris at the turn of the century lagged behind London, Glasgow, Chicago and New York, was in **underground transport**. First proposed in the 1870s, it took twenty years of furious debate before the Paris *métro* was finally realised in 1900. The design of the entrances was as controversial as every other aspect of the system, but the first commission went to Hector Guimard, renowned for his variations on the then current fashion in style. The whirling metal railings, Art Nouveau lettering and bizarre antennae-like orange lamps were his creation. But conservatives were not amused when it came to sites such as the Opéra: **Charles Garnier**, architect of that edifice, demanded classical marble and bronze porticoes for every station, and his line was followed, on a less grandiose scale, wherever the métro steps surfaced by a major monument. Thus Guimard was out of a job. Some of the early ones remain (**Place des Abbesses**, 18e, is one), as do some of the white-tiled interiors, replaced after World War II in central stations by bright paint with matching seats and display cases.

Art Nouveau designs also found their way on to buildings – the early department stores in Paris are the best example – but the new materials and simple geometry of the modern or International Style favoured the Art Deco look; again, you're most likely to come across them in the capital.

Skipping the miserable 1950s and 1960s buildings everywhere, France again becomes one of the most exciting patrons of international architecture in **present times**. The **Centre Beaubourg**, by **Renzo Piano and Richard Rogers**, derided, adored and visited by millions, maximises space by putting the service elements usually concealed in walls and floors on the outside. The visible ducts, cables and pipes are painted in accordance with the colour code of architectural plans. You might think the whole thing is a professional 'in' joke, but Beaubourg is one of the great contemporary buildings in western Europe – for its originality, popularity and practicality.

In **housing**, new styles and forms are to be seen in city suburbs and vacation resorts, many of them disastrous and visually unappealing but interesting to look at when you don't have to live there. The latest state-funded projects confirm French seriousness about innovative design – in Paris, the pyramid in the Louvre and the **Porte de la Villette** complex. The latter also exemplifies a new move away from demolition to clever restoration, in this case nineteenth-century abbatoirs and market halls. Throughout the country you'll see far older period streets, medieval and Renaissance, that look as though they've never been touched. More often than not, the restoration has been carried out by the **Maisons de Compagnonage**, the old craft guilds which have maintained traditional building skills, handing them down as of old from master to apprentice (and never to women), in addition to taking on new industrial skills.

Above all, though, bear in mind the extent and variety of architecture in France and don't feel intimidated by the established sights. If the empty grandeur of the Loire châteaux is oppressive, there are numerous smaller country houses open to the public, and such municipal buildings as the **Hôtels de Ville** tend to offer some charm or amusement, even in the smallest towns. It is also possible in France to experience whole towns as consistent places of architecture, not only Carcassonne and Aigues Mortes, Dinan and Nancy, but villages off the main roads in which time seems to have stopped long ago. And, besides, from any hotel bedroom, you can simply delight in what Le Corbusier called 'the magnificent play of forms seen in light', in the movement of morning sunlight over ordinary provincial tiles and chimneys.

Robin Salmon

BOOKS

TRAVEL

Donald Horne *The Great Museum: The Representation of History* (Pluto Press, 1984, £5.95). Original, stimulating analysis of the role of tourism, how it reflects history and ideology, and how we're affected by it. Not the most obvious book to carry around France but if you take it you'll read it, for the comments on Romanesque architecture, Verdun and the battle sites, revolutionary mementos . . . and 101 other insights.

Edwin Mullins *The Pilgrimage to Santiago* (1974, o/p). The main medieval pilgrim route to the shrine of St. James (Santiago) began in Paris on Rue St-Jacques. Mullins retraces the *Chemin* in this book, details the bizarre pilgrim-industry that peaked in the twelfth to fifteenth centuries, and points you to the churches along the way. Fascinating stuff, treating architecture (rightfully) as social history.

Freda White *Three Rivers of France* (Faber & Faber, 1984, £4.95), *West of the Rhone* (o/p), *Ways of Aquitaine* (o/p). Freda White spent a great deal of time in France in the 1950s – before tourism came along to the backwater communities that were her interest. These are all evocative books, slipping in the history and culture painlessly, if not always too accurately.

Rodney Gallop *A Book of the Basques* (1930, £8.95). Still the classic study of Basque life before the twentieth century destroyed its particularity, by an English clergyman who learned Basque and adopted the country as his own.

Eric Newby *On the Shores of the Mediterranean* (Picador, 1984, £4.95). Not Newby's best, and not largely about France, but with a short and wonderful chapter on dinner at the *Negresco* in Nice. Compulsive and vicarious pleasures.

Robert Louis Stevenson *Travels with a Donkey* (Century, £4.95). Mile-by-mile account of Stevenson's twelve-day trek in the Haute Loire and Cévennes uplands with a donkey, Modestine. One of the more readable 'travel classics' on France, and a journey interestingly reworked by Robert Holmes in *Footsteps* (Penguin £3.99). Persistent devotees of Stevenson's footpaths – and there are a surprising amount of both in France – might be interested in his first book, *Inland Voyage*, on the waterways of the north.

Laurence Sterne *A Sentimental Journey Through France and Italy* (Oxford University Press, 1984, £1.95). By the author of *Tristram Shandy*, the first bit of intentionally mad novel-writing. Despite the title, he never gets further south than Versailles.

Henry James *A Little Tour in France* (Penguin, £4.50). **Tobias Smollett** *Travels through France and Italy* (Oxford University Press, £4.95). **Hilaire Belloc** *The Pyrenees* (o/p). **Stendhal** *Travels in the South of France* (J. Calder, £9.95. The big names. But not all of them a lot more than that.

HISTORY

THE MIDDLE AGES

Emmanuel Le Roy Ladurie *Montaillou* (Penguin, 1984, £5.95). Village gossip of who's sleeping with whom, tales of trips to Spain and details of work, all extracted by the Inquisition from Cathar peasants of the eastern Pyrenees in the fourteenth century, and stored away until the last decade in the Vatican archives. Though academic and heavygoing in places, most of this book reads like an early novel.

Barbara Tuchman *A Distant Mirror* (Ballantine Books, 1980, o/p). The history of the fourteenth century – plagues, wars, peasant uprisings and crusades – told through the life of a sympathetic French nobleman whose career takes him through England, Italy and Byzantium and finally ends in a Turkish prison.

J. H. Huizinga *The Waning of the Middle Ages* (Penguin, £5.95). Primarily a study of the culture of the Burgundian and French courts – but a masterpiece that goes far beyond this, building up meticulous detail to recreate the whole life and the mentality of the fourteenth and fifteenth centuries.

Natalie Zemon Davis *The Return of Martin Guerre* (Harvard University Press, 1983, £11.95). A vivid account of peasant life in the sixteenth century and a perplexing and titillating hoax in the Pyrenean village of Artigat. Even better than the movie.

M. Uderzo and R. Goscinny *Asterix and the Goths* (Hodder, 1975, £2.95). Take it as present day French attitudes to their history, or as accurate portrayal of the Roman conquest – either way it's great reading.

REVOLUTIONS

Christopher Hibbert *The French Revolution* (Penguin, 1982, £5.95). Good, concise popular history of the period and events.

Thomas Paine *The Rights of Man* (Penguin, £2.99). Written in 1791 in response to English conservatives' views on the situation in France, this reasoned and passionate tract expresses the ideas of both the American and French revolutions. It was immediately banned on publication, and its author charged with treason, but enough copies had crossed the channel and been translated for Paine to be elected to the Convention by the people of Calais.

Gustave Flaubert *A Sentimental Education* (Penguin, 1970, £4.50). The novel that gives the best idea of what it was like to live in Paris through the 1848 revolution.

Karl Marx *Surveys from Exile* (Penguin, £3.95). *On the Paris Commune* (Lawrence and Wishart, U.K.). 'Surveys' includes Marx's speeches and articles around the time of the 1848 revolution, including an analysis, riddled with jokes, of Napoleon III's rise to power. 'Paris Commune', more rousing prose, has a history of the commune by Engels.

Alfred Cobban *A History of Modern France* (3 vols.: 1715–99, 1799–1871 and 1871–1962; Pelican Books, £3.95–4.50 each). Complete and very readable account of the main political, social and economic strands in French history from the death of Louis XIV to mid–de Gaulle.

NINETEENTH AND TWENTIETH CENTURIES

Theodore Zeldin *France 1845–1945* (Oxford University Press, 5 vols., £5.95–6.95). Five thematic volumes on all matters French. All good reads.

David Thomson *Democracy in France Since 1870* (Oxford University Press, o/p). An enquiry, sympathetic to the left, into why a country with such a strong socialist tradition should have had so many reactionary governments.

Alexander Worth *France 1940–55* (Beacon Press, Boston). Extremely good and emotionally engaged portrayal of the most taboo period in French history – the Occupation, followed by the Cold War and colonial struggle years in which the same political tensions and heart-searchings were at play.

Max Bloch *Strange Defeat* (Norton, 1968, New York). Moving personal study of the reasons for France's defeat and subsequent caving-in to fascism. Found among the papers of this Sorbonne historian after his death at the hands of the Gestapo in 1942.

Shari Benstock *Women of the Left Bank: Paris 1900-1940* (Virago, 1987, £9.99). Somewhat dry, academic style, but full of information about the crucial female contribution to the expatriate literary scene in Paris, and the founding of literary modernism.

SOCIETY AND POLITICS

John Ardagh *France Today* (Penguin, 1988, £6.99). Comprehensive overview up to 1987 – covering food, film education and holidays as well as politics and economics – from a social democrat and journalistic position. Very useful on details, lousy on feminism, and not a bad book to take to the seaside.

Theodore Zeldin *The French* (Collins, 1988, £6.95). A coffeetable book without the pictures, based on the author's extensive conversations with an extremely wide variety of people about money, sex, phobias, parents and everything else.

D. L. Hanley, A. P. Kerr and N. H. Waites *Contemporary France* (Methuen, 1984, o/p). Well-written and accurate academic textbook if you want to fathom the practicalities of power in France – the constitution, parties, trade unions, new policies, etc. It also has an excellent opening chapter on the period since the war.

Simone de Beauvoir *The Second Sex* Picador, 1988, £7.95). One of the prime texts of western feminism, written in 1949, covering women's inferior status in history, literature, mythology, psychoanalysis, philosophy and everyday life. The style is dry and intellectual but the subject matter easily compensates.

Claire Duchen *Feminism in France: from May '68 to Mitterrand* (Routledge, 1986, £8.95). Charts the evolution of the women's movement through to its present crisis, clarifying the divergent political stances and feminist theory that informs the various feminist groups, and placing them in the wider French political context.

Jolyon Howorth *The Politics of Peace* (Merlin Press, 1985, £1.95). Short, to the point, and utterly readable analysis of why the French peace movement is so behind its European neighbours.

Graham Greene *J'Accuse* (Bodley Head, 1982, £2.95). Greene's blistering attack on corruptions in Nice, for which, he says, he now has to sleep with a gun under his pillow.

Roland Barthes *Mythologies* (Paladin, 1973, £3.50). Completely brilliant description of how the ideas, prejudices and contradictions of French thought and behavior manifest themselves – in food, wine, cars, travel guides and other cultural offerings.

The New State of the World Atlas (Pluto, 1989, £6.95), One of the best reference books going not just for France, but for any country whose vital statistics you need to know: how much they pollute the earth; their wealth; their record on human rights and just about every other depressing detail.

VISUAL ARTS

Edward Lucie-Smith *A Concise History of French Painting* (Thames & Hudson, £5.95) If you're after an art reference book, this will do as well as any . . . though there are of course hundreds of books on particular French art movements. (Thames and Hudson do useful introductions to Impressionism, Expressionism, Symbolism etc.)

John Berger *Ways of Seeing* (BBC, 1972, £4.95). A book that can change how you look at paintings without making you feel ignorant or insensitive to the art – much of it, here, French.

Kenneth J. Comant *Carolingian and Romanesque Architecture, 800– 1200* (Penguin, 1974, £18.95). Good European study with concentration on Cluny and the Saint Jacques pilgrim route.

Norma Evenson *Paris: A Century of Change, 1878–1978* (Yale University Press, 1981, £17.95). The other end of the scale: a large illustrated volume that makes the development of urban planning and the fabric of Paris an enthralling subject – mainly because the author's ultimate concern is always with people, not panoramas.

Jacques-Henri Lartigue *Diary of a Century* (Penguin, 1978, o/p). Book of pictures by a great photographer, from the day he was given a camera in 1901 through the 1970s. Contains wonderful scenes of aristoratic leisure – on Normandy and Côte d'Azur beaches and racetracks – plus his own diary commentary.

Brassai *The Secret Paris of the Thirties* (Thames & Hudson, 1978, £12.50). Extraordinary photos of the capital's nightlife in the 1930s – brothels, music halls, street cleaners, transvestites and the underworld – each one a work of art and a familiar world (now long since gone) to Brassai and his friend Henry Miller who accompanied him on his night time expeditions.

FRENCH FICTION: A TOP 20

CLASSICS

1. **Gustave Flaubert** *Madame Bovary* (Penguin, £3.99).
2. **Emile Zola** *Germinal* (Penguin, £3.99).
3. **Emile Zola** *La Bête Humaine* (Penguin, £3.95).
4. **Victor Hugo** *Les Misérables* (Penguin, £5.95).
5. **Marcel Proust** *Remembrance of Things Past* (3 vols.; Methuen, £5.95).
6. **Honoré de Balzac** *Père Goriot* (Penguin, £3.50).
7. **Honoré de Balzac** *The Chouans* (Penguin, £4.95).
8. **Alexandre Dumas** *The Count of Monte Cristo* (Collins, £1.50).
9. **Lautreaumont** *Maldoror* (Allison & Busby, £3.95).
10. **Stendhal** *Scarlet and Black* (Penguin, £3.95).

MODERNS

1. **Jean Genet** *Thief's Journal* (Grove Press, £4.95).
2. **Henri Michaux** *Selected Writings* (New Directions, o/p).
3. **Marguerite Yourcenar** *Memoirs of Hadrian* (Penguin, £4.95).
4. **Jean-Paul Sartre** *Nausea* (Penguin, £3.50).
5 **Georges Simenon** Any of the *Maigret* books (Penguin).

6. **Simone de Beauvoir** *The Mandarins* (Fontana £5.95).
7. **André Gide** *The Immoralist* (Penguin, £5.95).
8. **Alain Robbe-Grillett** *The Erasers* (Calder, 1966, £7.95).
9. **Marguerite Duras** *The Lover* (Fontana, £3.50).
10. **Albert Camus** *The Plague* (Penguin, £3.99).

FRANCE IN FICTION

George Orwell *Down and Out in Paris and London* (Penguin, £2.50). Breadline living in the 1930s – Orwell at his best.

Anaïs Nin *The Journals 1914–1974* (7 vols., Quartet, 1967–80, £2.50–3.95 each). Not fiction, but a detailed literary narrative of French and U.S. fiction makers from the first half of this century (not least herself) in Paris and elsewhere. The more famous *Delta of Venus: Erotica* (Star books, 1979, £2.99) was also, of course, written in Paris – for porno connoisseurs. And if this is all you've read, get hold of *A Spy in the House of Love* (Penguin, 1985, £3.50), the finest of her excellent novels.

Henry Miller *Quiet Days in Clichy* (Allison & Busby, £3.99). *Tropic of Cancer* (Panther, £3.50), *Tropic of Capricorn* (Panther, £3.50). Nin's best Parisian chum, erratic, but with occasional flights of genius in describing 1930s, semen-stained Paris.

Lawrence Durrell The Avignon Quintet: *Monsieur, Livia, Constance, Sebastian,* and *Quinx* (Penguin, about £3.95 each). Miller's good friend, less prone to flights of genius but good on decaying grandeur in this evocation of the Nazi occupation of Avignon and surrounding countryside.

Jack Kerouac *Sartori in Paris* (Quartet £2.50) – and in Brittany, too. Typically inconsequential Kerouac experiences.

John Berger *Pig Earth* (Hogarth, 1988, £5.95). Best of Berger's trilogy drawn from the rural French village in which he lives.

Gertrude Stein *The Autobiography of Alice B. Toklas* (Penguin, £4.95). The goings-on at Stein's famous salon in Rue de Fleurus, Paris. This most accessible of her works, written from the ostensible point of view of Stein's long-time companion, gives an amusing account of the Paris art and literary scene of the 1910s and 1920s.

Eva Figes *Light* (Ballantine, 1983, o/p). It's summer 1900 and a day in the life of Claude Monet: Impressionism in words. Fun.

SPECIFIC GUIDES

Rob Hunter *Walking in France* (Oxford Illus, 1986, £4.95). Good account of the regional walking possibilities – with useful addresses if you're looking for new places to go.

Kev Reynolds *Walks and Climbs in the Pyrenees* (Cicerone, 1988, £7.95); **Andrew Harper** *The Tour of Mont Blanc* (Cicerone, 1982, £2.95). Reliable and detailed route descriptions for all levels of difficulty except serious climbers. Drivers might look at the same publisher's *France on Backroads* (1986, o/p), which offers more than 50 tours with sights and places to eat along the way.

Pyrenees West, Pyrenees East, Pyrenees Central (West Col, £6.95–8.95). These are more serious guides than the Cicerone ventures – but good stuff if you're committed. They again cover both hiking and climbing.

Topo Guides des Sentiers de Grande Randonnée (CNSGR, Paris). A series of route descriptions (in French, but not hard to follow) of all the major GR paths.

Georges Vernon *Haute Randonnée Pyrénées* (CAF, Paris). East-to-west description of the High Level route across the Pyrenees. Again in easy French.

W. Lippert *Fleurs des Montagnes, Alpages et Forêts* (Miniguide Nathan Tout Terrain). Best palm-sized, colour guide if you want something to pack away with your gear in the mountains.

Greg Ward *The Rough Guide to Brittany and Normandy* (Harrap, £4.95) Rightly hailed as a 'trailblazer' by the *Grimsby Evening Telegraph,* this beautifully-illustrated work is comprehensive and, if at times a little whimsical, a cracking good read.

Gai Guide (Gai Pied, Paris). Dependable listings of gay clubs, saunas, restaurants, places to listen to music and pick-up spots throughout France. Lesbian addresses are included though the photos are all male erotica. (See *Basics* for more information on guidebooks for gays.)

Gault et Millau: France (Gault et Millau £9.95) Now appearing in English, this is *the* French run-down on food and restaurants, as serious as a religious tract and an annual enticement to avarice, greed and (if you haven't got the readies) theft.

LANGUAGE

French is a far from easy language, despite the number of words shared with English, but the bare essentials are not difficult and make all the difference. Even just saying *"Bonjour Madame/Monsieur"* when you go into a shop and then pointing will usually get you a smile and helpful service. People working in hotels, restaurants, etc. almost always speak English and tend to use it even if you're struggling with French — be grateful, not insulted.

Differentiating words is the initial problem in **understanding spoken French** — it's very hard to get people to slow down. If, at last resort, you get them to write it down, you'll probably find you know half the words anyway.

PRONUNCIATION

One easy rule to remember is that consonants at the ends of words are usually silent. *Pas plus tard* (not later), for example, is pronounced "pa plu tarr." But when the following word begins with a vowel, you run the two together, thus: *pas après* (not after) becomes "pazapray."

Vowels are the hardest sounds to get right. Roughly:

a	as in **hat**
e	as in **get**
é	between **get** and **gate**
è	between **get** and **gut**
eu	like the u in **hurt**
i	as in mach**i**ne
o	as in h**o**t
ô, au	as in **o**ver
ou	as in f**oo**d
u	as in b**oo**t, said with pursed lips

More awkward are the combinations an/am, en/em, in/im, on/om, un/um at the ends of words or followed by consonants other than n or m. Again, roughly:

in/im	like the **an** in **an**xious
an/am, en/em	like the **a** in p**a**lm with a stuffy nose
on/om	like the **o** in d**o**n't with a stuffy nose
un/um	like the **u** in understand

Consonants are pretty much as the same as in English, except that: ch is always sh, c, is s, h is silent, th is the same as t, ll is like the y in yes, w is v, and r is growled.

QUESTIONS AND REQUESTS

The simplest way of asking a question is to start with *s'il vous plaît* (please), then name the thing you want in an interrogative tone of voice. For example:

Where is there a *bakery?*	*S'il vous plaît, la boulangerie?*
Can you show me the road to Lyon?	*S'il vous plaît, la route pour Lyon*

Similarly with requests

We'd like a room for *two*	*S'il vous plaît, une chambre pour deux*
Can I have a kilo of *oranges?*	*S'il vous plaît, une kilo d'oranges*

QUESTION WORDS

who	*qui*
where	*où*
how	*comment*
how many how much	*combien*
when	*quand*
why	*pourquoi*
at what time	*à quelle heure*
what is/which is	*quel est*

SOME BASIC WORDS AND PHRASES

French nouns are divided into masculine and feminine. This causes difficulties with adjectives, whose endings have to change to suit the gender of the nouns they are attached to. If you know some French grammar, you will know what to do. If not, stick to the masculine form, which is the simplest — it's what we have done in this glossary.

yes	*oui*
no	*non*
today	*aujourd'hui*
yesterday	*hier*
tomorrow	*demain*
in the morning	*le matin*
in the afternoon	*l'après-midi*
in the evening	*le soir*
at night	*la nuit*
now	*maintenant*
later	*plus tard*
at one o'clock	*à une heure*
at three o'clock	*à trois heures*
at ten-thirty	*à dix heures et demie*
at noon	*à midi*
man	*un homme*
woman	*une femme*
here	*ici*
there	*là*
this one	*ceci*
that one	*celà*
open	*ouvert*
closed	*fermé*
big	*grand*
small	*petit*
more	*plus*
less	*moins*
a little	*un peu*
a lot	*beaucoup*
cheap	*bon marché*
expensive	*cher*
good	*bon*
bad	*mauvais*
hot	*chaud*
cold	*froid*
with	*avec*
without	*sans*
day	*jour*
week	*semaine*
month	*mois*
year	*année*

TALKING TO PEOPLE

When addressing people you always use *Monsieur* for a man, *Madame* for a woman, *Mademoiselle* for a girl. Plain *bonjour* by itself is not enough. This isn't as formal as it seems, and you'll find it has its uses when you've forgotten someone's name or want to attract someone's attention.

Excuse me, do you speak English?	*Pardon, Madame, vous parlez anglais?*
How do you say in French?	*Comment ça se dit en français?*
What's your name?	*Comment vous appelez-vous?*
My name is . . .	*Je m'appelle . . .*
I'm English	*Je suis **anglais(e)***
Irish	***irlandais(e)***
Scottish	***écossais(e)***
Welsh	***gallois(e)***
I understand	*Je comprends*
I don't understand	*Je ne comprends pas*
Can you speak more slowly please?	*S'il vous plaît, parlez* moins vite
okay/agreed	*d'accord*
please	*s'il vous plaît*
thank you	*merci*
hello	*bonjour*
goodbye	*au revoir*
good morning/afternoon	*bonjour*
good evening	*bonsoir*
good night	*bonne nuit*
How are you?	*Comment allez-vous?/ Ça va?*
Fine, thanks	*Très bien, merci*
I don't know	*Je ne sais pas*
Let's go	*Allons-y*
See you tomorrow	*A demain*
See you soon	*A bientôt*
Sorry/Excuse me	*Pardon/Je m'excuse*
Leave me alone (aggressive)	*Fichez-mois la paix!*
Please help me	*Aidez-moi, s'il vous plaît*

ACCOMMODATION

a room for one/two/three people	*une chambre pour une/deux/trois personnes*
a double bed	*un lit double*
a room with a shower	*une chambre avec douche*

a room with a bath	*une chambre avec salle de bain*
Can I see it?	*Je peux la voir?*
for one/two/three nights	*pour une/deux/trois nuits*
hot water	*eau chaude*
cold water	*eau froide*
youth hostel	*auberge de jeunesse*
YHA card	*la carte internationale*
breakfast	*petit déjeuner*
Is breakfast included?	*Est-ce que le petit déjeuner compris?*
I would like breakfast	*Je voudrais prendre le petit déjeuner*
I don't want breakfast	*Je ne veux pas le petit déjeuner*
a room on the courtyard	*une chambre sur la cour*
a room on the streetside	*une chambre sur la rue*
first floor	*premier étage*
second floor	*deuxième étage*
with a view	*avec vue*
key	*clef*
to iron	*repasser*
do laundry	*faire la lessive*
sheets	*draps*
blankets	*couvertures*
quiet	*calme*
noisy	*bruyant*

GETTING AROUND

bus/car/train/ taxi/ferry/boat/plane	*autobus,bus,car/ voiture/train/ taxi/ferry/bateau/ avion*
bus station	*gare routière*
bus stop	*arrêt*
railway station	*gare*
platform	*quai*
What time does it leave?	*Il part à quelle heure?*
What time does it arrive?	*Il arrive à quelle heure?*
hitchhiking	*autostop*
on foot	*à pied*
how many km?	*combien de kilometres?*
how many hours?	*combien d'heures?*
Where are you going?	*Vous allez ou?*
I'm going to . . .	*Je vais à . . .*
I want to get off at . . .	*Je voudrais descendre à . . .*
the road to	*la route pour*
near	*près/pas loin*
far	*loin*
a ticket to . . .	*un billet pour . . .*
single ticket	*aller simple*
round-trip ticket	*aller retour*
validate your ticket	*composter votre billet*
ticket office	*vente de billets*
a book of bus/ métro tickets	*un carnet*
bus/métro pass	*carte orange*
weekly	*hebdomadaire*
monthly	*mensuel*
valid for	*valable pour*
street	*rue*
first street on the left	*premiere rue à gauche*
first street on the right	*premiere rue à droite*
traffic lights	*feux*
red light	*feu rouge*
green light	*feu vert*
on the corner of	*à l'angle de*
next to	*à côté de*
behind	*derrière*
in front of	*devant*
before	*avant*
after	*après*
under	*sous*
bridge	*pont*
to cross	*traverser*
on the other side of	*l'autre côté de*
straight ahead	*tout droit*

CARS

garage	*garage*
service	*service*
to park the car	*garer la voiture*
car park	*un parking*
no parking	*défense de stationner/ stationnement interdit*
petrol station	*poste d'essence*
petrol	*essence*
fill 'er up	*faire le plein*
oil	*huile*
air line	*ligne à air*
put air in the tyres	*gonfler les pneus*
battery	*batterie*
the battery is dead	*la batterie est morte*
plugs	*bougies*
to break down	*tomber en panne*
petrol can	*bidon*
insurance	*assurance*
green card	*carte verte*

for overseas driving registration	*carte grise*

HEALTH MATTERS

doctor	*médecin*
I don't feel well	*Je ne me sens pas bien*
medicines	*médicaments*
prescription	*ordonnance*
I feel sick	*J'ai mal au coeur*
headache	*J'ai mal á la tête*
stomach ache	*mal à l'estomac*
period	*règles*
pains	*douleurs*
it hurts	*ça fait mal*
aspirin	*aspirine*
chemist	*pharmacie*
hospital	*hôpital*

MONEY MATTERS

bank	*banque*
a one franc/five franc coin	*une pièce/d'un franc/de cinq francs*
exchange	*bureau de change*
a 100F note	*un billet de cent francs*
exchange rate	*cours de change*
travellers cheques	*chéques de voyage*
credit card	*carte de crédit*
money	*argent*
change	*la monnaie*
cashier	*caisse*

OTHER NEEDS

bakery	*boulangerie*
food store	*alimentation*
supermarket	*supermarché*
to eat	*manger*
to drink	*boire*
tobacconist	*tabac*
post office	*la Poste/bureau de poste*
stamps	*timbres*
toilet/washroom	*toilette*
police	*police*
telephone	*téléphone*
cinema	*cinéma*
theatre	*théâtre*
club/music	*une boîte/un club*
hairdresser	*coiffeur*
museum	*musée*
to reserve/book	*réserver*

NUMBERS AND DAYS

1	*un*	21	*vingt-et-un*
2	*deux*	22	*vingt-deux*
3	*trois*	30	*trente*
4	*quatre*	40	*quarante*
5	*cinq*	50	*cinquante*
6	*six*	60	*soixante*
7	*sept*	70	*soixante-dix*
8	*huit*	75	*soixante-quinze*
9	*neuf*	80	*quatres-vingt*
10	*dix*	90	*quatre-vingt-dix*
11	*onze*	95	*quatre-vingt-quinze*
12	*douze*	100	*cent*
13	*treize*	101	*cent-et-un*
14	*quatorze*	200	*deux cents*
15	*quinze*	300	*trois cents*
16	*seize*	500	*cinq cents*
17	*dix-sept*	1,000	*mille*
18	*dix-huit*	2,000	*deux milles*
19	*dix-neuf*	1,000,000	*un million*
20	*vingt*	1989	*dix-neuf-cent-quatre-vingt-neuf*

DAYS OF THE WEEK AND DATES

Sunday	*dimanche*
Monday	*lundi*
Tuesday	*mardi*
Wednesday	*mercredi*
Thursday	*jeudi*
Friday	*vendredi*
Saturday	*samedi*
first	*premier*
second	*deuxième*
third	*troisième*
fourth	*quatrième*
fifth	*cinquième*
sixth	*sixième*
seventh	*septième*
eighth	*huitième*
ninth	*neuvième*
tenth	*dixième*
September 1	*le premier septembre*
March 2	*le deux mars*
July 14	*le quatorze juillet*

PHRASEBOOKS AND DICTIONARIES

There are any number of French **phrasebooks** around, most of them adequate: *Hugo's French*

Phrasebook (Hunter, 1988, $3.25 is one of the most up to date.

More complete, is *French Keywords: The Basic 2000-Word Vocabulary Arranged by Frequency* (Oleander Press, 1983, $5.95). Among **dictionaries**, Harper and Row is the standard school dictionary; otherwise pick according to size and price. The *Dictionary of Modern Colloquial French* by Hérail and Lovatt (Routledge, Chapman and Hall, 1987, $14.95) makes great reading — as much for the English expressions as the French. It gives French-to-English only and includes the language of sex, crime, drugs — indeed all the words you ever wanted to understand.

LANGUAGE BOOKS

PHRASEBOOKS

Harrap's French Phrase Book (Harrap, £1.95). Good pocket reference – with useful contemporary phrases and a 5000-word dictionary of terms.

DICTIONARIES

Mini French Dictionary (Harap, £1.95). French-English and English-French, plus a brief grammar and pronunciation guide. Recommended.

French and English Slang Dictionary (Harrap, £9.95); ***Dictionary of Modern Colloquial French*** (Routledge, £15.00). Both volumes are a bit large to carry about, but they are the key to all the language you ever wanted to understand.

TEACH YOURSELF COURSES

Breakthrough French (Pan; book and two cassettes). Excellent, basic teach-yourself course.

A Vous La France; Franc Extra; Franc-Parler (BBC Publications; each course has a book and two cassettes). BBC radio courses, running from beginners' to fairly advanced language. Well geared to conversation.

FRENCH AND ARCHITECTURAL TERMS: A GLOSSARY

These are either terms you'll come across in the guide, or come up against on signs, maps, etc. while travelling round. For food items see *Basics*.

ABBAYE abbey
AMBULATORY covered passage round the outer edge of a choir of a church
APSE semi-circular termination at the east end of a church
ASSEMBLEE NATIONALE the French parliament
ARRONDISSEMENT district of a city
AUBERGE DE JEUNESSE (AJ) youth hostel
BAROQUE High Renaissance period of art and architecture, distinguished by extreme ornateness
BASTIDE medieval military settlement, constructed on a grid plan
BEAUX ARTS fine arts museum (and school)
CAR coach, bus
CAROLINGIAN dynasty (and art, sculpture, etc.) founded by Charlemagne; late eighth to early tenth century
CFDT Socialist trade union
CGT Communist trade union
CHASSE, CHASSE GARDEE hunting grounds (beware)
CHATEAU mansion, country house, or castle
CHATEAU FORT castle
CHEMIN DE ST-JACQUES medieval pilgrim route to the shrine of St James at Santiago de Compostela in northwest Spain
CHEVET end wall of a church
CIJ (*Centre d'Informations Jeunesse*) youth information centre
CLASSICAL architectural style incorporating Greek and Roman elements – pillars, domes, colonnades etc. – at its height in France in the seventeenth century and revived, as **neo-classical**, in the nineteenth century
CLERESTORY upper story of a church, incorporating the windows
CLUNIAC monastic movement and hence its architecture, derived from the Benedictine monastery at Cluny (see p.484)
CODENE French CND
CONSIGNE left luggage
COUVENT convent, monastery
DEGUSTATION tasting (wine or food)
DEPARTEMENT county – more or less
DONJON castle keep
EGLISE church
ENTREE entrance
FERMETURE closing period
FLAMBOYANT florid form of Gothic (see below)
FN (Front National) fascist party led by Jean–Marie Le Pen
FO Catholic trade union
FOUILLES archaeological excavations
FRESCO wall painting – durable through application to wet plaster
GALLO-ROMAIN period of Roman occupation of Gaul (A.D. 1c.–4c.)
GARE station; **ROUTIERE** – bus station; **SNCF** – train station
GITE D'ETAPE basic hostel accommodation primarily for walkers
GOBELINS most famous tapestry manufacturers, based in Paris, its most renowned period being in the reign of Louis XIV (17c.)
HALLES covered market
HLM publicly subsidised housing
HOTEL a hotel, but also an aristocratic town-house or mansion
HOTEL DE VILLE town hall
JOURS FERIES public holidays
MAIRIE town hall
MARCHE market
MEROVINGIAN dynasty (and art, etc.), ruling France and parts of Germany from sixth to mid–eighth centuries
NARTHEX entrance hall of church
NAVE main body of a church
PCF Communist party of France
PLACE square
PORTE gateway
PRESQU'ILE peninsula
PS Socialist party
PTT post office
QUARTIER district of a town
RELAIS ROUTIERS truckstop café-restaurants
RENAISSANCE art-architectural style developed in fifteenth-century Italy and imported to France in the early sixteenth century by François I (see *Contexts*)

RETABLE altarpiece
REZ DE CHAUSSEE (RC) ground floor
RN (*Route Nationale*) main road
ROMANESQUE Early medieval architecture distinguished by squat, rounded forms and naive sculpture
RPR Gaullist party led by Jacques Chirac
SI (*Syndicat d'Initiative*) tourist information office; also known as OT, OTSI and MAISON DU TOURISME
SNCF French railways
SORTIE exit
STUCCO plastic used to embellish ceilings, etc.
TABAC bar or shop selling stamps, cigarettes, etc.
TOUR tower
TRANSEPT cross arms of a church
TYMPANUM sculpted panel above a church door
UDF centre-right party headed by Giscard d'Estaing
VAUBAN Seventeenth-century military architect – his fortresses still stand all over France
VOUSSOIR sculpted rings in arch over church door
ZONE BLEUE restricted parking zone
ZONE PIETONNE pedestrian precinct

INDEX

HELP US UPDATE

We've gone to a lot of effort to ensure that this edition of the Rough Guide: France is completely up-to-date and accurate. However, things do change – restaurants and bars come and go, opening hours (as everywhere in Europe) are fickle – and we'd be the first to admit that France can never be fully 'covered' in any guide. Any suggestions, comments, or corrections toward the next edition would be much appreciated. We'll credit all contributions, and send a copy of the new book (or any other Rough Guide, if you prefer) for the best letters. Send them along to: The Rough Guides, 149 Kennington Lane, London SE11 4EZ.